$20.00
REF. SER. **SEP** 8 '87

A11703 324881

D0941137

I.B. CIPRIANI PINX.                                C. GRIGNION SCULP

GUIDO ARETINUS A BENEDICTINE MONK, HAVING REFORMED THE
SCALE OF MUSIC AND INVENTED A NEW METHOD OF NOTATION,
COMMUNICATES HIS IMPROVEMENTS TO POPE JOHN XX,
WHO INVITES HIM TO ROME AND BECOMES HIS DISCIPLE.

# A
# GENERAL HISTORY
## *of the*
# SCIENCE AND PRACTICE
## *of*
# MUSIC

*by*

SIR JOHN HAWKINS

With a New Introduction by
CHARLES CUDWORTH
Curator, Pendlebury Library of Music
University Music School, Cambridge, England

In Two Volumes

Volume II

DOVER PUBLICATIONS, INC.
NEW YORK        NEW YORK

Copyright © 1963 by Dover Publications, Inc.
All rights reserved under Pan American and
International Copyright Conventions.

Published in the United Kingdom by Constable
and Company Limited, 10 Orange Street, London
W. C. 2.

This new Dover edition, first published in 1963,
is an unabridged republication of the edition published by J. Alfred Novello in 1853.

In the 1853 edition, the portraits and other full-
page illustrations appeared as a separate volume; in
this Dover edition, all these illustrations are re-
produced in appropriate places within the two-volume
text.

This Dover edition also contains a new Introduc-
tion especially prepared for this edition by Charles
Cudworth, Curator, Pendlebury Library of Music,
University Music School, Cambridge, England.

Manufactured in the United States of America

Dover Publications, Inc.
180 Varick Street
New York 14, N.Y.

# List of Portraits in Volume Two

# A
# GENERAL HISTORY
### OF THE
# SCIENCE AND PRACTICE OF MUSIC.

## CHAPTER XCIX.

THOMAS MORLEY, one of the gentlemen of queen Elizabeth's chapel, the author of a well known treatise on the subject of practical music, was a disciple of Bird, for whom he ever entertained the highest reverence. He obtained a bachelor's degree in 1588, and was sworn into his place in the chapel July 24, 1592; he was the author of Canzonets or little short songs to three voices, Lond. 1593. The first book of Madrigals to four voices, Lond. 1594. Canzonets or little short Airs to 5 or 6 voices, Lond. 1595. Madrigals to 5 voices, Lond. 1595. Introduction to Music, Lond. 1597. The first book of Aires or little short Songes to sing and play to the lute with the bass viol, Lond. 1600. And the first book of Canzonets to two voices, Lond. 1595, and 1619. He also composed divine services and anthems, the words of some whereof are printed in James Clifford's Collection of divine services and anthems usually sung in cathedrals.* A service for the burial of the dead of his composition, the first of the kind, to the words of our liturgy, is printed in Dr. Boyce's Cathedral Music, vol. I. He also collected and published madrigals, entitled the Triumphs of Oriana, to five and six voices, composed by divers authors, Lond. 1601, and a set or two of Italian madrigals to English words; but the most valuable of all his works is his Plaine and easie Introduction to practicall Musicke, so often referred to in the course of this work, and of which an account is here given.

This valuable work is divided into three parts, the first teaching to sing; the second treating of Descant, with the method of singing upon a plain-song; the other of composition in three and more parts. Each of the three parts of this book is a several and distinct dialogue, wherein a master, his scholar, and a person competently skilled in music, are the interlocutors; and in the course of their conversation so many little particulars occur relating to the manners of the times,

* This book is very frequently referred to by Wood. It is a collection of the words only, of the services and anthems then usually sung, printed in duodecimo, 1664. The compiler was a native of Oxford, a chorister of Magdalen college there, and afterwards a minor canon of St. Paul's, and reader in some church near Carter-lane, and also chaplain to the society of Serjeant's Inn in Fleet-street. Athen. Oxon.

as render the perusal of the book in a great degree entertaining to those who are unacquainted with the subject of it; the truth of this observation will appear from the very introduction to the work, which is as follows :—

> ' POLYMATHES.
> ' PHILOMATHES.
> ' MASTER.

' POLYMATHES. Staye brother Philomathes, what haste? ' Whither go you so fast? PHILOMATH. To seek out an ' old friend of mine. POL. But before you goe I praie ' you repeat some of the discourses which you had yester- ' night at Master Sophobulus his banket, for commonly he ' is not without both wise and learned guestes. PHI. It ' is true indeed, and yesternight there were a number of ' excellent schollers, both gentlemen and others : but all ' the propose which was then discoursed upon was ' musicke. POL. I trust you were contented to suffer ' others to speake of that matter. PHI. I would that ' had been the worst; for I was compelled to discover ' mine own ignorance, and confesse that I knewe nothing ' at all in it. POL. How so? PHI. Among the rest ' the guestes by chance Master Amphron came thither ' also, who falling to discourse of musicke, was in an ' argument so quickly taken up and hotly pursued by ' Eudoxus and Calergus, two kinsmen of master Sopho- ' bulus, as in his own art he was overthrowne, but he still ' sticking in his opinion, the two gentlemen requested me ' to examine his reasons and confute them, but I refusing, ' and pretending ignorance, the whole company con- ' demned me of discurtesie, being fully persuaded that ' I had been as skilfull in that art as they took me to be ' learned in others; but supper being ended, and musicke ' bookes according to the custome, being brought to the ' table, the mistress of the house presented mee with a ' part, earnestly requesting me to sing, but when, after ' many excuses I protested unfeignedly that I could not, ' everie one began to wonder, yea some whispered to ' others, demanding how I was brought up : so that upon ' shame of mine own ignorance I goe nowe to seek out ' mine old friende master Gnorimus, to make myself his ' schollar. POL. I am glad you are at length come to ' be of that mind, though I wished it sooner, therefore ' goe, and I praie God send you such good successe as ' you would wish to yourself; as for me, I goe to heare ' some mathematical lectures, so that I thinke about one ' time wee may both meete at our lodging. PHI. Fare-

'well, for I sit upon thornes till I be gone, therefore I
'will make haste; but, if I be not deceived, I see him
'whom I seeke sitting at yonder doore, out of doubt it is
'hee. And it should seeme he studieth upon some point
'of musicke, but I will drive him out of his dumpe.
'Good morrow, Sir. MASTER. And you also good
'Master Philomathes, I am glad to see you, seeing it is
'so long ago since I sawe you, that I thought you had
'either been dead, or then had vowed perpetually to
'keep your chamber and booke to which you were so
'much addicted. PHI. Indeed I have been well affected
'to my booke, but how have you done since first I saw
'you? MAST. My health since you saw mee hath been
'so badd as, if it had been the pleasure of him who made
'all things, to have taken me out of the world I should
'have been very well contented, and have wished it more
'than once: but what business hath driven you to this
'end of the town? PHI. My errand is to you, to make
'myself your scholler; and seeing I have found you at
'such convenient leisure, I am determined not to depart
'till I have one lesson in musicke. MAST. You tell mee
'a wonder, for I have heard you so much speake against
'that art, as to terme it a corrupter of good manners,
'and an allurement to vices, for which many of your com-
'panions termed you a Stoic. PHI. It is true, but I am
'fo far changed, as of a Stoic I would willingly make a
'Pythagorean; and for that I am impatient of delay I
'praie you begin even now. MAST. With a good will;
'but have you learned nothing at all in musicke before?
'PHI. Nothing. Therefore I pray you begin at the very
'beginning, and teach me as though I were a childe.
'MAST. I will do so, and therefore behold here is the
'scale of musicke which we terme the Gam.' [Giving
him the gamut with the syllables.]

The master then proceeds to instruct his scholar
in the rudiments of song, in the doing whereof he
delivers to him the precepts of the plain and mensurable cantus, illustrated with examples in notes, to
some whereof, for the greater facility of utterance,
he has joined the letters of the alphabet, and these
are introduced by a distich, and concluded by a
direction to begin again, as here is shown :—

Christes crosse be my speede in all ver-tue to

procede A. b. c. d. e. f. g. h.

i. k. l. m. n. o. p. q. r. s. et

t. double w. v. x. with y. ez-od. et per se,

con per se. ti-tle, ti-tle, est Amen, When you have

done be-gin againe, be-gin a-gaine. Christes crosse

be my speede, in al ver-tue to pro-ceede.

A. b. c. d. e. f. g. h.*

The second part of the Introduction of Morley is
a treatise of Descant, as it was then called; the
meaning of the term, and the nature of the practice,
are explained in the following colloquy :—

'MASTER. Whom do I see afar off, is it not my scholar
'Philomathes? out of doubt it is he, and therefore I will
'salute him. Good morrow, scholler. PHI. God give
'you good morrow and a hundredth, but I marvayle not
'a little to see you so early, not only stirring, but out of
'doors also. MAST. It is no marvayle to see a snayle
'after a rayne to creep out of his shell and wander all
'about seeking the moisture. PHI. I pray you talk not
'so darkely, but let me understand your comparysons
'playnley. MAST. Then in plaine tearmes being over
'wearied with studie, and taking the opportunity of the
'fayre morning, I came to this place to snatch a mouth-
'ful of this holsome ayre, which gently breathing upon
'these sweet-smelling flowers, and making a whispering
'noise amongst these tender leaves, delighteth with re-
'freshing, and refresheth with delight my over weary
'senses; but tell me, I pray you, the cause of your hither
'coming; have you not forgotten some part of that
'which I shewed you at our last being together. PHI.
'No verily, but the contrary, I am become such a singer
'as you would wonder to heare me. MAST. How came
'that to passe? PHI. Be silent, and I will shew you;

* The practice of annexing words of a frivolous import to notes, for
the assistance of novices in the art of singing, was no new thing; the
Monks were the authors of it, and many of the examples of Glareanus
himself are either Hebrew names or Latin nonsense, set to very good
music; but in the example before us, the distich

        Christ's cross be my spede
        In all vertue to procede,

has a meaning which it will be the business of this note to enquire after.
    In the course of this work occasion has been taken to mention St.
Nicholas, and to shew that by those of the Romish communion he is
looked on as the patron of young scholars. In the homily against peril
of idolatry, which our church has directed to be read for the instruction
of the people, is a very particular enumeration of those saints, who,
either from a supposed power to heal certain diseases, or to confer
peculiar graces, or, in short, some way or other to favour mankind, were
the most common objects of private supplication; the passage referred
to is as follows :—
    'Every artificer and profession hath his special saint as a peculiar
'God. As for example, schollars have Saint Nicholas and Saint Gregory;
'Painters Saint Luke: neither lack soldiers their Mars, nor lovers their
'Venus amongst Christians. All diseases have their special Saints as
'Gods the curers of them. The pox Saint Roche, the falling evil St.
'Cornelis, the tooth ache St. Appollin, &c. Neither do beasts and cattel
'lack their gods with us, for Saint Loy is the horseleach [i. e. the horse-
'physician] and Saint Anthony the swineherd, &c. Where is God's
'providence and due honour in the mean season ? * * * if we remember
'God sometimes, yet because we doubt of his ability or will, to help us,
'we join to him another helper, as he were a noun adjective, using these
'sayings: such as learn, God and Saint Nicholas be my speed: such as
'neese, God help and Saint John : to the horse, God and Saint Loy save
'thee, &c.'
    From the above passage it appears that anciently 'God and Saint
'Nicholas be my spede,' was a customary ejaculation of young scholars;
and we can hardly suppose a more proper occasion for the use of it than
when infants of tender years are learning the rudiments of literature.
It is therefore not improbable that the distich
        'Saint Nicholas be my spede
        'In all vertue to procede,'
might be the introduction to the alphabet, and might be constantly repeated by the child previous to the beginning its lesson.
    The alphabet is frequently termed the Criss Cross, that is to say
Christ's cross row, because of a cross constantly placed before the letter
A, which sign was anciently a direction to the child to cross itself before
it began its lesson, as it is now in the mass-book for the same action in
different parts of the service.
    The use of the prayer to St. Nicholas may well be supposed to have
continued amongst us until the practice of praying to saints was condemned by our church as superstitious, which it was somewhat before
Morley's time; and after that, as our reformers had thought proper to
retain the use of the sign of the cross in some few instances, how
naturally did this variation suggest itself,
        Christ's cross be my spede
        In all vertue to procede.
which, as the reformation then stood, might well enough be deemed
a good Protestant prayer.

'I have a brother, a good scholar and a reasonable
'musition for singing, he at my first coming to you,
'conceived an opinion, I know not upon what reasons
'grounded, that I should never come to any meane
'knowledge in musicke, and therefore when he heard me
'practice alone he would continually mock me, indeed
'notwithstanding reason, for many times I would sing
'halfe a note too high, other while as much too lowe, so
'that he could not contain himself from laughing; yet now
'and then he would set me right, more to let me see that
'he could doe it, then that he ment any way to instruct
'me, which caused me so diligently to apply my prick-
'song booke, that in a manner I did no other thing but
'sing, practising to slip from one key to another, from
'flat to sharp, from sharp to flat, from any one place in
'the scale to another, so that there was no song so hard
'but I woulde venture upon it, no mood, nor proportion
'so strange but I would go through and sing perfectly
'before I left it; and in the end I came to such per-
'fection that I might have been my brother's maister, for
'although he had a little more practice to sing at first
'sight than I had, yet for the moods, ligatures, and other
'such things, I might set him to school. MAST. What
'then was the cause of your coming hither at this time?
'PHI. Desire to learne as before. MAST. What would
'you now learne. PHI. Beeing this last daye upon
'occasion of some businesse at one of my friends houses,
'we had some songs sung, afterwards falling to discourse
'of musicke and musitians, one of the company naming
'a friend of his owne, tearmed him the best Descanter
'that was to be found. Now, Sir, I am at this time come
'to knowe what Descant is, and to learne the same.
'MAST. I thought you had onely sought to know prickt
'song, whereby to recreate yourself, being wearye of
'other studies. PHI. Indeed when I came to you first
'I was of that minde, but the common proverb is in me
'verified, that much would have more; and seeing I have
'so far set foot in music, I doe not meane to goe backe
'till I have gone quite through all, therefore I pray you
'now, seeing the time and place fitteth so well, to dis-
'course with me what descant is, what parts, and how
'many it hath, and the rest. MAST. The heate in-
'creaseth, and that which you demand requireth longer
'discourse than you looke for, let us therefore go and sit
'in yonder shadie arbor to avoyde the vehementness of
'the sunne.—The name of Descant is usurped of the
'musitions in divers significations; some time they take
'it for the whole harmony of many voyces, others some-
'times for one of the voyces or partes, and that is when
'the whole song is not passing three voyces. Last of
'all, they take it for singing a part extempore upon
'a playne song, in which sense we commonly use it; so
'that when a man talketh of a descanter, it must be
'understood of one that can extempore sing a part upon
'a playne song. PHI. What is the meane to sing upon
'a playne song? MAST. To know the distances both
'of concords and discords. PHI. What is a concord?
'MAST. It is a mixt sound, compact of divers voyces, &c.'

Among the rules for extemporary descant, which
are in truth no other than the precepts of musical
composition, he explains the nature of that kind of
composition called two parts in one, which, as he
says, is when two parts are so made as that the
latter singeth every note and rest in the same length
and order as the leading part did sing before. From
hence he proceeds to declare the nature of canon
framed to a given plain-song; and of these he gives
sundry examples with the plain-song in various
situations, that is to say, sometimes above, sometimes
below, and at other times in the midst of the canon.

The third part of the Introduction treats of composing or setting of songs; and here the author
takes occasion to censure one master Boulde, an
ignorant pretender to music; and he does it in this
way, he supposes Philomathes by this time to have
profited so much by his master's instructions as to
have got the start of his brother Polymathes, and
that Polymathes, who is supposed to have learned
the little he knew of music of the above Master
Boulde, being sensible of this, is desirous of putting
himself under the tuition of his brother's master; the
master tenders him a plain-song, desiring him to
sing upon it a lesson of descant, which he does but
very indifferently, the faults in this and another
lesson or two which Polymathes sings, draws on
a discourse between him and his new master, wherein
he very humorously characterizes his former master,
Boulde.—'When,' says he, 'I learned descant of my
'maister Boulde, hee seeing me so toward and
'willing to learne, ever had me in his company; and
'because he continually carried a plaine song booke
'in his pocket, hee caused me to doe the like, and so
'walking in the fields he would sing the plainsong,
'and cause me to sing the descant, and when I sung
'not to his contentment he would shew me wherein
'I had erred; there was also another descanter,
'a companion of my maister's, who never came in
'my maister's company, though they were much
'conversant together, but they fell to contention,
'striving who should bring in the point soonest and
'make hardest proportions, so that they thought
'they had won great glory if they had brought in
'a point sooner or sung harder proportions the one
'than the other: but it was a worlde to heare them
'wrangle, everie one defending his owne for the best.
'What, saith the one, you keepe not time in your
'proportions; you sing them false, saith the other;
'what proportion is this, saith hee? Sesquipaltery,
'saith the other; nay, would the other say, you
'sing you know not what; it should seem you came
'lately from a barber's shop, where you had Gregory
'Walker* or a Coranta plaide in the new proportions
'by them lately found out, called Sesquiblinda and
'Sesqui-hearken after. So that if one unacquainted
'with musicke had stood in a corner and heard them,
'he would have sworne they had been out of their
'wittes, so earnestlie did they wrangle for a trifle.

* A note in the original. 'That name in derision they have given this
'quadrant Pavan because it walketh among barbers and fiddlers more
'common than any other.'
    This note of the author requires explanation. In Morley's time and
for many years after, a lute or viol, or some such musical instrument,
was part of the furniture of a barber's shop, which was used then to be
frequented by persons above the ordinary level of the people, who
resorted to the barber either for the cure of wounds, or to undergo some
chirurgical operations, or, as it was then called, to be trimmed, a word
that signified either shaving or cutting and curling the hair; these, together with letting blood, were the ancient occupations of the barber-
surgeon. As to the other important branch of surgery, the setting of
fractured limbs, that was practised by another class of men called bone-
setters, of whom there are hardly any now remaining. Peacham, in his
account of Maurice landgrave of Hesse before cited, says he was generally
accounted the best bone-setter in his country, whence it appears that
this faculty was sometimes exercised by men of condition and benevolent
tempers. But to return to the barber: the musical instruments in his
shop were for the entertainment of waiting customers, and answered the
end of a newspaper. At this day those who wait for their turn at the
barber's, amuse themselves with reading the news of the day or week;
anciently they beguiled the time with playing on a musical instrument,
which custom gave occasion to Morley to say of the quadrant Pavan
mentioned by him, that it was so common that it walked amongst the
barbers.

'And in truth I myselfe thought sometimes that
'they would have gone to round buffets with the
'matter, for the descant bookes were made angels,[*]
'but yet fistes were no visitors of eares, and therefore
'all parted friends. But to say the verie truth, this
'Poliphemus had a very good sight, especially for
'treble descant, but very bad utterance, for that his
'voice was the worst that ever I had heard; and
'though of others he was esteemed verie good in that
'kinde, yet did none think better of him then hee
'did of himself; for if one had named and asked his
'opinion of the best composers living at this time,
'hee would say in a vaine glory of his own sufficiencie
'tush, tush, for these were his words, he is a proper
'man, but he is no descanter, there is no stuffe in
'him, I wil not give two pinnes for him except he
'hath descant.'

In the course of his directions for composing and
setting of songs, Morley takes occasion to censure
Alfonso Ferabosco and Giovanni Croce for taking
perfect concords of one kind in succession, a practice
which he loudly condemns, and says of Fairfax,
Taverner, Shepheard, Mundy, White, Parsons, and
Bird, that they never thought it greater sacrilege to
spurn against the image of a saint than to take two
perfect chords of one kind together.

Speaking of the several kinds of composition
practised in his time, Morley gives the first place to
the motet.[†]

Next to the motet he places the madrigal, for the
etymology of which word he says he can give no
'reason.[‡] He says 'it is a kind of music made
'upon songs and sonnets, such as Petrarch and many
'other poets have excelled in, and that it is, next
'unto the motet the most artificial, and, to men of
'understanding, most delightful; and would not be
'so much disallowable if the poets who compose
'the ditties would abstain from some obscenities
'which all honest ears abhor, and from some such
'blasphemies as no man, at least who has any hope
'of salvation, can sing without trembling.' He then
enumerates the several kinds of composition and air
practised by the musicians of his time, mention
whereof will be made in a subsequent chapter.

It is to be remembered that the whole of this
work of Morley is in dialogue, and that by the
master, who is one of the interlocutors in it, he
means to represent himself, who having sufficiently
instructed his scholars dismisses them.

The dialogue being ended there follows what the
author calls the Peroratio, in which he discovers
much learning; in it he says that had it not been
for Boetius, the knowledge of music had not yet come
into our western part of the world, adding this as
a reason, 'The Greek tongue lying as it were dead
'under the barbarisme of the Gothes and Hunnes,
'and musicke buried in the bowels of the Greeke
'workes of Ptolomeus and Aristoxenus; the one of
'which as yet hath never come to light, but lies in

'written copies in some bibliothekes of Italie, the
'other hath beene set out in print, but the copies are
'everie where so scant and hard to come by, that
'many doubt if he have been set out or no.'

Next follow certain compositions of the author's
own, for three, four, and five voices, to Latin, Italian,
and English words, which have great merit.

The annotations at the end of the work are replete
with curious learning; in these Morley has not
spared to censure some ignorant pretenders to skill in
music, and, amongst the rest, the anonymous author
of a book entitled 'The Guide of the Path-Way to
'Music,' printed in 1596 in oblong quarto, for
William Barley, a great publisher of music books
about that time, of which he gives this character.
'Take away two or three scales which are filched
'out of Beurhusius,[§] and fill up the three first pages
'of the booke, you shall not finde one side in all the
'booke without some grosse errour or other. For
'as he setteth down his dupla, so doth he all his
'proportions, giving true definitions and false ex-
'amples, the example still importing the contrarie
'to that which was said in the definition.[||] But
'this is the worlde; every one will take upon him
'to write and teach others, none having more need
'of teaching than himselfe. And as for him of
'whom we have spoken so much, one part of his
'booke he stole out of Beurhusius, another out of

§ FREDERIC BEURHUSIUS, con-rector of the college of Dortmund, an
Imperial town in the circle of Westphalia. He wrote an Erotemata
Musicæ, which was published about the year 1580.

|| After this character of the book a particular account of its contents
will hardly be wished for; there are printed with it three books of
tablature, the first for the lute, the second for an instrument called the

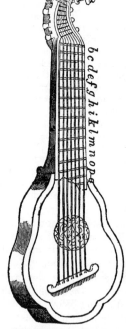

Orpharion, and the third for one called
the Bandore, concerning which two last
it may not be amiss here to speak, and
first of the Orpharion. It is of the following form, and is thus described by
the author:—
'The Orpharion is strung with more
'stringes than the lute, and also hath
'more frets or stops; and whereas the
'lute is struug with gut strings, the
'Orpharion is strung with wire strings,
'by reason of which manner of stringing,
'the Orpharion doth necessarilie require
'a more gentle and drawing stroke than
'the lute; I mean the fingers of the
'right hand must be easily drawn over
'the stringes, and not suddenly griped or
'sharpelie stroken as the lute is, for if
'yee should doo so, then the wire strings
'would clash or jarre together the one
'against the other, which would be a
'cause that the sound would be harsh
'and unpleasant. Therefore it is meete
'that you observe the difference of the
'stroke. And concerning the frets or
'stoppes, the difference doth consist in
'the different number that is between
'them, for the lute hath no further
'than i, and the Orpharion hath to q;
'but it is seldom that any lesson for the
'Orpharion doth passe the stops of L or
'M, yet those that are cunning can at
'their pleasure make use of all the
'stops.'
Among the lessons contained in this
book for the Orpharion, there is one named
Bockington's Pound, which seems to be
no other than that tune now called Pack-
ington's Pound, and to which is adapted
one of the songs in the Beggar's Opera.
The original composer of it appears to be
one Francis Cutting.

As to the Bandore, the figure whereof is also given in the following
page, the author says it is easy to play on, and is both commendable and
fit, either in consort or alone. He adds that the manner of tuning doth
a little differ from the lute and orpharion, but he has forgotten to mention
whether the strings are of wire, like those of the orpharion, or of catgut

* i. e. they flew about their ears as if they had wings.

† See an explanation of this word in page 388 of this work, in a note.

‡ See the conjectures of various authors concerning it in page 335
of this work, in a note.

'Lossius, perverting the sense of Lossius his wordes,
'and giving examples flatte to the contrarie of that
'which Lossius saith. And the last part of his book
'treating of Descant he took verbatim out of an old
'written booke which I have: but it should seeme
'that whatsoever or whosoever he was that gave it
'to the presse, was not the author of it himselfe,
'else would he have set his name to it, or then he
'was ashamed of his labour.'

In the annotations on the second part of Morley's
Introduction is the following curious note on the
term Descant. 'Thoughe I dare not affirme that
'this part was in use with the musitions of the
'learned Ptolemæus, or yet of that of Boetius, yet
'may I with some reason say that it is more auncient
'than pricksong, and only by reason of the name,
'which is contrapunto, an Italian word devised since
'the Gothes did overrun Italy, and changed the
'Latine tongue into that barbarisme which they now
'use. As for the word itselfe, it was at that time fit
'enough to express the thing signified, because no
'diversity of notes being used, the musicians instead
'of notes did set down their musicke in plain prickes
'or points; but afterwards, that custom being altered
'by the diversitie of forms of notes, yet the name is
'retained amongst them in the former signification,
'though amongst us it be restrained from the gene-
'rality to signifie that species or kind which of all
'others is the most simple and plaine; and instead
'of it we have usurped the name of descant. Also
'by continuance of time that name is also degene-
'rated into another signification, and for it we use
'the word setting and composing: and to come to
'the matter which now we are to intreat of, the word
'descant signifieth in our tongue the forme of setting
'together of sundry voices or concords for producing
'harmony; and a musician if he heare a song sung

like those of the lute. This instrument
is said by Stowe in his Annals, pag. 869,
to have been invented in the fourth year
of Queen Elizabeth, by John Rose,
citizen of London, living in Bridewell.

As to the instrument called the Orpharion, above described, it is necessary
to be observed that it cannot be the same
with the Orphion, mentioned in the
poems of Sir Aston Cockaine to have been
invented by Thomas Pilkington, one of
the queen's musicians, for Pilkington was
one of the musicians of Henrietta, the
consort of Charles I., and the Orpharion
appears to be of greater antiquity.

Pilkington died about 1660, at Wolverhampton, aged thirty-five, and lies there
buried. Besides an epitaph, Sir Aston
Cockaine wrote a poem to his memory,
in which are the following quibbling
lines :—

'Mastring all music that was known
    before,
'He did invent the Orphion, and gave
    more.
'Though he by playing had acquir'd
    high fame,
'He evermore escaped the gamester's
    name,
'Yet he at Gamut frequent was, and
    taught
'Many to play, till death set his Gam out.
'His flats were all harmonious; not like
    theirs
'Whose ebbs in prose or verse abuse our
    ears.
'But to what end praise I his flats, since
    that
'He is grown one himself, and now lies
    flat !'

'and mislike it, he will say the descant is nought;
'but in this signification it is seldom used, and the
'common signification which it hath is the singing
'extempore upon a plain-song, in which sense there is
'none who hath tasted the first elements of musicke
'but understandeth it. When descant did begin, by
'whom, and where it was invented, is uncertaine; for
'it is a great controversie amongst the learned if it
'were known to the antiquitie or no. And divers
'do bring arguments to prove, and others to disprove
'the antiquity of it; and for disproving of it they
'say that in all the works of them who have written
'of musicke before Franchinus, there is no mention
'of any more parts than one, and that if any did
'singe to the harpe, which was their most usual
'instrument, they sung the same which they plaied.
'But those who would affirme that the ancients knew
'it, saie: That if they did not know it, to what end
'served all those long and tedious discourses and
'disputations of the consonantes, wherein the most
'part of their workes are consumed? But whether
'they knew it or not, this I will say, that they had
'it not in halfe that variety wherein we now have it,
'though we read of much more strange effects of
'their musicke than of ours.'*

At the end of this book is the following list of
English musicians, the far greater part of whom
appear to have flourished before the reformation.
M. Pashe. Robert Jones. Jo. Dunstable. Leonel
Power. Robert Orwel. M. Wilkinson. Jo. Gwin-
neth. Robert Davis. M. Risby. D. Farfax. D.
Kirby. Morgan Grig. Tho. Ashwell. M. Sturton.
Jacket. Corbrand. Testwood. Ungle. Beech.
Bramston. S. Jo. Mason. Ludford. Farding.
Cornish. Pyggot. Taverner. Redford. Hodges.
Selby. Thorne. Oclande. Averie. D. Tye. D.
Cooper. D. Newton. M. Tallis. M. White. M.
Persons. M. Byrde.

By the compositions of Fairfax, Cornish, Taverner,
and Thorne, already given, a judgment may be
formed of the state of Music in those days. It
appears that many of the old English musicians were
men of learning in other faculties, particularly in
astronomy and physic, and what is strange, in logic.
Thorne of York lies buried in the cathedral of that
city, with the following inscription :—

Here lyeth Thorne, muſician moſt perfitt in his art,
In Logick's lore who did excell; all vice who ſet apart:
Whoſe lief and converſation did all men's love allure,
And now doth reign above the ſkies in joys moſt firm and pure.
        Who died Decemb. 7, 1573.

And in the same church is an inscription of the

* It seems by the conclusion of this passage that Morley was but little
acquainted with the effects of modern music, for there is extant a relation
to this purpose that surpasses all accounts of the power of ancient music
over the human mind. It is this: a musician of Ericus king of
Denmark, surnamed the Good, who reigned about the year 1130, a
hundred years after the time of Guido, having given out that he was
able by his art to drive men into what affections he listed, even into
anger and fury, and being required by the king to put his skill into
practice, played so upon the harp that his auditors began first to be
moved, and at last he set the king into such a frantic mood, that in a
rage he fell upon his most trusty friends and, for lack of weapon, slew
some of them with his fist, which when he came to himself he did much
lament. This story is recorded at large both by Krantzius and Saxo
Grammaticus, and is cited by Butler in his treatise on the Principles of
Music, pag. 7.

like import, celebrating the memory of another of his profession in these words :—

Muficus et logicus Wyrnal hic jacet ecce Johannes
Organa namque quafi fecerat ille loqui.

Thus humorously translated :—

Musician and logician both,
  John Wyrnal lieth here ;
Who made the organs erst to speak
  As if, or as it were.

## CHAP. C.

THE foregoing account may suffice to shew the design and method of Morley's Introduction to Music, a work for which all who love or practice the science are under the highest obligations to its author. John Caspar Trost, organist of the church of St. Martin at Halberstadt, a learned musician of the last century, translated it into the German language, and published it in folio, with the title of Musica Practica.

The particulars of Morley's life are no otherwise to be collected than from a few scattered notes concerning him in the Athenæ Oxonienses, and from his own work, throughout which he speaks the language of a sensible, a learned, and a pious man, a little soured in his temper by bodily infirmities, and more by the envy of some of his own profession, of which he complains in very feeling terms in the preface to almost every one of his publications. In that before his Introduction he speaks of the solitary life which he led, being compelled to keep at home, and that made him glad to find anything wherein to keep himself ex-

ercised for the benefit of his country : and in the course of his work he takes frequent occasion to mention the declining state of his health at the time of his writing it ; nevertheless he survived the publication of it some years, dying as it seems in the year 1604. Doni, in his ' Discorso sopra la per- 'fettione de Melodia,' printed with his treatise ' De' 'Generi e de' modi,' pag. 111, styles him ' Tommaso 'Morley, erudito musico Inglese.'

As a practical composer he has doubtless shown great abilities ; he was an excellent harmonist, but did not possess the faculty of invention in any very eminent degree. His compositions seem to be the effect of close study and much labour, and have in them little of that sweet melody which are found in those of Bennet, Weelkes, Wilby, Bateson, and some others ; nor in point of invention and fine contrivance are they to be compared with those of either Bird or Tallis. He composed a solemn burial service, the first perhaps of the kind ever known in England, and which continued to be performed at the interment of persons of rank till it gave way to that of Purcell and Croft, which will hardly ever be excelled.

After the expiration of the patent granted to Tallis and Bird, it seems that Morley had interest enough to obtain of queen Elizabeth a new one of the same tenor, but with ampler powers.* It was granted to him 40 Eliz. Anno Dom. 1598. Under this patent William Barley printed most of the music books which were published during the time that it continued in force.

The style of Morley may be judged of by the following composition, which is the fourteenth of his madrigals to four voices, published in 1594 :—

* Vide ante page 456.

THOMAS MORLEY.

## CHAP. CI.

WILLIAM BATHE, a person scarce known to the world as a writer on music, was nevertheless the author of a book with this title : ' A brief intro-
' duction to the true art of musicke, wherein are set
' downe exact and easie rules for such as seeke but to
' know the trueth, with arguments and their solutions,
' for such as seeke also to know the reason of the
' trueth : which rules be meanes whereby any by his
' owne industrie may shortly, easily, and regularly
' attaine to all such thinges as to this arte doe belong :
' to which otherwise any can hardly attaine without
' tedious difficult practice, by meanes of the irregular
' order now used in teaching, lately set forth by
' William Bathe, student at Oxenford. Imprinted
' at London by Abel Jeffes, dwelling in Sermon-lane
' neere Paules Chaine, anno 1584.' Small oblong quarto, black letter.

The authors of the Biographia Britannica, adding their own laborious researches to a few memorials in the Athen. Oxon. have given a much more satisfactory account than could be expected of this obscure person, for his name does not once occur in any treatise extant on the subject of music. The account they give of him is that he was born in Dublin anno 1564 ; that he was descended from a considerable family, who, what by rebellions, extravagance of heirs, and other misfortunes, were reduced to straight circumstances. They say of this William that he was of a sullen saturnine temper, and disturbed in his mind that his family was fallen from its ancient spendour ; that he was educated under a Popish school-master, but removed to Oxford, where he studied several years with indefatigable industry, but in what college, or whether he ever attained to any academical honours, Wood himself could never learn. That growing weary of the heresy, as he usually called the protestant faith professed in Eng-land, he quitted the nation and his religion together, and in the year 1596 was initiated amongst the Jesuits. That having spent some time among the Jesuits in Flanders, he travelled into Italy, and completed his studies at Padua, from whence he passed into Spain, being appointed to govern the Irish seminary at Salamanca. That at length taking a journey to Madrid to transact some business of his order, he died there on the seventeenth day of June, 1614, and was buried in the Jesuits' convent of that city.

In the estimation of his brethren he was a man of learning ; and Wood says of him that he had a most ardent zeal for the gaining of souls ; and that though of a temper not very sociable, he was much esteemed by those of his own persuasion for his extraordinary virtues and good qualities. He was the author of several books, the titles whereof are given in the Biographia Britannica.

His Introduction to Music is dedicated to his uncle Gerald Fitzgerald, earl of Kildare, and that for reasons which seem to betray somewhat of that saturnine temper above ascribed to him, for in it he thus expresses himself, ' being rhetorically persuaded
' to graunt to the publishing thereof, I forbore to do it
' till I had considered two thinges, whereof the one
' was the worthinesse of the matter. The other, the
' feeding of the common affections. But for the
' worthinesse, I thought it not to be doubted, seeing
' heere one set forth a booke of a hundred mery
' tales ; * another of the battaile between the spider
' and the fly ;† another De Pugnis Porcorum ;
' another of a monster born at London the second
' of January, hedded lyke a horse and bodied lyke
' a man, with other such lyke fictions ; and thinking
' this matter then some of these to be more worthy.
' As for the other, wich is to feede the common
' affections of the patient learned, I doubt not but it
' may soon be ; but he that wil take in hand to serve
' to the purpose of every petty pratler, may as soone
' by sprinckling water suffice the drienes of the earth,
' as bring his purpose to passe.'

The preface was doubtless intended by the author to recommend his book to the reader's perusal, but he has chosen to bespeak his good opinion rather by decrying the ignorance of teachers, and the method of instruction practised by them, than by pointing out any peculiar excellencies in his own work. He says that many have consumed a whole year before they could come at the knowledge of song only, but that he had taught it in less space than a month.

But how highly soever the author might value his own work, he thought proper some years after the first publication to write it over again in such sort,

* The author here means a translation of Les Centes Nouvelles nou-velles, which is mentioned by Ames to have been printed about this time. The original was published in 1455, by Louis XI. of France, then dauphin, during his retreat from his father's court to that of the duke of Burgundy.

† The Parable of the Spider and the Fly, quarto, 1556, in old English verse, by John Heywood.

as hardly to retain a single paragraph of the former edition. This latter edition was printed by Thomas Este, without a date, with the title of 'A brief Introduction to the skill of song: concerning the 'practice, set forth by William Bathe, gentleman.'

And here again the author, according to his wonted custom, censures the musicians of his time, and magnifies the efficacy of his own rules; for mark the modesty of his preface:—

'Olde musitions laid downe for song, manifold 'and crabbed confuse tedious rules, as for example; 'though there be in all but six names, UT RE MI FA 'SOL LA, having amongst them an easie order, yet 'could not they by rule declare, whether of these 'should be attributed to everie note, unlesse they 'had first framed the long ladder or skale of gamut, 'to which some added, thinking the ladder too short; 'some hewed off a peece, thinking it too long. Then 'would they have the learner be as perfect in coming 'down backward, as in going up forward, lest in his 'practice he should fall and break his necke. Then 'must he learne GAMUT in rule, A RE in space, ♮ MI 'in rule, C FA UT in space, &c. Then must he 'know GAMUT, how many cleves, how many notes. 'A RE how many notes, &c. Then must he know '♮ quadrij, proper-chant, and b mul, RE in A RE, 'whereby UT in C FA UT, whereby MI in A LA MI RE, 'whereby, &c. And when all have done, after their 'long circumstances of time, whereby they should be 'often driven to millibi, for notes standing in diverse 'places of gamut have names that the place where 'they stand comprehend not. Touching all the 'prolixe circumstances and needlesse difficulties that 'they use, it loathes me greatly that heere I should 'write them: and much more would it grieve the 'reader to learne them. Also many things are used 'in song for which they give no rules at all, but 'committed them to dodge at it, harke to it, and 'harpe upon it.'

The precepts for singing contained in this book are divided into ante rules, and post rules; the ante rules respect Quantity, Time, and Tune; the post rules, Naming, Quantity, Time and Tune; and, from the manifold objections of the author to the usual method of teaching, a stranger would expect that these were not only better calculated for the purpose of instruction, but also discoveries of his own; but nothing like this appears: his rule of teaching is the scale with the six syllables, and the cliffs of Guido; the mutations, the stumbling-block of learners, he leaves as he found them; and, in short, it may be truly said that not one of the 'prolixe 'circumstances or needlesse difficulties' that others use in teaching, is by him removed, obviated, or lessened: nevertheless, as a proof of the efficacy of his rules, he produces the following instances:—

'In a moneth and leese I instructed a child about 'the age of eight yeares to sing a good number of 'songs, difficult crabbed songs, to sing at the first 'sight, to be so indifferent for all parts, alterations, 'cleves, flats and sharpes, that he could sing a part 'of that kinde of which he never learned any song, 'which child for strangeness was brought before the 'lord deputie of Ireland to be heard sing, for there

'were none of his age, though he were longer at it, 'nor any of his time (though he were elder) known 'before these rules to sing exactly.

'There was another who by dodging at it, heark-'ning to it, and harping upon it, could never be 'brought to tune sharps aright, who so soone as hee 'heard these rules set downe for the same, could tune 'them sufficiently well. I have taught diverse others 'by these rules in lesse than a moneth what myselfe 'by the olde, obtained not in more than two yeares. 'Diverse other proofes I might recite which heere 'as needlesse I doe omit, because the thing will shew 'itselfe. Diverse have repented in their age that 'they were not put to sing in their youth; but 'seeing that by these rules, a good skill may be had 'in a moneth, and the wayes learned in four or five 'dayes: none commeth too late to learne, and 'especially if this saying be true: That no man 'is so olde but thinketh he may live one yeere 'longer. As Aristotle in setting forth his pre-'dicaments saw many things requisite to be entreated 'of, and yet unfit to be mixed with his treatise; he 'therefore made ante predicaments and post predica-'ments: so I for the same cause, desirous to abolish 'confusion, have added to my rules, ante rules and 'post rules. Vale.'

As to these rules, the best that can be said of them is that there is nothing like them to be met with in any writer on music, and of the perspicuity of his style let this, which is the first chapter of his post rules of song, as he calls them suffice for an example.

'The exceptions from the order of ascention and 'descention are diversely used according to the 'diversitie of place, and accordingly they are to 'be given, for each order in naming seemeth best to 'them that have been brought up withall.

'D is sometimes used in old songs as a cleve, and 'putteth UT down to the fifth place.

'In Italy as I understand, they change UT into 'SOL: in England they change RE into LA, when the 'next removing note before or after be under.'

The following is the third chapter of this ingenious author's post rules, and respects the singing of hard proportions:—

'In timing hard proportions that go odding, many 'take care only of the whole stroke, wholly kept 'without dividing it to the going up and then down 'agayne of the hand.

'Some keepe semibreefe time, as sufficient easie of 'itselfe, and do not divide it into minim time.'

'Three minim time is more difficult, and therefore 'some do divide it into minim time.'

But attend to a notable invention of this author for the measuring of time, and see what clear and intelligible terms he has chosen to express his meaning.

'Take a stick of a certaine length, and a stone of 'a certaine weight, hold the stick standing upon an 'end of some table: see you have upon the stick 'divers marks: hold the stone up by the side of the 'stick, then as you let fall the stone, instantly begin to 'sing one note, and just with the noyse that it maketh 'upon the table, begin another note, and as long 'as thou holdest the first note, so long hold the rest, 'and let that note be thy cratchet or thy minim, &c.,

' as thou seest cause, and thus maist thou measure
' the verie time itselfe that thou keepest, and know
' whether thou hast altered it or not.'

*The account above given affords occasion to
mention a musician who lived about this time,
equally obscure, of the name of Whythorne, the
author of a book, of which the following (taking it
from the Tenor Part) is the title, and a very
quaint one it is:* ' *Tenor of songs for 5 voices,
' composed and made by Thomas Whythorne, gent.
' The which songs be of sundry sorts, that is to say,
' some long, some short, some hard, some easie to be
' songe, and some plesant or mery: so that accord-
' ing to the skill of the singers (not being musitians)
' and disposition or delite of the hearers they may
' here finde Songes for their contentation and
' liking.* ꝺ *Now newly published A.D.* 1571,
' ꝺ *At the end of this book ye shall find an ad-
' vertisement concerning the use of the flats and
' sharps that are set with this musicke, also of the
' most needful faults to be amended that are escaped
' in the printing these five Books.'* *The book is of
an oblong form, printed in a neat black letter type
by old John Day. Whythorne's name does not
occur in any list of the musicians of this country,
and it is inferred that he attained to no degree of
eminence in his profession.*

JOHN MUNDY, organist, first of Eton college, and
afterwards of the free chapel of Windsor in queen
Elizabeth's reign, was educated under his father
William Mundy, one of the gentlemen of the chapel,
and an eminent composer. In 1586, at the same
time with Bull, Mundy the son was admitted to the
degree of bachelor of music at Oxford; and at the
distance of almost forty years after was created
doctor in the same faculty in that university. Wood
speaks of a William Mundy, who was a noted
musician, and hath composed several divine services
and anthems, the words of which may be seen in
Clifford's collection; this person was probably no
other than Mundy the father. John Mundy composed madrigals for five voices in the collection
entitled the Triumphs of Oriana, before spoken of,
and of which a particular account will be given
hereafter; was the author of a work entitled ' Songs
' and Psalmes composed into 3, 4, and 5 parts, for
' the use and delight of all such as either love or
' learne musicke,' printed in 1594. An excellent
musician undoubtedly he was, and, as far as can be
judged by the words he has chosen to exercise his
talent on, a religious and modest man, resembling in
this respect Bird. Wood says he gave way to fate
in 1630, and was buried in the cloister adjoining to
the chapel of St. George at Windsor.

## CHAP. CII.

THOMAS WEELKES, organist of Winchester, and,
as it should seem, afterwards of Chichester, was the
author of Madrigals to 3, 4, 5, and 6 voices, printed
in 1597. He also published in 1598 ' Ballatts and
' madrigals to five voices, with one to six voices ;'
and in 1600 ' Madrigals of six parts apt for the viols
' and voices.' Walther in his Lexicon mentions
that a monk of the name of Aranda published a
madrigal of Weelkes in a collection of his own
printed at Helmstadt in the year 1619. A madrigal
of his for six voices is published in the Triumphs of
Oriana. He also composed services and anthems,
which are well known and much esteemed. An anthem of his ' O Lord grant the king a long life,' is
printed in Barnard's collection.

There is extant also a work entitled ' Ayeres or
' phantasticke spirites for three voices, made and newly
' published by Thomas Weelkes gentleman of his
' majesties chapell, Bachelar of musicke, and Organest
' of the Cathedral church of Chichester.' Lond. 1608.

This collection contains also a song for six voices
entitled ' A remembrance of my friend M. Thomas
' Morley.'

The following most excellent madrigal of Weelkes
is the eleventh in the collection published by him
in 1597:—

THOMAS WEELKES.

By the Fasti Oxon. it appears that in 1602 William Weelkes of New College, Oxon. was admitted to the degree of bachelor; and Wood makes it a question whether the register of the university might not mistake the name of William, for that of Thomas Weelkes, which, considering the relation between New College and Winchester college, it is more than probable he did.

GILES FARNABY of Christ-Church college, Oxford, was in 1592 admitted bachelor of music. He was of Truro in Cornwall, and nearly related to Thomas Farnabie, the famous school master of Kent: there are extant of his composition, Canzonets to 4 voices, with a song of eight parts. Lond. 1598. A few of the Psalm-tunes in Ravenscroft's Collection, Lond. 1633, that is to say, the three additional parts to the tenor or plain-song, which is the ancient church tune, are of Farnaby's composition.

JOHN MILTON, the father of our celebrated epic poet, though not so by profession, was a musician, and a much more excellent one than perhaps will be imagined. He was born at Milton near Halton and Thame, in Oxfordshire, and, by the advice of a friend of the family, became a scrivener, and followed that business in a shop in Bread-street, London,* having for his sign the spread eagle, the device or coat-armour of the family. Under whom, or by what means he acquired a knowledge of music, the accounts that are given of him are silent, but that he was so eminently skilled in it as to be ranked among the first masters of his time there are proofs irrefragable.† *His son, in a Latin poem entitled "Ad Patrem," celebrates his skill in music; and in the following lines thereof, says of his father and himself, that the attributes of Phœbus, Music and Poetry, were divided between them:—*

'*Ipse volens Phœbus se dispertire duobus*
'*Altera dona mihi, dedit altera dona parenti,*
'*Dividuum que Deum genitor que puerque tenemus.*'

Among the Psalm-tunes composed into four parts by sundry authors, and published by Thomas Ravenscroft in 1633, there are many, particularly that common one called York tune, with the name John Milton; the tenor part of this tune is so well known, that within memory half the nurses in England were used to sing it by way of lullaby; and the chimes of many country churches have played it six or eight times in four and twenty hours from time immemorial. In the Triumphs of Oriana is a madrigal for five voices, composed by John Milton, and in a collection of musical airs and songs for voices and instruments entitled 'The Teares or 'lamentations of a sorrowful soule,' composed by Bird, Bull, Orlando Gibbons, Dowland, Ferabosco, Coperario, Weelkes, Wilbye, in short, by most of the great masters of the time, and set forth by Sir William Leighton, knight, one of the gentlemen pensioners in 1614, are several songs for five voices by John Milton, and among the rest, this :—

* The word scrivener anciently signified a mere copyist. Chaucer rebukes his amanuensis by the name of Adam Scrivenere. The writing of deeds and charters, making service-books, and copying manuscripts, was one of the employments of the regular clergy. After the dissolution of religious houses, the business of a scrivener became a lay profession; and 14 Jac. a company of scriveners was incorporated, about which time they betook themselves to the writing of wills, leases, and such other assurances as required but little skill in the law to prepare. It was at this time a reputable, and, if we may judge from the circumstances of the elder Milton, and the education which he gave his children, a lucrative profession; but after the fire of London the emoluments of it were greatly encreased by the multiplicity of business which that accident gave occasion to. Francis Kirkman the bookseller was put apprentice to a scrivener, and, in the account of his life, entitled The Unlucky Citizen, he relates that almost all the business of the city in making leases, mortgages, and assignments, and procuring money on securities of ground and houses, was transacted by these men, who hence assumed the name of money scriveners. The furniture of a scrivener's shop was a sort of pew for the master, desks for the apprentices, and a bench for the clients to sit on till their turn came to be dispatched. The following jest may serve to explain the manner in which this business was carried on: A country fellow passing along Cheapside, stopped to look in at a scrivener's shop, and seeing no wares exposed to sale, asked the apprentice, the only person in it, what they sold there? Loggerheads, answered the lad. By my troth, says the countryman, 'you must have 'a roaring trade then, for I see but one left in the shop.'

† We are told by Phillips, in his account of his uncle Milton, that he also was skilled in music. Mr. Fenton in his life of him adds that he played on the organ; and there can be but little reason to suppose, con-

sidering that he had his education in London, viz., in St. Paul's school, that he had his instruction in music from any other person than his father. From many passages in his poems it appears that Milton the younger had a deep sense of the power of harmony over the human mind. This in the Il Penseroso—

'But let my due feet never fail
'To walk the studious cloisters pale,
'And love the high embowed roof,
'With antique pillars massy proof,
'And storied windows richly dight,
'Casting a dim religious light.
'There let the pealing organ blow,
'To the full-voic'd choir below,
'In service high and anthems clear,
'As may with sweetness, through mine ear
'Dissolve me into extasies,
'And bring all Heav'n before mine eyes.'

shews that however he might object to choral service as a matter of discipline, he was not proof against that enthusiastic devotion which it has a tendency to excite. It may here be remarked that the lines above quoted present to the reader's imagination a view of an ancient Gothic cathedral, and call to his recollection such ideas as may be supposed to possess the mind during the performance of the solemn choral service; and it is probable that the poet became thus impressed in his youth by his frequent attendance at the cathedral of St. Paul, which was near his school, and in his father's neighbourhood, where the service was more solemn than it is now, and which cathedral, till it was destroyed by the fire of London, had perhaps the most venerable and awful appearance of any edifice of the kind in the world.

JOHN MILTON.

And lastly, it is said in the life of Milton the son, written by his nephew Edward Phillips, and prefixed to a translation of some of his Latin letters of state, printed in 1694, that Milton the father composed an In Nomine of no fewer than forty parts, for which he was rewarded by a Polish prince, to whom he presented it, with a golden medal and chain.*

## CHAP. CIII.

JOHN COPERARIO, a celebrated artist on the viol da gamba, and a good composer for that instrument, and also for the lute, was in great reputation about the year 1600. He excelled in the composition of fantasias for viols in many parts; he taught music to the children of James the First; and under him prince Charles attained to a considerable degree of proficiency on the viol; some of his vocal compositions are to be found in Sir William Leighton's collection, mentioned in the preceding article, and of

his fantasias there are innumerable in manuscript. He, in conjunction with Nicholas Laniere and others, composed songs in a masque written by Dr. Thomas Campion, on occasion of the marriage of Carr earl of Somerset and the lady Frances Howard, the divorced countess of Essex, and presented in the banquetting-room at Whitehall on St. Stephen's night, 1614. Mr. Fenton, in his notes on Waller, on what authority he does not mention, says that Henry Lawes having been educated under him, introduced a softer mixture of Italian airs than before had been practised in our nation, from which, and from his giving him the appellation of Signor, he seems to intimate that he was an Italian: but the fact is that he was an Englishman, and named Cooper, who having spent much of his time in Italy, Italianized his name to Coperario, and was called so ever after. Coperario composed fantasias for viols to a great number, which are extant in manuscript only. His printed works are, the songs composed by him in conjunction with Laniere on occasion of the above-mentioned marriage, and these that follow:—

'Funeral Teares for the death of the Right
'Honorable the Earle of Devonshire, figured in
'seaven songes, whereof six are so set forth that
'the wordes may be exprest by a treble voice alone
'to the lute and base viol, or else that the meane
'part may be added, if any shall affect more fulnesse

* A golden medal and chain was the usual gratuity of princes to men of eminence in any of the faculties, more especially law, physic, poetry, and music. Orlando de Lasso is always represented in paintings and engravings with this ornament about his neck, as are Matthiolus, Baudius, Sennertus, Erycius Puteanus, and many others. It seems that the medal and chain once bestowed as a testimony of princely favour, was ever after a part of the dress of the person thus honoured, at least on public occasions. So lately as the beginning of the present century the emperor Joseph I. presented Antonio Lotti of Venice with a gold chain, as a compliment for dedicating to him a book of Duetti Terzetti, &c. of his composition, in which was contained the famous madrigal 'In una Siepe ombrosa.' Letters from the Academy of ancient Music at London to Signor Antonio Lotti of Venice, 1732.

'of parts. The seaventh is made in forme of a dia-
'logue, and cannot be sung without two voices.
'Invented by John Coperario. Pius piè   Fol.
Lond. 1606.

'Songs of Mourning, bewailing the untimely
'death of prince Henry, worded by Thomas Cam-
'pion, and set forth to bee sung with one voice to
'the lute or violl by John Coperario.' Fol. Lond. 1613.

ELWAY BEVIN, a man eminently skilled in the knowledge of practical composition, flourished towards the
end of queen Elizabeth's reign. He was of Welsh
extraction, and had been educated under Tallis, upon
whose recommendation it was that on the third day
of June, 1589, he was sworn in, gentleman extraordinary of the chapel, from whence he was expelled
in 1637, it being discovered that he adhered to the
Romish communion. He was also organist of Bristol
cathedral, but forfeited that employment at the same
time with his place in the chapel. Child, afterwards
doctor, was his scholar. It is worthy of remark that
although Wood has been very careful in recording
eminent musicians, as well those of Cambridge as of
Oxford, the name of Bevin does not once occur in
either the Athenæ or Fasti Oxonienses. One of the
reasons for his care in preserving the memory of men
of this faculty was that himself was a passionate lover
of music, and a performer, and Bevin's merits were
such as intitled him to an eulogium, so that it is
difficult to account for this omission. The above
memoir however will in some measure help to
supply it. He has composed sundry services, some
of which are printed in Barnard's collection, and
a few anthems.

Before Bevin's time the precepts for the composition
of canon were known to few. Tallis, Bird, Waterhouse,
and Farmer, were eminently skilled in this most abstruse part of musical practice. Every canon as given
to the public, was a kind of enigma. Compositions
of this kind were sometimes exhibited in the form of
a cross, sometimes in that of a circle : there is now
extant one resembling a horizontal sun-dial ; and the
resolution as it was called of a canon, which was the
resolving it into its elements, and reducing it into
score, was deemed a work of almost as great difficulty
as the original composition ; but Bevin, with a view
to the improvement of students, generously communicated the result of many years study and experience in a treatise which is highly commended by
all who have taken occasion to speak of it.

This book was published in quarto, 1631, and
dedicated to Goodman, bishop of Gloucester, with
the following title :—' A briefe and short instruction
'of the art of musicke, to teach how to make discant
'of all proportions that are in use : Very necessary
'for all such as are desirous to attain to knowledge
'in the art ; and may by practice, if they can sing,
'soone be able to compose three, four, and five parts,
'and also to compose all sorts of canons that are
'usuall, by these directions of two or three parts in
'one upon the plain-song.'

The rules contained in this book for composition in
general are very brief ; but for the composition of
canon there are in it a great variety of examples of

almost all the possible forms in which it is capable
of being constructed, even to the extent of sixty
parts. In the course of his work the author makes
use of only the following plain-song—

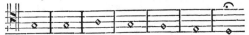

as the basis for the several examples of canon contained in his book, and it answers through a great
variety of canons, following at the stated distances of
a crochet, a minim, a semibreve, a breve, and three
minims, by augmentation and diminution, rectè et
retro and per arsin et thesin of three in one, four in
two, in the diatessaron and subdiatessaron, diapente
and subdiapente, and at various other intervals. But
what must be matter of amazement to every one
acquainted with the difficulties that attend this species
of composition is, that these few simple notes appear
virtually to contain in them all those harmonies which,
among a great variety of others, the following composition of this author is contrived to illustrate :—

CANON OF FIVE PARTS IN TWO, RECTE ET
RETRO ; ET PER ARSIN ET THESIN.

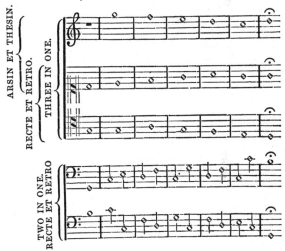

The author seems to have been a devout, but, in
some degree, a superstitious man, for speaking of
a canon of three parts in one, he makes use of these
words :—

'A Canon of three in one hath resemblance to the
'Holy Trinity, for as they are three distinct parts
'comprehended in one. The leading part hath
'reference to the Father, the following part to the
'Sonne, the third to the Holy Ghost.'

THOMAS BATESON, an excellent vocal composer,
was about the year 1600 organist of the cathedral
church of Chester. Wood says he was a person
esteemed very eminent in his profession, especially
after the publication of his English madrigals to
3, 4, 5, and 6 voices. About 1618 he became
organist and master of the children of the cathedral
church of the blessed Trinity in Dublin, and in the
university of that city it is supposed he obtained the
degree of bachelor of music. The following is one
of his madrigals for three voices :—

THOMAS BATESON.

THOMAS TOMKINS was of a family that seems to have produced more musicians than any in England. His father was Thomas Tomkins, Chanter of the choir of Gloucester, who discovering in his son a propensity to music, put him under the care of Bird, by whose instructions he so profited, that for his merits he was made a gentleman of the chapel royal, and afterwards organist thereof: some years after this he became organist of the cathedral church at Worcester, and composed songs of 3, 4, 5, and 6 parts, printed at London without a date, but conjectured to have been published before the year 1600. He was also the author of a work in ten books, intitled 'Musica Deo sacra et Ecclesiæ Anglicanæ,' consisting of anthems, hymns, and other compositions adapted to the church service. The words of others of his compositions of this kind may be seen in the collection of James Clifford before mentioned. The same James Clifford had what Wood calls a set of vocal church-music of four and five parts in manuscript, composed by Thomas Tomkins, which he gave to the collection of music in the library of Magdalen college, Oxford. Some of the madrigals in the Triumphs of Oriana were composed by Thomas Tomkins, the subject of the present article. The time both of his birth and death are uncertain, as are also the particular times when his works were severally published; all that can be said touching the time when he flourished is, that he was a scholar of Bird, that he was admitted to his bachelor's degree in 1607, being then of Magdalen college, and that he

was living, as Wood relates,* after the grand rebellion broke out. He had a son named Nathaniel, a prebendary of Worcester, and several brethren, among whom were Giles, organist of the cathedral church of Salisbury; John, organist of St. Paul's cathedral, and a gentleman of the chapel;† and Nicholas, one of the gentlemen of the privy-chamber to king Charles I., a person well skilled in the practice of music.

NICHOLAS LANIERE, LANIER, or LANEARE *(a Portrait),* for in all these ways is his name spelt, a musician of eminence in his time, though he lived and died in England, was born in Italy in the year 1568. He was a painter and an engraver, which two latter professions have entitled him to a place in the Anecdotes of Painting in England, published by Mr. Walpole, who has nevertheless considered him as a musician, and has given a brief but curious account of him.

During the reign of James I. the household musicians, those of the chapel, and many others of

* Fasti Oxon, vol. I. col. 176.

† In the old cathedral of St. Paul was the following inscription in 'memory of him :--Johannes Tomkins, Musicæ Baccalaureus, Organista 'sui temporis celeberrimus, postquam Capellæ regali, per annos duo-'decim, huic autem Ecclesiæ per novemdecem sedulo inserviisset, ad 'cœlestem chorum migravit, Septembris 27, Anno Domini, 1638. 'Ætatis suæ 52. Cujus desiderium mœrens uxor hoc testatur Mar-'more.' Dugd. Hist. St. Paul's Cath. edit. 1658. *Of this person Wood says, he was in high esteem for his admirable knowledge in the theoretical and practical part of his faculty. Among the poems of Phineas Fletcher, (the author of the " Purple Island,") is one in which, by the name of Thomalin he is celebrated, for the sweetness of his musical strains, with a tender reproof for his preferring court enjoyments to the pleasures of rural life ; and it is highly probable that Fletcher meant to characterise him in the second, sixth, and last of his piscatory eclogues, in each of which Thomalin is interlocutor.*

eminence, whom the patronage of Elizabeth had produced, were neglected, and very little of the royal favour was extended to any besides Laniere and Coperario; and for this it will not be difficult to assign a reason : the one was an Italian by birth, and the other had lived in Italy till his style, and even his very name, were so Italianized, that he was in general taken for a native of that country : these men brought into England the Stylo Recitativo, as it is called in the masque mentioned by Mr. Walpole, and which had then lately been invented by Jacopo Peri, and Giulio Caccini, and improved by Claudio Monteverde.

The masque at Lord Hay's for the entertainment of the Baron de Tour, in Ben Johnson's works, was, as therein is mentioned, composed by Laniere solely; but at a solemnity of a different kind, the infamous nuptials of Carr earl of Somerset with the lady Frances Howard, the divorced countess of Essex, he and Coperario lent their joint assistance, for in a masque, written by Dr. Thomas Campion and performed in the banquetting room at Whitchall on St. Stephen's night, 1614, on occasion of that marriage, and printed in the same year, their names occur as the composers of the music. The masquers were the duke of Lenox, the earls of Pembroke, Dorset, Salisbury, Montgomery ; the lords Walden, Scroope, North, and Hayes; Sir Thomas, Sir Henry, and Sir Charles Howard.

Many songs of Laniere are to be met with in collections published in the time of Charles I. but they seem to have little to recommend them.

An admirable portrait of himself, painted by his own hand, is yet in the music-school at Oxford, an engraving from which is inserted in the Appendix : at his right hand is a skull, in the mouth whereof is a label, containing a canon of his composition.

GEORGE FEREBE, master of arts of Magdalen college, Oxford, 1595, minister of Bishop's Cannings, Wilts, was a native of Gloucestershire, and well skilled in music. Wood, in the Fasti Oxon. vol. I. Col. 150, has given a curious account of him, which is here inserted in his own words :—' This person ' did instruct divers young men of his parish in the ' faculty of music, till they could either play or sing ' their parts. In the year 1613, Qu. Anne, the royal ' consort of K. James I. made her abode for some ' weeks in the city of Bath, purposely for the use of ' the waters there, in which time he composed a song ' of four parts, and instructed his scholars to sing it ' perfectly, as also to play a lesson or two which he ' had composed, upon their wind-instruments : on ' the 11th June, the same year, the queen in her ' return from Bath did intend to pass over the downes ' at Wensdyke, within the parish of Bishop's Cannings. ' Of which Ferebe having timely notice, dressed him- ' self in the habit of an old bard, and caused his ' scholars whom he had instructed, to be cloathed ' in shepherds' weeds. The queen having received ' notice of these people, she with her retinue made ' a stand at Wensdyke, whereupon these musicians ' drawing up to her, played a most admirable lesson ' on their wind-instruments ; which being done, they

' sang their lesson of four parts with double voices, ' the beginning of which was this :—

'Shine, O thou sacred shepherds' star
' On silly shepherd swains, &c.

' which being well performed also, the bard concluded ' with an epilogue, to the great liking and content of ' the queen and her company. Afterwards he was ' sworn chaplain to his majesty, and was ever after ' much valued for his ingenuity.'

## CHAP. CIV.

THE account herein before immediately given contains the succession of theoretic and practical musicians down to the end of the sixteenth century, at the commencement whereof, music, not to speak of that kind of it which was appropriated to divine service, from being the domestic recreation of private persons, and the entertainment of select companies, was introduced into the theatre, and made an auxiliary to dramatic performances. But before the history of this union and the subsequent progress of practical music can be given, it is necessary to review the past period, and ascertain the state of music in general at the close of it.

The compositions peculiar to the church, not to distinguish between one and the other of them, were, as has been related, the Mass, the Motet, the Anthem, and the Hymns for various occasions, such as the Stabat Mater, Salve Regina, A Solis ortu, Alma Redemptoris Mater, Ave Regina Cœlorum, and others to be found in the Romish Missal, the Antiphonary, and the Breviary ; the only species of vocal harmony calculated for private amusement hitherto mentioned, were the Madrigal, the Canon, and the Catch or Round, all which required a plurality of voices ; and of instrumental, the Fantazia for vio s and other instruments to a certain number. But besides these, the names of sundry other kinds of vocal and instrumental harmony and melody occur in Morley's Introduction, and other musical tracts, of which it is here proper to take notice ; and first of the Canzone.

The Canzone is a composition somewhat resembling, but less elaborate than the madrigal. It admits of little fugues and points, and seldom exceeds three parts, though the name is sometimes given to a song for one voice. Cervantes, in Don Quizote, calls the song of Chrysostom a Canzone.

The word Canzonet is a diminutive of Canzone, and therefore means a little or short canzone or song in parts. Luca Marenzio, though he in general applied himself to more elaborate studies, Giovanni Feretti, and Horatio Vecchi, are said to have excelled in this species of composition.

The Villanella, the lightest and least artificial kind of air known in music, is a composition, as Morley says, made only for the ditty's sake, in which he adds, many perfect chords of one kind, nay even disallowances, may be taken at pleasure, suiting, as he says, a clownish music to a clownish matter. Among the sonnets of Sir Philip Sidney is one said to be written to the air of a Neapolitan villanella.

NICHOLAS LANIERE,

MASTER OF THE BAND OF MUSIC

TO HIS MAJESTY CHA. I.

*From an original Painting in the Music-School, Oxford.*

The Ballet is a tune to a ditty, and which may likewise be danced to. Morley speaks also of a kind of Ballets called FA LA's, some whereof, composed by Gastoldi, he says he had seen and it seems imitated, for there is a collection of songs of this kind by Morley in five parts.

Morley mentions many other kinds of air in practice in his time, as namely, the Pavan,* the Passamezzo, the Galliard, the Courant, the Jig, the Hornpipe, the Scottish Jig, and others. It must be noted that these were all dance-tunes, and that the difference between the one and others of them lay in the difference of measure and the number of bars of which the several strains were made to consist.

But of vocal music the madrigal appears to have been most in practice of any kind at this time, as well in England as in other countries; it was some years after this species of harmony was invented, that the English musicians applied themselves to the study of it, for Bird seems to have been the first composer of madrigals in this country; his first essay of the kind was upon two stanzas of the Orlando Furioso, 'La Verginella,' which he set for five voices, and was received with the utmost degree of approbation.

Hitherto a madrigal to any other than Italian words was a thing not known; and it seemed to be a doubt among musicians whether the words of English poetry could with any degree of propriety be made to consist with the madrigal style of musical composition, till 1583, when a certain gentleman, whose name is unknown, for his private delight, made an essay of this kind, by translating the words of some most celebrated Italian madrigals into English verse, so as thus translated they might be sung to the original notes. These came to the hands of one

Nicholas Yonge, who kept a house in London for the reception of foreign merchants and gentlemen, and he in the year 1588 published them, together with others of the same kind, with the following title :—' Musica Transalpina, Madrigales translated ' of four, five, and sixe parts, chosen out of divers ' excellent authors; with the first and second part of ' La Verginella, made by maister Bird upon two ' stanzas of Ariosto,† and brought to speak English ' with the rest, published by N. Yonge, in favour of ' such as take pleasure in music of voices.' ‡

In this collection are the first, second, and third parts of the Thyrsis of Luca Marenzio, as Peacham calls it, translated from ' Tirsi morir volea, 'Chi fa ' hoggi il mio sole,' of the same author, to ' What ' doth my pretty darling ? The ' Susann' un jour,' of Orlando de Lasso, and the Nightingale of the elder Ferabosco, celebrated also by Peacham, with a number of other well chosen compositions from the best of the Italians. It was a work in great estimation; the picture of Dr. Heather, now in the music-school, Oxford, represents him with a book in

---

* The Pavan, from Pavo a peacock, is a grave and majestic dance; the method of dancing it was anciently by gentlemen dressed with a cap and sword, by those of the long robe in their gowns, by princes in their mantles, and by ladies in gowns with long trains, the motion whereof in the dance resembled that of a peacock's tail. This dance is supposed to have been invented by the Spaniards; and its figure is given with the characters for the steps in the Orchesographia of Thoinot Arbeau. Every Pavan has its Galliard, a lighter kind of air made out of the former.

Of the Passamezzo little is to be said, except that it was a favourite air in the days of queen Elizabeth. Ligon, in his History of Barbadoes, mentions a Passamezzo Galliard which in the year 1647 a Padre in that island played to him on the lute, the very same he says with an air of that kind which in Shakespeare's Henry the Fourth was originally played to Sir John Falstaff and Doll Tearsheet by Sneak, the musician therein named. This little anecdote Ligon might have by tradition, but his conclusion that because it was played in a dramatic representation of the history of Henry the Fourth, it must be as ancient as his time, is very idle and injudicious.

The Courant, the Jig, the Hornpipe, and a variety of other airs, will be spoken of hereafter. As to Scottish jigs, and indeed Scottish tunes in general, all men know that the style and cast of them is unaccountably singular. The vulgar notion is that this singularity arises from a commixture of the primitive rude melody of that country with the more refined air of the Italians; and that David Rizzio, the minion of Mary, queen of Scots, was not only the author of this improvement, but that many of the most admired Scottish tunes yet in use are of his composition. This is highly improbable, seeing that none of the writers on music take the least notice of him as a composer. Buchanan says that he was sent for into Scotland to entertain the queen in the performance of madrigals, in which he sang the bass part. Melvil says the same, and adds that he had a fine hand on the lute. Besides all which it will hereafter be shewn that the Scottish music, so far from borrowing from it, has enriched the Italian with some peculiar graces.

Henry Peacham, the author of the Compleat Gentleman, in a humorous little tract of his intitled the Worth of a Penny, takes notice that northern or Scottish tunes were much in vogue in his time; for describing a man dejected in his mind for want of money, he says that he cannot stand still, but like one of the Tower wild beasts, is still walking from one end of his room to another, humming out some new northern tune or other. Pag. 14. And again, giving the character of one Godfrey Colton, a tailor in Cambridge, of whom he tells a pleasant story; he says he was a merry companion with his tabor and pipe, and sang all manner of northern songs before nobles and gentlemen, who much delighted in his company. Pag. 29.

---

† These two stanzas are imitated from the Carmen Nuptiale of Catullus, and are as follow :—

> ' La Verginella è simile à la Rosa ;
> ' Ch' in bel giardin sù la nativa spina,
> ' Mentre sola, e sicura si riposa,
> ' Nè greggè, nè pastor se l'avvicina ;
> ' L'aura soave, e l'alba rugiadoso,
> ' L'acqua, la terra al suo favor s'inchina :
> ' Giovani vaghi, e donne inamorate,
> ' Amano haverne, e seni, e tempie ornate.

> ' Ma non si tosto dal maerno stelo
> ' Rimossa viene, e dal suo ceppo verde ;
> ' Che, quanto havea da gli huomini, e dal cielo
> ' Favor, gratia, e bellezza, tutto perde :
> ' La vergine, che 'l fior ; di che più zelo
> ' Che de begli occhi, e de la vita, haver de' ;
> ' Lascia altrui corre ; il pregio c'hauea innanti,
> ' Perde nel cor di tutti gl' altri amanti.'
>                     ORLANDO FURIOSO, Canto Primo.

The reader will at first sight discover that the air in the Beggar's Opera, ' Virgins are like the fair flower in its lustre,' is an imitation of the above stanzas.

‡ The history of this publication is contained in the dedication of the book to Gilbert lord Talbot, son and heir to George, earl of Shrewsbury, and is to this purpose ;—

' Since I first began to keep house in this citie, it hath been no small ' comfort unto mee, that a great number of gentlemen and merchants of ' good accompt (as well of this realme as of forreine nations) have taken ' in good part such entertainment of pleasure as my poore abilitie was ' able to afford them, both by the exercise of musicke daily used in my ' house, and by furnishing them with bookes of that kinde, yeerely sent ' me out of Itaiy and other places, which being for the most part Italian ' songs, are for sweetness of aire verie well liked of all, but most in ' account with them that understand that language ; as for the rest, they ' doe either not sing them at all, or at least with little delight. And ' albeit there be some English songs lately set forth by a great maister of ' musicke, which for skill and sweetness may content the most curious, ' yet because they are not many in number, men delighted with varietie ' have wished for more of the same sort. For whose cause chiefly ' I endevoured to get into my hands all such English songs as were ' praise-worthie, and amongst others I had the hap to find in the hands of ' some of my good friends, certaine Italian madrigales, translated most ' of them five yeeres agoe by a gentleman for his private delight (as not ' long before certaine Napolitans had been Englished by a very honour-' able personage, a councellour of estate, whereof I have seen some, but ' never possessed any.) And finding the same to be singularly well liked, ' not onely of those for whose cause I gathered them ; but of many ' skilful gentlemen and other great musicians who affirmed the accent of ' the words to be well maintened, the descant not hindred (though some ' fewe notes altred) and in everie place the due decorum kept : I was so ' bolde (beeing well acquainted with the gentleman) as to entreat the ' rest, who willingly gave me such as he had (for of some he kept no ' copies) and also some other more lately done at the request of his ' particular friends. Now when the same was seen to arise to a just ' number, sufficient to furnish a great set of bookes, diverse of my ' friendes aforesaid required with great instance to have them printed, ' whereunto I was as willing as the rest, but could never obtaine the ' gentleman's consent, though I sought it by many great meanes. For ' his answer was ever, that those trifles being but an idle man's exercise, ' of an idle subject written only for private recreation, would blush to be ' seen otherwise then by twilight, much more to be brought into the ' common view of all men.' He then relates that finding that they were about to be printed surreptitiously, he ventured to publish them himself.

his hand, on the cover whereof is written MUSICA TRANSALPINI.

In 1590 another collection of this kind was published with this title, 'The first set of Italian madri- 'galls, Englished, not to the sense of the original 'dittie, but after the affection of the noate, by 'Thomas Watson gentleman. There are also heere 'inserted two excellent madrigalls of Master William 'Byrd's, composed after the Italian vaine at the request 'of the said Thomas Watson.'

This book contains, among others, those madrigals of Luca Marenzio which Peacham has pointed out as excellent, viz., 'Veggo dolce mio ben,' or 'Farewell 'cruel and unkind.' 'Cantava,' or 'Sweet singing 'Amaryllis.' Those of Bird, which he composed at the request of the publisher, are both to the same words, viz., 'This sweet and merry month of May,' the one in four, the other in six parts, and are a compliment to queen Elizabeth.

The success of these several publications excited, as it was very natural to expect it would do, an emulation in the English musicians to compose original madrigals in their own language, which were so well received, that from thenceforth those of the Italians began to be neglected.

The first collection of this kind seems to be that of Morley, published in 1594, entitled 'Madrigalls 'to foure voyces newly published, the first book.'

In 1597, N. Yonge above-mentioned, who then called himself Nicholas, published a second collection of translated madrigals with the title of Musica Transalpina, the second part.

In the same year George Kirbye published a set of English madrigals for four, five, and six voices.

In 1597 also, Thomas Weelkes before named published 'Madrigals to three, four, five, and six voices;' and in 1598 'Ballets and Madrigals to five voyces, 'with one to six voyces.'

In 1598 Morley published with English words, 'Madrigals to five voyces, selected out of the best 'approved Italian authors.'

This collection contains madrigals of Alfonso Ferabosco, Battista Mosto, Giovanni Feretti, Ruggiero Giovanelli, Horatio Vecchi, Giulio Belli, Alessandro Orologio, Luca Marenzio, Hippolito Sabino, Peter Phillips, Stephano Venturi, and Giovanni di Macque, most of which are excellent in their kind, but no mention is made of the authors of the English words; it is therefore probable that they were written by Morley himself, who had a talent for poetry sufficient for the purpose. In the dedication of the book to Sir Gervis Clifton, is this remarkable aphorism, 'Whom God loveth not, they love not musique.'

In the same year, 1598, John Wilbye, a teacher of music, and who dwelt in Austin Friars, London, published 'Madrigals to three, four, five, and six voices.' most of which are excellent; this which follows is the tenth, and is thought little inferior to the best compositions of the kind of the Italian masters :—

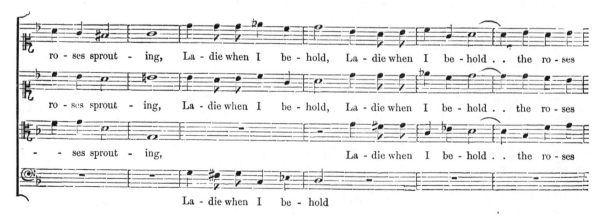

JOHN WILBYE.

The same Wilbye, in the year 1600, published 'A second set of Madrigals to 3, 4, 5, and 6 parts, 'apt both for viols and voices;' dedicated to the Lady Arabella Stuart.

## CHAP. CV.

IN 1599 JOHN BENNET published 'Madrigals to 'four voyces, being his first works.' He also composed a madrigal in the Triumphs of Oriana, and some of the songs contained in a book written by Thomas Ravenscroft, and published in 1614, entitled 'A briefe discourse of the true but neglected 'use of charact'ring the degrees by their perfection, 'imperfection, and diminution in mensurable musicke, 'against the common practice and custom of these 'times.' In the preface to which book he is styled a gentleman 'admirable for all kind of composures either in art or ayre, simple or mixt.'

Excepting the above short eulogium, we meet with no particulars relating to this person. Wood does not so much as mention him, from which circumstance alone it may not only be inferred that he was not a graduate in either university, but also that he was little known to the world in his profession. In the dedication of his book of Madrigals to Ralph Asheton, Esq. receiver of the queen's duchy revenues in the counties Palatine of Lancaster and Chester, it is hinted that the author was indebted to that gentleman both for his patronage and his education; but under what masters he received it we are at a loss to find.

The madrigals composed by Bennet, and printed in the collection above-mentioned, are seventeen in number; this which follows is the tenth of them; they are finely studied, and abound with all the graces and elegancies of vocal harmony; and it may be said of the work in general, that it is an honour to our country, and in no respect inferior to any collection of the kind published by the Italian or other foreign musicians.:—

JOHN BENNET.

JOHN FARMER, of whom mention has already been made, published in the same year, 1599, 'The first Sett of English Madrigals to four voices.' In the preface to this work the author professes to have so fully linked his music to number, as each give to other their true effect, which is to move delight; this virtue being, as he says, so singular in the Italians, as under that ensign only they hazard their honour.

The following madrigal is the first in the collection.

JOHN FARMER.

## CHAP. CVI.

The names of other composers of madrigals occur about this time, or within a few years after, the chief of whom were, Henry Youll, John Ward, Michael Este, bachelor of music, and master of the choristers in the cathedral of Lichfield, and Orlando Gibbons. And here it may be remarked, that of the authors above enumerated, some only appear to have been graduates in one or other university, or beneficed musicians in some cathedral or collegiate church ; as to the rest, the appellation assumed by them is simply that of practitioner in music. Youll and Farmer have no other adjunct to their respective names, and Bateson retained it till he acquired the degree of bachelor.

Besides the several collections of madrigals above mentioned, there is one, the title whereof is perpetually occurring in the Fasti Oxonienses. It is called the Triumphs of Oriana, and frequently in Wood's illiberal manner of expressing himself, the whole collection is called the Orianas. It seems by the work itself as if all the musicians of queen Elizabeth's time who were capable of composing, had endeavoured each to excel the other in setting a song, celebrating the beauty and virtues of their sovereign ; for to the Triumphs of Oriana it appears that the following musicians contributed, namely, Michael Este, Daniel Norcome,* John Mundy, Ellis Gibbons,† John Bennet, John Hilton,‡ George Marston,§ Richard Carleton, John Holmes,‖ Richard Nicholson,¶ Thomas Tomkins, Michael Cavendish, William Cobbold, Thomas Morley, John Farmer, John Wilbye, Thomas Hunt, Thomas Weelkes, John Milton,** George Kirbye, Robert Jones,†† John Lisley, and Edward Johnson. This collection was published by Morley with the title of 'The Triumphs of Oriana, to five and six voices, composed by divers authors. Lond. 1601.'

The occasion of this collection is said to be this : the lord high admiral, Charles Howard earl of Nottingham, was the only person who in the last illness of Elizabeth could prevail on her to go into and remain in her bed ;‡‡ and with a view to alleviate her concern for the execution of the earl of Essex, he gave for a prize-subject to the poets and musicians of the time, the beauty and accomplishments of his royal mistress, and by a liberal reward excited them severally to the composition of this work. This supposition is favoured by the circumstance of its being dedicated to the earl, and the time of its publication, which was in the very year that Essex was beheaded. There is some piece of secret history which we are yet to learn, that would enable us to account for the giving the queen this romantic name ;

* A clerk or singing-man at Windsor. Temp. Jac. I.
† Ellis Gibbons, organist of Salisbury, and brother of the famous Orlando Gibbons, mentioned hereafter.
‡ Bachelor of music, and organist of the church of St. Margaret, Westminster.
§ Mentioned in Sir Anthony Weldon's Court and Character of King James, pag. 106.
‖ Organist of Salisbury. Temp. Eliz.
¶ The first professor of music at Oxford under Dr. Heather's endowment.
** The father of the poet.
†† A famous lutenist and composer for the lute
‡‡ Vide Hist. View of the Negociations between the Courts of England and France, by Dr. Birch, pag. 208. Biogr. Brit. vol. IV. pag. 2678.

probably she was fond of it. Camden relates that a Spanish ambassador had libelled her by the name of Amadis Oriana, and for his insolence was put under a guard. Vide Rapin, vol. II. pag. 88.§§

In the reign of James I. the practice of singing madrigals declined so fast, that few, if any, collections of them were published after the year 1620, the reason of which may be, that the entertainments of his court were for the most part masques and other theatrical representations, with which music, at least that kind of it which required much skill in the composition, had little to do. The merit of these entertainments consisted either in the quaintness of the device or fable, if it may be so called, the magnificence of the scenes, the artificial construction of the machinery, or in the splendid decorations of the theatre or place of exhibition ; and it is well known that Jonson wasted much of his time in composing little interludes of this kind ; and that Inigo Jones was condemned to the task of studying decorations for them, and exercising his luxuriant invention upon no better materials than pasteboard and canvas.

Of the madrigal it has already been said, that it is a species of vocal harmony very elegant in its structure, and adapted to such poetry as was fit to be sung or uttered in the hearing of the most polite and

§§ In the Triumphs of Oriana, madrigal VIII. is the following passage:—
   'Thus Bonny Boots the birth-day celebrated
    'Of her, his lady deerest,
   'Fair Oriana which to his hart was nearest.'
And in Madrigal XXIV. this:—
   'For Bonny Boots that so aloft could fetch it,
   'Oh he is dead, and none of us can reach it.'
Again, in the first of Morley's canzonets of five and six voices, published in 1607, he is thus mentioned ;—
   'Fly love that art so sprightly,
   'To Bonny Boots uprightly,
   'And when in heaven thou meet him,
   'Say that I kindly greet him,
   'And that his Oriana
   'True widow maid still followeth Diana.'
And again his name occurs in the ninth canzonet in the same collection :—
   'Our Bonny Boots could toot it,
    'Yea and foot it,
   'Say lustie lads, who now shall Bonny Boot it ?
Bonny Boots seems to be a nick-name for some famous singer, who, because of his excellent voice, or for some other reason, had permission to call the queen his lady ; possibly the person meant might be one Mr. Hale, of whom mention is made by Sir William Segar, in his account of a solemn tilt or exercise of arms, held in the year 1590, before queen Elizabeth, in the Tilt-yard at Westminster, with emblematical representations and music, in which the above-mentioned Mr. Hale performed a part by singing the following song :—
   'My golden locks time hath to silver turn'd
   '(O time too swift, and swiftnes never ceasing)
   'My youth 'gainst age, and age at youth hath spurn'd.
   'But spurn'd in vaine ; youth waineth by encreasing,
   'Beauty, strength, youth, are flowers that fading beene,
   'Duety, faith, love, are rootes and ever greene.
   'My helmet now shall make an hive for bees,
   'And lovers songs shall turn to holy psalmes ;
   'A man at armes must now sit on his knees,
   'And feed on prayers that are old ages almes ;
   'And tho from court to cottage I depart,
   'My saint is sure of mine unspotted hart.
   'And when I sadly sit in homely cell,
   'I'll teach my swaines this carrol for a song :
   'Blest be the hearts that thinke my sovereigne well,
   'Curs'd be the soules that thinke to doe her wrong.
   'Goddesse, vouchsafe this aged man his right,
   'To be your beadsman now, that was your knight.'
Sir William Segar says of this person that he was 'her majesties 'servant, a gentleman in that arte excellent, and for his voice both 'commendable and admirable.' Treatise on Honour Military and Civill, lib. III. cap. 54. And Sir Henry Wotton in his Parallel between the Earl of Essex and the Duke of Buckingham, says that a sonnet of the earl's was upon a certain occasion sung before the queen by one Hales, in whose voice she took some pleasure. Reliquæ Wottonianæ, 8vo. 1685, page 165.

well-bred persons. Songs in this form, for three, four, and more voices, were the entertainment of persons of rank and fashion, young gentlemen and ladies, and, in a word, of the better sort.

Other kinds of vocal harmony there were, in which the humour of the words was more regarded than the goodness of the metre, justness of thought, propriety of expression, or any other the requisites of good poetry. Short poems of this kind, suited to the humours of the vulgar, were set to music in the form of canon in the unison, generally in three, and sometimes in four, five, six, and so on to many more parts. Besides which, we meet about this time with little compositions for three and four voices, called, for what reason it is not easy to say, Freemen's Songs.* The sentiments contained in these poetical compositions were in general not very favourable to good manners, for if they were not satirical, they were in general, exhortations to riot, dissipation, or incentives to lewdness, to drinking, and smoking tobacco, in a vein of humour adapted to a tavern or an ale-house.

Many ancient songs of this kind, set in the form of canon in the unison, or, as it was otherwise called, round, or catch, where the words of one part fell in with those of the other, are yet extant, so finely suited with apt melody and delightful harmony, that the best musicians of later times have in vain endeavoured to equal them.

Much of the humours and manners of the people of this country at different periods, is to be collected from vulgar and favorite song ballads. These were of various kinds, namely, amorous ditties, of which specimens have already been given, rhyming histories, and popular stories, some founded in truth, others mere fiction. Of these a collection is extant in the library of Magdalen college, Cambridge, made by Samuel Pepys, Esq. secretary of the admiralty in the reigns of Charles and James II.; but the most curious of the kind is that lately given to the world by the Rev. Dr. Thomas Percy, entitled Reliques of ancient English Poetry, which is not more valuable for its contents, than for the essays contained in it on the subjects of the ancient English minstrels, ancient metrical romances, the origin of the English stage, and the metre of Pierce Plowman's Vision.

To this latter collection the inquisitive reader is referred for the history of this species of poetry during a period of nearly three hundred years. All that is necessary to remark in this place is, that excepting ancient songs and catches, some of which will hereafter be inserted, the ballads above-mentioned, with many others of the like kind, were the entertainment of the common people : they were till the beginning of this century, and for about ten years after, printed on the old black letter type ; and were originally vended by persons who were capable of singing them to some well-known tune, who, in

London at least, did not wander about the streets for that purpose, but sold them in stalls.

Who was the author of the collection entitled Robinhood's Garland, no one has yet pretended to guess. As some of the songs have in them more of the spirit of poetry than others, it is probable it is the work of various hands ; that it has from time to time been varied and adapted to the phrase of the times is certain.

The legend of Robinhood is of great antiquity, for in the Vision of Pierce Plowman, written by Robert Langland or Longland, a secular priest, and a fellow of Oriel college, and who flourished in the reign of Edward III. is this passage :—

> I cannot perfitly my Pater nofter, as the prift it fingeth,
> I can rimes of Robenhod and Randal of Chefter,
> But of our Lorde or our Lady I lerne nothyng at all.

yet Ames takes no notice of any early impression of his songs. He mentions one only, entitled ' King Edward, Robinhood, and Little John,' printed by Caxton, or at least in his house, about the year 1500 ; the last edition of his Garland of any worth is that of 1719.

The history of this popular hero is but little known, and all the scattered fragments concerning him, could they be brought together, would fall far short of satisfying such an enquirer as none but real and well-authenticated facts will content. We must take his story as we find it. Stow in his Annals gives the following account of him :—

' In this time (about the year 1190, in the reign ' of Richard I.) were many robbers and outlawes, ' among which Robin Hood and little John, renowned ' theeves, continued in woods, despoyling and robb- ' ing the goods of the rich. They killed none but ' such as would invade them ; or by resistance for ' their own defence.

' The saide Robert entertained an hundred tall ' men and good archers, with such spoiles and thefts ' as he got, upon whom four hundred (were they ever ' so strong) durst not give the onset. He suffered ' no woman to be oppressed, violated, or otherwise ' molested : poore mens goods he spared, abundantlie ' relieving them with that which by theft he gat ' from abbies, and the houses of rich earles : whom ' Maior (the historian) blameth for his rapine and ' theft ; but of all theeves he affirmeth him to be the ' prince and the most gentle theefe.' Annals, pag. 159.

Bishop Latimer, in his Sermons, tells the following story relating to him :—

' I came once myselfe to a place, riding on a journey ' homeward from London, and I sent word over ' night into the town that I would preach there in ' the morning, because it was holyday, and methought ' it was an holidayes worke ; the church stoode in ' my way, and I took my horse and my company ' and went thither (I thought I should have found ' a great companye in the church) and when I came ' there the church doore was fast locked, I taryed ' there halfe an houre and more, and at last the key ' was found, and one of the parish comes to me and ' sayes Syr, this is a busie day with us. We cannot ' heare you, it is Robinhoodes daye. The parish are

---

* In a book entitled ' Deuteromelia : or the second part of Music's Melodie,' printed in 1609, are many of this kind. However difficult it may now be to account for this term, it was formerly well understood ; for Urry, in his Glossary to Chaucer, Voce VERILAYE, from the French Virelaie, upon the authority of Blount, interprets it a roundelay, country ballad or FREEMAN'S Song.

'gone abroad to gather for Robinhoode, I pray you
'let them not. I was fayne there to give place to
'Robinhoode: I thought my Rochet would have
'been regarded though I were not: but it would
'not serve, it was faine to give place to Robinhoodes
'men.' Sermon VI. before king Edward VI.
fol. 74. b.

Sir Edward Coke, in his third institute, pag. 197,
speaks of Robinhood, and says that men of his law-
less profession were from him called Roberdsmen:
he says that this notable thief gave not only a name
to these kind of men, but that there is a bay in the
river of    in Yorkshire, called Robinhood's
bay. He farther adds, that the statute of Winchester,
13 Edward I. and another statute of 5 Edward III.
were made for the punishment of Roberdsmen and
other felons.

Drayton in his Polyolbion, song 26, thus characterizes him:—

'From wealthy abbots' chests, and churches abundant
    store,
'What oftentimes he took, he shar'd amongst the
    poore.
'No lordly Bishop came in lusty Robin's way,
'To him before he went, but for his pass must pay.
'The widow in distress he gratiously reliev'd,
'And remedied the wrongs of many a virgin griev'd.'

Hearne in his Glossary to Peter Langtoft, voce
**trow,** inserts a manuscript note out of Wood, containing a passage cited from John Major, the Scottish
historian, to this purpose, that Robinhood was indeed
an arch-robber, but the gentellest thief that ever was;
and says he might have added, from the Harleian
MS. of John Fordun's Scottish Chronicle, that he
was, though a notorious robber, a man of great
devotion and charity.

He is frequently called Robert earl of Huntingdon;
and there is extant a dramatic history of his death
that gives him this title. There is also extant a
pedigree of his family, which shows that he had at
least some pretensions to the earldom. Nevertheless
the most ancient poems on him make no mention of
this title; and in a very old legend in verse, preserved in the archives of the public library of Cambridge, he is expressly asserted to have been simply
a yeoman.*

Dr. Stukeley, in his Palæographia Britannica, No. 11,
1746, has given an account of the descent of this
famous person, to this purpose; viz., that his true
name was Robert Fitz-Ooth, but that agreeably to
the practice in the north of England, the two last
letters of his name were contracted into d, whence he
was called Hood; that he was a man of rank, being
grandson of Ralph Fitz-Ooth, a Norman earl of
Kyme, whose name appears in the roll of Battell-
Abbey, and who came into England with William
Rufus.—That Robin Hood's maternal grandfather
was Gilbert de Gient, earl of Lincoln; his grandmother was the Lady Roisia de Vere, sister to the
earl of Oxford, and countess of Essex, from whom
the town of Royston, where she was buried, takes its
name. Robin Hood's father William was in those

* Vide **Reliques** of Ancient English Poetry, vol. I. pag. 81.

times of feudal dependance, a ward of Robert earl of
Oxford, who by the king's order gave to him in
marriage the third daughter of lady Roisia.

Robinhood had for his coat-armour Gules, two
bends engrailed, Or. The tragedy above-mentioned
makes him to die by poison, but the vulgar tradition
is, that being compelled to apply to a nun for assistance in a disorder that required bleeding, she
performed the operation so that he died under it.

At Kirklees in Yorkshire, now the seat of the
Armitage family, but which was formerly a Benedictine nunnery, and probably the very place where
he received his death's wound, is a grave-stone near
the park, under which, as it is said, Robinhood lies
buried. There is an inscription on it, now not
legible; but Mr. Ralph Thoresby, in his Ducatus
Leodiensis from the papers of Dr. Gale, dean of York,
gives the following as his epitaph:—

    Hear, undernead dis laitl stean,
    Laiz Robert, Earl of Huntingtun,
    Nea arcir ver az hie sa geude:
    An piple kauld im Robin Heud.
    Sic utlawz az hi, an iz men,
    Wil England never figh agen.
    Obiit 24 kal. Dekembris, 1247.

Dr. Percy doubts the genuineness of this epitaph,
and with good reason, for the affected quaintness of
the spelling, and the even pace of the metre, are
certainly ground for suspicion.

The same author has given, from a manuscript of
his own, a ballad of Robinhood and Guy of Gisborne,
which was never before printed, and, as he says,
carries the marks of much greater antiquity than any
of the common popular songs on the subject.

The songs above-mentioned, although many of
them are totally devoid of historical truth, being in
short metrical legends, were yet interesting enough
to engage the attention of the people, for either the
subject was of some dignity, or the catastrophe
affecting, or the poetry was level to the common
apprehension; in short, they fell in with the popular
humour; and in this way only can we account for
their transmission through a succession of ages, and
their existence at the present time. Too con-
temptuously therefore does the author of the Art
of English Poesy speak of our ancient songs and
ballads, when, comparing them to those grave and
stately metres which he takes occasion to commend,
he calls them 'small and popular musickes, song by
'these *Cantabanqui* upon benches and barrels' heads,
'where they have none other audience then boys or
'countrey fellowes that passe by them in the streete,
'or else by blind harpers, or such like taverne min-
'strels that give a fit of mirth for a groat, and
'their matters being for the most part stories of
'old time, as the tale of Sir *Topas*, the reportes
'of *Bevis of Southampton, Guy of Warwicke,*
'*Adam Bel,* and *Clymme* of the *Clough,* and such
'other old romances or historicall rimes, made pur-
'posely for recreation of the common people at
'Christmasse diners and brideales, and in tavernes
'and alehouses, and such other places of base resort;
'also they be used in carols and rounds, and such

'light or lascivious poemes, which are commonly
'more commodiously uttered by these buffons or
'vices in playes then by any other person.'

## CHAP. CVII.

Such was the general state of music in England
at the close of the sixteenth century; as to our
poetry, it had been gradually refining from the time
of Chaucer, and was arrived to great perfection,
when it received some little check from the attempts
of a few fantastic writers to improve it by certain
rules, teaching men to become poets, or makers, as
they affected to call them, rules that left scarce any
room for the exercise of those faculties with which it
is, though perhaps a little hyperbolically, said a poet
is born; much of this affected cant about poets and
makers is observable in the writings of Roger
Ascham, the preceptor to the children of Henry
VIII. somewhat of it in Sir Philip Sidney's elegant
little tract 'The Defence of Poesie,' and in the Discoveries, as they are called, of Ben Jonson, and more
in a work entitled 'The Arte of English Poetry con-
'trived into three bookes, the first of poets and
'poesie, the second of proportion, the third of orna-
'ment.' London, quarto, 1589.*

The author of this book, though some have ascribed it to Sir Philip Sidney, is in general believed
to be one Webster Puttenham, a gentleman pensioner
of Queen Elizabeth, a man not altogether destitute
of learning, but whose notions of the perfection of
poetry are such, as no degree of learning can justify.
What the author has said in his first book of poets
and poesy is common enough, and scarcely worthy
of remark; but his second book, intitled of Proportion poetical, is founded upon such principles, and contains such rules for writing poetry as could never
have entered into the head of a man who had any
taste or relish of that art which he professes to teach.
His arguments in favour of proportion poetical are
these :—'It is said by mathematicians that all things
'stand by proportion, and by the doctors of our
'theology that God made the world by number,
'measure, and weight.' As to poetical proportion,
'he says, 'it holdeth of the musical, because poesie
'is a skill to speak and write harmonically; and
'verses or rhyme be a kind of musical utterance by

* Three years before this, was published a Discourse of English
Poetry, a small tract in quarto, written by William Webbe; this is a very
curious book, and contains in it a proposal for the reformation of English poetry, by establishing a prosodia of versification in imitation of the
Greeks and Latins. Sir Philip Sidney, Sir Edward Dyer, Spenser, and
some others laboured to subject our poetry to some such rules as are
here prescribed, but without effect. The author gives a general account
of the English poets from Gower down to his own time, and speaks in
terms of very high commendation of Anthony Munday, an earnest
traveller in this art, in whose name he says he had seen very excellent
works, especially upon nymphs and shepherds, well worthy to be viewed
and to be esteemed as very rare poetry. He celebrates also Dr. Phaer
and Dr. Twine, the translators of Virgil, and Arthur Golding for his
labour in Ovid's Metamorphoses, and Dr. Gabriel Harvey, the brother of
the physician, an admired Latin poet. He speaks of certain compositions after the manner of the acrostic, by W. Hunnis, and says that the
earl of Surrey translated some part of Virgil into English hexameters.
A fuller account of this curious book is given in the British Librarian of
Mr. Oldys, No. 11.

About the same time, viz., in 1584, was printed at Edinburgh in quarto,
'The Essayes of a prentise in the divine art of Poesie.' This prentise
was James the Sixth of Scotland, and of England the first. The book
contains Sonnets, the Uranie of Du Bartas translated into English verse,
a poem entitled Phœnix, a version of Psalm CIV. and 'Ane schort
'Treatise conteining some reulis and cautelis to be observit and eschewit
'in Scottis poesie.'

'reason of a certain congruitie in sounds pleasing to
'the ear, though not perchance so exquisitely as the
'harmonical concents of artificial musicke, consisting
'in strained tunes, as is the vocal musicke, or that
'of melodious instruments, as lutes, harps, regals,
'records, and such like.' And, adds he, 'this our
'proportion poetical resteth in five points, staffe,
'measure, concord, situation and figure.'

All these are treated of in their order: as to staffe
or stanza, he exhibits it in various forms, viz., as
consisting of few or many verses, for the framing
whereof the rules given by him are so mechanical,
that they leave very little room for the exercise of
fancy or invention.

As to proportion in figure, it is a thing so little
heeded in poetry, or rather indeed so little understood, that we are necessitated to adopt the explanation of it by the author, and make use of his
own words :—

'Your last proportion is that of figure, so called
'for that it yelds an ocular representation, your
'meeters being by good symmetrie reduced into
'certaine geometrical figures, whereby the maker
'is restrained to keepe him within his bounds, and
'sheweth not onely more art, but serveth also much
'better for briefness and subtiltie of device, and for
'the same respect are also fittest for the pretie
'amourets in court to entertaine their servants and
'the time withal, their delicate wits requiring some
'commendable exercise to keepe them from idlenesse.
'I find not of this proportion used by any of the
'Greeke or Latine poets, or in any vulgar writer,
'saving of that one forme which they cal Anacreons
'egge. But being in Italie conversant with a certaine
'gentleman who had long travelled the oriental parts
'of the world, and seen the courts of the great
'princes of China and Tartarie, I being very in-
'quisitive to knowe of the subtilties of those countreys,
'and especially in matter of learning, and of their
'vulgar poesie; he told me that they are in all their
'inventions most wittie, and have the use of poesie
'or riming, but do not delight so much as we do in
'long tedious descriptions, and therefore when they
'will utter any pretie conceit, they reduce it into
'metrical feet, and put it in form of a lozange or
'square, or such other figure, and so engraven in
'gold, silver, or ivorie, and sometimes with letters
'of ametist, rubie, emeralde, or topas, curiousely
'cemented and peeced together, they send them in
'chaines, bracelets, collars, and girdles to their mis-
'tresses to weare for a remembrance; some fewe
'measures composed in this sort this gentleman gave
'me, which I translated word for word, and as near
'as I could, following both the phrase and the figure,
'which is somewhat hard to performe because of the
'restraint of the figure, from which ye may not
'digresse. At the beginning they wil seeme nothing
'pleasant to a English eare, but time and usage will
'make them acceptable inough, as it doth in all
'other newe guises, be it for wearing of apparell
'or otherwise.'

The geometrical figures recommended by him are
the lozenge, called Rombus, the fuzee or spindle

called Romboides, the triangle or tricquet, the square or quadrangle, the pillaster or cylinder, the spire or taper called Piramis, the rondel or sphere, the egge or figure ovall, the tricquet reversed, the tricquet displayed, the lozange reversed, the egg displayed, the lozange rabbated.

It is highly probable that the practice of composing verses resembling the form of eggs, altars, wings, and many other such quaint devices, now deservedly the subject of ridicule, had its foundation in the precepts contained in this book. The great proficients in this species of false wit were Withers, Quarles, Crashaw, Herbert, and some others, but they had but few followers; and notwithstanding the pains which Puttenham has taken to recommend it, the proportion of figure, as he terms it, has been little regarded.

The state of English poetry at this period is in general very well known to all that are conversant in English literature, but it may be thought necessary to be somewhat particular with respect to that species of it which is to be more immediately connected with music, and to give an account of a number of writers little known to the world, the authors of madrigals, sonnets, and other compositions for music, many whereof will be found to have great merit.

Puttenham has enumerated some of the most celebrated poets of his own time and of the age preceding, as namely, the earl of Surrey, Sir Thomas Wyat, Lord Vaux, Maister Chaloner, Maister Edward Dyer, N. Breton, George Gascoigne, Sir Philip Sidney, Sir Walter Raleigh, and others; but there are many writers of this class whose names scarce ever occur but in collections of songs and short lyric poems, at this time very little known. One of the first of this kind extant is the 'Paradyse of daynty 'Devises,' printed in 1577, the greater part by Richard Edwards before mentioned,* others by

Lord Vaux, Edward Vere Earl of Oxford, William Hunnys, Thomas Churchyard, Lodowic Lloyd, Jasper Heywood, and others.

The first of these collections is in the title-page said to contain 'sundry pithy preceptes, learned 'counsels, and excellent inventions, right pleasant 'and profitable for all estates;' besides these there are divers songs, many of which have been set to music, and certain verses of Edwards's in commendation of music, beginning 'Where griping grief the hart would wound,' alluded to in Shakespeare's Romeo and Juliet, act IV. scene 5.

Another collection of the same kind was printed in the year 1614. with the title of England's Helicon, or the Muses Harmony, a collection of songs. The names of the authors are as follows: Sir Phil. Sidney, Edmund Spenser, Michael Drayton, Edmund Bolton, Robert Greene, Thomas Lodge, Nich. Breton, Shepheard Tonie, George Peele, Howard Earl of Surrey, Thomas Watson,† John Wooton, W. Shakespeare, Bar. Yong,‡ Richard Barnefield, Earle of Oxenford, Sir Edward Dyer, N. Yong,§ M. N. Howell, Christopher Marlow, William Browne,‖ Christ. Brooke.

The other collection, namely, England's Helicon, is altogether in that vein of Poetry which Sir Philip Sidney introduced amongst us, and is celebrated for its pastoral simplicity. In it are in truth many very fine compositions, most of which are set to music by the ablest masters of the time, and chiefly in the form of madrigals.

Most of the persons above named were, in comparison of our English classics, obscure writers; they are nevertheless recorded, with many curious particulars relating to them, by Winstanley, Langbaine, Phillips, and Wood, and their merits are such as entitle them to the regard of such as wish to form a true judgment of English literature.

To this class of poets succeeded another, who deviating from their predecessors, introduced into their compositions, allegory and all the subtleties of metaphysics, and even school theology; these were Sir John Davies, Phineas Fletcher, author of the Purple Island, Dr. Donne, and a few others; this style of writing furnished very little employment for the musical composers of this time: as it was affected and obscure, it was short-lived, and gave way to that natural, elegant, and easy vein of poetry, which Spenser, Daniel, Carew, and Waller introduced and

---

* Of Edwards as a musician mention has already been made, see page 362, but besides his excellency in the faculty of music, it seems that he possessed a considerable talent in poetry. Wood says he was a member of Lincoln's Inn, and gives a farther account of him in the Athen. Oxon. vol. I. col. 151, to this purpose, viz. that he was the author of two comedies, Damon and Pythias, and Palemon and Arcite, often acted at court before queen Elizabeth, and in the university of Oxford, in the hall, for he was of Christ-church college.—That the queen was so delighted with the latter of these, that she sent for Edwards, and, after commending sundry passages in it, gave him many thanks, and a promise of a reward. This promise it seems she made good by appointing him first a gentleman of her chapel, and afterwards, upon the decease of Richard Bowyer, in 1561, master of the children. As a farther testimony of her favour, she formed the children of the royal chapel into a company of players, and granted to Edwards licence to superintend them. It is remarkable that the first regular establishment of a company of players was that of the children of Paul's in 1378; their theatre was the singing-school in or near the cathedral. The next was that of the parish-clerks of London at Skinner's-well; the next that of the children of the royal chapel above-mentioned; a few years after which another was established under the denomination of the children of the revels. These two companies of children last mentioned became very famous; all Lilly's plays, and many of Shakespeare's and Jonson's, were first acted by them; they were looked on with a jealous eye by the actors at the theatres; and Shakespeare alludes to the injudicious approbation of their performance in the following speeches of Rosencrantz and Hamlet:—
'—— There is an aiery of little children, little eyases [nestlings of 'an eagle or hawk] that cry out on the top of question, and are most 'tyrannically clapp'd for't: these are now the fashion; and so berattle 'the common stages (so they call them) that many wearing rapiers are 'afraid of goose-quills, and dare scarce come thither. HAM. What are 'they children? Who maintains them? How are they escoted? [paid] 'Will they pursue quality no longer than they can sing?' &c. HAMLET, act II. scene 2.
Among the children of queen Elizabeth's chapel was one named Sal. Pavey, who was it seems an excellent actor in the character of an old man. He died under the age of thirteen, and is celebrated by Ben Jonson in an epitaph printed with his epigrams.
Bishop Tanner, in his Bibliotheca, has an article for Edwards, in

which are mentioned some poems of his not printed in the Paradyse of daynty devises. He appears by the cheque book to have died on the last day of October, 1566.
WILLIAM HUNNIS, another of the authors above-mentioned, and who also wrote many of the poems printed in the Paradyse of daynty devises, and also translated some of David's Psalms into English metre, was likewise a musician and a gentleman of the chapel; his name occurs as such both in the list of Edward the Sixth's chapel establishment, and in that of queen Mary. He succeeded Edwards as master of the children, being appointed to that office on the fifteenth day of November, 1566, and died the sixth of June, 1597.

† Mentioned before as the publisher of the first Sett of Italian Madrigals Englished. From the circumstance of his having written poems printed in this collection, it is probable that he was the translator of the madrigals published by him.

‡ The translator of the Diana of George de Montemayor into English. Most of his poems in the England's Helicon are taken from this translation.

§ Nicholas Yong, before-mentioned as the publisher of the Musica Transalpina in two books.

‖ Author of Britannia's Pastorals. The rest may be met with in the Athenæ and Fasti Oxoniensis.

practised, and which lent to music as many graces as it borrowed from it.*

To the catalogue of English musicians herein before given, and continued down to the year 1600, the following additions may be made, of persons less noted for the number and variety of their publications, though perhaps not less excellent in their faculty, viz :—

RICHARD ALLISON, a private teacher of music in London, flourished in the reign of queen Elizabeth, and dwelt in Duke's Place near Aldgate. He was one of the ten authors that composed parts to the common Psalm tunes printed by Thomas Este in 1594, octavo. He also published the Psalms with this title ' The Psalmes of David in meter, the plaine ' song beeing the common tunne to be sung and plaid ' upon the Lute, Orpharyon, Citterne, or Base Viol, ' severally or altogether, the singing part to be ' either tenor or treble to the instrument, according ' to the nature of the voyce, or for foure voyces, with ' tenne short tunnes in the end, to which for the most ' part all the Psalmes may be usually sung, for the ' use of such as are of mean skill, and whose leysure ' least serveth to practise.'  Fol. London, 1599.

HUGH ASTON, an organist in the time of Henry VIII. composed a Te Deum for five voices, now in the music-school, Oxon.

THOMAS ASHWELL, a cathedral musician, lived in the reigns of Henry VIII. Edward VI. and queen Mary ; some of his compositions are in the music-school, Oxon.

EDWARD BLANCKS, one of the composers of the Psalms in four parts, printed by Este, and mentioned above.

AVERY BURTON, a cathedral musician in the reign of Henry VIII. an anthem of his in five parts is in the music-school, Oxon.

RICHARD CARLETON, bachelor of music, and in priest's orders, was the author of Madrigals to five voices, printed in 1601. He was one of the composers of the Triumphs of Oriana.

BENJAMIN COSYN, a famous composer of lessons for the harpsichord, and probably an excellent performer on that instrument, flourished about this time. There are many of his lessons extant that seem in no respect inferior to those of Bull. The name WILLIAM COSIN occurs in the Ashmolean manuscript list of musicians of Anthony Wood, and he is therein said

to have been organist of the Charter-house before the wars. It is probable that these persons were the sons of JOHN COSYN, who in 1585 published the Psalms in music of five and six parts.

HUGH DAVIS, bachelor of music, of New college, and afterwards organist of Hereford cathedral, is celebrated for his skill in church music. He died in 1644.

JOHN FARRANT, organist of Salisbury, another JOHN FARRANT, organist of Christ's hospital within Newgate, London ; and DANIEL FARRANT, supposed to be the son of Richard Farrant before mentioned ; all flourished about the year 1600 ; the latter is said to have been one of the first of those musicians who set lessons lyra-way, as it is called, to the viol, in imitation of the old English lute and Bandore.

JOHN FLOYD, of Welch extraction, bachelor of music, and a gentleman of the chapel, temp. Hen. VIII. He made a pilgrimage to Jerusalem, returned and died in the king's chapel, and was buried in the Savoy church with this inscription : Johannes Floyd virtutis et religionis cultor.  Obiit 3 Apr. 1523.

JOHN GILBERT, a bachelor of music of Oxon, 1510. JOHN GOODMAN, a noted composer, 1505. MATTHEW GOODWIN, 1585. WALTER HILTON, a Carthusian monk, and eminently skilled in music. He lived temp. Hen. VI. and wrote De Musica Ecclesiastica, lib. I. TOBIAS HUME, a soldier by profession, but an excellent performer on the Viol da Gamba ; he published in 1607, and dedicated to queen Anne, the consort of James I., a collection of songs entitled ' Captaine Hume's Poeticall Musicke, principally ' made for two basse violls, yet so contrived that it ' may be plaied 8 severall waies upon sundry in- ' struments with much facilitie.' MATTHEW JEFFRIES, ' a vicar choral of the cathedral of Wells, and bachelor ' of music of Oxon, 1593.  JOHN KEEPER of Hart ' hall : he published select Psalms in four parts 1574. HENRY NOEL, a gentleman pensioner of queen Elizabeth, and much favoured by her, for his skill in music.  FRANCIS PILKINGTON of Trinity college, Oxon, bachelor of music in 1595.  HENRY PORTER of Christ-church college, Oxon. bachelor of music in 1600.  RICHARD READ, bachelor of music in 1592. a composer of services.  JOHN SILVESTER, bachelor of music in 1521, an eminent musician.  ROBERT STEVENSON, created doctor in music, 1596.  HENRY STONING, a noted musician, temp. Eliz.

---

BOOK XII.          CHAP. CVIII.

FROM the foregoing deduction of the history of music a judgment may be formed, as well of the practice and the uses to which it was at different periods applied, as of the improvements from time to time made in the science. In particular it may be observed, that in all ages, and in almost all countries, it made a part of religious worship. Among

the Heathens and Jews, music was employed in sacrifices ; and these authorities in the opinion of the primitive fathers were deemed sufficient to justify the introduction of it into the ritual of the Christian church. From the middle of the fourth century to this time, music has therefore in some way or other made a part in the public worship of every church which acknowledges Christ for its head.

As to secular music, it may be remarked to have consisted either in that kind of it which is suited to triumphs, to shows and public spectacles, rejoicings

* In this view of poetry the sonnets of Shakespeare and the Amoretti of Spenser, surpass every thing of the kind in the English language; and it is to be wondered at that till about the year 1738, neither the one nor the other of them were ever set to music. A part of the Amoretti was then set, and published by Dr. Maurice Greene for a single voice, but the work did him little honour.

and festivities, or in that less vociferous kind, intended either for solitary practice or convivial recreation. In both of these the music was in general an auxiliar to poetry, or at least was made use of to enforce some sentiment, to awaken devotion, or inspire love. The principles of harmony were by this time sufficiently explored, and something like what we now call Air was discoverable in the melody of those times, the subsequent improvements in music respected chiefly, style, expression, and the power of exciting different passions by an artful combination and succession of corresponding sounds, and rendered it fit for a more intimate union and connection with poetry than had been known before; of which connection it is now time to speak.

It has already been shewn that the modern lyric poetry had its rise among the Provençals; and those who have undertaken to give the history of the theatre, seem more disposed to derive the origin of the principal theatrical entertainments now in use, from the same source, than from the more perfect models of ancient Greece and Rome. But here a distinction is to be made between tragedy and comedy on the one hand, and on the other those inferior species of dramatic poesy, namely, moralities, mysteries, mummeries, masques, serenatas, and above all the musical tragedy, or, as it has long been called, the Opera. The former of these have an undoubted claim to high antiquity, the latter it is conjectured had their rise in those times of ignorance and barbarism on which we look back with no other view than to estimate the degree of literary improvement in the course of a few centuries, and are in general of such a kind as scarce to merit a critical attention; the opera however will perhaps be thought so intimately connected with the subject of this work, as to require a very particular consideration.

The Italian writers have taken great pains to ascertain the origin of the musical drama or opera. Riccoboni in his 'Reflexions historiques et critiques sur les differens Théatres de l'Europe,' has collected their several opinions on the subject, and dates the public exhibition of operas from the year 1637, when, as he relates, the opera of Andromache was performed at the theatre of St. Cassan at Venice. This author seems to have made but a very indifferent use of the materials in his possession, and his account of the matter is very loose and unsatisfactory: it is to be observed that there is a diversity of opinions touching the origin of the musical drama, and he has adopted that which gives it the lowest degree of antiquity, the others carry it many years backwarder; these opinions shall severally be stated, and submitted to the reader's choice.*

First, it is said that the opera was invented by Johannes Sulpitius, surnamed Verulanus, a native of Veroli, a town in the Campania di Roma, and who flourished towards the end of the fifteenth century; this is asserted by Bayle in the article SULPITIUS, and his authority for it is Father Menestrier, who in his treatise 'Des Representations en Musique,' pag. 155, 156, has the following passage: 'Those remains of 'dramatic music which had been preserved in the 'church, served to restore it two hundred years ago; 'and Rome, (which had in a manner lost it, in order 'to bestow upon the recitation and declamation of 'actors, what the Grecians bestowed upon singing 'and harmony) brought it upon the stage towards 'the year 1480, as I learned from Sulpitius, in the 'epistle dedicatory prefixed to his notes upon Vitru-'vius,† which he presented to Cardinal Riari, great 'chamberlain of the church, and nephew of pope 'Sixtus IV. Sulpitius, praising the magnificence of 'the Cardinal, who had built many stately palaces in 'the neighbourhood of Rome, begs of him that he 'would erect public theatres for musical represen-'tations, of which Sulpitius calls him the restorer, 'having shewn at Rome a few years ago what had 'not been in use there for many ages. He tells the 'Cardinal in that epistle that Rome expects from 'him a theatre for such performances, because he has 'already given such an entertainment to the people 'upon a moveable theatre set up in a public place, 'and at other times in the castle of St. Angelo for 'the Pope's diversion, and in his palace for some 'Cardinals.'‡

Erythræus, in his Pinacotheca I. pag. 62, and Crescimbeni, ascribe the invention of the musical drama or opera to Emilio Cavaliere, who in the year 1590, exhibited in the palace of the grand duke at Florence, 'Il Satiro,' and 'La Disperazione di Fileno,' two dramas of the pastoral kind set to music.§ This relation, true as it may be, does not ascertain the original invention of the opera, which, according to

---

* Mr. Dryden, in the preface to his Albion and Albanius, confesses that he was not able by any search, to get any light either of the time when the opera began, or of the first author; but he professes, upon probable reasons, to believe that 'some Italians, having curiously observed 'the gallantries of the Spanish Moors at their Zambras, or royal feasts, '(where musick, songs, and dancing were in perfection; together with 'their machines at their running at the ring, and other solemnities) 'might have refined upon those Moresque amusements, and produced this 'pleasing kind of drama, by leaving out the warlike part, and forming a 'poetical design to introduce more naturally the machines, music and 'dances.' Then he proceeds to say, that however operas began, music has flourished principally in Italy; and that he believes their operas were first intended for the celebration of the marriages of their princes, or the magnificent triumphs of some general time of joy; and accordingly the expences upon these occasions were out of the purse of the sovereign or republic, as has been often practised at Turin, Florence, Venice, &c.

In a postscript to the above-mentioned preface, Dryden retracts this opinion, and says that possibly the Italians went not so far as Spain for the invention of their operas; for that they might have taken the hint at home, and formed this drama by gathering up the shipwrecks of the Grecian and Roman theatres, which were adorned with music, scenes, dances, and machines, especially the Grecian. And in the preface itself he observes that though the opera is a modern invention, yet it is built on the foundation of the Ethnic worship.

† Bayle remarks that Menestrier is mistaken in this description of Sulpitius's edition of Vitruvius; it is true that he published it during the pontificate of pope Innocent VIII. that is 'to say, between 1484 and 1492, but without notes or various readings. Bayle, SULPITIUS, note A.

‡ 'Tu enim primus tragœdiæ quam nos juventutem excitandi gratiâ 'et AGERE et CANTARE primi hoc ævo docuimus (nam ejusmodi actionem 'jam multis sæculis Roma non viderat) in medio foro pulpitum ad 'quinque pedum altitudinem erectum pulcherrimè exornasti. Eam-'demque postquàm in Hadriani mole Divo Innocentio spectante est acta, 'rursùs intrà tuos penates tamquam in media Circi caveâ toto confessu, 'umbraculis tecto, admisso populo, et pluribus tui ordinis spectatoribus 'honorificè excepisti. Tu etiam primus picturatæ scenæ faciem, quùm 'Pomponiani comœdiam agerent nostro sæculo ostendisti: quare à te 'theatrum novum tota urbs magnis votis expectat.'

It seems that the opera here spoken of, was set to music by Francesco Beverini, a learned musician who flourished in the pontificate of Sixtus IV. and that the subject of the drama was the conversion of St. Paul. It is remarkable that Sulpitius in his dedication styles himself only the reviver of this entertainment; by which expression he seems to intimate that it was in use among the ancients; and of that opinion Dryden appears at last to have been by the postscript to the preface to his Albion and Albanius before cited.

§ Crescimbeni, Commentarj. intorno all' Istoria della volgar Poesia, vol. I. lib. iv. page 234.

the above account, must have been in 1480, or, as Sulpitius intimates, still more early.

Notwithstanding these relations, it is insisted on by many that the musical drama or opera was invented by Ottavio Rinuccini, a native of Florence, a man of wit, handsome in person, polite, eloquent, and a very good poet.* He considerably enriched the Italian poetry with his verses, composed after the manner of Anacreon, and other pieces which were set to music and acted on the stage. His first composition of this kind was a pastoral called Daphne, which being but an essay or attempt to introduce this species of musical entertainment into practice, was performed only to a select and private audience; and the merit attributed to this peice encouraged him to write an opera called Eurydice.† The music both to the pastoral, Daphne, and the opera, Eurydice, was composed by Jacopo Peri, who on this occasion is said to have been the inventor of that well known species of composition, Recitative.‡ The Eurydice was represented on the theatre at Florence in the year 1600, upon occasion of the marriage of Mary de Medicis with Henry IV. of France. Rinuccini dedicated his opera to that queen, and in the following passage declares the sentiments he was taught to entertain of it by his friend Peri.

‘ It has been the opinion of many persons, most ‘ excellent queen, that the ancient Greeks and Romans ‘ sang their tragedies throughout on the stage, but ‘ so noble a manner of recitation has not that I know ‘ of been even attempted by any one till now; and ‘ this I thought was owing to the defect of the ‘ modern music, which is far inferior to the ancient; ‘ but Messer Jacopo Peri made me entirely alter my ‘ opinion, when upon hearing the intention of Messer ‘ Giacomo Corsi and myself, he so elegantly set to ‘ music the pastoral of Daphne, which I had com- ‘ posed merely to make a trial of the power of vocal ‘ music in our age, it pleased to an incredible degree ‘ those few that heard it. From this I took courage: ‘ the same piece being put into better form and re- ‘ presented anew in the house of Messer Peri, was ‘ not only favoured by all the nobility of the country,

‘ but heard and commended by the most serene grand ‘ duchess, and the most illustrious Cardinals dal ‘ Monte and Montalto. But the Eurydice has met ‘ with more favour and success, being set to music ‘ by the same Peri with wonderful art; and having ‘ been thought worthy to be represented on the stage, ‘ by the bounty and magnificence of the most serene ‘ grand duke, in the presence of your majesty, the ‘ cardinal legate, and so many princes and gentlemen ‘ of Italy and France; from whence, beginning to ‘ find how well musical representations of this kind ‘ were likely to be received, I resolved to publish ‘ these two, to the end that others of greater abilities ‘ than myself may be induced to carry on and im- ‘ prove this kind of poetry to such a degree, that we ‘ may have no occasion to envy those ancient pieces ‘ which are so much celebrated by noble writers.’

Father Menestrier confirms the above account, adding thereto some farther particulars in the following passage :—

‘ Ottavio Rinuccini, a Florentine poet, having a ‘ particular talent at expressing in his verses all kinds ‘ of passions, found means to adapt music and singing ‘ to them so well, that they neither destroyed any ‘ part of the beauty of the verses, nor prevented the ‘ distinct understanding of the words, which is often ‘ hindered by an affected multiplicity of divisions. ‘ He consulted in this Giacomo Corsi, a gentleman of ‘ Florence, well skilled in music and polite literature, ‘ and both calling in Giacomo Cleri,§ and Giulio ‘ Caccini, excellent masters in music, they together ‘ composed a drama entitled Apollo and Daphne, ‘ which was represented in the house of Messer Corsi, ‘ in the presence of the grand duke and duchess of ‘ Tuscany, and the cardinals Monti and Montalto, ‘ with so much success that he was encouraged to ‘ compose another, namely, his Eurydice, and caused ‘ it to be exhibited soon after at the same place. ‘ Claudio de Monteverde, an excellent musician, com- ‘ posed the music to the Ariadne on the model of ‘ these two; and being made chapel-master of St. ‘ Mark’s in Venice, introduced into that city these ‘ representations, which are now become so famous ‘ by the magnificence of the theatres and dress, by ‘ the delicacy of voices, harmony of concerts, and the ‘ learned compositions of this Monteverde, Soriano, ‘ Giovanelli, Teosilo, and other great masters.’ ‖

Count Algarotti, from a preface of Peri to the Eurydice, has given a very succinct relation of the occasion and manner of this invention in the following words : ‘ When he [Peri] had applied himself to ‘ an investigation of that species of musical imitation ‘ which would the readiest lend itself to the theatric ‘ exhibitions, he directed his researches to discover

---

* He entertained a wild passion for Mary de Medicis, and followed her into France, where he notwithstanding succeeded so well in obtaining the favour of Henry IV. to whom she was married, that he made him one of the gentlemen of his bedchamber. It is said of him that he had a singular propensity to amorous pursuits, but that his inclination for the queen having been greatly mortified by her wisdom and virtue, he was affected with a salutary shame, became a penitent, and applied himself to exercises of devotion, which he continued during the remainder of his life. His poems were collected by his son Peter Francis Rinuccini, and were printed in Florence in 1624, with a dedication to Lewis XIII. An account of this person is given by Johannes Victor Roscius in his Pinacotheca II. pag. 61, published under the name of Janus Nicius Erythræus.

† Nicius Erythræus ascribes to him two other operas, Arethusa and Ariadne.

‡ This is the general opinion, and it is the more likely to be true, as Peri has almost in terms related the process of the invention. Nevertheless some writers, and particularly Kircher, have given the honour of it to Giulio Caccini, a contemporary musician with Peri; his words are: ‘ Julius Caccinus was the first that restored the ratio of the recitative ‘ style in singing, so much in use among the ancients’ [Musurg. tom. I. pag. 510.] In this sentiment Kircher seems to be mistaken, though Peri himself, in his preface to the Eurydice, says that in the invention of it he imitated the practice of the ancient Greeks and Romans [Vide Crescimbeni, Commentarj intorno all’ Istoria della volgar Poesia, vol. I. lib. IV. pag. 233,] for in those few ancient musical compositions now extant, there are no melodies to be found that can be said to bear the least resemblance to the modern recitative; neither is it to be inferred from what the ancient harmonicians have said of the Melopoieia, that they were in the least acquainted with the nature of that progression, which constitutes the difference between recitative and song.

§ This should be Jacopo Peri.

‖ Des Representat. en Musique, pag. 163, et seq.
That Kircher should ascribe to Caccini rather than Peri the invention of Recitative, can only be accounted for by this circumstance, that Menestrier’s book was not published till thirty years after the writing of the Musurgia; and though he hints at Peri’s preface to the Eurydice, it does not appear that he had ever seen it.

That they were both excellent musicians is not to be doubted; of Caccini very little is known, except that he was by birth a Roman. Peri was a Florentine, and is celebrated by Nicius Erythræus, in his Pinacotheca I. pag. 144; by Crescimbeni, in his Commentarj intorno all’ Istoria della volgar Poesia, vol. I. pag. 233, and indeed by most writers that have taken occasion to mention him.

'the method of the ancient Greeks on similar oc-
'casions.  He carefully remarked what Italian words
'were, and what were not capable of intonation; and
'was very exact in minuting down the several modes
'of pronunciation, and the proper accents to express
'grief, joy, and all the other affections of the human
'mind, with a view to make the base move in proper
'time, now with more energy, now with less, ac-
'cording to the nature of each.  So scrupulous was
'he, that he attended to all the niceties and peculiari-
'ties of the Italian language, and frequently con-
'sulted with several gentlemen not less celebrated
'for the delicacy of their ears, than for their skill in
'the arts of music and poetry.

'The conclusion from this enquiry was, that the
'ground-work of the imitation proposed should be
'an harmony, following nature step by step, in a
'medium between common speaking and melody.
'Such were the studies of the musical composers in
'former times.  They proceeded in the improvement
'of their art with the utmost care and attention, and
'the effect proved that they did not lose their time
'in the pursuit of unprofitable subtleties.' *

These are the accounts which the writers of greatest
authority give of the invention of the musical drama
or opera, as it is called ;† and from this period it will
not be very difficult to trace its progress and farther
improvement.

In the extract herein before given from Menestrier,
it is said that the Ariadne of Rinuccini was set to
music by Claudio Monteverde ; this is in the highest
degree probable, not only because Monteverde was
at that time in high reputation, being then Maestro
di Cappella to the republic of Venice ;‡ but because
an opera of his entitled L'Orfeo, Favola in Musica,
is extant, which was represented at Mantua but a
very few years after the Eurydice, viz., in 1607,
corresponding most exactly with those set to music
by Peri ; that is to say, it consists of airs and
chorusses, with an intermixture of recitative ; answering to the description thereof in the passage above
cited from Algarotti, taken, as he asserts, from the
preface of Peri to the Eurydice.

This opera, for aught that can now be learned, was
the first ever printed with the music, and is supposed
to have been published soon after its representation.
A new edition of it was printed at Venice in 1615,
by Ricciardo Amadino.

The structure of this drama is so very unlike that
of the modern opera, as to render it a subject of
curious speculation ; for first it is to be observed that
in the performance of it no accompaniment of a
whole orchestra was required ; but the airs performed by the several singers were sustained by in-

* Saggio sopra l'Opera in musica del Signor Conte Algarotti, pag. 27.

† Formerly a common appellation to denote it was, 'Opera con intermedii.'  This appears by a passage in the life of Padre Paolo Sarpi,
wherein a relation is made of many attempts to murder that excellent
person, and of one in particular, wherein a friend of his, Padre Fulgentio,
was wounded, the assassins mistaking him for Father Paul.  The relater
says that these murderers escaped, and adds that by a strange accident
they were not pursued so quickly as they might have been, for that that
evening was presented at the theatre of St. Luigi an Opera con intermedii,
which occasioned so great a concourse of people, that the murderers
found means to retreat.

‡ The Ariadne of Monteverde is celebrated by Gio. Battista Doni in
his treatise De Præstantia Musicæ veteris, pag. 67.

struments of various kinds assigned to each character
respectively in the dramatis personæ, which stands
thus in the first page of the printed book :—

| Personaggi. | Stromenti. |
| --- | --- |
| La Musica Prologo | Duoi Grauicembani |
| Orfeo | Duoi contrabassi de Viola |
| Eurydice | Dieci Viole da brazzo |
| Choro di Ninfe e Pastori | Un Arpa doppia |
| Speranza | Duoi Violini piccoli alla Francese |
| Caronte | Duoi Chitaroni |
| Chori di spiriti infernali | Duoi Organi di legno |
| Proserpina | Tre Bassi da gamba |
| Plutone | Quattro Tromboni |
| Apollo | Un Regale |
| Choro de pastori che | Duoi Cornetti |
| fecero la Moresca | Un Flautina alla vigesima seconda |
| nel fine. | Un Clarino con tre trombe sordine§ |

By the first personage is to be understood the
Genius of music, who sometimes speaks in that
character at large.

The overture, if it may be called by that name,
is a short prelude, eight bars of breve time in length,
in five parts, for a trumpet and other instruments,
and consists of two movements, the last whereof is
termed Ritornello, a word signifying the same with
symphony.

This composition, which the author calls a Toccato,
from toccare, to touch, is directed to be sounded

§ The names of the several instruments above-mentioned require some
particular explanation ; and first it is to be observed, that the word
Grauicembani is misprinted, and should be Clavicembani, for the word
Clavicembano occurs frequently throughout the opera, and Grauicembani
never: as to Clavicembano, it is supposed to mean the same as Clavicembalo, the true Italian appellation for a harpsichord.

As to the Contrabassi de Viola, these are supposed to mean viols, of a
size between the tenor viol and violin.

The Viole da brazzo, of which it is to be observed there are ten required
in the performance of this opera, were clearly the arm-viol or tenor viol ;
the term da brazzo being used in contradistinction to da gamba, which is
appropriated to that species of base viol which in the performance on it
is placed between the legs.

The Arpa doppia seems to be the double-strung harp, an instrument,
which though by some said to have been invented by the Welsh, and by
others by the Irish, was very well known at this time.

The Violini piccoli alla Francese must in strictness signify small
violins ; and of these there are none now known but that contemptible
instrument called the Kit, which hardly any but dancing-masters are ever
known to touch ; it is therefore probable that by Violini piccoli we are to
understand common treble violins ; and this is the more likely, as violins
are no where else mentioned in the catalogue of instruments now under
consideration.

The noun Chitaroni is the nominative case plural of Chitarra, of which
the word Guitar is manifestly a corruption.

Organi di legno, of which two are here required, can signify nothing
but organs of wood, that is to say, organs with wooden pipes : for it is
well known that most organs are composed both of wooden and leaden
pipes.

The Bassi da gamba were clearly leg viols above described.

The Tromboni could be no other than trumpets, concerning which it
is unnecessary in this place to be particular.

The instrument against the name of Apollo, is Un Regale, a Regal,
which term has already been shown to mean a small portable organ, probably with pipes of metal.

The shepherds who sing the last chorus, dance also a Moresca ; this it
seems they do to the instruments mentioned in the last three lines of the
above catalogue.  The Cornet, though an instrument now out of use, is
very well described by Mersennus, Kircher, and other writers on music.
But the Flautino alla vigesima secondo, merits a very particular enquiry.

It is well known that of the flute Abec, which has already been described in this work, there are various sizes, smaller than that formerly
used in concerts, and which was therefore called the concert flute, and
that of these the lowest note, though nominally F, must in power
answer to that sound in the great system, to which it corresponds in a
regular course of succession upwards ; for this reason that sized flute
whose lowest note F was an unison with the note f in the acutes, was
called an octave flute.  Un Flautino alla vigesima secondo, by parity of
reason must therefore mean a treble octave flute, i. e. a flute whose
nominal F was by the smallness of the instrument removed three octaves,
measured by the interval of a twenty-second above its true and proper
situation in the scale.  A flute thus small could not be much bigger than
the oaten reed so frequently mentioned by the pastoral poets.

The word Clarino, as Altieri renders it, is a small trumpet, perhaps an
octave higher than the noble instrument of that name.

The Trombe sordine were probably trumpets of a less shrill and piercing
sound than those of this day ; but this is only conjecture.

three times 'Avanti il levar da la tela,' before the rising of the cloth or curtain.

To the overture succeeds the prologue, consisting of five speeches in recitative; it is spoken by the first of the personages named in the dramatis personæ, who represents the Genius of music, and sometimes speaks in that character at large, and at others in the person of a single performer, as thus, 'I su cetera d'or cantando soglio;' the purport of these speeches severally, is to declare the argument of the opera, to excite attention, and enjoin silence, not only on the audience, but on the birds, and even things inanimate, as in the following instance :—

'Hor mentre i canti alterno hor lieti hor mesti,
  'Non si mova Augellin fra queste piante,
  'Ne s'oda in queste rive onda sonante
'Et ogni auretta in suo camin s'arresti.'

The opera then begins with a speech in recitative by a shepherd, which is immediately succeeded by a chorus of five parts in counterpoint, directed to be sung to the sound of all the instruments. Other chorusses are directed to be sung to the sound of guitars, violins, and flutes, as particularly mentioned in the opera: solo airs there are none; but Recitatives, Chorusses, and Ritornellos, Terzetti, and Duetti, make up the whole of this opera, which concludes with what the author calls a Moresca; this is a composition in five parts, merely instrumental, and conjectured to be the tune of a dance a la Moresca, or after the fashion of the Moors, who it is well known long before this time settled in Spain, and introduced into that kingdom many customs which were adopted in other countries.

A specimen of recitative music, in the form in which it was originally conceived, cannot at this day but be deemed a curiosity; as must also an air in one of the first operas ever composed: for these reasons the following dialogue and duetto are inserted, taken from the fifth act of the Orfeo of Claudio Monteverde :—

APOLLO descende in una nuuola, cantando.

APOLLO ed ORFEO ascende al cielo, cantando.

CLAUDIO MONTEVERDE.

Notwithstanding that this kind of melody is said by the inventors of it to correspond with the method of enunciation practised by the ancient Greeks and Romans, it may well be questioned whether the difference between the one and the other was not very great, for this reason, that the inflections of the voice in the modern recitative do not preserve a medium between speaking and singing, but approach too nearly towards the latter to produce the effects of oratory.

There is no final chorus of voices to the opera from whence the above extracts are made, but the representation concludes with a dance to the following tune :—

MORESCA

CLAUDIO MONTEVERDE.

## CHAP. CIX.

THERE is very little doubt but that the Cantata Spirituale, or what we now call the Oratorio, took its rise from the Opera. Menestrier* attributes its origin to the Crusades, and says that the pilgrims returning from Jerusalem and the Holy Land, from St. James of Compostella, and other places to which pilgrimages were wont to be made, composed songs, reciting the life and death of the Son of God, and the mysteries of the Christian faith, and celebrating the achievements and constancy of saints and martyrs. This seems to be a mere conjecture of Menestrier; other writers render a much more probable account of the matter, and expressly say, that the Oratorio was an avowed imitation of the opera, with this difference only, that the foundation of it was ever some religious, or at least moral subject. Crescimbeni speaks of it in these terms :—

'The Oratorio, a poetical composition, formerly a 'commixture of the dramatic and narrative styles, 'but now entirely a musical drama, had its origin 'from San Filippo Neri,† who in his chapel, after 'sermons and other devotions, in order to allure 'young people to pious offices, and to detain them 'from earthly pleasure, had hymns, psalms, and 'such like prayers sung by one or more voices. 'These in process of time were published at Rome, 'and particularly in a book printed in 1585, with 'the title of *Laudi Spirituali, stampate ad istanza* 'de' RR. PP. della Congregazione dell' Oratorio; 'and another in 1603, entitled *Laudi Spirituali di* 'diversi, solite cantarsi dopo sermoni da' PP. 'della Congregazione dell' Oratorio. Among these 'spiritual songs were dialogues; and these entertain-'ments becoming more frequent, and improving 'every year, were the occasion that in the seventeenth 'century oratorios were first invented, so called from 'the place of their origin.‡ It is not known who

'was the first that gave them this name, not even by 'the fathers of the Congregation, who have been 'asked about it. We are certain however that 'Oratorios could not begin before the middle of 'the above-mentioned century; as we do not find 'any before the time of Francesco Balducci, who 'died about the year 1645, in whose collection of 'poems there are two, one entitled "La *Fede*, ove 'si spiega il Sagrifizio d' Abramo," the other "Il '*Trionfo* sopra la Santissima Vergine;" and although 'Giano Nicio Eritreo, who flourished even before '1640, speaking of Loreto Vettori, of Spoleto, an 'excellent musician and a good poet, says that on 'a certain night he heard him sing in the Oratory of 'the above-mentioned fathers, *Magdalenæ sua de-*'flentis crimina, seque ad Christi pedes abjicientis, '*querimonia*; which lamentation might be in that 'kind of poetry we are just speaking of; yet, as the 'author of it is unknown, and the time not certain 'when it was sung, we cannot say it preceded the 'Oratorios of Balducci.§

'These compositions in the beginning were a 'mixture of dramatic and narrative parts, for under 'the name of history, in those of Balducci or of Testo, 'as well as in all others, the poet has introduced the 'dramatis personæ; but although Testo's manner 'has been followed even in our days, at present it 'is quite abolished, and the Oratorio is a drama 'throughout. Of these some are ideal, others para-'bolical, and others with real persons, which are the 'most common, and others are mixed with both 'the above-mentioned kinds of persons: they are 'generally in two parts, and, being set to music, 'take up about two hours in the performance; yet 'Malatesta Strinati, and Giulio Cesare Grazini, both 'men of letters, published two Oratorios, the former 'on St. Adrian, divided into three acts, the latter on 'St. George, into five. No change of place or length 'of time is observed in them, for being sung without 'acting, such circumstances are of no service. The 'metre of them is like that of the musical drama, 'that is to say, the lines rhymed at pleasure; they 'are full of airs, and are truly very agreeable to hear 'when composed by good authors, such as Cardinal

* Des Represent. en Musique, pag. 153.

† St. Philip Neri was born at Florence in the year 1515. He was intended by his parents for a merchant, and to that end was sent to his uncle, who followed that employment, to be instructed therein, but he betook himself to study and exercises of devotion, and became an ecclesiastic. The congregation of the Fathers of the Oratory, founded by him, is an institution well known: in the first establishment of it he was assisted by Cæsar, afterwards Cardinal Baronius, who was his disciple. Baronius in his annals has borne an honourable testimony to his character and abilities, by styling him the original author and contriver of that great work. There is an account of St. Philip Neri in Ribadeneyra's Lives of the Saints, by means whereof, notwithstanding the many silly stories and palpable falsities related of him, it is easy to discover that he was both a devout and learned man.

‡ This though the true, is but an awkward etymology. The society

here spoken of, La Congregazione dei Padri' dell Oratorio, evidently derives its name from the verb Orare, an oratory being a place of prayer: in this instance the appellative Oratorio is transferred from the place to the exercise; a singular proof how inadequate the powers of language are to our ideas.

§ Jani Nicci Erythræi Pinac. altera lxviii. art. LORETUS VICTORIUS.

'Pier Matteo Petrucci, and Gio. Filippo Berninoa,
'prelate in the court of Rome, among the dead; and
'Cardinal Benedetto Pansilio, and Pietro Ottoboni,
'now living, who both in this, as well as in all kinds
'of poetry, are arrived at great excellency.

'But although Oratorios are at present so much in
'vogue, we have not lost entirely the manner of
'singing sacred things, for we hear some of them
'in those dialogues which are called Cantatas, and
'particularly in the summer, when the fathers of
'Vallicella perform their concerts in the garden of
'the monks of St. Onofrio. This custom is likewise
'followed with great splendour at particular times
'of the year by Cardinal Gio. Battista Spinola of
'St. Cecilia, who on Wednesdays has some very fine
'ones performed in his palace; for the most part the
'composition of Flaminio Piccioni, an eminent dra-
'matic poet. There is sung besides every year on
'Christmas eve in the pontiff's palace, a charming
'cantata, in the presence of the sacred college, for
'whom Giubileo da Pesaro, who died a few years
'ago, composed some very famous; as likewise Paolo
'Francesco Carli, a Florentine poet, not less cele-
'brated for his serious, than his comic productions: and
'this year the advocate Francesco Maria de Conti
'di Campello has favoured us with one, that for
'sweetness of versification, nobility of sentiment, and
'allusion to the present affairs of Italy, deserves to
'be highly commended.' *

To this account of Crescimbeni, Mons. Bourdelot
adds, that St. Philip Neri having prevailed upon the
most skilful poets and musicians to compose dialogues in Italian verse, upon the principal subjects
of the Holy Scripture, procured some of the finest
voices of Rome to sing, accompanied with all sorts
of instruments, and a band of music in the interludes.
—That these performances consisted of Monologues,
Dialogues, Duos, Trios, and Recitatives of four
voices; and that the subjects of some of them were
the conversation of the Samaritan woman with the
Son of God; of Job with his friends, expressing his
misery to them—The prodigal son received into his
father's house—Tobias with the angel, his father, and
wife—The angel Gabriel with the Virgin, and the
mystery of the incarnation.—That the novelty of
these religious dramas, and, above all, the exquisite
style of music in which they were composed, drew
together such a multitude of people as filled the
church boxes, and the money taken for admission
was applied in defraying the expences of the performance. Hence the origin of Oratorios as they
are now styled, or spiritual shows,† the practice

whereof is now become so general in Rome, that
hardly a day passes in which there are not one or
two such representations.‡

The deduction of the history of church-music,
herein before given, contains an account of the rise
and progress of antiphonal singing in the Greek and
Latin churches, the opposition it met with, the patronage given it by the Roman pontiffs at succeeding
periods, the form of the choral service exemplified
in the Cantus Gregorianus, with a general idea of
the musical offices directed by the ritual of the
church of Rome, as well on solemn as ordinary
occasions.

That the mode of religious worship, above described, prevailed in all the European churches till
the time of the Reformation, is not to be doubted:
the first deviation from it that we are now able to
trace, was that which followed the reformation by
Luther, who being himself a great proficient in, and
a passionate lover of music; and being sensible of its
use and importance in divine worship, in conjunction
with his friend Melancthon framed a ritual, little less
solemn, and calculated to engage the affections of the
people, than that of the church of Rome: and, to

* Crescimb. Comm. int. all' Istor. della volg. Poesia, vol. I. lib. iv.
pag. 256.

† This is a mistake; spiritual shows, though not with music and
recitative, are much more ancient than the time of St. Philip Neri. The
fraternity del Gonfalone, as it is called, was founded in 1264; and in their
statutes, printed in Rome in 1584, it is expressly declared that the
principal end of this institution was, that the members of the fraternity
should represent the passion of our Lord. It is true that this practice
was abolished in the pontificate of Paul III. that is to say, about the
year 1548; but we learn from Crescimbeni and other writers, that representations of this kind were common in Italy, and the practice of great
antiquity. Vasari, in his life of Buffalmacco the painter, gives an
account of a feast that was solemnized on the river Arno in the year 1304,
where a machine representing hell, was fixed on boats, and a sacred
history acted, supposed to be that of Lazarus. Comment. int. all' Istor.
della volg. Poesia, vol. I. lib. iv. pag. 241.

It is probable that this representation suggested to Pietro de Cosimo,

a Florentine painter, of whom Felibien has given an account, the idea of
a spectacle, the most whimsical, and at the same time the most terrifying
that imagination can conceive, which in the year 1510 he caused to be
exhibited at Florence. Felibien's relation of it is to this purpose:
'Having taken a resolution to exhibit this extraordinary spectacle at the
'approaching Carnival, Cosimo shut himself up in a great hall, and there
'disposed so secretly every thing for the execution of his design, that no
'one had the least suspicion of what he was about. In the evening of
'a certain day in the Carnival season, there appeared in one of the chief
'streets of the city a chariot painted black, with white crosses and dead
'men's bones, drawn by six buffalos; and upon the end of the pole stood
'the figure of an angel with the attributes of Death, and holding a long
'trumpet in his hands, which he sounded in a shrill and mournful tone,
'as if to awaken and raise the dead: upon the top of the chariot sat
'a figure with a scythe in his hand, representing Death, having under his
'feet many graves, from which appeared, half way out, the bare bones of
'carcases. A great number of attendants, clothed in black and white,
'masked with Death's heads, marched before and behind the chariot,
'bearing torches, which enlightened it at distances so well chosen, that
'every thing seemed natural. There were heard as they marched,
'muffled trumpets, whose hoarse and doleful sound served as a signal for
'the procession to stop. Then the sepulchres were seen to open, out of
'which proceeded, as by a resurrection, bodies resembling skeletons, who
'sang, in a sad and melancholy tone, airs suitable to the subject, as
'Dolor pianto e Penitenza, and others composed with all that art and in-
'vention which the Italian music is capable of: while the procession
'stopped in the public places, the musicians sang with a continued and
'tremulous voice the psalm Miserere, accompanied with instruments
'covered with crape, to render their sounds more dismal. The chariot was
'followed by many persons habited like corpses, and mounted upon the
'leanest horses that could be found, spread with black housings, having
'white crosses and death's heads painted at the four corners. Each of
'the riders had four persons to attend him, habited in shrouds like the
'dead, each with a torch in one hand, and a standard of black taffety
'painted with white crosses, bones, and death's heads in the other. In
'short, all that horror can imagine most affecting at the resurrection of
'the dead, was represented in this masquerade, which was intended to
'represent the triumph of Death. A spectacle so sad and mournful struck
'a damp through Florence; and although in a time of festivity, made
'penitents of some, while others admiring the ingenious manner in which
'every thing was conducted, praised the whim of the inventor, and the
'execution of a concert so suitable to the occasion.'

Crescimbeni, Comm. int. all' Istor. della volg. Poesia, vol. I. lib. iv.
pag. 243, speaking of those representations of sacred history, says that
he had met with one, namely, Abraham and Isaac, written by Feo
Belcari, and acted for the first time in the church of St. Mary Magdalen
at Florence in 1449.

These representations, however well intended, failed of producing the
end of their institution; Castelvetro says that in his time, and even at
Rome, Christ's passion was so acted as to set the spectators a laughing.
In France was a company of strollers, incorporated as it seems for the
same purposes as the fraternity del Gonfalone, with whom Francis I.
was much delighted; but the abuses committed by them were so numerous, that towards the end of his reign a process was commenced
against them, and in four or five years after his decease they were
banished France. Rymer, at the end of his Short View of Tragedy, has
given a copy of the parliament roll, containing the process at length.
He has also, because it contains a particular history of the stage, given
an abridgment of it in English.

‡ Hist. de la Musique, et de ses Effets, tom. I. pag. 256.

say the truth, the whole of the liturgy, as settled by him, appears to be, if not a reasonable, at least a musical service. The evidence of this assertion is a book intitled 'Psalmodia, hoc est Cantica sacra veteris Ecclesiæ selecta,' printed at Norimberg in 1553, and at Wittemberg in 1561. The publisher of it was Lucas Lossius, rector of the college at Lunenberg,* who has also given his own Scholia thereon.

To speak of this work in particular, it is prefaced by an epistle from Melancthon to the editor, whom he acknowledges as his intimate friend. This is followed by a dedication of the book to the brethren Frederick and John, sons of the reigning king of Denmark. The work is divided into four books, and the offices therein severally contained appear by the titles of each as they follow thus in order :—

Liber primus, continens Antiphonas, Responsoria, Hymnos et Sequentias, quæ leguntur diebus Dominicis, et festis Christi.

Liber secundus, continens cantica veteris ecclesiæ, selecta de præcipiis festis sanctorum Jesu Christi.

Liber tertius, continens cantiones missæ, seu sacri, ut vocant, præter Introitus, quos suprà in Dominicis, et festis diebus invenies suo loco.

Liber quartus, Psalmi cum eorum antiphonis ferialibus, et intonationibus, additis scholiis et lectionis varietate ex Psalterio D. Georg. majoris.

Calvin, whose separation from the church of Rome was founded in an opposition as well to its discipline as its tenets, in his establishment of a church at Geneva, reduced the whole of divine service to prayer, preaching, and singing; and this latter was by him laid under great restraints, for none of the offices in the Romish service, namely, the Antiphon, Hymn, and Motet, with that artificial and elaborate music to which they were sung, were retained; but all of music that was adopted by him, consisted in that plain metrical psalmody now in general use among the reformed churches, and in the parochial churches of this country. Not but there is reason to believe that the practice of psalmody had the sanction of Luther himself.

The opinion which Luther entertains of music in general, and of the lawfulness of it in divine worship, appears by those extracts from his Colloquia Mensalia herein before given; and there is good reason to believe, not only that those sweet Motetæ, which his friends sang at supper with him, were the composition of German musicians, but that German musicians were also the authors or composers of many of those melodies to which the Psalms then were, and even now are, usually sung. Sleidan informs us that upon a certain occasion, mentioned by him in his History of the Reformation of the Church, Luther paraphrased in the High German language, and set to a tune of his own composing, the forty-sixth Psalm, 'Deus noster refugium.' It is certain that he was a performer on the lute; and in the work above cited he speaks of his skill in music as an acquisition that he would not exchange for a great matter. Besides this, there is a tradition among the German

Protestants that he was the author of many of the melodies to which the Psalms are now usually sung in their churches;† and Bayle expressly says that to sing a Psalm was, in the judgment of the orthodox of that day, to be a Lutheran. All this considered, it is more than probable, though history is silent in this respect, that the practice of psalmody had its rise in Germany. We are not however to conclude from hence that it was admitted into the churches of the reformed, or that it made part of their public worship in the life-time of Luther; it rather seems to have been confined to family worship, and considered as a source of spiritual consolation; and to this purpose the many devout ejaculations with which the Psalms of David abound, render it with a remarkable degree of propriety applicable.

In this situation stood the matter about a year before the death of Luther; no vulgate translation of the Psalter had as then appeared in the world, and there was little reason to expect one from any country where the reformation had not got firm footing, much less was there to think that any such work, in a country where the established religion was the Romish, could possibly receive the sanction of public authority. But it fell out otherwise; and, however paradoxical it may sound, the protestant churches were indebted for this indulgence to a body of men whose tenets indeed forbad any such hopes, namely the college of the Sorbonne at Paris.

It happened about the year 1543, that there lived in France, Clement Marot, a man moderately endowed with learning, but extremely improved by conversation with men of parts and ingenuity, who with great success had addicted himself to the study of poetry; he had acquired great reputation by certain imitations of Tibullus, Propertius, and Catullus, and had by an elegant translation of the first book of Ovid's Metamorphosis into the French language, established the character of a good poet. This man being inclined to Lutheranism, was persuaded by a friend to publish at Paris a French version of the first thirty of David's Psalms, which he did by permission of the doctors of the Sorbonne, wherein they declare that the book contained nothing contrary to the Christian faith; soon after he added twenty more, but before he could complete his design, which was to have translated the whole in like manner, he died, and a version of the rest in French metre also, was supplied by his friend Theodore Beza.

Sleidan, from whom the above account is in part taken, has bestowed this eulogium on Marot: ' I ' thought it not amiss to commend the name of so ' excellent an artist to other nations also; for in ' France he lives to all posterity; and most are of ' opinion that hardly any man will be able to equal ' him in that kind of writing; and that, as Cicero said ' of Cæsar, he makes wise men afraid to write. ' Others and more learned men than he, have handled ' the same subject, but have come far short of the ' beauty and elegancy of his poems.'

---

* See an account of this person, pag. 397 of this work.

† Mr. Handel has been many times heard to say that the melody of our hundredth Psalm, which by the way is that of the hundred and thirty-fourth both of Goudimel and Claude le Jeune's Psalms, and certain other Psalm-tunes, were of Luther's composition. ,

This it is to be noted is the character of Marot and his book, drawn by a Protestant historian. Another writer, but of a different persuasion, Famianus Strada, has given a less favourable account of both; and yet perhaps, allowing for that prejudice which he could not but entertain against the author of such an innovation as this of Marot undoubtedly was, it is such as will justify the character that Sleidan has given of him; that of Strada is as follows:—

'Among the grooms of the bed-chamber to Francis ' I. of France, there was one Clement Marot, born at ' Douve, a village in the earldom of Namur, a man ' nuturally eloquent, having a rare vein in French ' poetry, wherewith the king was much taken, who ' therefore kept him as a choice instrument of his ' learned pleasures. But as his wit was somewhat ' better than his conditions, from his acquaintance ' with the Lutherans he was suspected to have changed ' his religion; and therefore fearing the king would ' be offended, he fled to his majesty's sister at Bern, ' the old sanctuary for delinquents; a while after, the ' king was pacified and he returned to Paris, where ' he was advised by his friend Franciscus Vatablus, ' the Hebrew lecturer, to leave the trifling subjects ' he wrote upon, and study divine poesy. Thereupon ' he began to translate the Psalms of the Hebrew ' prophet into French stanzas, but so ignorantly and ' perversely,* as a man altogether unlearned, that ' the king, though he often sang his verses, yet, upon ' the just complaints of the doctors of the Sorbonne, ' and their severe censure past on them, commanded ' that nothing of Marot in that kind should be from ' thenceforth published. But being forbid by pro- ' clamation, as it often happens, the longing of the reader, and fame of the work was increased so, that ' new tunes were set to Marot's rhymes, and they ' were sung like profane ballads. He in the mean ' time growing bold by the applauses of the people, ' and not able to forbear bragging, for fear of punish- ' ment, ran to Geneva; and flying from thence for ' new crimes committed, and first having been well ' whipped for them, he died at Turin. The success ' of this translation of the Psalms moved Theodore ' Beza, a friend of Marot, and who wrote an elegy ' in French on his death, to add to the fifty which ' Marot had published, a version in French of the ' other hundred made by himself, so the whole book ' of David's psalms was finished; and to make it ' pleasing to the people, tunes were set to them by ' excellent composers, that chimed so sweetly, that ' every one desired to have the new psalter; but ' many errors in it against religion being detected, ' and the work therefore prohibited, as well because ' the sacred verses of the prophet were published in ' a vulgar tongue by profane persons, as that they ' were *dolo malo* bound up with Calvin's catechism ' at Geneva: these singing psalms, though abhorred ' and slighted by the Catholics, remained in high ' esteem with heretics; and the custom of singing ' the Geneva psalms in French at public meetings, ' upon the highway, and in shops, was thenceforth ' taken for the distinctive sign of a sectary.'†

To this account of Strada may be added from Bayle, that the first publication of thirty of the psalms was dedicated to Francis I., that it was so well received by the people, that copies could not be printed so fast as they were sold off; that they were not then set to music as they are now, to be sung in churches, but every one gave such a tune as he thought fit; ' Each of the princes and courtiers,' says this author, ' took a psalm for himself: Hen. II. loved this, " Ainsi qu'on oit le cerf bruire," which he sang in ' hunting; Madam de Valentinois took this, " Du " fond de ma pensée." The queen chose the psalm " Ne vueilles pas ô Sire," which she sang to a merry ' tune; Anthony king of Navarre took this, " Revenge " moy, pren le querelle," and sang it to the tune of a ' dance of Poitou. In the mean time, Marot, fearing ' lest he should be sent to prison, fled to Geneva, ' where he continued his version as far as fifty psalms. ' Beza put the remaining hundred into verse; and the ' psalms which he rhymed in imitation of Marot's, ' were received by all men with great applause.'

## CHAP. CX.

No sooner was this version of the Psalms completed, than Calvin, who was then at the head of the church of Geneva, determined as it were to consecrate it, and introduce the practice of singing psalms amongst his people: for some time he stood in doubt whether to adopt the Lutheran choral form of singing in consonance, or to institute a plain unisonous melody in which all might join; at length he resolved on the latter, and to this end employed a musician, named Guillaume Franc, to set them to easy tunes of one part only, in which the musical composer succeeded so well, that the people became infatuated with the love of psalm-singing; at length, that is to say, in the year 1553, which was about seven after the version was completed, Calvin, to put the finishing hand to his design, divided the psalms into pauses or small portions, and appointed them to be sung in churches, and so made them a form of religious worship; soon after they were bound up with the Geneva Catechism, and from that time the Catholics, who had been accustomed to sing Marot's psalms in common with profane songs, were forbid the use of them under a severe penalty. The Protestants however continued the indiscriminate use of them at church; they considered the singing of psalms as an exercise of devotion; in the field it was an incentive to courage and manly fortitude, for in their frequent insurrections against their persecutors, a psalm sung by four or five thousand of them answered the end of the music of trumpets and other warlike instruments, and, in short, was among them the accustomed signal to battle.

To this purpose Strada mentions several notable instances that happened a few years after the publication of Marot's version; and first, speaking of the popular tumults in the Low Countries about the year

---

* Marot understood not the Hebrew language, but was furnished with a translation of the Psalms by Vatablus. Bayle, Marot, in not.

† Strada de Bello Belgico, lib. III. Sir Rob. Stapylton's translation. Ex Florimond de Remond in Hist. Ortu. &c. Hæres. lib. viii.

1562, he relates that 'two French Calvinist preachers
' in the night, the one at Valenciennes, and the other
' at Tournay, openly before a great assembly in the
' market-place, delivered their new gospel, and when
' they had done were followed through the streets by
' the multitude, to the number of an hundred at Va-
' lenciennes, and six hundred at Tournay, singing
' David's Psalms in French.* And in another place
' he says that on the 21st of August, 1566, the
' heretics came into the great church at Antwerp with
' concealed weapons, as if they resolved, after some
' light skirmishes for a few days past, to come now to
' battle, and waiting till evensong was done, they
' shouted with an hideous cry Long live the Gheuses ;†
' nay, they commanded the image of the blessed Virgin
' to repeat their acclamation, which if she refused to
' do, they madly swore they would beat and kill her ;
' and though Johannes Immersellius, prætor of the
' town, with some apparitors, came and commanded
' them to keep the peace, yet he could not help it,
' but the people running away to get out of the tumult,
' the heretics shut the doors after them, and as con-
' querors possessed themselves of the church. Now
' when they saw all was theirs, hearing the clock strike
' the last hour of the day, and darkness giving them
' confidence, one of them, lest their wickedness should
' want formality, began to sing a Geneva psalm, and
' then, as if the trumpet had sounded a charge, the
' spirit moving them altogether, they fell upon the
' effigies of the mother of God, and upon the pictures
' of Christ and his saints, some tumbled down and
' trod upon them, others thrust swords into their
' sides, or chopped off their heads with axes, with so
' much concord and forecast in their sacrilege, that
' you would have thought every one had had his
' several work assigned him ; for the very harlots,
' those common appurtenances to thieves and drunk-
' ards, catching up the wax candles from the altars,
' cast down the sacred plate, broke asunder the picture
' frames, defaced the painted walls ; part setting up
' ladders, shattered the goodly organs, broke the win-
' dows flourished with a new kind of paint. Huge
' statues of saints that stood in the walls upon pedes-
' tals, they unfastened and hurled down, among which
' an ancient great crucifix, with the two thieves
' hanging on each hand of our Saviour, that stood
' right against the high altar, they pulled down with
' ropes and hewed it to pieces, but touched not the
' two thieves, as if they only worshipped them, and
' desired them to be their good lords. Nay they pre-
' sumed to break open the conservatory of the eccle-
' siastical bread, and putting in their polluted hands,
' to pull out the blessed body of our Lord. Those
' base offscourings of men trod upon the deity, adored
' and dreaded by the angels. The pixes and chalices
' which they found in the vestry they filled with wine
' prepared for the altar, and drank them off in de-
' rision ; they greased their shoes with the chrisme or
' holy oil ; and after the spoil of all these things, laughed
' and were very merry at the matter.' ‡

* De Bello Belgico, lib. III.

† A name which *signifies a Vagrant, or rather a Beggar, but having
been applied to them by a nobleman, an enemy to their faction, they assumed
it as a defiance of him. Vide Strada, sub anno 1556.*

‡ De Bello Belgico, lib V.

Such were the effects produced by the introduction
of psalm-singing among those of the reformed religion ; and no one can be at a loss for a reason why
those of the Romish communion have expressed
themselves with the utmost bitterness against the
practice of it. Bayle in the article Marot, has given
a letter from a gentleman who had served the queen
of Navarre, to Catherine de Medicis, subscribed Vil-
lemadon, dated in August 1590, containing an account
of the reception of the psalms which Marot met with at
court, but abounding with such severe and scurrilous
invectives against the Calvinistical psalmody, and
those who were the friends of it, that the omission of
it in this place will, it is hoped, find a ready excuse.

From the several relations herein-before given it
would be difficult to form any judgment either of the
merit of Marot's version or of its author, but Bayle
has summed up his character, and, after bestowing
high commendations on his Psalms, ranks him among
the best of the French poets.

Having said thus much of the poetry, it now remains
to speak of the music of Marot's psalms : the common
notion is that they were originally set by Lewis
Bourgeois and Claude Goudimel, which is only so
far true as it respects the setting of them in parts ;
for it appears by an anecdote commuicated to Bayle
by a professor of Lausanne, and inserted in a note
on a passage of his life of Marot, that before this
they were sung to melodies of one part only in the
churches at Geneva, and that the composer of those
melodies was one Guillaume Franc ; and to this fact
Beza himself testifies in a kind of certificate, signed
with his own hand, dated Nov. 2, 1552. Bayle's
correspondent farther adds, that he had in his possession a copy of the Geneva psalms, printed in 1564,
with the name Guillaume Franc to it, whereto is prefixed the licence of the magistrate, signed Gallatin,
and sealed with red wax, declaring Guillaume Franc
to be the author of the musical notes to which the
psalms in that impression are set.

It seems that Bourgeois composed music to only
eighty-three of the Psalms, which music was in four,
five, and six parts ; these Psalms so set were printed
at Lyons in 1561. As to Goudimel, it is certain that
he set the whole in four and five parts, for the book
was printed at Paris in 1565, by Adrian Le Roy and
Robert Ballard. Nevertheless there is reason to
think that this or some other collection of Marot's
Psalms with the music, had made its appearance
earlier than 1565 ; and indeed express mention is
made of fifty of Marot's Psalms with the music,
printed at Strasburg with the liturgy in 1545 ; and
there is extant a preface to Marot's Psalms written by
Calvin himself, and dated June 10, 1543, wherein is
the following passage : ' All the psalms with their
' music were printed the first time at Geneva, with a
' preface concerning an agreement of the printers
' thereof, whereby they had engaged to appropriate a
' part of the profits arising from that and future im-
' pressions for the relief of the poor refugees at
' Geneva. §

§ Bayle, MAROT, in not. This agreement is alluded to by the deacons
of the church of Geneva, who in a note after the preface to the Sermons
of Calvin on Deuteronomy, published anno 1567, complain of the breach
of it, insisting that those who printed the psalms every day, could not

The name Guillaume Franc is hardly known among musicians, however, as the original melodies have never been ascribed to any other author, credit may be given to the anecdote above-mentioned to have been communicated to Bayle concerning them. What those original melodies were will hereafter be considered. It is certain that the honour of first composing music in parts to the Geneva psalms is due to Bourgeois and Goudimel; of the former very little is to be learned, but the character and unfortunate history of the latter remain on record.

CLAUDE GOUDIMEL, a supposed native of Franche Comté, was of the reformed religion; and in the Histoire Universelle of Mons. D'Aubigné is mentioned, among other eminent persons, to have been murdered in the massacre of Paris on St. Bartholomew's day, anno 1572: the circumstances of his death, as there related, are, that he, together with Mons. Perot, a civilian, were thrown out of a window, dragged along the streets and cast into the river; but this account is erroneous in respect of the place of his death; for Thuanus, in that part of his history where he takes occasion to mention the massacre of Lyons, has these words: 'The same fate [death] 'attended Claudius Goudimel, an excellent musician 'of our time, who set the psalms of David, translated 'into metre by Clement Marot and Theodore Beza, 'to various and most pleasing tunes.' In the Protestant Martyrology mention is made of Goudimel in these words: 'Claudius Goudimel, an excellent 'musician, and whose memory will live for ever for 'having composed tunes to the greater part of David's 'psalms in French.'

With respect to Goudimel's work, the music in four parts to the psalms, it was first published in the year     and has past a multitude of editions; one in 1602, printed at Delft, without any mention of Bourgeois, is intitled 'Les Pseaumes mis en rime 'Françoise. Par Clement Marot et Theodore de 'Beze; mis en musique à quatre parties par Claude 'Goudimel.' These psalms, for the greater facility in singing them, are of that species of musical composition called Counterpoint; but before his death Goudimel had meditated a noble work, viz., the psalms in five, six, seven, and eight parts, composed in the form of motets, with all the ornaments of fugue, and other inventions common to that kind of music; he had made a considerable progress in it, and, had not death prevented him, would quickly have completed the work.

The psalms of Marot and Beza were also set by another very eminent musician, Claude le Jeune, of whom an account has already been given.* He was a Protestant, a native of Valenciennes, and a favourite of Henry IV. of France. In the title-page of many of his works, published after his death, he is styled 'Phenix des musiciens;' and unquestionably he was in his art one of the greatest men of that day.

There are extant two collections of psalms with

the music of Claude le Jeune, both which appear to be posthumous publications; the one of these, most beautifully printed in separate books, of a small oblong form, at Paris, in 1613, and dedicated by his sister, Cecile le Jeune, to the Duke de Bouillon, contains the whole hundred and fifty psalms of Marot and Beza, with the music in four and five parts as it is said, but in truth the fifth part is frequently nothing more than a reduplication of some of the others in the octave above. A few of the psalms in this collection are plain counterpoint, the rest are of a more artificial contexture, but easy enough for the practice of persons moderately skilled in singing. There is extant also another collection, published at Paris in 1606, of a larger size than the former, entitled 'Pseaumes en vers mezurez, mis en Musique, 'A 2, 3, 4, 5, 6, 7, et 8 parties, par Claude le 'Jeune, natif de Valentienne, Compositeur de la 'musique de la chambre du Roy;' these are certain select psalms paraphrased by an unknown author, and as to the music, it abounds in all those ornaments of fugues, points, and varied motion, which distinguish the Canto figurato from the Canto fermo; so that thus set they might not improperly be styled Motets. This last collection of psalms was published by the author's sister, Cecile le Jeune, and dedicated by her to a friend and fellow-servant of her brother, one of the gentlemen of the chamber to Henry IV.

She also published in 1603, and dedicated to our king James I. a book entitled Le Printemps, containing compositions of her brother in three, four, five, six, seven, and eight parts, in the style of madrigals. By an advertisement prefixed to the book it seems that it was part of a work which the author had undertaken, and intended to adapt to the four seasons of the year. Another work of his was also published by the same Cecile le Jeune in 1606, intitled 'Octonaires de la vanité et inconstance du 'monde,' in three and four parts.

These two musicians, Goudimel and Claude le Jeune, are the most celebrated composers of music to the French psalms. But here it is necessary to remark, that though the common opinion is that they each composed the four parts, superius, contratenor, tenor, and bassus, of every tune, yet the tenor part, which at that time was of the most consequence, as it carried in it the air or melody of the whole composition, is common both to the tunes of Goudimel and le Jeune, and was in fact composed by another person, so that neither of them have done any thing more than given the harmony to a certain melody, which melody is in both authors one and the same.

It is very difficult to assign a reason for this conduct, unless we suppose that these melodies, to which the studies and labours of both these eminent men were but subservient, were on the score of their antiquity or excellence, in such estimation with the people, as to subject a modern musician that should reject them, to the imputation of envy or vanity; or, perhaps after all, and abstracted from every other claim to preference, the frequent use of them in the French protestant congregations might have occasioned such prejudices in their favour, as to render

with a good conscience do so without paying to their poor what was promised and agreed to be paid for their use before they were printed the first time.

    * Book X. chap. xc. of this work.

any others actually inadmissible among them. In either case our curiosity leads us to enquire who was the author of those melodies which two of the most eminent musicians of France condescended thus to honour. In short, recollecting what Bayle has related about the original French psalm-tunes of one part, and laying the above circumstances together, there is little reason to doubt but that those original melodies which constitute the tenor part, and are therefore the ground-work of Goudimel and Claude le Jeune's psalm-tunes, were those very original tunes which the above-cited author has ascribed to Guillaume Franc.

The psalms thus set by Goudimel and Claude le Jeune, were introduced into the public service of the church, not only at Geneva, but in France, Flanders, and most other countries where the reformation had got footing, and the service was in the French language; and continued to be sung until the version became obsolete; the church of Geneva, the first that received, was the first that forsook it and made use of another, begun by Mons. Conrart, and finished by Mons. Bastide; but the French churches, which since the revocation of the edict of Nantes became settled in foreign countries, continued and still use the version of Marot and Beza, revised and altered from time to time through a great number of editions, so as to correspond with those innovations and refinements to which the French and most other living languages are liable.*

Of the German psalmody very little can be said. It is imagined that the High Dutch version of the psalms was made very soon after Luther's time by some of the ablest of their ministers; but as the language is not very fit for poetry, whether it be good or bad the world has shewn very little curiosity to enquire. There are many excellent melodies sung in the German protestant congregations, which is no wonder, considering that that country has been famous for skilful musicians. They have a tradition among them that some of these melodies were composed by Luther himself; and as it is certain that he was skilled in music, that they were is highly probable.

## CHAP. CXI.

It remains now to show what part the church of England acted with respect to church music, and to account for its existence at this day: and here it may be observed, that the great revolutions of religion and government generally take a tincture from the characters of those under whose authority or influence they are brought about. The affection of Leo X. to music, was propitious to the final establishment of choral service in the Romish church; and that it is yet retained in this kingdom, notwithstanding the reformation, and the many efforts of its enemies to banish it, may be ascribed to the like disposition in

the four last princes of the Tudor family. For to instance in Henry VIII. it is certain that he was not only a lover of music, but profoundly skilled in it as a science.†

It will appear farther, that all the children of Henry were skilled in music; with respect to his son Edward, we are told by Cardan that he 'Cheli 'pulsabat;' and in Edward's manuscript Journal, written with his own hand, now in the British Museum, and which is printed in Burnet's History of the Reformation, mention is made of his playing on the lute to the French embassador.‡

As to Mary, her affection for the choral service might probably arise from her attachment to the Romish religion, yet she too was skilled in the practice of music, as appears by a letter from her mother queen Catherine to her, wherein she recommends to her the use of the virginals or lute if she have any.§

The skill in music which Elizabeth possessed is clearly evinced by the following passage in Melvil's Memoirs.‖ 'The same day, after dinner, my Lord 'of Hunsdean drew me up to a quiet gallery that 'I might hear some music, (but he said he durst not 'avow it) where I might hear the queen play upon 'the virginals. After I had hearkened a while I took 'by the tapestry that hung before the door of the 'chamber, and seeing her back was towards the door, 'I entered within the chamber, and stood a pretty 'space, hearing her play excellently well; but she 'left off immediately so soon as she turned her about 'and saw me. She appeared to be surprized to see 'me, and came forward, seeming to strike me with 'her hand, alledging she was not used to play before 'men, but when she was solitary to shun melancholy.'¶ To this passage it may not be improper to add a little anecdote, which perhaps has never yet appeared in print, and may serve to shew either that she had, or affected to have it thought she had, a very nice ear. In her time the bells of the church of Shoreditch, a parish in the northern suburbs of London, were much esteemed for their melody; and in her journies from Hatfield to London, as soon as she approached the town, they constantly rang by way of congratulation. Upon these occasions she seldom failed to stop at a small distance short of the church, and amidst the prayers and acclamations of

---

* This must be understood with an exception, for in some churches both here and abroad, the French protestants sing a paraphrase of the Psalms, by Antoine Godeau. This person was successively Bishop of Grasse and Venice, and died in 1672. The Psalms thus paraphrased are set in four parts by Jacques de Goiry, and were first published in Amsterdam in 1691; some years after they were reprinted by Pearson for the use of the French churches in London.

† See the foregoing volume, book VIII. chap. lxxvii. In a letter from Sir John Harrington to the lord treasurer Burleigh, mention is made of certain old Monkish rhymes called 'The Blacke Saunctus, or Monkes Hymn to Saunte Satane.' The father of Sir John Harrington, who had married a natural daughter of Henry VIII. named Esther, and was very well skilled in music, having learned it, as the letter says, 'in the fellow-'ship of good Maister Tallis, set this hymn to music in a canon of three 'parts; and the author of the letter says that king Henry was used 'in 'plesaunt moode to sing it.' Nugæ Antiquæ, printed for W. Frederick at Bath, 8vo, 1769, pag. 132.

‡ '19 July [1551]. Mons. le Mareschal St. Andre supped with me; 'after supper saw a dozen courses, and after I came and made me ready. '20. The next morning he came to me to mine arraying, and saw my 'bedchamber, and went a hunting with hounds, and saw me shoot, and 'saw all my guards shoot together; he dined with me, heard me play on 'the lute, ride; came to me to my study, supped with me, and so 'departed to Richmond.' Collection of Records, &c. in the Appendix to Burn. Hist. Reform. part II. pag. 31.

§ Burnet Hist. Reform. part II. Appendix pag. 142.

‖ Lond. 1752, pag. 99.

¶ It is also said that she played on an instrument strung with wire, called the Poliphant. Preface to Playford's Introduction to the Skill of Musick, edit. 1666.

the people, would listen attentively to and commend the music of the bells.

From these particulars it may reasonably be inferred, that the several princes to whom they relate were disposed to the retention of music in our solemn church service. It remains to shew on the other hand what were the sentiments of those who headed the reformation in England with respect to this part of divine service.

And first it appears that great complaints were made by many of the dignified clergy and others, of the intricacy and difficulty of the church music of those times. In consequence whereof it was once proposed that organs and curious singing should be removed from our churches.* Latimer, in his diocese of Worcester, went still farther, as appears by certain injunctions of his to the prior and convent of St. Mary, whereby he forbids in their service all manner of singing.†

By a statute of 27 Hen. VIII. cap. 15, power was given to the king to nominate two and thirty persons of his clergy and laity to examine all canons, constitutions, and ordinances provincial and synodical, and to compile a body of such ecclesiastical laws as should in future be observed throughout this realm. Nothing was done towards this necessary work during the life-time of Henry; but in the reign of his son the consideration of it was resumed, and a commission granted for the purpose to eight bishops, eight divines, eight civilians, and eight common lawyers. The deliberations of this assembly, composed of the ablest men in their several professions that the age afforded, terminated in a work, which though pr nted and exhibited to public view, is incomplete, and apparently defective in respect of authority, as wanting the royal sanction. It was published first in 1571, by Fox the Martyrologist, and by some other person, for very obvious reasons, in 1640, under the title of Reformatio Legum Ecclesiasticarum. Dr. Walter Haddon, a celebrated Latin scholar of that age, and Sir John Cheke, were employed in drawing it up, in the doing whereof they very happily imitated the style and form of the Roman civil law, as contained in the Pandects and Institutes of Justinian; but it seems the giving the work an elegant form was the whole of their merit, for virtually and in substance it was the work of Cranmer, who at that time was justly esteemed the ablest canonist in England.

Upon this work it may be observed that if ever choral music might be said to be in danger of being banished from our churches, the era of the compilation of the Reformatio Legum Ecclesiasticarum was of all others the time; and it may well be imagined that to those who were interested in the retention of the solemn church service, the years which were spent in framing that work, were a dreadful interval; however their fears were considerably abated when it was known that the thirty-two commissioners had not reprobated church music, but had barely condemned, by the name of figurate and operose music, that kind of singing which was productive of confusion, and rendered unintelligible to the auditory those parts of the service which required their strictest attention; at the same time the rule prescribed by the commissioners requires that certain parts of the service be sung by the ministers and clerks in a plain, distinct, and audible manner; which in effect was nothing more than reducing choral service to that state of purity and simplicity from which it had deviated.‡

In the book of Homilies we meet with a passage, which, whether intended to justify or reprehend the use of music in divine worship, has been a matter of controversy: an objection is put into the mouth of a woman, supposed to be discoursing with her neighbour on the subject of the reformed church service, which she utters in the following words:—' Alas, ' goffip, what fhall we now do at church, fince all the ' goodly fights we were wont to have are gone; fince we ' cannot hear the like piping, finging, chanting, and play-' ing upon the organs that we could before?' Upon which the preacher interposes, saying, ' But, dearly beloved, ' we ought greatly to rejoice and give God thanks that ' our churches are delivered out of all thofe things which ' difpleafed God fo fore, and filthily defiled his holy houfe ' and his place of prayer.' §

Upon a review of the censures on church-music contained in the decree of the council of Trent, heretofore mentioned, and in the Reformatio Legum Ecclesiasticarum, it will for the most part be found that they were occasioned rather by the abuses that for a long time had attended it, than any persuasion in the reformers of the unlawfulness of the practice. It is true that those of the English clergy, who in the persecution under queen Mary had fled to Francfort, and there laid the foundation of nonconformity, affected to consider it as superstitious and idolatrous; but the less rigid of their brethren thought it had a tendency to edification, and was sufficiently warranted by scripture and the practice of the primitive church.

The rule laid down for church music in England, almost a thousand years ago, was ' Simplicem ' sanctámque Melodiam, secundum morem Ecclesiæ, ' sectentur;'‖ with a view to this the thirty-two commissioners laboured to prevent the corruption of a practice that had at least the sanction of antiquity on its side, and to remove from the church what they as justly as emphatically termed ' curious ' singing.'

---

‡ 'In divinis capitibus recitandis, et Psalmis concinendis, ministri 'et clerici diligenter hoc cogitare debent, non solùm à se Deum laudari 'oportere, sed alios etiam hortatu et exemplo et observatione illorum 'ad eundem cultum adducendos esse. Quapropter partitè voces et dis-'tinctè pronuntient, et cantus sit illorum clarus et aptus, ut ad auditorum 'omnia sensum, et intelligentiam proveniant; itaque vibratam illam, 'et operosam musicam, quæ figurata dicitur, auferri placet, quæ sic in 'multitudinis auribus tumultuatur, ut sæpè linguam non possit ipsam 'loquentem intelligere. Tum auditores etiam ipsi sint in opere simul 'cum clericis et ministris certas divinorum officiorum particulas canentes, 'in quibus Psalmi primùm erunt, annumerabitur fidei symbolum, et gloria 'in excelsis, decem solemnia præcepta, cæteraque hujusmodi præcipua 'religionis capita, quæ maximum in communi fide nostra pondus habent: 'hiis enim piis divini cultus exercitationibus et invitamentis populus 'seipsum eriget, ac sensù quendam habebit orandi, quorum si nullæ nisi 'auscultandi partes sint, ita friget et jacet mens, ut nullam de rebus 'divinis vehementem et seriam cogitationem suscipere possit.' Reformatio Legum Ecclesiasticarum, tit. De Divinis Officiis, cap. 5.

§ Second part of the Homily of the Place and Time oi Prayer, pag. 209.

‖ Spelman. Concil. vol. I. pag. 248.

* Burn. Hist. Reform. part III. pag. 302, 304.
† Burnet Hist. Reform. part II. Collection of Records, book II. numb. 23.

There is an ambiguity in the expression 'curious singing' which might lead a stranger to the state of music at this period to suspect that it meant such a nicety, exactness, and volubility in the performance, as is at present required in the music of the theatre; but this seems not to have been the case. Morley, who is somewhat free in his censure of the choir singers of his time, acquits them of any such affected nicety in their singing as might lead men to say it was over curious: on the contrary, he represents their performance as slovenly to a great degree.* In short, the true object of those many censures which at different times were passed on choir service, was not curious singing, but intricate, elaborate, and unedifying music : *figurata* is the epithet by which it is characterised in the Reformatio Legum Ecclesiasticarum ; now *Cantus figuratus* is a term used in contradistinction to *Cantus planus* or *Cantus firmus*, and means that kind of song which abounds with fugues, responsive passages, and a commixture of various and intricate proportions, which, whether extemporary or written, is by musicians termed descant, and of this kind of music a specimen will be found in Appendix, No. 57.†

## CHAP. CXII.

THE above particulars sufficiently explain the term Curious Singing, and shew that the music of the church was, at the time above spoken of, extremely elaborate and artificial in its contexture. It also appears that those who had the direction of choral service in the several churches and chapels in this kingdom, were to a great degree solicitous about the performance of it; and to the end that every choir should be furnished with a competent number of singers, more especially boys, writs or placards were issued, empowering the officers to whom they were directed, to impress the male children of poor persons in order to their being instructed in music, and qualified for choir service. Tusser, the author of the Five hundred Points of good Husbandry, and who was born in the reign of Henry VIII. relates that being a child, and having been sent by his father to a music school, as was the practice in those times, he was removed to Wallingford college, where he remained till he was seized by virtue of one of those placards, which at that time were issued out to

sundry men, empowering them to impress boys‡ for the service of the several choirs in this kingdom; and that at last he had the good fortune to be settled at St. Paul's, where he had Redford, a skilful musician, for his master. The poor child seems to have had a hard time of it, as appears by his account in these words :—

### Stanza III.

It came to pas that born I was,
Of linage good and gentle blood,
In Eſſex laier in village faier
    That Rivenhall hight :
Which village lide by Banktree ſide,
There ſpend did I mine infancy ;
There then my name in honeſt fame
    Remained in ſight.

### IV.

I yet but yoong, no ſpeech of tong,
Nor teares withall that often fall
From mothers eies when child out cries
    To part her fro ;
Could pitty make good father take,
But out I muſt to ſong be thruſt ;
Say what I would, do what I could,
    His mind was ſo.

### V.

O painefull time ! for every crime
What tooſed eares, like baited beares !
What bobbed lips, what yerkes, what nips,
    What helliſh toies !
What robes ! how bare ! what colledge fare !
What bread how ſtale ! What penny ale !
Then Wallingford how wert thou abhor'd
    Of ſilly boies !

### VI.

Thence for my voice, I muſt (no choice)
Away of forſe like poſting horſe,
For ſundrie men had placards then
    Such child to take :
The better breſt, the leſſer reſt§
To ſerve the queere, now there now here ;
For time ſo ſpent I may repent,
    And ſorrow make.

### VII.

But marke the chance, myſelf to vance.
By friendſhip's lot to Paule's I got ;
So found I grace a certain ſpace
    Still to remaine
With Redford ‖ there, the like no where
For cunning ſuch and vertue much,
By whom ſome part of muſicke art
    So did I gaine.

* Introd. to Practicall Music, pag. 179.

† Dr. Brown, on the authority of Gassendi, asserts that some time, he says not how long, after the invention of counterpart by Guido, according to the natural tendency of this improvement, all the world ran mad after an artificial variety of parts. Dissertation on the Union, &c. of Poetry and Music, pag. 209. In this he seems to have made a twofold mistake, for neither was Guido the inventor of counterpoint, nor was it after a variety of parts that the world were running mad ; it was an affection for that curious and intricate music above spoken of that intoxicated the musicians, and which first the council of Trent, and afterwards the thirty-two commissioners, as above is related, endeavoured to reform. Nor is this author less unfortunate in his assertion that the Greeks that escaped from the taking of Constantinople brought a refined and enervate species of music into Italy from Greece. Ibid. Some ancient Greek manuscripts on music and other subjects were all they brought, and many of them have since been published ; that enervate species of music which he complains they brought to Rome, is no where taken notice of in history ; if by enervate he means elaborate, it is to be accounted for by supposing, that as the science improved, the musicians departed by degrees from that simplicity which distinguishes the songs of the Provençals, who, after all that can be said, were the fathers of the modern secular music, for as to ecclesiastical music, notwithstanding all that he has advanced, it was under the direction and management of the clergy.

‡ See a note of a commission, and also a letter directed to the master of the children of the chapel, Richard Gowre (query Bowyer mentioned infra page 542) Temp. Edward VI. in Strype's mem. eccles Vol. II., 538, 539, giving power to take up children for the king's use, and to serve in his chapel.

§ This expression is worthy of a critical observation :—
    'The better brest the lesser rest.'
In singing, the sound is originally produced by the action of the lungs ; which are so essential an organ in this respect, that to have a good breast was formerly a common periphrasis to denote a good singer. The Italians make use of the terms *Voce di Petto* and *Voce di Testa* to signify two kinds of voice, of which the first is the best. In Shakespeare's comedy of Twelfth Night, after the clown is asked to sing, Sir Andrew Aguecheek says :—
    'By my troth the fool has an excellent breast.'
And in the statutes of Stoke college in Suffolk, founded by Parker, archbishop of Canterbury, is a provision in these words: 'of which said 'queristers, after their breasts are changed [i. e. their voices broke] we 'will the most apt of wit and capacity be helpen with exhibition of forty 'shillings, &c.' Strype's Life of Parker, pag. 9.

‖ John Redford, organist and almoner of St. Paul's. See page 367 of this work.

VIII.

From l'aule's I went, to Eaton ſent
To learn ſtreightwaies the latin phraies,
Where fiftie three ſtripes given to mee
　　At once I had
For fault but ſmall or none at all,
It came to pas thus beat I was;
See Udall* ſee the mercie of thee
　　To me poore lad.

Such was the general state of cathedral music about the middle of the fifteenth century; the reformation in religion, which took place at that period, produced great alterations, as well in the discipline as doctrine of the Christian church; these, so far as they respect the Lutheran ritual, have been already mentioned; and those that relate to the Calvanists are purposely referred to another place. It remains then to trace the rise and progress of that formulary which at present distinguishes the church of England from the other reformed churches. And first it is to be noted, that until about the year 1530, the liturgy, as well here as in other countries then in subjection to the see of Rome, agreeably to the Roman ritual, was said or sung in Latin. In the year 1536 the Creed, Pater noster, and Ten Commandments were by the king's command put into English; and this, as Fuller observes, was the farthest pace which the reformation stepped in the reign of king Henry VIII.†

In the year 1548, being the second of the reign of Edward VI. a liturgy wholly in English was composed by Cranmer, archbishop of Canterbury, and other eminent divines, confirmed by a statute 2 and 3 of the same king, that imposed a penalty on such as should deprave the same, or neglect the use thereof, and printed in the year 1549, with the title of the 'Book of Common Prayer, &c.' as being framed as well for the use of the people as the priest, and in which all are required to join in common. Against this liturgy some objections were taken by Calvin, Beza, Fagius, Peter Martyr, Bucer, and others, upon which a statute was made in the fifth and sixth years of the same king, enacting that it should be faithfully and godly perused, explained, and made perfect. This was accordingly done, and, with some variations, the liturgy was published in 1552.

* This Udall was Nicholas Udall, styled by Bale 'Elegantissimus 'omnium bonarum literarum magister, et earum felicissimus interpres;' and that master of Eton school whose severity made divers of his scholars run away from the school for fear of beating. Roger Ascham tells the story in the preface to his Scholemaster; and a specimen of Udall's elegance both in verse and prose may be seen in the appendix to Ascham's works in quarto, published by John Bennet, 1761.

The life of this poor man [Tusser] was a series of misfortune; from Eton he went to Trinity hall in Cambridge, but soon left the university, and at different times was resident in various parts of the kingdom, where he was successively a musician, school-master, serving-man, husbandman, grazier, and poet, but never throve in any of these several vocations. Fuller relates 'that he traded at large in oxen, sheep, dairies, 'and grain of all kinds, to no profit; that whether he bought or sold he 'lost; and that when a renter he impoverished himself, and never 'enriched his landlord:' all which seems to be too true by his own showing, and is a proof of the truth of that saying in holy scripture that the battle is not to the strong, nor the race to the swift.

As to the Five hundred Points of Husbandry, it is written in familiar verse, and abounds with many curious particulars that bespeak the manners, the customs, and modes of living in this country from the year 1520, to about half a century after; besides which it discovers such a degree of œconomical wisdom in the author, such a sedulous attention to the honest arts of thriving, such a general love of mankind, such a regard to justice, and a reverence for religion, that we do not only lament his misfortunes, but wonder at them, and are at a loss to account for his dying poor, who understood so well the method to become rich.

† Church Hist. in Britaine, book VII. pag. 386.

In the first year of the reign of queen Elizabeth it underwent a second, and in the first of James a third revisal; but the latter of these produced only a small alteration in the rubric, so that we may date the final settlement of the English liturgy from the year 1559, when it was printed by Grafton, with this title, 'The Booke of Common Prayer and 'Administration of the Sacraments, and other Rites 'and Ceremonies of the Church of England.'

But notwithstanding these several alterations and amendments of the ritual, it will be found that the solemn service of our church is nearly coeval with the liturgy itself; for the rubric, as it stands in the first common prayer of Edward VI. prescribes in terms the saying or *singing* of mattens and even-song; and in the ministration of the communion that the clerks shall *sing* in English for the office or Introite, as it is called, a psalm appointed for that day. And again it directs that the clerks shall sing one or many of the sentences therein mentioned, according to the length and shortness of the time that the people be offering. Again, the rubric to the same first common prayer of Edward VI. directs that on Wednesdays and Fridays the English litany shall be said or *sung* in all places after such form as is appointed by the king's majesty's injunctions. These, together with the several directions contained in the rubric above-cited, for singing the post communions, Gloria in excelsis, and other parts of the service, sufficiently prove that, notwithstanding the objections against choral music, and the practice of some of the reformed churches, the compilers of the liturgy, and indeed the king himself, as may be gathered from his injunctions, looked upon the solemn musical service as tending to edification, and were therefore determined to retain it. And this opinion seems to be adopted by the statute of 2 and 3 Edw. VI. cap. 1. which though it contains no formal obligation on the clergy or others to use or join in either vocal or instrumental music in the common prayer, yet does it clearly recognize the practice of singing, and that in such terms, as cannot but preclude all question about the lawfulness of it with those who admit the authority of parliament to determine the form and order of public worship, for the statute enacts that 'if any manner of parson, 'vicar, or other whatsoever minister that ought to 'sing or should *sing* or say Common Prayer, ac- 'cording to the form then lately appointed, or shall 'refuse to use the same, or shall use any other form, 'he shall forfeit, &c.'

And section VII. of the same statute is a proviso that psalms or prayer taken out of the Bible may be used in due time, not letting or omitting thereby the service or any part thereof.‡ *This lets in the Jubilate, Magnificat, Nunc Dimittis, and Anthem, but not the Te Deum.*

The subsequent abolition of the mass, and the

‡ With respect to the manner of performing the solemn choral service at the beginning of the reign of Edward VI. we meet with the following note: 'On the eighteenth day of the moneth of September, 1547, the 'letany was sung in the English tongue in St. Paul's church between the 'quire and the high altar, the singers kneeling, half on the one side and 'half on the other. And the same day the epistle and gospel was also 'red at the high mass in the English tongue.' Heylin's History of the Reformation, pag. 42.

introduction of a new liturgy into the church, calculated to be either sung or said in churches, as it implied no less than a total repudiation of the ancient musical service, made it necessary for those who were concerned to maintain the dignity and splendour of divine worship to think of framing a new one. Many very excellent musicians were living about that time, but few of them had embraced the new religion, as it was called, and those of the old could not be expected immediately to assist in it. Dr. Tye, the king's preceptor in music, was a protestant, but he had undertaken, in emulation of Sternhold, to translate the Acts of the Apostles into English metre, and farther set them to music of four parts; notwithstanding all which, in less than two years after the compiling of king Edward's liturgy, a formule was composed, so perfect in its kind, that, with scarce any variation, it continues to be the rule for choral service even at this day.

The author of this valuable work was that John Marbeck or Merbecke, of whose persecution, grounded on a suspicion of heresy, an ample account has herein-before been given. This book was printed by Richard Grafton in 1550, and has this short title :—

### The Booke of Common Praier noted.

At the bottom of the last leaf is the name **John Merbeke,** by which we are to understand that he was the author or composer of the musical notes : these, so far as the liturgy of Edward VI. and that of Elizabeth may be said to correspond, are very little different from those in use at this day, so that this book may truly be considered as the foundation of the solemn musical service of the church of England.

A particular account of this curious work is here intended to be given, but first it is necessary to observe that it is formed on the model of the Romish ritual ; as first, it contains a general recitatory intonation for the Lord's Prayer, the Apostle's Creed, and such other parts of the service as are most proper to be read, in a certain key or pitch. To the Versicles, Responses, Introits, Kyries, Gloria in excelsis, Offertories, Prefaces, Sanctus, and Post-communions, melodies are adapted of a grave and decent form, and nearly as much restrained as those of St. Ambrose or Gregory ; and these have a harmonical relation to the rest of the service, the dominant of each being in unison with the note of the key in which the whole was to be sung.

After a short explanation of the musical characters that occur in the book, follows the order of Mattins, beginning with the Lord's Prayer,* which, as it is not required by the rubric to be sung, is set to notes that bespeak nothing more than a succession of sounds of the same name and place in the scale, viz., C sol fa ut, that being about the mean tone of a tenor voice. These notes are of various lengths, adapted to express the quantity of the syllables, which they do with great exactness.

For the reasons of this uniform kind of intonation

* It is to be remarked that the sentences from scripture, one or more whereof the minister at his discretion is directed to recite; the exhortation, general confession, and absolution, with which the order of Common Prayer now begins, were no part of King Edward's liturgy, but were first inserted in that of Queen Elizabeth.

it is necessary to recur to the practice of the church at the time when choral or antiphonal singing was first introduced into it, when it will be found that almost the whole of the liturgy was sung ; which being granted, the regularity of the service required that such parts of it as were the most proper for music, as namely, the Te Deum and other hymns, and also the evangelical songs, should be sung in one and the same key ; it was therefore necessary that this key, which was to pervade and govern the whole service, should be fixed and ascertained, otherwise the clerks or singers might carry the melody beyond the reach of their voices. As the use of organs or other instruments in churches was not known in those early times, this could no otherwise be done than by giving to the prayers, the creeds, and other parts of the service not so proper to be sung as read, some general kind of intonation, by means whereof the dominant would be so impressed on the ears and in the memories of those that sung, as to prevent any deviation from the fundamental key ; and accordingly it may be observed that in his book of the Common Praier noted, Marbeck has given to the Lord's Prayer an uniform intonation† in the key of C, saving a small inflexion of the final clause, which here and elsewhere he makes use of to keep the several parts of the service distinct, and prevent their running into each other. But this will be better understood by a perusal of the composition itself, which is as follows :—

### MATTINS.

*The* Quere *wyth the* Priest.

Priest. Glo - ry be to the Father and to the Sonne, and to the

† It is true that that uniform kind of intonation above described, especially in the precatory parts of divine service, is liable to exception, as being void of that energy which some think proper in the utterance of prayer ; yet when it is considered that the inflexions of the human voice are so various with respect to tone and cadence, that no two persons can in strictness be said to read alike, and that scarce any thing is more offensive to a nice and discerning ear than false emphasis or an affected pathos, it may well be questioned whether a grave and decent monotony is not upon the whole the best form of utterance, at least in public worship, as well for the other parts of the service required to be read, as the prayers.

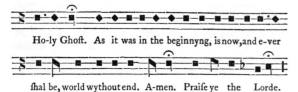

Ho-ly Ghoſt. As it was in the beginnyng, is now, and e-ver

ſhal be, world wythout end. A-men. Praiſe ye the Lorde.

The manner of intonating the psalms is directed to be the same as of the hymn Venite exultemus, the notes whereof are as follow :—

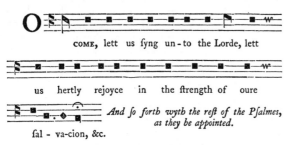

COME, lett us ſyng un-to the Lorde, lett

us hertly rejoyce in the ſtrength of oure

*And ſo forth wyth the reſt of the Pſalmes, as they be appointed.*

fal - va-cion, &c.

Next follows the Te Deum, which being a hymn of praise, deviates more from that tone of audible reading directed by the rubric than the preceding parts of the mattin-service. The Benedictus, which is directed to follow the second lesson, is noted in a different manner ; in short, it is set to a chanting tune, which is iterated as the several verses return. The same hymn, Benedictus, is set to other notes, but still in the form of a chant, and either of these, at the election of the priest, are allowed to be sung.*

Then follow the Kyrie and Christe Eleyson, and after them the Apostles' Creed and Lord's Prayer, both of which are intonated in C FA UT ; but in the intonation of the latter this particular is remarkable ; it is directed to be sung by the choir with the priest to the clause, 'And lead us not into temptation,' which the priest sings alone, and is answered by the choir in the last clause. The versicles,† responses, and collects follow immediately after ; the whole is thus intonated :—

PRIEST. And lead us not in-to tempta-cy-on, ANSW. But

de-li-ver us from e-vil. Amen. PRIEST. O Lorde, ſhew

* The practice of Chanting the Psalms, which doubtless is meant to imitate the ancient antiphonal singing instituted by Flavianus and Diodorus, is supposed to have had its rise at this time. In the English Psalter, to facilitate the practice of chanting, the text is constantly pointed in a manner no way reconcileable with the rules of Orthography, that is to say, with a colon as near the middle of the verse as possible, without the least regard had to the sense of it, as here, 'I am well 'pleased : that the Lord hath heard the voice of my prayer.' 'O how 'amiable are thy dwellings : thou Lord of hosts !' 'Behold now, 'praise the Lord : all the servants of the Lord.'
The Psalter referred to by the common prayer to be read in the daily service, is taken from the great Bible translated by Miles Coverdale and others ; and in the title page thereof the psalms are said to be pointed as they are to be sung or said in churches. In the great Bible the method of punctuation is that which the sense requires, but in the Psalter from queen Elizabeth's time downwards, the psalms are pointed in the manner above described. For the rule of chanting, before each verse of the psalm was thus divided, we are to seek.
† The versicles 'O Lord open thou my lips, &c.' and the responses are by the old church musicians improperly termed *Preces ;* and the versicles 'The Lord be with you, &c.' with their answers, preceding the litany, *Responses.* Vide The first Book of selected Church-Music published by John Barnard, Lond. 1641, fol. 83. 91.

thy mercy up-on us, ANSW. And graunt us thy ſalva-ci-on.

PRIEST. O Lorde ſave the kyng. ANSW. And mercifully heare

us when we call up-on thee. PRIEST. Indue thy miniſters

with righteouſnes. ANSW. And make thy cho-ſen peo-ple

joyfull. PRIEST. O Lorde ſave thy pe-ple, ANSW. And

bleſſe thyne inheritaunce. PRIEST. Give peace in our tyme

O Lord ; ANSW. Becauſe there is none other that fighteth

for us, but onely thou O God. PRIEST. O God make clene

our hertes within us, ANSW. And take not thine Ho - ly

Spi-rit from us. PRIEST. The Lord be with you. ANSW. And

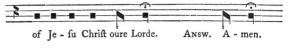

wyth thy ſpirit. PRIEST. Let us pray. *After the Collect for the day, theſe that follow :—*

GOD, which arte aucthor of peace and lover of concorde,

in know - ledge of whom ſtandeth our eternal life, whoſe ſervice is perfecte fredom : Defend us thy humble ſervauntes in all aſſaultes of our enemies, that we ſurely truſting in thy defence, maye not feare the power of any adverſaries : Through the might

of Je - ſu Chriſt oure Lorde. ANSW. A - men.

LORDE our heavenlye fa - ther, al - migh-tie

and everlyvyng God, which has ſafely brought us to the begynnyng of thys daye : defend us in the ſame wyth thy myghtye power, and graunt that this day we fall into no ſynne, neither runne into any kinde of daunger, but that all oure doynges may be ordred by thy governaunce, to do always that is righteous in thy ſight :

Through Je - ſus Chriſt our Lorde. ANSW. A - men.

And thus, ſaith the book, endeth Mattyns.

## CHAP. CXIII.

The Even-song, as it stood in the first liturgy of Edward VI. is noted in like manner. The versicles and responses, which are here called suffrages, correspond very nearly with the form of singing them at this day.

The hymn Benedicite, and the Athanasian Creed, which are occasionally sung in the morning service, appear also in this work of Marbeck with music of his composing.

In the Communion service occurs, first the Introite, which is thus intonated :—

### THE INTROITE.

*At the Communion.*

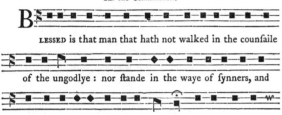

LESSED is that man that hath not walked in the counsaile

of the ungodlye : nor ftande in the waye of fynners, and

hath not fyt in the feate of the fcornefull, But his delight is, &c.

Then the Kyrie, intonated in the key of F FA UT :—

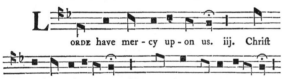

ORDE have mer - cy up - on us.  iij.  Chrift

have mer-cy up-on us.   iij.   Lord have mer-cy up-on us.

The Gloria in excelcis and Creed are composed as melodies, as are also the Offertories to the number of fifteen : The common and proper prefaces for Christmas, Easter, and Ascension days, and for Whit-Sundays and Trinity Sundays, follow next in order, and after them the Sanctus.*

### SANCTUS.

O L Y, Ho - ly, Ho - ly Lorde God of hoftes,

Heaven and earth are full of thy glo-ry.  Ofanna in the higheft.

LESSED is he that commeth in the name of the Lorde :

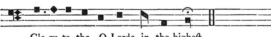

Glo-ry to the, O Lorde, in the higheft.

The prayer for the whole state of Christ's church, which has since been altered into a prayer for the whole state of Christ's church militant here on earth, with the last clause, is intonated in A RE, a fifth

---

* The SANCTUS is part of the communion office; nevertheless in Cathedrals, on Sundays and high festivals it is constantly sung at the end of morning prayer, and before that part of the service which is read by the Episteller and Gospeller while they are making their approach to the communion table.

---

above D SOL RE, the final note of the Sanctus. Then follows a prayer for the blessing of the Holy Spirit on the elements, with the intonation of the last clause, versicles, and responses, the Lord's prayer, Agnus Dei, Post-communions, and a thanksgiving ; which several parts of the service are either wholly omitted, or greatly altered in the liturgy of Elizabeth. These are chiefly noted as melodies. Marbeck's book contains also an office at the burial of the dead, which differs greatly from that now in use.

The objections of particular persons, and the censure of the thirty-two commissioners in the Reformatio Legum Ecclesiasticarum against curious singing had made it necessary that the new service should be plain and edifying. In order that it should be so, this of Marbeck was framed according to the model of the Greek and Latin churches, and agreeable to that tonal melody, which the ancient fathers of the church have celebrated as completely adequate to all the ends of prayer, praise, thanksgiving, and every other mode of religious worship.

The interval between the framing the first liturgy of Edward VI. and the setting it to musical notes, was but a year at most. It appears that at this time, besides an establishment of household musicians, consisting of singers and players on sundry different instruments, there was also one of gentlemen and children of the royal chapel, which had subsisted in succession from the time of Edward IV. The following is a list of both, with the salaries or stipends of the several officers as it stood in the reign of Edward VI. :—†

### MUSITIONS and PLAYERS.

| | | | £. | s. | d. |
|---|---|---|---|---|---|
| Trumpeters. Serjeante. | Benedict Browne | - - Fee | 24 | 6. | 8 |
| Trumpeters. | in No. 16, every of them having by the yere £24 6s. 8d. - | - Fee | 389 | 6 | 8 |
| Luters. | Philip Van Welder - / Peter Van Welder - | - Fee | 40 | 0 | 0 |
| Harpers. | William Moore - - / Bernard de Ponte - | - Fee / - Fee | 18 / 20 | 5 / 0 | 0 / 0 |
| Singers. | Thomas Kent - - / Thomas Bowde - | - Fee / - Fee | 9 / 9 | 2 / 2 | 6 / 6 |
| Rebeck. | John Severnecke | ·· - Fee | 24 | 6 | 8 |
| Sagbutts in number 6, whereof | 5 having £24 6s. 8d. by the yeere, and one at £36 10s. - - | - Fee | 158 | 3 | 4 |
| Vyalls in number 8, whereof | 6 at £30 8s. 4d. the yeere, and one at £20, and another at £18 5s. | - Fee | 220 | 15 | 0 |
| Bagpiper. | Richard Woodward - | - Fee | 12 | 3 | 4 |
| Minstrelles in number 9, whereof | 7 at £18 5s. a peece - / 1 at £24 6s. 8d. - / 1 at £3 6s. 8d. - | - Fee / - Fee / - Fee | 127 / 24 / 3 | 15 / 6 / 6 | 0 / 8 / 8 |
| Dromslades‡ in number 3, whereof | Robert Bruer, Master drummer / Alexander Pencax - / John Hodgkin - | Fee / - Fee / - Fee | 18 / 18 / 18 | 5 / 5 / 5 | 0 / 0 / 5 |
| Players on the flutes. | Oliver Rampons / Pier Guye - - | - Fee / - Fee | 18 / 34 | 5 / 8 | 0 / 4 |
| Players on virginals | John Heywoode - / Anthony de Chounte - / Robert Bewman - | - Fee / - Fee / - Fee | 50 / 30 / 12 | 0 / 8 / 3 | 0 / 4 / 4 |

† Vide extract from the Liber Niger Domus Regis at page 271, et seq.

‡ DRUMSLADE, idem quod DRUMMER, Minsh.

| Musicians Straungers | the 4 brethren Venetians, viz., John, Anthonye Jasper, and Baptiste | Fee | 16 | 6 | 8 |
| | Augustine Bassane | Fee | 36 | 10 | 0 |
| | William Trosses | Fee | 38 | 0 | 0 |
| | William Denivat | Fee | 38 | 0 | 0 |
| Players of interludes in number 8 | every of them at £3 6s. 8d. by yeere £26 13s. 4d. in Camera 7, £23 6d. 8d. in Sc̄cio one £3 6s. 8d. | Fee | 26 | 13 | 4 |
| Makers of instruments. | William Beton Organ-maker | Fee | 20 | 0 | 0 |
| | William Tresorer Regal-maker | Fee | 10 | 0 | 0 |

Summa totalis　　1732　5　0

Total number of persons　73

#### OFFICERS OF THE CHAPPELL.

|  |  | £ | s. | d. | | |
|---|---|---|---|---|---|---|
| Master of the children, Richard Bowyer | Fee | 40 | 0 | 0 | | |
| | Largesse to the children at high feasts | 9 | 13 | 4 | 65 | 13 | 4 |
| | Allowance for breakfast for the children | 16 | 0 | 0 | | |

| Gentlemen of the chappell 32, every of them 7d. ob. a day. | Emery Tuckfield | John Kye |
|---|---|---|
| | Nich. Archibald | John Angel |
| | William Walker | William Huchins |
| | R. Chamberleyn | Robert Phelipps |
| | W. Gravesend | Thomas Birde |
| | Richard Bowyer | Robert Perry |
| | William Barber | Thomas Wayte |
| | R. Richmounte | THOMAS TALLES |
| | Nicholas Mellowe | Thomas Wright |
| | John Bendebow | Robert Stone |
| | William Mawpley | J. SHEPHARDE |
| | George Edwards | WIL. HYNNES or HUNNIS |
| | Robert Morecock | Thomas Manne |
| | R. Alyeworth | Roger Kenton |
| | T. Palfreman | Lucas Caustell |
| | RICHARD FARRANT | Edward Addams |

365　0　0

2 at 4d. ob. a day either of them　13　13　9
5 at 4d. the daye every of them　30　8　4　} 46　2　1
Hugh Williams at 40s. a yeere　2　0　0

Summa totalis　476　15　5

1732　5　0　Musicians　　Number of persons 73
476　15　5　Officers of the Chappell　Number of persons 41

2209　0　5　Total of both　　　114

But all the labour and pains that had been bestowed in settling a ritual for the protestant service, were rendered vain; and the hopes that had been entertained of seeing the reformation of religion perfected, were defeated by the death of the king in 1553, and the succession to the throne of the lady Mary, from whose bigotry and natural gloominess of temper the protestants had every thing to fear. It is sufficiently known that this event was attended not only with an immediate recognition of the papal authority, but with the restoration of the Romish ritual, and that the zeal of this princess to undo all that had been done in the preceding reigns of her father and brother, was indefatigable. In particular she seems to have sedulously laboured the re-establishment of the Romish choral service, and directed the republication of a great number of Latin service-books,

among which were the Primer, Manual, Breviary and others, in Usum Sarum, which were reprinted at London by Grafton, Wayland, and other of the old printers, with the musical notes, for the use of her chapel.*

#### CHAP. CXIV.

THE accession of Elizabeth to the throne in 1558, was followed by an act of parliament, entitled an Act for the uniformity of the common prayer and service in the church, and administration of the sacraments, which, after reciting that at the death of Edward VI. there remained one uniform order of common service and prayer, which had been set forth and authorized by an act of the parliament holden in the 5th and 6th years of his reign, and that the same had been repealed by an act of parliament in the first year of queen Mary, to the great decay of the due honour of God, and discomfort to the professors of the trueth of Christes religion, Doth enact 'That the said statute of repeal, and every thing 'therein contained, only concerning the saide booke 'and service, &c. shall be void. And that all 'ministers shall be bounden to say and use the 'Mattens, Evensong, celebration of the Lord's sup-'per, and administration of the sacraments in such 'order and form as is mentioned in the said booke 'so authorized by parliament in the fifth and sixth 'yere of the reign of king Edward VI. with one 'alteration or addition of certaine lessens to be used 'on every Sunday in the yere, and the forme of the 'Letanie altered and corrected, and two sentences 'onely added in the deliverie of the sacrament to the 'communicants, and none other.'

By this statute the second liturgy of Edward VI with a few variations, was restored; but here we may note that correction of the litany which is referred to by the statute, for it indicates a temper less irascible than that which actuated the first reformers. In the litany of Henry VIII. continued in both the liturgies of Edward, is contained the following prayer: 'From all sedition and privy con-'spiracy, *from the tyranny of the bishop of Rome* '*and all his detestable enormities;* from all false 'doctrine and heresy, from hardness of heart, and 'contempt of thy word and commandment. Good 'Lord deliver us;' taken, with a very small variation, from this in the litany of the Lutherans, 'Ut ab 'hostium tuorum, Turcæ, et Papæ blasphemiis, cæde 'et libidinibus clementer nos conservare digneris.'†

The correction above-mentioned consisted in the recision of so much of the prayer for deliverance from sedition, &c. as related to the bishop of Rome and all his detestable enormities, as they are termed, and the addition of the words rebellion and schism, which are now a part of the prayer.

It is said of Elizabeth, that being a lover of state

* It is worthy of remark, that notwithstanding the fundamental difference in religion and the form of public worship in the two reigns, it appears by a record now in the possession of the Antiquarian Society, that with the variety of only a very few names, the list of Mary's chapel establishment was the same with that above given of her brother Edward's.

† In Psalmod. sive cant. sacra. vet. Eccles. select. per Luc. Lossium Luneberg.

and magnificence, she was secretly a friend, though not to the doctrines,* yet to the pomp and splendor of the Romish religion, and consequently to the ancient form of worship; and from principles of policy she might wish that the difference between the reformed and the Romish service might be as little as possible;† the effects of this disposition were visible in the reluctance with which she gave up the use of images and prayers for the dead, and the behaviour of those of the Romish communion, who made no scruple of attending the service of a church which had wrested the supremacy out of the hands of the pope.‡

At the beginning of her reign, those divines who had fled from the persecution under Mary, to Francfort, and other parts of Germany, and to Geneva, and had contracted a dislike to the discipline established in England, together with some of the principal courtiers, made some faint attempts towards a revival of the opposition to choral service; they insisted that the psalms of David in metre, set to plain and easy melodies, were sufficient for the purposes of edification; and for this they appealed to the authority of Calvin, and the practice of the churches under his direction.　But the queen, and those to whom she had committed the care of revising the liturgy, thought that the foreign divines had already meddled more in these matters than

---

* Nevertheless she seems to have entertained some opinions, which none of the reformed churches would ever acquiesce in.　When one of her chaplains, Mr. Alexander Nowel, dean of St. Paul's, had spoken less reverently in a sermon preached before her, of the sign of the cross than she liked, she called aloud to him from her closet window, commanding him to retire from that ungodly digression, and return to his text.　And when one of her divines, on Good Friday, anno 1565, had preached a sermon in defence of the real presence, she openly gave him thanks for his pains and piety.　Heylin's History of the Reformation, Eliz. pag. 124.　It seems that when she gave that shrewd answer to a Popish priest, who pressed her very hard to declare her opinion touching the presence of Christ in the sacrament:—

　　'Twas God the word that spake it,
　　　He took the bread and brake it;
　　And what the word did make it;
　　　That I believe, and take it.

she had either not settled, or was too wise to declare, her opinion touching the doctrine of transubstantiation.

† It is certain she had a crucifix in her chapel.　See a letter from Sandys, bishop of Worcester, to Peter Martyr, expressing his uneasiness at it.　Burn. Reform. III. 289. 291. and Records to book VI. No. 61. Heylin says that it remained there for some years, till it was broken to pieces by Patch the fool, no wiser man daring to undertake such a desperate service, at the solicitation of Sir Francis Knolles, a near relation of the queen.　Heylin's Hist. of the Reformation, Eliz. pag. 124.　Neal goes much farther, and says 'that the altar was furnished with rich 'plate, with two gilt candlesticks, with lighted candles, and a massy 'crucifix in the midst, and that the service was sung not only with 'organs, but with the artificial music of cornets, sacbuts, &c. on solemn 'festivals.　That the ceremonies observed by the knights of the garter 'in their adoration towards the alter, which had been abolished by 'Edward VI. and revived by queen Mary, were retained.　That, in 'short, the service performed in the queen's chapel, and in sundry 'cathedrals, was so splendid and showy, that foreigners could not dis-'tinguish it from the Roman, except that it was performed in the 'English tongue.'　By this method, he adds, most of the Popish laity were deceived into conformity, and came regularly to church for nine or ten years, till the pope, being out of all hopes of an accommodation, forbad them, by excommunicating the queen, and laying the whole kingdom under an interdict.　Hist. of the Puritans, vol. I. page 156.

‡ This fact is rather invidiously mentioned by Neal, in the passage cited from him in the preceding note; the authority for it is a letter from the queen to Sir Francis Walsyngham, dated 11. Aug. 1570, in which she says of the Roman Catholics, 'that they did ordinarily resort from 'the beginning of her reign in all open places to the churches, and to 'divine services in the church, without contradiction or shew of mis-'liking:' to the same purpose Sir Edward Coke, in a charge of his at Norwich assizes, asserted that for the first ten years of queen Elizabeth's reign the Roman Catholics came frequently to church; and in his speech against Garnet, and other conspirators, he affirmed this upon his own knowledge, giving an instance thereof in Bedingfield, Cornwallis, and several others of the Romish persuasion.　Collier's Ecclesiast. Hist. vol. II. pag. 436.

became them; the common prayer of her brother had been once altered to please Calvin, Bucer, Fagius, and others of them, and she seemed determined to make no more concessions, at least to that side, and therefore insisted on the retention of the solemn church service.

The declaration of her will and pleasure in this respect is contained in the forty-ninth of those injunctions concerning the clergy and laity of this realm, which were published by her in the first year of her reign, A. D. 1559; they were printed first by Jugge and Cawood, and are to be found in Sparrow's Collection of Articles, Injunctions, and Canons, in quarto, 1684.　That above referred to, entitled 'for 'continuance of syngynge in the church,' is in the words following:—

'Item, becaufe in dyvers collegiate, and alfo fome 'parifhe churches, there hath been lyvynges appoynted 'for the mayntenaunce of menne and chyldren, to ufe 'fyngynge in the churche, by meanes whereof the 'lawdable fcyence of muficke hath ben had in eftima-'tion, and preferved in knowledge:　The queenes 'majeftie, neyther meanynge in any wife the decaye ot 'any thynge that myght conveniently tende to the ufe 'and continuance of the faide fcience, neyther to have 'the fame in any parte fo abufed in the churche, that 'thereby the common prayer fhoulde be the worfe 'underftande of the hearers:　Wylleth and commandeth 'that fyrft no alteration be made of fuch affignementes 'of lyvynge as heretofore hath been appointed to the 'ufe of fyngynge or muficke in the churche, but that 'the fame fo remayne.　And that there bee a modefte 'and deyftynĉte fong fo ufed in all partes of the com-'mon prayers in the churche, that the fame may be as 'playnely underftanded as yf it were read without 'fyngyng.　And yet neverthelefe for the comforting 'of fuch as delite in muficke, it may be permytted that 'in the begynninge or in thend of common prayers, 'either at mornynge or evenynge, there may be funge 'an hymne or fuch lyke fonge, to the prayfe of Al-'mighty God, in the beft forte of melodye and muficke 'that may be convenienty devyfed, havynge refpeĉte 'that the fentence of the hymme may bee underftanded 'and perceyved.'

And yet, notwithstanding this express declaration of the queen's pleasure with regard to continuance of singing in the church, about three years after the publishing these her injunctions, six articles, tending to a farther reformation of the liturgy, were presented to the lower house of convocation, the last whereof was that the use of organs be removed from churches; which, after great debate, were so near being carried, that the rejection of them was owing to a single vote, and that, too, by the proxy of an absent member.§ Bishop Burnet has given from Strype, but without a direction where they are to be found, the heads of another proposal for a reformation, wherein it is insisted that organs and curious singing should be removed.||

In the resolution which queen Elizabeth maintained to continue the solemn musical service in the church,

---

§ Burn. Hist. Reform. part III. pag. 303.　　|| Ibid. 304.

it is supposed she was confirmed by Parker, whom she had then lately promoted to the see of Canterbury, a man of great learning and abilities, and, as it happened, eminently skilled in music. Strype, in his life of this prelate, says he had been taught in his youth to sing by one Love, a priest, and also by one Manthorp, clerk of St. Stephen's in Norwich. In his retirement from the persecution under queen Mary he translated into English verse the whole book of the psalms of David. In the foundation of his college at Stoke in Suffolk is a provision for queristers. He had a considerable hand in revising the liturgy of queen Elizabeth. Some of the particulars above related afford ground for a conjecture that Parker's affection to music might co-operate with his zeal for the church, and induce him to join with Elizabeth in her endeavours to reform the choral service, and consequently that its re-establishment was in some degree owing to him.

By the passing of the act of uniformity of the first of Eliz. cap 2, the common prayer and communion service were restored by such words of reference to the usage in her brother Edward's time, as would well warrant the use of that music which Marbeck had adapted to them; for which reason, and because it had been printed under the sanction of royal authority, the Booke of Common Praier noted by John Marbecke, was considered as the general formula of choral service: and to the end that the whole should be uniform and consistent, it is directed by the rubric of Elizabeth's liturgy, that in such places where they do sing, those portions of scripture which constitute the lessons for the day, as also the epistles and gospels, shall be sung in a plain tune, after the manner of distinct reading; the meaning whereof seems to be, that they should be uttered in a kind of monotony, with a reference to the dominant or key-note of the service, which for the most part lay in C FA UT, that being nearly the mean tone of a tenor voice: and most of the printed collections of services give as well the intonation of the lessons, as the melodies of the hymns and evangelical songs.

The settlement of religion, and the perfecting of the reformation, as it was of the utmost importance to the peace of the kingdom, and coincided with the queen's opinion, so was it the first great object of her attention. She succeeded to the crown on the seventeenth day of November, in the year 1558; on the twenty-eighth of April, 1559, the bill for the uniformity of the common prayer passed into a law, and was to take effect on the twenty-fourth day of June then next. Hitherto the Romish office was permitted to continue, the Latin mass-book remained, and the priests celebrated divine service for the most part as they had done in the time of queen Mary, during which interval were great and earnest disputes between the Protestant and Romish clergy touching the English service-book. It seems that the queen was so eager to hear the reformed service, that she anticipated its restoration; for whereas the act required that it should take place throughout the kingdom on St. John the Baptist's day, service in English was performed in her chapel on Sunday, May the second,* which was but four days after the use of it was enacted.

The liturgy of queen Elizabeth was printed in the first year of its establishment with this title, ' The ' Boke of common prayer and administration of the ' sacraments, and other rites and ceremonies of the ' church of England;' and the license contained in the rubrics, which declare that it may be said or sung, and direct that in choirs and places where they sing, the anthem shall follow certain parts of the service, is a plain intimation that this form of divine worship was calculated as well for choral as parochial service. The queen's injunctions, and also the act of uniformity, amounted to a tacit recognition of a solemn choral service; and under the authority of these, that of Marbeck was sung in the several choirs throughout the kingdom, but it was soon found that this formula, excellent as it was in its kind, was not adequate to all the purposes of framing it. In short, it was mere melody; the people, whose ears had been accustomed, as the homily above-cited expresses it, to piping, singing, chanting, and playing on the organs, could but ill brook the loss of those incentives to devotion; and in the comparison, which they could not but make between the pomp and splendour of the old form of worship, and the plainness and simplicity of the new, they were not a little disposed to prefer the former; the consideration whereof was probably the motive to the publication in the year 1560 of a musical service with this title, ' Certaine notes set forth in foure and ' three parts, to be song at the morning, communion, ' and evening praier, very necessarie for the church ' of Christe to be frequented and used: and unto them ' added divers godly praiers and psalmes in the like ' forme to the honor and praise of God. Imprinted ' at London, over Aldersgate, beneath S. Martins, by ' John Day, 1560.'

It does not appear by this book that any innovation was made in the service as formerly set to musical notes by Marbeck, and there is good reason to suppose that the supplications, responses, and method of intonating the Psalms, remained the same as he composed them. But it is to be remarked, that although the litany made a part of king Edward's first liturgy,† Marbeck had omitted or purposely forborne to set musical notes to it; and this is the rather to be wondered at, seeing that it was the ancient practice of the church, founded on the example of St. Gregory himself, to sing it; this omission however was soon supplied by the composer, whoever he was, of the

* Strype, in his Annals. vol. I. pag. 191, says the twelfth of May; but in this he must be mistaken, he having before, viz., pag. 77, said that the bill passed April the twenty-eighth. By a passage in the same volume of the Annals, page 134, it seems that the practice of singing psalms in churches had its rise a few months after, for he says 'On the      day of ' this month, September, [1559] began the true morning prayer at St. ' Antholin's, London, the bell beginning to ring at five, when a psalm ' was sung after the Geneva fashion, all the congregation, men, women, ' and boys singing together.'

Bishop Juel, in a letter written in March, 1560, seems to allude to this fact; his words are, 'the singing of psalms was begun in one church in ' London, and did quickly spread itself, not only through the city, but in ' the neighbouring places: sometimes at St. Paul's Cross there will be ' 6000 people singing together.' Vide Burnet Hist. Reform. part III. pag. 290. The foreign protestants had distinguished themselves by this practice some years before. Roger Ascham, in a letter from Augusta in Germany, dated 14 Maii, 1551, says 'three or four thousand, singing at a time in one church of that city is but a trifle.' Ascham's Works, published by James Bennet, 4to. pag. 382.

† See the twenty-second of king Edward's Injunctions.

litany in the book above described, and afterwards by Tallis, who composed the litany known by his name, which, by reason of its superior excellence, is the only one of many that have been made, that is used at this day. The great difference between Day's first book and that of Marbeck appears to be this. In Marbeck's the whole of the service was set to music of one single part, whereas in that published by Day, the offices in general were composed in four parts; the following is the order in which they stand, Venite exultemus, Te Deum laudamus, Benedictus Dominus, the Letanie, the Lorde's Praier; the Communion office, containing the Kyries after the commandments, Gloria in excelsis, Nicene Creed, Sanctus, the blessing of the minister upon the people.

The offices in the order of evening prayer set to music are only the Magnificat and Nunc dimittis.

Besides these, the book contains sundry prayers and anthems, composed also in four parts, in many of which this particular is remarkable, that the bass part is set for children.

The book also gives the names of many of those that composed the music; but it is to be observed that the litany has no name to it, neither does it in the least correspond with the litany of Tallis, so that we may suppose that he had not then set that office to music. Besides the name of Tallis, which occurs first at the end of the prayer ' Heare the voice and ' prayer of thy servants,' &c. we have these that follow. Thomas Cawston, M. [for Master] Johnson, Oakland, Shepard; and near the end of the book is inserted an In Nomine of Master Taverner, the bass part for children.

Five years after this, was published another collection of offices, with musical notes, with the following title, ' Mornyng and Evenyng prayer and Com-'munion set forthe in foure partes, to be song in 'churches, both for men and children, with dyvers 'other godly prayers and anthems of sundry men's 'doynges. Imprinted at London by John Day, 1565.'

The names of musicians that occur in this latter collection are Thomas Cawston, Heath, Robert Hasleton, Knight, Johnson, Tallis, Oakland, and Shepard.

Each of these works must be considered as a noble acquisition to the science of music; and had but the thought of printing them in score also occurred to those who directed the publication, the world had reaped the benefit of their good intentions even at this day; but being published as they are in separate parts, the consequence was that they could not long be kept together; and the books are now so dispersed, that it is a question whether a complete set of all the parts of either of these two collections is now to be found: and a farther misfortune is, that few persons are sufficiently skilled in music to see the evil of separating the parts of music books, or to attempt the retrieving them when once scattered abroad; on the contrary, many learned men have taken a single part for the whole of a musical work, and have thought themselves happy in the possession of a book of far less value than a mutilated statue. A single part of the Cantiones of Tallis and Bird, with the word Discantus at the top of the title-page, to dis-

tinguish it from the Superius, Medius, Bassus, and other parts, was in the possession of the late Dr. Ward, Gresham professor of rhetoric; and he, though one of the best grammarians of his time, mistook that for part of the title, and has given it accordingly. In like manner, Ames, a man of singular industry and intelligence in matters that relate to printing, having in his possession the Morning and Evening Prayer of 1565, above mentioned, has described it in his Typographical Antiquities by the title of the Common Prayer with musical notes Secundus Contratenor, never imagining that these two latter words were no part of the title, and that he had only one fourth part of a work which appeared to him to be complete.

Nevertheless the public were great gainers by the setting forth of the two collections of church-music above mentioned in print, one advantage whereof was, that the compositions therein contained were, by means of the press, secured against that corruption which inevitably attends the multiplication of copies of books by writing; and although it may be said of ancient manuscripts in general, that they are far more correctly and beautifully written than any since the invention of printing, it is easy to see that the increase of written copies must necessarily have been the propagation of error; and the fact is, that the ancient church-services, which before this time had been usually copied by monks and singing-men for the use of their respective churches, were, till they were corrected, and the text fixed by printed copies, so full of errors as to be scarce fit for use.

## CHAP. CXV.

Thus was the solemn choral service established on a legal foundation, and the people not only acquiesced in it, but thought it a happy temperature between the extremes of superstition and fanaticism; but the disciplinarian controversy, which had its rise in the preceding reign, and had been set on foot at Francfort and Geneva, whither many able divines had fled to avoid persecution, was pushed with great vehemence by some, who insisted on a farther reformation in matters of religion than had as yet taken place; these were the men called Puritans, of whom the leader at that time was one Thomas Cartwright.

This man, a bachelor of Divinity, a fellow of Trinity college, Cambridge, and Lady Margaret's professor in that university, in his public lectures, read in the year 1570, had objected to the doctrine and discipline of the church. Against the tenets of Cartwright, Dr. Whitgift, afterwards archbishop of Canterbury, preached; Cartwright challenged the doctor to a public disputation, which the latter refused unless he had the queen's licence for it; he however offered a private conference with him in writing, which the other declining, Whitgift collected from his lectures some of the most exceptionable propositions, and sent them to the queen, upon which Cartwright was deprived of his fellowship, and expelled the university. He then went abroad, and became minister to the English merchants at

Antwerp, and afterwards at Middleburg; in his absence the Puritans had drawn up a book entitled An Admonition to the Parliament, containing an enumeration of their grievances, the authors whereof, two Puritan ministers, Mr. Field and Mr. Wilcox, were committed to Newgate; soon after this, Cartwright returned, and drew up a second admonition,* upon which a controversy ensued, wherein Cartwright maintained that the holy scriptures 'were not only 'a standard of doctrine, but of discipline and govern-'ment, and that the church of Christ in all ages was 'to be regulated by them.'

Whitgift on the other hand asserted, that though the holy scriptures are a perfect rule of faith, they were not designed as a standard of church discipline or government; but that the forms of these are changeable, and may be accommodated to the civil government we live under: That the apostolical government was adapted to the church in its infancy, and under persecution, but was to be enlarged and altered as the church grew to maturity, and had the civil magistrate on its side.

In the course of this dispute, objections were made to the liturgy, and to the form and manner of cathedral service, particularly against 'the tossing the psalms from one side to the other,' a sarcastical expression which Cartwright frequently uses, with the intermingling of organs. Whitgift had defended this practice by the example of the primitive Christians, and upon the general principle that the church had a power to decree rites and ceremonies agreeably to the twentieth article of the church of England; and here the dispute rested for some time;† but

it was afterwards revived by Walter Travers, the lecturer at the Temple, a friend of Cartwright; and a formal examination and refutation of his tenets was undertaken by the learned and excellent Hooker, who at that time was Master of the Temple.

In the Ecclesiastical Polity, the objections of Cartwright and his adherents against the doctrine and discipline of the established church, are occasionally inserted in the margin of the book, but, which seems a strange omission in the publishers of it, without any reference to the particular book of Cartwright, to which it was an answer, or any intimation that he was the oppugner of Cartwright, other than the letters T. C. the initials of his Christian and surname, which are added to the several passages cited by Hooker.

The objections against singing in general, and also against antiphonal singing, are to this purpose: 'From whencesoever the practice [of antiphonal 'singing] came, it cannot be good, considering that 'when it is granted that it is lawfull for all the 'people to praise God by singing the Psalms of 'David, this ought not to be restrained to those few 'of the congregation who are retained in the service 'of the church for the sole purpose of singing; and 'where it is lawfull both with heart and voice to 'sing the whole psalm, there it is not meet that they 'should sing but the one half with their heart and 'voice, and the other with their heart only. For 'where they may both with heart and voice sing, 'there the heart is not enough; and therefore, besides 'the incommoding which cometh this way, in that 'being tossed after this sort, men cannot understand 'what is sung; those other two inconveniences come 'of this form of singing, and therefore it is banished 'in all reformed churches. And elsewhere, The 'singing of psalms by course, and side after side, 'although it be very ancient, yet it is not commendable,

* Fuller seems to be mistaken in his assertion that Cartwright drew up the first admonition; Neal ascribes it to the two persons above-named: both admonitions were rejected by the parliament; but the Puritans met with such favour from some of the members, that upon the dissolution of it, they presumed to erect a presbytery at Wandsworth in Surrey; this was in 1572, and from hence the origin of nonconformist or dissenting meeting-houses in this kingdom is to be computed. Vide Fuller's Church Hist. of Britain, Cent. XVI. book ix. pag. 103.

† It appears that Cartwright prosecuted this dispute many years after his return from abroad; and that in September, 1590, he was convened before the ecclesiastical commissioners; and for refusing to take the oath ex officio, was committed to the Fleet [Collier Eccl. Hist. vol. II. 626.] but was afterwards pardoned, and retired to an hospital at Warwick, of which he was master, and lived in friendship with the archbishop ever after. [Ib. 640.] Life of Hooker, 14. Nay, it is said that he changed his opinion, and sorely lamented the unnecessary troubles he had caused in the church by the schism which he had been the great fomenter of. Biogr. Brit. vol. VI. part II. pag. 4253. note KKK.

Contemporary with Cartwright was Robert Brown, a man descended of a good family in Rutlandshire, and a distant relation of the lord treasurer Burleigh; this man, though bred in Bennet college, Cambridge, entertaining a dislike to the doctrine and discipline of the established church, left England, and joined Cartwright's congregation at Middleburg, and, being a man of bold temper and turbulent disposition, laboured with all his might to widen the breach that Cartwright had made between the Puritans and the church, and to multiply the reasons against conformity; to this end he contended that church government was antichristian, that the rites of the church of England were superstitious, and its liturgy a mixture of popery and paganism: a summary of his doctrines, which are said to be the same in effect with those of the Donatists, is contained in a book printed by him at Middleburg, intitled a Treatise of Reformation, of which many copies were dispersed in England.

Returning hither soon after the publication of his book, Brown, together with one Richard Harrison, a country school-master, associated himself with some Dutchmen of the Anabaptist sect, and began a formal schism, in which he succeeded so well, that many separate congregations were set up in divers parts of the kingdom; at length his behaviour drew on him the censures of the church, which brought him to a partial recantation of his opinions, and procured him a benefice in Northamptonshire; but he soon after relapsed, and in an advanced age died in Northampton gaol, to which prison he had been committed for a breach of the peace, not being able to find sureties for his keeping it. Fuller, who was acquainted with him, and had heard him preach, gives the following circumstantial relation of the causes and manner of his commitment and death.

'As for his death in the prison of Northampton many years after, in

'the reign of king Charles, anno 1630, it nothing related to those opinions 'he did, or his followers do maintain, for, as I am credibly informed, 'being by the constable of the parish, who chanced also to be his god-'son, somewhat roughly and rudely required the payment of a rate, he 'hapned in passion to strike him. The constable not taking it patiently 'as a castigation from a god-father, but in anger, as an affront to his 'office, complained to Sir Rowland St. John, a neighbouring justice of 'the peace, and Brown is brought before him. The knight of himself 'was prone rather to pity and pardon than punish his passion, but 'Brown's behaviour was so stubborn, that he appeared obstinately 'ambitious of a prison, as desirous after long absence to renew his 'familiarity with his ancient acquaintance. His mittimus is made, and 'a cart with a feather-bed provided to carry him, he himself being too 'infirme (above eighty) to goe, too unweldie to ride, and no friend so 'favourable as to purchase for him a more comly conveyance. To North-'ampton jayle he is sent, where soon after he sickned, died, and was 'buried in a neighbouring churchyard; and it is no hurt to wish that his 'bad opinions had been interred with him.' Church Hist. Cent. XVI. book ix. page 168.

The same author relates that he boasted he had been committed to thirty-two prisons, some of them so dark, that in them he was not able to see his hand at noon-day.

The opinions which Brown had propagated were those which distinguished that religious sect, who after him were called Brownists. Not only Fuller and Collier, but Neal also represent him as a man of an idle and dissolute life, in no respect resembling either Cartwright or Travers, who dissented upon principle, and appear both, to have been very learned and pious men. These men were the first of those who opposed the liturgy, and were the occasion of those admirable arguments of Hooker in defence of church music, which here follow.

There is a passage in one of Howel's letters which seems to indicate that the tenets of Brown were grown very odious at the time when the former wrote, which for the singularity of it take in his own words :—

'Difference in opinion may work a disaffection in me, but not a detes-'tation; I rather pitty than hate Turk or Infidell, for they are the same 'metall, and bear the same stamp as I do, though the inscriptions differ: 'if I hate any it is those schismaticks that puzzle the sweet peace of our 'church, so that I could be content to see an Anabaptist go to hell on 'a Brownist's back.' Familiar Letters of James Howel, 1678, vol. I. sect. 6. Letter xxxii. To Sir Ed. B. Knt.

'and is so much the more to be suspected, for that
'the Devil hath gone about to get it so great
'authority, partly by deriving it from Ignatius time,
'and partly in making the world believe that this
'came from heaven, and that the angels were heard
'to sing after this sort, which as it is a mere fable,
'so is it confuted by historiographers, whereof some
'ascribe the beginning of this to Damasus, some other
'unto Flavianus and Diodorus.'

These are the principal arguments brought in
proof of the unlawfulness and impropriety of choral
antiphonal singing in the worship of God; in answer
to which it may be said, that its lawfulness, propriety,
and conduciveness to the ends of edification, have
been asserted by a great number of men, each as
fitly qualified to determine on a subject of this nature
as the ablest of their opponents. But the merits of
the controversy will best appear from that defence
of the practice in question contained in the Ecclesiastical Polity, of our countryman Hooker, who with
his usual temper, learning, eloquence, and sagacity, has
exhibited first a very fine eulogium on music itself,
and afterwards a defence of that particular application of it to divine service, which our national
church had recognized, and which it concerned him
to vindicate.

And first as to music in general, and its efficacy in
the exciting of devout affections, he uses these words:—

'Touching musical harmony, whether by instru-
'ment or by voice, it being but of high and low in
'sounds, a due proportionable disposition, such not-
'withstanding is the force thereof, and so pleasing
'effects it hath in that very part of man which is
'most divine, that some have been thereby induced
'to think that the soul itself by nature is, or hath in
'it harmony. A thing which delighteth all ages,
'and beseemeth all states; a thing as seasonable in
'grief as in joy; as decent, being added unto actions
'of greatest weight and solemnity, as being used
'when men most sequester themselves from action:
'the reason hereof is an admirable facility which
'music hath to express and represent to the mind
'more inwardly than any other sensible mean, the
'very standing, rising, and falling, the very steps
'and inflections every way, the turns and varieties of
'all passions whereunto the mind is subject; yea, so
'to imitate them, that whether it resemble unto us
'the same state wherein our minds already are, or
'a clean contrary, we are not more contentedly by
'the one confirmed, than changed and led away by
'the other. In harmony the very image and character
'even of virtue and vice is perceived, the mind de-
'lighted with their resemblances, and brought, by
'having them often iterated, into a love of the things
'themselves; for which cause there is nothing more
'contagious and pestilent than some kinds of har-
'mony, than some nothing more strong and potent
'unto good. And that there is such a difference of
'one kind from another we need no proof but our
'own experience, inasmuch as we are at the hearing
'of some more inclined unto sorrow and heaviness,
'of some more mollified and softened in mind; one
'kind apter to stay and settle us, another to move

'and stir our affections. There is that draweth to
'a marvellous grave and sober mediocrity; there is
'also that carrieth as it were into ecstasies, filling the
'mind with an heavenly joy, and for the time in
'a manner severing it from the body. So that al-
'though we lay altogether aside the consideration of
'ditty or matter, the very harmony of sounds being
'framed in due sort, and carried from the ear to
'the spiritual faculties of our souls, is, by a native
'puissance and efficacy, greatly available to bring to
'a perfect temper whatsoever is there troubled; apt
'as well to quicken the spirits, as to allay that which
'is too eager; sovereign against melancholy and
'despair; forceable to draw forth tears of devotion,
'if the mind be such as can yield them; able both to
'move and to moderate all affections. The prophet
'David having therefore singular knowledge, not in
'poetry alone, but in music also, judged them both
'to be things most necessary for the house of God,
'left behind him to that purpose a number of divinely
'indicted poems; and was farther the author of add-
'ing unto poetry, melody in public prayer, melody
'both vocal and instrumental for the raising up of
'men's hearts, and the sweetening of their affections
'towards God. In which considerations the church
'of Christ doth likewise at this present day retain it
'as an ornament to God's service, and an help to our
'own devotion. They which, under pretence of the
'law ceremonial abrogated, require the abrogation of
'instrumental music, approving nevertheless the use
'of vocal melody to remain, must shew some reason
'wherefore the one should be thought a legal cere-
'mony and not the other. In church music curiosity
'and ostentation of art, wanton, or light, or unsuitable
'harmony, such as only pleaseth the ear, and doth
'not naturally serve to the very kind and degree of
'those impressions, which the matter that goeth with
'it leaveth or is apt to leave in men's minds, doth
'rather blemish and disgrace that we do, than add
'either beauty or furtherance unto it. On the other
'side, these faults prevented the force and efficacy of
'the thing itself, when it drowneth not utterly, but
'fitly suiteth with matter altogether sounding to the
'praise of God, is in truth most admirable, and doth
'much edify, if not the understanding, because it
'teacheth not, yet surely the affection, because there-
'in it worketh much. They must have hearts very
'dry and tough, from whom the melody of the psalms
'doth not some time draw that wherein a mind re-
'ligiously affected, delighteth.'*

And to the objection against antiphonal singing,
'that the Devil hath gone about to get it authority,'
he thus answers:—

'Whosoever were the author, whatsoever the
'time, whencesoever the example of beginning this
'custome in the church of Christ; sith we are wont
'to suspect things only before tryal, and afterwards
'either to approve them as good, or if we find them
'evil, accordingly to judge of them; their counsel
'must need seem very unseasonable, who advise men
'now to suspect that wherewith the world hath had
'by their own account, twelve hundred years ac-

* Eccl. Polity, book V. sect. 38.

'quaintance and upwards; enough to take away
'suspicion and jealousie. Men know by this time,
'if ever they will know, whether it be good or evil
'which hath been so long retained. As for the
'Devil, which way it should greatly benefit him to
'have this manner of singing psalms accounted an
'invention of Ignatius, or an imitation of the angels
'of heaven, we do not well understand. But we
'very well see in them who thus plead, a wonderful
'celerity of discourse. For perceiving at the first,
'but only some cause of suspicion, and fear lest it
'should be evil, they are presently in one and the
'selfsame breath resolved that what beginning soever
'it had, there is no possibility it should be good.
'The potent arguments which did thus suddenly
'break in upon and overcome them, are First, that
'it is not unlawful for the people, all jointly to
'praise God in singing of psalms. Secondly, that
'they are not any where forbidden by the law of
'God to sing every verse of the whole psalm both
'with heart and voice quite and clean through-
'out. Thirdly, that it cannot be understood what is
'sung after our manner. Of which three, forasmuch
'as lawfulness to sing one way, proveth not another
'way inconvenient; the former two are true allega-
'tions, but they lack strength to accomplish their
'desire; the third so strong that it might persuade
'if the truth thereof were not doubtful. And shall
'this enforce us to banish a thing which all Christian
'churches in the world have received? a thing which
'so many ages have held: a thing which the most
'approved councils and laws have so oftentimes
'ratified; a thing which was never found to have
'any inconvenience in it; a thing which always
'heretofore the best men and wisest governours of
'God's people did think they never could commend
'enough; a thing which as Basil was persuaded did
'both strengthen the meditation of those holy words
'which are uttered in that sort, and serve also to
'make attentive, and to raise up the hearts of men;
'a thing whereunto God's people of old did resort
'with hope and thirst; that thereby, especially their
'souls might be edified; a thing which filleth the
'mind with comfort and heavenly delight, stirreth
'up fragrant desires and affections correspondent
'unto that which the words contain; allayeth all
'kind of base and earthly cogitations, banisheth and
'driveth away those evil secret suggestions which
'our invisible enemy is always apt to minister,
'watereth the'heart to the end that it may fructify,
'maketh the virtuous, in trouble full of magnanimity
'and courage, serveth as a most approved remedy
'against all doleful and heavy accidents which be-
'fall men in this present life. To conclude, so
'fitly accordeth with the apostle's own exhortation,
"Speak to yourselves in psalms and hymns and
"spiritual songs, making melody and singing to the
"Lord in your hearts;" that surely there is more
'cause to fear lest the want thereof be a maim, than
'the use a blemish to the service of God.'*

As to the merits of this controversy, every one is
at liberty to judge; and if any shall doubt at the

* Eccl. Polity, book V. sect. 39.

lawfulness and expediency of choral music after considering the arguments on both sides, there is little
hope of their being reconciled to it till an abler advocate than Hooker shall arise in its defence.

The form and manner of divine service being thus
far adjusted, an establishment of a chapel seemed to
follow as a matter of course, the settlement whereof
was attended with but very little difficulty. As
those gentlemen of the chapel who had served under
Edward VI. continued in their stations notwithstanding the revival of the mass, so when the Romish
service was abrogated, and the English liturgy restored, they manifested a disposition to submit to
those who seemed to be better judges of religious
matters than themselves; and notwithstanding that
in the time of queen Mary all persons engaged in the
chapel service must, at least in appearance, have been
papists, we find not that any of them objected to the
reformed service: this at least is certain, that both
Tallis and Bird, the former of whom had set the
music to many Latin motets, and the latter made
sundry masses and other compositions for queen
Mary's chapel, continued in the service of Elizabeth,
the one till the time of his death, and the other
during the whole of her reign, and the greater part
of that of her successor, he dying in 1623.

For the state of queen Elizabeth's chapel we are
in a great measure to seek: it is certain that Tallis
and Bird were organists of it, and that Richard
Bowyer was upon her accession to the crown continued one of the gentlemen of her chapel, who
dying, Richard Edwards was appointed master of
the children. This person, who has been mentioned
in a former part of this work, was a native of
Somersetshire, and a scholar of Corpus Christi college in Oxford, under George Etheridge, and at the
time of its foundation was made senior student of
Christ Church college, being then twenty-four years
of age. Wood, in the Athen. Oxon. has given a
curious account of the representation of a comedy of
his writing, entitled Palemon and Arcite, before
queen Elizabeth, in the hall of Christ Church college,
and of the queen's behaviour on the occasion. Edwards died on the thirty-first day of October, 1596;
and the fifteenth of November in the same year
William Hunnis, a gentleman of the chapel, and who
had been in that station during the two preceding
reigns, was appointed his successor; this person died
on the sixth day of June, 1597, and was succeeded by
Dr. Nathaniel Giles, of whom an account will hereafter
be given.

## CHAP. CXVI.

IT will now be thought time to enquire into the
rise and progress of psalmody in England; nor will
it be said that we were very remiss when it is known
how short the interval was, between the publication
of the French version and ours by Sternhold and
Hopkins, who as having been fellow-labourers in
this work of Reformation, are so yoked together,
that hardly any one mentions them asunder.

Thomas Sternhold is said to have been a native of
Hampshire. Where he received the rudiments of

literature is not known, but Wood says that he resided some time in the university of Oxford, and that he left it without the honour of a degree. By some interest that he had at court, he was preferred to the office of groom of the robes to Henry VIII. which he discharged so well, that he became a personal favourite of the king, who by his will left him a legacy of an hundred marks. Upon the decease of the king, Sternhold was continued in the same employment by his successor,; and having leisure to pursue his studies, he acquired some degree of esteem about the court for his vein in poetry and other trivial learning. He was a man of a very religious turn of mind, in his morals irreproachable, and an adherent to the principles of the reformation, and being offended with the amorous and immodest songs, which were then the usual entertainment of persons about the court, he undertook to translate the Psalms of David into English metre, but he died without completing the work. His will was proved the twelfth day of September, anno 1549; he is therein styled Groom of his Majesty's robes, and it thereby appears that he died seised of lands to a considerable value in Hampshire and in the county of Cornwall.

Fifty-one of the Psalms were all that Sternhold lived to versify and these were first printed by Edward Whitchurch, and published anno 1549, with the following title: 'All such Psalmes of David 'as Thomas Sternholde, late grome of the kinges 'majestyes robes did in his lyfe-tyme drawe into 'Englyshe metre.' The book is dedicated to king Edward VI. by the author, and was therefore probably prepared by him for the press. *In the dedication it is said that the king took pleasure in hearing these Psalms sung to him.* Wood is mistaken in saying that Sternhold caused musical notes to be set to his Psalms; they were published in 1549 and 1552, without notes; and the first edition of the Psalms with notes is that of 1562, mentioned hereafter.*

Ames takes notice of another work of the same author, entitled 'Certayne chapters of the Proverbs 'of Solomon drawn into metre;' this also was a posthumous publication, it being printed anno 1551, two years after Sternhold's decease.†

Contemporary with Sternhold was John Hopkins, originally a school-master, a man rather more esteemed for his poetical talents than his coadjutor: he turned

* It is worthy of remark that both in France and England the Psalms were first translated into vulgar metre by laymen, and, which is very singular, by courtiers. Marot was of the bed-chamber to Francis I. and Sternhold groom of the robes to Henry VIII and Edward VI; their respective translations were not completed by themselves, and yet they translated nearly an equal number of psalms, that is to say, Marot fifty, and Sternhold fifty-one.

† In the same year was published 'Certain Psalmes chosen out of the 'Psalmes of David, commonly called vii penytentiall Psalmes, drawen 'into Englyshe meter by Sir Thomas Wyat, Knyght, whereunto is added 'a prologe of the auctore before every Psalme, very pleasant and profett-'able to the godly reader. Imprinted at London, in Paules churchyarde, 'at the sygne of the Starre, by Thomas Raynald and John Harryngton, 'cum previlegio ad imprimendum solum, MDXLIX. The last day of 'December.'
And in 1550, 'Certayne Psalmes chosen out of the Psalter of David, 'and drawen furth into Engiysh meter by William Hunnis, servant to 'the ryght honorable Syr William Harberde, knight. Newly collected 'and imprinted. Imprynted at London in Aldersgate strete, by the wydowe of John Herforde for John Harrington, the yeare of our Lord 'M D and L. Cum privilegio ad imprimendum solum.'

into metre fifty-eight of the Psalms, which are distinguished by the initial letters of his name. Bishop Tanner styles him, 'Poeta, ut ea ferebant tempora, eximius;' and at the end of the Latin commendatory verses prefixed to Fox's Acts and Monuments, are some stanzas of his that fully justify this character.

William Whittyngham had also a hand in this version of the Psalms; he was a man of great learning, and one of those English divines that resided abroad during the persecution under queen Mary; preferring the order and discipline of the Genevan church to that of Francfort, whither he first fled; he chose the latter city for the place of his abode, and became a favourite of Calvin, from whom he received ordination. He assisted in the translation of the Bible by Coverdale, Goodman and others, and translated into English metre those Psalms, in number only five, which in our version bear the initials of his name; among these is the hundred and nineteenth, which is full as long as twenty of the others. He also versified the Decalogue, and the prayer immediately after it, and very probably the Lord's Prayer, the Creed, and the hymn Veni Creator, all which follow the singing psalms in our version. He was afterwards, by the favour of Robert earl of Leicester, promoted to the deanery of Durham; and might, if he had made the best of his interest, have succeeded Sir William Cecil, afterwards Lord Burleigh, in the employment of secretary of state. Wood, who has raked together many particulars concerning him, relates that he caused the image of St. Cuthbert, in the cathedral church of Durham, to be broke to pieces, and that he defaced many ancient monuments in that church.‡

The letter N. is also prefixed to twenty-seven of the Psalms in our English version; this is intended to denote Thomas Norton, of Sharpenhoe in Bedfordshire, a barrister, and, in Wood's phrase, a forward and busy Calvinist in the beginning of queen Elizabeth's reign, a man then accounted eminent for his poetry and making of tragedies. Of his merit in which kind of writing he has left us no proofs excepting the three first acts of a tragedy, at first printed with the title of Ferrex and Porrex, but better known by that of Gorbuduc, which it now bears, the latter two acts whereof were written by Thomas Sackville, lord Buckhurst earl of Dorset, lord high treasurer in the reign of James I. and the founder of the present Dorset family. This performance is highly commended by Sir Philip Sidney in his Defence of Poesy, and is too well known to need a more particular character.

Robert Wisdome translated into metre the twenty-fifth psalm, and wrote also that prayer in metre at the end of our version, the first stanza whereof is:—

'Preserve us Lord by thy dear word,
'From Pope and Turk defend us Lord,
'Which both would thrust out of his throne
'Our Lord Jesus Christ thy deare son.'

For which he has been ridiculed by the facetious bishop Corbet and others, though Wood gives him the character of a good Latin and English poet for

‡ Athen. Oxon. col. 195.

his time. He adds, that he had been in exile in queen Mary's reign; that he was rector of Settrington in Yorkshire, and also archdeacon of Ely, and had been nominated to a bishoprick in Ireland, temp. Edward VI. and that he died 1568.

The 70, 104, 112, 113, 122, 125, and 134 Psalms are distinguished by the initials W. K. *These denote William Keshe, a Scotch divine. See Warton's History of English Poetry, Vol. III. pag.* 418, *in note. Psalm* 136 *has the letters T. C., but for the name of this person we are to seek.*

The first publication of a complete version of the Psalms was by John Day, in 1562, it bears this title: 'The whole booke of Psalmes, collected into ' English metre by T. Sternhold, J. Hopkins, and ' others, conferred with the Ebrue; with apt notes to sing them withall.' *

* Another version of the Psalms, and that a complete one, but very little known, is extant, the work of archbishop Parker during his exile. In the diary of that prelate printed from his own manuscript, in Strype's life of archbishop Parker is the following memorandum:—' And still this ' 6 Aug. [his birth day] An. Dom. 1557, I persist in the same constancy ' upholden by the grace and goodness of my Lord and Saviour Jesus ' Christ, by whose inspiration I have finished the book of Psalms turned ' into vulgar verse.'

Strype says, ' What became of the Psalms I know not;' nevertheless it seems that they were printed, and that with the following title:—'The ' whole Psalter translated into English Metre, which contayneth an ' hundreth and fifty Psalmes. "Quoniam omnis terre Deus: Psallite ' "sapienter—Psal. 47. Imprinted at London by John Daye, dwelling over ' "Aldersgate beneath S. Martyn's." without a date. In a copy of this book, very richly bound, which was bought at the sale of the late Mr. West's library, is a memorandum on a spare leaf in the hand-writing of Dr. White Kennet, bishop of Peterborough, purporting that the archbishop printed this book of Psalms, and that though he forbore to publish it with his name, he suffered his wife to present the book fairly bound to several of the nobility; Dr. Kennet therefore conjectures that the very book in which this memorandum is made, is one of the copies so presented; and gives for a reason that he himself presented a like copy to the wife of archbishop Wake, wherein Margaret Parker in her own name and hand dedicates the book to a noble lady. Signed Wh. Peterb.

After the preface, which is in metre, and directs the singing of the psalms distinctly and audibly, is a declaration of the virtue of psalms in metre, and the self-same directions from St. Athanasius for the choice of psalms for particular occasions, as are prefixed to the version of Sternhold and Hopkins, and the rest, and at the conclusion of each psalm is a collect. They are printed without music, save that at the end are eight tunes in four parts, Meane, Contratenor, Tenor, and Basse, which, agreeably to the practice of the Romish church, are composed in the eight ecclesiastical tones, the tenor being the plain-song. It is said by Strype that Parker in the course of his education had been instructed in the practice of singing by two several persons, the one named Love, a priest, the other one Manthorp, clerk of St. Stephen's in Norwich, of the harshness of both which masters he felt so much, that he could never forget it. His affection to music in his mature age may be inferred from the provision made by him in the foundation of a school in the college of Stoke, in the county of Suffolk, of which he was dean; in which the scholars, besides grammar, and other studies of humanity, were taught to sing and play on the organ and other instruments: and also from the statutes of the same college, framed by himself, the last whereof is in these words: ' Item, to be found in the college henceforth ' a number of queristers, to the number of eight or ten or more, as may ' be born conveniently of the stock, to have sufficient meat, drink, broth, ' and learning. Of which said queristers, after their breasts be changed, ' we will the most apt of wit and capacity be helpen with exhibition of ' forty shillings, four marks, or three pounds a-piece to be students in ' some college in Cambridge. The exhibition to be enjoyed but six years.'

And that he had some skill in music appears by the following characteristic of the ecclesiastical tones, prefixed to the eight tunes abovementioned.

The nature of the eyght tunes.

1. The firſt is meeke: devout to ſee,
2. The ſecond ſad: in majeſty.
3. The third doth rage: and roughly brayth,
4. The fourth doth fawne: and flattry playth,
5. The fifth delight: and laugheth the more,
6. The ſixt bewayleth: it weepeth full ſore,
7. The ſeventh tredeth ſtoute: in froward race
8. The eighte goeth milde: in modeſt pace.

The Tenor of theſe partes be for the people when they will ſyng alone, the other partes put for the greater queers, or to ſuche as will ſyng or play them privately.

It is conjectured that the Psalms thus translated, with tunes adapted to them, were intended by the author to be sung in cathedrals, for at the

Notwithstanding some of these persons are celebrated for their learning, it is to be presumed that they followed the method of Marot, and rendered the Hebrew into English through the medium of a prose translation: the original motive to this undertaking was not solely the introduction of psalmsinging into the English protestant churches; it had also for its object the exclusion of that ribaldry which was the entertainment of the common people, and the furnishing them with such songs as might not only tend to reform their manners, but inspire them with sentiments of devotion and godliness; and indeed nothing less than this can be inferred from that declaration of the design of setting them forth, contained in the title-page of our common version, and which has been continued in all the printed copies from the time of its first publication to this day: ' Set forth and allowed to be sung in churches ' of the people together, before and after evening ' prayer, as also before and after sermon; and more-' over in private houses, for their godly solace and ' comfort, laying apart all ungodly songs and ballads, ' which tend only to the nourishment of vice and ' corrupting of youth.'

There is good reason to believe that the design of the reformers of our church was in a great measure answered by the publication of the Psalms in this manner; to facilitate the use of them they were

time when they were turned into verse, the church were put to great shifts, the compositions to English words being at that time too few to furnish out a musical service; and this is the more probable from the directions given by the archbishop for singing many of them by the rectors and the quier alternately. Who we are to understand by the rectors it is hard to say, there being no such officer at this time in any cathedral in this kingdom. If the word were of the singular number it might be interpreted chanter. These directions seem to indicate that till some time after queen Elizabeth's accession, the form and method of choral service was not settled, nor that distinction made between the singers on the dean's side and that of the chanter, which at this day is observed in all cathedrals.

Archbishop Parker's version of the Psalms may be deemed a great typographical curiosity, inasmuch as it seems to have never been published, otherwise than by being presented to his friends, it is therefore not to be wondered that it never fell in the way either of Strype, who wrote his life, or of Mr. Ames, that diligent collector of typographical antiquities. As to the book itself, the merits of it may be judged of by the following version of Psalm xxiii. extracted from it:—

The Lord ſo good: who geveth me food
    My ſhepeheard is and guide:
How can I want: or ſuffer ſcant
    Whan he defendth my ſide.

To feede my neede: he will me lead,
    In paſtures greene and fat:
He forth brought me in libertie,
    To waters delicate.

My ſoule and hart: he did convert,
    To me he ſheweth the path:
Of right wiſeneſs: in holines,
    His name ſuch vertue hath.

Yea though I go: through Death hys wo
    His vaale and ſhadow wyde:
I feare no dart: wyth me thou art,
    With ſtaff and rod to guide.

Thou ſhalt provyde: a table wyde,
    For me agaynſt theyr ſpite:
With oyle my head: thou haſt beſpred,
    My cup is fully dight.

Thy goodneſs yet: and mercy great,
    Will kepe me all my dayes:
In houſe to dwell: in reſt full well,
    Wyth God I hope alwayes.

printed ' with apt notes to sing them withall ;'* and from thenceforth the practice of psalm-singing became the common exercise of such devout persons as attended to the exhortation of the apostle ; ' if any was ' afflicted, he prayed ; if merry, he sang psalms.'

To enquire into the merits of this our translation might seem an invidious task, were it not that the subject has employed the pens of some very good judges of English poesy, whose sentiments are collected in a subsequent page : it may here suffice to

* To the earlier impressions of the Psalms in metre was prefixed a treatise, said to be made by St. Athanasius, concerning the use and virtues of the Psalms, wherein, among many other, are the following directions for the choice of psalms for particular occasions and exigencies.

' If thou wouldst at any time describe a blessed man, who is he, and ' what thing maketh him so to be: thou hast the 1, 32, 41, 112, 128 ' psalmes.

' If that thou seest that evill men lay snares for thee, and therefore ' desirest God's eares to heare thy praiers, sing the 5 psalme.

' If so again thou wilt sing in giving thanks to God for the prosperous ' gathering of thy frutes, use the 8 psalme.

' If thou desirest to know who is a citizen of heaven, sing the 15 ' psalme.

' If thine enemies cluster against thee, and go about with their bloody ' hand to destroy thee, go not thou about by man's helpe to revenge it, ' for al mens judgments are not trustie, but require God to be judge, for ' he alone is judge, and say the 26, 35, 43 psalmes.

' If they presse more fiercelie on thee, though they be in numbers like ' an armed hoast, fear them not which thus reject thee, as though thou ' wert not annointed and elect by God, but sing the 27 psalme.

' If they be yet so impudent that they lay wait against thee, so that it ' is not lawfull for thee to have any vocation by them, regard them not, ' but sing to God the 48 psalme.

' If thou beholdest such as be baptized, and so delivered from the ' corruption of their birth, praise thou the bountifull grace of God, and ' sing the 32 psalme.

' If thou delightest to sing amongst many, call together righteous men of godlie life, and sing the 33 psalme.

' If thou seest how wicked men do much wickednesse, and that yet ' simple folke praise such, when thou wilt admonish any man not to ' follow them, to bee like unto them, because they shall be shortly rooted ' out and destroid: speake unto thyselfe and to others the 37 psalme.

' If thou wouldst call upon the blind world for their wrong confidence ' of their brute sacrifices, and shew them what sacrifice God most hath ' required of them, sing the 50 psalme.

' If thou hast suffered false accusation before the king, and seest the ' divel to triumph thereat, go aside and say the 52 psalme.

' If they which persecute thee with accusations would betray thee, as ' the Phariseis did Jesus, and as the aliens did David, discomfort not ' thyselfe therewith, but sing in good hope to God, the 54, 69, 57 psalmes.

' If thou wilt rebuke Painims and heretiks, for that they have not the ' knowledge of God in them, thou maist have an understanding to sing ' to God the 86, 115 psalmes.

' If thou art elect out of low degree, especially before others to some ' vocation to serve thy brethren, advance not thyselfe too high against ' them in thine own power, but give God his glorie who did chuse thee, ' and sing thou the 145 psalme.'

The effects of these directions may be judged of by the propensity of the people, manifested in sundry instances to the exercise of psalm-singing.

The Protestants who fled from the persecution of the duke de Alva in Flanders, were mostly woollen manufacturers. Upon their arrival in England they settled in Gloucestershire, Somersetshire, Wiltshire, and a few other counties, where they distinguished themselves by their love of Psalmody. ' Would I were a weaver,' says Sir John Falstaff, [in Henry IV. part I. the first edition] ' I could sing psalms or any thing.'

As the singing of psalms supposes some degree of skill in music, it was natural for those who were able to do it to recreate themselves with vocal music of another kind ; and accordingly so early as the reign of James I. the people of these counties were, as they are at this day, expert in the singing of catches and songs in parts. Ben Jonson, in the Silent Woman, makes Cutberd tell Morose that the parson ' caught his ' cold by sitting up late, and singing catches with Clothworkers ;' and the old Gloucestershire three part song, ' The stones that built George Ridler's ' oven,' is well known in that and the adjacent counties.

And to speak of the common people in general, it may be remembered that the reading of the book of Martyrs, and the singing of psalms were the exercises of such persons of either sex, as being advanced in years, were desirous to be thought good christians ; and this not merely in country towns, villages and hamlets, where a general simplicity of manners, and perhaps the exhortations of the minister might be supposed to conduce to it, but in cities and great towns, and even in London itself ; and the time is not yet out of the memory of a few persons now living, when a passenger on a Sunday evening from St. Paul's to Aldgate, would have heard the families in most of the houses in his way occupied in the singing of Psalms.

' In the year 1646, king Charles I. being in the hands of the Scots, ' a Scotch minister preached boldly before the king at Newcastle, and ' after this sermon called for the fifty-second psalm, which begins, "Why " dost thou tyrant boast thyself, thy wicked works to praise." His majesty ' thereupon stood up, and called for the fifty-sixth psalm, which begins, " Have mercy Lord on me I pray, for men would me devour." The ' people waived the minister's psalm, and sung that which the king called ' for.' Whitelocke's Memorials, 234.

say, that so far as it tends to fix the meaning of sundry words, now for no very good reasons become obsolete, or exhibits the state of English poetry at the period when it was composed, it is one of those valuable monuments of literary antiquity which none but the superficially learned would be content to want. But it seems these considerations were not of force sufficient to restrain those in authority from complying with that humour in mankind which disposes them to change, though from better to the worse ; and accordingly such alterations have at different times been made in the common metrical translations of the singing Psalms, as have frustrated the hopes of those who wished for one more elegant and less liable to exception.

Thus much may suffice for a general account of the introduction of psalmody into this kingdom, and the effects it wrought on the national manners ; the order and course of this history naturally lead to an enquiry concerning the melodies to which the Psalms are, and usually have been sung, no less particular than that already made with respect to the French psalm-tunes.

Sternhold's Psalms were first printed in the year 1549 ; and the whole version, as completed by Hopkins and others, in 1562, with this title : ' The ' whole booke of Psalmes collected into English ' metre by T. Sternhold, J. Hopkins, and others, ' conferred with the Ebrue, with apt notes to sing ' them withall.' By these apt notes we are to understand the tunes, to the number of about forty, which are to be found in that and many subsequent impressions, of one part only, and in general suited to the pitch and compass of a tenor voice, but most excellent indeed for the sweetness and gravity of their melody ; and because the number of tunes thus published was less than that of the Psalms, directions were given in cases where the metre and general import of the words allowed of it, to sing sundry of them to one tune.

The same method was observed in the several editions of the Psalms published during the reign of queen Elizabeth, particularly in those of the years 1564, and 1577, which it is to be remarked are not coeval with any of the editions of the Common Prayer, to which they are usually annexed, for which no better reason can here be assigned than that the singing psalms were never considered as part of the liturgy ; and the exclusive privilege of printing the Common Prayer was then, as it is now, enjoyed by different persons. Nor do we meet with any impression of the Psalms suited, either in the type or size of the volume, to either of the impressions of the liturgy of Edward the Sixth, published in 1549 and 1552. In short, it seems that the practice of publishing the singing psalms by way of appendix to the Book of Common Prayer, had its rise at the beginning of the reign of queen Elizabeth ; for in 1562 that method was observed, and again in 1564 and 1577, but with such circumstances of diversity as require particular notice.

And first it is to be remarked that in 1576, though by a mistake of Jugge the printer, the year in the title-page is 1676, the liturgy was for the first time printed in a very small octavo size; to this are annexed Psalms of David in metre by Sternhold, Hopkins, and others, 'with apte notes to sing them withall,' imprinted by the famous John Daye, cum privilegio, 1577.

The publication of the Psalms in this manner supposed that the people, at least the better sort of them, could read; and by parity of reason it might be said that the addition of musical notes to the words implied an opinion in the publishers that they also could sing; but that they in fact did not think so at the time now spoken of, is most evident from the pains they were at in collecting together the general rudiments of song, which in the editions of 1564 and 1577, and in no other, together with the scale of music, are prefixed by way of introduction to the singing Psalms. Who it was in particular that drew up these rudiments, is as little known as the authors of the tunes themselves; they bear the title of 'A short Introduction into the Science of 'Musicke, made for such as are desirous to have the 'knowledge thereof for the singing of the Psalmes.'

As to the Introduction into the Science of Musicke, or, as it is called in the running title, 'The introduction to learn to sing,' it is not to be found in any of the impressions of the Common Prayer subsequent to that in 1577, which is the more to be wondered at, seeing the author, whoever he was, was so well persuaded of its efficacy as to assert, that 'by means 'thereof every man might in a few dayes, yea in 'a few houres, easily without all payne, and that also 'without all ayde or helpe of any other teacher, 'attain to a sufficient knowledge to singe any psalme 'contayned in the booke, or any other such playne 'and easy songes.' In which opinion the event shewed him to be grossly mistaken, as indeed, without the gift of prophesy, might have been foretold by any one who should have reflected on the labour and pains that are required to make any one a singer by notes to whom the elements of music are unknown; for in the year 1607 there came out an edition of the Psalms with the same tunes in musical notes as were contained in the former, with not only more particular directions for the sol-faing, but with the syllables actually interposed between the notes: this was in effect giving up all hope of instructing the people in the practice of singing, inasmuch as whatever they were enabled to do by means of this assistance, they did by rote.

Who was the publisher of this edition of 1607 does not appear; the title mentions only in general that it was imprinted for the company of stationers; the reasons for annexing the syllables to the notes are given at large in an anonymous preface to the reader, which is as follows :—

'Thou fhalt underftand (gentle reader) that I have '(for the helpe of thofe that are defirous to learne to 'fing) caufed a new print of note to be made, with 'letters to be joyned to every note, whereby thou 'maieft know how to call every note by his right 'name, fo that with a very little diligence (as thou art 'taught in the introduction printed heretofore in the

'Pfalmes) thou maieft the more eafily, by the viewing 'of thefe letters, come to the knowledge of perfect 'folfayeng : whereby thou maieft fing the Pfalmes the 'more fpeedilie and eafilie : the letters be thefe, U for 'Ut, R for Re, M for Mi, F for Fa, S for Sol, L for 'La. Thus where you fee any letter joyned by the 'note, you may eafilie call him by his right name, as 'by thefe two examples you may the better perceive :—

UT RE MI FA SOL LA LA SOL FA MI RE UT

UT RE MI FA SOL LA FA SOL LA

LA SOL FA LA SOL FA MI RE UT

'Thus I commit thee unto him that liveth for ever, 'who grant that we fing with our hearts unto the 'glorie of his holy name. Amen.'

And to exemplify the rule above given, every note of the several tunes contained in this edition has the adjunct of a letter to ascertain the sol-faing, as mentioned in the above preface.

After the publication of this edition in 1607, it seems that the company of stationers, or whoever else had the care of supplying the public with copies of the singing-psalmos, thought it best to leave the rude and unlearned to themselves, for in none of the subsequent impressions do we meet with either the introduction to music, or the anonymous preface, or, in a word, any directions for attaining to sing by notes.

## CHAP. CXVII.

GREAT has been the diversity of opinions concerning the merit of this our old English translation. Wood, in the account given by him of Sternhold, says that so much of it as he wrote is truly admirable; and there are others, who reflecting on the general end of such a work, and the absolute necessity of adapting it to the capacities of the common people, have not hesitated to say that, bad as it may be in some respects, it would at this time be extremely difficult to make a translation that upon the whole should be better. Others have gone so far as to assert the poetical excellence of this version, and, taking advantage of some of those very sublime passages in the original, which are tolerably rendered, but which perhaps no translation could possibly spoil, have defied its enemies to equal it.* On the other hand, the general poverty of the style, the meanness of the images, and, above all, the awkwardness of the versification, have induced many serious persons to wish that we were fairly rid of a work, that in their opinion, tends less to promote religion than to disgrace that reformation of it, which is

* See a defence of the book of Psalms collected into English metre by Thomas Sternhold, John Hopkins, and others, &c. by bishop Beveridge. Lond. 1710.

justly esteemed one of the greatest blessings of this country.

Another, but a very different class of men from those above enumerated, the wits, as they style themselves, have been very liberal in their censure of the English version of the Psalms. Scarce ever are the names of Sternhold and Hopkins mentioned by any of them but for the purpose of ridicule. Fuller alone, of all witty men the best natured, and who never exercises his facetious talent to the injury of any one, has given an impartial character of them and their works, and recommended a revision of the whole translation against all attempts to introduce a better in its stead.* His advice was followed, though not till many years after his decease, for in an impression of the Psalms of Sternhold and Hopkins, printed in 1696, we find the version accommodated to the language of the times, by the substitution of well-known words and familiar modes of expression in the room of such as were become obsolete, or not intelligible to the generality of the common people. But as the poet, whoever he was, was at all events to mend the version, its conformity with the original, if peradventure he could read it, could be with him but a secondary consideration. Neither does it seem that he was enough acquainted with the Engligh language to know that in the alteration of an old word for a new, the exchange is not always of the worse for the better. Hearne has given some shrewd instances of this kind in the Glossary to his Robert of Gloucester,† and very many more might be produced; however the first essay towards an emendation met with so little opposition from the people, that almost every succeeding impression of the Psalms was varied to the phrase of the day; and it is not impossible but that in time, and by imperceptible degrees, the whole version may be so innovated, as scarcely to retain a single stanza of the original, and yet be termed the work of its primitive authors.

A history of the several innovations in the metrical version of David's Psalms is not necessary in this place. It may suffice to remark, that in the first impression of the whole there is a variation from the text of Sternhold in the first stanza of the first psalm, which in the two editions of 1549 and 1552 reads thus :—

> The man is bleft that hath not gone
>     By wicked rede aftray,
> Ne fat in chayre of peftylence,
>     Nor walkte in fynners waye.

And that the edition of 1562 stood unaltered till 1683, as appears by Guy's copy printed at Oxford in folio that year. In 1696 many different readings are found, the occasion whereof is said to be this; about that time Mr. Nahum Tate and Dr. Nicholas Brady published a new version of part of the book of Psalms as a specimen of that version of the whole which was afterwards printed in 1696. In this essay of theirs they, in the opinion of many persons, had so much the advantage of Sternhold and Hopkins, that the company of stationers, who are possessed of the sole privilege of printing the Psalms, took the alarm, and found themselves under a necessity of meliorating the version of the latter, and for this purpose some person endued with the faculty of rhyming was employed by them in that very year 1696, to correct the versification as he should think proper; and since that time it has been still farther varied, as appears by the edition of 1726, but with little regard to the Hebrew text, at the pleasure of the persons from time to time intrusted with the care of the publication.

The effects of these sveral essays towards a reformation of the singing psalms are visible in the version now in common use, which being a heterogeneous commixture of old and new words and phrases, is but little approved of by those who consider integrity of style as part of the merit of every literary composition, and the result is, that the primitive version is now become a subject of mere curiosity. The translation of the Psalms into metre was the work of men as well qualified for the undertaking as any that the times they lived in could furnish; most of those which Norton versified, particularly psalms 109, 116, 139, 141, 145; and 104, 119, and 137 by Whittyngham, with a very small allowance for the times, must be deemed good, if not excellent poetry; and if we compare the whole work with the productions of those days, it will seem that Fuller has not greatly erred in saying, that match these verses for their ages, they shall go abreast with the best poems of those times.

With respect to the version as it stands accommodated to the language of the present times, it may be said, that whatever is become of the sense, the versification is in some instances mended; that the unmeaning monosyllable eke, a wretched contrivance to preserve an equality in the measure of different verses, is totally expunged; that many truly obsolete words, such as *hest* for *command, mell* for *meddle, pight* for *pitched, Saw* for *Precept,* and many others that have gradually receded from their places in our language, are reprobated; that many passages wherein the Divine Being and his actions are represented by images that derogate from his majesty, as where he is said to *bruise* the wicked with a *mace,* the weapon of a giant, are rendered less exceptionable than before; and where he is expostulated with in ludicrous terms, as in the following passage :—

> Why dooft withdraw thy hand aback,
>     And hide it in thy lappe,
> O pluck it out and be not flack
>     To give thy foes a rappe.‡

and this, which for its meanness is not to be defended :—

> For why their hearts were nothing bent
>     To him [*God*] nor to his trade.§

And where an expression of ridicule is too strongly pointed to justify the use of it in an address to God, as is this :—

> Confound them that apply,
>     And feeke to worke me fhame,
> And at my harme do laugh, and cry
>     So, fo, there goeth the game.‖

---

* Church Hist. of Britain, cent. XVI. book vii. pag. 406.
† Vocib. behet, rede.

‡ Psalm lxxiv. verse 12.      § Psalm lxxviii. verse 37.
‖ Psalm lxx. verse 3.

And where the rhymes are ill sorted like these :—

> Nor how he did commit their fruits
> Unto the caterpiller,
> And all the labour of their lands
> He gave to the grafhopper.*

And these others :—

> remembered } lord    } remember }
> offended †  } world ‡ } ever §   }

In these several instances the present reading is to be preferred, but, after all, what a late author has said of certain of his own works, may with equal truth and propriety be applied to the language of the modern singing-psalms. ' It not only is such as ' in the present times is not uttered, but was never ' uttered in times past; and if I judge aright, will ' never be uttered in times future : it having too ' much of the language of old times to be fit for the ' present; too much of the present to have been fit ' for the old, and too much of both to be fit for any ' time to come.'

There is extant a metrical translation of the Psalms by James I. which was printed, together with the Common Prayer and Psalter, in 1636, upon the resolution taken by Charles I. to establish the liturgy in Scotland ; some doubt has arisen whether this version was ever completed ; but, unless credit be denied to the assertion of a king, the whole must be allowed to be the work of the reputed author, for in the printed copy, opposite the title-page is the following declaration concerning it :—

> ' Charles R.
> 'Having caused this translation of the Psalmes ' (whereof our late dear father was author) to be ' perused, and it being found exactly and truly ' done, We do hereby authorize the same to ' be imprinted according to the patent granted ' thereupon, and do allow them to be sung in ' all the churches of our dominions, recommend-' ing them to all our good subjects for that effect.'

The Psalms have been either totally or partially versified by sundry persons, as namely, Sir Philip Sidney, Christopher Hatton, H. Dodd, Dr. Henry King, bishop of Chichester, Miles Smith, Dr. Samuel Woodford, John Milton, William Barton, Dr. Simon Ford, Sir Richard Blackmore, Dr. John Patrick, Mr. Addison, Mr. Archdeacon Daniel, Dr. Joseph Trapp, Dr. Walter Harte, Dr. Broome, and many others, learned and ingenious men, whose translations are either published separately, or lie dispersed in collections of a miscellaneous nature.  There are also extant two paraphrases of the Psalms, the one by Mr. George Sandys, the other by Sir John Denham.

The foregoing account respects solely the poetry of the English Psalms, and from thence we are naturally led to an enquiry concerning the melodies to which they now are, and usually have been sung. Mention has already been made of certain of these, and that they were first published in the version of the Psalms by Sternhold and Hopkins, in the year 1562, by the name of apt notes to sing them withal, but as many of them have been altered and sophis-

* Psalm lxxviii. verse 46·    † Psalm xiii. verse 1.
‡ Psalm lxxxiii. ver. ult.    § Psalm cxix. verse 49.

ticated, a few of them are here given as they stand in that edition, with the numbers of the psalms to which they are appropriated :—

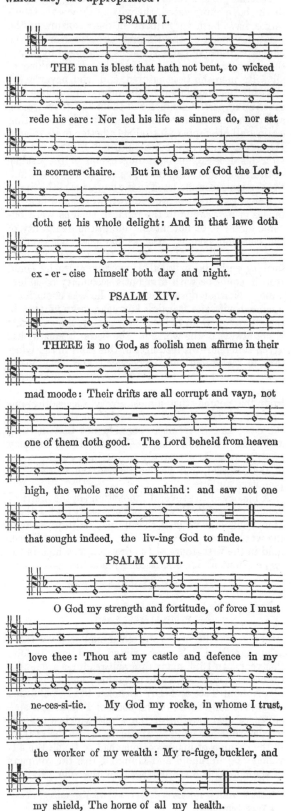

PSALM I.

THE man is blest that hath not bent,  to wicked rede his eare : Nor led his life as sinners do, nor sat in scorners chaire.    But in the law of God the Lor d, doth set his whole delight : And in that lawe doth ex - er - cise  himself both day and night.

PSALM XIV.

THERE is no God, as foolish men affirme in their mad moode : Their drifts are all corrupt and vayn, not one of them doth good.    The Lord beheld from heaven high, the whole race of mankind : and saw not one that sought indeed,  the liv-ing God to finde.

PSALM XVIII.

O God my strength and fortitude,  of force I must love thee : Thou art my castle and defence  in my ne-ces-si-tie.    My God my rocke, in whome I trust, the worker of my wealth : My re-fuge, buckler, and my shield, The horne of all my health.

PSALM LXXII.

LORD, give thy judgments to the king, therein

instruct him well: And with his sonne, that princely

thing, Lord, let thy justice dwell. That he may governe

uprightly, and rule thy folke a-right; And so defend

through e - qui - ty, the poor that have no might.

PSALM CXXIV.

NOW Is-ra-el may say and that truely, 1f that

the Lord had not our cause maintayned, If that the

Lord had not our right susteined, When all the world

a-gainst us furiously, made their uprores, and sayd

we should all dye.

Besides the tunes to the psalms, there are others appropriated to the hymns and evangelical songs, such as Veni Creator, The humble Suit of a Sinner, Benedictus, Te Deum, The Song of the three Children, Magnificat, Nunc dimittis, Quicunque vult, or the Athanasian Creed, the Lamentation of a Sinner, the Lord's Prayer, the Decalogue, the Complaint of a Sinner, and Robert Wisdome's Prayer, 'Preserve us Lord by thy dear word;' all which are versified and have a place in our collection of singing psalms.

The want of bars, which are a late invention,* might make it somewhat difficult to sing these tunes in time, and the rather as no sign of the mood ever occurs at the head of the first stave; but in general the metre is a sufficient guide.

With respect to the authors of those original melodies, published in the more early impressions of the version of Sternhold and Hopkins, we are

* The use of bars is not to be traced higher than the time when the English translation of Adrian le Roy's book on the Tablature was published, viz., the year 1574; and it was some time after that, before the use of bars became general. To come nearer to the point, Barnard's Cathedral Music, printed in 1641, is without bars; but bars are to be found throughout in the Ayres and Dialogues of Henry Lawes published in 1653, from whence it may be conjectured that we owe to Lawes this improvement.

somewhat to seek; it is probable that in so important a service as this seemed to be, the aid of the ablest professors of music was called in, and who were the most eminent of that time is easily known; but before we proceed to an enumeration of these, it is necessary to mention that some of the original melodies were indisputably the work of foreigners: the tunes to the hundredth, and to the eighty-first psalms are precisely the same with those that answer to the hundredth, and eighty-first in the psalms of Goudimel and of Claude le Jeune; and many of the rest are supposed to have come to us from the Low Countries. It is said that Dr. Pepusch was wont to assert that the hundredth psalm-tune was composed by Douland; but in this he was misunderstood, for he could hardly be ignorant of the fact just above-mentioned; nor that in some collections, particularly in that of Ravenscroft, printed in 1633, this is called the French hundredth psalm-tune; and therefore he might mean to say, not that the melody, but that the harmony was of Douland's composition, which is true. But if the insertion of this tune in the French collections be not of itself evidence, a comparison of the time when it first appeared in print in England, with that of Douland's birth, will go near to put an end to the question, and shew that he could hardly be the author of it. In the preface to a work entitled ' A Pilgrimes Solace,' published by Douland himself in 1612, he tells his reader that he is entered into the fiftieth year of his age, and consequently that he was born in 1563: now the tune in question appears in that collection of the singing-psalms above-mentioned to have been published in 1577, when he could not be much more than fourteen years old; and if, as there is reason to suppose, the tune is more ancient than 1577, the difference, whatever it be, will leave him still younger.

Of the musicians that flourished in this country about 1562, the year in which the English version of the Psalms with the musical notes first made its appearance, the principal were Dr. Christopher Tye, Marbeck, Tallis, Bird, Shephard, Parsons, and William Mundy, all men of eminent skill and abilities, and, at least for the time, adherents to the doctrines of the reformation.

There is no absolute certainty to be expected in this matter, but the reason above given is a ground for conjecture that these persons, or some of them, were the original composers of such of the melodies to the English version of the Psalms as were not taken from foreign collections; it now remains to speak of those persons who at different times composed the harmony to those melodies, and thereby fitted them for the performance of such as sung with the understanding.

The first, for aught that appears to the contrary, who attempted a work of this kind, seems to have been WILLIAM DAMON, of the queen's chapel, a man of eminence in his profession, and who as such has a place in the Bibliotheca of bishop Tanner. He it seems had been importuned by a friend to compose parts to the common church psalm-tunes; and having frequent occasion to resort to the house of this person, he so far complied with his request, as while he was there to compose one or more of the tunes at a time, till the whole was completed, intending thereby nothing more than to render them fit for the private use of him who had first moved him to the undertaking. Nevertheless this friend, without the privity of the author, thought fit to publish them with the following title :—' The Psalmes of David in Eng- ' lish meter, with notes of foure partes set unto them ' by Guilielmo Daman for John Bull,* to the use of ' the godly Christians for recreating themselves, in- ' stede of fond and unseemely ballades.' 1579.

It seems that neither the novelty of this work, nor the reputation of its author, which, if we may credit another and better friend of his than the former, was very great, were sufficient to recommend it : on the contrary, he had the mortification to see it neglected. For this reason he was induced to undertake the labour of recomposing parts, to the number of four, to the ancient church-melodies, as well those adapted to the hymns and spiritual songs, as the tunes to which the psalms were ordinarily sung. And this he completed in so excellent a manner, says the publisher, ' that by comparison of these and the ' former, the reader may by triall see that the auctor ' could not receive in his art such a note of disgrace ' by his friend's oversight before, but that now the ' same is taken away, and his worthy knowledge ' much more graced by this second travaile.' But the care of publishing the Psalms thus again composed, devolved to another friend of the author, William Swayne, who in the year 1591 gave them to the world, and dedicated them to the lord treasurer Burleigh. It is not impossible that either Damon himself, or his friend Swayne might buy up, or cause to be destroyed what copies of the former impression could be got at, for at this day the book is not to be found. This of 1591 bears the title of ' The former ' booke of the music of Mr. William Damon, late one ' of her Majesties musicians, conteyning all the tunes ' of David's Psalmes as they are ordinarily soung in ' the church, most excellently by him composed into ' 4 parts ; in which sett the tenor singeth the church- ' tune. Published for the recreation of such as de- ' lighte in musicke, by W. Swayne, Gent. Printed ' for T. Este, the assignè of W. Byrd, 1591.'

The same person also published at the same time with the same title, ' The second booke of the musicke ' of M. William Damon, containing all the tunes of ' David's Psalms, differing from the former in respect ' that the highest part singeth the church-tune.'

The tunes contained in each of these collections are neither more nor less than those in the earlier impressions of the Psalms, that is to say, exclusive of the hymns and spiritual songs, they are about forty in number ; the author has however managed, by the repetition of the words and notes, to make each tune near as long again as it stands in the original ; by which contrivance it should seem that he intended them rather for private practice than the service of the church ; which perhaps is the reason that none

of them are to be found in any of those collections of the Psalms in parts composed by different authors, which began to appear about this time.

By the relation herein before given of the first publication of the Psalms in metre with musical notes, and the several melodies herein inserted, it appears that the original music to the English Psalms was of that unisonous kind, in which only a popular congregation are supposed able to join. But the science had received such considerable improvements about the beginning of the seventeenth century, and the people by that time were so much accustomed to symphoniac harmony, that a facility in singing was no longer a recommendation of church tunes.

At this time cathedral and collegiate churches, and above all, the royal chapels, were the principal seminaries of musicians. The simplicity and parsimony that distinguished the theatrical representations afforded no temptation to men of that profession to deviate from the original design of their education or employment, by lending their assistance to the stage ; the consequence hereof was, that for the most part they were men of a devout and serious turn of mind, with leisure to study, and a disposition to employ their skill in celebrating the praises of their Maker.

It was natural for men of this character to reflect that as much attention at least was due to the music of the church as had been shown to that of the chamber ; the latter had derived great advantages from the use of symphoniac harmony ; whereas the former had been at a stand for near half a century ; and though it might be a question with some, whether the singing of the Psalms in parts was not in effect an exclusion of the majority of every congregation in the kingdom from that part of divine service ; it is to be noted that neither the law nor the rubric of our liturgy gives any directions in what manner the Psalms of David are to be sung in divine service ; and that they had the example of foreign churches, particularly that of Geneva, between which and our own there was then a better understanding than is likely ever to be again, to authorize the practice.

In short, with a view to promote the practice of psalmody, as well in churches as in private houses, the most eminent musicians of queen Elizabeth's time undertook and completed a collection of the ancient church-tunes, composed in four parts, and in counterpoint. In the execution of which purpose it is plain that they had the example of Goudimel and Claude le Jeune in view ; and that their design was not an elaborate display of their own invention, in such an artificial commixture of parts, as should render these compositions the admiration of the profoundly learned in the science, but an addition of such plain and simple harmony to the common church-tunes, as might delight and edify those for whose benefit they were originally composed ; and hence arose the practice, which in many country churches prevails even at this day, of singing the Psalms, not by the whole of the congregation, but by a few select persons sufficiently skilled in music to sing each by himself, the part assigned him.

---

* Called in the preface Citezen and Goldsmith of London : this person could not be Dr. Bull, who at this time was but sixteen years of age. Ward's Lives of Gresh. Prof. pag. 208, in not.

The names of those public-spirited persons who first undertook the work of composing the psalm-tunes in parts, is preserved in a collection, of which it is here meant to give more than a superficial account, as well on the score of its antiquity, as of its merit, namely, 'The whole booke of Psalmes, with their 'wonted tunes as they are sung in churches, com-posed into foure parts by X sondry authors; im-'printed at London by Thomas Est, 1594.' These authors were John Douland, E. Blancks, E. Hooper, J. Farmer, R. Allison, G. Kirby, W. Cobbold, E. Johnson, and G. Farnaby, who in the title page are said to have ' so laboured in this worke that the 'unskilful by small practice may attaine to sing 'that part which is fittest for their voice.' *

The book is very neatly printed in the size and form of a small octavo, with a dedication by the printer Thomas Est, to Sir John Puckering, knight, lord keeper of the great seal of England, wherein we are told, ' that in the booke the church-tunes are 'carefully corrected, and other short tunes added, 'which are sung in London, and most places of this 'realme.'

The former publications consisting, as already has been mentioned, of the primitive melodies, and those to the amount of forty only, gave but one tune to divers psalms; this of Est appears to be as copious as need be wished, and to contain at least as many tunes as there are psalms, all of which are in four parts, in a pitch for and with the proper cliffs to denote the cantus, altus, tenor, and bass, as usual in such compositions. It is to be observed, that throughout the book the church-tune, as it is called, holds the place of the tenor; and as the structure of the compositions is plain counterpoint, the additional parts are merely auxiliary to that, which for very good reasons is and ought to be deemed the principal.

It may here be proper to remark, that although in these tunes the church-tune is strictly adhered to, so far as relates to the progression of the notes, yet here for the first time we meet with an innovation, by the substituting semitones for whole tones in almost every instance where the close is made by an ascent to the final note; or, in other words, in form-ing the cadence the authors have made use of the sharp seventh of the key; which is the more to be wondered at, because in vocal compositions of a much later date than this, we find the contrary practice to prevail; for though the coming at the close by a whole tone below be extremely offensive to a nice ear, and there seems to be a kind of necessity for the use of the acute signature to the note below the cadence, yet it seems that the ancient composers, who by the way made not so free with this character as their successors, particularly the composers of instru-mental music, left this matter to the singer, trusting that his ear would direct him in the utterance to prefer the half to the whole tone.

But these compositions, however excellent in

themselves, were not intended for those alone whose skill in the art would enable them to sing with pro-priety; they were, though elegant, simple; in short, suited to the capacities of the unlearned and the rude, who sung them then just as the unlearned and the rude of this day do.

If then it was found by experience that the com-mon ear was not a sufficient guide to the true singing of the ancient melodies, it was very natural for those who in the task they had undertaken of composing parts to them, were led to the revisal of the originals by the insertion of the character above-mentioned, to rectify an abuse in the exercise of psalm-singing, which the authors were not aware of, and consequently had not provided against.

About five years after the publication of the Psalms by Est, there appeared a collection in folio, entitled, ' The Psalmes of David in meter, the plaine song 'beinge the common tune to be sung and plaide upon 'the lute, orpharion, citterne, or base violl, severally 'or altogether, the singing part to be either tenor or 'treble to the instrument, according to the nature of 'the voyce; or for foure voyces, with tenne short 'tunes in the end, to which for the most part all the 'psalmes may be usually sung, for the use of such as 'are of mean skill, and whose leysure least serveth 'to practize. By Richard Allison, Gent. practitioner 'in the art of musicke, and are to be sold at his 'house in the Dukes place neere Aldgate. Printed 'by William Barley, the assignè of Thomas Morley, '1599, cum privilegio regiæ majestatis.'

The above book is dedicated ' to the right honour-'able and most virtuous lady the lady Anne coun-'tesse of Warwicke.' Immediately following the dedication are three copies of verses, the first by John Douland, bachelor of musicke; the second a sonnet by William Leighton, esquire, afterwards Sir William Leighton, and the third by John Welton, all in com-mendation of the author and his most excellent worke. This collection being intended chiefly for chamber practice, the four parts are so disposed in the page, as that four persons sitting round a table may sing out of the same book; and it is observable that the author has made the plain-song or church-tune the cantus part, which part being intended as well for the lute or cittern, as the voice, is given also in those characters called the tablature, which are peculiar to those instruments.

There are no original melodies in this collection: the author confining himself to the church-tunes, has taken those of the hymns and spiritual songs and psalms as they occur in the earlier editions of the version by Sternhold and Hopkins.

To this collection of Allison succeeded another in 1621, with the title of ' The whole book of Psalmes 'with the hymnes evangelicall and songs spirituall, 'composed into four parts by sundry authors, to such 'severall tunes as have beene and are usually sung 'in England, Scotland, Wales, Germany, Italy, 'France, and the Netherlands. By Thomas Ra-'venscroft, Bachelor of Musicke,' in which is in-serted the following list of the names of the authors who composed the tunes of the psalms into four

* In the title-page Est is described as dwelling in Aldersgate-street, at the sign of the Black Horse. He therein styles himself the assignè of William Bird, who with Tallis, as before observed, had a joint patent from queen Elizabeth for the sole printing of music. Tallis died first, and this patent, the first of the kind, survived to Bird, who probably for a valuable consideration might assign it to Est.

parts: 'Thomas Tallis, John Douland, doctor of
'Musicke,* Thomas Morley, bachelor of Musicke,
'Giles Farnaby, bachelor of Musicke, Thomas Tom-
'kins, bachelor of Musicke, John Tomkins, bachelor
'of Musicke, Martin Pierson, bachelor of Musicke,
'William Parsons, Edmund Hooper, George Kirby,
'Edward Blancks, Richard Allison, John Farmer,
'Michael Cavendish, John Bennet, Robert Palmer,
'John Milton, Simon Stubbs, William Cranford,
'William Harrison, and Thomas Ravenscroft the
'compiler.'

In this collection, as in that of Est, the common
church-tune is the tenor part, which for distinction
sake, and to shew its pre-eminence over the rest, is
here in many instances called the tenor or plain-
song, and not unfrequently tenor or faburden.† Some
of the tunes in the former collection, as that to the
sixth psalm by George Kirby, that to the eighteenth
by William Cobbold, and that to the forty-first by
Edward Blancks, are continued in this; but the far
greater part are composed anew, and many tunes are
added, the melodies whereof are not to be found in
any other collection; and here we have the origin
of a practice respecting the names of our common
church tunes, that prevails among us to this day,
namely the distinguishing them by the name or
adjunct of a particular city, as Canterbury, York,
Rochester, and many others. It was much about
the time of the publication of this book that king
Charles I. was prevailed on by the clergy to attempt
the establishment of the liturgy in Scotland; and
perhaps it was with a view to humour the people
of that kingdom that some of these new-composed
tunes were called by the names of Dumferling,
Dundee, and Glasgow.

Among the new composed tunes in this collection,
that is to say such as have new or original melodies,
the composition of the author whose name they bear,
is that well-known one called York-tune, as also
another called Norwich-tune, to both whereof is
prefixed the name of John Milton; this person was
no other than the father of our great poet of that
name. The tune above spoken of called York-tune,
occurs in four several places in Ravenscroft's book,
for it is given to the twenty-seventh, sixty-sixth, and
one hundred and thirty-eighth psalms, and also to
a prayer to the Holy Ghost, among the spiritual
songs at the end of the book; but it is remarkable
that the author has chosen to vary the progression
of the notes of one of the parts in the repetition of the
tune; for the medius, as it stands to the words of
the one hundred and thirty-eighth psalm, and of the
prayer above-mentioned, is very different from the
same part applied to those of the twenty-seventh
and sixty-sixth.

Although the name of Tallis, to dignify the work,
stands at the head of the list of the persons who
composed the tunes in this collection, the only composition of his that occurs in it is a canon of two
parts in one, to the words 'Praise the Lord, O ye

'Gentiles;' and many of the tunes in Allison's collection are taken into this. Ravenscroft was a man
of great knowledge in his profession, and has discovered little less judgment in selecting the tunes than
the authors did in composing them.‡

Ravenscroft's book was again published in 1633,
and having passed many editions, it became the
manual of psalm-singers throughout the kingdom;
and though an incredible number of collections of
this kind have from time to time been published, the
compilations of those illiterate and conceited fellows
who call themselves singing-masters and lovers of
psalmody, and of divine music, yet even at this day
he is deemed a happy man in many places, who is
master of a genuine copy of Ravenscroft's psalms.

The design of publishing the Psalms in the manner above related was undoubtedly to preserve the
ancient church-tunes; but notwithstanding the care
that was taken in this respect, the same misfortune
attended them as had formerly befallen the ecclesiastical tones; and to this divers causes contributed,
for first, notwithstanding the pains that had been
taken by the publication of the Introduction into
the Science of Musike, prefixed to the earlier copies
of the Psalms in metre, to instruct the common
people in the practice of singing, these instructions
were in fact intelligible to very few except the minister and parish clerk, for we grossly mistake the
matter if we suppose that at that time of day many
of the congregation besides, could understand them.
In consequence of this general ignorance, the knowledge of music was not so disseminated among them
but that the poor and ruder sort fell into the usual
mistake of flat for sharp and sharp for flat.

Another cause that contributed to the corruption
and consequent disuse of the church tunes, was the
little care taken in the turbulent and distracted times
immediately following the accession of Charles I.
to appoint such persons for parish-clerks as were
capable of discharging the duty of the office. The
ninety-first of the canons, made in the year 1603,
had provided that parish-clerks should be sufficient
in reading and writing, and also of competent skill
in singing; but it is well known that instead of
rendering obedience to canons, those who at that
time were uppermost denied their efficacy. Nay, in
cases where a reason for the omission of a thing was
wanting, it was thought a good one to say that the
doing it was enjoined by the authority of the church.

The recognition of the office of a parish-clerk by
the church, and its relation to psalmody, naturally
lead us to enquire into the nature of that function,

---

* In the Fasti Oxon. it is noted that Douland was admitted to a
bachelor's degree at Oxford, 8 July 1588, but it does not appear that he
was ever created doctor.

† Of the term FABURDEN, see an explanation in page 256 of this work.

‡ It is in this collection of Ravenscroft that we first meet with the
tunes to which the Psalms are now most commonly sung in the parish
churches of this kingdom, for excepting those to the eighty-first,
hundredth, and hundred and nineteenth psalms, the ancient melodies
have given place to others of a newer and much inferior composition.
The names of these new tunes, to give them in alphabetical order,
are, Bath and Wells or Glastonbury, Bristol, Cambridge, Canterbury,
Chichester, Christ's hospital, Ely, Exeter, Gloucester, Hereford, Lincoln,
Litchfield and Coventry, London, Norwich, Oxford, Peterborough,
Rochester, Salisbury, Winchester, Windsor or Eaton, Worcester, Wol-
verhampton; and, to give what are styled northern tunes, in the same
order, they are Carlisle, Chester, Durham, Manchester, Southwell, and
York. The Scottish tunes are Abbey-tune, Duke's, Dumferling, Dundee,
Glasgow, Kings and Martyrs; and the Welch, St. Asaph, Bangor, St.
David's, Landaff, and Ludlow: so that the antiquity of these may be
traced back to the year 1621.

and the origin of the corporation of parish-clerks which has long existed in London.* Anciently parish-clerks were real clerks, but of the poorer sort; and of these every minister had at least one, to assist under him in the celebration of divine offices. By a constitution of Boniface archbishop of Canterbury, A. D. 1261, 45 Hen. III. it is ordained that the officer for the holy water shall be a poor clerk; and hence a poor clerk officiating under the minister is by the Canonists termed Aquæbajulus, a water-bearer. In the Register of archbishop Courtney the term occurs; and notwithstanding he was maintained by the parishioners, he was appointed to the office by the minister; and this right of appointment, founded on the custom of the realm, is there declared, and has in many instances been recognized by the common law. The offices in which the clerk was anciently exercised must be supposed to have respected the church-service, as the carrying and sprinkling holy water unquestionably did; and we are farther told that they were wont to attend great funerals, going before the hearse, and singing, with their surplices hanging on their arms, till they came to the church. Nevertheless we find that in the next century after making the above constitution, they were employed in ministring to the recreation, and, it may perhaps be said, in the instruction of the common people, by the exhibition of theatrical spectacles; and as touching these it seems here necessary to be somewhat particular

And first we are to know that in the infancy of the English drama, the people, instead of theatrical shows, were wont to be entertained with the representation of scripture histories, or of some remarkable events taken from the legends of saints, martyrs, and confessors; and this fact is related by Fitz-Stephen, in his description of the city of London, printed in the later editions of Stow's Survey, in these words: 'Lundonia pro spectaculis theatralibus, 'pro ludis scenicis, ludos habet sanctiores, repre-'sentationes miraculorum, quæ sancti Confessores 'operati sunt, seu representationes Passionum, quibus 'claruit constantia Martyrum.'

The same author, speaking of the Wells near London, says that on the north side thereof is a well called Clarks-Well; and Stow, assigning the reason for this appellation, furnishes us with a curious fact relating to the parish-clerks of London, the subject of the present enquiry; his words are these: 'Clarks-'well took its name of the parish-clerks in London, 'who of old time were accustomed there yearly to 'assemble, and to play some large history of holy 'scripture for example, of later time, to wit, in the 'year 1390, the 14th of Richard the Second, I read 'that the parish-clerks in London on the 18th of 'July plaid Enterludes at Skinners-well near unto 'Clarks-well, which play continued three days to-'gether, the king, queen, and nobles being present. 'Also in the year 1409, the tenth of Henry the 'Fourth, they played a play at the Skinners-well,

'which lasted eight days, and was of matter from the 'creation of the world; there were to see the same 'most part of the nobles and gentiles in England.'[†]

It is to be remarked that Fitz-Stephen does not speak of the acting of histories as a new thing, for the passage occurs in his account of the sports and pastimes in common use among the people in his time; and therefore the antiquity of these spectacles may with good reason be extended as far back as to the time of the Conquest. Of this kind of drama there are no specimens extant so ancient as the representation first above spoken of, but there are others in being, of somewhat less antiquity, from which we are enabled to form a judgment of their nature and tendency.

The anonymous author of a dialogue on old plays and old players, printed in the year 1699, speaks of a manuscript in the Cotton library, intitled in the printed catalogue 'A collection of Plays in old 'English Metre;'[‡] and conjectures that this may be the very play which Stow says was acted by the parish-clerks in the reign of Henry IV. and took up eight days in the representation; and it must be confessed that the conjecture of the author above-mentioned seems to be well warranted. By the character and language of the book it seems to be upwards of three hundred years old : it begins with a general prologue, giving the arguments of forty pageants or gesticulations, which are as so many several acts or scenes representing all the histories of both Testaments, from the creation to the choosing of St. Matthias to be an apostle. The stories of the New Testament are more largely related, viz., the Annunciation, Nativity, Visitation, the Passion of our Lord, his Resurrection, and Ascension, and the choice of St. Matthias. After which is also represented the Assumption and Last Judgment. The style of these compositions is as simple and artless as can be supposed; nothing can be more so than the following dialogue :—

### MARIA.

But hufband of a thyng pray you moft mekely,
I have knowing that your cofyn Elifabeth with childe is,
That it pleafe yow to go to her haftyly :
If ought we myght comfort her it were to me blys.

### JOSEPH.

A Goddys fake is fhe with child, fhe ?
Than will hir hufband Zachary be mery ;
In Montane they dwelle, far hencee fo mot yt be
In the city of Juda, I know it verily ;
It is hence I trowe myles two a fifty,
We are like to be wery or we come of the fame ;
I wole with a good wyll bleffyd wyff Mary
Now go we forth then in Goddys name, &c.

#### A little before the Resurrection.

Nunc dormient milites et veniet anima Christi de inferno, cum Adam et Eva, Abraham, John Baptist, et aliis.

---

* The office seems to have sprung out of that of Deacons, for in the early ages of Cristianity the Deacons exercised the functions thereof, helping the Priest in divine service. The subdeacons gave out the Psalms. Weever's Fun. Mon. 127, from the Summa Angelica Litera D.

† Survey of London, 4to. 1603, pag. 15.

‡ Sir William Dugdale, in his Antiquities of Warwickshire, pag. 116, cites it by the title of Ludus Coventriæ. The following is the title as it stands in the Catalogus Libror. Manuscript. Biblioth. Cotton, pag. 113. 'VIII. A Collection of Plays in old English Metre, h. e. Dramata sacra, 'in quibus exhibentur historiæ veteris et N. Testamenti introductis 'quasi in scenam personis illic memoratis, quas secum invicem collo-'quentes pro ingenio fingit Poeta videntur olim coram populo, sive ad 'instruendum sive ad placendum, à fratibus mendicantibus repræ-'sentata.'

## ANIMA CHRISTI.

Come forth Adam and Eve with the,
And all my fryendes that herein be
In paradyſe come forth with me,
　In blyſſe for to dwell :
The fende of hell that is your foo,
He ſhall be wrappyd and woundyn in woo,
Fro wo to welth, now ſhall ye go,
　With myrth ever mo to melle.

### ADAM.

I thank the Lord of thy grete grace,
That now is forgiven my gret treſpace,
Now ſhall we dwell yn blyſſful place.

The last scene or pageant, which represents the day of Judgment, begins thus :—

### MICHAEL.

*Surgite*, All men aryſe,
*Venite ad judicium*,
For now is ſet the high juſtice,
And hath aſſignyd the day of dome ;
Kepe you redyly to this grett aſſyſe,
Both grett and ſmall, all and ſum,
And of your anſwer you now adviſe,
What yow ſhall ſay when that yow come, &c.

Mysteries and moralites appear to have constituted another species of the ancient drama ; the first seem to have been representations of the most interesting events in the gospel-history ; one of this kind, intitled Candlemas-Day, or the Killing of the Children of Israel, is among the Bodleian manuscripts, and was bequeathed to the university by Sir Kenelm Digby ; the name of its author was Jhan Parfre, and it appears to have been composed in the year 1512.

The subject of this drama is tragical, notwithstanding which there are in it several touches of that low humour, with which the common people are ever delighted ; for in it the poet has introduced a servant of Herod, whom he calls Watkyn the messenger. This fellow, who is represented as cruel, and at the same time a great coward, gives Herod to understand that three strangers, knights, as he calls them, had been to make coffins at Bethlehem ; upon which Herod swears he will be avenged upon Israel, and commands four of his soldiers to slay all the children they shall find within two years of age ; which Watkyn hearing, intreats of Herod first that he may be made a knight, and next that he may be permitted to join the soldiers, and assist them in the slaughter. This request being granted, a pause ensues, the reason whereof will be best understood by the following stage-direction : Here the knyghts walke abought the place till Mary and Joſeph be conveied into Egipt.

Mary and Joseph are then exhorted by an angel to fly, and they resolve on it. The speech of Joseph concludes thus :—

Mary, you to do pleaſaunce without any let,
I ſhall brynge forth your aſſe without more delay,
Ful ſoone Mary thereon ye ſhall be ſett,
And this litel child that in your wombe lay,
Take hym in your armys Mary I you pray,
And of your ſwete mylke let him ſowke inowe.
Mawger Herowd and his grett fray :
And as your ſpouſe Mary I ſhall go with you.
　This ferdell of gere I ley upon my bakke ;
Now I am redy to go from this cuntre,
All my ſmale inſtruments is put in my pakke.

Now go we hens, Mary it will no better be,
For drede of Herowd apaas I high me ;
Lo now is our geer truſſed both more and leſſe,
Mary for to pleſe you with all humylite,
I ſhall go before, and lede forth your aſſe.

Et exeunt.

Then begins the slaughter, represented in the following dialogue :—

### 1 MILES.

Herke, ye wyffys, we be come your houſhold to viſite,
Though ye be never ſo wrath nor wood,
With ſharpe ſwoords that redely wyll byte,
All your chyldren within to years age in our cruel mood
Thurghe out all Bethleem to kylle and ſhed ther yong blood
As we be bound to the commaundement of the king,
Who that ſeith nay, we ſhall make a flood
To renne in the ſtretis by ther blood ſhedyng.

### 2 MILES.

Therefor unto us make ye a delyverance
Of your yong children and that anon ;
Or ells be Mahounde we ſhall geve a myſchaunce,
Our ſharpe ſwerds thurgh your bodies ſhall goon.

### WATKYN.

Therfor be ware for we wyll not leve oon
In all this cuntre that ſhall us eſcape,
I ſhall rather flee them everych oon,
And make them to lye and mowe like an ape.

### 1 MULIER.

Fye on you traitors of cruel tormentrye,
Wiche with your ſwerds of mortall violens——

### 2 MULIER.

Our young children that can no ſocoure but crie,
Wyll fle and devour in ther innocens.

### 3 MULIER.

Ye falſe traitors unto God ye do grete offens
To flee and morder yong children that in the cradell ſlumber ;

### 4 MULIER.

But we women ſhall make ageyns you reſiſtens,
After our power your malyce to encomber.

### WATKYN.

Peas you folyſhe quenys, wha ſhuuld you defende,
Ageyns us armyd men in this apparaile ?
We be bold men and the kyng us ded fende,
Hedyr into this cuntre to holde with you battaile.

### 1 MULIER.

Fye upon thee coward : of thee I will not faile
To dubbe thee knyght with my rokke rounde,
Women be ferſe when thei liſt to aſſaile,
Suche proude boyes to caſte to the grounde.

### 2 MULIER.

Avaunt, ye ſkowtys, I defye you everych one,
For I wole bete you all myſelf alone.

[Watkyn hic occidet per se.]

### 1 MULIER.

Alas, alas good coſynes, this is a ſorowfull peyn
To ſe our dere children that be ſo yong,
With theſe caytyves thus ſodeynly to be ſlayn ;
A vengeaunce I aſke on them all for this grett wrong.

### 2 MULIER.

And a very myſcheff mut come them amonge,
Whereſo ever thei be come or goon,
For thei have killed my yong ſone John.

### 3 MULIER.

Goſſippis, a ſhamefull deth I aſke upon Herowde our kyng,
That thus rygorouſly our chyldren hath ſlayn.

#### 4. MULIER.

I pray God bryng hym to an ille endyng,
And in helle pytte to dwelle ever in peyn.

#### WATKYN.

What ye harlotts? I have aſpied certeyn
That ye be tratorys to my lord the kyng,
And therfor I am ſure ye ſhall have an ille endyng.

#### 1 MULIER.

If ye abide, Watkyn, you and I ſhall game
With my diſtaffe that is ſo rounde.

#### 2 MULIER.

And yf I ſeas, thanne have I ſhame,
Tyll thu be fellid down to the grounde.

#### 3 MULIER.

And I may gete the within my bounde,
With this ſtaffe I ſhall make thee lame.

#### WATKYN.

Yee I come no more ther, be ſeynt Mahound,
For if I do, methynketh I ſhall be made tame.

#### 1 MULIER.

Abyde, Watkyn, I ſhall make thee a knyght.

#### WATKYN.

Thu make me a knyght! that were on the newe
But for ſhame my trouthe I you plight,
I ſhud bete your bak and ſide tyll it were blewe,
But be my god Mahounde that is ſo true,
My hert begynne to fayle and waxeth feynt,
Or ells be Mahounds blood ye ſhuld it rue,
But ye ſhall loſe your goods as traitors atteynt.

#### 1 MULIER.

What thu jabell, canſt not have do?
Thu and thi cumpany, ſhall not depart,
Tyll of our diſtavys ye have take part:
Therfor ley on goſſippes with a mery hart,
And lett them not from us goo.

Here thei ſhall bete Watkyn, and the knyghts ſhall come to
reſcue hym, and than thei go to Herowds hous.

Of Moralities, a species of the drama differing from the former, there are many yet extant, the titles whereof may be seen in Ames's Typographical Antiquities; the best known of them are one entitled Every Man, Lustie Juventus, and Hycke Scorner, an accurate analysis of which latter, Dr. Percy has given in his Reliques of ancient English Poetry, vol. I. pag. 130.

That such representations as these, namely, histories, mysteries, and moralities, were frequent, we may judge from the great number of them yet extant, and from the fondness which the people of this country have ever manifested for theatrical entertainments of all kinds; and that the parish-clerks of all other persons should betake themselves to the profession of players, by exhibiting such as these to the public, will not be wondered at, when it is remembered that besides themselves, few of the laity, excepting the lawyers and physicians, were able to read; and it might be for this reason that even the priests themselves undertook to personate a character in this kind of drama.

Of the fraternity of parish-clerks, Strype, in his edition of Stowe's Survey, book V. pag. 231, gives the following account: 'They were a guild or fra- 'ternity first incorporated by K. Hen. III. known 'then by the name of the brotherhood of St. Nicholas, 'whose hall was near St. Helens by Bishopsgate 'street, within the gate, at the sign of the Angel, 'where the parish-clerks had seven alms-houses for 'poor clerks' widows, as Stow shews. Unto this 'fraternity men and women of the first quality, 'ecclesiastical and others, joined themselves, who 'as they were great lovers of church-music in 'general, so their beneficence unto parish-clerks 'in particular is abundantly evident, by some ancient 'manuscripts at their common hall in Great Wood 'street, wherein foot-steps of their great bounty 'appear by the large gifts and revenues given for 'the maintenance and encouragement of such as 'should devote themselves to the study and practice 'of this noble and divine science, in which the parish- 'clerks did then excel, singing being their peculiar 'province.

'Some certain days in the year they had their 'public feasts, which they celebrated with singing 'and music, and then received into their society such 'persons as delighted in singing, and were studious 'of it. These their meetings and performances 'were in Guildhall college or chapel. Thus the '27th of September, 1560, on the eve thereof they 'had even-song, and on the morrow there was a 'communion; and after they had retired to Car- 'penter's-hall to dinner. And May 11, 1562, they 'kept their communion at the said Guildhall chapel, 'and received seven persons into their brotherhood, 'and then repaired to their own hall to dinner, and 'after dinner a goodly play of the children of West- 'minster, with waits and regals and singing.

'King Charles I. renewed their charter, and con- 'ferred upon them very ample privileges and im- 'munities, and incorporated them by the style and 'title of the Master, Wardens, and Fellowship of 'Parish-Clerks, of the city and suburbs of London 'and the liberties thereof, the city of Westminster, 'the borough of Southwark, and the fifteen out- 'parishes adjacent.'

## BOOK XIII.    CHAP. CXVIII.

THE principles of music, and the precepts of musical composition, as taught in the several countries of Europe about the middle of the sixteenth century, were uniformly the same; the same harmonies, the same modulations were practised in the compositions of the Flemish, the Italian, the German, the French, and the English musicians; and nothing character- istic of the genius or humour of a particular country or province, as was once the case of the Moorish and Provençal music, was discernible in the songs of that period, except in those of the Scots and Irish, the former whereof are in a style so peculiar, as borrow- ing very little from art, and yet abounding in that sweetness of melody, which it is the business of art to cultivate and improve, that we are driven to seek for the origin of this kind of music elsewhere than in the writings of those authors who have treated on the subject in general terms.

To speak of the Scots music in the first place; the common opinion is that it has received a considerable degree of infusion from the Italians, for that David Ricci or Rizzio, a lutenist of Turin, in the year 1564, became a favourite of Mary queen of Scots, and was retained in her service as a musician; and finding the music of the country of such a kind as rendered it susceptible of great improvement, he set himself to polish and refine it; and adopting, as far as the rules of his art would allow, that desultory melody, which he found to be its characteristic, composed most of those tunes to which the Scots songs have for two centuries past, been commonly sung.

Against this opinion, which has nothing to support it but vulgar tradition, it may be urged that David Ricci was not a composer of any kind. The historians and others who speak of him represent him as a lutenist and a singer; and Sir James Melvil, who was personally acquainted with him, vouchsafes him no higher a character than that of a merry fellow, and a good musician. 'Her majesty,' says he, 'had 'three valets of her chamber, who sang three parts, 'and wanted a bass to sing the fourth part. There- 'fore they told her majesty of this man, as one fit 'to make the fourth in concert. Thus was he drawn 'in to sing sometimes with the rest; and afterward 'when her French secretary retired himself to France, 'this David obtained the same office.'*

Melvil, in the course of his Memoirs, relates that Ricci engrossed the favour of the queen; that he was suspected to be a pensioner of the pope; and that by the part he took in all public transactions, he gave rise to the troubles of Scotland, and precipitated the ruin of his mistress.

Buchanan is somewhat more particular; the account he gives is, that Ricci was born at Turin; that his father, an honest but poor man, got a mean livelihood by teaching young people the rudiments of music. That having no patrimony to leave them, he instructed his children of both sexes in music, and amongst the rest his son David, who being in the prime of his youth, and having a good voice, gave hopes of his succeeding in that profession. That with a view to advance his fortune, Ricci went to the court of the duke of Savoy, then at Nice; but meeting with no encouragement there, found means to get himself admitted into the train of the Count de Moretto, then upon the point of setting out on an embassy to Scotland. That the Count, soon after his arrival in Scotland, having no employment for Ricci, dismissed him. The musicians of Mary queen of Scots were chiefly such as she had brought with her from France, on the death of the king her husband; and with these, as Buchanan relates, Ricci ingratiated himself by singing and playing among them, till he was taken notice of by the queen, soon after which he was retained in her service as a singer. From this station, by means of flattery and the most

abject arts of insinuation, he rose to the highest degree of favour and confidence; and being appointed her secretary for French affairs, became absorbed in the intrigues of the court, in the management whereof he behaved with such arrogance and contempt, even of his superiors, as rendered him odious to all about him.† The rest of his history is well known; he grew rich, and his insolence drawing on him the hatred of the Scottish nobility, he was on the ninth day of March, in the year 1566, dragged from the presence of the queen into an outer chamber of the palace, and there slain.

In such an employment as Ricci had, and with all that variety of business in which he must be supposed to have been engaged, actuated by an ambitious and intriguing spirit, that left him neither inclination nor opportunities for study, can it be thought that the reformation or improvement of the Scots music was his care, or indeed that the short interval of two years at most, afforded him leisure for any such undertaking? In fact, the origin of those melodies, which are the subject of the present enquiry, is to be derived from a higher source; and so far is it from being true, that the Scots music has been meliorated by the Italian, that the converse of the proposition may be assumed; and, however strange it may seem, an Italian writer of great reputation and authority has not hesitated to assert that some of the finest vocal music that his country can boast of, owes its merit in a great measure to its affinity with the Scots.

To account for that singularity of style which distinguishes the Scottish melodies, it may be necessary to recur to the account given by Giraldus Cambrensis of the music of the inhabitants of the northern parts of this kingdom, particularly near the Humber; and to advert to that passage in the ecclesiastical history of Bede, wherein he relates the arrival of John the Archchanter from Rome, his settlement among the Northumbrians; and the propensity of that people to music;‡ whose sequestered situation, and the little intercourse they must be supposed to have held with the adjacent countries, will account for the existence of a style in music truly original, and which might in process of time extend itself to the neighbouring kingdom.§

* Memoirs of Sir James Melvil of Halhill, 8vo. Lond. 1752, pag. 107.

† Buchan. Rer. Scotic. Hist. lib. xvii.    ‡ See pag. 138 of this work.

§ The ancient Scotch tunes seem to consist of the pure diatonic intervals, without any intermixture of those chromatic notes, as they are called, which in the modern system divide the diapason into twelve semitones; and in favour of this notion it may be observed that the front row of a harpsichord will give a melody nearly resembling that of the Scots tunes. But the distinguishing characteristic of the Scots music is the frequent and uniform iteration of the concords, more especially the third on the accented part of the bar, to the almost total exclusion of the second and the seventh; of which latter interval it may be remarked, that it occurs seldom as a semitone, even where it precedes a cadence; perhaps because there are but few keys in which the final note is preceded by a natural semitone; and this consideration will also furnish the reason why the Scots tunes so frequently close in a leap from the key-note to the fifth above. The particulars above remarked are obvious in those two famous tunes Katherine Ogie and Cold and raw, which are unquestionably ancient, and in the true Scots style. *The construction of the old Scotch tunes is this, that almost every succeeding emphatical note is a third, a fifth, an octave, or, in short, some note that is in concord with the preceding note. Thirds are chiefly used; which are very pleasing concords. I use the word emphatical to distinguish those notes which have a stress laid on them in singing the tune, from the lighter connecting notes, that serve merely like grammar articles in common speech to tack the whole together.*

*When we consider how these ancient tunes were first performed, we shall see that such harmonical succession of sounds was natural and even necessary*

How long it was that the popular melodies of Scotland continued to be propagated by tradition, it is not easy to ascertain, for it does not appear that that kingdom ever abounded with skilful musicians; however by the year 1400 the science had made such a progress there, that one of its princes, James Stuart, the first of his name, and the hundred and second in the list of their kings, attained to such a proficiency in it, as enabled him to write learnedly on music, and in his compositions and performance on a variety of instruments, to contend with the ablest masters of the time.

Bale and Dempster, and after them bishop Tanner, take notice of this prince in the accounts by them severally given of Scottish writers, and ascribe to him among other works, a treatise De Musica, and Cantilenas Scoticas.

Buchanan has drawn his character at full, and among many other distinguishing particulars, mentions that he was excellently skilled in music, more indeed, he adds, than was necessary or fitting for a king, for that there was no musical instrument on which he could not play so well, as to be able to contend with the greatest masters of the art in those days.*

The particulars of his story are related by all the Scottish historians, who, as do others, represent him as a prince of great endowments, being ignorant of no art worthy the knowledge of a gentleman; complete in all manly exercises, a good Latin scholar, an excellent poet, a wise legislator, a valiant captain, and, in a word, an accomplished gentleman and a great monarch. Notwithstanding which his amiable and resplendent qualities, a conspiracy was formed against him in the year 1436, by the earl of Athol, and others of his subjects, who broke into his chamber, he then being lodged in the Black Friars in Perth, and with many cruel wounds slew him in the forty-fourth year of his age, and the thirteenth of his reign.†

In the account given of James I. by bishop Tanner the brief mention of the Cantilenas Scoticas there

ascribed to him leaves it in some measure a question, whether he was the author of the words, or the music, of those Scots songs. That he was a poet is agreed by all; and Major, in his History de Gestis Scotorum, and bishop Nicholson,‡ mention a poem written by him on Joan daughter of the duchess of Clarence, afterwards his queen, and two songs of his writing, the latter of which is yet extant, and abounds with rural humour and pleasantry:§ but the evidence of his composing tunes or melodies is founded on the testimony of a well-known Italian author, Alessandro Tassoni, who in a book of his writing, entitled Pensieri diversi, printed at Venice in 1646, speaking of music, and first of the ancient Greek musicians, has this remarkable passage: 'We may reckon 'among the moderns, James, king of Scotland, who 'not only composed sacred poems set to music, but 'also of himself invented a new, melancholy, and 'plaintive kind of music, different from all other. 'In which he has since been imitated by Carlo 'Gesualdo, prince of Venosa, who in these our times 'has improved music with new and admirable com-'positions.' ‖

That the Scots melodies at the time when they were originally composed were committed to writing there can be no doubt; but it is to be feared that there are no genuine copies of any of them now remaining, they having for a series of years been propagated by tradition, and till lately existed only in the memory of the inhabitants of that kingdom. Nevertheless they seem not to have been corrupted, nor to have received the least tincture from the music of other countries, but retain that sweetness, delicacy, and native simplicity for which they are distinguished and admired. Some curious persons have of late years made attempts to recover and reduce them to writing; and such of them as were sufficiently skilled in music, by conversation with the Highlanders, and the assistance of intelligent people, have been able to reduce a great number of ancient Scots melodies into musical notes.

There are many fine Scots airs in the collection of songs by the well-known Tom Durfey, entitled 'Pills to purge Melancholy,' published in the year 1720, which seem to have suffered very little by their passing through the hands of those English masters who were concerned in the correction of that book; but in the multiplicity of tunes in the Scots style that have been published in subsequent collections, it is very difficult to distinguish betweeen the ancient and modern; those that pretend to be possessed of this discriminating faculty assert that the following, viz., Katherine Ogie, Muirland Willy,

---

*in their construction. They were composed to be played on the harp accompanied by the voice. The harp was strung with wire which gives a sound of long continuance, and had no contrivance like that in the modern harpsichord, by which the sound of the preceding could be stopped the moment a succeeding note began. To avoid actual discord it was therefore necessary that the succeeding emphatic note should be a chord with the preceding, as their sounds must exist at the same time. Hence arose that beauty in those tunes that has so long pleased, though men scarce know why. That they were originally composed for the harp, and of the most simple kind,—I mean a harp without any half notes, but those in the natural scale, and with no more than two octaves of strings from C to C,—I conjecture from another circumstance, which is, that not one of these tunes really ancient has a single artificial note in it; and that in tunes where it was not convenient for the voice to use the middle notes of the harp, and place the key in F, there the B, which if used should be a B♭, is always omitted by passing over it with a third.*

\* 'In musicis curiosius erat instructus, quam regem vel deceat, vel 'expediat, nullum enim organum erat, ad psallendi usum, comparatum, 'quo non ille tam scite modulabatur, ut cum summis illius ætatis 'magistris contenderet.' Buch. Rer. Scotic. Hist. lib. x. sect. 57.

In the continuation of the Scotichronicon of Johannes de Fordun, [Scotichron. à Hearne, vol. IV. pag. 1323,] is a character of James I. to the same purpose, but more particular; and in Hector Boethius is an eulogium on him, which is here given in the dialect of the country, from the translation of that historian by Ballenden. 'He was weil lernit to 'fecht with the swerd, to just, to turnay, to worsyl, to syng and dance, 'was an expert medicinar, richt crafty in playing baith of lute and harp, 'and sindry othir instrumentis of musik. He was expert in gramar, 'oratry, and poetry, and maid sae flowand and sententious versis, apperit 'weil he was ane natural and borne poete.'

† Buch. Rer. Scot. Hist. lib. x. Holinshed's Hist. of Scotland, pag. 384.

‡ In his Scottish Historical Library, pag. 55.

§ Tanner includes these in his account of his works. Allan Ramsay, in his Ever-Green, and also in his own poems, has ascribed that humorous Scots poem, 'Christ's Kirk on the Green,' to James I. and in his notes on it has feigned some circumstances to give a colour to the opinion that he was the author of it; but bishop Tanner with much better reason, gives it to James V. who also was a poet.

‖ 'Noi ancora possiamo connumerar trà nostri Jacopo Rè di Scozia, 'che non pur cose sacre compose in canto, ma trovò da se stesso una 'nuova, musica lamentevole, e mesta, differente da tutte' l' altre. Nel 'che poi è stato imitato da Carlo Gesualdo, Prencipe di Venosa, che in 'questa nostra età hà illustrata anch' egli la musica con nuove mirabili 'invenzioni.' Lib. X. cap. xxiii. Angelo Berardi in his Miscellanea Musicale, pag 50, acquiesces in this relation, and, without citing his authority, gives it in the very words of Tassoni.

and Cold and Raw,\* are of the highest antiquity, and that the Lass of Peatie's Mill, Tweed-side, Mary Scot, and Galloway Shiels, though perfectly in the Scots vein, bear the signatures of modern composition.†

Of the Irish music, as also of the Welch, alike remarkable with the Scotch for wildness and irregularity, but far inferior to it in sweetness of modulation, little is to be met with in the works of those who have written professedly on music. Sir James Ware has slightly mentioned it in his Antiquities of Ireland, and noted that the Irish harp is ever strung with brass wires. The little that has been said of the Welsh music is to be found in the Cambriæ Descriptio of Silvester Giraldus;‡ and mention is made of the Irish music, as also of the Scotch, in the continuation of the Scotichronicon of Johannes De Fordun, lib. 16. cap. 29. The passage is curious, as it contains a comparison of the music of the three countries with each other, and is in these words :—

'In musicis instrumentis invenio commendabilem 'gentis istius diligenciam. In quibus, præ omni 'nacione quam vidimus, incomparabiliter instructa 'est. Non enim in hiis, ut in Britannicis, quibus 'assueti sumus, instrumentis tarda et morosa est 'modulacio, verum velox et præceps, suavis tamen 'et jocunda sonoritas, miraque in tanta tam præ- 'cipiti digitorum rapacitate musica proporcio et 'arte per omnia indempni, inter crispatos modulos 'organaque multipliciter intricata, tam suavi velo- 'citate, tam dispari paritate, tam discordi concordia 'consona redditur et completur melodia, seu Dia-

\* This last air was wrought into a catch by John Hilton, which may be seen in his Collection of Catches, published in 1652. The initial words of it are 'Ise gae with thee my Peggy.' This tune was greatly admired by queen Mary, the consort of king William; and she once affronted Purcell by requesting to have it sung to her, he being present: the story is as follows. The queen having a mind one afternoon to be entertained with music, sent to Mr. Gostling, then one of the chapel, and afterwards subdean of St. Paul's, to Henry Purcell and Mrs. Arabella Hunt, who had a very fine voice, and an admirable hand on the lute, with a request to attend her; they obeyed her commands; Mr. Gostling and Mrs. Hunt sang several compositions of Purcell, who accompanied them on the harpsichord; at length the queen beginning to grow tired, asked Mrs. Hunt if she could not sing the old Scots ballad 'Cold and Raw,' Mrs. Hunt answered yes, and sang it to her lute. Purcell was all the while sitting at the harpsichord unemployed, and not a little nettled at the queen's preference of a vulgar ballad to his music; but seeing her majesty delighted with this tune, he determined that she should hear it upon another occasion : and accordingly in the next birth-day song, viz., that for the year 1692, he composed an air to the words, 'May her bright example chace Vice in troops out of the land,' the bass whereof is the tune to Cold and Raw; it is printed in the second part of the Orpheus Britannicus, and is note for note the same with the Scots tune.

† About the year 1730, one Alexander Munroe, a native of Scotland, then residing at Paris, published a collection of the best Scotch tunes fitted to the German flute, with several divisions and variations, but the simplicity of the airs is lost in the attempts of the author to accommodate them to the style of Italian music.

In the year 1733, William Thompson published a collection of Scotch songs with the music, entitled Orpheus Caledonius ; the editor was not a musician, but a tradesman, and the publication is accordingly injudicious and very incorrect.

Three collections of Scots tunes were made by      Mc Gibbon, a musician of Edinburgh, and published about twenty years ago with basses and variations ; and about the same time Mr. Francis Barsanti the father of Miss Barsanti, of Covent-Garden theatre, an Italian, and an excellent musician, who had been resident some years in Scotland, published a good collection of Scots tunes with basses of his own composition.

‡ It is said that the Welch music is derived from the Irish. In the Chronicle of Wales by Caradocus of Lhancarvan, is a relation to this purpose, viz., that Griffith Ap-Conan, king of North Wales, being by mother and grandmother an Irishman, and also born in Ireland, carried with him from thence divers cunning musicians into Wales, who devised in a manner all the instrumental music used there, as appears as well by the books written of the same, as also by the names of the tunes and measures used among them to this day. Vide Sir James Ware's Antiquities of Ireland, published by Walter Harris, Esq. chap. xxv. pag. 184.

'tessarone seu Diapente cordæ concrepent, semper 'tenera Bemol incipiunt, et in Bemol redeunt, ut 'cuncta sub jocunda sonoritatis dulcedine comple- 'antur, tam subtiliter modulos intrant et exeunt, sicque 'subtuso grossioris cordæ sonitu gracilium tinnitus 'licencius ludunt, latencius delectant, lasciviusque 'demulcent, ut pars artis maxima videatur arte velari, 'tamquam si lata ferat ars depressa pudorem. Hinc 'accidit, ut ea, quæ subtilius intuentibus, et artis 'archana decernentibus, internas et ineffabiles com- 'parent animi dilicias, ea non attendentibus, sed quasi 'videntibus non videndo, et audiendo non intelli- 'gentibus, aures pocius onerent quam delectant, et 'tam confuso et inordinato strepitu invitis audi- 'toribus fastidia parant tædiosa. Olim dicebatur, 'quod Scocia et Wallia Yberniam in modulis imitari 'æmula nitebantur disciplina. Hibernia quidem tan- 'tum duobus et delectatur instrumentis, cithara, 'viz. et tymphana, Scocia tribus, cythera, tympana 'et choro, Wallia, cythera, tibiis et choro. Æneis 'quoque utuntur cordis, non de intestinis vel corio 'factis. Multorum autem opinione hodie Scocia non 'tantum magistram æquiparavit Hiberniam, verum 'eciam in musica pericia longe jam prævalet et 'præcellit. Unde et ibi quasi fontem artis jam 'requirunt. Hæc ibi. Venerunt itaque periciores 'arte illa de Hibernia et Anglia, et de incom- 'parabili præcellencia et magisterio musicæ artis 'regiæ admirantes, eidem præ ceteris gradum attri- 'buunt superlativum. Ceterum quam diu hujus regni 'orbita volvitur, ejusdem prædicabilis practica, lau- 'dabilis rectoria, et præcellens policia accipient 'præconii incrementum.'

Towards the beginning of the seventeenth century, the principles of harmony being then generally known, and the art of composition arrived to great perfection, there appeared a great emulation among the masters throughout Europe in their endeavours towards the improvement of the science; and to speak with precision on the subject, it seems that the competition was chiefly between the Italians and the Germans. The former of these, having Palestrina for their master, had carried church-music to the highest degree of perfection; and in the composition of madrigals, for elegance of style, correctness of harmony, and in sweetness and variety of modulation, they were hardly equalled by the musicians of any country. Nevertheless it may be said that in some respects the Germans were their rivals, and, in the knowledge and use of the organ, their superiors. This people began very soon to discover the power and excellence of this noble instrument; that it was particularly adapted to music in consonance; that the sounds produced by it, not like those that answer to the touch of a string, were unlimited in their duration; that all those various graces and elegancies with which the music of the moderns is enriched, such as fugues, imitative and responsive passages, various kinds of motion, and others, were no less capable of being uttered by the organ, than by a number of voices in concert;§ and so excellent

§ Milton, who himself played on the organ, discovers a just sense of the nature and use of this noble instrument in that passage of his Tractate on education where he recommends, after bodily exercise, the recreating and composing the travailed spirits of his young disciples

were the Germans in this kind of performance on the organ, that towards the close of the fifteenth century, they seem almost to have exhausted its power; for in the year 1480, we are told that a German, named Bernhard, invented the pedal, thereby increasing the harmony of the instrument by the addition of a fundamental part.

But notwithstanding the competition above-spoken of, it seems that as the principles of music were first disseminated throughout Europe by the Italians, so in all the subsequent improvements in practice they seemed to give the rule: to instance in a few particulars, the church style was originally formed by them; dramatic music had its rise in Italy; Recitative was invented by the Italians; that elegant species of vocal composition, the Cantata, was invented by Carissimi, an Italian; Thorough-bass was also of Italian origin. These considerations determine the order and course of the present narration, and will lead us, after doing justice to our own country, by extending the account of English musicians to about the close of the sixteenth century, to exhibit a given series, commencing at that period, of Italian musicians; interposing, as occasion offers, such eminent men of other countries as seem to be entitled to particular notice.

The history of music as hitherto deduced, is continued down to a period, at which the science may truly be said to have arrived at great perfection. Abroad it continued to be encouraged and to flourish; but in this country it was so little regarded, as to afford, at least to the professors of it, a ground of complaint that music was destitute of patronage, and rather declined: the king, James I. was a lover of learning and field recreations; and though he had some genius for poetry, he had little relish for either music or painting. Indeed, had his love of music been ever so great, his own country afforded scarce any means of improvement in it; for we read of no eminent Scottish musicians either before or since his time. It is true his mother, as she was a very finely accomplished woman, was an excellent proficient, and during the time she was in France had contracted a love for the Italian vocal music; and it is recorded that upon her return to Scotland she took into her service David Ricci, a native of Turin, who had a very fine bass voice, to assist in the performance of madrigals for her own private amusement: Ricci was slain in the presence of the queen at the time when she was with child of the prince, afterwards James I. after which there was perhaps scarce any person left in her dominions capable of the office of preceptor to a prince in the science of music.*

with the solemn and divine harmonies of music: 'Either while the 'skilful organist plies his *grave* and *fancied descant*, in *lofty fugues*, or 'the whole symphony with artful and unimaginable touches adorn and 'grace the well-studied chords of some choice composer.' .

* Besides James I. of Scotland, we know of no person, a native of that country, who can with propriety be said to have been a musician; nevertheless it is to be observed that there is extant in the collection of the author of this work, a manuscript-treatise on music, written in the Scottish dialect, which appears to have been composed by some person eminently skilled in the science. It is of a folio size, and is entitled 'The Art of Music collectit out of all ancient Doctouris of Musick.' Pr. 'Qwhat is mensural musick?' It contains the rudiments of music, and the precepts of composition, with variety of examples, and a formula of the tones; from which circumstance it is to be conjectured that it was written before the time of the reformation in Scotland.

With respect to church-music, it is highly probable that James adhered to the metrical psalmody that had been instituted by Calvin, and adopted by many of the reformed churches; and of this his version of the Psalms may be looked upon as some sort of evidence; however upon his accession to the crown of England he was necessitated to recognize the form and mode of public worship established in this kingdom.

Notwithstanding the love which queen Elizabeth bore to music, and the affection which she manifested for the solemn choral service, it seems that the servants of her chapel experienced the effects of that parsimony, which it must be confessed was part of her character; they solicited for an increase of their wages; but neither the merits of Bull nor of Bird, both of whom she affected to admire, nor of Giles, or many other excellent musicians then in her service, were able to procure the least concession in their favour. Upon her decease they made the like application to her successor, having previously engaged some of the lords of the council to promote it. The event of their joint solicitation appears by an entry in the Cheque-book of the chapel-royal, of which the following is a transcript:—·*

5 December, 1604.

| | |
|---|---|
| The Lo. Charles Haward high admirall. | Be it remembered by all that shall succeed us, that in the year of our Lord God 1604, and in the second yeare of the reign of our most gracious sovereign |
| The Lo. Tho. Haward Lo. Chamberlaine | Lord JAMES, the first of that name, by the grace of God of Great Britaine, France, and Ireland, king. After a long and chargeable sute continued for increase |
| The Lo. Harrie Haward earle of Northampton | of wages in the end, by the furtherance of certaine honourable persons named in the margent, commissioners, and by the special favour and help of the right worshipfull doctor Montague, deane of |
| The Lo. Cecill vicount Cramborne | the chappel then beinge, and by the great paynes of Leonard Davies, sub-deane, and of Nathaniel Gyles, then master of the children, with other |
| The Lo. Knowles treasurer of houshold | auntients of the place, the king's most excellent majestie of his royall bountye and regard, pleased to add to the late intertainement of the chappell ten |

pounds per annum to every man: so increasinge there stipends from thirtie to fortie pounds per annum, and also augmented the twelve childrens allowance from six pence to ten pence per diem. And to the sergeant of the vestrie, was then geven increase of xl. per annum, as to the gent. and the two yeomen and the groome of the vestrie, the increase of fower pence per diem as to the twelve children. His royall majestie ordayninge that these several increases should be payd to the members of the chapell and vestrie in the nature of bourd wages for ever. Now it was thought meete that seeinge the intertainement of the chappell was

* This is the augmentation alluded to by Bird in the dedication of his Gradualia, part I, to Henry Howard earl of Northampton, above styled Lo, Harrie Haward, earl of Northampton, *and is recorded amongst the instances of king James the First's bounty in Stow's Annals, page* 1037.

Cursed be the partie that taketh this leafe out of this book. Amen.

not augmented of many years by any his majesties progenitors kinges and quenes raiginge before his highnes, that therefore his kinglie bountie in augmenting the same (as is before shewed) should be recorded, to be had ever in remembrance, that thereby not onlye wee (men and children now lyveinge) but all those also which shall succeede us in the chappell shuld daylye see cause (in our most devoute prayers) humblye to beseech the devine majestie to bless his highnes, our gracious queen Ann, prince Henrie, and all and everye of that royal progenie with blessings both spirituall and temporall, and that from age to age, and everlastynglye. And let us all praye Amen, Amen.

The names of the Gent. lyveing at the time of this augmentation graunted :—

Leonard Davies, Subdean.
Barthol. Mason  ⎫
Antho. Harrison  ⎪
Robert Stuckey  ⎬ Chaplaines
Steven Boughton  ⎪
William Lawes  ⎪
Antho. Kerbie  ⎭
Doctor Bull, Organist
Nathaniel Gyles, Master of the Children
Thomas Sampson, Clerke of the Cheque
Robert Stone
Will. Byrde
Rychard Granwell
Crue Sharp
Edmund Browne
Tho. Woodson
Henrie Eveseede
Robert Allison
Jo. Stevens

Jo. Hewlett
Richard Plumley
Tho. Goolde
Peter Wright
Will. Lawrence
James Davies
Jo. Amerye
Jo. Baldwin
Francis Wyborow
Arthur Cocke
George Woodson
Jo. Woodson
Edmund Shirgoold
Edmund Hooper.

The Officers of the vestrie then were—
Ralphe Fletcher, Sergeant
Jo. Patten  ⎫
Robert Lewis  ⎬ Yeomen
Harrye Allred, Groome.

## CHAP. CXIX.

THE recreations of the court during the reign of James I. were altogether of the dramatic kind, consisting of masques and interludes, in the composing and performance whereof the gentlemen, and also the children of the chapel, were frequently employed. Most of these dramas were written by Ben Jonson,* some in the lifetime of Samuel Daniel, laureate or court poet ; and others after Jonson, succeeded to that employment.†

* Speed's Chron. 725.
† The office of Poet Laureate is well known at this time. There are no records that ascertain the origin of the institution in this kingdom, though there are many that recognise it. The following is the best account that can here be given of it. As early as the reign of Henry III. who died in the year 1272, there was a court poet, a Frenchman, named Henry de Avranches, and otherwise 'Magistro Henrico Versificator,' Master Henry the Versifier, who from two several precepts, to be found in Madox's History of the Exchequer, is supposed to have had an assignment of a hundred shillings a year by way of salary or stipend. Vide Hist. of English Poetry by Mr. Thomas Warton, vol. I. pag. 47.
In the year 1341, Petrarch was crowned with laurel in the capitol by the senate of Rome. After that Frederic III. emperor of Germany, gave the laurel to Conradus Celtes ; and ever since the Counts Palatine of the empire have claimed the privilege solemnly to invest poets with the bays.
Chaucer was contemporary with Petrarch, and is supposed to have become acquainted with him while abroad. Upon his return to England he assumed the title of Poet Laureat ; and, anno 22 Rich. II. obtained a grant of an annual allowance of wine, as appears by the following docquet :—
 'Vigesimo secundo anno Richardi secundi concessum Galfrido
 'Chaucer unum dolium vini per annum durante vitâ, in portu
 'civitatis London, per manus capitalis pincernæ nostri.' Vide
 Fuller's Worthies, 27.
John Kay, in his dedication of the Siege of Rhodes to Edward IV.

The children of James were well instructed in music, and particularly in dancing, for their improvement in which latter accomplishment the king appears to have been very solicitous. In a letter from him to his sons, dated Theobalds, April 1, 1623, now among the Harleian manuscripts in the British Museum, Numb. 6987. 24, he desires them to keep up their dancing privately, 'though they whistle and 'sing to one another for music.'

Prince Charles was a scholar of Coperario, and by him had been taught the Viol da gamba ; and though Lilly the astrologer in his character of Charles I. contents himself with saying that the king was not unskilful in music, the fact is, that he had an excellent judgment in the science, and was besides an able performer on the above instrument.‡ As to prince Henry, it is highly probable that he had the same instructor with his brother : of his proficiency little is said in the accounts of his life ; but that he was however a lover of music, and a patron of men of eminence in the science, may be inferred from the following extract from the list of his household establishment, as contained in the Appendix to the Life of Henry Prince of Wales, by Dr. Birch :—

### MUSICIANS.

| | | |
|---|---|---|
| Dr. Bull | Mr. Ford | Valentine Sawyer |
| Mr. Lupo | Mr. Cutting | Matthew Johnson |
| Mr. Johnson | Mr. Stinte | Edward Wormall |
| Mr. Mynors | Mr. Hearne | Thomas Day |
| Mr. Jones | John Ashby | Sig. Angelo. |

A brief declaration of what yearly pensions, and to whom his highness did grant the same, payable out of his highness's treasure from the time of his creation until the first day of November, 1612 :—

| | £. | | £. |
|---|---|---|---|
| 1611 ⎱ June ⎰ To John Bull doctor of music ⎱⎰ | 40 | To John Ashby - - | 30 |
| | | To Edward Wormall | 20 |
| To Robert Johnson - | 40 | To Matthias Johnson | 20 |
| To Thomas Lupo - - | 40 | 1611 ⎱ To Thomas March ⎰ Ford one of his highness's musicians, by way of increase to his former pension. ⎱⎬⎰ | 10 |
| To John Mynors - - | 40 | | |
| To Jonas Wrench - - | 40 | | |
| To Thomas Day - - | 40 | | |
| To Valentine Sawyer - | 40 | | |
| To Thomas Cutting§ - | 40 | August. To Jerom Hearne one of his highness's musicians. ⎱⎬⎰ | 20 |
| To John Sturte - - - | 40 | | |
| To Thomas Ford - - | 30 | | |

subscribes himself his humble poet laureat ; and Skelton, who lived in the reigns of Henry VII. and VIII. styles himself Skelton Laureat.
At the beginning of the reign of James I. Samuel Daniel was laureat ; but though he was a man of abilities, Jonson was employed to write the court poems. Upon the death of Daniel, about the year 1619, Jonson was appointed his successor, who before this, viz., in February 1615, had obtained a grant of an annual pension of one hundred marks.
In the year 1630, by letters patent of Charles I. this pension was augmented to one hundred pounds per annum, with an additional grant of one terse of Canary Spanish wine, to be taken out of the king's store of wines yearly, and from time to time remaining at, or in the cellars within or belonging to his palace of Whitehall ; and this continues to be the establishment in favour of the poet laureate.
Upon these grants of wine it may be observed that the first of the kind seems to be that in a pipe-roll Ann. 36 Hen. III. to Richard the king's harper, and Beatrice his wife, in these words : ' Et in uno dolio vini 'empto et dato Magistro Ricardo, Citharistæ regis xl. fol. per Br. Reg. 'Et in uno dolio empto et dato Beatrici uxori ejusdem Ricardi.'
‡ Playford, who had good opportunities of information, speaking of the skill in music of some of our princes, says, ' Nor was his late sacred 'majesty and blessed martyr king Charles the First, behind any of his 'predecessors in the love and promotion of this science, especially in the 'service of Almighty God, and with much zeal he would hear reverently 'performed, and often appointed the service and anthems himself, 'especially that sharp service composed by Dr William Child, being by 'his knowledge in music a competent judge therein ; and would play his 'part exactly well on the bass-violl, especially of those incomparable 'fancies of Mr. Coperario to the organ.'
§ This Thomas Cutting was an excellent performer on the lute. In the year 1607 he was in the service of the Lady Arabella Stuart, when

Before the publication of Morley's Introduction the precepts of musical composition were known but to few, as existing only in manuscript treatises, which being looked upon as inestimable curiosities, were transmitted from hand to hand with great caution and diffidence ; so that for the most part the general precepts of music, and that kind of oral instruction which was communicated in the schools belonging to cathedral churches, and other seminaries of music, were the only foundation for a course of musical study ; and those who laboured to excel in the art of practical composition were necessitated either to extract rules from the works of others, or trust to their own powers in the invention of harmony and melody ; and hence it appears that Morley's work could not but greatly facilitate and improve the practice of musical composition.   The world had been but a few years in possession of Morley's Introduction before Thomas Ravenscroft, an author heretofore mentioned as the editor of the psalm-tunes in four parts, thought fit to publish a book of his writing with this title : ' A brief discourse of the true (but neglected) use of ' charact'ring the degrees by their Perfection, Imper- ' fection, and Diminution in Measurable Musicke

Christian IV. king of Denmark, begged him of his mistress. The occasion was probably this : Christian loved the music of the lute, and having while in England heard Douland, he obtained permission to take him with him to Denmark ; but Douland, after a few years stay at Copenhagen, imagining himself slighted, returned to England, and left the king without a lutenist ; in this distress Christian applied to his sister Ann, the wife of James I. and she, and also her son prince Henry interceded with the Lady Arabella to part with her servant Cutting, and obtained her consent.   It seems that Cutting stayed in Denmark but little more than four years, for he became a servant to Christian about March, 1607, and by the above list it appears that he was in the service of prince Henry in June, 1611. The following are the letters on the subject, the originals whereof are among the Harleian MSS. in the British Museum.   See the Catalogue, No. 6986. 42, 43, 44.

          Anna R.
   Wellbeloved cousine Wee greete you hartlye well ; Udo Gal, our deere brothers the king of Denmarks gentleman-servant, hath insisted with us for the licensing your servant thomas cottings to depart, but not without your permission, to our brother's service, and therefore we wryte these few lines to you, being assured your H. will make no difficultie to satisfie our pleasure and our deere brother's desires ; and so geving you the assurance off our constant favours, with our wishes for the conteneuance or convalescence of your helth, expecting your returne, we commit your H. to the protection of God.   From Whythall, 9 March 1607.

To our most honerable and wellbeloved
   cousine the Lady Arabella Stuart.

   MADAM, the queenes ma. hath commaunded me to signifie to your La. that shee would have Cutting your La. servant to send to the king of Denmark, because he desyred the queene that she would send him one that could play upon the lute, I pray your La. to send him back with ane answere as soon as your La. can.   I desyre you to commend me to my lo. and my la. shrewsbury, and also not too think me any thing the worse scrivenere that I write so ill, but to suspend your judgement till you come hither, then you shall find me, as I was ever,
A Madame Arbelle                          Your La. loving cousin
   ma Cousine.                                 and assured friend,
                                                          HENRY.

   May it please your Highnesse,
   I have received your Hs. letter whearin I am let to understand that the queene's majesty is pleased to command Cuttinge my servant for the king of Denmark : concerning the which your Highnesse requireth my answer to hir Majesty, the which I have accordingly returned by this bearer, referring him to hir Majesty's good pleasure and disposition. And although I may have some cause to be sorry to have lost the contentment of a good lute, yet must I confesse that I am right glad to have found any occasion whearby to expresse to her Majesty and your Highnesse the humble respect which I ow you, and the readinesse of my disposition to be conformed to your good pleasures : whearin I have placed a great part of the satisfaction which my heart can receive.  I have according lo your Hs. direction signified unto my uncle and aunt of Shrewsbury your Hs. gratious vouchsafeing to remember them, who with all duty present theyr most humble thancks, and say they will ever pray for your Hs. most happy prosperity : and yet my uncle saith that he carrieth the same splene in his heart towards your Hs. that he hath ever done.   And so praying to the Almighty for your Hs. felicity I humbly cease.   From Sheffeild the 15th of March, 1607.
                          Your Hs. most humble and dutifull
To the Prince his Highnesse,                       ARBELLA STUART.

' against the common practice and custome of these ' times.'   Quarto, 1614.*
   The author of this book had been educated in St. Paul's choir, under Master Edward Pearce, and was not only a good musician, but a man of considerable learning in his faculty ; the drift of it is to revive the use of those proportions, which, because of their intricacy, had long been discontinued.   To justify this attempt, he cites the authority of Franchinus, Glareanus, and Morley ; of which latter he says that he declared himself loth to break the common practice or received custom, yet if any would change that, he would be the first that would follow.
   This declaration of Morley naturally leads to the question whether, even at the time of his writing his Introduction, any change for the better could have been possibly effected ; since he himself has expressly said, that of the many authors who had written on mensurable music, and particularly on those branches of it, mood, time, and prolation, with their several varieties, hardly any two of them can be said to tell the same tale.
   Upon the whole, proportion is a subject of mere speculation ; and as to practice, there seems to be no conceivable kind of proportion, but in the present method of notation may be signified or charactered without regarding those distinctions of perfection, imperfection, and diminution of mood, time, and prolation, which this author labours to revive.
   To this discourse of Ravenscroft are added examples to illustrate his precepts, expressed in the harmony of four voices, concerning the ' Pleasure of ' five usual recreations : 1. Hunting ; 2. Hawking ; ' 3. Dancing ; 4. Drinking ; 5. Enamouring.' †
   In the year 1603, THOMAS ROBINSON published a book entitled ' The school of musicke, the perfect ' method of true fingering the Lute, Pandora, Or- ' pharion, and Viol da Gamba.'   It is a thin folio, and merits to be particularly noticed in this place. The style of it is remarkably quaint, and it is written, as the author expresses it, ' dialoguewise, betwixt a ' knight who has children to be taught, and Timo- ' theus who should teach them.'
   After a general eulogium on music, the author proceeds to his directions for playing on the lute, beginning with an explanation of that method of notation peculiar to it, called the Tablature, the precepts whereof seem to be nearly the same with those contained in the book of Adrian le Roy, an account whereof has herein before been given.   These are succeeded by a collection of easy lessons for the lute,

   * In this book it is asserted, on the authority of the' Præceptiones Musices Poeticæ seu de Compositione Cantus of Johannes Nucius,' that John Dunstable, of whom Morley takes notice, and who is also herein before mentioned, invented musical composition in parts ; and that Franchinus de Colonia invented mensurable music.   In this latter name Ravenscroft is mistaken, for it is to Franco, a scholastic or professor of Liege that the honour of this invention is due, though it is almost universally ascribed to Johannes de Muris.   With regard to the antiquity of musical composition in parts, Morley had his doubts about it, and declares his inability to trace it much farther back than the time of Franchinus, who lived some years after Dunstable ; and as to symphoniac music in general, there is no conclusive evidence that it existed before the time of Bede : and it is highly probable that it had its origin in that practice of extemporary descant described by Giraldus Cambrensis, and mentioned previously in this work.
   † This Thomas Ravenscroft was also the author of a collection of songs entitled ' Melismata, Musical Phansies fitting the Court, Citie, ' and Countrey-Humours, to 3, 4, and 5 voyces,' published in the year 1611.

and these latter by what the author calls rules to instruct you to sing, and a few psalm-tunes set in Tablature for the viol da gamba. This book of Robinson may be deemed a curiosity, as it tends to explain a practice which the masters of the lute have ever shewn an unwillingness to divulge.

In the year 1609 was published a book with this title: 'Pammelia, Musicks Miscellanie, or mixed 'varietie of pleasant Roundelayes and delightful 'Catches of 3. 4. 5. 6. 7. 8. 9. 10 parts in one. 'None so ordinarie as musical, none so musical as not 'to all very pleasing and acceptable. London, printed 'by William Barley for R. B. and H. W. and are to 'be sold at the Spread Eagle at the great North doore 'of Paules.' Quarto. It was again printed by Thomas Snodham, for Matthew Lownes and John Browne, in 1618.

This book, the oldest of the kind extant, fully answers its title, and contains a great number of fine vocal compositions of very great antiquity,* but, which is much to be lamented, without the names of the authors. Among the Rounds is the song mentioned in the character of Mr. William Hastings, written by the first earl of Shaftesbury, and printed in Peck's Collection of curious Historical Pieces, No. xxxiii. concerning which it is first to be observed, that, among numberless other singularities, respecting the diet and manner of living of this person, it is in the character said that he never wanted a London Pudding, and always sang it in with 'My pert eyes therein-a;' absolute nonsense! which the song itself here given will set to rights:—

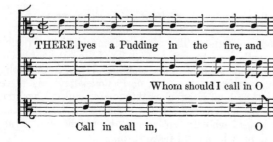

* The words to these compositions are for the most part on subjects of low humour, of which specimens are inserted in chap. LXVII., and here it may be observed that it was formerly a practice with the musicians to set the cries of London to music, retaining the very musical notes of them. In the collection entitled Pammelia, is a round to the cry of New oysters, Have you any wood to cleave? Orlando Gibbons set music of four parts to the Cries in his time, among which is one of a play to be acted by the scholars of our town; Morley set those of the Milliners' Girls in the New Exchange in the Strand, built in the reign of James I., and pulled down about thirty years ago: and among others equally unknown to the present times, these occur: Italian Falling Bands, French Garters, Roman Gloves, Rabatos, a kind of ruffs, Sister's, i.e., Nun's Thread, Slick-stones, Poking-sticks, these were made taper, and were of use to open and separate the plaits of those great ruffs then in fashion. In a play called Tarquin and Lucrece, these cries occur, a Marking-stone, Bread and Meat for the poor Prisoners, Rock-Samphire.

A few rounds from this collection are inserted by way of example of canons in the unison, in chap. LXVII. of this work; these that follow are of the same kind of composition, but to words of a different import:—

a Hassoc for your Pew, or a Pesocke to thrust your feet in, Lanthorne and Candle-light, with many others.

The cries of London in the time of Charles II. differed greatly from those of the preceding reigns; that of a Merry new Song, in the set of Cries designed by Lauron, and engraved by Tempest, is a novelty, as the singing of ballads was then but lately become an itinerant profession. The ancient printed ballads have this colophon: 'Printed by A. B., 'are to be sold at the stalls of the Ballad-singers;' but Cromwell's ordinance against strolling fiddlers, printed in Scobel's collection, silenced these, and obliged the ballad-singers to shut up shop.

EX - AU - DI Do - mi-

- ne, O - ra -

- ti - o -

- nem me - am.

QUIC - QUID pe - ti - e - ri-

- tis Pa -

- trem in no - mi - ne me -

- o da - bit vo - bis.

In the same year was published 'Deuteromelia, or 'the second part of Musick's Melodie, or melodious 'Musicke of pleasant Roundelaies, K. H. mirth or 'Freemens Songs,* and such delightful Catches, Qui 'canere potest canat, Catch that catch can. London, 'printed for Thomas Adams, dwelling in Paules 'church-yard, at the sign of the White Lyon, 1609.'

In this collection there are comparatively but few rounds or catches, it consisting chiefly of songs for three voices, in which all the stanzas are sung to the same tune like this, which is one of them:—

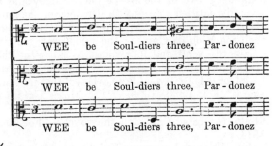

WEE be Soul-diers three, Par - donez

WEE be Soul-diers three, Par - donez

WEE be Soul-diers three, Par - donez

moy je vouz en prie: Late-ly come forth of the

moy je vouz en prie: Late-ly come forth of the

moy je vouz en prie: Late-ly come forth of the

* Of this term, FREEMEN'S SONGS no other interpretation can here be given than that of Cotgrave in his Dictionary, where it is used to explain the words Verilay and Round; and Verilay is elsewhere, by the same author, given as the signification of the word VAUDEVILLE, a country ballad or song, a Roundelay; from Vaudevire, a Norman town, wherein Olivier Bassell, the first inventor of this kind of air, dwelt. For the meaning of the letters K. H. we are yet to seek.

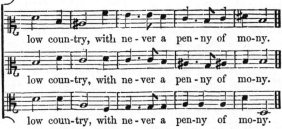

low coun-try, with ne - ver a pen-ny of mo-ny.

low coun-try, with ne - ver a pen-ny of mo-ny.

low coun-try, with ne - ver a pen-ny of mo-ny.

2. Here good fellow I drinke to thee,
   Pardonez moy je vouz en prie:
   To all good fellowes where ever they be.
   With never a penny of mony.

3. And he that will not pledge me in this,
   Pardonez moy je vouz en prie:
   Payes for the shot what ever it is,
   With never a penny of mony.

4. Charge it again boy, charge it againe,
   Pardonez moy je vouz en prie:
   As long as there is any incke in thy pen,
   With never a penny of mony.

## CHAP. CXX.

OF musicians who flourished in or about the reign of James I. not heretofore particularly mentioned, the following is a list, including in it notes of their respective publications.

JOHN AMNER, bachelor of music, organist of the cathedral church of Ely, and master of the children. There are extant of his composition, Sacred Hymns, of three, four, five, and six parts, for voices and viols, quarto, Lond. 1615; and some anthems, the words whereof are in Clifford's collection.

JOHN ATTEY, gentleman and practitioner in music, was the author of a work entitled, 'The first Booke 'of Ayres of four parts with Tablature for the Lute, 'so made that all the parts may be plaide together 'with the lute, or one voyce with the lute and bass 'violl.' Fol. Lond. 1622.

JOHN BARTLETT, gentleman, and practitioner in the art of music, was the author of a work with this title, 'A Booke of Ayres with a triplicitie of musicke, 'whereof the first part is for the lute or Orpharion, 'and the viol da Gamba, and 4 parts to sing. The 'second is for trebles to sing to the lute and viole; 'the third part is for the lute and one voyce, and the 'viole da Gamba.' Fol. Lond. 1606.

THOMAS BREWER, educated in Christ's Hospital London, and bred up to the practice of the viol, composed many excellent Fantasias for that instrument, and was the author of sundry rounds and catches, printed in Hilton's collection, as also of a celebrated song to the words 'Turn Amarillis to thy swain,' published in the earlier editions of Playford's Introduction, in two parts, and in his Musical Companion, printed in 1673, in three, and thereby spoiled, as some of the musicians of that day have not scrupled in print to assert.

THOMAS CAMPION was the author of two books of Airs, of two, three, and four parts. Wood, in the Fasti Oxon. vol. I. col. 229, styles him an admired

poet and musician, adding that Camden mentions him together with Spenser, Sidney, and Drayton. In Ferabosco's Aires, published in 1609, are commendatory verses signed Thomas Campion Dr. of Physic; there are also prefixed to Coriate's Crudities certain Latin verses by the person, who is there styled Medicinæ Doctor.  Farther, the entertainment at the nuptials of Carr with the lady Frances Howard, appears to have been written by Dr. Thomas Campion; there is also in the Bodleian library a book entitled 'Observations on the Art of English Poesy,' printed in 1602, by Thomas Campion, 12mo.  Again, there is extant a work entitled 'Songs bewailing the un-'timely death of Prince Henry,' written by Dr. Thomas Campion, and set to the viol and lute by Coperario. Lond, 1613, folio.  The same person was also the author of 'A new way of making fowre 'parts in Counterpoint by a most familiar and in-'fallible rule,' octavo, printed without a date, but dedicated to 'Charles, prince of Great Britaine.'*
This tract, but under the title of the 'Art of Descant, 'or composing of Musick in parts, with annotations 'thereon by Mr. Christopher Simpson,' is published by way of Appendix to the earlier editions of Playford's Introduction.  Wood mentions a Thomas Campion, of Cambridge, incorporated master of arts of Oxford, anno 1624, clearly a different person from him above-mentioned; but, which is strange, he does not so much as hint that Campion the poet and musician was a graduate in any faculty of either university.

WILLIAM CORKINE published 'Ayres to sing and 'play to the Lute and Basse Violl, with Pavins, 'Galliards, Almaines, and Corantes for the Lyra-'Violl. Fol. Lond. 1610.'  In 1612 he published a second part of this work.

JOHN DANYEL, M.B. of Christ-Church, 1604.  He was the author of 'Songs for the Lute, Viol, and Voice, 'in folio, Lond. 1606,' and is supposed to be the brother of Samuel Daniel, the poet laureate and historian, and the publisher of his works in 1623.

ROBERT DOWLAND, son of John, was the author of a work entitled 'A Musical Banquet,' folio, printed in 1610.

MICHAEL EST, bachelor of music, and master of the choristers of the cathedral church of Litchfield, was the author of sundry collections of Madrigals, and other vocal compositions, and of a madrigal of five parts, printed in the Triumphs of Oriana.  His publications are much more numerous than those of any author of his time : one of them, entitled 'The sixt 'Set of Bookes, wherein are Anthemes for Versus, 'and Chorus of 5 and 6 parts; apt for Violls and 'Voices,' is dedicated to Williams, bishop of Lincoln, and lord keeper, with an acknowledgement of his beneficence in granting to the author an annuity for his life.  It seems by the epistle that Est was an absolute stranger to the bishop, and that his lordship was

moved to this act of bounty by the hearing of some motetts of Est's composition.  It is probable that this person was the son of that Thomas Est who first published the Psalms in parts, and other works, assuming in many of them the name of Snodham, and the brother of one John Est, a barber, famous for his skill on the Lyra-Viol.

JOHN EARSDEN, together with George Mason composed the music in a work entitled 'The Ayres that 'were sung and played at Brougham castle in West-'moreland, in the King's entertainment, given by the 'right honourable the Earle of Cumberland, and his 'right noble sonne the Lord Clifford.'  Fol. Lond. 1618.

THOMAS FORD, the name of this person occurs in the list already given of Prince Henry's musicians, and also in certain letters patent purporting to be a grant of pensions or salaries to sundry of the king's musicians, 2 Car. I. herein after inserted.  He was the author of a work entitled 'Musicke of sundre 'kindes, set forth in two books, the first whereof are 'Aires for 4 voices to the Lute, Orpherion, or Basse 'Viol, with a dialogue for two voices, and two basse-'viols in parts, tunde the lute-way.  The second are 'Pavens, Galiards, Almaines, Toies, Jiggs, *Thumpes*,† 'and such like, for two basse Viols the liera way, so 'made as the greatest number may serve to play alone, 'very easy to be performed.' Fol. Lond. 1607.  The same Thomas Ford was the author of some Canons or Rounds printed in John Hilton's collection.

EDMUND HOOPER, organist of Westminster Abbey, and a gentleman of the chapel royal, where he also did the duty of organist.  He was one of the authors of the Psalms in four parts, published in 1594, and of sundry anthems in Barnard's Collection.  He died July 14, 1621.

ROBERT JONES seems to have been a voluminous composer ; two of the works published by him are severally entitled 'A musical Dreame, or the fourth 'book of Ayres ; the first part for the Lute, two voices, 'and the Violl da Gamba ; the second part is for the 'Lute, the Violl, and four voices to sing ; the third 'part is for one voyce alone, or to the Lute the basse 'Viol, or to both if you please, whereof two are Italian 'ayres.' Fol. Lond. 1609.  'The Muses Gardin for 'delights, or the fift booke of Ayres onely for the 'Lute, the basse Violl, and the voyce.'  Fol. Lond. 1611.

SIR WILLIAM LEIGHTON, Knight, one of the honorable band of gentlemen pensioners, published in 1614, 'The Tears or Lamentations of a sorrowful Soul, com-'posed with musical ayres and songs both for voices and divers instruments.'  These are compositions by himself and other authors, of whom an account has already been given.

---

* The proof of that singular fact that Campion was a doctor in physic, and not, as some have imagined, a doctor in music, might be rested on the particulars above-mentioned; but the dedication to this tract fixes it beyond doubt : for the author, after declaring himself to be a physician by profession, apologizes for his offering 'a worke of musicke to his 'Highnesse by the example of Galen,' who he says became an expert musician, and would 'needes apply all the proportions of music to the uncertaine motions of the pulse.'

† The word *Dump*, besides sorrow and absence of mind, which are the two senses which Dr. Johnson gives of it in his Dictionary, has also another, which has escaped him, viz., a melancholy tune; or, as Mr. Steevens, in a note on a passage in Romeo and Juliet, act IV. scene v. conjectures, an old Italian dance ; and considering the very licentious spelling of the time when this collection of Ford was printed, a suspicion might arise that the word *Thumpe* here noted was no other than the word *Dump*; but upon looking into the book, an air occurs, viz., the eleventh, wherein by a marginal note the performer on the lute is directed wherever he meets with one or two points under the letter a, which in the Tablature denotes an open string, to *thump* it with the first or second finger of the left hand : the use and effect of this strange practice is best known to the performers on the lute.

JOHN MAYNARD, a lutenist, was the author of a work with this title, 'The XII Wonders of the 'World, set and composed for the violl de gambo, 'the lute, and the voyce, to sing the verse, all three 'jointly, and none several; also lessons for the lute 'and base violl to play alone: with some lessons to 'play Lyra-wayes alone, or if you will to fill up the 'parts with another violl set lute-way, newly composed 'by John Maynard, lutenist at the famous schoole of St. 'Julian's in Hertfordshire.' Fol. Lond. 1611. These twelve wonders are so many songs exhibiting the characters of a courtier, a divine, a soldier, a lawyer, a physician, a merchant, a country gentleman, a bachelor, a married man, a wife, a widow, and a maid.

GEORGE MASON, see JOHN EARSDEN.

WILLIAM MEREDITH, organist of New College, Oxon. by Wood in his Hist. et Antiquit. Univ. Oxon. lib. II. pag. 157, styled 'Vir pius et facultate sua 'peritissimus,' is there said to have died anno 1637.

JOHN MUNDY, one of the organists of Queen Elizabeth's chapel, and also one of the organists of the free chapel of Windsor, was admitted to his bachelor's degree at Oxford in 1586, and to that of doctor in 1624. In the place of organist of Windsor he was the immediate successor of John Marbeck, of whose sufferings for religion, and providential escape from the flames, an account has herein before been given.* He was deeply skilled in the theory and practice of music, and published Songs and Psalms composed into three, four, and five parts, Lond. 1594; and was also the author of sundry anthems, the words whereof are printed in Clifford's Collection; and of a madrigal in the Triumphs of Oriana. He died anno 1630, and was buried in the cloister of St. George's chapel at Windsor.

WILLIAM MUNDY. Of this person Wood barely makes mention; he styles him one Will. Mundy, a noted musician, a composer of services and anthems, but no graduate. However it has been discovered that he was a composer as early as the year 1591, and was nevertheless the son of the former. In certain verses at the end of Baldwin's MS. cited in page 469 of this work containing the names of the several authors, whose compositions are therein inserted, are these lines:—

I will begine with White, Shepper, Tye, and Tallis,
Parſons, Gyles, Mundie th'oulde one of the queenes pallis
Mundie yonge, th'ould man's ſon  -  -  -  -  -

The old Mundy of the queen's palace was undoubtedly John, for in the Fasti, vol. I. col. 131, he is said to have been in 1586, or afterwards, one of the organists of her majesty's chapel; and Mundy the young is above expressly said to be the old man's son, and there are several compositions in Baldwin's MS. with the name Will. Mundie to them. The deduction from these particulars is, that William Mundy was the son of Dr. John Mundy, one of the

organists of queen Elizabeth's palace, or more properly of her royal chapel at Whitehall, and also organist of the chapel of St. George at Windsor. The name Will. Mundy is set to several anthems in Barnard's Collection, and, by a mistake, which Dr. Aldrich was at the pains of detecting, to that anthem of king Henry VIII. before mentioned, 'O God the 'maker of all things.'

MARTIN PIERSON or PEARSON, was master of the choristers at St. Paul's at the time when John Tomkins was organist there; he took his degree of bachelor in his faculty in 1613; and in 1630 published a work with this singular title, 'Mottects, or 'grave Chamber Musique, containing Songs of five 'parts of severall sorts, some ful, and some verse and 'chorus, but all fit for voyces and vials, with an 'organ part; which for want of organs may be performed on Virginals, Base-Lute, Bandora or Irish 'harpe. Also a mourning Song of sixe parts for the 'Death of the late Right Honorable Sir Fulke Grevil, 'Knight, composed according to the rules of art by 'M. P. batchelor of musique, 1630.' He died about the latter end of 1650, being then an inhabitant of the parish of St. Gregory, near the said cathedral, and was buried at St. Faith's church adjoining. He bequeathed to the poor of Marsh, in the parish of Dunnington, in the Isle of Ely, an hundred pounds, to be laid out in a purchase for their yearly use.

FRANCIS PILKINGTON, of Lincoln college, Oxford, was admitted a bachelor of music anno 1595. He was a famous lutenist, and one of the cathedral church of Christ in the city of Chester. Wood says he was father, or at least near of kin to Thomas Pilkington, one of the musicians of queen Henrietta Maria, celebrated in the poems of Sir Aston Cokaine. See page 493 of this work. He was the author of 'The 'first booke of Songs or Ayres of 4 parts, with 'Tablature for the lute or Orpherion, with the Violl 'da Gamba.' Fol. Lond. 1605.

PHILIP ROSSETER. This person was the author of a work entitled 'A booke of Ayres set foorth to be 'sang to the Lute, Orpherian, and base Violl, by 'Philip Rosseter, lutenist, and are to be sold at his 'house in Fleet-street, neere to the Grayhound.' Fol. Lond. 1601. In the preface to this book the author expresses in a humorous manner his dislike of those 'who to appeare the more deepe and singular in 'their judgment, will admit of no musicke but that 'which is long, intricate, bated with fugue, chained 'with sycopation, and where the nature of the word 'is precisely exprest in the note, like the old exploded 'action in comedies, when if they did pronounce '*Memini*, they would point to the hinder part of 'their heads; if *Video*, put their finger in their eye.'

WILLIAM STONARD, organist of Christ-Church Oxon. and created doctor in music anno 1608. Besides certain anthems, the words whereof are in Clifford's Collection, he was the author of some compositions communicated by Walter Porter to Dr. John Wilson, music-professor at Oxford, to be reposed and kept for ever among the archives of the music-school. Dr. Stonard was a kinsman either of Dr. Wilson or Porter; but Wood's account of him is so am-

* Marbeck is conjectured to have died about the year 1585. He had a son named Roger, a canon of Christ-Church, Athen. Oxon. vol. I. col. 152, and provost of Oriel college, and the first standing or perpetual orator of the university, and who in 1573 was created doctor in physic, and afterwards was appointed first physician to queen Elizabeth. He died in 1605, and, as Wood conceives, was buried in the church of St. Giles without Cripplegate, London, in which parish he died. Fasti Oxon. vol. I. col. 109.

biguously worded, that this circumstance will apply to either.

NICHOLAS STROGERS, an organist temp. James I.; some services of his are to be found in Barnard's Collection.

JOHN WARD was the author of a service and an anthem in Barnard's Collection, and also of Madrigals to three, four, five, and six voices; and a song lamenting the death of Prince Henry, printed in 1613, and dedicated to Sir Henry Fanshaw, by whom he was highly favoured.

MATTHEW WHITE, of Christ-Church college, Oxon. accumulated doctor in music in 1629; the words of some anthems composed by him are in Clifford's Collection: there was also a Robert White, an eminent church musician, the composer of several anthems in Barnard's Collection. Morley celebrates one of this name, but whether he means either of these two persons, cannot be ascertained.

About the end of James the First's reign, to speak of the progress of it in this country, music received a new and very valuable acquisition in the foundation of a music lecture in the university of Oxford by Dr. WILLIAM HEYTHER;* *(a Portrait,)* the occasion was this: he was an intimate friend of the famous Camden, who having a few years before his decease determined to found a history-lecture in the same university, sent his friend Mr. Heyther with the deed of endowment properly executed to the vice-chancellor Dr. Piers; this was on the seventeenth day of May, 1622; and Mr. Heyther having for some years before applied himself to the study of music, and signified an intention to be honoured with a degree in that faculty, he, together with his friend Mr. Orlando Gibbons, were suffered to accumulate the degrees both of bachelor and doctor in music; and on that or the next day, viz., the eighteenth of May, 1622, they were both created doctors.†

It seems that there was at Oxford a professorship or music lecture founded by king Alfred, but how endowed does not at this distance of time clearly appear, and we find it continued till after the Restoration; for Anthony Wood, in his life, has given the succession of music-lecturers, as he terms them, from the

year 1661 to 1681; but by his list of their names it does not seem that any of them were musicians; and perhaps the reading of the old lecture was a matter of form, and calculated merely to preserve the station of music among the liberal sciences. As to that of Dr. Heyther, it was both theoretic and practical, as appears by the following account of the circumstances of its foundation, extracted from the books of the university:—

' This matter was first moved and proposed in a
' convocation held the 5th May, 1626, and afterwards
' agreed upon by the delegates, and published in the
' convocation-house, as approved by them, together
' with Dr. Heyther's orders about it the 16th of
' November the same yeare; by his deed, bearing
' date 20 Feb. 2. Cha. I. he gave to the university for
' ever an annuity or yearly rent charge of 16*l.* 6*s.* 8*d.*,
' issuing out of divers parcells of land, situate and
' being within the parish of Chislehurst in Kent,
' whereof 13*l.* 6*s.* 8*d.* is to be employed in the music-
' master's wages, out of which he is to repair the
' instruments and find strings; and the other 3*l.* is to
' be employed upon one that shall read the theory of
' music once every term, or oftner, and make an
' English music-lecture at the Act time. Unto which
' 3*l.* Dr. Heyther requiring the ancient stipend of 40*s.*
' that was wont yearly to be given to the ordinary
' reader of music, to be added, or some other sum
' equivalent thereunto, the university thereupon agreed
' in a convocation that the old stipend of the morall
' philosophie reader, which was 45*s.*, should be con-
' tinued to the music-reader, and so by that addition
' he hath 5*l.* 5*s.* yearly for his wages.'‡ The first
professor under this endowment was Richard Nicholson, bachelor of music, and organist of Magdalen College.

The right of electing the professor is in the vice-chancellor, the dean of Christ-Church, the president of Magdalen College, the warden of New College, and the president of St. John's.

It further appears by the university books, that Dr. Heyther's professor was required to hold a musical praxis in the music-school every Thursday afternoon, between the hours of one and three, except during the time of Lent; to promote which he gave to the university an harpsicon, a chest of viols,§ and divers music-books both printed and written.

It is highly probable that Dr. Heyther was moved to this act of beneficence by Camden, who having been a chorister at Magdalen college, Oxford, may be supposed to have retained a love for music;‖ and that Camden had a great ascendant over him, might be inferred from the intimate friendship that subsisted between them for many years. They had both employments that obliged them to a residence in Westminster; for Camden was master of Westminster

---

* His name of his own signature in the cheque-book is spelt HEYTHER, notwithstanding which it is frequently spelt Heather and that even by Camden himself.

† By the Fasti Oxon. vol. I. col. 221, it appears that Wood had searched in vain to find out whether Orlando Gibbons had been admitted to any degree in music or not; but the following letter from Dr. Piers to Camden, in the Collection of Epistles to and from Camden, published by Dr. Thomas Smith in 1691, pag. 329, is decisive of the question, and proves that Heyther and Gibbons were created doctors on the same day:—

CCLXIII.
G. Piersius.   G. Camdeno.

' Worthy Sir,
' The university returns her humble thanks to you with this letter.
' We pray for your health and long life, that you may see the fruits of
' your bounty. We have made Mr. Heather a doctor in music; so that
' now he is no more Master, but Dr. Heather; the like honour for your
' sake we have conferred upon Mr. Orlando Gibbons, and made him
' a doctor too, to accompany Dr. Heather. We have paid Mr. Dr. Hea-
' ther's charges for his journey, and likewise given him the Oxford
' courtesie, a pair of gloves for himself, and another for his wife. Your
' honour is far above all these things. And so desiring the continuance
' of your loving favour to the university, and to me your servant, I take
' my leave.
' Oxon, 18 May              Yours ever to be commanded,
'   1622.                        ' WILLIAM PIERS.'

' Mr. Whear shall make his oration this term; and I shall write
' to you from time to time what orders the university will com-
' mend unto your wisdom concerning your history-lecture.'

‡ This stipend was afterwards augmented by Nathaniel Lord Crew, bishop of Durham.

§ A CHEST or set of VIOLS consisted of six viols, which were generally two basses, two tenors, and two trebles, each with six strings; they were the instruments to which those compositions called Fantasias were adapted. A more particular description of a chest of viols will be given hereafter.

‖ *By his Will published in the Appendix to Hearne's collection of Discourses written by eminent antiquaries, he gives six pounds to the singing men of the Collegiate Church of Westminster.*

WILLIAM  HEYTHER

MUS.  DOCT.  OXON.  MDCXXII.

*From an original Painting in the Music-School, Oxford.*

ORLANDO  GIBBONS

MUS. DOCT. OXON. MDCXXII.

school, and Heyther a gentleman of the king's chapel. In town they lived in the same house; and when in 1609 a pestilential disease having reached the house next to Camden and himself, Camden was seized with it, he retired to the house of his friend Heyther at Chislehurst, and by the help of Dr. Gifford, his physician, was cured. But of the friendly regard which Camden entertained for Dr. Heyther, he gave ample testimony, by appointing him executor of his will; and in the deed executed by Camden on the nineteenth day of March, 1621-2, containing the endowment of his history-lecture at Oxford, the grant thereby made of the manor of Bexly in Kent, is subjected to a proviso that the profits of the said manor, estimated at 400l. a year, should be enjoyed by Mr. William Heyther, his heirs and executors, for the term of ninety-nine years, to commence from the death of Mr. Camden, he and they paying to the history professor 140l. per annum; at the expiration of which term the estate was to vest in the university. Biog. Brit. CAMDEN, 133, in note.

It has been doubted whether Heyther had any skill in music or not, but it appears that he was of the choir at Westminster, and that on the twenty-seventh day of March, 1615, he was sworn a gentleman of the royal chapel. Farther, it appears by the Fasti Oxon. that on the fifth day of July, 1622, a public disputation was proposed, but omitted to be held between him and Dr. Nathaniel Giles on the following questions: 1. Whether discords may be allowed in music? Affirm. 2. Whether any artificial instrument can so fully and truly express music as the natural voice? Negat. 3. Whether the practice be the more useful part of music, or the theory? Affirm.

That he had little or no skill in practical composition may fairly be inferred from a particular which Wood says he had been told by one or more eminent musicians, his contemporaries, viz., that the song of six or more parts, performed in the Act for Heyther, was composed by Orlando Gibbons.*

Dr. Heyther was born at Harmondsworth, in Middlesex; he died the latter end of July, 1627, and was buried on the first of August in the broad or south aisle, joining to the choir of Westminster abbey. He gave to the hospital in Tothill-Fields, Westminster, one hundred pounds, as appears by a list of benefactions to the parish of St. Margaret in that city, printed in the *New* View of London, pag. 339.

There is now in the music-school at Oxford a picture of Dr. Heyther in his gown and cap, with the book of madrigals, intitled Musica Transalpina, in his hand; from this picture the portrait of him is taken.

ORLANDO GIBBONS, *(a Portrait,)* a native of Cambridge, was, as Wood says, accounted one of the rarest musicians and organists of his time. On the thirty-first day of March, 1604, he was appointed organist of the chapels royal in the room of Arthur Cock: some of his lessons are to be found in the collection herein before spoken of, intitled Parthenia.

He published Madrigals of five parts for Voices and Viols. Lond. 1612.† But the most excellent of his works are his compositions for the church, namely, services and anthems, of which there are many extant in the cathedral books. One of the most celebrated of his anthems is his Hosanna, one of the most perfect models for composition in the church-style of any now existing; and indeed the general characteristic of his music is fine harmony, unaffected simplicity, and unspeakable grandeur. He also composed the tunes to the hymns and songs of the church, translated by George Withers, as appears by the dedication thereof to king James I.; they are melodies in two parts, and in their kind are excellent. It has been for some time a question whether Orlando Gibbons ever attained to either of those academical honours due to persons of eminence in his profession; but it appears most evidently by the letter inserted in the preceding article of Dr. Heyther, that on the seventeenth, *or at farthest the eighteenth* of May, 1622, he accumulated the degrees of bachelor and doctor in his faculty; as also that this honour was conferred on him for the sake of Camden, who was his intimate friend. In 1625, being commanded to Canterbury to attend the solemnity of the marriage of Charles I. and Henrietta of France, upon which occasion he had composed the music, he was seized with the small-pox, and died on Whit-Sunday in the same year, and was buried in the cathedral church of Canterbury; his widow Elizabeth erected a monument over his grave with the following inscription:—

'Orlando Gibbons Cantabrigiæ inter Musas et
'Musicam nato, sacræ R. Capellæ Organistæ, Sphæ-
'rarum Harmoniæ Digitorum: pulsu æmulo Can-
'tionum complurium quæque eum non canunt minus
'quam canuntur conditori; Viro integerrimo et cujus
'vita cum arte suavissimis moribus concordissimè
'certavit ad nupt. C. R. cum M. B. Dorobern. accito
'ictuque heu Sanguinis Crudo et crudeli fato extincto,
'choroque cœlesti transcripto die Pentecostes A. D. N.
'MDCXXV. Elizabetha conjux septemque ex eo
'liberorum parens, tanti vix doloris superstes, mæren-
'tissimo mærentissima.   P. vixit A. M. D.' ‡

Over his monument is a bust with the arms of Gibbons, viz., three scallops on a bend dexter, over a lion rampant.

Dr. Orlando Gibbons left a son named Christopher, an excellent organist, who will be spoken of hereafter.

He had two brothers, Edward and Ellis, the one organist of Bristol, the other of Salisbury. Edward was a bachelor of Cambridge, and incorporated at Oxon in 1592. Besides being organist of Bristol, he was priest-vicar, sub-chanter, and master of the choristers in that cathedral. He was sworn a gentleman of the chapel March 21, 1604, and was master to Matthew Lock. In the triumphs of Oriana are two

---

* A manuscript copy of the exercise for Dr. Heyther's degree has been found, with the name of Orlando Gibbons to it. It is an anthem for eight voices, taken from the forty-seventh Psalm, and appears to be the very same composition with the anthem of Orlando Gibbons to the words 'O clap your hands together, all ye people,' printed in Dr. Boyce's Cathedral Music, vol. II. pag. 59.

† *In the dedication of the book to Sir Christopher Hatton, the author says that they were composed in the house of his patron; and that Sir Christopher furnished the words. This person was a collateral descendant of the Lord Chancellor Hatton: he died 13th Sept. 1619, and lies interred in St. John Baptist's, otherwise Jolip's Chapel, in Westminster Abbey.*

‡ The letters A. M. D. signify Annos, Menses, Dies, they were intended to have been placed at a distance from each other and to be filled up; but Mr. Dart, author of the antiquities of Canterbury Cathedral, has given a translation of the inscription, in which vixit A. M. D. is rendered 'he lived 1500.' Wood says he was not quite forty-five when he died.

madrigals the one in five, the other in six parts, composed by Ellis Gibbons. Wood styles him the admired organist of Salisbury. Of Edward it is said that in the time of the rebellion he assisted king Charles I. with the sum of one thousand pounds; for which instance of his loyalty he was afterwards very severely treated by those in power, who deprived him of a considerable estate, and thrust him and three grand-children out of his house, though he had then numbered more than fourscore years.

Nathaniel Giles was born in or near the city of Worcester, and took the degree of bachelor in 1585; he was one of the organists of St. George's chapel at Windsor, and master of the boys there. Upon the decease of William Hunnis, in 1597, he was appointed master of the children of the royal chapel, and was afterwards one of the organists of the chapel royal to king Charles I. He composed many excellent services and anthems. In 1607 he supplicated for the degree of doctor in his faculty, but for some unknown reason he declined performing the exercise for it till the year 1622, when he was admitted to it, at which time it was proposed that he should dispute with Dr. Heyther upon the certain questions, mentioned in the account above given of Dr. Heyther, but it does not appear that the disputation was ever held. Dr. Giles died January 24, 1633, aged seventy-five, and was buried in one of the aisles adjoining to St. George's Chapel at Windsor, under a stone with an inscription to his memory, leaving behind him the character of a man noted as well for his religious life and conversation, as his excellence in his faculty. He lived to see a son of his, named Nathaniel, a canon of Windsor and a prebendary of Worcester; and a daughter Margaret diposed of in marriage to Sir Herbert Croft, bishop of Hereford: she was living in the year 1695.

Upon the accession of Charles I. to the crown, Nicholas Laniere was appointed master of the king's music; and in Rymer's Fœdera, tom. XVIII. pag. 728, is the following grant in favour of him and other musicians, servants of the king:—

'Charles, by the grace of God, &c. To the
'treasurer and under-treasurer of our exchequer
'nowe being, and that hereafter for the tyme shall be,
'greetings, Whereas wee have beene graciously
'pleased, in consideration of service done, and to be
'done unto us by sundrie of our musicians, to graunt
'unto them the severall annuities and yearly pensions
'hereafter following, (that is to say) to Nicholas
'Laniere master of our music two hundred poundes
'yearly for his wages, to Thomas Foord fourscore
'poundes yearly for his wages, that is, for the place
'which he formerly held, fortie poundes yearely, and
'for the place which John Ballard late deceased, held,
'and now bestowed upon him the said Thomas Foord
'fortie poundes yearly, to Robert Johnson yearely for
'wages fortie poundes and for stringes twentie poundes
'by the yeare, to Thomas Day yearely for his wages
'fortie poundes and for keeping a boy twenty-fower
'poundes by the yeare, also to Alfonso Ferabosco,
'Thomas Lupo, John Laurence, John Kelly, John
'Cogshall, Robert Taylor, Richard Deering, John

'Drewe, John Laniere, Edward Wormall, Angelo
'Notary, and Jonas Wrench, to everie of them fortie
'poundes a peece yearly for their wages, and to
'Alfonso Bales and Robert Marshe, to each of them
'twentie poundes a-peece yearely for their wages.

'Theis are therefore to will and command you,
'out of our treasure in the receipt of our exchequer,
'to cause payment to be made to our said musicians
'above-mentioned, and to every of them severally
'and respectively, the said severall annuities and
'allowances, as well presently upon the sight hereof
'for one whole year ended at the feast of th' Annun-
'ciation of the blessed Virgin Mary last past before
'the date hereof, as alsoe from the feast hitherto, and
'soe from tyme to tyme hereafter at the fower usuall
'feasts or termes of the yeare, (that is to say) at the
'feast of the Nativity of St. John the Baptist, St.
'Michael, th' Archangell, the birth of our Lord God,
'and th' Annunciation of the blessed Virgin Mary,
'by even and equall portions, during their naturall
'lives, and the lives of everie of them respectively,
'together with all fees, profitts, commodities, allow-
'ances and advantages whatsoever to the said places
'incident and belonging, in as large and ample man-
'ner as any of our musicians in the same places
'heretofore have had and enjoyed the same; and
'theis presents, or the inrollment thereof, shall be
'your sufficient warrant and dischardge in this be-
'halfe. In witnes whereof, &c.

Witnes ourself at Westminster, the eleaventh day
of July.
'Per breve de privato sigillo, &c.'

Charles Butler, a native of Wycomb in the county of Bucks, and a master of arts of Magdalen College, Oxford, published a book with this title, 'The Principles of Musik, in singing and setting: 'with the twofold use thereof, ecclesiasticall and 'civil.' quarto, Lond. 1636. The author of this book was a person of singular learning and ingenuity, which he manifested in sundry other works, enumerated by Wood in the Athen. Oxon. among the rest is an English grammar, published in 1633, in which he proposes a scheme of regular orthography, and makes use of characters, some borrowed from the Saxon, and others of his own invention, so singular, that we want types to exhibit them. And of this imagined improvement of his he appears to have been so fond, that all his tracts are printed in like manner with his grammar;* the consequence whereof has been an almost general disgust of all that he has written. His Principles of Music is however a very learned, curious, and entertaining book; and, by the help of the advertisement from the printer to the reader, prefixed to it, explaining the powers of the several characters made use of by him, may be read to great advantage, and may be considered as a judicious supplement to Morley's Introduction. Its contents are in the general as follows:—

Lib. I. cap. 1. Of the moodes: these the author makes to be five, following in this respect Cassiodorus, and ascribing to each a different character and effect;

* A specimen of his orthography is inserted in Dr. Johnson's grammar prefixed to his Dictionary.

their names are the Doric, Lydian, Æolic, Phrygian, and Ionic. Cap. 2. Of Singing; and herein of the number, names, tune, and time of the notes, with their external adjuncts. Cap. 3. Of Setting, and herein of the parts of a song, of melody, harmony, intervals, concords, and discords, with the consecution of each: Of Ornaments, that is to say, Syncope, fugue, and formality. Cap. 4. Of the two ways of setting, that is to say, in counterpoint and in discant.

Lib. II. cap. 1. Of instruments and of the voice. Of ditty-music, and of mixt music, in which instruments are associated with the voice. Cap. 2. Of the divine use of music. Of the continuance of church-music; of objections against it. Of the special uses of divine music, with an apostrophe to our Levites. Cap. 3. Of the allowance of civil music, with the special uses thereof, and of the objections against it. Epilogue.

This book abounds with a great variety of curious learning relating to music, selected from the best writers ancient and modern, among which latter the author appears to have held Sethus Calvisius in high estimation.

## CHAP. CXXI.

Our church-music, through the industry of those who had set themselves to recover and collect the works of such musicians as flourished about the time of the Reformation; and the learning and ingenuity of those their successors who had laboured in producing new compositions, was by this time arrived at so high a degree of improvement, that it may be questioned, not only whether it was not then equal to that of any country; but whether it is if not even now, so near perfection, as to exclude the expectation of ever seeing it rivalled: and it is worthy of remark, that in the compositions of Tye, Tallis, Bird, Farrant, Gibbons, and some others, all that variety of melody, harmony, and fine modulation are discoverable, which ignorant people conceive to be the effect of modern refinement, for an instance whereof we need not seek any farther than to the anthem of Dr. Tye, 'I will exalt thee,' which a stranger to the music of our church would conceive to be a composition of the present day rather than of the sixteenth century. The same may be said of most of the compositions in the Cantiones Sacræ of Tallis and Bird, and the Cantiones Sacrarum and Gradualia of the latter, which abound with fugues of the finest contexture, and such descant, as, in the opinion of a very good judge, entitle them to the character of angelical and divine.

These considerations, aided by the disposition which Charles I. had manifested towards the church, and the favour shown by him to music and its professors, were doubtless the principal inducement to the publication in the year 1641, of a noble collection of church-music by one John Barnard, a minor canon of St. Paul's cathedral, the title whereof is as follows:—

'The first book of selected Church-music, consist-'ing of services and anthems, such as are now used 'in the cathedral collegiate churches of this kingdom,

'never before printed, whereby such books as were 'heretofore with much difficulty and charges tran-'scribed for the use of the quire, are now, to the 'saving of much labour and expence, published for 'the general good of all such as shall desire them 'either for publick or private exercise. Collected 'out of divers approved authors by John Barnard, 'one of the Minor Canons of the cathedral church 'of Saint Paul, London. London, printed by Edward 'Griffin, and are to be sold at the signe of the Three 'Lutes in Paul's alley. 1641.'

The contents of this book are services for morning and evening, and the communion, preces, and responses by Tallis, Strogers, Bevin, Bird, Orlando Gibbons, William Mundy, Parsons, Morley, Dr. Giles, Woodson; the Litany by Tallis, and anthems in four, five, and six parts, to a great number, by Tallis, Hooper, Farrant, Shepheard, Will. Mundy, Gibbons, Batten, Dr. Tye, Morley, Hooper, White, Dr. Giles, Parsons, Weelkes, Dr. Bull, and Ward: and here it may not be amiss to remark, that in this collection the anthem 'O God the maker of all things,' is ascribed to William Mundy, contrary to the opinion that has ever been entertained. It was probably this book that set Dr. Aldrich upon an inquiry after the fact, which terminated in a full conviction, founded upon evidence, that it is a composition of Henry VIII.

The book is dedicated to king Charles I. considering which, and the great expence and labour of such a publication, it might be conjectured that his majesty had liberally contributed towards it; but the contrary is so evident from a passage in the preface, where the author speaks of the charges of the work as an adventurous enterprize, that we are left at a loss which to commend most, his zeal, his industry, or the liberality of his spirit. For not to mention the labour and expence of collecting and copying such a number of musical compositions as fill a folio volume, not only the music, but the letter-press types appear to have been cast on purpose, the latter of which are in the character called by writing-masters, Secretary; with the initial letters in German text of a large size and finely ornamented.

A few years after the publication of Barnard's Collection, another was printed with this title, 'Musica 'Deo sacra et Ecclesiæ Anglicanæ, or music dedicated 'to the honour and service of God, and to the use 'of cathedrals and other churches of England, espe-'cially the chapel royal of king Charles I.' in ten books by Thomas Tomkins, bachelor of music, of whom an account has before been given.* This work consists of a great variety of services of different kinds, and anthems from three to ten parts, all of the author's own composition, many whereof are in great estimation.†

There was great reason to expect that the publications above-mentioned would have been followed

---

\* See page 507 of this work.

† It is much to be lamented that the thought of printing them in score did not occur to the publishers of these several collections; the consequence is, that, by the loss of part of the book, they at this day can scarcely be said to exist. Some years ago diligent search was made for a complete set of Barnard's books, and in all the kingdom there was not one to be found; the least imperfect was that belonging to the choir of Hereford, but in this the boys' parts were defective.

by others of the like kind not less valuable ; but the Puritans, who had long been labouring to abolish the liturgy, had now got the reins of government into their hands, and all hopes of this kind were frustrated by an ordinance which passed the House of Lords January 4, 1644, repealing the statutes of Edward VI. and Elizabeth, for uniformity in the Common Prayer ; and ordaining that the book of Common Prayer should not from thenceforth be used in any church, chapel, or place of public worship within the kingdom of England or dominion of Wales ; but that the directory for public worship therein set forth, should be thenceforth used, pursued, and observed in all exercises of the public worship of God.*

The directory referred to by the above ordinance was drawn up by the assembly of divines at Westminster,† who were the standing council of the parliament in all matters concerning religion ; the preface represents the use of the liturgy or service-book as ' burdensome, and a great hindrance to the preach- ' ing of the word, and that ignorant and superstitious ' people had made an idol of common prayer, and, ' pleasing themselves in their presence at that service, ' and their lip-labour in bearing a part in it, had ' thereby hardened themselves in their ignorance and ' carelessness of saving knowledge and true piety. ' That the liturgy had been a great means, as on the ' one hand to make and increase an idle unedifying ' ministry, which contented itself with set forms made ' to their hands by others, without putting forth them- ' selves to exercise the gift of prayer, with which our ' Lord Jesus Christ pleaseth to furnish all his servants ' whom he calleth to that office ; so on the other side it ' had been, and ever would be, if continued, a matter ' of endless strife and contention in the church.'

For these and other reasons contained in the preface, which represent the hearing of the word as a much more important duty of religion than prayer or thanksgiving, the directory establishes a new form of divine worship, in which the singing of Psalms is all of music that is allowed ; concerning which the following are the rules :—

' It is the duty of Christians to praise God pub- ' lickly by singing of psalms, together in the congre- ' gation, and also privately in the family. In singing ' of psalms the voice is to be tuneably and gravely ' ordered ; but the chief care must be to sing with ' understanding and with grace in the heart, making ' melody unto the Lord. That the whole congre- ' gation may join herein, every one that can read is ' to have a psalm-book, and all others, not disabled ' by age or otherwise, are to be exhorted to learn to ' read. But for the present, where many in the con- ' gregation cannot read, it is convenient that the ' minister, or some fit person appointed by him and ' the other ruling officers, do read the psalm line by ' line before the singing thereof.'

*The objection of the Puritans to the use of in- strumental Music in holy offices is, that it is both Jewish and Popish : upon which it may be remarked that the same may respectively be said of one at least*

of the ten Commandments and of the Lord's Prayer ; and Sir Edward Deering, who had the merit of bringing into the House of Commons the Bill for the abolition of Episcopacy, in the true spirit of his party has asserted in print that one single groan in the Spirit is worth the Diapason of all the Church music in the world. See his Declaration and Pe- tition to the House of Commons, Lond. 1644. The Directory seems to have compounded the matter by allowing the singing of Psalms, but has left it as a question to be agitated in future, whether the use of Organs in Divine worship be lawful or not ; ac- cordingly upon the Restoration of the Liturgy and the use of Organs in 1660, the Non-conformists de- clared against all instrumental music in Churches, and gave occasion to the publication of a discourse entitled ' The well-tuned Organ,' by one Joseph Brookband, a Clergyman, 4to, 1660, wherein the question is fully discussed and the Affirmative main- tained. In 1679, Dr. Edward Wetenhall, then Chanter of Christ Church, Dublin, and afterwards Bishop of Kilmore and Ross, published a discourse of Gifts and Offices, i. e. Prayer, Singing and Preaching, in the worship of God, 8vo. wherein the usage in the established church with respect to the points in question is with great learning and judg- ment defended. In 1698, upon the erection of an organ in the Parish Church of Tiverton, in the County of Devon, a sermon was preached by one Mr. Newte, which produced an anonymous answer in 4to, 1698. This was followed by a discourse concerning the rise and antiquity of Cathedral Worship, in a letter to a friend first printed in 1699, and afterwards in a collection of Tracts on the growth of Deism and other subjects, 8vo. 1709. This discourse includes a very severe censure of the practice in question ; but was suffered to remain without animadversion. In 1700, the learned Mr. Henry Dodwell published a treatise concerning the lawfulness of music in holy offices, in an octavo volume ; the preface written by the above Mr. Newte is a formal reply to the answer to the sermon ; and for upwards of four-score years this controversy, which began between Cartright and Hooker, has been at rest. Vide first note in chap. cxxv.

Thus was the whole fabric of the liturgy subverted, and the study of that kind of harmony rendered use- less, which had hitherto been looked upon as a great incentive to devotion. That there is a tendency in music to excite grave, and even devout, as well as lively and mirthful affections, no one can doubt who is not an absolute stranger to its efficacy ; and though it may perhaps be said that the effects of music are mechanical, and that there can be nothing pleasing to God in that devotion which follows the involuntary operation of sound on the human mind : this is more than can be proved ; and the scripture seems to inti- mate the contrary.

The abolition of the liturgy was attended not barely with a contempt of those places where it had been usually performed ; but by a positive exertion of that power which the then remaining reliques of the legis-

---

* Rushw. part II. vol. II. page 839.
† Pref. to vol. III. of Neal's Hist. of the Puritans.

lature had usurped, the Common Prayer had been declared by public authority to be a superstitious ritual. In the opinion of these men it therefore became necessary for the promotion of true religion that organs should be taken down ; that choral music-books should be torn and destroyed ; that painted glass windows should be broken ; that cathedral service should be totally abolished, and that those retainers to the church whose duty it had been to celebrate its more solemn service, should betake themselves to some employment less offensive to God than that of singing his praises. In consequence of these, which were the predominant opinions of those times, collegiate and parochial churches were spoiled of their ornaments ; monuments were defaced ; sepulchral inscriptions engraven on brass were torn up ; libraries and repositories were ransacked for ancient musical service-books, and Latin or English, popish or protestant, they were deemed equally superstitious and ungodly, and as such were committed to the flames or otherwise destroyed, and, in short, such havoc and devastation made, as could only be equalled by that which attended the suppression of religious houses under Henry VIII.

The sentiments of these men, who, to express the meekness and inoffensiveness of their dispositions, had assumed the name of Puritans, with respect to the reverence due to places set apart for the purpose of religious worship, were such as freed them from all restraints of common decency : that there is no inherent holiness in the stones or timbers that compose a cathedral or other church ; and that the ceremony of consecration implies nothing more than an exemption of the place or thing which is the subject of it from vulgar and common use, is agreed by the sober and rational kind of mankind ; and on the minds of such the ceremonies attending the dedication of churches have operated accordingly ; but, as if there had been a merit in contradicting the common sense and opinion of the world, no sooner were these men vested with the power, than they found the means to level all distinctions of place and situation, and to pervert the temples of God to the vilest and most profane uses.

To instance in one particular ; the cathedral church of St. Paul was turned into horse-quarters for the soldiers of the parliament, saving the choir, which was separated by a brick wall from the nave, and converted into a preaching place, the entrance to which was at a door formerly a window on the north side eastwards.* Hitherto many of the citizens and others were used to resort to hear Dr. Cornelius Burgess, who had an assignment of four hundred pounds a year out of the revenue of the church, as a reward for his sermons, which were usually made up of invectives against deans, chapters, and singing-men, against whom he seemed to entertain a great antipathy.† The noble Corinthian portico at the west end, designed by Jones, was leased out to a man of a projecting head, who built in it a number of small shops, which were letten by him to haberdashers,

glovers, semsters, as they were then called, or milliners, and other petty tradesmen, and obtained the name of St. Paul's Change.

Of musicians of eminence who flourished in the reign of king Charles I. the following are among the chief :—

Richard Deering was descended from an ancient family of that name in Kent. He was bred up in Italy, where he obtained the reputation of a most admirable musician. On his return to England, he practised for some time, but being straightly importuned, he became organist to the monastery of English nuns at Brussels ; upon the marriage of king Charles I. he was appointed organist to his consort Henrietta Maria, in which station he continued till he was compelled to leave England : he took the degree of bachelor of music as a member of Christ-Church college, Oxon, in 1610 ; he has left of his composition ' Cantiones sacræ quinque vocum, ' cum basso continuo ad Organum.' Antwerp, 1597 ; and ' Cantica sacra ad melodiam madrigalium elabo-' borata senis vocibus.' Antwerp, 1618. He died in the communion of the church of Rome about the year 1657.

John Hingston, a scholar of Orlando Gibbons,‡ was organist to Oliver Cromwell, who as it is said, had some affection for music and musicians.§ Hingston was first in the service of Charles I. but for a pension of one hundred pounds a year he went over to Cromwell, and instructed his daughters in music. He bred up under him two boys, whom he taught to sing with him Deering's Latin songs, which Cromwell greatly delighted to hear, and had often performed before him at the Cock-pit at Whitehall. He had concerts at his own house, at which Cromwell would

‡ Anthony Wood, from whose manuscript in the Ashmolean Museum the above account is partly taken, was not able to fill up the blank which he left therein for the name of Hingston's master ; but a manuscript in the hand-writing of Hingston, now extant, ascertains it. This relic is thus inscribed :—' My Masters Songs in score with some Fanta-' zias of 6 parts of my own.' The Fantazias stand first in the book, and are about six in number, some subscribed Jo. Hingston, Jan. 1640, and other dates ; the songs are subscribed Orlando Gibbons. Hence it is to be inferred that Orlando Gibbons was the master of Hingston : and this supposition is corroborated by the following anecdote, communicated by one of Hingston's descendants now living, to wit, that the Christian name Orlando, for reasons which they have hitherto been ignorant of, has in several instances been given to the males of the family. Note, that in the MS. above-mentioned one of Gibbons's songs has this memorandum, ' Made for Prince Charles to be sung with 5 voices to his wind ' instrument.'

§ There are many particulars related of Cromwell, which show that he was a lover of music : indeed Anthony Wood expressly asserts it in his life of himself, pag. 139, and as a proof of it relates the following story :— ' A. W. had some acquaintance with James Quin, M.A. one of the ' senior students of Christ Church, and had several times heard him ' sing with great admiration, His voice was a bass, and he had a great ' command of it ; t'was very strong, and exceeding trouling, but he ' wanted skill, and could scarce sing in consort. He had been turn'd out ' of his student's place by the visitors, but being well acquainted with ' some great men of those times that loved musick, they introduced him ' into the company of Oliver Cromwell the protector, who loved a good ' voice and instrumental musick well. He heard him sing with very ' great delight, liquor'd him with sack, and in conclusion said, " Mr. " Quin, you have done very well, what shall I do for you ?" To which ' Quin made answer with great complements, of which he had command, ' with great grace, " That your Highness would be pleased to restore me " to my student's place ;" which he did accordingly, and so kept it to ' his dying day.'

Cromwell was also fond of the music of the organ, as appears from the following remarkable anecdote :—In the grand rebellion, when the organ at Magdalen college in Oxford among others was taken down, Cromwell ordered it to be carefully conveyed to Hampton-Court, where it was placed in the great gallery ; and one of Cromwell's favourite amusements was to be entertained with this instrument at leisure hours. It continued there till the Restoration, when it was returned to its original owners, and was the same that remained in the choir of that college till within these last thirty years. Observations on the Fairy Queen of Spenser by Tho. Warton. Lond. 1772, vol. II. pag. 236, in not.

* Dugdale's Hist. of St. Paul's Cathedral, pag. 173
† Athen. Oxon. vol. II. col. 347.

often be present. In one of these musical entertainments Sir Roger L'Estrange happened to be a performer, and Sir Roger not leaving the room upon Cromwell's coming into it, the Cavaliers gave him the name of Oliver's fiddler ; but in a pamphlet entitled Truth and Loyalty vindicated, Lond. 1662, he clears himself from the imputation which this reproachful appellation was intended to fix on him, and relates the story in the words following :—

'Concerning the story of the fiddle, this I suppose 'might be the rise of it. Being in St. James's park, 'I heard an organ touched in a little low room of one 'Mr. Hinckson's ; I went in, and found a private 'company of five or six persons : they desired me to 'take up a viole and bear a part, I did so, and that a 'part too, not much to advance the reputation of my 'cunning. By and by, without the least colour of a 'design or expectation, in comes Cromwell. He 'found us playing, and as I remember so he left us.'

Hingston was Dr. Blow's first master, though the inscription on Blow's monument takes no notice of it, but says that he was brought up under Dr. Christopher Gibbons. He had a nephew named Peter, educated under Purcell, and who was organist of Ipswich, and an eminent teacher of music there and in that neighbourhood. A picture of John Hingston is in the music-school, Oxon.

JOHN HILTON, (a Portrait,) a bachelor in music of the university of Cambridge, was organist of the church of St. Margaret, Westminster, and also clerk of that parish.* He was the author of a madrigal in five parts, printed in the Triumphs of Oriana. In 1627 he published Fa La's for three voices ;† and in 1652, 'A choice Collection of Catches, Rounds, and Canons for 3 or 4 voyces,' containing some of the most excellent compositions of this kind any where extant, many of them by himself, the rest by the most eminent of his contemporaries.

There are extant in the choir-books of many cathedrals a morning and evening service of Hilton's composition, but they were never printed. He died in the time of the usurpation, and was buried in the cloister of the abbey-church of Westminster, with the solemnity of an anthem sung in the church before his corpse was brought out for interment ; an honour which he well deserved, for, though not a voluminous composer, he was an ingenious and sound musician.

WILLIAM LAWES, the son of Thomas Lawes, a vicar-choral of the church of Salisbury, and a native of that city, having an early propensity to music, was, at the expence of Edward earl of Hertford,

educated under Coperario. He was first of the choir at Chichester, but was called from thence, and on the first day of January, 1602, was sworn a gentleman of the royal chapel. On the sixth day of May, 1611 he resigned his place in favour of one Ezekiel Wood, and became one of the private musicians to king Charles I. Fuller says he was respected and beloved of all such persons who cast any looks towards virtue and honour ; and he seems to have been well worthy of their regard : his gratitude and loyalty to his master appear in this, that he took up arms for the king against the parliament, and though, to exempt him from danger, the general, Lord Gerrard, made him a commissary, yet the activity of his spirit disdained that security which was intended for him, and at the siege of Chester, in 1645, he lost his life by a casual shot. The king was so affected at his loss, that it is said he wore a particular mourning for him.‡

His compositions were for the most part Fantasias for viols and the organ. His brother Henry, in the preface to a joint work of theirs, hereunder mentioned, asserts that he composed above thirty several sorts of music for voices and instruments, and that there was not any instrument in use in his time but he composed so aptly to it as if he had only studied that. Many songs of his are to be met with in the collections of that day ; several catches and rounds, and a few canons of his composition are published in Hilton's Collection, but the chief of his printed works are, 'Choice Psalms put into Musick for three voices,' with a thorough-bass, composed to the words of Mr. Sandys's paraphrase, by him in conjunction with his brother Henry, and published in 1648, with nine canons of William Lawes printed at the end of the thorough-bass book.

HENRY LAWES, (a Portrait,) the brother of the former. Of his education little is known, except that he was a scholar of Coperario. By the cheque-book of the chapel royal it appears that he was sworn in Pisteller on the first day of January, 1625, and on the third day of November following a gentleman of the chapel ; after that he was appointed clerk of the cheque, and of the private music to king Charles I. Lawes is celebrated for having first introduced the Italian style of music into this kingdom, upon no better pretence than a song of his, the subject whereof is the story of Theseus and Ariadne, being the first among his Ayres and Dialogues for one, two, and three voices, Lond. fol. 1653, wherein are some passages which a superficial reader might mistake for recitative. The book however deserves particular notice, for it is published with a preface by Lawes himself, and commendatory verses by Waller,

---

* These two offices may seem incompatible, but upon searching the Parish Books it is found. The antient usage of the Parish of St. Margaret was to elect two persons to the office of Parish Clerk, and one of them to that of Organist. Hilton was elected Parish Clerk and Organist in 1628, and in the account of the Churchwardens his salary as Clerk is charged at £6. 13s. 4d. or ten Marks a year : his salary for officiating in the latter capacity does not appear. It is supposed that his employment of Organist ceased in 1644 ; for in that year by an ordinance of Parliament, Organs were taken down ; and the church seems to have been without one till after the Restoration, when Father Smith was employed to build that which is now in the above church, and was himself in 1676 elected Organist with a salary of £20. a year. It appears by the Parish Books, that, while the church was without an organ, it was the usage there to read, and not to sing the singing Psalms.

† Fa La's are short songs set to music, with a repetition of those syllables at the second and fourth line, and sometimes only at the end of every stanza. Morley composed many songs of this kind, but none equal to those of Hilton, which are remarkable for the goodness of the melody.

‡ The following quibbling lines were written on occasion of his death :—
On Mr. William Lawes, Musician, slain at the siege of West Chester.
> Concord is conquer'd ; in this urn there lies
> The Master of great Music's Mysteries ;
> And in it is a riddle like the cause,
> Will. Lawes was slain by those whose Wills were Laws.

Who was the author of them is hardly worth enquiry ; but it may be noted, that among the commendatory verses prefixed to the second edition of Playford's Musical Companion, printed in 1673, are certain lines written by Thomas Jordan, wherein is this couplet :—
> When by the fury of the good old cause,
> Will. Lawes was slain by such whose Wills were Laws.

This Thomas Jordan was a Dramatic Poet and a composer of city pageants : there is an article for him in Langbaine's account of the English Dramatic Poets, page 306.

JOHN HILTON

MUS.BACC.CANTAB. MDCXXVI.
*From a Picture in the Music-School, Oxford.*

HENRY LAWES SERVANT TO HIS MAJESTIE

KING CHA.I. IN HIS PUBLIC AND PRIVATE MUSIC.

Edward and John Phillips, the nephews of Milton, and other persons; besides, that the songs are, for the poetry, some of the best compositions of the kind in the English language; and, what is remarkable, many of them appear to have been written by young noblemen and gentlemen, of whose talents for poetry there are hardly any other evidences remaining; some of their names are as follow: Thomas earl of Winchelsea, William earl of Pembroke, John earl of Bristol, lord Broghill, Mr. Thomas Carey, a son of the earl of Monmouth, Mr. Henry Noel, son of lord Camden, Sir Charles Lucas, supposed to be he that together with Sir George Lisle was shot at Colchester after the surrender of the garrison; and Carew Raleigh, the son of Sir Walter Raleigh. In the preface to this book the author mentions his having formerly composed some airs to Italian and Spanish words; and speaking of the Italians, he acknowledges them in general to be the greatest masters of music: yet he contends that this nation had produced as able musicians as any in Europe. He censures the fondness of the age for songs sung in a language which the hearers do not understand: and to ridicule it, mentions a song of his own composition, printed at the end of the book, which is nothing else than an index containing the initial words of some old Italian songs or madrigals; and this index, which read together made a strange medley of nonsense, he says he set to a varied air, and gave out that it came from Italy, whereby it passed for an Italian song. In the title-page of this book is a very fine engraving of the author's head by Faithorne, a copy whereof, with the inscription under it, is inserted in the Portrait volume.

The first composition in this book is the Complaint of Ariadne, written by Mr. William Cartwright of Christ-Church college, Oxon. The music is neither recitative nor air, but is in so precise a medium between both, that a name is wanting for it. The song is in the key of C, with the minor third, and seems to abound with semitonic intervals, the use of which was scarcely known at that time. Whether it was this singular circumstance, or some other less obvious, that contributed to recommend it, cannot now be discovered, but the applauses that attended the publication of it exceed all belief.

In the year 1633, Henry Lawes, together with Simon Ives, were made choice of to compose the airs, lessons, and songs of a masque presented at Whitehall on Candlemas-night before the king and queen by the gentlemen of the four inns of court, under the direction of Noy the attorney-general, Mr. Edward Hyde, afterwards earl of Clarendon, Mr. Selden, Bulstrode Whitelocke,* and others. Of this ridi-

* Whitelocke made great pretensions to skill in music. In the manuscript memoirs of his life above-mentioned, he relates that 'with the 'assistance of Mr. Ives he composed an air, and called it Whitelocke's 'Coranto, which was first played publicly by the Black Friars music, 'then esteemed the best in London. That whenever he went to the 'playhouse there, the musicians would immediately upon his coming in 'play it. That the queen hearing it, would scarce believe it was com-'posed by an Englishman, because, as she said, it was fuller of life and 'spirit than the English airs, but that she honoured the Coranto and the 'maker of it with her majesty's royal commendation: and, lastly, that 'it grew to that request, that all the common musicians in this towne, 'and all over the kingdome, gott the composition of it, and played it 'publicly in all places for about thirty years after.' The reader may probably wish to peruse a dance tune the composition of a grave lawyer, one who was afterwards a commissioner of the great seal, and an ambassador, and which a queen of England vouchsafed thus to honour; and to gratify his curiosity it is here inserted by the favour of Dr. Morton of the British Museum, the possessor of the MS. from which it is taken:—

CORANTO.

LORD COMMISSIONER WHITELOCKE.

In the Journal of his embassy to Sweden, lately published from the above-mentioned MS. is this passage: 'Piementelle staying with 'Whitelocke above three howers, he was intertained with Whitelocke's 'musick; the rector chori was Mr. Ingelo, excellent in that and other 'faculties, and seven or eight of his gentlemen, well skilled both in 'vocall and instrumentall musicke; and Whitelocke himself sometimes 'in private did beare his part with them, having bin in his younger dayes 'a master and composer of musick.' Vol. I. page 289.
In the account which gave occasion to this note it is said that Lawes

and Ives had each an hundred pounds for composing the music to the masque: the same adds that proportionable rewards were also given to four French gentlemen of the queen's chapel, who assisted in the representation. Whitelocke's words are these: 'I invited them one 'morning to a collation at St. Dunstan's taverne, in the great roome, the 'Oracle of Apollo, where each of them had his plate layd for him covered, 'and the napkin by it; and when they opened their plates, they found 'in each of them forty pieces of gould of their master's coyne for the 'first dish.'

culous scene of mummery Whitelocke has given an account in his Memorials, but one much longer and more particular in certain memoirs of his life extant in manuscript, wherein he relates that Lawes and Ives had each an hundred pounds for his trouble, and that the whole charge of the music came to about one thousand pounds. *The masque was written by Shirley, it is entitled the Triumph of Peace, and is printed in 4to. like his plays. William Lawes joined with his brother and Ives in the composition of the music.*

Henry Lawes also composed tunes to Mr. George Sandys's excellent paraphrase on the Psalms, published first in folio in the year 1638, and in 1676 in octavo. These tunes are different from those in the Psalms composed by Henry and William Lawes, and published in the year 1648; they are for a single voice with a bass, and were intended for private devotion: that to Psalm lxxii. is now, and beyond the memory of any now living, has been played by the chimes of the church of St. Lawrence Jewry, London, at the hours of four, eight, and twelve.

Milton's Comus was originally set by Henry Lawes and was first published by him in the year 1637, with a dedication to Lord Bracly, son and heir of the earl of Bridgewater.

Of the history of this elegant poem little more is known than that it was written for the entertainment of the noble earl mentioned in the title-page of it, and that it was represented as a masque by his children and others; but the fact is, that it is founded on a real story: for the earl of Bridgewater being president of Wales in the year 1634, had his residence at Ludlow-castle in Shropshire; lord Bracly and Mr. Egerton, his sons, and lady Alice Egerton, his daughter, passing through a place called the Hay-Wood forest, or Haywood in Herefordshire, were benighted, and the lady for some short time lost; this accident being related to their father upon their arrival at his castle, furnished a subject which Milton wrought into one of the finest poems of the kind in any language; and being a drama, it was represented on Michaelmas night, 1634, at Ludlow-castle, for the entertainment of the family and the neighbouring nobility and gentry. Lawes himself performing in it the character of the attendant spirit, who towards the middle of the drama appears to the brothers habited like a shepherd, and is by them called Thirsis.*

Lawes's music to Comus was never printed, and there is nothing in any of the printed copies of the poem, nor in the many accounts of Milton now extant, that tends to satisfy a curious enquirer as to the form in which it was set to music, whether in recitative, or otherwise; but by a MS. in his own hand-writing it appears that the two songs, 'Sweet 'Echo,' and 'Sabrina Fair,' together with three other passages in the poem, 'Back, shepherds, back,' 'To 'the ocean now I fly,' 'Now my task is smoothly 'done,' selected for the purpose, were the whole of the original music to Comus, and that the rest of it being blank verse, was uttered with action in a manner conformable to the rules of theatric representation. The first of these songs is here given. At the end of it a quaint alteration of the reading occurs, which none but a musician would have thought of :—

* See the dedication of the original printed in 1637, and in Dr. Newton's edition of Milton's poetical works.

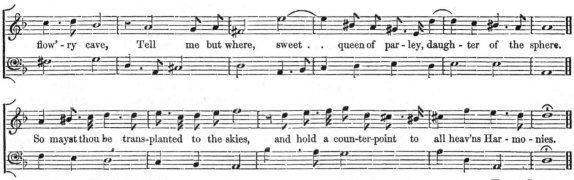

HENRY LAWES.

Lawes taught music in the family of the earl of Bridgewater, the lady Alice Egerton was in particular his scholar ;* he was intimate with Milton, as may be conjectured from that sonnet of the latter—

'Harry, whose tuneful and well-measured song.'

Peck says that Milton wrote his masque of Comus at the request of Lawes, who engaged to set it to music ; this fact needs but little evidence ; he fulfilled his engagement, adapting, as we may well suppose, the above song to the voice of the young lady whose part in the drama required that she should sing it.

The songs of Lawes to a very great number are to be found in the collections entitled 'Select musical ' Ayres and Dialogues,' by Dr. Wilson, Dr. Charles Colman, Lawes himself, and William Webb, fol. 1652 ; Ayres and Dialogues published by himself in 1653, and The Treasury of Music, 1669 ; and in various others printed about that time. Among them are most of the songs of Waller set by Lawes ; and Mr. Waller has acknowledged his obligation to him for one in particular which he had set in the year 1635, in a poem wherein he celebrates his skill as a musician, concluding with these lines :—

'Let those which only warble long,
'And gargle in their throats a song,
'Content themselves with UT, RE, MI,
'Let words and sense be set by thee.'

Mr. Fenton, in a note on this poem, says that the best poets of that age were ambitious of having their verses composed by this incomparable artist, who having been educated under Signor Coperario, introduced a softer mixture of Italian airs than before had been practised in our nation.† This assertion has no better a foundation than the bare opinion of its author, and upon a slight examination will appear to be a mistake ; Coperario was not an Italian, but an Englishman, who having visited Italy for improvement, returned to England, Italianized his name, and affected to be called Signor Giovanni Coperario,

instead of Mr. John Cooper. It appears by his compositions that he affected to imitate the style of the Italians, but that he introduced into our music any mixture of the Italian air, will hardly be granted by any that have perused his works. And as to Lawes, he has in the preface to his Ayres and Dialogues, intimated little less than a dislike of the Italian style, and in the last composition in that book done his utmost to ridicule it. The truth is, that not only in the time of Coperario, but in that of Lawes himself, the music of the English had scarce any air at all : and although in the much-applauded song of Lawes, his Ariadne, he has imitated the Italians by setting part of it in recitative ; there is nothing in the airs that distinguishes them from the songs of the time composed by English masters ; at least it must be confessed that they differ widely in style from those of Carissimi and Marc Antonio Cesti, who were the first that introduced into music that elegant succession of harmonic intervals which is understood by the term melody. This superiority of the Italian melody is to be ascribed to the invention of the opera, in which the airs are looked on as the most considerable part of the entertainment : it is but natural to suppose that when the stage was in possession of the finest voices of a country, every endeavour would be used to exhibit them to advantage ; and this could no way so effectually be done as by giving to the voice-parts such melodies as by their natural sweetness and elegant contrivance would most conduce to engage the attention of the judicious hearers.

But to return to Henry Lawes, he continued in the service of Charles I. no longer than till the breaking out of the rebellion ; after that he betook himself to the teaching of ladies to sing, and by his irreproachable life and gentlemanly deportment, contributed more than all the musicians of his time to raise the credit of his profession ; he however retained his place in the royal chapel, and composed the anthem for the coronation of Charles II. He died on the twenty-first day of October, 1662, and was buried in Westminster abbey.

If we were to judge of the merit of Lawes as a musician from the numerous testimonies of authors in his favour, we should rank him among the first that this country has produced ; but setting these aside, his title to fame will appear but ill-grounded. Notwithstanding he was a servant of the church, he contributed nothing to the increase of its stores : his

* She was also Countess of Carbery. See the Dedication to Lawes's Songs, 1653. Dr. Taylor preached her funeral sermon ; it is among his printed sermons. There is a song among the old collections entitled The Earl to the Countess of Carbery. Her sister Lady Mary married Lord Herbert of Cherbury. See the above Dedication, and Collins's Peerage—Egerton Duke of Bridgewater.

† Mr. Fenton, in the same note upon these lines of Waller, seems not to have understood the meaning of the two last. It was a custom with the musicians of those times to frame compositions, and those in many parts, to the syllables of Guido's hexachord, and many such are extant : Mr. Waller meant in the passage above-cited to reprehend this practice, and very emphatically says that while others content themselves with setting notes to syllables that have no meaning, Lawes employs his talent in adapting music to words replete with sentiment, like those of Mr. Waller.

talent lay chiefly in the composition of songs for a single voice, and in these the great and almost only excellence is the exact correspondence between the accent of the music and the quantities of the verse ; and if the poems of Milton and Waller in his commendation be attended to, it will be found that his care in this particular is his chief praise.

It will readily be believed that music flourished but very little during the time of the usurpation ; for although Cromwell was a lover of it, as appears by his patronage of Hingston, and other particulars of him above-noted ; yet the liturgy being abolished, those excellent seminaries of music, cathedrals, ceased now to afford a subsistence to its professors, so that they were necessitated to seek a livelihood by teaching vocal and instrumental music in private families ; and even here they met with but a cold reception, for the fanaticism of the times led many to think music an unchristian recreation, and that no singing but the singing of David's Psalms was to be tolerated in a church that pretended to be forming itself into the most perfect model of primitive sanctity.

Of the gentlemen of king Charles the First's chapel, a few had loyalty and resolution enough to become sharers in his fortunes ; and among these were George Jefferies, his organist at Oxford in 1643, and Dr. John Wilson ; of the latter Wood gives an account to this purpose :—

JOHN WILSON (*a Portrait,*) was born at Feversham in Kent. He seemed to value himself on the place of his nativity, and was often used to remark for the honour of that county, that both Alphonso Ferabosco and John Jenkins were his countrymen ; the former was born of Italian parents at Greenwich, and the latter at Maidstone ; they both excelled in the composition of Fantasias for viols, and were greatly esteemed both here and abroad. He was first a gentleman of his majesty's chapel, and afterwards his servant in ordinary in the faculty of music ; and was esteemed the best performer on the lute in England ; and being a constant attendant on the king, frequently played to him, when the king would usually lean on his shoulder. He was created doctor at Oxford in 1644, but upon the surrender of the garrison of that city in 1646, he left the university, and was received into the family of Sir William Walter, of Sarsden in Oxfordshire, who with his lady, were great lovers of music. At length, upon the request of Mr. Thomas Barlow, lecturer of Church-Hill, the parish where Sir William Walter dwelt, to Dr. Owen, vice-chancellor of the university, he was constituted music-professor thereof anno 1656, and had a lodging assigned him in Baliol college, where being assisted by some of the royalists, he lived very comfortably, exciting in the university such a love of music as in a great measure accounts for that flourishing state in which it has long subsisted there, and for those numerous private meetings at Oxford, of which Anthony Wood, in his life of himself, has given an ample and interesting narrative. After the Restoration he became one of the private music to Charles II. and one of the gentlemen of his chapel, succeeding in the latter capacity Henry Lawes, who

died on the twenty-first day of October, 1662. These preferments drew him from Oxford, and induced him to resign his place of professor to Edward Low, who had officiated as his deputy, and to settle in a house at the Horse-ferry, at Westminster, where he dwelt till the time of his death, which was in 1673, he then being near seventy-nine years old : he was buried in the little cloister of St. Peter's church, Westminster. A picture of him is yet remaining in the music-school at Oxford, and the engraving (as in separate Volume) is taken from it. The compositions of Dr. Wilson are ' Psalterium Carolinum, the Devotions of 'his sacred Majestie in his solitudes and sufferings 'rendered in verse, set to musick for three voices and 'an organ or theorbo,' fol. 1657. ' Cheerful Airs or 'Ballads; ' first composed for one single voice, and since 'set ' for three voices. Oxon. 1660.' 'Airs for a voice 'alone to a Theorbo or Bass Viol;' these are printed in a collection entitled ' Select Airs and Dialogues,' fol. 1653. ' Divine Services and anthems,' the words whereof are in James Clifford's Collection, Lond. 1663. He also composed music to sundry of the odes of Horace, and to some select passages in Ausonius, Claudian, Petronius Arbiter, and Statius, these were never published, but are extant in a manuscript volume curiously bound in blue Turkey leather, with silver clasps, which the doctor presented to the university with an injunction that no person should be permitted to peruse it till after his decease. It is now among the archives of the Bodleian library.

It appears that Dr. Wilson was a man of a facetious temper, and Wood has taken occasion from this circumstance to represent him as a great humourist, and a pretender to buffoonery : most people know that a humourist and a man of humour are two very different characters, but this distinction did not occur to Anthony. Henry Lawes has given a much more amiable, and probably a truer portrait of him in the following lines, part of a poem prefixed to the Psalterium Carolinum :—

' From long acquaintance and experience, I
' Could tell the world thy known integrity ;
' Unto thy friend ; thy true and honest heart,
' Ev'n mind, good nature, all but thy great art,
' Which I but dully understand.'

## CHAP. CXXII.

BENJAMIN ROGERS was the son of Peter Rogers of the chapel of St. George at Windsor ; he was born at Windsor, and was first a chorister under the tuition of Dr. Nathaniel Giles, and afterwards a clerk or singing-man in that chapel : after that he became organist of Christ-Church, Dublin, and continued in that station till the rebellion in 1641, when being forced thence, he returned to Windsor, and again became a clerk in St. George's chapel ; but the troubles of the times obliging him to quit that station, he subsisted by teaching music at Windsor, and on an annual allowance, which was made him in consideration of the loss of his place. In 1653, he composed Airs of four parts for Violins, which were presented to the archduke Leopold, afterwards

IOHN WILSON

MUS. DOCT. OXON.

MDCXLIV.

*From an original Painting in the Music-School, Oxford.*

emperor of Germany, and were often played before him to his great delight; he being himself an excellent musician.

Mr. Rogers was favoured in his studies by Dr. Nathaniel Ingelo, a fellow of Eton college, who in the year 1653 being appointed chaplain to lord commissioner Whitelocke, embassador to Sweden, took with him thither some compositions for instruments, which were oftentimes played before queen Christina, and greatly admired, not only by her majesty, but by the Italian musicians her servants.\* Afterwards, viz., in the year 1658, the same Dr. Ingelo recommended his friend Rogers to the university of Cambridge, and having obtained a mandate from Cromwell for that purpose, he was admitted to the degree of bachelor in music of that university.

In the year 1662, October 21, Mr. Rogers was again appointed a clerk of St. George's chapel at Windsor, with an addition of half the salary of a clerk's place beside his own, and also an allowance of twenty shillings per month out of the salary of Dr. Child, in consideration of his performing the duty of organist whenever Child was absent; and about the same time he was appointed organist of Eton college.† All these places he held until a vacancy happening in Magdalen college, he was invited thither by his friend Dr. Thomas Pierce, and appointed organist there; and in 1669, upon the opening the new theatre, he was created doctor in music. In this station he continued till 1685, when being ejected, together with the fellows, by James II. the society of that house allowed him a yearly pension, to keep him, as Wood says, from the contempt of the world, adding, that in that condition he lived in his old age in a skirt of the city of Oxon. unregarded.

The works of Dr. Rogers enumerated by Wood are of small account, being only some compositions in a collection entitled 'Court Ayres, consisting of 'Pavans, Almagnes, Corants, and Sarabands of two 'parts,' by him, Dr. Child, and others, Lond. 1655, octavo, published by Playford; and some hymns and anthems for two voices in a collection entitled Cantica Sacra, Lond. 1674, and others in the Psalms and Hymns of four parts, published by Playford. But his services and anthems, of which there are many in our cathedral books, are now the most esteemed of his works, and are justly celebrated for sweetness of melody and correctness of harmony.

Wood concludes his account of him in these words: ' His compositions for instrumental music, whether ' in two, three, or four parts, have been highly valued, ' and were always 30 years ago or more, first called ' for, taken out and played, as well in the public ' Music-school, as in private chambers; and Dr. ' Wilson the professor, the greatest and most curious ' judge of music that ever was, usually wept when ' he heard them well performed, as being wrapt up

' in an extacy, or if you will, melted down, while ' others smiled, or had their hands and eyes lifted up ' at the excellency of them.'

Upon the restoration of Charles II. the city of London having invited the king, the dukes of York and Gloucester, and the two houses of parliament to a feast at Guildhall, Mr. Rogers was employed to compose the music; Dr. Ingelo upon this occasion wrote a poem entitled Hymnus Eucharisticus, beginning ' Exultate justi in Domino,' this Mr. Rogers set in four parts,‡ and on Thursday the fifth day of July 1660, it was publicly performed in the Guildhall, and Mr. Rogers was amply rewarded for his excellent composition.

JOHN JENKINS, a native of Maidstone in Kent, was one of the most celebrated composers of music for viols during the reigns of Charles the First and Second. He was patronized by          Deerham of Norfolk, Esq. and by Hamon L'Estrange of the same county, a man of very considerable erudition. In the family of this gentleman, Jenkins resided for a great part of his life, following at the same time the profession of a private teacher of music. His compositions are chiefly Fantasias for viols of five and six parts, which, as Wood asserts, were highly valued and admired, not only in England, but beyond seas. He set to music some part of a poem entitled Theophila, or Love's Sacrifice, written by Edward Benlowes, Esq., and printed at London, in folio, 1651; and many songs.

Notwithstanding that Jenkins was so excellent a master, and so skilful a composer for the viol, he seems to have contributed in some degree to the banishment of that instrument from concerts, and to the introduction of music for the violin in its stead. To say the truth, the Italian style in music had been making its way into this kingdom even from the beginning of the seventeenth century; and though Henry Lawes and some others affected to contemn it, it is well known that he and others were unawares betrayed into an imitation of it; Walter Porter published ' Airs and Madrigals with a Thorough-bass for the Organ, or Theorbo-lute, the Italian way;' even

---

\* Whitelocke in the account of that embassy lately published, frequently mentions the applause given by the queen and her servants to what he calls his music, but he has forborne to mention to whom that applause was due, or even hinted that the author of it was Dr. Rogers. Whitelocke pretended to skill in music; he says that while he was in Sweden he had music in his family, and frequently performed a part. Vide page 579, in not. an air of his composition.

† *Vide State Trials, Vol. IV., p. 274.*

‡ Of this hymn, those stanzas which are daily sung by way of grace after meat at Magdalen college, Oxford, are part: they begin at ' Te Deum Patrem colimus.' Of the other compositions above spoken of, and of the reception they met with abroad, mention is made in a letter from Mr. Rogers to his intimate friend Anthony Wood, dated April 9, 1695, from his house in New-Inn, Hall-lane, Oxon., from which the following is an extract:—

' According to your desire when you were at my house last week, I ' have herewith made some addition to what I formerly gave you, viz.—

' That Dr. Nathaniel Ingelo going into Sweedland as chaplaine to the ' lord ambassador to Christina the queen, he did then present to the said ' queen two sets of musique which I had newly made, being four parts, ' viz., two treble violins, tenor, bass in Elami key, which were played ' often to her Majesty by the Italians, her musicians, to her great ' content.

' There are also several setts of his of two parts for the violins ' called Court-masquing Ayres, printed by John Playford, at the Inner ' Temple, in the year 1662, which were sent into Holland by the said John ' Playford, and played there by able masters to the States General at the ' conclusion of the treaty of peace, when the Lord Hollis went over ambassador there; which were so well liked off, that the noblemen and ' others at the playing thereof did drink the great rummer of wine to ' Minehere Rogers of England: this account I had of Mr. John Ferris ' of Magdalen college, who was there at that time, and one of the performers thereof.'

The letter above written is signed Ben. Rogers, and directed to his worthy friend Anthony Wood, at his house over-against Merton College; the design of the letter is evidently to satisfy Wood in a request to have an account of the doctor's compositions; and therefore, notwithstanding the use of the pronoun *his* for *mine*, the compositions of two parts for violins abovementioned, must be understood to be the doctor's own, and as such they are mentioned in Wood's account of him in the Fasti Oxon vol. II. col. 174.

Dr. Child, whose excellence lay in the composition of church-music, disdained not to compose psalms after the Italian way, and Deering gave wholly into it, as appears by his Cantiones Sacræ, and his Cantica Sacra, the one published in 1597, the other in 1618. Others professed to follow the Italian vein, as it was called ; and to favour this disposition a collection of Italian airs was published about the beginning of king Charles the Second's reign, by one Girolamo Pignani, then resident in London, entitled ' Scelta di Canzo- ' nette Italiane de piu autori : dedicate a gli amatori ' della musica ;' after which the English composers, following the example of other countries, became the imitators of the Italians.

In compliance therefore with this general prepossession in favour of the Italian style, Jenkins composed twelve Sonatas for two violins and a bass, with a thorough-bass for the organ, printed at London about the year 1660, and at Amsterdam in 1664 ; and these were the first compositions of the kind by an Englishman. Jenkins lived to about the year 1680. He is mentioned in terms of great respect by Christopher Simpson, in his compendium of Practical Music ; and there is a recommendatory epistle of his writing, prefixed to the first edition of that work printed in 1667. Wood says he was a little man, but that he had a great soul.

Musicians of eminence in the reign of Charles I. besides those already noticed were :—

ADRIAN BATTEN, a singing-man of St. Paul's and a celebrated composer of services and anthems, of which there are many in Barnard's Collection ; as are also the words of many anthems composed by him in that of Clifford.

JOHN CAERWARDEN, a native of Hertfordshire, of the private music to king Charles I. a noted teacher on the viol but a harsh composer.

RICHARD COBB, organist to Charles I. till the rebellion, when he betook himself to the teaching of music.*

DR. CHARLES COLMAN, a gentleman of the private music to king Charles I. after the rebellion he taught in London, improving the lyra-way on the viol. Dr. Colman, together with Henry Lawes, Capt. Cook, and George Hudson, composed the music to an entertainment written by Sir William D'Avenant, intended as an imitation of the Italian opera, and performed during the time of the usurpation at Rutland-house in Charter-house-yard. Dr. Colman died in Fetter-lane, London.

WILLIAM CRANFORD, a singing man of St. Paul's, the author of many excellent rounds and catches in Hilton's and Playford's Collections. He composed that catch in particular to which Purcell afterwards put the words ' Let's lead good honest lives, &c.'

JOHN GAMBLE, apprentice to Ambrose Beyland, a noted musician, was afterwards musician at one of the play-houses ; from thence removed to be a cornet in the king's chapel. After that he became one in

* This name occurs in the Ashmolean manuscript ; but is probably mistaken for John Cobb, the composer of an elegy on William Lawes, printed among the Psalms of Henry and William Lawes, 4to. 1648, in which he is styled Organist of his Majesty's Chapel-Royal. Sundry catches and canons of his composition appear in Hilton's collection mentioned in page 578.

Charles the Second's band of violins, and composed for the theatre. He published ' Ayres and Dialogues to the Theorbo and bass Viol,' fol. Lond. 1659. Wood, in his account of this person. Fasti, vol. I. col. 285, conjectures that many of the songs in the above collection were written by the learned Thomas Stanley, Esq. the author of the History of Philosophy, and seemingly with good reason, for they resemble. in the conciseness and elegant turn of them, those poems of his printed in 1651, containing translations from Anacreon, Bion, Moschus, and others.

WILLIAM HOWES, born near Worcester, where he was bred up with the waits, became one of the choir of Windsor till the rebellion, when he followed the king to Oxon. and was a singing man of Christ-Church ; he returned after the wars to Windsor, and had a soldier's pay allowed him to subsist on, till the restoration resettled him, in both places, he was afterwards a cornet in the king's chapel. He died at Windsor, and was buried in St. George's chapel yard.

GEORGE JEFFERIES, organist to Charles I. when he was at Oxon. 1643, servant to Lord Hatton of Kirby in Northamptonshire, where he had lands of his own, was succeeded in the king's chapel by Edward Low. His son Christopher Jefferies, a student of Christ-Church, played well on the organ.

RANDAL or RANDOLPH JEWIT, a scholar of Orlando Gibbons, and bachelor in music of the university of Dublin, was organist of Christ-Church Dublin, succeeding in that station Thomas Bateson, before spoken of. In 1639 he quitted it, and Benjamin, afterwards Dr. Rogers, was appointed in his room, upon which Jewit returned to England, and became organist of Winchester, where he died, having acquired great esteem for his skill in his profession.

EDWARD LOW, originally a chorister of Salisbury, afterwards organist of Christ-Church, Oxon. and professor of music, first as deputy to Dr. Wilson, and afterwards appointed to succeed him. He succeeded George Jefferies as organist of the chapel royal, he died at Oxford the eleventh of July, 1682, and lies buried in the Divinity chapel joining to Christ-Church there. He published in 1661 ' Short directions for the performance of Cathedral Service,' of which, as also of the author, there will be farther occasion to speak.

RICHARD NICHOLSON, organist of Magdalen college, Oxford, was admitted to the degree of bachelor in music of that university in 1595. He was the first professor of the musical praxis in Oxford under Dr. Heyther's endowment, being appointed anno 1626. He died in 1639, and was the author of many madrigals, and of one of five parts, printed in the Triumphs of Oriana.

ARTHUR PHILLIPS was made a clerk of New College, Oxford, at the age of seventeen ; after that he became organist of Magdalen college, took the degree of bachelor of music in that university, and upon the decease of Richard Nicholson, Dr. Heyther's professor, in 1639, was elected to succeed him. Upon the breaking out of the rebellion he went abroad, and after changing his religion for that of Rome, was retained by Henrietta Maria queen of England, then in France, as her organist, but being dismissed her service, he returned hither, and was entertained in the family of          Caryl, a gentleman of the Romish persuasion in Sussex. His vocal compositions of two and three parts are said to have great merit, but we know not that any of them are extant in print. Wood asserts that this person was nearly related to, if not descended from, the famous Peter Phillips, organist to the archduke and archduchess Albert and Isabel, of whom an account is herein before given.

WALTER PORTER, a gentleman of the chapel royal to Charles I. and master of the choristers at Westminster. He suffered in the time of the rebellion, and was patronized by Sir Edward Spencer: his works are 'Airs and Madrigals for two, three, four, 'and five voices, with a thorough-bass for the organ 'or Theorbo-lute, the Italian way,' printed in 1639; Hymns and Motets for two voices, 1657; and the Psalms of Mr. George Sandys composed into music for two voices, with a thorough-bass for the organ, printed about the year 1670.

THOMAS WARWICK, organist of the abbey-church of St. Peter's Westminster, and also one of the organists of the royal chapel. This person, as Tallis had done before him, composed a song of forty parts, which was performed before king Charles I. about the year 1635, by forty musicians, some the servants of his majesty, and others, of whom Benjamin, afterwards Dr. Rogers, was one. He was the father of the noted Sir Philip Warwick, secretary of the treasury in the reign of Charles II.

During that period, which commenced at the beginning, and terminated with the middle of the seventeenth century, the English seem to have possessed a style of their own; at least it may be said that till towards the year 1650 our music had received no stronger a tincture from that of Italy than must be supposed necessarily to result from the intercourse between the two countries; and this too was considerably restrained by those civil commotions which engaged the attention of all parties, and left men little leisure to enjoy the pleasures of repose, or to cultivate the arts of peace. Upon the restoration of the public tranquillity, the manners of this country assumed a new character; theatrical entertainments, which had long been interdicted, ceased to be looked on as sinful, and all the arts of refinement were practised to render them alluring to the public. To this end, instead of those obscure places, where tragedies and comedies had formerly been represented, such as the Curtain near Shoreditch,* the Magpye in Bishopsgate-street, and the Globe on the Bank-side, Black-Friars, theatres were erected with scenical decorations, and women were introduced as actors on the stage.

The state of dramatic music among us was at this time very low, as may well be inferred from

the compositions of Laneare, Coperario, Campion, and others to court masques in the reign of king James I. and from the music to Milton's Comus by Lawes; and yet each of these was in his time esteemed an excellent musician: this general disparity between ecclesiastical and secular music is thus to be accounted for: in this country there are not, as in Italy and elsewhere, any schools where the latter is cultivated; for, to say the truth, the only musical seminaries in England are cathedral and collegiate foundations; and it is but of late years that the knowledge of the science was to be attained by any other means than that course of education and study which was calculated to qualify young persons for choral service; it is notorious that the most eminent composers for the theatre for some years after the Restoration, namely, Lock, Purcell, and Eccles, had their education in the royal chapel; † and till the time of which we are now speaking, and indeed for some years after, he was held in very low estimation among musicians, who had not distinguished himself by his compositions of one kind or other for the church. From this propensity to the study of ecclesiastical music it naturally followed that the national style was grave and austere; for this reason, the blandishments of the Italian melody were looked on with aversion, and branded with the epithets of wanton and lascivious, and were represented as having a tendency to corrupt the manners of the people. It is very difficult to annex correspondent ideas to these words, as they respect music; we can only observe how the principle operated in the compositions of those masters who affected to be influenced by it; and here we shall find that it laid such restrictions on the powers of invention, that all discrimination of style ceased. In all the several collections of songs, airs, and dialogues published between the years 1600 and 1650, the words might, without the least injury to the sense, be set to any airs of a correspondent measure; and with regard to melody, he must have no ear that does not prefer a modern ballad tune to the best air among them.

The defects in point of melody under which the music of this country so long laboured, may justly be ascribed to the preference given to harmony; that is to say, to such compositions, namely, madrigals and fantasias for viols in five and six parts, as were the general entertainment of those who professed to be delighted with music; and these had charms sufficient to engage the attention not only of learned, but even of vulgar ears: The art of singing had never been cultivated in England with a view to the improvement of the voice, or the calling forth those powers of expression and execution, of which we at this time know it is capable; and as to solo-compositions for instruments, the introduction of such among us was at a period not much beyond the reach of the memory of persons yet living.

In Italy the state of music was far different; the

* At this theatre Ben Jonson was an actor; it was situated near the north-east corner of Upper Moorfields, and behind Hog-lane; the whole neighbourhood, for want of another name, is called the Curtain, which some have mistaken for the term Curtain used in fortification, imagining that some little fortress was formerly erected there, but it is taken from the sign of the theatre, which was a green curtain. Vide Athen. Oxon. vol. I. col. 608.

† This circumstance gave occasion to Tom Brown to say that the men of the musical profession hang between the church and the playhouse like Mahomet's tomb between the two loadstones. Works of Mr. Thomas Brown, vol. II. page 301, in a letter of Dr. Blow to Henry Purcell, in answer to one feigned to be written from among the dead.

invention of the opera had introduced a new species, differing from that of the church, in regard that it admitted of all those graces and ornaments, which, as they tended rather to gratify the sense than improve the affections, it had been the business of councils, and the care of bishops and pastors, to exclude from divine worship. In the musical entertainments of the theatres it was found that the melody of the human voice, delightful as it naturally is, was in males capable of improvement by an operation which the world is at this day well aware of; as also that in the performance on single instruments the degrees approaching towards perfection were innumerable, and were generally attained in a degree proportioned to the genius and industry of all who were candidates for the public favour.

The applauses, the rewards, and other encouragements given to distinguished performers, excited in others an emulation to excel; the effects whereof were in a very short time discerned. It was about the year 1590 that the opera is generally supposed to have had its rise; and by the year 1601, as Scipione Cerreto relates,* the number of performers celebrated for their skill in single instruments, such as the lute, the organ, viol d'arco, chittarra, viol da gamba, trumpet, cornet, and harp, in the city of Naples only, exceeded thirty.†

* Della Prattica Musica, pag. 157.

† In Coriat's Crudities the author mentions his hearing in the year 1608, at St. Mark's church at Venice, the music of a treble viol, so excellent that no man could surpass it. He also gives a description of a musical performance in the same city in honour of St. Roche, at which he was also present; and celebrates as well the skill and dexterity of many of the performers as the music itself, which he says was such as he would have gone an hundred miles to hear. The relation is as follows:—

'This feast consisted principally of musicke, which was both vocall 'and instrumentall, so good, so delectable, so rare, so admirable, so 'superexcellent, that it did even ravish und stupifie all those strangers 'that never heard the like. But how others were affected with it 'I know not; for mine owne part I can say this, that I was for the time 'even rapt up with St. Paul into the third heaven. Sometimes there 'sung sixteene or twenty men together, having their master or mode- 'rator to keepe them in order; and when they sung, the instrumentall 'musicians played also. Sometimes sixteene played together upon their 'instruments, ten sagbuts, foure cornets, and two violdegambaes of an 'extraordinary greatnesse; sometimes tenne, sixe sagbuts, and foure 'cornets; sometimes two, a cornet and a treble violl. Of those treble 'viols I heard three severall there, whereof each was so good, especially 'one that I observed above the rest, that I never heard the like before. 'Those that played upon the treble viols, sung and played together, and 'sometimes two singular fellowes played together upon Theorboes, to 'which they sung also, who yeelded admirable sweet musicke, but so 'still that they could scarce be heard but by those that were very neare 'them. These two Theorbists concluded that night's musicke, which 'continued three whole howers at the least. For they beganne about 'five of the clocke, and ended not before eight. Also it continued as 'long in the morning: at every time that every severall musicke played, 'the organs, whereof there are seven faire paire in that roome, standing 'al in a rowe together, plaid with them. Of the singers there were 'three or foure so excellent that I thinke few or none in Christendome 'do excell them, especially one, who had such a peerelesse and (as 'I may in a manner say) such a supernaturall voice for sweetnesse, 'that I thinke there was never a better singer in all the world, insomuch 'that he did not onely give the most pleasant contentment that could be 'imagined, to all the hearers, but also did as it were astonish and amaze 'them. I alwaies thought that he was an eunuch, which if he had beene, 'it had taken away some part of my admiration, because they do most 'commonly sing passing wel; but he was not, therefore it was much the 'more admirable. Againe it was the more worthy of admiration, because 'he was a middle-aged man, as about forty yeares old. For nature doth 'more commonly bestowe such a singularitie of voice upon boyes and 'striplings, then upon men of such yeares. Besides it was farre the 'more excellent, because it was nothing forced, strained, or affected, but 'came from him with the greatest facilitie that ever I heard. Truely 'I thinke that had a nightingale beene in the same roome, and contended 'with him for the superioritie, something perhaps he might excell him, 'because God hath granted that little birde such a priviledge for the 'sweetnesse of his voice, as to none other; but I thinke he could not 'much. To conclude, I attribute so much to this rare fellow for his 'singing, that I thinke the country where he was borne, may be as 'proude for breeding so singular a person as Smyrna was of her Homer, 'Verona of her Catullus, or Mantua of Virgil: but exceeding happy may

It was scarce possible but that a principle thus uniformly operating through a whole country, should be productive of great improvements in the science of melody, or that the style of Italy, where they were carrying on, should recommend itself to the neighbouring kingdoms; the Spaniards were the first that adopted it, the French were the next, and after them the Germans.

In England, for the reasons above given, it met at first with a cool reception, and Coperario, who went to Italy purposely for improvement, brought very little back but an Italian termination to his name. Lawes disclaimed all imitation of the Italians, though he was the first who attempted to introduce recitative amongst us, a style of music confessedly invented by Giulio Caccini, a musician of that country, Lawes's favourite song of Ariadne in Naxos is no other than a cantata, but how inferior it is to those of Cesti and others any one will determine who is able to make the comparison.

Other of our musicians who were less attached to what was called the old English style, thought it no diminution of their honour to adopt those improvements made by foreigners which fell in with that most obvious distinction of music into divine and secular, and which had before been recognized in this kingdom in compositions of Allemands, Corantos, Pavans, Passamezzos, and other airs borrowed from the practice of the Germans and the Italians. Even the grave Doctors Child and Rogers, both church-musicians, and Jenkins, who is said to have been the glory of his country, disdained not to compose in the Italian vein as it was called; the first of these published Court Ayres after the manner of the Italians, as did also Rogers, and Jenkins composed Sonatas for two violins and a bass, a species of music invented in Italy, and till the time of this author unknown in England. From the example of the e men ensued in this country a gradual change in the style of musical composition; that elaborate con-texture of parts which distinguish the works of Tye, Tallis, Bird, and Gibbons, was no longer looked on as the criterion of good music, but all the little graces and refinements of melody were studied. To answer particular purposes, the strict rules of harmony were occasionally dispensed with; the transitions from key to key were not uniformly in the same order of succession; and in our melody, too purely diatonic, chromatic passages were introduced to aid the expression, and give scope for variety of modulation; in short, the people of this country, about the middle of the seventeenth century, began to entertain an idea of what in music is termed fine air, and seemed in earnest determined to cultivate it with as much zeal as their neighbours.

Nor are we to look on this propensity to innovation as arising from the love of novelty, or that caprice which often leads men to choose the worse for the better; the improvements in melody and harmony

'that citie, or towne, or person bee that possesseth this miracle of nature. 'These musicians had bestowed upon them by that company of Saint 'Roche an hundred duckats, which is twenty three pound six shillings 'eight pence starling. Thus much concerning the musicke of those 'famous feastes of Saint Lawrence, the Assumption of our Lady, and 'Saint Roche.' Coriat's Crudities, page 250.

are reciprocal, and both have a necessary tendency to introduce new combinations, and thereby produce variety.

## CHAP. CXXIII.

THE efforts from time to time made by the Italians in the improvement of music, have been deduced to the year 1600; and its progress in other countries has been traced to the same period: it is necessary to observe the same course through the succeeding century, and by memoirs of the lives and works of the most eminent theoretic and practical musicians who flourished during that period, to relate the subsequent refinements, as well in the theory as the practice of the science.

BENEDETTO PALLAVACINO, a native of Cremona, and an eminent composer, was maestro di capella to the duke of Mantua about the year 1600. He is highly celebrated by Draudius, in his Bibliotheca Classica, pag. 1630. His works are chiefly madrigals for five and six voices, and in general are very fine.

DOMENICO PEDRO CERONE, a native of Bergamo, and maestro di capella of the royal chapel at Naples, was the author of a very voluminous work written in the Spanish language, and published at Naples in the year 1613, with this title, 'El Melopeo y Maestro. 'Tractado de musica theorica y pratica: en que se 'pone por extenso, lo que uno para hazerse perfecto 'musico ha menester saber: y por mayor facilidad, 'comodidad, y claridad del lector, esta repartido en 'xxii libros.'*

This book, perhaps the first of the kind ever written in the language of Spain, is a musical institute, and comprehends in it the substance of Boetius, Franchinus, Glareanus, Zarlino, Salinus, Artusi, Galilei, and, in short, of most of the writers on music who had gone before him. In it are treated of the dignity and excellency of music, of the necessary qualifications in a teacher of the science, and of the reciprocal duties of the master and disciple; in what cases correction may be administered to advantage, and of the reverence due from disciples to their masters: these, and a great number of other particulars still less to the immediate purpose of teaching music, and yet supported by a profusion of references to the scriptures, the fathers, and to the Greek and Latin classics, make up the first book.

The titles of the several books are as follow:—
Lib. i. De los Atavios, y Consonancias morales. Lib. ii. De las Curiosidades y antiguallas en Music. Lib. iii. Del Cantollano Gregoriano ò Ecclesiastico. Lib. iv. Del Tono para cantar las Orac. Epist. y Evang. Lib. v. De los Avisos necess. en Cantollano. Lib. vi. Del Canto metrico, mensural, ò de Organo. Lib. vii. De los Avisos necess. en canto de Organo. Lib. viii. De las glosas para glosar las obras. Lib. ix. Del Contrapunto comun y ordinario. Lib. x. De los Contrapuntos artificiosos y doctus. Lib. xi. De los movimientos mas observados en la Comp. Lib. xii. De los Avisos necessarios para la perf. Comp.

Lib. xiii. De los Fragmentos Musicales. Lib. xiv. De los Canones, Fugas, y de los Contr. à la xij. &c. Lib. xv. De los Lugares comunes, Entradas y Clausulas, &c. Lib. xvi. De los Tonos en Canto de Organo. Lib. xvii. Del Modo, Tiempo, y Prolacion. Lib. xviii. Del valor de las notas en el Ternario. Lib. xix. De las Proporciones, y comp. de diversos Tiempos. Lib. xx. La declaracion de la Missa Lomme armè de Prenestina. Lib. xxi. De los Conciertos, e instrum. music y de su temple. Lib. xxii. De los Enigmas musicales.

In the fifty-third chapter of his first book Cerone enquires into the reasons why there are more professors of music in Italy than in Spain; and these he makes to be five, namely, 1. The diligence of the masters. 2. The patience of the scholars. 3. The general affection which the Italians entertain for music; and this he illustrates by an enumeration of sundry persons of the nobility in Italy who had distinguished themselves by their skill in music, and had been the authors of madrigals and other musical compositions, particularly the Count Nicolas De Arcos, the Count Ludovico Martinengo, the Count Marco Antonio Villachara, Geronimo Branchiforte Conde de Camerata, Carlo Gesualdo Principe de Venosa, Alexander Gonzaga, duke of Mantua, and Andrew Aquaviva, duke of Atri, the author of a learned treatise on music published in 1528. Under this head he takes occasion to celebrate the liberality of Philip III. the then reigning king of Spain towards musicians; as an instance whereof he says that of chapel-masters and organists under him, some had salaries of three hundred, and some of five hundred ducats a year. The fourth reason assigned by him is the great number of academies in Italy for the study of music, of which he says there are none in Spain, excepting one founded by Don Juan de' Borja, Major-domo to the empress Donna Maria de Austria, sister of Philip II. king of Spain. The fifth reason he makes to be the continual exercise of the Italian masters in the art of practical composition.

These reasons of Cerone sufficiently account for the small number of musicians which Spain has produced in a long series of years; but though it be said that during that interval between the time when St. Isidore, bishop of Sevil lived, and that of Salinas, we meet with no musician of eminence a native of Spain excepting Bartholomeus Ramis, the preceptor of Spataro, already mentioned, and Don Blas, i. e. Blasias Rosetta,† Christopher De Morales, and Thomas a Sancta Maria; nor indeed with any intimation of the state of the science in that country, yet at the time that Salinas published his treatise De Musica the Spaniards are remarked to have applied themselves to the study of the science with some degree of assiduity. The first musician of

---

* It seems also to have been published in 1619 at Antwerp. Walth. 152.

† Rosetta was the author of a treatise published in 1529, entitled 'Rudimenta Musices, de triplici musices specie; de modo debite solvendi 'divinum pensum: et de auferendis nonullis abusibus in templo Dei.' Christopher Morales was an excellent composer of madrigals about the year mentioned before. Thomas a Sancta Maria was a native of Spain, being born at Madrid, and a Dominican monk; he lived a very few years before Salinas, and in the year 1565 published at Valladolid a work entitled 'Arte de tanner fantasia para tecla viguela y todo instrumendo de tres o quatro ordines.'

eminence among the Spaniards after Salinas seems to have been Gonçalo Martinez, and after him Francesco de Montanos : this person was a portionist or pensioner and maestro di cappella in the church of Valladolid for the space of thirty-six years ; he was the author of a treatise entitled 'Arte de Musica theorica y practica,' published in 1592 ; and of another entitled 'Arte de Contollano,' published at Salamanca in 1610, to whom succeeded Sebastian Raval, a celebrated composer.

After this apology for the low state of music in his country, Cerone proceeds to explain the nature of the ancient system of music, making use of the several diagrams that occur in the works of Franchinus, Glareanus, Salinas, Zarlino, and other writers ; he then proceeds to teach the precepts of the Cantus Gregorianus, following herein that designation of the ecclesiastical tones, and the method of singing the offices which is to be found in the works of Franchinus. From these he proceeds to the practice of singing, and the Cantus Mensurabilis, next to the precepts of Counterpoint, or plain and figurate Descant, and then to fugue and canon.

Towards the end of this book he treats of the proportions in music, giving the substance of all that is said by other writers on that branch of the musical science.

In the twenty-first book he speaks of musical instruments, which he divides into three classes, namely, the pulsatile, which he calls Instrumentos de golpe, comprehending the Atambor, Symphonia, Gystro, Crotal, Ciembalo, Tintinabulo, Pandero, and Ataval. Under the head of wind-instruments he ranks the Chorus, Tibia or Flute, the Sambuca, Calamo, Sodelina or Gayta, the Syringa or Fistula, the Chirimia, Trompeta, Sacabuche, Corneta, Regal, Organo, Fagote, Cornamusa, Cornamuda, Dulçayna, and Doblado. Lastly, in the class of stringed instruments he places the Sistro comun, Psalterio, Accetabulo, Pandura, Dulcemiel, Rebequina or Rabel, Vihuela, Violon, Lyra, Cythara or Citola, Quitarra, Laud, Tyorba, Arpa, Monochordio, Clavichordio, Cymbalo, and Spineta. He speaks also of the temperature of the lute, and delivers the sentiments of the various writers on that controverted subject.

The twenty-second and last book is affectedly mysterious ; it consists of a great variety of musical enigmas as he calls them, that is to say, Canons in the forms of a cross, a key, and a sword, in allusion to the apostles Peter and Paul ; others that have a reference to the figure of a balance, a piece of Spanish coin, a speculum, a chess-board, and one resolvable by the throwing of dice.

It appears very clearly from this work of Cerone that the studies of the Spanish musicians had been uniformly directed towards the improvement of church-music ; and for this disposition there needs no other reason than that in Spain, music was a part of the national religion ; and how tenacious they were of that formulary which St. Gregory had instituted for the use of the Latin church, may be inferred from a fact related in a preceding part of this history, to wit, that a contest for its superiority

divided the kingdom, and was at length determined by the sword.

With this predilection in favour of ecclesiastical, it cannot be supposed that secular music could meet with much encouragement in Spain. In this huge volume, consisting of near twelve hundred pages, we meet with no compositions for instruments, all the examples exhibited by the author being either exercises on the ecclesiastical tones, or motets, or Ricercatas,* and such kind of compositions for the organ ; neither does he mention, as Scipione Ceretto, Mersennus, Kircher, and others have done, the names of any celebrated performers on the lute, the harp, the viol, or other instruments used in concerts.

The common musical divertisements of the Spaniards seem to have been borrowed from the Moors, who in a very early period had gained a footing in Spain, and given a deep tincture to the manners of the people ; these appear to be songs and dances to instruments confessedly invented by the Arabians, and from them derived to the Moors, such as the Pandore, the protatype of the lute ; and the Rebec, a fiddle with three strings, and to which most of the songs in Don Quixote are by Cervantes said to have been sung. As to their dances, excepting the Pavan, which whether it be of Spanish or Italian original is a matter of controversy, the most favourite among the Spaniards till lately have been the Chacone and Saraband† and that these were brought into Spain by the Moors, seems to be agreed by all that have written on music.

In the enumeration of instruments by Cerone mention is made of the guitar, Ital. Chittara, an appellation well known to be derived from the word Cithara. The form of the guitar is exhibited by Mersennus in his Harmonics, lib. I. De Instrumentis harmonicis, pag. 25, and is there represented as an instrument so very broad as to be almost circular ; the same author also gives the figure of an instrument longer in the body than the former, and narrower in the middle than at the extremities, somewhat resembling a viol, and this he calls the Cithara Hispanica or Spanish Guitar.‡

This instrument by numberless testimonies appears for some ages back to have been the common amusement of the Spanish gentlemen : Quevedo, an eminent Spanish writer of the last century, relates the adventures of a very accomplished gentleman, but a great humourist, one who in the day time constantly kept within doors, excluding the light of heaven from his apartments, and walked the streets of Madrid by

* RICERCATA, a term derived from the Italian verb Ricercare, to search or enquire into, signifies in the language of musicians, though improperly, a prelude or Fantasia for the organ, harpsichord, or Theorbo ; they are generally extempore performances, and in strictness, when committed to writing. should, as should also voluntaries, be distinguished by some other appellation. Vide Dictionaire de Musique par Brossard.

† Besides the dances abovementioned there is one called the Fandango, which the Spaniards are at this time fond of even to madness, the air of it is very like the English hornpipe ; it is danced by a man and woman, and consists in a variety of the most indecent gesticulations that can be conceived.

‡ About the year 1730 a teacher of the guitar, an Italian, arrived at London, and posted up in the Royal Exchange a bill inviting persons to become his scholars : it began thus : 'De delectabl music calit Chittara 'fit for te gantlman e ladis camera ;' the bill had at the top of it the figure of the instrument miserably drawn, but agreeing with that in Mersennus. The poor man offered to teach at a very low rate, but met with none that could be prevailed on to learn of him.

night with his guitar, on which he had arrived at great perfection, imitating in this particular the practice of the young nobility and gentry of Spain, who followed it as the means of recommending themselves to the notice and favour of their mistresses.

For this instrument there are extant many collections of lessons composed by Spaniards and others. Mersennus mentions one published in 1626 by Ludovico de Briçenneo, entitled 'Tanner è Templar la 'Guitarra;' another written by Ambrosius Colonna of Milan, published in 1627, entitled 'Intavolatura 'di Cithara Spagnola,' containing many airs, viz., Passacalli tam simplices quam Passegiati, Chiacone, Zaravande, Folias, Spagnolette,* Pavagnilie Arie, Monache, Passe-mezzi, Romanescha, Corrente, Gagliarda, Toccata, Nizarda, Sinfonia, Balletto, Capricio, and Canzonette.

ROMANO MICHIELI, [Lat. Michaelius Romanus,] maestro di cappella in the church at Venice called Cathedrale de Concordia. He published at Venice a Compieta for six voices. This author is celebrated for his skill in the composition of canon, an example whereof in a canon for nine choirs or thirty-six voices is inserted in Kircher's Musurgia, tom. I. pag. 584. But his most celebrated work is a book entitled 'Musica vaga ed artificiosa,' published at Venice in 1615, in which the subject of canon is very learnedly discussed and explained by a variety of examples. In the preface to this book are contained memoirs of the most celebrated musicians living in Italy at the time of writing it.

JOHANN WOLTZ, organist of Heilbrun, an imperial town in the dukedom of Wirtemberg, and also a burgher thereof, was the publisher of a work printed at Basil in 1617, entitled 'Novam musices organices 'tabulaturam,' being a collection of motets and also fugues and canzones, gathered from the works of the most famous musicians and organists of Germany and Italy. In the dedication of this book to the magistrates of Heilbrun the author takes notice that he had been organist there forty years, and that his son had succeeded him. He was esteemed one of the most skilful organists of his time; nevertheless there are no compositions of his own extant, a circumstance much to be lamented.

LUDOVICO VIADANA, maestro di cappella at first of the cathedral church of Fano, a small city situate in the gulph of Venice in the duchy of Urbino, and afterwards of the cathedral of Mantua, is celebrated for having about the year 1605 improved music by the invention of the figured or thorough-bass. Printz has given a relation of this fact in the following terms: 'In the time of Viadana, Motets abounded 'with fugues, syncopations, the florid and broken 'counterpoint, and indeed every kind of affectation 'of learned contrivance; but as the composers seemed 'more to regard the harmony of the sounds than the 'sense of the words, adjusting first the one, and 'leaving the other to chance, such confusion and 'irregularity ensued, that no one could understand 'what he heard sung; which gave occasion for many 'judicious people to say, "Musicam esse inanem "sonorum strepitum.' Now this ingenious Italian 'organist and skilful composer, (who, as Christopher 'Demantius relates, was able to raise more admiration 'in the minds of the hearers with one touch upon 'the organ, than others with ten) perceiving this, he 'took occasion to invent monodies and concerts, in 'which the text, especially aided by a distinct pro-'nunciation of the singer, may well and easily be 'understood. But as a fundamental bass was neces-'sarily required for this purpose, he took occasion 'from that necessity to invent that compendious 'method of notation which we now call continued 'or thorough-bass.'

Draudius has mentioned several works of Viadana, among which are the following: 1. 'Opus musicum 'sacrorum Concentuum, qui et unica voce, nec non 'duabus, tribus, et quatuor vocibus variatis conci-'nentur, una cum basso Cont. ad Organum applicato,' an. 1612. 2. 'Opera omnia sacrorum Concentuum, '1, 2, 3, et 4 vocum cum Basso continuo et generali, 'Organo applicato, novâque inventione pro omni 'genere et sorte Cantorum et Organistarum accom-'modatâ. Adjunctâ insuper in Basso generali hujus 'novæ inventionis instructione et succinctâ expli-'catione. Latine, Italice, et Germanice, an. 1613 '(item an. 1620).'†

CLAUDIO MONTEVERDE, maestro di cappella of the church of St. Mark at Venice,‡ was a famous composer of motets and madrigals, and flourished about the end of the sixteenth and the beginning of the last century. In the year 1600 he became engaged in a dispute with some of the ablest musicians of his time, occasioned by certain madrigals of his, in which the dissonances were taken in a manner not warranted by the practice of other musicians. The particulars of this controversy are related by Artusi in the second part of his treatise 'De Imperfettioni della moderna Musica.' Monteverde is celebrated for his skill in recitative, a style of music of which he may be said to have been one of the inventors; at least there are no examples of recitative more ancient than

---

* Of the several airs above enumerated a particular description will be given hereafter, at present it may not be improper to mention that the Chacone is supposed to have been invented by the Arabians, and the Saraband by the Moors; the Follia is so particularly of Spanish original, that in music-books it is frequently called Follia di Spagna. Grassineau has given a very silly description of it, styling it a particular sort of air called Fardinal's Ground, which mistake is thus to be accounted for: about the year 1690 there resided at the court of Hanover, in quality of concert-master, a musician named Farinelli. Corelli being then at Hanover, Farinelli gave him a ground to compose on; and the divisions by him made thereon, to the number of twenty-four, make the twelfth of his solos, termed FOLLIA. Corelli had the practice of the Spanish musicians in his eye, the Follia di Spagna, being nothing else than a certain number of airs in different measures composed on a ground bass. Vivaldi also has composed a sonata consisting of divisions on the same ground, and called it Follia. See his Sonatas for two violins and a bass opera prima.

† It does not appear by the date of any of the above publications that Viadana invented thorough-bass so early as 1605. But as Printz has expressly asserted it, and his testimony has never yet been controverted, it would be too much at this distance of time to question it; nevertheless it may be remarked that within two years as early as the period above assigned, it was practised by another author, namely, Gregory Aichinger, a German, and a voluminous composer, who in 1607 published at Augsburg, 'Cantiones Ecclesiasticas a 3 et 4 voc. mit. 'einem G. B.' says the relator, i. e. with a general or thorough bass. Walth. 18.

Farther, it has been discovered that the practice of figuring basses was known before the beginning of the seventeenth century: in a work of our countryman Richard Deering, entitled 'Cantiones Sacræ quinque vocum,' published at Antwerp in 1597, the bass part is figured with a 6th wherever that concord occurs.

‡ Upon a comparison of times it seems probable that he was the immediate successor in that station of Zarlino, who himself succeeded Adrian Willaert.

are to be found in his opera of Orfeo, from which an extract is inserted in a subsequent part of this work ; and indeed it may with truth be said that Monteverde was the father of the theatric style. It seems that before his advancement to the dignity of chapel-master of St. Mark's he was chapel-master to the duke of Mantua, for he is so styled in his fifth book of madrigals represented at Venice in the year 1612. Monteverde was one of the original members of the Accademia Filomusi, erected at Bologna in the year 1622. Some very fine madrigals of his composition are extant in the collections published by Pietro Phalesio and others, about the year 1600.

ANTONIO CIFRA, a Roman educated in the school heretofore mentioned to have been instituted by Palestrina and Nanino, for the instruction of youth in music ; after he had finished his studies was taken into the service of the archduke Charles of Austria, brother of the emperor Ferdinand II. After that he became director of the music in the German college at Rome, and about the year 1614 was appointed maestro di cappella of the church of Loretto. He composed altogether for the church, and made a great number of masses and motets. Milton is said to have been very fond of his compositions, and to have collected them when he was in Italy.

PIETRO FRANCESCO VALENTINI, a Roman, and of a noble family, was educated under Palestrini and Gio. Maria Nanino, in the school instituted by them at Rome ; he was an excellent theorist, and, notwithstanding the nobility of his birth, was necessitated to make music his profession, and even to play for hire. He was the author of many compositions of inestimable value, among the rest is the canon entitled 'Canon Polymorphus,' inserted in page 303 of this work, which may be sung two thousand ways ; this composition was once in the possession of Antimo Liberati, who esteemed it as a very great curiosity ; not knowing perhaps that the author had given it to Kircher, who published it in his Musurgia. Valentini was the author of a work published in 1645, entitled 'La Transformatione di Dafne, Favola morale con 'due intermedii ; il primo contiene il ratto di Pro-'serpina, il secondo la cattività nella rete di Venere 'e Marte. La Metra Favola Græca versificata ; con 'due intermedii ; il primo rappresentante l'uccisione 'di Orfeo, ed il secondo Pitagora, che ritrova la 'Musica.'

PAOLO AGOSTINO, (a Portrait,) a disciple of the same school, was successively organist of Sancta Maria Trastevere, St. Laurence in Damaso, and lastly of St. Peter's at Rome. For invention he is said to have surpassed all his contemporaries. His compositions for four, six, and eight choirs are said to have been the admiration of all Rome. He died in 1629, aged thirty-six, and lies buried in the church of St. Michael in Rome. He left a daughter, married to Francesco Foggia, who will be spoken of hereafter.

GIROLAMO DIRUTA was a Franciscan friar, and the author of a work entitled 'Il Transilvano, Dialogo 'sopra il vero modo di sonar Organi ed Istromenti 'da penna,' printed at Venice in folio in the year 1625. The author styles himself Organista del Duomo di Chioggia. The design of this his work is to teach the method of playing on the organ and harpsichord. After explaining the scale of music and the characters used in the Cantus Mensurabilis, he remarks the distinction between the organ and the other instruments which are the subject of his discourse : the organ he observes is to be sounded gravely, and at the same time elegantly ; other instruments used in concerts and in dancing he says are to be played on with spirit and vivacity. And here he drops a hint that the profane and lascivious music, forbidden to be used in the church by the decree of the council of Trent, consisted in airs resembling dance-tunes, i. e. 'Passemezzi, ed altre 'sonate da ballo.'

After some general directions respecting the position of the hand, and the application of the fingers to the instrument, he exhibits a variety of lessons or Toccatas upon the ecclesiastical tones, some by himself, and the rest by other masters, as namely, Claudio Merulo, Andrea Gabrieli, Luzzasco Luzzaschi, Paolo Quagliati, Gioseffo Guami, and others.

In the course of this dialogue the author takes occasion to mention in terms of the highest respect, Claudio Merulo and Andrea Gabrieli, who seem to have been joint organists of the church of St. Mark at the time of the first publication of this book.

In the year 1622 Diruta published a second part of the Transilvano ; this is divided into four books, the first is said to be 'Sopra il vero modo de intavolare ciaschedun Canto.' The second teaches the rules of counterpoint, and the method of composing Fantasias, of which kind of music he gives a variety of examples, the composition of Luzzasco Luzzaschi, Gabriel Fattorini, and Adriano Bianchieri. The third part treats of the ecclesiastical tones, and of the method of transposing them, and other matters necessary to be known by every organist. The fourth book treats of the method of accompanying in choral service, with the use of the several registers or stops, as they are now called, of the organ.

MICHAEL PRÆTORIUS, a musician eminent both in the theory and practice, was a native of Creutzberg, a city, castle, and bailiwick on the river Wena in Thuringia, belonging to the duke of Saxe Eisenach, where he was born on the fifteenth day of February, 1571. Having made a great proficiency in music, he was appointed by Henry Julius, duke of Brunswick, chapel-master, and chamber-organist of his court, and also chamber or private secretary to Elizabeth his consort ; after which, being an ecclesiastic by profession, he became prior of the Benedictine monastery of Ringelheim or Ringeln, situated between Goslar and Lichtenburg, in the bishopric of Hildesheim. In the year 1596 he was the forty-eighth of fifty-three organists who were appointed to make trial of an organ then lately erected in the castle-church of Groningen. He was also, but in what part of his life is not ascertained, chapel-master of the electoral court of Dresden ; this appears by the superscription of a congratulatory ode in Latin, composed by John Steinmetz, prefixed to the first volume of the Syn-

PAOLO AGOSTINO

DA VALLERANO,

COMPOSITORE.

tagma Musicum of Prætorius. The musical compositions of Prætorius are very numerous, and consist of motetts, masses, hymns, and other offices in the church service. Besides these he composed a work, intended to consist of four volumes in quarto, but only three were printed, it is entitled Syntagma Musicum, and contains a deduction of the progress of ecclesiastical music from its origin to the author's own time, with a description of the several instruments in use at different periods. In the dedication of this work Prætorius complains of the many troubles and fatigues which he had undergone; and perhaps it is to be imputed to these that he left the work imperfect. He died at Wolfenbuttle on the fifteenth day of February, 1621, which day of the month was also that of his nativity, he having just completed the fiftieth year of his age.

HEINRICH SCHUTZ was born on the eighth day of October, 1585, at Kosteritz, a village on the river Elster in Voightland. His grandfather Albrecht Schutz, a privy-councellor, dying in 1591, at Weissenfeils, and leaving considerable possessions, Christopher his son removed with his family thither, and was elected a burgomaster of that city. In the year 1599, Heinrich having made a considerable proficiency in music, and having a very fine voice, was introduced to the Count Palatine Moritz at his court of Hesse Cassel, where having distinguished himself, he was by the direction of the Count instructed in languages and the arts. Having perfected himself in the rudiments of literature and the sciences, he in the year 1607, together with a brother of his, named George, and a son of his father's brother named Heinrich, went to the university of Marpurg, and prosecuted the study of the law. In the short space of two years Heinrich Schutz had made so good use of his time, that at the end of it he maintained a public disputation de Legatis, and gained great applause for his learning and acuteness. Soon after this his patron Count Moritz coming to Marpurg, Heinrich waited on him, and the Count discovering in him the same propensity to music that had first recommended him to his notice, proposed to him the leaving of the university in order to study music under Giovanni Gabrieli, a most celebrated musician at Venice, promising to bear his expences, and maintain him there. This offer of grace was no sooner made than accepted, Schutz went to Venice, and continued there till the death of his master in 1612. Having made a progress in his studies equal to any of his fellow disciples, he returned back to Hesse Cassel, and the Count Palatine settled on him a pension of two hundred guilders per annum; but not having determined to make music his profession, he betook himself again to the study of the law, which he pursued with great eagerness till the year 1615, when the elector of Saxony, John George, upon occasion of the baptism of the young prince Augustus his son, invited him to his court, and invested him with the dignity of director of his music, at the same time honouring him with a gold chain and medal. Being now settled in an honourable and lucrative employment, Schutz, on the first day of June, 1619, married Magdalen, a young woman

whom the original author of this account has distinguished by the description of Christian Wildeck of Saxony's land steward's book-keeper's daughter,* and by her had two daughters.

In the year 1625 Schutz became a widower; and in the year 1628, having a desire to revisit Italy, he obtained permission for that purpose. While he was abroad his father and also his wife's father died, the one in August, 1631, the other in October in the same year. During his abode at Venice, viz., in 1629, he published a collection of Latin motets with the title of Sagillarius.

Soon after his return to Dresden the electorate of Saxony became the seat of war; not choosing therefore to make that city his residence, Schutz, with the permission of the elector, in the year 1634 accepted an invitation of his Danish majesty to settle at Copenhagen; from thence in 1638 he removed to Brunswic Lunenburgh, and in 1642 returned to Denmark, where he was appointed director of the king's music. Towards the end of his life he became in a great measure deaf, after which misfortune he went very little abroad, betaking himself to the reading of the holy scriptures and the study of theology; yet he did not renounce the study of music, for in this his retirement he composed several very noble works, as namely, some of the Psalms, particularly the hundred and nineteenth, also the history of the Passion as recorded by three of the Evangelists. In his latter years he was afflicted with a diarrhæa, with which he struggled for a long time, till at length on the sixth day of November, 1672, a violent attack of that disorder put a period to his days, he being then eighty-seven years and twenty-nine days old, fifty-seven years whereof he had been chapel-master at the court of Saxony.

The works of Schutz are **Historie der Aufersttehung Jesu Christi** in seven books, published at Dresden in 1623, **Kleinen geistlichen Concerten,** for 1, 2, 3, 4, and 5 voices, Leipsig, 1636. Symphoniarum Sacrarum, the first part, published at Friburg in 1629, by George Hofman, a friend of the author, while he was abroad, dedicated to the elector John George. Symphoniarum Sacrarum the second part, published at Dresden by Johann Klemme, organist to the elector of Saxony, and Alexander Herings, organist of Bautzen in the year 1647, it is called his tenth work, and is by them dedicated to Christian V. king of Denmark. Symphoniarum Sacrarum, the third part, 1650. In the year 1661 all the works of Schutz were reprinted at Dresden by the express command of John George II. who committed the care of revising them to one Cornelius Becker.

JOHANN KLEMME, a celebrated organist and church musician, a Saxon by birth, was distinguished for his early proficiency in singing and knowledge of music by the elector of Saxony, Christian II. It seems that, agreeably to the custom of Germany and other countries, that prince was used to be entertained at his meals with vocal music, and that he had discovered in Klemme singular readiness and dexterity in the practice of descant: to encourage a genius so

* A Designatio Personæ almost as verbose as that with which the visitors of Don Saltero's Museum are amused, when they are shewn Pontius Pilate's wife's chamber-maid's sister's hat.

hopeful, he committed him to the tuition of the ablest masters in the court of Dresden, under whom he was instructed and maintained at the expence of the elector, for the space of six years, at the end of which his patron died. Fortunately for Klemme, John George the succeeding elector, entertained an equal affection for music with his predecessor, and having discovered in Klemme a strong propensity to improvement, he placed him for his farther instruction under Christian Erbach, a famous organist and composer at Augsburg, under whom he studied three years. At the expiration of this term Klemme returned to Dresden, and soon after was appointed master of the electoral chapel, and organist to the elector, by the recommendation of Schutz, who had held the former office fifty-seven years, and now resigned it on account of his age.

The works of Klemme are Fugues for the Organ, in number thirty-six, published at Dresden, 1631. He also in conjunction with Alexander Herings, organist of Bautzen, published in the year 1647, the second part of the Symphoniarum Sacrarum of Heinrich Schutz, and dedicated it to Christian V. king of Denmark, the first part of which work had been published at Friburg by some other friend of the author during his absence in the year 1629, with a dedication to the elector John George.

TARQUINIO MERULA, a cavalier, and also accademico filomuso in Bologna, was also maestro di cappella of the cathedral of Bergamo in the year 1639. His compositions are of various kinds, and consist as well of instrumental as vocal music ; he published several collections of Masses and Psalms to be performed either with or without instruments : one of his works is entitled ' Canzoni overo sonate concertate per ' Chiesa e Camera, a 2, e 3 Stromenti, lib. 1, 2, 3, e 4.' Tarquinio Merula was one of those musicians who introduced instruments other than the organ, that is to say, viols and also violins, into the church in aid of choral singing ; and, which is worth remarking, he appears by the work, the title whereof is above given at length, to have composed sonatas both for the church and the chamber as early as the year 1637, beyond which, in respect of antiquity, it will be found very difficult to carry the invention of this species of musical composition, since it is certain that for some years after that time, the only concert-music in practice either in France or England were

those fantasias for viols already described in the course of this work. Among the vocal compositions of Merula is one singularly humorous in its kind : it is the grammatical declension of the Latin pronoun hic, set to musical notes in the form of a fugue, or, as it is vulgarly called, a canon in the unison. It seems the office of chapel-master at Bergamo was not the first of Merula's preferments, for in a work of his entitled ' Concerti Spirituali, con alcune sonate à 2, 3, 4, e 5 voci,' printed at Venice in 1628, he is styled ' Organista nella Chiesa Collegiate di S. Agata, ' e Maestro di Cappella nella Cathedrale di Cremona.'

MARCO SCACCHI, a Roman by birth, and a celebrated musician, was maestro di cappella to Sigismund III. and Uladislaus IV. successively kings of Poland. Angelo Berardi, the author of the Miscellanie Musicali, Documenti Armonici, and other tracts on music, acknowledges that in the compilation of them he received great assistance from his friend Marco Scacchi. He was the author of a treatise published in 1643 with this title, ' Cribrum musicum ' ad triticum Siferticum, seu Examinatio succincta ' Psalmorum, quos non ita pridem Paulus Siferdus, ' Dantiscanus, in æde Parochiali ibidem Organædus, ' in lucem edidit, in quâ clarè et perspicuè multa ' explicantur, quæ summè necessaria ad artem melo- ' poeticam esse solent, Autore Marco Scacchio, Ro- ' mano, Regiæ Majestatis Poloniæ et Sueciæ Capellæ ' magistro. Venetiis apud Alexandrum Vincentium.'

In the year 1647 Scacchi published ' Cantilena ' V. voc. et lachrymæ sepulchrales,' containing a motet composed on occasion of the death of Johannes Stobæus ; and certain canons entitled ' Canones sive ' Lachrimæ sepulchrales ad Tumulum Johannis ' Stobæi ;' prefixed to the book is an eulogium celebrating the praises of Stobæus, of whom the author says that he was ' inter sui seculi musicos facilè ' princeps.' This person was a Prussian by birth, and chapel-master of the church of Koningsberg in Regal Prussia.

The musical compositions of Scacchi are greatly esteemed by the Italians for the exceeding closeness of their contexture, and that ingenious and artificial contrivance, which manifests itself to the curious observer. As a specimen of these his excellencies, Berardi, in the Documenti Armonici, has published two madrigals, the one in four, the other in five parts, the latter whereof is here inserted :—

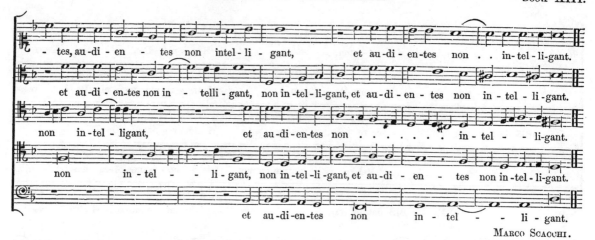

-tes, au-di-en - tes non intel-li-gant, et au-di-en-tes non .. in-tel-li-gant.

et au-di-en-tes non in - telli - gant, non in-tel-li-gant, et au-di-en - tes non in-tel-li-gant.

non in-tel - ligant, et au-di-en-tes non . . . . . . . . in - tel - - li-gant.

non in-tel - - li-gant, non in-tel-li-gant, et au-di - en - tes non in-tel-li-gant.

et au-di-en-tes non in - tel - - li - gant.

MARCO SCACCHI.

GREGORIO ALLEGRI, (a Portrait,) a disciple of Gio. Maria Nanino, and a fellow student under him and Palestrina, with Bernardino Nanino, the nephew of Gio. Maria, Antonio Cifra, Pier Francesco Valentini, and Paolo Agostino, was a singer in the papal chapel, being admitted as such on the sixth day of December, 1629. He was besides, as a scholar of his, Antimo Liberati, relates, a celebrated contrapuntist. Andrea Adami, surnamed da Bolsena, who has given a brief account of him, says that he was but an indifferent singer; but that he was distinguished for his benevolent disposition, which he manifested in his compassion for the poor, whom he daily relieved in crowds at his own door, and in daily visits to the prisons of Rome, and communications with those confined there, whose distresses he enquired into and relieved to the extent of his abilities. Allegri was a man of very devout temper: his works are chiefly for the service of the church; nevertheless he sometimes composed for instruments:* among his compositions in the church style is a Miserere in five parts in the key of G, with the minor third, which by reason of its supposed excellence and pre-eminence over all others of the like kind, has for a series of years been not only reserved for the most solemn functions, but kept in the library of the pontifical chapel with a degree of care and reserve that none can account for.†

Andrea Adami, who might be a good singer, but was certainly a very poor writer, and, as may be collected from many passages in his book, less than a competent judge of the merits of musical composition, has given a character of this work in the following words: 'Among those excellent com- 'posers who merit eternal praise, is Gregorio Allegri, 'who with few notes, but those well modulated, and 'better understood, has composed a Miserere, that

'on the same days in every year is sung, and is the 'wonder of our times, being conceived in such pro- 'portions as ravish the soul of the hearer.'

The above eulogium, hyperbolical as it is, will be found to mean but little when it is considered that most men express delight and admiration, rapture and astonishment in the strongest terms that imagination can suggest. The Miserere of Allegri is in its structure simply counterpoint, a species of composition which it must be allowed does not call for the utmost exertions of genius, industry, or skill; and it might be said that the burial service of Purcell and Blow may well stand in competition with it; if not, the Miserere of Tallis, printed in the Cantiones Sacræ of him and Bird in the year 1575, in the opinion of a sober and impartial judge, will be deemed in every respect so excellent, as to suffer by the bare comparison of it with that of Allegri.

This person died on the eighteenth day of February, in the year 1652, and was buried near the chapel of St. Filippo in the Chiesa nuova, in the place of sepulture appropriated to the singers in the pope's chapel.

BARBARA STROZZI, otherwise STROZZA, a Venetian lady,‡ flourished towards the middle of the last century, and was the author of certain vocal compositions, containing an intermixture of air and recitative, which she published in 1653, with the title of 'Cantate, Ariette, e Duetti,' with an advertisement prefixed, intimating that she having invented this commixture, had given it to the public by way of trial; but though the style of her airs is rather too simple to be pleasing, the experiment succeeded, and she is allowed to be the inventress of that elegant species of vocal composition the Cantata.

GIACOMO CARISSIMI, maestro di cappella of the church of St. Apollinare in the German college at Rome, is celebrated by Kircher and other writers as one of the most excellent of the Italian musicians. He is reputed to be the inventor of the Cantata, which is borrowed from the opera, but which in the

* A composition of his for two violins, a tenor and bass viol, is published in the Musurgia of Kircher, tom. I. pag. 487.

† The few copies of the Miserere of Allegri till lately extant are said to be incorrect, having been surreptitiously obtained, or written down by memory, and the chasms afterwards supplied: such it is said is that in the library of the Academy of Ancient Music, but one in every respect complete, and copied with the utmost care and exactness, was about three years ago presented as an inestimable curiosity by the present pope to an illustrious personage of this country.
The French church-musicians have a Miserere, which is highly valued among them, the production of their own country, composed by Allouette, of the church of Nôtre Dame in Paris, a celebrated composer of motets, and a disciple of Lully.

‡ This lady is not to be confounded with another of her own sex, Laurentia Strozzia, a Dominican nun of Florence, who lived near fifty years after her, and wrote on music. She was very learned, understood the Greek language, and wrote Latin Hymns, which were translated into French, and set to music by Jacques Mauduit, a French musician, celebrated by Mersennus in his Harmonie Universelle Des Instrumens de Percussion, page 63.

GREGORIO ALLEGRI

ROMANO

CANT. DELLA CAPP. PONT.

MDCXXIX.

preceding article is shewn to have been invented by Barbara Strozzi, a lady his contemporary, and in truth was only first applied by Carissimi to religious subjects, and by him introduced into the church: a remarkable composition of his in this kind is one on the last Judgment, which begins with a recitative to the words 'Suonare l'ultima tromba.' One of the most finished of his compositions is his Jephtha, a dialogue of the dramatic kind, and adapted to the church service; it consists of recitatives, airs, and chorus, and for sweetness of melody, artful modulation, and original harmony, is justly esteemed one of the finest efforts of musical skill and genius that the world knows of. Kircher in his Musurgia, tom. I. page 603, speaks with rapture of this work, and after pointing out its beauties, gives the chorus of virgins 'Plorate filiæ Israel,' for six voices in score and at length.

Another work of Carissimi, of the same kind, and not less excellent than that abovementioned, is his Judicium Salomonis, to which may be added his dialogue between Heraclitus and Democritus, in which the affections of weeping and laughing are finely contrasted in the sweetest melodies that imagination ever suggested.*

To Carissimi is owing the perfection of the recitative style; this species of music was invented by Jacopo Peri and Giulio Caccini, but reduced to practice, and greatly improved by Claudio Monteverde; Carissimi excelled in imitating the inflections of the human voice, and in uniting the charms of music with the powers of oratory.

He was likewise the inventor of moving basses, in which he was imitated by a famous composer of Cantatas, Pier Simone Agostino, Colonna, Bassani, and lastly by Corelli. He was also among the first of those that introduced the accompaniment of violins and other instruments with the voices in the performance of motets, a practice which he took from the theatre, and was afterwards adopted by Colonna, Bassani, Lorenzani, and other Italians. A disciple of his, Marc Antonio Cesti, who will be spoken of in the next article, introduced the Cantata on the stage and into secular performances. Mattheson calls this a profanation, but with little reason, for the Cantata was never appropriated to church-service, and in its original design was calculated for private entertainment.

Kircher in the strongest expressions of gratitude acknowledges his having received great assistance from Carissimi in the compilation of the Musurgia, particularly in that part of it which treats of Recitative, in which style he asserts that Carissimi had not his equal.

Dr. Aldrich has adapted English words to many of Carissimi's motets; one of them, 'I am well pleased,' is well known as an anthem, and is frequently sung in the cathedrals of this kingdom: and here it may be noted that the chorus in Mr. Handel's oratorio of Samson, 'Hear Jacob's God,' is taken from that in Jephtha 'Plorate filiæ Israel.'

Among the Harleian manuscripts is a volume of musical compositions, said by Mr. Humphrey Wanley, who drew up the Catalogue as far as No. 2407, to have been bought of himself, the first whereof is entitled 'Ferma, lascia, ch'io parli Sacrilego Ministro, 'Cantata di Giacomo Carissimi,' upon which is the following note: 'This Giacomo Carissimi 'was in his time the best composer of church- 'music in all Italy. Most of his compositions were 'with great labour and expence collected by the late 'learned dean of Christ-Church, Dr. Henry Aldrich. 'However, some things of Carissimi I had the luck 'to light upon, which that great man could not 'procure in Italy, of which this Cantata was one. 'Carissimi living to be about ninety years old, com- 'posed much, and died very rich as I have heard.'†

Marc Antonio Cesti was first a disciple of Carissimi, and afterwards a monk in the monastery of Arezzo in Tuscany. The emperor Ferdinand III. made him his maestro di cappella, notwithstanding which, and his religious profession, he composed but little for the church, for which he has been censured; nay he composed for the theatre, operas to the number of five; one entitled Orontea was performed at Venice about the year 1649, and another entitled La Dori some years after. His Cantatas, as has been mentioned in the article of Carissimi, were all of the secular kind, and the invention of the Cantata di Camera is therefore by some ascribed to him, while others contend that the honour of it is due to Carissimi his master; neither of these opinions have any foundation in historical truth; the Cantata, as above is related, was originally invented by Barbara Strozzi; and there are some of her compositions now extant which bear the name of Cantatas, and are so in fact, as consisting of recitative and airs for the voice; it is true that the evidences of art and skill in the contrivance of them are but few, however they are prior in respect of time to those of Carissimi and Cesti, and must therefore be looked on as the earliest compositions of the kind. One of the most celebrated Cantatas of Cesti is that to the words 'O cara Liberta;' some of his airs are printed in a collection published in London about the year 1665 by Girolamo Pignani, entitled 'Scelta di Canzonette 'Italiane de piu Autori.' The following sprightly duet is also of his composition

CA-RA ca-ra'e dol-ce,          ca-ra ca-ra'e dol-ce, ca-ra'e dol-ce Li-ber

CA-RA ca-ra'e dol - - ce Li-ber-ta,      ca-ra'e, ca-ra'e dol-ce, ca-ra'e dol-ce-

* Pietro Torri, chapel-master of the church of Brussels in the year 1722, composed a duet on the same subject.          † Harleian Catalogue, No. 1265.

MARC ANTONIO CESTI.

ESTHER ELIZABETH VELKIERS may justly be thought to merit a place in a work of this kind, for her excellence in the faculty of music. She was a native of Geneva, and was born about the year 1640, but before she was a twelvemonth old, through the carelessness of a servant, was suffered to go so near a heated oven, that she was in an instant almost totally deprived of her sight. As she grew up, her father discovering in her a strong propensity to learning, taught her the use of letters by means of an alphabet cut in wood, and had her instructed in the Latin, German, French, and Italian languages. Being thus furnished, she applied herself to the study of the mathematics, natural and experimental philosophy, and lastly, theology; in all which sciences she acquired such a degree of knowledge as rendered her the wonder and admiration of the ablest professors. As a relief to her severer studies, she betook herself to music, the knowledge whereof she acquired with great facility. She had a good voice and a very fine hand, which she exercised on the harpsichord. She had scarce any remains of sight, but had nevertheless attained the power of writing a hand very legible. Nothing of her composition is remaining, nor any other memorials of her extraordinary genius and abilities, than are to be found in some of the German

Lexicons, in which she is mentioned in terms of great respect.[*]

JOHANN CASPAR KERL, was a native of Saxony, and having in his early youth made great proficiency in music, was called to Vienna by the archduke Leopold, and appointed organist at his court, where discovering signs of an extraordinary genius, he was for his improvement committed to the care of Giovanni Valentini, maestro di cappella at the Imperial court, and after that sent to Rome for instruction under Carissimi: upon his return great offers were made him to enter into the service of the Elector Palatine, but he declined them, chusing rather to settle at Bavaria, where he became maestro di cappella to the elector Ferdinando Maria. His principal work is his 'Modulatio Organica super Magnificat octo 'Tonis Ecclesiasticis respondens,' engraved and printed in folio at Munich in 1687. Kerl is justly esteemed one of the most skilful and able organists that the world ever produced. In a competition that he had with some Italian musicians at the court of the elector of Bavaria, he composed a piece for that instrument of wonderful contrivance, and which none but himself could execute.

The following is given as a specimen of Kerl's style of composition for the organ.

* *Bishop Burnet in 1685, when abroad on his travels, saw and had long conversations with this extraordinary person.*

CANZONA.

JOHANN CASPAR KERL.

FABIO COLONNA, of the illustrious family of that name at Rome, was a celebrated mathematician, naturalist, and speculative musician. He was born at Naples in the year 1567, and flourished at the beginning of the succeeding century. He acquired great reputation by his skill in botany, and by the publication at different times of three books of Plants with figures, and remarks on the writings of Theophrastus, Pliny, Dioscorides, and Matthiolus : he was a member of the society called Accademia Lyncæi, established by the Duke De Aqua Sparta ; the first of those institutions for the improvement of science and literature, which are now so numerous in Italy and other parts of Europe. In the year 1618 he published in the Italian language a work in three books, entitled ' Della Sambuca Lincea, overo dell' instrumento musico perfetto, which instrument he named Lincea, and also Pentecontachordon, as consisting of fifty strings.

In this work of Colonna is contained the division of the diapason, which many have confounded with that of Vicentino, and makes the octave to consist of thirty-two sounds or thirty-one intervals.

Salinas asserts, and as it seems Mersennus once thought, that the two systems of Vicentino and Colonna were one and the same, as they both divide the tone into five parts, three whereof are given to the greater semitone, and two to the lesser. Salinas's words are these : ' I should not pass over a certain ' instrument, which was begun to be fabricated in ' Italy about forty years since, and was by its in-' ventor, let him be who he will, called Archicymba-' lum, in which all the tones are found to be divided ' into five parts, three whereof are given to the greater ' semitone, and two to the lesser one.'

And Mersennus remarks that that division cannot be called a new one which began to be made ninety-seven years before the time of his, Mersennus's, writing, viz., in the year 1634 ; between which time, and the time when Salinas published his book, fifty years elapsed : wherefore says Mersennus, as Colonna is a very old man, and confesses that he received this invention from another, it agrees very well with what Salinas has remarked.*

But in the Harmonie Universelle, livre III. Des Genres de la Musique, Prop. XI. Mersennus exhibits Colonna's system, which has no one circumstance in common with that of Vicentino, excepting only the division of the tone into five parts, as appears by the following description :—

' Fabio makes use of a monochord of the length of ' seven feet between the two bridges, and divides it ' into 200 equal parts, by means of an iron wheel, ' of the size of a Julio, an Italian coin worth five ' pence, this wheel has forty teeth, and being placed

' in a collateral situation with the string, and rolled ' along, in fifty revolutions marks 200 points.

' As to the degrees of the different species of the ' Diatonic, which he endeavours to find in the division ' of the octave into thirty-eight intervals, they prove ' that the Greeks have groped in the dark for that ' which they might easily have found if they had ' followed nature.

' The design of Fabio is to prove that the tone ' ought to be divided into five parts, but this may ' be done, as we have elsewhere said, by a division ' of 19 parts.'†

' The table here ex-' hibited shews all the ' chords, and intervals in ' the octave of Fabio. Its ' two columns contain all ' the chords of the octave, ' and shew the different ' points of the monochord ' on which the bridge is ' to be placed, to find ' every degree and every ' interval, as well against ' the whole chord, as a-' gainst the residue ; and ' for this purpose the right ' hand column contains a ' number, which, together ' with its correspondent ' number on the left, com-' pletes the number 2000, ' representing the whole ' chord.

' For example, the num-' bers 1000 and 1000 at ' the top of each column, ' make up the number ' 2000 ; the numbers in ' the sixth place from the ' top, that is to say, 1200 ' and 800 in like manner ' complete the number ' 2000 ; and the same ' thing will come to pass ' in all the rest of the num-' bers in the two columns, ' whose addition will al-' ways give the number ' 2000, the sum of the ' divisions contained in ' the whole chord.

' It is easy to know ' what every residue ' makes with the whole ' chord, or with the other

| | | | | |
|---|---|---|---|---|
| A | 1000 | | 1000 | |
| | 1063 | $\frac{14}{17}$ | 936 | $\frac{3}{17}$ |
| G | 1090 | $\frac{10}{11}$ | 909 | $\frac{1}{11}$ |
| | 1111 | $\frac{1}{9}$ | 888 | $\frac{8}{9}$ |
| #f | 1142 | $\frac{6}{7}$ | 857 | $\frac{1}{7}$ |
| F | 1200 | | 800 | |
| E | 1250 | | 750 | |
| | 1333 | $\frac{1}{3}$ | 666 | $\frac{2}{3}$ |
| | 1538 | $\frac{6}{13}$ | 461 | $\frac{7}{13}$ |
| | 1411 | $\frac{13}{17}$ | 588 | $\frac{4}{17}$ |
| | 1428 | $\frac{4}{7}$ | 571 | $\frac{3}{7}$ |
| D | 1454 | $\frac{6}{11}$ | 545 | $\frac{5}{11}$ |
| #c | 1500 | | 500 | |
| | 1600 | | 400 | |
| | 1739 | $\frac{3}{23}$ | 260 | $\frac{20}{23}$ |
| C | 1658 | $\frac{18}{29}$ | 341 | $\frac{11}{29}$ |
| | 1666 | $\frac{2}{3}$ | 333 | $\frac{1}{3}$ |
| ♮ | 1684 | $\frac{4}{9}$ | 315 | $\frac{5}{9}$ |
| | 1714 | $\frac{2}{7}$ | 285 | $\frac{5}{7}$ |
| | 1777 | $\frac{7}{9}$ | 222 | $\frac{2}{9}$ |
| | 1860 | $\frac{20}{43}$ | 139 | $\frac{23}{43}$ |
| | 1811 | $\frac{17}{53}$ | 188 | $\frac{36}{53}$ |
| | 1818 | $\frac{2}{11}$ | 181 | $\frac{9}{11}$ |
| | 1828 | $\frac{4}{7}$ | 171 | $\frac{3}{7}$ |
| | 1840 | $\frac{2}{13}$ | 153 | $\frac{11}{13}$ |
| | 1882 | $\frac{6}{17}$ | 117 | $\frac{11}{17}$ |
| | 1937 | $\frac{59}{83}$ | 62 | $\frac{24}{83}$ |
| | 1900 | $\frac{100}{101}$ | 99 | $\frac{1}{101}$ |
| | 1904 | $\frac{16}{21}$ | 95 | $\frac{5}{21}$ |
| #a | 1910 | $\frac{30}{67}$ | 89 | $\frac{37}{67}$ |
| | 1920 | | 80 | |
| | 1939 | $\frac{13}{33}$ | 60 | $\frac{20}{33}$ |
| | 1963 | $\frac{31}{163}$ | 36 | $\frac{132}{163}$ |
| | 1949 | $\frac{47}{197}$ | 50 | $\frac{150}{197}$ |
| | 1951 | $\frac{9}{41}$ | 48 | $\frac{32}{41}$ |
| | 1954 | $\frac{20}{131}$ | 45 | $\frac{11}{131}$ |
| | 1959 | $\frac{9}{49}$ | 40 | $\frac{40}{49}$ |
| | 1969 | $\frac{3}{13}$ | 30 | $\frac{10}{13}$ |
| A | 2000 | | | |

* Harmonici, lib. VI. De Generibus et Modis, Prop. xiii.

† Vide Harmon. lib. V. De Dissonantiis, Prop. xix.

'remaining part, that is to say, what every number
'of each column makes when compared with its
'opposite number, or with that of the whole chord,
'for example :—

'The sixth step of the first column, 1200, and the
'sixth of the second, 800, make the fifth, but 800
'with 2000, the greater tenth, and 1200 with 2000,
'the greater sixth. The rest of the relations are
'seen in this table, in which I have put the letters
'A, ♭, C, &c. that is A, RE, ♭ MI, C FA UT, and so
'on opposite the numbers answering to them. For
'example, the A with the ♭, or 2000 with $1777\frac{7}{9}$
'makes the greater tone 9 to 8, for there is no
'number which makes the lesser tone, viz., 10 to 9
'with 2000, since 1800 is not there, which is to
'2000 as 9 to 10. Now I begin this system with
'our A RE, because it answers to the Proslambano-
'menos of the Greeks, and I put the other letters ♭
'MI, C FA UT, &c. with those feigned ones having
'this character ♯, ascending to the octave, A LA MI
'RE, opposite to the numbers which answer to these
'syllables, although you might begin from C UT, D
'RE, or any other syllable or harmonical letter.
'I really wonder that Colonna and others have
'laboured so much at the division of the octave
'without first ascertaining the true intervals that are
'necessary to be used in singing, for the C SOL UT FA
'at the bottom, marked 2000,* has no greater tone
'above it ; the D LA RE SOL makes the greater tone ;
'and he should have put the number 1750 to make
'the greater tone, without which it is not possible to
'obtain the justness of the consonants ; he has also
'left out the B FA, that is 1125, which should make
'the greater semitone with A marked 1200, and the
'fourth with F marked 1500 ; he has no ♭ MI, which
'should make the fifth with E, or 1600, as does the
'number $1066\frac{2}{3}$. I omit several other harmonical
'intervals which cannot be found in his octave, both
'consonant and dissonant, but must observe that he
'has made the measures of his system so difficult,
'that out of the thirty-nine numbers there are only
'six that are not fractional, and these I could not
'reduce into less whole terms than those which are
'to be seen in the 12th proposition of the sixth book
'of the Harmonics, de Generibus et Modis, which
'are so prodigiously great, that there are but few who
'would not rather for ever quit all the pleasure of
'music than examine them, and proportion the chords
'of instruments to their intervals and ratios.

'But as the principal design of Colonna was to
'determine the several intervals by the monochord
'on every chord, and consequently to give a system
'which might serve for C SOL UT FA, or D LA RE SOL,
'E MI LA, F UT FA, G RE SOL UT, A MI LA RE, B FA,
'♭ MI, this invention should not be suffered to be
'buried in oblivion. The division of the tone into
'five equal parts is noted by four different characters
'called dieses ; the first of these is made by two lines
'crossing each other obliquely, the second has four
'lines, the third six, and the fourth eight, as in this
'example :—

1   2      3      4      5 6 7    8    9 10  11 12

'in which he puts the first diesis of the first note to
'the second, and so on, until he comes to the sixth
'note, which is a tone above the first, and a diesis
'above the fifth ; and certainly if the tone could in
'reality be divided into five equal parts, the invention
'of these characters for distinguishing them is in-
'genious enough, because the number of crossing
'lines shews how many dieses we must ascend or
'descend in singing ; for the first cross points out an
'ascent by one diesis, the second by two, &c.; and
'if the tone were capable of a division into eight
'commas, as some imagine, some such like characters
'might be made use of, or indeed the common
'numbers. But it is certain that the tone cannot be
'divided into five equal dieses by numbers, for as the
'diesis is the difference between the greater and
'lesser semitone, which last Colonna supposes equal
'to two dieses, it follows that all his divisions are
'false, for two dieses are greater than the lesser
'semitone $\frac{2591}{15625}$, as may be demonstrated by the
'rule of proportion, since the ratio of two dieses is
'16384 to 15625, and these two numbers are to one
'another as $25 \frac{2591}{15625}$ to 24, when that of the lesser
'semitone is as 25 to 24.

'But this author seems not to have understood
'the perfect theory of music, because he takes no
'notice of the greater semitone, an essential interval
'in music, for the number, $1871\frac{1}{4}$ which makes that
'semitone with the first or greatest number of his
'monochord, that is to say, 2000, is not in his division,
'and had it been there, should have been placed
'between $1882\frac{6}{17}$ and $1840\frac{2}{13}$. And if the characters
'are truly marked, he puts the greater semitone
'2000 to $1882\frac{6}{17}$, and consequently makes it greater
'than it is.

'The following example will shew how he divides
'the octave by the chromatic and enarmonic degrees,
'opposite to which are placed the numbers of his
'monochord :—

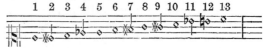

| 2000 | $1949\frac{47}{197}$ | 1920 | $1882\frac{6}{17}$ | $1818\frac{2}{11}$ | $1777\frac{7}{9}$ | $1714\frac{2}{7}$ | $1666\frac{2}{3}$ | 1600 | 1500 | $1428\frac{4}{7}$ | $1333\frac{1}{3}$ | 1250 | 1200 | $1111\frac{1}{9}$ | $1090\frac{1}{11}$ | 1000 |

'But the octave, divided as under into twelve
'equal semitones, answers all the ends of his division.

1 2 3 4 5 6 7 8 9 10 11 12 13

Mersennus has given so copious a description of
Colonna's system, that he has left very little to be
said on the subject, except that it has never been
adopted in any of the proposals for a temperature :
neither indeed has that of Vicentino, which he has
investigated with great ingenuity. On the contrary,
the above division of the octave into thirteen sounds
and twelve intervals, which is the same with that

mentioned in pag. 401 of this work, in not. and which Mersennus has particularly recommended in the Harmonie Universelle, liv. III. Des Genres de la Musique, Prop. XII. seems to prevail, as having hitherto resisted all attempts towards a farther improvement.

### CHAP. CXXV.

Marin Mersenne, *(a Portrait,)* [Lat. Marinus Mersennus,] a most learned French writer, was born on the eighth day of September, 1588, at Oyse in the province of La Maine. He received his instruction in polite literature at the college of Flêche, but quitting that seminary, he went to Paris, and after having studied divinity some years in the college of the Sorbonne, entered himself among the Minims, and on the seventeenth day of July, 1611, received the habit. In September, 1612, he went to reside in the convent of that order at Paris, where he was ordained priest, and performed his first mass in October, 1613. Immediately upon his settlement he applied himself to the study of the Hebrew language under the direction of father John Bruno, a Scots Minim, and having acquired a competent degree of skill therein, he became a teacher of philosophy and theology in the convent of Nevers. In this station he continued till the year 1619, when he returned to Paris, determined to spend the remainder of his life in study and conversation, as indeed he did, making them his whole employment. In the pursuit of his studies he established and kept up a correspondence with most of the learned and ingenious men of his time. During his stay at la Flêche he had contracted a friendship with Des Cartes, which he manifested in many instances, of which the following may be reckoned as one. Being at Paris, and looked on as the friend of Des Cartes, he gave out that that philosopher was erecting a new system of physics upon the foundation of a Vacuum; but finding the public were indifferent to it, he immediately sent intelligence to Des Cartes that a Vacuum was not then the fashion, which made that philosopher change his system and adopt the old doctrine of a Plenum. The residence of Mersennus at Paris did not hinder him from making several journies into foreign countries, for he visited Holland in the middle of the year 1629, and Italy four times, viz , in 1639, 1641, 1644, 1646. In the month of July, 1648, and in the dog-days, having been to visit his friend Des Cartes, he returned home to his convent excessively heated; to allay his thirst he drank cold water, and soon after was seized with an illness which produced an abscess on his right side. His physicians imagining his disorder to be a kind of pleurisy, he was bled several times to no purpose; at last it was thought proper to open his side, and the operation was begun, but he expired in the midst of it on the first day of September, 1648, he being then about the age of sixty. He had directed the surgeons, in case of a miscarriage in the operation, to open his body, which they did, and found that they had made the incision two inches below the abscess.

The author of Mersennus's life, Hilarion de Coste, gives this farther character of him and his writings.

He was a man of universal learning, but excelled particularly in physics and the mathematics; on these subjects he published many books, and one in particular entitled 'Questiones celeberimæ in Genesim, 'cum accuratâ textûs explicatione : in quo volumine 'athæi et deistæ impugnantur, &c.'* Paris 1623 It abounds with long digressions, one on the subject of music, in which, and indeed in many other parts of his book, he takes occasion to censure the opinions of Robert Fludd, an Englishman, a doctor in physic, and a fellow of the college of physicians in London, but a crack-brained enthusiast, of whom, as he was a writer on music, an account will hereafter be given.

The character of Mersennus as a philosopher and a mathematician is well known in the learned world. To that disposition which led him to the most abstruse studies, he had joined a nice and judicious ear, and a passionate love of music, these gave a direction to his pursuits, and were productive of numberless experiments and calculations tending to demonstrate the principles of harmonics, and prove that they are independent on habit or fashion, custom or caprice, and, in short, have their foundation in nature, and the original frame and constitution of the universe.

In the year 1636 Mersennus, published at Paris, in a large folio volume, a work entitled Harmonie Universelle, in which he treats of the nature and properties of sound, of instruments of various kinds, of consonances and dissonances, of composition, of the human voice, and of the practice of singing, and a great variety of other particulars respecting music.

This book consists of a great number of separate and distinct treatises, with such signatures for the sheets and numbers for the pages as make them independent of each other. The consequence whereof is, that there are hardly any two copies to be met with that contain precisely the same number of tracts, or in which the tracts occur or follow in the same order, so that to cite or refer to the Harmonie Universelle is a matter of some difficulty. The titles of the tracts are as follow : De l'Utilité de l'Harmonie. De la Nature et des Proprietez du Son. Des Consonances. Des Dissonances. Des Instrumens. Des Instrumens à chordes. Des Instrumens à vent. Des Instrumens de Percussion. Des Orgues. Des Genres de la Musique. De la Composition. De la Voix. Des Chants. Du Mouvement des Corps. Des Mouvemens et du son des Chordes. De l'Art de bien chanter, and herein des Ordres de Sons, de l'Art d'embellir la Voix, les Recits, les Airs, ou les Chants. De la Rythmique.

As the substance of these several treatises is contained in the Latin work of Mersennus herein spoken of, it is not necessary to give any thing more than a general account of the Harmonie Universelle ; nevertheless some material variations between the Latin and the French work will be noted as they occur.

In the year 1648, Mersennus published his Harmonie Universelle in Latin, with considerable addi-

* The title of the book as entered in the Bodleian Catalogue is Questiones et Explicatio in sex priora capita Geneseως, quibus etiam 'Græcorum et Hebræorum Musica instauratur.' Par. 1623. It seems that the Harmonie Universelle and Harmonici, contain in substance the whole of what he has said in it relating to music.

C. Grignion sculp.

MARIN MERSENNE

DE L'ORDRE DES PERES MINIMES

MDCXXXVI.

tions and improvements, with this title, 'Harmoni-
'corum libri xii. in quibus agitur de sonorum natura,
'causis, et effectibus : de consonantiis, dissonantiis,
'rationibus, generibus, modis, cantibus, compositione,
'orbisque totius harmonicis instrumentis.'    This
work, though the title does not mention it, is divided
into two parts, the first containing eight, and the
second four books, thus distinguished : Lib. i. De
natura et proprietatibus sonorum.    ii. De causis
sonorum, seu de corporibus sonum producentibus.
iii. De fidibus, nervis et chordis, atque metallis, ex
quibus fieri solent.   iv. De sonis consonis, seu consonantiis.  v. De musicæ dissonantiis, de rationibus,
et proportionibus ; deque divisionibus consonantiarum.
vi. De speciebus consonantiarum, deque modis, et
generibus.   vii. De cantibus, seu cantilenis, earumque
numero, partibus, et speciebus.   viii. De compositione
musica, de canendi methodo, et de voce.

The several chapters of the second part are thus
entitled :—

Lib. i. De singulis instrumentis ενTATOɩς seu
εγχορδοɩς hoc est nervaceis et fidicularibus.  ii. De
instrumentis pneumaticis.   iii. De organis, campanis,
tympani, ac cæteris instrumentis κρονομενοɩς, seu que
percutiuntur.   iv. De campanis, et aliis instrumentis
κρονομενοɩς seu percussionis, ut tympanis, cymbalis, &c.

The titles of these several books do in a great
measure bespeak the general contents of them severally ; but the doctrines delivered by Mersennus
are founded on such a variety of experiments touching the nature and properties of sound, and of chords,
as well of metal as those which are made of the
intestines of beasts ; and his reasoning on these
subjects is so very close, and withal so curious, that
nothing but the perusal of this part of his own
original work can afford satisfaction to an enquirer,
for which reason an abridgment of it is here forborne.

In the fourth and fifth books he treats of the
consonances and dissonances, shewing how they are
generated, and ascertaining with the utmost degree
of exactness the ratios of each ; for an instance
whereof we need look no farther than his fifth book,
where he demonstrates that there are no fewer than
five different kinds of semitone, giving the ratios of
them severally.

His designation of the genera contained in his
sixth book, De Generibus et Modis, is inserted in
page 34 of this work.   Previous to his explanation
of the modes, he exhibits a view of the scale of
Guido in a collateral position with that of the ancient
Greeks, making Proslambanomenos answer to A RE,
and Nete hyperboleon to aa, LA MI RE.   Of the
ancient modes he says very little, but hastens to
declare the nature of the modern, or as they are
otherwise termed the ecclesiastical tones, and these
with Glareanus he makes to be twelve.   This book
contains also his examen and censure of the division
of the monochord by Fabio Colonna.

In his seventh book, De Cantibus, in order to
shew the wonderful variety in music, he exhibits
tables that demonstrate the several combinations or
possible arrangements of notes in the forming a Can-

tilena ; and in these the varieties appear so multifarious, that the human mind can scarce contemplate
them without distraction ; in short, to express the
number of combinations of which sixty-four sounds
are capable, as many figures are necessary as fill
a line of a folio page in a small type ; and those
exhibited by Mersennus for this purpose are thus
rendered by him :—

'Ducenti viginti et unus vigintioctoiliones, 284
'vigintiseptemiliones, 59 vigintisexiliones, 310 vigin-
'tiquinqueiliones, 674 vigintiquatuoriliones, 795 vi-
'gintitresiliones, 878 vigintiduoiliones, 785 viginti
'et unusiliones, 453 vigintiliones, 858 novemdeci-
'miliones, 545 octodecimiliones, 553 septemdecimi-
'liones, 220 sexdecimiliones, 443 quindecimiliones,
'327 quatuordecimiliones, 118 tredecimiliones, 855
'duodecimiliones, 467 undecimiliones, 387 decimi-
'liones, 637 noviliones, 279 octiliones, 113 septi-
'liones, 59 sexiliones, 747 quintiliones, 33 quadri-
'liones, et sexcenti triliones.'*

In his book intitled De Instrumentis harmonicis,
Prop. II. he takes occasion to speak of the chords of
musical instruments, and of the substances of which
they are formed ; and these he says are metal and
the intestines of sheep or any other animals.   He
says that the thicker chords of the greater viols and of
lutes are made of thirty or forty single intestines,
and that the best of this kind are made in Rome
and some other cities in Italy, and this superiority
he says may be owing to the air, the water, or the
herbage on which the sheep of Italy feed : he adds
that chords may be also made of silk, flax, or other
materials, but that the animal chords are far the best.
Chords of metal he says are of gold, silver, copper,
brass, or iron, which being formed into cylinders, are
wrought into wires of an incredible fineness ; these
cylinders he says are three, or four feet long, and by
the power of wheels, which require the strength of
two or three men to turn them, are drawn through
plates with steel holes, which are successively changed
for others in gradual diminution, till the cylinders
are reduced to slender wires.

To demonstrate the ductility of metals, particularly
silver and gold, he says that he tried a silver chord,
so very slender, that six hundred feet of it weighed
only an ounce, and found that it sustained a weight
of eight ounces before it broke ; and that when it
was stretched by the same weight on a monochord
eighteen inches in length, it made in the space of
one second of time a hundred vibrations : as to gold,
he says that an ounce may be converted into sixteen
hundred leaves, each at least three inches square,
and that he remembered a gold-beater that by mere
dint of labour hammered out such a leaf of gold till
it covered a table like a table-cloth.   He mentions
also the covering cylinders or chords of silver or
copper with gold, and demonstrates that an ounce of
gold being beaten into leaves, may be made to gild
a wire two hundred and sixty-six leagues long.

In Prop. VIII. of the same book, the author

* According to the computation of ringers, the time required to ring
all the possible changes on twelve bells is seventy-five years, ten months,
one week, and three days.

treats of the Cithara or Lute, and of the Theorbo, which he calls the Cithara bijuga, thus represented by him :—

After having explained the construction of these two several instruments, and shewn the tuning, and the method of playing on each, as also the mechanical operations of the workmen in making them, he directs the application of the hands and fingers, and describes the several little percussions or graces in the performance on the lute.

And here, to avoid confusion, it may be proper to note the difference between the above two instruments: the first is the primitive French lute improved by an additional number of strings from that represented in page 418 of this work. The other is the Theorbo or Cithara bijuga, so called from its having two necks, though we ought rather to say that it has two nuts, which severally determine the lengths of the two sets of strings. When the strings of the latter are doubled, as among the Italians they frequently are, the instrument is called Arcileuto, the Arch-lute. See page 418 of this work, in not. The use of it then is chiefly in thorough-bass. In the earlier editions of Corelli's Sonatas, particularly of the third opera, printed at Bologna in 1690, the principal bass part is entitled Violone, ò Arcileuto. In the Antwerp editions it is simply Violone, from whence it may be inferred that in Flanders the Arch-lute was but little, if at all, in use.

In Prop. XIII. he explains the tablature for the lute as well by figures as letters, illustrating the latter method in a subsequent proposition by a Cantilena of Mons. Boësset, master of the chamber-music to the king of France.

Prop. XIX. contains a description of another instrument of the lute-kind, which he calls the Pandura, of the following form :— and seems to be an improvement of the instrument

called the Bandore, invented by John Rose,* and spoken of in pag. 493 of this work.

* The right name of this person seems to have been Ross. He had a son, a famous viol-maker. Mace, in his Musick's Monument, pag. 245, says that one Bolles and Ross were two of the best makers of viols in the world, and that he had known a bass-viol of the former valued at one hundred pounds.

In Prop. XX. are given the figure, concentus, and tablature of the Mandura or lesser lute, an instrument of this form ;—

In Prop. XXI. the following representation of the Cithara Hispanica, or Spanish Guitar.†

In Prop. XXII. are exhibited the form and concentus of the instrument called the Cistrum, thus delineated :—

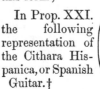

This instrument Mersennus says is but little used, and is held in great contempt in France, as indeed it has been till very lately in this country. The true English appellation for it is the Cittern, notwithstanding it is by ignorant people called the Guitar : the practice on it being very easy, it was formerly the common recreation and amusement of women and their visitors in houses of lewd resort. Many are the allusions to this instrument in the works of our old dramatic poets : whence it appears that the Cittern was formerly the symbol of a woman that lived by prostitution. Another proof of the low estimation in which it was formerly held in England is that it was the common amusement of waiting customers in barbers' shops.‡

Prop. XXIV. exhibits the form and use of an instrument resembling the Cittern in the body, but having a neck so long as to make the distance between the nut and the bridge six feet. The general

† According to the well-known maxim 'Additio probat minoritatem,' the appellation Cithara Hispanica, which we render the Spanish Guitar, supposes a guitar of some other country, but the case is not so, although a certain instrument now in fashion, and which is no other than the Cistrum or Cisteron of Mersennus, or the old cittern, is ignorantly termed a guitar. This confusion of terms is to be thus accounted for: almost every instrument of the lute-kind is in Latin called Cithara, and by the Italians Cetera, and sometimes Chittarra; the Spaniards pronounce this latter word Guitarra, and sometimes, as in Cerone, Quitarra. So that upon the whole the simple appellative, Guitar, is a sufficient designation of the Cithara Hispanica or Spanish lute, which differs greatly from that of the French and Italians in its form, as may be seen by comparing their respective diagrams above exhibited.

‡ This fact is alluded to in Jonson's Comedy of the Alchemist, and also in his Silent Woman, in which Morose finding that instead of a mute wife he has got one that can talk, cries out of Cutberd, who had recommended her to him, 'That cursed barber! I have married his Cittern that is common to all men.' It seems that formerly a barber's shop, instead of a newspaper to amuse those that waited for their turn, was furnished with a musical instrument, which was seldom any other than the Cittern, as being the most easy to play on of any, and therefore might be truly said to be common to all men : and when this is known, the allusion of the poet appears to be very just and natural; as to the fact itself, it is ascertained in one of those many little books written by Crouch, the bookseller in the Poultry, and published with the initial letters R. B. for Robert Burton, entitled Winter Evening Entertainments, 12mo. 1687, it consists of ten pleasant relations, and fifty riddles in verse, each of which has a wooden cut before it; Numb. XLIV. of these riddles is explained a barber; the cut prefixed to it represents his shop with one person under his hands, and another sitting by and playing on a cittern. *This instrument grew into disuse about the beginning of this century.* Dr. King, taking occasion to mention the barbers of his time, says that turning themselves to periwig making they had forgot their cittern and their music. Works of Dr. William King, Vol. 2, page 79.

name of it is the Colachon; but it is also called the Bichordon or Trichordon, accordingly as it is strung; the use of it is to play songs in two or three parts, which Mersennus says may be performed on it with all the varieties of fugues, Syncopes, and other ornaments of figurate music. He adds that the table or belly of this instrument may be of parchment or copper, or even of glass.

The several instruments above enumerated are of that genus which is characterized by the appellation of the Cithara, or as it is usually rendered, the Lute. Another class is included in the general denomination of the Barbiton, and of these there appear to be two species, the Violin and the Viol; these Mersennus particularly characterizes, but first he describes an instrument of a singular form, and a very diminutive size, which, for want of a better name, he calls the Lesser Barbiton;* this is a small violin invented for the use of the dancing-masters of France, of such a form and dimension, as to be capable of being carried in a case or sheath in the pocket. There are two forms of this instrument by him thus exhibited :—

He then describes the violin properly so called; that is to say, the common treble violin, and from thence proceeds to the greater, called by the Italians the Violone, and of late years the Violoncello. He gives also a representation of the violin: to each of these instruments he assigns a tuning by fifths, but the ambit of the former differs from that of the modern Violoncello.

Mersennus speaks also of the tenor and contratenor violin, which he says differ only in magnitude from the treble violin. He adds that these instruments are severally strung with four chords, each acuter than the other in the progression upwards by a diapente.

Mersennus having treated thus largely of the violin species, and shewn what is to be understood by a concert of violins,† he proceeds to a description

of the viol species; and first he treats of the greater viol, which he says has six chords; the form of this instrument is thus represented by him :—

Speaking of that little pillar of wood placed under the belly of the viol and other instruments, which we call the sound-post, Mersennus makes it a question, why it is placed under the slenderest, rather than the thickest chord, which seems most to require a support, and recommends to the enquiry of ingenious persons the reason of this practice.‡

In Prop. xxii. Mersennus treats of an instrument which he calls the new, or rather the ancient lyre, but whether properly or not, almost any one is able to judge.

It is an instrument of a very singular kind as may be seen by the following representation of it :—

'pleasanter. If you have a mind to hear the upper part only, what can
'be more elegant than the playing of Constantinus? what more vehement
'than the enthusiasm of Bocanus? what more subtile and delicate than
'the little percussions or touches of Laxarinus and Foucardus? If the
'bass of Legerus be joined to the acute sounds of Constantinus, all the
'harmonical numbers will be compleated.'

At present we have no such instruments in use as the contratenor violin. It seems that soon after this arrangement it was found unnecessary, inasmuch as the part proper to it might with ease be performed on the violin, an instrument of a more sprightly sound than any other of the same species; and it may accordingly be observed, that in concertos, overtures, and other instrumental compositions of many parts, the second violin is in truth the countertenor part.

Mersennus has taken no notice of the instrument now used in concerts, called by the Italians and French the Violone, and by us in England the double bass; it seems that this appellation was formerly given to that instrument which we now call the Violoncello; as a proof whereof it may be remarked, that in the earlier editions of Corelli's Sonatas, particularly that of Opera III. printed at Bologna in 1690, that bass part which is not for the organ is entitled Violone, whereas in the latter, printed at Amsterdam by Estienne Roger, the same part is entitled Violoncello; hence it appears that the name Violone being transferred to the greatest bass of modern invention, there resulted a necessity of a new denomination for the ancient bass-violin, and none was thought so proper as that of Violoncello, which is clearly a diminutive of the former.

The Violone or double bass is by Brossard and others said to be double in its dimensions to the Violoncello, and consequently that its ambit is precisely an octave more grave; but this depends upon the number of strings, and the manner of tuning them, some performers using four strings, and others only three, and in the tuning of these there is a difference among them.

The true use of the Violone is to sustain the harmony, and in this application of it has a noble effect; divided basses are improper for it, the strings not answering immediately to the percussion of the bow; these can only be executed with a good effect on the Violoncello, the sounds whereof are more articulate than distinct.

It is much to be doubted whether the countertenor violin ever came into England; Anthony Wood, in his Life, speaking of the band of Chas. II. makes no mention of the contratenor violin, the following is his description of it: 'Before the restoration of K. Ch. 2, and especially 'after, violins began to be out of fashion, and only violins used, as treble 'violin, tenor and bass violin; and the king, according to the French 'mode, would have 24 violins playing before him while he was at meals, 'as being more airie and brisk than viols.'

* In England this instrument is called a Kit, it is now made in the form of a violin; its length, measuring from the extremities, is about sixteen inches, and that of the bow about seventeen. Small as it is, its powers are co-extensive with those of the violin. Mr. Francis Pemberton, a dancing-master of London, lately deceased, was so excellent a master of the Kit, that he was able to play solos on it, exhibiting in his performance all the graces and elegancies of the violin, which is the more to be wondered at as he was a very corpulent man.

† We have here a perfect designation of a concert of violins, as contradistinguished from one of viols, usually called a chest of viols, by means whereof we are enabled to form an idea of that band of twenty-four violins established by Lewis XIV. which as Mons. Perrault and others assert, was the most famous of any in Europe.

The common opinion of this band is, that it consisted of four and twenty treble violins, thus ridiculously alluded to by Durfey in one of his songs,

'Four and twenty fiddlers all in a row.'

But the fact is that it was composed of Bass, Tenor, Contratenor, and Treble instruments, all of which were included under the general denomination of violins. Mersennus gives a very particular description of Lewis's band in the following passage :—' Whoever hears the 24 fidicinists 'of the king with six Barbitons to each part, namely, the bass, tenor, 'contratenor, and treble, perform all kinds of Cantilenas and tunes for 'dancing, must readily confess that there can be nothing sweeter and

‡ The figure here given represents the true form of the viol, but great confusion arises from the want of names whereby to describe the instruments of which we are now speaking; Mersennus could find no term to signify the Viol but the Barbiton and the Lyre; the former of these names he gives also to all the instruments included in the violin species; nay the Italians and others call a tenor violin Viola, and as to the Lyre, Galilei uses it for the lute, and by others of the Italian writers it is made to signify most other instruments of that class, but the true distinction between the viol and the violin species, arises from the difference of their form, and the number of their strings respectively, the viol, meaning that for concerts, of what size soever it be, having six strings, and the violin, whether it be the treble, the tenor, or the bass, having uniformly four.

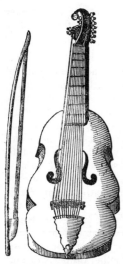

It is mounted with fifteen chords, sustained by a bridge which forms a segment of a very large circle, and of consequence is nearly flat: it is capable of performing a concentus of four, and even five parts. It seems that Mons. Bailif, a French musician, used this instrument in accompaniment to his voice. Mersennus calls him the French Orpheus.

The subject matter of Prop. xxxiii. is so very curious, that it will not admit of an abridgment. The proposition is entitled 'Explicare quamobrem 'nervus quilibet percussus 'plures simul sonos edat, qui 'faciunt inter se Diapason, Disdiapason, duodecimam, 'decimamseptimam,' &c. and is to this effect :—

'This proposition opens a wonderful phenomenon, 'and throws a light on the 8, 11, 12, 13, and other 'problems of Aristotle contained in his nineteenth 'section, in which he demands "Why do the graver "sounds include the acuter." And here it may be 'noted that Aristotle seems to have been ignorant 'that every chord produces five or more different 'sounds at the same instant, the strongest of which 'is called the natural sound of the chord, and alone 'is accustomed to be taken notice of, for the others 'are so feeble, that they are only perceptible by 'delicate ears. Some things therefore are here to be 'discussed, when some most certain and true experi'ments have been premised, the first of which is, 'that a chord of brass or metal produces as many 'sounds precisely as one made of gut; the second 'is that these several different sounds are more easily 'perceived in the thicker than the slenderer chords 'of instruments, for this reason, that the former 'are more acute; the third experiment teaches that 'not only the Diapason and Disdiapason, the latter 'of which is more clearly and distinctly perceived 'than the octave, but also the twelfth and greater 'seventeenth are always heard; and over and above 'these I have perceived the greater twenty-third, 'about the end of the natural sound.'* The fourth ex-

'periment convinces us that all these sounds are not 'perceived by some persons, although they imagine 'they have delicate and learned ears. The fifth 'shews that the sounds which make the twelfth and 'the seventeenth are more easily distinguished than 'the others, and that we very often imagine we 'perceive the diapente and the greater tenth, mis'taking for them their replicates, that is to say, the 'twelfth and seventeenth. Lastly, the sixth experi'ment teaches us that no chord produces a sound 'graver than its primary or natural sound.

'These things being premised, we are now to 'investigate the cause why the same chord should 'produce the sounds above-mentioned, and expressed 'in these lesser numbers, 1, 2, 3, 4, 5, for the dia'pason is as 1 to 2, the twelfth as 1 to 3, the Dis'diapason as 1 to 4, and the greater seventeenth as '1 to 5. These phenomena cannot be referred to 'any other causes than the different motions of the 'air; but it is very difficult to explain by what 'means the same chord or air is moved at the same 'time once, twice, thrice, four, and five times; for 'as it is struck but once, it is impossible that it can 'be moved twice or three times, &c. unless we allow 'that there is some motion of the chord or the air, 'greater than the rest, and of an equal tenor from 'the beginning to the end, while other intermediate

* The Diapason, Disdiapason, twelfth, greater seventeenth, and greater twenty-third here mentioned, are with respect to the octave or diapason, subordinate or secondary sounds: the four first arise from the respective vibrations of certain parts, ex. gr. a half, a fourth, a third, and a fifth of the chord, coinciding with the vibrations of the same chord in an harmonical ratio of 1 to 9. Mersennus at the close of the above proposition leaves it as a desideratum. Of these partial vibrations of a chord mention is made in some of the papers communicated to the Royal Society by Dr. Wallis and others, published in the Philosophical Transactions [Vide. page 407 in not. n et infra .] But Mons. Sauveur, of the Academy of Sciences at Paris, has pursued this discovery by a distinction of his own invention between harmonical and inharmonical sounds. According to him, harmonical sounds are such as make a determinate number of vibrations in the time that some other fundamental sound to which they are referred makes one vibration; and these are produced by the parts of chords which vibrate a certain number of times, while the whole chord vibrates once. By this circumstance the harmonical sounds are distinguished from the thirds major and minor, and fifth, where the relations of the vibrations are respectively 4 to 5, 5 to 6, 2 to 3. And whereas the ratios of sounds had before the time of Mons. Sauveur, been contemplated in the following series of numbers, 1 to 2, 2 to 3, 3 to 4, 4 to 5, measuring respectively the intervals of an octave, a fifth, a fourth, and a third major, he took the numbers in their natural order, 1, 2, 3, 4, 5, 6, &c. and found that as 1 to 2 is the ratio of the octave, 1 to 3 a twelfth, 1 to 4 a fifteenth or double octave, 1 to 5 a seven-

teenth major, 1 to 6 a nineteenth, meaning by the first number of these several ratios the whole of the chord, and by the second the parts thereof corresponding with such number; so while a general vibration of the whole chord was going on, other vibrations of the several parts thereof denoted by the above numbers exceeding the unit were making that produced subordinate sounds in consonance with their fundamental, and these he called harmonical sounds. Vide. Chamber's Dict. Voce Harmonical Sounds, and see the original tract of M. Sauveur in the History of the Academy of Sciences for the year 1701.

The parts of a bell, besides the general sound which is excited by the stroke of the clapper, do in like manner in certain proportions at the same time yield subordinate and acuter sounds in consonance therewith, which a nice ear will clearly distinguish. The same may be observed of that useful and most accurate instrument, the tuning fork as now constructed, the slightest percussion of which will bring out a variety of subordinate harmonical sounds; though here it must be remarked that the secondary sounds of bells are very frequently dissonant, as may be observed in the bell of almost any house clock; and in a peal of hand-bells tuned in respect of their primary sounds, with the utmost nicety, it has been discovered that being heard at such a distance as to render their secondary sounds predominant, viz., at that of fifty yards or thereabouts, these latter have been most offensively discordant. [Vide infra .] Of these subordinate or secondary sounds, more especially such as are produced from a chord or the tuning fork, the least acute which we hear is an octave with the whole sound, the next that follows is a twelfth, the next a seventeenth, till they grow too acute for the ear to perceive them. As to the greater twenty-third, it is an interval compounded of the Trisdiapason and tone, or in other words, the Triplicate of the second, and being therefore a Dissonant, is not to be accounted for upon the principles here laid down; and it may be observed that as it was the last sound of the five mentioned by him, that Mersennus was able to hear, it might possibly be the necessary result of languid and expiring vibrations, resembling as himself hints the departing smoke of a candle. Upon all which it is remarked that upon the percussion of a chord, no subordinate or secondary sound is produced that makes a fifth, or a third major or minor, with the fundamental or primary sound; nor in short, any that does not coincide in respect of its vibrations with every single vibration of the whole chord or sonorous body whatever it be.

The doctrine of subordinate sounds, so far as they are produced by the vibration of a chord, is by this discrimination clearly investigated, and we learn by it how far nature unassisted by art will go in the production of consonances; but on what principle those are founded that arise from the percussion of a bell, or the stroke of a tuning fork, on which the proportions of the subvibrating parts are unaiscoverable, and by consequence their proportions immensurable, remains yet to be discovered.

Mons. Sauveur asserts that the structure of the organ, by which he must be supposed to mean the combination of pipes therein, depends upon this so long-unknown principle; but we should rather say it is resolvable into it; in like manner as we must suppose the wedge of the pulley and the lever, which were in use before the principles on which they severally act were investigated; for in the construction of the organ, meaning thereby the Diapason or full concentus or symphony of the greater or lesser pipes, it was sufficient for the fabricators of that instrument to know, that they could not long be ignorant of it that the acuter sounds in the harmonical ratios above enumerated would coincide with, and also did, the fundamental or graver; and it remained for philosophers and speculative musicians to discover the physical causes of this wonderful coincidence.

'motions are made more frequent, almost in the same
'manner as, according to the Copernican system, the
'earth makes three hundred and sixty-five daily
'revolutions, while it makes only one round the sun.

'But it appears from experience that a chord of
'an hundred foot long, composed of any materials
'whatsoever, has not the two above-mentioned mo-
'tions, but only one, whereby it makes its courses
'backwards and forwards: wherefore the cause of
'this phenomenon is to be sought from other motions,
'unless it is to be imputed to the different surfaces
'of the chords, the upper one whereof might produce
'a graver, and the others that follow, as far as the
'centre of the chord, acuter sounds; but as these
'surfaces constitute only one continued homogeneous
'body, as appears from chords made of pure gold or
'silver, and are therefore moved by the same action
'and vibrated backwards and forwards by the same
'number of courses, they cannot produce the different
'sounds, wherefore I imagine that the air which is
'first affected by the percussion of the chord, vibrates
'quicker than the chord itself, by its natural tension
'and aptitude for returning, and therefore produces
'an acuter sound, or rather that the same air being
'driven by the chord to the right side for example,
'returns at first with the same celerity, but is again
'repelled, and is agitated with a double velocity, and
'thus produces a Diapason with the primary and
'principal sound of the chord, which being still more
'agitated by the different returns of the chord, and
'returning more frequently itself, acquires a triple,
'quadruple, and quintuple celerity, and so generates
'the twelfth, fifteenth, and greater seventeenth. These
'first consonances must occur, nor can the air receive
'any other motions, as it should seem, before it is
'affected by them. But by what means it makes the
'twenty-third, or 1 to 9, let them who have leisure
'enquire, and I advise them to lend a most attentive
'ear to the chords, that they may be able to catch or
'perceive both the above sounds, and any others that
'may be produced.

'To this phenomenon of chords may be referred
'the different sounds produced at the same time by
'the greater bells, as is well known by every one;
'and the leaps and intervals of the trumpet and litui,
'which imitate the sounds of the above-mentioned
'chords. Add to these the various sounds of glass
'vessels when their edges are pressed or rubbed by
'the finger, also the different figures and periods
'of smoke ascending from the flame of a candle;
'and the pipes of organs which make two sounds at
'one time.'

Prop. XXXVI. contains a description of the instrument called by the author, Vielle, and by Kircher
Lyra Mendicorum; a figure of this instrument is to
be seen in the Musurgia of Ottomarus Luscinius, and
in a preceding part of this work. Mersennus says
that the construction of it is little understood, by
reason that it is only used by blind men and other
beggars about the streets. He makes it to consist of
four chords, that is to say, two which pass along the
belly of the instrument, and are tuned in unison to
each other, but are an octave lower than the former

two. All the four strings are acted upon by a wheel
rubbed with powder of rosin, which does the office of
a bow. The middle strings are affected by certain
keys which stop them at different lengths, and produce
the tones while the others perform the part of a mono-
phonous bass, resembling the drone of a bagpipe.
Mersennus says that there were some in his time
who played so well on this contemptible instrument,
that they could make their hearers laugh, or dance,
or weep.

Mersennus next treats, viz. in Prop. xxxvii. of that
surprising instrument, the Trumpet Marine, here
delineated, con-
cerning which he
thus delivers his
sentiments:—

'The instrument commonly called the Marine
'Trumpet, either because it was invented by seamen,
'or because they make use of it instead of a trumpet,
'consists of three boards so joined and glued
'together, that they are broad at the lower end, and
'narrow towards the neck, so that it resembles a tri-
'lateral pyramid with a part cut off; a neck with
'a head is added to this pyramid in order to contain
'the peg that commands the chord; near the greater
'end of the instrument is a stay, to which the chord
'is fastened by a knot under the belly, and detains it.
'To the left of the stay is the movable bridge which
'bears up the chord, and determines with the little
'bridge or nut at the smaller end, the harmonical
'length of the chord. The bow is necessary to strike
'the chord, and consists of silk, and a stick, as has
'been said in the discourse on the Barbitons.

'The most remarkable thing that occurs in this
'instrument is that little stud of ivory, bone, or other
'matter which is fastened into the left foot of the
'bridge, under which a square little piece of glass is
'placed, and fastened to the belly, that when it is
'agitated by the different strokes of the stud it may
'communicate a tremor to the sounds of the chord,
'and that by this means this instrument may imitate
'the military trumpet, for when the chord is rubbed
'by the bow, the left leg beats against the glass plate
'with repeated strokes, and impresses a peculiar
'quality or motion into the sounds of the chord, com-
'posed of the triple motion, namely of the stud, the
'chord, and the bow.

'The manner of using the trumpet marine is this,
'its head is turned towards the breast of the per-
'former, and leans thereon while he passes the bow
'across the chord, and lightly touches with the
'thumb or the fore-finger those parts of the chord
'which are marked by the divisions; but the bow
'is to be drawn over the chord between the thumb
'which the chord is touched by, and the little bridge,
'not but that it might be drawn at any other place,
'but at that above directed it strikes the chord a
'great deal more easily and commodiously.

'Of the six divisions marked on the neck of the
'instrument, the first makes a fifth with the open
'chord, the second an octave, and so on for the rest,
'corresponding with the intervals of the military
'trumpet.'

Mersennus says that Glareanus has taken notice of the trumpet marine, and that he distinguishes it by the appellation of the Citharisticum; to which we may add, that there are many curious particulars both in the Dodecachordon of Glareanus, and the Harmonics of Mersennus, as also in the Harmonie Universelle of the latter, concerning this instrument.*

Prop. XXXIX. treats of the Spinnet, or, as Mersennus terms it, the Clavicymbalum; the figure which he has given of it resembles exactly the old English virginal, in shape a parallelogram, its width being to its depth in nearly the proportion of two to one; from whence it may be inferred that the triangular spinnet now in use is somewhat less ancient than the time of Mersennus. He makes it to consist of thirteen chords and keys, including twelve intervals; that being the number contained in an octave, divided according to the modern system into seven tones and five semitones. He says that the tuning of this instrument is by many persons held a great secret, nevertheless he reveals it by explaining

* In the Philosophical Transactions for 1692, is a discourse on the trumpet and trumpet marine by the Hon. Francis Roberts, and a copious extract from it in the Abridgment of Lowthorp and Jones, vol. I. pag. 607, wherein are many curious particulars concerning this instrument. As an introduction to his discourse the author observes of the military or common trumpet, that its ordinary compass is from double C FA UT to c SOL FA in alt, but that there are only some notes in that series which it will give; and farther that the 7th, 11th, 13th, and 14th notes in that progression, viz., B b, f, aa, and bb are out of tune.

To account for these defects he adverts to the trumpet marine, which though very unlike the common trumpet, has a wonderful agreement with it; as resembling it most exactly in sound, yielding the self same notes, and having the same defects.

He refers to the known experiment of two unison strings, and observes upon it that not only the unison will answer to the touch of a correspondent string, but also the 8th and 12th in this manner:—

If an unison be struck, it makes one entire vibration in the whole string, and the motion is most sensibly in the midst, for there the vibrations take the greatest scope.

If an 8th is struck it makes two vibrations, the point in the midst being in a manner quiescent, and the most sensible motion the middle of the two subdivisions.

If a 12th be struck it makes three vibrations, and the greatest motion at the midst of the three subdivisions, the points that divide the string into three equal parts being nearly at rest, so that in short the experiment holds when any note is struck which is an unison to half the string, and a 12th to the third part of it.

In this case (the vibrations of the equal parts of a string being synchronous) there is no contrariety in the motion to hinder each other, whereas it is otherwise if a note is unison to a part of a string that does not divide it equally, for then the vibrations of the remainder not uniting with those of the other parts, immediately make confusion in the whole.

Now, adds he, in the Trumpet Marine you do not stop close as in other instruments, but touch the string gently with your thumb, whereby there is a mutual concurrence of the upper and lower part of the string to produce the sound. This is sufficiently evident from this, that if any thing touches the string below the stop, the sound will be as effectually spoiled as if it were laid upon that part which is immediately struck with the bow. From hence therefore we may collect that the Trumpet Marine yields no musical sound but when the stop makes the upper part of the string an aliquot of the remainder, and consequently of the whole, otherwise, as we just now remarked, the vibrations of the parts will stop one another, and make a sound suitable to their motion altogether confused.

The author then demonstrates with great clearness that these aliquot parts are the very stops which produce the trumpet notes, and that the notes which the trumpet will not hit are dissonant, merely because they do not correspond with a division of the monochord into aliquot parts.

Having before premised that the trumpet and trumpet marine labour each under the same defects as the other, he applies this reasoning to the trumpet in these words:—

'Where the notes are produced only by the different force of the breath, 'it is reasonable to imagine that the strongest blast raises the sound by 'breaking the air within the tube, into the shortest vibrations, but that 'no musical sound will rise unless they are suited to some aliquot part, 'and so by reduplication exactly measure out the whole length of the 'instrument; for otherwise a remainder will cause the inconvenience 'before-mentioned to arise from conflicting vibrations; to which if we 'add that a pipe being shortened according to the proportions we even 'now discoursed of in a string, raises the sound in the same degrees, 'it renders the case of the trumpet just the same with the monochord.'

To these remarks of Mr. Roberts another not less curious and difficult to account for, may be added, viz., that the chord of the trumpet marine is precisely equal in length to the trumpet, supposing it to be one continued uninflected tube.

the method of tuning the spinnet, agreeable to the practice of the present times.

From the spinnet he proceeds in Prop. XL. to shew the construction of the Organocymbalum, in French called the Clavecin, and in English the harpsichord, an instrument too well known at this day to need a description. But it seems that in the time of Mersennus there were two kinds of harpsichord, the one of the French above spoken of, and the other of the Italians, called by him the Manichordium. Of this he treats at large in Prop. XLII.

In this instrument the diapason is said by the author to be divided according to the three genera; it resembles in shape the spinnet described by Mersennus, but is considerably larger, having fifty keys. He adds that the use of it is for the private practice of those who choose not to be heard; but he gives no reason for the difference between this and other instruments of the like kind in the division of the diapason.

He next proceeds to describe an instrument which he calls the Clavicytherium or harp with keys; this is no other than the upright harpsichord, which of late has been introduced into practice, and made to pass with the ignorant for a new invention.

Prop. XLIII. contains an explanation of the figure, parts, harmony, and use of the Chinor, Cinyra, or harp, which he exhibits in the form of a harp of our days. His description of this instrument is brief, and rather obscure, but in the Harmonie Universelle he is more particular, and delivers his sentiments of it to this effect: 'Many difficulties 'have been started relating to this instrument, among 'others whether the harp of David resembled this of 'ours; but as there are no vestiges of antiquity re-'maining, whereby we can conclude any thing about 'it, it must suffice to describe our own,' and this he does by a figure of it.

The verbal description which follows the figure of the instrument imports that this harp is triple strung, and that the chords are brass wire. The first row, and also the third, consist of twenty-nine chords, and are tuned in unison; the intermediate row consists of semitones, and contains a less number. In the Harmonie Universelle, which contains a much fuller description of the harp than the book now quoting, Mersennus speaks of a French musician, Mons. Flesle, who in his time touched the harp to such perfection, that many preferred it to the lute, over which he says it has this advantage, that all its chords are touched open, and besides, its accordature or tuning comes nearer to truth than that of the lute; and as to the imperfection complained of, that the vibrations of the chords sometimes continue so long as to create dissonance; he observes that a skilful performer may with his fingers stop the vibration of the chords at pleasure.

Prop. XLIV. contains an explanation of the figure, parts, concentus, and use of the Psalterium, together with a proposal of a mundane instrument. The instrument first above spoken of, as exhibited by Mersennus, is in truth no other than that common instrument known by the name of the Dulcimer.

The little rod or plectrum with which it is struck, is by him said to be made of the wood of the plumb, the pear, or the service-tree. He adds that two of these may be used at a time for the playing of Duos and Cantilenas in consonance.

The mundane instrument above-mentioned is more largely spoken of in the Harmonie Universelle; the figure of it is apparently taken from the Utriusque Cosmi Historia of Dr. Robert Fludd, a book of which a large account will hereafter be given. The conceit of a mundane instrument is certainly one of the wildest that madness ever formed; Mersennus says Γ answers to the earth, A to the water, ♮ to the air, and so on for the rest till G, which answers to the sun, supposed to be the centre of our system, and from thence in a progression of tones and semitones upwards to the heavens.

## CHAP. CXVI.

THE book of Mersennus entitled De Instrumentis Harmonicis is subdivided into two, the first whereof treats of nervaceous or stringed, and the second of pneumatic or wind instruments. In preface to this latter the author waives the consideration of the nature of wind, and refers to the Historia Ventorum of our countryman Lord Verulam.

In Prop. I. he describes an instrument resembling the Syringa of Pan, formed of reeds in different length conjoined with wax. The instrument exhibited is of this form, and it consists of twelve tubes of tin, the lesser being subtriple in its ratio to the greater. This instrument he says is used by 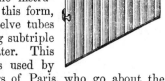 the braziers or tinkers of Paris, who go about the streets to mend kettles, and advertise the people of their approach by the sound of it.

He next speaks of the lesser Tibiæ, and those of few holes, here delineated, which he thus describes: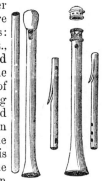
' The first of these instruments, viz.,
' that on the left hand is perforated
' both above and below, and is made
' of the rind or bark of a tree, or of
' a branch of the elder-tree, having
' the pith taken out; or of the wood
' of the box-tree excavated, or even
' of iron, or any other matter. The
' second has three apertures, that is
' to say, one at the top, where the
' breath is blown into it, another in
' front, below it, where the sound is made, and a third
' at the bottom where the wind goes out. The third
' and fifth figures represent pipes of reed or wheat-
' straw, on which the shepherds play, wherefore the
' instrument is called "tenuis avena," "calamus agres-
" tis," and "stipula," and those who play on the barley-
' straw are called ραπαταυλαι because ραπατη is the
' same as καλαμις, as Salmasius on Solinus observes.
' But whether these pipes may be called Gingrinæ,
' a kind of short pipes of goose bones, that yield

' a small doleful sound, and those who play on them
' Gingritores; and whether they are said, jugere, to
' cry like a kite, I leave to the judgment of the
' critics, who also dispute whether the right and the
' left-hand pipes had the same number of holes, such
' as those we give in the sixth proposition, or whether
' they were unequal in the number of their holes.
' A very late translator of Vopiscus, concludes that
' they were unequal, and attributes more holes to the
' left tibia than to the right, that the former might
' sound more acute; and that the left or Tyrian, sung
' after, or followed, the right or Lydian in singing;
' and also that the Adelphi, Andria, and Heauton-
' timorumenos of Terence were acted with these, and
' that in such manner as never to sing together.
' Moreover you may justly call the pipe which comes
' next in Prop. II. with three holes, the right-hand
' pipe, and the flajolet the left, if any person has
' a mind to sing the Cantus of Terence's comedies
' with these pipes; I shall however add that the left-
' hand pipe, though not equal to it in the number of
' holes, was shorter than the right-hand one, in order
' to sound more acute; pipes of this kind are usually
' made after two manners, namely, with a little tongue
' placed in the middle of the reed, which appears in
' the third figure, so that while the mouth com-
' prehends the little tongue, the left hand stops and
' opens with any finger the upper hole, as the right
' hand does the lower; or the tongue is cut in the
' upper part, as in the fifth figure, and then when the
' mouth blows therein the fingers of the right hand
' open and shut the holes to form the different sounds.
' There now remains the fourth pipe, which is
' commonly called the Eunuch. This sings rather by
' speaking than by blowing, for it returns a sound or
' voice of the same acumen with which it is prolated,
' and which is reflected with a bombus or humming
' sound like a drone, from a very thin or fine sheep-
' skin or onion-peel, and acquires a new grace. This
' slender skin covers the orifice at the upper extremity,
' and like the head of a drum is stretched or strained
' on the pipe, and tied round with a thread, and the
' cap or cover, which is represented over it, and
' which has several holes in it, is put over it, but the
' sound comes freely out of the hole at the bottom.
' There are some persons who recite songs of four or
' more parts with these pipes. We must not omit
' that pipes of this kind may be made of the bones
' of mules or other animals well cleansed, or of those
' of birds, nay even of the middle stalk of an onion,
' of glass, wax, &c. and of these materials some have
' constructed organ-pipes.'

Prop. II. contains a description of the small flute, or pipe with three holes, with which the tabor or little drum is used in accompaniment. Its form is here delineated.

Upon this instrument Mersennus makes some curious observations, as that though it has but three holes, eighteen sounds may be produced from it. He says that the gravest sound is prolated when all the holes are stopped, and that the three next in succession are made by lifting up the fingers, so that the fourth note is the sound of the instrument when open. The other sounds, and which make up the number eighteen, he says are produced by stronger blasts of the breath, accommodated to the different degrees of acuteness required; and this variety of blowing is also observed in the other tibiæ and fistulæ, of which he afterwards speaks. Mersennus says he had heard an Englishman, John Price by name, by the sole variety of blowing on this instrument, ascend to the compass of a ter-diapason or twenty-second. He adds, that there are some things concerning this pipe which are wonderful. First, that after the graver sounds, g, a, b, c, which are produced by the least blast, the blowing a little stronger gives the fifth above: and yet it is impossible to produce from this instrument the three intermediate sounds which occur between the fourth note c, and the fifth gg, viz., d, e, f, that so the first octave might be perfect, as is the second: and this defect he says is peculiar to this instrument only. Secondly, that it leaps from its gravest sound to a diapason when the wind is a little increased, and again to a second diapason if the wind be increased to a greater degree.*

From the pipe with three holes, the associate of the tabor, Mersennus proceeds to what he calls the lesser tibia or Flajolet, here delineated.

Of this instrument Mersennus observes that it need not exceed the length of the little finger. He says that at the aperture near the top the impelled wind goes out, while the rest passes through the open holes and the lower orifice. He observes that the white circles marked on the instrument resembling a cypher, denote the holes on the back part of it, and that the uppermost of these is stopped by the thumb of the left hand, and the lowermost or fifth from the top, by the thumb of the right hand: the black circles represent the holes in the front of the instrument. He adds that in his time one Le Vacher was a celebrated performer on this instrument, and in his French work he intimates that he was also a maker of flajolets.

In the Harm. Univer. Des Instrumens à Vent, Prop. VII. Mersennus speaks more fully of the flajolet. He says that there are two ways of sounding this instrument; and all such as have the lumiere, i. e. the aperture under the tampion; the first is by simple blowing, the other by articulation and the action of the tongue; the former he says imitates the organ, the latter the voice: one is practised by villagers and apprentices, the other by masters.

The ambit of the flajolet, according to the scale exhibited by Mersennus, is two octaves from g SOL RE UT upwards. At the end of his description of the instrument, both in the Latin and French work, he gives a Vaudeville for flajolets in four parts† by

Henry le Jeune, who he says composed the examples for the other wind-instruments described in his book, as knowing very well their power and extent.

Prop. V. treats of the Fistula Dulcis, seu Anglica, called also the flute Abec; ‡ the figure of it is here represented. §

Of the two figures adjacent to the instrument at length, the uppermost shews the aperture for the passage of the wind between the tampion or plug and the beak; the other represents the end of the flute with a view of the beak and the tampion. This instrument has eight holes in the front, and one behind, which is stopped by the thumb; as to the lower or eighth hole, Mersennus remarks that there are two so numbered; for this reason, that the instrument may be played on either by right or left-handed persons, one or other of the two holes being stopped with wax. ‖

Mersennus observes that flutes are so adjusted by their different sizes as to form a concentus of treble, contratenor, tenor, and bass; and that the treble-flute is more acute than the contratenor by a ninth or a diapason, and a tone. The contratenor he makes to be a diapente more acute than the bass, as is also the tenor; for he supposes the contratenor and tenor to be tuned in unison, in the same manner as they are in several other harmonies of instruments.¶

In this, which is his Latin work, Mersennus does not mention the sizes of the several flutes, but in the Harmonie Universelle he is more particular, for he says that the length of the bass-flute is two feet and three quarters, that of the tenor one foot five inches, and the treble only eleven lines.**

From the scale or diagram for the flute exhibited by Mersennus, it appears that the ambit or compass of the instrument is a disdiapason or fifteen notes, and that the lowest note of the system for the treble-flute is C FA UT; but this system, as also those of the tenor and bass-flute, is adapted to what is called by him and other French writers, le petit Jeu; nevertheless there is a flute known by the name of the concert-flute, the lowest note whereof is F; †† indeed

---

* This observation applies to flutes of almost all kinds; in the flute Abec, by stopping the thumb hole, and certain others with the fingers, a sound is produced, but half stopping the thumb-hole without any other variation, gives an octave to such sound. The octaves to most of the sounds of the Fistula Germanica, or German flute, are produced only by a more forcible blast. This uniformity in the operations of nature, though it has never yet been accounted for, serves to shew how greatly the principles of harmony prevail in the material world.

† It is a kind of Gavot, having four bars in the first strain, and eight in the last. The air at the end of the fifth Sonata of the fourth Opera of Corelli answers precisely to this description. For the inventor of this kind of air, and the etymology of the word VAUDEVILLE, see page 569 of this work, in not.

‡ For the reason of this appellation see page 331 of this work, in not.

§ Flutes are mentioned in the works of St. Evremond with great encomiums on the French performers thereon, and in Sir George Etherege's Comedy of the 'Man of Mode.'

‖ From hence it is evident that the practice of making the flute in pieces, that so the lower hole, by turning the piece about, might be accommodated to the hand, was not known when Mersennus wrote.

¶ Particularly the viol and violin, in neither of which species there is any distinction between the tenor and contratenor; perhaps in the concentus of flutes the contratenor part was given to the tenor, in that of the violin it is the second treble.

** This is a mistake of the author which we know not how to correct: a line is but a twelfth part of an inch.

†† The true concert flute is that above described; but there are also others introduced into concerts of violins of a less size, in which case the method was to write the flute part in a key correspondent to its pitch; this practice was introduced by one    Woodcock, a celebrated performer on this instrument, and by an ingenious young man, William Babell, organist of the church of Allhallows Bread-street, London, about the year 1710, both of whom published concertos for this instrument, in which the principal part was for a sixth flute, in which case the lowest note, though nominally F, was in power D, and consequently required a transposition of the flute-part a sixth higher, viz., into the key of D.

But these attempts failed to procure for the flute a reception into concerts of various instruments, for which reason one Thomas Stanesby, a very curious maker of flutes and other instruments of the like kind, about the year 1732, adverting to the scale of Mersennus, in which the lowest note is made to be C FA UT, invented what he called the new

ever since the introduction of the flute into concerts, the lowest note of the flute, of what size soever it be, has been called F, when in truth its pitch is determinable only by its correspondence in respect of acuteness or gravity with one or other of the chords in the Scala Maxima or great system.

Mersennus next proceeds to what he calls Fistulas regias, royal flutes,* or those of the Grand Jeu as he calls it; meaning thereby, as it is supposed, those that are tuned in unison with their respective notes in the Scala Maxima, respective forms whereof are thus represented by him :—

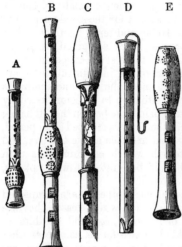

B　C　D　E　The Instruments here delineated are thus described by the author: The flute A, has a key, which by the pressure of the little finger opens the hole which is under it in the box. The fistula B, has three boxes, a greater and two lesser; the first of these is represented apart by C, that all the springs which are any way necessary to open and shut the holes may appear; below that part of the instrument, resembling in its form a barrel, are two keys which command two holes below them, and being pressed with the little finger, open either the one or the other of them. Beneath these are seen springs contained in the two lower boxes of the instrument B, but as they are too far distant from the hands, the little square pieces of brass which appear in the lower part of fig. C, are pressed down by the foot, in order to lift up the springs, as is seen in the tail of the lower spring, which being pushed down, lifts up the plate, and opens a great hole like a window, and nearly equal to the breadth of the fistula.

system, in which by making the flute of such a size as to be a fifth above concert pitch, the lowest note became C SOL FA UT; by this contrivance the necessity of transposing the flute part was taken away; for a flute of this size adjusted to the system above mentioned, became an octave to the violin.

To further this invention of Stanesby, one Lewis Merci, an excellent performer on the flute, a Frenchman by birth, but resident in London, published about the year 1735, six Solos for the flute, three whereof are said to be accommodated to Mr. Stanesby's new system, but the German flute was now become a favorite instrument, and Stanesby's ingenuity failed of its effect.

There were two persons, flute-makers, of the name of Stanesby, the father and the son, the Christian-name of both was Thomas; they were both men of ingenuity, and exquisite workmen; the father dwelt many years in Stonecutter-street leading from Shoe-lane to what is now the Fleet-market, and died about the year 1734; the son had apartments and his workshop over the Temple Exchange, in Fleet-street: he died in 1754, and lies buried in St. Pancras church-yard near London, where is a stone with the following incription to his memory :—'Here lies the body of the 'ingenious Thomas Stanesby, musical wind instrument maker; esteemed 'the most eminent man in his profession of any in Europe. A facetious 'companion, a sincere friend; upright and just in all his dealings; ready to serve and relieve the distressed; strictly adhering to his word, even 'upon the most trivial occasions, and regretted by all who had the hap-'piness and pleasure of his acquaintance. Obiit, 2 Mart. 1754, ætat suæ, 62.'

* In the Harmonie Universelle, Des Instrumens, à Vent, Mersennus says that these flutes were a present from England to one of the kings of France, which perhaps is his reason for calling them royal flutes.

The figures D and E, represent a flute of the larger size in two separate pieces, the springs being concealed by the perforated box, which in fig. C, for the purpose of exhibiting the springs, must be supposed to be slipped up above the forked keys, the station whereof is above the box, as is seen in fig. B. The little tube with a curvature at each end, is inserted into the top of the instrument, and hooks into a hole of a piece of wood, which appears opposite the second hole in fig. B, that the mouth of the flute, which cannot be reached by the mouth of the performer, may be as it were transferred to the end of the tube opposite the second hole, fig. D. This contrivance is necessary only in flutes of the larger size, the bass especially, which are from seven to eight feet long.

After exhibiting a gavot of four parts as an example of a concentus for English flutes, Mersennus remarks that a performer on this instrument, at the same time that he plays an air, may sing a bass to it; but without any articulation of the voice, for that the wind which proceeds from the mouth while singing is sufficient to give sound to the flute, and so a single person may perform a duo on this instrument.

Prop. VI. treats of the German flute, and also of the Helvetian flute or fife, each whereof is represented as having only seven holes, including that aperture which is blown into, from which it should seem that the eighth hole, or that which is now opened by means of a key, is a late improvement of this instrument.

Mersennus gives this figure† as an example of a treble-instrument, which he says ought to be one foot ten inches long, measuring from the bottom of the tampion, signified by the dotted circle, to the lower extremity: those for the other parts he observes should be longer, and also thicker. For example, he says that to produce the most grateful sounds of a concentus, or, as he otherwise expresses it in the Harm. Univer. Des Instrumens à Vent, Prop. IX. page 241, to make the octave or fifteenth, the flute should be twice or four times as long and as thick, as the treble-flute. He adds that flutes of this kind are made of such woods as are easily excavated, and will best polish, as namely, plumb-tree, cherry-tree, and box; and that they may be made of ebony, crystal, and glass, and even of wax.

The system of this instrument is of a large extent, comprehending a disdiapason and diapente, or nineteen sounds; Mersennus has given two scales, the one commencing from G, and the other from D, a fifth higher. The first of these scales it seems was adjusted by one Quiclet, Lat. Kicletus, a French cornetist, and the other by Le Vacher, already mentioned; the method of stopping is apparently different in these two scales in many instances, that is to say, the same sound that is produced by the opening and shutting of certain holes in the diagram of Quiclet, is produced by the opening and shutting of others in that of Le Vacher; and it is to be remarked that in the latter, no one sound of the instrument is directed

† It is to be observed that the instrument from which this figure was taken, was by accident become crooked, nevertheless Mersennus, in the Harm. Univer. Des Instrumens à Vent, pag. 241, says that he chose to give it thus deformed, it being one of the best flutes in the world.

to be produced by unstopping all the holes, from whence it appears that the present practice has its foundation in the example of Quiclet.

It is worthy of remark that neither of these persons had discovered that the diapason of any of the sounds in the first septenary was to be produced by a stronger blast of the breath; as is observed in the English flute, and at this day in the German flute; for to produce the notes in the second septenary, and so upwards, a different method of stopping is required than for their octaves below. This peculiarity, as also the reason why the ambit of this instrument is so much more extensive than that of other flutes, Mersennus recommends as a useful and entertaining subject of enquiry. *

In this proposition Mersennus treats also of the Tibia Helvetica, or Fife; this is in truth an instrument precisely of the same species with the former, but proportionably less in every respect; wherefore says the author, 'it sounds more acutely and vehe-'mently, which it ought to do, least the sound of it 'should be drowned by that of the drum.'

Speaking of a concentus for German flutes, Mersennus says that it can consist of only three parts, for that in a bass German flute the distance of the holes would be so great that no finger could command them, for which reason he says that in a concentus of four parts the bass is either the Sacbut or bassoon.

Propositions VII. and VIII. comprehend a description and explanation of the Hautboy, a treble-instrument, invented by the French, and of the instruments used in concentus with it, namely the Bassoon, Bombardt, Fagot, Courtaut, and Cervelat.

The hautboy described by Mersennus is by him given in two forms, viz., the treble and tenor; the first is the least, and has ten holes, the latter only seven, the lowest whereof is opened by a key.

In his description Mersennus notes a diversity between the holes for the fingers and those for the egress of the wind, therefore of the ten holes in the treble hautboy, nine only are to be reckoned harmonical; and of the eight in the tenor, which number includes that concealed under the box, and that on either side below it, the last serve only for the emission

of the wind, so that the number of harmonical holes is seven. Of the intermediate figures the upper shews the mouth-piece of the tenor called the Pirovette, in which the reed is inserted, in a larger size, the under is the box open and with the key exposed.

He gives also a representation of the bass-hautboy of the form in the margin.

This instrument Mersennus says, is in length five feet, and being so long, is inspired by means of the tube at the top of it, in which a small tongue or reed is inserted for the same purpose as in the treble and tenor hautboy. The number of holes contained in it are eleven: of these seven are seen in the upper part of the instrument, three are contained under the box, and another is placed below it, in a situation to be commanded by that key which appears below the box on the left hand; the three holes within the box are stopped and opened, by three of the keys that are seen above the box, and that below by the fourth, which communicates with that below. The box is perforated in many places, to give egress to the sound.

Prop. VIII. treats of such pipes as are compacted together in a little bundle, for which reason they are called Fagots; and of Bassoons, &c. and exhibits an instrument of this kind in two forms, as also another called by the French the Courtaut. They are severally represented by the following figures:—

These figures are described by Mersennus in the order of their situation, the first has three keys, that on the left hand naked, the two on the right covered with boxes. The brazen tube has a mouth-piece at the extremity, by means whereof the instrument is inflated; the funnel at the top is moveable, and the instrument, though apparently consisting of two tubes, is in effect one, the two being bound together with hoops of brass, and the cavities of each stopped with a peg, as is seen in the under of the two short figures, in which are two white spots denoting two pegs that stop the cavities of the two tubes in such manner that the wind may not escape till it arrives at the upper hole under the funnel, except when either of the holes short of it is unstopped.

The second figure represents an instrument, called, by reason of its shortness, the Courtaut.† This Mersennus says is made of one cylindrical piece of wood, and has eleven holes. The upper of the two short figures shews that the Courtaut has two bores, which

---

* In the Harm. Univer, pag. 243, speaking of the flute, Mersennus says that in Sicily and elsewhere, there are persons who introduce into the mouth, and sound at one time, two and even three flutes of reed or cane; and he adds that if men had laboured as industriously and curiously to perfect instruments of this kind, as they have the organ, they might perhaps have found out some method of playing four or five parts with one and the same breath of the mouth; and if they were to take the pains to pierce them in such manner that the diatonic genus being on one side, as it is in effect, the chromatic and enarmonic might be on two other sides, and they might easily execute all that the Greeks knew with a bit of wood.

† Courtaut, from the adjective Court, short; the French dictionaries explain it a short bassoon. We have a verb, curtail, that signifies to shorten, and a noun, Curtail, interpreted a bass to the hautboy. Phillips.

are concealed under the moveable box into which the tube is inserted; the holes in those tampions called by Mersennus, Tetines, which project from each side of the instrument are for the fingers, and by being doubled are adapted for the use of either right or left-handed persons. The two light holes are on the opposite side of the instrument, the upper one is for the egress of the wind after all the rest are stopped. Mersennus adds that there are some persons, who by excavating a stick or walking-staff, have wrought it into an instrument of this latter kind, thereby making of it a kind of Bourdon, like those used by the pilgrims to the body of St. James at Compostella, for the purpose of recreating themselves on a walk.

For a description of the third instrument we must refer to the Harm. Universelle Des Instrumens à Vent, Prop. XXXII. where it is said to be the same with the first, but without the funnel.

The Bassoon, according to Mersennus, is an instrument exceeding in magnitude all others of the Fagot kind,* to which it is a bass, and therefore it is called the Bassoon; though there is another kind of bassoon which he calls the Cervelat, a word signifying a sausage; this strange instrument is inflated by means of a reed resembling that of a hautboy, but of a larger size. The instrument itself is but five inches in height, and yet is capable of producing a sound equally grave with one of forty inches in length. Within it are eight canals or ducts, answering to the number of holes in the lid or upper surface; these canals it seems have a communication with each other, and yet are affected by the stopping of those on the surface of the cylinder; some of them corresponding to one canal and others to others, in the same manner as if all were reduced into one continued tube.† The white circles denote the holes on the opposite side. The two bassoons are exhibited by Mersennus in this form :—

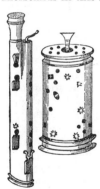

Prop. X. treats of the Tibia Pictavia or Hautbois de Poictou, a very slender hautboy; and also of the Cornamusa or bagpipe, consisting of a Bourdon or drone, a small pipe in which is inserted a wheaten straw, and another pipe called the Calumeau, with seven holes. These two pipes are inserted into the neck of a calf-skin bag, resembling in shape a chemist's retort, on the back whereof is fixed the drone above mentioned, as also a short pipe, through which the whole instrument is inflated by the mouth of the performer. There is no need to insert a figure of this instrument, as it differs but very little from the Scotch bagpipe.

* FAGOTTO is a word used by the Italians to signify a bassoon, but it appears above that it is common to that and all such other instruments as by being compacted together, resemble a fagot.

† Stanesby who was a diligent peruser both of Mersennus and Kircher, and in the making of instruments adhered as closely to the directions of the former as possible, constructed a short bassoon or Cervelat, such a one as is above described, for the late earl of Abercorn, then lord Paisley, and a disciple of Dr. Pepusch, but it did not answer expectation: by reason of its closeness the interior parts imbibed and retained the moisture of the breath the ducts dilated, and broke. In short the whole blew up.

Mersennus adds that in France the country people make use of this instrument on holidays, and in their songs and dances at weddings; nay, that they sing their vespers to it in churches where there are no organs. In the next proposition he describes an instrument of an elegant form and richly decorated, called the Musette, the bagpipe of the French.

In Prop. XIV. he describes the Italian bagpipe, called by him the Surdeline; this is a much larger and more complicated instrument than either of the former, and consists of many pipes and conduits for the conveyance of the wind, with keys for the opening of the holes by the pressure of the fingers: this instrument, as also the Musette, is inflated by means of bellows, which the performer blows with his arm, at the same time that he fingers the pipe.

## CHAP. CXXVII.

MERSENNUS next proceeds to treat of those instruments which serve for ecclesiastical harmony; and first he describes the cornet. He says the use of it is to supply the acuter sounds, which he says in this instrument vibrate after the manner of lightning. The form of the Cornet in its various sizes is thus represented by him :—

The first figure is of a treble cornet, the second shews the lower part of the tenor, the third is the bass, of the serpentine form, and is four or five feet in length. Mersennus says that the sounds of the cornet are vehement, but that those who are skilful, such as Quiclet, the royal cornetist, are able so to soften and modulate them, that nothing can be more sweet. He adds that the true and genuine bass of the cornet is the Serpent. Of this instrument Mersennus gives a particular description in Prop. XVI. And first he exhibits it in this form :—

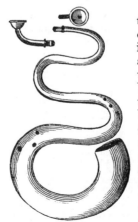

The Serpent he says is thus contorted to render it commodious for carriage, its length being six feet and one inch. As it is usually made of a very brittle wood, namely nut-tree, and its thickness being but one line, or the twelfth of an inch; it is usually covered with leather, and also strengthened with sinews of oxen glewed round the first curve, which is the part by which it is held when transported from one place to another, though these precautions are unnecessary, when, as is frequently the case, this instrument is made of brass or silver.

Mersennus mentions some peculiar properties of this instrument, and, among others, that the sound of it is strong enough to drown twenty robust voices, being animated by the breath of a boy, and yet the sound of it may be attempered to the softness of the sweetest voice. Another peculiarity of this instrument is, that great as the distance between the third and fourth hole appears, yet whether the third hole be open or shut, the difference is but a tone.

After a description of the Hunting-horn, Mersennus proceeds in Prop. XVIII. to explain the figure, parts, system, tones, and use of that noble instrument the trumpet : * he says that the system of this instrument is wonderful, as indeed it appears to be from his description of it, in which he remarks that its first or lowest sound is C FA UT, and its next towards the acute, G SOL RE ; and that it cannot by any means whatever be made to utter the intermediate sounds RE MI FA. Again he says the third sound is C FA UT in the acute, making a diatessaron to the second. He endeavours in a long discourse to assign reasons for the defects in this instrument ; but they are better accounted for in a passage above-cited from a paper in the Philosophical Transactions, written by the Hon. Mr. Roberts, describing the trumpet marine.

But, notwithstanding these defects in the trumpet, Mersennus, in Prop. XX. speaking of a trumpet somewhat different from the former, intimates that they may in a great measure be overcome by practice ; and says that his imagination of the possibility of so doing is strongly encreased by certain letters by him received from Mons. Bourdelot, a most learned physician, resident at Rome, who therein asserts that a famous performer on the trumpet, Hieronymo Fantino by name, had actually produced from his instrument all the tones within its compass without intermission, joining them with those of the organ of St. Peter's church at Rome, Girolamo Frescobaldi, the organist of that church, playing on it at the same time. It is true, Mersennus says, that the trumpeters of the duke de Crequi, the French embassador, objected to these tones as inordinate, and indeed spurious ; but whether they are necessarily to be deemed so or not, or, in other words, whether a regular succession of intervals on the trumpet be repugnant to the order of nature or not, he recommends as a question well worthy of consideration.†

* The trumpet is said by Vincentio Galilei, in his Dialogo della Musica, page 146, to have been invented at Nuremberg ; and there is extant a memoir which shews that trumpets were made to great perfection by an artist in that city, who was also an admired performer on that instrument, it is as follows : ' Hans Meuschel of Nuremberg, for his ' accuracy in making trumpets, as also for his skill in playing on the ' same alone, and in the accompaniment with the voice, was of so great ' renown, that he was frequently sent for to the palaces of princes the ' distance of several hundred miles. Pope Leo X. for whom he had made ' sundry trumpets of silver, sent for him to Rome, and after having been ' delighted with his exquisite performance, dismissed him with a ' munificent reward.'

† The French horn is no other than a wreathed or contorted trumpet : it labours under the same defects as the trumpet itself, but these of late have been so palliated, as to require no particular selection of keys for this instrument. In the beginning of the year 1773, a foreigner named Spandau played in a concert at the Opera-house a concerto, part whereof was in the key of C with the minor third, in the performance whereof all the intervals seemed to be as perfect as in any wind-instrument ; this

Prop. XXI. contains a description of the Tuba tractilis or Sacbut, so called from its being capable of being drawn out ; it is elsewhere said by Mersennus to be the true bass of the military trumpet, and indeed the similarity of sound in both seems to indicate no less.

In the concluding Proposition in this book, viz., that numbered XXII. he describes a Chinese instrument, which he says was sent him by an English gentleman named Hardy ; it consists of a large cane excavated and fixed to the necks of two Cucurbites, hollow and without bottoms ; along the surface of the cane, but a little distant from it, chords are strained by the means of pins ; he adds that the method of performing on this instrument is by iron plectra fastened to the ends of the fingers.

He also describes another instrument, which he says was sent to him from Rome by Giovanni Battista Doni, secretary to Cardinal Barberini. It was constructed of the half of an Indian fruit of the melon kind, cleared from its contents, and afterwards covered on the top with a serpent's skin like a kettle-drum : to this was affixed on the belly of the instrument a handle made of an Indian reed, about twice the length of the body. He describes also other Chinese and Indian instruments, equally barbarous and ill-constructed with those above-mentioned.

In the succeeding book, entitled De Organis, Campanis, Tympanis, ac cæteris Instrumentis κρουομενοις, seu quæ percutiuntur, Mersennus enters into a most minute investigation of the natures and properties of these several instruments, and with respect to the organ in particular, he is so very precise, that were the art of organ-building lost to the world, there is very little doubt but that it might be recovered by means of this book.

It is impossible so to abridge this elaborate and curious tract, as to render it of any use to the generality of readers, it must therefore suffice to say that it contains a description of the several parts of an organ, of the materials and dimensions of the several orders of pipes, with the division of the Abacus or key-board, and the temperament of the instrument.

Speaking of pipes, he distinguishes between such as are stopped at the ends and such as are open ; as also between pipes of wood and metal. Assigning the effects of these different materials in the production of tones of various kinds, he shews also the use of that tongue, which being inserted into the mouth of any pipe, causes it to yield a sound like that of a reed. As to the proportion between the length and circumference of pipes, he says it is a very difficult thing to ascertain, but that experience shews that the quadruple ratio is the cause of the best sound. This proportion is not taken from the diameter of the tube, but from the width of the plate, supposing it to be of metal, of which it is formed, which when reduced to a cylinder, bears a ratio of about 7 to 22 to its circumference. Nevertheless he says that in the first order of pipes the largest is sixteen feet in length ; he adds that he had seen pipes

improvement was effected by putting his right hand into the bottom or bell of the instrument, and attempering the sounds by the application of his fingers to different parts of the tube.

thirty-two feet long, but that it is not in the power of the ear to form a judgment of the sounds which these produce ; and these pipes he resembles to chords of such an enormous length, as make but twelve returns and a half in the space of a second of time.

The difference of pipes in respect of the acumen and gravity of their sounds, depends upon their size, for the longer the pipe is, the slower are its vibrations, and consequently the graver is its sound ; and, what is much to be wondered at, a pipe stopped at the end will produce a sound an octave lower than when open.*

From these particulars respecting the pipes of an organ, their ratios, and the sounds produced by them, Mersennus proceeds to explain the mechanism of this noble instrument by a verbal description of its several parts, and representations thereof in diagrams. Such a minute description as this was necessary in a work that professes no less than to teach the art of making the several instruments of which it treats. In a work such as is the present, the same degree of precision will hardly be required, especially as a very accurate description of the organ is contained in the Facteur d'Orgues, which makes part of the Descriptions des Arts et Métiers, now publishing at Paris ; and a very satisfactory one is extant in the Principles of Mechanics of Mr. W. Emerson, Lond. quarto, 1758 ; nevertheless such a general description of the organ is here given as is consistent with the nature of the present work.

From what has already been said of the organ, it appears that it is to be considered in the several views of a machine and a musical instrument ; the former of these belong to the science of mechanics, and such as are skilled therein may with wonder contemplate this noble effort of ingenuity and industry ; such will be delighted to observe the means by which an instrument of this magnitude is inflated, and those contrivances of ducts and canals, whereby a due proportion of wind is distributed to thousands of pipes of different forms and magnitudes, and by what means is it so communicated as to be in readiness to obey the touch of the finger, they will wonder at the variety of sound produced by pipes formed of the same materials differently constructed, and at the regular and artful arrangement of these for the purpose of occupying the whole of a given space ; and lastly, they will be astonished at the general and universal concent of parts, which renders the whole of this stupendous machine obedient to the will of the performer.

In the consideration of the organ as a musical instrument, it is to be noted that the sounds produced by it are of various kinds, that is to say, some resemble those of the flute or pipe, allowing for the difference of shrillness and mellowness arising from different degrees of magnitude ; others have a sound arising from the tremulous motion of the air re-sembling the human voice, others imitate the clangor of the trumpet ; and those orders of pipes, whether simple or compounded, that in the construction of the instrument are connected together or rendered subservient to one touch of the key, are called stops.

The simple stops are those in which only one pipe answers to the touch of the key, these are the Diapason, † Principal, Tierce, Twelfth, Fifteenth, Flute, Block-Flute, Trumpet, Clarion, Nazard, Vox-humana, Krumhorn, and some others. The compound stops are the Cornet, the Sesquialtera, Mixture, Furniture and sundry others ; and are so called for that in them several pipes are made to speak at the touch of a single key, as in the Sesquialtera three, in the Cornet five, in the Mixture and in the Furniture three, four, or more ; and the full organ or chorus is compounded of all.

Among pipes a distinction occurs, not only with respect to the materials of which they are formed,‡ but also between those in which the wind is cut by the tongue, which is visible in the aperture of pipes of that class, and others where the percussion is against a reed as it is called, though made of brass, inserted in the body of the pipe, and which answers to the Glottis or upper part of the human larynx ; and of pipes thus constructed are composed the stops called the Vox-humana, Regal, Krumhorn, Trumpet, Clarion, Hautboy, and many others. The figures here exhibited represent these Glottides in different views, as also a pipe with the glottis affixed to it.

Fig. A shews the glottis of a trumpet-pipe in front ; the wire is doubled at top, and one end thereof is bent down, and made to form a bar ; the front of the glottis is of thin brass and very elastic ; the bar pressing hard against this plate, being moved upwards or downwards by the wire, opens or closes the aperture, making the sound either flatter or sharper, and this is the method of tuning pipes of this kind. Fig. B is a side view of a glottis with the aperture. In Fig. C the pipe containing the glottis is mounted on a canal or duct, which being placed on the wind-chest, conveys the wind to the aperture, which cutting against the end of the spring, is the immediate cause of that reedy tone which distinguishes pipes of this class.

Of the pipes in an organ those called the Diapasons § are to be considered as the basis or foundation ; above these succeed in regular order other

---

* Mersennus in another place seems to contradict himself, saying that a covered pipe of the same height and breadth with an open one, does not produce a perfect diapason or octave, but one that is diminished by a semitone, and that the same when twice as wide makes an octave increased by a semitone. The organ-builders, in order to avoid this, make the breadth of the covered pipes sesquialtera to that of the open ones, in order to constitute a perfect octave.

† This is an improper term to signify a single order of pipes: the organ-makers are betrayed into the use of it by the consideration that it is the foundation of the harmony of the instrument, the pitch of all the other orders of pipes being accommodated to it. See the true sense of the word Diapason in a subsequent note.

‡ Pipes are made of either wood or metal, some have mouths like flutes, others have reeds ; the smallest pipes are made of tin, or of tin and lead ; the sound of wooden and leaden pipes is soft, short pipes are open and the long ones are stopped : the mouths of large square wooden pipes are stopped with valves of leather. Metal pipes have a little ear on each side of the mouth to tune them, by bending it a little in or out. Whatever note any open pipe sounds, when the mouth is stopped it will sound an octave higher, and a pipe twice its capacity will sound an octave lower.

§ These are of two kinds, the open and the stoped, the latter are of wood, and are so called from their being stopped with a tampion or plug of wood clothed with leather.

simple stops, tuned in harmonical intervals to the diapasons, as the tierce or third, the sesquialtera in the ratio of 3 to 2, or the fifth ; some in the octave, others in the tenth, which is the replicate of the third, the twelfth the replicate of the fifth, the bis-diapason, and so on to the twenty-second. By means of the Registers that command the several orders of pipes, the wind is either admitted into or excluded from them severally ; and we accordingly hear the cornet, the flute, or the trumpet, &c. at the will of the performer. When all the stops are drawn, and the registers open, the wind pervades the whole instrument, and we hear that full and complete harmony, that general and universal concent, which, as being per omnes, is what the ancient writers mean to express by the term Diapason.*

And here it is wonderful to consider that notwithstanding that surd quantity in the musical system, which renders it impossible precisely to adjust the intervals that compose the diatessaron, and which, as Boetius observes, makes the amount of six sesquioctave tones to exceed the diapason, by the commixture of pipes in the manner above-mentioned, all the irregularities hence arising are reconciled, and in effect annihilated.

Of the stops of an organ, the most usual are the Diapasons, the open and stopped, the Tierce, Sesquialtera, Flute, Cornet, Tenth, Twelfth, Fifteenth, Principal, Furniture, Mixture, Trumpet, Clarion, Hautboy, Larigot, Vox-humana, Krumhorn, and Nazard. The foreign organs, especially those of Germany, have many more, particularly that in the abbey church of Weingarten, a town in the Upper Palatinate, which has sixty-six, and contains no fewer than six thousand six hundred and sixty-six pipes.† The organ at Haerlem is said to have sixty stops, many of them but little known to the English workmen, among which are the Bourdon, Gemsen-horn, the Quintadena, Schalmey, Dulciana, Buzain, and Zink.‡

* The following passages in some of our best poets fully justify the above sense of these words :—

And 'twixt them both a quadrate was the base,
Proportion'd equally by seven and nine ;
Nine was the circle set in heaven's place,
All which compacted, made a goodly *Dyapase*.
        FAERIE QUEENE. book II. canto ix. stanza 22.

  *      *      *      *      *      *

Jarr'd against nature's chime, and with harsh din
Broke the fair music that all creatures made
To their great Lord, whose love their motion sway'd
In perfect *Diapason* while they stood
In first obedience and their state of good.
        MILTON, at a solemn music.

Many a sweet rise, many as sweet a fall,
A full-mouth'd *Diapason* swallows all.     CRASHAW.

From harmony from heav'nly harmony
This universal frame began ;
   From harmony to harmony
Through all the compass of the notes it ran,
The *Diapason* closing full in man.
        DRYDEN, Song for St. Cecilia's day, 1687.

† Of this instrument, the most elegant and superb of any in the world, the figure, with a particular description, is given in the Facteur d'Orgues above-mentioned.

‡ The names, as also the etymologies of these appellations are but little understood, and many of them have so departed from their primitive significations, that they may be said to be arbitrary ; to instance in the Tierce and Sesquialtera, the former can mean nothing but a third above the diapasons, and the latter must signify the interval expressed by that term which signifies the whole and its half, viz., the ratio of 3 to 2, or, in the language of musicians, the diapente or fifth ; whereas it has long been the practice to tune the Tierce a seventeenth, *i. e.* a double octave and a third, and to compound the Sesquialtera of the unison third and fifth.

Many of the above names bespeak their signification, others require

The German organs have also keys for the feet, called Pedals, an invention of a German, named Bernhard, about the year 1400. These command certain pipes, which, to encrease the harmony, are tuned below the diapasons.

Among the modern improvements of the organ the most remarkable are the Swell and the Tremblant, the former invented by an English artificer, consists in a number of pipes placed in a remote part of the instrument, and inclosed in a kind of box, which being gradually opened by the pressure of the foot, increases the sound as the wind does the sound of a peal of bells, or suppresses it in like manner by the contrary action. The Tremblant is a contrivance by means of a valve in the Port-vent or passage from the wind-chest, to check the wind, and admit it only by starts ; so that the notes seem to stammer, and the whole instrument to sob, in a manner very offensive to the ear. In the organ at the German chapel in the Savoy, is a Tremblant.

In cathedral churches where there are generally two organs, a large and a small, the latter the French distinguish by the epithet Positif, the reason whereof we are to seek, the term being only proper and belonging to organs fixed to a certain place, and is used in contradistinction to portatif, a term applied to those portable ones, which, like the Regal, may be carried about. We in England call it the choir, and by corruption the choir organ.

The foregoing account, intended to supersede the

to be explained ; the Larigot means a flajolet. The Krumhorn is an imitation of a pipe described by Ottomarus Luscinius, in his Musurgia, lib. I. pag. 20, and also in page 331 of this work, and is often corrupted into Cremona, from the notion that the sound of this stop resembles that of a Cremona violin.

The Nazard, or, as Mersennus terms it, the Nasutas, from its snuffling tone, resembles the singing of those who utter sounds seemingly through the nose.

The word Bourdon signifies the drone of a bagpipe ; the Latin word for it is Bombus, as also Bombyx. Hoffman. Lex. Univer. in Art. Mersennus in his Latin work uses the latter. At Manchester, and also at Coventry, is an organ with this stop.

The Gemsen-horn is a small pipe made of the horn of a quadruped called the Gems, a Shamoy or wild goat. Luscinius describes it, and the stop so named is an imitation of it. See page 331 of this work.

The appellation of Quintadena, corruptly spelt Quintadeena, quasi Quinta ad una, or five to one. This is the ratio of the greater seventeenth, which the word Quintadena was doubtless intended to bespeak, and the diapasons are the acute terms, consequently the pitch of this stop is a double octave and a third major below the diapasons. In the organ of Spitalfields church, made by Bridge, is a stop which he improperly, as it should seem, called a Quintadena, the pitch of it being only a fifth above the diapasons. However it is the only one of the kind in England.

The word Schalmey is derived from Chalumeau, and the latter from Calamus. The Schalmey is described by Luscinius, Musurgia, lib. I. pag. 19, and is a kind of hautboy, very long and slender. See the figure of it in page 331 of this work.

The Dulcian is probably an imitation of an instrument of Moorish original, called the Dulçana, a kind of tenor-hautboy, or, as Brossard describes it, a small bassoon. Mention is made of this instrument by Cerone, lib. XXI. cap. i. and by Cervantes in Don Quixote, 'Entre Moros—se usa un genero de Dulçaynas que paracen nuestras Chirimias.' See page 444 of this work, in not. Or it might signify a stop called the Dulciana, consisting of very long and narrow pipes in unison with the diapason, but that the latter is said to be a very recent invention.

The word Buzain is a corruption of Busaun, or, as it is now spelt, Posaune, which signifies a Sacbut or bass-trumpet, and the stop so named is an imitation of that instrument, which see represented in page 332 of this work.

The Zink, corruptly spelt Cink, is an imitation of the Zinken horn, a very small pipe, or rather a whistle, described and delineated from Luscinius, page 331 of this work. It is made of a small branch of a deer's horn.

The desire of variety in the stops of an organ has been indulged to a ridiculous degree. In the organ of Weingarten are stops intended to imitate the sound of bells, the voice of the cuckow, and the roaring of the sea. Other absurd fancies have intruded into this noble instrument, such as figures that beat time, alluded to by Dr. Donne in these lines :—

' As in some organs, puppets dance above,
' And bellows pant below, which them do move.'   **Satire II.**

necessity of giving at large Mersennus's description, may serve for a general idea of the organ. The early fabricators of this instrument are as little known as celebrated by their works; Zarlino mentions two persons at Rome, Vincenzo Colombi and Vincenzo Colonna, famous organ-makers in his time; but before them, viz., towards the end of the fifteenth century, there flourished Rudolphus Agricola, an admirable artist, who made the organ at Groningen.* Ralph Dallans, Bernard Smith, and Renatus Harris, are names well known in Germany, France, and England, as excellent organ-makers. Of these an account will hereafter be given. In the mean time it may be observed that there is no method of estimating the improvement of the manual arts so satisfactory as that of comparing the works of modern artificers with those of the ancient. The mechanism of an organ at this day proves it to be a wonderful machine, constructed with great ingenuity, and most elegantly wrought. The following figure represents an organ in the time of king Stephen, taken from a manuscript Psalter of Eadwine in the library of Trinity college, Cambridge. Insig. R. 17. 1.

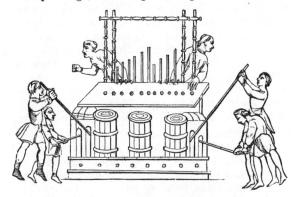

The eighth and last book of the harmonics treats of bells and other instruments of percussion, including therein drums of various kinds, as also Castanets, the Claquebois or regals of wood described page 330 of this work; and descending even to the Cymbalum Orale, or Jew's-harp.

With respect to bells, Mersennus treats of the different metals of which they are formed, of their figure, crassitude, and degrees of ponderosity as they respect each other in any given series. He describes also those peals of bells in the towers of many churches in Germany, called Carillons, on which, by the help of a contrivance of ropes fastened to the clappers, and collected together at the lower ex-

tremities, tunes are played at stated hours of the day. This kind of practice on bells is in effect tolling, and not ringing, an art which seems to be peculiar to England, which for this reason is termed the ringing island.

The ringing of bells is a curious exercise of the invention and memory; and though a recreation chiefly of the lower sort of people, is worthy of notice. The tolling a bell is nothing more than the producing a sound by a stroke of the clapper against the side of the bell, the bell itself being in a pendant position and at rest. In ringing, the bell, by means of a wheel and a rope, is elevated to a perpendicular; in its motion to this situation the clapper strikes forcibly on one side, and in its return downwards, on the other side of the bell, producing at each stroke a sound. The music of bells is altogether melody, but the pleasure arising from it consists in the variety of interchanges and the various succession and general predominance of the consonances in the sound produced.†

† The invention of bells, that is to say, such as are hung in the towers or steeples of Christian churches, is by Polydore Virgil and others, ascribed to Paulinus bishop of Nola, a city of Campania, about the year 400; it is said that the names Nolæ and Campanæ, the one referring to the city, the other to the country, were for that reason given to them. In the time of Clothair II. king of France, and in the year 610, the army of that king was frighted from the siege of the city of Sens by ringing the bells of St. Stephen's church. Vincent, Spec. Hist. lib. XXIII. cap. ix. Bede relates that about the year 670, 'Audivit subito in aëre notum 'Campanæ sonum, quo ad orationes excitari vel convocari solebant.' Hist. Eccl. lib. IV. cap. xxiii. Ingulphus mentions that Turketulus, abbat of Croyland, who died about the year 870, gave a great bell to the church of that abbey, which he named Guthlac, and afterwards six others, viz., two which he called Bartholomew and Bettelin, two called Turketul and Tatwin, and two named Pega and Bega, all which rang together: the same author says, 'Non erat tunc tanta consonantia 'campanarum in totâ Angliâ.' Ingulph. Hist. fol. 889, edit. Franc. Not long after, Kinseus, archbishop of York, built a tower of stone to the church of St. John at Beverly, and placed therein two great bells, and at the same time provided that other churches in his diocese should be furnished with bells. J. Stubbs, Act. Pont. Eborc. fol. 1700. See more about bells in Spelman's Glossary, voce CAMPANA, and in Bingham's Antiquities of the Christian Church, book VIII. chap. vii. sect 15.

Mention is made by St. Aldhelm, and William of Malmesbury, of bells given by St. Dunstan to the churches in the West.

In the times of popery bells were baptised and anointed Oleo Chrismatis; they were exorcised and blessed by the bishop, from a belief that when these ceremonies were performed they had a power to drive the devil out of the air, to calm tempests, to extinguish fire, and to recreate even the dead. The ritual for these ceremonies is contained in the Roman pontifical; and it was usual in their baptism to give to bells the name of some saint. In Chauncy's History of Hertfordshire, page 383, is a relation of the baptism of a set of bells in Italy with great ceremony, a short time before the writing that book. The bells of the parish church of Winnington in Bedfordshire had their names cast about the verge of every one in particular, with these rhyming hexameters :—

Nomina Campanis hec indita sunt quoque nostris.
1. Hoc signum Petri pulsatur nomine Christi.
2. Nomen Magdalene campana sonat melode.
3. Sit nomen Domini benedictum semper in euum.
4. Musa Raphaelis sonat auribus Immanuelis.
5. Sum Rosa pulsata mundi que Maria vocata.
Weev. Fun. Mon. 122.

By an old Chartulary, once in the possession of Weever the antiquary, it appears that the bells of the priory of Little Dunmow in Essex, were, anno 1501, new cast, and baptised by the following names :—

Prima in honore Sancti Michaelis Archangeli.
Secunda in honore S. Johannis Evangeliste.
Tertia in honore S. Johannis Baptiste.
Quarta in honore Assumptionis beate Marie.
Quinta in honore sancte Trinitatis, et omnium sanctorum.
Fun. Mon. 633.

The bells of Osney abbey near Oxford were very famous; their several names were Douce, Clement, Austin, Hautecter [potius Hautcleri] Gabriel and John. Appendix to Hearne's Collection of Discourses by Antiquaries, Numb. XI.

Near Old Windsor is a public house vulgarly called the Bells of Bosely; this house was originally built for the accommodation of bargemen and others navigating the river Thames between London and Oxford. It has a sign of six bells, i. e. the bells of Osney.

In the Funeral Monuments of Weever, are the following particulars relating to bells :—

' Bells had frequently these inscriptions on them :—

' Funera plango, Fulgura frango, Sabbata pango,
' Excito lentos, Dissipo ventos, Paco cruentos.   Page 122.

* RUDOLPHUS AGRICOLA was born at Bafflen in Friesland, two miles from Groningen. He was a learned divine, philosopher, poet, and musician, and also an excellent mechanic. *Those who would know more of him than can here be mentioned may consult Bayle in art. Blount's Censura Celebrium Auctorum, and Dr. Jortin's Life of Erasmus.* There are of his composition Songs in his native language to music in four parts : he is also said to have sung well, and to have had a fine hand on the lute. Melchior Adamus has celebrated him for his extensive learning and skill in music. That he made the organ at St. Martin's church is uniformly believed throughout the Netherlands upon better authority than bare tradition; Benthem, in his Hollandischen Kirch-und Schulen-Staat, expressly asserts it; and with him Walther agrees in the relation of the fact. The organ of Agricola is yet remaining in St. Martin's church : some additions have been made to it since his time, but they are no more to be considered as improvements, than the additions to the organs of Father Smith, which serve but as a foil to the unimproved part of the instrument.

The Harmonie Universelle contains in substance the whole of the Harmonici, but is in some measure improved in the latter. There are nevertheless some tracts, and many curious particulars in the French which are not to be found in the Latin work. To instance, in Livre Septiesme, entitled Des Instrumens de Percussion; in this is an account of a French musician born in 1517, named Jacques Mauduit, and who, though not mentioned by any other writer on music, was styled Pere de la Musique. Mersennus gives him a most exalted character, and exhibits a Requiem in five parts of his composition.

## BOOK XIV.　CHAP. CXXVIII.

JOHN KEPLER, a great astronomer and mathematician, was born at Wiel in the duchy of Wirtemberg, on the twenty-seventh of December, 1571. His father, Henry Kepler, was descended from a family

<small>' In the Little Sanctuary at Westminster, king Edw. erected a ' Clochier, and placed therein three bells for the use of St. Stephen's ' chapel: about the biggest of them were cast in the metal these words :—</small>

<small>　　　' King Edward made mee thirtie thousand weight and three,
　　　' Take me down and wey mee, and more you shall fynd mee.</small>

<small>' But these bells being to be taken down in the raigne of king Hen. VIII. ' one writes underneath with a coale :—</small>

<small>　　　　　' But Henry the eight,
　　　　　' Will bait me of my weight.'　Ibid. 492.</small>

<small>This last distich alludes to a fact mentioned by Stow in his Survey of London ward of Farrindon Within, to wit, that near to St. Paul's school stood a Clochier, in which were four bells called Jesus bells, the greatest in all England, against which Sir Miles Partridge staked a hundred pounds, and won them of king Henry VIII. at a cast of dice.</small>

<small>It is said that the foundation of the Corsini family in Italy was laid by an ancestor of it, who, at the dissolution of religious houses, purchased the bells of abbey and other churches, and by the sale of them in other countries, acquired a very great estate.</small>

<small>*Somerset the protector was a great spoiler of churches and chapels, and attempted to pull down the bells in all parish churches, and leave but one in a steeple, whereat the old commonally were offended and ready to rebel. Howe's Preface to his edition of Stow's Annals, edit. 1631.*</small>

<small>*The exportation of bell metal was temp. Hen. VIII. and Edw. VI., prohibited by statute and also by proclamation, from an apprehension that our enemies might cast it into great guns. Strype's Eccl. Mem. Vol. II. page 45.*</small>

<small>*It is said by some author that upon the surrender of a town, the first act of the besiegers is to seize the bells.*</small>

<small>Nevertheless it appears that abroad there are bells of great magnitude. In the steeple of the great church at Roan in Normandy, is a bell with this inscription :—</small>

<small>　　　Je suis George de Ambois,
　　　Qui trente cinque mille pois,
　　　Mes lui qui me pesera,
　　　Trente six mill me trovera.</small>

<small>　　　I am George of Ambois,
　　　Thirtie five thousand in pois :
　　　But he that shall weigh me,
　　　Thirtie six thousand shall find me.　Ibid.</small>

<small>And it is a common tradition that the bells of King's college chapel, in the university of Cambridge, were taken by Henry V. from some church in France, after the battle of Agincourt. They were taken down some years ago, and sold to Phelps the bell-founder in White-Chapel, who melted them down.</small>

<small>The practice of ringing bells in change is said to be peculiar to this country, but the antiquity of it is not easily to be ascertained : there are in London several societies of ringers, particularly one known by the name of the College Youths; of this it is said Sir Matthew Hale, lord chief justice of the court of King's Bench, was, in his youthful days, a member; and in the life of this learned and upright judge, written by bishop Burnet, some facts are mentioned which favor this relation.</small>

<small>Mersennus has said nothing of the ringing of bells in changes; nor has Kircher done any thing more than calculate the possible combinations arising from a given number. In England the practice of ringing is reduced to a science, and peals have been composed which bear the names of the inventors. Some of the most celebrated peals now known were composed about fifty years ago by one Patrick; this man was a maker of barometers: in his advertisements he styled himself Torricellian Operator, from Torricelli, who invented instruments of this kind.</small>

<small>In the year 1684, one Abraham Rudhall, of the city of Gloucester, brought the art of bell-founding to great perfection. His descendants in succession have continued the business of casting bells; and by a list published by them, it appears that at Lady day, 1774, the family, in peals and odd bells, had cast to the amount of 3594. The peals of St. Dunstan's in the East, and St. Bride's, London, and St. Martin's in the Fields, Westminster, are in the number.</small>

<small>*It seems that formerly the usual number of a peal of bells was five. Stow's Annals, 1003. In the year 1430, a sixth bell was added to the peal of five, in the Church of St. Michael's, Cornhill, after which it was accounted the best ring of bells for harmony and sweetness of tone in England. Stow's Survey, 4to., in Cornhill Ward.*</small>

<small>*It has been remarked, that the compleatest and most perfect ring of bells is a peal of six, in which whether ascending or descending the semitone holds the middle position, as it does in both the natural and the duram hexachord. In the molle hexachord the tritonus intervenes. Vide D. V. Holder's Treatise on the natural grounds of Harmony.*</small>

which had raised itself under the emperors by military desert, and was himself an officer of rank in the army, but, after a series of misfortunes, was reduced to the necessity of keeping a public house for the support of himself and his family. He died in 1590, leaving his son John in a very helpless and forlorn condition.

The necessitous circumstances of Kepler's father would not allow of his giving his children such an education as might tend to repair the ruined fortunes of the family : his son John, however, discovered an early propensity to learning, and found means, upon the death of his father, to put himself into a course of study in the university of Tubingen, where, after he had acquired a competent degree of knowledge in physics, he betook himself to the mathematics under the direction of Michaël Moestlin, a famous professor there. In this branch of science Kepler made so rapid a progress, that in the year 1593 he was invited to teach the mathematics at Gratz in Styria. Being settled there, he applied himself wholly to the study of astronomy, and published his works from time to time.

In the year 1597 he married, and became involved in a vexatious contest for the recovery of his wife's fortune, and the year after was banished from Gratz on account of his religion, but was soon recalled; however, the growing troubles and the confusions of that place inclined him to think of a residence elsewhere; and as Tycho Brahe, having settled in Bohemia, and obtained from the emperor a great number of instruments for carrying on his pursuits in astronomy, had often solicited Kepler to come and abide with him, he left the university of Gratz, and removed into Bohemia with his family and library in the year 1600. Kepler in this journey was seized with a quartan ague, which continued seven or eight months; upon his recovery he set himself to assist Tycho Brahe with all his power, but there was but little cordiality between them : Kepler was offended at Tycho for the great reserve and caution with which he treated him, and for refusing to do some services to his family, which he had requested of him. Tycho Brahe died in 1601, but in the performance of the engagement which he had entered into with Kepler to induce him to settle at Prague, he had, on his arrival in that city, introduced him to the emperor Rudolphus, who received him very kindly, and made him his mathematician, upon condition that he should serve Tycho by making arithmetical calculations for him; in consideration thereof he was honoured with the title of mathematician to the emperor. Upon the decease of Tycho Brahe, Kepler received a command from the emperor to finish those tables begun by Tycho, which are known by the name of the Rudolphine tables, and he applied himself very vigorously to it; but such difficulties arose in a short time, partly from the nature of the work, and partly from the delay of the treasurers entrusted with the management and disposal of the fund appropriated for carrying it on, that they were not completed till the year 1627. Kepler complained that from the year 1602 he was looked upon by the treasurers with a very invidious eye; and that when in 1609 he had published a noble specimen of the work, and the emperor had given orders that, besides the expence of the edition, he should be immediately paid the arrears of his pension, which he said amounted to four thousand crowns, he in vain knocked at the doors of the Silesian and Imperial chambers, and it was not till two years after, that the generous orders of Rudolphus in his favour were obeyed. He met with no less discouragement from the financiers under the emperor Matthias than under Rudolphus, and therefore, after struggling with poverty for ten years at Prague, he began to think of removing thence, which the emperor hearing, stationed him at Lintz, and appointed him a salary from the states of Upper Austria, which was paid for sixteen years. In the year 1613 he went to the assembly at Ratisbon, to assist in the reformation of the Calendar, but returned to Lintz, where he continued to the year 1626.* In November in that year he went to Ulm, in order to publish the Rudolphine Tables; and afterwards in 1629, with the emperor's leave, settled at Sagan in Silesia, where he published the second part of his Ephemerides, for the first had been published at Lintz in the year 1617. In the year 1630 he went to Ratisbon to solicit the payment of the arrears of his pension, but being seized with a fever, which it is said he brought upon himself by too hard riding, he died there in November, in the fifty-ninth year of his age.

Before the time of Kepler the opinion of astronomers was, that the orbits of the heavenly bodies were circular, but in 1609 he shewed from the observations

* In a letter from Sir Henry Wotton to Lord Bacon is the following curious relation respecting Kepler, to whom Sir Henry, then being our ambassador to some one of the princes of Germany, had made a visit. ' I lay a night at Lintz, the metropolis of the Higher Austria, but then in ' very low estate, having been newly taken by the duke of Bavaria, who, ' blandiente fortunâ, was gone on to the late effects : there I found Kepler, ' a man famous in the sciences, as your Lordship knows, to whom I pur- ' pose to convey from hence one of your books, that he may see we have ' some of our own that can honour our king, as well as he hath done with ' his Harmonica. In this man's study I was much taken with the draught ' of a landskip on a piece of paper, methoughts masterly done ; whereof ' inquiring the author, he bewrayed with a smile, it was himself ; adding ' he had done it, Non tanquam Pictor, sed tanquam Mathematicus. This ' set me on fire : at last he told me how. He hath a little back tent (of ' what stuff is not much importing) which he can suddenly set up where ' he will in a field, and it is convertible (like a wind-mill) to all quarters ' at pleasure, capable of not much more than one man, as I conceive, and ' perhaps at no great ease ; exactly close and dark, save at one hole, about ' an inch and a half in the diameter, to which he applies a long per- ' spective trunk, with a convex glass fitted to the said hole, and the ' concave taken out at the other end, which extendeth to about the ' middle of this erected tent, through which the visible radiations of all ' the objects without are intromitted, falling upon a paper, which is ' accommodated to receive them, and so he traceth them with his pen in ' their natural appearance, turning his little tent round by degrees till he ' hath designed the whole aspect of the field. This I have described to ' your Lordship, because I think there might be good use made of it for ' Chorograpy ; for otherwise to make landskips by it were illiberal : though ' surely no painter can do them so precisely.' Reliquæ Wottonianæ, Lond. 1685, page 299.

It does not appear that Kepler claimed the honour of this invention, which, though Sir Henry Wotton seems not to have known it, is ascribed to Baptista Porta.

of Tycho Brahe, that the planet Mars described an ellipsis about the sun, placed in the lowermost focus, and collected the same to be the case of the rest.† He also discovered this great law observed by nature in the revolutions of the heavenly bodies, viz. that the squares of their periodical times are as the cubes of their mean distances.‡ Kepler is also said to have been the first investigator of the true cause of tides, as arising from the principle of gravitation, though Sir Isaac Newton so far improved upon his discoveries on that subject, as to make the doctrine in a manner his own.§

The most celebrated of Kepler's works are his Prodromus Dissertationum de Proportione Orbium cœlestium, and his Mysterium Cosmographicum, in which latter, as it is said, the sublime secret of the five regular bodies is laid open. Of this latter work the author thought so highly, that in a conversation with one of his friends, Thomas Lansius, he declared that if the electorate of Saxony were offered him on condition of his renouncing the honour of the discoveries contained therein, he would not accept it.

Besides these and many other books on astronomy and other mathematical subjects, Kepler was the author of a work entitled Harmonices Mundi, which he dedicated to our king James I., the third book whereof, as it is on the subject of musical harmony, it materially concerns us so far to take notice of, as to mention its general contents, and point out those singularities which distinguish it.

The third book of the Harmonices Mundi is on the subject of those proportions which we term harmonical, having for its title De Ortu proportionum harmonicarum, deque natura et differentiis rerum ad cantum pertinentium. The titles of the several chapters are as follow :—

Caput I. Ortus consonantiarum ex causis suis propriis. II. De septem chordæ sectionibus harmonicis, totidemque formis consonantiarum minorum. III. De medietatibus harmonicis ; et trinitate consonantiæ. IV. Ortus et denominatio intervallorum usualium seu concinnorum. V. Secto et denominatio consonantiarum per sua intervalla usualia. VI. De cantus generibus, dûro et molli. VII. Proportio omnium octo sonorum usualium unius diapason. VIII. Abscissio semitoniorum, et ordo minimorum intervallorum in diapason. IX. De diagrammate, lineis, notis, literisque sonorum indicibus ; de systemate, clavibus et scala musicâ. X. De tretrachordis et syllabis, UT, RE, MI, FA, SOL, LA. XI. De compositione systematum majorum. XII. De consonantiis adulterinis, ex compositione ortis. XIII. De cantu concinno simplici. XIV. De modus seu tonis. XV. Qui modi, quibus serviant affectibus. XVI. De cantu figurato seu per harmoniam.

In the introduction to this treatise Kepler observes that the antiquity of music may be inferred from the mention of the harp and organ in the book of Genesis ;

† See his Tabulæ Rudolphinæ, and Comment. de Stella Martis ; as also Costard's History of Astronomy, pag. 173, 174. Kepler's problem, and the solution of it by Sir Isaac Newton, are inserted in Keill's Introduction to Astronomy. Lect. xxiii. xxiv.

‡ Maclaurin's Account of Sir Isaac Newton's Philosophical Discoveries, page 50.

§ Cost. Hist. of Astronomy, page 957

and that from the similarity in the sound of the names and the attributes commonly ascribed to both, there is ground to conjécture that Jubal and Apollo were one and the same person ; and that, for the same reasons, the like may be said of Tubal Cain and Vulcan. He then digresses to the contemplation of the Pythagorean Tetractys, and points out the mysterious properties of the number four.* He also takes notice that Ptolemy was the first that vindicated the sense of hearing against the Pythagoreans, and received among the concinnous intervals not only the diatessaron, diapente, and diapason, but also the sesquioctave for the greater, and the sesquinona for the lesser tone, and the sesquidecima for the semitone ; and added not only other superparticulars that were approved of by the ear, as the sesquiquarta and sesquiquinta, but also introduced some of the superbipartients. By this means, he adds, Ptolemy indeed amended the Pythagorean speculation, as repugnant to the origin of harmonical proportions, but did not entirely reject it as false ; yet he remarks that this same person, who had restored the judgment of the ears to its dignity, did however again desert it, he himself also insisting on and abiding by the contemplation of abstract numbers; wherefore he denied that the greater and lesser thirds and sixths are consonances, and admitted in their stead other proportions.

Chapter I. contains some of the principal axioms in Harmonics, upon which the author animadverts in a strain of philosophy that distinguishes his writings, to this purpose :

' The speculation concerning these axioms is sub-
' lime, Platonic, and analogous to the Christian faith,
' and regards metaphysics and the doctrine of the soul;
' for geometry, which has a relation to musical har-
' mony, suggested to the divine mind in the creation
' of the world what was best, most beautiful, and
' nearest resembling God himself, and the images of
' God the creator, as are all spirits, souls, and minds
' which actuate bodies, and govern, move, increase, and
' preserve them. These by a certain instinct delight
' in the same proportions which God himself made
' use of in the formation of the universe, whether
' they are impressed on bodies and motions, or arise
' from a certain geometrical necessity of matter, divi-
' sible in infinitum, or from motions excited by matter;
' and these harmonical proportions are said to consist
' not in Esse, but in Fieri. Nor do minds delight
' only in these proportions, but they also make use of
' the same as laws, to perfect or perform their offices,
' and to express these same proportions in the motions
' of bodies where it is allowable. Of this the follow-
' ing books produce two most luculent examples, the
' one of God himself the Creator, who has regulated
' the motions of the heavens by harmonical propor-
' tions ; the other of that soul which we usually call
' the sublunary nature, which stirs up the meteors ac-

' cording to the laws or prescripts of those proportions
' which occur in the radiations of the stars. A third
' example is that of the human soul, and the souls of
' beasts in some measure, for they delight in the har-
' monical proportions of sounds, and are sad or dis-
' pleased with such as are not harmonical; from which
' affections of the soul, the former are termed conso-
' nances, and the latter dissonances ; but if another
' harmonical proportion of voices and sounds, to wit,
' the metrical ratio of quantities long and short be also
' added, these affect the soul, and stir up the body to
' dancing or leaping, and the tongue to pronunciation,
' according to the same laws ; to this workmen adapt
' the strokes of their hammers, and soldiers their pace.
' All things live when harmonies subsist, but deaden
' when they are disturbed.'

As touching the nature of harmony, and that determination which the senses make between concinnous and inconcinnous intervals, Kepler, as do indeed most other writers on the subject, resolves it into the coincidence of vibrations.

Chap. II. contains a series of proportions tending to shew that for producing the consonances, seven sections of a chord are all that can be admitted ; in answer to which it need only be said that in the Sect o Canonis of Euclid and Aristides Quintilianus, the contrary is demonstrated.

In Chap. VI. the author declares his sentiments with respect to the hard and soft genera of Cantus ; the first he says is called the soft cantus, because in it the intervals of the third and sixth from the lowest note are soft, and that the other is called the hard cantus for the contrary reason ; upon which he remarks, that this distinction is recognized by God himself in the motions of the planets.

In Chap. VII. in which the author undertakes to demonstrate the natural order of the concinnous intervals contained in the octave, he asserts, without taking notice of the division of the diapason into tetrachords, that it seems most agreeable to nature that whenever we make choice of a section, the greater intervals should converge towards the grave sounds. In his section therefore he observes this order, greater tone 8, 9, lesser tone 9, 10, semitone 15, 16, which he says is sufficient to stand forth against the authorities of Ptolemy, Zarlino, and Galileo, who make the lesser tone the lowest in position.†

Chap. VIII. proposes a section of the monochord for the Testudo or lute, in which he censures that of Vincentio Galileo, declaring it to be an injudicious essay towards a temperament, and that the author was ignorant of the demonstrative quantity of sounds.

Chap. IX. treats of the modern method of notation by lines and the letters of the alphabet, and contains the author's opinion touching the origin of the cliffs,

---

* The Pythagoreans maintained that in the first of the five regular solids, viz., the Tetrahedron or Pyramid, the Tetractys is to be found, for that a point answers to unity, a line to the number two, a superficies to three, and solidity to four. Farther they say that the judicative power is fourfold, and consists in mind, science, opinion, and sense. In short, in physics, metaphysics, ethics, and theology, they made the number four an universal measure ; and scrupled not to assert that the nature of God himself is typified by the Tetrad.

† Kepler, with all his acuteness, seems to have been bewildered in this abstruse speculation : indeed so far as not to be able to distinguish between the friends and the adversaries of his doctrine; for this very arrangement of the greater and lesser tone, that is to say the greater first, and the second next, constitutes the intense diatonic of Ptolemy, which had been received by Ludovico Fogliano, and recognized by Zarlino: nor were there any of the moderns, excepting Vincentio Galileo, who disputed it, and he contended for an equality of tones; notwithstanding which Kepler enumerates Galileo among the friends of Ptolemy, and, by a mistaken consequence, among the adversaries of himself. See Dr. Wallis's Appendix to Ptolemy, page 318 ; and see also page 401 of this work, in not.

which he with great ingenuity proves to be gradual deviations from the respective letters F C and G; he delivers his sentiments in these words :—

'Some things offer themselves to our observation 'concerning these letters; for first, all the letters are 'not written on the lines and spaces which their sta-'tions require, but only these, F G C, as often as there 'is a place for one of them on the line, B also when 'it has its sound in a space.

'Moreover the letter C has a different character, 'namely, the following ⧦; I suppose that this arose 'from the distortion of the ancient letter C, for as the 'writers used broad-pointed pens, most of the notes 'were made square for dispatch in writing; nor could 'a round C be described with these pens: so that they 'made the C of three little lines, one slender, and the 'other two thick, in the room of the horns; the pen 'being drawn broadways thus ◼, the fine little line, 'on account of their expeditious writing, was made 'longer, and was carried above and below beyond the 'horns thus ⧦; but, in order to terminate the horns, 'they drew little lines parallel to the first thus ⧦, and 'at length these two lines were made one, and the 'whole character became of this form ⧦, but by the 'gaping of the quill it was frequently and at length 'generally made hollow or open thus ⧉.

'It may nevertheless be questioned whether or no 'the term musical scale might not suggest to the in-'ventors the character of a figure resembling a ladder, 'such as is used by the moderns, to denote the station 'of C in the scale.'

The conjectures of Kepler with regard to the origin of the character used to denote the tenor cliff are in-genious, but he seems to have failed in his attempt to account for the form of the character 𝄢, which gives the F FA UT wherever it is placed; for first he sup-poses it to have been originally the small γ, and, secondly, that the two points behind it were intended to signify a reduplication of the note Γ; in this he certainly errs, for the station of the bass cliff on the fourth line is but a seventh from GAMUT, the replicate whereof is G SOL, RE, UT, and not F FA UT. It must be owned that for the origin of the above character we are greatly to seek, but is highly probable that it is a corruption of the letter F; and that for this reason Guido, when he reformed the scale, found it necessary, in order to ascertain the denominations of the several chords contained in it, to affix some certain character to the lowest of them; for this purpose he made choice of the Greek Γ: succeeding musicians found it necessary in practice to ascertain the place of c SOL FA UT, which they did by the letter C; and the same motive induced them to point out also g SOL RE UT, by g, stationing it on the third line above that whereon C stood: a thought then suggested itself that a cliff on the third line below C, would give the whole a uniform appearance, by placing the cliffs in the middle of the scale, and making them equidistant from each other; and this was no sooner done by placing F three lines below C, than the whole character Γ on the first line of the

stave became useless; for the note GAMUT is as clearly determined by the station of F on the fourth line, as by its original character.

Touching the origin and use of the flat and sharp signatures, these are the sentiments of Kepler :—

'As to the first, b, its presence, whether it falls 'upon a line or a space, denotes the soft cantus, and 'its absence the hard; and by a certain abuse the letter b is used for the character of the semitone or syllable FA.

'When a semitone is extraordinarily constituted in 'the place of a tone, and the syllable MI in the place 'of the syllable FA, then the letter b, or the character 'derived from it, is prefixed to the note, for the 'ancients without doubt described it thus ♮, but we 'instead thereof thus ♯ or ×, which, as Galileus 'imagines, should seem to say to the reader the same 'thing as the Greek word Diaschisma formerly did, 'for it evidently expresses a splitting, and points out 'to us the cutting of the semitones.'

Chap. X. contains a comparison of the hexachords of the moderns with the tetrachords of the ancient Greeks, very clearly demonstrating the superior ex-cellence of the hexachord system; and here by the way it is to be observed that he differs from Doctor Wallis and many other authors, who have expressed their wishes that Guido, instead of six, had taken seven syllables into this system: further he censures that German, whoever he was, that introduced the seven syllables BO, CE, DI, GA, LO, MA, NI.

Chap. XIII. the author speaks of the manner of singing, which he says the Turks and Hungarians are accustomed to, and resembles the noises of brute animals rather than the sounds of the human voice; but this kind of melody, rude as it is, he supposes not fortuitous, but to be derived from some instru-ment concinnously formed, which had led the whole nation into the use of such intervals in singing as nature abhors. To this purpose he relates that being at Prague, at the house of the Turkish ambassador, at a time when the accustomed prayers were sung by the priests, he observed one on his knees frequently striking the earth with his hand, who appeared to sing by rule, for that he did not in the least hesitate, though the intervals he sung were wonderfully un-accustomed, mangled, and abhorrent, which, that his reader may judge of them, he gives in the following notes :—

Touching that long-agitated question, whether the music of the ancient Greeks was solitary or in con-sonance, Kepler, chap. XVI, thus delivers his sen-timents :—

'Although the word Harmony was anciently used 'to signify a Cantus, yet we are not to understand 'by it a modulation by several voices in consonance; 'for that this is an invention of modern date, and 'was utterly unknown to the ancients, needs not to 'be proved.' He adds, 'It is indeed objected, that 'in the republic of Plato a tying together of the 'cantus by harmony is mentioned as if it had at that 'time been made use of;* but this passage is to be 'understood of instruments, such as the Syringa, the 'Cornamusa, and Testudo, when one sound intonates 'in consonance with another.'

The author concludes his third book of the Harmonices Mundi with what he calls a political digression concerning the three kinds of mediation, taken in part from Bodinus, who appears to be no less fond than himself of such fanciful analogies.

As there are three forms of policy or civil government, namely, Democracy, Aristocracy, and Monarchy, he compares Democracy to arithmetical proportion, Aristocracy to the geometrical, and Monarchy to the harmonical. He farther remarks that as all the rules of governing are comprehended under justice, of which there are two kinds, viz., commutative justice, which is implied in the arithmetical equality, and distributive in the geometrical similitude,† so there is a third species of justice made up of both. He says that the poets, who feign the three daughters of Justice to be Equity, Law, and Peace, do as it were make them the tutelars severally of arithmetical, geometrical, and harmonical proportion: and that the laws concerning marriage afford an example of the three proportions, for says he 'If patricians marry patrician wives, and plebeians 'plebeian wives, then it is the geometrical similitude; 'where it is allowed to marry promiscuously, without 'any manner of restriction, then the arithmetical 'equality is found; but if, as in the case of factions, 'the poorest patricians are permitted to marry with 'the richer plebeians, then that gives the harmonical 'proportion as being convenient for both.'

Kepler pretends also to discover an analogy between the three kinds of proportion above enumerated, and the order observed in the arrangement of persons, distinguishing between senators and plebeians at feasts and at public shows. In the pursuit of this argument he insists on a variety of topics drawn from the Roman civil law, and pretends to trace resemblances which never did exist but in his own bewildered imagination.

He concludes this digression with a remark that Bodinus beautifully compares the arithmetical equality to the iron ruler Polycletus, which may be broken before it can be bent; the geometrical similitude to the leaden Lesbian ruler, which was accommodated to all angles; and the harmonical proportion to a wooden ruler which indeed may be bent, but immediately returns back.

Such singularities as are discoverable in the writings of Kepler, could hardly fail to draw on him the censures of those who were engaged in the same course of study with himself. Ismael Bullialdus says he abounds in fictions; and Martinus Schookius, who allows him to be an able astronomer and mathematician, says that where he affects to reason upon physical principles, no man talks more absurdly,‡ and expresses his concern that a man, in other respects so excellent, should disgrace the divine science of mathematics with his preposterous notions; for, says he, what could an old woman in a fever, dream more ridiculous than that the earth is a vast animal, which breathes out the winds through the holes of the mountains, as it were through a mouth and nostrils? Yet he writes expressly thus in his Harmonices Mundi, and attempts also seriously to prove that the earth has a sympathy with the heavens, and by a natural instinct perceives the position of the stars.

The absurdities of Kepler were such as have exposed him and his writings to the ridicule of many a less able mathematician than himself. Mr. Maclaurin has remarked that he was all his life in pursuit of fancied analogies; but he adds, that to this disposition we owe such discoveries as are more than sufficient to excuse his conceits.§ Upon which it may be observed, that had he made no greater discoveries in mathematics than he has done in music, it is highly probable that the conceits had remained, and the discoveries been forgotten.

## CHAP. CXXIX.

ROBERT FLUD, Lat. de Fluctibus, a very famous philosopher and a writer on music, was the son of Sir Thomas Flud, knight, some time treasurer of war to queen Elizabeth in France and the Low Countries, and was born at Milgate, in the parish of Bearsted, in Kent, in the year 1574. He was admitted of St. John's college in the university of Oxford, in 1591, at the age of seventeen; and having taken both the degrees in arts, applied himself to the study of physic, and spent six years in travelling through France, Spain, Italy, and Germany, in most of which countries he not only became acquainted with several of the nobility, but even read lectures to them. After his return, in the year 1605, being in high repute for his knowledge in chemistry, he proceeded in the faculty of physic, took the degree of doctor, was admitted a fellow of the college of physicians, and practised in London. He was esteemed by many both as a philosopher and a physician, though it may be objected, that as he was of the fraternity of the Rosicrucians, as they are called, his philosophy was none of the soundest. His propensity to chemistry served also to mislead him, and induced him to refer to it not only the wonders of nature, but miracles, and even religious mysteries. His works,

---

* The passage here alluded to is that which gave rise to the controversy between Mons. Fraguier and Mons. Burette. See page 102, in not.

† Great confusion appears among the writers on Ethics in their division of justice, and their definitions of its several species. Grotius as here, and also Puffendorf distinguishes it into distributive and commutative; and Gronovius, the Commentator on the former, assigns to distributive justice the geometrical, and to commutative the arithmetical Ratio. Vide Grotius de Jure Belli ac Dacis à Gronovis lib. I. cap. i. sect. 8. Puffendorf de Officio Hominis à Carmichael, lib. I. cap. ii, sect. 14. Dr. More dividing Justice into distributive and corrective, gives to the former the geometrical ratio 6, 2, 12, 4, and to the latter the arithmetical 5, 7, 9, 11. Enchirid Eth. lib. II. cap. 6, sect. 6. These analogies thus recognised are become scientific. Nevertheless the relation between qualities and quantities, moral actions and mathematical proportions, is not clearly discernible; the latter are measurable, the former not.

‡ The singularity in Kepler's method of reasoning may be remarked in his endeavours to torture and strain the three kinds of proportion, that is to say, geometrical, arithmetical, and harmonical, to a resemblance of the three forms of civil policy, and the practice of the Romans in their marriages, and the order of seating the spectators of public shows and solemnities; and there are many other instances in the Harmonices Mundi, which, though they have escaped observation, are no less ridiculous, as where he says, speaking of the terms Αγωγη and Πλοκη, made use of by Euclid, that the Πλοκη wanders about the Αγογη 'ut canis circa viatorem,' i. e. as a dog about a traveller.

§ Account of Sir Isaac Newton's Philosophical Discoveries, page 47.

which are very many, amounting to near twenty tracts, are in Latin; and it is said, that as he was a mystic in philosophy, and affected in his writings a turgid and obscure style, so was his discourse, particularly to his patients, so lofty and hyperbolical, that it resembled that of a mountebank more than of a grave physician, yet it is said that he practised with success, and what is more, that Selden held him in high estimation. Mosheim asserts that the reading his books turned the brain of Jacob Behmen; and at present it is their only praise, that for some time they were greatly admired and sought after by alchemists, astrologers, searchers after the philosophers' stone, and, in short, by all the madmen in the republic of letters both at home and abroad.

Some of his pieces were levelled against Kepler and Mersennus, and he had the honour of replies from both. He wrote two books against Mersennus, the first intitled, 'Sophiæ cum Moriæ certamen, in quo, 'lapis Lydius a falso structore, Fratre Marino Mer-'senno monacho, reprobatus, celeberrima voluminis 'sui Babylonici in Genesin figmenta accurate exa-'minat.' Franc. 1629, fol. The second, 'Summum 'bonorum quod est verum Magiæ Cabalæ, Alchymæ 'Fratrum Rosæ crucis verorum veræ subjectum, in 'dictarum scientiarum laudem, in insignis calumni-'atoris Fr. Mar. Mersenni dedecus publicatum per 'Joachim Frizium,' 1629, fol. Mersennus desiring Gassendus to give his judgment of these two books of Flud against him, that great man drew up an answer divided into three parts, the first of which sifts the principles of Flud's whimsical philosophy as they lie scattered throughout his works; the second is against 'Sophiæ cum Moriæ certamen, &c.' and the third against 'Summum bonorum, &c.' This answer, called Examen Fluddanæ Philosophiæ, is dated February 4, 1629, and is printed in the third volume of the works of Gassendus in folio. In the dedication to Mersennus is a passage in substance as follows, viz., 'Although I 'am far from thinking your antagonist a match for 'you, yet it must be owned that he is really a man of 'various knowledge, known to all the learned of the 'age, and whose voluminous works will shortly have 'a place in most libraries. And in the present dis-'pute will have one great advantage over you, namely, 'that whereas your philosophy is of a plain, open, 'intelligible kind, his, on the contrary, is so very ob-'scure and mysterious, that he can at any time conceal 'himself, and, by diffusing a darkness round him, 'hinder you from discerning him, so far as to lay hold 'of him, much less to drag him forth to conviction.'

Dr. Flud died at his house in Coleman-street, London, in the year 1637, and was buried in the church of Bearsted, the place of his nativity. In the Athenæ Oxonienses is an account of him and a catalogue of his writings, but of the many books he wrote, the only one necessary to be taken notice of in this work is that entitled 'Utriusque Cosmi, Majoris scilicet et 'minoris, metaphysica, physica, atque technica histo-'ria in duo volumina, secundum Cosmi differentiam 'divisa. Tomus primus de Macrocosmi Historia in 'duos tractatus divisa.' * This work was printed at

* It seems that the second volume was never published.

Oppenheim, in a thick folio volume, and published in 1617. It abounds with plates and diagrams of the most fantastic kind, and though the author was beholden to a foreign press for its publication, is recommended to the patronage of his rightful sovereign James the First.

As to the work itself, the nature and tendency of it are unfolded in the following analytical distribution of its parts :—

| | | |
|---|---|---|
| Tractatus | Primus de | Metaphysico Macrocosmi et Creaturarum illius ortu. |
| | | Physico Macrocosmi ingeneratione et corruptione progressu. |
| | Secundus de arte naturæ simia in Macrocosmo producta et in eo nutrita et multiplicata, cujus filias præcipuas hîc anatomiâ vivâ recensuimus, nempe : | Arithmeticam. |
| | | Musicam. |
| | | Geometriam. |
| | | Perspectivam. |
| | | Artem Pictoriam. |
| | | Artem Militarem. |
| | | Motus } Scientiam. Temporis } |
| | | Cosmographiam. |
| | | Astrologiam. |
| | | Geomantiam. |

The third book of the first tract is intitled De Musica Mundana. In this discourse the author supposes the world to be a musical instrument, and that the elements that compose it, assigning to each a certain place according to the laws of gravitation, together with the planets and the heavens, make up that instrument which he calls the Mundane Monochord, in the description whereof he thus expresses himself:

'We will take our beginning from the matter of 'the world, which I have made to resemble the chord 'of the monochord, whose great instrument is the 'Macrocosm itself, as a certain scale or ladder whereby 'the difference of the places lying between the centre 'and periphery of the mundane instrument is distin-'guished, and which difference of places we shall 'aptly compare to the musical intervals, as well the 'simple as the compound. Wherefore it is to be 'known that as the chord of an instrument in its 'progression from Γ is accustomed to be divided into 'intervals by metrical proportions, so likewise I have 'distributed both the matter and its form into degrees 'of quantity, and distinguished them by similar pro-'portions, constituting musical consonances; for if a 'monochord be supposed to extend from the summit 'of the empyrean heaven to the basis of the earth 'itself, we shall perceive that it may be divided into 'parts constituting consonances; and if the half part 'thereof were touched or struck, it would produce 'the consonant diapason in the same manner as the 'instrumental monochord.

'But it is to be considered that in this mundane 'monochord the consonances, and likewise the proper 'intervals, measuring them, cannot be otherwise de-'lineated than as we divide the instrumental mono-'chord into proportional parts; for the frigidity, and 'also the matter itself, of the earth, as to the thickness 'and weight thereof, naturally bears the same propor-'tion to the frigidity as the matter of the lowest 'region, in which there is only one fourth part of the 'natural light and heat, as 4 to 3, which is the ses-

'quitertia proportion ; in which proportion a diates-
'saron consists, composed of three intervals, namely,
'water, air, and fire ; for the earth in mundane music
'is the same thing as Γ in music, unity in arithmetic,
'or a point in geometry ; it being as it were the term
'and sound from which the ratio of proportional
'matter is to be calculated. Water therefore occupies
'the place of one tone, and the air that of another
'interval more remote ; and the sphere of fire, as it
'is only the summit of the region of the air, kindled
'or lighted up, possesses the place of a lesser semi-
'tone. But in as much as two portions of this matter
'are extended upwards as far as to the middle heaven,
'to resist the action of the supernatural heat ; and the
'same number of parts of light, act downwards
'against these two portions of matter, these make up
'the composition of the sphere of the sun, and natu-
'rally give it the attribute of equality, and by that
'means the sesquialtera proportion is produced, in
'which three parts of the lower spirit or matter of
'the middle heaven are opposed to the two parts of
'the solar sphere, producing the consonant diapente :
'for such is the difference between the moon and the
'sun, as there are four intervals between the convexity
'of this heaven and the middle of the solar sphere,
'namely, those of the entire spheres of the moon,
'Mercury, and Venus, compared to full tones, and
'the half part of the solar sphere, which we have
'compared to the semitone. But as the consonant
'diapason is constituted of the diatessaron and dia-
'pente, therefore this consonant diapason must neces-
'sarily be there produced ; and this is the most perfect
'consonance of matter, which can by no means acquire
'its perfection unless it fills up its appetite in the
'solar form. Moreover, this middle heaven, though
'its most perfect consonance ends in its heart, namely,
'the sun, and thence begins its motion to the formal
'diapason, yet it sounds out nothing else than the
'consonant diapente in its concavity, as well above its
'sphere of equality as below it ; which consonant
'therefore suits better with this place than any of the
'other consonants, because it is less perfect, and is
'placed in the middle between the perfect and imper-
'fect : thus also this heaven, although it be perfect
'and free from corruption, is said to be less perfect
'with regard to the upper heaven, and obtains the
'middle situation between both heavens, namely, the
'perfect and imperfect.'

The definition which Boetius gives of mundane
music, so far as relates to the motion of the celestial
orbs, is founded in the Pythagorean notion of the
music of the spheres, and in this sense it has a literal
signification ; but when he speaks of the composition
of the elements, the order of time, and the succession
of the seasons, and of the regularity, order, and harmony observable in the operations of nature, it is
evident he makes use of the term in a figurative sense.
In like manner do those who speak of human music,
moral music, and, as Kepler and others do, of political music ; but this author not only supposes the
world to be a musical instrument, but proceeds without any data, to assign to the four elements and to the
planets, certain stations, and to portion out the heavens
themselves ; and having distributed the several parts

of the creation according to the suggestions of his
own fancy, he pretends to discover in this distribution
certain ratios or proportions in strict analogy with
those of music, which he exhibits in the following
diagram :—

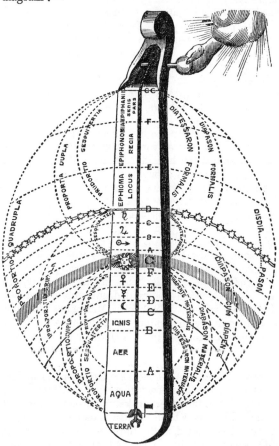

The mundane monochord thus adjusted and divided
into systems of diatessaron, diapente, and diapason,
is not to be considered as a subject of mere speculation ; and it will be perceived that the author has not
been at the pains of stringing his instrument for nothing ; for the soul or spirit of the world, according
to him, is a formal substance, striking on the chord
of the mundane instrument, which is a material substance, produces music : light therefore, says our
author, acts on the mundane instrument just as the
breath or spirit of a man acts on the air when he sings.

In Chap. IV. the author undertakes to demonstrate his whimsical hypothesis by the figure
of a pipe or flute in this form, from which he
says it appears that the true proportion of the
whole world may be collected ; this boasted
demonstration is in the words following :—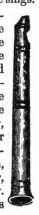
'The pipe here spoken of is divided into three
'regions or parts, the two lower whereof have
'each three holes, denoting the beginning,
'middle, and end of each region ; but the upper
'region, consisting of one great hole only, ex-
'presses the nature of the empyrean heaven,
'whose every part is of the same condition, or,
'as it were, most replete with the divine unity.
'But as this instrument is not moved by its

HIERONYMUS FRESCOBALDUS
FERRARIENSIS,
ORGANISTA ECCLESIÆ D.PETRI IN VATICANO.
ÆTAT. SUÆ XXXVI.

'own nature, nor sounds of itself without a moving
'soul, so neither can the world, or the part of the
'world move but by the immense mind or soul: as
'therefore the highest mind, God, is the summit of
'the whole machine, and as it were beyond the ex-
'treme superficies of the world, makes the joints of
'the world to exhibit his music, graver in the lower
'part, and acuter and clearer the nearer the parts
'approach to the summit itself; so likewise when
'the musician blows life and motion beyond the con-
'tent of the pipe, and in its summit, the farther the
'holes are from that blowing power, the more grave
'are the sounds that are produced; and the higher
'they ascend towards the point of inspiration, the
'more are they acute. And in the same manner as
'the great aperture near the top of the pipe gives as
'it were life and soul to the lower ones, so likewise
'the empyrean heaven gives soul to all the lower
'spheres. O how great and how heavenly is this
'contemplation in a subject seemingly so trivial,
'when it is diligently and profoundly considered by
'an intelligent mind!'

Were it possible to convey an idea in words of the
nature of that folly and absurdity which are discoverable in the writings of this enthusiast, the foregoing
extract from this work of his might be spared; but
his notions, as they elude all investigation, so cannot
they even be stated in any words but his own, and
this must be the apology for inserting them.

Tract II. part ii. of this work, agreeably to the
analysis above given of it, is on practical music. In
this he enters largely into the subject, and from the
manuscript of Waltham Holy Cross, which it is evident he had made use of, gives the whole doctrine of
the Cantus Mensurabilis, with the diagrams relating
to it, and among the rest that of the triangular shield,
exhibited in page 248 of this work, the invention
whereof he ascribes to one Robert Brunham, a monk.

He describes also the musical instruments of the
moderns, namely, the Barbiton or lute, the Orpharion
and Pandora; and under the pneumatic class, the
Regals, as also pipes of various kinds. Of the Sistrena or Cittern these are his words: 'Sistrena est
'instrumentum musicum ex quatuor chordis metallis
'duplis consistens, et tonsoribus commune;' most
exactly corresponding with what has been already
observed on this silly instrument, which is now become the recreation of ladies, and by the makers is
ignorantly termed the Guitar.

The rest of this tract, excepting those whimsical
devices, such as musical dials, musical windows, musical colonnades, and other extravagancies with which
the author has thought proper to decorate his work,
contains very little that deserves notice.

Upon the whole Flud appears to have been a man
of a disordered imagination, an enthusiast in theology
and philosophy: as such he is classed by Butler, with
Jacob Behmen and the wildest of the mystic writers:

'He Anthroposophus and Flud,
'And Jacob Behmen understood;'
          HUDIBRAS, Part I. Canto i.

Notwithstanding which, Webster, in his Displaying

of supposed Witchcraft, asserts that he was a man
acquainted with all sorts of learning, and one of the
most Christian philosophers that ever wrote.

## CHAP. CXXX.

GIROLAMO FRESCOBALDI *(a Portrait)*, a native of
Ferrara, was born in the year 1601, and at the age of
about twenty-three was organist of the church of St.
Peter at Rome. He is not less celebrated for his
compositions for the organ, than for his exquisite skill
in that instrument. He was the first of the Italians
that composed for the organ in fugue; and in this
species of composition, originally invented by the
Germans, he was without a rival.

Of many musicians it has been said, that they were
the fathers of a particular style, as that Palestrina
was the father of the church style, Monteverde of
the dramatic, and Carissimi of the chamber style: of
Frescobaldi it may as truly be said that he was the
father of that organ-style which has prevailed not
less in England than in other countries for more than
a hundred years past, and which consists in a prompt
and ready discussion of some premeditated subject in
a quicker succession of notes than is required in the
accompaniment of choral harmony. Exercises of
this kind on the organ are usually called Toccatas,
from the Italian Toccare, to touch; and for want of
a better word to express them, they are here in
England called Voluntaries. In the Romish service
they occur at frequent intervals, particularly at the
elevation, post communions, and during the offerings;[*]
and in that of our church, in the morning prayer,
after the psalms and after the Benediction, or, in other
words, between the first and second service; and in
the evening service after the psalms.[†]

In the year 1628, Bartolomeo Grassi, organist of
St. Maria in Acquirio in Rome, and who had been a
disciple of his, published a work of Frescobaldi entitled 'In partitura il primo libro delle canzoni a una
'due tre e quatro voci. Per sonare con ogni forte di
'stromenti.' At the end of the book is an advertisement from Grassi, in which he says that the compositions contained in it are in the grand gusto, and,
having been universally applauded, are to be looked
on as models of perfection. It seems from the title
of the work that these originally were vocal compositions, but that, for the improvement of the studious
in music, Grassi had published them in score, rejecting the words, and in this form they met with such a
favourable reception, that he expressly tells us he had
printed them three times.

The following composition is taken from a work of
Frescobaldi printed at Rome in 1637, entitled 'Il
'secondo libro di Toccata, Canzone, Versi d'Hinni,
'Magnificat, Gagliarde, Correnti et altre Partite d'In-
'tavolatura di Cimbalo et Organo,' and is the third
Canzone in that collection.

---

[*] A collection of this kind was published in the year 1716, by Domenico
Zipoli, organist of the Jesuits' church at Rome with this title, 'Sonate
'd'Intavolatura per Organo, e Cimbalo, parte prima, Toccata, Versi,
'Canzone, Offertorio, Elevazioni, Post-Communio, e Pastorale.'

[†] This order was settled at the Restoration. See The divine Services
and Anthems usually sung in his Majesties Chapel, and all Cathedrals,
&c. by James Clifford, Lond. 1664.

CANZONA.

GIROLAMO FRESCOBALDI.
2 s

RENE' DES CARTES, the famous French philosopher and mathematician, the particulars of whose life and character are very well known, was the author of a treatise entitled Musicæ Compendium, written when he was very young, and in the year 1617, and, which is very extraordinary, while he was engaged in the profession of a soldier, and lay in garrison at Breda. The subject matter of this tract is distributed under the following heads : De numero vel tempore in sonis observando.   De sonorum diversitate circa acutum et grave.   De consonantiis.   De octavâ.   De quintâ. De quartâ.   De ditono, tertiâ minore, etsextis. De gradibus sive tonis musicis.   De dissonantiis. De ratione componendi et modis.   De modis.

The above-mentioned tract, although comprehended in fifty-eight small quarto pages, contains a great number of very curious particulars relating to the science of music.* The observations of the author on the effects of various measures, as contained in the following passages, are new and judicious, and in the words of his translator are these :—

' We say in the generall that a slow measure doth ' excite in us gentle and sluggish motions, such as ' a kind of languor, sadnesse, fear, pride, and other ' heavy and dull passions : and a more nimble and ' swift measure doth proportionably excite more ' nimble and sprightly passions, such as joy, anger, ' courage, &c. the same may also be sayd of the ' double kind of percussion, viz., that a quadrate, or ' such as is perpetually resolved into equals, is slower ' and duller than a tertiate, or such as doth consist ' of three equal parts.   The reason whereof is, because ' this doth more possesse and employ the sense, ' inasmuch as therein are more, namely 3, members ' to be adverted, while in the other are only 2.'

In his enumeration of the consonances, he, contrary to the sense of all other writers, from John De Muris down to Mersennus, excludes the unison, and for this very good reason, that ' therein is no difference of ' sounds as to acute and grave ; it bearing the same ' relation to consonances, as unity doth to numbers.

Of the two methods by which the diapason or octave is divided, the arithmetical and geometrical, the author, for the reasons contained in the sixth of his Prænotanda, prefers the former ; and for the purpose of adjusting the consonances, proposes the division of a chord, first into two equal parts, and afterwards into smaller proportions, according to this table :—

| $\frac{1}{2}$ | Eighth | | | | | | | | | |
|---|---|---|---|---|---|---|---|---|---|---|
| $\frac{1}{3}$ | Twelfth | $\frac{2}{3}$ | Fifth | | | | | | | |
| $\frac{1}{4}$ | Fifteenth | $\frac{2}{4}$ | Eighth | $\frac{3}{4}$ | Fourth | | | | | |
| $\frac{1}{5}$ | Seventeenth | $\frac{2}{5}$ | Tenth Major | $\frac{3}{5}$ | Sixth Major | $\frac{4}{5}$ | Ditone | | | |
| $\frac{1}{6}$ | Nineteenth | $\frac{2}{6}$ | Twelfth | $\frac{2}{6}$ | Eighth | $\frac{4}{6}$ | Fifth | $\frac{5}{6}$ | Third Minor |

The advantages resulting from the geometrical division appear in the Systema Participato, mentioned by Bontempi, which consisted in the division of the diapason or octave into twelve equal semitones by eleven mean proportionals ; but Des Cartes rejects this division for reasons that are very far from satisfactory.

A translation of this book into English was, in 1653, published by a person of honour, viz., William Lord Brouncker, president of the Royal Society, and the first appointed to that office, with animadversions thereon, which show that his lordship was deeply skilled in the theory of the science ; and although he agrees with his author almost throughout the book, he asserts that the geometrical is to be preferred to the arithmetical division : and, as it is presumed, with a view to a farther improvement of the Systema Participato, he proposes a division of the diapason by sixteen mean proportionals into seventeen equal semitones ; the method of which division is exhibited by him in an algebraic process, and also in logarithms.

ANDREAS HAMMERSCHMIDT, a Bohemian, born in 1611, and organist, first of the church of St. Peter at Freyburg, and afterwards of that of St. John at Zittau, is celebrated for his assiduity in the cultivation and improvement of the church-style in Saxony, Thuringia, Lusatia, and other provinces in Germany.   Mattheson applauds in the highest terms that zeal for the glory of God, which he has manifested in his Motets for four, five, and six voices. He died in 1675 ; and in the inscription on his monument in the great church at Zittau, of which he was organist, he is styled the German Orpheus.

JOHANN ANDREAS HERBST [Lat. Autumnus,] was born at Nuremberg in the year 1588.   In the year 1628 he was appointed chapel-master at Francfort on the Maine, and continued in that station till 1641, when he was called to the same office at Nuremburg. However, in 1650, he thought fit to return to Francfort, at the solicitation of the magistrates and others his friends ; and, being by them reinstated in his former dignity, he continued in that station till the time of his death, in the year 1660.   He was excellently skilled in the theory of music ; and in the art of practical composition had few equals, and was besides, like most of the Germans, a sound and judicious organist.   In the year 1643 he published in the German language a book entitled Musica Poetica ; and ten years after, a translation either from the Latin or the Italian, for it is extant in both languages, of the Arte prattica e poetica of Giov. Chiodino, in ten books.   Herbst was also the author of a tract entitled ' Musica moderna prattica, overo ' maniere del buon canto,' printed at Francfort in 1658, in which he recommends the Italian manner of singing.   His other works are a small tract on Thorough-bass, and a discourse on Counterpoint, containing directions for composing ' à mente non à penna.'   Of his musical compositions, the only ones

' man the most grateful of all other sounds, that it holds the greatest con-
' formity to our spirits.   Thus also is the voice of a friend more grateful
' than that of an enemy, from a sympathy and dispathy of affections : by
' the same reason, perhaps, that it is conceived that a drum headed with
' a sheep's skin yields no sound though strucken, if another drum headed
' with a wolf's skin be beaten upon in the same room.'

* There are nevertheless some singularities in it, of which the following may serve as a specimen : ' This only thing seems to render the voice of

extant in print are Meletemata sacra Davidis, and Suspiria S. Gregorii ad Christum, for three voices; these were printed in 1619, as was also a nameless composition of his for six voices. Vid. Draudii. Bibl. Class. pag. 1649.

JOHANN JACOB FROBERGER, a disciple of Frescobaldi, and organist to the emperor Ferdinand III. flourished about the year 1655. He was a most admirable performer on, and composer for the organ and harpsichord. Kircher, in the Musurgia, vol. I. page 466, has given a lesson of his upon UT, RE, MI, FA, SOL, LA, abounding with a great variety of fuguing passages that manifest his skill in the instrument. Mattheson ascribes to him the power of representing on the organ, by a certain imitative faculty, which he possessed in an eminent degree, even the histories of particular transactions; as an instance whereof he refers to an allemand of his where the passage of Count Thurn over the Rhine, and the danger he and his army were in, is very lively represented to the eye and ear by twenty-six cataracts or falls in notes, which it seems Froberger was the better able to do, he having been present with the Count at the time.* Mattheson takes notice that Froberger, in the composition of his lessons, made use of a stave of six lines for the right, and one of seven for the left hand; to which he might have added, that his master Frescobaldi used a stave of eight lines for the left hand.†

JOHANNES HIERONYMUS KAPSBERGER, a German of noble birth, celebrated by Kircher and others, was not more famous for the number and variety of his compositions, than for his exquisite skill and performance on almost all instruments, more particularly the Theorbo-lute, which appears to be a modern invention. The author of it was a Neapolitan musician, of whose name no account remains. As to the instrument, it is well known to be of the lute-kind; and as the improvements made in it wrought no essential change in its form, it might well have retained its primitive name; but the person, whoever he was, that improved it, by doubling the neck, and lengthening the chords, thought himself warranted in giving it the appellation of the Theorbo, for no better reason than its resemblance to an utensil, a kind of mortar used by glovers for the pounding of perfumes, and which is called Tiorba. The instrument thus improved seemed to rival the Clavicymbalum or harpsichord; Kapsberger laboured to recommend and bring it into practice, and in this he succeeded, for Kircher says that in his time it was deservedly pre-

ferred to all other instruments; no one being so adapted to the diatonic, chromatic, and enarmonic division. He assisted Kircher in the compilation of the Musurgia.

It appears by a list which Walther gives of his works, that Kapsberger was both a voluminous and a multifarious composer. Many of his compositions are for the lute in tablature, others for the church, as masses, litanies, and motets; others for the theatre, and some for public solemnities. Several of his vocal compositions are to poems and verses of Cardinal Maffeo Barberini, afterwards pope Urban VIII. and there is of his composition a work entitled 'Coro 'musicale in nuptiis D D. Thaddei Barberini et 'Annæ Columnæ,' printed at Rome in 1627, from which particulars it might be inferred that he stood in some degree of favour with the Barberini family. Nevertheless he is represented by Doni, who being so much with the cardinal, must have known Kapsberger very well, as a man of great assurance, which he manifested in his attempts to get banished from the church the compositions of Palestrina. The method he took to effect this purpose is related in page 427 of this work.

## CHAP. CXXXI.

GERARDUS JOHANNES VOSSIUS, a native of a town in the neighbourhood of Heidelberg, a man of universal learning and great abilities, published at Amsterdam, in 1650, a work entitled De quatuor Artibus popularibus, in which is a chapter De Musice. Great erudition is manifested in this tract, and also in another of his entitled De universæ Mathesios Natura et Constitutione. The titles of the several chapters therein contained relating to music are as follow, viz., Cap. XIX. De musicæ contemplativæ objecto; ac duplici ejus κριτηρίῳ; et pro eo variantibus musicorum sectis. XX. De musices antiquitate; et quantum ea Pythagoræ debeat, et quis primus de musicis scripserit. Item alii aliquot veteres musices scriptores: sed qui injuriâ temporum deperierint. XXI. De utilitate musices. XXII. De musices partibus, generibus; ac præcipuis ejus, quos habemus, scriptoribus. LIX. De musicis Græcis priori hujus operis parte indictis. LX. De musicis Latinis antea omissis. In these tracts are contained a great variety of curious particulars relating to music and musicians, and such as have written on the science, in chronological succession, from the earliest times down to his own. In the course of his studies at Dort, which he began about the year 1590, he made a considerable progress in the science of music, for which he seems to have entertained a more than ordinary affection. An intimate friendship subsisted during the whole of his life between him and Erycius Puteanus, a fellow student with him at Dort, who being eminently skilled in the theory of music, is supposed to have assisted him in his researches into those authors who have treated on the subject. About the year 1600 he was chosen director of the college of Dort, being then but twenty-three years of age; and in 1614 he was appointed director of the theological college which the States of Holland had then lately founded in the

---

* It seems that many of the German musicians affected imitations of this kind. Dietrich Buxtehude of Lubeck, in six suits of lessons for the harpsichord, has attempted to exhibit the nature and motions of the planets: and Johann Kuhnau of Leipsic published six sonatas entitled *Biblische-Historien*, wherein, as Francis Lustig asserts, is a lively representation in notes of David manfully fighting with Goliah. Musikkunde, page 278.

† The studies of Frescobaldi and Froberger contributed greatly at this time to bring the harpsichord into general use, which before had been almost appropriated to the practice of ladies; as did also the exquisite workmanship of the Ruckers, harpsichord-makers of Antwerp, their contemporaries: there were three of the name and family, viz., the father, named Hans, and two sons, Andreas and Hans, who, for distinction sake, wrote his Christian name as the Germans do, Johann, and assumed for the initial of it, J. instead of H. The harpsichords of the Ruckers have long been valued for the fullness and sweetness of their tone, but are at this time less in use than formerly, on account of the narrowness of their compass, compared with the modern ones.

university of Leyden. Vossius, before this appointment, had attached himself to the profession of divinity, and had taken the side of Arminius at the famous synod of Dort, held in 1618. The principles which he avowed, and, above all, a history of the Pelagian Controversy, which he published in that year, recommended him to the favour of Laud, who being archbishop of Canterbury in 1629, procured for him of Charles I. a prebend in the church of Canterbury, with permission to hold it notwithstanding his residence at Leyden. Upon this promotion he came over to England to be installed ; and having taken the degree of doctor of laws at Oxford, returned to Leyden, from whence he removed, in 1633, to Amsterdam, and became the first professor of history in the college then newly founded in that city. He died at Amsterdam anno 1649, aged seventy-two years.

Giovanni Battista Doni, a Florentine by birth, and descended from a noble family, though not a musician by profession, is celebrated for his skill in the science. He was much favoured by Cardinal Barberini,* and, at his recommendation, was appointed secretary to the college of cardinals. Being a man of very extensive learning and great ingenuity, and finding the fatigues of his employment a great interruption to his studies, he quitted it, and retired to the city of his nativity, and ended his days there, being not much above fifty years of age. It appears by an account which Doni has given of himself and of his studies, that in his younger days he learned in France to play on the flageolet and the lute ; and, in his more advanced age, to sing, to which end he made himself perfect in the practice of solmisation ; that he also attained to some proficiency on the harpsichord ; and, notwithstanding the little time he had to spare from his important occupation, he applied himself with an uncommon degree of assiduity to the study of the science of harmony, in the course whereof he, partly at his own, and partly at the expence of others, constructed a great number of instruments of his own invention.

In this account which he gives of himself, Doni professes to have directed his studies towards the restitution of the ancient practice, for which it must be confessed he seems to have entertained too great a fondness. He ascribes to the envy and malice of the world the ill reception that his labours met with, and intimates a resolution that he had taken of laying down his employment, and retiring to Florence, with a view to prosecute his studies, and keep up the remembrance of his family, which was become desolate by the immature death of two brothers.

In the Notitia Auctorum of Cardinal Bona is this character of Doni, ' De musica, modisque musicis ' antiquis et novis doctissime scripsit, doctius scrip- ' turus si Græca eruditione præditus suisset.' And Meibomius, in the preface to his edition of the ancient

musicians, expressly says that he did not understand the Greek language.

In the year 1635 Doni published at Rome a discourse entitled ' Compendio del Trattato de' Generi ' e de' Modi della Musica, con un Discorso sopra la ' perfettione de' Concenti,' and dedicated it to his patron Cardinal Barberini. The following are the titles of the several chapters of the Compendium. Cap. I. Quanto mal' intesa sia hoggi la materia de' generi e de' modi. II. Quanto sia grande la diversità tra i modi antichi ed i moderni. III. Altre differenze tra i modi antichi ed i nostri. IV. Che per la restauratione de' generi, e de' modi gl' instrumenti d' archetto sono piu à proposito de gl' altri : e dell' origine dell' organo. V. Con quali mezzi i generi, e modi si possino anch' hoggi pratticare. VI. Come nelle viole suddette si debbono segnare le voci ed intavolarle. VII. Della vera differenza de' tuoni e modi ; e dell' intavolatura, e connessione loro, con le giuste distanze. VIII. Quanto sia commoda et utile, la predetta divisione. IX. Altre considerationi intorno le dette viole. X. Della divisione de gl' organi ed altri instrumenti di tasti per l' uso de' generi e de' tuoni. XI. Della divisione harmonica de gl' instrumenti di tasti. XII. Dell' uso et utilità di questa divisione. XIII. Del modo d' accordare l' organo perfetto. XIV. Catalogo delle consonanze di ciascuna voce de' tre sistemi. XV. Sommario de' Capi più principali, che si contengono nell' opera intera.

This book is of a very miscellaneous nature ; the avowed design of it is to shew that the music of the ancients is to be preferred to that of the moderns ; and in the course of the argument many particulars occur worthy of notice. The author censures Vicentino for his arrogance and his vain attempt to introduce into practice the genera of the ancients, but commends Domenico Zampieri the painter, better known by the name of Dominichino, for a like attempt, and for the invention of a kind of viol much better calculated for that purpose than the archicembalo of Vicentino. He says that Hercole Bottrigaro understood the doctrine of the Genera better than any other of the moderns; and of Zarlino and Salinas, that the first was the prince of practical, as the other was of theoretic musicians.

Together with this treatise is printed a tract entitled Discorso sopra la Perfettione delle Melodie, at the beginning whereof the author treats of the madrigal-style in musical composition, and of those particulars that distinguish the Canto Figurato from the Canto Ecclesiastico ; the invention of which last he says necessarily followed from the use of the organ. The passage is curious, and is as follows :—

' It is not difficult to trace the origin of this kind ' of music, for as organs in churches have been in use ' ever since the time of pope Vitalianus, to which ' instrument this kind of harmony, the Concenti ' Madrigaleschi, seems to belong, seeing that the ' voices may be lengthened at pleasure, and fugues, ' imitations, and such like artifices introduced as on ' the organ ; it is very probable that the symphony ' peculiar to the organ might by degrees be transferred

---

* Cardinal Barberini, afterwards pope Urban VIII., as appears by many passages in his writings, was a lover of music. When Milton was at Rome he was introduced to him by Lucas Holstenius, the keeper of the Vatican library ; and the Cardinal, at an entertainment of music performed at his own expence, received him at the door, and taking him by the hand, brought him into the assembly. Toland's Life of Milton, 8vo. 1761, page 13.

' to vocal performance, taking for a theme or subject
' some motet, anthem, or other sacred words, in a rude
' and awkward kind of counterpoint. That this was
' the case I am very certain, having remarked that
' concenti of this kind were called Organa. In a
' volume in the Vatican library marked No. 5120,
' containing, among others, sundry treatises on coun-
' terpoint, is one with this title :

" Sequitur Regula Organi."

' And a little after it is explained, according to the
' way of those times, Organum, Cantus factus et ordi-
' natus ad rectam mensuram, videlicit, quod unus
' punctus sit divisus ab alio : that is to say, that a
' note, for notes at that time were marked with points,
' whence proceeds the word Contrapunto, in one part
' should not correspond with a note in the other, nor
' be of the same measure. Hence we may see that
' by Organum, in that age they meant the Contrapunto
' diminutivo,* which, according to Bede and more
' ancient writers, is better called Discantus; for where
' he says that music is practised " concentu, discantu,
" organis," I should think he means material organs,
' as he makes use of the plural number. But when
' Guido, who lived between the time of Bede and that
' anonymous author, whom I am now citing, says, as
' he does in the Micrologus, chap. xviii. " Diaphonia,
" vocum disjunctio sonat, quam nos organum voca-
" mus ;" it seems he can mean nothing but that style
' of vocal composition in which diverse airs are given
' to the different parts, according to the meaning of
' the above-mentioned contrapuntist. But, as we have
' presupposed with others, that this kind of music
' cannot be much more than two hundred years old,
' we may believe that Guido understood the term
' Contrapunto diminutivo in the sense which the
' Greek word Diaphonia, signifying Dissonance, seems
' to imply, and in which Franchinus uses the word
' Organizare. This modern kind of concentus how-
' ever does not in reality consist in this, nor in the
' connection of several airs together, but in the sing-
' ing of musical words artfully ranged, and different
' passages at the same time, with many repetitions,
' fugues, and imitations, in such a manner, that in
' regard to the material part of the concentus, viz.,
' the sounds and consonances, one can hardly hear any
' thing more delightful. But that which gives form
' and soul to music suffers remarkable imperfections,
' for by the utterance of many things together the
' attention of the hearer is disturbed, and then so
' many repetitions are frivolous and seem affected ;
' words also are curtailed, and the true pronunciation
' thereof spoiled. I do not dispute whether this kind
' of music has been properly introduced, but this I
' know very well, that it has been in use only these
' few centuries ; for as in ancient times nothing but
' the plain and simple cantus was heard in churches,
' and that rather by connivance than under the sanc-
' tion of public authority ; so even now it is rather
' tolerated than approved of by the church in sacred
' subjects, in which it seems to have had its origin.'
He ascribes to Giulio Caccini the invention of

Recitative, and for the practice of it celebrates Giuseppe Cenci, detto Giuseppino, as he does Ludovico
Viadana for the invention of thorough-bass.

He censures the old German musicians for setting
to music such words as these, Liber Generationis Jesu
Christi Filii David, &c. as also the use of such forms
of speech as the following, which it seems were
common at Rome in his time, Le Vergini del Palestrina, Le Vergini dell' Asola, instead of Le Vergini
del Petrarca, modulate ò messe in musica dal Palestrina, dall' Asola, &c. He says that the Canzones of
Petrarch, Guarini, Tasso, and Marino, as set to music
in the form of madrigals, are the finest of modern
vocal compositions : and he mentions the following
of Petrarch as peculiarly excellent, ' Italia mia,'
' Tirsi morir volea,' and ' Felice chi vi mira.' † He
intimates that for accompanying the human voice, the
Tibia is the fittest instrument ; and concludes with
the mention of an instrument invented by himself,
and called the Lyra Barberini, which participates of
the sweetness of both the harp and lute ; at the end
of this tract is a sonnet written by the author's patron,
Cardinal Barberini, who while the book was printing
was elected pope and assumed the name of Urban
VIII., set to music, at the instance of Doni, in four
parts, by Pietro Eredia ; and, as it is said, in the
ancient Dorian and Phrygian modes.

In the year 1640 Doni published his ' Annotazioni
' sopra il compendio de' generi, e de' modi della mu-
' sica,' and, together with these, sundry tracts and
discourses, that is to say, ' Trattato de' tuoni o modi
' veri,' inscribed to his friend Pietro della Valle.
' Trattato secondo de' tuoni, o harmonie de gl' antichi,
' Al rev. P. Leon Santi. Discorso primo dell' inutile
' osservanza de' tuoni, ò modi hodierni ; Al Signor
' Galeazzo Sabbatini a Bergamo. Discorso secondo,
' sopra le consonanze ; Al Padre Marino Mersenne a
' Parigi. Discorso terzo, sopra la divisione eguale
' attribuita ad Aristosseno; Al Signor Piero de' Bardi
' de' Conti di Vernio à Firenze. Discorso quarto,
' sopra il Violone Panarmonico ; Al Signor Pietro
' della Valle. Discorso quinto, sopra il Violino
' Diarmonico ed la Tiorba a tre manichi, A' Signori
' Dominico e Virgilio Mazzocchi.' In this last discourse the author describes an instrument of his own
invention, resembling in shape the Spanish guitar,
but having three necks, each of them double, like the
Theorbo and Arch-lute; the use of which instrument
is by a different temperature or disposition of the
frets on each of the three necks, to enable the performer to play at his election in either the Dorian, the
Phrygian, or the Hypolydian mode. ' Discorso sesto,
' sopra il Recitare in scena con l' accompagnamento
' d' Instrumenti musicali ; All' illustriss. et excel-
' lentiss. Signore il Sig. Don Camillo Colonna. Dis-
' corso settimo, della Ritmopeia de' versi Latini e
' della melodia de' Cori Tragichi ; Al Signor Gio.
' Jacomo Buccardi.' The annotations, and also the
tracts abound with curious particulars relating to the
music and musicians of the author's time.

---

* CONTRAPUNTUS DIMINUTUS is a term used by Kircher and others to
signify that kind of music where a given plain-song is broken or divided
into notes of a less value: it is the same with Contrapunctus floridus, an
example whereof is given in page 228 of this work.

† The second of these madrigals, set by Luca Marenzio for five voices,
is printed in the Harmonia Celeste, and, with the English words ' Thirsis
to die desired,' in the Musica Transalpina. It is divided into three parts,
and is one of those madrigals of Luca Marenzio which Peacham has
celebrated.

## CHAP. CXXXII.

In the year 1647 Doni published a treatise entitled De Præstantia Musicæ veteris, in three books; this work is written in dialogue, and is a very learned disquisition on the subject of music, as well ancient as modern; the interlocutors are Charidorus, by whom is characterized the author himself; Philoponus, a man of learning, Polyaenus, a friend of both, and Eumolpus a singer.

In this curious and entertaining work the subject is discussed in the way of free conversation, wherein, although the author professes himself a strenuous advocate for the ancients, great latitude is given in the arguments of his opponents, and particularly of Philoponus, who is no less a favourer of the moderns. The argument insisted on in the course of this work is, that the musical faculty was treated of more skilfully by the ancient Greeks and by the Romans than at this day; and that in the construction and use of such instruments as the Cythara and Lyra, and pipes of all kinds, they were equal at least to the moderns; but in such as are made to sound by mutual percussions, as the Cymbala and Crotala, they far exceeded them.

The data required and granted for this purpose are, first, that almost all the more elegant arts and faculties, and among those that of music, grew obsolete, and at last entirely perished by the incursions and devastations of the Barbarians, who miserably over-ran and laid waste Greece and Italy, and all the provinces of the Roman empire. Secondly, that by so many plunderings, burnings, slaughters, and subversions, and changes of languages, manners, and institutions, the greatest part of the ancient books in all kinds of learning perished; so that not even the thousandth part escaped; and those that were saved were almost all maimed and defective, or loaded with errors, as they came down to us; and, as it always happens, the best were lost, and the more unworthy shared a better fate in this general shipwreck. Thirdly, that those who are to be called ancients, as far as relates to this subject of enquiry, are only such as flourished in Greece and Italy before these devastations; for those who lived between them and our forefathers, in whose time literature and music began again to flourish, are not properly to be called ancients, nor are they worth regarding.

As this treatise is written in dialogue, it is somewhat difficult so to connect the speeches of the several interlocutors, as to give them the form of an argument. The principal question agitated by them is simply this, Whether the music of the ancients or of the moderns is to be preferred: Doni, in the person of Charidorus, takes the part of the ancients; and Philoponus is a no less strenuous advocate for the moderns. Indeed the whole force of the argument rests in the speeches of these two persons, those of the other two being interposed merely for the sake of variety, and to enliven the conversation. For this reason it will perhaps be thought that the best method of abridging this tract will be by giving first the substance of Charidorus's argument in favour of the ancients, and opposing to it that of Philoponus in defence of the moderns, and this is the course we mean to pursue.

Charidorus asserts that as Pythagoras was the parent and founder of music, we are not to wonder that the most learned writers on the subject of harmonics were those of his school. Of these he says Archytas of Tarentum, Philolaus of Crotona, Hippasus Metapontinus, and Eubulides were the chief. He adds that the Platonics also, and many of the Peripatetics were great cultivators of the science of harmony; but that of the writings of these men there are no remains, excepting one little book, the nineteenth of the problems of Aristotle. Of the later philosophers he mentions Plutarch, who he says wrote a book on music, yet extant, full of things most worthy to be known. Of Aristoxenus he speaks with rapture, styling him the prince of musicians, and cites St. Jerome's opinion of him, that he was by far the most learned philosopher and mathematician of all the Greeks. He highly applauds Ptolemy of Pelusium, whose three books of Harmonics he says are full of excellent learning, but rather obscure, notwithstanding the noble commentaries of Porphyry on the first of them. With him he joins Aristides Quintilianus, Alypius, Bacchius, Gaudentius, Cleonides, Pappus Alexandrinus, Theo Smyrnæus, Diophantus, Adrastus, Diocles, Gemimus, Nichomachus, and others. He greatly commends the five books, De Musica, of Boetius as a very elegant, ingenious, and learned work. He says it was drawn from the manual of Nichomachus, and laments that the author did not live to complete it. As to the rest of the Latin writers, St. Augustin, Martianus Capella, Cassiodorus, and Bede, whom he reckons among the semi-ancients, he says their writings contain nothing either learned or notable; and that Varro, Apuleius, Albinus, and other Romans that laboured in this field, and whose works are since extinct, were more learned than any of them.

To the more ancient of the monkish writers on music, namely, Odo of Cluni, Berno the abbat, and Guido Aretinus, Notgerus, Hucbaldus, and some others, Charidorus allows some degree of merit; but of Franco of Cologne,* Philippus de Caserta, Marchettus Paduanus, Prosdocimus Beldimandus, Johannes de Muris, Anselmus Parmensis, and others of the old Italian writers, he says they did not even dream of what eloquence or polite learning was: nor does he scruple to censure even Franchinus himself for making use of the word Manerium instead of Modum, Tritechordium, Baritonantem, Altisonantem, and some others, as he does also Glareanus for the same reason.

He mentions also a certain modern author, but conceals his name, who in treating of the genera, asserts that the enarmonic genus is so called, for that it is as it were without harmony, ignorantly supposing the syllable *en* to be privative like *in*, as when we say ineptus insulsus, &c. and of another, who in a pretty large volume says that the diatonic was so

* Franco was of Liege, not of Cologne. See page 176 of this work.

called, because Dia in Greek signifies the number Six, and Tonicum resounding.

He censures severely Nicola Vicentino for his absurd opinions, and for arrogating to himself the title of Archimusicus; the passage is given at length, in page 396 of this work.

He says that Gaffarel, a most learned Frenchman, had commented on the music of the Jews; and praises the two books of Mersennus in French and in Latin, which he says the author sent him as a present; and adds that the same person translated Bacchius into French.

Then follows a curious account of a musical impostor, and of his attempt to introduce a new tuning of the organ in one of the principal churches in Rome, in these words: 'You remember that a certain 'ragged old man came into this city not long since, 'who knew nothing more than to play tolerably on 'the Polyplectrum, and yet would obtrude as a new 'and most useful invention that equality of the semi-'tones which is commonly, but unjustly attributed to 'the Aristoxeneans, and is falsely imagined to be 'found in the division of the keys of the organ, and 'that he attemperated his instrument accordingly. 'You know what crouds he gathered together, and 'what a noise he made, and when he had insinuated 'himself into the acquaintance of Chærilus, whom 'you know to be a most audacious and impudent man, 'that boasts of a certain counterfeit species of erudi-'tion, but chiefly of his proficiency in the study of 'poetry and music, in the circles and courts of princes, 'what think you he did? He extorted money from 'the French orator, whom he worked for on that 'foolish and tedious drama, which was exhibited on 'the birth-day of the Dauphin by the chorus of the 'Roman singers; and when the good singers were 'fretting and fuming, as resenting such roguery, and 'the best of them were so incensed, as to be ready to 'tear off their cassocks for being compelled to sing 'to such ill temperated organs, he at length, by 'prayers, promises, small gifts, and boasting speeches, 'drew the musurgists over to his opinion, and so 'softened, by frequent and gratuitous entertainments, 'that noble organist Psycogaurus, who presided over 'the music of the palace, that he was not ashamed, 'contrary to the faith of his own ears, to extol to the 'best of princes this invention: and he also reported 'abroad that the old man had been presented with a 'golden chain of a large price, that by this lie the 'imposter might gain credit among the unskilful. 'And that the farce might be the better carried on, 'the same person introduced to his friends this old 'man rather burdened than honoured with a chain of 'great weight, hired from some Jewish banker. But 'you will say that this is ridiculous: yet ought we 'rather to weep than laugh at it; for he had prevailed 'so far that the same prince, who, as chance would 'have it, was repairing at that time the choir and 'music-gallery in one of the chief and most ancient 'cathedrals in the city, gave orders for the reducing 'of the noble organ in the same to that dissonant 'species of temperature; and it actually had been 'executed had not our Donius prevented it.'

Doni then relates an attempt of Kapsberger to introduce his own music into the chapel of a certain bishop in prejudice to that of Palestrina, an account whereof has been given in the life of Palestrina, herein before inserted in this work.

After some very severe reflections on the conduct of Kapsberger, he proceeds to censure Fabio Colonna in these words: 'But lest I should seem to attack 'this our age too fiercely, hear what had liked to have 'happened in the Borghesian times.* Fabio Colonna, 'a man well known, and a diligent searcher into na-'ture, died lately at Naples; he, incited by an imma-'ture and depraved ambition, being at that time but 'a young man, published a certain book relating to 'theorical music, entitled Sambuca Lyncea; and I do 'not know that a more foolish or unlearned one has 'appeared for some time before; and there were not 'wanting some unskilful judges who persuaded pope 'Paul to send for this man from Naples, and allow 'him a large stipend for superintending the construc-'tion of an organ in the Vatican church, at a large 'expence, according to his own system; and the 'thing would have been done, had not that prince 'refused to be at the expence of it.'

Charidorus then breaks out into an eulogium on Olympus, the reputed inventor of the enarmonic genus, whose music he says was pathetic and divine. He then appeals to one of the interlocutors in these words: 'You best can judge, O Philoponus, whether 'this character be due to the symphonies of Iodocus 'and Johannes Mouton, and the rest of that class; 'for I am persuaded you are conversant in their 'works, remembering that I once saw a collection of 'Masses composed by them severally, and printed by 'the direction of pope Leo X. in curious types, lying 'on a table in your study.' Philoponus answers, 'There is really nothing of this kind to be found in 'them, yet the authors you mention were possessed 'of the faculty of harmony; and a marvellous felicity 'in modulating and digesting the consonances, afford-'ing great delight to the hearing; but the elocution 'is barbarous and inconcinnous; and as for moving 'the affections, they never so much as dreamt of it.'

Charidorus again recurs to the ancient musicians, of whom he gives a long account from Homer, Plato, Plutarch, Cicero, Quintilian, Seneca, Athenæus, and other writers. Speaking of the moderns, he cele-brates Ercole as a skilful organist; but, as to the modern theorists, he says, that excepting Jacobus Faber Stapulensis, Salinas, Zarlino, Vincentio Galilei, Michael Prætorius, Mersennus, Bottrigaro, and some very few others, their works contain only trivial and common things, and what had been said a hundred times over. He adds that nobleness of birth and a liberal education in musicians conduce much to the elegance of their modulations; as a proof whereof he says, some have observed that the compositions of the prince of Venosa, and of Thomas Pecius, a patrician of Sienna in Tuscany,† had in them some-

---

* Paul V. who at that time was Pope, was of the Borghesian family, being son of Antonio Borghese of Sienna; he was elected anno 1605, and died in 1621. See Rycaut's Lives of the Popes, page 227.

† TOMASO PECCI, though but little known, is celebrated by Kircher as an excellent musician: there is extant of his composition a book of Madrigals, published at Venice in 1609.

what that was not vulgar nor plebeian, but that sounded elegant and magnificent.

Charidorus complains of the want of some severe law to repress that effeminate and light music which then prevailed; and says that that most wise pope Marcellus II. had determined to correct the licentiousness of the musicians according to the opinion of the holy council of Trent. But that he suffered himself to be imposed on by the cunning of one musician,* and the glory of such a work to be snatched out of his hands.

Book II. contains the argument of Philoponus, in which he undertakes to point out the defects of the ancient music, and to shew the superiority of the modern. To this end he infers that the ancients must have been unacquainted with music in consonance from this circumstance, that they never looked on the ditone and trihemitone, nor the greater and lesser sixth, as consonants; and in support of his opinion adduces the testimony of Zarlino and Galilei, both of whom say that, among the ancients, if at any time two singers were introduced, they did not sing together, but alternately. Philoponus next observes that the ancient musicians were ignorant of those graces and ornaments which we call Passaggios, and of those artful and ingenious contrivances, fugues, imitations, canons, and double counterpoints; and that the superiority of the modern music may be very justly gathered from the great plenty, variety, and excellence of instruments now in use, more especially the organ; whereas among the ancients the principal were the lyre and the cithara, which were mounted with very few chords.

As another proof of the superiority of the modern music, he mentions the extension of the scale by Guido Aretinus to the interval of a greater sixth beyond that of the Greeks, his invention of the syllables, and, lastly, the modern notation or method of writing down music.

Philoponus proceeds to celebrate the modern writers on music, namely, Salinas, Zarlino, and Galilei, as also the composers of songs both sacred and profane, that is to say, Adrian Willaert, Palestrina, Cristoforo Morales, Luca Marenzio, Pomponio Nenna, Tomaso Pecci, and the prince of Venosa, Cyprian de Rore, Felice Anerio, and Nanino, Filippo de Monte, and Orlando de Lasso. For the invention and improvement of Recitative he applauds Giulio Caccini, Jacopo Peri, and Claudio Monteverde; and for their singing, Suriano, and another named Theophilus; as also two very fine female singers, Hadriana Baroni, and her daughter Leonora, in these words 'If by chance we bring women into this 'contest, how great will be the injury to compare 'either Hadriana or her daughter Leonora† with the

'ancient Sappho? or if, besides the glory of well 'singing, you think a remarkable skill in music is 'necessary, there is Francesca, the daughter of Caccini, 'whom I have just now praised.'

He then celebrates Frescobaldi as an admirable performer on the organ, and others of his time for their excellence on other instruments; and remarks on the great concourse of people at the churches of Rome on festival days upon the rumour of some grand musical performance, especially when new motetti were to be sung.

Charidorus to these arguments of Philoponus replies; and first he asserts that although the ditone, trihemitone, and the two sixths were not known to the ancients as consonances; and for this he cites the testimony of Galilei, and Salinas, lib. II. cap. ii. page 60, who indeed says the same thing, but gives this awkward reason for not enumerating these intervals among the consonances, namely, that those who thought them such were unwilling to contradict

'omnes hic Romæ, quotquot ingenio et poëticæ facultatis laude præstant, 'carminibus, tum Etrusce tum Latinè scriptis, singulari ac prope divino 'mulieris illius canendi artificio tanquam faustos quosdam clamores et 'plausius edunt; legi, inquam, unum Lælii (Guidiccionis) epigramma, 'ita purum, ita elegans, ita argutum, ita venustum, prope ut dixerim, 'nihil me vidisse, in eo genere, elegantius neque politius.'

Fulvio Testi has also celebrated her in the following sonnet:—

Se l' Angioletto mia tremolo, e chiaro,
   A le stelle, onde scese, il canto invia,
   Ebbra del suono, in cui sè stessa obblia,
   Col Ciel pensa la Terra irne del paro.

Ma se di sua Virtù non ponto ignaro
   L' occhio accorda gli sguardi à l' armonia,
   Trà il concento, e il fulgor dubbio è se sia
   L' udir più dolce, ò il rimirar più caro.

Al divin lume, â le celesti note
   De le potenze sue perde il vigore
   L' alma, e dal cupo sen suelta si scote.

Deh, fammi cieco, ò fammi sordo, Amore:
   Che distratto in più sensi (oimè) non pote
   Capir tante dolcezze un picciol core.

   Poesie Liriche del Conte D. Fulvio Testi, Ven. 1691, pag. 361.

Among the Latin poems of Milton are no fewer than three entitled 'Ad Leonoram Romæ canentem,' wherein this lady is celebrated for her singing, with an allusion to her mother's exquisite performance on the lute. Doni was acquainted with them both; and it may be supposed that they severally performed in the concerts at the Barberini palace. Mention has already been made of Milton's being introduced to one of these entertainments by the Cardinal himself; and it is more than probable that at this or some other of them he might have heard the mother play and the daughter sing.

A fine eulogium on this accomplished woman is contained in a Discourse on the Music of the Italians, printed with the life of Malherbe, and some other treatises at Paris, 1672, in 12mo, at the end of which are these words: 'This discourse was composed by Mr. Maugars, prior of 'St. Peter de Mac, the king's interpreter of the English language, and 'besides so famous a performer on the viol, that the king of Spain and 'several other sovereign princes of Europe have wished to hear him. 'The character given by this person of Leonora Baroni is as follows: "She is endowed with fine parts; she has a very good judgment to dis-"tinguish good from bad music; she understands it perfectly well; and "even composes, which makes her absolute mistress of what she sings, "and gives her the most exact pronunciation and expression of the "sense of her words. She does not pretend to beauty, neither is she "disagreeable, or a coquet. She sings with a bold and generous modesty, "and an agreeable gravity; her voice reaches a large compass of notes, "and is exact, loud, and harmonious; she softenes and raises it without "straining or making grimaces. Her raptures and sighs are not las-"civious; her looks have nothing impudent, nor does she transgress "a virgin modesty in her gestures. In passing from one key to another "she shews sometimes the divisions of the enharmonic and chromatic "kind with so much art and sweetness, that every body is ravished with "that fine and difficult method of singing. She has no need of any "person to assist her with a Theorbo or viol, one of which is necessary "to make her singing complete; for she plays perfectly well herself on "both those instruments. In short, I have had the good fortune to hear "her sing several times above thirty different airs, with second and "third stanzas composed by herself. I must not forget to tell you that "one day she did me the particular favour to sing with her mother and "her sister. Her mother played upon the lute, her sister upon "the harp, and herself upon the Theorbo. This concert, composed of "three fine voices, and of three different instruments, so powerfully "transported my senses, and threw me into such raptures, that I forgot "my mortality, and thought myself already among the angels enjoying "the felicity of the blessed.'" Bayle, Art. BARONI, in not.

---

* Who this cunning musician was we are at a loss to guess. It is said of Palestrina, that pope Marcellus II. being about to banish music out of the church, was induced to depart from a resolution which he had taken for that purpose by that fine mass of his composing, entitled Missa Papæ Marcelli. See page 421 of this work.

† ADRIANA of Mantua, for her beauty surnamed the Fair, and her daughter LEONORA BARONI: the latter of these two celebrated persons is by Bayle said to have been one of the finest singers in the world; a whole volume of poems in her praise is extant with this title, 'Applausi 'poëtica alle glorie della Signora Leonora Baroni. Nicius Erythræus,' in his Pinacotheca II. page 427, 12mo. Lips. 1712, alludes to this work, saying, 'Legi ego, in theatro Eleonoræ Baronæ, cantricis eximiæ, in quo

the doctrines of the Pythagoreans, who allowed of no other consonances than the diatessaron, diapente, and diapason ; yet upon this foundation he scruples not to assert, and that in terms the most positive, that the ancients were acquainted with and practised music in consonance.

He then enters into a long discourse on the Tibiæ of the ancients, the genera and their species, and other particulars of the ancient music.  To what Philoponus had advanced in favour of Suriano and Theophilus, Charidorus answers that the complaint of Ariadne, written by Ottavio Rinuccini, and set to music by Claudio Monteverde, is more to be esteemed than any canon of either of them.

He commends that triumvirate, meaning, as it is supposed, Giulio Caccini, Jacopo Peri, and Claudio Monteverde, who revived the monodical or recitative style, but he adds, that what they did was not so much the effect of their own judgment and industry, as of the advice and assistance of the learned men then at Florence.

Of symphonetic music, the excellencies of which Philoponus had so strongly insisted on, Charidorus seems to entertain no very high opinion ; for he says that were the musicians in general to make their compositions as fine as those of Cypriano de Rore ; yet because the melody is required to be distributed through all the several parts, for if one part be highly finished, the rest will sing unhandsomely, the grace and beauty of the work will not shine forth.  And as to that variety of motion and difference in the time of notes, and those sundry points and passages which constitute the difference between figurate and plain descant, he says that they produce nought but confusion, and that they render only an enervate kind of music ; and that as those who labour under a fever have an inordinate and inconstant pulse, so in this kind of harmony, the numbers being inordinate and confused, that energy which so greatly affects and delights our ears and minds is wanting, and the whole becomes a confused jargon of irregular measures.*

In the course of his reasoning Charidorus frequently cites Plato, Aristotle, Nichomachus, Aristides Quintilianus, Aristoxenus, Bacchius, Plutarch, Ptolemy, and others of the Greek writers on music ; and after collecting their sentiments, he opposes to them those of Guido Aretinus, Bartolomeo Ramis, Spataro, and Steffano Vanneo ; for as to Franco and Johannes De Muris, and the rest of that class, he says they are half ancient, and totally barbarous ; and adds, that among the ancients the very women were skilled in harmonics, for that Porphyry, in his Commentaries on the Harmonics of Ptolemy, mentions one Ptolemais, a certain woman, who treated accurately on the elements of the Pythagorean music. Speaking of the metrical part of music, he says that the ancients were very exact and curious in their phrase, and in their pronunciation, and examined the momenta of times, accents, letters, and syllables, but

that the moderns pay but little attention to these matters : yet he says that through the endeavours of the Florentine Academy, a more distinct and elegant pronunciation in the monodical cantus or recitative began to be esteemed.   He adds, that recitative thus improved was introduced by a young man named Loretus, before-named, whom Nicola Doni, a relation of the author, very kindly entertained at his house for some years, and caused to be assisted in his musical studies.

Charidorus then bewails the fate of modern music, in that it is no longer as it was wont to be, the sister of poetry ; and observes that the ecclesiastical songs are deficient both in purity of phrase and elegance of sentiment : and as to harmony of numbers, he says it is not to be looked for, for that they are written in prose, in which so little regard is paid to concinnity or aptness of numbers, that there have not been wanting musicians who have set to music in parts, the genealogy of Jesus Christ, consisting wholly of Hebrew names.†

He then enters largely into the consideration of the Melopoeia and Rythmopoeia of the ancients, and next of the Progymnastica, or rudiments of music ; he says that the practice of singing was much more aptly and expeditiously taught by the ancient Greeks than by the modern Latins, with the help of the six syllables invented by Guido, or by the later Germans and French with that of seven : and he asserts, with the greatest degree of confidence, that the noviciate of the younger students in music would be much shortened were two of the six syllables of Guido cut off ; and as to the practice of solmisation, his sentiments are as follow : 'What that monk Aretinus 'boasts of his invention, saying that it greatly con-'tributed to facilitate the learning of music, is 'partly true and partly false : it is true when com-'pared with the ages next immediately before him, 'in which the ancient progymnastical syllables were 'out of use ; but false when compared with the prac-'tice of the ancient Greeks and Romans, who made 'use of these four syllables, TA, TA, TE, TE ; and if, 'following their example, the system of Guido were 'reduced to the ancient measure, it would be far 'more commodious.'

In the third and last part, Doni, in the person of Charidorus, cites from Suetonius a passage wherein it is related of Nero, that in order to enable him to sing the better, he not only abstained from fruit and such kind of food as had a tendency to hurt his voice ; but to improve it suffered a leaden plate to be fixed on his breast, and made use of vomits and clysters.‡

To this discipline of Nero, ridiculous as it was severe, and the servile condition of singers in ancient Greece and Rome, Charidorus opposes the licentious and disorderly lives of those of modern Italy, of whom he gives the following account :—

'In these our days the singers are generally of the

---

* This objection lays a ground for a suspicion that Doni was an incompetent judge of the merits of musical composition ; for who does not see, with respect to the power of moving the affections, the difference between mere melody and music in consonance, and the preference due to the latter ?

† Doni here alludes to a composition in Glareanus of Iodocus Pratensis, to the words of the first chapter of the Gospel of St. Matthew.

‡ The author gives not the least intimation to favour the notion that the practice of castration, with a view to the preservation of the voice, was in use among the ancients ; but he speaks of the practice of infibulation for a similar purpose, as mentioned by Juvenal, and refers to Celsus for a particular description of the method of performing the operation.

'lower class, yet are their masters unable to keep 'them under restraint; and their insolence is such as 'scarcely to be borne with. You see those nice 'eunuchs, who every one of them make more money 'than ten singing masters, how daintily they live, 'how much they boast of themselves, what little ac- 'count they make of other men, and that they even 'deride such as are learned. I say nothing of their 'morals, since what is seen by every body cannot be 'denied. When the princes Barberini have on certain 'festival days given to the public musical dramas, 'have you not seen some of them contesting with 'those lords, impudently thwarting them, and endea- 'vouring to get admitted whomsoever they pleased 'into the theatre? when tickets of admission were 'made out they have not been content with a few, but 'were ready to tear more out of the hands of such 'as were appointed to distribute them.'

He says that Vitruvius relates that he had been told by the son of Masinissa, king of Numidia, who made him a visit, and stayed some days at his house, that there was a certain place in Africa, Pliny calls it Zama, where were fountains of such a nature, that those who were born there and drank of the water had excellent voices for singing; and that he himself, at Luneburg, a city of Savoy, seated under the very Alps, had been at a fountain, the water whereof pro- duced similar effects; and that coming there on a certain festival in the evening, he found some of the inhabitants singing praises to God with voices sweet and musical to a wonderful degree, and such as he conceives those of the singers in ancient Greece and Rome to have been.

He says that notwithstanding the great number of singers at Rome, there were in his time very few whose voices were perfect and sweet. He adds that the silence of the ancients in this particular implies that the practice of castration, for the purpose of meliorating the voice, was not in use among the an- cient Greeks and Romans; but contradicts the vulgar opinion of its effect, insisting that the voices of women and boys are in general more sweet than those of eunuchs, the singing of whom together in large companies he resembles to the noise of a troop of wethers.

Philoponus having in his argument insisted largely on the exquisite performance of many modern musi- cians on various instruments, Charidorus replies that the best of them are not to be compared to those among the ancients, who played on the lyre and the tibia. He says that the English are allowed to excel on the flute; and that there are many in that king- dom good performers on the cornet, yet he cannot believe that the English artists are equal to the an- cient players on the tibia, namely, Antigenides, Pronomus, and Timotheus.

Speaking of instruments, he says there are many particulars relating to the construction of them, which are unknown to the modern artificers, as namely, that the best strings are made when the north, and the worst when the south wind blows; and that the bel- lies of lutes and viols, and other instruments of the fidicinal kind, should be made of fir, cloven and not sawed, lest the fibres should be cut across in smoothing.*

He says it is no wonder that the tibiæ of the an- cients excelled so greatly those of the moderns, seeing that the old Greeks and Romans were most diligent and curious about them; for they were constructed of box, the wood of the Lote-tree, of silver, and of the shank-bones of certain animals, that is to say, deer and asses, and of a Grecian reed, still in use among the nations of the East, excelling all the rest in sweetness, as he judges from having once heard an Englishman play on a pipe of this kind.

He greatly laments, that although Vitruvius has given a description of the ancient hydraulic organ, we, at this distance of time, are incapable of under- standing the terms made use of by him for explaining it, and that the diagrams representing the several parts of it are lost. He adds, that the organ men- tioned by Zarlino in his Sopplimenti, affords no argument to conclude that those of the ancients were not greatly superior to it.

He next proceeds to censure the musicians of his time for the licentiousness and levity of their compo- sitions, in these words, 'Despising the most sweet 'motets of Prenestinus and Morales, and others which 'they call too old, and studying novelty, they daily 'obtrude their own symphonies, which they steal here 'and there, and afterwards tack together in a pitiful 'manner. Who taught them,' exclaims he, 'to adapt 'to a joyful modulation and concentus, that sad and 'mournful petition of Kyrie Eleison? Or, on the 'other hand, to make sad and mournful that clausula 'of Mary's song, the Gloria Patri, which is full of 'exultation? yet this they daily practise.'†

At the end of this treatise of Doni, De Præstantia Musicæ veteris, is a catalogue of the author's writings on the subject of music, amounting to no fewer than twenty-four tracts, reckoning many that were never published, and a few that he did not live to complete.

From the account above given of Doni it must appear that he was very deeply skilled in musical science, and that he had diligently perused as well the writings of the ancients as the moderns on the subject. Pietro della Valle, the famous traveller, who was intimately acquainted with him, bears a very honourable testimony to his character, for he says he had 'congiunta a gran bontà e integrità di costumi 'profondissima erudizione, con esatta notizia della 'lingua Greca, delle mattematiche, della teoria musi- 'cale, della poesia, dell' istoria, e di ogni altra facoltà 'che a ciò possa giovare; con l' ajuto e comodità che 'ha avuto di vedere molti bei libri reconditi e non

---

* This remark, if attended to, will be found to amount to nothing; for the fibres of the wood are as much cut across by the smoothing or work- ing the belly of such an instrument as by sawing.

† Both the objections implied in these queries are well founded, but the latter only of them will hold at this day; for the public ear is too depraved to bear pathetic music. As to the former objection, it arose from the practice of assimilating the music of the church to that of the theatre: and this abuse has so prevailed, that the Kyrie Eleison is now frequently set to a movement in jig-time. In a mass of Pergolesi, one of the most pathetic of modern composers, the Gloria Patri is a fugue in chorus, and the Amen a minuet. Graun's celebrated Te Deum is of a lighter cast than any opera of Lully, Bononcini, or Handel: in it that most solemn clause, 'Te ergo quæsumus, tuis famulis subveni, quos 'pretioso sanguine redemisti,' is set to a movement in triple time, in the lightest of all the keys, viz. E ♮ with the greater third, and with an accompaniment by a German flute. The church-music of Perez of Lisbon is for the most part in the same style.

'pubblicati alle stampe, massimamente autori antichi 'Greci nella Vaticana e in molt' altre librerie famose.'

This character of Doni, given by one who was intimate with him, and well knew the estimation he was held in at Rome, is in some measure confirmed by Meibomius, although he had no other foundation for his opinion than that intrinsic evidence of learning, industry, and ingenuity contained in the writings of Doni; for he says that none of the age he lived in had written with more learning or elegance than he had done; and that had he been better skilled in Greek literature, and known at least the first principles of the mathematics, he would have performed greater things. A few years ago the musical tracts of Doni were collected, and published in Italy, in two volumes folio, with a portrait of him.

## CHAP. CXXXIII.

ATHANASIUS KIRCHER was born at Fulda in Germany, on the second day of May, 1601. At the age of seventeen he entered into the society of the Jesuits, and, after going through a regular course of study, during which he shewed most amazing parts and industry, he became a teacher of philosophy, mathematics, and the Hebrew and Syriac languages, in the university of Wirtzburg in Franconia. In the year 1631, when the Suedes entered Germany under Gustavus Adolphus, he retired into France, and settled in the Jesuits' college at Avignon, and remained there till 1635. He was then called to Rome to teach mathematics in the Roman college, which he did six years; afterwards he became professor of the Hebrew language in that city, and died there in the month of November, 1680, having written and published twenty-two volumes in folio, eleven in quarto, and three in octavo. The chief of his works are, the Musurgia Universalis. Primitiæ Gnomicæ Catoptricæ. Prodomus Copticus. Ars Magnetica. Thesaurus Linguæ Ægyptiacæ. Ars magna Lucis et Umbræ. Obeliscus Pamphilius. Oedipus Ægyptiacus, tom. IV. Itinerarium Extaticum. Obeliscus Ægyptiacus. Mundus subterraneus, tom. II. China Illustrata. Phonurgia nova. Kircher was more than ordinarily addicted to the study of hieroglyphical characters; and it is said that certain young scholars caused to be engraved some unmeaning fantastic characters or figures upon a shapeless piece of stone, and buried it in a place which was shortly to be dug up; upon digging the place the stone was found, and was by the scholars that had hid it, carried to Kircher as a most singular antique, who, quite in raptures, applied himself instantly to explain the hieroglyphics, and, as he conceived, made it intelligible.

As the Musurgia is dispersed throughout Europe, and is in the hands of many persons, a general view of it may suffice in this place. It is dedicated to Leopold, archduke of Austria, afterwards emperor of Germany, who was not only a patron of music, but an excellent performer on the harpsichord. Of its nature and contents an accurate judgment may be formed by the perusal of the following Synoposis prefixed to the first volume.

SYNOPSIS

MUSURGIÆ UNIVERSALIS,

IN X. LIBROS DIGESTÆ.

Quorum septem primi Tomo 1. Reliqui tres Tomo II. comprehenduntur.

Liber I.   Physiologicus, soni naturalis Genesin, naturam et proprietatem effectusque demonstrat.

Liber II.   Philologicus, soni artificialis, sive Musicæ primam institutionem propagationemque inquirit.

Liber III.   Arithmeticus, motuum harmonicorum scientiam per numeros et novam Musicam Algebraicam docet.

Liber IV.   Geometricus, intervallorum consono dissonorum originem per monochordi divisionem Geometricam, Algebraicam, Mechanicam, multiplici varietate ostendit.

Liber V.   Organicus, Instrumentorum omnis generis Musicorum structuram novis experimentis aperit.

Liber VI.   Melotheticus, componendarum omnis generis cantilenarum novam et demonstrativam methodum producit: continetque quicquid circa hoc negotium curiosum, rarum et arcanum desiderari potest.

Liber VII.   Diacriticus, comparationem veteris Musicæ cum moderna instituit, abusus detegit, cantus Ecclesiastici dignitatem commendat, methodumque aperit, qua ad patheticæ Musicæ perfectionem tandem perveniri possit.

Liber VIII.   Mirificus, novam artem Musarithmicam exhibet, qua quivis etiam Musicæ imperitus, ad perfectam componendi notitiam brevi tempore pertingere possit, continetque Musicam Combinatoriam, Poeticam, Rhetoricam, Panglossiam Musarithmicam omnibus linguis novo artificio adaptat.

Liber IX.   Magicus, reconditiora totius Musicæ arcana producit; continetque Physiologiam consoni et dissoni; Præterea Magiam Musico-medicam, Phonocampticam, sive perfectam de Echo, qua mensuranda, qua constituenda doctrinam, Novam Tuborum oticorum, sive auricularium, fabricam; item Statuarum, ac aliorum Instrumentorum Musicorum Autophonorum, seu per se sonantium, uti et sympathicorum structuram curiosis ac novis experientiis docet. Quibus adnectitur Cryptologia musica, qua occulti animi conceptus in distans per sonos manifestantur.

Liber X.   Analogicus, decachordon naturæ exhibet, quo Deum in 3 Mundorum Elementaris, Cœlestis, Archetypi fabrica ad Musicas proportiones respexisse per 10. gradus, veluti per 10. Naturæ Registra demonstratur.

Registrum 1.   Symphonismos Elementorum, sive Musicam Elementarem.

Registrum 2.   Cœlorum admirandam Symphoniam in motibus, influxibus effectibusque.

Registrum 3.   Lapidum, Plantarum, Animalium, in Physico, Medico, Chymico negotio.

Registrum 4.   Musicam Microcosmi cum Megacosmo, id est minoris cum majori mundo.

Registrum 5.   Musicam Sphigmicam, sive pulsuum in venis arterisque se manifestantem.

Registrum 6.   Musicam Ethicam in appetitu sensitivo et rationali elucescentem.

Registrum 7.   Musicam Politicam, Monarchicam, Aristocraticam, Democraticam, Oeconomicam.

Registrum 8.   Musicam Metaphysicam, sive Potentiarum interiorum ad Angelos et Deum comparatam.

Registrum 9.   Musicam Hierarchicam, sive Angelorum in 9 choros distributorum.

Registrum 10.   Musicam Archetypam, sive Dei cum universa natura concentum.

} exhibet.

In the preface to the Musurgia the author relates that he had been assisted by many professors of the musical science in the compiling of his work, that is to say, by Antonio Maria Abbattini, chapel-master of St. John de Lateran and St. Lawrence in Damasus, and afterwards of St. Maria Maggiore, and to Pietro Heredia of Rome, in the ecclesiastic and motetic styles; by Pietro Francesco Valentini, and Francesco Picerli, in what relates to canon; by Hieronymus Kapsberger in the organic style; and by Giacomo Carissimi in the recitatives and the more abstruse parts of musical composition; and for this assistance he makes a grateful acknowledgment.

He apologizes for writing on music, himself not being a musician, by the example of the prince of Venosa, who, though not a musician by profession, was admirably skilled in the science, and was also an excellent composer: he adds, that neither Ptolemy nor Alphonsus were astronomers or musicians by profession, and yet the one wrote on Harmonics, and the other compiled Astronomical tables. For his own part, he says, that from his youth he had assiduously applied himself, not only to learning and the sciences, but to practical music, his skill in which can only be judged of by the contents of his work; nor is it, he says, the practice alone that he has laboured to cultivate, but he has treated largely of the theory, without which the knowledge acquired by practice will be of little avail.

He takes notice that Mersennus had then lately given to the world a large volume entitled Harmonie Universelle, which he says is a most excellent work, but that it does not so much regard the practical musician as the philosopher.

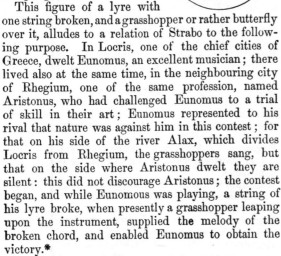

Before we proceed to an account of this elaborate and entertaining work, it may be observed that even the title-page suggests a subject of enquiry sufficient to awaken curiosity, namely, the following emblematical device, which Kircher found engraven on an antique gem.

This figure of a lyre with one string broken, and a grasshopper or rather butterfly over it, alludes to a relation of Strabo to the following purpose. In Locris, one of the chief cities of Greece, dwelt Eunomus, an excellent musician; there lived also at the same time, in the neighbouring city of Rhegium, one of the same profession, named Aristonus, who had challenged Eunomus to a trial of skill in their art; Eunomus represented to his rival that nature was against him in this contest; for that on his side of the river Alax, which divides Locris from Rhegium, the grasshoppers sang, but that on the side where Aristonus dwelt they are silent: this did not discourage Aristonus; the contest began, and while Eunomus was playing, a string of his lyre broke, when presently a grasshopper leaping upon the instrument, supplied the melody of the broken chord, and enabled Eunomus to obtain the victory.*

In Chap. II. of the same book Kircher gives the anatomy of the ear; and delineates, with seemingly great exactness, the organ of hearing in a man, a calf, a horse, a dog, a hare, a cat, a sheep, a goose, a mouse, and a hog.

From the organs of hearing he proceeds, Chap. XI. to describe the vocal organs in the human species, and in Chap. XIV. those of other animals and insects, particularly the frog and the grasshopper: he is very curious in his disquisitions touching the voice and the song of the nightingale, which he has endeavoured to render in notes borrowed from the musical scale.† In the same manner he has exhibited the crowing of the cock, the voice of the hen after laying, her clucking or call to her chickens, the note of the cuckow, and the call or cry of the quail.

In the same chapter he also takes notice, but without assenting to it, of that general opinion, that swans before death sing most sweetly, which besides that it is of very great antiquity, has the authority of Plato in its favour, and is upon relation delivered by Aldrovandus, concerning the swans on the river Thames near London. Notwithstanding which, from the difference in opinion of writers about it, who severally affirm that some swans sing not till they die, others that they sing, yet die not; and for other reasons, Sir Thomas Brown hesitates not to reject it as a vulgar error in these words: 'When therefore ' we consider the dissention of authors, the falsity of ' relations, the indisposition of the organs, and the ' immusical note of all we ever beheld or heard of; ' if generally taken, and comprehending all swans, or ' of all places, we cannot assent thereto. Surely he ' that is bit with a Tarantula shall never be cured by ' this musick;‡ and with the same hopes we expect ' to hear the harmony of the spheres.'§

In Book II. Kircher treats of the music of the Hebrews, and exhibits the forms of sundry of their instruments; from hence he proceeds to the music of the Greeks, of which in this place he gives but a very general and superficial account.

In Book III. he enters very deeply into the doctrine of Harmonics, first explaining the several kinds of proportion, and next demonstrating the ratios of the intervals. In Chap. VIII. of this book he exhibits the ancient Greek scale and that of Guido in a collateral situation, thereby demonstrating the coincidence of each with the other. This book contains also a system of musical arithmetic, drawn from the writings of Boetius and others, in which are contained rules for the addition, subtraction, multiplication, and division of intervals by means of characters adapted to the purpose.

* Heylin, in his Cosmography, edit. 1703, page 63, relating this story, says he does not insist on the belief of the reader, but he asserts that very good authors have said that on the Locrian side of the river Alax the grasshoppers do merrily sing; and that towards Rhegium they are always silent. He adds, that the story, whether true or false, is worthy to have been celebrated by the Muse of Strada in the person of the poet Claudian.

† The song of the nightingale, as given by Kircher, is very elaborate, and must have cost him much pains to get it into any form; it seems to correspond very well, with respect to the measure or time of the notes which constitute the several strains; but the division of our scale is too gross for the intervals, which are smaller than any to be found either there or in the more minute divisions of the ancients, the enarmonic not excepted.

‡ Sir Thomas Brown, though he rejected the fable of the singing of swans, gave credit to that other of the Tarantula

§ Enquiry into vulgar Errors, book III. chap xxvii.

This book contains also a very precise designation of the genera with their several colours or species, as they are found in the writings of the Greek harmonicians.

From the Genera Kircher proceeds to the modes of the ancients, which, with Ptolemy, he makes to be equal with the species of diapason; from hence he digresses to those of the moderns, which, with Glareanus, he makes to be twelve in number.

Book IV. is wholly on the division of the monochord, and directs the method of finding the intervals by various geometric and algebraic processes.

Book V. entitled De Symphoniurgia, contains directions for the composition of music in consonance, a practice, which, after a very laborious search and enquiry, he pronounces the ancient Greeks to have been absolutely ignorant of. To the examples of ancient notation, by points on the lines, and not the spaces of a stave, which he had found in the Dialogo della Musica of Vincentio Galilei, he adds another, which he had procured from a friend of his, the abbot of the monastery of Vallombrosa, consisting of a stave of two lines only, with points on each, and at different stations on the space; this example, which is inserted in a former part of this work,* he makes to be of greater antiquity than the improvement of the stave by Guido.

From this method of notation he says the term Counterpoint, so well understood at this day, is derived. And here Kircher takes occasion to mention John de Muris as the original inventor of the characters for notes of different lengths. Enough has been said in the course of this work in refutation of that popular error, and to prove that the invention is not to be ascribed to De Muris, but to Franco of Liege, who flourished in the same century with Guido.

In this book Kircher explains with sufficient exactness the nature of Counterpoint, both simple and figurate; as also of Fugue, by him termed Contrapuntus Fugatus; and delivers in general terms the precepts for composition in two, three, four, and more parts.

In the course of this book he gives various examples of the ecclesiastic and theatric styles, and celebrates for their skill in the former, Orlando de Lasso, Arcadelt, Iodocus Pratensis, Palestrina, Suriano, Nanino, Christopher Morales, Cifra, and many more; and for the madrigal-style the prince of Venosa, Horatio Vecchi, and others.

Towards the close of this book he speaks of that spurious kind of fugue called Fuga in Nomine; and not only explains the nature of canon, but gives examples of canons, wonderful in their contrivance, and mentions one that may be sung by twelve million two hundred thousand voices.

In Book VI. he treats of instrumental music, and of the various instruments in use among the moderns. Almost the whole of this book is taken from the Latin work of Mersennus, and it is but in few instances that Kircher differs from his author. At the end of this book, following the order of Mersennus,

* Page 158.

he treats of bells, and gives a particular description of the great bell at Erfurth; he says it was cast in the year 1497, by Gerard Wou de Campis, at the expence of the neighbouring princes and noblemen, and citizens of Erfurth; that it is in thickness a quarter and half quarter of an ell, its height is four ells three quarters, and its exterior periphery fourteen ells and a half, and its weight two hundred and fifty-two hundred.

Kircher says that it requires twenty-four men to ring or strike this bell, besides two others, who on each side shove forward the tongue or clapper,† and that the sound of it is plainly to be heard at the distance of three German leagues; he says that its fundamental note is D sol re, but that it gives also F fa ut, making a consonance of a minor third.‡

In Book VII. is a comparison between the ancient and modern music: with respect to the former the following are his sentiments :—

'The whole of the Greek monuments of the 'ancients that are extant are the writings of Aristides 'Quintilianus, Manuel Briennius, Plutarch, Aristotle, 'Callimachus, Aristoxenus, Alypius, Ptolemy, Euclid, 'Nichomachus, Boetius, Martianus Capella and some 'others, who flourished in the last age; several of 'whose Greek manuscripts are bound up together in 'one huge tome, in the library of the Roman college, 'where they are kept as a great treasure; and if you 'carefully compare all those authors together, as 'I have done, you will find nothing so different in 'any of them but what may be found in all the 'rest. For except the analogous, cœlestial, humane, 'and divine music, they all, in the first place, dwell 'on the various composition, division, and mixture 'of the tetrachords and systems of the diapason: 'secondly, they all apply themselves with great care 'to the determination of the different tones or modes: 'and, thirdly, all their industry is employed in com-'pounding and determining the three genera, the 'diatonic, chromatic, and enarmonic; and in sub-'dividing the most minute intervals. Boetius seems 'to have snatched the palm from them all by his 'most exact and ingenious description; for he has 'so fully delivered the precepts of the ancient musi-'cians, so clearly explained what was obscure, and 'so dexterously supplied what was defective, and 'written so perfectly in that most learned work of 'his, that while he shews he let none of the ancient 'music be hid, he seems not only to have described, 'but also to have restored the music of the ancients,

† Kircher's expression in the original is, 'Ut plene exaudiatur, et 'sufficienter concutiatur à 24 hominibus compulsanda est, præter quos 'bini alii requiruntur, qui ex utroque latere linguam impellant;' and this suggests a doubt whether in fact this bell is ever rung at all or not; to ring a bell, in propriety of speech, is by means of the rope and the wheel to raise it on its axis, so as to bring it to a perpendicular situation, that is to say, with its rim upwards; the pull for this purpose gives a stroke of the clapper on one side of the bell, and its descent to its original pendent situation occasions another on the other side. The action of twenty-four men in Kircher's account is not clearly described, but that of the two men whose employment it is to shove the clapper against the side of the bell, does most plainly bespeak the act of tolling and not ringing, a practice which it is said to be peculiar to England, which for that reason, and the dexterity of its inhabitants in composing and ringing musical peals wherein the sounds interchange in regular order, is called the ringing island.

‡ Whoever is desirous of knowing more about bells, may consult Hieronymus Magius, De Tintinnabulis. Amstel. 1664, in which book are many curious particulars relating to them.

'by adding to the inventions of those that went
'before him several things discovered by himself;
'so that whatever is dispersed in all the rest, may
'be seen collected, encreased, and digested with
'exquisite care in Boetius.'

In this book he gives from Alypius some fragments of antiquity as specimens of the characters
for the notation of music in use among the ancient
Greeks; these are inserted in an earlier part of this
work. Here also he takes occasion to describe the
various kinds of dancing-air in practice in his time; as
namely, the Galliard, Courant, Passamezzo, the Alle-

mand, and Saraband; of all which he gives examples,
composed purposely by his friend Kapsberger.

This book is of a very miscellaneous nature; and
it must here suffice to say, that besides a general
enumeration of the most eminent musicians of the
author's time, it contains a great variety of fine
compositions selected from their works; among which
are a madrigal of five parts, composed by the emperor
Ferdinand III., and an air in four parts by Lewis
XIII. king of France, which he found in Mersennus,
and is here inserted :—

LEWIS XIII. KING OF FRANCE.

He mentions also that his Catholic majesty, the then
king of Spain, had with great ingenuity composed
certain litanies, but that he could not procure them
time enough to insert in his work.*

The second volume begins with Book VIII. en-

* The above air is inserted both in the Harmonici and Harmonie
Universelle of Mersennus, and is by him termed a royal Cantilena: he
gives it in two forms, viz., simply, as originally composed by the king,
and with variations on the two first strains by the Sieur de la Barré,
organist to the king and queen. These variations, consisting of dimin-
utions to the amount of sixty-four notes to one measure or semibreve,
are calculated for the harpsichord, and reduce the air to the form of
a lesson. And here, to obviate a doubt of the possibility of depressing
sixty-four keys in so short a time, Mersennus assures his reader that he
had frequently seen Barré do it. He also celebrates another excellent
performer, who, excepting Barré, he says had not his equal in the world,
the younger Cappella, styled le Baron de Chaubonniere: the father of
this person was living at the time when Mersennus wrote his book; he
was then fourscore years of age, and had been clavicymbalist to Henry IV.
The son told Mersennus that in his performance on the harpsichord he
had been much more skilful and able than himself; and that he despaired
of attaining to the same degree of perfection, or of ever meeting with
his equal.

titled De Musurgia Mirifica; in this are contained
tables of the possible combinations of numbers as
they respect the musical intervals; as also a very
minute investigation of the rythmic art, in which the
quantities which constitute the various kinds of metre
in the Greek and Latin poetry are explained and
illustrated by the characters used in musical notation; with some curious observations on the Hebrew,
Syriac, and Arabic poetry, and also on that of the
Samaritans, Armenians, and other Orientals.

In Book IX. is a chapter intitled De Sympathiæ et
Antipathiæ sonorum ratione; the experiment therein
described is wonderfully curious. It supposes five
drinking-glasses of the same magnitude and capacity;
the first filled with aqua vitæ, the second with wine,
the third with aqua subtilis, and the fourth with
some thick fluid, as sea-water or oil, and the fifth or

middle one with common water; in which case, if a finger be wetted and rubbed round the edge of the water-glass the following effects will be produced, viz., the aqua vitæ in the first glass will be prodigiously agitated, the wine in the second but gently shaken, the aqua subtilis in the third shaken in a less degree, and the sea-water or other fluid in the fourth scarcely at all. From this experiment it may be supposed the invention of music on glasses is derived. He then produces a great variety of instances of the wonderful effects wrought by music, beginning with the dispossession of Saul as recorded in sacred writ, which he endeavours to account for mechanically. In the same manner he reasons upon the fall of the walls of the city of Jericho at the sound of the trumpets of the priests; ascribing all to physical or mechanical causes; and, in short, arguing upon principles that tend to destroy in both instances the credit of the narration. But to prove that music has power as well to excite as to subdue evil affections, he by way of contrast to the case of Saul, cites from Olaus Magnus and Krantzius the story of Ericus king of Denmark, already related in page 493 of this work.

Seeing how particular Kircher is in his relation of the effects of music on the human mind, it can hardly be supposed he would omit to mention that instance of the wonderful efficacy of it in the cure of the frenzy, which is said to be occasioned by the bite of the Tarantula; and accordingly he describes the various symptoms that are brought on by the bite of that insect, and refers to histories where an absolute cure had been wrought by the sole power of music.*

* Kircher has illustrated his account of the Tarantula by histories of cases; and first he speaks of a girl, who being bitten by this insect, could only be cured by the music of a drum. He then proceeds to relate that a certain Spaniard, trusting to the efficacy of music in the cure of the frenzy occasioned by the bite of the Tarantula, submitted to be bitten on the hand by two of these creatures, of different colours, and possessed of different qualities; the venom was no sooner diffused about his body, than the symptoms of the disorder began to appear; upon which harpers, pipers, and other musicians were sent for, who by various kinds of music endeavoured to rouse him from that stupor into which he was fallen: but here it was observed that the bites of the two insects had produced contrary effects, for by one he was incited to dance, and by the other he was restrained therefrom: and in this conflict of nature the patient expired.

The same account of the Tarantula is given in the Phonurgia nova of Kircher, with the addition of a cut representing the insect in two positions, the patient in the action of dancing, together with the musical notes of the tune or air, by which in one instance the cure was effected.

In the Musurgia Kircher attempts mechanically to account for the cure of the bite of the Tarantula by music: he says of the poison, that it is sharp, gnawing, and bilious, and that it is received and incorporated into the medullary substance of the fibres. With respect to the music, he says that the sounds of chords have a power to rarify the air to a certain harmonical pitch; and that the air thus rarified, penetrating the pores of the patient's body, affects the muscles, arteries, and minute fibres, and incites him to dance, which exercise begets a perspiration, in which the poison evaporates.

Unsatisfactory as this theory appears, the belief of this strange phenomenon has prevailed among the ablest of modern physicians. Sir Thomas Brown, so far from disputing it, says that since many attest the fact from experience, and that the learned Kircherus hath positively averred it, and set down the songs and tunes solemnly used for the cure of the disease; and since some also affirm that the Tarantula itself will dance at the sound of music, he shall not at all question it. Enquiries into Vulgar Errors, book III. chap. xxviii.

Farther, that eminent Italian physician of the last century, Baglivi, a native of Apulia, the country where the Tarantula is produced, has written a dissertation 'De anatomia morsu et effectibus Tarantulæ.' In this he describes the region of Apulia, where the Tarantula is produced, with the anatomy and figure of the insect and its eggs, illustrated by an engraving; he mentions particularly the symptoms that follow from the bite, and the cure of the disease by music, with a variety of histories of cures thus wrought, many of them communicated by persons who were eye-witnesses of the process.

Ludovicus Valetta, a Celestine monk of Apulia, published at Naples in the year 1706, a treatise upon this Spider, in which he not only answers the objections of those who deny the whole thing, but gives,

The account which he, and indeed other writers, gives of the process, is in short this: the symptoms of the disorder appearing, which in general are violent sickness, difficulty of breathing, and universal faintness; a musician is brought, who tries a variety of airs, till at last he hits upon one that rouses the patient from his stupor, and urges him to dance, the violence of which exercise produces a proportionable agitation of the vital spirits, attended with a consequent degree of perspiration, the certain presage of a cure.

The remaining part of this book is a disquisition on Echos; and to this purpose the author relates from Cardan a pretty story, which does not shock our credulity like many others in his work; and is here given in the words of the relater: 'A certain friend from his own knowledge, several instances of persons who had suffered this way, some of whom were of great families, and so far from being dissemblers, that they would at any rate, to avoid shame, have concealed the misfortune which had befallen them.

The honourable Mr. Robert Boyle, in his treatise of languid and unheeded Motions, speaking of the bite of the Tarantula, and the cure of the disease which follows it, by means of music, says that having himself had some doubts about the matter, he was, after strict enquiry, convinced that the relations in the main were true.

Lastly, Dr. Mead, in his Mechanical Account of Poisons, Lond. 1747. has given an essay on the Tarantula, containing the substance of the above relations, which he endeavours to confirm by his own reasoning thereon.

Notwithstanding the number and weight of these authorities, and the general acquiescence of learned and ingenious men in the opinion that the bite of the Tarantula is poisonous, and that the cure of the disorder occasioned by it is effected by music, we have reason to apprehend that the whole is a mistake.

In the Philosophical Transactions for the year 1672, page 4066, is an extract of a letter from Dr. Thomas Cornelio, a Neapolitan physician, to John Doddington, Esq. his majesty's resident at Venice, communicated by the latter, in which, speaking of his intention to send to Mr. Doddington some Tarantulas, he says, 'Mean while I shall not omit to impart 'to you what was related to me a few days since by a judicious and un-'prejudicate person; which is, that being in the country of Otranto, 'where those insects are in great numbers, there was a man, who thinking 'himself stung by a Tarantula shewed in his neck a small speck, about 'which in a very short time there arose some pimples full of a serous 'humour; and that in a few hours after that poor man was sorely 'afflicted with very violent symptoms, as syncopes, very great agitations, 'giddiness of the head, and vomiting; but that without any inclination 'at all to dance, and without all desire of having any musical instru-'ments, he miserably died within two days.

'The same person affirmed to me that all those who think themselves 'bitten by Tarantulas, except such as for evil ends feign themselves to 'be so, are for the most part young wanton girls, whom the Italian 'writer calls Dolce di Sale; who, by some particular indisposition falling 'into this melancholy madness, persuade themselves, according to the 'vulgar prejudice, to have been stung by a Tarantula. And I remember 'to have observed in Calabria some women, who, seized on by some such 'accidents, were counted to be possessed with the Devil, it being the 'common belief in that province that the greatest part of the evils which 'afflict mankind proceed from evil spirits.'

He mentions also a particular kind of tumour to which the people of Calabria are subject, called in their language Coccia Maligno; and which, if attended with certain symptoms, brings on death. He says that the common opinion of this distemper is, that it befalls those only who have eaten the flesh of animals that have died a natural death; which notion he affirms to be false, with a remark, that of many strange effects we daily meet with, the true cause not being known, some one is assigned upon no better ground than vulgar prejudice, which he believes to be the only foundation for the common opinion touching the cause of that distemper, which appears in those that think themselves stung by the Tarantula.

Dr. Serao, an Italian physician, as it seems has written an ingenious book, in which he has effectually exploded this opinion as a popular error; and in the Philosophical Transactions, No. LX. for the year 1770, pag. 236, is a letter from Dominico Cirillo, M.D. professor of natural history in the university of Naples, wherein taking notice of Serao's book, he says that having had an opportunity of examining the effects of this animal in the province of Taranto, where it is found in great abundance, he finds that the surprizing cure of the bite of the Tarantula by music, has not the least truth in it; and that it is only an invention of the people, who want to get a little money by dancing when they say the Tarantism begins. He adds, 'I make no doubt but sometimes the 'heat of the climate contributes very much to warm their imaginations, 'and throw them into a delirium, which may be in some measure cured 'by music; but several experiments have been tried with the Tarantula, 'and neither men nor animals after the bite have had any other com-'plaint than a very trfling inflammation upon the part, like those pro-'duced by the bite of a scorpion, which go off by themselves without any 'danger at all. In Sicily, where the summer is still warmer than in any 'part of the kingdom of Naples, the Tarantula is never dangerous. And 'music is never employed for the cure of the pretended Tarantism.'

' of mine having set out on a journey, had a river to
' cross, and not knowing the ford, cried out *Oh*, to
' which an echo answered *Oh*; he imagining it to be
' a man, called out in Italian *Onde devo passar?* it
' answered *passa*; and when he asked *qui?* it replied
' *qui*; but as the waters formed a deep whirlpool
' there, and made a great noise, he was terrified, and
' again asked *Devo passar qui?* The echo returns
' *passa qui*. He repeated the same question often,
' and still had the same answer. Terrified with the
' fear of being obliged to swim in case he attempted
' to pass there, and it being a dark and tempestuous
' night, he concluded that his respondent was some
' evil spirit that wanted to entice him into the torrent,
' wherefore he returned, and relating the story to
' Cardan, was convinced by him that it was no demon,
' but the sport of nature.'

From this account of a natural, Kircher proceeds
to a description of an artificial echo, namely, that in
the Villa Simonetta near Milan; and of a building
at Pavia, mentioned by Cardan in his treatise De
Subtilitate, which would return a sound thirty times.
As also that at Syracuse, by some called the Prison,
and by others the Ear of Dionysius, described by
Mirabella in his Ichnography of Syracuse.

From Phonic and Acoustic buildings, Kircher
proceeds to a description of Phonotactic machines,
which by the rotation of a cylinder produce music
from bells, and organs constructed for the purpose;
and here he gives a very particular description of
what he calls a Cymbalarian machine, in the form of a
star, in the church of the monastery of Fulda, so contrived, as that by the motion of a cylinder round its
axis, music is produced from a number of small bells.

He next describes an instrument, contrived to resemble in the sound of it a concert of viols; it is in
fact a harpsichord with a circular belly, under which
is a wheel, one sixth part whereof rises above the
belly of the instrument. The strings, which are required to be of the intestines of animals, like those
of the harp, are strained into contact with the edge
of this wheel, which being rubbed with powder of
rosin, produces from each a sound like that of a viol.

In this chapter Kircher mentions a contrivance of
his own, an instrument which a few years ago was
obtruded upon the public as a new invention, and
called the harp of Æolus, of which he thus speaks.

' As the following instrument is new, so also is it
' easy to construct and pleasant, and is heard in my
' museum, to the great admiration of every one. It
' is silent as long as the window, in which it is placed,
' remains shut, but as soon as it is opened, behold an
' harmonious sound on the sudden arises that asto-
' nishes the hearers; for they are not able to perceive
' from whence the sound proceeds, nor yet what kind
' of instrument it is, for it resembles neither the sound
' of a stringed, nor yet of a pneumatic instrument,
' but partakes of both. The instrument is made of
' pine wood; it is five palms long, two broad, and
' one deep; it may contain
' fifteen or more chords, all
' equal, and composed of
' the intestines of animals,
' as appears in this figure.

' The instrument is A B C D, the pegs C A, the
' bridges I K and that at the other end parallel with
' it: the chords being put round the pegs, and ex-
' tended over the bridges, are fastened to keys at B V:
' the roses are F F F; and near S is a handle by
' which it may be suspended. The method of tuning
' it now remains, which is not, as in other instruments,
' by thirds, fourths, fifths, or eighths, but all the chords
' are to be tuned to an unison, or in octaves. It is
' very wonderful, and nearly paradoxical, that chords
' thus tuned should constitute different harmony. As
' this musical phenomenon has not as yet been ob-
' served by any one that I know of, I shall describe
' the instrument very minutely, to the end that it may
' be searched into more narrowly, and the effects pro-
' duced by it accounted for. But first I shall shew
' the conditions of the instrument, and where it
' ought to be fixed.

' The instrument is to be situated in a close place,
' yet so that the air may on either side have free
' access to it: in order to which it may be observed
' that the wind may be collected by various methods;
' first by canals that are made in the form of cones
' or shells, or else by valves; for example, let there
' be two valves, E F and
' B V C D, as in the
' figure below, so joined
' together in F and V
' D, that they may how-
' ever leave a passage for
' the wind into the space
' between the two parallel
' boards F R and V D.

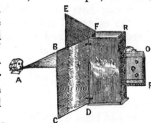

' Let the valves be placed on the outside, and the
' parallel boards on the inside of the room, at the
' back of which the instrument is to be fixed, at the
' chink S N, but so as to be turned against the chink
' in an oblique situation, that the wind being collected
' by the valves, and forced between the narrow part
' between the boards B V and E F, and going out
' through the chink, may strike all the chords of the
' instrument S O N P. When it is thus disposed
' you will perceive an harmony in the room in pro-
' portion as the wind is weaker or stronger; for
' from time to time all the chords having a tremulous
' motion impressed upon them, produce a corres-
' pondent variety of sounds, resembling a concentus
' of pipes or flutes, affecting the hearers with a strange
' pleasure.' *

In this book we also meet with a discourse on the
ancient hydraulic organ, which, from the description
of it by Vitruvius, Kircher laboured to construct;
but both his explanation, and the figure of the instrument, which he was at the pains of delineating,
and has given in the book, appear to be nothing
more than an exercise of that imagination, which
was ever at work and employed in solving difficulties.

Book X. is on the subject of Analogical music,

* It may here be remarked that many instruments, supposed to be of
very late invention, are to be found described in the writings of Mersennus and Kircher. The short bassoon, and the perpendicular harpsichord are instances to this purpose. The Lyrichord, as it is called, lately
constructed by Plenius, is evidently borrowed from an instrument
mentioned in a preceding page; and the harp of Æolus, so much celebrated as a modern discovery, is no other than the instrument here
described by Kircher.

as the author affects to term it, and tends to demonstrate the harmony of the four elements, and of the planetary system. He labours also to prove that the principles of harmony are discoverable in the proportions of our bodies, and in the passions and affections of the mind; and even in the seven sacraments of the Romish church. From these he proceeds to the consideration of political and metaphysical harmony; and, lastly, to that harmony, if any one can understand what it means, which subsists in the several orders of intellectual beings, and which is consummated in the union between God and the universe.

In the year 1673 Kircher published his Phonurgia Nova, a work in which he explains the nature, properties, powers, and effects of sound.

In the Phonurgia Nova, Sect. VI. Cap. i. the author gives a very circumstantial account of that useful instrument which we call the Speaking Trumpet, the invention whereof is generally ascribed to a native of this country, Sir Samuel Moreland,* but Kircher claims it as his own.

And first he relates that the motives for his attempt were drawn from that branch of the science of optics called catoptrics, and the structure of those tubes, by the help whereof curious men make observations on the sun; and that he conceived a possibility of magnifying sound by methods similar to those whereby bodies are, at least to our view, encreased beyond their true dimensions. How far his reasoning was just, or whether the sciences of optics and acoustics are founded on the same principles or not, it is not necessary here to enquire, but that he succeeded in his endeavours, and was the inventor of the instrument here spoken of, he does most positively assert.

He says, that in order to attain the end proposed, he made experiments with cylindrical, conic, and elliptic tubes, both simple and contorted, or twisted like a screw, but that he found that one of a cylindrical form succeeded best; and that this he improved by continuing it in length beyond that proportion which at first he thought sufficient for his purpose. His description of the instrument, and his relation of its effects are not a little curious, and are in these words:

* Of this instrument an account was published at London in the year 1671, wherein the author relates several experiments made by him with this instrument, the result thereof was, that a speaking trumpet constructed by him, being five feet six inches long, twenty-one inches diameter at the greater end, and two inches at the smaller, being tried at Deal castle, was heard at the distance of three miles, the wind blowing from the shore. Together with the book, which is a thin folio, entitled Tuba Stentoro-Phonica, printed for the famous Moses Pitt, bookseller in St. Paul's church-yard, was sold at his shop, the instrument itself, price 2l. 5s.

In the Philosohical Transactions, No. 141, for the year 1678, is a letter from Mr. J. Conyers, containing an account of what he calls a Reflecting Trumpet, consisting of two parts, the outermost a large concave pyramid, about a yard long, open at the base, and closed with a flat but concave head at the top, the figure then resembling a tall and very slender bell. Within this it is said a tube was fastened, which was continued from the top of the cone some inches below the base, and then returned at right angles. The letter says that this instrument was tried at Arundel-house in the Strand, where the meetings of the Royal Society were then held; and although the wind was contrary, and very strong, the sound thereof was distinctly heard across the garden of the said house, even to the other side of the Thames; whereby it appeared, that a reflecting trumpet made after this, or some like manner, of wood, tin, pewter, stone, earth, or of bell-metal, would carry the voice as far, if not farther, than the long one, invented by Mr. Samuel Moreland.

The same person attempted to improve the speaking-trumpet, by constructing it with three angular arches, instead of one reaching almost from one end to the other: but he found that little was gained by this variation of the instrument from its original form.

'There was a repository in my museum, in our 'college at Rome, parted from the rest of the build-'ing by a wall that had a gate in it; and at the end 'of the repository was a window of an oval form, 'looking into the college garden, which garden was 'about three hundred palms square. In this window 'I fixed a conic tube, composed of iron plates, 'twenty-two palms in length, the aperture whereof 'for speaking, exceeded not a quarter of a palm; 'the body of the tube was about one palm in diameter, 'but it was gradually encreased towards the further 'end to the diameter of three palms. The instru-'ment thus constructed was placed in the window in 'a direction towards the garden.

'The Janitors or porters of our college had fre-'quent occasions to speak to me, either to notify the 'approach of a stranger, or upon matters of a do-'mestic concern; and as it was inconvenient for 'them to be continually coming to me, they called 'to me from the gate, and I, being in my chamber, 'heard them clearly and distinctly, and answered 'them through the tube, and was heard by them.'†

'To those who visited my museum, and were 'astonished to hear the effect of this instrument, 'I explained the contrivance of it; and it is scarce 'credible how many persons were drawn from distant 'cities to see and hear it.'

After having given this history of the invention of the Speaking-Trumpet, Kircher proceeds to refute the opinion that it was first discovered in England, in these words: 'I have here thought proper to 'communicate to the reader a description of this 'instrument, that he might not persuade himself that 'this was a new invention, brought out of England, 'but that it was exhibited by me in our college at 'Rome twenty-four years before the time when it is 'said to have been invented in England; and this 'many persons now living, both our own fathers, and 'also strangers, who deigned to visit my museum 'filled with rare curiosities, are able to testify.'‡

He then proceeds to relate that having been compelled to remove his museum to another part of the college called the Gallery, he made improvements in the tube, adapted to that place; and that he made a statue, the lips and eyes whereof, by a secret contrivance, were made to move, and that by means of the tube, he uttered through it feigned and ludicrous consultations, with a view to shew the fallacy and imposture of ancient oracles.

He says that, with a desire of knowing the efficacy and power of the conic tube, he ascended the very high mountain of St. Eustachius, and took with him one of fifteen palms in length; and that in speaking through the same, he and his companions made themselves heard at different stations, two, three,

† This passage is very obscure in the original, and leaves it a question whether Kircher and the porters spoke through one or different instruments of the same kind; the latter is the most probable.

‡ To corroborate this assertion, sundry passages, extracted from the writings of other persons, are prefixed to the Phonurgia, as namely Jacobus Albanus Ghibbesius, Gaspar Schottus, and Franiscus Eschinardus; these import that the instrument called the Tuba Stentorophonica was invented by Kircher twenty years before the time when a description of it was published at London by Sir Samuel Moreland.

Kircher's museum was, as he intimates, a very curious one. A catalogue of it was published at Rome in the year 1709.

four, and five Italian miles distant from the place whence the sound was uttered; and that by means of the tube alone they called to the people of the neighbouring villages for necessaries, and were supplied; and farther, invited above two thousand of them, as by a voice from heaven, to ascend the mountain, and celebrate the feast of Pentecost, during which solemnity Kircher and his companions sung litanies through tubes of this kind constructed by him.

The works of Kircher are either on subjects of the most remote antiquity, or such as from their very nature seem to elude all enquiry; nevertheless, for his Musurgia Universalis, the world is under great obligations to him. In thus availing himself of the researches of other learned men, and also of all the assistance that he could possibly derive from an extensive correspondence, and the communications of persons the most eminent of his time in the theory and practice of music, he has exhibited such a fund of instruction and entertainment; such a diversity of curious particulars relating to the principles and gradual progress of the science, and such a number of curious anecdotes respecting the professors of his time, and the opinions entertained of their works, that we know not which to admire most, his ingenuity or industry.

But notwithstanding the merits of Kircher in these and other instances, the Musurgia soon after its publication was very severely censured by a man who had pursued the study of music with no small degree of assiduity, namely, Marcus Meibomius, of Amsterdam, of whom and his writings here follows an account.

## CHAP. CXXXIV.

Marcus Meibomius, a celebrated philologist and critic, was a native of Tonningen, in Holstein. In his advanced years he settled at Stockholm, and became a favourite of Christina, queen of Sweden. Having made a deep research into the works of the Greek writers on music, he contracted an enthusiastic fondness for the music of the ancients, and entertained an opinion not only of its superiority to that of the moderns, but that he was able to restore and introduce it into practice. The queen, who by frequent conversations with him had been made to entertain the same sentiments on the subject as himself, was easily prevailed on to listen to a proposal of his, which was to exhibit a performance of music, under his direction strictly conformable to the practice of the ancients; and, to crown all, he, who had but a bad voice, and had never in his youth been exercised in the practice of vocal music, was to sing in it. To this end instruments of various kinds were made at the expence of the queen, and under the directions of Meibomius; and public notice was given of a musical performance that was to captivate and astonish all that should be so happy as to hear it. On the appointed day Meibomius appeared, and addressing himself to sing, was heard with patience for a short time; but his performance and that of his auxiliaries was past enduring: neither the chromatic nor

the enarmonic genus suited the ears of his illiterate auditory, and the Lydian mood had lost its soothing power. In short, his hearers, unable to resist the impulses of nature, expressed their sense of the performance by general laughter.

Whatever were the feelings of the people, Meibomius was but little disposed to sympathize with them: their mirth was his disgrace, and he felt it but too sensibly: for seeing in the gallery Mons. Bourdelot the younger, a physician, and a rival of his in the queen's favour, he immediately imputed the behaviour of the people to some insinuations of his to the prejudice of the performance; and without being restrained by the presence of the queen, ran up to him, and struck him a blow on the neck; and, to avoid the consequences of his rashness, quitted the city before he could be called to account for it, and took up his residence at Copenhagen. In this latter city Meibomius was well received, and became a professor at Sora, a college in Denmark for the instruction of the nobility. Here he was honoured with the title of counsellor to the king; and soon after was called to Elsineur, and advanced to the dignity of Architeloni, or president of the board of maritime taxes or customs; but neglecting the duty of his employment, he was dismissed, and upon that occasion quitted Denmark. Soon after this he settled at Amsterdam, and became professor of history in the college there; but refusing to give private instruction to the son of a burgomaster of that city, alledging that he was not used to instruct boys but students, he was dismissed from that station. Upon this he quitted Amsterdam, and visited France and England, but afterwards returned to Amsterdam, and led a private life, and died in 1710 or 1711, having attained to a great age. He assisted in the publication of an edition of Vitruvius at Amsterdam, in 1643, wherein he has endeavoured to rectify such passages as related to music, and were misunderstood by former editors. But his great work was his edition of the seven Greek authors who had wrote on music, namely, Aristoxenus, Euclid, Nicomachus, Alypius, Gaudentius, Bacchius, and Aristides Quintilianus, of which it is here proposed to give a brief account. It was published at Amsterdam in the year 1652, and contains a general preface to the whole, and also a preface to each of the treatises as they occur, with a Latin translation of the Greek text, and copious notes, tending to reconcile various readings, and explain the meaning of the several authors. The work is dedicated to Christina, queen of Sweden, in an epistle that abounds with flattery, and is not more hyperbolical than pedantic; for, after enumerating her virtues, and celebrating her wisdom and learning, he says of her, 'tibi Hypatæ Diapason, Diapente, ac 'Diatessaron consonent.' In the general preface the author is very severe on the modern musurgists; and takes occasion to mention Kircher, whom he taxes with ignorance of Grecian literature. He then proceeds to relate that Vitruvius, in his treatise De Architectura, lib. V. cap. v. had promised a short but solid doctrine of harmonics, drawn from Aristoxenus, in order to determine the consonances of those echoing vessels which he proposed to place in the theatres of Rome; which doctrine, by a fate common to the works of ancient authors, came to the hands of Meibomius obscured with foul defects, and that he laboured for three years to restore it; but that Kircher, who also applied himself to the same laudable endeavour, has rendered the whole doctrine of Vitruvius erroneous. He farther censures Kircher for disregarding the niceties of grammar, and for the use of what he calls barbarous terms, such as Sesqui-tertias, Sesquiquartus, Sesquioctavus, instead of Super-tertias, Superquartus, Superoctavus. He adds that the word Musurgia, the title of Kircher's work, and which he uses for Opus de Musica, is not warranted by the authority of any one Greek writer, but is repugnant to the analogy observed in the formation of compound words, and signifies a musical operation. Again he censures Kircher for this passage in the Musurgia, page 133, 'Aristoxenus semitonia putat 'esse dimidia tonorum. Hunc secutus Martianus 'Felix turpiori adhuc errore lapsus deprehenditur, 'qui non modo tonum in duas œquales, sed in 3 et 4 'dirimit atque secat partes.' 'What fouler error,' says Meibomius, 'could this man, Kircher, fall into, 'than to imagine that Martianus Capella, who was 'a mere copier of Aristides Quintilianus, and not 'a very exact one neither, should be the inventor of 'any thing new in music? Did Kircher,' exclaims Meibomius, 'ever read Aristoxenus, or any of the 'ancients? Did he ever read Boetius, who in express 'words attributes this division to Aristoxenus, in 'lib. V. cap. xv?' He proceeds to censure Kircher for his ignorance in the Greek language, as also for the many errors which he says are to be found in that plate in the Musurgia which exhibits the ancient Greek musical characters. And here Meibomius takes occasion to mention a visit which Ismael Bullialdus made him at Amsterdam, in the autumn previous to the publication of his book, and of the conversation between them: he says that Bullialdus informed him that Mersennus was then employed in translating Bacchius into the French language; and that upon Meibomius's shewing him many remarks which he had made on Bacchius, Gaudentius, Euclid, and other ancient writers, Bullialdus generally acquiesced in his opinions. He remarks that Kircher, in the Musurgia, page 139, mentions Archytas, Didymus, Eratosthenes, and other authors, whose manuscripts he says he has in possession: 'I think,' says Meibomius, 'he must in this particular be 'mistaken; for, excepting their several divisions of 'the three genera, which are to be found at the end 'of Ptolemy's second book of Harmonics, there are 'no writings on music of either of these three persons 'recorded to be extant,' and he wishes that Kircher would publish them for the satisfaction of himself and others.* He says that the world is greatly mistaken in supposing that Guido enlarged the ancient system by the addition either of chords below or above it; for he asserts that they assumed a chord below Proslambanomenos, and afterwards rejected it, as producing a confused and undistinguishable

* This remark is justly founded, for the authors therein mentioned are enumerated among the Scriptores perditi.

sound; but that Guido reassumed it, and marked it with the Greek letter Γ; and that the ancients proceeded farther in the acutes than Guido did, he says is evident from the tables of the three genera.

In this preface Meibomius takes occasion to introduce the Te Deum with ancient musical notes, concerning which he says there is no doubt but that this melody was used by St. Augustine and St. Ambrose, though perhaps it may have been corrupted in some measure since their time. At the close of this general preface he mentions that French translation of Bacchius by Mersennus, of which he had received information from Ismael Bullialdus, and says that immediately upon notice of it he sent to Paris for the book. He charges Mersennus with having omitted many difficult passages and mistaken others; and concludes, that if he had seen this translation before he had finished his notes on Bacchius, they would have been much fuller by his observations on the errors of Mersennus.

Besides the general preface of Meibomius, he has given one also to each of the Greek authors published by him: these chiefly relate to certain manuscripts of each, with which he was furnished by many learned men his contemporaries, whom he celebrates; among whom are Daniel Heinsius, Claudius Salmasius, and our countrymen Selden and Dr. Gerard Langbaine.

To his edition of the seven Greek authors Meibomius has added a treatise De Musica of Martianus Mineus Felix Capella, that is to say, lib. IX. of that author's work, entitled De Nuptiis Philologiæ et Mercurii. Martianus Capella has in some sort abridged Aristides Quintilianus; and it seemed right to Meibomius to give the work at large, and also the abridgement, with notes on each. The treatise De Nuptiis Philologiæ et Mercurii is in Latin; an account of it, as also of its author, is elsewhere given in this work. The edition published by Meibomius of the seven Greek authors, with a translation, and also of Martianus Capella with notes, was doubtless a very considerable acquisition to the science of music: the manuscripts of each of them had been brought into Europe by those learned Greeks who escaped at the sacking of Constantinople, and settling in Italy, became the revivers of learning; these were by accidents of various kinds dispersed; copies were made of them, which inevitably multiplied various readings; few persons knew where to find them; and they never having been brought together into one point of view, the very existence of some of the tracts which Meibomius has given to the world was a matter of doubt with the learned.

But notwithstanding the care and industry of Meibomius, manifested in the publication of this work, his manner of introducing it is justly reprehensible; for his general preface abounds with invectives against all who presumed to think less highly of the ancient music than himself, more especially Kircher. The Musurgia of Kircher is to be considered as an original work, very comprehensive in its extent, and formed from a great variety of materials; in the compilation of it, it must be supposed that the author attended more to the subject matter of it than to the style : it appears therefore a very pedantic and froward behaviour in Meibomius to object to the Musurgia, which abounds with learning, and a great variety of curious and entertaining particulars, the want of that grammatical nicety and exactness, which few, except men of narrow and contracted minds, are apt to excel in.

But it is not of Kircher alone that Meibomius affects to speak in terms of contempt : Mersennus, who was possesed of more musical science than any man of his time, has hardly escaped his censure for errors pretended to be made by him in his translation of Bacchius; nor has his friend Ismael Bullialdus met with better treatment in respect of his version of Theo. Smyrnæus. Indeed little less than such behaviour to those who differed from him was to be expected from a man so bigoted as Meibomius appears to have been, and whose irascible temper seems, by the relation contained in the account of his life, to have been incapable of restraint within the bounds of decency.

## CHAP. CXXXV.

Pietro Mengoli, a musician and mathematician of Bologna, was the author of a work entitled Speculationi di Musica, printed at Bologna in the year 1670. In the proem to this book he gives an account of himself and the course of his studies to the following effect, viz., that he began to sing when he was ten years old; and being arrived at the age of eighteen, applied himself very closely to the study of the theory of music; and at the end of fourteen years, that is to say, in the year 1658, having, as he conceived, made very important discoveries, he undertook to read public lectures on music in several schools, wherein, besides his own doctrines, he endeavoured to explain those which Zarlino and Galileo had taught before him : That having instructed a gentleman, namely, Signor Ercole Zani, in the elements of music, this person directed a monochord to be made for the purpose of discovering the nature of consonance and dissonance, and the physical causes that render them severally grateful, or the contrary, 'o the sense of hearing; but that in this enquiry they could never satisfy themselves, they having all along taken that for granted which they found to be wrong, namely, that concord arises from the frequent union of two sounds striking at the same instant the external drum of the ear : That Signor Ercole being however resolved to find out the truth, proposed what should have been thought of before, that is to say, to see and examine the organ of hearing; they therefore applied to Gio. Galeazzo Manzi, a skilful anatomist, and a doctor of physic in the university of Bologna, who demonstrated to them that in the human ear there are three small bones bound together; and that in the ear are contained not only one Tympanum, as other professors have thought, but two drums, the one, with respect to its situation in the ear, external, the other internal : and that the same person likewise shewed to them the cavity of the ear and its mouth; and that after having made his

observations thereon, the author began to commit to writing his speculations, which he encreased afterwards by degrees, adding thereto whatever he thought necessary to the elucidation of his subject.

The proem to this work is succeeded by what the author terms the Natural History of music, in which are many curious particulars, the result of his anatomical researches; the purport of it, as it is given in the Philosophical Transactions, is as follows :—

' A sound begins from the collision of two parts of ' the air, which separating, make a vacuum as to the ' air, in which vacuum two other parcels of air meet ' and strike each other; and because the two first ' parcels of air incline to return to the centre of the ' collision, but cannot, because their room is taken ' up, they part from the centre by lines curved, and ' as it were recurring to their first place; in the ' doing whereof they make a collision with those ' parts of the air, which have possessed themselves ' of their room, and thus the species of sound are multiplied and extended. These curved lines are more ' waving near the centre of the collision, as being ' more stretched long-ways than spirally, and less ' waving where they are farther from the centre; in ' which latter lines the inclination to return towards ' the centre is prevalent above the impetus of receding ' from it; so that at last they return back towards ' the centre. Thus of the species of sound there is ' filled a sphere of air, or such a part of a sphere of it, ' as this motion of the air can without impediment ' spread itself through. In the like manner two ' sounds from two centres, one within the sonorous ' sphere of the other, begin and are distributed ' through the small particles of the air, in such a ' manner, that some of the pulses are affected by one ' sound, and others, without confusion, by another; ' and that the pulses of the acuter sound are swifter, ' and complete their pulses in a shorter time than ' those of a grave sound, which are slower and longer. ' The Aura or subtile matter in which these motions ' of the air are made, according to its comparable ' subtility, and that property it has of being altogether ' indifferent to any condition of bodies, and suited ' exactly to represent any motion, or stamp, or weight ' of other bodies, among which it is found; this Aura ' does not impede, but assists the two motions produced by these two sorts of pulses, it being affected ' by all the intermediate motions. There may be ' also more sounds than two distributed through the ' particles of the air, yet not without some confusion; ' and the more sounds there are, the more irregular ' will the distribution of the pulses be, especially near ' the centres themselves where the sounds begin. ' The ear is an organ by which a man placed in a ' sonorous sphere perceives and judges of sounds and ' their habitudes, whether of consonance or dissonance. ' This organ has three parts, the exterior, without ' the cavity of the ear, and visibly extant on the ' head; the middlemost, which is the cavity itself; ' and the innermost, which being within the cavity, ' is a bone, resembling in substance a spunge, in ' which is a cavern recurring to the hollow part of ' the ear, and shaped like a knot of ribbons; and in

'all the holes of this spungy-like bone are found
'webs stretched out, that inclose the air.  The
'middle part is closed up by two membranes, called
'drums, which are stretched over the cavity of the
'ear; and of these two the one is external, at the
'bottom of the exterier part of the air; and the
'other internal, upon the mouth of the cavern:
'between these drums are three small bones tied to
'one another, and to the drums, and fastened in two
'points to the sides of the cavity, and movable, so
'that if the outward drum be made to shake, the
'inward must shake also, and that twice as often.
'The inclination of these two drums is to move in
'duple proportion,* but the exigency of the instru-
'ment moves them differently from their inclinations:
'so that this is the sensitive organ in which the soul
'perceives what is acted there.  Between these
'drums is no air,† properly so called, but only an
'Aura,‡ which seconding the inclinations of the
'drums to motion, and the motions themselves,
'preserves all the intermediate inclinations and
'motions; and the mind is able to contemplate the
'intermediate inclinations and motions of the Aura.
'If the ear be within a sonorous sphere, the particles
'of the air affected by the sound enter at the ex-
'ternal part of the ear one after another, passing in
'order through the spiral ways that are there to the
'bottom of the ear, and striking the drum, after
'which they issue out by other spiral ways, and give
'place to other particles of air.  The external drum
'being struck once, shakes frequently, and, by means
'of these three little bones the internal drum answers
'to it in a double frequency; and the Aura in the
'cavern of the internal part of the ear, goes and
'comes alternately through its knot-like passage;
'spreading itself through the other ways of the
'spungy-like bone, and, being repercussed to the
'webs that inclose it, rebounds and multiplies the
'sound, until another parcel of air follows and strikes
'the drum, and causes the shaking as before.  But
'if the ear be within two sonorous spheres, the
'affected pulses that cause the sound succeed the
'one the other, and by turns strike the outward
'drum; and, by the exigencies of the alternations,
'the ratios that are not expressible by numbers, are
'yet by the shakings of the drum rendered capable of
'being numbered.'

The above extracts contain in substance the
doctrines delivered in that part of the work now
under consideration, which the author calls his
Natural history of music; and these being premised, he gives a very particular description of the
ear, together with the phenomena of sound, and of
the hearing of sounds, especially two together, in
which description occur many new principles, by
him laid down as the chief foundation of the whole

* Ital. Proportione dimidiati della doppia.

† Though the author will admit of no air properly so called between
the drums, yet he admits of air in the caverns, and within the Os
petrosum, the inward part of the ear, because the drums would have no
motion at all if there were nothing but Aura; forasmuch as this Aura,
though it may be moved by any other thing, yet it cannot be a means to
convey motion from one body to another: It is, says he, the internal
instrument of the mover that lodges there within, but not of any mover
that is without.

‡ AURA, a gentle gale or blast of wind, Altieri.

work: after which he treats of musical intervals,
their perfections, and measure; explicating his doctrine by many theorems, giving withal definitions of
the several intervals, and taking particular notice of
six sorts of them, for which having found no names,
he has thought fit to borrow names from colours.
Next he discourses at large of the true numbers for
the musical intervals, shewing withal between what
numbers the species of each interval are most perfect.
Further he treats of musical chords; then of singing,
and of the modulations of tune; which latter he
distinguishes from singing in general, by observing
that modulation is a succession of sounds, impressing
itself so strongly upon the sense that we are able to
repeat it.

Besides this the author discourses amply of consonance, and of harmonical proportions; as also of
the passions of the soul, shewing how they are concerned in, and wrought upon by music; after which
he gives a table of the several musical chords suited
to the several affections, and concludes with a brief
discourse on the music of the moderns.§

JOHANN ROSENMULLER was a Saxon by birth, and
a joint professor of music with Tobias Michaelis in
the academy of St. Thomas at Leipsic, until, being
suspected of an unnatural vice, he was imprisoned;
but he found means to escape, and fled to Hamburg.
After some stay in that city he went to Italy, where
he was greatly esteemed for his skill and performance
on the organ, and published many compositions,
particularly Sonate da Camera à 5 Stromenti, and
a collection of airs of various kinds.  At length he
became chapel-master in the great church at Wolfenbuttle, and died in the year 1685.

JOHANN THEIL, of Naumburg, was the son of
a tailor, and was born on the twenty-ninth day of
July, 1646.  He received his first instructions in
music from           Scheffler, at that time the principal
musician of that city, and completed his studies in
the universities of Halle and Leipsic.  From thence
he went to Weissenfels in Saxony; and under Schutz,
the chapel-master there, perfected himself in the art
of composition.  Being thus qualified, he removed to
Stettin in Pomerania, and became a teacher of music;
and, among many others, had for his pupils Dietrich
Buxtehude, afterwards the famous organist of the
church of St. Mary in Lubec; and Zachau, the first
preceptor of Handel.  In the year 1673 Thiel became
chapel-master at Gottorp; but being driven thence
by the wars, he went and settled at Hamburg, where
he continued for some years to teach the science of
music.  In the year 1685 he accepted a call from the
magistracy of Wolfenbuttle to the office of chapel-
master, in the room of Rosenmuller, then lately

§ An account of this treatise of Mengoli is given in the Philosophical
Transactions, vol. VIII. No. C. page 6194, which, for the purpose of the
above article, has been compared with the original.  At the close of the
account is this singular passage: 'Now whether this author has by all
'these speculations and pains given a perfect scale of music according
'to the true proportions of sounds (which is a great desideratum in
'music) we must leave to the judgment of the great masters, especially
'the judicious and extraordinary skilful musician Mr. John Birchensha,
'who it is still hoped, if he be competently encouraged and assisted, will
'in due time publish a complete system of music.'  Of this man an
account will hereafter be given, as also of the boasting proposal here
alluded to, which, for want of encouragement, or perhaps other reasons,
was never fulfilled.

deceased, and held it for some years; after which he went into the service of Christian II. duke of Merseburg, and continued therein till the death of that prince. In the course of these his employments he made a great variety of compositions for the church, most excellent in their kind. For one mass of his, which was performed in the chapel of the Imperial court, he received at the hands of Heer Schmeltzer, a present of an hundred Rix-dollars. Many other presents he received from the emperor Leopold, and the queen of Prussia, both of whom entertained a great regard for him, and set a great value on his works. His compositions are chiefly masses, in some of which he professes to imitate the elegant and majestic style of Palestrina. He was also the author of a most valuable work, of which the following is the title at large. 'Novæ Sonatæ 'rarissimæ artis et suavitatis musicæ, partim 2 vocum, 'cum simplis et duplo inversis Fugis; partim 3 'vocum, cum simplis, duplo et triplo inversis Fugis; 'partim 4 vocum, cum simplis, duplo et triplo et 'quadruplo inversis Fugis; partim 5 vocum, cum 'simplis, duplo, triplo, quadruplo aliasque variegatis 'inventionibus et artificiosis Syncopationibus. Summa '50 Sonatæ. Accedunt 50 Præludia 2, 3, 4 et 5 'vocum, cum simplo, et duplo syncopato Contra-'puncto. 50 Allem. et totidem Cour. 2, 3 et 4 'vocum, cum brevibus Fugis similibusque aliis in-'ventionibus suavissimis. 50 Ariæ et 50 Sarab. 2, '3 et 4 vocum, singularis gratissimæque suavitatis. '50 Ghique 2, 3, 4 et 5 vocum, cum simplicis et 'duplo variique generis inversis Fugis.'

From the clear evidence of deep learning and a prolific invention contained in these his works, Theil is justly ranked among the first of the German musicians. He had a son named Benedict Frederic, who had been a theorbist in the chapel of the duke of Wolfenbuttle, and afterwards became organist of the church of St. Wentzel in Naumburg, at whose house in that city Thiel died, in the year 1724, having attained the age of near fourscore, leaving behind him the character of a sound musician, and a virtuous and good man.

There was another famous musician contemporary with him above named, Andrew Theil, the author of a fine collection of lessons, entitled 𝕹𝖊𝖚𝖊𝖗 𝕮𝖑𝖆𝖇𝖎𝖊𝖓 𝖀𝖇𝖚𝖓𝖌, published in the year 1696, of whom notice is taken by Walther.

Friedrich Wilhelm Zachau, born at Leipsic in the month of November, 1663, was the son of a musician, and was by him instructed in the rudiments of music till he was of an age sufficient to entitle him to a reception into the public school at Leipsic, where he attained to a competent skill in the science, and became an excellent performer on the organ and other instruments. He finished his studies in music under Theil at Stettin, and in the year 1684 was called to the office of organist of the church of Our Lady, at Halle in Saxony, and continued therein till the day of his death, which was the fourteenth of August, 1721. He composed many pieces for the church, and some lessons for the clavier or harpsichord. His eminence in his faculty occasioned

a great resort of young persons to him for instruction; and it is no small addition to his reputation that he was the master of Mr. Handel.

Johann Philip Krieger, the son of an eminent merchant of Nuremberg, born the twenty-sixth day of February, 1649, began to learn the clavier or harpsichord when he was but eight years of age, of Johann Drechsel who had been a disciple of Froberger. At the age of sixteen he was placed under the care of Johann Schroder of Copenhagen, organist of the church of St. Peter in that city: after five years continuance there, during which time he received considerable improvement under the royal chapel-master Forster, he went to Holland, and from thence to Bareith, where he became first chamber-organist to the Margrave, and afterwards chapel-master in that city. In the year 1672 he went to Italy, and at Rome considerably improved himself by the instructions of Abbatini, and Pasquini the famous performer on the harpsichord. On his return homewards he stayed some time at Naples, and took lessons from Rovetta, the organist of the church of St. Mark in that city. After a stay of some months he returned to Germany, determined to settle at Vienna, where he had no sooner arrived than he was invited by the emperor to court, who, after hearing him, presented him with a purse of ducats and a gold medal and chain: he continued in the service of the emperor some years, retaining, with the permission of the Margrave, his place of chapel-master of Bareith. Afterwards being invited to settle at Halle, he went thither, and at length became chapel-master to the elector of Saxony at the court of Weissenfels, which function he exercised near forty years, and died in the month of February, 1727.

The works of Krieger are of various kinds; they consist of Sonatas for the violin and viol da gamba, Field Music, or Overtures for trumpets and other sonorous instruments; Latin and German Psalms set to music; and, lastly, Songs in the several dramatic entertainments composed by him, entitled Flora, Cecrops, and Procris. Lessons of his for the harpsichord are also to be met with in manuscript, which have a masterly appearance; but it is no where said that he published any compositions for that instrument.

## CHAP. CXXXVI.

Jean Baptiste Lully (*a Portrait*), a celebrated musician, was born at Florence in the year 1634, of obscure parents; but discovering, even in his infancy, a propensity to music, a Cordelier, who had taken notice of him, undertook, for no other consideration than the hope of making him one day eminent in the science, to teach him the practice of the guitar, an instrument then much in use in most parts of Italy.

It happened that while Lully was under the tuition of this benevolent ecclesiastic, a French gentleman, the Chevalier Guise, then upon his travels, arrived at Florence; this person, upon his taking leave of Mademoiselle de Montpensier, a *cousin* of Lewis XIV.

JEAN BAPTISTE LULLY,

SECRETAIRE DU ROY ET SURINTEN-

DANT DE SA MUSIQUE.

at Paris, had been requested by her to find out some pretty little Italian, to be about her person in quality of a page ; and though the countenance of Lully did by no means answer to the instructions he had received, his vivacity and ready wit, and, above all, the proficiency which he had attained to on an instrument as much the favorite of the French as of the Italians, made him forget all other considerations ; and, trusting to these recommendations, he easily persuaded Lully, then about ten years of age, to follow him to Paris.  Upon his arrival there, Lully met with but a cool reception from the lady for whose service he was intended.  She liked not his appearance, which was mean and unpromising ; and, declining to retain him as a servant about her person, she assigned him a station which she thought best suited with his appearance, in her kitchen, and commanded the officers of her household to enter him in their books as her under-scullion.

Neither the disappointment which he had met with, nor the sordid employment to which he was destined, affected the spirit of Lully : in the moments of his leisure from the kitchen he used to scrape upon a scurvy fiddle, which the strong propensity that impelled him to music made him contrive to procure.  A person about the court, the Count de Nogent, as it is said, happened to hear him, and informed the princess that her scullion had both talents and a hand.  She thereupon employed a master to teach him the violin ; and Lully in a few months became so good a proficient, that he was sent for up to the chamber from whence his figure had before banished him ; and now behold him in the rank of musicians.  But an unlucky accident, and his own indiscretion, occasioned his discharge from her service. The following stanza of Bardou will explain it :—

> Mon cœur outré de déplaisirs,
> Etroit si gros de ses soûpirs ;
> Voyant vôtre cœur si farouche :
> Que l'un d'eux se voyant réduit
> A ne pas sortir par la bouche,
> Sortit par un autre conduit.

A sigh of this nature, which had escaped his mistress in her private closet, was very plainly heard by Lully in his chamber, and he was foolish enough not only to mention it, but to set to music the verses above quoted, which had been scribbled on the occasion, and was very deservedly dismissed for his pains.

The lady did not follow her resentment, and Lully found means to get himself entered among the king's violins : some say that at first he was only their boy, that carried their instruments ; be that as it may, he plied his studies so closely, that in a little time he became able to compose ; and some of his airs being noticed by the king, he called for the author, and was so struck with his performance of them on the violin, on which instrument Lully was now become a master, that he created a new band, called Les petits Violons, and placed him at the head of it ; and under his direction it soon surpassed the famous band of twenty-four, till then the most celebrated in Europe.  This was about the year 1660, at which

time the favorite entertainments at the French court, were representations of the dramatic kind, called Ballets ; these consisted of dancing, intermixed with action, and speaking in recitative ; and to many of them Lully composed the music.

Entertainments of this kind suited not those ideas of grandeur and magnificence that filled the mind of the king : an academy had been established at Venice for the performance of operas, and Lewis determined as to have one in France that should if possible exceed it.  Cardinal Mazarine encouraged this disposition ; accordingly in the year 1669 the king granted to the Abbé Perrin, master of the ceremonies to Philip duke of Orleans, a privilege for the purpose of conducting an opera, to be performed in the French language, but after the model of that at Venice.

Perrin had a talent for poetry ; he immediately engaged with Cambert, the organist of St Honoré ; this person had been sur-intendant de la musique to the queen mother, Ann of Austria, and the Marquis de Sourdeac, and was esteemed the best musician in France : the fruit of their joint labours was the opera of Pomone, which was performed in March, 1670, with universal applause ; but Lully having by this time gotten possession of the public, and indeed of the king's ear, and having been appointed Sur-intendant de la musique de la chambre du Roy, he soon found means to make the situation of Cambert so very uneasy, that he was glad for a consideration in money, backed with the injunctions of his sovereign to quit it, and Lully was immediately appointed to fill his place.*  Upon this Lully associated himself with Quinault, who was appointed to write the operas : and being now become composer and joint director of the opera, he did not only detach himself from the former band, and instituted one of his own, but he determined on the building a new theatre near the Luxemburg palace, and in a short time accomplished it, agreeably to a design of Vigarini, an Italian architect.

The first musical performance in this newly erected theatre was in the month of November in the same year, 1670, of an entertainment consisting of a variety of detached pieces, included under the title of Le Combat de l'Amour et de Bacchus.

From the day that the king made him superintendent of his music Lully neglected the violin so much, that he even had not one in his house : whether it was vanity that made him put away from his sight

---

* Cambert retired to England in 1672, and was favoured by Charles II. he performed his Pomone here, but with indifferent success ; and died with grief, as it is said, in 1677.  His death is thus accounted for by Bourdelot, ' Mais l'envie, qui est inséparable du mérite, lui abregea les ' jours. Les Anglois ne trouvent pas bon qu'un etrangér se mêle de ' leur plaire et de les instruire.  Le pauvre garçon mourut là un peu ' plutôt qu'il ne seroit mort ailleurs.'  Hist. de la Musique et de ses Effets, tom. III. pag. 164.  A modest reflection in the mouth of a man whose country has produced fewer good musicians than any in Europe.

Perhaps one reason of the dislike of the English to Cambert's Pomone, was that the opera was a kind of entertainment to which they had not been accustomed ; another might be that the levity of the French musical drama is but ill suited to the taste of such as have a relish for harmony.  The operas of Lully consist of recitatives, short airs, chiefly gavots, minuets, and courants, set to words ; and choruses in counterpoint, with entrées, and splendid dances, and a great variety of scenery ; and, in short, were such entertainments as none but a Frenchman could sit to hear, and it was never pretended that those of Cambert were at all better.

an instrument that could not but recall to his remembrance his employment in her highness's kitchen; or whether his attachment to his studies, and the duties of his station, and the obligation he was under to gratify the call for new compositions, induced him to free himself from his subjection to an instrument that requires assiduity and unremitted practice, it is difficult to determine : be this as it will, his performance on the violin, even in this state of desuetude, was so excellent as to attract the admiration of all who heard him; though it must be confessed, that after he was appointed to the direction of the opera, these were very few; his usual answer, even to such persons of rank about the court, as requested to hear from him an air on the violin, being, that he looked upon himself as engaged to acknowledge only one master, the Marshal de Grammont, who alone had the power to make him play from time to time upon it. This nobleman had a servant named La Lande, whom he afterwards made his valet, and who became one of the best performers on the violin of any in Europe; one day at the end of a meal the Marshal desired Lully to hear his valet, and give him a few instructions; La Lande came and played, and, without doubt, to the best of his power, but Lully, more attentive to his defects than his excellencies, whenever he erred would snatch the instrument out of his hand, and, under the notion of teaching him, would indulge the enthusiastic spirit that at the instant seized him, and play on it sometimes for three hours, and at length became so enraptured with the music, as to lay down the instrument with regret.*

On the other hand, to the guitar, a trifling instrument, Lully retained throughout his life such a propensity, that for his amusement he resorted to it voluntarily; and to perform on it, even before strangers, needed no incentive. The reason of this seeming perverseness of temper is thus accounted for : the guitar is an instrument of small estimation among persons skilled in music, the power of performing on it is attained without much difficulty; and, so far as regards the reputation of the performer, it is of small moment whether he plays very well on it; but the performance on the violin is a delicate and an arduous energy; this Lully knew, and he set too high a value on the reputation he had acquired when in constant practice, to risk the losing it.

In the year 1686 the king was seized with an indisposition that threatened his life, but, recovering from it, Lully was required to compose a Te Deum for the celebration of so providential an event; accordingly he did compose one, which is not more remarkable for its excellence than for the unhappy accident that attended the performance of it. He had neglected nothing in the composition of the music, and the preparations for the executing of it; and, the better to demonstrate his zeal, he himself beat the time : with the cane he used for this purpose he struck himself in the heat of action, a blow upon the end of his foot; this caused a small blister to arise thereon, which encreasing, Mons. Alliot, his

physician, advised him immediately to have his little toe cut off, and, after a delay of some days, the foot, and at length the whole limb : at this juncture an adventurer in physic presented himself, who hardily offered to cure the patient without an amputation. The family of Vendome, who loved Lully, promised this quack two thousand pistoles in case he should accomplish the cure; but this act of beneficence, and the efforts of the empiric, were in vain. Lully died on the twenty-second day of March, 1687, and was interred in the church of the discalceat Augustines at Paris, where a fine monument for him is yet remaining. His wife was the daughter of Michael Lambert, an excellent performer on the lute, and composer and Maître de la Musique de la Chambre du Roy. He had by her, living at his decease, three sons and three daughters.

A story is related of a conversation between Lully and his confessor in his last illness, which proves the archness of the one, and the folly of the other, to this purpose : for some years before the accident that occasioned his illness, Lully had been closely engaged in composing for the opera; the priest took occasion from hence to insinuate, that unless, as a testimony of his sincere repentance for all the errors of his past life he would throw the last of his compositions into the fire, he must expect no absolution. Lully at first would have excused himself, but after some opposition he acquiesced; and pointing to a drawer wherein the draft of Achilles and Polixene lay, it was taken out and burnt, and the confessor went away satisfied. Lully grew better, and was thought to be out of danger. One of the young princes, who loved Lully and his works, came to see him; and 'What, Baptiste,' says he to him, 'have you thrown your opera into ' the fire? you were a fool for giving credit thus to ' a dreaming Jansenist, and burning good music.' ' Hush, hush, my Lord,' answered Lully in a whisper, ' I knew very well what I was about, I have a fair ' copy of it.' Unhappily this ill-timed pleasure was followed by a relapse; the gangrene increased, and the prospect of inevitable death threw him into such pangs of remorse, that he submitted to be laid upon a heap of ashes, with a cord about his neck. In this situation he expressed a deep sense of his late transgression; and, being replaced in his bed, he, farther to expiate his offence, sung. to an air of his own composing, the following words :—

Il faut mourir pécheur il faut mourir.

With respect to his person, Lully was of a thicker and shorter make than his prints represent; in other respects they sufficiently resemble him. His countenance was lively and singular, but by no means noble; his complexion was black, eyes small, nose big, and mouth large and prominent; and his sight was so short, that he could hardly distinguish the features of those whom he conversed with. In his temper there was a mixture of dignity and gentleness; and it must be said to his praise that he behaved without pride or haughtiness to the lowest musician; and yet he had less of what is generally denominated politeness in his manner, than was to be expected from a man who had lived a

---

* Many stories of the like kind are related of Geminiani whose temper was such as renders them credible.

long time in a refined court. He had the gaiety of a Frenchman, with a little of the libertine, as far as regards wine and food, and no farther; for it was never known that he had any criminal connexion with women; but he was so far from being without a tincture of avarice, that in some instances it is said he was sordid; and that this disposition moved him to fall out with Fontaine, whom he contrived to curtail of his pay because he had inserted in an opera some words that Lully disliked. This at least must be allowed, that he knew the value of wealth, for it is said that he left behind him in ready money the sum of six hundred and thirty thousand livres.

The courtiers called Lully a miser, not because he did not often entertain them, but because he entertained them without profusion; the excuse he made was that of a man of sense: he declared that he would not imitate those who prepare costly banquets for noblemen, and are laughed at by them for their pains. He had a vivacity fertile in sallies of original wit, and told a story with admirable humour. These are the particulars of his life and general character, it now remains to speak of him as a musician.

At the time when Lully was placed at the head of the little band of violins, not half the musicians in France were able to play at sight: he was accounted an excellent master that could play thorough-bass on the harpsichord or theorbo in accompaniment to a scholar; and, with respect to composition, nothing can be conceived more inartificial than the sonatas and airs for violins of that time. The treble part contained the whole of the melody; the bass and the interior part were mere accompaniment, and the

whole was a gross and sullen counterpoint. The combinations of sounds then allowed of were too few to admit of sufficient variety; and the art of preparing and resolving discords was a secret too precious to be communicated. In every of these respects did Lully improve the music of France; farther in his overtures he introduced fugues, and in chorusses he first made use of the side and kettle-drum.

To speak of his style is a matter of some difficulty. He quitted Italy before he was old enough to receive any impressions either of melody or harmony, so that his cannot be said to be the style of the Italians; nor could it be that of the French, for at the time of his arrival at Paris there was among them no style at all; in short, his style was his own, original, self-formed, and derived from no other source than the copious fountain of his own invention.

After the account above given, it would be needless to mention that the compositions of Lully were chiefly operas, and other dramatic entertainments: these, though excellent in their kind, would give but little pleasure at this day, the airs being very short, formed of regular measures, and too frequently interrupted by the recitatives; the reason whereof is, that Lewis XIV. was very fond of dancing, and had no taste for any music but airs, in the composition whereof a stated and precise number of bars was the chief rule to be observed; of harmony, or fine melody, or of the relation between poetry and music, he seems to have had no conception.* The following composition, taken from his Roland, may serve as a specimen of the style of Lully's opera airs:—

ROLAND, cou - rez aux ar - mes, aux ar - - mes, cou - rez aux

ar - mes, Que la Glo - ire a de char-mes! Que la Glo-ire a de char - - mes! L'Amour de ses

di - vins ap - pas Fait vivre au de la du tré - pas, L'Amour de ses di - vins ap - pas Fait

* In a contest between *Baptistin*, a scholar of Corelli, and one of the French band, an ordinary performer, Lewis preferred an air in Cadmus, an opera of Lully, and none of his best, to a solo, probably of Corelli, played by the former, saying, 'Voila mon goût, à moi: Voila mon goût.' Hist. Mus. et ses Effets, tom III. page 321. And it is said of Lully, that to comply with the taste of his master, he laboured as much in composing the dances as the airs of his operas. Ib. 209. *The person* above-mentioned, *a Florentine by birth, whether because of the smallness of his stature, or with reference to Lully, whose name was Baptiste, is by the French called le petit Baptiste. He was a scholar and the adopted son of Corelli, and is said to have first introduced the Violoncello into France. He composed three operas, Melagre, Mants la Fee, and Polydore; but is most celebrated for his cantatas; one whereof, viz., Democrite et Heraclite, the French hold in great estimation. He died so lately as the year 1740.*

JEAN BAPTISTE LULLY.

The merit of Lully is therefore to be judged of by his overtures, and works of a more serious nature than his operas. Some motets of his are extant, though not in print; and Mons. Perrault, in his account of Lully among the Eloges Historiques, mentions a Tenebræ* of his, which at the performance of that solemn service, of which it is a part, excited such an universal approbation, that, for the merit of having composed it, the king was prevailed on to appoint him Sur-Intendant of his music, and to confer on him some honours that seem to be little more than titular.†

His opera and other compositions for the theatre were from time to time printed in folio, in a fine character, as they were performed; the following is the list which the authors of the Nouveau Dictionnaire Historique-Portatif have given of them, viz., Cadmus, Alceste, Thesée, Atys, Psyche, Bellerophon, Proserpine, Persée, Phaëton, Amadis, Roland, Armide, these are tragedies in five acts. Les Fêtes de l'Amour et de Bacchus, Acis et Galathée, pastorals in three acts; Le Carnaval, a masque with entrées; Le Triomphe de l'Amour, a ballet with entrées; L'Idyle de la Paix, et L'Eglogue de Versailles, and Le Temple de la Paix, a ballet with entrées. He also composed the music to some of the comedies of Moliere, particularly l'Amour Médecin, Pourceaugnac, and Le Bourgeois Gentilhomme, in which latter he performed the part of the Mufti with great applause.

He composed also Symphonies for violins in three parts, but it does not appear that they were ever published. One observation more respecting this extraordinary person shall conclude the account of him. Lully may be said to be the inventor of that species of instrumental composition, the Overture; more particularly that spirited movement the Largo, which is the general introduction to the fugue; ‡ for

though it may be said that the symphonies and preludes of Carissimi, Colonna, Bassani, and others, are in effect overtures, yet the difference between them and those of Lully is apparent; the former were compositions of the mild and placid kind, and stole upon the affections insensibly; the latter are animated, and full of that energy which compels attention.

## CHAP. CXXXVII.

Wolfgang Caspar Printz, was born the tenth day of October, 1664, at Weildthurn, a small city situate in the Upper Palatinate, on the frontiers of Bohemia, where his father was a principal magistrate, and a receiver of the public revenues, until, on account of his religion, he quitted that station, and removed to Vohenstraus, a small town in the territory of Furstenburg. Discovering an inclination to music, Printz was committed to the tuition of Wilhelm Stockel, a celebrated organist from Nuremburg, by whom he was taught the elements of the science, and the principles of composition. For his master on the Clavier or harpsichord and the violin he had Andrew Paul Vander Heyd, a Bohemian; and having finished his exercises under these persons, he frequented the school at Weyden from the year 1655 to the year 1659, having for his instructor on the harpsichord John Conrad Mertz, an organist, and a skilful composer; and on certain wind instruments John George Schober, after which he went to the university at Altdorff, where he continued till the year 1661.

Anno 1662, about Easter, having been recommended by Francesco Santi, a musician from Perugia, to Count Promnitz at Dresden, he was engaged in his service as music-director and court composer. With this nobleman, then a captain of foot in the Imperial service, he travelled through Silesia, Moravia, and Austria, and was with him at the encampment near Altenburg, in the month of June, 1663; from which, the Count being taken with a dangerous illness, Printz departed in October in the same year, and arrived at Sorau, a town in the circle of Upper Saxony.

Upon the decease of Count Promnitz, Printz was invited to the office of chanter in the church of a town named Triebel, where he married; but, after a year's

---

* An office in the Romish church, celebrated about four or five in the afternoon, on Maundy-Thursday, Good Friday, and other solemn days, to commemorate the darkness that overspread the face of the earth at the time of the crucifixion.

† In the titles of his operas he is styled Escuyer, Conseiller, Secretaire du Roy, Maison Couronne de France et de ses Finances; et Sur-Intendant de la Musique de sa Chambre.

‡ It is said that the overtures of Lully were in such esteem, that they are to be found prefixed to many manuscript copies of Italian operas; and Mattheson asserts that Mr. Handel in the composition of his overtures professed to imitate those of Lully. And indeed whoever will make the comparison, will find good reason to be of that opinion. Those to the operas of Theseus, Alexander, Muzio Scævola, and Ariodante are much in his cast; and this may be remarked of the fugues in the overtures of Lully, that they are generally in the time of six crotchets in a bar, equally divided by the Tactus or beat.

continuance in that employment, being called to the same office in the church at Sorau, he entered upon it at Whitsuntide, 1665. In the year 1682 he was appointed to the direction of the choir of the same church; and, as it is supposed, continued in that station till the time of his death.

The works of this author are many, and are enumerated by Walther in his Lexicon. Among them is a history of music, published at Dresden, in quarto, in the year 1690, with the title of **Historiche Beschreibung der edelen Sing=und kling=kunst,** of which it may be expected some account should here be given.

It is written in chronological order; the author begins his history with the invention of the harp and organ by Jubal, founding his relation on the authority of the holy scriptures, and those testimonies respecting the ancient Jewish musicians, which Kircher has collected from the rabbinical writers. He is very exact in his delineations of the Hebrew instruments, which for the most part are taken from Johannes Schütterus, the author of Collectaneis Philologicis. For want of better materials he adopts the fictions of the poets in the stories by them related of Orpheus, Amphion, and Arion. He relates the invention of the Mercurian Lyre from Nicomachus, Boetius, and other writers; and continues the succession of the Greek musicians in short extracts from a variety of authors, nearly down to the Christian æra. He then, from Eusebius, Theodoret, Sozomen, and other ecclesiastical writers, explains the practice of antiphonal singing introduced among the primitive Christians by Flavianus and Diodorus; and, from other authorities, the final establishment of church music by St. Ambrose and St. Gregory. He speaks of the invention of the organ, and the introduction of that instrument into the church-service by pope Vitalianus; and celebrates Bede and Rabanus Maurus among the most eminent musicians of their time.

He dates the invention of music in consonance from the year 940, and with great formality of circumstance ascribes it to St. Dunstan, archbishop of Canterbury. The following is a translation of the author's own words:—' In the year of Christ ' 940, Dunstan, otherwise Dunstaphus, an English- ' man, being very young, betook himself to the study ' of music, and thereby became of immortal memory. ' He was the first that composed songs in different ' parts, namely, Bass, Tenor, Discant, and Vagant or ' Alt.' A little farther on in his work he is some- what more particular. He says that in the time of Dunstan the method of notation was by points placed on lines, of which method he gives a specimen, the same with that herein before inserted, page 158, from Galilei. He says that at this time the music of the church was very simple, and that Dunstan was the first that found out the harmony of four different voices, though he proceeded no farther in it than the Contrapunctus Simplex. But that it was not till some years after this invention that the practice of singing in consonance became general.*

The rest of this book contains a brief deduction of the history of the science, and a particular enu- meration of such persons as have excelled in it, down to his own time; concluding with an account of himself and his studies, from which the foregoing particulars of his life are taken. Printz appears to have been a very able man in his profession, and to have bestowed great pains in the compilation of this work, the brevity of which is its only fault. Walther says the author had written it also in Latin, but that he did not live to publish it in that language.

Mattheson, in his **Forschendes Orchestre,** page 242, relates that during the last illness of Printz he wrote a book entitled De Instrumentis in toto Orbe musicis; and Walther adds that he died on his birth- day, viz., the tenth of October, in the year 1717.

JOHANN CHRISTOPHER DENNER is celebrated for his exquisite skill and ingenuity in the construction of flutes, and other instruments of the like kind; he was born at Leipsic on the thirteenth day of August, 1655; and at the age of eight years was taken to Nuremburg, in which city his father, a com- mon turner in wood, had then lately chose to settle with his family. After a very few years stay there, the younger Denner, having been instructed like other boys of his age, in the rudiments of music, betook himself to his father's trade, and in particular to the fabrication of flutes, hautboys, and other wind instruments, which, by the help of a nice ear, added to the skill he had acquired in music, and the proficiency he had attained to in playing on them, he tuned so exquisitely, that his instruments were sought for from all parts. He is said to have greatly improved the Chalumeau, an instrument resembling the hautboy, and described by Mersennus

* Printz professes to have taken the above account of the invention of music in consonance from one or both of the authors cited by him, namely, David Chytræus, and Conrad Dieterich; nevertheless Walther, who appears to have been very well acquainted with Printz's writings, seems to give very little credit to this relation; for he cites a book written by Salomon Van Til, entitled ' SING-DICHT-UND SPIEL-KUNST, page 125, wherein it is said that the invention of music in consonance is of an older date than the time of St. Dunstan, though he admits that Dunstan might have introduced it among his countrymen.

The truth of the above relation is at this day so little questioned, that the modern writers on music seem generally agreed to acquiesce in it. Francis Lustig of Groningen and　　Marpourg of Berlin, have ex- pressly asserted that St. Dunstan was the inventor of Counterpoint, the one in a treatise entitled ' MUSIK KUNDE,' the other in a book printed in quarto at Berlin in 1766, entitled Traité de la Fugue et du Contrepoint, part II. sect. 7. But upon a careful enquiry after the evidence of the fact, there appears none to support it; on the contrary, the relation in- volves in it a series of the grossest blunders, as shall here be de- monstrated.

In the year 1613, one Johannes Nucius, an ecclesiastic of Gorlitz in Lusatia, published a book with the title of Musices Poeticæ, sive de Compositioni Cantus Præceptiones absolutissimæ, wherein, on what authority we know not, he asserts that John of Dunstable, of whom an account is given page 274 of this work, was the inventor of musical composition. His words are an answer to the question, ' Quem dicimus ' Poeticum Musicum?' and are these: ' Qui non solum præcepta musicæ ' apprimè intelligit, et juxta ea rectè ac benè modulatur, sed qui proprij ' ingenij penetralia tentans, novas cantilenas cudit et flexibiles sonos pio ' verborum pondere textibus aptat. Talem artificem Glareanus Sym- ' phonetæ appellatione describit. Sicut Phonasci nomine cantorem ' insinuat. Porrò tales artifices clarverunt, primum circa annum Christi ' 1400 aut certè paulò post. Dunastapli Anglus à quo primum figuralem ' musicam inventam tradunt.' Mus. Poet. cap. I.

It is extremely difficult to find out any sense in which the above re- lation can be said to be true; for if by the term Figuralem musicam we are to understand, as all men do, the Cantus figuratus or mensurable music, it is certain that that was in use some centuries before the time of John of Dunstable: if it be taken for music in consonance, the invention of that, though at this time it is impossible to fix precisely the æra of it, is at least as ancient as the time of Bede, who makes use of the word Discantus. See page 188.

But taking the relation of Nucius for true, it refers to John of Dunstable, who flourished about the year 1400, whereas his invention or improvement, whatever it was, is by Printz, Lustig, and Marpourg, the two last of whom are now living, ascribed to Dunstan, died about the year 1000.

and Kircher; and to have been the original inventor of another instrument, which neither of them do so much as mention, namely, the Clarinet. He died on the twentieth day of April, 1707, leaving behind him two sons, who followed the business of their father, and, like him, were excellent performers on most of the instruments they professed to make.*

A son of one of these Denners betook himself to painting, and became remarkable for the singularity of his style. His studies were only heads, and those in general of old persons; his colouring was very fine, and his portraits were so close a copy, that he represented the defects and decays of nature, and even the ravages of disease in the human countenance. His pictures were so elaborate, and of consequence his price so high, that few, without the hope of a more favourable likeness than it was his practice to paint, would choose to sit to him. About the year 1745 a portrait of his, the head of an old man, was exhibited to public view in London, at the rate of half a crown each person, and many resorted to see it. Notwithstanding his ill success, a disciple of Denner, one Van Smissen, ventured to pursue the same course of study, and practised the same style of painting. Trusting to the propensity which, as he had been told, the English have to favour foreigners, he came over to England, and took lodgings in St. Martin's Lane, London; his paintings on canvas were like enamel, but he had no idea of grace or elegance; and meeting with but little encouragement, after a short stay he left this country.

ALESSANDRO STRADELLA, one of the great Italian musicians in his time, flourished about the middle of the seventeenth century; he was both a very fine singer and an exquisite performer on the harp, an instrument in which he greatly delighted; over and above which qualifications, he possessed a talent for vocal composition, sufficient alone to have rendered him famous to all posterity. He was for some time composer to the opera at Venice, under an appointment of the magistrates of that republic, and frequently sang on the stage, cantatas and other of his own compositions, accompanying himself on the harp.

His character as a musician was so high at Venice, that all who were desirous of excelling in the science were solicitous to become his pupils. Among the many whom he had the instruction of, was one, a young lady of a noble family of Rome, named Hortensia, who, notwithstanding her illustrious descent, submitted to live in a criminal intimacy with a Venetian nobleman. The frequent access of Stradella to this lady, and the many opportunities he had of being alone with her, produced in them both such an affection for each other, that they agreed to go off together for Rome. In consequence of this resolution they embarked in a very fine night, and by the favour of the wind affected their escape.

Upon the discovery of the lady's flight, the Venetian

had recourse to the usual method in that country of obtaining satisfaction for real or supposed injuries; he dispatched two assassins, with instructions to murder both Stradella and the lady, giving them a sum of money in hand, and a promise of a larger if they succeeded in the attempt. Being arrived at Naples, the assassins received intelligence that those whom they were in pursuit of were at Rome, where the lady passed for the wife of Stradella. Upon this they determined to execute their commission, wrote to their employer, requesting letters of recommendation to the Venetian embassador at Rome, in order to secure an asylum for them to fly to, as soon as the deed should be perpetrated.

Upon the receipt of letters for this purpose, the assassins made the best of their way towards Rome; and being arrived there, they learned that on the morrow, at five in the evening, Stradella was to give an oratorio in the church of San Giovanni Laterano. They failed not to be present at the performance, and had concerted to follow Stradella and his mistress out of the church, and, seizing a convenient opportunity, to make the blow. The performance was now begun, and these men had nothing to do but to watch the motions of Stradella, and attend to the music, which they had scarce begun to hear, before the suggestions of humanity began to operate upon their minds; they were seized with remorse, and reflected with horror on the thought of depriving of his life a man capable of giving to his auditors such pleasure as they had but just then felt. In short, they desisted from their purpose, and determined, instead of taking away his life, to exert their endeavours for the preservation of it; they waited for his coming out of the church, and courteously addressed him and the lady, who was by his side, first returning him thanks for the pleasure they had received at hearing his music, and informed them both of the errand they had been sent upon; expatiating upon the irresistible charms, which of savages had made them men, and had rendered it impossible for them to effect their execrable purpose; and concluded with their earnest advice that Stradella and the lady should both depart from Rome the next day, themselves promising to deceive their employer, and forego the remainder part of their reward, by making him believe that Stradella and his lady had quitted Rome on the morning of their arrival.

Having thus escaped the malice of their enemy, the two lovers took an immediate resolution to fly for safety to Turin, and soon arrived there. The assassins being returned to Venice, reported to their employer that Stradella and Hortensia had fled from Rome, and taken shelter in the city of Turin, a place where the laws were very severe, and which, excepting the houses of embassadors, afforded no protection for murderers; they represented to him the difficulty of getting these two persons assassinated, and, for their own parts, notwithstanding their engagements, declined the enterprize. This disappointment, instead of allaying, served but to sharpen the resentment of the Venetian: he had found means to attach to his interest the father of Hortensia, and by various

---

* It is somewhat remarkable that many excellent performers on such wind instruments as the flute and hautboy, have also been makers of them. Denner, Le Vacher, and Quiclet, so much celebrated by Mersennus, are instances of this; to whom may be added Meuschel of Nuremburg, a maker of trumpets.

arguments, to inspire him with a resolution to become the murderer of his own daughter. With this old man, no less malevolent and vindictive than himself, the Venetian associated two ruffians, and dispatched them all three to Turin, fully inspired with a resolution of stabbing Stradella and the old man's daughter wherever they found them. The Venetian also furnished them with letters from Mons. l'Abbé de Estrades, then embassador of France at Venice, addressed to the marquis of Villars, the French embassador at Turin. The purport of these letters was a recommendation of the bearers of them, who were therein represented to be merchants, to the protection of the embassador, if at any time they should stand in need of it.

The duchess of Savoy was at that time regent; and she having been informed of the arrival of Stradella and Hortensia, and the occasion of their precipitate flight from Rome; and knowing the vindictive temper of the Venetians, placed the lady in a convent, and retained Stradella in her palace as her principal musician. In a situation of such security as this seemed to be, Stradella's fears for the safety of himself and his mistress began to abate, till one evening, walking for the air upon the ramparts of the city, he was set upon by the three assassins abovementioned, that is to say, the father of Hortensia, and the two ruffians, who each gave him a stab with a dagger in the breast, and immediately betook themselves to the house of the French embassador as to a sanctuary.

The attack on Stradella having been made in the sight of numbers of people, who were walking in the same place, occasioned an uproar in the city, which soon reached the ears of the duchess: she ordered the gates to be shut, and diligent search to be made for the three assassins; and being informed that they had taken refuge in the house of the French embassador, she went to demand them. The embassador insisting on the privileges which those of his function claimed from the law of nations, refused to deliver them up; he nevertheless wrote to the Abbé de Estrades to know the reason of the attack upon Stradella, and was informed by the Abbé that he had been surprized into a recommendation of the three men by one of the most powerful of the Venetian nobility. In the interim Stradella was cured of his wounds, and the marquis de Villars, to make short of the question about privilege, and the rights of embassadors, suffered the assassins to escape.

From this time, finding himself disappointed of his revenge, but not the least abated in his ardour to accomplish it, this implacable Venetian contented himself with setting spies to watch the motions of Stradella. A year was elapsed after the cure of his wounds; no fresh disturbance had been given to him, and he thought himself secure from any further attempts on his life. The duchess regent, who was concerned for the honour of her sex, and the happiness of two persons who had suffered so much, and seemed to have been born for each other, joined the hands of Stradella and his beloved Hortensia, and they were married. After the ceremony Stradella and

his wife having a desire to visit the port of Genoa, went thither with a resolution to return to Turin: the assassins having intelligence of their departure, followed them close at their heels. Stradella and his wife it is true reached Genoa, but the morning after their arrival these three execrable villains, rushed into their chamber, and stabbed each to the heart. The murderers had taken care to secure a bark which lay in the port; to this they retreated, and made their escape from justice, and were never heard of more.

Mr. Wanley, who in the Catalogue of the Harleian manuscripts, No. 1272, has given a short account of Stradella, says that the lover of this lady, whom he calls the baroness or countess, was the heir of either the Cornaro or Colonna family; and that after the murder of Stradella, which he says was in the year 1670, she was sent for to France by the then king; and that she had been heard to sing both in Italy and France by a friend of Mr. Wanley, Mr. Berenclow, who said she was a perfect mistress of the best manner, for which, with her, he only admired Cornelio Galli, and the two eunuchs, Tosi and Sifacio.*

The truth of this relation is very questionable: in the above account, taken from a French writer, Mons. Bourdelot, author of the Histoire de la Musique et de ses Effets, it is said that, in full gratification of the malice of their enemy, both Stradella and the lady were murdered. There was about that time a lady, but a German, as it is supposed; a fine singer, who sang in the operas abroad, and even at London,† known by no other name than the Baroness; and it is not improbable that Mr. Barenclow might be deceived into an opinion that she was the relict of Stradella.

The same person says that when the report of Stradella's assassination reached the ears of Purcell, and he was informed jealousy was the motive to it, he lamented his fate exceedingly; and, in regard of his great merit as a musician, said he could have forgiven him any injury in that kind; which, adds

---

* This Mr. Berenclow was a musician of some eminence in queen Anne's reign, and the son of a Dr. Bernard Martin Berenclow, of whom Mr. Wanley, in the Harleian Catalogue, No. 1265. 19, gives the following account: 'Dr. Berenclow was born in the duchy of Holstein near 'Toninghen; his mother was a Berchem, a family sufficiently eminent 'both in the Upper and Nether Germany. He married Katherine, one 'of the daughters of Mr. Laneir, clerk of the closet to king Charles the 'First. He was professor of physic in the university of Padua, and 'practised with success and reputation in Italy, France, Germany, 'Holland, Flanders, and England. And, notwithstanding his frequent 'journies and removals, died rich in ready money, jewels, plate, pictures, 'drawings, &c. of great price and curiosity; which his widow, notwith- 'standing (by true pains-taking) made a shift to overcome, and utterly 'squander away in about five years after his decease.'
    Cornelio Galli was a native of Lucca, and one of the gentlemen of the chapel to Catherina, the consort of Charles II. He is said to have first introduced a fine manner of singing into England. Vide Harleian Catalogue, No. 1264.
    Pier-Francesco Tosi was an Italian by birth, but travelled much, and resided at different times at most of the courts in Europe. He was in England in the several reigns of king James, king William, and king George I. and was patronized by the earl of Peterborough. He lived to the age of fourscore; and, besides sundry elegant cantatas, was the author of a tract entitled 'Opinioni de' Cantori antiche e moderna, o sieno 'Osservazioni sopra il Canto figurato,' printed at Bologna in 1723, which Mr. Galliard translated into English, and published in 1743.
    Sifacio. The true name of this person is unknown: this, which he was generally called by, was given him on occasion of his performing the part of Syphax in an Italian opera. He was in England, and a singer in the chapel of king James II., but, returning to Italy, was assassinated.

    † She performed the part of Lavinia in the opera of Camilla, represented at Drury-Lane theatre in 1706, and that of Eurilla. in the Triumph of Love, at the Hay-market, some time after.

the relator, 'those who remember how lovingly 'Mr. Purcell lived with his wife, or rather what a 'loving wife she proved to him, may understand 'without farther explication.'

It may be questioned whether any of the compositions of Stradella were ever published; Walther has given no catalogue of them, nor has any been

met with in the accounts of him by other writers. Many of his pieces in manuscript are in the library of the Academy of ancient Music, particularly an oratorio entitled San Giovanni Battista, and sundry madrigals, among which is a very fine one for five voices, to the words ' Clori son fido amante,' &c.

## BOOK XV.   CHAP. CXXXVIII.

Gio. Andrea Angelini Bontempi, a native of Perugia, was the author of a work entitled Historia Musica. He it seems was a practical musician; and, in the earlier part of his life, was chapel-master to the elector of Saxony. He was a man eminently learned in his profession, as appears by a tract of his writing, entitled Nova quatuor Vocibus componendi methodus, printed at Dresden in 1660; but the work by which he is best known is his History of Music, printed in folio at Perugia in 1695.

This book is divided into three parts, which are thus entitled, Della Teorica, Della Pratica antica, Della Pratica moderna, from whence it may be conjectured, that, in the judgment of the author, there could be no theory of the moderns properly so called. Each of these three titles is subdivided into two parts, so as to render it difficult to cite the book otherwise than by the pages.

Discoursing on music at large at the beginning of his work, Bontempi takes notice of that analytical division of it by Aristides Quintilianus in his first book, and mentioned in a preceding page of this work; but this division Bontempi seems here to reject, preferring the scholastic division into mundane, humane, political, rythmical, metrical, and harmonical music. The former however he seems to have adopted, merely in compliance with the method of the Latin and Italian writers, for he hastens to the latter branch of his subdivision. On the subject of rythmical or metrical music he is very elaborate; and, with a view to reduce the precepts delivered by him into practice, he exhibits an oratorio written by himself, founded on the history of the life and martyrdom of St. Emilianus, bishop of Trevi, the poetry whereof is conformable to those metrical rules which the author endeavours to recommend. The History of Music begins with the title Musica Harmonica; and, after giving different etymologies of the word Music, Bontempi, from Boetius, Polydore Virgil, Alstedius, and other writers, ascribes to a variety of personages, deities, semideities, heroes and others, the invention of the several instruments in use among the ancients.

The invention of the lyre by Mercury, the improvement of it by Terpander, with the formation of the Systema maxima by Pythagoras, are faithfully related by this author from Nicomachus, and other ancient writers; but here he fails not to mention that egregious mistake in the relation of the discovery of the consonances by means of hammers of different weights, which we have before noted; and having it seems seen the detection of this error in

the writings of Galileo Galilei, he, prompted by curiosity, as he himself relates, made an experiment of chords distended by weights in the ratios of 12, 9, 8, 6, which, instead of consonances, produced irrational intervals.*

After having treated largely on the music of the Greeks, and given the substance of what the several writers have said on the subject, he gives a very decisive opinion that the ancients were strangers to music in consonance, notwithstanding the assertion of Vincentio Galilei and others to the contrary.†

In the second division of his first part Bontempi continues to discourse on the theory of the ancients, in his explanation whereof he follows the division of Aristides Quintilianus, making music to consist of seven parts, that is to say, 1. sounds, 2. intervals, 3. the genera, 4. systems, 5. the tones or modes, 6. the mutations, 7. the melopoeia.‡

In the first subdivision of the second part, Della Pratica antica, he endeavours to explain the practice of the ancients by a commentary on some select passages of Aristoxenus relating to the measure of intervals, and the constitution of the genera, and their colours or species.

He then takes occasion to celebrate Virgilio Mazzochi, maestro di cappella of the church of St. Pietro in Vaticano, and professor in the college or school instituted at Rome for the education of youth for the service of the papal chapel; and gives an account of their exercises and method of study. He says that one hour in a day is spent in the practice of difficult passages; another in the Trillo or shake; another in singing in the presence of the master, and before a looking-glass, in order to prevent bad habits, and distortions of the features, and to regulate the actions of the muscles; and that these are the exercises of the morning. In the afternoon he says a small portion of time is employed in the study of the theory of music; that one hour is given to the framing of counterpoints on a Canto fermo; that another is spent in hearing from the master, and committing to writing the precepts of counterpoint at large, or practical composition; and another in reading, as in the morning; and that the remainder of the day is devoted to the practice of the Clavicembalo, and the framing some composition, for instance, a psalm, a motet, a canzonet, or a song, best suited to the genius of the students. On those

* Page 54.
† Che gli Antichi cantassero in consonanza, come vuole il Galilei nel suo Discorso intorno all' Opere del Zarlino, è una favola de' Moderni, che senza Greca letteratura, camina unitamente con l' altre.
‡ Page 83.

days on which they are permitted to go out of the college, he says the scholars are wont to sing at a certain place without the Porta Angelica, near the Mount of Marius, where is an echo, which, as it is pretended, returns the sound of their voices in such a manner as to enable them to discover their defects in singing. At other times, says he, they resorted to the churches in Rome, and either assisted in the service, or attended to the performance of those excellent singers and musicians who flourished during the pontificate of Urban VIII. After which they returned to the school or college, and, making exercises on what they had heard, communicated them and their observations to their master, who in return, in lectures delivered and explained to them the precepts of science and practice.*

He then proceeds to exhibit from Franchinus, or, as he calls him, Gaffaro, and Vanneo, the constitution of the four ecclesiastical tones of St. Ambrose, which he shews to be derived from the Dorian, Phrygian, Lydian, and Mixolydian modes of the ancient Greeks. After which he proceeds to relate that St. Gregory increased the number of the ecclesiastical tones to eight, by adding thereto four others, derived as he says, from the Hypodorian, Hypophrygian, Hypolydian, and Hypermixolydian, distinguishing the eight ecclesiastical tones into authentic and plagal.†

In the first subdivision of the third part, Della Pratica Moderna, he considers the practice of the moderns, founding it on the reformation of the scale by Guido Aretinus; of whose invention of a method of determining the place of the semitones in the diapason, by the use and application of the syllables, he has given a just account.‡

The syllables of Guido, as they were invented solely for the purpose of assisting the voice in the discrimination between the tones and semitones, determine nothing as to the ratios or measures of those intervals; and it is obvious that a succession of tones precisely equal with the semitones, interposed in their natural order, had been productive of those inconveniences, arising from a surd quantity in the constitution of the diatessaron, which it had been the endeavour of many writers to palliate, and which had given rise to that controversy between Zarlino and Galilei, whether the ditonic diatonic of Ptolemy, or rather of Pythagoras, or the intense or syntonous diatonic of the former was to be preferred.

To remedy this inconvenience, a system had been invented which divided the octave into thirteen sounds or chords, and twelve intervals, that is to say, semitones, of which Bontempi speaks to the following purpose: ' This was that sublime and ' memorable operation, which so improved the noble ' science of counterpoint; for a very skilful man, ' whose name, and even the age he lived in, is not ' known, having found that the diatessaron and dia- ' pente would admit of a small variation without offence to the ear, he reformed those intervals. ' Besides this he first interposed in the middle of ' each tetrachord the Spesso Cromatico; § and after-

* Page 170.    † Page 172.    ‡ 182, et seq.
§ By the Spesso Cromatico Bontempi means the chromatic or double diesis, or, in other words, the lesser semitone, consisting of four commas,

' wards, at other distances, an interval never known ' before in the orders of tetrachords, marked thus ✗, ' or thus b, according as the modulation was either ' of the sharp or flat kind; thus he formed a system ' of sounds, separated from each other by the interval ' of a semitone, and thereby united the chromatic ' with the diatonic genus, and of the two formed one.' ||

Bontempi has said that the name of the author of this last and great improvement of the musical system, as also the age in which he lived, are unknown, and refers to Polydore Virgil, lib. III. cap. xviii. Polydore Virgil's book De Inventoribus Rerum, contains little more respecting music than a brief account of the invention of it, and of a few instruments, such as the harp, the organ, and the lyre; and it seemed strange that he who has mentioned in particular no one system, should take notice of the improvement of any; his work has therefore been recurred to, and all that he says on the subject is found to be contained in the following words: ' Multa insuper novissimis temporibus instrumenta ' musica inventa sunt, quorum autores jam in ob- ' livionem venerunt. Ex quibus propter suavitatem ' concentus omni admirationi et laude digna sunt ' illa, quæ organa nuncupant, valde quidem ab illis ' dissimilia, quæ David Judæorum rex fecerat, qui- ' bus Levitæ sacros hymnos concinerent, sicut nos ' his pariter canimus. Item alia id genus sunt, ' quæ monochordia clavicymbala varieq; nominantur,

denoted by a double cross, which is the common sharp signature. Vide Brossard Dict. de Musique, DIESIS.

|| Page 186.
Brossard has given an account of this improvement, which, as it is much more full and satisfactory than that of Bontempi, is here inserted:—
' It being found that there was a chord placed between the Mese and ' Paramese of the ancients, or our A and B, which divided the interval of ' a tone, that was between them, into two semitones: it was thought ' that chords also might be added, as well between those that were at the ' like distance from each other, i. e. had a tone between them; the ' author of this improvement therefore not only inserted the B mol, as ' in Guido's system, but also the chromatic chords of the diatonic scale, ' that is those which divide the tones major of each tetrachord into ' semitones; and this he did by raising the lowest chord a semitone, by ' means of a double diesis ♯, which was placed immediately before the ' note so to be raised, or on the same degree with it after the cliff: again, ' it having been found that the tones minor terminating the tetrachords ' upwards, were no less capable of such division, he, by the help of the ' chromatic chords, divided them also; so that the octave then became ' composed of thirteen sounds and twelve intervals, eight whereof are ' diatonic or natural, distinguished by white notes thus ○, and five ' chromatic thus, by black ones ◆; and the diesis prefixed.' Dict. de Musique, voce SYSTEMA.

Brossard elsewhere observes, that in the several systems of the diatonic genus for which he refers to Bontempi, page 93, the tetrachord is composed of three intervals, that is to say, semitone, tone major, and tone minor; and that Ptolemy and Didymus, among all their reformations, taking it for granted that the tone minor was indivisible into semitones, interposed but one chromatic sound in the tetrachord, thereby dividing the tone major into semitones, the one major and the other minor, leaving the tone minor as they found it. But he says that it having afterwards been found necessary to divide the tone minor in like manner, and also to extend the diatessaron and contract the diapente; a very learned man, whose name is not mentioned in history, perceiving that the ear was not displeased if the fifth was a little diminished, that is, if it was not quite of so great an extent, found out an admirable temperament, which rendered the second tone of the fourth equal to the first, by giving the fourth a little greater extent than it naturally had from its mathematical form of 3, 4, which tone consequently admitted one chromatic chord, that divided it into two semitones. This system is called by the Italians Systema Temperato. He observes that by means of this addition of the chromatic chord the octave becomes divisible into twelve semitones, without any chasm in or between the two tetrachords that compose it; and also that thereby two of the genera, that is to say, the chromatic and diatonic, are brought into one system, which, for that reason, is by Bontempi and other of the Italian writers, called Systema Participato. Vide Brossard, voce TEMPERAMENTO.

'eorum, tamen æque inventores magno quidem suæ
' gloriæ damno in nocte densissima delitescunt.'*

In the second subdivision of the third part, della
Practica Moderna, Bontempi deduces the practice of
counterpoint from the time of its supposed invention
by Guido down to the time of Johannes de Muris,
who lived about three hundred years after.  Impli-
citly relying on Gaffurius, Vanneo, and Kircher, he
ascribes to De Muris the invention of the Cantus
Mensurabilis, and says that it was adopted and improved by Prosdocimus, Tintor, Franco, Caserta,
Anselmo da Parma, and other contrapuntists.  He says
that in the original invention of counterpoint the
sounds in consonance were distinguished in writing,
by an opposition of note against note, but that by
the introduction of the Cantus Mensurabilis, which
was signified by certain characters, of dissimilar
forms, that which was originally termed counterpoint
assumed the name of Canto figurato.†

In treating on the science of counterpoint, this
author, following the method of the Italians, divides
it into five parts, namely, 1. the figures or characters
used to denote the sounds and their measures ; 2. the
degrees of mode, time, and prolation, signified by
their respective characters ; 3. the proportions ; 4.
Contrapunto semplice ; 5. Contrapunto florido.‡  In
the discussion of each of these he is very accurate ;
and in his discourse on the last two heads delivers
the precepts for the composition of a cantilena in
consonance both in the Contrapunto florido and the
Contrapunto semplice, according to the practice of
his time.

In the course of his work he celebrates two of his
countrymen, namely, Lemme Rossi§ and Baldassare
Ferri, both of Perugia ; the former of these had
written a treatise on music, from which Bontempi
has given many copious extracts ; the latter was
a singer, of whom he gives a great character.

The Historia Musica of Bontempi is a work of some
merit ; but, to speak ingenuously, it seems little
calculated for instruction ; the author appears to have
read a great deal on the subject of music ; nevertheless it is apparent in many instances that the
knowledge he had attained was not derived from
the genuine source.  That he had perused the Greek
writers in the edition of Meibomius cannot be doubted,
for he cites the book, though he has not adopted all
the prejudices of the editor.  But his great fault is
a too ready acquiescence in the authorities of Franchinus, Steffano Vanneo, and Kircher in matters
respecting the theory and practice of music among
the moderns, under which comprehensive term he
properly enough includes not only Guido, the inventor
of the modern system, but St. Gregory and St.
Ambrose, who, from the modes of the ancients,
instituted for the purpose of religious worship, that

formula of vocal melody comprized in the eight
ecclesiastical tones.  In a discourse on this important
branch of musical history, it was requisite that the
author should have recurred to original materials,
such as are to be found in public repositories, not to
say in Italy only, but in almost every city and
university in Europe : the neglect of this method
has led Bontempi to adopt the errors of former
writers, who seem to have founded their reports on
mere popular tradition, and to become the propagator
of many errors, which, as a historian, it was his duty
to detect and explode.  To enumerate instances of
this kind is an invidious office, but those contained in
his relation of the invention of music in consonance
by Guido, and of the Cantus Mensurabilis by Johannes de Muris, are of such importance, that they
merit particular notice.  With respect to the former
assertion, there is not the least authority for it either
in the Micrologus or the Argumentum novi Cantus
inveniendi of Guido, or in his epistle to his friend
Michael of Pomposa ; and, from the superficial account
which he gives of Guido and his improvements, there
is reason to think that Bontempi had never perused
any of his writings ; and as to the Cantus Mensurabilis, no one can read the relation of its invention
by Franco of Liege, as given by the learned Bene-
dictines, the publishers of the Histoire Literaire de
la France, but must conclude that the names De
Muris, Prosdocimus, Tintor, Franco, Caserta, and
Anselmo da Parma, are cited by rote from the
margin of the Practica Musicæ of Franchinus, or
rather from the Systema Musica of his compatriot
Lemme Rossi, whose name occurs in almost every
page of his work.  Indeed it is easy to discover
where the materials of this author failed him ; for
while he had the Latin version of the Greek writers
on music lying before him, he was able to give an
account of the original constitution of the lyre of
Mercury, and of the names of the several persons
who at different times increased the number of
chords of which it consisted, from four to seven,
as also of the subsequent extention of the system to
fifteen chords, with other improvements ; but no
sooner does he dismiss these materials, than his
narration is interrupted, and a chasm ensues, which
he attempts to supply by citations from Alstedius
and other chronological writers, the bare recorders
of memorable events ; and from materials so scanty
as these we are not to wonder if he found himself
unable to furnish many particulars respecting that
history, the deduction whereof is the object of his
work.

The invention of the several musical instruments
in use among the moderns, and the successive improvements made in them at different periods, is
surely a very essential part of musical history ; and
it would be but a weak answer to any one who
should object that Bontempi is silent on this head,
to say that a great deal to the purpose is to be found
in the Musurgia of Ottomarus Luscinius, the Dialogo
della Musica of Vincentio Galilei, in the writings of
Mersennus, the Musurgia of Kircher, and in the
History of Music of Wolfgang Caspar Printz.  And

---

* Polyd. Virgil. De Invent. Rer. Lib. VIII. Basil. apud Johan.
Froben. 1521.

† Page 199.        ‡ 205.

§ Lemme Rossi was an eminent mathematician and philosopher, and
professor of the Greek language in the university or academy of Perugia.
He appears to have been deeply skilled in the theory of music by the work
above alluded to, which was published at Perugia in the year 1666,
and is entitled 'Systema Musica, overo Musica speculativa, dove si
' spiegano i piû celebri di tutti trè generi.'

FRANCESCO FOGGIA ROMANO,

COMPOSITORE.

ANTIMO LIBERATI MUSICO NELLA CAPPELLA PONTIFICIA

MAESTRO DI CAPPELLA NELLA CHIESA DELLA SANTISSIMA

TRINITA DE PELLEGRINI, E MAESTRO DI CAPPELLA ED ORGANISTA

NELLA CHIESA DI S. MARIA DELL ANIMA DELLA NATIONE TUETONICA.

here it may be remarked, that an unjustifiable partiality for the country where the author was born distinguishes this work ; for, among the moderns whom he has taken occasion to mention, the name of any musician not an Italian, scarcely occurs.   In a word, the information contained in the Historia Musica of Bontempi is just sufficient to awaken that curiosity which it is the end of history to gratify.   In those who are ignorant of the subject it may excite approbation ; but that it falls short of affording satisfaction to a learned and curious enquirer, every one of that character must feel when he reads it.

LORENZO PENNA, of Bologna, a Carmelite monk, and a professor of music, was the author of a work entitled Albori Musicale, printed at Bologna in 1672, divided into three parts, the first treating of the elements or principles of the Canto Figurato ; the second on Counterpoint ; and in the third, of the precepts or rules, to use the author's own expression, ' per suonare l'Organo sopra la parte.'

In this book, which is one of the best of those many on the subject written by Italians, and published after the year 1600, the scale of Guido with the use of the syllables * and the cliffs, and the nature of the mutations are explained in a very concise and intelligible manner, as are also the characters used in the Cantus Mensurabilis.   Of the rules for counterpoint laid down by this author, little can be said other than that they are perfectly consistent with the laws of harmony.   In the course of his directions for the composition of counterpoint, examples in notes are contained, teaching the student the use and application of various passages, with cautions for avoiding such as the rules of harmony prohibit.

Under the head of Contrapunto Fugato his directions are very concise and perspicuous.   Of Canon he gives a variety of examples, both in Partito and in Corpo, with rules for the composition of canon in the unison, the second, the third major and minor, and so on to the diapason.

The third part is in effect a treatise on thoroughbass or the art of accompanyment, and is drawn from the works of Luzzasco Luzzaschi, Claudio Merula, Frescobaldi, and other celebrated organists of Italy.

The second part of the Albori Musicale was published at Venice in the year 1678, but whether by the author or some one else does not appear. The publication of one part only of the three which the Albori Musicale contains, is perhaps to be accounted for by the circumstance of its utility to students in the musical faculty, an intimation whereof is given by the words ' Per li Studiosi,' in the titlepage of the second impression.

FRANCESCO FOGGIA *(a Portrait)*, is celebrated as one of the most eminent of the Italian musicians of the last century.   He was born about the year 1604, and was a disciple, and also the son-in-law of Paolo Agostino, as having married his daughter.   Very early in his life, being distinguished for his skill in ecclesiastical harmony, he was appointed maestro di cappella of the church of San Giovanni Laterano in

Rome.   Kircher, in the Musurgia, lib. VII. cap. vi. page 614, has spoken of him in terms of high commendation.   He was living in the year 1684, the year in which Antimo Liberati published his letter in answer to one of Ovidio Persapegi, in which is the following character of him—' essendo il sostegno, ' e 'l padre della musica, e della vera harmonia ' ecclesiastica, come nelle stampe hà saputo far vedere, ' e sentire tanta varietà di stile, ed in tutti far cog-'noscere il grande, l' erudito, il nobile, il polito, il ' facile, ed il dilettevole, tanto al sapiente, quanto all' ' ignorante ; tutte cose, che difficilmente si trovano ' in un solo huomo, che dovrebbe esser' imitato da ' tutti i seguaci di buon gusto della musica, come io ' hò cercato di fare colla mio debolezza, essendo stato ' sempre invaghito, innamorato di quella nobilissima ' maniera di concertare.'

ANDREAS LORENTE, of Alcala, organist of the principal church there, published in the year 1673, a work in folio in the Spanish language, entitled El Porque de la Musica, in four books, the first containing the elements of plainsong ; the second treating of consonance and the Cantus Mensurabilis, the third of counterpoint, and the fourth of the composition of music.   This book, of which the late Mr. Geminiani was used to say it had not its fellow in any of the modern languages, is questionless a very learned work ; it is in truth a musical institute, and may be said to contain all that is necessary for a practical composer to know.   From the method of solmisation directed by this author, it is evident that the Spaniards, as well as the French and others, have for some time past solfaed by heptachords ; or in other words, they have added a syllable to the six of Guido.   It has been already said that the French use SI after LA ; Lorente directs to sing BI in the same place.   In the course of the work are interspersed a great number of compositions of his own and other authors, from three to five parts ; that is to say, hymns and offices for the church, and some motets, which shew great skill and invention.

GIO. PAOLO COLONNA, maestro di cappella nella Basilica di S. Petronio in Bologna, Accademico Filaschisi, e Filarmonico, flourished at this time. His compositions, which are very numerous, are altogether for the church, consisting of Motets, Litanies, Masses, Psalms, and Offices for the dead, many whereof he published at Bologna, between the years 1681 and 1694.   Like the motets of Carissimi, Bassani, and other of the church-musicians of the last century, his are usually with instrumental parts. His style is at once pathetic and sublime ; and in the composition of church-music he stands among the first of the Italians.

## CHAP. CXXXIX.

ANTIMO LIBERATI, *(a Portrait)*, when a youth, served in the Imperial chapel of Ferdinand III. and his brother Leopold.   Afterwards he became a singer in the pontifical chapel, and maestro di cappella, and organist of the church della Santissima Trinità de' Pellegrini ; and, lastly, maestro di cappella and

---

* This author makes use of the syllable DO instead of UT, and speaks of it as a modern practice in his time.

organist of the church di Santi Maria dell' Anima della Natione Teutonica at Rome. In this quality he wrote a letter dated the fifteenth of October, 1684, with the following title: ' Lettera scritta dal Sig. Antimo Liberati in risposta ad una del Sig. Ovidio Persapegi,' the occasion whereof was as follows: about the middle of the year 1684 the place of maestro di cappella of the metropolitical church of Milan being vacant, Persapegi, by the direction, as it is presumed, of those who had the appointment to that office, wrote to Liberati for his opinion touching the pretensions of five persons, who at that time were candidates for it. Who they were does not appear by the answer of Liberati; nor is it certain that Persapegi's letter is extant in print.*

After discussing the merits of the several compositions tendered by the candidates as evidence of their abilities, he proceeds to trace the rise and progress of music from the time of Pythagoras downwards, taking particular notice of Guido's invention, and the completion of it by Johannes de Muris. Among the less ancient practical musicians he celebrates Johannes Okenheim, the disciple of Iodocus Pratensis He mentions, from Glareanus, the circumstance of his having made a composition for thirty-six voices or nine choirs, to obviate an opinion of some professors of his time, that music for so many voices was a modern invention. Besides this he asserts that fugue, canon, and double counterpoint were invented by the same Okenheim.

He says that from these two great men, Iodocus Pratensis and Johannes Okenheim, sprang many excellent masters, who erected musical academies in different kingdoms and provinces; that many of them settled in Italy and in Rome; and that the first who gave public instructions for singing and harmonic modulation was Gaudio Mell, Flandro, a man of great talents, and of a sweet flowing style, who opened at Rome a noble and excellent school for music, where many pupils distinguished themselves in that science, but, above all, Gio. Pierluigi Palestrina,† who, as if marked by nature herself, he says surpassed all other rivals, and even his own master. With him he joins Gio. Maria Nanino, the intimate friend of Palestrina, and corrector with him in the musical school by them established at Rome. Among many eminent musicians educated in this seminary, he mentions Bernardino Nanino, the youngest brother of Gio. Maria Nanino, Antonio Cifra, Pier Francesco Valentini, Gregorio Allegri, and Paolo Agostino, of whom he gives a very high character. Of Allegri he says that he wrote for

* Walther speaks of the letter of Liberati as a great curiosity. It seems he was never able to get a sight of it, and therefore was content with an extract of it, with which he was furnished by a friend of his, Gottfried Heinrich Stoltzels, chapel-master to the duke of Saxe Gotha, and from it has inserted the character of Francesco Foggia in its place. Better success has attended the researches of the author of this work, who thinks himself warranted in saying that the letter, which is now lying before him, abounds with very many curious particulars of musical history, which it would have been scarcely possible to supply from any other materials; and of this opinion it seems was Andrea Adami, who, in his Osservazioni per ben regolare il Coro de i Cantori della Cappella Pontificia, has followed Liberati very closely, and even adopted some of his mistakes.

† See a detection of this error in the account of Palestrina, given in page 419, et seq.

the pontifical chapel, where he was a singer, and that from him he, Liberati, received his instructions in music. Of Agostino he says that in music he surpassed all of his time, and that he died in the flower of his youth; and that from him sprang Francesco Foggia, then living, and eighty years of age. He mentions also another disciple of Agostino, Vincenzo Ugolino, famous for his skill in teaching, and for having been the master of Lorenzo Ratti and Horatio Benevoli, who for many years was maestro di cappella nella Basilica di San Pietro.

Liberati says that at the time of writing his letter there were living three disciples of Horatio Benevoli, of whom the oldest was himself; the next in age Ercole Bernabei, who succeeded Benevoli at St. Peter's, and went afterwards to Bavaria, invited thither by the elector; the youngest he says was Giovanni Vincenti, for many years maestro di cappella della Santa Casa di Loretto, but who then lived in perfect ease, enjoying his patrimony, and the fruits of his studies.

ANGELO BERARDI, a canon of the collegiate church of St. Angelo di Viterbo, was the author of many musical tracts, and, amongst the rest, one entitled Documenti Armonici, in the composing whereof he was assisted, as himself confesses, by Marco Scacchi, chapel-master to the king of Poland. It was printed at Bologna in 1687, and is divided into three books, containing the precepts for the composition of counterpoint, fugue, and canon, illustrated by a great variety of examples, among which are sundry compositions of Adrian Willaert, Iodocus Pratensis, and others, well deserving the attention of the curious.

In the year 1689, Berardi published, at Bologna, Miscellanea Musicale, in three parts; the first is a collection from Boetius, Zarlino, Kircher, and other writers, containing, it must be confessed, few particulars relating to the state of music at different times, that are not to be found in every treatise on the subject that has been written within these last hundred years.

He takes occasion to enumerate many princes who have been distinguished, as well for their skill in music, as their affection for it; and, among the rest, James I. king of Scotland, concerning whom he cites verbatim from Alessandro Tassoni the passage inserted in the account herein before given of that prince, and his improvement of the Scots music.

In the second part he relates the invention of the syllables,‡ and the reformation of the scale by Guido, as also the institution of the Cantus Mensurabilis by John de Muris; but, as he professes to follow Vincentino, it is no wonder that his account is erroneous in many particulars.

The third part contains a variety of examples of

‡ Brossard relates that Berardi very ingeniously comprised the syllables of Guido in the following line:—

UT RElevet MIserum FAtum SOLitosque LAbores.

But it does not appear in this place, nor is it to be found in any of the tracts above spoken of; but it may be remarked that the sign of the printer at Bologna who published Corelli's Opera terza, is a violin with this verse round it.

counterpoint, and a series of exercises on the twelve tones.

In 1693, Berardi being then maestro di cappella of the church di Santa Maria in Trastevere, published at Bologna ' Il Perche Musicale overo Staffetta Armonica ;' and, in 1706, Arcani Musicali ; and these, according to Walther, are all his works.

The writings of this author abound with particulars worthy the attention of a student in music. He appears to have been an ingenious, and certainly was a modest man, for, although a canon, and maestro di cappella of a cathedral, he governed himself according to the directions of his friend Marco Scacchi, and submitted his works to his inspection ; and of his friendly disposition towards those of his own profession a judgement may be formed from the tract entitled Il Perche Musicale, which is divided into sections, many of which are dedicated to contemporary musicians in terms of great esteem and affection.

Isaac Vossius, a man of considerable parts and learning, was the son of Gerard John Vossius, already spoken of. He was born at Leyden in the year 1618, and, having his father for his instructor, soon became distinguished for his proficiency in academical learning, and was honoured with the favour of Christina, queen of Sweden, who corresponded with him by letters, and invited him to her court, and was taught by him the Greek language ; but, about the year 1652, having incautiously intended a design to write against Salmasius, who at that time stood very high in her favour, the queen withdrew her regard from Vossius, and dismissed him from any further attendance on her.

After the death of his father, Isaac Vossius was by the university of Leyden complimented with the offer of the history professor's chair, but thought proper to decline it. In the year 1670 he came into England, and was created doctor of laws in the university of Oxford. In 1673 king Charles II. appointed him a canon of Windsor, and assigned him lodgings in the castle, where he died in 1688, leaving behind him a library, which for a private one, was then supposed to be the best in the world.

Of his works, which are not near so numerous, nor indeed so valuable as those of his father, the most popular is his treatise ' De Poematum cantu et ' viribus Rythmi,' printed at Oxford in 1673, of which here follows an account :—

It begins with a remark that music is of two kinds, that is to say, it is either naked and simple, consisting of mere sounds, or of sounds joined to words ; and that although many think them to be poets who are able to sing verses, because anciently poets were also musicians, he held a different opinion, because poets were not the only singers of poems ; the distinction between the two being that those who made verses were called poets, and those that sung them singers, or, by a more honourable name, musicians. He says that the primitive verses wanted feet, and were therefore ungraceful, but that metre and rythmus were afterwards invented, which are as it were the very soul of poetry, and of these he

speaks to the following purpose. The beauty and elegance of verse consist in an apt disposition of different numbers and their symmetry. The Greeks first observed that it was not sufficient that the verses should run with an equal number of syllables, without a ratio of time, and therefore divided the syllables into long, short, and ambiguous : afterwards finding that those verses did not move concinnously which wanted members, they distributed the syllables into classes, and composed feet of two, three, or more, that the motion of the cantus and verses might be distinguished by measures and intervals. But as it was not sufficient for the members to be moved unless they had motions suited to the affections which they were designed to express, they invented feet of different times and modes, by which they represented in so lively a manner, not only the conspicuous motions of the body, but the dispositions of the mind, that there was scarce any thing existing that they could not express in their cantus and numbers.

After a brief enumeration of the various kinds of metrical feet, he proceeds in his observations on the force and efficacy of that particular arrangement and interchange of quantities, which he calls the Rythmus, ascribing to that only those wonderful effects which are said to have been wrought by the music of the ancients. He says that the ancient manner of reciting verses differed but little from the practice of scanning ; though he admits a difference between the cantus of singing, and recitation or common speech ; in the latter whereof he says it was ever esteemed a fault for the voice to ascend higher than the Diapente. He adds, that among the ancient musicians there was a threefold method of prolation, namely, continuous, diastemical or distinguished by intervals ; and another in a medium between both ; and that Aristides Quintilianus, Martianus Capella, and Boetius uniformly assigned the latter to the recitation of verses ; on the contrary, he says Dionysius Halicarnassæus and Nichomachus make no distinction between the voice of recitation and common speech.

To manifest his contempt of modern music and musicians, he cites, from Saxo Grammaticus, the relation of the effects of music on Ericus king of Denmark, already mentioned in the course of this history, but insists it is a fable borrowed from the story of Alexander and Timotheus. He says that the power of exciting the affections by music has ceased above these thousand years, that is to say, from the time that the knowledge and use of the rythmus was lost ; and that now, when music is much more flourishing than it was at the time when Ericus lived, no musician would dare attempt what his citharedist is said to have effected.

After observing that there is a rythmus in the arterial pulse, and bestowing a few commendations on Galen for his diligent enquiries on that subject in his book ' De Natura et Differentiis Pulsuum,' he asserts that the Chinese, as they excel the Europeans in many things, so do they in the medicinal art; for that without enquiring of their patients whether their head, their stomach, their shoulders, or any other part of their body gives them pain, they feel both pulses at the same instant, and, without ever failing, pronounce the nature of the disorder with which the patient is afflicted.

Upon that controverted question, namely, whether the ancients were acquainted with music in consonance or not, the author, with his usual temerity, delivers these as his sentiments :—

'Some have arrived to such a pitch of folly as to
'assert in their writings that the Concentus of several
'voices was utterly unknown to the ancients ; and
'that what they called Symphony, was nothing more
'than the Concentus sung alternately. Can any
'person be so ignorant of Greek and Latin, as not
'to see that even the terms Harmony, Symphony,
'and Concentus testify the contrary ? Who can
'there be so foolish as to think that the chorusses of
'singers and troops of symphonists under a Choro-
'didasculus, did not sing together but alternately ?
'Surely if this had been the case, Seneca must have
'lied when he spoke thus in Epistle 84. "Non
"vides, quam multorum vocibus chorus constet ?
"Unus tamen ex omnibus sonus redditur. Aliqua
"illic acuta est, aliqua gravis, aliqua media. Ac-
"cedunt veris feminæ, interponuntur tibiæ. Singu-
"lorum ibi latent voces, omnium apparent."* What
'need I bring down Plato, Aristotle, Cicero, and
'an infinite number of others, who all with one
'unanimous consent teach us, that harmony or con-
'centus was made when several voices, differing in
'the acumen and gravity of sound, were equally
'mingled together ? I make no mention of the
'manifold concentus of the tibiæ, or the harmonical
'fullness of the hydraulic organ, being ashamed to
'dwell any longer on a thing that is so manifest.'

He says that the patrons of this age infer the ignorance of the ancients with respect to music in consonance, from this circumstance, to wit, that they did not reckon the ditone, and trihemitone, or semi-ditone, nor either of the two sixths, namely, the greater and the less, among the consonants ; but that this argument is no better than that other adduced to prove that the modern music is more complete than the ancient, namely, that the system of the ancients contained only fifteen chords, which is less by a hexachord than that of Guido ; but he says that many of the improvements ascribed to Guido are erroneously attributed to him ; for that in the framing of the scale he did but follow the example of the organs and harps of his time, which consisted respectively of twenty pipes or strings, as a writer more ancient than Guido by some ages testifies.

The application of the syllables UT, RE, MI, &c. he makes to be an invention of no worth ; nevertheless he says that the Egyptians prolated their musical sounds by the vowels, which he conceives to be the more convenient practice ; and that the very Barbarians distinguished their sounds by such

like syllables or diminutive words, long before the time of Guido.†

The arguments of the imperfection of the ancient music, arising from the form of their instruments, he endeavours, but in vain, to refute ; and hastens to a description of the ancient hydraulic organ, the representation whereof, as given by him, seems to be but a creature of his own imagination. After describing this instrument, he censures Kepler for affirming that the ancient organists were no better than the modern Utricularii, or mendicant bag-pipers: an appellation which he says more properly belongs to the modern organists. As to the cantus of the tibia blown on by the mouth, he thinks it may be truly said that the modern performers know no more of it than the ancient shepherds ; and that, if we except the Chinese, who alone excel in this kind of music, we shall find none in this age that can please even a moderate ear.

Speaking of the ratios of chords, and of pipes, he refutes an error of the elder Galileo, in his dialogues De Motu, which it seems had been adopted by Mersennus and Des Cartes, namely, that, cæteris paribus, the thinner chords yield the acuter sounds ; the contrary whereof he affirms to be the fact.

After having treated very copiously on the Tibiæ of the ancients, and, without the least evidence from history, discriminated them into species, some as peculiar to the Phrygian, others to the Dorian, and others to the Ionian mood, he proceeds to consider the instruments of the moderns, as namely, the Harp, the Testudo or lute, the Barbiton or viol, and the Pandura or violin, the invention of all which he ascribes to Barbarians, for this notable reason, that the necks of these several instruments are divided by those transverse chords which we term frets ; whereas no such appear in the instruments of the ancients. He adds, that these Compendia are evidences of ignorance in the modern musicians ; and, lamenting the deplorable state of music in his time, professes to question whether since that of Charlemagne, the science has not sustained a loss more than equal to all the improvements of the moderns.

He censures very severely those Plasmata or divisions, which he says distinguish the modern music ; and adds, that both the Italian and French singers abound in flexions ; but that the Italians use the longer, and are therefore laughed at by the French, who, to do them justice, he says, observe the rythmus, which is the reason that in many of their songs we meet with concinnous and very elegant motions. He commends the Italians and Spaniards for their distinct articulation in singing.

After such a laboured encomium on the rythmus of the ancients as this of Vossius appears to be, it cannot be expected but that he should treat the invention of the Cantus Mensurabilis, its substitute, with the greatest contempt ; and accordingly he

---

* 'Do you not see how many voices the chorus consists of ? yet there
'is but one sound rendered by them all; some voices are acute, some
'grave, and some in the medium ; women are joined with the men, and
'the tibiæ are interposed. In this case the voice of either person is not
'to be distinguished, but those of all may be heard.'

† It is evident from this passage that Vossius was ignorant of the use of the syllables. All men are sensible that musical sounds are most easily prolated by vowels associated with consonants, but none but a person skilled to some degree in music knows that it was for the purpose of ascertaining the stations of the two semitones in the diapason that the syllables of Guido were taken.

has delivered his sentiments of it in the following terms : 'To comprehend many things in a few 'words, all the notes of which modern music con-'sists are, the Maxima, Longa, Breve, Semibreve, 'Minim, Semiminim, Fusa, and Semifusa, which 'as they are barbarous names, so are they also 'barbarous and foolish inventions. If we have 'a mind that the cantus should be elegant and con-'cinnous, it should be ordered so that every syllable 'should answer to a correspondent syllable. But 'as there are no syllables which are not either long 'or short, and of these, as I have often said before, 'the short consists only of one time, and the long 'of two; so also should there be no more nor no 'fewer notes introduced than two sorts, to agree 'with the minim and semiminim, as they are com-'monly called; for who is there that ever dreamt 'of syllables of eight, or sixteen, or thirty-two 'tones, or of others so short, that no speech can 'possibly express them; who does not laugh at the 'sound of one syllable prolated so slowly, that two 'or three heroic verses may be most commodiously 'uttered in the same time? Away therefore with 'these elgancies; and, if we have any love for 'music, let us follow the example of the ancients 'in this as in other things; for if we restore the 'Rythmus, joined to a distinct pronunciation of the 'words, so that the ancient form and beauty of 'music may return, all these common ornaments of 'the modern cantus, I mean the small flexions, 'teretismata or iterations, fugues, syncopes, and 'other such foolish artifices, will vanish as shades 'and clouds on the appearance of the sun.'*

In the course of this work, which is nothing better than an unintelligible rhapsody, the author is very lavish in his censures of the ignorance and folly of other writers on the subject of music; and there are many who think that his enthusiasm and extreme bigotry have justly rendered him liable to the imputation of the latter; for the proof whereof the following most curious passage is selected from page 62 of his work, and submitted to the reflection of the impartial reader. 'Many people take delight 'in the rubbing of their limbs, and combing of their 'hair; but these exercises would delight much 'more, if the servants at the baths and of the 'barbers were so skilful in this art, that they could 'express any measures with their fingers. I re-'member that more than once I have fallen into the 'hands of men of this sort, who could imitate any 'measure of songs in combing the hair, so as some-'times to express very intelligibly Iambics, Trochees, 'Dactyls, &c. from whence there arose to me no 'small delight.'†

In a word, the above-mentioned treatise abounds with evidence of that gross credulity for which the

author was remarkable ;‡ nor is this the only weak-ness with which he is justly charged; his partiality for the ancients, his bold and hasty conclusions, his affected contempt of all modern improvements in science, his insolent treatment of such as differed from him in opinion, and, above all, his vanity, have placed him in the foremost rank of literary coxcombs. As to his work, it may upon the whole be said to be a very futile and unsatisfactory disquisition.

GIOVANNI MARIA BONONCINI, a disciple of Gio. Paolo Colonna, maestro di cappella in the church of San Petronio in Bologna, was a celebrated composer, and the author of a treatise printed at the same place in the year 1673, entitled 'Musico prattico, 'che brevemente dimostra il modo di giungere alla 'perfetta cognizione di tutte quelle cose, che con-'corrono alla composizione de i Canti, e di ciò ch' 'all' Arte del Contrapunto si ricerca.'

In the compilation of this treatise the author appears to have availed himself of the writings and compositions of the most celebrated Italian musicians, as well theorists as practical composers, of whom he gives a numerous list at the beginning of his book. About the year 1695 he published a second part, which was translated into the German language, and printed at Stutgard in the year 1701. The subject matter of these two books is, first, an intro-duction to the science of music, and next the pre-cepts of musical composition; the author appears to be eminently skilled in the science, but his work contains scarce any thing but may be found in the writings of others who had treated the subject before him : and indeed his censure is so justly applicable to the Italian writers from the time of Franchinus downward, that the bare mention of their works of this kind must suffice in our future memoirs of them.

Of his musical compositions there are extant 'Cantate per Camera à voce sola,' dedicated to Francesco II. d'Este, reigning duke of Modena, printed at Bologna in 1677. In the dedication to this work he promises in a short time to publish Madrigals for five voices, on the twelve modes, with the title of Composizione da Tavolino,§ but whether

---

* Page 128.

† 'Gaudent complures membrorum frictione et pectinatione capillorum, 'verum hæc ipsa multò magis juvant si balnearii et tonsores adeo in 'arte sua fuerint periti, ut quosvis etiam numeros suis possint explicare 'digitis. Non semel recordor me in ejusmodi incidisse manus, qui 'quorumvis etiam canticorum motus suis imitarentur pectinibus, ita ut 'nonnunquam iambos vel trochæos, alias dactylos vel anapæstos, non-'nunquam amphibraches aut pæonas quam scitissime experimerent, 'unde haud modica oriebatur delectatio.'

‡ His credulity, and also the singularity of his character, will appear from the following particulars, which Mons. des Maizeaux has recorded of him in his Life of St. Evremont. He says that Vossius understood most of the languages in Europe, without being able to speak one of them well; that he was intimately acquainted with the genius and customs of antiquity, but an utter stranger to the manners of his own times. That he published books to prove that the Septuagint version was divinely inspired, yet discovered in conversation, and by his behaviour in his last moments, that he believed no revelation at all: that in other respects he was the weakest and most credulous man alive, being ever ready to credit any extraordinary and wonderful re-lation, though ever so fabulous or ill-grounded. St. Evremont was used to spend the summers with the court at Windsor; he knew, and fre-quently conversed with Vossius ; the above is his character of him, and Des Maizeaux has added to it many more particulars respecting Vossius to the same purpose.

Mons. Renaudot in his Dissertations added to the Anciennes Relations des Indes et de la Chine, relates that Vossius, having had frequent con-ferences with Father Martini, while he was in Holland, superintending the printing of his Atlas Chinois, made no scruple of believing all which that father told him concerning the wonderful things in China; and that he did not stop where Martini stopped, but proceeded farther, even to infer as a certain fact the antiquity of the Chinese accounts above that of the books of Moses. King Charles II. who knew his nature and character well, used to call him the strangest man in the world, for 'there is nothing,' the king would say, 'which he refuses to believe, 'except the Bible.' It is said that Lord Shaftesbury alludes to this in-consistent character of Vossius in his advice to an Author. Vide Characteristics, vol. I. page 345.

§ By this term we are to understand such vocal compositions as are usually sung by divers persons in a chamber, or sitting at a table : in the

he ever published them or not we are unable to say. 'Sinfonie a 5, 6, 7, a 8 Instromenti, con alcune à 'una e due Trombe, servendo ancora per Violini,' dedicated to his master Gio. Paolo Colonna, Bologna 1685. 'Sinfonie à tre Instromenti, col Basso per l' 'Organo.' Bologna 1686. Both these collections are in fact Sonate da Chiesa, and, like the first and third operas of Corelli, consist of slow movements, with fugues of various measures intermixed. Masses for eight voices, dedicated to Orazio Maria Bonfioli, abbat of the church di S. Giovanni in Monte, of which the author was maestro di cappella.

There were three other eminent musicians of the name of Bononcini, the sons of the above person; the one named Antonio resided at Modena; his name is to be found subscribed to a recommendatory epistle prefixed to Marcello's Psalms, printed at Venice in 1723. Gio. Battista, another of them, settled at Vienna, was composer to the emperor in 1703. Giovanni Bononcini is supposed to have been the younger of the three brothers; he also is one of those many eminent musicians who joined in the recommendation of Marcello's Psalms. He spent some years of his life in England; and, having been for a time composer to the opera at London, and the rival of Mr. Handel, a farther account of him will be given hereafter.

CLAUDE FRANCOIS MENESTRIER, a French Jesuit, wrote and published at Paris, in the year 1681, a treatise entitled 'Des Representations en Musique anciennes et modernes.' In this book, among a great variety of curious particulars, is contained a brief enquiry into the music of the Hebrews, in which the author cites the testimony of Origen to prove that the Song of Solomon is a poem of the dramatic kind, viz., an epithalamium on occasion of the nuptials of that prince, and was a representation in music, and enforces the argument with his own observations on the poem itself. He asserts that dramatic music was introduced into France in the time of the crusades, by the pilgrims, who returning from the Holy Land, formed themselves as it were into choirs, and exhibited spectacles of devotion, accompanied with music and songs, in which were declared the achievements and sufferings of saints and martyrs, with suitable elogies. Menestrier is very circumstantial in this relation; and, notwithstanding what is said in page 529 of this work, there seems, upon a review of the passage, no reason to doubt the truth of it; and his information is the more worthy of note, for that it leads us to a practice, which it is highly probable suggested to St. Philip Neri the introduction into Italy of the oratorio or sacred drama, of which it is generally said he was the inventor.

He relates that in the year 1647, Cardinal Mazarine being desirous of introducing into France the divertisements of Italy, procured a company of comedians to represent at the Palais Royal the drama of Orpheus and Eurydice, in Italian verse, with the music. And that in 1669 Lewis XIV.

Miscellanea Musicale of Angelo Berardi, parte prima, page 41, is the following passage: 'Lo stile da camera si divide, e si considera sotto tre 'stili. I. Madrigali da tavolino. II. Madrigali concertati con il basso 'continuo. III. Cantilene concertate con varie sorti di strumenti.'

having concluded the treaty of the Pyrennées, and thereby given peace to Europe, and being at leisure to cultivate the arts, he, by the advice of the Cardinal, established academies of painting, sculpture, architecture, philosophy, and mathematics; and by his letters patent of the twenty-eighth of June, 1669, granted liberty to the Sieur Perrin to establish at Paris, and in other cities, academies of music for the public performance of musical dramas agreeable to the practice in Italy, Germany, and England. He says that under this patent Perrin continued for a few years to exhibit entertainments of this kind, but that afterwards the same was revoked, and another granted to Lully in the following terms :—

'Louis par la grace de Dieu, Roi de France et de 'Navarre, à tous presens et à venir, salut. Les 'Sciences et les Arts étant les ornemens les plus 'considèrables des Etats, nous n'avons point eu de 'plus agreables divertissemens depuis que nous avons 'donné la paix à nos peuples, que de les faire revivre, 'en appellant prés de nous tous ceux qui se sont 'acquis la reputation d'y exceller, non seulement 'dans l'étenduë de nôtre Royaume; mais aussi dans 'les Pays étrangers : et pour les obliger d'avantage 'de s'y perfectionner, nous les avons honorés des 'marques de nôtre estime, et de nôtre bienveillance : 'et comme entre les Arts Liberaux, la Musique y 'tient un des premiers rangs, nous aurions dans le 'dessein de la faire reussir avec tous ces avantages, 'par nos Lettres patentes du 28 Juin, 1669, accordé 'au Sieur Perrin une permission d'établir en nôtre 'bonne Ville de Paris, et autres de nôtre Royaume, 'des Academies de Musique pour chanter en public 'de pieces de Theatre, comme il se pratique en 'Italie, en Allemagne, et en Angleterre. Mais ayant 'été depuis informé que les peines et les soins que 'ledit Perrin a pris pour cét établissement, n'ont pû 'seconder pleinement nôtre intention et élever la 'Musique au point que nous nous l'étions promis ; 'nous avons crû pour mieux réüssir qu'il étoit à 'propos d'en donner la conduite à une personne, 'dont l'experience, et la capacité nous fussent connuës, 'et qui eût assez de suffisance pour fournir des éleves 'tant pour bien chanter, et actionner sur le Theatre, 'qu'à dresser des bandes de Violons, Flûtes, et 'autres instrumens. A ces Causes bien informez de 'l'intelligence, et grande connoissance que s'est acquis 'nôtre cher et bien-amé Jean Baptiste Lully, au fait 'de la Musique, dont il nous a donné, et donne 'journellement de tres-agreables preuves depuis 'plusieurs années, qu'il s'est attaché à nôtre service, 'qui nous ont convié de l'honorer de la charge de 'Surintendant, et Compositeur de la Musique de 'nôtre chambre ; Nous avons au dit Sieur Lully, 'permis et accordé, permettons et accordons par ces 'presentes, signées de nôtre main d'établir une 'Academie Royale de Musique dans nôtre bonne 'Ville de Paris, qui sera composée de tel nombre, 'et qualité de personnes qu'il avisera bon être, que 'nous choisirons et arréterons, sur le rapport qu'il 'nous en fera pour faire des representations devant 'nous, quand il nous plaira, des pieces de Musique 'que seront composées, tant en vers François qu'au-

'tre langues ètrangeres, pareilles, aux Academies
'd'Italie, &c.'

This book farther contains many curious accounts of public spectacles, dramatic and musical representations in sundry courts of Europe, upon occasion of the marriages and births of princes, and other solemnities.

Menestrier also published, in 1682, a tract entitled 'Des Ballets anciens et modernes selon les Regles du Theatre.' The general contents whereof are inserted in the Act. Erudit. Lipsiæ. The author died on the twenty-first day of January, 1705.

JOHANN PACHELBEL, a celebrated organist and composer of music, was born at Nuremburg on the first day of September, 1653. Discovering in his early youth a strong inclination to liberal studies, particularly music, he was provided by his parents with the ablest instructors that could be procured. His master for the harpsichord was Heinrich Schemmern, of Nuremberg, under whose tuition he remained for a few years; after which he went to Altdorff, meaning there to have finished his studies, but, finding himself straitened in his circumstances, having obtained permission of absence for one year, he, for the sake of a better subsistence, and greater improvement, removed to the Gymnasium Poeticum in Regensburg, where he remained three years, prosecuting his studies particularly in music, with so much diligence, that the fame of his proficiency spread throughout Germany. Upon his quitting Regensburg he went to Vienna, and became vicar to the organist of the church of St. Stephen in that city. This situation, though attended with but little profit, was very agreeable to him, as it procured him the acquaintance and friendship of the famous Johann Caspar Kerl then chapel-master at Vienna. In 1675, Pachelbel had a call to Eisenach, which he readily accepted, and upon his arrival was preferred to the dignity of court organist. In 1678 he removed to Erfurth, and for twelve years was eminently distinguished in that city. In 1690 he was invited to Stutgard, but that city being threatened with an invasion of the French, he quitted it soon after his arrival, and settled at Gotha. In 1695, George Caspar Wecker, who had been for many years organist of Nuremburg, died, and Pachelbel received an invitation to succeed him, which he readily embraced, being desirous of a settlement in his native country; and in that station he continued till the day of his death, which was the third of March, 1706, or, as Walther rather thinks, about Candlemas, 1705. Pachelbel is celebrated as one of the most excellent of those German Organists, of whom Kerl is accounted the father. He laboured in the improvement of the grand and full style on the organ, and was no less solicitous to perfect the vocal music of the church. The works published by him are but few, being only four Funeral Hymns, composed at Erfurth in the time of the pestilence that then raged there, and published at the same place; and seven Sonatas for two violins and a bass, and Airs with variations, both printed at Nuremberg.

JOACHIM MEYER was a doctor of laws, and professor in the university of Gottingen, where, in the year 1686, he was also appointed professor of music, and Cantor Figuralis. These employments he held for the space of about ten years, when retaining to himself the bare title of professor of music, he relinquished the practice of it, and gave lectures on history and public law. Upon the death of Justus Dranszfeld he became rector of the college, but at the end of three years quitted that honorable station on account of his age and infirmities, when, as the reward of his great merit, he was permitted to receive and enjoy all his salaries and emoluments, with the addition of a pension. He nevertheless continued to reside in his college, and, being esteemed one of the ablest lawyers of his time, was frequently called on to assist at consultations with the members of the state, and those of that profession, till the year 1732, in which he died. In the year 1726 he published a tract entitled 'Unvorgreiffſiche Gedancken uber die Neuliche ingeriſſene Theatriliſche-kirchen-MUSIC,' in which he very severely censures sundry of his contemporaries, who, by the levity of their compositions, had confounded the ecclesiastic with the theatric style.

JOHANN KUHNAU, the son of a fisherman of Geysingen, a town near Altenberg, on the borders of Bohemia, four miles distant from Dresden, was an eminently learned and skilful musician. In the year 1684 he was organist of the church of St. Thomas at Leipsic; and, while he was in that station wrote a dissertation De Juribus circa Musicos Ecclesiasticos, and afterwards defended it against the censures of his adversaries. In 1689 he published lessons for the harpsichord in two volumes, and, in 1696, seven Sonatas, entitled Clavier-Fruchte, that is to say, fruits of the Clavier; and, in 1700, six sonatas entitled Bibliſche Hiſtorien;* and, in the same year, to silence the clamours of some ignorant men of his profession, who envying his merit and reputation, had libelled him, he wrote a small tract, which he entitled the Musical Quacksalver. In the same year, 1700, Kuhnau was appointed Director Musices of the university of Leipsic, in which station he died on the fifth day of June, 1722, in the sixty-third year of his age, and was succeeded in that honourable post by John Sebastian Bach. Ernest Wilhelm Hertzog, a German count palatine, and a magistrate of Merseburg, has celebrated the memory of Kuhnau in a discourse entitled 'Memoria 'beate defuncti directoris chori musices Lipsiensis, 'Dn. Johannis Kuhnau, polyhistoris musici, et 'reliqua, summopere incluti, &c.' printed at Leipsic in 1722, and therein extols him for his skill 'in 'Theologiâ, in Jure, in Oratoriâ, in Poësi, in 'Algebrâ et Mathesi, in Linguis exoticis, et in Re 'Musicâ.' He left behind him two manuscripts in Latin, which have never yet been published, the one entitled 'Tractatus de Monochordo, seu Musica 'antiqua ac hodierna, occasione Tetrachordi, non ad

* A modern author, Francis Lustig, of Groningen, in a treatise entitled 'Inleiding tot de Musykkunde,' takes notice of this work, and says that in it is a lively representation, in musical notes, of David manfully combating Goliah.

' Systema tantum, sed et Melopœiam accommodati,
' cum prævio Præludio e penu Matheseos puræ
' depromto, ac lectorem ad intelligenda, quæ in hoc
' opere tractantur, præparante.' The other manuscript abovementioned is entitled 'Disputatio de
Triade Harmonicâ.'

JOHANN KROPFFGANTZ was the son of a burgomaster of a small town in Germany named Arnshaug,
who was himself a good musician and lutenist.
He was born in the year 1668, at Neustadt on the
Orla in Osterland. At nine years of age he began
to play on the lute; and, having been removed to
Leipsic for farther instruction, he, at the age of
twelve, became a great proficient on that instrument. Being intended by his father for the profession of a merchant, and not a musician, Kropffgantz laid aside his instrument, and applied himself
to business, and, in a course of years, became
a merchant at Breslau. After some years continuance in trade, he was moved by an irresistible
desire to betake himself again to music; and took
lessons in the theory, and also in the practice, on
his favourite instrument, from the ablest masters,
namely, Schuchart and Meley, who was then lately
returned from Paris, and others no less eminent.
He continued in this course for twenty-five years,
till, having the misfortune to dislocate his right
hand, he had nothing left to employ him but the
study of the theory of music, which he pursued
with great ardour. The time of his death is uncertain; he left three children, viz., two sons and
a daughter, who were all excellent performers on
the lute; the latter, named Johanna Eleonora, was
born on the fifth of November, 1710; and it was
for many years a kind of fashion for the nobility
and strangers, whose occasions drew them to Breslau,
to visit her, and be entertained with her fine
performance.

GABRIEL NIVERS was one of the four organists of
the chapel of Lewis XIV. and also organist of the
church of St. Sulpice, at Paris; he was the author
of a very learned and curious tract, entitled Dissertation sur le Chant Gregorien, published at Paris
in 1683.* The occasion of writing this book was,
that the Cantus Gregorianus, in the course of so
many years as had elapsed since its original institution, had been greatly corrupted. Nivers
undertook to restore it to its original purity, in
order to which he had recourse to anicent manuscripts, and particularly those numerous tracts on
the modes or tones from the time of Guido and
Berno the abbot, down to the end of the fifteenth

century, of which mention has been made in the
course of this history; and in this laborious task
Nivers succeeded so well, that he restored the
church-music of France to its original purity and
simplicity; and, agreeably to his corrections, the
antiphonary of the Gallican church was republished
by the express command of the king himself.

The Dissertation sur le Chant Gregorien is a
small octavo volume, divided into eighteen chapters,
entitled as follows :—

Chapitre I. De l'origine, et de l'excellence du
Chant Gregorien. Chap. II. Du l'utilité du Chant
de l'Eglise, et de ses effets. Chap. III. Contre les
Heretiques et tous ceux qui blasment le Chant de
l'Eglise. Chap. IV. Que le Chant Gregorien ou
Romain, ayant esté communiqué, et s'estant répandu
dans toutes les Eglises des Diocèses et des Ordres
Religieux, a esté changé et corrompu en plusieurs
parties. Chap. V. Que le Chant Romain, ou le
Chant Gregorien mesme à Rome, a esté corrompu
en quelques parties, quoy que neantmoins il y soit
resté le plus pur et le plus correct de tous. Chap.
VI. De la facilité qu'il y avoit de corrompre le
Chant Gregorien, et de la necessité qu'il y a de le
corriger. Chap. VII. Des abus qui se sont glissez
dans la maniere de chanter le Pleinchant. Chap.
VIII. Des abus commis au Chant Gregorien dans
plusieurs parties de l'Office divin, contre les Regles
de la science, prouvez par les termes de l'Epistre
de saint Bernard, conformémert aux mesmes Regles.
Chap. IX. Du nombre, des figures, et de l'usage des
Caracteres du Pleinchant. Chap. X. De la quantité
des Notes. Chap. XI. Du commencement de l'Office
divin. Chap. XII. Des Antiennes. Où il est traité
a fond des huit Tons de l'Eglise. Chap. XIII. Des
Pseaumes. Où il est traité a fond de leurs Ter-
minaisons differentes et specifiques selon les huit
Tons du Chant Gregorien. Chap. XIV. Des Capi-
tules et des Respons. Chap. XV. Des Hymnes.
Chap. XVI. Des Cantiques. Chap. XVII. Des
autres Parties de l'Office divin. Chap. dernier.
Que le Chant Gregorien est le plus authentique, et
le plus considerable de tous les Chants Eccle-
siastiques.

At the end of the Dissertation are the forms of
the offices, with the musical notes adjusted according
to the rules laid down by the authors. These are
entitled ' Formulæ Cantus ordinarii Officii divini,'
they direct the intonation of the prayers, the books
of the prophets, the epistles, the gospels, the
versicles, the office for the dead, and other parts
of divine service; and are followed by a short
discourse, entitled 'Tractatus de modis canendi
Psalmos et Cantica, secundum octo Cantûs Gre-
goriani tonos,' including a formula of the eight
tones, entitled Tabula Tonorum. After these follow
six litanies, the Stabat Mater, sundry anthems to
the Virgin Mary, and a prayer for the king, all
with musical notes.

The author of this book appears to have been
well skilled in ecclesiastical history, and to have
read to good purpose the writings of Amalarius
Fortunatus, St. Bernard, Durandus, Cardinal Bona,

---

* Before this time, but at what particular period is not ascertained,
a French ecclesiastic, named Jumillac, published a tract entitled 'La
Science et Pratique du Pleinchant,' esteemed the best of its kind. Hist.
Mus. tom. IV. page 80. In 1678 an author named Gerolamo Cantone,
Maestro de' Novizi, e Vicario nel Convento di Francesco di Torino,
published a tract entitled 'Armonia Gregoriana,' containing the rudiments
of the Cantus Ecclesiasticus. In 1682 was published a work entitled
'Cantore addotrinato,' by Matteo Coferati, the preface to which is a
discourse 'dell' origine e progressi del Canto Ecclesiastico,' written by
Francesco Cionacci, a priest of Florence. In 1686 was published at
Milan, 'Il Canto Ecclesiastico,' by Marzio Erculeo, in which, besides the
necessary instructions for the Cantus Ecclesiasticus, are contained the
forms of the most solemn functions in the Romish service. But the
most copious treatise on the subject is one with the title of 'Istruzioni
Corali, by Domenico Scorpione, maestro di cappella, e del Canto nel
Sagro Seminario di Benevento,' printed at Benevento in 1702.

MATTEO SIMONELLI ROMANO,

CANT. DELLA CAPP. PONT.

MDCLXII.

and other of the Roman ritualists. In short, the Dissertation sur le Chant Gregorien is a most entertaining and valuable work, and is the best history of church-music any where extant.

In the year 1697 Nivers published at Amsterdam, Traité de la Composition de Musique. This work was printed with a Dutch translation by Estienne Roger, and is dedicated to a merchant at Amsterdam, named Abraham Maubach. In the general catalogue of books printed at Paris, published in the year 1729, quarto, the two following articles are ascribed to Nivers, Le premier Livre des Motets, and Le premier Livre des Pieces d'Orgue.

## CHAP. CXL.

MATTEO SIMONELLI, *(a Portrait)*, was a singer in the pontifical chapel in the year 1662, and was, in the language of the Italian writers, a grand contrapuntist; for which reason, as also for his excellency in the church style, of which he gave proofs in a variety of compositions for the most solemn of the pontifical functions, he was styled the Palestrina of his time. Nor was he more celebrated for learning and skill in his profession, than for his assiduity and success in teaching the science and practice of music to others. He was the instructor of a great number of pupils, and had the honour to be the first master to Corelli. It does not appear that any compositions of his were ever pubished, but his works are preserved with great care in the college of the pontifical singers at Rome.

GIOVANNI LEGRENZI was organist of the church of Santa Maria Maggiore in Bergamo, afterwards maestro di cappella in the church della Spirito Santo in Ferrara: and in his latter years maestro di cappella of the church of St. Mark at Venice. The works of this author consist of Masses, Motets, Sonate per Chiesa and da Camera, Psalms, Litanies, and Cantatas. His opera XIV. is entitled ' Echi ' di Riverenza di Cantate, e Canzoni a gli Applausi ' festeggianti ne gli Himenei delle Altezze Sereniss. ' di Maria Anna Arciduchessa d' Austria, e Gio. ' Guglielmo Prencipe Co. Palatino del Reno, &c.' ' being twenty-four Cantatas, à voce sola, published at Bologna in 1678. The last of his publications is his Opera XVII. entitled ' Motetti Sacri à Voce sola con tre Stromenti,' published in 1692. Legrenzi was the master of Antonio Lotti, of Venice, his successor in the chapel of St. Mark; and also of Michael Angelo Gasparini, a brother, as it is supposed, of Francesco Gasparini, both of whom resided in the house of Legrenzi in the year 1686, for the purpose of receiving his instructions.

GIOVANNI BATTISTA BASSANI, maestro di cappella of the cathedral church of Bologna, was a very voluminous composer of music, having given to the world no fewer than thirty-one different works. He is equally celebrated both as a composer for the church and for concerts, and was besides a celebrated performer on the violin, and, as it is said, taught Corelli on that instrument. His compositions consist of Masses, Psalms, Motets with instrumental parts, and Sonatas for violins; his fifth opera in part cular, containing twelve Sonatas for two violins and a bass, is much esteemed; it is written in a style wonderfully grave and pathetic, and abounds with evidences of great learning and fine invention. The first and third operas of Corelli are apparently formed after the model of this work.

Bassani was one of the first who composed motets for a single voice, with accompaniments of violins; a practice which is liable to objection, as it assimilates church-music too nearly to that of the chamber: and of his solo-motets it must be confessed that they differ in style but little from opera airs and cantatas; two operas of them, viz., the eighth and the thirteenth, were printed in London, by Pearson, above fifty years ago, with the title of Harmonia Festiva: many of the masters here gave them to their scholars as lessons; and there are ladies now living, who had Mr. Robinson, the late organist of Westminster abbey, for their master, who yet sing to the harpsichord those two favourite airs of Bassani, Quid Arma, quid Bella, and ' Alligeri Amores.'

ERCOLE BERNABEI, a Roman by birth, and a disciple of Horatio Benevoli, succeeded Kerl as chapelmaster to the elector of Bavaria, Ferdinando Maria. After that he was called to the same office in the church of San Luigi de' Francesi in Rome; and at length, upon the decease of Benevoli, maestro di cappella of the pontifical chapel. He was the master of Steffani, and died about the year 1690. In the year 1669 he published at Rome a fine collection of Madrigals for three and four voices. At his decease, viz., in 1691, a collection of Motets, composed by Bernabei, was published at Munich, and, some years after, another at Amsterdam.

AGOSTINO STEFFANI was born about the year 1650, at Castello Franco, a small frontier town in the territory of Venice.* Of his family or descent nothing certain is known; nor is there any further ground for conjecture, than his having in his infancy been a singer in some neighbouring cathedral church or chapel; a circumstance, from which we may at least conclude that his parents were not distinguished for their rank in life.

His want of the advantages of birth and fortune was however amply recompensed by those extraordinary talents that nature had endowed him with, among which an excellent voice was perhaps not the least. He had not served above two years in the choir, when a nobleman of Germany, who had been at Venice to be present at the diversions of the carnival, happened upon some public occasion to hear him sing, and was so pleased with his voice and appearance, that, upon application to the chapelmaster, he procured his discharge from the choir, and took him to Bavaria, the place of his residence. At the expence of this beneficent person was Steffani maintained, and instructed in all the branches of useful and ornamental learning: the direction of his

* Walther says he was born at Leipsic, though his name seems to indicate that he was an Italian; but Mr. Handel, who knew him intimately, and furnished most of the particulars contained in his memoir, gave the author the above account of the place of his nativity.

musical studies in particular was committed to Signor Ercole Bernabei, then chapel-master to the elector of Bavaria, and one of the most considerable masters of his time. What proficiency he made under him will best appear from his works; and what opinion of his merit his tutor entertained, may be inferred from that strict friendship, which for many years subsisted between them. It is needless, as Steffani was a native of Italy, to say that he was of the Romish persuasion; however it must not be omitted, that, in compliance with the request of his munificent patron, who was desirous of making the learned education he had bestowed on him the means of some further advantage, our author at the proper age received ordination, and soon afterwards became entitled to an appellation, by which indeed he is now most commonly distinguished, viz. that of Abbate or Abbot.

In the course of his studies he had composed several Masses, Motets, Hymns, Kyries, Magnificats, and other essays in the church-style, which he thought proper now to exhibit, and they were occasionally performed in the chapel at Munich, so greatly to his reputation, that Ernestus Augustus, duke of Brunswic, the father of king George I. though a protestant prince, being a passionate lover of music, invited him to the court of Hanover, and, it is said, conferred on him the employment of master of his chapel,* and committed to his care the management of the opera, an entertainment which had then but lately found its way into Germany. The latter trust, however agreeable it might be to his inclination, was the occasion of great uneasiness to him; for, whether it was owing to the ignorance or petulance of the persons employed to sing, it was sometimes with great difficulty that they could be prevailed on to study their parts, so as to do justice to the composer; and even when their condescension was greatest in this respect, so many feuds and jealousies were continually arising among them, as frequently disappointed an illustrious audience of their entertainment. This particular is in some degree verified by what is related of the elector's son, the late king Geo. I. who, upon some such occasion as this, prevailed on our author to resign his charge for a short time to him, imagining perhaps that his rank and quality might give him a better title to command this set of people, than even the great merit of their manager; but he was soon convinced of the difficulty of the undertaking, for in a few days he quitted it, and left them to themselves, declaring that he could with much more ease command an army of fifty thousand men, than manage a company of opera singers.

The earlier compositions of Steffani were for the church, and consisted of Masses and Motets; but, being settled in Germany, he applied himself wholly to the study of secular music, and composed sundry operas, as namely, Alexander the Great, Orlando, Enrico, Alcides, Alcibiades, Atalanta, Il Trionfo

del Fato, and Le Rivali Concordi, which being translated from the Italian into the German language, were performed at Hamburg between the years 1694 and 1700. He also composed a few madrigals in five parts; a very fine one of his, 'Gettano il 'Re,' is frequently performed in the Academy of ancient Music, as is also one of his motets, 'Qui 'diligit Mariam,' the scores whereof were presents from himself to the society. A short duet, and an air from some of his operas were introduced into the English opera of Thomyris Queen of Scythia, performed at Drury-lane theatre in 1708, and adapted severally to the words, 'Prithee leave me,' and 'Farewell love.'

But the most celebrated of all his works are his duets, composed for two voices, with no other accompaniment than a bass calculated simply to sustain the harmony without increasing in effect the number of parts. It is probable that he might apply his studies so much to this species of composition, in compliance with the taste of the ladies about the court; for it is observable that the poetry of them is altogether of the amatory kind;† and it appears by little memorandums in several copies, that many of his duets were composed at the request of divers ladies of distinction; and that some of them were made for their own private practice and amusement. Who the particular persons were we are at a loss to discover, as they are distinguished only by initial letters, denoting their quality, except in the instance of the two duets beginning 'Inquieto mio cor,' and 'Che volete,' these appearing to have been made for and sung by her highness the electress of Brandenburg.‡

Of these compositions it is their least praise that Mr. Handel professed but to imitate them, in twelve duets which he composed for the practice of the late queen Caroline. Mattheson remarks of Steffani's duets, that they are imitations in the unison and octave, and for the most part they are so. By this circumstance they stand eminently distinguished from those desultory compositions that bear the name of duets, in which the air, whatever it be, is deserted before it has well reached the ear; as also from those other, in which the accompaniment is no better than the insipid harmony of thirds and sixths.§

The characteristic of these compositions is fine and elegant melody, original and varied modulation,

---

* It is rather to be supposed that Steffani's employment was director of the elector's chamber music; for he was of the Romish communion, and it is well known that the service in the electoral chapel is according to the Lutheran ritual.

† The words of these poems were composed by the Marquis de Ariberti, Sig. Conte Palmieri, Abbate Guidi, hereafter mentioned in the life of Corelli, Sig. Averara, and Abbate Hortensio Mauro: this last named person wrote also the words for twelve duets, which Mr. Handel composed for the practice of the late queen Caroline when she was princess of Wales, who greatly admired this kind of composition.

‡ This must have been the admired lady Sophia Charlotta, only daughter of the aforesaid duke of Brunswic, and sister to the late king, and the person whom Corelli has honoured with the patronage of his Opera quinta. In the year 1684 she was married to Frederic III. marquis of Brandenburg, by whom she had issue the father of the present king of Prussia.

§ *Frederick prince of Wales had a collection of Steffani's duets in ten or twelve volumes in small oblong quarto, finely written, and the initial letters ornamented. It was probably made for the princess Sophia or the elector her son (George I.) and contained about one hundred duets. This collection, excepting two volumes that were left behind by accident, the prince gave to the lady of Signor Capello, ambassador from the Republic of Venice, about the year 1744.*

and a contexture of parts so close, that in some instances canon itself is scarcely stricter; and, which is very remarkable, this connection is maintained with such art as not to affect the air materially, or superinduce the necessity of varying it in order to accommodate it to the harmony. But as these compositions exceed the power of verbal description, the following must testify to their merits:

ABBATE STEFFANI.

It may be remembered that in the account herein before given of Antimo Liberati, mention is made of a letter from him to Ovidio Persapegi. In this letter the author seems to adopt the notions respecting music, of Sextus Empiricus, in his treatise adversus Mathematicos, and of Cornelius Agrippa, in his discourse de Incertitudine et Vanitate Scientiarum, and affects to doubt whether the principles of music have any foundation in nature or not, or, in short, whether the pleasure arising from the contemplation of musical harmony is not resolvable into mere fancy, and a previous disposition of the mind to approve it. To obviate this silly notion, Steffani, in the year 1695, published a series of letters with this title, 'Quanta certezza abbia da suoi principii la musica,' which Andreas Werckmeister, a most excellent musician, and organist of the church of St. Martin at Halberstadt, translated and published at Quedlinburg, in the year 1700. Mattheson, in his Orchestra, page 300, 302, mentions two persons, namely, John Balhorn and      Weigweiser, as the authors of observations on these letters of Steffani; but, according to Mattheson's account, neither of them was either able to read the original, or in the translation to distinguish between the sense of the author, as delivered in the text, and the opinions of the translator, contained in the notes.

The musical talents of our author, however extraordinary, were far from being the only distinguishing part of his character: he had great natural endowments, and these he had considerably improved by study, and the conversation of learned and polite

men. Nor did he confine his pursuits merely to those branches of learning that are immediately connected with his profession; but he applied himself to the study of the constitution and interests of the empire, by which he became enabled to act in a sphere that very few of his profession were ever known to attain—politics and the business of the public. It is therefore not to be wondered at that he was frequently employed in negociations to foreign courts, or that he should on such occasions be honoured with all the marks of distinction usually paid to public ministers. Among other transactions, he had a considerable share in concerting with the courts of Vienna and Ratisbon the scheme for erecting the duchy of Brunswic Lunenberg into an electorate; a step which the critical situation of affairs in the year 1692 rendered necessary to the preservation of a proper balance between the interests of the house of Austria and its adversaries, who, by the accession of the Newburg family to the electorate of the Rhine, were now thought to be too formidable. This important service could not fail of recommending him to the friends of the Austrian family; accordingly the elector, as a testimony of his regard, assigned him a pension of fifteen hundred rix-dollars per annum; and the pope, Innocent XI., promoted him to the bishopric of Spiga.* Though as the advantages resulting from this event could but very remotely, if at all, affect the interests of the Roman

* SPIGA is situate in Anatolia or Asia Minor, and is one of those nominal bishoprics which are said to be in partibus infidelium. Anciently it was a city of great eminence, and called Cyzicus. Vide Heyl. Cosmogr. page 610, Edit. 1703.

catholics in the empire, some have been induced to think that this signal instance of favour shown by the pontiff himself must have been the reward of a negociation more favourable to their cause, viz., the procuring liberty for those of that persuasion to erect a church at Hanover, and publicly to exercise their religion there; a privilege which, till the time Steffani solicited for it, had been denied them, and which at this juncture it was not thought prudent any longer to refuse.

He was now considered as a statesman, and was besides a dignitary of the church; and having a character to sustain, with which he imagined the public profession of his art not properly consistent, he forebore the setting his name to his future compositions, and adopted that of his secretary or copyist, Gregorio Piua.   Influenced perhaps by the same motives, in the year 1708 he resigned his employment of chapel-master in favour of Mr. Handel.

About the year 1724 the Academy of ancient Music in London was become so famous as to attract the notice of foreigners; and Steffani, as a testimony of his regard for so laudable an institution, having presented that society with many of his own valuable compositions, the Academy, in return for so great a favour, unanimously elected him their president,* and received from him a very polite letter, acknowledging the honour done him.

In the year 1729, an inclination to see his relations and the place of his nativity, determined him to take a journey into Italy, from whence, after he had staid a winter, and visited the most eminent masters then living, he returned to Hanover.   He had not remained long in that city, before some occasion called him to Francfort, and soon after his arrival he became sensible of the decay of his health; being of a constitution which the slightest disorder would affect, and consequently little able to endure the infirmities incident to old age, after an indisposition of a few days he died.

When he was last in Italy, he resided chiefly at the palace of Cardinal Ottoboni, with whom it had long been a custom on Monday in every week to have performances of concerts; or of operas, oratorios, and other grand compositions: on these occasions, in the absence of a principal singer, it has many times fallen to the lot of Steffani to be a performer; and it is said by some, whose good fortune it has been to be present at such an accident, that when he sang he was just loud enough to be heard, but that this defect in his voice was amply recompensed by his manner, in the chasteness and elegance of which he had few equals.   As to his person, he was less than the ordinary size of men, of a tender constitution of body, which he had not a little impaired by intense study and application.   His deportment is said to have been grave, but tempered with a sweetness and affability that

rendered his conversation very engaging; he was perfectly skilled in all the external forms of polite behaviour, and, which is somewhat unusual, continued to observe and practise them at the age of fourscore.

Besides the letters above-mentioned, there are extant in print the following works of Steffani, viz., Psalmodia Vespert. 8. Voc. Romæ, 1674; a collection of Motets entitled Sacer Janus Quadrifrons, 3. Voc. Monachii, 1685; and a collection of Airs taken from his operas: the latter is not to be regarded as a genuine publication, though of Estienne Roger of Amsterdam, for the title bears not his Christian name, and his surname is mis-spelt Stephani; besides this, the title is 'Sonate da Camera, à tre, due Violini, alto Viola e Basso,' but the book itself is in truth no other than a collection of overtures, symphonies, entrés, dance-tunes, and airs for instruments, in which kind of composition it is well known Steffani did not excel.†

## CHAP. CXLI.

ANDREAS WERCKMEISTER, the son of a brewer at Bennickenstein, a small town in Thuringia, was born on the thirtieth day of November, in the year 1645.   He was instructed for two years in music by his father's brother, Christian Werckmeister, organist at Bennungen; but in the month of August, 1660, he was removed to a school at Nordthausen, where he staid for two years.   From thence he went to Quidlenburg, in the college whereof another brother of his father, Victor Werckmeister, was cantor, and having greatly improved himself in the study and practice of music, received an invitation from the council of Hasselfelde, a city on the river Hartz, in the principality of Blankenburg, to become their organist, which he accepted.   While he was in this employment he had a like call to Ellrich, but was prevented from complying with it by the duke Rudolphus Augustus, who desired to keep him in the district of Blankenburg.   However, being invited, in the year 1674, to Elbingerod, by the offer of the employments of organist, and also recorder of that town, he was permitted to accept them.   In the year 1696 he was appointed organist of the church of St. Martin at Halberstadt, in which station he died on the twenty-sixth day of October, 1706.   In a sermon, preached at his funeral by John Melchior Gotzens, and printed in 1707, it is mentioned that he was Royal Prussian Inspector of the organs in the principality of Halberstadt. Mr. Handel, who was well acquainted with him, was used to speak of him in terms of great respect; and he was doubtless a learned and very skilful musician: his works are, 𝕺𝖗𝖌𝖊𝖑=𝕻𝖗𝖔𝖇𝖊, printed in 1681; Musicæ Mathematicæ Hodegum curiosum, 1687; Sonatas for a Violin, with a thorough-bass, 1689; 𝕸𝖚𝖘𝖎𝖈𝖆𝖑𝖎𝖘𝖈𝖍𝖊 Temperatur, 1691; a Treatise in German on the use and abuse of music, printed

* ' Huic ut annumerentur Societati, petiisse non dedignati sunt primi ' Ordinis Viri, Musicæ studio dediti, Praxeosque periti; inter quos ' semper meminisse juvabit Abbatem Steffani, Spigæ Episcopum, qui ' dum nomen suum nostris Tabulis inscribi rogavit, Præses unanimi ' omnium consensu est electus.'   Letters from the Academy of Ancient Music at London to Signor Antonio Lotti of Venice, with his Answers and Testimonies, Lond. 1732.

† Dr. Cooke has twelve motets of Steffani for three voices, as has also Professor Aylward.   They are manuscript, and are probably these.   Among them are two that are exquisitely fine—' Qui pacem amatis' and ' Cingit floribus.'

in the same year, Hypomnemata Musica, 1697; **Erweiterte Orgel=Probe**, 1698; Cribrum Musicum, 1700; a translation of Steffani's Letters abovementioned with notes, 1700; Reflections on Thorough-bass, in German, without a date; Harmonologiam Musicam, 1702; Organum Gruningense Redivivum, 1705; **Musicalische** Paradoxal Discurse, published the year after his decease.

SEBASTIAN DE BROSSARD, an eminent French musician, in the former part of his life had been prebendary and chapel-master of the cathedral church of Strasburg, but afterwards became grand chaplain, and also Maître de Chapelle in the cathedral of Meaux. There is extant of his a work entitled ' Prodromus Musi-'calis, ou Elevations et Motets à Voix seule, avec une Basse-continue.' The first edition printed in the second in 1702. 'Elevations et Motets à 'ii et iii Voix, et à Voix seule, deux dessus de 'Violon, ou deux Flûtes avec la Bass-continuë,' 1698, being the second part of the Prodromus Musicalis. He was the author also of a very useful book, entitled ' Dictionaire de Musique, contenant une explica-'tion des termes Grecs, Latins, Italians, et François 'les plus usitez dans la Musique,' printed at Amsterdam, in folio, in 1703, and afterwards at the same place in octavo, without a date. At the end of this book is a catalogue of authors, ancient and modern, to the amount of nine hundred who have written on music, divided into classes, wherein are interspersed many curious observations of the author relating to the history of music. By Mr. Boivin's Catalogue general des Livres de Musique for the year 1729, it appears that Brossard was the author of two sets of motets, as also of nine Leçons de Tenebres therein mentioned.

It seems that these several publications were at a time when the author was far advanced in years; for Walther takes notice that in the Mercure Galante he is mentioned as an abbé and componist so early as the year 1678.

PAOLO LORENZANI, a Roman by birth, and a pupil of Horatio Benevoli, was maestro di cappella, first in the Jesuits' church at Rome, and afterwards in the cathedral of Messina in Sicily; from whence he was invited by Lewis XIV. to Paris, where he was greatly caressed by the king and all the nobility. He composed and published at Paris a collection of very fine motets. In the year 1679, the king sent him to Italy to engage singers for his chapel; and it is said that he returned with five, who had scarce their equals in Europe.

ARCANGELO CORELLI (*a Portrait*), a native of Fusignano, a town situated near Imola, in the territory of Bologna, was born in the month of February, 1653. His first instructor in music was Matteo Simonelli, a singer in the pontifical chapel, mentioned in a preceding article, by whom he was taught the rudiments of the science, and the art of practical composition; but the genius of Corelli leading him to prefer secular to ecclesiastical music, he afterwards became a disciple of Giovanni Battista Bassani, who, although maestro di cappella of the church of Bologna, was celebrated for his excellence in that species of

composition which Corelli most delighted in, and made it the study of his life to cultivate.

We may reasonably suppose that to facilitate his studies Corelli had been taught the Clavicembalo and organ; nevertheless he entertained an early propensity to the violin, and, as he advanced in years, laboured incessantly in the practice of that instrument. About the year 1672 his curiosity led him to visit Paris, probably with a view to attend the improvements which were making in music under the influence of Cardinal Mazarine, and in consequence of the establishment of a Royal Academy; but, notwithstanding the character which he brought with him, he was driven back to Rome by Lully, whose jealous temper could not brook so formidable a rival as this illustrious Italian. In the year 1680 he visited Germany, and met with a reception suitable to his merit from most of the German princes, particularly the elector of Bavaria, in whose service he was retained, and continued for some time. After about five years stay abroad, he returned again to Rome, and there pursued his studies with great assiduity.

In the year 1686, our king James II. being disposed to cultivate a good understanding with pope Innocent XI., sent the earl of Castlemain, with a numerous train, his embassador to the court of Rome. Upon this occasion Christina, who had then lately resigned the crown of Sweden, and taken up her abode at Rome, entertained the city with a musical drama of the allegoric kind, written by Alessandro Guidi of Verona, a fine Italian poet, and set to music by Bernardi Pasquini.*

The proficiency of Corelli on his favourite instrument, the violin, was so great, that the fame of it reached throughout Europe; and Mattheson has not scrupled to say that he was the first performer on it in the world; and Gasparini styles him 'Virtuosis-'simo di violino, e vero Orfeo de nostri tempi.'† It does not, however, appear that he had attained to a power of execution in any degree comparable to that of later professors; and it may well be supposed that the just and rational notions which he entertained of the instrument, and of the end and design of music in general, aided by his own good sense, restrained him from those extravagances, which have no other tendency than to disgust the judicious, and excite the admiration of the ignorant. The style of his performance was learned, elegant, and pathetic, and his tone firm and even: Mr. Geminiani, who was well

---

* It is printed in the Poems of Guidi, octavo, Verona, 1726, with this title, ' Accademia per Musica fatta in Roma nel real Palazzo della ' Maestà di Cristina Regina di Suezia per Festiggiare l'assonzione al ' trono di Jacopo Re d' Inghilterra. In occasione della solenne Am-' basciata mandata da S. M. Britannica alla Santita di nostro Signore ' Innocenzo XI.
     ' Personnaggi.
' Londra, Tamigi, Fama, Genio Dommante, Genio Ribelle, Cori di ' Cento Musici.'
And at the bottom of the page is the following note: ' Bernardo ' Pasquini, Compositore della Musica, Arcangelo Corelli Capo degl' ' Istromenti d' arco, in numero di Centocinquanta.'

† L'Armonico Prattico al Cembalo, cap. vii. This appellation seems to have been generally given him, and is recognized in the following verses under the prints of him :
     ' Liquisse Infernas jam credimus Orphea Sedes
     ' Et terras habitare, hujus sub imagine formæ
     ' Divinus patet ipse Orpheus, dum numine dignâ
     ' Arte modos fingit, vel chordas mulcet, utramque
     ' Agnoscit laudem, meritosque Britannus honores.'

ARCANGELUS CORELLIUS

DE FUSIGNANO,

DICTUS BONONIENSIS.

acquainted with and had studied it, was used to resemble it to a sweet trumpet. A person who had heard him perform says that whilst he was playing on the violin, it was usual for his countenance to be distorted, his eyes to become as red as fire, and his eyeballs to roll as in an agony.

About the year 1690 the opera was in great perfection at Rome; Pasquini was the great dramatic composer: Mattheson infers the excellence of this entertainment from this circumstance, that Pasquini, Corelli, and Gaetani were performers in the Roman orchestra at the same time, the first being at the harpsichord, the second at the head of the band, and the latter performing on the lute.

While he was thus engaged at Rome, Corelli was highly favoured by that great patron of poetry and music, Cardinal Ottoboni. Crescembini says that he regulated the musical academy held at the palace of his eminence every Monday afternoon. Here it was that Mr. Handel became acquainted with him; and in this academy a Serenata of Mr. Handel, entitled Il Trionfo del Tempo, was performed, the overture to which was in a style so new and singular, that Corelli was confounded in his first attempt to play it.*

The merits of Corelli as a performer were sufficient to attract the patronage of the great, and to silence, as indeed they did, all competition; but the remembrance of these is at this day absorbed in the contemplation of his excellencies as a musician at large, as the author of new and original harmonies, and the father of a style not less noble and grand, than elegant and pathetic.

The works of Corelli are solely compositions for instruments, and consist of six operas,† entitled as follows :—

Suonate a trè due Violini, e Violone, col Basso per l' Organo Opera prima.

Sonate da Camera a trè, doi Violini, e Violone, ò Cimbalo. Opera Seconda.

Suonate a trè, doi Violini, e Violone, ò Arcileuto col Basso per l' Organo. Opera Terza.

Suonate da Camera a trè, doi Violini, e Violone ò Cimbalo. Opera Quarta.

Sonate à Violino e Violone ò Cembalo. Opera Quinta, Parte Prima : Parte Seconda, Preludii, Allemande, Correnti, Gighe, Sarabande Gavotte, e Follia.

This work was first published at Rome, with a dedication by the author to Sophia Charlotta, electress of Brandenburg, dated the first day of January, 1700.

Concerti Grossi con duoi Violini e Violoncello di Concertino obligati e duoi altri Violoni, Viola e Basso di Concerto Grosso ad arbitrio che si potranno radoppiare.‡

The four operas of Sonatas were published, as they were completed, at different times; the first edition of the first opera has escaped a diligent search, but those of the second, third, and fourth have been recovered : the second Opera, printed at Rome in 1685, is dedicated to Cardinal Panfilio; the third, printed at Bologna in 1690, to Francis II. duke of Modena; the fourth, also printed at Bologna, in 1694, to Cardinal Ottoboni, in whose palace at Rome the author then resided ' col spetioso carattere d' attuale servitore' of his eminence, as the dedication expresses it. These early editions, and also the subsequent ones published at Antwerp, were printed on the old lozenge-headed note, with the quavers and semiquavers disjoined from each other, forming a very obscure and illegible character.§

About the year 1720 Estienne Roger of Amsterdam printed a fine edition of the four Operas of Sonatas, stamped on copper, in the same character with the rest of his numerous publications.

Of the Concertos, the first is that beautiful one printed at Amsterdam for Estienne Roger and Michael Charles Le Cene, with a frontispiece before it, designed by Francesco Trevisani, of a muse playing on and singing to the lute.‖ The dedication of this work to John William, Prince Palatine of the Rhine, bears date at Rome the third day of December, 1712.

During the residence of Corelli at Rome, besides those of his own country, many persons were ambitious of becoming his disciples, and learning the practice on the violin from the greatest master of that instrument the world had then heard of. Of these it is said the late Lord Edgecumbe was one; and that the fine mezzotinto print of Corelli by Smith, was scraped from a picture painted by Mr. Hugh Howard at Rome for that nobleman.¶

---

* This Serenata, translated into English, and entitled The 'Triumph of Time and Truth,' was performed at London in 1751. The overture is in the printed collection of Mr. Handel's overtures, and it is conjectured, that the first movement was what appeared difficult to Corelli.

† There are two collections of Sonatas, printed at Amsterdam, not included in the above enumeration, the one entitled 'Sonate a trè, doi ' Violini e Basso per il Cimbalo, si crede che Siano State Composte di ' Arcangelo Corelli avanti le sue altre Opere, Opera Settima. Stampate ' à Spesa di Michele Carlo Le Cene;' the other 'Sonate a trè, due Violini 'col Basso per l' Organo di Arcangelo Corelli di Fusignano, Ouvrage ' posthume,' published by Estienne Roger and the above Le Cene. Of the authenticity of the posthumous work there is not the least evidence; and as to the Opera Settima, there is the fullest to prove it the work of another. In short, these Sonatas, in the title-page whereof the reader is told that they are believed to have been composed by Arcangelo Corelli before his other works, are no other than nine of twelve Sonatas for two violins and a bass, composed by a countryman of ours resident in Italy, and which were published with this title, 'Sonate a trè, doi Violini 'Violone, ò Arcileuto col Basso per l'Organo. Dedicate all' Altezza 'Serenissima di Ferdinando III. Gran Prencipe di Toscana. Da Giovanni Ravenscroft, alias Rederi, Inglese, Opera Prima. In Roma, per ' il Mascardi, 1695.

There is extant also in the book entitled the Division Violin, part II. a Solo in the key of G, with the lesser third, said to be of Corelli, but it wants authority.

‡ Of this species of musical composition we are told that Giuseppe Torelli, of Bologna, was the inventor.

§ Of the Antwerp editions the following only have come to hand, Opera Prima Nuovamente Ristampata. In Anversa Stampato in Casa di Henrico Aertssens al Monte Parnasso, anno 1688. Opera Terza Nuovamente Ristampata, by the same person, 1691. But such was the parsimony of the printers of these subsequent editions, that the dedications are omitted, which might have ascertained the time of the first publication of each Opera, and possibly furnished some particulars respecting the author, as that to the original edition of the fourth does, whereby we are informed that Corelli was a domestic of Cardinal Ottoboni, that the work which it precedes was composed in his palace, and that the pieces contained in it were frequently performed in the academy there held.

The Italian and Flemish editions were so little fit for use, that the demand for Corelli's works being very great in England, many persons acquired a subsistence by copying in writing the Sonatas of Corelli in a legible character; in particular Mr. Thomas Shuttleworth, a teacher of music, and who was living in Spitalfields in the year 1738, by his industry in this practice was enabled to bring up a numerous family.

‖ For want of attention in the engraver, the print is the reverse of the painting, and the muse is made to finger the instrument with her left hand.

¶ This picture was painted between 1697 and 1700, for in that interval it appears that Mr. Howard was abroad. Anecdotes of Painting in England by Mr. Horace Walpole, vol. III. page 144. That Corelli sat to Mr. Howard for it is certain, for in the print after it is this inscription : 'H. Howard ad vivum pinxit.' Mr. Howard was no very extraordinary painter, but being an Englishman, and the English being celebrated for

Corelli died at Rome about six weeks after the publication of his Opera Sesta, that is to say, on the eighteenth day of January, 1713, and was buried in the church of the Rotunda, otherwise called the Pantheon, in the first chapel on the left hand of the entrance. Over the place of his interment is a sepulchral monument to his honour, with a marble bust thereon, erected at the expense of Philip William, Count Palatine of the Rhine, under the care and direction of Cardinal Ottoboni.* The following is the inscription thereon :—

D. O. M.

ARCANGELO CORELLIO A FUSIGNANO

PHILIPPI WILLELMI COMITIS PALATINI RHENI

S. R. I. PRINCIPIS AC ELECTORIS

BENEFICENTIA

MARCHIONIS DE LADENSBURG

QUOD EXIMIIS ANIMI DOTIBUS

ET INCOMPARABILI IN MUSICIS MODULIS PERITIA

SUMMIS PONTIFICIBUS APPRIME CARUS

ITALIÆ ATQUE EXTERIS NATIONIBUS ADMIRATIONI FUERIT

INDULGENTE CLEMENTE XI. P. O. M.

PETRUS CARDINALIS OTTOBONUS S. R. E. VIC. CAN.

ET GALLIARUM PROTECTOR

LIIRISTE CELEBERRIMO

INTER FAMILIARES SUOS JAM DIU ADSCITO

EJUS NOMEN IMMORTALITATI COMMENDATURUS

M. P. C.

VIXIT ANNOS LIX. MENS. X. DIES XX.

OBIIT IV. ID. JANUARII ANNO SAL. MDCCXIII.

For many years after his decease, this excellent musician was commemorated by a solemn musical performance in the Pantheon, on the anniversary of his death. In the year 1730 an eminent master, now living, was present at that solemnity, who relates that at it the third and the eighth of his Concertos were performed by a numerous band, among whom were many who had been the pupils of the author. He adds, that these two pieces were performed in a slow, distinct, and firm manner, without graces, and just as they are wrote ; and from hence concludes that this was the manner in which they were played by the author himself.

He died possessed of a sum of money equal to about six thousand pounds sterling. He was a passionate admirer of pictures,† and lived in an uninterupted friendship with Carlo Cignani and Carlo

portrait- painting, it is imagined that he left behind him one other picture of Corelli, painted by himself, or at least a copy of the former ; for the bust on the monument of Corelli in the Rotunda at Rome, does in every respect most exactly correspond with the mezzotino print of Smith.

* It is commonly said here that the Jig in the fifth Sonate in the Opera Quinta, is engraven on Corelli's monument ; but it is in the following sense only that this assertion is true. The bust represents him, as the print does, with a music-paper in his hand, on which are engraven certain musical-notes, which, upon a near inspection, appear to be a few bars of that fine air.

† It may serve as an argument to prove the affinity of the sister arts of music and painting, that the love of each to an equal degree has in many instances centered in the same person. Mr. Handel, though not a collector, was a lover of pictures, and for many years before his death frequented, for the purpose of viewing them, all collections exposed to sale : Geminiani, in the latter years of his life, was absorbed in the love of painting, and once declared to the author of this work, that he loved it better than music. Nicholas Laniere, though celebrated as one of the first musicians in his time, has rendered his character so ambiguous by his excellence in painting, that both faculties claim him ; and in Mr. Walpole's Anecdotes he stands ranked among the painters, and with very good reason ; his own portrait in the music-school at Oxford, painted by himself, being a masterly work. On the other hand, there are instances of painters who have been no less excellent in the practice of music, as were Leonardo da Vinci, Domenichino, and Sir Godfrey Kneller ; Guido Reni, and our countryman Mr. Samuel Cooper were famous for their skill and performance on the lute.

Maratti : these two eminent painters were rivals for his favour, and for a series of years presented him at times with pictures, as well of other masters as of their own painting. The consequence hereof was, that Corelli became possessed of a large and valuable collection of original paintings, all which, together with the sum above-mentioned, he bequeathed to his dear friend and patron, Cardinal Ottoboni, who, reserving the pictures to himself, generously distributed the rest of the effects among the relations of the testator.

Corelli is said to have been remarkable for the mildness of his temper and the modesty of his deportment ; the lineaments of his countenance, as represented in his portrait, seem to bespeak as much ; nevertheless he was not insensible to the respect due to his skill and exquisite performance. Cibber, in the Apology for his Life, page 340, relates that when he was playing a solo at Cardinal Ottoboni's, he discovered the Cardinal and another person engaged in discourse, upon which he laid down his instrument ; and being asked the reason, gave for answer, that he feared the music interrupted conversation. He was censured by some who were acquainted with him for his parsimony, upon no better ground than the accustomed plainness of his garb, and his disinclination to the use of a coach or other carriage. Mr. Handel had remarked these two little particulars in his conduct, and would sometimes, when he spoke of him, add, but without a view to depreciate his character, that his ordinary dress was black, and his outer garment a plain blue cloak.

That he was a man of humour and pleasantry may be inferred from the following story, related by Walther, in his account of Nicolas Adam Strunck, violonist to Ernestus Augustus, elector of Hanover. This person being at Rome, upon his arrival made it his business to see Corelli ; upon their first interview Strunck gave him to understand that he was a musician ; 'What is your instrument ?' asked Corelli ; 'I can play,' answered Strunck, 'upon the 'harpsichord, and a little on the violin, and should 'esteem myself extremely happy might I hear your 'performance on this latter instrument, on which I 'am informed you excel.' Corelli very politely condescended to this request of a stranger ; he played a solo, Strunck accompanied him on the harpsichord, and afterwads played a Toccata, with which Corelli was so much taken, that he laid down his instrument to admire him. When Strunck had done at the harpsichord, he took up the violin, and began to touch it in a very careless manner, upon which Corelli remarked that he had a very good bow-hand, and wanted noting but practice to become a master of the instrument ; at this instant Strunck put the violin out of tune, and, applying it to its place, played on it with such dexterity, attempering the dissonances occasioned by the mis-tuning of the instrument with such amazing skill and dexterity, that Corelli cried out in broken German, 'I am called 'Arcangelo, a name that in the language of my 'country signifies an Archangel ; but let me tell 'you, that you, Sir, are an Arch-devil.'

Our observations on the works of Corelli may properly enough be classed under two heads, that is to say, their general history, and their peculiar character; as to the first, it is confidently asserted that they were composed with great deliberation; that they were revised and corrected from time to time; and, finally, submitted to the inspection of the most skilful musicians of the author's time. Of the Sonatas it may be remarked that the first and third Operas consist of fugues and slow movements, without any intermixture of airs; these are termed Sonate da Chiesa, in contradistinction to those in the second and fourth operas, which are styled da Camera: the former, we are told by Mattheson, were usually played in the churches abroad after divine service; and the whole four operas for many years furnished the second music before the play at both the theatres in London. The fifth opera consists of those solo-sonatas which the author himself was accustomed to perform on special occasions; there is one edition of them in two distinct parts, viz. one for the violin, and the other for the violoncello or harpsichord; and another with the graces to the adagio movements, which some have suspected to be spurious, but they are in one of the Amsterdam editions; and to obviate a doubt of their genuineness, the publisher, Estienne Roger, has, in one of his printed catalogues, signified that the original copy of them, as also some letters of the author on the subject, were open to the inspection of the curious at his shop. The last of the twelve is a set of divisions, twenty-four in number, on a favourite air, known in England by the name of Farinelli's Ground,* and is called by Corelli, Follia. The twelfth Sonata of Vivaldi's Opera Prima is a praxis on the same melody.

So much for the general history of his works; as to their peculiar character, it may be said that to enumerate the various excellencies of this great master would require a particular examen of his several compositions; of his Sonatas Mattheson remarks, that there is more art and contrivance in them than in his Overtures, i. e. his Concertos; but in this he certainly is mistaken. The first opera is but an essay towards that perfection to which he afterwards arrived; there is but little art and less invention therein; the third, eighth, and ninth Sonatas therein contained are almost the only ones in practice. The second opera carries with it the evidences of a genius matured by exercise; the second, the fifth, the eighth, and the eleventh Sonatas are both learned and elegant. The third opera is the most elaborate of the four, as abounding in fugues. The first, the fourth, the sixth, and the ninth Sonatas of this opera are the most distinguished; the latter has drawn tears from many an eye; but the whole is so excellent, that, exclusive of mere fancy, there is scarce any motive for preference. The fourth opera is, in its kind, equal to the former two; the second and eleventh Sonatas excite a melancholy, soothing and of the most pathetic kind. The third, sixth,

and tenth are gay and lively in an eminent degree; they do not provoke mirth, but they inspire cheerfulness, gaiety, and every species of good humour short of it. Of his Solos, the second, the third, the fifth, and the sixth are admirable; as are the ninth, the tenth, and, for the elegant sweetness of the second movement, the eleventh. A very good musician, Giorgio Antoniotti, has remarked of the fugue in the first, that the melody of the subject is but indifferent,† but every one must own that the subject itself is well sustained.

The sixth opera, though composed at a time when the faculties of the author might be supposed to have been on the decline, affords the strongest proof of the contrary; nothing can exceed in dignity and majesty the opening of the first Concerto, nor, for its plaintive sweetness, the whole of the third. And he must have no ears, nor feeling of the power of harmony, or the effects of modulation, who can listen to the eighth without rapture. ‡

The compositions of Corelli are celebrated for the harmony resulting from the union of all the parts; but the fineness of the airs is another distinguishing characteristic of them: the Allemand in the tenth Solo is as remarkable for spirit and force, as that in the eleventh is for its enchanting delicacy: his jigs are in a style peculiarly his own; and that in the fifth Solo was never equalled. In the Gavot-movements in the second and fourth operas, the melody is distributed with great judgment among the several parts. In his minuets alone he seems to fail; Bononcini, Mr. Handel, and Giuseppe Martini have excelled him in this kind of air.

It is said there is in every nation a style both in speaking and writing, which never becomes obsolete; a certain mode of phraseology, so consonant and congenial to the analogy and principles of its respective language, as to remain settled and unaltered.§ This, but with much greater latitude, may be said of music; and accordingly it may be observed of the compositions of Corelli, not only that they are equally intelligible to the learned and unlearned, but that the impressions made by them have been found to be as durable as general. His music is the language of nature; and for a series of years all that heard it became sensible of its effects; of this there cannot be a stronger proof than that, amidst all the innovations which the love of change had introduced, it continued to be performed, and was heard with delight in churches, in theatres, at public solemnities and festivities in all the cities of Europe for near forty years. Men remembered, and would refer to passages in it as to a classic author; and even at this day the masters of the science, of whom it must be observed, that though their studies are regulated by the taste of the public, yet have they a taste of their own, do not hesitate to pronounce of the compositions of Corelli, that, of fine harmony and elegant modulation, they are the most perfect exemplars.

† In a treatise entitled L'Arte Armonica, published at London in 1760, page 95.

‡ This concerto was composed on occasion of a solemnity peculiar to the Romish church, the celebration of the Nativity; the printed copies. having this advertisement, 'Fatto per la Notte di Natale.'

§ Dr. Sam. Johnson's preface to his edition of Shakespeare.

* This ground was composed by        Farinelli, uncle of the famous singer Carlo Broschi Farinelli, and componist, violinist, and concertmaster at Hanover about the year 1684. He was ennobled by the king of Denmark, and was by king George I. appointed his resident at Venice.

The natural and familiar style of Corelli's music, and that simplicity which is one of its characteristics, betrayed many into an opinion that it was easily to be imitated; and whoever considers that from harmonies such as his are, a rule or canon might be drawn that would give to any music, composed in conformity to it, a similar appearance, would entertain the same notion; but the experiment has been made, and has failed. Ravenscroft professed to imitate Corelli in those Sonatas which Roger published, and hoped to make the world believe were some of the earliest of his works. The airs indeed of Albinoni, Torelli, Giuseppe Valentini, and Mascitti, especially the Allemands, Courants, and Jigs, seem to have been cast in Corelli's mould; but an Englishman, named James Sherard, an apothecary by profession,* composed two operas of Sonatas, which an ordinary judge, not knowing that they were the work of another, might mistake for compositions of this great master.

ALESSANDRO SCARLATTI of Naples, and a Cavaliero, a most voluminous composer, is celebrated as having perfected the theatric style. It is said that he composed near a hundred operas; and oratorios, serenatas, and cantatas to an incredible number; and farther, that his invention was so fertile, and his application so intense, that his copyist was not able to write so fast as he composed. Of his numerous compositions we know of but two works in print, viz. 'Cantate à una e due Voci,' and 'Motetti à una, 'due, tre, e quattro Voci con Violini.'† He is said to have first introduced into his airs accompaniments for the violin, and symphonies, which both enrich the melody and give relief to the singer. He had a son named Domenico, who was formerly chapel-master in some church of Rome, but in the year 1728 was taken into the service of the king of Portugal, who it is said, upon his arrival at Lisbon, to defray the expense of his journey, presented him with two thousand dollars, since which time he has applied himself to the composition of lessons for the harpsichord, of which there are a great number in print.

TOMASO ALBINONI, a Venetian, was originally a maker of cards, but having an early propensity to music, and having been taught the violin in his youth, he became not only an excellent performer on that instrument, but also an eminent composer. The titles of such of his works as are in print may be seen in the Dutch Catalogues; they consist solely of music for instruments, viz. Concertos and Sonatas for Violins, and Cantate da Camera, and a Collection

of Airs, entitled 'Balletti à tre, due Violini e Vio-'loncello col Basso da Tomaso Albinoni, Dilettante 'Veneto, Opera terza,' which were sundry times printed, and at length became so familiar in England, that many of the common fiddlers were able to play them. In the year 1690 we find him associated with Gasparini, mentioned in the next article, in the composition of an opera called Engelberta, performed at the theatre di San Cassiano at Venice. Albinoni was living about the year 1725, and was known to a person who furnished the above facts concerning him.

FRANCESCO GASPARINI, born at Lucca about the year 1650, Accademico filarmonico, and director of the choir in the hospital della Pietà at Venice, was one of the finest vocal composers of the last century. He excelled equally in the composition of chamber and theatrical music, his Cantatas being esteemed among the finest of the kind ever published; and his operas, of which he composed a great number, are scarcely exceeded by those of Scarlatti. An opera of his, entitled Merope, was performed in Italy, not so long ago as to be beyond the remembrance of a very able musician lately deceased, who relates that he was present at the representation of it, and that one recitative without instruments, sung by Merope and her son, produced a general effusion of tears from a crowded assemby of auditors. He joined with Albinoni in the composition of an opera entitled Engelberta, mentioned in the preceding article, and was living at Rome in the year 1723, as appears by a letter of his writing, prefixed to the Psalms of Marcello, in answer to one of the author. The works of Gasparini in print are, Cantate da Camera à Voce sola, printed at Lucca in 1697; and a treatise, published at Venice in 1708, entitled L'Armonico Prattico al Cimbalo, regole per ben suonare il basso.

It is needless to observe upon the foregoing deduction of facts, that music was arrived at a great degree of perfection towards the end of last century; and it must appear from the accounts already given in the course of this work, of eminent professors in different ages, and of various countries, that the science owes much of the perfection to which it has been brought to the Italians and Germans. In what degree the English contributed to its improvement, can only be judged of by their works, and the suffrages of those writers, and, among others, Erasmus, who have borne testimony to the general disposition of the people of this country to favour the practice of it; to which may be added one farther testimony, viz., the declaration of Lewis XIV. in his grant to Lully, before inserted, wherein he recites that he had granted to Perrin licence to establish academies of music, in which should be sung theatrical dramas, 'comme il se pratique en Italie, en 'Allemagne, et en Angleterre;' from whence it seems that, in the opinion of the French in the year 1669, the dramatic music of the English was of such a kind as to be at least worthy of imitation, and that by a people who were endeavouring to form a taste after the purest models of perfection.

This consideration, as also another, to wit, that

---

* This person lived in Crutched-Friars, London; he was the brother of Dr. Sherard the botanist, author of the Hortus Elthamensis. The Sonatas of Sherard were printed at Amsterdam, and published by Estienne Roger.

† An opera of his, entitled 'Pyrrhus and Demetrius,' was translated into English, and, with some additional airs and an overture, by Nicolini Haym, was performed at the Haymarket theatre in 1708, and printed with both the Italian and English words. The original opera was performed with universal applause at Rome, Naples, and other places, and is said to be the finest in its kind of all Scarlatti's works.
In the English opera the airs of Haym are distinguished from those of Scarlatti by their superior excellence; and also by this circumstance, that the latter have the Italian printed under the English words. The air 'Vieni o Sonno,' is celebrated as divine; and that of 'Veder parmi un ombra nera,' as also another not printed, are, in the opinion of a very good judge, who was living at the time of the performance, two of the most masterly airs that were ever composed for the theatre. See a Comparison between the French and Italian Music and Operas, translated from the French, with remarks. Page 15, in not. and page 75.

the succession of English musicians has, in this work, hitherto been continued down no further than to about the middle of the last century, makes it necessary to recur some years backward, and to take a view of the state of music in that gloomy period, during which a sullen abstinence from innocent and elegant delights was looked upon as conducive to the glory of God and the interests of religion; and this naturally leads us to the history of the theatre, which will be found to involve in it, at least for a considerable number of years, the history of music also.

## CHAP. CXLII.

THE intelligent reader need not be told, that during the time of the usurpation stage plays were an abomination; the first writer who endeavoured to possess the world with the belief that theatrical entertainments were inconsistent with the purity of the christian religion, was one Stephen Gosson, rector of St. Botolph's without Bishopsgate, a man of wit and learning, who himself had written some few things for the stage, but falling in with the principles of the puritans, he changed the course of his studies, and became a bitter enemy to plays, players, and pipers, by whom he means musicians in general, as appears by a little book published by him 1579, entitled ' The School of Abuse, containing ' a pleasant invective against poets, pipers, plaiers, ' jesters, and such like catterpillers, of a common ' welth; setting up the flagge of defiance to their ' mischievous exercise, and overthrowing their bul- ' warkes by prophane writers, natural reason, and ' common experience.'

Gosson's book, notwithstanding the severity of the satire, is in truth what he calls it, a pleasant invective, for it abounds with wit and humour, and exhibits a very lively picture of the manners of the age in which it was written. The author soon after published a small tract, entitled, ' Plays confuted in ' five Actions. proving, that they are not to be ' suffered in a christian common weale; by the ' waye, both the cavils of Thomas Lodge,* and the ' Play of Playes, written in their defence, and other ' objections of players frendes are truely set downe, ' and directly aunswered,' wherein are several severe reflections, as well on musicians, as on the authors and frequenters of stage entertainments.

The quarrel which Gosson had commenced against plays and players, was prosecuted with all the malevolence that fanaticism could suggest, by that hotbrained zealot William Prynne, in his book entitled ' Histrio-Mastix, the Players Scourge, or Actors ' Tragædie, in which it is pretended to be evidenced, ' that stage playes, (the very pompes of the divell, ' which we renounce in baptisme, if we believe the ' fathers) are sinful, heathenish, lewde, ungodly ' spectacles, and most pernicious corruptions; con- ' demned in all ages as intolerable mischiefes to ' churches, to republickes, to the manners, mindes, ' and soules of men. And that the profession of

* Dr. Lodge, the author of sundry pastoral poems in England's Helicon, and other elegant compositions.

' play-poets, of stage players, together with the ' penning, acting, and frequenting of stage players ' are unlawfull, infamous, and misbecoming christians. ' All pretences to the contrary are here likewise fully ' answered, and the unlawfulnes of acting or beholding ' academicall enterludes briefly discussed, besides ' sundry other particulars concerning dancing, dicing, ' health-drinking, &c.'†

The prosecution of Prynne for publishing this book and the consequences of it, are well known to every person conversant with English history; but the effects it wrought upon the minds of the people in general, were such as put a total stop to stage exhibitions of every kind. The public could but ill brook the total interdiction of dramatic representations, which, under proper regulations might, and indeed have been rendered subservient to the purposes of morality; and the dissatisfaction that was expressed on this occasion suggested to Sir William Davenant, the thought of an entertainment resembling the Italian opera, in which he was encouraged by no less a person than the famous Sir John Maynard, Serjeant at Law, and several citizens. That this entertainment was in the Italian language, though Wood calls it an Italian opera, is much to be doubted; but whatever it was, it was performed at Rutland House, in Charterhouse-yard or Square, on the 23rd day of May, 1656.‡ It is highly probable, it was no other than that drama published among Sir William Davenant's Works, page 341, entitled, ' the First day's Entertainment at Rutland House, ' declamations and music, after the manner of the ' ancients,' and if so, it had not the least claim to the title of an opera. It consists of several orations in prose, intermixed with vocal and instrumental music, which in a note at the end, we are told, was composed by Dr. Charles Coleman, Mr. Henry Lawes, and Mr. George Hudson.

Wood says, that this opera, as he calls it, was afterwards translated to the Cockpit in Drury-lane, and delighting the eye and ear extremely well, was much frequented for many years.

But notwithstanding these attempts in its favour, the forbidding the use of the liturgy, and the restraints on the stage, amounted in effect, to a proscription of music from the metropolis, and drove the professors of it to seek protection where they were most likely to find it. It will easily be conceived, that the prohibition of cathedral service left a great number of musicians, as namely, organists, minor canons, lay-clerks, and other persons attendant on choirs, without employment; and the gloomy and sullen temper of the times, together with the frequent hostilities that were carried on in different parts of the kingdom, during the usurpation, had driven music to a great degree out of private families. The only place which these men could, as to an asylum, resort, was to Oxford, whither the King

† It is pretended that Prynne meant by this book, to libel Queen Henrietta Maria, the consort of Charles I. who, about the time of its publication, had acted a part in a pastoral at Somerset House; but Whitelock asserts, that it was published six weeks before that pastoral was acted. See his Memorials and Athen. Oxon. 434.

‡ Athen. Oxon. vol. II. col. 412.

had retired; there went with him thither, Dr. Wilson, one of the Gentlemen of his chapel, and he had an organist with him named George Jeffries; these and a few others, with the assistance of the University people, made a stand against the persecution of the times; choral service was performed there after a very homely fashion, and concerts of vocal and instrumental music were sometimes had in the rooms of the Gentlemen of the University for the entertainment of each other. But this lasted only till the surrender of the garrison in 1646, when the King was obliged to leave the place; however, the spirit that had been excited in favour of music during his residence there, and the continuance of Dr. Wilson in the University, who was professor, and a man of a cheerful disposition, contributed to an association of Gentlemen of the University, with the musicians of the place, and these together established a weekly concert. The place of greatest resort for this purpose was the house of one William Ellis, formerly organist of Eton College, and, at the time now spoken of, organist of St. John's. Of this meeting, and of the persons who frequented it Wood gives a very particular account in his life, published by Hearne, at the end of his edition of Caii Vindiciæ Antiq. Acad. Oxon. 1730, and again at Oxford in 1772; and in the manuscript of his in the Ashmolean Museum, mentioned in vol. III. page 258, in not. is the following memoir relating to it :—

‘After Cathedrals and Organs were put down in ‘the grand Rebellion, he [Ellis] kept up a weekly ‘Meeting in his house opposite to that Place where ‘the Theatre was afterwards built, which kept him ‘and his wife in a comfortable Condition. The ‘Meeting was much frequented and many Masters ‘of Musick were there, and such that had belonged ‘to Choirs, being out of all Employ, and therefore ‘the Meeting, as all other Musick Meetings, did ‘flourish; and Musick, especially vocal, being dis-‘countenanced by the Presbyterians and indepen-‘dents, because it favoured much the Cathedrals and ‘Episcopacy, it was the more used. But when ‘King Charles was restored and Episcopacy and ‘Cathedrals with it, then did the Meetings decay, ‘especially for this Reason, because the Masters of ‘Musick were called away to Cathedrals and Col-‘legiate Choirs.’

Of the meeting itself the following is Wood's account in his own words :—*

* Wood may be credited in whatever he relates touching music, for he was passionately fond of it; and was besides, a good proficient on the violin, as appears by the following extract from his life, page 70, edit. 1772 :—

‘This yeare [1651] A. W. began to exercise his natural and insatiable ‘Genie he had to Musick. He exercised his Hand on the Violin, and ‘having a good eare to take any tune at first hearing, he could quickly ‘draw it out from the Violin, but not with the same tuning of Strings ‘that others used. He wanted Understanding, Friends, and Money, to ‘pick him out a good Master, otherwise he might have equal'd in that ‘Instrument, and in singing, any person then in the Universitie. He had ‘some companions that were musical, but they wanted instruction as ‘well as he.’

Elsewhere [page 74] he says, ‘that being taken ill he retired to Cassing-‘ton, and there learn't to ring on the six Bells, then newly put up; and ‘having had from his most tender years, an extraordinary ravishing ‘Delight in Musick, he practised privately there, without the help of an ‘Instructer, to play on the Violin. It was then that he set and tuned ‘his strings in Fourths, and not in Fifths, according to the manner: ‘And having a good eare, and being ready to sing any Tune upon hearing

‘By this time, [viz. anno 1656,] A. W. had some ‘genuine skill in Musick, and frequented the ‘Weekly Meetings of Musitians in the house of ‘Will. Ellis, late Organist of S. John's Coll. situat ‘and being in a House, opposite to that place ‘whereon the Theater was built. The usual Com-‘pany that met and performed their parts were (1) ‘Joh. Cock, M. A. Fellow of New Coll. by the ‘Authority of the Visitors. He afterwards became ‘Rector of Heyford-Wareyne neare Bister,† and ‘marrying with one of the Woodwards of Wood-‘stock, lived an uncomfortable Life with her. (2) ‘Joh. Jones, M. A. Fellow of the said Coll. by the ‘same Authority. (3) George Croke, M. A. Fellow ‘of the said Coll. also by the same Authority. He ‘was afterwards drown'd, with Brome, son of Brome ‘Whorwood of Halton near Oxon. in their passage ‘from Hampshire to the Isle of Wight, 5. Sept. 1657. ‘(4) Joh. Friend, M. A. Fellow also of the said ‘House, and by the same Authority. He died in ‘the Country, an. 1658. (5) George Stradling, ‘M. A. Fellow of Alls. Coll. an admirable Lutinist, ‘and much respected by Wilson the Professor. ‘(6) Ralph Sheldon, Gent. a Rom. Catholick of ‘Steple-Barton in Oxfordshire, at this time living in ‘Halywell neare Oxon. admired for his smooth and ‘admirable way in playing on the Viol. He died ‘in the City of Westminster....165 , and was ‘buried in the Chancel of the Church of S. Martin in ‘the Fields. (7) Thom. Wren, a yonger son of ‘Matthew Wren, Bishop of Ely, a Sojourner now in ‘the House of Franc. Bowman, Bookseller, living ‘in S. Marie's parish in Oxon. (8) Tho James, ‘M. A. of Magd. Coll. would be among them, but ‘seldome played. He had a weekly Meeting in ‘his Chamber at the Coll. practised much on the

‘it once or twice, he would play them all in short time with the said ‘way of Tuning, which was never knowne before.’

In the year 1653 he put himself under the tuition of a master, of whom, and his proficiency under him, he gives the following account :—
‘After he [A. W.] had spent the Summer at Cassington in a lonish ‘and retir'd condition, he return'd to Oxon, and being advised by some ‘persons, he entertain'd a Master of Musick to teach him the usual way ‘of playing on the Violin, that is, by having every String tuned 5 notes ‘lower than the other going before. The Master was Charles Griffith, ‘one of the Musitians belonging to the City of Oxon. whom he thought ‘then to be a most excellent Artist; but when A. W. improv'd himself ‘in that Instrument, he found him not so. He gave him 2s. 6d. entrance, ‘and 10s. quarterly. This person after he had extreamly wondered how ‘he could play so many Tunes as he did by Fourths, without a Director ‘or Guide, he then tuned his Violin by Fifths, and gave him Instructions ‘how to proceed, leaving then a Lesson with him to practice against his ‘next coming. Ibid. 76.
‘Whereas A. W. had before learned to play on the Violin by the In-‘struction of Charles Griffith, and afterwards of Jo. Parker, one of the ‘Universitie Musitians, he was now advis'd to entertaine one Will. ‘James, a Dancing-Master, by some accounted excellent for that Instru-‘ment; and the rather, because it is said, that he had obtained his ‘knowledge in Dancing and Musick in France. He spent in all half ‘a yeare with him, and gained some improvement from him; yet at ‘length he found him not a compleat Master of his facultie, as Griffith ‘and Parker were not: and, to say the Truth, there was yet no compleat ‘Master in Oxon. for that Instrument, because it had not been hitherto ‘used in Consort among Gentlemen, only by common Musitians, who ‘played but two Parts. The Gentlemen in privat Meetings, which A. W. ‘frequented, play'd three, four and five Parts with Viols, as Treble-Viol, ‘Tenor, Counter-Tenor and Bass, with an organ, Virginal, or Harpsicon ‘joyn'd with them: and they esteemed a Violin to be an Instrument ‘only belonging to a common Fidler, and could not endure that it should ‘come among them, for feare of making their Meetings to be vaine and ‘fidling. But before the Restoration of K. Ch. 2. and especially after, ‘Viols began to be out of fashion, and only Violins used, as Treble-‘Violin, tenor and Bass-Violin; and the King, according to the French ‘Mode, would have 24 Violins playing before him, while he was at Meales ‘as being more airie and brisk than Viols.’ Ibid. 96.

† Wood is very licentious in his spelling: the place here meant is Bicester, a market-town in Oxfordshire.

'Theorbo Lute; and Gervace Westcote being often
'with him as an Instructor, A. W. would sometimes
'go to their Meeting and play with them.

'The Musick Masters, who were now in Oxon.
'and frequented the said meeting, were (1) Will.
'Ellis, Bach. of Musick, owner of the House
'wherein the Meeting was. He alwaies play'd his
'part either on the Organ or Virginal. (2) Dr.
'Joh. Wilson, the public Professor, the best at the
'Lute in all England. He sometimes play'd on
'the Lute, but mostly presided at the Concert. (3)
'        Curteys, a Lutinist, lately ejected from
'some Choire or Cath. Church. After his Majes-
'tie's Restoration he became Gent. or singing-man
'of Ch. Church in Oxon. (4) Tho. Jackson, a
'Bass-Violist; afterwards one of the Choire of S.
'John's Coll. in Oxon. (5) Edw. Low, Organist
'lately of Ch. Church. He play'd only on the
'Organ; so when he performed his part Mr. Ellis
'would take up a Counter-Tenor Viol, and play, if
'any person were wanting to performe that part.
'(6) Gervace Littleton *alias* Westcot, or Westcot
'*alias* Littleton,* a Violist. He was afterwards a
'singing man of S. John's Coll. (7) Will. Glexney,
'who had belonged to a Choire before the Warr.
'He was afterwards a Gent. or singing-man of
'Ch. Ch. He play'd well upon the Bass-Viol, and
'sometimes sung his part. He died 6 Nov. 1692,
'aged 79 or thereabouts. (8)        Proctor, a
'yong man and a new Commer. He died soon
'after. * * * * John Parker, one of the Uni-
'versitie Musitians, would be sometimes among
'them, but Mr. Low, a proud man, could not
'endure any common Musitian to come to the
'Meeting, much less to play among them. Among
'these I must put Joh. Haselwood an Apothecary,
'a starch'd formal Clisterpipe, who usually play'd
'on the Bass-Viol, and sometimes on the Counter-
'Tenor. He was very conceited of his Skil (tho he
'had but little of it) and therefore would be ever
'and anon ready to take up a Viol before his betters:
'which being observed by all, they usually call'd
'him *Handlewood.* * * * *

'- - - - Proctor died in Halywell, and was
'buried in the middle of the church there. He
'had been bred up by M. Joh. Jenkyns, the Mir-
'rour and Wonder of his Age for Music, was ex-
'cellent for the Lyra-Viol and Division-Viol, good
'at the Treble-Viol and Treble-Violin, and all
'comprehended in a man of three or 4 and twentie
'yeares of age. He was much admired at the
'Meetings, and exceedingly pitied by all the faculty
'for his loss.'†

* The grandfather of Littleton, the famous lawyer and judge, temp.
Edw. IV. Thomas de Littleton, took his name from the place of his
birth. He had issue a daughter Elizabeth, his only child, who was
married to Thomas Westcote, Esq. but, as Lord Coke observes, 'she
'being fair, and of a noble spirit, and having large possessions and
'inheritance, resolved to continue the honour of her name; and there-
'fore prudently, whilst it was in her power, provided by Westcote's assent
'before marriage that her issue inheritable should be called by the name
'of de Littleton.' Pref. to Lord Coke's first Institute. And accordingly
Littleton is by Camden, in his Britannia, named Thomas Littleton alias
Westcote. The person above-mentioned was doubtless a descendant of
this family; and hence it appears how long it was before the Littletons
renounced their paternal, in favour of their maternal name, as deeming
the latter the more honourable.

† Life of Anthony à Wood, Oxf. 1772, page 88, et seq.

The state of music in Oxford, the only part of the
kingdom in which during this melancholy period it
could be said to receive any countenance, is farther
related by Wood in the following passages contained
in his life of himself:—

'In the latter end of this yeare, 1657, Davis
'Mell, the most eminent Violinist of London,‡ being
'in Oxon. Peter Pett, Will. Bull, Ken. Digby, and
'others of Allsoules, as also A. W. did give him a
'very handsome entertainment in the Taverne cal'd
'*The Salutation* in S. Marie's parish Oxon. own'd
'by Tho. Wood, son of - - - - Wood of Oxon.
'sometimes servant to the father of A. W. The
'Company did look upon Mr. Mell to have a pro-
'digious hand on the Violin, and they thought that
'no person, as all in London did, could goe beyond
'him. But when Tho. Baltzar, an Outlander, came
'to Oxon. in the next yeare, they had other thoughts
'of Mr. Mell, who tho he play'd farr sweeter than
'Baltzar, yet Baltzar's hand was more quick, and
'could run it insensibly to the end of the Finger-
'board. §

'1658. A. W. entertain'd two eminent Musitians
'of London, named Joh. Gamble and Tho. Pratt,
'after they had entertain'd him with most excellent
'Musick at the Meeting House of Will. Ellis.
'Gamble had obtained a great name among the
'Musitians of Oxon. for his book before publish'd,
'entit. *Ayres and Dialogues to be sung to the
'Theorbo-Lute or Bass-Viol*;‖ the other for se-
'veral compositions; which they played in their
'consorts.

'Tho. Baltzar, a Lubecker borne, and the most
'famous Artist for the Violin that the World had
'yet produced, was now in Oxon. and this day
'A. W. was with him and Mr. Ed. Low, lately
'Organist of Ch. Church, at the Meeting-House of
'Will. Ellis. A. W. did then and there, to his very
'great astonishment, heare him play on the Violin.
'He then saw him run up his Fingers to the end of
'the Finger-board of the Violin, and run them
'back insensibly, and all with alacrity and in very
'good tune, which he nor any in England saw the
'like before. A. W. entertain'd him and Mr. Low
'with what the House could then afford, and after-
'wards he invited them to the Tavern; but they
'being engag'd to goe to other Company, he could
'no more heare him play or see him play at that
'time. Afterwards he came to one of the weekly
'Meetings at Mr. Ellis's house, and he played to the
'wonder of all the auditory: and exercising his
'Fingers and Instrument several wayes to the
'utmost of his power, Wilson thereupon the public
'Professor (the greatest Judg of Musick that ever

‡ Of this person mention is made in the Miscellanies of John Aubrey,
Esq. under the article Miranda. He is there styled the famous Violinist
and Clock maker. The story related by Aubrey is, that a child of his,
crookbacked, was cured by the touching or rubbing of a dead hand. In
the diary of Wood he is called 'Davie or Davis Mell the eminent Violinist
'and Clockmaker.' Life of Wood 1772, pag. 108, in note.

§ Ibid. page 108.

‖ Gamble was one of the playhouse musicians, and of king Charles
the Second's band: he was a man of considerable note in his time. The
words of the above Ayres and Dialogues are supposed to have been
written by Mr. Stanley, author of the History of Philosophy. Vide ante,
page 584.

'was) did, after his humoursome way, stoop downe
'to Baltzar's Feet, to see whether he had a Huff *
'on, that is to say, to see whether he was a Devil or
'not, because he acted beyond the parts of a man.†

'About that time it was, that Dr. Joh. Wilkins,
'Warden of Wadham Coll. the greatest Curioso of
'his time, invited him and some of the Musitians to
'his Lodgings in that Coll. purposely to have a
'consort, and to see and heare him play. The In-
'struments and Books were carried thither, but
'none could be perswaded there to play against
'him in Consort on the Violin. At length the
'Company perceiving A. W. standing behind in a
'corner neare the dore, they haled him in among
'them, and play, forsooth, he must against him.
'Whereupon he being not able to avoid it, he took
'up a Violin, and behaved himself as poor Troylus
'did against Achilles. He was abash'd at it, yet
'honour he got by playing with and against such a
'grand Master as Baltzar was. Mr. Davis Mell
'was accounted hitherto the best for the Violin in
'England, as I have before told you; but after
'Baltzar came into England, and shew'd his most
'wonderful parts on that instrument, Mell was not
'so admired; yet he play'd sweeter, was a well-bred
'Gentleman, and not given to excessive drinking
'as Baltzar was.‡

'All the time that A. W. could spare from his
'beloved Studies of English History, Antiquities,
'Heraldry and Genealogies, he spent in the most
'delightful facultie of Musick, either instrumental
'or vocal: and if he had missed the weekly
'Meetings in the House of Will. Ellis, he could not
'well enjoy himself all the week after. All or
'most of the Company, when he frequented that
'Meeting, the names of them are set downe under
'the yeare 1656. As for those that came in after,
'and were now performers, and with whome A. W.
'frequently playd, were these: (1) Charles Perot,
'M. A. Fellow of Oriel Coll. a well bred Gent.
'and a person of a sweet nature. (2) Christop.
'Harrison, M. A. Fellow of Queen's Coll. a maggot-
'headed person and humourous. He was afterwards
'Parson of Burgh under Staynsmore in Cumberland,
'where he died in the Winter time *an.* 1694. (3)
'Kenelm Digby, Fellow of Alls. Coll. He was
'afterwards LL.Dr. and dying in the said Coll. on
'Munday night Nov. 5. *an.* 1688, was buried in the
'Chappel there. He was a Violinist, and the two
'former Violists. (4) Will. Bull, Mr. of Arts,
'Bach. of Phys. and Fellow of Alls. Coll. for the
'Violin and Viol. He died 15 Jul. 1661. aged 28
'yeares, and was buried in the Chappel there. (5)
'Joh. Vincent, M. A. Fellow of the said Coll.
'a Violist. He went afterwards to the Inns of
'Court, and was a Barrester. (6) Sylvanus Taylor,
'somtimes Com. of Wadh. Coll. afterwards Fellow
'of Allsoules, and Violist and Songster. He went
'afterwards to Ireland, and died at Dublin in the
'beginning of Nov. 1672. His elder brother, capt.
'Silas Taylor, was a Composer of Music, playd and
'sung his part;§ and when his occasions brought

* *i. e.* a hoof.       † Life of Wood, page 111.

‡ Life of Wood, 112.

The account given by Wood of Baltzar may seem a little exaggerated; and, so far as regards his performance, we must take it upon the credit

of the relator; but were it to be judged of by the style and manner of his compositions, of which there are some in print, it must have been admirable. The following Allemand of his is taken from the Division-Violin, part II. published in 1693, and is the first air of the book:—

## ALLEMAND.

THOMAS BALTZAR.

§ Of the elder of these two young men, Silas Domville or D'omville alias Taylor, there is an account in the Athen. Oxon. vol. II. col. 623. He was, by the testimony of Wood, a man of learning and ingenuity, and well versed in the history and antiquities of this country, as appears by a history of Gavelkind written by him, and published in 1663, 4to. He was also well skilled in music. Wood says that he composed two or more anthems, which being sung in his majesty's chapel, and well per-

formed, his majesty was pleased to tell the author he liked them. A composition of his in two parts is printed in Playford's Collection of Court Ayres, &c. He set to music Cowley's translation of an ode of Anacreon, 'The thirsty earth,' &c. for two voices: it is printed in Playford's 'Musical Companion,' edit. 1673, page 78, and wrote also rules for the composition of music, which were never published; a manuscript copy thereof is in the collection of the author of this work. At the

' him to Oxon, he would be at the Musical Meetings,
' and play and sing his part there. (7) Hen. Langley,
' M. A. and Gent. Com. of Wadh. Coll. a Violist and
' Songster. He was afterwards a worthy Knight,
' lived at Abbey-Foriat neare Shrewsbury, where he
' died in 1680. (8) Samuel Woodford, a Commoner
' and M. A. of the said Coll. a Violist.* He was
' afterwards a celebrated Poet, beneficed in Hamp-
' shire, and Prebendary of Winchester. (9) Franc.
' Parry, M. A. Fellow of Corp. Ch. Coll. a Violist
' and Songster. He was afterwards a Traveller, and
' belonged to the Excise Office. (10) Christop.
' Coward, M. A. Fellow of C. C. Coll. He was
' afterwards Rector of Dicheat in his native County
' of Somersetshire, proceeded D. of D. at Oxon. in
' 1694. (11) Charles Bridgeman, M. A. of Queen's
' Coll. and of Kin to Sr. Orlando Bridgeman. He
' was afterwards Archdeacon of Richmond. He died
' 26 Nov. 1678, and was buried in the Chap. belong-
' ing to that Coll. (12) Nathan. Crew, M. A. Fellow
' of Linc. Coll. a Violinist and Violist, but alwaies
' played out of Tune, as having no good eare. He
' was afterwards, thro several Preferments, Bishop of
' Durham. (13) Matthew Hutton, M. A. Fellow of
' Brasnose Coll. an excellent Violist. Afterwards
' Rector of Aynoe in Northamptonshire. (14) Thom.
' Ken of New Coll. a Junior.† He would be some-
' times among them, and sing his part. (15) Christop.
' Jeffryes, a junior Student of Ch. Church, excellent
' at the Organ and Virginals or Harpsichord, having
' been trained up to those Instruments by his Father
' Georg Jeffryes, Steward to the Lord Hatton of
' Kirbie in Northamptonshire, and Organist to K.
' Ch. I. at Oxon. (16) Rich. Rhodes, another junior
' Student of Ch. Church,‡ a confident Westmonas-
' terian, a Violinist to hold between his Knees.

' These did frequent the Weekly Meetings, and
' by the help of publick Masters of Musick, who
' were mixed with them, they were much improv'd.
' Narcissus Marsh, M. A. and Fellow of Exeter

instance of his father he took part with the usurpers, and became a
captain under colonel Edward Massey, and after that a sequestrator for
the county of Hereford, but exercised his power with so much humanity
and courtesy, that he was beloved of all the king's friends.

* Afterwards DD. Upon his leaving the university he went to the
Inner Temple, and was chamber-fellow with Thomas Flatman the poet.
He paraphrased the Psalms and the Canticles ; the former is commended
by Mr. Richard Baxter, and was also the author of a few original poems.
See more of him in Athen. Oxon. vol. II. col. 1098.

† Afterwards bishop of Bath and Wells, and one of the seven bishops
that were sent to the Tower. His conscience not permitting him to
take the oaths at the revolution, he was deprived, and spent the remainder
of his days in retirement. He was so eminently distinguished for piety
and benevolence, that Dryden is said to have intended for him that
character of a good parson, which he has imitated from Chaucer. During
his retreat bishop Ken amused himself with poetry: many of his compositions were published, together with his life, in 1713, by a relation of
his, William Hawkins of the Middle Temple, Esq., and in the Harmonia
Sacra, book II. is an Evening Hymn, written by him and set to music
by Jeremiah Clark.

‡ ' Richard Rhodes, a Gentleman's Son of London, was educated in
' Westminster School, transplanted thence to Ch. Ch. and soon after was
' made Student thereof, being then well grounded in Grammar and in
' the Practical Part of Music. He wrote and composed Flora's Vagaries,
' a Comedy, which, after it had been publickly acted by the Students of
' Ch. Ch. in their common Refectory on the 8th of Jan. 1663, and at the
' Theatre Royal by his Maj. Servants, was made publick at London 1670,
' and afterwards in 1677. This person, who only took one Degree in
' Arts, [at which time he made certain Compositions in Musick of two
' or more Parts, but not as I conceive, extant] went afterwards into
' France, and took, as I have heard, a Degree in Physick at Mountpelier.
' But being troubled with a rambling Head, must needs take a Journey
' into Spain, where, at Madrid, he died, and was buried in 1668.' Athen.
Oxon. vol. II. col. 419.

' Coll.§ would come sometimes among them, but
' seldome play'd, because he had a weekly Meeting
' in his Chamber in the said Coll. where Masters of
' Musick would come, and some of the Company
' before mention'd. When he became Principal of
' S. Alban's hall, he translated the Meeting thither,
' and there it continued when that Meeting in Mr.
' Ellis's house was given over, and so it continued
' till he went into Ireland, and became Mr. of Trin.
' Coll. at Dublin. He was afterwards Archb. of
' Tuam in Ireland.

' After his Majestie's Restoration, when then the
' Masters of Musick were restored to their several
' places that they before had lost, or else if they
' had lost none, they had gotten then preferment, the
' weekly Meetings at Mr. Ellis's house began to
' decay, because they were held up only by Scholars,
' who wanted Directors and Instructors, &c. so that
' in a few yeares after, the Meeting in that house
' being totally layd aside, the chief Meeting was at
' Mr. (then Dr.) Marshe's Chamber, at Exeter Coll.
' and afterwards at S. Alban's hall, as before I have
' told you.

' Besides the Weekly Meetings at Mr. Ellis's
' house, which were first on Thursday, then on Tues-
' day, there were Meetings of the Scholastical Musi-
' cians every Friday Night, in the Winter time, in
' some Colleges: as in the Chamber of Hen. Langley,
' or of Samuel Woodford in Wadham Coll. in the
' Chamber of Christop. Harrison in Queen's Coll. in
' that of Charles Perot in Oriel, in another at New
' Coll. &c. to all which some Masters of Musick
' would commonly retire, as Will. Flexney, Tho.
' Jackson, Gervas Westcote, &c. but these Meetings
' were not continued above 2 or 3 yeares, and I think
' they did not go beyond the yeare 1662.'

## CHAP. CXLIII.

PRYNNE, who in his Histrio-Mastix has made
stage-plays the principal object of his satire, is not
less bitter in his censure of music, especially vocal.
He asserts that one unlawful concomitant of stage-
plays is amourous, obscene, lascivious, lust-provok-
ing songs, and poems, which he says were once so
odious in our church, that in the articles to be
enquired of in visitations, set forth in the first
yeere of queene Elizabeth's raigne, Art. 54, churchwardens were enjoined to enquire ' whether any
' minstrels or any other persons did use to sing or
' say any songs or ditties that be vile and uncleane.'
And as to instrumental music, he cites Clemens
Alexandrinus to prove that ' cymbals and dulcimers
' are instruments of fraud ; that pipes and flutes
' are to be abandoned from a sober feast; and that
' chromaticall harmonies are to be left to impudent
' malapertnesse in wine, to whorish musicke crowned
' with flowers :' with a deal of such nonsense.

In these bitter invectives Prynne does but speak
the language of the sectaries of his time. Gosson

§ Of this person there is a fuller account in Athen. Oxon. vol. II.
col. 960. Among other things there mentioned he is said to have
written ' An introductory Essay to the Doctrine of Sounds,' printed in
the Philosophical Transactions, and of which an account will herein after
be given.

and Stubs talk in the same strain: the latter calls those, baudy pipers and thundering drummers and assistants in the Devil's Daunce, who play to the Lord of Misrule and his company in country towns and villages upon festivals.* The consequence of the hatred excited by these and other writers against the recreations of the people, were an almost total interdiction of stage-plays and other theatrical entertainments,† and such a general reprobation of music, as in a great measure banished it from the metropolis, and drove it, as has been related, to Oxford, where it met with that protection and encouragement which has ever been shown it by men of liberal and ingenious minds.

The necessary connection between dramatic entertainments and music we have hitherto forborne to speak of; reserving the subject for this place. That this connection is nearly as ancient as the drama itself few need be told, it being well known that the scenic representations, as well of the Greeks as Romans, were accompanied with music, both vocal and instrumental. In the old English Moralities, which were dramas of a religious kind, songs were introduced in the course of the representation; thus in the old morality intitled Lusty Juventus, written in the reign of Edward VI. a song is introduced. In the comedy of Gammer Gurton's Needle, the most ancient in our language, the second act begins with a song, which, though it has been greatly corrupted, is at this time not unknown in many parts of England.‡ In the comedy of King Cambises musicians play at the banquet. In the tragedy of Ferrex and Porrex, otherwise called Gorbuduc, written about the year 1556, the order of the dumb show before each act requires severally the music of violins, cornets, flutes, hautboys, and of drums and flutes together. In the Statiro-Mastix or the Untrussing of the humourous Poet, by Thomas Dekker, in the advertisement ad Lectorem it is intimated to have been customary for the trumpet to sound thrice before the beginning of a play. In the Return from Parnassus, act V. begins with a concert. In the pleasant comedy called Wily beguiled, nymphs and satyrs enter singing; and in a word, the plays of Shakespeare, Beaumont and Fletcher, Jonson, and others written before the time of the usurpation, afford such abundant evidence of the union of music with theatrical representations, as proves little less than that they are necessarily co-existent, and that the banishment of the one from the stage was a proscription of the other.

The Restoration was followed by a total change in the national manners; that disgust which the rigour of the preceding times had excited, drove the people into the opposite extreme of licentiousness; so that in their recreations and divertisements they were

* Anatomie of Abuses, page 107.

† There was nevertheless a sort of connivance at these entertainments in favour of friends, and to a limited degree; as in the instance of Sir William Davenant's entertainment at Rutland house, which was patronised by Serjeant Maynard, and of a licence granted in 1659 to Rhodes the bookseller for acting plays at the Cockpit in Drury-lane; but the restraints under which the stage was laid were such, that Whitelocke thought it a bold action of Sir William Davenant to print his entertainment. Vide Whitel. Mem. of Engl. Affairs sub anno 1656.

‡ See it in page 373.

hardly to be kept within the bounds of moderation the theatres, which in the reign of king James I. to speak of London only, were seventeen in number,§

§ The author of the preface to Dodsley's collection of old Plays, has given the following enumeration of as many of them as he was able to recover.

'St. Paul's singing-school, the Globe on the Bankside, Southwark, the 'Swan and the Hope there; the Fortune between Whitecross-street and 'Golden-lane, which Maitland tell us was the first playhouse erected in 'London; the Red Bull in St. John's Street, the Cross-Keys in Grace-'church-street, Juns, the Theatre, the Curtain, the Nursery in Barbican, 'one in Black-Friers, one in White-Friers, one in Salisbury Court, and 'the Cockpit, and the Phœnix in Drury-Lane.'

The same person seems to think that, having continued his account of the English theatre down to the year 1629, it becomes immediately connected with that given by Cibber in his life, which commences a little after the restoration. But in his history there is a chasm, which no one has thought of supplying, so that we can have but a very confused notion of the number and situation of the playhouses in the time of Charles I. But by the help of a pamphlet, now become very scarce, entitled 'Roscius 'Anglicanus or a Historical Review of the Stage,' written by Downes, who at first was an actor in, and afterwards prompter to that which was called the Duke's theatre, we are enabled to connect the two accounts, to correct many mistakes in our theatrical history, which we have hitherto passed unnoticed, and to bring the whole of it into one point of view.

This author relates 'that in the reign of king Charles I. there were 'six playhouses allow'd in town: the Black-Friars Company, his 'Majesty's Servants; the Bull in St. John's Street; another in Salisbury 'Court; another call'd the Fortune; another at the Globe; and the sixth 'at the Cockpit in Drury Lane; all which continu'd acting till the 'beginning of the said Civil Wars. The scattered remnant of several 'of those houses, upon King Charles's Restoration, fram'd a Company, 'who acted again at the Bull, and built them a new house in Gibbons 'Tennis Court in Clare market, in which two places they continu'd acting 'all 1660, 1661, 1662, and part of 1663. In this time they built them a 'new Theatre in Drury Lane; Mr. Thomas Killegrew gaining a Patent 'from the King in order to create them the King's Servants; and from 'that time they call'd themselves his Majesty's Company of Comedians 'in Drury Lane.'

Touching Drury-lane theatre, it may be observed that it was permitted in the time of the usurpation, for Downes in his pamphlet, page 17, says, 'in the year 1659 General Monk marching then his army out of Scotland 'to London, Mr. Rhodes a Bookseller being Wardrobe-keeper formerly '(as I am inform'd) to king Charles the first's Company of Comedians 'in Black Friars, getting a License from the then Governing State, fitted 'up a House then for Acting called the Cock-pit in Drury Lane, and in 'a short time compleated his Company.'

Cibber, in his Apology for his Life, 4to. page 53, 54, says that the patent for Drury-lane was granted to Sir William Davenant, and that another was granted to Henry Killigrew, Esq. for that company of players which was called the Duke's Company, and acted at the Duke's theatre in Dorset Garden. In this he is egregiously mistaken, Sir William Davenant never had any concern in the theatre at Drury-lane, nor had Killigrew any with the Duke's company, who acted first in Lincoln's Inn fields, and afterwards in Dorset Garden. He farther informs us, page 240, that the new theatre in Drury-lane was designed by Sir Christopher Wren. The description he gives of it is such, as joined with our own feelings, must make us regret those alterations in that edifice which the thirst of gain has from time to time suggested to the managers.

Downes mentions that the theatre in Drury-lane opened on Thursday in Easter week, being the eighth day of April, 1663, with the comedy of the Humorous Lieutenant.

The theatre in Drury-lane was called the King's theatre: of that called the Duke's, the following is the history. King Charles I. by his letters patent, bearing date the twenty-sixth day of March, in the fifteenth year of his reign, grants to Sir William Davenant, his heirs and assigns, licence to errect upon a parcel of ground behind the Three Kings ordinary in Fleet-street, in the parish of St. Dunstan in the West, or St. Bride's, London, or in any other place to be assigned him by the Earl Marshall, a theatre or playhouse, forty yards square at the most, wherein plays, musical entertainments, scenes, or other the like presentments may be presented. The patent is extant in Rymer's Fœdera, tom. XX. page 377.

It does not appear that any theatre was erected by Sir William Davenant on the spot described in the above licence; it seems that he engaged with Betterton, who had been an apprentice to Rhodes the bookseller above-mentioned, and was afterwards a player under him, and also with the rest of Rhodes's company, to build one elsewhere. Sir William having thus formed a company of actors, obtained from Charles II. licence to erect a new theatre in Lincoln's Inn fields. Downes says that by this patent Betterton, who was then but twenty-two years of age, and the rest of Rhodes's company were created the King's Servants, and were sworn by the earl of Manchester, then lord chamberlain, to serve his royal highness the duke of York at the theatre in Lincoln's Inn fields. Rosc. Angl. 19.

While this theatre was building, Sir William Davenant wrote the Siege of Rhodes, in two parts, and that excellent comedy the Wits, which were rehearsed at Apothecary's Hall; and upon opening the house in 1662, these were the first plays acted there. Rosc. Angl. 20.

After a few years continuance at Lincoln's Inn fields, Sir William Davenant erected a magnificent theatre in Dorset Garden, in a situation between Salisbury Court, and the Thames, and determined to remove thither with the players under him. But he died in 1668, probably before it was compleated, and his interest in the patent devolved to his widow, lady Davenant, and Mr. Betterton.

Cibber says that the actors both at the King's and the Duke's theatre were, it is true, reduced to two, namely, the King's in Drury-lane, and the Duke of York's in Dorset Garden, but these latter exceeded the former in splendour and magnificence so greatly, that the difference between the one and the other in these respects was immeasurable. The old playhouses were either a large room in a noted alehouse, or a slight erection in a garden or place behind an alehouse; the pit unfloored, in which the spectators either stood, or were badly accommodated with benches to sit on; the music was seldom better than that of a few wretched fiddles, hautboys, or cornets; and to soothe those affections which tragedy is calculated to excite, that of flutes was also made use of: but the music of these several classes of instruments when associated being in the unison, the performance was far different from what we understand by concert and symphony; and upon the whole mean and despicable.

The modern playhouses above-mentioned were truly and emphatically styled theatres, as being constructed with great art, adorned with painting and sculpture, and in all respects adapted to the purposes of scenic representation. In the entertainments there exhibited music was required as a

were masters of their art. In each there were also women; Downes says that four of Sir William Davenant's women actresses were boarded at his own house. Rosc. Angl. 20.

This passage in Downes's narrative ascertains the time when female actors first appeared on the stage. In the infancy of the English theatre it was held indecent for women thus to expose themselves, and, to avoid the scandal thence arising, it was the custom for young men dressed in female habits to perform the parts of women; but this was exclaimed against by puritan writers, particularly Prynne, who in his 'Histrio-Mastix,' page 169, cites St. Chrysostom and other of the fathers to prove that the dressing up a youth to represent the person of a tender virgin, is a most abominable act. So that at this time the former was looked upon as the lesser evil. This gave occasion to Sir William Davenant to solicit for permission to employ females; and accordingly in his patent was the following clause: 'And whereas the women's parts in plays have 'hitherto been acted by men in the habits of women, at which some have 'taken offence, we do permit and give leave, for the time to come, that 'all women's parts be acted by women.'

Cibber relates that in the contest between the two companies for the public favour, that of the king had the advantage; and that therefore, these are his words, 'Sir William Davenant, master of the Duke's 'Company, to make head against their success, was forc'd to add spectacle 'and musick to action; and to introduce a new species of plays, since 'called Dramatick Operas, of which kind there are the Tempest, Psyche, 'Circe, and others, all set off with the most expensive decorations of 'scenes and habits, with the best voices and dancers.' Life of Cibber, 57.

It is to be feared that in this relation Cibber, without recurring to authentic memorials, trusted altogether to the reports of others; for not one of the plays above-mentioned were represented under the direction, or even during the life-time of Sir William. The fact stands thus: Sir William died in 1668; the theatre in Dorset Garden was opened on the ninth day of November, 1671, with the comedy of Saint Martin Marr-all. In 1673 was represented the Tempest, made into an opera by Shadwell, and set to music by Matthew Lock. In February in the same year came forth the opera of Psyche, also written by Shadwell, and set to music by Lock and Sign. Baptist Draghi; and in 1676 was performed Circe, an opera, written by Dr. Charles Davenant, a son of Sir William, and set to music by Mr. John Banister.

These representations are related to have been made at a prodigious expense, in music, dancing, machinery, scenes, and other decorations, and were intended to rival those of the French stage; and some of the best French dancers, namely, L' Abbeè, Balon, and Mademoiselle Subligny, performed at them. At length, in the year 1682, according to Downes, but, as Cibber says, in 1684, the Duke's company not being able to subsist, united with the King's, and both were incorporated by the name of the King's Company of Comedians.

For about ten years that at Drury-lane was the only theatre in London. But Mr. Betterton obtained a licence from king William to erect a theatre within the walls of the tennis court in Lincoln's-Inn fields, and, by the help of a liberal subscription of the nobility and gentry, opened it in 1695, with a new comedy of Mr. Congreve, viz. Love for Love. Cibber's Life, 113, 114.

The theatre in Lincoln's-Inn fields was rebuilt by William Collier, Esq. a lawyer, and member for Truro in Cornwall, and in 1714 opened with the comedy of the Recruiting Officer. The subsequent history of the two theatres, as also the erection of that in the Haymarket, now the Opera-house, are related at large by Cibber in the Apology for his Life.

The patent for Lincoln's Inn fields theatre came afterwards into the hands of Mr. Christopher Rich, whose son, the late Mr. John Rich, built the present theatre in Covent-Garden. Mr. Shepherd was the architect who designed it.

necessary relief, as well to the actors as the audience, between the acts: compositions for this purpose were called Act-tunes, and were performed in concert; instruments were also required for the dances and the accompaniment of songs. Hence it was that, upon the revival of stage-entertainments, music became attached to the theatres, which from this time, no less than, formerly the church had been, became the nurseries of musicians; insomuch, that to say of a performer on any instrument that he was a playhouse musician, or of a song, that it was a playhouse song, or a playhouse tune, was to speak of each respectively in terms of the highest commendation.

It must be confessed that this exaltation of the stage did not immediately follow the restoration: a work of greater importance engaged the attention of all serious men, to wit, the restoration of the liturgy, and the revival of that form of religious worship which had been settled at the reformation, and which by the ordinance that abolished the use of it, and by the preface to the directory substituted in its place, had been stigmatized as vain, superstitious, and idolatrous. In what manner this great purpose was effected, and in particular the methods which were taken to restore cathedral service, will hereafter be related, as will also the prosecution of that design, which has been hinted at in the relation herein before given of an entertainment at Rutland-house, intended by the author, Sir William Davenant, as an imitation of the opera, and the subsequent progress of music in its connection with the drama; but first it will be necessary, by way of explanation of Wood's account of the state of music at Oxford during a period of near twenty years, to describe particularly those concerts which were so well attended, and afforded such entertainment to the members of the university.

## CHAP. CXLIV.

WHAT is to be understood by a concert of viols, such as Wood speaks of, is now hardly known: we are therefore necessitated to recur to a book published by old John Playford in the year 1683, entitled 'An Introduction to the Skill of Music, the tenth 'edition, for a description of the bass, the tenor, and 'the treble viol, with the respective tunings of each;' and from thence we learn that the bass-viol had six strings, the first called the treble; the second the small mean; the third the great mean; the fourth the counter-tenor; the fifth the tenor or gamut string, and the sixth the bass: and that the tuning these was as follows, viz. the first or treble string, D LA SOL RE; the second, A LA MI RE; the third, E LA MI; the fourth, C FA UT; the fifth, GAMUT; and the sixth double D SOL RE.

The Tenor-viol, which also had six strings, was tuned to the same intervals, the sixth or greatest string answering to GAMUT on the bass, and the first to G SOL RE UT on the treble viol, which had its tuning precisely an octave higher than the bass-viol.[*]

* We have here a perfect designation of the order and tuning of a set of viols, and this will explain what is meant by a chest of viols, which generally consisted of six in number, and were used for playing Fantazias

The bass-viol was originally a concert instrument, and used in the performance of Fantazias from two to six parts, but it was frequently played on alone, or as an accompaniment to the voice, in the manner of the lute. In the first case it was called the Concert-viol, in the other the Viol da gamba. It was fretted with more or fewer frets, according to the use to which it was employed; when used in concert, four were generally sufficient, but when alone, or to accompany the voice, seven were requisite.

Concerning compositions of many parts adapted to viols, of which there are many, it is to be observed, that when the practice of singing madrigals began to decline, and gentlemen and others began to excel in their performance on the viol, the musicians of the time conceived the thought of substituting instrumental music in the place of vocal; and for this purpose some of the most excellent masters of that instrument, namely Douland, the younger Ferabosco, Coperario, Jenkins, Dr. Wilson, and many others, betook themselves to the framing compositions called Fantazias, which were generally in six parts, answering to the number of viols in a set or chest, as it is called in the advertisement in the preceding note, and abounded in fugues, little responsive passages, and all those other elegancies observable in the structure and contrivance of the madrigal. In what manner a set of these instruments was tuned for the purpose of performing in concert, has been already mentioned. It now remains to speak of the Bass-viol or Viol da Gamba.

To the instructions respecting the bass, the tenor, and the treble viol contained in the second book of Playford's Introduction, are added brief directions for the treble violin, the tenor violin, and the bass violin, which, as they are each strung with four strings, appear clearly a species separate and distinct from the viol. And here it is to be noted,

that the bass-violin, which is also described by Playford, and had the tuning of its first or highest string, in G sol re ut, its second in C fa ut, and its third in FF fa ut, and its fourth in BB mi, appears clearly to have been an instrument different from the Violoncello, now the associate of the treble and tenor violin in concerts, into which it was first introduced by the Italians. But we are now speaking of the viol species; and of this it is to be observed, that the method of notation proper to it was by the characters common to both vocal and instrumental music, but that about the time of king James I. the notation for the lute called the tablature, was by Coperario transferred to the Bass-viol. The tablature as adapted to the Bass-viol consisted in a stave of six lines, representing the six strings of the instrument, with letters of an antique form, signifying the place of the tones and semitones on each string. The first of these methods was calculated for the performance on the viol in concert. the compositions for that instrument called Fantazias being uniformly written in the notes of the Gamut. The Lyra-way,* as it was called, was adapted to the tablature, and by that method the viol was rendered capable, without a variation of the characters, of performing lute lessons.

In either way the instrument, consisting of six strings, was tuned according to the following directions of Playford: ' The treble, being raised as high ' as it will conveniently bear, is called D la sol re; ' then tune your second four notes lower, and it is ' A la mi re; the third four notes lower, is E la mi; ' the fourth three notes lower is C fa ut; the fifth ' four notes lower is Gamut; and the sixth four ' notes lower than the fifth, is double D sol re.'† The instrument being fretted with five frets for the first or treble string, and four for each of the others, the progression on each string will be as follows:—

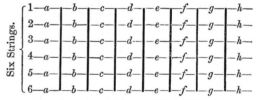

Open   First   Second   Third   Fourth   Fifth   Sixth   7th Fret.

The frets which cross the stave in the above example, together with the letters adjoining to them, determine the station of the tones and semitones on each string; thus, to instance in the first string, *a* stands for D, which has the sound for the string open or unstopped; *b* for D , *c* for E, *d* for F, *e* for F♯, *f* for G, *g* for G♯, and *h* for A; and this explanation will apply to the other strings on the instrument. As to the frets, they were nothing more than pieces of very small catgut string dipped in warm glue and tied round the neck of the instru-

in six parts. To this purpose old Thomas Mace of Cambridge speaks, in that singularly humorous book of his writing, 'Musick's Monument.' page 245. 'Your best provision (and most compleat) will be a good ' chest of viols, six in number (viz.) 2 Basses, 2 tenors, and 2 trebles, all ' truly and proportionably suited. Of such there are no better in the ' world than those of Aldred, Jay, Smith, yet the highest in esteem are ' Bolles and Ross (one bass of Bolles's I have known valued at 100*l*.) ' these were old, but we have now very excellent workmen, who (no ' doubt) can work as well.'

In a collection of airs, entitled 'Tripla Concordia, published in 1667 ' by John Carr, living at the Middle Temple gate in Fleet Street,' is the following advertisement:—

'There is two Chests of Viols to be sold, one made by Mr. John Ross, ' who formerly lived in Bridewell, containing two trebles, three tenors, ' and one bass: the chest was made in the year 1298.

'The other being made by Mr. Henry Smith, who formerly lived over- ' against Hatton-house in Holbourn, containing two trebles, two tenors, ' two basses. The chest was made in the year 1633. Both chests are ' very curious work.'

The John Ross mentioned in the above advertisement, was the son of the person mentioned in the Annals of Stowe by the name of John Rose, to have invented 4to. Eliz. the instrument called the Bandora. See page 493, in not.

Concerts of viols were the usual entertainments after the practice of singing madrigals grew into disuse: and these latter were so totally excluded by the introduction of the violin, that, at the beginning of this century, Dr. Tudway of Cambridge was but just able to give a description of a chest of viols, as appears by the following extract from a letter to his son, written for the purpose of instructing him in music:—

'A chest of viols was a large hutch, with several apartments and ' partitions in it; each partition was lined with green bays, to keep the ' instruments from being injured by the weather; every instrument was ' sized in bigness according to the part played upon it; the least size ' played the treble part, the tenor and all other parts were played by a ' larger sized viol; the bass by the largest size. They had six strings ' each, and the necks of their instruments were fretted. Note, I believe ' upon the treble-viol was not higher than G or A in alt, which is nothing ' now.'

* Playford calls the method of playing on the Bass-viol by the Tablature the Lyra-way, and the instrument played on in this manner the Lyra-viol. Introduction to the Skill of Musick, page 96, 87, edit. 1683.

† The six lines above, as they answer to the strings of the instrument, have not the least relation to the stave of Guido; the letters and not the lines represent the notes in succession; and as to the characters to denote their several lengths, they are referred to above.

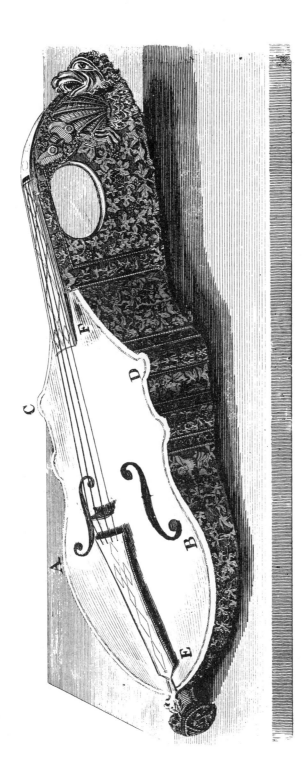

ment, at proper distances; and in stopping them it was required that the extremity of the finger should be behind, but in immediate contact with the fret.

The notation by the tablature determines nothing as to the time or value of notes, and therefore requires the aid of other characters for this purpose; those in use when the viol was in greatest esteem were such as were originally adapted to the tablature for the lute, and are described in page 419. But afterwards they were changed to those characters that are used in the notation according to the Gamut.*

It has already been mentioned that the practice of singing madrigals, which had prevailed for many years throughout Europe, gave way to concerts of viols, such as are above described; but the languor of these performances, which consisted of Fantazias of five and six parts, was not compensated by that sweet and delicate tone which distinguishes the viol species; the violin, though it had long been in the hands of the vulgar,† and had been so degraded that the appellation of Fiddler was a term of reproach, was found to be an instrument capable of great improvement; and the softness and delicacy of the violin tone, and the occasional force and energy of the instrument itself, were such recommendations of it as determined the Italian masters, about the beginning of the seventeenth century, to introduce it into practice.

The treble violin, the tenor violin, and the violoncello, have a necessary connection with each other, and form a species of fidicinal instruments distinct from that of the viol: the introduction of these into concerts is therefore to be considered as a new era in musical history, and may justify a retrospect to the circumstances that preceded and contributed to this event.

What kind of an instrument the ancient violin or fiddle mentioned by Chaucer was, we are at a loss at this distance of time to discover; but what the fiddle was about the year 1530, appears by the figure of it in the Musurgia of Ottomarus Luscinius, hereinbefore exhibited. Notwithstanding this certainty, there is good reason to suppose that towards the end of the sixteenth centry the shape of it was rather vague and undetermined, for at a sale by auction of the late duke of Dorset's effects, a violin was bought, appearing to have been made in the year 1578, which, though of a very singular form, and encumbered with a profusion of carving, was essentially the very same instrument with the four-

stringed violin, as appears by the following representation of it :—‡

To the above engraving, taken immediately from the instrument itself, a verbal description of it will be deemed but a necessary adjunct.

The dimensions of the instrument are as follow. From the extremity of the tail-pin to the dragon's head, two feet. From A to B seven inches and a half. From C to D six inches. Length of the belly thirteen inches. Thickness at E one inch, at F four and a half. Over the pins is a silver gilt plate, that turns upon a hinge, and opens from the nut downwards; thereon are engraved the arms of England, and under them, encircled by a garter with the usual motto, the bear and ragged staff,§ and an earl's coronet at top; in the tail-pin is inserted a gilt silver stud, to which the tail-piece is looped, with a lion's face curiously wrought on the top; this is secured by a nut, which screws to it on the under side of the instrument, whereon are engraven these letters and figures I $\frac{15}{78}$ P supposed to signify the year when it was made, and the initials of the maker's name. The subject of the carving on the deepest part, and on the side above presented to view, is a man with an axe, standing on the ground, and working upon some fallen branches of an oak tree: on the opposite part are represented hogs under an oak tree, and a man beating down acorns; the rest of the carving is foliage; the whole is in alto relievo. Under the carving is a foil of tinsel or silver gilt. The back of the instrument is not curved, but forms a very obtuse angle; and from the bottom of the back, extending to the back of the dragon's head, the carving, which is very bold, consists of oak foliage.

Notwithstanding the exquisite workmanship of it, the instrument produces but a close and sluggish tone, which considering the profusion of ornament, and the quantity of wood with which it is incumbered, is not to be wondered at.

But, notwithstanding the diversities in the shape of the violin at different periods, that the modern violin had assumed the form which it now bears, almost as early as the beginning of the seventeenth century, is indisputable, for of the violins of Cremona, so long celebrated for the beauty of their shape and fineness of tone,‖ there are great numbers that

---

* These have been considerably improved both in England and Holland since their first invention, for originally the quavers and semiquavers, though ever so numerous in succession, were all distinct; but about the year 1660 Playford invented what he called the new tyed note, wherein by one or two strokes continued from the bottom of each note to the next, the quavers and semiquavers were formed into compages of four or six, as the time required, a contrivance that rendered the musical characters much more legible than before. The Dutch followed this example soon after the English had set it; and afterwards the French, and after them the Germans; but so lately as the year 1724, when Marcello's Psalms were published in a splendid edition at Venice, the Italians printed after the old manner, and so did the Spaniards till within these very few years.

† Dr. Tudway, in his letter to his son, says that within his remembrance it was scarce ever used but at wakes and fairs, and that those who played on it travelled about the country with their instrument in a cloak-bag.

‡ A larger plate of this instrument will be found in the Supplementary Volume of Portraits.

§ The bear and ragged staff was the cognizance of the Nevils earls of Warwick. Robert Dudley, earl of Leicester, who derived his pedigree from them, took it for his crest. See Fuller's Worthies in Warwickshire, 118. This agrees with a tradition concerning it, that the instrument was originally queen Elizabeth's, and that she gave it to her favourite the earl of Leicester, which is not improbable, seeing that her arms are also upon it.

‖ There were three persons of the name of Amati, natives of Cremona, and makers of violins, that is to say, Andrew, Jerome, and Antony his

appear to have been made before year 1620, and yet it does not appear that the violin was used in concert till some years after.

Scipione Cerreto, in his treatise De Prattica musicale, enumerates the many excellent composers and performers on various instruments living at Naples in the year 1601; and it is worthy of note that among the latter are mentioned only Sonatori excellenti del Liuto, d'Organo, di Viola d'arco, di Chittara a sette chorde, di Lira in gamba, di Tromboni, di Ciaramelle e Cornetti, and dell' Arpa à due ordini, from whence it may be inferred that at that time the violin in Italy, as in England and other countries, was an instrument of little account, and deemed fit only for the entertainment of the vulgar; nevertheless we find that in a very few years after it rose so high as to be admitted into the theatre: indeed it may be said to be coeval with the opera itself. It has already been mentioned that the most ancient opera in print is the Orfeo of Claudio Monteverde, represented at Mantua in 1607, and published at Venice in 1615; to this is prefixed the personages of the drama, and the names and numbers of the instruments used in the performance; and among the latter occur duoi Violini piccoli alla Francese: now the diminutive, piccoli, supposes an instrument of the same species, of a larger size than itself, i. e. a violin; but this it seems was not admitted into the performance, perhaps for this reason, that the Viola da brazzo, i. e. the treble viol, held its place: and if it be asked what then was the use of the Violino piccoli? it may be answered, perhaps for a particular accompaniment, the imitation of the singing of birds for instance; or for a like purpose as the Flauto alla vigessima seconda, viz. a treble octave flute. However it is certain that at the beginning of the sixteenth century the practice of the violin was cultivated in Italy with uncommon assiduity; so that in a few years after it became the principal of concert instruments. From Italy it passed into France, and from thence into England. At first it was used in accompaniment with the voice, and was confined to the theatre; but the good effects of it, in giving to the melody a force and expression which was wanting in the sound of the voice, and extending the limits of the harmony in the chorus, recommended it also to the church.

The motetts and hymns that made a part of divine service, had hitherto been composed for voices, with no other accompaniment than that of the organ; and this kind of music, which corresponds with the practice of the primitive church, is still retained in the pope's chapel; but no sooner were the advantages discovered that resulted from the union of voices and instruments, than all the objections arising from the seeming profanation of the temples of God, by admitting into them such instruments as had hitherto been appropriated to theatrical representations, vanished.

This innovation gave rise to a new church-style, in which the principal end of the composer was rather to display the excellencies of either some fine singer or instrumental performer, than to inspire the auditory with those sentiments which should accompany divine worship. For examples of this kind we need look no farther than the motets of Carissimi, Colonna, and Bassani, in which the solo vocal parts are wrought up to the highest degree of perfection; and the instrumental accompaniments abound with divisions calculated to shew the powers of execution in the performers.

Whether vocal music gains more than it loses by being associated with such instruments as it is usually joined with, may admit of a question: it is universally agreed, that of all music that of the human voice is the sweetest; and it may be remarked, that in a chorus of voices and instruments the sounds never coalesce or blend together in such a manner, as not to be distinguishable by the ear into two species; while in a chorus of voices alone, well sorted, and perfectly in tune, the aggregate of the whole is that full and complete union and consent, which we understand by the word Harmony, as applied to music. On the other hand it may be said that what is wanting in harmony is made up by the additional force and energy which is given to vocal music by its union with that of instruments; but it is worthy of consideration whether music, the end whereof is to inspire devotion, stands in need of such aids, or rather indeed whether such aids have not a tendency to defeat its end.

This at least is certain, that the theatric and ecclesiastic styles are discriminated by the very nature and tendency of each, and that the confusion of the one with the other has for upwards of a century been considered by the ablest defenders of choral service as one of the great abuses of music.

## CHAP. CXLV.

It is now time to speak of the revival of choral service upon the restoration of king Charles the Second. At this time no more than nine of the bishops of the church of England were living; these immediately on the king's return took possession of their respective bishoprics; and such sees as were vacant were immediately filled up, either by translations or new appointments. The sequestered clergy severally entered upon the livings which they had been ejected from, and dispossessed the incumbents whom they found there. Heads and fellows of colleges were also reinstated, and the government and discipline of the church were reduced to the legal form.

No sooner was the liturgy re-established, than

sons, and Nicolas, the son of the latter. Andrew flourished about the year 1600.

Besides these there were two persons of the name of Stradivarius of Cremona, admirable artisans; the latter was living at the beginning of this century: his signature was 'Antonius Stradivarius Cremonensis Faciebat Anno          A†S.'

Andrew Guarnier, also of Cremona, signed thus, 'Andreas Guarnerius, 'fecit Cremonœ sub titulo Sancta Teresæ, 1680.'

The violins of Cremona are exceeded only by those of Stainer, a German, whose instruments are remarkable for a full and piercing tone; his signature is as follows:—

'Jacobus Stainer, In Absam prope Oenipontum 1647.' Oenipons is the Latin name of Insprunck in Germany, the chief city of Tyrol.

Matthew Albani, also a Tyrolese, signed thus 'Matthias Albanus fecit in Tyrol Bulsani 1654.'

the bishops and clergy became sensible of the necessity of reviving the choral service; but here they were greatly at a loss. By an ordinance made in the year 1644, organs in churches and chapels had been commanded to be taken down;* and the fury of the rabble was not less remarkable in their demolition, than in that impious zeal which prompted them to despoil churches of their ornaments, and, as far as it was in their power, by the destruction of funeral monuments, to efface from the remembrance of mankind those virtues of the illustrious dead, which it is the end of monuments and sepulchral inscriptions to perpetuate.

Organs being thus destroyed, and the use of them forbidden in England, the makers of those instruments were necessitated to seek elsewhere than in the church for employment; many went abroad, and others betook themselves to such other occupations for a livelihood, as were nearest related to their own; they became joiners and carpenters, and mixed unnoticed with such as had been bred up to those trades; so that, excepting Dallans, Loosemore of Exeter, Thamar of Peterborough, and Preston of York, there was at the time of the restoration scarce an organ-maker that could be called a workman in the kingdom. Some organs had been taken down, and sold to private persons, and others had been but partially destroyed; these, upon the emergency that called for them, were produced, and the artificers above named were set to work to fit them up for use; Dallans indeed was employed to build a new organ for the chapel of St. George at Windsor, but, whether it was through haste to get it finished, or some other cause, it turned out, though a beautiful structure, but an indifferent instrument.

The next step towards the revival of cathedral service, was the appointment of skilful persons for organists and teachers of music in the several choirs of the kingdom; a few musicians of eminence, who had served in the former capacity under the patronage of Charles I. namely Child, Christopher Gibbons, Rogers, Wilson, Low, and others, though advanced in years, were yet living; these were sought out and promoted; the four first named were created doctors, and Child, Gibbons, and Low were appointed organists of the royal chapel; Gibbons was also made master of the children there, and organist of Westminster Abbey. Rogers, who had formerly been organist of Magdalen college at Oxford, was preferred to Eton; Wilson had a place both in the chapel and in Westminster choir; and Albertus Bryne was made organist of St. Paul's.

By this method of appointment the choirs were provided with able masters; but great difficulties, arising from the late confusion of the times, and the long intermission of choral service, lay behind. Cathedral churches, from the time of the suppression of monasteries, had been the only seminaries for the instruction of youth in the principles of music; and as not only the revenues appropriated for this purpose were sequestered, but the very institution itself was declared to be superstitious, parents were deprived both of the means and the motives to qualify their children for choral duty, so that boys were wanting to perform those parts of the service which required treble voices. Nay, to such streights were they driven, that for a twelvemonth after the restoration the clergy were forced to supply the want of boys by cornets,† and men who had feigned voices. Besides this, those of riper years, whose duty it had been to perform choir service, namely, the minor canons and lay-clerks of the several cathedrals, had upon their ejection betaken themselves to other employments; some went into the king's army, others taught the lute and virginals; and others psalmody, to those whose principles restrained them from the use of any other music in religious worship.

In consequence hereof, and of that inaptitude which follows the disuse of any faculty, when the church-service was revived, there were very few to be found who could perform it; for which reason the universities, particularly that of Oxford, were very sedulous in their endeavours to promote the study of practical music: and, to render the church-service familiar, a book, written by Edward Low, was printed at Oxford in 1661, entitled ' Some short directions for the performance of Cathedral Service.' This Edward Low‡ came from Salisbury, having been brought up under John Holmes, the organist of that cathedral. In the year 1630 he

---

* The words of the ordinance are ' all organs, and the frames or cases ' wherein they stand, in all churches and chappels [i. e. cathedral, 'collegiate, or parish churches or chappels] shall be taken away and ' utterly defaced, and none other hereafter set up in their places.' Scobell's Collection of Arts, 1651, page 181. *Bishop Sanderson, in one of his sermons, says, that the Puritans objected to the use of instrumental music in divine worship, deeming it unlawful: this opinion was adopted by the Nonconformists at the Restoration, and in general seems to be still retained by them. At the close of the last century, upon occasion of erecting an organ in a parish church at Tiverton, in the county of Devon, a sermon was preached by one Mr. Newte, which was remarked on in an anonymous pamphlet, entitled ' a letter to a friend in the country concerning the use of instrumental music in the worship of God, 4to. 1698. To this letter the preacher replied in the preface to a treatise by the learned Mr. Dodwell on the lawfulness of instrumental music in holy offices, 8vo. 1700. The preface and the tract that follows it contain a full and decisive vindication of the practice in question, and so far prevailed with some of the more moderate of the Dissenters, that Dr. Edmund Calamy was once heard to say that in his Meeting Place in Long Ditch, Westminster, he should have no objection to the erection of an organ.*

† These instruments had been introduced into the choral service before, for in the Statutes of Canterbury Cathedral, provision is made for players on sackbuts and cornets. And the same appears by the following passage in the Life of Archbishop Whitgift, as given in the Biographia Britannica, page 4255, respecting the service at Canterbury Cathedral. ' There happily ' landed an intelligencer from Rome, who wondered to see an Archbishop or ' Clergyman in England so reverenced and attended, and being present also ' the Sunday following at service at the Cathedral in Canterbury, where ' seeing his grace attended with his gentlemen and servants, as also the Dean, ' Prebendaries, and Preachers, in their Surplices and scarlet hoods, and ' hearing the solemn music, with the voices and organs, cornets and sackbuts, ' he was struck with amazement and admiration, and declared that they ' were led in great blindness at Rome by our own nation, who made the ' people there believe, that there was not in England either Archbishop or ' Bishop, or Cathedral or any church or Ecclesiastical government; but that ' all was pulled down to the ground, and that the people heard their Minister ' in woods and fields, among trees and brute beasts; but for his own part he ' protested that, unless it were in the Pope's chapel, he never saw a more ' solemn sight, or heard a more heavenly sound.' And we are told that at the churching of the queen, after the birth of lady-Mary, daughter of James I. in the Royal Chapel sundry Anthems were sung with organ, cornets, sackbuts, and other excellent instruments of music. Vide Stow's Annals, 864. Lastly Charles I. when at Oxford, had service at the Cathedral with organs, sackbuts, recorders, cornets, &c. From a tract entitled ' The well tuned Organ,' by Joseph Brookband, 4to, 1660.

‡ Of this person mention has already been made. Vide ante pag. 584 et 681, and Wood in his life takes frequent occasion to speak of him.

Soon after the restoration he was appointed one of the organists of the chapel royal. He died on the eleventh of July, 1682, and was buried at the upper end of the divinity chapel, on the north side of the cathedral of Christ Church, near to the body of Alice, his sometime wife, daughter of Sir John Peyton the younger, of Doddington in the Isle of Ely, Knight. Fasti, vol. I. coll. 178. Henry Purcell succeeded him in the place of organist of the royal chapel, July 14, 1682, as appears by the Cheque-Book.

succeeded Dr. Stonard as organist of Christ Church, Oxford. He was also for some years deputy music professor for Dr. Wilson, but, upon Wilson's leaving the university, was appointed professor in his own right. Wood says that though not a graduate, he was esteemed a very judicious man in his profession. Fasti, vol. I. col. 178. The book above-mentioned was again published in duodecimo, anno 1664, under the title of 'A Review of some short directions for performance of Cathedral Service,' with a dedication to Dr. Walter Jones, subdean of the chapel royal, and a preface, addressed to all gentlemen that are true lovers of cathedral service, wherein he informs them, which is strictly true, that the versicles, responses, and single tunes of the reading psalms then in use, and which he has published, are exactly the same that were used in the time of Edward VI., for which he refers to another copy, printed anno 1550, which can be no other than the book entitled 'The Booke of Common Praier noted,' by John Marbeck, of which an account has herein before been given.

As the formulary contained in this book of Low is adapted to the liturgy established in the reign of queen Elizabeth, and continued, with a few inconsiderable variations, to this time, it necessarily follows that it must differ in many respects from that of Marbeck, which was adapted to the common prayer of Ewd. VI. To enumerate all the particulars in which they differ will hardly be thought necessary; it may suffice to say that the versicles and responses are very nearly the same in each: besides these, the author has inserted a variety of chanting tunes for the Psalms, Venite exultemus, &c. some of which it is conjectured were composed by Dr. Child, of Windsor, as is also a Te Deum of four parts in counterpoint, there also given. The litany seems to be that of Tallis in four parts :* it is followed by a burial service in four parts of Mr. Robert Parsons, and a Veni Creator, the author unknown, which concludes the book.

The places of organist and master of the children in the several cathedrals were no sooner filled up with able men, than those on whom they were bestowed, as also the gentlemen of the king's chapel, laboured incessantly in the composition of services and anthems; thereby endeavouring to make up the loss which church-music had sustained in the preceding period of near twenty years, so that in the short space of two years a great number of each were composed by them, as appears by James Clifford's Collection of divine Services and Anthems usually sung in his Majesties Chappell, and in all the Cathedrals and Collegiate Choires of England and Ireland. Lond. 1664, duod.

This James Clifford was a native of Oxford, being born in the parish of St. Mary Magdalen there. He was educated in Magdalen college school, and became a chorister of that college, but took no degree in the university of Oxford. After the restoration he was a minor canon of St. Paul's cathedral, and reader in some church near Carter-

*It is Tallis only in part.*

lane; and after that chaplain to the honourable society of Serjeants-Inn in Fleet-street, London.[†] He died about the year 1700, leaving a widow, who survived him some years; she dwelt in Wardrobe-court, in Great Carter-lane, London, and had a daughter, who taught a school of little children.[‡] Besides the above collection, he published a Catechism, and a preparation Sermon; and these seem to be the whole of his writings.

To the collection of Services and Anthems above-mentioned is a dedication to Dr. Walter Jones, subdean of the chapel royal, and two prefaces, the one whereof seems to have been published with an earlier edition of the book, the other containing chanting tunes for the Venite, Te Deum, Benedicite, Jubilate, Magnificat, Cantate Domino, Nunc Dimittis, Deus Misereatur, the Psalms, and Quicunque vult.. After these follow 'Brief directions for the 'understanding of that part of the divine service 'performed with the organ in St. Paul's cathedral 'on Sundayes, &c.' The particulars most worthy of regard among these directions are the following : 'After the Psalms, a voluntary upon the organ 'alone.' 'After the third collect "O Lord our "heavenly father, &c." is sung the first anthem.' 'After the blessing "The grace of our Lord Jesus "Christ, &c" a voluntary alone upon the organ.§ In the second or communion service nothing remarkable occurs ; but after the sermon follows another anthem, which concludes the morning service.

At evening service, 'After the psalms a voluntary 'alone by the organ.' After the third collect, "Lighten our darkness, &c." is sung the first, and "after the sermon the last anthem.'

At the end of the book is a short address to the reader, in which it is intimated that the best musicians of later times had found it expedient to reduce the six syllables used in solmisation to four, by permutation of UT, RE, into SOL, LA. At the end of this postscript the author professes to exhibit a table, containing, as he terms it, 'that very basis or foun-'dation of music which had long before been com-'piled for the instruction of youth in the rudiments 'of musick, by that most worthy and excellent 'author thereof, Ralph Winterton, Dr. of Physick 'and Regius Professor of the same in the university 'of Cambridge, in his own words and methode ;' 'but, by some unaccountable mistake, this table or basis, whatever it be, is omitted in all the copies of the book that have come to our hands, and instead thereof is inserted 'A Psalm of Thanksgiving to be 'sung by the Children of Christ's Hospital on 'Monday and Tuesday in Easter holydaies at St.

† Athen. Oxon. vol. II. col. 1019.

‡ These particulars were communicated by a person now living, who was one of the daughter's little pupils, and, though turned of fourscore, retains a remembrance of his person.

§ This was the usage in cathedrals for many years, but in some, particularly St. Paul's and Canterbury, and at Westminster, the practice has been, and still is, instead of a voluntary, to sing the Sanctus to solemn music in the interval between morning prayer, concluding with the Benediction, and the second or communion service, which is certainly a change for the better. In the Temple church, which by the way is neither a cathedral nor parochial church, a voluntary is introduced in this part of the service, but at no other in London.

' Maries Spittle, for their founders and benefactors,
' composed to Music by Thomas Brewer.'

This book, as it contains not the music, but only
the words of the services and anthems in use at the
time of its publication, is so far at least valuable, as
it serves to show what was the stock of music which
the church set out upon at the restoration, as also
who were the composers of greatest eminence in that
and the preceding time. The names that occur in
this collection are, William Bird, Thomas Tallis,
Thomas Weelks, Richard Farrant, Edmund Hooper,
William Mundy, John Shepherd, Orlando Gibbons,
Adrian Batten, Dr. Tye, Robert White, Dr. Giles,
Robert Parsons, Thomas Morley, John Ward, John
Hilton, Dr. Bull, Richard Price, Albertus Bryne, or-
ganist of St. Paul's cathedral; Michael East, Henry
Lawes, Henry Smith, Mr. Cob, Henry Molle, Mr.
Johnson, Thomas Tomkyns, Christ. Gibbons, Law-
rence Fisher, Mr. Stonard, Henry Loosemore, Mr.
Jeffries, Randolph Jewett, Mr. Bennett, Mr. Wil-
kinson, Mr. Gibbs, John Amner, John Holmes, Mr.
Coste, Mr. Cranford, Dr. Wilson, Richard Gibbs,
organist of Christ Church in Norwich; Mr. Wig-
thorpe, Leonard Woodson, Richard Hutchinson, Mr.
Rogers, Martin Peerson, Mr. Mudde, John Heath,
Dr. Child, Edward Smith, Peter Stringer, organist
of Chester cathedral; Richard Hinde, Richard Portman, George Mason, John Hingestone, Richard
Carre, Giles Tomkins, William Lawes, Edward
Low, Pelham Humfrey, John Blow, and Robert
Smith, the three latter children of his majesty's
chapel; Henry Cook, Esq., master of the children,
and one of the gentlemen of his majesty's chapel
royal; Matthew Lock, Esq. Sir William Leighton,
Robert Jones, Alphonso Ferabosco.

The number of workmen in England being found
too few to answer the demand for organs, it was
thought expedient to make offers of encouragement
for foreigners to come and settle here; these brought
over from Germany Mr. Bernard Schmidt and
Harris; the former of these, for his excellence in
his art, and the following particulars respecting him,
deserves to live in the remembrance of all such as
are friends to it.

BERNARD SCHMIDT, (a Portrait), or, as we pronounce the name, Smith, was a native of German,
but of what city or province in particular is not
known. Upon the invitations of foreign workmen
to settle here, he came into England, and brought
with him two nephews, the one named Gerard, the
other Bernard; and, to distinguish him from these,
the elder had the appellation of Father Smith. Immediately upon their arrival Smith was employed
to build an organ for the royal chapel at Whitehall,
but, as it was built in great haste, it did not answer
the expectations of those who were judges of his
abilities. He had been but a few months here
before Harris arrived from France, bringing with
him a son named Renatus, who had been brought up
in the business of organ-making under him; they
met with little encouragement, for Dallans and
Smith had all the business of the kingdom; but

upon the decease of Dallans in 1672,* a competition
arose between these two foreigners, which was attended with some remarkable circumstances. The
elder Harris was in no degree a match for Smith,
but his son Renatus was a young man of ingenuity
and spirit, and succeeded so well in his endeavours
to rival Smith, that at length he got the better of
him.

The contest between Smith and the younger
Harris was carried on with great spirit; each had
his friends and supporters, and the point of preference between them was hardly determined by
that exquisite piece of workmanship of Smith, the
organ now standing in the Temple church; of the
building thereof the following is the history, as
related by a person who was living at the time, and
intimately acquainted with both Smith and Harris.

' Upon the decease of Mr. Dallans and the elder
' Harris, Mr. Renatus Harris and Father Smith
' became great rivals in their employment, and
' several tryals of skill there were betwixt them on
' several occasions; but the famous contest between
' these two artists was at the Temple church, where
' a new organ was going to be erected towards the
' latter end of K. Charles the second's time : both
' made friends for that employment; but as the
' society could not agree about who should be the
' man, the Master of the Temple and the Benchers
' proposed they both should set up an organ on each
' side of the church, which in about half a year or
' three quarters of a year was done accordingly;
' Dr. Blow and Mr. Purcell, who was then in his
' prime, shewed and played Father Smith's organ on
' appointed days to a numerous audience; and, till
' the other was heard, every body believed that
' Father Smith certainly would carry it.

' Mr. Harris brought Mr. Lully,† organist to
' Queen Catherine, a very eminent master, to touch
' his organ, which brought Mr. Harris's organ into
' that vogue; they thus continued vying with one
' another near a twelvemonth.

' Then Mr. Harris challenged Father Smith to
' make additional stops against a set time; these
' were the Vox-humane, the Cremona or Violin
' stop, the double Courtel or bass Flute, with some
' others I may have forgot.

' These stops, as being newly invented, gave great
' delight and satisfaction to the numerous audience;
' and were so well imitated on both sides, that it
' was hard to judge the advantage to either. At last
' it was left to my Lord Chief Justice Jeffries, who
' was of that house, and he put an end to the con-
' troversy by pitching upon Father Smith's organ;
' so Mr. Harris's organ was taken away without loss
' of reputation,‡ and Mr. Smith's remains to this

* An inscription on a stone in the old church of Greenwich ascertained
nearly the time of his death; Strype gives it in these words: ' Ralph
' Dallans, Organ-maker, deceased while he was making this organ;
' begun by him Feb. 1672. James White his partner finished it, and
' erected this stone 1673.' Circuit Walk. Greenwich. The organ at
New College, Oxford, as also that in the music-school there, were made
by Dallans.

† Qy. Draghi, whose christian name Baptist, might mislead Dr. Tudway,
the author of this account,

‡ Harris's organ was afterwards purchased for the cathedral of Christ
Church at Dublin, and set up there; but about twenty years ago Mr.

'day.***** Now began the setting up of organs 'in the chiefest parishes of the city of London, where 'for the most part Mr. Harris had the advantage of 'Father Smith, making I believe two to his one; 'among them some are reckoned very eminent, viz. 'the organ at Saint Bride's, Saint Lawrence near 'Guildhall, Saint Mary Ax, &c. *

Notwithstanding the success of Harris, Smith was considered as an able and ingenious workman; and, in consequence of this character, he was employed to build an organ for the cathedral of St. Paul;† *in which undertaking he narrowly escaped being a great sufferer, for on the 27th day of February, 1699, a fire broke out in a little room, at the west end of the North aisle of the church, enclosed for the organ builder's men, which communicating itself towards the organ, had probably consumed the same and endangered at least one side of the choir; but it was timely extinguished, though not without damage to two of the pillars and some of the fine carving by Gibbons. Vide New View of London, 457. The vulgar report was, that the Plumbers or some others employed in soldering or repairing the metal pipes, had been negligent of their fire; but the true cause of the accident was never discovered. The organs made by Smith,* though in respect of the workmanship they are far short of those of Harris, and even of Dallans, are justly admired, and for the fineness of their tone have never yet been equalled.*

The name of Smith occurs in the lists of the chapel establishment from 1703 to 1709, inclusive, as organ-maker to the chapel, and also to queen Anne. He had a daughter, married to Christopher Schrider, a workman of his, who about the year 1710 succeeded him in his places.‡

The organ of St. Paul's, erected soon after the

year 1700, had established the character of Smith as an artist; whether Harris had been his competitor for building an instrument for that church, as he had been before at the Temple, does not now appear; but in the Spectator, No. 552, for December 3, 1712, is a recommendation of a proposal of Mr. Renatus Harris, organ-builder, in these words: 'The ambition of this artificer is to errect an organ in St. 'Paul's cathedral, over the west door, at the entrance 'into the body of the church, which in art and 'magnificence shall transcend any work of that kind 'ever before invented. The proposal in perspicuous 'language sets forth the honour and advantage such 'a performance wou'd be to the British name, as 'well that it would apply the power of sounds in 'a manner more amazingly forcible than perhaps 'has yet been known, and I am sure to an end 'much more worthy. Had the vast sums which 'have been laid out upon operas without skill or 'conduct, and to no other purpose but to suspend or 'vitiate our understandings, been disposed this way, 'we should now perhaps have an engine so formed, 'as to strike the minds of half a people at once in 'a place of worship with a forgetfulness of present 'care and calamity, and a hope of endless rapture, 'joy, and Hallelujah hereafter.'

In the latter part of his life Renatus Harris retired to Bristol, and, following his business there, made sundry organs for the churches in that city, and in the adjacent parishes, as also for churches in the neighbouring counties. He had a son named John, bred up under him, who followed the business of organ-making, and made a great number of very fine instruments.§ In the Mercurius Musicus for September and October, 1700, is a song inscribed 'Set by Mr. René Harris.'

## CHAP. CXLVI.

IMMEDIATELY upon the restoration the utmost endeavours were exerted for the establishment of a

Byfield was sent for from England to repair it, which he objected to, and prevailed on the chapter to have a new one made by himself, he allowing for the old one in exchange. When he had got it he would have treated with the parishioners of Lynn in Norfolk for the sale of it; but they disdaining the offer of a second-hand instrument, refused to purchase it, and employed Snetzler to build them a new one, for which they paid him 700l. Byfied dying, his widow sold Harris's organ to the parish of Wolverhampton for 500l. and there it remains at this day. One of two eminent masters now living, who were requested by the churchwardens of Wolverhampton to give their opinions of this instrument, declares it to be the best modern organ he ever touched.

Mr. Francis Piggot was the first organist of the Temple church. This person had been an organist extraordinary of the chapel royal, but, upon the decease of Dr. Child, was appointed to succeed him as organist in ordinary, and was sworn in accordingly, 10 Apr. 1697. He died in 1704, and was succeeded at the Temple by his son, who died about the year 1736. As the church is common to both the societies of the Inner and Middle Temple, there have for many years past been two organists of it.

* Dr. Tudway's letter to his son above cited.

† He also made the organ for the theatre, and Christ Church, and for the church of St. Mary at Oxford; and at London he made that of St. Mary at Hill, St. Clement Danes, and of St. Margaret's Westminster. That at the theatre was taken down, and removed to the church of St. Peter in the East at Oxford, and a new one, made by Byfield and Green, erected in its stead.

‡ On this person there is the following humorous Epitaph in print:—

Here rests the musical Kit Schrider,
Who organs built when he did bide here;
With nicest ear he tuned 'em up;
But Death has put the cruel stop:
Tho' breath to others he convey'd,
Breathless, alas! himself is laid,
May he who us such keys has given,
Meet with St. Peter's Keys of Heaven!
His Cornet, twelfth, and Diapason
Could not with air supply, he weasoned;
Bass, Tenor, Treble, Unison,
The loss of tuneful Kit bemoan.
    Webb's Collection of Epitaphs, vol. II. page 76.

§ The subsequent history of organ-makers and of organ-making in this country lies in so short a compass, that it may briefly be continued down from the time when Dr. Tudway's account ends, to nearly the present.

Smith's nephews, Gerard and Bernard, worked chiefly in the country, as did also one Swarbrick, bred up under the elder Harris, and one Turner of Cambridge; their employment was more in the repairing of old than the building of new organs. About the year 1700, one Jordan, a distiller, who had never been instructed in the business, but had a mechanical turn, and was an ingenious man, betook himself to the making of organs, and succeeded beyond expectation. He had a son named Abraham, whom he instructed in the same business; he made the organ for the chapel of the Duke of Chandois at Canons near Edgware, and many organs for parish churches. Byfield and Bridge were two excellent workmen; the former made the organ for Greenwich hospital, and the latter that noble instrument in the church of Spitalfields, for which he had only 600l. These are all now dead. In the latter part of their lives, to prevent their underworking each other, there was a coalition between them; so that whoever was the nominal artificer of any instrument, the profits accruing from the making of it were divided among them all.

Contemporary with these men was one Morse of Barnet, an apothecary by profession, who would needs be a maker of organs. He made an organ for the church of St. Matthew Friday-street, and another for that of St. James Clerkenwell; they were both wretched instruments, and were taken down in a very few years after they were set up. One Griffin a barber in Fenchurch-street, also pretended to make organs: he dealt with a few parishes in London in a very singular way: in consideration of an annuity granted to him for his life, he built for the contracting parish an organ, and engaged to pay a person for playing it as long as the annuity should be payable: encouraged by his success in three or four instances of the kind, this man stood for Gresham professor of music against a person well skilled in the science, and, being a common-council man, and the electors also common-council men of London, he was chosen.

BERNARD SMITH

ORGAN — MAKER.

*From a Picture in the Music-School, Oxford.*

choir in the royal chapel : three organists were appointed, namely, Dr. Child, Dr. Christopher Gibbons, and Mr. Edward Low. These had also other places ; for Child was organist of Windsor, Gibbons of Westminster Abbey, and Mr. Low of Christ church, Oxford ; and, as they attended by monthly rotation, their foreign places were rendered tenable with those at the chapel. Henry Cook was made master of the children : this person had been bred up in the king's chapel, but quitted it at the commencement of the rebellion, and went into the king's army. In the year 1642 he obtained a captain's commission, and ever after was called Captain Cook. Not his loyalty alone, but that and his skill in music recommended him to the favour of Charles II. A hymn of his composing in four parts was performed instead of the litany, in the chapel of St. George at Windsor, by order of the sovereign and knights of the garter, on the seventeenth day of April, 1661.

The establishment of the chapel of king Charles II. appears by the following entry in the Cheque-book :—

' The names of the Subdean, Gentlemen, and others of his
' Majesty's Chapel Royal, at the time of the Coronation of
' King Charles the Second.

April 23d, being St. George's Day, 1661.

Dr. Walter Jones, Subdean.

Roger Nightingale, Ralph Amner, Philip Tinker, John Sayer, Durant Hunt, George Low, Henry Smith, William Tucker — Ministers.

Edward Lowe, William Child, Christ. Gibbons — Organists.

Henry Cook, Master of the Children.

Henry Lawes, Clerk of the Cheque.

Thomas Piers, Thomas Hazzard, John Harding — Gents.

William Howes, Thomas Blagrave, Gregory Thorndell, Edward Bradock, Henry Purcell, James Cobb, Nathaniel Watkins, John Cave, Alphonso Marsh, Raphael Courteville, Edward Coleman, Thomas Purcell, Henry Frost, John Goodgroom, George Betenham, Matthew Pennell — Gents.

Thomas Haynes, Serjeant of the Vestry.
William Williams, Yeoman.
George Whitaker, Yeoman.
Augustine Cleveland, Groom.

' At which time every gentleman of the chapel in orders
' had allowed to him for a gown five yards of fine scarlet ; and
' the rest of the gentlemen, being laymen, had allowed unto
' each of them foure yards of the like scarlet.'

The stock of music which they set out upon consisted chiefly of the anthems and services contained in Barnard's collection, and such others in manuscript as could be recovered and made perfect : these lasted about three or four years ; but the king perceiving a genius in many of the young people of the chapel, encouraged them to compose themselves ; and many of this first set, even while they were children of the chapel, composed anthems and services which would do honour to a mature age. These were sung to violins, cornets, and sacbuts, the performers on which were placed in the organ-loft ; and, by the king's special order, had Symphonies and Ritornellos adapted to those instruments.

The salaries of the gentlemen of the chapel had

been augmented both by James I. and Charles I., and in the year 1663 Charles II., by a privy-seal, farther augmented them to seventy pounds a year, and granted to Mr. Cook and his successors in office thirty pounds a year, for the diet, lodging, washing, and teaching each of the children of the chapel royal. A copy of this grant is entered in the cheque-book ; in the margin thereof is a memorandum purporting that it was obtained at the solicitation of Mr. Cook.*

The encouragement given to church music by king Charles II. had an effect upon all the choirs in the kingdom. In cathedrals that were amply endowed, as St. Paul's for instance, in which a maintenance is assigned for minor canons and lay singers, the performance was little inferior to that of the royal chapel :† in other cathedrals, where the revenues were so small as to reduce the members of the church to the necessity of taking mechanics and illiterate persons to assist in the choral service, it was proportionably inferior. But the most obvious effect of it was a variation in the church style. It

* Charles the Second had some knowledge of music ; he understood the notes, and sang, to use the expression of one who had often sung with him, a plump bass ; but it no where appears that he considered music in any other view than as an incentive to mirth. In a letter of his to Henry Bennet, afterwards earl of Arlington, dated from Bruges, August 18, 1655, he says, ' Pray get me pricked down as many new ' Corrants and Sarrabands and other little dances as you can, and bring ' them with you, for I have got a small fidler that does not play ill on ' the fiddle.' See the account of the preservation of King Charles II. after the battle of Worcester, page 150.

And in another letter to the same person, dated Sept. 1, 1656, he says ' You will find by my last, that though I am furnished with one small ' fidler, yet I would have another to keep him company ; and if you can ' get either he you mention, or another that plays well, I would have you ' do it.' Ibid. page 168.

His taste for music seems to have been such as disposed him to prefer a solo song to a composition in parts ; though it must be confessed that the pleasure he took in hearing Mr. Gostling sing, is a proof that he knew how to estimate a fine voice. This gentleman came from Canterbury, and in 1678 was sworn a gentleman extraordinary, and in a few days afterwards, a vacancy then happening by the death of Mr. William Tucker above mentioned, a gentleman in ordinary of the royal chapel. He was afterwards subdean of St. Paul's, and his memory yet lives in that cathedral. Purcell made sundry compositions purposely for him, and, among others, one, of which the following is the history :—
The king had given orders for building a yacht, which, as soon as it was finished, he named the Fubbs, in honour of the Duchess of Portsmouth, who we may suppose was in her person rather full and plump. The sculptors and painters apply this epithet to children, and say for instance of the boys of Fiammengo, that they are fubby. Soon after the vessel was launched the king made a party to sail in this yacht down the river, and round the Kentish coast ; and, to keep up the mirth and good humor of the company, Mr. Gostling was requested to be of the number. They had got as low as the North Foreland, when a violent storm arose, in which the king and the duke of York were necessitated, in order to preserve the vessel, to hand the sails, and work like common seamen ; by good providence however they escaped to land : but the distress they were in made an impression on the mind of Mr. Gostling, which was never effaced. Struck with a just sense of the deliverance, and the horror of the scene which he had but lately viewed, upon his return to London he selected from the psalms those passages which declare the wonders and terrors of the deep, and gave them to Purcell to compose as an anthem, which he did, adapting it so peculiarly to the compass of Mr. Gostling's voice, which was a deep bass, that hardly any person but himself was then, or has since been able to sing it ; but the king did not live to hear it : this anthem, though never printed, is well known. It is taken from the 107th psalm ; the first two verses of the anthem are the 23rd and 24th of the psalm. ' They that go down to the sea in ships, ' and occupy business in great waters. These men see the works of the ' Lord, and his wonders in the deep.'
King Charles II. could sing the tenor part of an easy song ; he would oftentimes sing with Mr. Gostling ; the duke of York accompanying them on the guitar.

† About this time it was very common for persons of rank to resort in the afternoon to St. Paul's to hear the service, and particularly the anthem ; and to attend a lady thither was esteemed as much an act of politeness, as it would be now to lead her into the opera. In the life of Mary Moders, the famous pretended German princess, who was executed in the year 1673, for a capital felony in stealing plate, and who had been married to many husbands, it is related that whilst Mr. Carleton, one of them, was courting her, and in the infancy of their acquaintance, he invited her to honour him with her company to St. Paul's to hear the organ, and certain excellent hymns and anthems performed by rare voices.

has already been remarked, that the services and anthems contained in Barnard's collections were the stock which the church set out upon at the restoration; these were grown familiar after a few years' practice; the king was in the flower of his age, and the natural gaiety of his disposition rendered him averse to the style of our best church music; in short, he had not solidity of mind, nor skill sufficient to contemplate the majesty and dignity, nor taste enough to relish that most exquisite harmony, which distinguish the compositions of Tye, of Tallis, Bird, Farrant, Gibbons, and many others. This was soon discovered by the young people of the chapel, and gave such a direction to their studies, as terminated in the commencement of what may very truly and emphatically be called a new style of church music.*

Amongst those that affected to compose in the light style of church music, Mr. Pelham Humphrey,† Mr. Blow, and Mr. Michael Wise were the chief; these were children of the chapel, educated under Captain Cook; they were all three young men of genius, and were not more distinguished for the novelty and originality of their style, than for their skill in the principles of harmony.

The restoration of monarchy, and the re-establishment of ecclesiastical discipline, induced many devout persons to attempt a revival also of that knowledge which is necessary to the decent and orderly performance of parochial music or psalmody; and to that end John Playford published a new edition of his 'Introduction to the Skill of Musick,' originally printed during the usurpation, viz., in 1655, which was followed by a collection entitled 'Psalms and 'Hymns in solemn musick, in foure parts, on the 'common tunes to the psalms in metre used in parish 'churches. Also six hymns for one voice to the 'organ,' by the same John Playford; printed by W. Godbid, and dedicated to Sancroft, dean of St. Paul's. Fol. 1671.

In the preface to this work, which carries with it an air of seriousness that distinguishes the writings of this honest old man, the testimony of some of the fathers and the example of the primitive church are adduced in favour of the practice of psalm-singing. The author cites a passage from Comenius, which shows that in his time the Bohemians, besides the Psalms of David, had no fewer than seven hundred hymns in use. He then gives a short history of the custom of singing psalms; and, speaking of our old version, and the reception it met with, says it was made by men whose piety exceeded their poetry, but that, such as it was, it was ranked with the best English poesy at that time; that the Psalms, translated into English metre, and having apt tunes set to them, were at first used and sung only for devotion in private families, but that soon after by permission

they were brought into churches; that for many years this part of divine service was skilfully and devoutly performed with delight and comfort by many honest and religious people, and is still continued in our churches, but not with that reverence and estimation as formerly, some not affecting the translation, others not liking the music, both which he confesses need reforming; that those many tunes formerly used to these psalms, for excellency of form, solemn air, and suitableness to the matter of the Psalms, are not inferior to any tunes used in foreign churches, but that the best and almost all the choice tunes are lost and out of use in our churches; the reason whereof he gives in these words:—'In and about this great 'city, in above one hundred parishes, there is but 'few parish-clerks to be found that have either 'ear or understanding to set one of these tunes 'musically as it ought to be; it having been a custom 'during the late wars, and since, to chuse men into 'such places more for their poverty than skill and 'ability, whereby this part of God's service hath 'been so ridiculously performed in most places, that 'it is now brought into scorn and derision by many 'people.'

For these reasons he professes, through the assistance of Almighty God, to have undertaken the publication of this work, and therein to have selected all the best and choicest tunes, to the number of forty-seven, to which, with a bass he has composed two contratenors, making four parts, all which are fitted to men's voices.

Playford appears to have been no admirer of the old version of the Psalms, and therefore he has selected from a translation by Dr. Henry King, bishop of Chichester, and from another by one Mr. Miles Smith, and also from the poems of Mr. George Herbert, such psalms and hymns, as for elegance of style, smoothness of language, and suitableness to the tunes, he thinks excel those contained in the former.

There are few positions in this preface of Playford but what will be readily assented to, except that which relates to the loss of the best and almost all the choice tunes anciently used in our churches; for, though in a great measure out of use, they exist even at this day in the collections of Este, Ravenscroft, Allison, and other authors, as has been shewn.

The same Playford soon after published in octavo, 'The whole Book of Psalms: with the usual Hymns 'and Spiritual Songs. Together with the ancient 'and proper Tunes sung in Churches, with some 'of later use. Composed in three parts, Cantus, 'Medius, and Bassus, in a more plain and useful 'method than hath been formerly published.' In this collection the author, varying from the rule observed by him in the former, has given the church-tune to the cantus part, and has contrived the medius so as not to rise above the cantus, to the end that the air of the church-tune should predominate; farther he has placed the two upper parts in the G SOL' RE UT cliff, an innovation which it is easier to make than defend.

We meet here with a great variety of tunes now

---

* The particular instances of innovation were solo anthems and movements in courant time, which is a dancing measure, and which the king had acquired a great fondness for while he was in France.

† Of Humphrey it is said in particular that his proficiency in music, and the presages of his becoming a great man in his profession, gave great uneasiness to his master, Captain Cook. In the Ashmolean Manuscript, mentioned in page 455, it is said by the author, Anthony Wood, of Cook that he was the best musician of his time, till Pell. Humphries came up, after which says the MS. he died in discontent.

in common use, which are not contained in Ravenscroft, namely, St. James's, London New, St. Mary's, and others called Proper Tunes, which, for ought that appears to the contrary, we may conclude were composed by Playford himself.

From the reasons deducible from the above account of his works, Playford is looked upon as the father of modern psalmody; but, notwithstanding his labours, it does not appear that the practice has much improved since his time; one cause whereof may possibly be the use of the organ in parish churches, which within this last century has increased to so great a degree, that in most of the cities and great towns in the kingdom it is a sign of great poverty in a parish for a church to be without one. The consequence whereof is, that the conduct of this part of the service devolves to the organist: he plays the thorough-bass, or, in other words, the whole harmony of the tune, while the clerk and the congregation sing the tenor, which they remember and sing by ear only, in which kind of performance not the least skill in music is necessary.*

Besides what are to be found in the collections before enumerated, there are extant many other musical compositions to the words of David's Psalms, either closely or paraphrastically rendered, which lie dispersed in the works of the musicians who flourished about the latter end of the sixteenth, and the beginning of the last century: to mention a few instances, a collection entitled Certaine Pfalmes felect out of the Pfalmes of David, and drawn into Englyfhe Metre, with notes to everie Pfalme in foure partes to fynge, was published by Francis Seager, 12mo. 1553. John Keeper, of Hart Hall, Oxon. published in 1574, 'Select Psalms of David set to musicke of foure 'parts;' and in 1585 one John Cosin published the Psalms in musicke of five and six parts.

In 1594 Dr. John Mundy, organist of the chapel of Windsor,† published 'Songs and Psalmes com- 'posed into 3 and 4 parts for the use and delight of 'all such who either love or learne musicke.' As to the songs, they are to every intent madrigals; and for the psalms, some are prose, as they stand in the old Bible translation, the rest are of the version of Sternhold and Hopkins, to the amount of about twenty in the whole.

Some years after, a person, of whom nothing more than the initials of his name, R. H. is known, published a translation of an Italian paraphrase of the seven penitential psalms, written by Francesco Bembo, with the music of Giovanni Croce, Maestro di Cappella of the church of St. Mark at Venice, a celebrated composer of that time,‡ and whom

Morley mentions as such in his Introduction. The title of the book is 'Musica Sacra to six voyces, 'composed in the Italian tongue by Giovanni Croce, 'new Englished,' printed by Este in 1608. The motives of the publication of this book, which are said to be the excellence of the songs, and the promotion of piety, are given at large in the dedication of the work 'to the vertuous lovers of musicke.'

These compositions are in a style greatly superior to those contained in the former collections, which, as they were intended solely for popular use, were, as has been mentioned, of that species of musical composition distinguished by the name of Counterpoint: On the contrary, these of Mundy and Cosin, and more eminently those of Byrd are descant, and that of a very artificial contexture.

The paraphrase of the Psalms by George Sandys was, and that very deservedly, in great estimation about the beginning of the last century; and this induced the two brothers, Henry and William Lawes, the great musicians of that day, to set many of them to music. Sandys's Psalms are also set to music for two voices, with a thorough-bass, by Mr. Walter Porter.

A paraphrase of some select psalms by Sir John Denham, Mr. Addison, and others, was set to music for a single voice with instrumental parts, by Mr. Andrew Roner, a teacher of music in London, and published about the year 1730.

## CHAP. CXLVII.

The practice of music had suffered no less than the profession of it during the usurpation. King Charles I. soon after his accession, had shewn a disposition to encourage the liberal arts, and particularly music, as appears by his charter granted to Nicholas Laniere and others, herein before inserted.§ He had also in the eleventh year of his reign granted a charter to divers persons, the most eminent musicians, incorporating them by the style of Marshall, Wardens, and Cominalty of the Arte and Science of Musick in Westminster, in the County of Middlesex, and invested them with sundry extraordinary powers and privileges, which charter was by the same king confirmed in the fourteenth year of his reign.

This charter had lain dormant from the time of granting it to the restoration, that is to say, above twenty-five years, but immediately after that event, the persons named in it, or such of them as were then living, determined to rescue music from the disgrace into which it had fallen, and exert their authority for the improvement of the science and the interest of its professors.

The history of this company lies in a short compass; the minutes of their transactions are extant among the Harleian manuscripts, in a book formerly Mr. Wanley's, numbered in the catalogue 1911. As there is no entry in this book of the charter, recourse has been had to the patent-roll, in the chapel of the Rolls: the purport whereof is as follows :—

* In country parishes, where the people have not the aid of an instrument to guide them, such young men and women as nature has endowed with an ear and a tolerable voice, are induced to learn to sing by book as they call it; and in this they are generally assisted by some poor ignorant man, whom the poring over Ravenscroft and Playford has made to believe that he is as able a proficient in psalmody as either of those authors. Such men as these assume the title of singing-masters and lovers of divine music, and are the authors of those collections which are extant in the world, and are distinguished by the titles of 'David's 'Harp new strung and tuned,' 'The Harmony of Sion,' 'The Psalm- 'singer's Companion,' and others of the like kind, to an incredible number.

† Mentioned page 571 of this work.

‡ See an account of him in page 442.

§ Page 574 of this work.

The charter bears date 15 Jul. 11 Car. and recites that king Edw. 'IV. by his letters patent under the 'greate seale of his realme of England, bearing date 'the foure and twentieth day of Aprill, in the nynth 'yeare of his raigne, did for him and his heires give 'and graunt licence unto Walter Haliday* Marshall

*,Sic Orig. The Christian name of Marshall is Robert, as appears by the charter itself, which as a singular curiosity is here inserted from Rymer's Fœdera, tom. XI.

'*Pro Fraternitate Ministrallorum Regis.*
'Rex Omnibus, ad quos &c. Salutem.
'Sciatis quòd, ex Querelosa Insinuatione, Dilectorum Nobis, *Walteri* '*Haliday* Marescalli, *Johannis Cliff, Roberti Marshall, Thomæ Grene,* '*Thomæ Calthorn, Willielmi Cliff, Willielmi Christean,* Et *Willielmi* '*Eyneysham,* Ministrallorum nostrorum accepimus qualiter nonnulli, 'rudes Agricolæ et Artifices diversarum Misterarum Regni nostri Angliæ, 'finxerunt se fore Ministrallos,
'Quorum aliqui Liberatam nostram, eis minimé datam, portarent, 'Seipsos etiam fingentes esse Ministrallos nostros proprios,
'Cujus quidem Liberatæ ac dictæ Artis sive Occupationis Ministral-'lorum colore, in diversis Partibus Regni Nostri prædicti, grandes 'Pecuniarum Exactiones de Ligeis nostris deceptivè colligunt et re-'cipiunt,
'Et licet Ipsi in Arte sive Occupatione illa minimè Intelligentes vere 'Experti existant, et diversis Artibus et Operationibus Diebus Ferialibus 'sive Profestis utuntur, et Victum suum inde sufficienter Percipiant, de 'Loco tamen ad Locum in Diebus Festivalibus·discurrunt, et Pecunia 'illa totaliter percipiunt, e quibus Ministralli nostri prædicti, et cæteri 'Ministralli nostri pro tempore existentes, in Arte sive Occupatione 'prædicta sufficienter Eruditi et Instructi, nullisque aliis Laboribus, 'Occupationibus, sive Misteris utentes, vivere deberent,
'Nedùm in Artis sive Occupationis illius nimiam Verecundiam, ac 'ipsorum Ministrallorum nostrorum, eadem Arte sive Occupatione ut 'prædictum est utentium, Deteriorationem multiplicem et manifestam, 'verùm etiam in Populi nostri in hujusmodi Agricultura sua et aliter 'Dampnum ut accepimus non modicum et Gravamen,
'Unde iidem Ministralli nostri Nobis humilimè supplicârunt ut Nos 'eis de Remedio congruo in hac parte ex Gratia nostra speciali providere 'dignaremur,
'Nos, Præmissa considerantes ac Supplicationi suæ rationabili in ea 'parte favorabiliter inclinati, de Gratia nostra prædicta, ac ex certa 'Scientia et mero Motu nostris, *Concessimus* et *Licentiam dedimus,* ac 'per Præsentes *Concedimus* et *Licentiam damus,* pro Nobis, et Hæredibus 'nostris, quantum in Nobis est, præfatis, *Waltero Haliday* Marescallo, *Jo-* '*hanni Cliff Roberto Marshalle, Thomæ Grene, Thomæ Calthorn, Willielmo* '*Christean,* Et *Willielmo Eneysham,* Ministrallis nostris quòd Ipsi, ad 'Laudem et Honorem Dei, et ut specialiùs exorare teneantur pro salubri 'Statu nostro et Præcarissimæ Consortis nostræ *Elizabethæ Reginæ* '*Angliæ* dùm agimus in humanis, et pro Animabus nostris cùm ab hac 'luce migraverimus, necnon pro Anima Carissimi Domini et Patris 'nostri *Richardi* nuper *Ducis Eborum,* et Animabus inclitorum Pro-'genitorum nostrorum, et omnium Fidelium Defunctorum, tàm in 'Capella beatæ Mariæ Virginis infra Ecclesiam Cathedralem Sancti 'Pauli Londoniæ, quàm in Libera Capella nostra Regia Sancti Anthonii 'in eadem Civitate nostra Londoniæ, quandam FRATERNITATEM *sive* 'GILDAM perpetuam (quam, ut accepimus, Fratres et Sorores Fraterni-'tatis Ministrallorum Regni nostri prædicti, retroactis temporibus, 'Inierunt, Erexerunt, et Ordinârunt) Stabilire, Continuare, et Augmen-'tare, ac quascúmque Personas, tàm Homines, quàm Mulieres, eis 'grato animo Adhærentes, in FRATRES et SORORES FRATERNITATIS 'sive GILDÆ *prædictæ* Recipere, Admittere, et Acceptare possent et 'valeant,
'Et quòd Marescallus et Ministralli nostri prædicti per Se sint et esse 'debeant, Jure et Nomine UNUM CORPUS et UNA COMMUNITAS PER-'PETUA, ac Habiles et Capaces in Lege, Habeantque Successionem 'perpetuam,
'*Et quod* tàm Ministralli prædicti, qui nunc sunt, quàm cæteri 'Ministralli nostri et Hæredum nostrorum qui exnunc erunt imper-'petuum, ad eorum libitum Nominare possint, Eligere, Ordinare, et 'successivè Constituere de Seipsis UNUM MARESCALLUM habilem et 'idoneum, pro Termino Vitæ suæ in Officio illo permansurum, ac etiam 'quolibet Anno DUOS CUSTODES *ad Fraternitatem sive Gildam prædictam* '*Regendum et Gubernandum.*
'*Et, ulterius, Volumus* et per Præsentes *Concedimus,* pro Supportatione 'et Augmentatione *Fraternitatis sive Gildæ prædictæ,* quòd nullus 'Ministrallus Regni nostri prædicti, quamvis in hujusmodi Arte sive 'Occupatione sufficienter Eruditus existat, eadem Arte sive Occupatione 'infra Regnum nostrum prædictum de cætero, nisi de *Fraternitate sive* '*Gilda prædicta* sit et ad eandem Admissus fuerit et cum cæteris Con-'fratribus ejusdem contribuerit, aliquo modo utatur, nec eam palàm seu 'publicè excerceat (ita tamen quòd nullus prædictorum Ministrallorum, 'sic ut prædicitur admittendum, solvat pro hujusmodi Ingressu sive 'Admissione ultra *Tres Solidos et Quatuor Denarios)* et si secus fecerit, 'seu quoquo modo contravenerit, per præfatos Marescallum et Mini-'strallos nostros et Hæredum nostrorum prædictorum, pro tempore 'existentes, juxta eorum Discretiones Amerciatur,
'Et quòd prædicti *Marescallus et Ministralli* nostri, ac *Custodes* et '*Successores* sui *Congregationes et Communicationes licitas* et honestas de 'Seipsis, ac *Statuta et Ordinationes licita* pro salubri Gubernatione et 'Commodo *Fraternitatis sive Gildæ prædictæ,* quoties et quando opus 'fuerit, licitè et impunè Incipere, Facere, et Ordinare valeant,
'*Et, si* aliquis hujusmodi Ministrallorum nostrorum vel Hæredum 'nostrorum prædictorum Decesserit vel Obierit, seu ob Demerita vel 'Offensas sua, aut aliâ Causâ quacúmque, a Servitio nostro prædicto 'Exoneratus, Amotus, sive Depositus fuerit, adtunc *Marescallus et*

'and John Cliff, and others, then minstrells† of the 'said king, that they by themselves should be in 'deed and name one body and cominalty, perpetual 'and capable in the lawe, and should have perpetual 'succession; and that as well the minstrells of the

'*cæteri Ministralli nostri,* et Hæredum nostrorum pro tempore exis-'tentes, alium Ministrallorum idoneum et in Arte sive Occupatione illa 'Expertum sufficienter et Eruditum, ubicùmque loco infra Regnum 'nostrum prædictum tàm infra Libertates quàm extra eum inveniri 'contigerit (Comitatu Cestriæ Excepto) Vice et Loco hujusmodi sic 'Descendentis Exonerati, Amoti, sive Depositi, ex parte nostra Eligere, 'Nominare, et in unum Ministrallorum nostrorum et Hæredum nos-'trorum penes Nos Retinendum Habilitare, ac ad Vadia nostra, nostro 'Regio Assensu superinde habito, Admittere et Acceptare possint et 'valeant.
'*Et, insuper, Volumus* et per Præsentes *Concedimus* præfatis Mare-'scallo et Ministrallis nostris, quòd Ipsi et Successores sui de cætero 'Potestatem habeant et Facultatem Inquirendi, omnibus viis modis et 'mediis rationabilibus et legitimis quibus meliùs sciverint, per totum 'Regnum nostrum prædictum, tàm infra Libertates quàm extra (dicto 'Comitatu Cestriæ Excepto) de omnibus et singulis hujusmodi Personis 'fingentibus se fore Ministrallos, et dictam Liberatam nostram surreptivè 'portantibus, ac Arte sive Occupatione illâ, ut prædictum est, indebitè 'et minus justè utentibus, seu eandem exercentibus, aut *de Fraternitate* '*sive Gilda prædictâ* non existentibus, et de omnibus aliis Articulis et 'Circumstantiis Præmissa qualitercúmque concernentibus,
'Ac ad omnes et singulas hujusmodi Personas, prædictam Artem et 'Occupationem Ministrallorum Excercentes, de tempore in tempus, 'quotiens necesse fuerit, tàm infra Libertates quàm extra (dicto Comitatu 'Cestriæ ut præmittitur Excepto) Supervidendum, Scrutandum, Re-'gendum, et Gubernandum, et earum quamlibet, ob Offensas et Defectus 'suos in Præmissis factos, justè et debitè Corrigendum et Puniendum,
'Ac quæcúmque Amerciamenta, Fines, Forisfacturas, et Deperdita '(si quæ prætextu hujusmodi Inquisitionis Supervisûs seu Scrutinii, 'ratione Præmissorum, super quascúmque Personas, se ut præfertur 'Ministrallos fingentes, seu aliter Delinquentes, debitè et probabiliter 'invenerint Adjudicata, Assessa, sive Afferata) ad Usum et Proficuum '*Fraternitatis prædictæ,* pro continua et perpetua Sustentatione certarum 'Candelarum cerearum, vulgariter nuncupatarum *Tapers,* ad Sumptus 'ejusdem Fraternitatis in Capellis prædictis ad præsens existentium de 'cætero existere contingentium, Levandum, Applicandum, et Dis-'ponendum,
'*Habenda et Occupanda, Excercenda et Gaudenda,* omnia et singula 'prædicta Inquisitionem, Scrutinium, Supervisum, Regimen, Guber-'nationem, Correctionem, Punitionem, ac cætera Præmissa modis et 'formis supradictis, præfatis *Waltero, Johanni, Roberto, Thomæ Grene,* '*Thomæ Calthorn, Willielmo Cliff, Willielmo Cristean,* et *Willielmo* '*Eynesham,* Ministrallis nostris, et Successoribus suis Ministrallis 'nostris et Hæredum nostrorum prædictorum imperpetuùm, sine 'Occasione, Impedimento, Impetitione, Molestatione, Perturbatione, 'seu Calumnia Nostri, vel Hæredum nostrorum, Justiciariorum, Es-'cætorum, Vicecomitum, aut aliorum Ballivorum seu Ministrorum 'nostrorum, vel Hæredum nostrorum et aliorum quorumcúmque,
'Et hoc absque Fine vel Feodo Magno seu Parvo, in Hanaperio 'Cancellariæ nostræ seu alibi, ad usum nostrum seu Nomine nostro, 'pro Præmissis faciendis aut solvendis,
'Eo quòd expressa mentio de vero Valore seu Certitudine Præ-'missorum, sive eorum alicujus, in Præsentibus minimè facta existit, 'aut aliquo Statuto, Actu, sive Ordinatione in contrarium factis, editis, 'seu provisis, non obstantibus.
'In cujus &c.
'Teste Rege apud *Westmonasterium* Vicesimo quarto die Aprilis.
'*Per Breve de Privato Sigillo et de Data, &c.*'
The above Walter Haliday, Robert Marshall, and John Cliff, together with one William Wykes, had it seems been minstrels of the king's predecessor Hen. VI. and were impowered by him to impress minstrels 'in solatium regis,' as the writ expresses it. This singular precept appears in Rymer's Fœdera, tom. XI. page 375, and is in this form:—
'*De Ministrallis propter Salatium Regis providendis.*
'Rex, dilectis sibi, *Waltero Halyday, Roberto Marshall, Willielmo* '*Wykes,* et *Johanni Clyffe,* Salutem.
'Sciatis qnòd Nos, considerantes qualiter quidem Ministralli nostri 'jam tardè Viam universæ Carnis sunt ingressi, aliisque, loco ipsorum, 'propter Salatium nostrum de necesse indigentes, Affignavimus vos, 'conjunctim et divisim, ad quosdam Pueros, Membris Naturalibus 'Elegantes, in Arte Ministrellatûs instructos, ubicùnque inveniri po-'terint, tàm infra Libertates, quàm extra, Capiendum, et in Servitio 'nostro ad Vadia nostra Ponendum, &c.'
It is highly probable that the placards for impressing children for the service of the choir, mentioned by Tusser, and under which he himself was taken from his father's house, [See page 537,] were founded on the authority of this precedent.

† *It appears by this charter, as also by the list of the household establishment of Edw. IV. see page 271, that in the reign of that prince Circa 1461,* Minstrel *was the common appellation of one that played on any musical instrument; and we find that such persons continued to be so denominated down to the time of the latest English translation of the Bible. In the 2nd book of Kings, Chapter III. verse 15, it is related that the prophet Elisha upon a certain occasion called for a* minstrel *to compose his mind and fit it for divine inspiration. And 9 Matt. 22 we read that when Jesus came into the ruler's house in order to raise his daughter then dead, and about to be carried to her funeral, he saw the Minstrels. Men of this profession have been for many years past, and now are called* Musicians, *a term which, as Boetius has clearly shewn, belongs to the higher order of speculatists in the science.*

'said king, which then were, as other minstrells of
'the said king, and his heires which should be
'afterwards, might at their pleasure name, chuse,
'ordeine, and successively constitute from amongst
'themselves, one Marshall, able and fitt to remaine
'in that office during his life, and alsoe twoe wardens
'every yeare, to governe the said fraternity and guild.'

It also recites that 'certeine persons, suggesting
'themselves to be freemen of a pretended society
'of minstrells in the cittie of London, in prejudice
'of the liberties and priviledges aforesaid in the said
'recited letters patents mencioned and intended to
'the minstrells and musicians of the said king and
'his heires, did by untrue suggestions procure of
'and from king James of ever blessed memory,
'letters patent under his greate seale of England,
'bearing date the eight day of July, in the second
'yeare of his raigne, to incorporate them by the
'name of master, wardens, and cominalty of the arte
'or science of the musicians of London. And,
'amongst divers other priviledges, to graunt unto
'them the survey, scrutiny, correction, and govern-
'ment of all and singular the musicians and minstrells
'within the said cittie of London, suburbs, liberties
'and precincts of the said cittie, or within three
'miles of the same cittie. By colour whereof they
'endeavoured to exclude the musicians and minstrells
'enterteyned into the king's service, and all others
'expert and learned in the said art and science of
'musick, from teaching and practising the same
'within the said cittie, and three miles thereof,
'that would not subject themselves unto theire said
'pretended fraternity, or purchase their appro-
'bation thereunto, although greate part of them
'were altogether unskilfull in the said art and science
'of musick.'

It farther recites that 'at the prosecution of
'Nicholas Lanier, Thomas Ford, Jerome Lanier,
'Clement Lanier, Andrewe Lanier, Thomas Day,
'John Cogshall, Anthony Roberts, Daniell Farrant,
'John Lanier, Alfonso Ferabosco, Henry Ferabosco,
'Edward Wormall, and John Drewe, musicians en-
'terteyned in the king's service, a Scire Facias had
'bin brought in the king's name against the said
'pretended master, wardens, and cominalty of the
'art or science of the musicians of London, in the
'high court of chauncery, for the cancelling and
'making voide of the said letters patent; and that
'judgement at theire said prosecution had been had
'and given by the said court accordingly, and the
'said letters patent vacated and cancelled thereupon.'

The king, therefore, 'for and in consideration of
'the good and faithfull service which his said mu-
'sicians had done and performed unto him, and in
'pursuance of the intent and meaning of the said
'king Edward the Fourth, in his said recited letters
'patent mentioned, of his speciall grace, certeine
'knowledge, and meere motion, DOTH for him, his
'heires, and successors, will, ordeine, constitute,
'declare, and graunt that the said Nicholas Lanier,
'Thomas Ford, Jerome Lanier, Clement Lanier,
'Andrewe Lanier, Thomas Day, John Cogshall,
'Anthony Roberts, Daniel Farrant, John Lanier,

'Alfonso Ferabosco, Henry Ferabosco. Edward
'Wormall, John Drewe, John Stephens, Thomas
'Tompkins, Ezechiell Wade, Roger Nightingall,
'Walter Porter, John Frost senior, John Frost
'junior, Ralph Amner, Henry Lawes, John Tom-
'kins, William Lanier, Jeronimo Bassano, Robert
'Baker, Anthony Bassano, William Gregory, Robert
'Parker, John Mason, Christopher Bell, John
'Adson, Frauncis Farmelowe, Thomas Mell, Moun-
'sieur Gaultier,* Nicholas Du Vall, John Kelly,
'Giles Tomkins, Robert Taylor, William Lawes,
'John Wilson, Phillip Squire, Morrice Webster,
'Stephen Noe, John Woodington, Davis Mell,†
'Thomas Lupo, Daniell Johnson, and Theophilus
'Lupo, his said musicians, and all such persons as
'are, or shall be the musicians of him, his heires,
'and successors, shall from thenceforth for ever, by
'force and vertue of the said graunt, be a body cor-
'porate and politique, in deed, fact, and name, by
'the name of Marshall, Wardens, and Cominalty of
'the arte and science of musick, in Westminster in
'the county of Middlesex, and by the same name
'have perpetual succession, and be capable in the
'law to implead and be impleaded: And that they
'have a common seale.'

The charter goes on to appoint Nicholas Lanier
the first marshal for life, Thomas Ford and Jerome
Lanier first wardens until Midsummer day next
ensuing the date of the patent, and Clement Lanier.
Andrew Lanier, Thomas Day, John Cogshall,
Anthony Roberts, Daniel Farant, John Lanier,
Alfonso Ferabosco, Henry Ferabosco, Edward
Wormall, and John Drewe to be the first assistants, and continue in the same office for their
natural lives, with power to elect a marshal, warden,
and assistants in future.

The other powers granted by this charter are,
that the corporation shall meet in or near the city of
Westminster from time to time. That they make
bye-laws and impose fines on such as transgress
them, which fines they shall have to their own use,
after which is a clause in these words:—

'And for the better government and ordering of
'all such person or persons as doe or shall at any
'time hereafter, professe and exercise the said art
'and science of musique within our said realme of
'England, our county palatine of Chester only ex-
'cepted,‡ Wee doe hereby, for us, our heires, and
'successors, further will, give, and graunt unto the
'said marshall, wardens, and cominalty of the said
'art and science of musique in Westmister, in the
'county of Middlesex, and theire successors, that the
'said marshall, wardens, and assistants, and theire
'successors, or the greater part of them, for the tyme
'being, for ever hereafter. shall have the survey,
'scrutinie, correction, and government of all and
'singuler the musicians within our said kingdome of

* JACQUES GOUTER. a Frenchman. and a celebrated lutenist. There
is extant a very fine etching of him, of which see an account in Granger's
Biogr. Hist. vol. I. page 538. The author of that work is mistaken in
saying that he is represented holding two lutes in his left hand, for the
instrument he holds is a theorbo, which has two necks, and is therefore
termed Cithara bijuga.

† The famous violinist mentioned page 681.

‡ For the reason of this exception see page 191, et seq.

'England, the said county palatine of Chester onely
'excepted. And wee doe for us, our heires, and suc-
'cessors, give and graunt unto the said marshall,
'wardens, and cominalty of the art and science of
'musique, in Westminster in the county of Mid-
'dlesex, and their successors, that it shall and may
'be lawfull to and for the said marshall, wardens,
'and cominalty, and every person and persons that
'shall be at any tyme hereafter admitted to be a
'member of theire said fraternity and corporation, or
'shall be, upon due examination and tryall had of
'theire sufficiency and skill in the said art or science,
'allowed thereunto by the said marshall, wardens,
'and assistants, or the greater part of them, to use,
'exercise, and practise the said arte and science of
'musique in and within the cittie of London, and
'suburbs and liberties thereof, or elsewhere soever
'within our said kingdome of England, our said
'county palatine of Chester onely excepted, any act,
'ordinance, or constitution of common council of the
'said citty of London, or any other matter or thing
'whatsoever to the contrary thereof in any wise not-
'withstanding.'

In pursuance of the powers above granted, the
corporation hired a room in the house of one Mr.
Ganley, situated in Durham-yard, in the Strand, and
within the city and liberty of Westminster. Their
first meeting was on the twenty-second day of October, 1661, Nicholas Laniere then being marshal,
from which day they proceeded to make orders, of
which the following are the most remarkable .—

'1662. Jan. 20. Ordered that Edward Sadler, for
'his insufficiency in the art of musique, be from
'henceforward silenced and disabled from the exer-
'cise of any kinde in publique houses or meetings.'

Some orders signed 'Hen. Cooke, Dep. Marshall.'

'Feb. 3. Richard Graham, appointed their soli-
'citor at law.'

19. It appears they licensed teachers of music.

'1663. Nov. 24. Symon Hopper resigns his
'office of assistant, John Banister elected in his
'room.

'Jan. 13. Ordered that Matthew Lock, Christopher
'Gibbons, Dr. Cha. Colman, and William Gregory,
'do come to the chamber at Durham-yard on Tuesday
'next, at two of the clock in the afternoon, and
'bring each of them ten pounds, or show cause to the
'contrary.

'March 1. Ordered that there be a petition pre-
'sented to the king's majestie for the renewing of
'their former patent.

'1664. May 13. Ordered that Henry Cooke,
'George Hudson, John Hingston, and John Lilly
'do meete fower of the musique of the cittie of
'London, to treat upon such matters and things as
'concern the good of the said corporation.

'June 14. Proceedings at law ordered against all
'such persons that make any benefit or advantage of
'musique in England and Wales, and that do not
'obey the grant under the great seale to the cor-
'poration.

'June 21. Ordered that John Hill, Francis
'Dudeny, John Dunstan, James Saunders, and

'others, now waites of the cittie of Westminster, do
'appear before this corporation at Mr. Ganley his
'house in Durham-yard, in the county of Middlesex,
'on Tuesday next at 10 of the clock in the morning,
'as they tender obedience to his majesties letters
'patent in that behalf graunted.

'July 2. Ordered that Richard Hudson, the clerk
'of the corporation, doe summon all the common
'minstrells from tyme to tyme to come before the
'corporation.

'July 9. Thomas Purcell chosen an assistant in
'the room of Dr. Charles Colman, deceased.

'Same day. Ordered that all his majesties mu-
'sique do give their attendance at the chamber at
'Durham-yard for practise of musique, when the
'master of the musique shall appoint them, upon for-
'feiture of 5l. each neglect.

'1670. Jan. 21. Pelham Humphrey chosen an
'assistant.

1670. *From Monday, August 22, to Thursday,
August 25. Whereas His Sacred Majesty hath
been pleased, after the example of his Royal Ancestors, to incorporate the Musitians of England
for its encouragement of that excellent science, and
the said corporation to have power over all that profess the same, and to allow and make free all such
as they shall think fit: This is to give notice to all
persons concerned in Musique that the Corporation
sits the Saturday in every week at their Hall in
Durham-yard in the Strand, in pursuance of the
trust and authority to them committed by His
Most Gracious Majesty, and that they have granted
several deputations into several counties to execute
the same.—London Gazette, No. 498, page 173.*

'1672. June. 24. Henry Cooke, Esq. being mar-
'shall of the corporation of musique in Westminster,
'in the county of Middlesex, resigns by reason of
'sicknesse, and Thomas Purcell appointed in his
'room. Signed, John Hingeston, deputy marshal,
'and by the wardens and assistants.

'July 18. John Blow chosen assistant.

'1675. Dec. 17. Mr. Nicholas Staggins chosen an
assistant, and admitted deputy marshal.'

The meetings of the corporation after this time
appear by the entries in their minute-book to have
been very few; the last was at the Three Tuns
tavern, on the second day of July, 1679, when John
Moss was chosen an assistant in the room of John
Lilly. It seems that they were incapable, otherwise
than by their own particular studies, of affecting
any thing for the improvement of the science, and
that they held it the wisest course to leave the
matter as they found it. By a note of Mr. Wanley
on this manuscript in the Harleian Catalogue, it
appears that at the time of making it the corporation
was extinct.*

* There can be no doubt that this corporation is extinct, and there is
good ground to suppose that the London company of musicians are in
a condition but little better; their charter appearing to have been
obtained by untrue suggestions, and to have been vacated by a judgment
of the court of chancery. The law it is true recognizes as corporations
those fraternities that subsist by prescription, but it requires as a condition to this title that their exercise of corporate functions shall have
been from time immemorial; but as to that of London, its origin may
be traced to the time of Ja. I. which in a legal sense is within time of
memory.

A very remarkable particular occurs in Strype's Continuation of Stowe's

## BOOK XVI.　CHAP. CXLVIII.

MEETINGS of such as delighted in the practice of music began now to multiply, and that at Oxford, which had subsisted at a time when it was almost the only entertainment of the kind in the kingdom, flourished at this time more than ever. In that general joy, which the restoration of public tranquility had produced, an association was formed of many of the principal members of the university, heads of houses, fellows, and others, in order to promote the study and practice of vocal and instrumental harmony in the university. The occasion and circumstances of this laudable design can only now be made appear by a list of the contributors to it, now extant in the music-school, and also by a written table, exhibiting an account of the expenditure of divers sums of money, which had been given to promote it, these are as follow :—

### I.

The list of those noble and worthy benefactors who have contributed to the refurnishing the publique Musick Schoole in this university with a new organ, harpsecon, all sortes of the best authors in manuscript for vocall and instrumentall music, and other necessaryes to carry on the practicall music in that place. All the old instruments and bookes left by the founder, being either lost, broken, or imbeasled in the time of rebellion and usurpation. This collection began in the yeare 1665. and was carried on in part of the two following yeares, and then ceased by reason of the first Dutch warr, but now compleated in this yeare 1675.

| Noblemen in 1665. | | Dr. Gardner, Chr. Ch. | - £2 |
|---|---|---|---|
| Ld. Annesley gave - | - £5 | Dr. Allestrey, Chr. Ch. | - 2 |
| Sr. Seamour Shirley - | 5 | Dr. Mayne - - - | - 2 |
| Mr. Crew now Bp. - | 3 | Dr. Mew, Bp. - | - 2 |
| Drs. in 1665. | | Dr. Yates, Prin. Braz. | - 2 |
| Dr. Blandford, vice chanc. | 3 | Dr. Jenkins, Princ. Jes. | - 1 |
| Dr. Fell, Deane Chr. Ch. | 4 | Masters in 1665. | |
| Dr. Merredeth, All. S. - | 3 | Mr. Houghton, Braz. | - 1 |
| Dr. Woodward, N. Coll. | 3 | Mr. R. Hill, Chr. Ch. | - 1 |
| Dr. Dolbin, now Bp. - | 2 | Mr. R. South, Chr. Ch. | - 1 |
| Dr. Dickenson - - | 2 | Mr. H. Bagshaw, Chr. Ch. | 1 |
| Dr. Pierce, Pre. Mag. - | 2 | Mr. Martin, Chr. Ch. | - 1 |
| Dr. Barlow, now Bp. | - 2 | Mr. Coward, Cp. Christi | - 1 |

Survey of London; that author, under the head of Temporal Government, exhibits the arms of the several companies of London, with a short history of them severally, beginning with the day and year of their incorporation. In the instance of the Musicians, book V. chap. xxv. he gives the arms of that company, but says not a word of the corporation itself. This omission he endeavours to supply in the second appendix to his work, page 16, by a letter from Mr. Mauduit, Windsor herald, containing an account of some incorporations not expressed in the Survey. In this letter Mr. Mauduit, speaking of the company of Musicians, says 'that the time of their incorporation was refused by the clerk of the company to be given.' He however supposes that they were incorporated by James I. by the name of Master, Wardens, and Commonalty. Of their arms he says that they were granted them by patent by William Camden Clarencieux, An. 1614.

The reason for this refusal may be collected from the recitals in the preamble to the above patent, but it is not so easy to account for the exercise of those powers which the London company of musicians even at this day claim, particularly that by which they exclude from performances within the city such musicians as are not free of their company. A remarkable instance of this kind happened in the year 1737. One Povey, a whimsical man, and known to the world by his having been the original projector of the Penny-post office, engaged a number of musicians, some from the opera, to play at a weekly concert, for which he obtained subscriptions, to be held in a great room in an old house in a court in St. Martin's le Grand. The first night of performance was the Saturday after the interment of queen Caroline; the bills and advertisements announced that an oration would be delivered, deploring the death of that princess, but in the midst of the performance such of the musicians as were known to be foreigners were arrested at the suit of the company of musicians of London; a proceeding, which had it been contested, could scarcely have been warranted, seeing that St. Martin's le Grand is not part of the city of London, but a liberty of Westminster.

| | | | | |
|---|---|---|---|---|
| Mr. Sterry, Merton - | - £1 | Mr. T. Spratt, Wad. | - £1 | |
| Mr. Denton, Queens | 10s. | Noblemen in 1675. | | |
| Mr. Parry, Cor. Christi | - £1 | Sr. J. Parsons, Chr. Ch. - | 2 | |
| Mr. J. Price, St. Johns | 10s. | Sr. J. Chichester, Exeter | 2 | |
| Mr. J. Price, New Coll. | - £1 | Sr. C. Yelverton - - | 3 | |
| Mr. T. Tomkins, All. S. | 1 | Sr. T. Isham - - | 3 | |
| Mr. J. Tomkins, Bal. - | 1 | Drs. in 1675. | | |
| Mr. Hutton, Braz. - | 1 | Dr. Bathurst, Vice chanc. | 3 | |
| Mr. Lowe, New Coll | 1 | Dr. Lockey, Chr. Ch. - | 2 | |
| Mr. Thomas, New Coll. | 10s. | Dr. Wallis - - - | 1 | |
| Mr. Hawkins, Bal. - | - £1 | Dr. Smith - - - | 2 | |
| Mr. Fairfax, Mag. - | 1 | Masters in 1675. | | |
| Strangers in 1665. | | Mr. Bernard, St. Johns - | 1 | |
| Bp. H. King - - | - 5 | Mr. Thornton, Wad. - | 1 | |
| Dr. Franklin - - | 1 | Mr. Old, Chr. Ch. - | - | |
| Mr. Hannes - - | 1 | Mr. Aldrich, Chr. Ch. | - | |
| Mr. Tinker - - | 10s. | Strangers in 1675. | | |
| Mr. Sayer - - | 10s. | Mr. C. Harris - - | 2 | |
| Mr. Hodges - - | 10s. | G. Lowe, Esq. - - | 2 | |
| Mr. Stratford, Trin. - | - £1 | J. Lowen - -, | £1. 10s. | |

### II.

The account of instruments, books, and other necessaries bought for the use of the music school, with money contributed for that use from those noble and worthy benefactors nominated on the other side, as also what instruments, books, &c., have been given by others.

| | | |
|---|---|---|
| 1 upright organ with 4 stopps, made by Ralph Dallans, for which he received 48l. (abating 10l. for the materials of the old organ) and for painting and gilding to Mr. Taylor painter in Oxford 3l. 10s. in all - | 51 10 0 | |
| Sets of choice books for instrumental music, ii. whereof are the composition of Mr. John Jenkins, for 2. 3. 4. 5 and 6 parts for the organ and harpsecon, and 6 sets more composed by Mr. Lawes, Coprario, Mr. Brewer, and Orlando Gibbons, all bought of Mr. Wood, which cost - - - - | 22 0 0 | |
| 2 violins with their bowes and cases, bought of Mr. Comer in the Strand; cost 12l. 10s. and are at 2nd hand, * * * * which was Mr. Bull's of All Soulds cost 2l. 10s. In all | 15 0 0 | |
| 1 set of books, the composition of Mr. Baltzar (commonly called the Swede) for violins, viol, and harpsicon; as also the compositions of Dr. Christopher Gibbons, his famous Ayres and Galliards for violins, viol, and organ, both sets together cost - - | 5 0 0 | |
| 7 desks to lay the books on for the instruments and organ, bought of John Wild at 2s. a piece - - - - - - | 0 14 0 | |
| To Mr. Taylor the painter for the long picture in the music schoole of our Saviour and the woman of Samaria - - - | 3 0 0 | |
| By charge in procuring the several pictures of those great masters in the facultie of music, carriage of them hither, frames to some of them, boarding all of them behinde to secure them from the dampe wall, &c. - - | 10 0 0 | |
| The several disbursements then in the year 1667 was and deducting what was allowed for the materials of the old organ, there rests - - - - - | 101 4 0 | |

Mr. Henry Lawes, Gent. of his majesty's chappell royal and of his private music, gave to this school a rare Theorbo for singing to, valued at * * * with the earl of Bridgewater's crest in brass just under the fingerboard, with its case, as also a set of * * *

Dr. Will. Child, Gent. of his majesty's chappell royal, and organist of the free chapp. at Windsor, gave his own picture from * * * * taffaty curtain * * * * the whole charge amounting to     -     -     -     6  9  6

The paper containing the above accounts being pasted on a wainscot board, has been so much injured by the damp, that no more of the writing is legible.

This at Oxford was the first subscription concert of which any account is to be met with: indeed it seems to have been the only association of the sort in the kingdom; the reason of this might be, that the pretenders to the love of music were not then so numerous as they have been of late years. A concert was formerly a serious entertainment, at which such only as had a real and genuine affection for music assembled, for the purpose of enjoying the pleasures of harmony, and contemplating the effects of it in a silent approbation: such as had no ear for music, and these are by far the majority of the human species, were then ingenuous enough to confess it, and that a concert was an entertainment that afforded them no kind of pleasure; and we may accordingly suppose that concerts were the entertainment of such select companies only, and that at the houses of persons of distinction, the avowed patrons of the science of harmony, and its professors.

The first assembly of the kind deserving the name of a concert in London, was established under circumstances that tended rather to degrade than recommend such an entertainment, as being set on foot by a person of the lowest class among men in this country, in a suburb of the town, difficult of access, unfit for the resort of persons of fashion, and in a room that afforded them scarce decent accommodations when they had escaped the dangers of getting at it. In short, it was in the dwelling of one Thomas Britton, a man whose livelihood was selling about the streets small coal, which he carried in a sack on his back, that a periodical performance of music in parts was first exhibited, and that gratis too, to the inhabitants of this metropolis. The house of this man was situate in Aylesbury-street, leading from Clerkenwell-green to St. John's-street; the room of performance was over his small-coal shop, and, strange to tell, from the year 1678, when he first began to entertain the public, to the time of his death in 1714, Tom Britton's concert was the weekly resort of the old, the young, the gay and the fair of all ranks, including the highest order of nobility.

The history of this extraordinary person will find a place in a subsequent part of this work, where an account will be given of sundry persons eminent in music, from whose assistance his concert derived its reputation; that it is here mentioned will scarce need any other apology, than that the order of narration seemed to require it.

For the common and ordinary sort of people there were entertainments suited to their notions of music; these consisted of concerts in the unison, if they may be so called, of fiddles, of hautboys, trumpets, &c.; these were performed in booths at fairs held in and about London, but more frequently in certain places

called music-houses, of which there many in the time of Charles II.* The first of this kind was one known by the sign of the Mitre, situate near the west end of St. Paul's; the name of the master of this house was Robert Hubert, *alias* Forges. This man, besides being a lover of music, was a collector of natural curiosities, as appears by the following title of a pamphlet published in duodecimo, anno 1664, ' A Catalogue of ' the many natural rarities, with great industry, cost, ' and thirty years travel into foreign countries, col-' lected by Robert Hubert, *alias* Forges, Gent. and ' sworn servant to his majesty, and daily to be seen ' at the place called the Musick-House at the Mitre, ' near the west end of St. Paul's church.†

Another place for entertainment of the like kind was the music-house at Stepney, situated in the row of houses fronting the west end of Stepney church; it had for a sign the head of Charles II. and was the resort of seafaring people and others. In a great room of this house was an organ‡ and a band of fiddles and hautboys, to the music whereof it was no unusual thing for parties, and sometimes single persons, and those not of the very inferior sort, to dance.

Ward, in his London Spy, Part XIV. has given a particular description of a music-house which he visited in the course of his ramble, surpassing all of the kind in or about London. Its situation was in Wapping, but in what part of that suburb we are not told. The sign was that of the Mitre, and by the account which this author gives of it, the house, which was both a tavern and a music-house, was a very spacious and expensive building. He says that the music-room was a most stately apartment, and that no gilding, carving, painting, or good contrivance were wanting in the decoration of it; the seats, he says, were like the pews in a church, and the upper end being divided by a rail, appeared to him more like a chancel than a music-loft. Of the music he gives but a general account, saying only that it consisted of violins, hautboys, and an organ.

* Edward Ward, in his London Spy, Part XI. page 255, mentions these, as also the music-houses and music-booths in Bartholomew fair, which, as he relates, were very numerous so late as about the year 1700; but it seems that upon his visit to the fair, he liked this kind of music so little, that he professes he had rather have heard an old barber ring Whittington's bells upon a cittern, than all that these houses afforded. London Spy, Part XI. page 255.

† In a manuscript of the late Mr. Oldys, being a collection relating to the city of London and its history, mention is made of this pamphlet with the following note. ' I have been informed by Sir Hans Sloane ' that this collection, or a great part of it, was purchased by him into his ' noble museum of the like curiosities, which now with his library is ' removed from his late house by Bloomsbury-square to his larger house ' at Chelsea.'

It is conjectured that this house was situated in London-house Yard, at the north-west end of St. Paul's church, and on the very spot where now stands the house known by the sign of the Goose and Gridiron; for the tradition is that it was once a music-house. It seems that the successor of Hubert was no lover of music, but a man of humour, and it is said that in ridicule of the meetings formerly held there, he chose for his sign a goose stroking the bars of a gridiron with his foot, and called it the Swan and Harp.

‡ *It seems that in the usurpation, when the Liturgy and the use of organs in divine service was abolished, these instruments, being removed from the churches, were set up in such houses as that above described, and to this purpose the anonymous author, a Frenchman, of a character of England, translated by Mr. Evelyn, and published with an answer 24to 1659 has these words: ' they have translated the organs out of their churches and set ' them up in Taverns chanting their dithyrambics and bestial Bacchanalias ' to the tune of those instruments which were wont to assist them in the ' celebration of God's praises,' page 30.*

§ *Probably in Shadwell. On the South side of that street, is a place called Music house-court, New View of London 57. See it in the Plan of St. John's, Wapping, and St. Paul's, Shadwell. Strype's Stow. Book IV. page 47.*

The house being a tavern, was accommodated as well to the purpose of drinking as music; it contained many costly rooms, with whimsical paintings on the wainscotting. The kitchen was railed in to prevent the access to the fire of those who had nothing to do at it, and overhead was what this author calls an harmonious choir of canary birds singing.

The owner of this house had, according to Ward's account, used every method in his power to invite guests to it; and, under certain circumstances, appeared to be not less solicitous for their safety than their entertainment; for he had contrived a room under ground, in which persons were permitted to drink on Sundays, even during the time of divine service, and elude the search of the churchwardens.*

Another music-house, and which subsists even at this day, but in a different form, was that of Sadler's Wells, concerning which a pamphlet was published in the year 1684, with this title, 'A true and exact account of 'Sadler's Wells lately found at Islington, treating of 'its natures and vertues; together with an enumera-'tion of the chief diseases which it is good for, and 'against which it may be used, and the manner and 'order of taking it, published for the good of the 'publick by T. G., Doctor in Physick.'†

The music performed at these houses of entertainment was such as, notwithstanding the number of instruments, could scarcely entitle it to the name of a concert. For the most part it was that of violins, hautboys, or trumpets, without any diversity of parts, and consequently in the unison; or if at any time a bass instrument was added, it was only for the purpose of playing the ground-bass to those divisions on old ballad or country-dance tunes which at that time were the only music that pleased the common people. Some of the most admired of these were then known, and are still remembered by the following names :—John Dory ;‡ Paul's Steeple ; Old

Simon the King ; Farinel's Ground ;§ Tollet's Ground ; Roger of Coverly ; John come kiss me, a tune inserted in the earlier editions of Playford's Introduction ;|| Johnny cock thy Beaver, a tune to the song in D'Urfey's Pills to Purge Melancholy, 'To Horse brave Boys,' &c. ; Packington's, quasi Bockington's Pound ; Green Sleeves, which is the tune to the air in the Beggar's Opera, 'Though laws are made for every degree'; The Old Cebell, composed by Signor Baptist Draghi, and printed with a song to it in dialogue, sung in an opera called the Kingdom of the Birds, written by D'Urfey, and printed in the first volume of his Pills to purge Melancholy ; a sweet air composed by Mr. Solomon Eccles, with divisions, printed as a country-dance tune, and called Bellamira, in the 'Dancing Master,' published by Henry Playford in 1701, page 149.

Besides these there occasionally came into practice divers song and dance-tunes that had been received with applause at the theatres, and which by way of eminence were called play-house tunes, such as Genius of England, Madam Subligny's minuet, the Louvre, and many others. The principal composers of this kind of music not already named, were Mr. John Reading,¶ John Banister, Godfrey Finger,** Mr. Bullimore, John Lenton, Christopher Simpson, Matthew Lock, Henry and John Eccles, Raphael Courteville, and other less eminent musicians.

This, as far as it can be now traced, was the state of popular music about the end of the last century. Of the gradual refinements in the practice of it at large, and of the introduction of the opera into this kingdom, the following is the history :—

The restoration of king Charles II. must be considered as a remarkable epoch in the history of music in two respects ; first as the re-establishment of choral service, and the commencement of a new style in church-music is to be dated from thence ; and, secondly, as it gave a new form to that kind of music, which, in contradistinction to that of the church, is usually termed secular music. The instruments commonly used in this latter appear to have been the lute, the harp, the fiddle, cornets, pipes of various kinds, and, lastly, viols, the latter of which were at length so adjusted with respect to size and tuning, that a concert of viols became a technical term in music.

Hitherto in England the viol had never been con-

---

* Within the time of memory it was customary for the churchwardens in London and the suburbs, to perambulate their parishes on Sundays, during the time of divine service, and search the taverns and alehouses; and if they found any persons drinking therein, to turn them out, and deal with the keepers of such houses according to law.

† The author says the water of this well was before the reformation very much famed for several extraordinary cures performed thereby, and was thereupon accounted sacred, and called Holywell. The priests belonging to the priory of Clerkenwell using to attend there, made the people believe that the virtues of the water proceeded from the efficacy of their prayers. But upon the reformation the well was stopped up, upon a supposition that the frequenting of it was altogether superstitious; and so by degrees it grew out of remembrance, and was wholly lost, until found out by the labourers which Mr. Sadler, who had newly built the musick-house there, and, being surveyor of the highways, had employed to dig gravel in his garden, in the midst whereof they found it stopped up, and covered with a carved arch of stone, in the year 1683. It is here also said to be of a ferruginous taste, somewhat like that of Tunbridge, but not so strong of the steel. It is recommended for opening all obstructions, and also for purging and sweetening of the blood, &c. And Dr. Morton had that summer advised several of his patients to drink it, as the owner also was to brew his beer with it.

After the decease of Mr. Sadler above mentioned, one Francis Forcer, a musician, and the composer of many songs printed in the 'Theater of Music,' published by Henry Playford and John Carr in the years 1685, 1686, and 1687, became the occupier of the Wells and music-house. His successor therein was a son of his, who had been bred up to the law, and, as some said, a barrister; he was the first that exhibited there the diversions of rope-dancing, tumbling, &c. He was a very gentlemanly man, remarkably tall and athletic, and died in an advanced age, about the year 1730, at the Wells, which for many years had been the place of his residence.

‡ The song of John Dory, with the tune to it, is printed in the Deuteromelia, or the second part of 'Musick's Melodie,' 1609. The legend of this person is, that being a sea-captain, or perhaps a pirate, he engaged to the king of France to bring the crew of an English ship bound as captives to Paris, and that accordingly he attempted to make prize of an English vessel, but was himself taken prisoner. The song

of John Dory, and the tune to it were a long time popular in England : in the comedy of the Chances, written by Beaumont and Fletcher, Antonio, a humorous old man, receives a wound, which he will not suffer to be dressed but upon condition that the song of John Dory be sung the while.

§ Mentioned page 677 of this work, to have been composed by Farinelli of Hanover, and to have been made the subject of Corelli's twelfth Solo.

|| This was a very favourite tune : in the first part of the Division Violin there are two sets of divisions on it, the one by Mr. Davis Mell, the other by Baltzar the Lubecker, of whom Anthony Wood speaks so highly in his life. Most of the tunes above mentioned, together with many others of great antiquity, in a style peculiar to this country, are inserted in an appendix to this work.

¶ A scholar of Dr. Blow; organist of Hackney, and afterwards of St. Dunstan in the West, and St. Mary Woolnoth. He published a book of anthems by subscription, and died but a few years ago.

** A native of Olmutz in Moravia, and of the chapel to James II. He composed several Operas of Sonatas for violins, and also for flutes, the titles whereof are in the Catalogue of Estienne Roger. Lenton, the two named Eccles, and Banister, were of the band to king William; Banister was his first violin ; of him, as also of Simpson and Lock, mention will be made hereafter.

sidered as an instrument proper for a concert, or indeed of any other use than as an incentive to dancing, and that kind of mirth which was anciently the concomitant of religious festivity, particularly at Christmas, in the celebration whereof fiddlers were deemed so necessary, that in the houses of the nobility they were retained by small stipends, as also cloaks and badges, with the cognizance or arms of the family, like certain other domestic servants.* From the houses of great men to wakes, fairs, and other assemblies of the common people, the transition of these vagrant artists was natural. Bishop Earle has given a very humorous character of a common fiddler, which exhibits this particular of ancient local manners in a strong point of view.†

* This usage is mentioned in the Dialogue on old Plays and Players, and is alluded to in an old comedy entitled ' Ram-Alley,' or Merry Tricks, written by Lodowic Barrey, and printed in 1611, in which Sir Oliver Small-shanks says to the fiddlers that attend him,

' This yeare you shall have my protection,
' And yet not buy your liverie coates yourselves.'

The retainer of these servants, like watermen at this day, might possibly leave them at liberty, as occasion offered, to seek a livelihood elsewhere than in the families to which they properly belonged ; and they might nevertheless be itinerants in some degree, as may be collected from the following speech in the old play of the Return from Parnassus or the Scourge of Simony, to a company of fiddlers, who desire to be paid for their music:

' Faith fellow fiddlers, here is no silver found in this place ; no not ' so much as the usual Christmas entertainment of musicians, ' a black jacke of beer, and a Christmas pye.'

† ' A poor fiddler is a man and fiddle out of case, and he in worse case ' than his fiddle. One that rubs two sticks together (as the Indians ' strike fire) and rubs a poor living out of it ; partly from this, and partly ' from your charity, which is more in the hearing than giving him, for ' he sells nothing dearer than to be gone. He is just so many strings ' above a beggar, though he have but two; and yet he begs too, only ' not in the downright for God's sake, but with a shrugging God bless ' you, and his face is more pin'd than the blind man's. Hunger is the ' greatest pain he takes, except a broken head sometimes, and the ' labouring John Dory. Otherwise his life is so many fits of mirth, and ' 'tis some mirth to see him. A good feast shall draw him five miles by ' the nose, and you shall track him again by the scent. His other ' pilgrimages are fairs and good houses, where his devotion is great to ' the Christmas, and no man loves good times better. He is in league ' with the tapsters for the worshipful of the inn, whom he torments next ' morning with his art, and has their names more perfect than their ' men. A new song is better to him than a new jacket, especially if ' baudy, which he calls merry, and hates naturally the Puritan, as an ' enemy to his mirth. A country wedding and Whitson ale are the two ' main places he domineers in, where he goes for a musician, and over-' looks the bagpipe. The rest of him is drunk and in the stocks.'

In the times of puritanical reformation, the profession of a common fiddler was odious ; Butler has spoken the sentiments of the party in the invectives of Hudibras against Crowdero and his profession ; and by the way the following lines in his poem,

' He and that engine of vile noise,
' On which illegally he plays,
' Shall dictum factum both be brought
' To condign punishment as they ought.'

are a plain allusion to an ordinance made in 1658, in which is the following clause :—

' And be it further enacted by the authority aforesaid, that if any ' person or persons, commonly called fiddlers or minstrels, shall at any ' time after the said first day of July, [1657] be taken playing, fiddling, ' and making musick in any inn, ale-house, or tavern, or shall be taken ' proffering themselves, or desiring, or intreating any person or persons ' to hear them play, or make musick in any of the places aforesaid, that ' every such person and persons so taken, shall be adjudged, and are ' hereby adjudged and declared to be rogues, vagabonds, and sturdy ' beggers, and shall be proceeded against and punished as rogues, ' vagabonds, and sturdy beggers within the said statute, any law, statute, ' or usage to the contrary thereof in any wise notwithstanding.'

Of Whitson-ales, mentioned in the above character, as also of Church-ales, little is now known besides the name. In the Anatomie of Abuses by Philip Stubs, a book already cited, is the following description of both :—

' In certaine towns where drunken Bacchus beares swaie, against ' Christmas and Easter, Whitsunday, or some other time, the church-' wardens, (for so they call them) of every parish, with the consent of ' the whole parish, provide halfe a score or twenty quarters of mault, ' whereof scme they buy of the church stocke, and some is given them ' of the parishoners themselves ; every one conferring somewhat according ' to his ability : which mault being made into strong ale or beere, is set ' to sale eyther in the church, or in some other place assigned to that ' purpose. Then when this Nippitatum, this Huffecappe (as they call ' it) and this Nectar of life is set abroach, well is he that can get the ' soonest to it, and spend the most at it, for he that sitteth the closest

' to it, and spendes the most at it, hee is counted the Godliest man of all ' the rest, and most in God's favour, because it is spent uppon his church ' forsooth : but who either for want cannot, or otherwise for feare of God's ' wrath will not, stick to it, he is counted one destitute both of vertue ' and godlinesse. In so much as you shall have many poore men make ' hard shift for money to spende thereat. And good reason for being put ' into this Corban, they are perswaded it is meritorious and a good ' service to God. In this kinde of practise they continue six weekes, ' a quarter of a yeare, yea halfe a yeare together, swilling and gulling ' night and day, til they be as drunke as swine and as mad as March ' hares.'

The above passage may serve for an explanation of the word BRIDALE, which differs from BRIDAL, a nuptial festival, and may possibly signify the distribution of drink to a neighbourhood upon occasion of a nuptial solemnity.

The same author says, that to justify these disorderly practises, it is pretended that the money received at these assemblies is expended by the churchwardens, &c. in the repair of their respective churches and chapels, and that with it they buy ' bookes for service,' Cuppes for the ' celebration of the Sacrament, Surplesses for Sir John, and other ' necessaries, and maintaine other extraordinarie charges in their ' parishes besides.'

See a description of Church-ales, as also an apology for them in Carew's Survey of Cornwall, 68 et seq.

From the Antiquarian Repertory.
Customs of Church Ale. From a MS. in the library of Thomas Astle, Esq.
Inter MSS. Dodsworth in Bib. Bod. Vol. 158, p. 97.

This is the agreement betwixt the inhabitants of the towns and parishes of Elvaston, Thurlaston, and Ambaston of the one part, and the inhabitants of the town of Okebrook within the said parish of Elvaston, in Com. Derby, on the other part, by John, Abbot of the Dale, Ralph Saucheverell, Esq., John Bradshaw, and Henry Tithel, Gent., Witnesseth, that the inhabitants, as well of the said parish of Elvaston, as of the said town of Okebrook, shall brew four ales, and every ale of one quarter of malt, and at their own costs and charges, betwixt this and the feast of St. John Baptist next coming— And that every inhabitant of the said town of Okebrook shall be at the several ales, and every husband and his wife shall pay twopence, every cottager one penny, and all the inhabitants of Elvaston, Thurlaston, and Ambaston shall have and receive all the profits and advantages coming of the said ales to the use and behoof of the said church of Elvaston ; and the inhabitants of the said towns of Elvaston, Thurlaston, and Ambaston, shall brew eight ales betwixt this and the feast of St. John the Baptist, at the which ales, and every one of them, the inhabitants of Okebrook shall come and pay as before rehearsed ; and if he be away at one ale, to pay at the t'oder ale for both, or else to send his money. And the inhabitants of Okebrook shall carry all manner of tymber being in the dale wood now felled, that the said prestchyrch of the said towns of Elvaston, Thurlaston, and Ambaston shall occupye to the use and profit of the said church.

N. B. This appears to have been the old method of paying money for the repair of country churches.

Custom of Bride Ale.
From the Court Rolls of Hales-owen Borough in Com. Salop, in the hands of Thomas Lyttleton, Lord of the said Borough, de Anno. 15 Eliz. R.

Item, a payne is made, that no person or persons that shall brewe any weddyn ale to sell, shall not brewe above twelve strike of malt at the most, and that shall sell persons so married shall not keep nor have above eight messe of persons at his dinner within the burrowe : and before his brydall daye he shall keep no unlawfull games in hys house, nor out of hys house, on pain of 20 shillings.

Communicated by Thomas Astle, Esq.

But farther to show in how small estimation the violin was formerly held in this country : it appears that at the time when Anthony Wood was a young man, viz., about the year 1650, that the tuning of it was scarcely settled ; for in the account by him given of his learning to play on that instrument, he says that he tuned it by fourths, and the notation was borrowed from the tablature of the lute, which had then lately been transferred to the viol da gamba. But the king, soon after his return to England, having heard Baltzar's exquisite performance on the violin, took him into his service, and placed him at the head of a band of violins, but he dying in 1663, was succeeded by Mr. John Banister, who had been bred up under his father, one of the waits, as they are called, of the parish of St. Giles in the Fields, near London ; this person was sent by Charles II. to France for improvement, but soon after his return was dismissed the king's service for saying that the English violins were better than the French.‡

‡ It seems that he had good reason for saying so, for at the time when Lully was placed at the head of a band of violins, created on purpose for him by Lewis XIV. and called Les petits Violons, in contradistinction to that of twenty-four, not half the musicians in France were able to play at sight.

By means of this circumstance, and the several particulars before enumerated, respecting the taste of Charles II. for music, we are enabled to trace with some degree of certainty the introduction of the violin species of instruments into this kingdom, and to ascertain the time when concerts, consisting of two treble violins, a tenor, and a bass violin or violoncello, came into practice;* that they had their origin in Italy can scarce admit of a question; and it is no less certain that they were adopted by the French; though it is not easy to conceive the use of a band wherein were twenty-four performers on the same instrument; nor indeed how so many could be employed to advantage in any such concerts as were known at that time.

Indeed the idea of a performance, where the instruments for the bass and intermediate parts were in number so disproportionate to the treble, seems to be absurd; and there is reason to suspect that the song 'four and twenty fiddlers all on a row,' in D'Urfey's Pills to purge Melancholy, was written in ridicule of that band of twenty-four violins, which, as the French writers assert, was the most celebrated of any in Europe.†

During the residence of Charles at the court of France, he became enamoured of French manners and French music; and upon his return to England, in imitation of that of Lewis, he established a band of violins, and placed at the head of it, at first Baltzar the Lubecker, and after him Banister, who, for a reason above assigned, was removed from the direction of it.

Besides the person that presided over the violins, who can hardly be supposed to have been any other than he that played the principal violin part, there was also a master or director of the king's music; the person who first occupied this station was Nicholas Laniere, as appears by a grant of Charles I. herein before inserted. Upon the death of Laniere, who lived some years after the restoration, Matthew Lock was appointed to that office, with the same allowance of 200l. a year; but about the year 1673, Cambert, a French musician, who had been master of music to the queen mother Ann of Austria, and the Marquis de Sourdeac, and also joint manager of the opera at Paris, came into England, and by Charles II. was made superintendent of his music.

Cambert, though he died in 1677, lived here long enough to exhibit an opera of his composition, entitled Pomone, which had been received at Paris with general applause, and to introduce into concerts

the violins, and those other instruments of that species, the tenor violin and violoncello, the characteristic whereof is that they have uniformly four strings tuned in fifths. To these were adapted compositions of a new structure, namely, Sonatas, the invention of some of the most eminent performers on the violin among the Italians; these were of two kinds, viz., Sonate da Chiesa, and Sonate da Camera; the first consisted of slow solemn movements, intermixed with fugues; the other of preludes and airs of various forms, as Allemands, Courants, Sarabands, Gavots, and Jigs.

But here a distinction is to be noted between the airs abovementioned, and those of the age preceding, and this will require a particular specification of each.

The word Air is rather a modern term in music; it had its original among the Italian masters; Lord Bacon makes use of it in his essay on Beauty, saying that the sweetest airs in music are made by a kind of felicity, and not by rule. These were the Passamezzo, the Pavan, the Galliard, the Allemand, the Coranto, the Jig, and some others, which may be termed old airs.

The PASSAMEZZO, from *passer* to walk, and *mezzo* the middle or half, is a slow dance, little differing from the action of walking. As a Galliard‡ consists of five paces or bars in the first strain, and is therefore called a Cinque Pace; the Passamezzo, which is a diminutive of the Galliard, has just half that number, and from that peculiarity takes its name.

The PAVAN is by some writers said to be an air invented in Padua. This is founded on no better authority than mere etymological conjecture; the word is derived from the Latin Pavo, a peacock, and signifies a kind of dance, performed in such a manner, and with such circumstances of dignity and stateliness, as show the propriety of the appellation.§

The GALLIARD is a lively air in triple time;

‡ In lessons for the harsichord and virginal the airs were made to follow in a certain order, that is to say, the slowest or most grave first, and the rest in succession, according as they deviated from that character, by which rule the Jig generally stood last. In general the Galliard followed the Pavan, the first being a grave, the other a sprightly air; but this rule was not without exception. In a manuscript collection of lessons composed by Bird, formerly belonging to a lady Neville, who it is supposed was a scholar of his, is a lesson of a very extraordinary kind, as it seems intended to give the history of a military engagement. The following are the names of the several airs in order as they occur. 'The 'Marche before the battell, The Souldiers Sommons, The Marche of 'foot-men, The Marche of horse-men: Now folowethe the Trumpets, 'The Bagpipe and the Drone, the Flute and the Drome, the Marche to 'the Fighte, Here the battells be joyned, The Retreate, Now folowethe 'a Galliarde for the victory.' There is also in the same collection a lesson called the Carman's Whistle.

The airs composed about the time of queen Elizabeth, however excellent in their kind, seem to have derived their reputation from their being the tunes of dances actually performed at court, or at public assemblies for the purpose of feasting and recreation. In a work entitled 'Lachrymæ or Seaven Teares figured in seaven passionate Pavans with 'divers other Pavans, Galiards, and Almands by John Dowland,' the several airs are distinguished by appellations which seem to indicate their being the favourites of particular persons, as in these instances: 'M. John Langton's Pavan, the King of Denmark's Galiard, the Earl of 'Essex Galiard, Sir John Souch his Galiard, M. Henry Noell his Galiard, 'M. Giles Hoby his Galiard, M. Nicho. Gryffith his Galiard, M. Thomas 'Collier his Galiard with two trebles, Captaine Piper his Galiard, M. 'Bucton his Galiard, Mr. Nichols Almand, Mr. George Whitehead his 'Almand.'

Of this fact it is some sort of proof that the airs above enumerated are in the title-page of the book said to be set forth for the lute, viols, or violins; and it is certain that in Dowland's time the latter of these instruments was appropriated to the practice of dancing. Farther it is expressly said by Christopher Simpson, in his Compendium of Practical Music, page 143, that fancies and symphonies excepted, instrumental music in its several kinds was derived from the various measures in dancing.

§ See page 215 of this work.

* Of the French concerts there are few memorials remaining, other than some scattered passages in Mersennus, cited or referred to in the course of this work. In this kingdom the music for concerts of violins, before the invention of the Sonata, consisted altogether of airs in three, and sometimes four parts. Of these sundry collections were published by Playford, and others: some of the most celebrated of them were those entitled 'Court Ayres, Pavins, Almains, Corants, and Sarabands,' by Dr. Child, Dr. Coleman, Dr. Rogers, Will. Lawes, Jenkins, and others, published by Playford in 1656, 'Tripla Concordia, or a Choice Collection 'of new Airs in three parts for treble and Basse Violins,' by Matthew Lock, Robert Smith, William Hall, John Banister, Robert King, and Francis Forcer: printed for John Carr, 1977, obl. quarto; and a collection of airs by Matthew Lock, called his little Consort.

† Notwithstanding this establishment and the pains that Lewis XIV. took to introduce the opera into France, it is to be doubted whether the scenery, the decorations, and, above all, the dances, were not the principal object of his regard in these splendid representations: and it is said of Lully, that to gratify his master he laboured as much in composing the dances as the airs of the opera. Hist. de la Musique et de ses Effets, tom. III. page 321.

Brassard intimates that it is the same with the Romanesca, a favourite dance with the Italians.

The ALLEMAND, ALMAND, or ALMAIN, as its name imports, is an air originally invented by the Germans; it is of a grave and serious cast, yet full of spirit and energy, arising from the compass of notes which it takes in; the measure of it is duple time of four crotchets in a bar; the air consists of two strains, with a repetition of each; and those that define it with exactness say that it ought to begin with an odd quaver or semiquaver, or with three semiquavers. Walther says that in this species of instrumental composition, especially the Allemand for the dance, the Germans excel all other nations; but this assertion seems rather too bold; the Allemands of the Italian masters, particularly Corelli, Albinoni, and Geminiani, being inferior to none that we know of: that in the tenth solo of Corelli may be looked upon as one of the most perfect models for this kind of air.

The CORANTO, Courant, Fr. Corrente, Ital. Currens saltatio, Lat., is a melody or air consisting of three crotchets in a bar, but moving by quavers, in the measure of $\frac{3}{4}$, with two strains or reprises, each beginning with an odd quaver. Walther, who describes it, assigns to it no determinate number of bars; nor is there any precise rule that we know of for the measure of it, save that the number of bars, whatever it be, is the multiple of 8. Of dance-tunes it is said to be the most solemn.

The SARABAND is an air of great antiquity; the Spaniards write it Zarabanda, and this orthography seems to confirm the opinion of those who derive it from the Moors, saying that they brought it into Spain, and that from thence it was diffused throughout Europe.*

The CHACONE, a less common air than any of those above enumerated, is said by some, who take it for granted that the word is derived from the Italian cieco, blind, to be the invention of some blind musician; but others assert that, like the Saraband, it is of Moorish original; and those who would carry it still higher, suggest that the word is derived from the Persian Schach, which signifies a king; and that Chacone might signify a royal dance: from the Persians, say these, it might pass to the Saracens, and from them to the Moors. The characteristic of the Chacone is a bass or ground, consisting of four measures, of that kind of triple wherein three crotchets make the bar, and the repetitions thereof with variations in the several parts from the beginning to the end of the air, which, in respect of its length, has no limit but the discretion of the composer. The whole of the twelfth Sonata of the second opera of Corelli is a Chacone.

There is another air in music called by the Italians the PASSACAGLIO, and by the French Passacaille, which, like the Chacone, consists in a variety of divisions on a given ground bass; the only essential difference between the one and the

other of the two is, that the Chacone is ever in the major, and the Passacaille in the minor third of the key. In Mr. Handel's lessons for the harpsichord, Suite Septieme is an air of the sort last above described.

The JIGG is supposed by some to have been invented by the English, but its derivation from the Teutonic GIEG, or, as Junius writes it, GHIJGHE, a fiddle, is rather against this opinion. Mattheson speaks of the Jigs of this country as having in general a pointed note at the beginning of every bar; but for this distinction there seems not to be the least authority. The same author seems to think that originally the Jig was a dance tune, and of English invention: nevertheless it has been adopted by most nations in Europe; for not only in England, but in Italy, Germany, and France it appears to have been a favourite species of air. Its characteristic is duple time, thus marked, $\frac{6}{8}$ or $\frac{12}{8}$. The air itself consists of two strains, undetermined as to the number of bars †

To speak now of the airs of the moderns, and first of the Gavot.

The Gavot, so far as regards the general practice of it, is hardly to be traced further backwards than to the time of Lully, that is to say about the year 1670. Huet says that the appellation is derived from the Gavots, a people inhabiting a mountainous district in France called Gap.‡ It signifies a dance-tune in duple time, consisting of two strains, the first whereof contains four bars, and the latter eight, and sometimes twelve, each beginning with two crotchets, or the half of a bar, with a rise of the hand in beating, and ending also with two crotchets that begin the last bar. Walther says it is required that the first strain of a Gavot should have its cadence in the third or fifth of the key, for that if it be in the key-note itself, it is not a Gavot but a Rondeau; and in this opinion both Brossard and Mattheson concur.§

The invention of the MINUET, Fr. Menuet, seems generally to be ascribed to the French, and particularly to the inhabitants of the province of Poictou; the word is said by Menage and Furetiere to be de-

---

* Within the memory of persons now living, a Saraband danced by a Moor was constantly a part of the entertainment at a puppet shew; this particular may be considered as an additional circumstance in proof that this dance is of Moorish original. See page 216.

† The Jigs of Corelli abound with fine melody: that in the sixth of his Solos is celebrated throughout Europe. In the fourth of Mr. Handel's Concertos for the organ is an example of a jig movement interwoven with one in andante time, and the contrast has a remarkably fine effect.

‡ 'GAVOTE. Sorte de danse. M. Huet, dans son Traité curieux de 'l' Origine des Romans, page 124. *Les Martegales et Madrigaux ont pris 'leur nom des* MARTEGAUX, *peuples montagnards de Provence; de même 'que les Gavots, peuples montagnards du pays de Gap, ont donné le nom 'à cette danse que nous appellons* Gavote. Cette ètymologie me paroît 'très véritable.' M. Menage, article GAVOTE.

§ The Gavots of Corelli, Albinoni, Vivaldi, and others of the Italians, correspond with these rules as far as they relate to the measure, the number of bars in each strain, and the cadences; but in respect to the initial notes of the air, they deviate from it; for they sometimes begin with a whole bar, as that in the first Sonata of the second Opera of Corelli, and the fifth of his fourth Opera, and yet they are termed Gavots, as are also those airs of the Gavot-kind in the tenth of his Solos, and the ninth of his Concertos, each whereof begins with an odd quaver. As to those airs of his which are said to be tempo di Gavotta, such as that in his ninth Solo, and those in the fifth and eighth of his second, and the third and tenth of his fourth Opera, they are not Gavots, but movements in the time of the Gavot, with a general imitation of the air.

After all, the Gavot, strictly so called, is an air that disgusts by its formality; those Gavots only have a pleasing effect in which the middle and final closes are suspended by a varied and eloquent modulation, of which the Gavot in the overture of Semele, and the last movement in the third of Mr. Handel's Concertos for the organ, are remarkable instances.

rived from the French Menuë or Menue, small or little, and in strictness signifies a small pace. The melody of this dance consists of two strains, which, as being repeated, are called reprises, each having eight or more bars, but never an odd number. The measure is three crotchets in a bar, marked thus, $\frac{3}{4}$, though it is commonly performed in this time, $\frac{3}{8}$. Walther speaks of a minuet in Lully's opera of Roland, each strain of which contains ten bars, the sectional number being 5, which renders it very difficult to dance.

The PASPY, Fr. Passe-pied, from passer to walk, and pied a foot, is a very brisk French dance, the measure $\frac{3}{8}$, and often $\frac{6}{8}$. It has three or more strains or reprises, the first consisting of eight bars. It is said to have been invented in Bretagne, and is in effect a quick minuet.

The BOUREE is supposed to come from Auvergne in France; it seldom occurs but in compositions of French masters; its time is duple, consisting of twice four measures in the first strain, and twice eight in the second.

The SICILIANA is an air probably invented in Sicily, of a slow movement, thus characterised, $\frac{12}{8}$; it consists of two strains, the first of four, and the second of eight bars or measures.

The LOUVRE is a mere dance-tune; the term is not general, but is applied singly to a French air, called L'amiable Vainqueur, of which Lewis XIV. was extremely fond; the French dancing masters composed a dance to it, which is well known in England.

That the HORNPIPE was invented by the English seems to be generally agreed: that it was not unusual to give to certain airs the names of the instruments on which they were commonly played, may be instanced in the word Geig, which with a little variation is made to signify both a fiddle and the air called a Jig, and properly adapted to it. Indeed we have no such instrument as the hornpipe, but in Wales it is so common that even the shepherd-boys play on it. In the Welsh language it has the name of the Pib-corn, i. e. the Hornpipe; and it is so called as consisting of a wooden pipe, with holes at stated distances, and a horn at each end, the one to collect the wind blown into it by the mouth, and the other to carry off the sounds as modulated by the performer. A very learned and curious antiquary, the Hon. Daines Barrington, has lately communicated to the world a description, as also the form of this rustic instrument, and with no small appearance of probability conjectures that it originally gave the name to the air called the Hornpipe.*

The measure of the Hornpipe is triple time of six crotchets in a bar, four whereof are to be beat

* See the Archæologia of the Antiquarian Society, vol. III. page 33. That there was anciently a musical instrument called the Hornpipe is evident from the following passage in Chaucer, in which it is mentioned with the flute:—

Controve he would, and foule faile
With Hornpipes of Cornwaile.
In floites made he discordaunce,
And in his mufike with mifchaunce
He would feine, &c.
ROMAUNT OF THE ROSE, Fo. 135. b. edit. 1561.

with a down, and two with an up hand. There occurs in the opera of Dioclesian, set to Music by Purcell, a dance called the CANARIES: of this, and also another called TRENCHMORE, it is extremely difficult to render a satisfactory account. The first is alluded to by Shakespeare in the following passage:—

'Moth. Master, will you win your love with a French 'brawl?†
'Arm. How meanst thou? brawling in French?
'Moth. No, my compleat master: but to jig off a tune 'at the tongue's end, canary to it with your feet, humour 'it with turning up your eyelids,' &c.
LOVE'S LABOUR LOST, Act III. Scene 1.

As to the air itself, it appears by the example in the opera of Dioclesian to be a very sprightly movement of two reprises or strains, with eight bars in each. The time three quavers in a bar, the first pointed. That it is of English invention, like the country-dance, may be inferred from this circumstance, that none of the foreign names that distinguish one kind of air from another correspond in the least with this. Nay, farther, the appellation is adopted by Couperin, a Frenchman, who among his lessons has an air which he entitles Canaries.

Of the dance called Trenchmore frequent mention is made by our old dramatic writers: thus in the Island Princess of Beaumont and Fletcher, Act V. one of the townsmen says—

'All the windows i' th' town dance a new Trenchmore.

In the Table talk of Selden, tit. KING OF ENGLAND, is the following humorous passage:

'The court of England is much alter'd. At 'a solemn dancing, first you had the grave measures, 'then the Corantoes and the Galliards, and this kept 'up with ceremony; and at length to Trenchmore, 'and the Cushion dance: Then all the company 'dances, lord and groom, lady and kitchen-maid, no 'distinction. So in our court in queen Elizabeth's 'time, gravity and state were kept up. In king 'James's time things were pretty well. But in king 'Charles's time there has been nothing but Trench-'more and the Cushion-dance, omnium gatherum, 'tolly polly, hoite come toite.'

And in the comedy of the Rehearsal, the Earth, Sun, and Moon are made to dance the Hey to the tune of Trenchmore: from all which it may be inferred that the Trenchmore was also a lively movement ‡

The COUNTRY-DANCE is also said to have had its origin with us. Indeed Mr. Weaver, one of the best teachers of dancing in the kingdom of the last age, and who appears to have been well acquainted with the history of his art, has asserted it in express terms. He says that the country-dance is the peculiar growth of this nation, though it is now transplanted into almost all the courts of Europe, and it is become in the most august assemblies one of the favourite diversions.§

† i. e. the dance called the Brawl or Brauls, mentioned page 215.
‡ In the Dancing Master, or Directions for dancing Country-dances, with the tunes to each dance. published by Henry Playford in 1698, page 44, is a tune entitled 'Trenchmore,' inserted in the Appendix to this work.
§ Essay towards a History of Dancing by John Weaver. Lond. 8vo. 1712, page 170.
For the composition of country-dance tunes no rule is laid down by

We meet also among the compositions of the English masters of the violin who lived in the time of Charles II. with an air called the Cebell, an appellation for which no etymology, nor indeed any explanation, is attempted by any of our lexicographers : for this reason we are necessitated to resort for satisfaction to those few exemplars of this kind of air now remaining, and by these it appears to have been an air in duple time of four bars or measures, only repeated in division at the will of the composer, but with this remarkable circumstance, that the several strains are alternately in the grave and the acute series of notes in the musical scale.*

That elegant species of composition the Sonata, had its rise about the middle of the seventeenth century : who were the original inventors of it is not certainly known, but doubtless those that excelled most in it were Bassani and Corelli. The first essay towards the introduction of the Sonata into England was a collection of Sonatas for two violins and a bass, by Mr. John Jenkins ; these it is true were in three parts only ; and compositions of this kind must be said to have been wanting in that variety of harmony which is produced by a concert of six viols ; but this defect was soon remedied by giving to the violoncello one bass part, and to the organ, harpsichord, or arch-lute another ; and, lastly, by the invention of the Concerto Grosso, consisting of two choruses, with an intermediate part, so necessary in all symphoniac music, for the tenor violin. It is said that we are indebted for this great improvement in instrumental music to Giuseppe Torelli, and from about the year 1700, until almost the present time, the designation of a full concert for violins has been, two principal and two second violins, a tenor violin, and a violoncello, with a thorough-bass for the harpsichord, and of consequence the viol species of instruments has grown into disuse.

The lute, notwithstanding the great improvements which the French had made of it, as well by varying its form as by increasing the number of chords, thereby rendering it in some respects the rival of the harpsichord, was nevertheless now declining in the estimation of the world. Waller suggests as a reason for it, an opinion, which, although it is controverted by Mace and other masters, had very probably its foundation in truth : it was suspected that the practice of the lute had a tendency to bring on deformity in ladies and persons of deli-

cate habits,† an evil which was not to be feared from the erect and graceful posture required in playing on the harpsichord. But whoever considers the structure of the lute, the labour of stringing it, and the attention requisite to keep it in order, over and above the incessant practice necessary to acquire a fine hand on it, need not look far for reasons why it has given place to the harpsichord, of all musical instruments ever invented the most easy.

## CHAP. CXLIX.

The Italian opera having undergone a gradual refinement, was now arrived at great perfection, and, notwithstanding the early prejudices of the French against Italian music, had found its way to Paris. Lewis XIV. in the year 1669, had established the Academie Royal de Musique ; Corneille, Quinault, and other the best poets of France, composed the drama of many operas, and first Cambert, and afterwards Lully, set them to music. The public taste, and the posture of affairs in this country, were not then so favourable to theatrical representations of this kind, as to enable us to emulate our neighbours in the exhibition of them : some faint attempts of imitation had indeed been made by the introduction of vocal and instrumental music into some of our plays, as particularly Macbeth and the Tempest, composed by Matthew Lock, in which were a few airs and choruses, distributed at proper intervals through the five acts, with a few short recitatives ; but for want of a proper fable, of machinery, and other requisites, and, above all, a continued recitative to connect and introduce the airs, these representations could hardly be said to bear more than a very faint resemblance of the Italian opera properly so called.

The above two plays of Macbeth and the Tempest, altered from Shakespeare, the one by Sir William Davenant, and the other by Shadwell, were performed at the theatre in Lincoln's-Inn fields ; the latter was wrought into the form of an opera ; the applause with which they were severally received gave encouragement to Shadwell to compose a drama named Psyche, which, though he would have it thought he took it from Apuleius, is in a great measure a translation of the Psyche of Quinault, which was set to music by Lully in 1672, in the manner of the Italian opera. Lock had succeeded beyond expectation in the music to Macbeth and the Tempest, and he, together with Gio. Battista Draghi, composed the music to this opera of Psyche. The following advertisement in the preface of Shadwell to Psyche will show the part which each of them took, as also what other persons assisted in the work.

'All the instrumental music (which is not min-'gled with the vocal) was composed by that great 'master, Signior Gio. Battista Draghi, master of the

---

any of the writers on music, perhaps for this reason, that there is in music no kind of time whatever but may be measured by those motions and gesticulations common in dancing ; and in fact there are few song-tunes of any account within these last hundred years that have not become also country-dances. Simpson in his Compendium of ' Practical Musick,' page 144, says of country-dances, and indeed of some other airs, that they are so easy to compose, that he has known some ' who by ' a natural aptness, and by the accustomed hearing of them, would make ' such like, being untaught, although they had not so much skill in ' music as to be able to write them down in notes.'

\* Examples of this species of air occur in the Division Violin, a book which has already been mentioned. But the most celebrated of any that we know of, is that called the Old Cebell, which some very old persons now living remember to have been one of the most popular tunes at the beginning of this century. It is printed as a song with words to it in D'Urfey's Pills to purge Melancholy, vol. I. page 139 ; the author of it is there said to be Sig. Baptist, by whom some have understood Lully, whose christian names were Jean Baptiste, but the person meant is Sig. Giovanni Battista Draghi, of whom an account will hereafter be given.

† See in his works the letter following that to Lady Lucy Sidney. Mace in answer to the objection, which it seems was a common one, asserts that in his whole time he never knew any person that grew awry by the practice of the lute. Musick's Monument, page 46.

'Italian music to the king. The dances were made
' by the most famous master of France, Monsieur St.
' Andrée. The scenes were painted by the ingenious
' artist, Mr. Stephenson. In those things that con-
' cern the ornament or decoration of the play, the
' great industry and care of Mr. Betterton ought to
' be remembered, at whose desire I wrote upon this
' subject.'

This opera was performed at the theatre in Dorset
Garden in February, 1673; Downes, the prompter,
says that the scenes, machines, cloths, and other
necessaries and decorations, cost upwards of 800l.
He adds that it was performed eight days together,
but did not prove so beneficial to the undertakers as
the Tempest.

In the year 1677, Charles Davenant, the elder son
of Sir William Davenant,* wrote an opera entitled
Circe, the music to which was composed by Mr.
John Banister; it was performed at Lincolns-Inn
fields theatre, and was well received.

In 1685, the year in which king Charles II. died,
Mr. Dryden wrote an allegorical drama, or, as he
calls it, an opera, entitled Albion and Albanius; it
was set to music by Monsieur Louis Grabu, a French
musician, and performed at the theatre in Dorset
Garden: it appears by the preface to have been
written during the life-time of the king, but was not
represented till some months after his decease. As
this opera is printed among the dramatic works of
Mr. Dryden, with a preface, in which the composer
of the music is complimented to the prejudice of
Purcell, and the rest of the English musicians, it
may here suffice to say that it is a satire against
sedition, with a view to the conduct of the earl of
Shaftesbury,† who then, though in a declining state
of health, headed the opposition to the court measures. It abounds with ridiculous pageantry, such
as Juno drawn by peacocks, and the representation
of a rainbow, or some such meteor, which had then
lately been seen in the heavens, and was exhibited
at an expense that far exceeded the amount of the
money taken for admittance. Downes says it was
performed on a very unlucky day, viz., that on which
the duke of Monmouth landed in the west; and he
intimates that the consternation into which the
kingdom was thrown by this event was a reason

* This gentleman was first an actor on the stage in Dorset-Garden,
under his mother Lady D'avenant, Mr. Betterton, and Mr. Harris, and
removed with them to the theatre in Lincoln's-Inn-fields. He afterwards took the degree of Doctor of Laws, and obtained the post in the
Custom-house of inspector general of the exports and imports. He was
extremely well skilled in political arithmetic, and matters relating to the
revenue, and wrote many valuable tracts on those subjects.

† This appears by a device of machinery thus described : ' Fame rises
' out of the middle of the stage, standing on a globe, on which is the
' arms of England: the globe rests on a pedestal : on the front of the
' pedestal is drawn a man with a long, lean, pale face, with fiends' wings,
' and snakes twisted round his body: he is encompassed by several
' phanatical rebellious heads, who suck poison from him, which runs
' out of a tap in his side.'

The wit of this satire at this day stands in some need of an explanation.
The earl of Shaftesbury was afflicted with a dropsy, and had frequent
recourse to the expedient of tapping; and such was the malevolence of
his enemies, that although they had their choice of numberless particulars by which he might have been distinguished, that of the tap
appeared to them the most eligible. Some time before his death it was
a fashion in taverns to have wine brought to guests, and set upon table
in a wooden or silver vessel shaped like a tun, with a cock to it, and this
was called a Shaftesbury.

why it was performed but six times, and was in
general ill received.‡

After an interval of about five years, Mr. Betterton
made another attempt to introduce the opera on the
English stage. To that end he prevailed on Mr.
Dryden to write King Arthur, which having in it a
great deal of machinery and dancing, and being
finely set to music by Purcell, succeeded very well,
and encouraged him to alter the Prophetess of
Beaumont and Fletcher into the resemblance of an
opera; and this he did by retrenching some of the
seeming superfluities, and introducing therein musical interludes and songs to a great number, all
which, together with the dances, which were composed by Mr. Priest, were set to music by Purcell,
and was performed with great applause. The same
method was practised with the Midsummer Night's
Dream of Shakespeare, which was altered into a
drama called the Fairy Queen. To this also Mr.
Priest composed the dances, and Purcell the music.

Of these entertainments it is observed that they
were in truth only plays with songs intermixed with
the scenes, and that there could be no pretence for
calling them operas, other than because chorusses and
dances were introduced in them after the manner of
the French.

CHRISTOPHER SIMPSON (a Portrait), was a musician
of considerable eminence, and flourished about this
time. He was greatly celebrated for his skill on the
viol, and was the author of two treatises, of which an
account will shortly be given. Of his birth or education we find nothing recorded; nor are there any
particulars extant of him, save that in his younger

‡ The following humorous ballad was written in ridicule of this drama,
and in particular of Grabu's music to it :—

From Father Hopkins, whose vein did inspire,
  *Bayes* sends this raree-show to publick view;
Prentices, fops, and their footmen admire him,
  Thanks patron, painter, and Monsieur *Grabu*.

Each actor on the stage his luck bewailing,
  Finds that his loss is infallibly true;
*Smith*, *Nokes*, and *Leigh* in a Feaver with railing,
  Curse poet, painter, and Monsieur *Grabu*.

*Betterton, Betterton*, thy decorations,
  And the machines were well written we knew;
But all the words were such stuff we want patience,
  And little better is Monsieur *Grabu*.

D— me, says *Underhill*, I'm out of two hundred,
  Hoping that rainbows and peacocks would do;
Who thought infallible Tom could have blunder'd,
  A plague upon him and Monsieur *Grabu*.

*Lane*, thou hast no applause for thy capers,
  Tho' all without thee would make a man spew;
And a month hence will not pay for the tapers,
  Spite of Jack Laureat and Monsieur *Grabu*.

*Bayes*, thou wouldst have thy skill thought universal,
  Tho' thy dull ear be to musick untrue;
Then whilst we strive to confute the Rehearsal,
  Prithee learn thrashing of Monsieur *Grabu*.

With thy dull prefaces still wouldst thou treat us,
  Striving to make thy dull bauble look fair;
So the horn'd herd of the city do cheat us,
  Still most commending the worst of their ware.

Leave making operas and writing Lyricks,
  'Till thou hast ears and canst alter thy strain;
Stick to thy talent of bold Panegyricks,
  And still remember the breathing the vein.

Yet if thou thinkest the town will extol 'em,
  Print thy dull notes, but be thrifty and wise;
Instead of angels subscrib'd for the volume,
  Take a round shilling, and thank my advice.

In imitating thee this may be charming,
  Gleaning from Laureats is no shame at all;
And let this song be sung next performing,
  Else ten to one but the prices will fall.

days he was a soldier in the army raised by William Cavendish, duke of Newcastle, for the service of Charles I. against the parliament; that he was of the Romish communion, and patronised by Sir Robert Bolles, of Leicestershire, whose son, a student in Gray's Inn, Simpson taught on the viol. He dwelt some years in Turnstile, Holborn, and finished his life there. In the year 1665, Simpson published in a thin folio volume a book entitled Chelys Minuritionum; in English, the Division Viol, printed in columns, viz. in Latin, with an English translation; Editio secunda, dedicated to Sir John Bolles, son and heir of Sir Robert Bolles above mentioned.

In the dedication of this second edition, the author, among the reasons which he gives for recommending the former edition to the patronage of this young gentleman's father, represents his circumstances in these terms:—' All the motives that could enter into ' a dedication of that nature did oblige me to it. ' First, as he was a most eminent patron of music and ' musicians; secondly, as he was not only a lover of ' music, but a great performer in it, and that the ' treatise had its conception, birth, and accomplish- 'ment under his roof in your minority; lastly, as he ' was my peculiar patron, affording me a cheerful ' maintenance, when the iniquity of the times had ' reduced me, with many others in that common ca- ' lamity, to a condition of needing it.'* In the same epistle dedicatory he scruples not to say of this young gentleman, Sir John Bolles, that the book recommended to his patronage, as it was written for his instruction, so had it made him not only the greatest artist, but the ablest judge of the contents of it of any person in Europe, being a gentleman, and no professor of the science; and in support of this assertion he refers to a paper of verses printed at Rome, occasioned as he says by the rare expressions on the viol of this his pupil and patron at a music meeting, in which were present ' not only divers grandees of ' that court and city, with some embassadors of ' foreign states, but also the great musicians of Rome, ' all admiring his knowledge of music, and his excel- ' lence upon that instrument.'†

* It should seem by this that Simpson had been of some choir, and that at the usurpation he was turned out of his place, for that was the common calamity which befel the musicians of that time.

† The verses above mentioned are these that follow:—

Eximiæ Nobilitati, Doctrinæ, Virtuti, cum summa Musices harmonia consono adolescenti, illustrissimo Domino, D JOANNI BOLLES, Anglo, Roberti Baronet. Hæredi Filio. Mirificam suavitatem ejusdem et argutiam in tangenda Britannica Chely, quam vulgò dicunt Violam Majorem stupori Romæ fuisse.

O D E.

Jacobi Albani Ghibbesii, Med. Doct. ac in Romana Sapientia Eloq. Prof. Primarii.

Res suas dicam sibi habere Phœbo,
Te modis aures retinente nostras:
Quale solamen Samius negârit
　　　　Doctor Olympo.

Quantus Alcides animos triumphas,
Gallico major! trahat ille vulgus:
Roma Te vidit stupefacta primos
　　　　Ducere patres:

Roma tormentum fidium insecuta
Dulce, concentus licèt ipsa mater.
Allobrox miræ Venetusque plausit
　　　　Nuntius arti.

Vividum claro, celebrémque alumno
Laudo Simpsonum: vaga fama quantum
Thessali cultu juvenis magistrum
　　　　Distulit orbi.

The epistle containing this remarkable anecdote concludes with an intimation, somewhat obscurely worded, that the Latin translation of the book was made by Mr. William Marsh, some time a scholar of the author, for the purpose of making it intelligible to foreigners.

The book has the like imprimatur with others published about that time; but the licenser, Sir Roger L'Estrange, has superadded to his allowance a preface recommending it in terms that import much more than a compliment to his friend the author, as Sir Roger was a very fine performer on the instrument which is the subject of it.

As to the book itself, the design of it is to render familiar a practice which the performers on the Viol da Gamba, about the time of its publication, were emulous to excel in, namely, the making extemporary divisions on a ground-bass; but as this was not to be done at random, and required some previous skill in the principles of harmony, the author undertakes to unfold them in his treatise.

It is divided into three parts: the first contains instructions at large for the performance on the instrument; the second teaches the use of the concords and discords, and is in truth a compendium of descant; the third part contains the method of ordering division to a ground, a practice which the author thus explains:—

' Diminution or division to a ground, is the break- 'ing either of the bass or of any higher part that ' is applicable thereto. The manner of expressing it ' is thus:—

' A ground, subject, or bass, call it what you ' please, is prick'd down in two several papers; one ' for him who is to play the ground upon an organ, 'harpsichord, or what other instrument may be apt ' for that purpose; the other for him that plays upon ' the viol, who having the said ground before his ' eyes as his theme or subject, plays such variety of ' descant or division in concordance thereto as his ' skill and present invention do then suggest unto ' him. In this manner of play, which is the perfec- 'tion of the viol or any other instrument, if it be ' exactly performed, a man may show the excellency ' both of his hand and invention, to the delight and ' admiration of those that hear him.

' But this you will say is a perfection that few ' attain unto, depending much upon the quickness of ' invention as well as quickness of hand. I answer ' it is a perfection which some excellent hands ' have not attained unto, as wanting those helps ' which should lead them to it; the supply of which ' want is the business we here endeavour.'

Hactenùs plectrum, citharamque vates
Noverint; Arcu Violaque freti
Concinent posthac: nequè Thressa certet
　　　　Chorda Britannæ.

O virûm felix, et opima rerum
Albion, sedes placitura Musis!
O poli sidus mihi, quò remotam
　　　　Dirigo puppim!

à Museo nostro, Kal. April 1661.　　Monumentum, et pignus amoris.

Of this Dr. Gibbes there is an account in the Fasti Oxon. vol. II, col 192, by which it appears that he was born of English parents at Roan in Normandy; that he became poet laureat to the emperor Leopold, and was by diploma declared doctor in physic of the university of Oxford. He died anno 1676, and was buried in the Pantheon at Rome.

I. Carwarden pinxit.    C. Grignion sculp.

CHRISTOPHORI SIMPSON EFFIGIES.

MDCLXVII.

After giving sundry examples of grounds, with the method of breaking or dividing them, the author proceeds to treat of descant division, which he thus defines :—

'Descant division is that which makes a different 'concording part unto the ground. It differs from 'the former in these particulars : That breaks the 'notes of the ground ; This descants upon them : 'That takes the liberty to wander sometimes be- 'neath the ground ; This, as in its proper sphere, 'moves still above it ; That meets every succeeding 'note of the ground in the unison or octave ; This in 'any of the concords. But in the main business of 'division they are much the same ; for all division, 'whether descant or breaking the bass, is but a 'transition from note to note, or from one concord 'to another, either by degrees or leaps, with an ad- 'mixture of such discords as are allowed in com- 'position.'

However difficult the practice may seem of making a division extempore upon a given ground, preserving the melody without transgressing the rules of harmony, this author speaks of two viols playing together in division, and for this exercise he gives the following rules :—

'First let the ground be prick'd down in three 'several papers, one for him who plays upon the 'organ or harpsichord, the other two for them 'that play upon the two viols ; which for order and 'brevity we will distinguish by three letters, viz., A 'for organist, B for the first bass, and C for the 'second.

'Each of these having the same ground before 'him, they may all three begin together, A and B 'playing the ground, and C descanting to it in slow 'notes, or such as may suit the beginning of the 'musick. This done, let C play the ground, and B 'descant to it, as the other had done before, but with 'some little variation. If the ground consists of two 'strains, the like may be done in the second ; one 'viol still playing the ground, whilest the other 'descants or divides upon it.

'The ground thus play'd over, C may. begin 'again, and play a strain of quicker division ; which 'ended, let B answer the same with another, some- 'thing like it but of a little more lofty ayre ; for the 'better performance whereof, if there be any dif- 'ference in the hands or inventions, I would have the 'better invention lead, but the more able hand still 'follow, that the musick may not seem to flaccess or 'lessen, but rather increase in the performance.

'When the viols have thus, as it were vied and 'revied one to the other, A, if he have the ability 'of hand, may, upon a sign given him, put in his 'strain of division ; the two viols playing one of 'them the ground, and the other slow descant to it ; 'A, having finished his strain, a reply thereto may 'be made, first by one viol and then by the other.

'Having answered one another in that same man- 'ner so long as they think fit, the two viols may 'divide a strain both together. In which doing, let 'B break the ground, by moving into the octave up-

'ward or downward, and returning from thence 'either to his own note, or to meet the next note in 'the unison or octave ; by this means C knowing B's 'motion, he knows also to avoid running into the 'same, and therefore will move into the third or fifth, 'or sixth where it is required, meeting each succeed- 'ing note in some one of the said concords, until he 'come to the close : where he may, after he has divi- 'ded the binding, meet the close note in the octave ; 'which directions well observed, two viols may move 'in extempory division a whole strain together, 'without any remarkable clashing in the consecution 'of fifths or eighths.

'When they have proceeded thus far, C may begin 'some point of division, of the length of a breve or 'semibreve, naming the same word, that B may know 'his intentions ; which ended, let B answer the same 'upon the succeeding note or notes, to the like quan- 'tity of time ; taking it in that manner one after 'another, so long as they please. This done they 'may betake themselves to some other point, a new 'variety.

'This contest in breves, semibreves, or minims, 'being ended, they may give the signe to A, if as I 'said he have the ability of hand, that he may begin 'his point, as they had done one to another, which 'point may be answered by the viols, either singly or 'jointly ; if jointly it must be done according to the 'former instructions of dividing together, playing 'still slow notes, and soft whilest the organist di- 'vides ; for that part which divides should always be 'heard lowdest.

'When this is done both viols may play another 'strain together, either in quick or slow notes, which 'they please ; and if the music be not yet spun out to a 'sufficient length, they may begin to play triplas 'and proportions answering each other, in whole 'strains or parcels, and after that join together in a 'thundering strain of quick division, with which they 'may conclude ; or else with a strain of slow and 'sweet notes, according as may best sute the circum- 'stance of time and place.'*

To illustrate the practice which it is the design of the book to recommend, Simpson has inserted, by way of appendix to it, sundry grounds with divi- sions on them, composed by himself, and among others the following :—

* The practice of extempory descant, either by the voice or with an instrument, is now unknown in music. Of vocal descant Morley has given his sentiments at large in the following words :—
'Singing extempore upon a plainsong is indeede a peece of cunning, 'and very necessarie to be perfectly practised of him who meaneth to be 'a composer, for bringing of a quick sight ; yet it is a great absurditie so 'to seeke for a sight, as to make it the end of our studie, applying it to 'no other use ; for as a knife or other instrument not being applied to 'the end for which it was devised (as to cut) is unprofitable, and of no 'use ; even so is descant, which being used as a helpe to bring readie 'sight in setting of parts, is profitable ; but not being applied to that 'ende, is of itselfe like a puffe of wind, which being past cometh not 'againe, which hath beene the reason that the excellent musitians have 'discontinued it, although it be unprofitable to compose without it, but 'they rather employ their time in making of songes, which remain for 'the posterity then to sing descant, which is no longer known then the 'singer's mouth is open expressing it, and for the most part cannot be 'twise repeated in one manner.' Introduction to Practical Music, page 121.
The same reflections must arise upon the practice of extempory descant by instruments. As to the descant of viols, we know no more of it than is contained in this elaborate treatise ; and for aught that appears to the contrary, it began and ended with this author.

## DIVISION ON A GROUND.

CHRISTOPHER SIMPSON.

In 1667 Simpson published A Compendium of practical Musick, in 5 parts, containing 1. The rudiments of Song. 2. The principles of composition. 3. The use of discord. 4. The form of figurate Descant. 5. The contrivance of Canon.

This book is dedicated to William Duke of Newcastle, the author of the celebrated treatise on Horsemanship, who was also a great lover of music, and is strongly recommended by two prefatory epistles, the one of Mathew Lock, and the other by John Jenkins.

The first part contains little more than is to be found in every book that professes to teach the precepts of singing.

The second teaches the principles of composition, and treats of Counterpoint, Intervals, and Concords, with their use and application; of the key or tone, and of the closes or cadences belonging to the key. By the directions here given it appears, as indeed it does in those of Dr. Campion, that the ancient practice in the composition of music in parts was to frame the bass part first.

He begins his rules for composition with directions how to frame a bass, and how to join a treble to a bass, after which he proceeds to composition of three parts, concerning which his directions are as follow:—

'First, you are to set the notes of this part in 'concords different from those of the treble. 2. 'When the treble is a 5th to the bass, I would have 'you make use either of a 3d. or an 8th for the other 'part; and not to use a 6th therewith, untill I have 'shewed you how, and where a 5th and a 6th may 'be joyned together. 3. You are to avoid 8ths in 'this inner part likewise, so much as you can with 'convenience. For though we use 5ths as much as 'imperfects, yet we seldom make use of 8ths in three 'parts. The reason why we avoid 8ths in two or 'three parts is, that imperfect concords afford more 'variety upon accompt of their majors and minors: 'besides imperfects do not cloy the ear so much as 'perfects do.

'Composition of four parts. If you design your 'composition for four parts, I would then have you 'join your Altus as near as you can to the treble; 'which is easily done by taking those concords note 'after note which are next under the treble, in 'manner as follows.

'Make the altus and the treble end in the same

'tune ; which in my opinion is better than to have
' the treble end in the sharp 3d. above ; the key of
' the composition being flat, and the sharp third more
' proper for an inner part at conclusion.'

For the adding a fourth part, viz. a tenor, he
gives the following rules : 'First, that this part
' which is to be added be set in concords, different
' from the other two upper parts ; that is to say, if
' those be a 5th and 3d, let this be an 8th ; by which
' you may conceive the rest.

'Secondly, I would have you join this tenor as
' near the Altus as the different concords do permit ;
' for the harmony is better when the three upper
' parts are joined close together.

'Thirdly, you are to avoid two 8ths or two 5ths
' rising or falling together, as well amongst the
' upper parts, as betwixt any one part and the bass ;
' of which there is less danger by placing the parts
' in different concords.'

From hence the author proceeds to compositions
in five, six, seven and eight parts, and to compositions for two choirs each.

The third part of the book teaches the use of
the discords, and shows the nature of Syncopation,
and relation inharmonical. Here he takes notice of
the three scales of music, the diatonic, the chromatic,
and the enharmonic, of which he gives a concise
but clear definition.

He inclines to the opinion that the modern scale,
in which the octave is divided into twelve semitones,
is in fact a commixture of the diatonic and the chromatic, touching which he delivers these his sentiments :—

' Now as to my opinion concerning our common
' scale of musick, taking it with its commixture of
' the chromatick, I think it lies not in the wit of man
' to frame a better as to all intents and purposes for
' practical musick. And as for those little dissonances,
' for so I call them for want of a better word to ex-
' press them, the fault is not in the scale, whose
' office and design is no more than to denote the dis-
' tances of the concords and discords, according to
' the lines and spaces of which it doth consist, and
' to shew by what degree of tones and semitones a
' voice may rise or fall :

' For in vocal musick those dissonances are not
' perceived, neither do they occur in instruments
' which have no frets, as violins and wind instru-
' ments, where the sound is modulated by the touch
' of the finger ; but in such only as have fixed stops
' or frets, which being placed and fitted for the
' most usual keyes in the scale, seem out of order
' when we change to keys less usual ; and that as I
' said doth happen by reason of the inequality of
' tones and semitones, especially of the latter.'

The fourth part teaches the form of figurate descant, and treats first, in a very concise but perspicuous manner, of the ancient modes or tones. In
his directions for figurate descant the author shews
how they are made to pass through each other, and
speaks of the consecution of fourths and fifths, thirds
and sixths. He next explains the nature of fugue
in general, and gives directions for constructing a
fugue per arsin et thesin, and also of a double fugue.

He next treats of music composed for voices ;
upon which he observes that it is to be preferred to
that of instruments, and for this opinion refers to
the testimony of Des Cartes, who in the beginning
of his Compendium asserts that, of all sounds, that of
the human voice is the most grateful.

Of the different kinds of vocal music in use in his
time he thus speaks :—

' Of vocal music made for the solace and civil de-
' light of man, there are many different kinds, as
' namely, Madrigals, in which fugues and all other
' flowers of figurate musick are most frequent.

' Of these you may see many sets of 3, 4, 5, and
' 6 parts, published both by English and Italian
' authors. Next the dramatic or recitative musick,
' which as yet is something a stranger to us here in
' England. Then Cansonets, Vilanellas, Airs of all
' sorts, or what else poetry hath contrived to be set
' and sung in musick. Lastly Canons and Catches,
' which are commonly set to words ; the first to such
' as be grave and serious, the latter to words designed
' for mirth and recreation.'

For accommodating notes to words he gives the
following rules :—

' When you compose musick to words, your chief
' endeavour must be that your notes do aptly ex-
' press the sense and humour of them. If they be
' grave and serious, let your musick be such also :
' if light, pleasant, or lively, your musick likewise
' must be suitable to them. Any passion of love,
' sorrow, anguish, or the like is aptly expressed by
' chromatick notes and bindings. Anger, courage,
' revenge, &c. require a more strenuous and stirring
' movement. Cruel, bitter, harsh, may be expressed
' with a discord ; which nevertheless must be brought
' off according to the rules of composition. High,
' above, heaven, ascend ; as likewise their contraries,
' low, deep, down, hell, descend, may be expressed
' by the example of the hand, which points upward
' when we speak of the one, and downward when we
' mention the other ; the contrary to which would be
' absurd. You must also have respect to the points
' of your ditty, not using any remarkable pause or
' rest, untill the words come to a full point or pe-
' riod : Neither may any rest, how short soever, be
' interposed in the middle of a word ; but a sigh or
' sob is properly imitated by a crochet or quaver
' rest.

' Lastly you ought not to apply several notes, nor
' indeed any long note, to a short syllable, nor a
' short note to a syllable that is long. Neither do I
' fancy the setting of many notes to any one syllable,
' though much in fashion in former times, but I would
' have your musick to be such, that the words may
' be plainly understood,'

He next speaks of music designed for instruments ;
and this he says abounds no less than vocal music
with points, fugues, and all other figures of descant.
He describes the several kinds of instrumental music
in use at the time of writing his book, in these
words :—

' Of this kind the chief and most excellent for art
' and contrivance, are fancies of 6, 5, 4, and 3 parts
' intended commonly for viols. In this sort of

'musick the composer, being not limited to words,
'doth employ all his art and invention solely about
'the bringing in, and carrying on of these fugues.

'When he has tried all the several ways which he
'thinks fit to be used therein, he takes some other
'point and does the like with it; or else for variety
'introduces some chromatick notes with bindings
'and intermixtures of discords; or falls into some
'lighter humour, like a madrigal, or what else his
'fancy shall lead him to: but still concluding with
'something that hath art and excellency in it.

'Of this sort you may see many compositions
'made heretofore in England by Alfonso Ferabosco,
'Coperario, Lupo, White, Ward, Mico, Dr. Colman,
'and many more now deceased. Also by Mr.
'Jenkins, Mr. Lock, and divers other excellent men,
'doctors and bachelors in musick yet living.

'This kind of musick, the more is the pity, is now
'much neglected, by reason of the scarcity of audi-
'tors that understand it: their ears being better
'acquainted and more delighted with light and airy
'music.

'The next in dignity after a fancy is a Pavan,
'which some derive from Padua in Italy; at first
'ordained for a grave and stately manner of dancing,
'as most instrumental musicks were in their several
'kinds, fancies and symphonies excepted, but now
'grown up to a height of composition made only to
'delight the ear.

'A Pavan, be it of 2, 3, 4, 5, or 6 parts, doth
'commonly consist of three strains, each strain being
'played twice over. Now as to any peice of music
'that consists of strains take these following obser-
'vations.

'All musick concludes in the key of his compo-
'sition, which is known by the bass, as hath been
'shown; this key hath always other keys proper to
'it for middle closes. If your Pavan or what else,
'be of three straines, the first strain may end in the
'key of the composition as the last doth; but the
'middle strain must always end in the key of a
'middle close.

'Sometimes the first strain does end in a middle
'close, and then the middle strain must end in some
'other middle close; for two strains following imme-
'diately one another, ought not to end in the same
'key. Therefore when there are but two strains let
'the first end in a middle close, that both strains
'may not end alike.'

The fifth and last part is on the subject of Canon,
a species of composition in which the author says
divers of our countrymen have been excellent; and
here he takes notice of Mr. Elway Bevin, who he says
professes fair in the title-page of his book, and gives
us many examples of excellent and intricate canons
of divers sorts, but not one word of instruction how
to make such like.

He then proceeds to explain the method of composing canon in two or three parts, as also canon in
the unison; syncopated or driving canon; canon a
note higher or lower; canon rising or falling a note
each repetition; retrogade canon, or canon recte et
retro; double descant, in which the parts are so

contrived that the treble may be the bass, and the
bass the treble: and canon on a given plain song,
with examples of each.

Lastly, he gives directions for the composition
of Catch or Round, by some called Canon in the
Unison.

Simpson was also the author of Annotations on
Dr. Campion's little tract on Composition, mentioned
page 560 of this work, and which is reprinted in
some of the earlier editions of Playford's Introduction, particularly that of 1660, but omitted in
the latter ones, to make room for a tract entitled
'An Introduction to the Art of Descant,' probably
written by Playford himself, but augmented by
Purcell.

## CHAP. CL.

EDMUND CHILMEAD, an excellent Greek and Latin
scholar, and mathematician, was also well skilled in
the theory and practice of music, and was the author
of a tract entitled 'De Musicâ antiquâ Græcâ,'
printed in 1672, at the end of the Oxford edition of
Aratus, as also of annotations on three Odes of
Dionysius, there also published,* with the ancient
Greek musical characters.

This person was born at Stow in the Wold in
Gloucestershire, and became one of the clerks of
Magdalen college. About the year 1632 he was
one of the petty canons or chaplains of Christ Church;
but being ejected by the Parliament visitors in 1648,
he came to London, and, being in great necessity,
took lodgings in the house of that Thomas Este, a
musician, and also a printer of music, of whom
mention is made in a preceding part of this work;
this man dwelt at the sign of the Black Horse in
Aldersgate-street, and having in his house a large
room, Chilmead made use of it for a weekly music
meeting, deriving from the profits thereof the means
of a slender subsistence.

Being an excellent Greek scholar, Chilmead was
employed to draw up the Catalogus Manuscriptorum
Græcorum in Bibliotheca Bodleiana. In the catalogue
which Wood gives of his works, he mentions a
treatise 'De Sonis,' which does not appear to have
ever been published. The rest of his works seem
to have been chiefly translations, amongst which is
that well-known book of Jacques Gaffarel, entitled
'Curiosités inovies sur la Sculpture Talismanique
'des Persans,' and in the translation 'Unheard of
'Curiosities,' &c. He died in the year 1653, in the
forty-third year of his age, having for some years
received relief in his necessities from Edward Byshe,
Esq. Garter King at Arms, and Sir Henry Holbrook,
knight, the translator of Procopius. He was interred
in the church of St. Botolph without Aldersgate,
but no inscription to his memory is there to be
found.†

Together with the Oxford edition of Aratus is
published the ΚΑΤΑΣΤΕΡΙΣΜΟΙ of Eratosthenes,
whose division of the genera is to be seen among

* See page 32, in a note.
† Vide Athen. Oxon. vol. I. col. 169.

CHRISTOPHER GIBBONS

MUS.DOCT.OXON. MDCLXIV.

*From an original Painting in the Music-School, Oxford.*

WILLIAM CHILD

MUS. DOCT. OXON. MDCLXIII.

*From an original Painting in the Music-School Oxford*

others of the ancient Greek writers in the Harmonics of Ptolemy.

The editor of this book, seeming to consider it as a fragment necessary to be preserved, has given from Ptolemy this division; and, to render it in some degree intelligible, annexes three odes of Dionysius, which Dr. Bernard, a fellow of St. John's college, had found in Ireland among the papers of Archbishop Usher, with the annotations of Chilmead thereon; as also a short treatise, ' De Musicâ antiquâ Græcâ,' by the same person. This tract contains a designation of the ancient genera agreeable to the sentiments of Boetius, with a general enumeration of the modes; after which follow the odes, with the Greek musical characters, which Chilmead has rendered in the notes of Guido's scale; and at the end of the book is inserted a fragment of an ode of Pindar, with the ancient musical characters and modern notes, found by Kircher in the library of the monastery of St. Salvator in Sicily, and inserted in the Musurgia, and also in a preceding part of this work.*

WILLIAM TUCKER was a gentleman of the chapel royal in the reign of king Charles II. and junior priest there at the time of the coronation, and also a minor canon in the collegiate church of St. Peter at Westminster. He was a good church musician, and composed sundry anthems, the most celebrated whereof are ' Praise the Lord O ye servants,' ' This ' is the day that the Lord hath made,' and ' Unto ' thee O Lord.' He died on the twenty-eighth day of February, 1678, and was succeeded in his place by the Rev. John Gostling, A. M. from Canterbury.

WILLIAM GREGORY, also a gentleman of the chapel royal in the same reign, was a composer of anthems, of which those of best note are ' Out of the deep ' have I called,' and ' O Lord thou hast cast us out.' In the music-school Oxon. is a portrait of him.

CHRISTOPHER GIBBONS, *(a Portrait)*, the son of the celebrated Dr. Orlando Gibbons, was bred up from a child to music, under his uncle Ellis Gibbons, organist of Bristol; he had been favoured by Charles I. and was of his chapel. At the restoration he was appointed principal organist of the king's chapel, organist in private to his majesty, and organist of Westminster-abbey. In the year 1664 he was licensed to proceed Doctor in music of the university of Oxford in virtue of a letter from the king in his behalf, in which is a recital of his merits in these words, ' the bearer Christopher Gibbons, one of our ' organists of our chappell royal, hath from his youth ' served our royal father and ourself, and hath so ' well improved himself in music, as well in our ' judgment, as in the judgment of all men skilled in ' that science, as that he may worthily receive the ' honour and degree of doctor therein.' He completed his degree in an act celebrated in the church of St. Mary at Oxford on the eleventh day of July in the year above-mentioned.†

Dr. Christopher Gibbons was, as Dr. Tudway

asserts, more celebrated for his skill and performance on the organ than for his compositions; nevertheless there are many anthems of his extant, though we know of none that have ever been printed. Those of most note are ' God be merciful unto us,' ' Help ' me O Lord,' ' Lord I am not high-minded,' and ' Teach me O Lord.' It is said that he had a principal hand in a book entitled ' Cantica Sacra,' containing Hymns and Anthems for two voices to the organ, both Latin and English. Lond. 1674, fol. He died in the parish of St. Margaret, Westminster, on the twentieth day of October, anno 1676.‡

ALBERTUS BRYNE was a scholar of John Tomkins, and his successor as organist of St. Paul's cathedral, being appointed to that office immediately upon the restoration. He was an eminent church-musician, and a composer of services and anthems, and as such his name occurs in Clifford's Collection. He died in the reign of Charles II. and was buried in the cloister of Westminster Abbey, but there is no inscription to be found there to ascertain precisely the time of his death, or the place of his interment.

WILLIAM CHILD, *(a Portrait)*, a native of Bristol, was educated in music under Elway Bevin, organist of the cathedral of that city. In the year 1631, being then of Christ Church college Oxford, he took his degree of bachelor in that university; and in 1636 was appointed one of the organists of the chapel of St. George at Windsor, in the room of Dr. John Mundy, and soon after one of the organists of the royal chapel at Whitehall. After the restoration he was appointed to the office of chanter of the king's chapel, and became of the private music to Charles II. In 1663 he obtained licence to proceed Doctor in his faculty, and on the thirteenth day of July in the same year completed his degree at an act celebrated in St. Mary's church, Oxon. Dr. Child died in the year 1696, having attained the age of ninety years, and was succeeded in his place of organist of the king's chapel by Mr. Francis Piggot.

His works are ' Psalms of three voices, &c. with ' a continual bass either for the Organ or Theorbo, ' composed after the Italian way,' Lond. 1639. Catches and Canons, published in Hilton's collection entitled ' Catch that Catch can.' Divine Anthems and compositions to several pieces of poetry, some of which were written by Dr. Thomas Pierce of Oxford. Some compositions of two parts, printed in a book entitled ' Court Ayres,' mentioned in a preceding page. The engraving is taken from a whole length picture of him now in the music-school Oxon. (See Portrait volume).

---

* It is there said that the Oxford edition of Aratus was published by Chilmead, but upon better information it is conjectured that Dr. Aldrich was the editor of it.

† Fasti Oxon. vol. II. col. 158.

‡ Wood says that Dr. Christopher Gibbons was master of the singing-boys belonging to Charles the Second's chapel; but in this he seems to be mistaken. By the Cheque-book it appears that Capt. Cook, who had been appointed to that office at the restoration, died in 1672, and that he was succeeded in it by Humphrey. It farther appears by a subsequent entry in the same book, that Humphrey died in July 1674, and that in his place as master of the children came Mr. John Blow. Gibbons died in 1676, and it is well known that Blow held the place till the time of his death, which was in 1708. Farther, the entry of Gibbons's death in the Cheque-book, styles him only organist of the chapel, from all which it must be concluded that Gibbons was never master of the children. The only remaining difficulty arises from the inscription on Dr. Blow's monument, in which it is said that he was a scholar of Dr. Christopher Gibbons. This asertion may either be founded on the mistaken authority of Wood, or it may mean that he was taught the principles of music at large, or the practice of the organ by Dr. Gibbons.

He composed many services and anthems, none of which appear to have been printed, except his service in E with the lesser third, and that famous one in D with the greater third, and three fine anthems; and those only in Dr. Boyce's Cathedral Music. His style was in general so remarkably natural and familiar that it sometimes gave offence to those whose duty it was to sing his compositions. Being at Windsor, he called the choir to a practice of a service that he had newly composed, which the choirmen found so easy in the performance, that they made a jest of it. This fact is said to have occasioned his composing his famous service in D♯, which in some parts of it is remarkably intricate and difficult,* but upon the whole is delightfully fine. Playford, in the preface to his Introduction, edit. 1683, says that king Charles I. often appointed the service and anthems himself, especially that sharp service composed by Dr. William Child.

The memory of Dr. Child is celebrated for an act of beneficence that was hardly to be expected from one in his station of life: it seems that he was so ill paid for his services at Windsor, that a long arrear of his salary had incurred, which he could not get discharged: after many fruitless applications to the dean and chapter, he told them that if they would pay him the sum in arrear he would new pave the choir of their chapel for them: they paid him his money, and the doctor performed his promise; neither they, nor the knights companions of the most noble order of the garter interposing to prevent it, or signifying the least inclination to share with a servant and dependant of theirs in the honour of so munificent an act.

He lies interred in the chapel of St. George at Windsor: the following is the inscription on his gravestone :—

' Here lies the body of William Child, doctor in music,
' and one of the organists of the chapel royal at White-
'hall, and of his majesty's free chapel at Windsor 65
' years. He was born in Bristol, and died here the 23d
' of March 1696-7 in the 91st year of his age. He paved
'.the body of the choir.

      ' Go, happy soul, and in the seats above
      ' Sing endless hymns of thy great Maker's love.
      ' How fit in heavenly songs to bear thy part,
      ' Before well practic'd in the sacred art ;
      ' Whilst hearing us, sometimes the choire divine,
      ' Will sure descend, and in our consort join ;
      ' So much the music, thou to us hast given,
      ' Has made our earth to represent their heaven.'

He gave twenty pounds towards building the town-hall at Windsor, and fifty pounds to the corporation, to be disposed of in charitable uses at their discretion.

JOHN BANISTER was the son of one of that low class of musicians called the Waits, of the parish of St. Giles near London; but having been taught by his father the rudiments of music, he became in a short time such a proficient on the violin, that by king Charles II. he was sent to France for im-

provement, and upon his return was made one of his band ; but having taken occasion to tell the king that the English performers on that instrument were superior to those of France, he was dismissed from his service. He set to music the opera of Circe, written by Dr. Davenant, and performed in the year 1676, at the theatre in Dorset Garden ; as also sundry songs printed in the collections of his time. He died on the third day of October, 1679, and lies buried in the cloister of Westminster Abbey, as appears by an inscription on a marble stone in the wall of the west ambulatory thereof, yet remaining legible. He left a son of both his names, a fine performer on the violin, of whom an account will be given hereafter.

MATTHEW LOCK (*a Portrait*), was originally a chorister in the cathedral church of Exeter, while William Wake was organist there: he was afterwards a scholar of Edward Gibbons, and became so eminent that he was employed to compose the music for the public entry of King Charles II. Although bred in a cathedral, he seems to have affected the style of the theatre, and to have taken up dramatic music where Henry Lawes left it. Downes says he composed the music to the tragedy of Macbeth, as altered by Sir William Davenant. Nevertheless, there are extant of his many compositions that are evidence of his great skill and ingenuity in the church style, as, namely, two anthems, ' Not unto us, O Lord,' and ' Turn thy face from my sins ;' and one for five voices, in Dr. Boyce's collection, ' Lord, let me know my end.' He appears to have been a man of a querulous disposition, and therefore it is not to be wondered at that he had enemies. Being composer in ordinary to the king, he composed for the chapel a morning service, in which the prayer after each of the ten commandments had a different setting; this was deemed an inexcusable innovation, and on the first day of April, 1666, at the performance of it before the king, the service met with some obstruction, most probably from the singers.

The censures which this small deviation from the ancient practice had drawn on him, and the disgrace he had suffered in the attempt to gratify the royal ear with a composition that must have cost him some study, reduced Lock to the necessity of publishing the whole service ; and it came abroad in score, printed on a single sheet, with the following vindication of it and its author by way of preface :—

' Modern Church Musick pre-accused, censured,
' and obstructed in its performance before his
' majesty, April 1, 1666. Vindicated by the
' author, Matt. Lock, composer in ordinary to
' his majesty.

' He is a slender observer of humane action, who
' finds not pride generally accompanied with igno-
' rance and malice, what habit soever it wares. In
' my case zeal was its vizor, and innovation the
' crime. The fact, changing the custome of the
' church, by varying that which was ever sung in
' one tune, and occasioning confusion in the service
' by its ill performance. As to the latter part of the
' charge, I must confess I have been none of the

* Dr. Tudway says that from this circumstance it was in his time questioned whether Dr. Child was really the author of it; but this doubt has long subsided.

MATTHEW LOCK,

COMPOSER IN ORDINARY TO HIS MAJESTY
CHA. II.

fortunatest that way; but whether upon design or 'ignorance of some of the performers it so happen'd, 'I shall neither examine nor judge, (they are of age 'to understand the value of their own reputation, 'and whom they serve): nor is it my business to 'find eyes, ears, or honesty to any, or answer for 'other men's faults : but, that such defects should 'take their rise from the difficulty or novelty of the 'composition, I utterly deny ; the whole, being a 'kind of counterpoint, and no one change, from the 'beginning to the end, but what naturally flows 'from, and returns to its proper center, the Kay. 'And for the former, the contrary is so notoriously 'manifest, that all relating to the church know that 'that part of the liturgy assigned for musick, was 'never but variously compos'd by all that under-'took it : witness the excellent compositions of Mr. 'Tallis, Byrd, Gibbons, (and other their and our co-'temporaries) on the Te Deum, Commandments, 'Preces, Psalms Magnificat, &c. in use to this day, 'both in his majesties chappel, and the cathedralls in 'this nation.   And to speak rationally, should it be 'otherwise, art would be no more art, composers 'useless, and science pinion'd for destruction.   If 'therefore, in imitation of them, I have according 'to art, and the nature of the words, contrived and 'varied this little composition ; and, as to the true 'manner of speaking, conducted it in the mid-way 'between the two extremes of gravity and levity; 'I hope I may without ostentation affirm myself 'guiltless, and return the crime from whence it 'came : Æsop's maunger.   And here might I fairly 'take notice of a thing lately crawl'd into the world, 'under the notion of composition, which in the 'height of its performance is both out of time, out 'of tune, and yet all to the same tune, had I the 'itch of retaliation ; but since the accuser has been 'pleased to passe a publick censure on the tender of 'my duty, I shall only at present take the freedom '(though it was never intended for a publick view) 'in this manner to expose it ; that all capable of 'judging, may see, there's neither heresie, nor schism, 'nor any thing of difficulty as to performance either 'in the matter or form of it.   In fine, this vindica-'tion offers at no more, than denying those to be 'judges in science, who are ignorant of its principles.'

The singularity of this service consisted in this, that whereas it had been the practice to make the Preces to all the commandments except the last, in the same notes, here they are all different; in other respects there is nothing singular in the com-position : it is in the key of F, with the major third, and all counterpoint, except the Nicene Creed, which is what the musicians term Canto figurato.

About the year 1672 Lock became engaged in a controversy with one Thomas Salmon, the occasion of which was as follows : this man was a master of arts of Trinity college, Oxford, and at length rector of Mepsall in Bedfordshire, and had written a book entitled ' An essay to the advancement of music, by 'casting away the perplexity of different cliffs, and 'uniting all sorts of music, lute, viol, violins, organ, 'harpsichord, voice, &c. in one universal character :'

in which he substitutes in the place of the usual cliffs, the letters B for the bass, M for the mean or middle part, and Tr. for the treble, proposing thereby to facilitate the practice both of vocal and instrumental music.

This in a general view of it is the design of the book, but with the help of an abridgment of it, by one who seems to have taken great pains to under-stand the design of the author, we are enabled to give a summary of his proposal in the following few lines :—

'Mr. Salmon reflecting on the inconveniences 'attending the use of the cliffs, and also how useful 'it would be that all music should be reduced to one 'constant cliff, whereby the same writing of any 'piece of musick would equally serve to direct the 'voice and all instruments ; a thing one should 'think to be of very great use : he proposes in his 'Essay to the Advancement of Musick, what he calls 'an universal character, which I shall explain in a 'few words.   In the first place he would have the 'lowest line of every particular system constantly 'called g, and the other lines and spaces to be 'named according to the order of the seven letters ; 'and because these positions of the letters are 'supposed invariable, therefore he thinks there is 'no need to mark any of them ; but then, secondly, 'that the relations of several parts of a composition 'may be distinctly known, he marks the treble with 'the letter T at the beginning of the system, the 'mean with M, and the bass with B ; and the gs 'that are on the lowest line of each of these systems, 'he supposes to be octaves to each other in order. 'And then for referring these systems to their 'corresponding places in the general system, the 'treble g, which determines all the rest, must be 'supposed in the same place as the treble cliff of the 'common method ; but this difference is remarkable, 'that tho' the g of the treble and bass systems are 'both on lines in the general system, yet the mean 'g, which is on a line of the particular system, is on 'a space in the general one ; because in the pro-'gression of the scale, the same letter, as g, is 'alternately upon a line and a space ; therefore the 'mean system is not a continuation of any of the 'other two, so as you could proceed in order out of 'the one into the other by degrees, from line to 'space, because the g of the mean is here on a line, 'which is necessarily upon a space in the scale ; and 'therefore in referring the mean system to its proper 'relative place in the scale, all its lines correspond 'to spaces of the other, and contrarily ; but there 'is no matter of that if the parts be so written 'separately, as their relations be distinctly known, 'and the practice made more easy ; and when we 'would reduce them all to one general system, it is 'enough we know that the lines of the mean part 'must be changed into spaces, and its spaces into 'lines.   Thirdly, if the notes of any part go above 'or below its system, we may set them as formerly 'on short lines drawn on purpose : but if there are 'many notes together above or below, Mr. Salmon 'proposes to reduce them within the system, by

'placing them on the lines and spaces of the same
'name, and prefixing the name of the octave to
'which they belong. To understand this better,
'consider he has chosen three distinct octaves fol-
'lowing one another; and because one octave needs
'but four lines, therefore he would have no more in
'the particular system; and then each of the three
'particular systems expressing a distinct octave of
'the scale, which he calls the proper octaves of these
'several parts, if the song run into another octave
'above or below, it is plain; the notes that are out
'of the octave peculiar to the system, as it stands by
'a general rule marked T, or M, or B, may be set
'on the same lines and spaces; if the octave they
'belong to be distinctly marked, the notes may be
'very easily found, by taking them an octave higher
'or lower than the notes of the same name in the
'proper octave of the system. For example, if the
'treble part runs into the middle or bass octave, we
'prefix to these notes the letter M or B, and set
'them on the same lines and spaces, for all the three
'systems have in this hypothesis the notes of the
'same name in the same correspondent places; if
'the mean run into the treble or bass octaves, prefix
'the signs T or M. And lastly, because the parts
'may comprehend more than three octaves, therefore
'the treble may run higher than an octave, and the
'bass lower; in such cases the higher octave for the
'treble may be marked T t, and the lower for the
'bass B b. But if any body thinks there be any
'considerable difficulty in this method, which yet
'I am of opinion would be far less than the changing
'of cliffs in the common way, the notes may be con-
'tinued upward and downward upon new lines and
'spaces, occasionally drawn in the ordinary manner.
'And tho' there may be many notes far out of the
'system above or below, yet what is the inconveniency
'of this? Is the reducing the notes within 5 lines,
'and saving a little paper, an adequate reward for
'the trouble and time spent in learning to perform
'readily from different cliffs?

'As to the treble and bass, the alteration by this
'new method is very small; for in the common posi-
'tion of the bass cliff the lowest line is already g,
'and for the treble it is but removing the g from the
'second line, its ordinary position, to the first line;
'the greatest innovation is in the parts that are set
'with the c cliff.'

These are the sentiments of Malcolm touching
Salmon's proposal for rejecting the cliffs from the
scale of music; but it must be presumed that he had
never perused the arguments of Lock and Playford
against it, in which it is demonstrated to be im-
practicable.

Salmon's book, for what reason it is hard to guess,
was not published by the author himself, but by
John Birchensha, a noted musician in his time, who
recommends it in a preface of his own writing. If
Salmon had understoood more of music than it
appears he did, he never would have thought the
knowledge of the cliffs so difficult to attain, nor
would he have attempted, by the establishment of a
new and universal character, to have rendered unin-

telligible to succeeding generations the many inestimable compositions extant in his time: notwithstanding this, there is in his manner of writing such
an air of pertness and self-sufficiency, as was enough
to provoke a man of Lock's temper; and accordingly
he published in the same year a book entitled 'Observations upon a late book entitled an Essay, &c.,'
which, as Wood says, lying dead upon the booksellers's hands, had another title prefixed to it, viz.,
'The present practice of music vindicated against
'the exceptions and new way of attaining music,
'lately published by Tho. Salmon,' to which, continues Wood, was added a very scurrilous, abusive,
and buffooning thing entitled 'Duellum Musicum,
'written by John Phillips, and a letter from John
'Playford to Mr. Thomas Salmon, by way of confu-
'tation of his essay.' Lond. 1673, 8vo.*

As to the observations of Lock, above mentioned
to have lain dead on the bookseller's hands, the book
is now grown so scarce, that after twenty years'
inquiry not one copy has been to be found; nevertheless, the merits of this controversy may be judged
of from Lock's 'Present Practice of Music Vindicated,' and Playford's letter at the end of it, in
both which it is demonstrated that Salmon's scheme
would introduce more difficulties in music than it
would remove, and that in some instances it cannot
possibly be applied to practice. And as to Wood's
censure of the Observations that they are scurrilous
and abusive, it may be said that if they are more
scurrilous and abusive than the answer to it, entitled 'A Vindication of an Essay to the advancement of musick from Mr. Lock's observations,' they
must in truth be a great curiosity.†

* Athen. Oxon. vol. II. col. 1075.

† Salmon was also the author of a treatise entitled ' A proposal to per-
'form Musick in perfect and mathematical Proportions,' Lond. 4to 1688,
divided into three chapters.

In Chap. I. the author, after lamenting 'that fatal period when the
'North swarmed with barbarous multitudes, who came down like a
'mighty torrent, and subdued the best nations of the world, which were
'forced to become rude and illiterate, because their new masters and
'inhabitants were such,' observes that 'amidst these calamities it is no
'wonder that music perished.' 'All learning,' says he, 'lay in the dust,
'especially that which was proper in the times of peace.' But he tells us
'that this darkness was not perpetual, for that the ages at last cleared up,
'and from the ruins of antiquity brought forth some broken pieces, which
'were by degrees set together, and by this time of day are arrived near
'their ancient glory. Guido has been refining above six hundred years.'

He then, in a style equally vulgar and affected with the passage above
cited, felicitates the world on the publication of the ancient Greek
writers on music by Meibomius, and of Ptolemy by Dr. Wallis; and also
of those two fragments of ancient Greek music published with Chilmead's
notes, at the end of the Oxford edition of Aratus.

Chap. II. contains some few observations on the practice of music in
the author's time, with a remark that for the last twenty years before
the time of writing this book, the internal constitution of the octave had
been twofold, that is to say, either with the greater third, sixth, and
seventh, or a lesser third, sixth, and seventh; which progressions
severally constitute the flat and sharp keys, of the one whereof he makes
that of A to be the prototype, as that of C is the other.

Chap. III. contains an account of his tables of proportion. It seems
that the divisions therein contained are adapted to the practice of the
viol; for he gives his reader the choice of any one of several strings for
the two divisions of the octave recommended by him. The whole of his
proposal terminates in a contrivance of changeable finger-boards, differently fretted according to the key, by means whereof, those dissonances, which in some keys arise and are discoverable in the organ
and harpsichord, when perfectly tuned, are palliated.

It is difficult to discover in what sense proportions thus adjusted can
be termed mathematical. All men know that it has been the labour of
mathematicians for many ages to effect an equal division of the octave,
and that all their endeavours for that purpose have been baffled by that
surd quantity which has remained in every mode of division that the
wit of man has hitherto suggested; it may therefore be inferred that no
proportions strictly mathematical can be found by which a division, such
as the author pretends to have discovered, can be effected.

After all, this proposal is not mathematical, but simply practical
and as all the inconveniences that this author proposes to remove by the
use of changeable finger-boards for the viol arise, from the frets, so by

Wood is greatly mistaken in the account by him given of this dispute; for the observations of Lock on Salmon's book, and 'The present Practice of Music Vindicated,' by the same author, with the 'Duellum Musicum' of Phillips, and the letter from Playford, are two separate and distinct publications. The following is the true history and order of the controversy:—

I. Essay to the advancement of music by Thomas Salmon.

II. Observations thereon by Matthew Lock.

III. A vindication of an Essay to the advancement of Music from Mr. Matthew Lock's observations inquiring into the real nature and most convenient practice of that Science, by Thomas Salmon, M.A. of Trin. Coll. Oxon.

This vindication is in the form of a letter to Dr. John Wallis, Savilian professor of geometry in the university of Oxford, and begins with thanks for a letter from that person to the author, testifying his approbation of the essay, and an acknowledgment of the honour done him by the Royal Society, who in their Transactions, No. 80, published in February, 1671-2, had upon their judgments recommended it to public practice.

These several tracts were all published in the year 1672. In the following year came forth

IV. The present practice of music vindicated, with the Duellum Musicum and Playford's letter, which closes the dispute.

The subject-matter of this controversy is not now so important as to require a minute detail of the arguments; it may suffice to say, that with a studied affectation of wit and humour, it abounds with the most abusive scurrility that ever disgraced controversy.

Wood, who seems to have entertained an unjustifiable partiality for Salmon and his proposal, intimates that he had the best of the argument; but the contrary may be presumed from the total silence of Salmon, after the last publication against him by Lock and his associates, and from the opinion of the public, who have never acquiesced in the proposal to reject the cliffs, from a well-grounded persuasion that the substituting of letters in their places would introduce rather than prevent confusion; so that the method of notation contended for by Lock continues to be practised, without the least variation, to this day; and Mr. Thomas Salmon, together with his essay to the advancement of music, by casting away the cliffs, and uniting all sorts of music in one universal character, are now very deservedly forgotten.

Mention has been made in a preceding page of the introduction of the opera into this kingdom, and of the opera of Psyche, written by Shadwell, and composed by Lock; this entertainment seems to have been well received by the public, for in 1675 he published it in score, together with the music in the Tempest, before mentioned, with a preface in his usual style, and a dedication to James duke of Monmouth.

It appears by Lock's preface that the instrumental music, before and between the acts, of Psyche, was composed by Sig. Giovanni Battista Draghi, a musician in the service of queen Catherine, and who is mentioned in the next succeeding article.

The world is indebted to Lock for the first rules ever published in this kingdom on the subject of continued or thorough-bass; a collection of these he has given to the world in a book entitled Melothesia, Lond. oblong quarto, 1673. It is dedicated to Roger L'Estrange, Esq., afterwards Sir Roger L'Estrange, a man eminently skilled in music, and an encourager of its professors, and contains, besides the rules, some lessons for the harpsichord and organ by himself and other masters. He was also the author of a collection of airs entitled 'A little Consort of three parts for Viols or Violins,' printed in 1657, and of the music to sundry songs printed in the Treasury of Music, the Theater of Music, and other collections of songs. In the latter of these is a dialogue, 'When death shall part us from these kids,' which he set to music, and, together with Dr. Blow's 'Go, perjured man,' was ranked amongst the best vocal compositions of the time.

Lock was very intimate with Silas Taylor, the author of a History of Gavelkind, who himself was a good musician,* as also an antiquary. Their acquaintance commenced through Lock's wife, who was of the same county with Taylor, viz. Hereford: her maiden name was Gammons. It is to be presumed that at the time when he composed his morning service he was of the chapel royal, and consequently a protestant; but it is certain that he went over to the Romish communion, and became organist to queen Catherine of Portugal, the consort of Charles II. and that he died a papist in 1677.†

GIOVANNI BATTISTA DRAGHI was an Italian by birth, and was probably a brother of Antonio Draghi, maestro di capella at Vienna, and of Carlo Draghi, organist to the emperor Leopold. He is supposed to have been one of those musicians who came into England with Mary d'Este, princess of Modena, the consort of James II. He was a very fine performer on the harpsichord, and composed and published in England lessons for that instrument. He joined with Lock in composing the music to the opera of Psyche, and upon his decease in 1677, succeeded him in the place of organist to the queen.‡

---

the removal of the frets the inconveniences are removed: and we find by experience that persons having a good ear, and nature only for their guide, do in all cases divide the octave most accurately.

At the end of the proposal is a letter of Dr. Wallis to the author, approving in general of his design, but attended with some such shrewd remarks on it, as tend to show that Salmon was far from equal to the task he had undertaken. At the close of the remarks is a very curious passage, containing an assertion of Dr. Wallis, that there are manifest places in Ptolemy that the frets, μαγαδια, of the ancients were moveable, not in tuning only, but even in playing, which is a strong argument against the opinion that in the ancient modes the tones and semitones followed in succession as they arise in the scale, and that of seven modes or keys, five are lost; so that only two, viz. A and C, are remaining.

* An anthem of his, 'God is our hope and strength,' is well known among the church musicians.

† It is probable that his residence was at Somerset-house, the palace of the queen dowager, for his last publication is dated from his lodgings in the Strand.

‡ The queen was permitted the exercise of her own religion; and it is probable that in some part of Whitehall she might have a chapel, in which mass was celebrated, with an organ, and something like a choir. This is certain, that when, upon the death of Charles II. she went to reside at the palace of Somerset-house, she had an ecclesiastical establishment, which included in it an organist and three chapel-boys, as appears

Although Draghi was an Italian, and there are many compositions of his extant, particularly a Madrigal among the Harleian manuscripts in the British museum, 'Qual spaventosa Tromba,' which are altogether in the Italian style, he seems during his long residence in this country to have, to a remarkable degree, assimilated his style to that of the old English masters, as appears by an anthem of his, 'This is the day that the Lord hath made,' and more evidently in sundry old ballad airs and dance-tunes composed by him, the melodies whereof are singularly excellent.

During the reigns of Charles II. and James II. Draghi seemed to be a favourite court musician. Mr. Wanley, a faithful narrator of facts, and who, being a musical man, might possibly have been personally acquainted with him, says that Draghi was music-master to our most excellent queen Anne;* meaning, it is presumed, that the queen, when young, and of a suitable age, had been taught music by this person, as was probably her sister, the princess Mary.

Towards the latter end of his life he composed the music to an opera written by D'Urfey, 'The Wonders in the Sun, or the Kingdom of Birds.' This whimsical drama was performed at the Queen's Theatre in the Hay-market, in the month of July, 1706. It is said that the songs in this opera, of which there are a great number, were written by several of the most eminent wits of the age, who lent the author their assistance; and it is probable that for this reason he dedicated it to the Kit Kat Club. Among others that seem to be the production of a genius superior to D'Urfey, is that excellent song known by the name of the 'Dame of Honour.' This song was set by Draghi, and it is difficult to say which is most to be admired, the song for the sentiments, or the air for the sweetness of its melody. There are also in it the famous tune called the 'Old Cebell;' as also another very fine one to the words 'Tell me, Jenny, tell me roundly;' and, lastly, a tune which, some years after the exhibition of the opera, became a country-dance, and in the printed collections of country-dance tunes is called the Czar.

Downes, the prompter, says of this opera that the singers in it were Mr. Cook, Mr. Laroon, Mr. Lawrence, Mr. Hudson, and others, and the dancers, Mons. De Bargues, Mons. L'Abbé's brother, Mr. Fair-

bank, Mr. Elford,† and others; and that it lasted only six days, not answering half the expense of it.

We meet in the printed collections many songs with the name Signor Baptist to them; this subscription means uniformly Baptist Draghi, and not Baptist Lully, as some have supposed.

Pelham Humphrey was one of the first set of children after the restoration, and educated, together with Blow and Wise, under Captain Cook. He was admitted a gentleman of the chapel Jan. 23, 1666, and distinguished himself so greatly in the composition of anthems as to excite the envy of his master, who, it is confidently asserted, died of discontent at seeing paid to him that applause which was but due to his merit.‡ Cook died on the thirteenth day of July, 1672, and on the thirtieth of the same month Humphrey was appointed master of the children in his room. This honourable station he held but a short time, for he died at Windsor on the fourteenth day of July, 1674, in the twenty-seventh year of his age, and was succeeded as master of the children by his condisciple Blow. He lies interred in the east ambulatory, reaching from north to south of the cloister of Westminster Abbey. On his gravestone was the following inscription, but it is now effaced:—

HERE LIETH INTERRED THE BODY OF
PELHAM HUMPHREY,
WHO DIED THE XIVTH OF JULY, ANN. DOM. MDCLXXIV,
AND IN THE XXVIITH YEAR OF HIS AGE.

In Dr. Boyce's Collection of Cathedral Music are two very fine anthems of Humphrey, 'O Lord my God,' and 'Have mercy upon me.' In conjunction with Dr. Blow and Dr. Turner he composed the anthem 'I will alway give thanks.' He also composed tunes to many of the songs in the Theater of Music, the Treasury of Music, and other collections in his time, particularly that to the song 'When Aurelia first I courted,' which was the favourite of those times; and another to a song said to have been written by king Charles II. 'I pass all my hours in an old shady grove,' printed with the music in the appendix to this work.

Pietro Reggio, a native of Genoa, was of the private music to Christina, queen of Sweden, and was greatly celebrated for his performance on the lute.§ Upon the queen's resignation of the crown he came to England, and choosing Oxford for the place of his residence, in the year 1677 published there a little tract entitled 'A Treatise to sing well any Song

---

by the following list in Chamberlayne's present state of England, printed in 1694.

Lord Almoner, Cardinal Howard of Norfolk; Mr. Paulo de Almeyda, Mr. Emanuel Diaz, Almoners; Confessor, Father Christopher de Rozario; Father Huddlestone, and Father Michael Ferreyra, Chaplains; three Portugal Franciscan Friars, called Arrabidoes, and a lay brother; Mr. James Martin, Mr. Nicholas Kennedy, Mr. William Hollyman, Chapelboys; Mr. John Battista Draghi, Organist; Mr. Timothy de Faria, Mr. James Read, Mr. Anthony Fernandez, Virgers.

Queen Catherine's chapel at Somerset-house was remaining till the year 1733, when it was destroyed to make room for the Prince of Orange, when he came over to marry the Princess Anne. A gentleman, who remembers it, says that adjoining to it was a bed-chamber, with a small window, contrived that the queen when in bed might see the elevation of the Host. *The window was at the top above the bedstead, so that she might hear the service but could see nothing. I have been in that room.* —Horace Walpole.

* Queen Anne played on the harpsichord. She had a spinnet, the loudest and perhaps the finest that ever was heard, of which she was very fond. She gave directions that at her decease this instrument should go to the master of the children of the chapel royal for the time being, and descend to his successors in office: accordingly it went first to Dr. Croft, and is now in the hands of Dr. Nares, master of the children of the royal chapel.

† Mr. Richard Elford was educated in the choir of Lincoln, and was afterwards of the choir at Durham, but coming to London, be became a singer on the stage. His person being, as Dr. Tudway relates, awkward and clumsy, and his action disgusting, he quitted the theatre, and was admitted a gentleman of the chapel royal, and to the places of a lay-vicar in St. Paul's cathedral and Westminster abbey. His voice was a fine countertenor. As a gentleman of the chapel he had an addition of an hundred pounds a year to his salary. Mr. Weldon's six Solo Anthems, published with the title of 'Divine Harmony,' were composed on purpose for him; and in the preface the author celebrates Mr. Elford for his fine performance of them. He had a brother, also a singer, who by the interest of Dean Swift was preferred to a place in one of the cathedrals in Dublin.

‡ Captain Henry Cook was made master of the children at the restoration. He was esteemed the best musician of his time to sing to the lute, till Pelham Humphries came up, after which he died with discontent. Ashmolean MS. art. Cook.

§ Whitelock, when embassador at Stockholm, heard him sing and accompany himself on the Theorbo, with great applause. Ashmolean MS.

whatsoever.' He also set to music for a single voice, with a thorough-bass, those love-verses of Cowley called the Mistress.

After some years residence in Oxford, he removed to London, and died in the parish of St. Giles in the Fields, on the twenty-third day of July, 1685. The following inscription to his memory was remaining till about the year 1735, when the church was pulled down in order to be rebuilt:—

PETRUS REGGIO
CUJUS CORPUS EX ADVERSO JACET
NATUS GENUÆ DIVINAM MUSICÆ
SCIENTIAM A CLARISSIMIS IN SUA
PATRIA ATQUE A DEO IN TOTO
ORBE MAGISTRIS EXCULTAM
AB IPSO ULTERIUS ORNATAM
EX ITALIA ET COELO DICERES TRANSALPES
IN HISPANIAM GERMANIAM
SUECIAM ET GALLIAM
DEINDE IN ANGLIAM TRANSTULIT
POSTREMO AD COELESTES CHOROS
SECUM EVEXIT
DIE XXIII JULII MDCLXXXV.

MICHAEL WISE, a most sweet and elegant composer, born in Wiltshire, was one of the first set of children of the royal chapel after the restoration: he became organist and master of the choristers in the cathedral church of Salisbury in 1668; and on the sixth of January, 1675, was appointed a gentleman of the chapel royal in the room of Raphael Courtville, deceased. On the twenty-seventh of January, 1686, he was preferred to be almoner and master of the choristers of St. Paul's. He was much favoured by Charles II. and being appointed to attend him in a progress which he once made, claimed as the king's organist pro tempore, to play the organ at whatsover church the king stopped at: it is said that at one church he presumed to begin his voluntary before the preacher had finished his sermon; a very unwarrantable and indecent exertion of his right, how well soever founded. It is possible that some such indiscreet behaviour as this might draw on him the king's displeasure; for upon his decease he was under a suspension, and at the coronation of James II. Edward Morton officiated in his room.

He composed several very fine anthems, namely, 'Awake up my glory,' 'Prepare ye the way of the Lord,' 'Awake, put on thy strength,' and some others. He also composed that well-known two-part song, 'Old Chiron thus preached to his pupil Achilles,' and some Catches, printed in the Musical Companion, which are excellent in their kind. He was a man of great pleasantry, but ended his days unfortunately; for being with his wife at Salisbury in the month of August, 1687, some words arose between him and her, upon which he went out of the house in a passion, and, it being towards midnight, he was stopped by the watch, with whom he began a quarrel, in which he received a blow on the head with a bill, which fractured his skull and killed him.

The advantages were very great which music derived from the studies of these men: they improved and refined upon the old church-style, and formed a new one, which was at once both elegant and solemn;

and from the many excellent compositions of the musicians of king Charles the Second's reign now extant, it may be questioned whether the principles of harmony, or the science of practical composition, were ever better understood than in his time; the composers for the church appearing to have been possessed of every degree of knowledge necessary to the perfection of the art. Other improvements, it is true, lay behind, but these regarded the philosophy of sound in general, and in the division of the science of physics are comprehended under the term Phonics.

The first, at least among modern philosophers, that have treated on the generation and propagation of sound is Lord Verulam, who in his Natural History, Century II. has given a great variety of very curious experiments touching music in general, and in particular touching the nullity and entity of sounds. II. The production, conservation, and dilation of sounds. III. The magnitude and exility and damps of sounds. IV. Of the loudness or softness of sounds, and their carriage at longer or shorter distance. V. Touching the communication of sounds, &c.

The Royal Society, which was instituted at London immediately after the restoration, for the improvement of natural knowledge, seems to have prosecuted this branch of it with no small degree of ardour, as appears by a great variety of papers on the subject of sound, its nature, properties, and affections, from time to time published in the Philosophical Transactions. Besides which there are extant a great variety of tracts on this subject, written by the members of that society, and published separately, some of the most distinguished of which are, 'A Philosophical Essay on Music,' published in quarto, 1677, without the name of the author, but which it is certain was written by Sir Francis North, Lord Chief Justice of the Court of Common Pleas, and afterwards Lord Keeper of the Great Seal;* a translation of 'Des Cartes de Musica,' by a person of honour, Henry Lord Brouncker, president of the Royal Society, with learned notes by the translator; an 'Introductory Essay to the Doctrine of Sound, containing some proposals for the improvement of Acousticks,' by Narcissus, bishop of Ferns and Leighlin; and a 'Discourse on the natural Grounds and Principles of Harmony,' by William Holder, D.D. London, octavo, 1694.

A short abstract from two of the discourses above mentioned will suffice to show the nature and tendency of each. Of the others mention is elsewhere made in the course of this work.

The general purport of the treatise written by Sir Francis North is as follows:—

It begins with an inquiry into the cause of sounds: in order thereto the author states those phenomena of sound which he thinks most considerable, as, first, that it may be produced in the Toricellian vacuity. 2. That it causes motion in solid bodies. 3. That it is diminished by the interposition of solid bodies; and 4. If the bodies interposed are very

* This is expressly asserted in the Life of the Lord Keeper North, written by his brother, the Hon. Roger North, Esq. page 297.

**thick,** its passage is wholly obstructed.   5. That it **seems** to come to the ear in straight lines, when the object is so situated that it cannot come in straight lines to the ear.   6. That when there is a wind, the sphere is enlarged on that part on which the wind blows, and diminished on the contrary part.   8 That it arrives not to the ear in an instant, but considerably slower than sight.   9. That it comes as quick against the wind as with it, though not so loud, nor so far.

Hence he raises the following hypothesis; he supposes the air we breathe in to be a mixture of divers minute bodies, of different sorts and sizes, though all of them are so small as to escape our senses: the grosser of them he makes elastical, and to be resisted by solid bodies, altogether impervious to them : the smaller parts he supposes to pass through solid bodies, though not with that ease ; but that upon a sudden and violent start of them they shock the parts of solid bodies that stand in their way, and also the grosser parts of the air.   Lastly, he supposes there may be another degree of most subtle ethereal parts, with which the interstices of these and all other bodies are replete, which find a free passage everywhere, and are capable of no compression, and consequently are the medium and cause of the immediate communication of sound.

Now, of these three, he esteems the middle sort to be the medium and cause of sound, and supposes that at any time when the grosser air is driven off any space, and leaves it to be possessed by these and other more subtle bodies, and returns by its elasticity to its former place, then are these parts extruded with violence, as from the centre of that space, and communicate their motion as far as the sound is heard : or that where any solid body is moved with a sudden and violent motion, these parts must be affected thereby ; for as these parts are so much resisted by solid bodies as to shock them, so on the contrary they must needs be moved by a sudden starting of solid bodies.

So that, according to him, sound may be caused by the trembling of solid bodies, without the presence of gross air; and also by the restitution of gross air, when it has been divided by any sudden force, as by the end of a whip, having all the motion of a whip contracted in it, and by a sudden turn throwing off the air ; or by ascension, as in thunder and guns ; or by any impression of force, carrying it where other air cannot so forcibly follow, as upon compressing of air in a bladder till it breaks, or in a potgun, a sudden crack will be caused.

Having laid down this hypothesis, and left his reader to apply it to the before-mentioned phenomena, he proceeds to discourse of music itself, and labours to show how this action that causes sound is performed by the several instruments of music.

His definition of a tone is adapted to his hypothesis, and will be thought somewhat singular: 'A tone,' says he, 'is the repetition of cracks or pulses 'in equal spaces of time, so quick, that the interstices ' or intervals are not perceptible to sense.'

He observes that the compass of music extends from such tones, whose intervals are so great, that the several pulses are distinguishable by sense, to those whose interstices are so very small, that they are not commensurate with any other.

Speaking of the production of tones, and of the assistances to sound by instruments, he says that wherever a body stands upon a spring that vibrates in equal terms, such a body put in motion will produce a tone, which will be more grave or acute according to the velocity of the returns ; and that therefore strings vibrating have a tone according to the bigness or tension of them ; and bells that vibrate by cross ovals produce notes according to the bigness of them, or the thickness of their sides ; and so do all other bodies, whose superficies being displaced by force, result or come back by a spring that carries them beyond their first station.   And here he observes that it is easy to comprehend how every pulse upon such vibrations causes sound ; for that the gross air is thrown off by the violence of the motion, which continues some moment of time after the return of the vibrating body ; whereupon some space must be left to that subtle matter, which upon the result of the air starts as from a centre, which action being the same as that which our author supposes to be the cause of sound, is repeated upon every vibration.

But finding it more difficult to show how tones are made by a pipe, where there are no visible vibrations, he considers the frame of a pipe, and the motion of the air in it, and thereby attempts to find the cause of the tone of a pipe, and the pulse that gives it sound.

His doctrine on this head is delivered in these words : ' To shew how the pulses are caused, ' whereby the included air is put into this motion, it ' is necessary to observe the frame of a pipe, which ' chiefly consists in having a long slit, through which ' the air is blown in a thin film against, or very near, ' a solid edge that is at some distance opposite to it, ' in such manner that the intermediate space is ' covered by the stream of air.   This film of air on ' the one side is exposed to the outward air, and on ' the inside is defended from it by the sides of the ' pipe, within which the air inclosed in the pipe ' stagnates, whilst the outward air is by the blast ' put into a vortical motion.

' The vortical motion or eddy on the outside is so ' strong, that there not being a balance to that force ' on the inside, the film of air gives way, and ' the eddy bears into the pipe, but is immediately ' overcome by the blast, which prevails until the ' eddy overcomes it again ; and so there is a crossing ' of streams by turns and pulses, which causes the ' voice of the pipe, the gross air of one stream being ' thrown off by the interposition of the other.

' These vicissitudes or terms will answer the tone ' of the pipe according to the gage of its cavity : for ' the spring of the included air helps towards the ' restitution of the blast and eddy in their turns, ' which causes those turns to comply with the tone of ' the pipe ; and therefore the same blast will cause ' several tones, if the gage or measure of the included ' air be changed by apertures in the side of the pipe.

' But there must be some proportion between the

'mouth, so I call that part of the pipe where the
'voice is, and the gage of the pipe; for though the
'pulses will be brought to comply with the tone of
'the pipe in any reasonable degree, yet when there
'is great disparity it will not do so; as if the pipe be
'too long for the proportion of the diameter, the
'pulses at the mouth cannot be brought to so slow
'terms as to answer the vibrations of the included
'air; therefore the pipe will not speak unless it can
'break into some higher note.  If the slimy stream
'of air be too thick, the pipe will not speak, because
'the eddy cannot break through; if the opposite
'edge be too remote, the stream cannot entirely cover
'the aperture, for it mixes with the outward air,
'and is more confused the further it is from the vent
'or passage, whereby some outward air may have
'communication to make an opposite eddy on the
'inside of the stream.  For the same reason, if there
'be the least aperture in the region of the mouth of
'the pipe, it will not speak at all.

'Hence it is that the voice of organ pipes is so
'tender and nice : but shrill whistles depend not
'upon this ground; for they are made in any small
'cavity, where the blast is so applyed that the erum-
'pent air must cross it, whether the stream be thick
'or thin.  Therefore the bore of a key, a piece of
'nut-shell, or any other cavity will make a whistle,
'whose tone will be according to the quantity of the
'included air; for the less that is, the harder it is to
'be compressed, and the quicker and stronger it
'must break forth.

'Another kind of whistle is, when a hollow body
'with a small cavity is perforated by opposite holes,
'a blast either way will cause a tone, which seems
'to be made in this manner.

'The air that is violently drawn or thrust through
'these holes, is straitned at the passage by the swift-
'ness of the motion, and within the cavity is some-
'what enlarged, and consequently its force is directed,
'and it presses beyond the compass of the opposite
'aperture, whereupon it bears of all sides into the
'cavity; hereby the air within the cavity is com-
'pressed until it breaks forth by crossing the stream,
'which being done by vicissitudes, causes a tone :
'this kind of action, as I imagine, is performed when
'men whistle with their lips.

'In some pipes the pulses are caused by springs,
'as the Regal stop of an organ, which is commonly
'tuned by shortening the spring, whereby it becomes
'stronger, but the note will be changed by the alter-
'ation of the cavity; and therefore to make them
'steddy, some that stand upon very weak springs
'have pavilions set to them.

'A rustick instance may be given of the compliance
'of a spring, in taking such vibrations as are pro-
'portionable to the cavity; it is a Jews-harp, or
'Jews-trump, the tongue whereof has natural vibra-
'tions according to the strength and length of the
'of the spring, and so is fitted to one particular tone ;
'but countrymen framing their breath and their
'mouth to several notes make a shift to express a
'tune by it.

'In a shawm or hautboy the quill at the mouth is

'a kind of spring, but so weak and indifferent, that it
'complies with any measure*, and therefore the tone
'will be according to the apertures of the pipe.

'The fluttering and jarring of discording sounds,
'which I did before observe, is so regular, and
'the sounds take their turns with equal interstices,
'which makes the joining of them produce a harsher
'sound than either had before; whereby organ-
'makers imitate the hautboy or trumpet without any
'spring or quill, by joining discording pipes.†

'In a Sacbut the lips of a man do the same office as a
'quill does in a Shawm or hautboy; when the inclu-
'ded air is lengthened, the tone varies ; nevertheless
'they can produce several notes that are in chord to
'the tone of the instrument by strengthening the blast
'without lengthening the cavity : and in a trumpet
'which is the same kind of instrument, only not
'capable of being lengthened, they can sound a whole
'tune, which is by the artificial ordering the blast
'at the mouth, whereby the sound breaks into such
'notes as are to be used.'

Having thus shown how tones are produced by
instruments of music, the author proceeds to take
notice of other assistances which instruments give to
sound, in these words :—

'In violins and harpsicords the tones are made
'wholly by the vibrating strings, but the frame of
'the instrument adds much to the sound ; for such
'strings vibrating upon a flat rough board, would
'yield but a faint and pitiful sound.

'The help that instruments give to the sound, is
'by reason that their sides tremble and comply with
'any sound, and strike the air in the same measure
'that the vibrations of the music are, and so consi-
'derably increase the sound.

'This trembling is chiefly occasioned by the con-
'tinuity of the sides of the instrument with the
'vibrating string; therefore if the bridge of a violin
'be loaded with lead, the sound will be damp; and
'if there be not a stick called the sound post to
'promote the continuity between the back and belly
'of the instrument, the sound will not be brisk and
'sprightly.

'Such a continuity to the nerve of hearing will
'cause a sense of sound to a man that hath stopped
'his ears, if he will hold a stick that touches the
'sounding instrument between his teeth.‡

'The sound of itself, without such continuity,
'would occasion some trembling; but this is not
'considerable in respect of the other, though it be all
'the assistance that the structure of a chamber can
'give to musick, except what is by way of echo.

* *Sig. Orig.* but Quere if not pressure ?
† In this sentiment the author is mistaken : discordant pipes are made
use of by the organ-makers to imitate the kettle-drum; and the best for
this purpose are F♯ and GAMUT, but the hautboy and trumpet are
imitable only by reed pipes of the same form as those instruments
respectively, that is to say, having the greater end spreading with a
curve like a bell, in a greater or less degree.
‡ Thomas Mace, a writer of whom there will shortly be occasion to
speak, and a lutenist, having almost lost his hearing, invented a double
lute, which he contrived to make the loudest instrument of the lute
kind he had ever heard ; nevertheless he was not able to hear all that he
played on it, except by means of such a contrivance as is above suggested.
In short, as he relates, he heard by the help of his teeth, which when he
played he was wont to lay close to the edge of the instrument, where the
lace is fixed, and thereby derived, as he expresses it, with thankfulness
to God, one of the principal refreshments and contentments that he
enjoyed in this world.  Musick's Monument, page 203.

' This tremble of the instruments changes with
' every new sound; the spring of the sides of the in-
' strument standing indifferent to take any measure,
' receives a new impression; but a vibrating string
' can take no measure but according to its tension.

' Therefore instruments that have nothing to stop
' the sounding strings, make an intolerable jangle to
' one that stands near, as bells to one that is in
' the steeple, and hears the continuing sound of
' dissonant tones; such is the Dulcimer: but the harp-
' sichord, that hath rags upon the jacks, by which
' the vibration of the string is staid, gives no distur-
' bance by the sonorousness of the instrument, for
' that continues not the sound after the vibrations
' determined, and another tone struck, but changes
' and complies with the new sound.'

Next he treats of the varying and breaking of
tones into other tones, both in strings and in pipes.
In his discourse on this part of music there occur
divers pertinent observations concerning the motions
of pendulums, the nature of the trumpet marine, and
of the true trumpet, and of the sacbut. And having
shown that sound causes a motion, not only of solid
bodies, but of the grosser parts of the air, within
the sphere of it, he considers that if the air which
is moved by being inclosed, stands upon such a
degree of resistance to compression, that it hath a
spring vibrating in the same measure with the sound
that puts it into motion, there will be the same effect
as when two strings are tuned in unison; that is, the
motion will be so augmented by succeeding regular
pulses, that the inclosed air may be brought to ring,
and produce a tone. And here he takes notice of the
advice of Vitruvius in his Architecture, importing
that in the structure of a theatre there should be
vases or hollow pots of several sizes, to answer all
the notes of music, placed upon the stage; in such
a manner that the voice of them which sing upon
the stage may be augmented by the ringing of them;
Vitruvius mentioning divers ancient theatres where
such were, in some of brass, in some of earth.

After this he proceeds to consider the nature of
the keys in music, and of a single tune, which he
says consists in the succeeding notes having a due
relation to the preceding, and carrying their proper
emphasis by length, loudness, and repetition, with
variety that may be agreeable to the hearer. Next
he treats of Schisms, and the scale of music, showing
that the latter is not set out by any determinate
quantities of whole notes or half notes, though the degrees are commonly so called; but that the degrees of
the musical scale are fixed by the ear in these places
where the pulses of the tones are coincident, without
any regard to the quantity; and here he endeavours,
by a division of the monochord, corresponding as it
seems very nearly with that of Lord Brouncker, in his
translation of Des Cartes, to show how all notes come
into the scale by their relation and dignity; whence
he thinks it is obvious why, for easiness of instruction
and convenience, the scale of degrees of music is
made as musicians now exhibit it.

He next proceeds to the consideration of music
consisting of several parts, which, as he expresses it,
is made up of harmony, formality, and conformity.

Lastly, he speaks of time, or the measure of music,
the due observation whereof he says is grateful, for
the reasons given by him for the formality of a single
tune, because the subsequent strokes are measured by
the memory of the former; and if they comprehend
them, or are comprehended by them, it is alike
pleasant, for that the mind cannot choose but compare the one with the other, and observe when the
strokes are coincident with the memory of the
former. Wherefore he says it is that the less the
intervals are, the more grateful the measure; because
it is easily and exactly represented by the memory;
whereas a long space of time, that cannot be comprehended in one thought, is not retained in the memory
in its exact measure, nor can abide the comparison,
the time past being always shortened by so much as
it is removed from the time present.

He concludes his discourse with two observations,
first, that it plainly appears how music comes to be
so copious, for, considering the species of keys, the
number of them, the variety of chords, the allowable
mixture of discords, and the diversity of measure,
it is not to be wondered at, that it should, like
language, afford every age and nation, nay, every
person, particular styles and modes. Secondly, it
appears that tones or modes of music in ancient
time could not be of other kinds than they are now,
since there can be no other in nature; whereof the
great effects it then had, if truly related, must be
imputed to the rarity of it, and the barbarity of the
people, who are not transported with anything
after it becomes common to them.

A farther account of this scarce and curious tract
is given in that singular book The Life of the Lord
Keeper Guilford, written by the honourable Roger
North,* a brother of his lordship, which, as it

* This person wrote also the lives of his two brothers, the honourable
Sir Dudley North, Knight, commissioner of the customs, and afterwards
of the treasury to Charles II. and the hon. and rev. Dr. John North,
master of Trinity college in Cambridge; as also an Examen or Enquiry
into the Credit and Veracity of the compleat History of England, compiled by Bishop Kennet, 4to. 1740. The Life of the Lord Keeper is
a curious book, as it contains the history of Westminster Hall, with
a great variety of entertaining particulars of the most eminent practisers
from the year 1650 to 1680; but the style of it, like that of the author's
other writings, is exceedingly quaint and affected. Nor are his opinions
of men and things, particularly of law and justice, less singular, as will
presently be shown.
Sir Dudley North was a Turkey merchant, and, being one of the
English factory at Constantinople, had the management of a great
number of lawsuits; how he managed them, and what were the
sentiments of his brother touching his conduct, and particularly of the
obligation of an oath, the following passage will show :—
' Another scheme of our merchants law conduct was touching proofs.
' The Turkish law rigidly holds every person to prove all the facts of his
' case by two Turkish witnesses, which makes the dealing, with a view
' of dispute, extremely difficult; for which reason the merchants usually
' take writing; but that hath its infirmity also, for the witnesses are
' required to prove not only the writing, which with us is enough, but
' they must prove every fact contained in it to be true, or else the evidence
' is insufficient. It fell out sometimes that when he had a righteous
' cause, the adversary was knavish, and would not own the fact, and he
' had not regular and true witnesses to prove it; he made no scruple in
' such case to use false ones; and certain Turks that had belonged to the
' factory, and knew the integrity of their dealings, would little scruple to
' attest facts to which they were not privy, and were paid for it. I have
' heard the merchant say he had known that at trials Turks standing by
' unconcerned, have stept forwards to help a dead lift (as they tell of
' a famous witnessing attorney, who used to say at his trial, ' Doth it
' stick? give me the book),' as these expect to be paid, and the merchants
' fail not to send them the premio, else they may cause great incon-
' veniences. Nay, a merchant there will directly hire a Turk to swear the
' fact, of which he knows nothing, which the Turk doth out of faith he
' hath in the merchant's veracity; and the merchant is very safe in it, for
' without two Turks to testify, he cannot be accused of subornation. This
' is not as here accounted a villainous subornation, but an ease under an
' oppression, and a lawful means of coming into a just right. The
' Christian oath is not in the case, so there is no profanation: and (upon
' the whole) the morality of the action seems to depend on the pure

contains a summary of the doctrines laid down in the Philosophical Essay of Music, as also some particulars relating to his lordship's musical studies, is here inserted in the words of the author :—

'Now to illustrate his lordship's inclination to ingenious arts, and sciences, I have two subjects to ' enlarge upon. 1. Musick. 2. Picture. As for his ' musick, I have already mentioned his exquisite ' hand upon the Lyra and Bass-Viol, and the use he ' made of it to relieve his solitude in his chamber. ' He had a desire to use also the Theorbo and violin. ' He scarce attempted the former, but supplied the ' use of it by the touch of his Lyra Viol upon his ' knee, and so gained a solitary consort with his ' voice.* He attempted the violin, being ambitious ' of the prime part in consort, but soon found that ' he began such a difficult art too late ; and his profit ' also said nay to it, for he had not time for that kind ' of practice. It was great pity he had not naturally ' a better voice, for he delighted in nothing more ' than in the exercise of that he had, which had ' small virtue but in the tuneableness and skill. He ' sang anything at first sight, as one that reads in a ' new book, which many, even singing-masters, ' cannot do. He was a great proller of songs, espe- ' cially duets, for in them his brother could accom- ' pany him ; and the Italian songs to a thorough-bass ' were choice purchases, and if he liked them he ' commonly wrote them out with his own hand ; ' and I can affirm that he transcribed a book of ' Italian songs into a volume of the largest quarto, ' and thicker than a Common Prayer Book. And this ' was done about the time he had received the Great ' Seal ; for if he would discharge his mind of ' anxieties, he often took the book of Songs, and ' wrote one or two of them out ; and as he went ' along he observed well the composition and ele- ' gancies, as if he not only wrote but heard them, ' which was great pleasure to him.

'His lordship had not been long master of the ' viol, and a sure consortier, but he turn'd composer, ' and from raw beginnings advanced so far as to ' complete divers concertos of two and three parts, ' which at his grandfather's house, were perform'd ' with masters in company, and that was no small ' joy and encouragement to him. But it was not to ' be expected he should surmount the style and mode ' of the great musick-master Mr. Jenkins, then in

' use where he came. And, after his capacity reach'd ' higher, he had no time to be so diverted. Yet ' while he was Chief Justice, he took a fancy to set ' to musick, in three parts, a Canzon of Guarini, ' beginning thus, "Cor mio del," &c. In that he ' aimed to compass what he thought a great per- ' fection in consort-musick, ordering the parts so ' that every one shall carry the same air, and how- ' ever leading or following, the melody in each part ' is nearly the same, which is in composing no ' easy task.

' Not many years before his lordship was preferred ' to the Great Seal, he fell upon a pleasing specula- ' tion of the real mechanism whereby sounds are dis- ' tinguished into harmony and discord, or disposed ' to please or displease our sense of hearing. Every ' one is sensible of those effects, but scarce any know ' why, or by what means they are produced. He ' found that tones and accords might be anatomised ' and by apt schemes be presented to the eye as well ' as to the ear, and so musick be demonstrated in ' effigie. After he had digested his notions, and ' continued his schemes, he drew up a short tract, ' which he entitled A Philosophical Essay of Musick, ' not with the form and exactness of a solemn writer, ' but as the sense of a man of business, who minds ' the kernel and not the shell. This was printed by ' Mr. Martin, printer to the Royal Society, in 1677. ' The piece sold well, and in a few years it was out ' of print, and ever since is scarce to be met with but ' in private hands. If I may give a short account of ' his lordships's notion, it is but this : all musical ' sounds consist of tones, for irregular noises are ' foreign to the subject. Every tone consists of dis- ' tinct pulses or strokes in equal time, which being ' indistinguishably swift, seem continual. Swifter ' pulses are, accordingly, in sound sharper, and the ' slower flatter. When diverse run together, if the ' pulses are timed in certain proportions to each ' other, which produce coincidences at regular and ' constant periods, those may be harmonious, else dis- ' cord. And in the practice of musick, the stated ' accords fall in these proportions of pulsation, viz. ' $\frac{2}{1}, \frac{3}{2}, \frac{4}{3}, \frac{5}{4}, \frac{6}{5}$. Hence flow the common denomina- ' tions of 8th, 5th, 4th, 3d, 2d ; and these are produced ' upon a monochord by abscission of these parts, ' $\frac{1}{2}, \frac{1}{3}, \frac{1}{4}, \frac{1}{5}, \frac{1}{6}$. Of all which the fuller demonstration ' is a task beyond what is here intended.

' But to accomplish an ocular representation of ' these pulses, his lordship made a foundation upon ' paper by a perpetual order of parallel lines, and ' those were to signify the flux of time equably. ' And when a pulse happened, it was marked by ' a point upon one of those lines, and if continued ' so as to sound a base tone, it was marked upon ' every eighth line ; and that might be termed the ' Base. And then an upper part, which pulsed as ' $\frac{2}{1}$, or octave, was marked, beginning with the first ' of the base, upon every fourth line, which is twice ' as swift : and so all the other harmonious pro- ' portions, which shewed their coincidences, as well ' with the base as with one another. And there ' was also shewed a beautiful and uniform aspect in

'justice and right, and not upon the regularity (in a Christian sense) of 'the means. The Turks in their country are obliged, as we are here, by 'the rules of common justice. But it is to be supposed that being here, 'they would not regard our forms, but would get their right if they 'might by infringing them all. So we in that country are obliged in 'common honesty to observe even their law of right and equity, but have 'no reason to regard their forms; and the compassing a right by any means 'contrary to them all, is not unreasonable. But to apprehend these 'diversities one must have a strong power of thought, to abstract the 'prejudices of our domestic education, and plant ourselves in a way of 'negotiating in heathen remote countries.

'Our merchant found by experience that in a direct fact a false 'witness was a surer card than a true one; for if the judge has a mind 'to baffle a testimony, an harmless honest witness, that doth not know 'his play, cannot so well stand his many captious questions as a false 'witness used to the trade will do, for he hath been exercised, and is 'prepared for such handling, and can clear himself when the other will 'be confounded; therefore if there be true witness, circumstances may 'be such as shall make the false ones more eligible.' Life of the Hon. Sir Dudley North, page 46.

* The nature of the Lyra-Viol, and the practice of the Viol Lyra way are fully explained in the account herein after given of John Playford.

'the composition of these accords when drawn
'together. This as to Times. The ordinary col-
'lation of sounds is commonly made by numbers,
'which, not referred to a real cause or foundation
'in nature, may be just, but withal very obscure,
'and imparting of no knowledge. Witness the
'mathematicians musical proportions. His lordship
'did not decline numbers, but derived them from
'plain truths. He found 360 the aptest for those
'subdivisions that musick required, and, applying
'that to an open string or monochord, each musical
'tone, found by abscission of a part of the string, is
'expressible by those numbers so reduced in pro-
'portion. As $\frac{1}{2}$ of the string pinched off is as $\frac{2}{1}$, or
'180, an octave ; and $\frac{1}{3}$ as $\frac{3}{2}$ 240 ; and so of the
'rest down to the tone or second, which cuts off $\frac{1}{9}$,
'and the semitone a $\frac{1}{16}$, &c.'* Life of Lord Keeper
Guilford, page 296.

The discourse of Dr. Marsh is of a different kind,
and treats altogether of the philosophy of sound,
without intermeddling with either the theory or
practice of music. Of the author mention has been
made in a preceding page. From the account given
of him by Wood it appears that he was well skilled
in the practical part of music ; and that while he
was a fellow of Exeter college, and principal of
Alban-hall, he had a weekly meeting or concert of
instrumental, and sometimes vocal music at his
lodgings : and to the account of his subsequent
preferments given by Wood, may be added, that
from the archiepiscopal see of Cashell he was translated to that of Dublin, and from thence to that of
Armagh, and that he died in 1713.

In his discourse on Acousticks the Doctor treats
very largely on Vision, and the improvements thereof by means of glasses and tubes of various kinds,
and from the principles laid down in the preceding
part of his discourse, he concludes that considerable
improvements may also be made in Acousticks,
which improvements he distributes into two classes,
viz. improvements of hearing as to its object, which
is sound, and the improvements of the organ of
hearing, and the medium through which sound is
propagated. Under these two several heads he
treats at large of the imitation of the voices of
sundry animals, as quails and cats ; and of those
sounds which are produced by the collision of solid
bodies ; of the speaking-trumpet, and of reflected
audition by echoes, which he says is capable of great
improvement, one whereof he thus describes :—

* The author of this book was himself well acquainted with the
principles of music, and entertained some doubts on the division of the
monochord, of which he could find no solution in the method of division
proposed by his brother in the essay above cited. Among the papers of
Dr. Pepusch was found the following quære in his own hand-writing, as
also the answer to it in the hand-writing of the Doctor.

Quære. The sound arising by the abscission of $\frac{8}{9}$ths is a tone, and
more remote from perfection of consonance than that of $\frac{7}{8}$ths ; why then
is the former accepted in music, and not the latter, which is abhorred ?
Dic et eris Apollo.

Answer. Considering only the numbers, it is true that $\frac{7}{8}$ is nearer to
concordance than $\frac{8}{9}$, but as they are both discords, $\frac{8}{9}$ is allowed, having
a natural and immediate relation to the concords, which $\frac{7}{8}$ having not,
is absolutely rejected. For the same reason, all relations compounded of
the numbers 2, 3, 5, are musical, all others $\frac{7}{8}$, $\frac{11}{10}$, $\frac{13}{12}$, &c. are contrary to it.

'As speculas may be so placed, that reflecting one
'upon or into the other, either directly or obliquely,
'one object shall appear as many : after the same
'manner ecchoing bodies may be so contrived and
'placed, as that reflecting the sound from one to
'another, either directly and mutually, or obliquely
'and by succession, out of one sound shall many
'echoes be begotten, which in the first case will be
'altogether, and somewhat involved and swallowed
'up by each other, and thereby confused, as a face
'in a looking-glass obverted ; in the other they will
'be separate, distinct, and succeeding one another,
'as most multiple ecchoes do.
'Moreover a multiple eccho may be made by so
'placing the ecchoing bodies at unequal distances,
'that they reflect all one way, and not one on the
'other, by which means a manifold successive sound
'will be heard, not without astonishment ; one clap
'of the hand like many ; one Hah ! like laughter ;
'one single word like many of the same tone and
'accent, and one viol like many of the same kind,
'imitating each other.†
'Furthermore, as Speculas may be so ordered,
'that by reflection they will make one single object
'appear many ; as one single man to seem many
'men differing in shape and complexion, or a com-
'pany of men ; so may ecchoing bodies also be
'ordered, that from any one sound given they shall
'produce as many ecchoes, different both as to their
'tone and intension ; the grounds whereof have
'elsewhere been laid down in a treatise concerning
'the sympathy of lute-string.
'By this means a musical room might be so con-
'trived, that not only one instrument play'd in it
'shall seem as many of the same sort and size, but
'even a concert of somewhat different ones, only by
'placing certain ecchoing bodies, so that any note
'played shall be return'd by them in third, fifth,
'and eighth.'

There is very little doubt but that the writings of
Mersennus and Kircher, and probably the various
discoveries of Lord Bacon, and the hints suggested
by him in his Natural History, gave this direction
to the studies of philosophical men of this time. It
seems that the Academy Del Cimento had for some
time been making experiments on the philosophy
of sound, many of which are referred to in the
Transactions of the Royal Society : the result of
these appears with great advantage in a very learned
treatise written by Padre Daniello Bartoli, of the
Society of Jesus, printed at Rome in the year 1679,
entitled 'Del Suono de Tremori Armonici e dell'
udito.' The pursuits of the Royal Society of
London were directed to the same object : in the
Philosophical Transactions are sundry papers on the
nature and properties of sound, and others expressly
on the subject of music, among which is one entitled
'The Theory of music reduced to arithmetical and
'geometrical proportions, by Thomas Salmon.'

† It is the opinion of some that the sound of words may be imprisoned
and let loose so as to articulate. Of this persuasion the papists endeavour
to avail themselves when they produce, as they are said to do, a most
precious relic, the Hah! of Joseph the husband of the blessed Virgin,
uttered by him when fetching a stroke with his axe, hermetically sealed, in a
glass viol. Vide Bp. Wilkin's Secret and Swift Messenger, Chap. XVII.

This paper seems to contain in substance that proposal to perform music in perfect and mathematical proportions, of which mention has been made in the preceding account of this person, and refers to a musical experiment said to have been made before the society, for the purpose, as it seems, of trying the truth of his proportions. The nature of this experiment will best appear from the author's own words, which are these :—

'To prove the foregoing propositions, two viols 'were mathematically set out, with a particular fret 'for each string, that every stop might be in a per-'fect exactness : upon these a sonata was perform'd 'by Mr. Frederick and Mr. Christian Stefkins; 'whereby it appeared that the theory was certain, 'since all the stops were owned by them to be per-'fect. And that they might be proved agreeable to 'what the best ear and the best hand perform in 'modern practice, the famous Italian, Signor Gas-'parini,* plaid another sonata upon the violin in 'consort with them, wherein the most compleat har-'mony was heard.'

The result of this experiment was a conviction, at least of the author, that the harmony resulting from his division was the most complete that ever had been heard, and that by it the true theory of music was demonstrated, and the practice of it brought to the greatest perfection. Vide Philosoph. Trans. No. 302, page 2072. Jones's Abridgm. vol. IV. part II. page 469.

JOHN ABELL, one of the chapel in the reign of King Charles II. was celebrated for a fine counter-tenor voice, and for his skill on the lute. The king admired his singing, and had formed a resolution to send him, together with one of his chapel, Mr. Gostling, to the Carnival at Venice, in order to show the Italians what good voices were produced in England ; but the latter signifying an unwilling-ness to go, the king desisted from his purpose. He continued in the chapel till the time of the revolu-tion, when he was discharged as being a papist. Upon this he went abroad, and distinguished himself by singing in public in Holland, at Hamburg, and other places, where acquiring considerable sums of money, he lived profusely, and affected the expense of a man of quality, moving about in an equipage of his own, though at intervals he was so reduced as to be obliged to travel, with his lute slung at his back, through whole provinces. In rambling he got as far as Poland ; and upon his arrival at Warsaw, the king having notice of it, sent for him to his court. Abell made some slight excuse to evade going, but upon being told that he had everything to fear from the king's resentment, he made an apology, and re-ceived a command to attend the king next day. Upon his arrival at the palace, he was seated in a chair in the middle of a spacious hall, and imme-diately drawn up to a great height ; presently the king with his attendants appeared in a gallery oppo-

site to him, and at the same instant a number of wild bears were turned in ; the king bade him then choose whether he would sing or be let down among the bears : Abell chose the former, and declared afterwards that he never sang so well in his life. This fact is alluded to in a letter from Pomigny de Auvergne to Mr. Abell of London, singing-master, among the letters from the dead to the living in the works of Mr. Thomas Brown, vol. II. page 189.[†]

Mattheson, in his Vollkommenen Cappellmeister, takes notice of Abell, and says that he sang in Hol-land, and at Hamburg, with great applause. He adds that he was possessed of some secrets, by which he preserved the natural tone of his voice to an ex-treme old age.

About the latter end of Queen Ann's reign Abell was at Cambridge with his lute, but he met there with poor encouragement. How long he lived after-wards is not known, but the account of his death was communicated to the gentleman who furnished many of the above particulars by one, who, having known him in his prosperity, assisted him in his old age, and was at the expense of his funeral.

After having rambled abroad for many years, it seems that Abell returned to England, for in 1701 he published at London a Collection of Songs in several languages, with a dedication to King William, wherein he expresses a grateful sense of his majesty's favours abroad, and more especially of his great cle-mency in permitting his return to his native country. In this collection is a song of Prior, ' Reading ends in melancholy,' published among his posthumous works, and there said to have been set by Mr. Abell. Mention is made in the Catalogue of Estienne Roger of Amsterdam, of a work of Abell, entitled ' Les Airs d'Abell pour le Concert du Duole ;' and in the ' Pills to purge Melancholy,' vol. IV. are two songs, set by Abell to very elegant tunes.

## CHAP. CLI.

JOHN BIRCHENSHA was probably a native of Ireland ; at least it is certain that he resided at Dublin in the family of the Earl of Kildare, till the rebellion in the year 1641 drove him from thence hither : he was remarkable for being a very genteel man in his person and behaviour ; he lived in London many years after the restoration, and taught the viol. Shadwell, in his comedy of the Humourists, act III. puts this speech into the mouth of a brisk fantastical coxcomb, 'That's an excellent Corant ; really I must ' confess that Grabu is a pretty hopeful man ; but ' Birkenshaw is a rare fellow, give him his due ; for ' he can teach men to compose that are deaf, dumb, ' and blind.' [walks about combing his peruke.[‡]

* FRANCESCO GASPARINI, of whom an account is given in page 678 of this work. The two persons of the name of Stefkins were of the king's band in 1694, as appears by Chamberlayne's present State of England, published in that year, and were the sons of Theodore Stefkins, a very fine performer on the lute, celebrated by Salmon in his essay to the Advancement of Music.

† In this letter are many intimations that Abell was a man of intrigue; there are in it also allusions to some facts not particularly mentioned, as that the king of France presented him with a valuable diamond for singing before him, which was stolen from him by an Irishman ; and that he received a sum of money from the Elector of Bavaria for some particular purpose, and went off with it ; and in Abell's answer he is made to confess the fact, by his apology that it was but spoiling the Egyptians. In another letter of the same person from Henry Purcell to Dr. Blow, Abell is celebrated as a fine singer. Brown's Works vol. II. page 297.

‡ Combing the peruke, at the time when men of fashion wore large wigs, was even at public places an act of gallantry. The combs for this

The last sentence of the above speech has an allusion to a proposal of his, hereunder mentioned, for printing by subscription a work entitled Syntagma Musicæ. He published in 1664, Templum Musicum, or the Musical Synopsis of Johannes Henricus Alstedius,* and a small tract in one sheet, entitled Rules and Directions for composing in Parts.

In the Philosophical Transactions for the year 1672, page 5153, is the following pompous advertisement respecting a book which Birchensha was about to publish. 'There is a book preparing for the press ' entituled Syntagma Musicæ, in which the eminent ' author, John Birchensha, Esq. treats of music ' philosophically, mathematically, and practically. ' And because the charge of bringing this book to ' the press will be very great, especially the several ' cuts therein, with their printing off, amounting by ' computation to more than 500l. besides other great ' expenses for the impression of the said book, divers ' persons, for the encouragement of the said author ' have advanced several sums of money, who for ' every 20s. so advanced are to receive one of the ' said books fairly bound up; the author engaging ' himself under his hand and seal to deliver to each ' of the subscribers and advancers of so much money ' one of the said books, at or before the 24th March, ' 1674. In which excellent work there will be :—

' 1st. A discovery of the reasons and causes of ' musical sounds and harmony. A complete scale ' of music never before perfected. The proportions ' of all consonant and dissonant sounds useful in ' music, demonstrated by entire numbers, which the ' author says hath not been done by any. The ' different opinions of musical authors reconciled. ' Of sounds generated and diffused in their medium. ' Of their difference to the organ of hearing; together ' with their reception there, and wonderful effects. ' Of the matter, form, quantity, and quality of musical ' bodies or sounds: that musical sounds are originally ' in the radix or unison; and of their fluxion out of ' it. Of the general and special kinds, differences, ' properties, and accidents of sounds. Of the truth ' and falsehood of sounds.

' 2. Of the mathematical principles of music. ' Of the whole and parts of the scale of music. ' Of sounds equal and unequal. Of the numeration,

' addition, subtraction, multiplication, and division ' of musical sounds. Of musical proportions and ' their various species. What a musical body or ' sound mathematically considered, viz. as numerable, ' is. Of musical medieties, scilicet, arithmetical, ' geometrical, and harmonical; together with eight ' other musical medieties, of which no mention is ' made by any musical author. Of the radixes of ' musical numbers; and that by their powers all ' those numbers, and no other, which demonstrate ' the proportions of sounds do arise. Of music ' diatonic, chromatic, and enharmonic. Of the prin- ' cipals of a musical magnitude: What and how ' manifold they are; how they are conjoin'd. Of ' the contact, section, congruity, and adscription of ' a musical body. Of the commensurability thereof. ' In what respect a musical sound may be said to be ' infinite, and how to bound that infinity.

' 3. Of musical systems, characters, voice or ' key. Of the transposition of keys. Of the mu- ' tations of musical voice. Of musical pauses and ' periods. Of the denomination of notes. Of the ' moods and intervals. Of pure and florid counter- ' point. Of figurate music. Of fugues, canons, ' double descant, syncope, of the mensuration of ' sounds called time; the reason thereof. Of choral ' musick both Roman and English. Of the rythmical ' part of music. Of solmization, and the reason ' thereof.

' 4. The abstruse and difficult terms of this science ' are explained. The unnecessary and mystical sub- ' tleties into which the causes both of the theory ' and practice of music were reduced, to the great ' obscuring this art, are omitted: the principles of ' philosophy, mathematicks, grammar, rhetoric, and ' poetry are applied to musical sounds, and illustrated ' by them; the generation of such sounds is discoursed ' of, and particularly demonstrated.

' 5. An easy way is by this author invented for ' making airy tunes of all sorts by a certain rule, ' which most men think impossible to be done; and ' the composing of two, three, four, five, six, and ' seven parts, which by the learner may be performed ' in a few months, viz. in two months he may exqui- ' sitely, and with all the elegancies of music, compose ' two parts; in three months three parts, and so ' forward, as he affirms many persons of honour and ' worth have often experienced, which otherwise ' cannot be done in so many years.

' 6. Whatsoever is grounded upon the several ' hypotheses and postulata in this book, is clearly ' demonstrated by tables, diagrams, systems,' &c.

This book was either never published, or is become very scarce; for after a very careful search, and much inquiry, a copy of it has not been found.

Birchensha was also the publisher of that book written by Thomas Salmon, which gave rise to the controversy between the author and Matthew Lock, of which an account has already been given. The preface to it is subscribed John Birchensha.

THOMAS MACE (a Portrait), a practitioner on the lute, one of the clerks of Trinity college, Cambridge, stands distinguished among the writers on music by

---

purpose were of a very large size, of ivory or tortoise-shell curiously chased and ornamented, and were carried in the pocket as constantly as the snuff-box: at court, on the mall, and in the boxes, gentlemen conversed and combed their perukes. There is now in being a fine picture by the elder Laroon, of John duke of Marlborough at his levee, in which his grace is represented dressed in a scarlet suit, with large white satin cuffs, and a very long white peruke, which he combs while his valet, who stands behind him, adjusts the curls after the comb has passed through them.

* ALSTEDIUS was a German divine of the reformed religion, and one of the most voluminous writers of the last century. He was for many years professor of theology and philosophy at Herborn, in the county of Nassau, and after that at Alba-Julia in Transylvania; and was one of the divines that assisted at the synod of Dort. He laboured for the greatest part of his life to reduce the several branches of science into systematical order, in which, according to the opinion of most men, he succeeded well. Nevertheless it must be said of the Templum Musicum that it is so formal as to resemble a logical more than a musical treatise. Of the many works which he was the author of, his encyclopædia and his Thesaurus Chronologicus are deemed the most valuable. He was a Millenarian, and published in 1627 a treatise De Mille Annis, wherein he taught that the faithful shall reign with Jesus Christ upon earth a thousand years, at the end whereof would be the general resurrection and last judgment; and he asserted that this reign would commence in the year 1694. He died at Alba-Julia in the year 1638, being fifty years of age.

EFFIGIES THO: MACE TRIN.

COL. CANTABR. CLERICI

ÆTAT. SUÆ LXIII.

a work entitled ' Musick's Monument, or a Remem-
' brancer of the best practical Musick both divine
' and civil, that has ever been known to have been
' in the world,' folio, 1676.

This person was born in the year 1613: under
whom he was educated, or by what means he became
possessed of so much skill in the science of music,
as to be able to furnish out matter for a folio volume,
he has no where informed us: nevertheless his book
contains so many particulars respecting himself, and
so many traits of an original and singular character,
that a very good judgment may be formed both of
his temper and ability. With regard to the first, he
appears to have been an enthusiastic lover of his
art; of a very devout and serious turn of mind, and
cheerful and good-humoured under the infirmities
of age, and the pressure of misfortunes. As to the
latter, his knowledge of music seems to have been
confined to the practice of his own instrument, and
so much of the principles of the science, as enabled
him to compose for it; but for his style in writing
he certainly never had his fellow.

As to the book itself, a singular vein of humour
runs through it, which is far from being disgusting,
as it exhibits a lively portraiture of a good-natured,
gossiping old man, and this may serve as an apology
for giving his sentiments in many instances in his
own phrase.

The four first chapters of his first book are an
eulogium on psalmody and parochial music; the
fifth contains a recommendation of the organ for that
purpose; and the sixth, with its title, is as follows:—

' How to procure an Organist.

' The certain way I will propose shall be this,
' viz., first, I will suppose you have a parish clark,
' and such an one as is able to set and lead a psalm,
' although it be never so indifferently.

' Now this being granted, I may say that I will,
' or any musick master will, or many more inferiours,
' as virginal players, or many organ makers, or
' the like; I say any of those will teach such a
' parish clark how to pulse or strike most of our
' common psalm-tunes, usually sung in our churches,
' for a trifle, viz. 20, 30, or 40 shillings, and so well
' that he need never bestow more cost to perform
' that duty sufficiently during his life.

' This I believe no judicious person in the art will
' doubt of. And then, when this clark is thus well
' accomplished, he will be so doated upon by all the
' pretty ingenuous children and young men in the
' parish, that scarcely any of them but will be begging
' now and then a shilling or two of their parents to
' give the clark, that he may teach them to pulse a
' psalm-tune; the which any such child or youth
' will be able to do in a week or fortnight's time
' very well.

' And then again, each youth will be as ambitious
' to pulse that psalm-tune in publick to the congre-
' gation, and no doubt but shall do it sufficiently well.

' And thus by little and little the parish in a short
' time will swarm or abound with organists, and
' sufficient enough for that service.

' For you must know, and I intreat you to be-

' lieve me, that seriously it is one of the most easie
' pieces of performances in all instrumental musick,
' to pulse one of our psalm-tunes truly and well after
' a very little shewing upon an organ.

' The clark likewise will quickly get in his money
' by this means.

' And I suppose no parent will grutch it him, but
' rather rejoyce in it.

' Thus you may perceive how very easily and cer-
' tainly these two great difficulties may be overcome,
' and with nothing so much as a willing mind.

' Therefore be but willingly resolved, and the
' work will soon be done.

' And now again methinks I see some of you
' tossing up your caps, and crying aloud, " We will
" have an organ, and an organist too; for 'tis but
" laying out a little dirty money, and how can we
" lay it out better than in that service we offer up
" unto God? and who should we bestow it upon, if
" not upon him and his service?"

' This is a very right and an absolute good resolve,
' persist in it and you will do well, and doubtless
' find much content and satisfaction in your so doing.

' For there lies linked to this an unknown and un-
' apprehended great good benefit, which would re-
' dound certainly to all or most young children, who
' by this means would in their minorities be so
' sweetly tinctured or seasoned, as I may say, or
' brought into a kind of familiarity or acquaintance
' with the harmless innocent delights of such pure
' and undefilable practices, as that it would be a great
' means to win them to the love of virtue, and to
' disdain, contemn, and slight those common, gross,
' ill practices which most children are incident to
' fall into in their ordinary and accustomed pursuits.'

But lest his arguments in favour of the general
use of the organ should fail, this author shows in
Chap. VIII. how psalms may be performed in
churches without that instrument; his method is
this:—

' Wheresoever you send your children to the
' grammar-school, indent so with the master, that
' your children shall be taught one hour every day
' to sing, or one half day in every week at least,
' either by himself, or by some music-master whom
' he shall procure; and no doubt but if you will pay
' for it the business may be effected.

' For there are divers who are able to teach to
' sing, and many more would quickly be, if such a
' general course were determined upon throughout
' the nation.

' There would scarcely be a schoolmaster but
' would or might be easily able himself to do the
' business once in a quarter or half a year; and
' in a short time every senior boy in the school will
' be able to do it sufficiently well.

' And this is the most certain, easie, and substantial way that can possibly be advis'd unto.

' And thus, as before I told, how that your organists
' would grow up amongst you as your corn grew in
' the fields; so now, if such a course as this would
' be taken, will your quiresters increase even into
' swarms like your bees in your gardens; by which

'means the next generation will be plentifully able
'to follow St. Paul's counsel, namely, to teach and
'admonish one another in psalms, and hymns and
'spiritual songs, and so sing with a grace in their
'hearts and voices unto the Lord, and to the setting
'forth of his glorious praise.'

Chap. X. the author mentions the time and place
when and where was heard, as he professes to believe,
the most remarkable and excellent singing of psalms
known or remembered in these latter ages; in his
judgment far excelling all other either private or
public cathedral musick, and infinitely beyond all
verbal expression or conceiving.

'The time when was in the year 1644, the place
'where, was in the cathedral church of the royal
'city York.* * * * The occasion of it was the great
'and close siege which was then laid to the city,
'and strictly maintain'd for eleven weeks space, by
'three very notable and considerable great armies,
'viz. the Scotch, the Northern, and the Southern;
'whose three generals were these, for the Scotch,
'the old Earl Leven, viz. David Lessley, alias
'Lashley; for the Northern, the old Ferdinando
'Lord Fairfax; for the Southern, the Earl of
'Manchester: and whose three chief commanders
'next themselves were, for the Scotch, Lieutenant
'General ————; for the Northern, Sir Thomas
'now Lord Fairfax; and for the Southern, Oliver
'Cromwell, afterwards Lord Protector.

'By this occasion there were shut up within that
'city abundance of people of the best rank and
'quality, viz. lords, knights, and gentlemen of the
'countries round about, besides the soldiers and
'citizens, who all or most of them came constantly
'every Sunday to hear publick prayers and sermon
'in that spacious church.

'And indeed their number was so exceeding great,
'that the church was, I may say, even cramming or
'squeezing full.

'Now here you must take notice, that they had
'then a custom in that church, which I hear not in
'any other cathedral, which was, that always before
'the sermon the whole congregation sang a psalm,
'together with the quire and the organ: and you
'must also know, that there was then a most ex-
'cellent, large, plump, lusty, full-speaking organ,
'which cost, as I am credibly informed, a thousand
'pounds.

'This organ I say, when the psalm was set before
'the sermon, being let out into all its fullness of stops,
'together with the quire began the psalm.

'But when that vast concording unity of the
'whole congregational-chorus, came, as I may say,
'thundering in, even so as it made the very ground
'shake under us; Oh the unutterable ravishing
'soul's delight! in the which I was so transported
'and wrapt up in high contemplations, that there was
'no room left in my whole man, viz., body, soul,
'and spirit, for any thing below divine and heavenly
'raptures: nor could there possibly be any thing on
'earth to which that very singing might be truly
'compared, except the right apprehensions or con-
'ceivings of that glorious and miraculous quire, re-

'corded in the scriptures at the dedication of the
'temple, of which you may read in the 2 Chron.
'ch. 5, to the end; but more particularly eminent
'in the two last verses of that chapter, where king
'Solomon, the wisest of men, had congregated the
'most glorious quire that ever was known of in all
'the world: and at their singing of psalms, praises,
'or thanksgivings, the glory of the Lord came
'down amongst them, as there you may read.* * * *
'But still further that I may endeavour to make
'this something more lively apprehended, or under-
'stood to be a real true thing.

'It would be considered that if at any time or
'place such a congregated number could perform
'such an outward service to the Almighty, with
'true, ardent, inward devotion, fervency, and affec-
'tionate zeal, in expectation to have it accepted by
'him; doubtless it ought to be believed that it
'might be and was done there and then.

'Because that at that time the desperateness and
'dismaidness of their danger could not but draw
'them into it, in regard the enemy was so very
'near and fierce upon them, especially on that side
'the city where the church stood; who had planted
'their great guns so mischievously against the
'church, and with which constantly in prayers time
'they would not fail to make their hellish dis-
'turbance, by shooting against and battering the
'church, insomuch that some times a canon bullet
'has come in at the windows, and bounced about
'from pillar to pillar, even like some furious fiend
'or evil spirit, backwards and forwards, and all
'manner of side ways, as it has happened to meet
'with square or round opposition amongst the
'pillars, in its returns or rebounds, untill its force
'has been quite spent.

'And here is one thing most eminently remarkable,
'and well worth noting, which was, that in all the
'whole time of the siege there was not any one
'person, that I could hear of, did in the church re-
'ceive the least harm by any of their devilish cannon
'shot; and I verily believe that there were con-
'stantly many more than a thousand persons at that
'service every Sunday during the whole time of
'that siege.'

In Chapters XI. and XII. this author treats of
cathedral music, and after asserting that we have in
this nation a large collection of compositions for
the church, so magnificently lofty and sublime, as
never to be excelled by art or industry, he laments
the paucity of clerks in the several choirs of this
kingdom, and the inability of many of them; and
assigns as a principal reason for the decline of
cathedral service, that the lay clerks are necessitated
to be barbers, shoemakers, tailors, and smiths, and
to follow other still inferior occupations, having no
better a provision than the ancient statutable wages;
the hardship of which restraint he says himself had
been an experimental witness of during more than
fifty years' service in the church; and upon this
occasion he tells a story to the following purpose,
of which he says he was both an eye and ear witness:
a singing man, a kind of pot-wit, very little skilled

in music, had undertaken in his choir to sing a solo anthem, but was not able to go through with it : as the dean was going out, and the clerk was putting off his surplice, the dean rebuked him sharply for his inability ; upon which with a most stern, angry countenance, and a vehement rattling voice, such as made the church ring, shaking his head at him, he answered the dean, 'Sir, I'd have you know that 'I sing after the rate of so much a year,' naming his wages, 'and except ye mend my wages, I am re-'solved never to sing better whilst I live.'

The second part of this work treats of the lute, and professes to lay open all the secrets of that instrument, which till the author's time were known only to masters ; and to this their closeness, and extreme shyness in revealing the secrets of the lute, he attributes it that the instrument is so little understood. On this occasion he complains of the French, who he says are generally accounted great masters, for that they would seldom or never write their lessons as they played them, much less reveal any thing that might tend to the understanding of the art of the instrument, so that there have seldom been at any time above one or two excellent or rare artists in this kind.

In the second chapter he endeavours to refute the common objections against the lute, such as that it is the hardest instrument in the world ; that it will take up the time of an apprenticeship to play well upon it ; that it makes young people grow awry ; that one had as good keep a horse as a lute for cost ; that it is a woman's instrument ; and that it is out of fashion. Under the objection of difficulty he takes notice that it is chiefly grounded on the number of strings on the lute, which he makes to be twelve, only six whereof are used in grasping or stopping ; the other six, being basses, and are struck open with the thumb : and the easiness of hitting them, he demonstrates by what he calls an apt comparison ; for he supposes a table with six or seven ranks of strings, such, he says, as many country people have at the end of some cupboards, fastened on with nails at each end, with small stones or sticks to cause them to rise and sound from the wood : he says that an ingenious child might strike these six or seven strings in order, resembling the bells, and then out of order, in changes ; and to these ranks of strings on the country people's cupboards does he resemble the six ranks of the lute-basses. The objection that the lute is a costly instrument, he answers by an affirmation that all his life long he never took more than five shillings the quarter to maintain a lute with strings, nor for the first stringing more than ten shillings.

Chap. III. contains directions how to know and choose a good lute ; the author says that the lutes most esteemed in his time were those made by Laux Maller, two whereof he says he had seen, pitiful, old, battered, cracked things, valued at one hundred pounds a-piece ; one of these he says was shown him by Goutier, the famous lutenist,* which the king had paid that sum for : the other he says was

* JACQUES GOUTER, vide page 697 of this work.

the property of Mr. Edward Jones, one of Goutier's scholars, who being minded to dispose of it, made a bargain with a merchant that desired to have it with him in his travels, that on his return he should either pay Mr. Jones a hundred pound as the price of it, or twenty pound for his use of it in the journey.

After a multiplicity of directions for ordering the lute, and particularly for taking off the belly, which he says is generally necessary once in a year or two, he proceeds in Chap. VI. to give directions for stringing the lute, and describes very minutely the various kinds of strings, and for the choice of a true length gives the following direction, which he calls a pretty curiosity :—

'First draw out a length or more, then take the 'end, and measure the length it must be of within 'an inch or two, for it will stretch so much at least 'in the winding up ; and hold that length in both 'hands, extended to a reasonable stiffness ; then 'with one of your fingers strike it, giving it so 'much liberty in slackness as you may see it vibrate, 'or open itself ; which, if it be true, it will appear 'to the eye just as if there were two strings ; but 'if it shews more than two it is false, and will sound 'unpleasantly upon your instrument ; nor will it ever 'be well in tune, either stopt or open, but snarle.'†

Chap. IX. contains an explanation of that kind of notation called the Tablature, in which each of the six strings of the lute are represented by a line, and the several frets or stops by the letters a, b c, d, e, f, g, h, y,‡ k, the letter a ever signifying the open string in all positions.§

With the same precision and singularity of style he describes the characters for the time of notes, calling the semibreve the master note ; and for the more easy division of it, calling that a groat, the minim two pence, the crotchet a penny, the quaver a half penny, and the semiquaver a farthing. From thence he proceeds to directions for the fingering, as also for the graces, one whereof, by him called the nerve-shake, he says he was not able to make well, and that for a reason, which with his usual pleasantry he gives in these words :—

'Some there are, and many I have met with, who 'have such a natural agility in their nerves, and 'aptitude to that performance, that before they could 'do anything else to purpose, they would make 'a shake rarely well. And some again can scarcely 'ever gain a good shake, by reason of the unaptness 'of their nerves to that action, but yet otherwise 'come to play very well.

'I for my own part have had occasion to break 'both my arms, by reason of which I cannot make

† This direction is given by Adrian Le Roy in his instructions for the lute. See page 420 of this work, and is adopted both by Mersennus and Kircher. Indeed this experiment is the only known test of a true string, and for that reason is practised by such as are curious at this day.

‡ y is used by him in preference to i, as being a more conspicuous character.

§ Of the notation by the tablature frequent mention has been made in the course of this work ; from the nature of it, it is obvious that it has not the least relation to the musical characters properly so called ; and the fact is, that many persons have been good performers on the lute, and at the same time totally ignorant of the notes of the Gamut, and yet there are masters of the lute who play by them ; and this is supposed in those compositions of Corelli's in particular, where the thorough-bass is said to be for the organ, harpsichord, or arch-lute.

' the nerve-shake well nor strong; yet by a certain
' motion of my arm, I have gained such a contentive
' shake, that sometimes my scholars will ask me how
' they shall do to get the like? I have then no
' better answer for them than to tell them they must
' first break their arm as I have done, and so possibly
' after that, by practice they may get my manner
' of shake.'

Among a variety of lessons of the author's composition, inserted in this his work, is one which he
calls his Mistress, as having been composed a short
time before his marriage, and at the instant when,
being alone, he was meditating on his intended wife.
It is written in tablature, but is here rendered in the
characters of musical notation :—

Thomas Mace.

The occasion of his composing it, and the reasons
for giving it the name of his Mistress, are related
in the following singular history :—

' You must first know that it is a lesson, though
' old yet I never knew it disrelished by any; nor is
' there any one lesson in this book of that age as it
' is; yet I do esteem it in its kind, with the best
' lesson in the book, for several good reasons which
' I shall here set down.

' It is, this very winter, just 40 years since I made
' it; and yet it is new, because all like it; and
' then, when I was past being a suitor to my best
' beloved, dearest, and sweetest living mistress, but
' not married, yet contriving the best and readiest
' way towards it: and thus it was.

' That very night, in which I was thus agitated
' in my mind concerning her, my living mistress,
' she being in Yorkshire, and myself at Cambridge,
' close shut up in my chamber, still and quiet, about
' 10 or 11 a clock at night, musing and writing
' letters to her, her mother, and some other friends;
' in summing up and determining the whole matter
' concerning our marriage: You may conceive I
' might have very intent thoughts all that time, and
' might meet with some difficulties; for as yet I had
' not gained her mother's consent, so that in my
' writings I was sometimes put to my studyings.
' At which times, my lute lying upon my table,
' I sometimes took it up, and walked about my
' chamber, letting my fancy drive which way it
' would, for I studied nothing at that time as to
' musick; yet my secret genius or fancy prompted
' my fingers do what I could into this very humour,
' so that every time I walked and took up my lute
' in the interim betwixt writing and studying, this
' ayre would needs offer itself unto me continually;
' insomuch that at the last, liking it well, and lest
' it should be lost, I took paper and set it down,
' taking no further notice of it at that time; but
' afterwards it passed abroad for a very pleasant and
' delightful ayre amongst all; yet I gave it no name
' till a long time after, nor taking more notice of it
' in any particular kind, than of any other my com-
' posures of that nature.

' But after I was married, and had brought my

' wife home to Cambridge, it so fell out that one
' rainy morning I stay'd within, and in my chamber,
' my wife and I were all alone; she intent upon her
' needle-works, and I playing upon my lute at the
' table by her. She sat very still and quiet, listning
' to all I played without a word a long time, till at
' last I happened to play this lesson, which so soon
' as I had once play'd, she earnestly desired me to
' play it again; for, said she, that shall be called
' my lesson.

' From which words so spoken with emphasis and
' accent, it presently came into my remembrance the
' time when, and the occasion of its being produced,
' and returned her this answer, viz., That it may very
' properly be called your lesson, for when I composed
' it you were wholly in my fancy, and the chief
' object and ruler of my thoughts; telling her how
' and when it was made; and therefore ever after
' I thus called it my Mistress; and most of my
' scholars since call it Mrs. Mace to this day.'

This relation is followed by a kind of commentary
on the lesson itself in these words :—

' First, observe the two first bars of it, which will
' give you the fugue, which fugue is maintained quite
' through the whole lesson.

' Secondly, observe the form and shape of the
' whole lesson, which consists of two uniform and
' equal strains, both strains having the same number
' of bars.

' Thirdly, observe the humour of it, which you
' may perceive by the marks and directions is not
' common.

' These three terms or things ought to be con-
' sidered in all compositions and performances of
' this nature, viz., ayres or the like.

' The fugue is lively, ayrey, neat, curious, and
' sweet like my mistress.

' The form is uniform, comely, substantial, grave,
' and lovely like my mistress.

' The humour is singularly spruce, amiable, plea-
' sant, obliging, and innocent like my mistress.'

He afterwards composed a second part of this
' lesson, so contrived, as to be, as he calls it, a Consort-
' lesson to the former, to be played upon another
' equal lute, or as a lone lesson.

THOMAS MACE.

Touching the performance of which, he gives a direction, purporting that when the second part is played with the first, the performer is to rest the two last notes of the fourth bar, and the three first notes of the fifth.

The remainder of the second part consists of directions for the composition of lessons for the lute, as namely, Preludes, Fancies, and Voluntaries, Pavans, Almains, Galliards, Corantos, Sarabands, Tattle de Moys,* Chacones, Toys or Jigs, Common tunes,† and Grounds, with examples of each; and concludes with a comparison between two tunings of the lute, the one called by him the flat tuning, and the other the new tuning, though he says it was in his time at least forty years old: the latter of these he endeavours by a variety of examples to prove is the best, and concludes his argument with this assertion, 'The flat tuning is a most perfect, full, 'plump, brisk, noble, heroic tuning; free and copious, 'fit, aptly and liberally to express any thing in any 'of the 7 keys; but that new tuning is far short of 'these accommodations, and is obviously subject to 'several inconveniences.'

The third part treats of the viol, and of music in general; and here he takes occasion to lament the abuse of music in the disproportionate numbers of bass and treble instruments in the concerts of his time, in which he says it was not unusual to have but one small weak-sounding bass-viol, and two or three violins, scolding violins, as he calls them; nay he says that he has frequently heard twenty or more violins at a sumptuous meeting, and scarce half so many basses, which latter he says should in reason be the greater number.

Of the concerts which he had been accustomed to hear in his youth, and before the violin became a concert instrument, he never speaks but in such

terms of rapture, as shew him to have been thoroughly susceptible of the charms of music. The following is his description of them, and refers to about the beginning of the last century :—

'In my younger time we had musick most ex-'cellently choice and most eminently rare, both 'for its excellency in composition, rare fancy, and 'sprightly ayre; as also for its proper and fit per-'formances; even such, as if your young tender ears 'and fantasies, were but truly tinctured therewith, 'and especially if it possibly could but be cry'd up 'for the mode or new fashion, you would embrace 'for some divine thing.

'And lest it should be quite forgot, for want of 'sober times, I will set down, as a remembrancer 'and well-wisher to posterity, and an honourer of 'the memory of those most eminent worthy masters 'and authors, who some of them being now de-'ceased, yet some living, the manner of such musick 'as I make mention of, as also the nature of it.

'We had for our grave musick Fancies of 3, 4, 5, 'and 6 parts to the organs, interposed, now and then, 'with some Pavins, Allmaines, solemn and sweet 'delightful ayres, all which were, as it were, so many 'pathetical stories, rhetorical and sublime discourses, 'subtil and acute argumentations, so suitable and 'agreeing to the inward, secret, and intellectual 'faculties of the soul and mind, that to set them forth 'according to their true praise, there are no words suf-'ficient in language; yet what I can best speak of them 'shall be only to say, that they have been to myself, 'and many others, as divine raptures, powerfully cap-'tivating all our unruly faculties and affections for the 'time, and disposing us to solidity, gravity, and a 'good temper, making us capable of heavenly and 'divine influences.

''Tis great pity few believe thus much; but far 'greater that so few know it.

'The authors of such like compositions have been 'divers famous Englishmen and Italians, some of 'which for their very great eminency and worth in 'that particular faculty, I will name here, viz., Mr.

---

* This is the name of an air invented by himself, much like a Saraband, but having as he expresses it, more of conceit in it, and speaking in a manner those very words.

† These tunes he says are such as the boys and common people sing about the streets, many whereof were then as the common song-tunes have since been, most excellent.

' Alfonso Ferabosco, Mr. John Ward, Mr. Lupo, Mr.
' White, Mr. Richard Deering, Mr, William Lawes,
' Mr. John Jenkins, Mr. Christopher Simpson, Mr.
' Coperario, and one Monteverde, a famous Italian
' author; besides divers and very many others, who
' in their late time were all substantial, able, and pro-
' found composing masters in this art, and have left
' their works behind them, as fit monuments and
' patterns for sober and wise posterity, worthy to be
' imitated and practised: 'tis great pity they are so
' soon forgot and neglected, as I perceive they are
' amongst many.

' And these things were performed upon so many
' equal and truly-siz'd viols, and so exactly strung,
' tuned, and played upon, as no one part was any
' impediment to the other; but still, as the composi-
' tion required, by intervals, each part amplified and
' heightened the other, the organ evenly, softly, and
' sweetly according to all.

' We had, beyond all this, a custom at our meet-
' ings, that commonly after such instrumental music
' was over, we did conclude all with some vocal
' music to the organ, or, for want of that, to the
' Theorboe.

' The best which we ever did esteem, were those
' things which were most solemn and divine, some of
' which I will for their eminency name, viz. Mr.
' Deering's Gloria Patri, and other of his Latin songs,
' now lately collected and printed by Mr. Playford,
' a very laudable and thank-worthy work, besides
' many other of the like nature, Latin and English,
' by most of the above-named authors and others,
' wonderfully rare, sublime, and divine beyond all
' expression.

' But when we would be most ayrey, jocond,
' lively, and spruce, then we had choice and singular
' consorts, either for 2, 3, or 4 parts, but not to the
' organ, as many, now a days, improperly and unad-
' visedly perform such like consorts with, but to the
' harpsicon; yet more properly and much better to
' the pedal, an instrument of a late invention, con-
' trived, as I have been inform'd, by one Mr. John
' Hayward of London, a most excellent kind of in-
' strument for a consort, and far beyond all harpsicons
' or organs that I yet ever heard of, I mean either
' for consort or single use; but the organ far beyond
' it for those other performances before mentioned.'

Of the pedal above mentioned he gives a brief description, which seems to indicate that it was a kind
of harpsichord with stops to be governed by the
feet. He says that the pedal was not commonly
used or known, because few could make of them
well, and fewer would go to the price of them, twenty
pounds being the ordinary price of one, but that the
great patron of music in his time, Sir Robert Bolles,
whom in the university he had the happiness to
initiate in the high art of music, had two of them,
the one at thirty pounds, and the other at fifty pounds.

He then proceeds to give directions for procuring
and maintaining the best music imaginable, and exhibits first the plan of a music-room contrived by
himself for concerts, with galleries for auditors,
capable of holding two hundred persons. Among
the instruments proper for a great concert to be
performed in this room, he recommends a table-
organ, as being far more reasonable and proper than
an upright organ. He says that two table organs
were in being at the time when he wrote his book,
that they were of his own contrivance, and were
for his own use, as to the maintaining of public
concerts, &c. and that he did design to erect such
a music-room as he has described, but that it
pleased God to disappoint and discourage him,
chiefly by the loss of his hearing, and the consequent emptiness of his purse; but concludes his
account with an advertisement, that although it had
been his unhappiness to be compelled to part with
these instruments, yet that one of them was then to
be sold, and that if any person would send to him
about it, he would find it a very, very, jewel. He
next recommends as the properest instruments for
a concert, a chest of viols, a description whereof,
as the term is at this day scarcely understood, is here
given in his own words :—

' Your best provision and most compleat will be
' a good chest of viols, six in number, viz., two
' basses, two tenors, and two trebles, all truly and
' proportionably suited.

' Of such there are no better in the world than
' those of Aldred, Jay, Smith, yet the highest in
' esteem are Bolles and Ross; one bass of Bolles
' I have known valued at 100l. These were old,
' but we have now very excellent good workmen,
' who no doubt can work as well as those, if they
' be so well paid for their work as they were; yet
' we chiefly value old instruments before new; for
' by experience they are found to be far the best.
' * * * * * * But if you cannot procure an intire
' chest of viols, suitable, &c. endeavour to pick up
' here or there so many excellent good odd ones, as
' near suiting you as you can, every way, viz., both
' for shape, wood, colour, &c. but especially for size.

' And to be exact in that, take this certain rule,
' viz. let your bass be large : Then your trebles
' must be just as short again in the string, viz., from
' bridge to nut, as are your basses, because they
' stand eight notes higher than the basses, therefore
' as short again; for the middle of every string is
' an eighth. The tenors in the string just so long
' as from the bridge to F fret, because they stand
' a fourth higher than your basses, therefore so long.

' Let this suffice to put you into a compleat order
' for viols either way; only note, that the best place
' for the bridge is to stand just in the three quarter
' dividing of the open cuts below, though most,
' most erroneously suffer them much to stand too
' high, which is a fault.

' After all this you may add to your press a pair
' of violins, to be in readiness for any extraordinary
' jolly or jocund consort occasion; but never use
' them but with this proviso, viz., be sure you make
' an equal provision for them, by the addition and
' strength of basses, so that they may not out-cry
' the rest of the musick, the basses especially; to
' which end it will be requisite you store your press
' with a pair of lusty, full-sized Theorboes, always

'to strike in with your consorts or vocal musick, to
'which that instrument is most naturally proper.

'And now to make your store more amply com-
'pleat, add to these three full-sized Lyra-viols, there
'being most admirable things made, by our very best
'masters for that sort of musick, both consort-wise,
'and peculiarly for two or three Lyres.

'Let them be lusty, smart-speaking viols; because
'that in consort they often retort against the treble,
'imitating, and often standing instead of that part,
'viz., a second treble.

'They will serve likewise for Division-viols very
'properly.

'And being thus stored, you have a ready enter-
'tainment for the greatest prince in the world.'

He next proceeds to give directions for the practice of the viol, together with a few lessons by way
of example; and concludes with a chapter on music
in general, but which contains nothing more than
some reflections of the author on the mysteries of
music, which he says have a tendency to strengthen
faith, and are a security against the sin of atheism.

Mace does not appear to have held any considerable rank among musicians, nor is he celebrated
either as a composer or practitioner on the lute;
nevertheless his book is a proof that he was an
excellent judge of the instrument, and contains such
a variety of directions for the ordering and management thereof, as also for the performance on it, as
renders it a work of great utility. In it are many
curious observations respecting the choice of stringed
instruments, the various kinds of wood of which
they are made, the method of preserving them, and
the preference due to the several kinds of strings imported hither from Rome, Venice, Pistoja, Lyons,
and other places. In another view of it his work
must be deemed a great curiosity, as containing in it
a full and accurate description of that kind of notation called the Tablature, of the truth and accuracy
whereof proof has been made by persons ignorant of
the lute, in the translation of some of his lessons
into the characters of musical notation. The singularity of his style, remarkable for a profusion of
epithets and words of his own invention, and tauto-
logy without end, is apt to disgust such as attend less
to the matter than the manner of his book; but on
others it has a different effect, as it exhibits, without
the least reserve, all the particulars of the author's
character,* which the reader will easily discern was
not less amiable than singular.

The engraving given of Mace (see Portrait
Volume) is taken from one of Faithorne, prefixed to
his book, the inscription under which bespeaks him
to have been sixty-three years of age in 1676. How
long he lived afterwards is not known. It seems
that he had children, for in his book he speaks of

his youngest son named John, who, with scarce any
assistance from his father, had attained to great proficiency on the lute by reading his book.†

## CHAP. CLII.

JOHN PLAYFORD (a Portrait), born in the year
1613, was a stationer and seller of musical instruments, music-books, and music-paper. What his
education had been is not known, but that he had
attained to a considerable proficiency in the practice
of music and musical composition is certain. In the
Ashmolean Manuscript it is said he was clerk of the
church belonging to the Temple, and that he dwelt
near the Inner Temple gate. This latter assertion
is erroneous in two respects, for in the first place
many of the title-pages of books published by him
describe his shop as situated in the Temple near the
church-door; and it may be thence conjectured that
it was at the foot of the steps, either on the right
hand or on the left, descending from the Inner
Temple-lane to the cloisters. As to his dwelling,
it was in Arundel-street in the Strand.

In the year 1655 he published an introduction to
the skill of music, which appears to be extracted from
Morley's Introduction, Butler's Principles of Music,
and other books on the subject of music; it is divided into three books, the first containing the
principles of music, with directions for singing; the
second, instructions for the bass, treble, and tenor
viol, and also for the treble violin, with lessons for
each; and the third the art of descant, or composing
of music in parts.

Wood says that in the drawing up of this book
Playford had the assistance of Charles Pidgeon of
Grays-Inn; and that Dr. Benjamin Rogers also
assisted him in many of his vocal compositions, of
which there are many extant. Be this as it may,
the Introduction of Playford, as it was written in
a plain and easy style, succeeded so well, that in
the year 1683 was published a tenth edition of it,
considerably improved and enlarged by the author
and his friends. This is the edition referred to
here and elsewhere in this work, its character being
that it is fuller than some editions, and more correct
than any.

The explanation given by this author of the scale
of music, and of the several kinds of time, are no
other than are to be found in most books on the
subject; but what he says of the graces proper in
singing is entire new matter, and is taken from
a tract with this title: 'A brief discourse of the
'Italian manner of singing, wherein is set down the
'use of those graces in singing, as the Trill and
'Gruppo, used in Italy, and now in England;
'written some years since by an English gentleman
'who had lived long in Italy, and, being returned,
'taught the same here.'‡

* The most remarkable of these are that affected precision with which
he constantly delivers himself, and his eager desire to communicate to
others, even to the most hidden secrets, all the knowledge he was
possessed of. In the relation he gives of the occasion of composing that
lesson of his called Mrs. Mace, and the tenderness and affection with
which he speaks of her who had been his wife more than forty years,
who does not see the portrait of a virtuous and kind-hearted man? To
which we may add, that the book throughout breathes a spirit of devotion; and, agreeably to his sentiments of music, is a kind of proof that
his temper was improved by the exercise of his profession.

† Page 45. To this instance of the efficacy of his book in teaching
the practice of the lute, it may here be added, that the late Mr. John
Immyns, lutenist to the chapel royal, had the like experience of it.
This person, who had practised on sundry instruments for many years,
and was able to sing his part at sight, at the age of forty took to the lute,
and by the help of Mace's book alone, became enabled to play thorough-
bass, and also easy lessons on it, and by practice had rendered the
tablature as familiar to him as the notes of the scale.

‡ Who was the author of this discourse is not known. He says of

Of the graces here treated on, the Trill, or plain shake, and the Gruppo are the chief: the first is defined to be a shake upon one note only, in the making whereof the scholar is directed to sing the first of these examples :—

beginning with the first crotchet, and beating every note with the throat upon the vowel o to the last breath. The Gruppo as defined by this author, appears to be no other than the shake now practised, and which consists in the alternate prolation of two tones in juxta position to each other, with a close on the note immediately beneath the lower of them. The second of the above examples is intended to explain it. The first of these graces, called the Trill, or plain shake, is farther described in the following note of Playford relating to it :—

'Our author having briefly set forth this chief or
'most usual grace in singing called the Trill, which,
'as he saith very right, is by a beating in the throat
'on the vowel o; some observe that it is rather the
'shaking of the Uvula or palate on the throat in
'one sound upon a note: for the attaining of this
'the most sure and ready way is by imitation of
'those who are perfect in the same; yet I have
'heard of some that have attained it after this manner,
'in singing a plain-song of six notes up and six
'down, they have in the midst of every note beat or
'shaked with their finger upon their throat, which
'by often practice came to do the same notes exactly
'without. It was also my chance to be in company
'with some gentlemen at a musical practice, which
'sung their parts very well, and used this grace,
'called the Trill, very exactly. I desired to know
'their tutor, they told me I was their tutor, for they
'never had any other but this my Introduction.
'That, I answered, could direct them but in the
'theory, they must needs have a better help in the
'practice, especially in attaining to sing the Trill
'so well. One of them made this reply, which
'made me smile; I used, said he, at my first learn-
'ing the Trill to imitate the breaking of a sound in
'the throat, which men use when they lure their
'hawks, as he-he-he-he, which he used slow at first,
'and after more swift on several notes, higher and
'lower in sound, till he became perfect therein.
'The Trill being the most usual grace, is usually
'made in closes or cadences, and when on a long
'note exclamation or passion is expressed, there the

'Trill is made in the latter part of such note; but
'most usually upon binding notes, and such as pre-
'cede the closing note. To those who once attain
'to the perfect use of the Trill, other graces will be-
'come easie.*'

Of the other graces in singing mentioned by this author, the exclamation is the chief, and which is nothing more than an increase of the voice to some degree of loudness at the extremity of an ascending passage.

After sundry examples of short songs for the practice of learners, and a few of the most common psalm tunes, follows the order of performing the divine service in cathedrals and collegiate chapels, taken from Edward Low's treatise on that subject, of which an account has already been given. The second book consists of an introduction to the playing on the bass viol or viol da gamba, as also on the other instruments of that species, namely, the treble and tenor viol; this is followed by a like introduction to the treble violin, including the tuning of the tenor or bass violin. What the author has said respecting the first of these two classes of instruments has been given in a preceding page, and the following extracts from his book will show the system of the latter, as also the manner of teaching the violin in the author's time.

It has already been related that the notation by the tablature had been transferred from the lute to the viol. This method had been found so easy and convenient for those who were content to be small proficients, that it was applied also to the violin, and may be understood by the following scale and example of a tune called Parthenia, set in that manner :—

The First or Treble.      The Second or small Mean.

The Third or great Mean.      The Fourth String or Bass.

---

himself that he had been taught that noble manner of singing which he professes to teach others, by the famous Scipione del Palla in Italy; and that he had heard the same frequently practised there by the most famous singers, men and women. He speaks also of airs of his composition, which, as also this discourse, were by him intended for publication. Playford, in his Introduction, edit. 1666, says that the publication of it by the author was prevented by his death, but that the manuscript fortunately coming to his hands, he was by some of the most eminent masters encouraged to print it.

* Notwithstanding all that is above said of it, the trill must appear to be somewhat very different from a grace or ornament in singing; nay, that the practice of it approaches to a defect; for it is nothing less than an intermitted prolation of a single tone. As to the Gruppo or shake, properly so called, it is the chief grace, as well in instrumental as vocal performance; nevertheless it is not once mentioned by Morley or Butler, or any of the old English writers on music, and seems to have been unknown among us at the time when Playford wrote; which is much to be wondered at, seeing that it had been practised in Italy long before, as appears by Doni's treatise 'De Præstantia Musicæ veteris,' page 59, where Philoponus, one of the interlocutors, speaking of the graces and elegancies of modern music, makes use of these words: 'Hinc fre-
'quentes argutissimorum ac prædulcium melismatum usurpationes; et
'Compismorum in clausulis jucundissimus usus.' The directions above given point out very properly where the shake may be used, but they were little heeded in England till the practice of the opera singers had taught us the true use of it. Those who can recollect Mr Phillip Hart,

JOHANNIS PLAYFORD EFFIGIES.

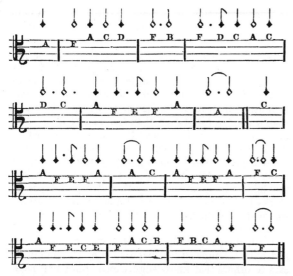

Which tune, according to the rule before given, respecting the lute and the viol, viz., that if a crotchet be over any letter, the following letters are to be crotchets also till the note be changed, and the like of other notes, is thus to be rendered in the characters of musical notation :—

Parthenia.

The third part of Playford's Introduction consists of rules for composing music in parts; but this has been varied from time to time in the several editions, as occasion offered. In that of 1660, the third part consisted solely of Dr. Campion's tract entitled 'The art of Descant, or composing music in parts, with the annotations of Christopher Simpson;' but in that of 1683 Campion's tract is rejected, and instead thereof we have 'A brief Introduction to the art of Descant, or composing music in parts,' without the name of the author, and probably written by Playford himself. In the subsequent editions, particularly that of 1713, this is continued, but with very considerable additions, said to have been made by Mr. Henry Purcell.

Playford appears to have possessed the friendship of most of the eminent musicians of his time, and in consequence thereof was the publisher of a very great number of music-books between the years 1650 and 1685. He was a good judge of music, had some skill in composition, and was very industrious in his vocation, contributing not a little to the improve-

ment of the art of printing music from letter-press types, by the use of what he calls in some of his publications the new tied note, of the invention whereof it may not be improper here to take some notice.*

The musical characters formerly in use in this kingdom were wrought from metal types: the notes were distinct from each other, and the quavers and semi-quavers were signified by single and double tails, without any mark of colligation or connection whatever. In the Melothesia of Matthew Lock, published by John Carr in 1673, the quaver and semi-quaver are joined by single and double tails. But it is to be noted that the music in that work is printed from copper-plates; from hence it is supposed Playford took the hint, and transferred the practice to letter-press types.

Of the numerous publications of Playford, the collection of Catches by John Hilton, entitled 'Catch that Catch can,' printed in 1652, seems to be the first. Playford was then clerk of the Temple church, and the book was sold at his shop near the church-door. In 1667 it was published with the additional title of the Musical Companion, with very considerable additions; and a second part, containing Dialogues, Glees, Ayres, and Ballads for two, three, and four voices. This edition was dedicated to Charles Pigeon, Esq. and other members of a music society and meeting in the Old Jewry, London. Before it are recommendatory verses in Latin and English, by the said Pigeon, who appears to have been a member of the society of Gray's Inn. In 1673 the Musical companion was published with still farther additions: and in 1687 a second book; and after that a few additional sheets without a title, but called the third part. The catches, rounds, and canons in this collection were composed by Hilton himself, Henry and William Lawes, Holmes, Nelham, Cranford, Ellis, Brewer, Webb, Jenkins, Dr. Child, Ives, Dr. Wilson, Ford, Dr. Rogers, Captain Cooke, Lock, and others, the most eminent musicians of that time; and it is not too much to say that they are the best of the kind extant.†

* In page 380 of this work, it is remarked that the first musical types used in this country appear in Higden's Polychronicon, printed by Wynkyn de Word, in the year 1495: and their introduction being thus ascertained, it may be thought necessary to continue the history of music printing, at least in this country, down to that period to which we have brought the history of the science itself: and here it is to be noted that after Wynkyn de Word, Grafton appears to have used musical types, and after him old John Day of Aldersgate; but in queen Elizabeth's reign letters patent were obtained by Tallis and Bird, granting to them and their assigns the sole privilege of printing music: neither Tallis nor Bird were printers in fact, but they employed to print their Cantiones, in 1575, Thomas Vautrollier of Black Friars, and after him Thomas East, Est, or Este, who about the year 1600 changed his surname to Snodham.

In the year 1598 a patent, with ampler powers than were contained in the former, was granted to Thomas Morley, author of the Introduction; after the expiration of which it seems the business of music printing lay under no restraints, but was exercised by the printers in common, that is to say, by John Windet, William Barley, William Godbid, and many others, for various booksellers and publishers till the time of the restoration, soon after which the sellers of musical instruments took to the business of selling music books also.

† In this collection is a Three Part Song, ' The Glories of our Birth and State,' set by Edward Coleman, which was formerly much sung at Oxford and elsewhere, by the friends of king Charles I. as being thought to allude to his unhappy catastrophe. It was reputed to have been written on that occasion by Butler; and as such is printed among his Posthumous Works in three little volumes. Further to recommend it, the last stanza has very much the appearance of a version of a passage in the Eikon Basilike Sect. 15. Yet after all, the whole of it was written, and probably before

organist of the church of St. Mary Undershaft, and Mr. Bernard Gates, master of the children of the chapel royal, must have remarked in the playing of one and the singing of the other, such a frequent iteration of the shake, as destroyed the melody: and that even the last set of boys educated by the latter, sang in the manner their great grandfathers must be supposed to have done.

Another publication of Playford merits also particular notice in this place, as it explains a practice to which we at this day are strangers. The book here meant is entitled 'Musick's Recreation on the Viol Lyra-way,' concerning which the following advertisement is given in the preface :—

'The Lero or Lyra-Viol is so called from the
'Latin word Lyra, which signifies a harp, alluding
'to the various tuning under the name of Harp-way,
'&c. This way of playing on the viol is but of late
'invention; an imitation of the old English lute or
'bandora, whose lessons were prickt down by certain
'letters of the alphabet, upon six lines or rules;
'which six lines did allude to the six course of
'strings upon those instruments, as they do now
'unto the six single strings upon the viol. The first
'authors of inventing and setting lessons this way to
'the viol were Mr. Daniel Farrant, Mr. Alphonso
'Ferabosco, and Mr. John Coperario, alias Cooper,
'who composed lessons not only to play alone, but
'for two or three Lyra-viols together in consort;
'and since it hath been much improved by the
'excellent inventions and skill of famous masters,
'viz., Mr. William Lawes, Dr. Colman, Mr. Jenkins,
'Mr. Ives, Mr. Hudson, Mr. Withie, Mr. Bates, Mr.
'Lillie, Mr. Gregory, Mr. Mosse, Mr. Wilson, and
'others.'

Playford says the Lyra-viol has six strings, as also frets or stops to the number of seven, on the neck of the instrument, to which are assigned seven letters of the alphabet, viz., b, c, d, e, f, g, h, the letter a answering to the open string wherever it occurs. It seems that there were sundry methods of tuning the Lyra-viol, which were severally adopted by the masters of the instrument, the most usual whereof were those termed harp-way sharp and harp-way flat, high harp-way sharp and high harp-way flat, and of these the book contains examples.

The two methods of notation for the viol and other stringed instruments, by the letters and by the notes, are severally distinguished by the terms Lyra-way and Gamut-way, with this exception, that the literal notation for the lute is ever called the Tablature; concerning which, as also the notation by letters in general, it may be observed that they do not imply the least degree of skill in the system or scale of music, and are therefore a very inartificial practice; the same may be said of the old method of notation for the flute and flageolet by dots, of which, as a matter of curiosity, an account will hereafter be given.

Playford's skill in music was not so great as to entitle him to the appellation of a master. He knew nothing of the theory of the science, but was very well versed in the practice, and understood the rules of composition well enough to write good harmony; of this he has given proofs in a great number of songs in two, three, and four parts, printed in the Musical companion, as also in his Psalms and Hymns in solemn Music, in four parts, printed in folio,* and

in that collection in octavo entitled the 'Whole Book of Psalms, with the usual Hymns and spiritual Songs, composed in three parts.' In the compiling of his Introduction it is apparent that he was assisted by men more knowing than himself; for in the preface to the later editions of it, particularly that of 1666, are sundry curious particulars relating to music which indicate a greater degree of learning than a man in his station of life could be supposed to be possessed of. Doubtless the book itself was of great benefit to the public, as it disseminated the knowledge of music among the common people; many learned to sing, and to play on the viol and the fiddle, in a homely way it is true, and parish clerks in the country acquired a competent skill in psalmody, having no other instructor than Playford's Introduction.

With such talents as Playford was possessed of, and with a temper that disposed him to communicate to others that knowledge which could not have been attained without much labour; and being besides an honest and friendly man, it is not to be wondered at that he lived upon terms of friendship with the most eminent professors of music his contemporaries, or that he should have acquired, as he appears to have done, almost a monopoly in the publication of music-books. He lived to near the age of fourscore. His memory is celebrated in two or three short poems on his death, and in an elegy by Nahum Tate, the then poet laureat, *which was set to music by Henry Purcell, and published in* 1687.

Playford had a son named John, a printer of music, and a younger named Henry, who followed the business of his father, at first in the shop near the door of the Temple-church, but afterwards in the Temple Exchange, Fleet-street. His dwelling-house was that which had been his father's in Arundel-street in the Strand. The music books advertised by him were but few in number compared with those published by his father. Among them were the Orpheus Britannicus, and the ten Sonatas, and the airs of Purcell. The printers employed by him were John Heptinstall and William Pearson; the latter greatly improved the art of printing music on metal types; he dwelt in Aldersgate-street, near the end of Long-lane, and was living after the year 1735.

Henry Playford published in 1701 what he called the second book of the 'Pleasant musical Companion,
'being a choice collection of Catches for three and
'four Voices; published chiefly for the encourage-
'ment of the musical societies, which will be speedily
'set up in all the chief cities and towns in England.'
The design of this publication is more fully explained in the preface to the book, particularly in the following passage :—

'And that he [the publisher] may be beneficial to
'the publick in forwarding a commendable society,
'as well as the sale of his book, he has prevailed with
'his acquaintance and others in this city to enter

---

*the Eikon Basilike, as a solemn funeral song in a play of Shirley's, entitled 'The Contention of Ajax and Ulysses.' Vide Percy's Reliques of Ancient English Poetry, vol. I. page 270.*

* It is worth remarking, that in the preface to this book it is said that

the ancient practice in the singing of psalms in church was for the clerk to repeat each line; probably because at the first introduction of the psalms into our service, great numbers of the common people were unable to read.

'into several clubs weekly, at taverns of convenient
'distance from each other, having each house a par-
'ticular master of musick belonging to the society
'established in it, who may instruct those, if desir'd,
'who shall be unskilled, in bearing a part in the
'several catches contained in this book, as well as
'others; and shall perfect those who have already
'had some insight in things of this nature, that they
'shall be capable of entertaining the societies they
'belong to abroad. In order to this he has provided
'several articles to be drawn, printed, and put in
'handsome frames, to be put up in each respective
'room the societies shall meet in, and be observed
'as so many standing rules, which each respective
'society is to go by; and he questions not but the
'several cities, towns, corporations, &c. in the king-
'doms of Great Britain and Ireland, as well as foreign
'plantations, will follow the example of the well-
'wishers to vocal and instrumental musick in this
'famous city, by establishing such weekly meetings
'as may render his undertaking as generally received
'as it is useful. And if any body or bodies of gentle-
'men are willing to enter into or compose such
'societies, they may send to him, where they may
'be furnished with books and articles.'

This project was recommended in certain verses
written by Tom Brown, and dated from Mr. Steward's,
at the Hole in the Wall in Baldwin's Gardens,
inscribed to his friend Mr. Playford on his book of
Catches, and his setting up a weekly club for the
encouragement of music and good fellowship. It
had some success in promoting the practice of catch-
singing in and about London, and also at Oxford;
but it does not appear that in other parts of the
kingdom any such musical clubs or societies were
formed, as it was the drift of the proposal to
recommend.

It is conjectured that Henry Playford survived
his father but few years, for we meet with no publication by him after the year 1710, about which
time Mr. John Young was become a man of note in
the business of selling musical instruments and music
books. The shop of this person was at the corner
of London-House-yard in St. Paul's church-yard,
and was much frequented by the choir-men of St.
Paul's. Edward Ward, in his London Spy, says
that there was perpetual fiddling in it to draw in
customers, and that the door used to be crowded
with hearers; this Mr. John Young was the father
of a musical family, and of Mr. Talbot Young, a fine
performer on the violin, the founder of the Castle
concert in Paternoster-row, of whom there will be
occasion to speak hereafter.

## CHAP. CLIII.

THE flute appears to be an instrument of great
antiquity in this kingdom; it is frequently mentioned
by Chaucer; and it seems by the description of it
in Mersennus, that there was a species of it, which
by himself and other foreigners was termed the
English Flute, 'Fistula dulcis seu Anglica.'* The

* See page 608 of this work.

proper and most discriminating appellation for it is
that of the Flute à bec, or beaked flute;† nevertheless we meet with ancient books of instructions
for the instrument, wherein it is termed, but very
improperly, as it is conceived, the Recorder. Milton
could never mean that they were one and the same
instrument, when in the same line he mentions

'Flutes and soft Recorders.'

Among bird-fanciers the word record is used as
a verb to signify the first essays of a bird in singing;‡
and it is well known that Bullfinches and other birds
are taught to sing by a flajolet. Lord Bacon, in his
Natural History, Cent. III. Sect. 221, speaks of
Recorders and Flutes at the same instant, and says
that the Recorder hath a less bore and a greater,
above and below; and elsewhere, Cent. II. Sect.
187, he speaks of it as having six holes, in which
respect it answers to the Tibia minor or flajolet of
Mersennus. From all which particulars it should
seem that the Flute and the Recorder were different
instruments, and that the latter in propriety of
speech was no other than the flajolet.§

Nevertheless the terms are confounded; and in
a book of instructions and lessons for the flute, so
old that the notation is by dots, the instructions
for the instrument are entitled directions for the
Recorder.

We are now to speak of the method of notation
by dots, which will easily be understood by such as
have ever had occasion to look into the books published for the instruction of learners on the flute,
German flute, or hautboy, for it consists simply of
a stave of eight lines, answering to the number of
holes on the instrument, whereon dots are placed to
signify when the holes are to be stopped, the uppermost line answering to the thumb-hole; so that dots
on all the eight lines bespeak the note F, and dots
on all the lines but the lowest, G; and so of the
rest: and as to the time, it was signified by such
characters as were used for the same purpose in the
tablature for the lute. The like way of playing by
dots was used for the flajolet, as appears by a book
entitled 'The Pleasant Companion, or new Lessons
'and Instructions for the Flagelet by Thomas
'Greeting, Gent.' printed for John Playford in 1675.

The last publication of this kind was a book
called The New Flute Master, printed in 1704, in
which are sundry preludes by Mr. John Banister,
the grandson of that Banister mentioned before to
have been sent to France by king Charles II. for
improvement on the violin; in this the learner is

† See an explanation of this term page 331, in note.

‡ Nevertheless the pastoral poets use it for the singing of birds in
general, as in these instances:—

Sweet Philomel, the bird,
That hath the heavenly throat,
Doth now alas! not once affoord,
*Recording* of a noate.
N. BRETON, in ENGLAND'S HELICON.

Now birds *record* new harmonie,
And trees do whistle melodies;
Now every thing that nature breeds,
Doth clad itself in pleasant weedes.
THO. WATSON, in the same collection.

§ *Thirlby, bishop of Westminster, while a scholar of Trinity Hall,
Cambridge, had a chamber under that of Bilney the martyr; at which time
he used often to play on his recorder for his diversions, and then good
Bilney would go to his prayers. Strype's Eccles. Mem. Vol. II. 464.*

furnished with directions for playing either Dot-way or Gamut-way, for these were the terms of distinction, and is left to his choice of either.

After what has been said of the tablature, and of the notation by dots, it must appear that the playing at sight after either of these methods was scarcely practicable, and that the rejection of them both is but a consequence of the great improvements of music within this last century.

From the account herein before given of the progress of music, it appears that through every stage of improvement, besides that it was the profession of persons educated to the practice of it, it was the recreation of gentlemen: among the latter, those of a more grave and serious turn betook themselves to the practice of the lute and viol da gamba,* resorting to it as a relief from study, and as an incentive to sober mirth. Others, less sensible of the charms of harmony and melody, looked upon music as a mere accomplishment, and were content to excel only on those instruments on which a moderate degree of proficiency might be attained with little labour and application; and these seem to have been the Flute à bec and the Flageolet: the latter of these was for the most part the amusement of boys; it was also used for the purpose of teaching birds, more particularly bullfinches, to sing easy tunes; for which reason one of the books of instructions for the flageolet now extant, is entitled The Bird-fancier's Delight; but the flute, especially of the larger size, was a more solemn instrument, and was taken to by the fine gentlemen of the time, whose characters were formed after that model of good breeding exhibited in the French court towards the end of the last century.

Cibber, in the Apology for his Life, page 214, has with great propriety marked the character of the beaux of his time, who he says were of a quite different cast from the modern stamp, and had more of the stateliness of the peacock in their mein, than which now seems to be their highest emulation, the pert air of a lapwing; to which remark we may add, that the character of a gentleman, in the vulgar apprehension, consisted then in the assemblage of such external qualifications, as served to recommend him to the favour of those who looked no farther than the mere outside; among which some small skill in music was thought as necessary as the accomplishment of dancing.

As the French mode of behaving and conversing had been adopted here, so were in some degree their recreations and amusements. From the time of making that present of English flutes to the king of France, which Mersennus speaks of, the flute became a favourite instrument among the French, and many gentlemen were notable proficients on it; and though the instrument had passed from England to France, the general practice of it by persons of fashion was then derived from thence to us.† That

the flute was formerly the instrument of a gentleman may be inferred from the following circumstance: in that species of graphical representation called Still Life, we observe a collection of implements and utensils thrown in disorder on a table, exhibiting a group of various forms, contrasted with each other, at the will of the artist. He that shall carefully attend to pictures of this kind, will seldom fail to find a lute, and also a flute, frequently with a book of lessons for one or the other instrument; but if this particular fail to prove that the flute was the recreation of gentlemen, what shall be said to a portrait of one of our poets, who died above fifty years ago, drawn when he was about twenty, wherein he is represented in a full trimmed blue suit, with scarlet stockings rolled above his knees, a large white peruke, and playing on a flute near half an ell in length; or to this, which is the frontispiece to a book of instructions and lessons for this instrument, published about the year 1700.

And to come nearer to our own times, it may be remembered by many now living, that a flute was the pocket companion of many who wished to be thought fine gentlemen. The use of it was to entertain ladies, and such as had a liking for no better music than a song-tune, or such little airs as were then composed for that instrument; and he that could play a solo of Schickhard of Hamburg, or Robert Valentine of Rome, was held a complete master of the instrument. A description of the mutual compliments that attended a request to one of these accomplished gentlemen to perform, or a recital of the forms of entreaty or excuse, with a relation of the apologies, the bows, the congees that passed upon such an occasion, might furnish matter for a diverting scene in a comedy; but here it

---

* In the will of Sir Henry Wotton, printed in his remains, is a bequest of his viol da gamba to one of his friends. Sir John Bolles, Sir Francis North, and Sir Roger L'Estrange, as above related, were excellent performers on this instrument.

† The flageolet had also its admirers: in that most ingenious and entertaining book, Dr. More's divine Dialogues, Hylobares one of the interlocutors, at intervals during the conversation, entertains his friends with the music of the Flageolet, as does another of them, Bathynous, on the Theorbo. On this latter instrument we are told the author himself was a performer, and that the power of the music thereof, aided by his own rapturous thoughts, was frequently so great as forced him to desist. See his Life by the Rev. Mr. Richard Ward, and the Biog. Brit. Art. More [Henry.]

may suffice to say, that in the present state of manners, nothing of the kind is to be found amongst us.*

As the French had set us the example for the practice of the flute à bec, so did they for the German or traverse flute, an instrument of little less antiquity. The Sieur Hotteterre le Romain of Paris was the first that published instructions for it; and these were considerably improved in a treatise entitled 'Methode pour apprendre aisèment à joüer de la Flute traversiere,' by Mons. Corrette: the former of these books was published about the year 1710; and from that time the practice of the flute à bec descended to young apprentices of tradesmen, and was the amusement of their winter evenings; the German or traverse flute still retains some degree of estimation among gentlemen, whose ears are not nice enough to inform them that it is never in tune.†

Nicholas Staggins, a man bred under his father, a common musician in London, had interest enough to procure himself the place of composer to Charles II. and afterwards to be master of the band of music to William III. In the year 1664, more by the favour of Dr. James, the vice-chancellor, than any desert of his own, he attained to the degree of doctor in music. His exercise should have been a vocal composition in five or six parts, and also one for instruments, but the former, as being the more difficult work, was dispensed with. The partiality shown to this man seems to have occasioned great murmurings, and to silence them the following advertisement was published in the Gazette for the year 1664, No. 1945:—'Cambridge, July 6. Dr. Nicholas Staggins, 'who was some time since admitted to the degree of 'Dr. of music, being desirous to perform his exercise 'upon the first public opportunity for the said 'degree, has quitted himself so much to the satisfac-'tion of the whole university this commencement, 'that by a solemn vote they have constituted and 'appointed him to be a public professor of music 'there.'

At Cambridge is no endowment for a music professor, so that the appointment here mentioned must have been merely honorary; however, in virtue of it Dr. Tudway succeeded to the title upon the death of Dr. Staggins, and it has been continued down to the present time.

In a collection entitled 'Choice Ayres, Songs, and 'Dialogues to sing to the Theorbo-Lute or Bass-'Viol,' published in 1675, is a song composed by Dr. Staggins, to the words 'While Alexis;' and in Playford's Dancing Master is a country-dance tune called Dr. Staggins's Jig; a few other such compositions may possibly be found, but it does not appear that he ever composed anthems or services, or

indeed any works that could render him justly eminent in his faculty.

John Wallis, an eminent divine and mathematician, was born at Ashford in Kent on the twenty-third day of November, 1616. From a grammar-school at Felsted in Essex he went to Emanuel college in Cambridge, and became a fellow of Queen's college before a vacancy happened in his own. About the year 1640 he was admitted to holy orders, and, leaving the university, became domestic chaplain to Sir Richard Darly of Yorkshire, and the Lady Vere, the dowager of Lord Horatio Vere. In 1664, he was chosen one of the scribes or secretaries to the assembly of divines at Westminster. Having made a considerable progress in mathematics and natural philosophy, he was in 1649 appointed Savalian professor of geometry at Oxford; upon which occasion he entered himself at Exeter college, and was admitted to the degree of master of arts, and in 1654 to that of doctor of divinity: soon after which, upon the decease of Dr. Gerrard Langbaine, he was appointed Custos Archivorum of the university.

In his younger years he invented the art of deciphering, and by his great penetration and ingenuity discovered and established those principles which have been the rule of its professors ever since, and have entitled him to the appellation of the father of the art. His singular readiness in developing the sense of secret writing, drew upon him the suspicion of having deciphered the letters of Charles I. taken at the battle of Naseby; but he fully cleared himself in a letter to Dr. Fell, bishop of Oxford, dated April 8, 1685, an extract whereof is published in the preface to Hearne's edition of Peter Langtoft's Chronicle.

Dr. Wallis was one of those persons whose private meetings for the improvement of philosophy by experiments, gave occasion to the institution of the Royal Society; and after its establishment he was a constant attendant, and frequent correspondent of the society, communicating from time to time his discoveries in various branches of natural philosophy and the mathematics, as appears by his publications in the Philosophical Transactions.

The learning of Dr. Wallis was not less deep than extensive. A singular degree of acuteness and penetration is discoverable in all his writings, which are too multifarious to be here particularized; and the rather as a copious account of them is given in his life in the Biographia Britannica. Those which it concerns us here to take notice of, are his edition of Ptolemy, with the appendix entitled 'De veterum 'harmonia ad hodiernam comparata;'‡ as also 'Por-'phyrii in Harmonica Ptolemæi Commentarius, ex 'cod. MSS. Græce et Latine editus;' and 'Manuelis 'Bryennii harmonica ex cod. MSS.,' which are contained in the third and last volume of his works in folio, printed at Oxford in 1669. These pieces of ancient harmonics, with those before published by

---

* This account will not seem exaggerated to those who remember such old gentlemen as had been the scholars of Banister, Woodcock, Baston, and other masters of the flute.

† This is an objection that lies in common against all perforated pipes; the best that the makers of them can do is to tune them to some one key, as the hautboy to C, the German flute to D, and the flute à bec to F; and to effect this truly, is a matter of no small difficulty. The flutes of the latter kind of the younger Stanesby approach the nearest of any to perfection; but those of Bressan, though excellent in their tone, are all too flat in the upper octave. For these reasons some are induced to think, notwithstanding what we daily hear of a fine embouchure, and a brilliant finger, terms equally nonsensical applied, as they are, to the German flute, that the utmost degree of proficiency on any of these instruments is scarcely worth the labour of attaining it.

‡ The reduction of the ancient system of music to the modern, which makes the Greek scale, as far as it goes, correspond with that of Guido, though an arduous undertaking, Dr. Wallis has happily effected in his appendix to Ptolemy; and in his notes on that work he has gone very near to demonstrate an exact correspondence between the modes of the ancients and keys of the moderns.

Meibomius, complete the whole of what the ancient Greek writers have left upon that subject.

Dr. Wallis was also the author of sundry papers printed in the Philosophical Transactions, particularly A Discourse on the Trembling of consonant Strings ;* another on the division of the monochord ;† another on the imperfection of the organ ;‡ and a fourth on the strange effects reported of music in former times.§

Many particulars of the life of this great man are related in a letter from him to Dr. Thomas Smith, printed in the preface to Hearne's edition of Peter Langtoft's Chronicle ; at the end of which letter is a very serious vindication of himself from the calumnies of his enemies.  What is related of him in the Athen. Oxon. is little to be regarded, for it is evident that Wood hated him for no other reason than the moderate principles which he professed, and which show Dr. Wallis to have been a much wiser man than himself.

He died on the twenty-eighth day of October, 1703, in the eighty-eighth year of his age, and was buried in the church of St. Mary at Oxford, in which is a handsome monument to his memory.

## CHAP. CLIV.

John Blow (a Portrait), a native of North Collingham, in the county of Nottingham, was one of the first set of children after the restoration, being bred up under Captain Henry Cook.  He was also a pupil of Hingeston, and after that of Dr. Christopher Gibbons.  On the sixteenth day of March, 1673, he was sworn one of the gentlemen of the chapel in the room of Roger Hill; and in July, 1674, upon the decease of Mr. Pelham Humphrey, was appointed master of the children of the chapel.  In 1685 he was made one of his majesty's private music, and composer to his majesty, a title which Matthew Lock had enjoyed before him, but which seems to have been at that time merely honorary.  He was also almoner and master of the choristers of the cathedral church of St. Paul, being appointed to those places upon the death of Michael Wise, in 1687, who had been admitted but in the January preceding ; but he resigned them in 1693, in favour of his scholar Jeremiah Clark.  Blow was not a graduate of either university ; but archbishop Sancroft, in virtue of his own authority in that respect, conferred on him the degree of doctor in music.  Upon the decease of Purcell in 1695, he became organist of Westminster-Abbey.  In the year 1699 he was appointed composer to his majesty, with a salary of forty pounds a year, under an establishment, of which the following is the history.  After the revolution, and while king William was in Flanders, the summer residence of queen Mary was at Hampton Court.  Dr. Tillotson was then dean of St. Paul's and the reverend Mr.

Gostling sub-dean, and also a gentleman of the chapel. The dean would frequently take Mr. Gostling in his chariot thither to attend the chapel duty ; and in one of those journeys, the dean talking of church music, mentioned it as a common observation, that ours fell short of what it had been in the preceding reign, and that the queen herself had spoken of it to him.  Mr. Gostling's answer was, that Dr. Blow and Mr. Purcell were capable of composing at least as good anthems as most of those which had been so much admired, and a little encouragement would make that appear.  The dean mentioned this to her majesty, who approved of the thought, and said they should be appointed accordingly, with a salary of 40l. per annum,‖ adding that it would be expected that each should produce a new anthem on the first Sunday of his month of waiting.¶

This conversation, according to the account above given, which was communicated by the son of Mr. Gostling now living, was had in the life-time of Purcell, that is to say, before the year 1695, but it did not take effect till four years after, and then only as to one composer,** as appears by the following entry in the Cheque-book :—

'1699.  Upon a new establishment of a com-
'poser's place for the chapel royal, Dr. John
'Blow was admitted into it by a warrant
'from the right reverend dean, and sworn in
'by me          'Ralph Battell, Subdean.'

Blow was a composer of anthems while a chapel-boy, as appears by Clifford's collection, in which are several subscribed ' John Blow, one of the children of his majesty's chapel;' and on the score of his merit was distinguished by Charles II.  The king admired very much a little duet of Carissimi to the words ' Dite o Cieli,' and asked of Blow if he could imitate it.  Blow modestly answered he would try, and composed in the same measure, and the same key of D with a minor third, that fine song, ' Go perjured man.'††  That the reader may be able to draw a comparison between the two compositions, that of the Italian is here inserted.  Blow's is known to every Englishman conversant in music.

---

* Philos. Trans. No. 134, pag. 839, Mar. anno 1677.

† Ibid. No. 238, pag. 80, Mar. anno 1698.

‡ Ibid. No. 242, pag. 249, July, anno 1698.

§ No. 243, pag. 297, Aug. anno 1698.   Lowthorp and Jones's Abridgm. edit. 1732, chap. x. pag. 606, et seq.

‖ These salaries have since been augmented to 73l. per annum, and thereby made equal to those of the gentlemen of the chapel.

¶ Dr. Tillotson's interest with queen Mary, which was very great, is thus to be accounted for.  Upon her marriage, the prince of Orange and she were hurried out of town so fast (there being a secret design to invite them to an entertainment in the city which the court did not like), that they had scarce time to make provision for their journey.  Being come to Canterbury, they repaired to an inn, where, through haste, they came very meanly provided.  Upon application by Mr. Bentinck, who attended them, to borrow money of the corporation, the mayor and his brethren, after great deliberation, were afraid to lend them any.  Dr. Tillotson, then dean of Canterbury, hearing of this, immediately got together his own, and what other plate and money he could borrow, and went to the inn of Mr. Bentinck with the offer of what he had.  This was highly acceptable to the prince and princess, and the dean was carried to wait upon them.  By this lucky accident he began that acquaintance and correspondence with the prince and Mr. Bentinck, which advanced him afterwards to the archbishoprick.  Echar's Hist. of Eng. Appendix, page 11.  Rapin, vol. II. page 683.  This fact is related by Dr. Birch in his life of archbishop Tillotson, page 49, with this additional circumstance, that it is drawn from a manuscript account taken from the archbishop's own mouth.

** There was no appointment of a second composer till 1715, when Mr. John Weldon was admitted and sworn into that place.

†† He afterwards composed another, little inferior, also printed in the Amphion Angelicus, to the words ' Go perjured maid.'

GIACOMO CARISSIMI.

The song of 'Go perjured man' was first published singly, and some years after in the fourth and last book of the Theater of Music, printed for Henry Playford in 1687. It was again published with the addition of instrumental parts, in the Amphion Anglicus of Dr. Blow, *but in none of the copies are the words sense. The song is to be found in a book for the extreme scarcity of which no reason can be assigned, other than that it was never thought* *worthy of a second impression. It is a Collection of Poems much in the cast of those of Cleveland, and is entitled ' Hesperides,' by Robert Herrie, 8vo. 1648. The words, such as they are, are as under.**

* Go, perjur'd man, and if thou e'er return
To see the small remainder of my Urn,
When thou shalt laugh at my religious dust,
And ask where's now the colour, form, and trust
Of woman's beauty ? and with hand more rude
Rifle the flowers which the virgins strew'd,
Know, I have pray'd to fury, that the wind
May blow my ashes up and strike thee blind.

The Orpheus Britannicus of Purcell had been published by his widow soon after his decease, and contained in it some of that author's finest songs: the favourable reception it met with was a motive with Blow to the publication, in the year 1700, of a work of the same kind, entitled 'Amphion Anglicus, 'containing compositions for one, two, three, and 'four voices, with accompanyments of instrumental 'music and a thorough-bass figured for the organ, 'harpsichord, or theorbo-lute.'

This book was dedicated to the princess Anne of Denmark; in the epistle the author gives her royal highness to understand that he was preparing to publish his church services and divine compositions, but he lived not to carry his design into effect. To the Amphion Anglicus are prefixed commendatory verses by sundry persons, many of whom had been his scholars, as namely, Jeremiah Clark, organist of St. Paul's cathedral; William Croft, organist of St. Anne, Soho, and John Barret, music-master to the boys in Christ's hospital, and organist of St. Mary at Hill. Among them is an ode addressed to the author by one Mr. Herbert, in a note on which it is said that an anthem of Bird, in golden notes, is preserved in the Vatican library; and in the second stanza are the following lines respecting Blow:—

'His Gloria Patri long ago reach'd Rome,
'Sung and rever'd too in St. Peter's dome;
'A canon will outlive her jubilees to come.'

The canon here meant is that fine one to which the Gloria Patri in Dr. Blow's Gamut service is set.* That it should be sung in St. Peter's church at Rome may seem strange, but the fact is thus accounted for: Dr. Ralph Battell, subdean of the royal chapel, and a prebendary of Worcester, being at Rome in the reign of James II. was much with Cardinal Howard, then protector of the English nation, as Cardinal Albani is now, and being upon his return to England, the Cardinal requested of him some of our church-music, particularly the compositions of Blow and Purcell, which he said he had been told were very fine; the doctor answered he should readily oblige his eminence, and desired to know how he should send them; the Cardinal replied in William Penn's packet.† And there can be little doubt but that so

* The whole service is printed in the first volume of Dr. Boyce's Cathedral Music, page 263, and the Canon alone, in the editions of Playford's Introduction after the year 1700.

† This was the famous William Penn, the Quaker, who from the favour shown him by James II. and other circumstances, was strongly suspected to be a concealed papist. The imputation he affected to consider as greatly injurious to his character; and accordingly entered into a very serious debate with the archbishop Tillotson on the subject, which he did not give over till by his letters he had fully convinced him that the charge was groundless. If the above anecdote does not stagger the faith of those who have read Penn's Letters, it is possible the following story may:—
The same Dr. Battell being a prebendary of Worcester, was, as his duty required, annually resident there for a certain portion of the year; the gaoler of the city was a man of such a character, as procured him admittance into the best company. By this person, Dr. Battell was told that he had once in his custody a Romish priest, who lamenting the troubles of James the Second's reign, told his keeper that the misfortunes of that prince were chiefly owing to Father Petre and Father Penn. Dr. Battell recollecting that Penn was frequently with Sherlock, then dean of St. Paul's, was determined to sift him about it; accordingly he applied to Dr. Sherlock, with whom he was well acquainted, and told him the story; the Doctor said that Mr. Penn dined with him once a week, and that he should be glad to be satisfied touching the truth or falsehood of the insinuation; that he would mention it to Penn, and engage Dr. Battell to meet him at the deanery and state the fact as he had heard it; but Penn evaded an appointment and from that time forbore his visits to Dr. Sherlock.

excellent a composition as that above mentioned was in the number of those sent.

Of the work itself little is to be said; in the songs for two, three, and four voices, the harmony is such as it became so great a master to write; but in the article of expression, in melody, and in all the graces and elegancies of this species of vocal composition, it is evidently defective.

Dr. Blow set to music an Ode for St. Cecilia's day, 1684, the words by Mr. Oldham, published together with one of Purcell on the same occasion, performed in the preceding year. He also composed and published a collection of lessons for the harpsichord or spinnet, and an ode on the death of Purcell, written by Mr. Dryden. There are also extant of his composition sundry hymns printed in the Harmonia Sacra, and a great number of Catches in the latter editions of the Musical Companion.

This great musician died in the year 1708, and lies buried in the north aisle of Westminster Abbey. On his monument is the canon above mentioned, engraven on a book under the following inscription:—

Here lieth the body
Of JOHN BLOW, Doctor in MUSICK,
Who was organist, composer, and
Master of the children of the chapel
Royal for the space of 35 years,
In the reigns of
K. Cha. II. K. Ja. II.
K. Wm. and Q. Mary, and
Her present majesty Q. Anne,
And also organist of this collegiate church,
About 15 years.
He was scholar to the excellent musician
Dr. Christopher Gibbons,
And master to the famous Mr. H. Purcell,
and most of the eminent masters in musick since.
He died Oct. 1, 1708, in the 60th year of his age.
His own musical compositions,
Especially his church musick,
Are a far nobler monument
To his memory,
Than any other can be raised
For him.

He married Elizabeth, the only daughter of Edward Braddock, one of the gentlemen, and clerk of the cheque, of the royal chapel, one of the choir, and master of the children of Westminster Abbey. She died in childbed on the twenty-ninth day of October, 1683, aged thirty. By her he had four children, viz., a son, named John, and three daughters, Elizabeth, married to William Edgeworth, Esq. Catherine, and Mary. John died on the second day of June, 1695, aged fifteen; he lies buried in the north ambulatory of the cloister of Westminster Abbey, next to his mother, with an inscription, purporting that he was a youth of great towardness and extraordinary hopes. Elizabeth died on the second day of December, 1719; Catherine the nineteenth of May 1730, and Mary the nineteenth of November 1738.

Dr. Blow was a very handsome man in his person, and remarkable for a gravity and decency in his deportment suited to his station, though he seems by some of his compositions to have been not altogether insensible to the delights of a convivial hour

JOHN BLOW MUS. DOCT. MDCC.

VERA EFFIGIES

HENRICI PURCELL.

ÆTAT. SUÆ XXIV.

He was a man of blameless morals, and of a benevolent temper; but was not so insensible of his own worth, as to be totally free from the imputation of pride. Such as would form a true estimate of his character as a musician, must have recourse to his compositions for the church, which are very many; and to them we are very judiciously referred by the author of his epitaph; for it is not in his songs, a few excepted, that we find much to admire; the reason whereof may be that his studies had been uniformly directed to the expression in musical language of the most sublime sentiments. Notwithstanding the encomiums contained in the verses prefixed to the Amphion Anglicus, the publication of that work drew on Blow the censures of Dr. Tudway and others of his friends, some of whom ascribed it to no better a motive than a desire to emulate Purcell; though whoever shall compare it with the Orpheus Britannicus, must be convinced that in point of merit the difference between the two is immeasureable. For this reason the friends of Dr. Blow's memory may wish that this collection of songs had never been published, but for their consolation let them turn to those heavenly compositions, his services and anthems, particularly his services in E la mi and A re, his Gamut service above mentioned, and the anthems 'God is our hope and 'strength,' 'O God, wherefore art thou absent,' and 'I beheld and lo a great multitude,'* printed in Dr. Boyce's Cathedral Music, which afford abundant reason to say of Dr. Blow, that among church musicians he has few equals, and scarce any superior.

## CHAP. CLV.

Henry Purcell (a Portrait), was the son of Henry Purcell,† and the nephew of Thomas Purcell, both gentlemen of the chapel at the restoration of Charles II.‡ The former died on the eleventh day of August, 1664,§ his son being then but six years old; the latter survived, and continued in his station till the day of his death, which was the thirty-first of July, 1682.‖ At the time of the decease of the elder Henry, Capt. Cook was master of the children of the chapel, and having been appointed to that charge immediately upon the restoration, had educated one set of children, who for distinction sake are called the first set of chapel children after that

* Touching the last of the above-mentioned anthems there is an anecdote, which, as it was communicated by Mr. Weeley of the king's chapel, who had been a scholar of Blow, we may venture to give as authentic. In the reign of king James II. an anthem of some Italian composer had been introduced into the chapel, which the king liking very much, asked Blow if he could make one as good; Blow answered he could, and engaged to do it by the next Sunday, when he produced the anthem 'I beheld,' &c. When the service was over the king sent Father Petre to acquaint Blow that he was much pleased with it. 'But,' added Petre, 'I myself think it too long:' 'That,' answered Blow, 'is 'the opinion of but one fool, and I heed it not.' The Jesuit was so nettled at this expression of contempt, that he meditated revenge, and wrought so with the king, that Blow was put under a suspension, which however he was freed from by the Revolution, which took place very shortly after.

† Ashmol. MS.

‡ Vide page 693, the list of the gentlemen and officers of the chapel at the time of the coronation of king Charles II. being St. George's day, 1661. Thomas Purcell was the author of that fine chant printed in Dr. Boyce's collection, vol. I. page 289, No. II. called the Burial Chant.

§ Ashmol. MS.          ‖ Cheque Book.

event. Among these were Blow, Wise, Pelham Humphrey, and others.

Purcell was one of the second set, and is said to have been educated under Blow; but considering that Purcell was born in 1658, and that Blow was not appointed master of the children till sixteen years after, it can hardly be thought that Blow was his first instructor. It may with a great appearance of probability be supposed that Purcell was at first a scholar of Cook, who came in at the restoration, and died in 1672; and the rather as it is certain that he was a scholar of Humphrey, who was Cook's immediate successor. To reconcile these several facts with the inscription on Blow's monument, in which it is expressly said that Blow was Purcell's master, the only way is to suppose that Purcell, upon quitting the chapel, might, for the purpose of completing his studies, become the pupil of Blow, and thereby give occasion to what is generally reported touching the relation between them of master and scholar.

Being very diligent and attentive to the instructions of his teachers, Purcell became an early proficient in the science of musical composition, and was able to write correct harmony at an age, when to be qualified for the performance of choral service is all that can be expected. And here it may be noted that among the first set of children of the chapel after the restoration, were several, who while they were in that station were the composers of anthems; and Purcell, who was of the second set, gave proofs of his genius by the composition of several of those anthems of his, which are now sung in the church.

Upon the decease of Dr. Christopher Gibbons in the year 1676, Purcell, being then but eighteen years of age, was appointed organist of the collegiate church of Saint Peter at Westminster; and in the year 1682, upon the decease of Mr. Edward Low, he became his successor as one of the organists of the chapels royal. *In the beginning of the year 1689 he became engaged in a dispute with Dr. Sprat, the then Dean, and the Chapter of Westminster, the occasion whereof was this. It seems that at the coronation of king William and queen Mary, he had received and claimed as his right, the money taken for admission into the organ loft of persons desirous of being near spectators of that ceremony, which for the following reasons must be supposed to have amounted to a considerable sum; the profit arising to the owner of one of the houses at the west end of the Abbey, where only the procession could be viewed, amounted at the last coronation to five hundred pounds. The organ in Purcell's time was on the north side of the choir, and was much nearer the altar than now, so that spectators from thence might behold the whole of that august ceremony.*

*A sum like that which this must be presumed to have been was worth contending for, and if Purcell had the authority of precedent for his support, he was right in retaining it as a perquisite arising from his office; but his masters thought otherwise, and insisted on it as their due, for in an old chapter book I find the following entry: '18 April, 1689,*

'*Mr. Purcell, the organ blower, to pay to Mr.*
'*Needham such money as was received by him for*
'*places in the organ loft, and in default thereof his*
'*place to be declared null and void, and that his*
'*stipend or sallary be detained in the Treasurer's*
'*hands until further orders.*' *Upon which it may
be observed that the penning of it is an evidence of
great ignorance or malice, in that it describes him
by the appellation of organ blower who was organist
of their own church, and in truth the most excellent
musician of his time.*

*What the issue of this contest was does nowhere
appear. It may be supposed either that he refunded
the money or compounded the matter with the Dean
and Chapter, it being certain that he continued to
execute his office for some years after.*

It has been remarked by one who was intimately
acquainted with him, that Purcell in his earlier
compositions gave into that style which King Charles
II. affected: this is true so far as it respects the
melody of his compositions, and for so doing he had
the authority of Wise and Humphrey; though, to
say the truth, the taste of the king, and the example
of these his predecessors did but coincide with his
own ideas of music. There is a vulgar tradition
that Mary D'Este of Modena, the consort of king
James II., upon her arrival in England brought with
her a band of musicians of her own country, and that
Purcell, by acquaintance and conversation with them,
and sometimes joining with them in performance,
contracted an affection for the Italian style; but for
this assertion there is no foundation, for before this
time he had looked very carefully into the works of
the Italian masters, more especially Carissimi, Cesti,
Colonna, Gratiani, Bassani, and Stradella, of which
latter he could never speak without rapture.

There is but very little doubt that the study of the
works of these excellent masters was the motive with
Purcell for introducing into his compositions a more
elegant and pathetic melody than had been known in
England; of the good effects whereof he was so soon
well persuaded, that in the year 1683 he published
twelve Sonatas for two violins and a bass, for the organ
or harpsichord, in the preface to which he gives the following as his sentiments of the Italian music:—* * *
'For its author he has faithfully endeavoured a just
'imitation of the most famed Italian masters, prin-
'cipally to bring the seriousness and gravity of that
'sort of musick into vogue and reputation among our
'countrymen, whose humour 'tis time now should
'begin to loath the levity and balladry of our neigh-
'bours. The attempt he confesses to be bold and
'daring; there being pens and artists of more emi-
'nent abilities, much better qualified for the imploy-
'ment than his or himself, which he well hopes
'these his weak endeavours will in due time provoke
'and enflame to a more accurate undertaking. He
'is not ashamed to own his unskilfulness in the
'Italian language, but that is the unhappiness of his
'education, which cannot justly be counted his fault;
'however he thinks he may warrantably affirm that
'he is not mistaken in the power of the Italian notes,
'or elegancy of their compositions.'

From the structure of these compositions of Purcell,

it is not improbable that the sonatas of Bassani, and
perhaps of some other of the Italians, were the
models after which he formed them: for as to Corelli,
it is not clear that any of his works were got abroad
so early as the year 1683. Be that as it may, the
sonatas of Purcell have manifestly the cast of Italian
compositions; each begins with an adagio movement:
then follows what we should call a fugue, but which
the author terms a canzone; then a slow movement,
and last of all an air. Before the work is a very
fine print of the author, his age twenty-four, without
the name of either painter or engraver, but so little
like that prefixed to the Orpheus Britannicus, after
a painting of Closterman, at thirty-seven, that they
hardly seem to be representations of the same person.

It should seem that this work of Purcell met
with encouragement, for afterwards he composed ten
Sonatas, in four parts, among which is one in F FA
UT, that for its excellence has acquired the appellation of the Golden Sonata. These were not published till after his decease, and will therefore be
spoken of hereafter.

As Purcell had received his education in the
school of a choir, the natural bent of his studies was
towards church music: services he seemed to
neglect, and to addict himself to the composition of
anthems, a kind of music which in his time the
church stood greatly in need of.

And here it is proper to mention an anthem of
his, 'Blessed are they that fear the Lord,' as being
composed on a very extraordinary occasion. Upon
the supposed pregnancy of king James the Second's
queen in 1687, a proclamation was issued for a thanksgiving to be observed on the fifteenth day of January,
in London and twelve miles round; and on the
twenty-ninth day of the same month throughout
England, for joy of this event; and Purcell, being
then one of the organists of the royal chapel, was
commanded to compose an anthem, and he did it
accordingly for four voices with instruments. The
original score in his own hand-writing is yet extant.

The anthem 'They that go down to the sea in
'ships,' was composed at the request of the Rev.
Mr. Subdean Gostling, who being at sea with the
king and the duke of York in the Fubbs yacht, and
in great danger of being cast away, providentially
escaped.*

Among the letters of Tom Brown from the dead
to the living, is one from Dr. Blow to Henry
Purcell, in which it is humorously observed, that
persons of their profession are subject to an equal
attraction of the church and the playhouse, and are
therefore in a situation resembling that of the tomb
of Mahomet,† which is said to be suspended between
heaven and earth. This remark of Brown does so
truly apply to Purcell, that it is more than probable
his particular situation gave occasion to it; for he
was scarcely known to the world before he became,
in the exercise of his calling, so equally divided
between both the church and the theatre, that
neither the church, the tragic, nor the comic muse
could call him her own.

* For the particulars of this deliverance, vide ante, page 693, in not.
† Works of Mr. Thomas Brown, vol. II. page 301.

In the pamphlet, so often referred to in the course of this work, entitled ' Roscius Anglicanus,' or an ' Historical View of the Stage,' written by Downes the prompter, and published in 1708, we have an account of several plays and entertainments, the music whereof is by that writer said to have been composed by Purcell. It does not appear that he had any particular attachment to the stage, but a occasional essay in dramatic music drew him into it. One Mr. Josias Priest, a celebrated dancing-master, and a composer of stage dances, kept a boarding school for young gentlewomen in Leicester-fields ; * and the nature of his profession inclining him to dramatic representations, he got Tate to write, and Purcell to set to music, a little drama called Dido and Æneas ;† Purcell was then of the age of nineteen, but the music of this opera had so little appearance of a puerile essay, that there was scare a musician in England who would not have thought it an honour to have been the author of it. The exhibition of this little piece by the young gentlewomen of the school to a select audience of their parents and friends was attended with general applause, no small part whereof was considered as the due of Purcell.

At this time Banister and Lock were the stage composers ; the former had set the music to Dr. D'avenant's opera of Circe, and the latter to Macbeth ; but the fame of Dido and Æneas directed the eyes of the managers towards Purcell, and Purcell was easily prevailed on by Mr. Priest to enter into their service. He composed the music to a variety of plays mentioned in Downes's account, of which the following is an abstract :—

Theodosius or the Force of Love, written by Nat. Lee, the music by Mr. Henry Purcell, being the first he ever composed for the stage. King Arthur, an opera written by Dryden, the musical part set by Mr. Henry Purcell, and the dances composed by Mr. Josiah‡ Priest. The Prophetess, an opera written by Mr. Betterton, the vocal and instrumental music by Mr. Henry Purcell, and the dances by Mr. Priest. The Fairy Queen, an opera altered from the Midsummer Night's Dream of Shakespeare, the music by Mr. Purcell, the dances by Mr. Priest.

These are all the plays to which, according to Downes's account, Purcell composed the music. But it appears by the Orpheus Britannicus that he made the music to very many others, namely, Timon of Athens, Bonduca, the Libertine, Œdipus, the Tempest, as altered from Shakespeare by Dryden and Sir William Davenant ; and composed many of the songs in that most absurd of all dramatic representations, the History of Don Quixote, in three parts, by Tom D'Urfey ; farther, that collection of Airs composed for the Theatre, published by his widow in 1697, contains the overtures and airs to the following operas and plays : Dioclesian,§ King Arthur,

* He removed in 1680 to the great school-house at Chelsea, formerly Mr. Portman's, Vide Gazette, Nunb. 1567.

† The song in the Orpheus Britannicus ' Ah ! Belinda,' is one of the airs in it. In the original opera the initial words are ' Ah ! my Anna.'

‡ Sic Orig.

§ Called also the Prophetess ; it was not written by Betterton, but was altered by him from Beaumont and Fletcher.

Fairy Queen, the Indian Queen, the Married Beau,‖ Old Bachelor, Amphitryon, and Double Dealer, comedies; and to the Princess of Persia,¶ the Gordian Knot untied,** Abdelazor, or the Moor's Revenge,†† and Bonduca,‡‡ tragedies, and the Virtuous Wife, a comedy.§§

The opera of Dioclesian in score was published by Purcell himself in the year 1691, with a dedication to Charles duke of Somerset, in which he observes that ' Music is yet but in its nonage, a forward ' child, which gives hope of what he may be hereafter ' in England, when the masters of it shall find more ' encouragement;' and ' that it is now learning ' Italian, which is its best master, and studying ' a little of the French air, to give it somewhat more ' of gaiety and fashion.'

In the year 1684 Purcell published ' A musical ' entertainment performed on November 22, 1683, it ' being the festival of St. Cecilia, a great patroness of ' Music.'

The rest of Purcell's compositions in print are chiefly posthumous publications by his widow, and consist of ' A Collection of Ayres composed for the Theatre, and upon other occasions, 1697.' The ten Sonatas above mentioned, the ninth whereof is that which for its excellence is called the Golden Sonata in F FA UT, printed also in 1697. Lessons for the Harpsichord, Orpheus Britannicus, in two books, a work not more known than admired, sundry hymns and four anthems in the Harmonia Sacra, and part of the solemn burial service, which was completed by Dr. Croft, and is printed at the end of his book of anthems. The compositions above mentioned, as also a great number of songs and airs, rounds and catches, and even dance-tunes, set by him, are a proof of Purcell's extensive genius; but neither the allurements of the stage, nor his love of mirth and good-fellowship, of which he seems to have been very fond, were strong enough to divert his attention from the service of the church.

The Te Deum and Jubilate of Purcell are well known to all persons conversant in cathedral music. The general opinion has long been that he composed these offices for the musical performance at St. Paul's for the benefit of the sons of the clergy,‖‖ grounded perhaps on the uniform practice of performing them on that occasion until about the year 1713, when they gave way to the Te Deum and

‖ By Crowne.     ¶ By Elkanah Settle.     ** The author unknown.
†† By Mrs. Behn.     ‡‡ By Beaumont and Fletcher.     §§ By D'Urfey.

‖‖ Of this benevolent institution the history is as follows. In the time of the usurpation a sermon was preached at St. Paul's, Nov. 8, 1658, to the sons of ministers solemnly assembled, by George Hall, minister at St. Botolph Aldersgate, *son of the famous bishop Hall, and afterwards bishop of Chester.* It is supposed that the design of this discourse was to promote charitable contributions in favour of the sons of the clergy, since the corporation created for that purpose date their origin from the time above-mentioned. Whether before the restoration sermons of this kind were annual we know not, but afterwards a charter was granted, bearing date the first day of July, 1678, whereby a body politic and corporate was constituted by the name of the Governors of the Charity for the Relief of the poor Widows and Children of Clergymen, with licence to possess any estate not exceeding the yearly value of 2000*l.* Afterwards, upon the accession of Dr. Thomas Turner's gift, which amounted to about 18,000*l.* the governors, Dec. 16, 1714, obtained an augmentation of the said grant, by a licence to possess the yearly value of 3000*l.* over and above all charges and reprises, as also over and above the said 2000*l.* per annum. To promote the design of this institution, a sermon was preached at the anniversary meeting of the sons of clergymen in the church of St. Mary le Bow on the seventh day of November,

Jubilate of Mr. Handel, which had been composed for the thanksgiving on the peace of Utrecht, but the fact is otherwise, as will be shown.

Soon after the restoration of Charles II., when the civil commotions that had long disturbed the peace of this realm were at an end, the people gave into those recreations and amusements which had been so severely interdicted during the usurpation. Plays were not only permitted to be acted, but all the arts of scenical representation were employed to render them the objects of delight, and musical associations were formed at Oxford, and in other parts of the kingdom.

The first voluntary association of gentlemen in London, for the purpose of musical recreation, and which could properly be called a concert, seems to have been that at the house of Britton, the small-coal man, established about the year 1678, an acount whereof, as also of concerts given by masters, and which were uniformly notified in the London Gazette, will hereafter be given; but the lovers of music residing in this metropolis had a solemn annual meeting at Stationers' Hall on the twenty-second day of November, being the anniversary of the martyrdom of St. Cecilia,* from the time of re-

building that edifice after the fire of London. The performances on occasion of this solemnity being intended to celebrate the memory of one who, for reasons hard to discover, is looked on as the tutelar saint and patroness of music, had every possible advantage that the times afforded to recommend them: not only the most eminent masters in the science contributed their performance, but the gentlemen of the king's chapel, and of the choirs of St. Paul's and Westminster, lent their assistance, and the festival was announced in the London Gazette :† *and to give it a greater sanction, a sermon was annually for some years preached at the Church of St. Bride, Fleet-street.*

For the celebration of this solemnity Purcell composed his Te Deum and Jubilate, and also the

most curious painting of the saint, as also a stately monument, with a cumbent statue of her with her face downwards.

St. Cecilia is usually painted playing either on the organ or on the harp, singing as Chaucer relates thus :—

> And whiles that the organs made melodie,
> To God alone thus in her herte fong fhe,
> O Lorde my foul and eke my body gie
> Unwemmed left I confounded be.

Over and above this account there is a tradition of St. Cecilia, that she excelled in music, and that the angel, who was thus enamoured of her, was drawn down from the celestial mansions by the charms of her melody; this has been deemed authority sufficient for making her the patroness of music and musicians.

The legend of St. Cecilia has given frequent occasion to painters and sculptors to exercise their genius in representations of her, playing on the organ, and sometimes on the harp. Raphael has painted her singing with a regal in her hands; and Domenichino and Mignard singing and playing on the harp. And in the vault under the choir of St. Paul's cathedral, against one of the middle columns on the south side, is a fine white marble monument for Miss Wren, the daughter of Sir Christopher, wherein that young lady is represented on a bass relief, the work of Bird, in the character of St. Cecilia playing on the organ, a boy angel sustaining her book, under which are the following inscriptions :—

'M. S.

'Desideratissimæ Virginis Janæ Wren Clariss. Dom. Christophori 'Wren Filæ unicæ, Paternæ indolis literis deditæ, piæ, benevolæ, 'domisidæ, Arte Musica peritissimæ.

'Here lies the body of Miss. Jane Wren, only daughter of Sir 'Christopher Wren, Kt. by Dame Jane his wife, daughter of William 'Lord Fiz-William, Baron of Lifford in the kingdom of Ireland. Ob. 29 'Decemb. anno 1702, Ætat. 26.'

In this vault lies interred also Dr. Holder, who will be spoken of hereafter. As few are acquainted with this place of sepulture, this opportunity is taken to mention that in a book entitled ' A new View of London,' in two volumes octavo, 1708, it is said to be probably one of the most capacious, and every way curious vaults in the world.

A few words more touching the above-mentioned book are here added for the information of the curious reader, and will conclude what it is feared may by some be thought a tedious note.

It was written by Mr. Edward Hatton, surveyor to one of the Fire-offices in London, and the author of Comes Comercii, an Index to Interest and useful books. The duty of the author's employment obliged him to make surveys of houses in all parts of the city, and in the discharge thereof he took every opportunity of remarking what appeared to him most worthy of note. His View of London contains the names of squares, streets, lanes, &c., and a description of all public edifices; among these are the churches, which, he being very well skilled in architecture, are no where else so accurately described; and although in the book the monumental inscriptions are sometimes erroneously given, no one can see it, as he may almost every day, exposed to sale on stalls, but must regret that a work of such entertainment and utility is held so cheap.

† Of the several poems written on occasion of this solemnity, Dryden's Alexander's Feast has unquestionably the preference; though it has been remarked that the two concluding lines have the turn of an epigram. Without pretending to determine on their respective merits, here follows a list of as many others of them as are to be found in Dryden's Miscellany.

A Song for St. Cecilia's day, 1687. By Mr. Dryden, part IV. page 331. Set to music by Mr. Handel many years after it was written.

A Song for St. Cecilia's day, 1690. Written by Tho. Shadwell, Esq., composed by Mr. King, part IV. page 93.

An Ode for St. Cecilia's day, 1690, part VI. page 130.

An Ode for St. Cecilia's day, 1693, written by Mr. Tho. Yalden, and composed by Mr. Daniel Purcell, part IV. page 35.

A Hymn to Harmony, written in honour of St. Cecilia's day, 1701, by Mr. Congreve, set to music by Mr. John Eccles, master of her majesty's music, part IV. page 308.

A Song for St. Cecilia's day at Oxford. By Mr. Addison, part IV. page 20.

Besides these there is extant an Ode for St. Cecilia's day, 1708, by Mr. Pope, printed among his works.

---

1678, by Dr. Thomas Sprat, afterwards bishop of Rochester, in which, upon a reference to it, it appears that these solemnities had been usual before they were encouraged by a royal establishment.

The sermons continued to be preached at Bow church till the year 1697, when Dr. George Stanhope preached his sermon for the benefit of this charity at the cathedral church of St. Paul, at which time, as it is imagined, the thought was first suggested of a grand musical performance, as a joint motive to devotion and pity, with the eloquence of the preacher.

The annual feast of the sons of the clergy appears to be prior to their incorporation. In the London Gazette of November 22, 1677, is an advertisement of the annual feast of the sons of the clergy, to be held at Merchant Taylors' hall, on Thursday the twenty-ninth day of November then next.

Since the year 1697 there has been constantly an annual sermon, and also a grand musical service at the cathedral church of St. Paul to promote the ends of this charity; the most eminent divines of our church have in succession been the preachers, and the musical performance has received all the advantages that could possibly be derived from the assistance of the ablest of the faculty. For many years past it has been the practice of the stewards of the corporation to have at St. Paul's on the Tuesday preceding the day of the sermon, what is called a rehearsal of the performance, as also a collection for the charity.

* St. Cecilia, among Christians, is esteemed the patroness of music, for the reasons whereof we must refer to her history, as delivered by the notaries of the Roman church, and from them transcribed into the Golden Legend, and other books of the like kind. The story says that she was a Roman lady, born of noble parents, about the year 225. That notwithstanding she had been converted to Christianity, her parents married her to a young Roman nobleman named Valerianus, a pagan, who going to bed to her on the wedding night, *as the custom is,* says the book, was given to understand by his spouse that she was nightly visited by an angel, and that he must forbear to approach her, otherwise the angel would destroy him. Valerianus somewhat troubled at these words, desired he might see his rival the angel, but his spouse told him that was impossible, unless he would be baptised and become a Christian, which he consented to: after which returning to his wife, he found her in her closet at prayer, and by her side, in the shape of a beautiful young man, the angel cloathed with brightness. After some conversation with the angel, Valerianus told him that he had a brother named Tiburtius, whom he greatly wished to see a partaker of the grace which he himself had received; the angel told him that his desire was granted, and that shortly they should both be crowned with martyrdom. Upon this the angel vanished, but soon after showed himself as good as his word; Tiburtius was converted, and both he and his brother Valerianus were beheaded; Cecilia was offered her life upon condition that she would sacrifice to the deities of the Romans, but she refused, upon which she was thrown into a cauldron of boiling water, and scalded to death; though others say that she was stifled in a dry bath, *i. e.* an inclosure from whence the air was excluded, having a slow fire underneath it; which kind of death was sometimes inflicted among the Romans upon women of quality who were criminals. See the second Nonne's Tale in Chaucer, the Golden Legend, printed by Caxton, and the Lives of Saints by Peter Ribadeneyra, Priest of the Society of Jesus. Printed at St. Omer's in 1699.

Upon the spot where her house stood is a church, said to have been built by pope Urban I. who administered baptism to her husband and his brother; it is the church of St. Cecilia in Trastevere. Within is a musical entertainment performed for St. Cecilia's day above mentioned; the lattter was published, together with a second musical entertainment of Dr. Blow for the same anniversary, in the following year. The former was printed under the direction of Mrs. Purcell, but on so coarse a type, and with such evidences of inattention, as have subjected those who had the care of the publication to censure.*

The several works above-mentioned were composed with great labour and study, and with a view to the establishment of a lasting reputation; but there are others that is to say, hymns, in the Harmonia Sacra,† and single songs and ballad tunes to a very great number, in the printed collections of his time, which alone shew the excellencies of Purcell in vocal composition; even his rounds and catches, many whereof were composed and sung almost at the same instant, have all the merit which can be ascribed to that species of harmony. And here it may not be improper to mention an anecdote respecting one of them, which the communication of a friend to this work has enabled the author to give. The reverend Mr. Subdean Gostling played on the viol da gamba, and loved not the instrument more than Purcell hated it. They were very intimate, as must be supposed, and lived together upon terms of friendship; nevertheless, to vex Mr. Gostling, Purcell got some one to write the following mock eulogium on the viol,‡ which he set in the form of a round for three voices.

> Of all the instruments that are,
> None with the viol can compare :
> Mark how the strings their order keep,
> With a whet whet whet and a sweep sweep sweep;
> But above all this still abounds,
> With a zingle zingle zing, and a zit zan zounds.

Though the unsettled state of public affairs at the time when he lived, obliged almost every man to attach himself to one or other of the two contending parties, Purcell might have availed himself of that exemption which men of his peaceable· profession have always a right to insist on, but he seemed not disposed to claim it. In James the Second's time he sang down the Whigs, and in that of William, the Tories. It is true he did not, like William Lawes, sacrifice his life to the interests of a master who loved and had promoted him, but he possessed a kind of transitory allegiance; and when the former had attained to sovereignty, besides those gratuitous effusions of loyalty which his relation to the court disposed him to, could as easily celebrate the praises of William as James.

> ' His billet at the fire was found,
> ' Whoever was depos'd or crown'd.'

* Vide Preface to Dr. Croft's Anthems.

† The Harmonia Sacra is a collection in two books, of divine hymns and dialogues, set to music by music by Lock, Humphrey, Blow, Purcell, and others. The third edition, printed in 1714, is by far the best. In it are four anthems by Purcell, and three by Croft, Blow, and Clark. To the second book are verses addressed to Blow and Purcell by Dr. Sacheverell. Tate collected the words, and published them in a small volume without the music.

‡ It was first printed in the second book of the 'Pleasant Musical Companion,' published in 1701, and has been continued in most of the subsequent collections of Catches.

This indifference is in some degree to be accounted for by that mirth and good humour, which seem to have been habitual to him; and this perhaps is the best excuse that can be made for those connexions and intimacies with Brown and others, which show him not to have been very nice in the choice of his company. Brown spent his life in taverns and ale-houses; the Hole in the Wall in Baldwin's Gardens§ was the citadel in which he baffled the assaults of creditors and bailiffs, at the same time that he attracted thither such as thought his wit atoned for his profligacy. Purcell seems to have been of that number, and to merit censure for having prostituted his invention, by adapting music to some of the most wretched ribaldry that was ever obtruded on the world for humour. The house of Owen Swan, a vintner‖ in Bartholomew-lane, humorously called Cobweb-hall, was also a place of great resort with the musical wits of that day; as also a house in Wych-street, behind the New Church in the Strand, within time of memory known by a sign of Purcell's head, a half length; the dress a brown full-bottomed wig, and a green night-gown, very finely executed. the name of the person who last kept it as a tavern was Kennedy, a good performer on the bassoon, and formerly in the opera band.

But notwithstanding the intimacies above mentioned, he had connections that were honourable. The author of the Life of the Lord Keeper North, speaking of his lordship's skill in the science, and the delight he took in the practice of music, says that at his house in Queen-street his lordship had a concert, of which Mr. Purcell had the direction; and at that time of day concerts were so rare, that it required the assistance of no less than a master to keep four or five performers together : his scholars were the sons and daughters of the nobility and principal gentry in the kingdom, a circumstance which alone bespeaks the nature of his connexions, and the rank he held in his profession.

Of his performance on the organ we are able to say but little, there being no memorials remaining that can tend to gratify our curiosity in this respect, save a humorous rebus in Latin metre, written by one Mr. Tomlinson, and here inserted; in which it is intimated that he was not less admired for his performance than his compositions. The verses above alluded to were set to music in the form of a catch by Mr. Senton; they were first printed in

§ *A pretended privileged place. See Northhook.*

‖ In the Pleasant Musical Companion, printed in 1726, is a catch on this person, the words whereof are written by himself. A gentleman now living, who knew him, relates that the sign of his house was the Black Swan, and that he was parish-clerk of St. Michael's in Cornhill; that failing in his trade as a vintner in his latter years, he removed to a small house in St. Michael's-alley, and took to the selling of tobacco, trusting to the friendship of a numerous acquaintance; and that on his tobacco papers were the following lines composed by himself:—

> The dying Swan in sad and moving strains,
> Of his near end and hapless fate complains,
> In pity then your kind assistance give,
> Smoke of Swan's best, that the poor bird may live.

A like exhortation to lend assistance to this poor old man, is contained in the following epigram, written by one of his friends:—

> The aged Swan, opprest with time and cares,
> With Indian sweets his funeral prepares ;
> Light up the pile, thus he'll ascend the skies,
> And, Phœnix like, from his own ashes rise.

the second book of the Pleasant Musical Companion, published in 1701, and are as follow :—

> Galli marita, par tritico seges,
> Prænomen est ejus, dat chromati leges ;
> Intrat cognomen blanditiis Cati,
> Exit eremi in Ædibus stati,
> Expertum effectum omnes admirentur.
> Quid merent Poetæ ? ut bene calcentur.

Thus translated and set to music :—

> A mate to a cock, and corn tall as wheat,
> Is his Christian name who in musick's compleat :
> His surname begins with the grace of a cat,
> And concludes with the house of a hermit ; note that.
> His skill and performance each auditor wins,
> But the poet deserves a good kick on the shins.

Purcell died on the twenty-first day of November, 1695.* There is a tradition that his death was occasioned by a cold which he caught in the night, waiting for admittance into his own house. It is said that he used to keep late hours, and that his wife had given orders to his servants not to let him in after midnight : unfortunately he came home heated with wine from the tavern at an hour later than that prescribed him, and through the inclemency of the air contracted a disorder of which he died. If this be true, it reflects but little honour on Madam Purcell, for so she is styled in the advertisements of his works ; and but ill agrees with those expressions of grief for her dear lamented husband, which she makes use of to Lady *Elizabeth* Howard in the dedication of the Orpheus Britannicus.† It seems probable that the disease of which he died was rather a lingering than an acute one, perhaps a consumption ; and that, for some time at least, it had no way affected the powers of his mind, since one of the most celebrated of his compositions, the song ' From rosy bowers,' is in the printed book said to have been the last of his works, and to have been set during that sickness which put a period to his days. He was interred in Westminster Abbey. On a tablet fixed to a pillar, before which formerly stood the organ,‡ placed there by his patroness the

Lady Elizabeth Howard, is an inscription, which has been celebrated for its elegance, and is as follows :—

> ' Here lyes
> ' Henry Purcell, Esq. ;
> ' Who left this life,
> ' And is gone to that blessed place,
> ' Where only his harmony
> ' can be exceeded.
> ' Obiit 21mo. die Novembris,
> ' Anno Ætatis suæ 37mo,
> ' Annoq ; Domini 1695.'

Lady *Elizabeth* Howard had been a scholar of Purcell ; she was the eldest daughter of Thomas earl of Berkshire, and the wife of Dryden, who is plainly alluded to in the dedication of the Orpheus Britannicus. Many of his best compositions were made for her entertainment, and were recommended by her own performance. Purcell had set the music to King Arthur, and many other of Dryden's dramatic works. Dryden wrote an ode on his death which Dr. Blow set to music ; and Lady *Elizabeth* erected the tablet. From all these particulars the inference is not unnatural that Dryden was the author of the above inscription. On a flat stone over his grave was the following epitaph, now totally effaced :—

> Plaudite, felices superi, tanto hospite ; nostris
>    Præfuerat, vestris additur ille choris :
> Invida nec vobis Purcellum terra reposcat,
>    Questa decus seêli, deliciasque breves.
> Tam cito decessisse, modos cui singula debet
>    Musa, prophana suos religiosa suos.
> Vivit Io et vivat, dum vicina organa spirant,
>    Dumque colet numeris turba canora Deûm.

Thus translated :—

> Applaud so great a guest celestial pow'rs,
> Who now resides with you, but once was ours ;
> Yet let invidious earth no more reclaim
> Her short-liv'd fav'rite and her chiefest fame ;
> Complaining that so prematurely dy'd
> Good-nature's pleasure and devotion's pride.
> Dy'd ? no he lives while yonder organs sound,
> And sacred echos to the choir rebound.

The dwelling-house of Purcell was in a lane in Westminster, beyond the abbey, called St. Anne's lane, situated on the south side of Tothill-street, between Peter's-street and the east end of Orchard-street.§ It is presumed that he married young ; at least it is certain that he was a housekeeper at the age of twenty-five, for his first Sonatas, published in 1683, are in the London Gazette of June 11, in that year, advertised to be sold at his house above mentioned.

Of the circumstances of his family we have no kind of intimation, other than the acknowledgement of his widow to Lady Howard that her generosity had extended itself to his posterity, and that the favours she had entailed upon them were the most valuable part of their inheritance : from hence we may conclude that he had children living at the time

---

* Dr. Boyce, in the account of Purcell prefixed to his Cathedral Music, vol. II. says that he resigned his place of organist of Westminster-Abbey in 1693 ; but in this particular he seems to have been misinformed ; upon searching the treasurer's accounts for 1694, Purcell appears to have been then organist. Farther he is a subscribing witness to an agreement dated 20th July, 1694, between the dean and chapter of Westminster and Father Smith for repairing the abbey organ, and is therein called organist of the said church. The treasurer's accounts for 1695 are not to be found ; nor can any entry be found in the books or accounts of the abbey that will determine the question whether Purcell resigned or died in the office ; but upon the evidence above stated the latter is the more eligible supposition. As organist of the chapel royal he was succeeded by Mr. Francis Piggot, organist of the Temple ; and as organist of Westminster Abbey by Dr. Blow, who was his senior, and had been his master.

† Mr. Wanley in the Harleian Catalogue, No. 1272, giving an account of Stradella, says that when Purcell, who had only seen two or three of his compositions, heard that he was assassinated, and upon what account, he lamented him exceedingly ; nay, so far as to declare that he could have forgiven him an injury in that kind ; and then adds this reflection of his own, ' which those who remember how lovingly Mr. Purcell lived ' with his wife (or rather what a loving wife she proved to him) may ' understand without farther explication.'

‡ The customary place of interment for an organist is under the organ of his church. In Purcell's time, and long after, the organ of Westminster Abbey stood on the north side of the choir, and this was anciently the station of the organ in all churches. In Hollar's fine view of the inside of old St. Paul's in Sir William Dugdale's history of that cathedral, the organ is so situated, as it is at this day at Canterbury and the king's chapel. The reason of it was that the organist should not be obliged to turn his back to the altar. But this punctilio is now disregarded, and, which is extraordinary, even at the embassador's chapel in Lincoln's-Inn fields, where the organ stands at the west end, as in most churches in this kingdom.

§ There is a sort of curiosity in some readers which it is possible may be gratified by the following note. Dr. Heyther lived at Westminster in the same house with Camden. Dr. Christopher Gibbons in New-street, betwixt the Ambry [Almonry] and Orchard-street, Westminster. In the Gazette for July 6, 1671, he advertises the loss of a silver tankard from thence. Dr. Blow's house was in the Broad Sanctuary, Westminster : Jeremy Clark's dwelling was in St. Paul's churchyard, where now the Chapter-house stands.

of his decease, and that they were but ill provided for.* Of these we have been able to trace one only, viz., a son named Edward, who was bred to music, and in July 1726 was elected organist of the church of St. Margaret, Westminster.† He was also organist of the church of St. Clement, Eastcheap, London, and dying in the year 1740, was succeeded in that place by his son Henry, who had been bred up in the king's chapel under Mr. Gates. This Henry became also organist of the church of St. Edmund the King, London, and afterwards of that of St. John, Hackney. He died about twenty-five years ago. His father was a good organist, but himself a very indifferent one. Henry Purcell had two brothers, the one named Edward, whose history is contained in a monumental inscription on his grave-stone in the chancel of the church of Wightham, near Oxford, and here inserted ‡ The other was Daniel, a musician, who will be the subject of the next article.

The premature death of Purcell was a great afflic-tion to the lovers of his art. His friends, in conjunc-tion with his widow, for whom and his family he had not been able to make any great provision, were anxious to raise a monument of his fame. To that end they selected, chiefly from his compositions for the theatre, such songs as had met with a favourable reception, and by the help of a subscription of twenty shillings each person, published in the year 1698 that well-known work the Orpheus Britannicus, with a dedication to the author's good friend and patroness the above-mentioned Lady Howard, and commenda-tory verses by his brother Daniel, Mr. J. Talbot, fellow of Trinity college, Cambridge, Henry Hall, organist of Hereford, and other persons.§

It is conceived that the Orpheus Britannicus suffered not a little from the impatience of those who were contributors to the expense of it; for had due time been allowed, there would have been found among the author's compositions, particularly his music for plays, a great number of songs, for the omission whereof no reason but that above can be assigned. To go no farther, in the Tempest are many recita-tives and songs equally good with the best in the Orpheus Britannicus; and if this should be doubted, let the following, taken from that drama, and which has never yet been printed, speak for itself:—

AE - OLUS, you must ap - pear, my great commands to hear, rough . . . AE - o-lus ap-

1mo. & 2ndo.

- pear.

While these pass o'er the

---

* His will, dated the first day of November, 1695, recites that at the time of making it he was very *ill in constitution*, but of sound mind. In it no particular mention is made of his estate or effects, or of his children: it is in short a general devise to his loving wife Frances, and an appointment of her his executrix, and was proved by her in the prerogative court of the archbishop of Canterbury, on the seventh day of December, 1695.

† Upon an inspection of the parish books for the purpose of ascertain-ing this fact, it appears that the organ of this church was built by Father Smith in 1676, and that himself was the first organist there, and played for a salary.

‡ 'Here lyeth the body of EDWARD PURCELL, eldest son of Mr. 'PURCELL, gentleman of the royal chapel, and brother to Mr. HENRY 'PURCELL; so much renowned for his skill in musick. He was 'gentleman-usher to king Charles the 2nd. and lieutenant in Col. 'Trelawney's regiment of foot. in which for his many gallant actions in 'the wars of Ireland and Flanders, he was gradually advanced to the

'honour of lieutenant-colonel. He assisted Sir GEORGE ROOK in the 'taking of Gibraltar, and the prince of HESSE in the memorable 'defence of it. He followed that prince to Barcelona, was at the taking 'of Mount-joy, where that brave prince was killed; and continued to 'signalize his courage in the siege and taking of the city in the year '1705. He enjoyed the glory of his great services till the much 'lamented death of his late mistress queen ANNE, when, decayed with 'age, and broken with misfortunes, he retired to the house of the Right 'Hon. Montague earl of Abingdon, and died June 20th, 1717. Aged 64.

§ A second edition of the Orpheus Britannicus was published in 1702, in a better character than the former, and with the addition of above thirty songs; to make room for which some in the first edition are omitted. The additional songs were communicated by the Rev. Mr. George Lluellyn. This person had been a page of the back stairs in the reign of Charles II., and at court became acquainted with Purcell. Afterwards he entered into holy orders, and had a living near Shrewsbury.

HENRY PURCELL.

In the year 1702 was published a second edition of the Orpheus Britannicus, and also a second book; the editor of this latter was Henry Playford. It is dedicated to Charles Lord Halifax, and contains songs in the Fairy Queen, the Indian Queen, birthday songs,\* and other occasional compositions, together with that noble song, ' Genius of England.' This latter composition, which has an accompaniment for a trumpet, and is said to have been sung by Mr. Freeman and Mrs. Cibber, leads us to remark that Purcell was the first who composed songs with symphonies for that instrument; and that it is to be inferred from the many instances in the Orpheus Britannicus of songs so accompanied, that he had a great fondness for it, which is thus to be accounted for :—

In the royal household is an establishment of a sergeant and office of trumpets, consisting of the sergeant and sixteen trumpets in ordinary. The origin of this office may be traced back to the time of Edw. VI., when Benedict Browne was sergeant-trumpeter, with a salary of £24 6s. 8d. per ann. (see page 541 of this work.) The salary was afterwards augmented to £100, and so continues; but even thus increased, it bears but a small proportion to the perquisites or fees of office, some of which arise from creations of nobility, and even from the patents by which sheriffs are appointed.

In Purcell's time the serjeant was Matthias Shore. This man had a brother named William, a trumpeter, and also a son named John, who by his great ingenuity and application had extended the power of that noble instrument, too little esteemed at this day, beyond the reach of imagination, for he produced from it a tone as sweet as that of a hautboy. Matthias Shore had also a daughter, a very beautiful and amiable young woman, whom Purcell taught to sing and play on the harpsichord. Cibber was well acquainted with John Shore, and being one day on a visit to him at his house, happened to hear his sister at her harpsichord, and was so charmed with

\* Among these is the song ' May her blest example chase,' the bass whereof is the melody of the old ballad ' Cold and raw.' For the history of this composition vide ante page 564, in note.

her that he became her lover and married her. Cibber was then not quite twenty-two years of age, and, as himself confesses,† had no other income than twenty pounds a year allowed him by his father, and twenty shillings a week from the theatre,‡ which could scarce amount to above thirty pounds a year more. The marriage having been contracted against the consent of the lady's father, she and her husband were by him left to shift for themselves; upon which she took to the stage; and in a part in Don Quixote, together with Mr. Freeman, sang the song abovementioned, her brother performing the symphony on the trumpet.

## CHAP. CLVI.

To entertain an adequate idea of the merits of Purcell, we must view him in the different lights of

† Of this family the following is the farther history. William Shore succeeded Matthias, and survived him but a few years. By a note in Strype, [St. Martin's in the Fields, page 73,] it appears that he was buried in the old church of that parish. Old Mr. Shore was afterwards so far reconciled to his daughter, Mrs. Cibber, that he gave her a small fortune; the rest of what he was possessed of, he laid out in building a house on the bank of the Thames, which was called Shore's Folly, and has been demolished several years. John Shore the son succeeded his uncle in the office of Serjeant Trumpeter; and by the lists of the royal household it appears that in 1711 he had a place in the queen's band. At the public entry of king George I., in 1714, he rode as Serjeant Trumpeter in cavalcade, bearing his mace; and on the eighth day of August, 1715, upon a new establishment of gentlemen and additional performers in the king's chapel, was sworn and admitted to the place of lutenist therein. He was a man of humor and pleasantry, and was the original inventor of the tuning-fork, an instrument which he constantly carried about him, and used to tune his lute by, and which whenever he produced it gave occasion to a pun. At a concert he would say, ' I have ' not about me a pitch-pipe, but I have what will do as well to tune by, ' a pitch fork.' Some of his contemporaries in office, now living, give him the character of a well-bred gentleman, extremely courteous and obliging to all. It is said that he had the misfortune to split his lip in sounding the trumpet, and was ever after unable to perform on that instrument, and also to be engaged in contentious suits for the ascertaining of his fees; and that his bad success in some of them, disordered his understanding, insomuch that meeting one day with Dr. Croft in the Park, he would needs fight him. He died in the year 1753, and was succeeded in his place of Serjeant Trumpeter by Mr. Valentine Snow, and in that of lutenist to the chapel by Mr. John Immyns. His sister, Mrs. Cibber, was very much afflicted with an asthma, and died about the year 1730. These particulars respecting Cibber's marriage, and his wife's father, are related by his daughter, Mrs. Charlotte Charke, in a narrative of her life, published in 1755. *Mr. Snow died about ten years ago, and is the subject of the following humorous epitaph :—*
    *Thaw every breast, melt every eye with woe,*
    *Here's dissolution by the hand of death;*
    *To dirt, to water's turn'd the fairest Snow,*
    *O! the king's Trumpeter has lost his breath.*
             *Webb's Collection of Epitaphs Vol. II. page 4.*

‡ Apology for his Life, quarto, page 107.

a composer for the church, the theatre, and the chamber. He was not fond of services, and, excepting that sublime composition, his Te Deum and Jubilate, his services in B♭, and what is called his second or Benedicite service, in the same key, we know of no work of his of this kind extant. Anthems afforded more exercise for his invention, and in these his excellencies are beyond the reach of description: that of his to the words 'O give thanks,' is esteemed the most capital of them; but there are others, namely, 'O God thou art my God,' 'O God thou hast cast us 'out,' 'O Lord God of hosts,' 'Behold I bring you 'glad tidings,' 'Be merciful unto me O God,'* and 'My song shall be alway of the loving kindness of 'the Lord,' a solo anthem, composed on purpose for Mr. Gostling; which are in a style so truly pathetic and devout, that they can never be heard without rapture by those who are sensible of the powers of harmony: and so finely were his harmonies and melodies adapted to the general sense of mankind, that all who heard were enamoured of them. Brown in one of his Letters mentions that the cathedrals were crowded whenever an anthem of Purcell was expected to be sung.

Of his compositions for the theatre we are enabled to form some judgement, from those parts of them that are published in the Orpheus Britannicus; of these the music to King Arthur seems to have been the most admired: the frost scene in that drama, and the very artful commixture of semitones therein, contrived to imitate that shivering which is the effect of extreme cold, have been celebrated by the pen of Mr. Charles Gildon, in his Laws of Poetry; but doubtless the most perfect of his works of this sort are the music to the Tempest, the Indian Queen, and Œdipus. The former of these plays, in compliance with the very corrupt taste of the times, was altered by Sir William D'avenant and Dryden from Shakespeare, who, as if they had formed their judgment of dramatic poesy rather on the precepts of Mons. Quintinye, than of Aristotle, and thought that the exact regularity observed in the planning of the gardens of that day, afforded a good rule for the conduct of the drama, chose that the characters of Caliban and Miranda should each have a counterpart, and accordingly have given us a Sycorax, a female savage; and Hyppolito, a man that never saw a woman.

It is said that Dryden wrote his Alexander's Feast with a view to its being set by Purcell, but that Purcell declined the task, as thinking it beyond the power of music to express sentiments so superlatively energetic as that ode abounds with. The truth of this assertion may well be questioned, seeing that he composed the Te Deum, and scrupled not to set to music some of the most sublime passages in the Psalms, the Prophecy of Isaiah, and other parts of holy scripture; not to mention that Mr. Thomas Clayton, he that set Mr. Addison's opera of Rosamond, who was the last in the lowest class of musicians, saw nothing in Alexander's Feast to deter him from setting and performing it at the great room in

Villiers-street, York-buildings, in 1711, Sir Richard Steele and he being then engaged in an undertaking to perform concerts at that place for their mutual benefit.† But Clayton's composition met with the contempt it deserved; and the injury done by him to this admirable poem was amply repaired by Mr. Handel.

As to the chamber-music of Purcell, it admits of a division into vocal and instrumental; the first class includes songs for one two and three voices; those for a single voice, though originally composed for the stage, were in truth Cantatas, and perhaps they are the truest models of perfection in that kind extant; among the principal of these are 'From rosy bowers,' sung by Mrs. Cross in the character of Altisidora, in the third part of Don Quixote; and that other 'From silent shades;' to which we may add the incantation in the Indian Queen, 'Ye 'twice ten hundred deities,' with the song that follows it, 'Seek not to know what must not be revealed;' and that bass song sung by Cardenio in Don Quixote, 'Let the dreadful engines of eternal will.'‡ Nor can less with justice be said of his songs for two voices, particularly 'Sing all ye Muses,' 'When 'Myra sings,' 'Fair Chloe my breast so alarms,' and others: as to his dialogues 'Since times are 'so bad,' and 'Now the maids and the men,' they are songs of humour, and in a style so peculiarly his own, that we know not to what test of comparison they can be brought, or how to judge of them, otherwise than by their own intrinsic excellence.

Other compositions of his there are of a class different from those above mentioned, as ballads and catches, of which he made many. The air 'What 'shall I do to show how much I love her,' in the opera of Dioclesian; 'If love's a sweet passion,' in the Fairy Queen;§ and another printed in Comes Amoris, book IV. song I. to the words 'No, no, 'poor suff'ring heart,' are ballads, and perhaps the finest of the kind ever made. Of Catches it may be said that they are no more the test of a musician's abilities than an epigram is of a poet's; nevertheless each has its peculiar merit: and of the catches of Purcell it may be said, that they have every excellence that can recommend that species of vocal harmony.

As Purcell is chiefly celebrated for his vocal compositions, it may perhaps be conceived that in the

---

† Life of Mr. John Hughes prefixed to his poems.

‡ Of the two compositions last above mentioned we are able here to give the judgment of foreigners. When the Italian musicians, who came hither with the princess of Modena, king James the Second's queen, became acquainted with our language, they discovered great beauties in Purcell's recitative; and it is said on very good authority, that the notes to the words in the song, 'Seek not to know, &c.,

    'Enquire not then who shall from bonds be freed,

    'Who 'tis shall wear a crown, and who shall bleed,'

charmed them to astonishment.

And touching the other, a reverend divine, a member of a cathedral choir, a great lover and an excellent judge of music, communicates the following anecdote. 'A very eminent master in London told me that a 'disciple of his, who went by his advice to Italy for improvement of his 'studies in music, at his first visit to him after his return mentioned his 'having heard Purcell talked of as a great composer, and desired his 'opinion of him; for an answer the master sat down to the harpsichord, 'and performed this song. The young gentleman was so struck when 'he heard the passage "Can nothing warm me," that he did not know 'how to express his admiration, but by crying out he had never heard 'music before.'

* Usually sung at Westminster Abbey on the 30th of January.

§ Printed among his Ayres, page 12.

original performance of them they derived considerable advantages, and that the singers, like the actors of that day, had abilities superior to those of the present; but this, as far as the inquiry can be traced, was not the fact: before the introduction of the Italian opera into England the use of the vocal organs was but little understood; and as to what is called a fine manner, the best singers were as much strangers to it as they were to the shake, and those many nameless graces and elegances in singing now so familiar to us; for which reason it is that we see in many of Purcell's songs the graces written at length, and made a part of the composition. From all which it may be inferred that the merit of the singers in and about this time rested chiefly in that perfection which is common to all ages, a fine voice. Those among them who seem to have been most liberally endowed with this gift, were, of men, Mr. James Bowen, Mr. Harris, Mr. Freeman, and Mr. Pate, all actors and singers at the theatres;* and Mr. Damascene, Mr. Woodson, Mr. Turner, and Mr. Bouchier, gentlemen of the chapel;† and of women, Mrs. Mary Davis, Miss Shore, afterwards Mrs. Cibber, Mrs. Cross, Miss Campion, and Mrs. Anne Bracegirdle.‡

* None of the men abovementioned are greatly celebrated as singers, their chief praise being that they were excellent actors, especially Harris, who is highly spoken of by Downes.

† The gentlemen of the chapel about this time were used occasionally to assist in musical performances on the stage, but queen Anne, thinking the practice indecent, forbad it.

‡ Mrs. Davis was one of those female actresses who boarded with Sir William D'avenant in his house. Downes relates that she acted the part of Celania, a shepherdess, in a play called the Rivals, said to have been written by him; and in it sang, in the character of a shepherdess mad for love, the following song:—

> My lodging it is on the cold ground,
>   and very hard is my fare;
> But that which troubles me most is
>   the unkindness of my dear;
> Yet still I cry, O turn love,
>   and I prethee love turn to me,
> For thou art the man that I long for,
>   and alack what remedy!
>
> I'll crown thee with a garland of straw then,
>   and I'll marry thee with a rush ring,
> My frozen hopes shall thaw then,
>   and merrily we will sing;
> O turn to me my dear love,
>   and I prethee love turn to me,
> For thou art the man that alone canst
>   procure my liberty.
>
> But if thou wilt harden thy heart still,
>   and be deaf to my pittyful moan,
> Then I must endure the smart still,
>   and tumble in straw all alone;
> Yet still I cry, O turn love,
>   and I prethee love turn to me,
> For thou art the man that alone art
>   the cause of my misery.

Which king Charles the Second hearing, he was so pleased that he took her off the stage, and had a daughter by her, who was named Mary Tudor, and was married to Francis lord Ratcliffe, afterwards earl of Derwentwater. Mrs. Davis was also a fine dancer; she danced with Mr. Priest an Entrée in a masque in the last act of Dryden's comedy of Feigned Innocence, or Sir Martin Mar-all, and was greatly applauded. Of Miss Shore mention has already been made. Mrs. Cross was a celebrated actress, especially in those characters in which singing was required. She acted the part of Altisidora in the third part of Don Quixote, and in that character sang the song 'From rosy bowers.' The history of Mrs. Bracegirdle is well known. She it seems had a fine voice, and acted the part of Marcella in the second part of Don Quixote, and in it sang the song 'I burn, I burn,' set to music by Mr. John Eccles. In the Orpheus Britannicus is a song in which she is celebrated for her performance of this character. Miss Campion was a young woman of low extraction, unhappy in a beautiful person and a fine voice. William the first duke of Devonshire took her off the stage, and made her his mistress. She died in May 1706, in the nineteenth year of her age; and the duke, who was then in his sixty-sixth, buried her in the church of Latimers, the seat of his family in the county of Bucks. In the chancel of that church he erected a monument for her, on which is a Latin inscription, importing that she was wise above her years, bountiful to the poor, even beyond her abilities; and at the playhouse, where she sometime acted, modest

His music for instruments consists of overtures, act-tunes, and dance-tunes composed for the theatre, and the two sets of Sonatas for violins, of the publication whereof mention is above made. These compositions are greatly superior to any of the kind published before his time; and if they fall short of his other works, the failure is to be attributed to the state of instrumental music in his time, which was hardly above mediocrity. For although Ferabosco, Coperario, and Jenkins, in their compositions for viols had carried the music for those instruments in concert to great perfection, upon the introduction of the violin into this kingdom these were disregarded, and the English musicians, namely, Rogers, Porter, Child, Lock, and others, set themselves to compose little airs in three and four parts for violins and a bass. Jenkins indeed composed a set of Sonatas for those instruments, and so did Godfrey Finger some years after; but of these works the chief merit was their novelty.

Neither does it appear that in Italy the improvements in instrumental had kept an equal pace with those of vocal music. In a general view of the state of instrumental music towards the end of the last century, it will appear to have been wanting in spirit and force: in the melody and harmony it was too purely diatonic; and, in regard to the contexture of parts, too nearly approaching to counterpoint. In France Lully invented that energetic style which distinguishes his overtures, and which Handel himself disdained not to adopt; and in Italy Corelli introduced a variety of chromatic, or at least semitonic combinations and passages, which, besides that they had the charm of novelty to recommend them, gave a greater latitude to his modulation, and allowed a wider scope for invention: nor was the structure of his compositions less original than delightful; fugues well sustained, and answering at the properest intervals through all the parts; fine syncopations, and elegant transitions from key to key; basses, with the sweetest harmony in the very melody; these are the characteristics of Corelli's compositions, but these Purcell lived rather too early to profit by. Doubtless, therefore, Lully and Corelli are to be looked on as the first great improvers of that kind of instrumental harmony which for full half a century

and untainted; that, being taken with a hectic fever, with a firm confidence and christian piety she submitted to her fate, and that William duke of Devonshire upon her beloved remains had erected that tomb as sacred to her memory. Dr. White Kennet, afterwards bishop of Peterborough, preached the funeral sermon of this noble personage, and published memoirs of his family, representing him in both, as also in his complete History of England, as no less distinguished by his virtues than his titles, the chief reason whereof, seems to be that the duke styled himself a hater of tyrants, and was a great instrument in the Revolution. Notwithstanding which, a general indignation rose in the minds of all sober and good men against the duke and his panegyrist, the one for the shameless insult on virtue and good manners, contained in the above inscription, the other for his no less shameless prostitution of his eloquence, in an endeavour to confound the distinctions between moral good and evil, and represent as worthy of imitation a character, which in one very essential particular is justly to be abhorred. It is said that the duke repented of his past life, and it is to be hoped, though there is no evidence of it, that in the number of his errors his conduct in the above instance was included.

To the account already extant of Mrs. Bracegirdle it may be added, that in the latter part of her life she dwelt in the family of Francis Chute, Esq., one of his majesty's learned counsel, his house being then in Norfolk-street in the Strand. She died on the twelfth day of September, 1748, in the eighty-fifth year of her age, and lies buried in the east ambulatory of the cloister of Westminster Abbey, under a black marble stone, the inscription on which is all, except her name, effaced.

has been practised and admired throughout Europe. The works of the latter of these were not published until a few years before Purcell's death, so that unless we suppose that he had seen them in manuscript, it may be questioned whether they ever came to his hands ;* and therefore who those famed Italian masters were whom he professes to have imitated in the composition of his first sonatas, we are at a loss to discover.

And yet there are those who think that, in respect of instrumental composition, the difference between Purcell and Corelli is less than it may seem. Of the Golden Sonata the reputation is not yet extinct ; there are some now living who can scarce speak of it without rapture : and Dr. Tudway of Cambridge, in that letter of his to his son, which has so often been quoted in the course of this work, has not scrupled to say of it that it equals if not exceeds any of Corelli's sonatas. Which sentiment, whether it be just or not, the reader may determine by the help of the score here inserted :—

## SONATA.

* In the London Gazette,' Numb. 3116, for September 23, 1695, is the following advertisement : 'Twelve Sonatas (newly come over from Rome) 'in 3 parts, composed by Signeur Archangelo Corelli, and dedicated to 'his Highness the Elector of Bavaria, this present year 1694, are to be 'had fairly prick'd from the true original, at Mr. Ralph Agutter's, Musical 'Instrument Maker, over-against York-Buildings in the Strand, London.' Upon the face of this advertisement it may be questioned whether the book to which it refers was then printed or not, but it is pretty clear from the expression ' prick'd from the true original,' which means the notation of music by writing, in contradistinction to printing, that the copy above mentioned was a manuscript one. And it is certain that for some years, that is to say, till about 1710, when the elder Walsh first printed them on pewter plates, the Sonatas of Corelli were circulated through this kingdom in manuscript copies.

HENRY PURCELL.

Whatever encomiums may have been bestowed elsewhere, as namely, on Coperario, Lawes, Laneare, and others, it is certain that we owe to Purcell the introduction amongst us of what we call fine air, in contradistinction to that narrow, contracted melody, which appears in the compositions of his predecessors : the first effort of this kind was the Ariadne of Henry Lawes, between which and the ' Rosy bowers' of Purcell the difference in point of merit is immeasurable. It has already been mentioned, and Purcell has expressly said, that in his compositions he imitated the style of the Italians;* and there is good ground to suppose he sedulously contemplated the works of Carissimi and Stradella: how far he profited by their example, and to what degree of perfection he improved vocal music in this countr , those only know who are competently skilled in this divine science, and have studied his works with that care and attention which they will ever be found to merit.

DANIEL PURCELL was a brother of the former, and from him derived most of that little reputation which as a musician he possessed. It does not appear that he was educated in any choir, or that he stood in any

degree of relation to the church other than that of organist; so that unless we suppose him to have been a scholar of his brother, we are at a loss to guess who was his instructor in the science. He was for some time organist of Magdalen college, Oxford, and afterwards of St. Andrew's Church in Holborn.† He was one of the candidates for a prize payable out of the sum of 200l. raised by some of the nobility, to be distributed amongst musicians. The design of this act of bounty will be best explained by the following advertisement respecting it, published in the London Gazette, No. 3585, for March 21, 1699 :—'Several persons of quality having ' for the encouragement of musick advanced 200 ' guineas, to be distributed in 4 prizes, the first of ' 100, the second of 50, the third of 30, and the ' fourth of 20 guineas, to such masters as shall

* The very explicit declarations to this purpose in the dedication of his first sonatas. and of his opera of Dioclesian, are enough to silence for ever those, who, knowing nothing either of him or his works, assert that the music of Purcell is different from the Italian, and entirely English.

† The occasion of his coming to London was as follows : Dr. Sacheverell, who had been a friend of his brother Henry, having been presented to the living of St. Andrew Holborn, found an organ in the church, of Harris's building, which, having never been paid for, had from the time of its erection in 1699, been shut up. The doctor upon his coming to the living, by a collection from the parishioners, raised money to pay for it, but the title to the place of organist was litigious, the right of election being in question between the rector, the vestry, and the parish at large: Nevertheless he invited Daniel Purcell to London, and he accepted it; but in February, 1717, the vestry, which in that parish is a select one, thought proper to elect Mr. Maurice Greene, afterwards Dr. Greene, in preference to Purcell, who submitted to stand as a candidate. In the year following Greene was made organist of St. Paul's, and Daniel Purcell being then dead, his nephew Edward was a candidate for the place, but it was conferred on Mr. John Isum, who died in June 1726.

'be adjudged to compose the best; this is therefore 'to give notice, that those who intend to put in for 'the prizes are to repair to Jacob Tonson at Grays-'Inn-gate, before Easter next day, where they may 'be further informed.'

It is conjectured that the earl of Halifax was a liberal contributor to the fund out of which these sums were proposed to be paid.* The poem given out as the subject of the musical composition was the Judgment of Paris, written by Mr. Congreve. Weldon, Eccles, and Daniell Purcell were three of the competitors;† the two former obtained prizes, and we may suppose that the latter was in some degree successful, seeing that he was at the expense of publishing his work in score.

Daniel Purcell composed also the music to an opera entitled Brutus of Alba, or Augusta's Triumph, written by George Powell, the Comedian, and performed in 1697 at the theatre in Dorset-garden. A collection of single songs from this opera, with the music, is in print. He composed also songs for plays to a very great number; sundry of them, but without the basses, are in the Pills to purge Melancholy. In general they have but little to recommend them, and Daniel Purcell is at this day better known by his puns, with which the jest-books abound, than by his musical compositions.

## CHAP. CLVII.

WILLIAM HOLDER (a Portrait), doctor in divinity, a canon of Ely, a residentiary of St. Paul's, and subdean of the chapel royal, a person of great learning and sagacity, was the author of a treatise of the natural grounds and Principles of Harmony, octavo, 1694; as also a tract entitled the Elements of Speech, and a discourse concerning time, with application of the natural day, lunar month, and solar year. He is said to have taught the use of speech to a young gentleman, Mr. Alexander Popham, born deaf and dumb, by a method which he relates in an apendix to his Elements of Speech; but it seems that Mr. Popham was afterwards sent to Dr. Wallis, who had done the same thing by another young person; and upon Mr. Popham's being made able to speak, Dr. Wallis claimed the merit of it in a paper published in the Philosophical Transactions, which Dr. Holder answered.ᵇ The wife of Dr. Holder, Susanna, the sister of Sir Christopher Wren, was not less famous than her husband for cures of another kind, it being related of her in the inscription on her sepulchral monument that 'in compassion to the 'poor she applied herself to the knowledge of me-'dicinal remedies, wherein God gave so great a 'blessing, that thousands were happily healed by 'her, and no one ever miscarried; and that king 'Charles the Second, queen Catherine, and very 'many of the court had also experience of her suc-'cessful hand.§

It will appear by the account hereafter given of Dr. Holder's treatise on harmony, that he was very deeply skilled in the theory, and well acquainted with the practice of music. In the chapel and the cathedrals where his duty required him to attend, he was a strict disciplinarian, and, for being very exact in the performance of choral service, and frequently reprimanding the choir-men for their negligence in it, Michael Wise was used to call him Mr. Snub-dean. He died at his house in Amen-corner, in London, on the twenty-fourth day of January, 1696, aged eighty-two, and lies buried in the vault under the choir of St. Paul's cathedral, with a marble monument, on which is the following inscription :—

'H. S. E.

'Gulielmus Holder, S. T. P. Sacelli Regalis Sub-'decanus Sereniss. Regiæ Majestati Subeleemosi-'narius Ecclesiæ Sti Pauli et Eliens. Canonicus, 'Societatis Regiæ Lond. Sodalis, &c. Amplis quidem 'Titulis donatus amplissimis dignus. Vir per ele-'gantis et amœni ingenii Scientias Industriâ suâ 'illustravit, Liberalitate promovit, egregie eruditus 'Theologicis, Mathematicis, et Arte Musica, Me-'moriam excolite posteri et â Lucubrationibus suis 'editis Loquelæ Principia agnoscite et Harmoniæ. 'Obiit 24 Jan. 1697.'

The treatise of the natural grounds and principles of harmony is divided into chapters. In the first the author treats of sound in general, how it is produced and propagated.

Chap. II. is on the subject of sound harmonic, the first and great principle whereof is shewn to be, that the tune of a note, to speak in our vulgar phrase, is constituted by the measure and proportion of vibrations of the sonorous body, that is to say, of the velocity of those vibrations in their recourses, whether the same be a chord, a bell, a pipe, or the animal larynx. After explaining with great perspicuity Galileo's doctrine of pendulums, he supposes for his purpose the chord of a musical instrument to resemble a double pendulum moving upon two centres, the nut and the bridge, and vibrating with the greatest range in the middle of its length.

Chap. IV. He makes a concord to consist in the coincidence of the vibrations of the chords of two instruments, and speaks to this purpose :—If the vibrations correspond in every course and recourse, the concord produced will be the unison, if the ratio of the vibrations be as 2 to 1, in which case they will unite alternately, viz., at every course, crossing at the recourse, the concord will be the octave. If the vibrations be in the ratio of 3 to 2, their sounds will consort in a fifth, uniting after every second, i. e. at every other or third course; and if as 4 to 3, in a diatessaron or fourth, uniting after every third recourse, viz., at every fourth course, and so of the other consonances according to their respective ratios.

---

* This is hinted at in the dedication of the second book of the Orpheus Britannicus.

† Jerry Clark being asked why he did not compose for the prize, gave for answer that the nobility were to be the judges, leaving the querist to make the inference.

‡ Fasti Oxon. vol. II. col. 139.

§ This inscription seems to allude to a cure which corresponds with the following anecdote. Mrs. Holder was recommended to Charles II. to cure a sore finger that he had; the king put himself under her care, and while she was dressing it, the serjeant surgeon came in, and enquiring what she was about, the king gave him his finger; the surgeon upon looking at it, said 'Oh, this sore is nothing:' 'I know very well (said 'the king) it is nothing, but I know as well that of it you would have 'made something, which was what I meant to prevent, by committing 'myself to the care of this good lady.'

GUILIELMUS HOLDER S.T.P. SACELLI REGALIS SUBDECANUS SERENISSIMI

REGIÆ MAJESTATI SUBELEEMOSYNARIUS ECCLESIARIUM

SANCTI PAULI ET ELIENSIS CANONICUS SOCIETATIS REGIÆ

LONDINENSIS SODALIS MDCLXXXIII.

MRS. ARABELLA HUNT.

In Chap. V. he treats of the three sorts of proportion, namely, arithmetical, geometrical, and that mixed proportion resulting from the former two, called harmonical proportion. Under the head of geometrical proportion, the author considers the three species of multiplex, superparticular, and superpartient, already explained in the course of this work, and gives the rules for finding the habitudes of rations or proportions, as also a medium or mediety between the terms of any ration, by addition, subtraction, multiplication, and division of rations, forming thereby a praxis of musical arithmetic.

In Chap. VI. entitled of Discords and Degrees, the author digresses to the music of the ancients, touching which he seems to acquiesce in the opinion of Kircher and Gassendus, that the Greeks never used concert music, i. e. of different parts at once, but only solitary, for one single voice or instrument; which music he says by the elaborate curiosity and nicety of contrivance of degrees, and by measures, rather than by harmonious consonancy and by long studied performance, was more proper to make great impressions upon the fancy, and operate accordingly as some historians relate. Whereas, adds he, ours more sedately affects the understanding and judgment, from the judicious contrivance and happy composition of melodious consort. He concludes this sentiment with an assertion that the diatonic genus of music is founded in the natural grounds of harmony; but not so, or not so regularly, the chromatic or enarmonic kinds, of which nevertheless he gives an accurate designation, concluding with a scheme from Alypius of the characters used in the notation of the ancient Greek music, with their several powers.

In the conclusion of this work he gives as a reason why some persons do not love music, a discovery of the famous Dr. Willis, to wit, that there is a certain nerve in the brain which some persons have and some have not.

The above-mentioned treatise of Dr. Holder is written with remarkable accuracy; there is in it no confusion of terms; all that it teaches is made clear and conspicuous, and the doctrines contained in it are such as every musician ought to be master of; and much more of the theory of music he need not know.

It appears that besides a profound knowledge in the theory of music, Dr. Holder was possessed of an eminent degree of skill in the science of practical composition. In a noble collection of church-music, in the hand-writing of Dr. Thomas Tudway, now in the British Museum, of which an account will hereafter be given, is an anthem for three voices in the key of C with the greater third, to the words 'Praise our God ye people,' by Dr. William Holder.

MRS. ARABELLA HUNT, *(a Portrait )*, celebrated for her beauty, but more for a fine voice and an exquisite hand on the lute, lived at this time, and was the person for whom many of the songs of Blow and Purcell were composed. She taught the princess Anne of Denmark to sing; and was much favoured by queen Mary, who, for the sake of having Mrs.

Hunt near her, bestowed on her an employment about her person, and would frequently be entertained in private with her performance, even of common popular songs.* A gentleman now living, the son of one who used frequently to sing with her, remembers to have heard his father say, that Mrs. Hunt's voice was like the pipe of a bullfinch. She was unfortunate in her marriage : nevertheless she lived irreproachably, and maintained the character of a modest and virtuous woman; the reputation whereof, together with her accomplishments, rendered her a welcome visitant in the best families in the kingdom. In the summer season she was much at the house of Mr. Rooth, at Epsom. This gentleman had married the dowager of the second earl of Donegal, and being very fond of music, had frequent concerts there. In a letter from Mr. Rooth to Mr. John Hughes, the author of the Siege of Damascus, he tells him that Mrs. Hunt is at his house, and waits to see him, and hopes he will bring Signor Corelli with him.†

Mrs Hunt died on the twenty-sixth day of December, 1705. Mr. Congreve has celebrated her in an ode entitled 'On Mrs. Arabella Hunt singing,' and in the following lines, written after her decease, under the picture of her by Kneller :—

> Were there on earth another voice like thine,
> Another hand so blest with skill divine,
> The late afflicted world some hopes might have
> And harmony retrieve thee from the grave.

In the foregoing account respecting the English church musicians, frequent occasion has occurred to mention their appointments to places in the royal chapel. The term royal chapel means in general the chapel in each of the royal palaces, but in common speech it is taken for that of Whitehall. This makes it necessary to relate a melancholy accident that happened near the end of the last century, which was followed by a translation of the royal residence, and may in some sort be considered as a new era in the history of church-music.

The palace of Whitehall was originally built by Cardinal Wolsey. On his attainder it became forfeited to the crown, and was the town residence of our princes from Henry VIII. down to William and Mary : it was a spacious building, in a style somewhat resembling Christ Church college, Oxford, and the chapel was a spacious and magnificent room. On the fifth day of January, 1698, by the carelessness, as it is said, of some of the servants in the laundry, the whole of it was consumed,‡ and the king and queen necessitated to take up their residence at St.

---

* Vide ante, page 564, in note, the story of her singing, at the queen's request, the old ballad of 'Cold and raw,' and Purcell's revenge on the queen for it.

† Meaning the Sonatas of Corelli, then but lately published.

‡ This edifice narrowly escaped a total demolition by fire on the ninth day of April, 1691. The circumstances are thus related in a letter from Mr. Pulteney to Sir W. Colt, cited in the Continuation of Rapin's History of England, vol. I. page 171. 'It began about eight o'clock at night, by 'the negligence of a maid servant, who (to save the pains of cutting a 'candle from a pound) burnt one off, and threw the rest down carelessly 'before the flame was out, at the lower end of the stone gallery, in those 'lodgings which were the duchess of Portsmouth's, and burnt very vio- 'lently till four the next morning, during which time almost all the stone 'gallery and buildings behind it, as far as the Thames, were consumed, 'and one or two men killed by the buildings that were blown up.'

James's, where there was neither room sufficient to receive, nor accommodations for, half the household.*

Concerning the palace of St. James, it is said by Stow, Newcourt, and others, that it was formerly, even before the time of the Conquest, an hospital founded by the citizens of London for fourteen sisters, maidens that were leprous, living chastely and honestly in divine service.

' This hospital was surrendered to king Hen. VIII. ' in 23 of his reign, being then valued at 100l. per ' ann.   The sisters being compounded with, were al- ' lowed pensions for term of their lives, and the king

' built there a goodly mannor, annexing thereunto a ' park, inclosed about with a wall of brick, now ' called St. James's Park, which hath been of late ' years (to wit) soon after the restauration, very much ' improved and beautified with a canal, ponds, and ' curious walks between rows of trees, by king ' Charles II. and since that very much enlarged, and ' the whole encompassed round with a brick wall by ' the same king, and serves indifferently to the two ' palaces of St. James and White-hall.'   Newcourt's Repertorium, vol. I. page 662.   Stow's Survey, edit. 1633, page 495.

## BOOK XVII.

In tracing the progress of music in this country, it is found that the compositions of our most celebrated masters were calculated either for the service of the church, for theatric entertainment, or for private chamber practice.  Those persons who understood or professed to love music had their meetings in divers

* The places of the royal residence from time to time are very indistinctly noted by our historians, the inquiry into them is a subject of some curiosity, and not unworthy the attention of an antiquary : the most ancient that we know of was the palace of Edward the Confessor, adjoining to the monastery of Westminster, the site whereof is now called Old Palace yard.  In this was the Aula Regia, in which were holden the courts of justice.  William Rufus built Westminster-hall, as it is said, to rid his house of so great and troublesome assemblies ; and it is further said that he meditated building near it a new palace, which design of his gave name to New Palace-yard.  Nevertheless the succeeding kings down to Henry VIII. continued to dwell in the old palace.

Whitehall was originally built by Hubert de Burgh, earl of Kent, and justiciary of England, and afterwards became the inn or town residence of the archbishops of York.  Wolsey re-edified it, but being convicted of a premunire, anno 1529, it was, 21 Henry VIII. by Sir Thomas More, lord chancellor, the duke of Norfolk, and certain other great officers, recovered to them and their heirs for the use of the king against the cardinal, by the name of York-place, and they by charter delivered and confirmed the same to the king, which charter, dated 7 Feb. 21 Hen. VIII. is now extant among the records at Westminster.  Strype, book VI. page 5.

After this, Henry VIII. removed his dwelling from the old palace near the monastery of St. Peter Westminster to Whitehall, and that because the old palace was then, and had been a long time before, in utter ruin and decay, as it is expressed in an act of parliament, 28 Hen. VIII. cap. 12, and that the king had lately obtained this Whitehall, which is styled in the same act, ' One great mansion, place and house, being parcel of ' the possessions of the archbishoprick of York, situate in the town of ' Westminster, not much distant from the same ancient palace ; and that ' he had lately upon the soil of the said mansion, place and house, and ' upon the ground thereunto belonging, most sumptuously and curiously ' builded and edified many and distinct beautiful, costly, and pleasant ' lodgings, buildings, and mansions, for his grace's singular pleasure, ' comfort, and commodity, to the honour of his highness and his realm. ' And thereunto adjoining had made a park, walled and environed with ' brick and stone ; and there devised and ordained many and singular ' commodious things, pleasures, and other necessaries, apt and convenient ' to appertain to so noble a prince for his pastime and solace.'

By the said act the whole limits of the royal palace are set out and described, namely, ' That all the said soil, ground, mansion, and buildings, ' and the park, and also the soil of the ancient palace, should be from ' thenceforth the king's whole palace at Westminster, and so be taken, ' deemed, and reputed, and to be called and named the king's palace at ' Westminster for ever.   And that the said palace should extend, and be ' as well within the soil and places before limited and appointed, as also ' in all the street or way leading from Charing Cross unto the Sanctuary- ' gate at Westminster ; and to all the houses, buildings, lands, and ' tenements on both sides of the same street or way from the said Cross ' unto Westminster-hall, between the water of the Thames on the east ' part, and the said park-wall on the west part, and so through all the ' limits of the old palace.'

Before this time, besides the old palace at Westminster, our princes had sundry places of residence, as namely the Tower, the Old Jewry, where Henry VI. dwelt ; Baynard's Castle, the habitation of Henry VII. Tower Royal, of Rich. II. and Stephen ; the Wardrobe in Carter-lane, of Rich. III.   Hen. VII. lived also at Bridewell, and Elizabeth at Whitehall, and also at Somerset House.  Of their summer palaces, namely Windsor, Hampton-Court, Shene, Greenwich, Eltham, and others, frequent mention is made in history.

In the reign of James I. Inigo Jones made a design for a new palace at Whitehall, but the only part of it ever built was the Banqueting-house as it now appears.  One Cavendish Weedon, a member of Lincoln's-Inn, of whom farther mention will be made hereafter, published a proposal for rebuilding it in seven years, at an expence not exceeding 600,000l. as also a scheme for raising the money.  Vide Strype's Continuation of Stow's Survey of London, book VI. page 6.

## CHAP. CLVIII.

parts of the kingdom for the practice of vocal and instrumental music ; but till the establishment of those weekly musical meetings at Oxford of which an account has herein before been given, we meet with no voluntary associations for musical recreation, till some time after the restoration.  The first of the kind in London had its rise in a very obscure part of the town, viz., at Clerkenwell, in such a place, and under such circumstances, as tended more to disgrace than recommend such an institution.   In short it was in the house, or rather hovel of one Thomas Britton, a man who for a livelihood sold small-coal about the streets, that this meeting was held, the first of the kind in London, as beginning in the year 1678, and the only one that corresponded with the idea of a concert.

An account of this extraordinary man, and of the meetings at his house, is referred to a future page. His concert is here mentioned as that which gave rise to other meetings for a similar purpose, of which there were many towards the end of the last century.

In the interim it is proposed to speak of those musical performances with which the people in general were entertained at places of public resort, distinguishing between such as were calculated for the recreation of the vulgar, and those which for their elegance come under the denomination of concerts.   The first of these were no other than the musical entertainments given to the people in Music-houses, already spoken of, the performers in which consisted of fiddlers and others, hired by the master of the house ; such as in the night season were wont to parade the city and suburbs under the denomination of the Waits.†   The music of these men could scarcely be called a concert, for this obvious reason, that it had no variety of parts, nor commixture of different instruments : half a dozen of fiddlers would scrape Sellenger's Round, or John come kiss me, or Old Simon the King with divisions, till themselves and their audience were tired, after which as many players on the hautboy would in the most harsh and discordant tones grate forth Green Sleves, Yellow Stockings, Gillian of Croydon, or some such common dance-tune, and the people thought it fine music.

But a concert, properly so called, was a sober re-

† It was the ancient custom for the waits to parade the streets nightly during the winter.  Now they go about a few nights only before Christmas to furnish a pretence for asking money at the return of that festival.

recreation; persons were drawn to it, not by an affectation of admiring what they could not taste, but by a genuine pleasure which they took in the entertainment. For the gratification of such, the masters of music exerted their utmost endeavours; and some of the greatest eminence among them were not above entertaining the public with musical performances, either at their own houses, or in places more commodious; receiving for their own use the money paid on admission. And to these performances the lovers of music were invited by advertisements in the London Gazette, the form and manner whereof will appear by the following extracts.

Numb. 742. Dec. 30, 1672. 'These are to give 'notice, that at Mr. John Banister's house (now called 'the Musick-school) over against the George tavern 'in White Fryers, this present Monday, will be mu- 'sick performed by excellent masters, beginning 'precisely at 4 of the clock in the afternoon, and 'every afternoon for the future, precisely at the same 'hour.'

Numb. 958. Jan. 25, 1674. Mr. John Banister advertises that he is removed to Shandois-street, Covent Garden, and there intends entertainment as formerly on Tuesday then next, and every evening for the future, Sundays only excepted.

Numb. 961. Feb. 4, 1674. 'A rare concert of 'four Trumpets Marine, never heard of before in 'England. If any persons desire to come and hear 'it, they may repair to the Fleece tavern near St. 'James's, about two of the clock in the afternoon, 'every day in the week except Sundays. Every 'concert shall continue one hour, and so begin again. 'The best places are one shilling, and the other 'sixpence.'

Numb. 1154. Dec. 11, 1676. 'On Thursday 'next, the 14th instant, at the Academy in Little 'Lincoln's-Inn-fields, will begin the first part of the 'Parley of Instruments, composed by Mr. John 'Banister, and perform'd by eminent masters, at six 'o'clock, and to continue nightly, as shall by bill or 'otherwise be notifi'd. The tickets are to be deli- 'ver'd out from one of the clock till five every day, 'and not after.'

Numb. 1356. Nov. 18, 1678. 'On Thursday 'next, the 22d of this instant November, at the 'Musick-school in Essex-buildings, over-against St. 'Clement's church in the Strand,* will be continued 'a consort of vocal and instrumental musick, be- 'ginning at five of the clock every evening, composed 'by Mr. John Banister.'

Banister died in the year 1679, as has been already related; he left a son named John, a fine performer on the violin, who was one of king William's band, and played the first violin at Drury-lane theatre when operas were first performed there, and will be spoken of hereafter.

Numb. 2088. Nov. 23, 1685. An advertisement of the publication of several Sonatas, composed after the Italian way, for one and two bass-viols, with a thorough-bass, by Mr. August Keenell, and of their

* Viz., in the great house a few doors down on the right hand, now occupied by Mr. Paterson, the auctioneer.

being to be performed on Thursday evenings at the dancing-school in Walbrook, next door to the Bell inn; and on Saturday evenings at the dancing-school in York-buildings, at which places will be also some performance on the Baritone by the said Mr. August Keenell.

About this time we also find that concerts were performed in Bow-street, Covent Garden, for in the Gazette, Numb. 2496, Oct. 14, 1689, is an advertisement that the concerts that were held in Bow-street and York-buildings were then joined together, and would for the future be performed in York Buildings.

Numb. 2533. Feb. 20, 1689. The music meeting that was lately held in Villiers-street, York-build- ings,* is advertised to be removed into Exeter Change in the Strand; but in a subsequent advertisement of March 10, in the same year, it is said to be removed back to Villiers-street.

Numb. 2599. Oct. 9, 1690. 'Mr. Franck's con- 'sort of vocal and instrumental musick will be 'performed to-morrow, being the 10th instant, at the '2 Golden Balls, at the upper end of Bow-street, 'Covent-Garden, at 7 in the evening; and next 'Wednesday at the Outroper's* office in the Royal 'Exchange, and will be continued all the ensuing 'winter.'

Numb. 2637. Feb. 19, 1690. 'The consort of 'musick lately in Bow-street is removed next 'Bedford-gate in Charles-street, Covent Garden, 'where a room is newly built for that purpose, and 'by command is to begin on Friday next the 20th 'instant, where it is afterwards to be continued 'every Thursday, beginning between 7 and 8 in the 'evening.'

Numb. 2651. April 9, 1691. 'The consort of 'vocal and instrumental musick, lately held in York- 'Buildings, will be performed again at the same 'place and hour as formerly, on Monday next, 'being Easter Monday, by the command, and for 'the entertainment of Her Royal Highness the 'Princess of Denmark.'

Numb. 2654. April 20, 1691. 'The concert of 'vocal and instrumental music in Charles-street, 'Covent Garden, by their Majesties' authority will 'be performed on Tuesday next, the 23d instant, 'and so continue every Thursday by command.'

Numb. 2746. March 6, 1691. 'A concert of 'musick, with several new voices, to be performed

† In Villiers-street, York-buildings, was formerly a great room used for concerts and other public exhibitions. In the Spectator are sundry advertisements from thence. About the year 1711 Sir Richard Steele and Clayton were engaged in a concert performed there; and since their time it has been used for the like purposes. The house of which it was part was on the right hand side of the street, near the bottom, and adjoining to what is now called the water-office, but within these few years it was pulled down, and two small houses have been built on the site of it.

‡ For the etymology of the appellative OUTROPER we are to seek; but the following clause in the charter granted by Charles II. to the citizens of London, will go near to explain the meaning of it. 'Also we will, 'and for us our heirs and successors do erect and create in and through 'the said city, &c. a certain office called Outroper or common cryer, to 'and for the selling of houshold stuff, apparel, leases of houses, jewels, 'goods, chattels, and other things of all persons who shall be willing 'that the said officers shall make sale of the same things by public and 'open clamour, commonly called Outcry, and sale in some common and 'open place or places in the said city, &c.' And in the London Gazette, Numb. 2404, is an order of the Mayor and Aldermen of London for re- viving the said office of Outroper, for the benefit of the orphans to whom the chamber of London is indebted, and that Thomas Puckle be admitted thereto: And that the West Pawn of the Royal Exchange be the place for such sales.

' on the 10th instant at the Vendu in Charles-street,
' Covent Garden.' *

Numb. 2834. Jan. 9, 1692. ' The Italian lady,
' (that is lately come over that is so famous for her
' singing) has been reported that she will sing no
' more in the concert in York-buildings : This is to
' give notice that next Tuesday, being the 10th in-
' stant, she will sing in the concert in York Buildings,
' and so continue during this season.'

Numb. 2838. Jan. 23, 1692. ' These are to give
' notice that the musick meeting, in which the Italian
' woman sings, will be held every Tuesday in York-
' buildings, and Thursdays in Freeman's-yard, in
' Cornhill, near the Royal Exchange.

Numb. 2858. April 3, 1693. ' On next Thurs-
' day, being the 6th of April, will begin Signor
' Tose's † consort of musick, in Charles-street, Covent-
' garden, about eight of the clock in the evening.

Numb. 2917. Oct. 26, 1693. ' Signor Tosi's con-
' sort of musick will begin on Monday, the 30th
' instant, in York-buildings, at eight in the evening,
' to continue weekly all the winter.'

Numb. 2926. Nov. 27, 1693. ' In Charles-street,
' in Covent-garden, on Thursday next, the 30th in-
' stant, will begin Mr. Franck's consort of musick,
' and so continue every Thursday night, beginning
' exactly at eight of the clock.'

Numb. 2943. Jan. 25, 1693. ' At the consort-
' room in York-buildings, on this present Thursday,
' at the usual hour, will be performed Mr. Purcell's
' Song, composed for St. Cecilia's Day in the year
' 1692, together with some other compositions of his,
' both vocal and instrumental, for the entertainment
' of his Highness Prince Lewis of Baden.'

Numb. 2945. Feb. 1, 1693. ' At the consort in
' York-buildings, on Monday next, the 5th instant,
' will be performed Mr. Finger's St. Cecilia's Song,
' intermixed with a variety of new musick, at the or-
' dinary rates.'

Numb. 2982. June 11, 1694. ' On Thursday
' will be a new consort of musick in Charlest-street,
' Covent-garden, where a gentlewoman sings that
' hath one of the best voices in England, not before
' heard in publick, to be continued every Thursday
' for a month.'

Numb. 3027. Nov. 15, 1694. ' A consort of
' musick, composed by Mr. Grabue,‡ will be per-
' formed on Saturday next at Mr. Smith's, in Charles-
' street, Covent-garden, between the hours of seven
' and eight.'

Numb. 3030. Nov. 26, 1694. ' The consort of
' musick in Charles-street, Covent-garden, will
' begin again next Thursday, with the addition of
' two new voices, one a young gentlewoman of 12
' years of age, the room being put in good condition,
' and there to continue this season.'

Numb. 3250. Jan. 1696. ' The musick that was
' performed of St. Cecilia's Day, composed by Signor
' Nicola, § will be performed on Thursday night in
' York-buildings, being the 7th instant.'

Numb. 3286. May 10, 1697. ' On Thursday
' next, being the 13th instant, will be performed in
' York-buildings an entertainment of vocal and in-
' strumental musick, composed by Dr. Staggins.'

Numb. 3356. Jan. 10, 1697. ' In York-buildings,
' this present Monday, the 10th instant, at the re-
' quest of several persons of quality, will be a con-
' sort of vocal and instrumental music never per-
' formed there before, beginning at the usual hour,
' for the benefit of Mr. King and Mr. Banister.' ||

Numb. 3366. Feb. 14, 1697. ' An entertainment
' of new musick, composed on the peace by Mr. Van
' [Vaughan] Richardson, organist of Winchester
' cathedral, will be performed on Wednesday next,
' at 8 at night, in York-buildings.'

Numb. 3374. March 14, 1697. ' Wednesday
' next, being the 16th instant, will be performed in
' York-buildings a consort of new musick, for the
' benefit of Dr. Blow and Mr. Paisible, beginning at 8.'

Numb. 3377. March 24, 1698. ' Monday next,
' the 28th instant, will be performed in York-build-
' ings, a new consort of musick by the chiefest masters
' in England, where Signior Rampony, an Italian
' musician belonging to the prince of Vaudemont, at
' the request of several persons of quality, will for
' once sing in the same in Italian and French. Half
' a guinea entrance.'

Numb. 3388. May 2, 1698. ' Wednesday next,
' the 4th of May, will be performed, in York-build-
' ings, the Song which was sung before her royal
' highness on her birth-day last. With other va-
' riety of new vocal and instrumental musick, com-
' posed by Dr. Turner,¶ and for his benefit.'

Numb. 3390. May 9, 1698. ' On Tuesday next,
' the 10th instant, will be performed in York-build-
' ings an entertainment of vocal and instrumental
' musick, being St. Cecilia's Song, composed by Dr.
' Blow, and several other new songs, for the benefit
' of Mr. Bowman and Mr. Snow.'

Numb. 3396. May 30, 1698. ' This present
' Monday, being the 30th of May, Mr. Nicola's con-
' sort of vocal and instrumental musick will be per-
' formed in York-buildings.'

Numb. 3454. December 19, 1698. ' On Friday
' next will be performed, in York-buildings, a new
' entertainment of vocal musick by Signeur Fidelio,
' beginning exactly at 7 at night.'

Numb. 3458. Jan. 2, 1698. ' On Wednesday next
' will be performed in York-buildings Mr. Daniel
' Purcell's musick made for last St. Cecilia's feast, for
' the benefit of Mr. Howell and Mr. Shore, with an
' addition of new vocal and instrumental musick, be-
' ginning at 7 at night.'

It appears also that concerts were occasionally
performed at the theatre in Drury-lane. In Dryden's

---

* The Vendu, by an advertisement in the preceding Gazette, appears
to have been a place for the sale of paintings, and to have been situate
next Bedford-gate in Charles-street.

† PIER-FRANCESCO TOSI, a fine singer, mentioned in page 653,
in note, and of whom occasion will be taken to speak hereafter. It may
be remarked that the spelling in all these advertisements is very
incorrect, and the notification in the most awkward terms.

‡ The person who set to music Dryden's Albion and Albanius. See
page 707, in note.

§ Supposed to be Nicola Matteis, the author of two collections of airs
for the violin.

|| The younger Banister : the elder died about eight years before.

¶ Of the royal chapel : he lived far into the present century, and is
therefore referred to a subsequent page.

Miscellany, part III. page 151, are verses thus entitled, ' Epilogue to the ladies, spoken by Mr. Wilks ' at the musick-meeting in Drury-lane, where the ' English woman* sings.    Written by Mr. Man- ' waring, upon occasion of their both singing before ' the queen and K. of Spain at Windsor.†'

About this time a man of a projecting head, one Cavendish Weedon, a member of Lincoln's Inn, had formed a design of an establishment for the relief of poor decayed gentlemen, and for erecting a school for the education of youth in religion, music, and accounts.    To this end he had a performance of divine music at Stationers' Hall, January the 31st, 1701, for the entertainment of the lords spiritual and temporal, and the honourable House of Commons. This performance consisted of an oration written by himself, two poems by Nahum Tate, and three anthems, one composed by Dr. Blow, the two others by Dr. Turner.    The words of the whole are extant in a quarto pamphlet printed at the time.

He had also another performance of the same kind, and for the same purpose, at Stationers' Hall, in the month of May, 1702 : the oration was written by Jeremy Collier ; the music was an anthem and a Te Deum, both composed by Dr. Blow.

Besides this benevolent design, the author entertained another, in which he seems to have been desirous of emulating Amphion, and by the power of harmony to erect public edifices.    To this end he projected a musical service of voices and instruments, to be performed in Lincoln's Inn chapel every Sunday at eleven o'clock, except during Lent and the vacation, under the direction of Dr. Edward Maynard, by subscription, the proposals for which were engraved on a folio sheet, and on two others the plan of Lincoln's Inn-fields, with the figures of the twelve apostles, and water-works at each corner, to be supplied from Hampstead water, and the model of St. Mary's chapel, to be erected in the centre *for praise*, as he terms it, after a design of Sir Christopher Wren, engraved by Sturt in 1698.‡

Strype, in his continuation of Stowe's Survey, book IV. page 74, mentions a proposal of the same person which, whether it be included in the above or was another does not there appear, for building the Six Clerks' office, and other Chancery offices at the east side of Lincoln's Inn garden.

## CHAP. CLIX.

HENRY ALDRICH, *(a Portrait)*, an eminent scholar and divine, the son of Henry Aldrich of Westminster, Gent., was born there in the year 1647, and educated in the college school in that city under the famous Dr. Richard Busby.    In 1662 he was admitted of Christ Church college, Oxon. and having been elected

a student under that foundation, took the degree of master of arts April 3, 1669.    Entering soon after into holy orders, he distinguished himself by his great proficiency in various branches of divine and human learning, and became a famous tutor in his college.    On the fifteenth of February, 1681, he was installed a canon of Christ Church, and the second of May following accumulated the degrees of bachelor and doctor in divinity.    In the controversy with the papists during the reign of king James II. he bore a considerable part, and thereby rendered his merit so conspicuous, that when at the revolution Massey the popish dean of Christ Church fled beyond sea, his deanery was conferred on Dr. Aldrich, who was therein established the seventeenth of June, 1689.    In this eminent station he presided with a dignity peculiar to his person and character, behaving with great integrity and uprightness, attending to the interests of his college, and the welfare of those under his care, and promoting to the utmost of his abilities learning, religion, and virtue.

The learning of Dr Aldrich, and his skill in polite literature were evinced by his numerous publications, particularly of many of the Greek classics, one whereof he generally published every year as a gift to the students of his house.    He also wrote a system of logic for the use of a pupil of his, and printed it ; but he possessed so great skill in architexture and music, that his excellence in either would alone have made him famous to posterity.    The three sides of the quadrangle of Christ Church college, Oxford, called Peck-water square, were designed by him, as was also the elegant chapel of Trinity college, and the church of All Saints in the High-street, to the erection whereof Dr. Ratcliff, at his solicitation, was a liberal contributor.

Amidst a variety of honourable pursuits, and the cares which the government of his college subjected him to, Dr. Aldrich found leisure to study and cultivate music, particularly that branch of it which related both to his profession and his office.    To this end he made a noble collection of church-music, consisting of the works of Palestrina, Carissimi, Victoria, and other Italian composers for the church, and by adapting with great skill and judgment English words to many of their motets, enriched the stores of our church, and in some degree made their works our own.§

With a view to the advancement of music, and the honour of its professors, Dr. Aldrich had formed a design of writing a history of the science, which, had he lived to complete it, would have superseded the necessity of any such work as the present.    The materials from which he proposed to compile it are yet extant in the library of his own college.    Upon a very careful perusal of them it seems that he had noted down everything he had met with touching music and musicians, but that no part of them had been wrought into any kind of form.

* Supposed to be Mrs. Tofts.

† Of the arrival of this prince mention is made in Salmon's Chronological Historian in the following passage.  ' Dec. 23, [1703] King Charles ' III. arrived at Spithead.    The duke of Somerset, master of the horse, ' brought him a letter from her majesty, and invited him to Windsor, ' where he arrived the 29th, and on the 31st returned with the duke of ' Somerset to his seat at Petworth in Sussex.  He set sail for Portugal ' the 5th of January, but being put back by contrary winds, it was the ' 27th of February before he arrived at Lisbon.'

‡ Anecdotes of British Topography, page 312.

§ Instances of this kind are the anthems ' I am well pleased,' from Carissimi, and ' O God king of glory,' from Palestrina.  To improve himself in the practice of composition, he was very industrious in putting into score the works of others.   The author of this work has in his collection four books of the madrigals of the Prencipe di Venosa, copied by the late Mr. John Immyns from a score in the hand-writing of Dr Aldrich.

The abilities of Dr. Aldrich as a musician rank him among the greatest masters of the science: he composed many services for the church, which are well known, as are also his anthems, to the number of near twenty.

In the Pleasant Musical Companion, printed in 1726, are two catches of Dr. Aldrich, the one, 'Hark the bonny Christ-church bells,' the other entitled 'A Smoking Catch, to be sung by four men smoking their pipes, not more difficult to sing than diverting to hear.'*

That he was a lover of mirth and pleasantry may be inferred from the above and numberless other particulars related of him. The following stanzas of his composition are a version of a well known song, and evidence of a singular vein of humour, which he possessed in an eminent degree :—

Miles et navigator,
Sartor, et ærator,
Jamdudum litigabant,
De pulchrâ quam amabant,
     Nomen cui est Joanna.

Jam tempus consummatum,
Ex quo determinatum,
Se non vexatum iri,
Præ desiderio viri,
     Nec pernoctare solam.

Miles dejerabat,
Hanc prædâ plus amabat,
Ostendens cicatrices,
Quas æstimat felices,
     Dum vindicavit eam.

Sartor ait ne sis dura,
Mihi longa est mensura,
Instat æris fabricator,
Ut olla sarciatur,
     Rimaque obstipetur.

Dum hi tres altercantur,
Nauta vigilantur,
Et calide moratur,
Dum prælium ordiatur,
     Ut agat suam rem.

Perinde ac speratur,
Deinceps compugnatur,
Et sæviente bello,
Transfixit eam telo
     Quod vulneravit cor.

The publication of Lord Clarendon's History of the Rebellion was committed to the care of Dr. Aldrich jointly with Dr. Sprat, bishop of Rochester, and upon no better testimony than the hearsay evidence of a zealous patriot, Mr. John Oldmixon, they were charged with having altered and interpolated that noble work.

In 1702 Dr. Aldrich was chosen prolocutor of the convocation; and on the fourteenth day of December, 1710, to the unspeakable grief of the whole university, he died at his college of Christ Church, being then in the sixty-third year of his age. He continued in a state of celibacy all his lifetime, and as he rose in the world, disposed of his income in works of hospitality and charity, and in the encouragement of learning. Notwithstanding that modesty and humility for which he was remarkable, and which he manifested by withholding his name from his numerous learned publications, he exerted a firm and steady conduct in the government of his college. Pursuant to his directions before his death, he was buried in the cathedral of Oxford, near the place where bishop Fell lies, and without any memorial of him, other than that character which he had justly acquired, of a deep scholar, a polite gentleman, a good churchman, and a devout Christian.

* Dr. Aldrich's excessive love of smoking was an entertaining topic of discourse in the university, concerning which the following story among others passed current. A young student of the college once finding some difficulty to bring a young gentleman his chum into the belief of it, laid him a wager that the dean was smoking at that instant, viz., about ten o'clock in the morning. Away therefore went the student to the deanery, where being admitted to the dean in his study, he related the occasion of his visit. To which the dean replied in perfect good humour, 'You see you have lost your wager, for I'm not smoking but 'filling my pipe.' The catch above mentioned was made to be sung by the dean, Mr. Sampson Estwick, then of Christ church, and afterwards of St. Paul's, and two other smoking friends. Of this Mr. Estwick, who is plainly pointed out by the words in the above catch 'I prithee 'Sam fill,' an account will be given in the next ensuing article.

The smoking catch gave occasion to another on snuff, which for the singular humour of it is here inserted. Tom Brown wrote the words, and Robert Bradley, a composer of songs in the collections of that time, set them to the following notes :—

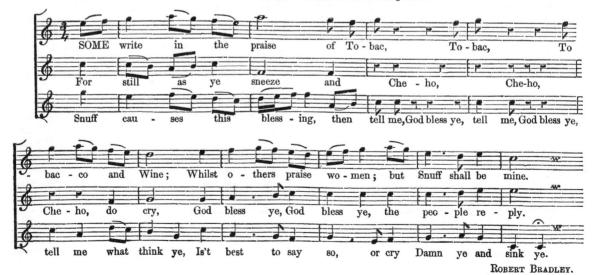

SOME write in the praise of To-bac, To-bac, To-
For still as ye sneeze and Che-ho, Che-ho,
Snuff cau - ses this bless-ing, then tell me,God bless ye, tell me, God bless ye,

-bac-co and Wine; Whilst o-thers praise wo-men; but Snuff shall be mine.
Che-ho, do cry, God bless ye, God bless ye, the peo-ple re-ply.
tell me what think ye, Is't best to say so, or cry Damn ye and sink ye.

ROBERT BRADLEY.

HENRICUS   ALDRICH S.T.P.

ECCLESIÆ CHRISTI   OXON. DECANUS.

SAMPSON ESTWICK was one of the first set of children after the restoration, and educated under Captain Henry Cook. From the king's chapel he went to Oxford, and entering into holy orders, became a chaplain of Christ Church, where he was honoured with the friendship of Dr. Aldrich, his intimacy with whom may be inferred from the famous smoking catch mentioned in the preceding article. Upon the decease of Dr. Aldrich he came to London, and was appointed one of the minor canons, and afterwards a cardinal of St. Paul's.* After he had been some time in the choir, he was presented to the rectory of St. Michael, Queenhithe, London. Nevertheless he continued to perform choral duty till near the time of his decease, when he was a little short of ninety years of age. In the former part of his life, viz., soon after his settlement in London, he was a candidate for Gresham professor of music, but without success. He died in the month of February, 1739. In a character given of him in one of the public papers, he is styled a gentleman universally beloved for his exemplary piety and orthodox principles.

This venerable servant of the church still survives in the remembrance of many persons now living. Bending beneath the weight of years, but preserving his faculties, and even his voice, which was a deep bass, till the last, he constantly attended his duty at St. Paul's, habited in a surplice, and with his bald head covered with a black satin coif, with grey hair round the edge of it, exhibited a figure the most awful that can well be conceived. Some compositions of his are extant, but not in print.

Besides the several English musicians who lived after the restoration, of whom an account has been given in the foregoing pages, there were many others of whom few memorials are now remaining; these may be classed under three heads, namely, composers whose works exist only in manuscript; performers on particular instruments, whose merits could not long survive themselves; and gentlemen of the chapel, distinguished by remarkable circumstances. Of these it is here thought proper to give an account, commencing about the middle, and continued down to the end of the last century.

SAMUEL AKEROYD, of the Yorkshire family of that name. He composed many songs in the Theater of Music, a collection of Songs in four books, published in the years 1685, 1686, and 1687.

THOMAS BALTZAR. This person is mentioned in a preceding page; he was born at Lubec, and was esteemed the finest performer on the violin of his time. He came into England in the year 1658,

and lived about two years in the house of Sir Anthony Cope, of Hanwell, in Oxfordshire. In the memoranda of Anthony Wood concerning musicians, it is said that Baltzar commenced bachelor of music at Cambridge, which is rather improbable, seeing that he resided chiefly at Oxford; but to ascertain the fact, recourse has been had to the register of the university of Cambridge, and in a list of graduates in music, extracted from thence, his name does not appear. He was the great competitor of Davis Mell, who, though a clock maker by trade, was, till Baltzar came hither, allowed to be the finest performer on the violin in England; and after his arrival he divided with him the public applause, it being agreed that Mell exceeded in the fineness of his tone and the sweetness of his manner, and Baltzar in the power of execution and command of the instrument. Moreover, it is said of the latter that he first taught the English the practice of shifting, and the use of the upper part of the finger-board. Baltzar was given to intemperance, and is said to have shortened his days by excessive drinking: he was buried in the cloister of Westminster-abbey on the twenty-seventh day of July, 1663, as appears by the register of that church.†

JOHN BISHOP was a scholar of Daniel Rosingrave, organist of Salisbury Cathedral, and a lay singer in King's college chapel, Cambridge, but removing thence, he became organist of the cathedral and college of Winchester. He published a collection of airs for two flutes, entitled Harmonia Lenis, and composed some things for the church.

THOMAS BLAGRAVE, a gentleman of the chapel of Charles II., and a performer on the cornet there,‡ was of the Berkshire family of that name; a few songs of his are printed in ' Select Ayres and Dialogues,' folio. 1669. His picture is in the music school, Oxford.

RICHARD BRIND, educated in St. Paul's choir, and afterwards organist of that cathedral, and Dr. Greene's master. He composed two thanksgiving anthems, now scarcely known.

WILLIAM CÆSAR, alias SMEGERGILL, composed sundry songs, printed in Playford's Musical Companion, the Treasury of Music, published in 1669, and other collections of that time.

JULIUS CÆSAR, a physician of Rochester, descended from an ancient family of that city, was well skilled in music. Two catches of his composition are published in the Pleasant Musical Companion, 1726, and are inferior to none in that collection.

EDWARD COLMAN, son of Dr. Charles Colman, a

---

* ' The church of Saint Paul had before the time of the Conqueror ' two Cardinalls, which office still continues. They are chosen by the ' deane and chapter out of the number of the twelve petty canons, and ' are called Cardinales chori; their office is to take notice of the absence ' or neglect of the quire, and weekely to render accompt thereof to the ' deane and chapter. These two Cardinalls doe minister ecclesiasticall ' sacraments to the ministers of the church and their seruants, as well to ' the healthfull as to the sieke. They heare confessions, and appoint ' comfortable penance: and lastly, they commit the dead to some conue- ' nient sepulture. These Cardinalls haue the best preheminence in the ' quire above all next to the Subdeane, and the best stalls.' Weever's Funeral Monuments, page 384; and see the Statutes of St. Paul's in the Appendix to Dugdale's History of that Cathedrall, tit. De Cardinalibus chori.—*Vide Fuller's Worthies, Chapter 4, Page 13.*

† Ashmol. MS.

‡ Upon the revival of choral service, in the royal chapel especially, they were necessitated, for want of treble voices, to make use of cornets; [See page 689]: and on particular occasions sacbuts and other instruments were also employed. Besides this, as Dr. Tudway relates, king Charles II. commanded such as composed for the chapel to make also Symphonies and Ritornellos to many of the anthems in use, which were performed by a band of instruments placed in the organ-loft. The knowledge of this fact will in some measure account for the places in the procession at the coronation, which performers on these instruments have sometimes had. At that of James II. and also that of Geo. I. walked two of the king's musicians in scarlet mantles, playing each on a sacbut, and another, clad in like manner, playing on a double curtal or bassoon. The organ-blower had also a place in the two processions above mentioned, having on him a short red coat, with a badge on his left breast, viz., a nightingale of silver, gilt, sitting on a sprig.

singing master in London, and also a teacher of the lute and viol.*

JOHN COURTEVILLE was the author of sundry songs printed in the Theater of Music.

RAPHAEL COURTEVILLE was a gentleman of the chapel in the reign of Charles II., and the first organist of the church of St. James, Westminster, and is supposed to have been the brother of him mentioned above. He composed Sonatas for two flutes, and sundry songs printed in the collections of his time. A son of his, named also Raphael, succeeded him as organist of St. James's. The latter of these was the reputed author of the Gazetteer, a paper written in defence of Sir Robert Walpole's administration, and was by the writers on the side of opposition stigmatized with the name of Court-evil.†

ALEXANDER DAMASCENE, one of the gentlemen of the chapel royal in the reign of William and Mary, composed sundry songs published in the Theater of Music.

THOMAS DEAN, organist of Warwick and Coventry. Some airs of his composition are printed in the Division-Violin. He flourished at the beginning of this century, and accumulated the degrees of bachelor and doctor in his faculty of the university of Oxford in 1731.

JOHN EST, a barber. It has been before observed that the profession of music had some sort of connexion with the trade of a barber, and that a cittern was part of the furniture of a barber's shop.‡ This man was first a small proficient on that instrumen, but afterwards took to the Lyra-viol, and became so famous a performer on it as to give occasion to the following verses, which are here inserted, not for their goodness, but because they are evidence of a fact that has been frequently asserted in the course of this work :—

> In former time 't hath been upbrayded thus,
> That barber's musick was most barbarous,
> For that the cittern was confin'd unto
> The Ladies Fall, or John come kiss me now,
> Green Sleeves, and Pudding Pyes, with Nell's delight,
> Winning of Bolloigne, Essex' last good night.§
>    But, since reduc'd to this conformity,
> And company became society,
> Each barber writes himself, in strictest rules,
> Master, or bachelor i' th' musick schools,
> How they the mere musitians do out-go,
> These one, but they have two strings to their bow.
> Barber musitians who are excellent,
> As well at chest, as the case instrument,
> Henceforth each steward shall invite his guest
> Unto the barber's and musitian's feast,
> Where sit ye merry, whilst we joy to see
> Art thus embrac'd by ingenuity.

* Formerly there were in London many masters who taught the practice of singing by the syllables: the profession is alluded to in some of the comedies written about the time of Charles II. But singing follows so naturally the smallest degree of proficiency on any instrument, that the learning of both is unnecessary; and in fact those that teach the harpsichord are now the only singing-masters, that we know of, except a few illiterate professors, who travel about the country, and teach psalmody by the notes, at such rates as the lower sort of people are able to pay.

† In a weekly paper, now deservedly forgotten, entitled the Westminster Journal, Numb. 54, for Saturday, December 4, 1742, is a fictitious letter subscribed, 'Ralph Courtevil, Organ-blower, Essayist, and 'Historiographer.'

‡ A song to this purpose in the 'Pills to purge Melancholy.'

§ Popular tunes so called.

THOMAS FARMER, originally one of the waits in London, was nevertheless admitted to the degree of bachelor in music of the university of Cambridge in 1684. He composed many songs printed in the collections of his time, and particularly in the 'Theater of Music' and the 'Treasury of Music,' and was the author of two very fine collections of airs, the one entitled 'A Consort of Music in 'four parts, containing thirty-three lessons, beginning 'with an overture,' and another 'A second Consort 'of Music in four parts, containing eleven lessons, 'beginning with a Ground,' both printed in oblong quarto, the one in 1686, the other in 1690. In the Orpheus Britannicus is an elegy on his death, written by Tate and set by Purcell, by which it appears that he died young. His dwelling house was in Martlet-court in Bow-street, Covent-garden.

DANIEL FARRANT, supposed to be a son of Richard Farrant, mentioned page 522, of this work, was one of the first of those musicians who set lessons lyraway for the viol, in imitation of the old English lute and Bandore.

JOHN GOODGROOME, bred a chorister at Windsor, a gentleman of the chapel in the reigns of Charles II. and William and Mary, composed songs, printed in the 'Treasury of Music.' One of the same name, probably his son, was about fifty years ago organist of the church of St. Peter in Cornhill, London.

RICHARD GOODSON, bachelor in music, organist of New college and Christ Church, Oxford, elected professor in that university the nineteenth of July, 1682. He lies buried in the chapel adjoining to the choir of Christ Church, on the south side thereof, under a stone, on which is the following inscription :—

> 'H. S. E.
> 'Richardus Goodson,
> 'Hujus Ecclesiæ organista,
> 'Hujus Academ. Mus. Prælector
> 'Utriq ; Deliciæ et Decus.
> 'Ob. Jan. 13, 1717-8.'

He was succeeded as professor and organist of Christ Church by his son Richard Goodson, who was also a bachelor in music, and the first organist of Newbery. He died Jan. 9, 1740-1, and lies buried near his father.

WILLIAM HALL, one of the royal band, temp. Gul. & Mar. composed sundry airs published in a collection entitled Tripla Concordia. He died in 1700, and lies buried in the church-yard of Richmond in Surrey. On his grave-stone he is styled William Hall, a superior violin.

## CHAP. CLX.

HENRY HALL, born about the year 1655, the son of Capt. Henry Hall, of New Windsor, was educated in the royal chapel, and had for his last master Dr. Blow. His first promotion was to the place of organist of Exeter. After that he became organist of Hereford, and also a vicar choral in the same church. He died March 30, 1707, and lies buried under a stone inscribed to his memory in the cloister of the college of the vicars of Hereford cathedral. He had a son of both his names, who was a vicar and also organist of Hereford, and dying Jan. 22 1713, was buried near his father in the above mentioned cloister. The similar situation of these two persons, and the small difference of six years between the time of the death of both father and son, make it somewhat difficult to distinguish them, and this difficulty is increased by the additional circumstance that each had a talent of poetry. The elder was a sound musician, and composed sundry anthems, well known to those who are conversant in church-music. He also wrote commendatory verses to both books of the Orpheus Britannicus : in those to the first, are these lines, which bespeak him to have been a fellow-disciple with Purcell under Blow, and consequently the elder of the two.

> ' Hail ! and for ever hail harmonious shade !
> ' I lov'd thee living, and admire thee dead.
> ' Apollo's harp at once our souls did strike,
> ' We learnt together, but not learnt alike :
> ' Though equal care our master might bestow,
> ' Yet only Purcell e'er shall equal Blow :
> ' For thou, by heaven for wondrous things design'd,
> ' Left'st thy companion lagging far behind.'

Prefixed to the Amphion Anglicus are commendatory verses, subscribed Henry Hall, organist of Hereford, addressed to his esteemed friend Dr. Blow upon publishing his book of Songs, upon which it may be observed that as they are written in a very familiar style, and contain not the least intimation that the relation of master and scholar ever subsisted between them, it is to be inferred that these were written by the younger Hall. The following are the concluding lines of this address :—

> ' Thus while you spread your fame, at home I sit,
> ' Amov'd by fate, from melody and wit,
> ' The British bard on harp a Treban* plays,
> ' With grated ears I saunter out my days ;
> ' Shore's most harmonious tube ne'er strikes my ear,†
> ' Nought of the bard besides his fame I hear :
> ' No chanting at St. Paul's regales my senses,
> ' I'm only vers'd in Usum Herefordensis.
> ' But if by chance some charming piece I view,
> ' By all caress'd because put forth by you ;
> ' As when of old, a knight long lost in love,
> ' Whose Phillis neither brine nor blood cou'd move,
> ' Throws down his lance, and lays his armour by,
> ' And falls from errantry to elegy :
> ' But if some mighty hero's fame he hears,
> ' That like a torrent all before him bears,
> ' In haste he mounts his trusty steed again,
> ' And led by glory, scow'rs along the plain ;
> ' So I with equal ardour seize my flute,
> ' And string again my long neglected lute.'

The above lines are far from being destitute of merit, but there are verses of the same author that have gained him rank among our poets. A ballad of his on the Jubilee in 1700 found its way into a collection in two volumes, printed by Lintot, and called Pope's Miscellany, as containing in it Windsor Forest, the Rape of the Lock, Eloisa to Abelard, and other of his best poems ; and in a collection entitled the Grove, consisting of original poems and translations by Walsh, Donne, Dryden, Butler, Suckling, and others, published in 1721,‡ are as many of Hall's poems as probably could be found. Among them is that well-known ballad beginning ' All in the land of cyder,' and these verses that follow, addressed to Mr. R. C., who every year sent him a Dun a little before St. Paul's day :—

> ' If rhime for rhino could atone,
> ' Or wit stave off an ardent dun,
> ' If words in sweetest numbers chose,
> ' Would but wipe off our tickling prose,
> ' How blest a life would poets lead,
> ' And, ah ! how punctual you'd be paid !
> ' But since the greatest stroke of wit,
> ' Will not compound the meanest debt,
> ' Nor fifty feet in Congreve's muse
> ' Tick with old Tranter § for two shoes ;
> ' Nor all the rhymes great Dryden wrote,
> ' Prevail to trust him for a coat ;
> ' Know, Robin, I design you money,
> ' To face the fair now falling on you.‖
> ' But of the Saints both great and small,
> ' There's none torments me like Saint Paul,
> ' Who yearly persecutes the poor,
> ' As he did Christians heretofore :
> ' For still about that holy tide,
> ' When folk to fair of Bristol ride,
> ' More dunning bills to me are brought,
> ' Than e'er the Saint epistles wrote.
> ' But here the difference is, we see,
> ' He wrote to Heathens, they to me.
> ' Nor can I blame their cleanly calling,
> ' So often from their faith for falling,
> ' Since many a one thro' sly deceivers
> ' Have been undone by being believers.
>    ' But, Robin, this is not your case,
> ' Whom heav'n some coin has giv'n, and grace ;
> ' Who gruff when sober, bright when mellow,
> ' Art in the main a pretty fellow.'

In the same collection are the following lines of his on the Vigo expedition :—

> ' Whilst this bumper stands by me brim full of cydero,
> ' A fig for king Philip and Portocarrero ;
> ' With the smoke of my pipe thus all my cares vanish,
> ' Whilst, with their own silver, we purchase the Spanish,¶
> ' And since the whole Flota is taken or sunk, boys,
> ' We'll be, as becomes us, exceedingly drunk, boys.'

Most of the musical compositions with the name Henry Hall are to be ascribed to the elder of the two of that name, for it is not clear that the younger was the author of any ; and indeed it seems that his character of a musician is lost in that of a poet.

STEPHEN JEFFRIES, *a pupil of Michael Wise, in 1680, being then but twenty years of age, was elected organist of Gloucester Cathedral, which office he held thirty-four years. He composed that fine melody which the chimes of the above-mentioned church continue to play to this day, and which, for*

---

* The Treban, called also the warrior's song, is a tune of great antiquity among the inhabitants of Wales: the words to it are in stanzas of three lines, each of seven syllables. The Treban of South Wales, called Treban morganisg, has the same character, but is conjectured to be less ancient. Ex. Rel. Mr. Edw. Jones, the harper and publisher of a late Collection of Welch Poetry and Music.

† The trumpet of Serjeant Shore, who is mentioned page 752 of this work.

‡ In this collection are sundry poems, written by     Kenrick, a doctor both in divinity and physic. He wrote for Purcell those two songs in the Orpheus Britannicus, ' When Teucer from his father fled,' and ' Nestor who did to thrice man's age attain,' which are printed in the collection abovementioned.

§ A shoemaker.     ‖ Bristol fair.

¶ Spanish tobacco: In Dr. Aldrich's smoking catch the concluding words are ' a pipe of Spanish.'

*the singular contrivance of it, deserves remark—for it is to be observed that the bells thereof are eight in number, descending by a major sixth and third from d to D, and that the clock bell is a minor third lower than the tenor bell, viz., B♮. The tune, which is a very solemn one, is so contrived as to take in every bell in the peal, and, by an artful evasion of the semitone below D, which there is no bell to answer, to make the clock bell the final note, thereby constituting a series of tones and semitones proper to the key of B. The notes of this singular melody are given below.**

*This person died in 1712, and lies buried in the east ambulatory of the cloister adjoining to his church, as appears by an inscription on his gravestone.*

*The choirmen of Gloucester relate that, to cure him of a habit of staying late at the tavern, his wife drest up a fellow in a winding-sheet, with directions to meet him with a lanthorn and candle in the cloisters through which he was to pass on his way home; but that, on attempting to terrify him, Jeffries expressed his wonder only by saying, 'I thought all you spirits had been abed before this time.'*

*That Jeffries was a man of singular character we have another proof in the following story related of him. A singer from a distant church, with a good voice, had been requested and undertook to sing a solo anthem in Gloucester Cathedral, and for that purpose took his station at the elbow of the organist in the organ-loft. Jeffries, who found him trip in the performance, instead of palliating his mistake and setting him right, immediately rose from his seat, and leaning over the gallery, called out aloud to the choir and the whole congregation, 'He can't sing it.'*

WILLIAM HINE *succeeded to the place of organist of Gloucester Cathedral upon the decease of Stephen Jeffries in 1712. He joined with one of the Halls in that composition which is known by the name of Hall and Hine's Service, and was so much esteemed for skill in his faculty and his gentlemanly qualities, that his salary was, by the dean and chapter of his church, increased twenty pounds a year. He was the musical preceptor of Mr. Richard Church, late organist of Christ Church, Oxford, and also of Dr. William Hayes, late professor of music in that university. He died at the age of forty-three, in August, 1730.*

WILLIAM INGLOTT, organist of the cathedral church of Norwich, should have have had a place in a preceding page, as having lived at the beginning of the last century; nevertheless, rather than omit it, a memoir of him is here inserted. He lies buried in the above-mentioned cathedral, and, by an inscription to his memory, seems to have been in his

day a famous organist, at least Dr. Croft may be supposed to have thought so when he repaired his monument, on which are the following lines :—

    ' Here William Inglott organist doth rest,
    ' Whose art in musick this cathedral blest,
    ' For descant most, for voluntary all,
    ' He past on organ, song and virginall :
    ' He left this life at age of sixty-seven,
    ' And here 'mongst angells all sings first in heav'n,
    ' His fame flies far, his name shall never die,
    ' See art and age here crown his memorie.

     ' Non digitis Inglotte tuis terrestria tangis ;
       ' Tangis nunc digitis organa celsa poli.
          ' Anno Dom. 1621.

' Buried the last day     This erected the 15th day
' of December 1621.               of June 1622.

     ' Ne forma hujusce monumenti injuriâ
     ' Temporum penè deleti, dispereat, exculpi
     ' Ornavit Gul. Croft, Reg. Capellæ in
     ' Arte Musicâ Discipul. Præfectus.'

SIMON IVES was a lay vicar in the cathedral of St. Paul, till driven from thence by the usurpation, when he became a singing-master and a teacher in private families. He and Henry Lawes were made choice of to compose the airs, lessons, and songs of the masque presented by the four inns of court before king Charles I. and his queen at Whitehall, on Candlemas night 1633.[†] Many catches and rounds of Ives are to be found in Hilton's collection, and in Playford's Musical Companion, as are also single songs among the Ayres and Dialogues published in his time. He died in the parish of Christ Church, London, 1662. Whitelock in his Memorials gives him the character of an excellent musician and a worthy man.

WILLIAM KING, organist of New College, Oxford, set to music Cowley's Mistress, and published it with this title, 'Poems of Mr. Cowley and others ' composed into songs and ayres, with a thorough-' basse to the Theorbo, Harpsecon, or Base-violl.' fol. Oxford 1668.

ROBERT KING, bachelor in music, of Cambridge, 1696, one of the band of William and Mary. He composed sundry airs printed in the Tripla Concordia ; and set to music many songs printed in the Theater of Music.

JOHN LENTON, one of the band of king William and queen Mary, was a master of the flute. He composed and published, in conjunction with Mr. Tollet, hereafter mentioned, a work entitled ' A con-' sort of musick in three parts.' Some catches of his composition are printed in the Pleasant Musical Companion. *He was also author of a tract, entitled ' the Gentleman's Diversion, or the violin explained,' oblong 4to, no date : at the end are sundry fine airs by himself and other masters of his time. A second edition of it with an appendix, but without the airs, was published in 1702, under the title of ' The ' useful instructor on the violin.' In the directions for ordering the bow and instrument, the learner is cautioned, as well against holding the latter under the chin, as against a most unaccountable practice,*

---

\* *The tune as it is set to the proper key of the bells, by Mr. Abraham Rudhall, bell founder, in Gloucester.*

*viz., the holding it so low as the girdle; which he says some do in imitation of the Italians: so that we must conclude he means that the violin should rest on the breast of the performer. It is also remarkable that in neither of the editions of the book is there any mention, nay the least hint about shifting, and that the scale therein exhibited reaches but to C on the second line above the stave; a proof of the comparatively small degree of proficiency to which the masters of the instrument were at that period arrived; and yet at the end of his book the author says, that this nation was never so well provided with able performers, as at the time of its publication.*

HENRY LOOSEMORE, bachelor in music of Cambridge, 1640, and organist first of King's college, Cambridge, and afterwards of the cathedral of Exeter. He composed services and anthems. One of this name, a lay singer or organist of Exeter cathedral, is said to have built the organ which was erected in that church at the restoration.

GEORGE LOOSEMORE, bachelor in music of Trinity college, Cambridge.

ALPHONSUS MARSH was a gentleman of the chapel in the reign of Charles II. Sundry songs of his composition, as also of a song of his, of both his names, are extant, in the 'Treasury of Musick,' and other collections of that time.

JOHN NEWTON, doctor in divinity, and rector of Ross in Herefordshire, a person of great learning and skill in the mathematics, was the author of the 'English Academy, or a brief Introduction to the 'seven liberal Arts,' in which music, as one of them, is largely treated of. It was published in octavo, anno 1667. Vide Athen. Oxon. col. 632.

ROGER NIGHTINGALE, a clergyman, and one of the chapel at the restoration, was then an old man. He had been of the chapel to Charles I. and, even before the commencement of that king's reign, distinguished as a singer. He dwelt with Williams, bishop of Lincoln, at Bugden in Huntingdonshire, the episcopal seat; and when that prelate was translated to York, he took Nightingale with him to Cawood-castle, and, as a mark of his favour, gave him a lease worth £500 to be sold.*

FRANCIS PIGGOT, bachelor in music of the university of Cambridge, 1698, and first organist of the Temple church. He succeeded Purcell as one of the organists of the royal chapel. An anthem of his, 'I was glad,' is extant in many cathedrals. He had a son, who succeeded him as organist of the Temple, and was also organist of Windsor chapel, but coming into a large fortune upon the decease of a relation, Dr. John Pelling, rector of St. Anne, Westminster, he retired to Windsor, and either resigned his places, or did his duty by deputies.

JOHN READING, a scholar of Dr. Blow, was a lay vicar, and also master of the children in the cathedral church of Lincoln. Removing from thence, he became organist of the parish church of St. John,

Hackney, and afterwards St. Dunstan in the West, and St. Mary Woolnoth, London. He published a collection of anthems of his composition with this strange title, 'By subscription a Book of new Anthems, containing a Hundred Plates fairly engraven, with a Thorough Bass figured for the 'Organ or Harpsichord with proper Retornels. By 'John Reading, Organist of St. John's, Hackney; 'educated in the Chapple Royal, under the late 'famous Dr. John Blow. Price 10 Shillings.' He died a few years ago, in a very advanced age.

VAUGHAN RICHARDSON, a scholar of Dr. Blow, and organist of the cathedral of Winchester. He published, in the year 1706, A Collection of Songs for one two, and three voices, accompanied with instruments, and composed sundry anthems, which are well known in most cathedrals.

DANIEL ROSINGRAVE, educated in the chapel royal, and a fellow-disciple of Purcell, became organist of Salisbury, and afterwards of St. Patrick's, Dublin. He had two sons musicians, one of whom, named Thomas, having been sent by his father into Italy to study, in the year 1710, returning to England, was elected organist of the parish church of St. George, Hanover-square; the other remained in Ireland, and was his father's successor.

THEODORE STEFKINS, one of the finest performers on the lute in his time, and as such he is celebrated by Salmon in his Essay to the Advancement of Music. There were two other persons of this name, Frederic and Christian, sons of the former, who were of the band of William and Mary; the latter was living in 1711.

WILLIAM THATCHER, born at Dublin, and bred there under Randal Jewit, came into England and taught on the virginals before and after the restoration. He died in London about 1678.

THOMAS TOLLET. This person composed that well-known ground known by his name, and published directions to play on the French flageolet. In conjunction with John Lenton, mentioned above, he composed and published, about the year 1694, a work entitled A Consort of Musick in three parts. A daughter of his was a dancer at Goodman's-fields playhouse about the year 1728, when that theatre was first opened.

To these may be added the following names of famous organists, celebrated performers on particular instruments, and composers of music of various kinds, who flourished during the above period.

ISAAC BLACKWELL. This person composed songs, printed in a collection entitled 'Choice Ayres, Songs, and Dialogues to sing to the Theorbo-lute and Bass-viol,' fol. 1675. There are some compositions of his for the church in the books of the royal chapel, and in those of Westminster Abbey. BOWMAN, organist of Trinity college, Cambridge. JAMES COOPER, organist of the cathedral of Norwich, and there buried. COTTON, also organist of the same cathedral, and there buried. WILLIAM DAVIS, one of the choir, and master of the children of the cathedral of Worcester. EDWARD and JOHN DYER, dancing masters by profession, but both excellent musicians:

---

* Bishop Williams was very beneficent to musicians. Happening to hear some compositions of Michael Est, to whom he was quite a stranger, he settled an annuity on him for his life, moved by no other consideration than his merit in his profession. See page 560 of this work.

they lived about the time of the restoration, and had their dwelling in Shoe-lane, London. JAMES HART, a gentleman of the chapel in the reign of king William and queen Mary. JAMES HAWKINS, the father and son, the one organist of the cathedral of Ely, the other that of Peterborough. WILLIAM HINE, organist of Gloucester. GEORGE HOLMES, organist of Lincoln. BENJAMIN LAMB, organist of Eton college, and verger of the chapel of St. George at Windsor: he composed many anthems. JOHN Moss, composer of sundry songs in the Treasury of Music. NORRIS, master of the children of the same cathedral of Lincoln. PAISIBLE, a famous master of the flute, and a composer for that instrument. THOMAS PLEASANTS, organist of the cathedral of Norwich, and there buried. CHARLES QUARLES, bachelor in music of Cambridge, 1698, and organist of Trinity college there. JOHN ROGERS, servant to Charles II., a famous lutenist, lived near Aldersgate, and died about the year 1663. ANTHONY WAKELEY, organist of the cathedral of Salisbury. JOHN WALTER, organist of the collegiate church at Windsor. THOMAS WANLESS, bachelor in Music of Cambridge, 1698, and organist of York cathedral. THOMAS WILLIAMS, organist of St. John's college, Cambridge.

GIUSEPPE TORELLI, a native of Verona, academico filarmonico di Bologna, and a famous performer on the violin, was concert master at Anspach about the year 1703. After that he removed to Bologna, and became maestro di capella in the church of San Petronio in that city. He composed and published sundry collections of airs and Sonatas for violins, but the most considerable of his works is his eighth opera, published at Bologna by his brother, Felice Torelli, after the death of the author, viz., in 1709, entitled 'Concerti grossi con una pastorale, per il santissimo natale,' consisting of twelve concertos, 'à due violini concertini, due violini ripieni, viola e cembalo.' He is said to have been the inventor of that noble species of instrumental composition the Concerto grosso.

ZACCARIA TEVO, a native of Saccha, a city in Sicily, a Franciscan monk, bachelor in divinity, and a professor or master of music in Venice, published in the year 1706, in quarto, a work entitled Il Musico Tesore, containing in substance the whole of what has been written on the subject by Boetius, Franchinus, Galilei, Mersennus, Kircher, and, in short, almost every other author on the subject of music. As the works of these have been mentioned in order as their names have occurred, there seems to be but little occasion for a more particular account of Tevo's book than the following Index, containing the heads of the several chapters, will furnish. Nevertheless it may be remarked, that he is so liberal in his quotations from the Margarita Philosophica of Gregory Reisch,* that almost the whole of the tract on music therein contained is inserted in the Musico Tesore of Tevo:—

### PARTE PRIMA.

Cap 1. Del Titolo dell' Opera; 2. Della Definitione, e Divisione della Musica; 3. Della Musica

* See the account of this book in page 306 of this work.

Mondana; 4. Della Musica Humana; 5. Della Musica Armonica; 6. Della Musica Metrica, e Ritmica; 7. Della Musica Organica; 8. Della Musica Piana, e Mesurata; 9. Della Musica Teorica, & Inspettiva; 10. Della Musica Prattica, & Attiva; 11. Dell' Inventione della Musica; 12. Della Propagatione della Musica; 13. Qual fosse l'Antica Musica; 14. Quanto fosse rozza l'Antica Musica; 15. Degl' effetti della Musica; 16. Dell' inventione del Cantar in consonanza; 17. Del detrimento della Musica; 18. A che fine si deve imparare la Musica; 19. Qual sii il vero Musico; 20. Della difesa della Musica, e Cantar moderno.

### PARTE SECONDA.

Cap. 1. Delle Voci, e suoni in Commune; 2. Della definitione delle Voci, e suoni; 3. Della formatione della Voce; 4. Della varietà delle Voci, e suoni; 5. Della formatione, e propagatione de suoni nell' Aria; 6. Come vengono comprese le voci, e suoni dal senso dell' udito; 7. Dell' inventione delle Figure Musicali; 8. Del Tuono, e Semituono; 9. Che cosa sii Musico intervallo; 10. Delli Tetracordi, e Generi della Musica; 11. Del Sistema Greco, & antico, sua inventione, e divisione; 12. Del Sistema di Guido Aretino; 13. Del Sistema principato comparato alle quattro Parti, & alla tastatura dell' Organo; 14. Della Melopeia; 15. Della proprietà del Canto; 16. Delle quattro parti Musicali, e loro natura; 17. Delle Mutationi; 18. Della Battuta; 19. Degl' Essempii di qualsivoglia Battuta; 20. Degl' Affetti causati dalla modulatione delle Parti.

### PARTE TERZA.

Cap. 1. Che sii contrapunto, consonanza, dissonanza, numero sonoro; 2. Delle consonanze, de dissonanze in particolare, e loro formatione in ordine Pratico; 3. Della consideratione del Numero in ordine Armonico; 4. Delle proportioni in ordine Armonico; 5. Delle dimostrationi delle consonanze, e dissonanze in ordine Teorico; 6. Del modo di formare li Passaggi; 7. Che non si possino fare due conzonanze perfette del medesimo genere; 8. Delli passaggi del Unisono; 9. Delli passaggi della terza maggiore, e minore; 10. Delli passaggi della Quinta; 11. Delli passaggi della Sesta maggiore, e minore; 12. Delli passaggi dell' Ottava; 13. Delle dissonanze in commune; 14. Delli passaggi della Seconda; 15. Delli passaggi della Quarta; 16 Delli passaggi della quarta superflua, e della Quinta diminuta; 17. Delli passaggi della Settima; 18. Delle Legature, e delle Sincope; 19. Delle due dissonanze, e delle due Negre; 20. Di alcune osservationi per le parte di mezzo.

### PARTE QUARTA.

Cap. 1. Di alcune regole generali del Contrapunto; 2. Delle spetie del Contrapunto; 3. Modo di formare l'Armonial Testura a due, e più voci per Contrapunto semplice; 4. Delli Tuoni, ò Modi Armoniali secondo gl' Antichi; 5. Delli Tuoni, ò Modi Armoniali secondo li Moderni; 6. Del modo di formare il Contrapunto a due, e più voci, e delle sue cadenze; 7. Delle regole per la formatione del Contrapunto sopra il Basso; 8. Delle Cadenze degli otto Tuoni delli Moderni; 9. Della natura, e proprietà delli Tuoni; 10. Del Contrapunto Fugato in genere; 11. Della Fuga in particolare, e delle sue Specie; 12. Delle Imitationi; 13. Delli Duo, e Fughe per tutti li Tuoni; 14. Delli Canoni; 15. Della formatione di più soggetti; 16. Delli Contrapunti doppii; 17. Del modo di rivoltare le Parti, e Soggetti; 18. Del modo di formare le Compositioni con Voci, Instrumenti; 19. Della Musica Finta, e Trasportatione delli Tuoni; 20 & Ultimo. Congedo dell' Auttore al suo Musico Testore.

It has already been remarked of the several treatises on music by Italian authors, from the time of Franchinus downwards, that the latter have for the most part been but repetitions of the former; and this might be objected to Tevo's book; but when it is considered that, notwithstanding the copiousness of the subject, it is concise, and at the same time perspicuous, it may well be considered as a valuable abridgment, abounding with a great variety of learning and useful instruction.

## CHAP. CLXI.

PIETRO TORRI, an Italian by birth, was, in the younger part of his life, chamber musician to the Margrave of Bareith; after that he became chapel master of the great church at Brussels. It is said that he was a disciple of Steffani, which is probable, seeing that his compositions are chiefly duets and close imitations of the style of that master. One of the most celebrated of his compositions of this kind is a duet entitled Heraclitus and Democritus, in which the affections of laughing and weeping are contrasted and expressed with singular art and ingenuity. He died about the year 1722. The fame of his excellence was very great throughout all Flanders; and it is said that in queen Anne's time, while we were at war with the French, his house being in some danger, the duke of Marlborough gave particular orders that it should be protected from violence; in gratitude for which instance of generosity, he presented the duke with a manuscript, containing some of the most valuable of his compositions, which are yet remaining in the family library.

About the beginning of the present century music flourished greatly under the patronage of the emperor Leopold, who was himself not only a judge, but a great master of the science; as an evidence whereof there are yet extant many compositions made by him for the service of his own chapel. He was a great friend of Kircher, as also to Thiel of Naumburg, mentioned in a former part of this work. To the latter he made many presents in reward of his excellent compositions.

The anonymous author of the life of this prince, published at London in 1708, in the character which he gives of him, speaks particularly to his affection for music, and represents the personal indignities to which his love of it sometimes exposed him, in the following passage :—

'This person was versed in most of the specula-'tive sciences, and understood musick to perfection, 'and had several pieces of his own composing sung in 'his own chapel, and therefore he had several musicians, especially Italians, about him, who showed 'themselves very insolent upon divers occasions, and 'more than once refused to sing in the face of the 'emperor himself and his court, upon pretence their 'salaries were not well paid them; and this, upon a 'representation to his Imperial majesty, what punishment they deserved, gave him occasion jestingly to 'answer, that these fellows, when they are deprived 'of their virility, might at the same time lose part of 'their brains. The impertinence of these eunuchs 'may be judged of by the behaviour of one of them 'a little before the emperor's death. This person 'crouding into the chapel where he had at that time 'no part of the music, and pressing upon a foreign 'knight to make way for him, which the other was 'not forward to do, the eunuch angrily said to him, "Ego sum Antonius M. Musicus sacræ Cæsareæ "majestatis."

The principal musicians in the court of the emperor Leopold were, his chapel-master Fux, and his vice chapel-masters Caldara and Ziani, all three very great men, but differently endowed, the first being a theorist, the others mere practical musicians. Here follows an account of them severally :—

JOHANN JOSEPH FUX was a native of Stiria, a province of Germany in the circle of Austria. In 1707 he published at Nuremberg a work of his composition, entitled 'Concentum musico-instrumentale in 7 partitas divisum,' and also composed an opera called Eliza, for the birth of the empress Elizabeth Christiana, which was printed at Amsterdam by Le Cene. But he is better known to the world by his 'Gradus 'ad Parnassum, sive manuductio ad compositionem 'musicæ regularem, methodo novâ ac certâ, nondum 'antè tam exacto ordine in lucem edita,' printed in the year 1725, and dedicated to the emperor Charles VI., who defrayed the whole expense of the publication. This work is printed in a folio volume, divided into two books, and merits particular notice.

In the preface he gives as reasons for writing his book, that many learned men have written on the speculative part of music, but few on the practice,[*] and that the precepts of these latter are not sufficiently clear. For these reasons, he says, and farther, because many young students of his acquaintance had testified an ardent desire of knowledge in the science, but were not able to attain it for want of proper instructors, he at first gave lectures to such, and continued so to do for near thirty years, during which time he had served three emperors of the Romans. At length, recollecting that sentiment of Plato recorded by Cicero, viz., that we were not born for ourselves, but for our country, our parents, and our friends, he determined to give his labours to the world, and now offers them to the public, with an apology for the work, that he was frequently interrupted in the progress of it by sick-

[*] In this assertion Fux is grossly mistaken: Franchinus, Zarlino, Zaccone, Artusi, Berardi, the elder Bononcini, Gasparini, and many others, whom we have enumerated, have written expressly on the subject of practical music.

ness, and the necessary attendance in the discharge of his function.

The first book is altogether speculative, its principal subject being number, with the proportions and differences thereof. The proportions that respect music the author makes to be five, namely, multiple, superparticular, superpartient, multiple-superparticular, and multiple-superpartient.

The division of proportion he says is threefold, namely, into arithmetical, harmonical, and geometrical, of all which an explanation has been given in the foregoing part of this work. He next describes the several operations for the multiplication, addition, and subtraction of ratios; applying the rules laid down by him to the discovery of the ratios of the several intervals contained in the octave.

Towards the conclusion of this book the author observes that the genera of the ancient Greeks were three; but that the moderns had restrained them to two, namely, the diatonic and chromatic, the commixture of which he says he does not disapprove: but he most earnestly dissuades the musicians of his time against the use of the mixed genus in the composition of church-music, having as he says, by long practice and experience found that the diatonic alone is most suitable to this style.

The second book is written in the form of a dialogue, the interlocutors in which are Aloysius a master, and Joseph a disciple. The author's reason for assuming those names is to be found in the preface, where he says that by Aloysius he means Prænestinus or Palestrina, to whom he owns himself indebted for all his knowledge in music, and whose memory he professes to reverence with the most pious regard; wherefore we are to understand by Joseph, Fux himself, whose Christian names were John Joseph.

In this conversation the author, in the person of Aloysius, delivers the precepts of musical composition, beginning with simple counterpoint, i. e. that which consists in the opposition of note to note, with various examples of compositions on a plain-song in two and three parts. From thence he proceeds to the other kinds, explaining as he goes along the use of the dissonances. From simple he proceeds to florid counterpoint, the doctrine of which he illustrates by a variety of exercises in four parts on a given plain-song.

Having delivered and illustrated by examples the precepts of counterpoint, the author goes on to explain the doctrine of fugue, which denomination he contends is applicable only to those compositions, where a certain point is proposed by one part, and answered by another, in intervals precisely the same, that is to say, such as may be proved by the sol-misation. This obliges him to lay down the order in which the tones and semitones succeed each other in the several modes or keys, and terminates in a very obvious distinction between fugues properly so called, in which the points in the several parts sol-fa alike, and those other where the sol-misation is different; these latter, though to the eye

they may appear fugues, being in fact no other than imitations.*

This explanation of the nature of fugue in general, is succeeded by rules for the composition of fugues in two, three, and four parts, and of double counterpoint, a kind of composition so constructed, as that the parts are converted the one into the other; that is to say, the upper becoming the under, and è converso; with many other varieties incident to this species, such as diminution, inversion, and retrograde progression.

At the end of this discourse on fugue, Aloysius reprehends very severely the singers in his time for those licentious variations which it was the practice with them to make.

Discoursing on the modes, he cites a passage from Plato in his Timæus, to show that the music of the ancient Greeks was originally very deficient in respect of the number of the intervals. He says that the ancient modes borrowed their names from those countries in which they were respectively invented or most in use, but that the true distinction between them arises from the different succession of the tones and semitones in each, from the unison to the octave. In short, he supposes the modes and the species of diapason to be correlative, and making the latter to be six in number, viz., D, E, F, G, A, C, he pronounces that, notwithstanding other authors reckon more, the modes are in fact only six.†

But here it is to be noted, that he admits of the distinction of the modes into authentic and plagal, the first of which two classes consists in the harmonical, the other in the arithmetical division of the diapason; and had he admitted B as a species of diapason, he would, agreeably to the sentiments of Glareanus, Zarlino, Artusi, and most of the succeeding writers, have brought out twelve modes, that is to say, six authentic, and six plagal; instead of which latter he gives but five, namely, C, D, E, G, A, passing over F, as incapable of an arithmetical division, by reason of the tritone arising at b. So that upon the whole he makes but eleven modes, agreeing in this particular with no one author that has written on the subject of music.

For the distinction between the authentic and plagal modes he cites the opinion of Zarlino, who says that the beginnings and endings, or closes, are the same in both, and that the sole difference between them consists in the nature of the modulation, which in the authentic modes is in the acute, and in the plagal in the grave part.

Having before assumed that there are but six species of diapason or octave, and having justly remarked that the distinction of authentic and plagal respects chiefly the ecclesiastical tones, he proceeds to point out, by means of the flat and sharp signatures, several successions of tones and semitones, which he says are transpositions from the several modes: a needless labour as it seems, seeing that the use

* This distinction is very accurately noted in Dr. Pepusch's Short Introduction to Harmony.

† The species of diatessaron are three, and of diapente four; and these added together form seven species of diapason. See page 130 of this work; and Wallisii Append. in Ptolemæi Harmonicis, 4to. page 310, 311.

of six modes, in the sense in which the term is strictly understood, is unknown to the moderns, who look upon the word as synonymous with the word key; and of these there seem to be in nature but two, viz., those whose respective finals are A and C,* the one having its third minor, and the other major; and into one or other of these all that variety of keys, included under the denomination of Musica ficta, or, as the Italians call it, Musica finta, that is to say, feigned music, are demonstrably resolvable.

Towards the conclusion of his work he treats of the ecclesiastical style, which he says is of two kinds, to wit, that of the chapel, and that proper for a full choir. With respect to the former he observes that in the primitive times the divine offices were sung without the aid of instruments; and that the same practice prevails in many cathedral churches, and also in the court of the emperor during the time of Lent. But that notwithstanding the primitive practice, the organ, and a variety of other instruments were introduced into the chapel service, and continued to be used, with the exceptions above noted, in his time. He recommends in the composition of music for the service of the chapel, the pure diatonic genus, without any mixture of the chromatic, and celebrates Palestrina as the prince of composers in the chapel style, referring to a motet of his, ' Ad te ' Domine levavi animam meam,' as a composition admirably adapted to the sense of the words, and in other respects most excellent.

After this he gives some directions for compositions for the chapel, wherein the organ and other instruments are employed. In these he says the restrictions are fewer than in the former; and adds, that the first and second violin parts should ever be in the unison with the cantus, as the trumpets are with the altus and tenor.

Of the mixed style, or that which is proper for a full choir, he says but little, and proceeds to the recitative style, for composing in which he gives a few general rules; and is most particular in pointing out those rests and clausules which best correspond with the points or stops in written speech, namely, the comma, semicolon, colon, and period; as also with the notes of interrogation and admiration, and with these he concludes his discourse.

Upon a careful survey of this work of Fux, it may be said to be sui generis, for it is of a class a little superior to those many introductions to music, heretofore mentioned to have been written for the instruction of children, and published in Germany above two centuries ago, under the titles of Enchiridion Musicæ, Musicæ Isagoge, Erotemata Musicæ, Compendium Musices,† &c. and greatly below those more elaborate works that treat of the science at large.

Antonio Caldara, one of the vice-chapel-masters of the emperor Leopold, under Fux, is celebrated for the sublimity of his style, which he has manifested in two oratorios of his composition, the one

entitled Giuseppe, performed in the year 1722; the other ' Il Ré del dolore, in Giesu Cristo Signor ' nostro, coronato di spine.' He published two operas of sonatas for two violins and a bass, printed at Amsterdam, and 'Cantate da Camera à voce sola,' printed at Venice.

Mark Antonio Ziani, the other vice-chapel-master of the Emperor Leopold, composed sundry operas and oratorios, which, being extant only in manuscript, are no where to be found but in the collections of the curious, though there are sonatas of his extant, printed by Roger. The three persons above named are spoken of in terms of great respect in a collection of Letters from the Academy of Ancient Music at London to Sig. Antonio Lotti of Venice, with his answers and testimonies, published at London 1732.

Antonio Lotti was organist of the ducal chapel of St. Mark at Venice. In the year 1705 he published at Venice, and dedicated to the emperor Joseph, a work entitled 'Duetti Terzetti e Madrigali.' In this collection is a madrigal for five voices, inscribed ' La Vita Caduca,' beginning ' In una Siepe ombrosa.' The history of this composition is attended with some peculiar circumstances: the words of it were written by Abbate Pariati, and the music to it composed at his request: in return for some compositions of Ziani, Lotti sent to that master a copy of this madrigal, which he caused to be sung before the emperor Leopold, who highly approved of it; upon which Lotti determined to publish his Duetti Terzetti, &c., and dedicated it to the emperor; but he dying before it was finished, he dedicated it to the emperor Joseph, who honoured him with a present customary on those occasions, a gold chain and medal.

Many years after the publication of the book, this madrigal was produced in manuscript in the Academy of Ancient Music at London, as a composition of Giovanni Bononcini, then resident here. But it being known to some of the members that it had been published among other of Lotti's works, Bononcini's title to it was disputed; and he refusing to clear up the matter, an appeal was made to the author himself, he being then living, which terminated in the utter confusion of Bononcini and his adherents. The particulars of this controversy will be given in a subsequent page, among other transactions of the Academy of Ancient Music.

Excepting the above work, we know of no compositions of Lotti in print, but there are very many in manuscript, which shew him to have been a very fine composer of church-music. He married Signora Santini, a celebrated singer, who had appeared in most of the courts in Germany. Lotti was living at Venice in the year 1731, as appears by his correspondence with the Academy above mentioned.

Francesco Conti, a celebrated theorbist, was, upon the decease of Ziani, appointed vice-chapel-master to the emperor of Germany. He composed an opera entitled ' Archelao Rè di .Cappadocia,' the words whereof were written by Abbate Pariati, as also

* Vide ante, page 60 of this work, et seq.
† See page 397 of this work, et seq.

the opera of Clotilda, performed at London in the year 1709.

The misfortunes of this person, arising from an inconsiderate indulgence of his resentment, have excited compassion in some, who would otherwise perhaps have envied the reputation and honours which he enjoyed. In the year 1730, upon some provocation given him by a secular priest at Vienna, he revenged the insult by blows, and was sentenced to a most severe punishment. The particulars of his sentence are contained in the following extract of a letter from Ratisbon, dated October 19, 1730.

'Vienna, Sept. 10. The Imperial composer, 'Franc. Conti, in pursuance of a decree of a church-'ban pronounced against him, was sentenced to 'stand at the door of the cathedral church of St. 'Stephen. His Imperial majesty indeed, with his 'usual clemency, reduced the standing three times 'to once only; but as he behaved so ill the first 'time of standing in the presence of many hundred 'people, he was ordered to stand again at the said 'door the 17th of Sept. for the second time, in 'a long hair coat, called a coat of penitence, between 'twelve peace-officers, forming a circle about him, 'with a black lighted torch in his hand, for an hour, 'which he is to do again on the 24th. His allowance 'is bread and water, so long as he is in the hands of 'the spiritual court, and as soon as he shall be 'delivered to the temporal he will be fined to pay '1000 florins to the clergyman he struck, and all 'the costs and damages besides, and to be imprisoned 'four years, and afterwards banished for ever from 'the Austrian dominions, because he behaved so 'rude and scandalously the first time of his standing 'before the church door.

'The following epigram was made on this occasion:—

'Non ea musa bona est nec musica, composuisti
　'Quam Conti, tactus nam fuit ille gravis;
'Et bassus nimium crassus neque consona clavis:
　'Perpetuo nigras hic geris ergo notas.'

It evidently appears by the foregoing account of the progress of music, that among the moderns the great improvements both in science and practice were made by the Italians; and that these were in general adopted by the Germans, the French, the English, and indeed almost every other nation in Europe. The French, even so early as the time of Charlemagne, appear to have been extremely averse to innovations, at least in their church-music; since that they have been very backward in adopting the improvements of their neighbours; and it was not till about the middle of the last century that music flourished in any considerable degree among them. But soon after that time, in consequence of the studies of Mersennus, and the practice of Lully, a style was formed in France, which by other countries was thought worthy of imitation.

Of Cambert and Lully, Nivers and Brossard, an account has already been given. Here follow memoirs of such other French musicians as are most distinguished for skill either in the theory or practice of the science.

## CHAP. CLXII.

HENRI DUMONT, chapel-master to Louis XIV. is celebrated by the French writers as a masterly performer on the organ. He was born in the diocese of Leige in 1610, and was the first French musician that introduced thorough-bass into his compositions. There are extant some of his motets, which are in great estimation; as also five grand masses, called royal masses, which are still performed in some of the convents in Paris, and in many provincial churches of France. Dumont died at Paris in the year 1684.

MICHEL LAMBERT was born in 1610, at Vivonne, a small village of Poitou. He had an exquisite hand on the lute, and sang to it with peculiar grace and elegance. His merit alone preferred him to the office of master of the king's chamber music; upon which he became so eminent, that persons of the highest rank became his pupils, and resorted to his house, in which he held a kind of musical academy. Lambert is reckoned the first who gave his countrymen a just notion of the graces of vocal music. His compositions however are of but small account, consisting only of some little motetts, music for the Leçons de Ténebres, and a collection containing sundry airs of one, two, three, and four parts, with a thorough-bass. Lambert had a daughter, who was the wife of Lully. He died at Paris in the year 1690.*

GAUTHIER, surnamed the Elder, was also an admired French lutenist. He, together with a cousin of his, Pierre Gauthier, mentioned in the next article, published a collection entitled 'Livre 'de tableau des pieces de Luth sur différens modes.' The authors have added some rules for playing on this instrument. The principal piece of the elder Gauthier are those lessons of his entitled l'Immortelle, la Nonpareille, le Tombeau de Mezangeau. There was also a Denis Gauthier, who composed lessons much admired by performers on the lute, of which the most esteemed are those entitled l'Homicide, le Canon, and le Tombeau de Lenclos.

PIERRE GAUTHIER, a musician of Ciotat, in Provence, was director of an opera company, which exhibited by turns at Marseilles, Montpellier, and Lyons. He embarked at the Port de Cette, and perished in the vessel, at the age of fifty-five, in 1697. There is extant of his composition a collection of duos and trios, which is much esteemed.

LOULIÉ, a French musician, was the author of an ingenious and useful book, published in 1698 by Estienne Roger of Amsterdam, entitled 'Elements ou Principes de Musique mis dans un nouvel ordre,' in which, after teaching the method of solmisation according to the French manner, in which the syllable SI is assumed for the last note of the septenary, he explains the nature of transposition, and suggests the method of reducing music in any of the keys denoted by either the acute or grave signatures into the original or radical keys,

* In Sir George Etherege's comedy of the Man of Mode, Sir Fopling says, 'I learned to sing at Paris, of Lambert, the greatest master in the 'world, but I have his own fault, a weak voice.'

from which they are respectively transpositions; which practice is explained at large in Chapter XII of this work. A discovery the more worthy of notice, as some pains have been taken to conceal it.*

In the course of his work the author lays down an easy rule for the division of the monochord, and assigns the proportions of the natural sounds in the octave, distinguishing between the greater and lesser tone. Towards the end of the book is a description of an instrument called by him the Chronometer, contrived for the measuring of time by means of a pendulum. The form of the instrument, as exhibited by him, is that of an Ionic pilaster, and is thus described by Malcolm in his Treatise of Music, page 407 :—

'The Chronometer consists of a large ruler or
' board six foot or seventy-two inches long, to be
' set on end; it is divided into its inches, and the
' numbers set so as to count upwards; and at every
' division there is a small round hole, through whose
' center the line of division runs. At the top of
' this ruler, about an inch above the division 72,
' and perpendicular to the ruler, is inserted a small
' piece of wood, in the upper side of which there is
' a groove, hollowed along from the end that stands
' out to that which is fixt in the ruler, and near
' each end of it a hole is made : through these holes
' a pendulum chord is drawn, which runs in the
' groove; at that end of the chord that comes
' through the hole furthest from the ruler the ball
' is hung, and at the other end there is a small
' wooden pin, which can be put in any of the holes
' of the ruler; when the pin is in the upmost hole
' at 72, then the pendulum from the top to the center
' of the ball, must be exactly seventy-two inches;
' and therefore whatever hole of the ruler it is put
' in, the pendulum will be just so many inches as
' that figure at the hole denotes. The manner of
' using the machine is this; the composer lengthens
' or shortens his pendulum till one vibration be
' equal to the designed length of his bar, and then
' the pin stands at a certain division, which marks
' the length of the pendulum; and this number
' being set with the clef at the beginning of the
' song, is a direction to others how to use the
' chronometer in measuring the time according to
' the composer's design; for with the number is set
' the note, crotchet or minim, whose value he would
' have the vibration to be; which in brisk duple
' time is best a minim or half a bar, or even a whole
' bar, when that is but a minim; and in slow time
' a crotchet. In triple time it would do well to be
' the third part, or half or fourth part of a bar; and
' in the simple triples that are allegro, let it be a

' whole bar. And if in every time that is allegro,
' the vibration is applied to a whole or half bar,
' practice will teach us to subdivide it justly and
' equally. And mind that to make this machine of
' universal use, some canonical measure of the divi-
' sions must be agreed upon, that the figure may
' give a certain direction for the length of the
' pendulum.'

JEAN BAPTISTE MOREAU, a musician of Angers, was led by his musical talents to try his fortune in Paris; and having succeeded in a bold attempt to get unperceived into the closet of Madame the Dauphiness Victoire de Baviere, who was fond of music, he had the assurance to pull her by the sleeve, and ask permission to sing to her a little air of his own composing; the dauphiness, laughing, permitted him; he sang without being disconcerted, and the princess was pleased. The story came to the king, and he desiring to see him, Moreau was introduced to his majesty in the apartment of Madame Maintenon, and sang several airs, with which the king was so well pleased, that he immediately ordered him to compose a musical entertainment, which was performed at Marli two months after, and applauded by the whole court. He was also engaged to compose the interludes for the tragedies of Esther, Athalie, Jonathas, and several other pieces for the house of St. Cyr. His chief excellence consisted in his giving the full force of expression to all kinds of words and subjects assigned him. The poet Lainez, with whom he was intimate, furnished him with songs and little cantatas, which he set to music, but none of them are published.

MARC ANTOINE CHARPENTIER was superintendant of the music of the duke of Orleans, and his instructor in the art of musical composition. He has left several operas, one of which, viz., his Medèe, was in its time highly celebrated. He composed another called Philomele, which was thrice represented in the Palais Royal. The duke of Orleans, who had composed part of it, would not suffer it to be published. Charpentier died at Paris in 1704.

LOUIS LULLY, and JEAN LOUIS LULLY, sons of Jean Baptist Lully, were also musicians. They composed in conjunction the music to the opera of Zephire et Flore, written by Michel du Boullai, secretary to the grand prior of Vendôme, and represented in the Academie Royal on the twenty-second day of March, 1688. They also set the opera of Orpheus, written by the same person, and an opera called Alcide.

PASCAL COLASSE, chapel-master to Louis XIV., was born at Paris 1636. He was a pupil of Lully and took him for his model in all his compositions, as the following lines testify :—

Colasse de Lulli craignit de s'écarter,
Il le pilla, dit-on, cherchant à l'imiter.

But it is said that whether he imitated Lully or not, his opera of Thetis and Peleus will always be esteemed an excellent production. There are besides of his composition, motets and songs. Colasse destroyed both his fortune and health in an infatuated

---

* In Dr. Pepusch's Short Introduction to Harmony is a whole chapter on the subject of transposition, referring to a plate with a diagram of six keys, viz., three with the minor, and three with the major third, with the flats and sharps in order as they arise. Over this is a stave of lines which he calls the slider, with the letters signifying the cliffs placed thereon. To enable the student to reduce any transposition to its original key, he is directed to cut off the slider, and apply it to the diagram, which process will terminate in the annihilation of the flat and sharp signatures, and shew the original key from whence the transposition is made. For the reason of the whole the student is to seek; but the secret is revealed by Loulié in the twenty-ninth page of his book above mentioned.

pursuit of the Philosopher's Stone, and died at Versailles in the year 1709.

N. ALLOUETTE, conductor of the music in the church of Notre Dame at Paris, is known for his motets and a very fine Miserere. Lully was his master.

GUILLAUME MINORET was one of the four masters of, or composers to the chapel of Louis XIV.* He composed many motets, which, though greatly admired, have never yet been printed. Those in greatest esteem are 'Quemadmodum desiderat,' 'Lauda Jerusalem Dominum,' 'Venite exultemus,' 'Nisi Dominus ædificaverit domum.' Minoret died in the year 1716 or 1717, in a very advanced age.

ANDRE' CAMPRA, born at Aix in Provence in 1660, was at first a chorister in the cathedral of that city, having for his instructor in music William Poitevin, a preacher to that church. Soon after his leaving the choir he became distinguished by his motets, which were performed in churches and private concerts, and so well received that they procured him the rank of director of the music in the Jesuits' church at Paris, and some other preferment in that metropolis. His genius having been too much confined while restrained to the narrow limits of a motet, he set himself to compose for the stage, and made the music to sundry operas. His progress in this new course of study was answerable to his industry, and by following the manner of Lully he acquired a degree of excellence but little inferior. His Europe Galante, Carnaval de Venise, and Fêtes Venitiennes; his Ages, his Fragmen de Lully, which are ballets, his operas of Hesione, Alcide, Telephé, Camille, and Tancrede, were greatly applauded, and are still admired. The grace and vivacity of his airs, the sweetness of his melody, and, above all, his strict attention to the sense of the words, render his compositions truly estimable.

JEAN GILLES, of Tarascon, in Provence, was director of the music, or chapel-master in the church of St. Stephen in Thoulouse. He possessed the Christian virtue of charity in so great a degree, and had such a disposition to relieve the distresses of others, as tended to the impoverishment of himself. He was a singer in the choir of the cathedral of Aix, and a fellow-pupil, with the celebrated Campra, of William Poitevin, mentioned in the preceding article. Gilles's abilities soon became so conspicuous, that Bertier, bishop of Rieux, who particularly esteemed him, solicited for him the place of chapel-master in the church of St. Stephen in Thoulouse; but the chapter had already conferred it on Farinelli,† who, on being told that Gilles was a candidate for it,

sought out his competitor, and obliged him to acquiesce in his resignation of the office—an instance of generosity equally honourable to both. There are of Gilles many fine motets; several of them have been performed in the Concert Spirituel at Paris with great applause, particularly his 'Diligam te.' But his capital work, however, is a Messe des Morts, in which, at the first time of performing it, he sang himself.

MICHEL RICHARD DE LALANDE, born at Paris in the year 1657, was the fifteenth child of his parents, and discovering in his infancy a strong propensity to music, he was entered a chorister in the church of St. German l'Auxerrois, and was there distinguished for the fineness of his voice. At the age of puberty his voice left him, but before that time, by diligent application, and frequently spending whole nights in practice, he attained to great perfection on various instruments, and on the violin in particular he played with great facility and judgment. Being thus qualified, he applied to Lully, requesting to be taken into the opera, but being rejected, he broke his instrument, and renounced the use of it for ever.‡ After this discouragement he betook himself to the organ and harpsichord, and was soon solicited to accept of several churches, but at length was chosen by the duke de Noailles to instruct his eldest daughter. This nobleman, who never suffered any opportunity to escape him of bearing testimony to the merit of Lalande, embraced an occasion of recommending him to Louis XIV., and did it with so much honest warmth that the king chose him to instruct his daughters, Mademoiselle de Blois and Mademoiselle de Nantes, on the harpsichord. He frequently composed in obedience to the orders, and sometimes even in the presence of Louis, little musical pieces, and so much was the king delighted with him that he loaded him with favours. He enjoyed in succession the two offices of music-master of the king's chamber, the two of composer, that of superintendent of music and the four offices of the royal chapel. His motets, which were always performed before Louis XIV. and Louis XV. with great applause, have been collected and published in two volumes in folio. The Cantate, the Dixit, and the Miserere, are principally admired. He died at Versailles in 1726.

J. THEOBALDE, called THEOBALDO GATTI, was born at Florence. It is said of him, that, being charmed with the music of Lully, which had reached him even in his native country, he went to Paris to compliment that celebrated musician, and in all his compositions studied to emulate him, and at length discovered himself to be a meritorious pupil of that great man, by two operas which he caused to be represented in the Royal Academy of Paris, viz., Coronis, a pastoral in three acts, the words by Mons. Baugé; and Scylla, a tragedy in five. He died at Paris in the year 1727, at an advanced age, having for fifty years been a performer on the bass viol in the orchestra of the opera, and was interred in the church of St. Eustache.

---

* The others were Colosse, Lalande, and Coupillet. They were all chosen upon great deliberation, for upon the death of Dumont in 1680, or thereabouts, the king instead of two composers for his chapel would have four; and to that end he directed circular letters to be sent into all the provinces of France, inviting musicians to Versailles, in order to give proof of their abilities. Le Seur was a candidate for one of the places, but lost it by his unhappy setting of two words in a motett, and Coupillet succeeded by fraud; for after he was elected it was discovered that the composition by which he obtained the place was not his own, but the work of Desmarets, a young man then unknown, but who afterwards became one of the first musicians in France.

† This might possibly be that Farinelli already spoken of as concertmaster or director of the music in the electoral palace of Hanover, and whom Mattheson in his Vollkommenen Capellmeister expressly asserts to have been the uncle of Carlo Broschi Farinelli, the famous singer in the opera at the Haymarket.

‡ He had been valet to the Marshal de Grammont, and by him was introduced to Lully. See page 648 of this work.

JEAN FRANCOIS LALOUETTE, a disciple of Lully, successively conducted the music in the churches of St. Germain l'Auxerrois and Notre Dame. He composed many motets for a full choir, which are much admired; but none of his compositions have been published, except some motets for the principal anniversary festivals, for one, two, and three voices, with a thorough bass. He died at Paris in 1728, at the age of 75.

MARIN MARAIS, born at Paris in 1656, made so rapid a progress in the art of playing on the viol, that Sainte-Colombe, his master, at the end of six months would give him no farther instructions. He carried the art of playing on this instrument to the highest pitch of perfection, and was appointed one of the chamber music to the king. Marais was the first that thought of adding to the viol three strings of brass wire to deepen the tone. He composed several pieces for the viol, and sundry operas, namely, Alcide, Ariane, Bacchus, Alcione, and Semelé, the most celebrated of which is the Alcione. There is a tempest in it particularly admired, and which produces an astonishing effect; a rumbling and doleful sound joining with the sharp notes of a flute and other instruments, presents to the ear all the horrors of a tempestuous ocean and the whistling of the wildest winds. His works bear the pregnant marks of a fertile genius, united to an exquisite taste and judgment. This celebrated musician died in 1728, in the Fauxbourg S. Marceau, and lies buried in the church of St. Hyppolite. He has left behind him of his composition three collections of pieces for the bass viol.*

ELIZABETH CLAUDE JACQUETTE DE LA GUERRE, a female musician, the daughter of Marin de la Guerre, organist of the chapel of St. Gervais in Paris, was born in that city in 1669, and instructed in the practice of the harpsichord and the art of composition by her father. She was a very fine performer, and would sing and accompany herself with so rich and exquisite a flow of harmony as captivated all that heard her. She was also an excellent composer, and, in short, possessed such a degree of skill, as well in the science as the practice of music, that but few of her sex have equalled her. An opera of her composition, entitled Cephale et Procris, was represented in the Royal Academy of Paris in the year 1694, and is extant in print. She died in the year 1729, and lies buried in the church of St. Eustache in Paris.

SALOMON, a native of Provence, was admitted into the band of the chapel royal to play on the bass viol, an instrument on which he excelled. This man, who was very plain and simple in his appearance, seemed to possess no other talent than that of playing with exactness and precision; yet he composed an opera entitled Medèe et Jason, which was performed in the Royal Academy in 1713 with great applause, and is in print. At the first night of

the representation he went disguised into the crowd, and was a silent witness of the praises and censures passed upon the piece. Salomon died at Versailles in the year 1731, being seventy years of age.

JEAN LOUIS MARCHAND was a native of Lyons, and an organist of some church in that city; when, being very young, he would needs go to Paris, and strolling as by accident into the chapel of the college of St. Louis le Grand, a few minutes before service was to begin, he obtained permission to play the organ; and so well did he acquit himself, that the Jesuits taking pains to find him out, retained him amongst them, and provided him with every requisite to perfect himself in his art. Marchand would never give up his office in that college, though he was tempted to it by advantageous offers. He died at Paris in 1732, aged sixty-three, and left of his composition two books of lessons for the harpsichord, which are greatly admired.

FRANCOIS COUPERIN, organist of the chapel to Louis XIV. and his successor, the late king, and also of his chamber-music, in which he had the charge of the harpsichord, was a very fine composer for this latter instrument.

The family of Couperin has produced a succession of persons eminent in music; the following is a brief account of it. There were three brothers of the name of Louis, Francis, and Charles, natives of Chaume, a little town in Brie. Louis, the eldest, was become eminent for his performance on the organ, and in consequence thereof obtained the place of organist of the king's chapel. In reward of his merit a post was created for him, namely, that of Dessus-de-viole. He died about the year 1665, at the age of thirty-five, and has left of his composition three suites of lessons for the harpsichord, in manuscript, which are to be found only in the collections of the curious.

Francis, the second of the three brothers, was a master of the harpsichord, but no composer: he practised and taught his scholars the lessons of his brother. At the age of seventy he had the misfortune to be overturned in a carriage in one of the streets of Paris, and lost his life by the accident. He had a daughter named Louisa, who sang and played on the harpsichord with admirable grace and skill, and who, notwithstanding her sex, was in the number of the king's musicians, and in that capacity received an annual pension or salary. She died in the year 1728, at about the age of fifty-two.

Charles, the youngest, was a celebrated organist: he died in 1669, leaving one son, namely, Francis Couperin, above spoken of, and who was indeed the glory of the family, being, perhaps, the finest composer for the harpsichord that the French have to boast of. The lessons for this instrument, published by himself, make four volumes in folio; among them is one entitled 'Les Goûts réunis, ou l'Apothéose de Lulli et de Corelli,' and the following allemande, which may serve as a specimen of his style :—

* Catalogue de la Musique, imprimée à Amsterdam chez Etienne Roger, page 42.

Francois Couperin.

The foregoing air is entitled ' Les Idées Heureuses,' agreeably to the practice of the French composers of lessons for the harpsichord. See the article        Gauthier, ante page 776.

This Couperin, whom we must call the younger Francis, died in 1733, aged sixty-five, leaving two daughters, equally celebrated for their performance on that which appears to have been the favourite instrument of the family ; the one a nun in the abbey of Maubuisson ; the other is the successor of her father in the charge of the harpsichord in the king's chamber, an employment which, except in this instance, was never known to have been conferred on any but men.

## CHAP. CLXIII.

THE establishment of the Royal Academy at Paris contributed greatly to the improvement of the French music, but it failed of answering the ultimate end of its institution. It appears to have been the design of Cardinal Mazarine and Louis XIV. to introduce a style in France corresponding with that of the Italians : but for reasons arising from the temper and genius of the people, or perhaps some other inscrutable causes, it gradually deflected from its original, and in the space of a few years assumed a character so different from that of the Italian music, that it afforded ground for a dispute which of the two was entitled to the preference, and gave rise to a controversy which is scarely yet at an end. It began as follows :—

In the year 1704 was published a small tract entitled ' Paralele des Italiens et des François, en ce qui regarde la Musique et les Opera,' in which the pretensions of each are thus stated :—

On the part of the French it is asserted, that the French operas are, in respect of the poetry, regular coherent compositions, perfectly consistent with the laws of the drama ; and as to the music, that the French have the advantage of bass voices, so proper in the character of gods, kings, and heroes ; that the French opera derives still farther advantages from the chorusses and dances ; that the French masters excel those of Italy in their performance on the violin, the hautboy, and the flute ;* the latter of whom, says this author, have taught the instrument to lament in so affecting a manner in the mournful airs, and to sigh so amorously in those that are tender, that all are moved by them. Besides these advantages he mentions others on the side of the French, as, namely, their habits and their dances ; he says that the Combatans and the Cyclopes in Perseus, the Trembleurs and the Forgerons in Isis, and the Songes Funestes in Atys, all operas of Lully, as well in respect of the airs as of the stops adapted thereto by Beauchamp, are originals in their kind. And lastly, that the conduct and economy of a French opera is through the whole so admirable, that no person of common understanding will deny that it affords a more lively representation than the Italian, and that a mere spectator cannot but be much better pleased in France than Italy.

* Here the author celebrates as fine performers on the flute, Philbert, Philidor, Descoteaux, and les Hoteterres.

In behalf of the Italian music the author observes, that the language itself, abounding with vowels that are all sonorous, whereas above half the French vowels are mute, or at least are seldom pronounced, is more naturally adapted to music than that of the French. That in their respective compositions the invention of the Italians appears to be inexhaustible ; that of the French narrow and constrained. That the French in their airs affect the soft, the easy, and the flowing ; but the Italians pass boldly from sharp to flat, and from flat to sharp, venturing on the most irregular dissonances, and the boldest cadences ; so that their airs resemble the compositions of no other nation in the world : and that a like boldness is discoverable in the Italian singers, who, having been taught from their cradles to sing at all times, and in all places, sing the most irregular passages with the same assurance as they would the most orderly, uttering everything with a confidence that secures them success. He says that the Italians are more susceptible of the passions than the French, and by consequence express them more strongly in their music ; as an instance whereof the author refers to a symphony in a performance at the Oratory of St. Jerome at Rome, on St. Martin's day, in the year 1697, upon these two words, ' mille saette,' of which he speaks to this purpose. ' The air consisted of ' disjoined notes, like those in a jig, which gave the ' soul a lively impression of an arrow ; and that ' wrought so effectually on the imagination, that ' every violin appeared to be a bow, and their bows ' were like so many flying arrows darting their ' pointed heads upon every part of the symphony.' From simple airs the author proceeds to the consideration of compositions in several parts, in which he says the Italians have greatly the advantage ; for that whereas in the French music the melody of the upper part is only regarded, in the Italian it is so equally good in all the parts, that we know not which to prefer. He concludes his remarks on the general comparison of the French and Italian music, with an observation that Lully was an Italian ; and that he excelled all the musicians in France, even in the opinion of the French themselves ; and that therefore, to establish an equality between the two nations, an instance ought to be produced of a French musician who has in the like degree excelled those of Italy ; but this he says is impossible. He adds that Italy produced Luigi, Carissimi, Melani, and Legrenzi, and after them Scarlatti, Bononcini, Corelli, and Bassani, who were living at the time of his writing, and charmed all Europe with their excellent productions.

From this general comparison the author proceeds to one more particular, viz., that of the French with the Italian opera. He confesses that the French recitative is to be preferred to the Italian, which he says is close and simple, with very little inflection of the voice, and therefore too nearly approaches common speech ; but he says that accompanying their recitatives with such fine harmony as the Italians use, is a practice not to be met with in any other part of the world whatsoever. Having mentioned in the foregoing part of his discourse the advantage which the music of France derives from the number of bass voices with which that country abounds, he observes that this is small in comparison with the benefit which the opera in Italy receives from the castrati, who are there very numerous; and on the comparative excellence of these over women, in respect of the sweetness, flexibility, and energy of the voice, he expatiates very largely, adding, that whereas the voices of women seldom continue in perfection above twelve years, those of castrati will continue for forty: he adds, that the latter are fitter in general to represent female characters than even women themselves, for that they usually look handsomer on the stage; as an instance whereof he mentions Ferini, who performed the part of Sybaris, in the opera of Themistocles at Rome, in 1685. He says that all the towns in Italy abound with actors of both sexes; and that himself once saw at Rome a man who understood music well; and who, though he was neither a musician nor a comedian by profession, but a procurator or solicitor, that had left his business in the carnival time to perform a part in the opera,* acquitted himself as an actor as well as either the French Harlequin or Raisin could have done upon such occasion.

He says that the Italians have the same advantage over the French in respect of their instruments and the performers, as of their singers and their voices. That their violins are much larger strung, and their bows longer.† That the arch-lutes of the Italians are as large again as the theorboes of the French, as are also their bass-viols. That in Italy, youths of fourteen or fifteen play at sight over the shoulders of perhaps two or three persons standing between them and the book, such symphonies as would puzzle the best French masters, and this correctly, without having the time measured to them; whereas nothing of the kind is to be seen at Paris. But the reason he gives for the exquisite performance in the Italian bands is, that the greatest masters are not above appearing in them. 'I have,' says this author, ' seen Corelli, Pasquini, and Gaetani play all together ' in the same opera at Rome; and they are allowed ' to be the greatest masters in the world on the ' violin, the harpsichord, and Theorbo or Arch-lute; ' and as such they are generally paid 3 or 400 ' pistoles a-piece for a month or six weeks at most; ' whereas in France the profession of music is ' despised.'

He concludes his comparison with a description of some very extraordinary representations on the Italian stage, of which he says he was an eye-witness; which description is here given in the words of a very judicious person,‡ the translator of

the book into English. 'To conclude all, the Italian ' decorations and machines are much better than ' ours; their boxes are more magnificent; the open-' ing of the stage higher, and more capacious; our ' painting, compared to theirs, is no better than ' daubing; you will find among their decorations ' statutes of marble and alabaster, that may vie with ' the most celebrated antiques in Rome; palaces, ' colonnades, galleries, and sketches of architecture, ' superior in grandeur and magnificence to all the ' buildings in the world; pieces of perspective that ' deceive the judgment as well as the eye, even of ' those that are curious in the art; prospects of ' a prodigious extent, in spaces not thirty feet deep; ' nay, they often represent on the stage the lofty ' edifices of the ancient Romans, of which only the ' remains are now to be seen; such as the Colossus ' which I saw in the Roman college in the year 1698,§ ' in the same perfection in which it stood in the reign ' of Vespasian its founder; so that these decorations ' are not only entertaining but instructive.

'As for their machines, I cannot think it in the ' power of human wit to carry the invention farther. ' In the year 1697 I saw an opera at Turin, wherein ' Orpheus‖ was to charm the wild beasts by the ' power of his voice: of these there were all sorts ' introduced on the stage; nothing could be more ' natural, or better designed; an ape among the ' rest played an hundred pranks, the most diverting ' in the world, leaping on the backs of the other ' animals, scratching their heads, and entertaining ' the spectators with the rest of his monkey-tricks. ' I saw once at Venice an elephant discovered on ' the stage, when, in an instant, that great machine ' disappeared, and an army was seen in its place; ' the soldiers having, by the disposition of their ' shields, given so true a representation of it, as if ' it had been a real living elephant.

'The ghost of a woman, surrounded with guards, ' was introduced on the theatre of Capranica at Rome ' in the year 1698; this phantom extending her arms, ' and unfolding her cloaths, was, with one motion, ' transformed into a perfect palace, with its front, its ' wings, its body, and court-yard, all formed by ' magical architecture; the guards striking their ' halberds on the stage, were immediately turned ' into so many water-works, cascades, and trees, ' that formed a charming garden before the palace. ' Nothing can be more quick than were those changes, ' nothing more ingenious or surprising: and, in ' truth, the greatest wits in Italy frequently amuse

---

* The name of the person here alluded to was Paciani, a man well known at Rome at the latter end of the last century; his performances on the theatre were gratuitous, and the mere result of his fondness for the profession of an actor.

† The bow of the violin has been gradually increasing in length for these last seventy years; it is now about twenty-eight inches. In the year 1720, a bow of twenty-four inches was, on account of its length, called a Sonata bow; the common bow was shorter; and by the account above given the French bow must have been shorter still.

‡ Supposed to be Mr. Galliard.

§ ' The Colossus the author mentions was painted by father Andrea ' Pozzo the Jesuit, who, as well for his painting in the church of St. ' Ignatius belonging to his order, and other pieces, but especially for his ' book of perspective, in folio, printed at Rome, is worthily esteemed as ' the first man in that kind, by all those that have any skill in that ' science.'
The intelligent reader needs hardly be told that both in the passage above, and in this note, the translator has mistaken his author in rendering the word Colisée Colossus, instead of Coliseum, the name of the amphitheatre of Vespasian, the ruins whereof are yet to be seen at Rome.

‖ This opera of Orpheus was afterwards performed at Rome, but not succeeding, the undertakers were obliged to have recourse to the opera of Roderigo, which they had presented just before. This opera of Roderigo was composed by Francesco Gasparini, and was universally applauded. Both these were performed on the theatre della Pace, and the principal parts were done by Biscione, Maurino, and Valentino, he who afterwards sang in the opera in London.

'themselves with inventions of this nature: people
'of the first quality entertain the publick with such
'spectacles as these, without any prospect of gain
'to themselves.* Signor Cavaliero Acciaioli, brother
'to the cardinal of that name, had the direction
'of those on the theatre Capranica in the year 1698.
'This is the sum of what can be offered on behalf
'of the French or Italian musick by way of parallel.
'I have but one thing more to add in favour of the
'operas in Italy, which will confirm all that has
'been already said to their advantage; which is,
'that though they have neither chorusses nor other
'diversions in use with us, their entertainments last
'five or six hours together,† and yet the audience is
'never tired; whereas after one of our representations,
'which does not hold above half so long at most,
'there are very few spectators but what grow suffi-
'ciently weary, and think they have had more than
'enough.'

The author of this discourse, though he affected
concealment, was soon after its publication discovered
to be the Abbé Raguenet, a native of Rouen, the
author of 'Les Monumens de Rome, ou description

* On this passage the English translator of the Parallel makes the
following note. 'Besides the machines mentioned by the author in this
'place, we saw several others at Rome of the same Cavaliero Acciaioli's
'contrivance, as la Frescatane on the theatre of Torre di Nona, the
'Colonnato of Lapis Lazuli, the funeral in Penelope, and many
'more equally surprizing. Upon the theatre of Capranica the same
'artist contrived Il Gigante, &c. But the most famous of all on that
'theatre was the Intermede of Hell, in the opera of Nerone Infante,
'which I will endeavour to describe with as much brevity as I am able,
'it being impossible to express it in such words as it deserves. At the
'sound of a horrid symphony, consisting of Corni, Serpentoni, and Regali,
'part of the floor of the stage opened and discovered a scene underneath,
'representing several caves full of infernal spirits, that flew about in
'a prodigious number, discharging fire and smoak at their nostrils and
'their mouths: at some distance likewise was observed a great number
'of damned spirits, labouring under their several torments; and in
'another side was discovered a river of Lethe with Charon's boat, on
'board of which was Mercury, Cupid, and the soul of one who had lately
'died for love. Upon their landing a prodigious monster appeared,
'whose mouth opening, to the great horror of the spectators covered
'the front wings, and the remaining part of the stage: within his jaws
'were discovered a throne composed of fire, and a multitude of monstrous
'serpents, on which Pluto sate, with a crown of fire on his head, and
'habited in other royal ornaments of the same nature. The singer that
'performed this part was one of those deep basses which, in the author's
'opinion are so rarely found in Italy. After Cupid had demanded justice
'of Pluto upon those old women, who in the preceding intermede, had
'cut his wings for making Agrippina, Nero's mother, in love; and several
'other passages belonging to this intermede, the mouth of the monster
'closed, at which instant Cupid endeavouring to fly off was arrested by
'a little devil, who seized on his foot; upon which Cupid giving himself
'a little turn shot the devil with one of his darts; whereupon the devil
'was transformed into a curling smoke that disappeared by degrees, and
'Cupid escaped. After this the great monster expanding his wings
'began to move very slowly towards the audience; under his body
'appeared great multitudes of devils, who formed themselves into a
'ballet, and plunged one after another into the opening of the floor before
'mentioned; out of which a prodigous quantity of fire and smoke was
'discharged. After this the great monster being got as far as the
'musick-room, and whilst all the spectators were intent upon what was
'doing, and began to fear he would come into the pit, he was in an in-
'stant transformed into an innumerable multitude of broad white
'butterflies, which flew all into the pit, and so low that some of them
'touched the hats of several of the spectators; at which some seemed
'diverted, and others not a little terrified, till by degrees they lodged
'themselves on different parts of the theatre, and at length disappeared.
'During this circumstance, which sufficiently employed the eyes of the
'spectators, the stage was refitted, and the scene changed into a beautiful
'garden, with which the third act begun. This representation was so
'extraordinary in its nature, so exactly performed, and so universally
'admired and applauded, that great numbers of foreigners came to
'Rome on purpose to behold it; and confessed when they had seen it,
'that it far exceeded the expectations fame had given them of it. And
'it must be confessed it gave the spectators a more perfect instructive
'idea of hell, than 'tis possible for the most artful flowing fancy to de-
'lineate. So that the author was not mistaken when he said that these
'sorts of entertainments are no less instructive than agreeable.'

† The Italian operas do not usually last five or six hours, as this author
imagines, the longest being not above four: it is true that sometimes at
Vienna the late emperor Leopold would have operas of the length the
author mentions, provided they were good, being a great admirer of the
Italian music: besides he composed himself, and played on the harpsichord to perfection.

'des plus beaux ouvrages de Peinture, de Sculpture,
'et d'Architecture de Rome, avec des observations.'
Paris, 1700 et 1702; 'L'Histoire d'Olivier Cromwel,'
and other works; upon which Mons. Jean-Laurent
le Cerf de la Vieuville de Freneuse, undertook
a refutation of the Parallel in three dialogues,
entitled 'Comparaison de la Musique Italienne, et
'de la Musique François.' Brux. 1704.

The Comparaison consists of three dialogues, in
which the several passages in the Parallel that tend
either to the praise of the Italian or the censure of
the French music, are made to undergo a severe
examination. In the comparison between the
musicians of the two countries, Charpentier and
Colasse are opposed to Luigi, i. e. Palestrina, and
Carissimi; Lully is placed above all competition,
and Bassani and Corelli below it. Of the compositions of the latter, he says that they are harsh
and irregular, abounding with dissonances; that he
has seen a piece of Corelli in which were fourteen
fourths together, and that in the eleventh sonata of
his fourth opera the reader may discern twenty-six
sixths in succession.

After a long eulogium on Lully, in which the
most celebrated airs in his operas are pointed
out, the author takes notice of a passage in the
Parallel, in which the voices of the Italian castrati
are compared to those of nightingales; and of another
that follows it, wherein it is asserted, that from the
particular circumstances that distinguish persons of
this kind, they are better actors of female characters
than even women themselves. To refute an assertion so wild as this, requires no great force of
argument; nevertheless this author takes great
pains to render it ridiculous, and has succeeded in
the attempt.

To his instance of the Roman procurator, who left
his employment in carnival time, and became an
actor on the public stage, he opposes the example of
Mons. Destouches, whose profession it seems was that
of a soldier, un mousquetaire, notwithstanding which,
for his pleasure he studied music, and was the composer of many fine operas.

To that passage in the Parallel, in which the
author asserts that he has seen at Rome, Corelli,
Pasquini, and Gaetani perform together in the same
opera, he answers, that at Paris the great masters do
the same; and that Rebel, Theobald, and La Barre
were wont to appear in the orchestra, whenever
a performance of theirs required their attendance;
and notwithstanding that exquisite piece of machinery
devised by the Cavalier Acciaioli, mentioned in the
Parallel, he says that the French are more ingenious
than the Italians in representations of this kind; and
that in the decorations of the theatre they excel all
other nations. And for this assertion, as also for the
superiority of the French machinery, he appeals to
the testimony of Misson and St. Evremont, who both
say something to the same purpose.

At the end of the dialogues is a letter from the
author to an anonymous friend, dated 3 April, 1704,
to the same effect with the rest of the work.

It appears that the Abbé Raguneet replied to the

Comparaison, and that Le Cerf defended it in an answer and two other pieces, which were reprinted some years after the first publication of them, and are extant in an edition of the Histoire de la Musique et de ses effets, printed in the year 1725. Thus the controversy ended as between the parties; but a French physician named Andri, who about the time wrote in the Journal de Sçavans, after commending the first of Le Cerf's publications, turned into ridicule the two last; upon which Le Cerf being greatly irritated, published a pamphlet entitled 'L'Art de décrier ce qu'on n'entend point; ou le Médecin Musicien.' The piece was full as bitter as its title seemed to indicate, and it seems that its bitterness was its most remarkable characteristic; for Fontaine, upon reading of it, pronounced, that if any one deserved to be called a complete fool, it was Le Cerf: But to qualify this severe censure, the Abbé Trublet, from whom this anecdote is taken, says that folly does not imply a total privation of reason and penetration; and that Le Cerf had a great share of both; but that his great defect was that want of common sense, which will sometime expose a man to the ridicule of his inferiors in understanding.

The succession of eminent English musicians from that period at which we were constrained to interrupt it by the above account, is as follows.

## CHAP. CLXIV.

JEREMIAH CLARK was educated in the royal chapel, under Dr. Blow, who entertained so great a friendship for him, as to resign in his favour the place of master of the children and almoner of St. Paul's; and Clark was appointed his successor in 1693, and shortly after he became organist of that cathedral. In July, 1700, he and his fellow-pupil were appointed gentlemen extraordinary of the royal chapel; and in 1704 they were jointly admitted to a place of organist thereof in the room of Mr. Francis Piggot. Clark had the misfortune to entertain a hopeless passion for a very beautiful lady in a station of life far above him; his despair of success threw him into a deep melancholy: in short, he grew weary of his life, and on the first day of December, 1707, shot himself.*

The compositions of Clark are few: his anthems are remarkably pathetic, at the same time that they preserve the dignity and majesty of the church

* He was determined upon this method of putting an end to his life by an event, which, strange as it may seem, is attested by the late Mr. Samuel Weeley, one of the lay-vicars of St. Paul's, who was very intimate with him, and had heard him relate it. Being at the house of a friend in the country, he took an abrupt resolution to return to London: his friend having observed in his behaviour marks of great dejection, furnished him with a horse and a servant. Riding along the road, a fit of melancholy seized him, upon which he alighted, and giving the servant his horse to hold, went into a field, in a corner whereof was a pond, and also trees; and began a debate with himself whether he should then end his days by hanging or drowning. Not being able to resolve on either, he thought of making what he looked upon as chance, the umpire, and drew out of his pocket a piece of money, and tossing it into the air, it came down on its edge and stuck in the clay: though the determination answered not his wish, it was far from ambiguous, as it seemed to forbid both methods of destruction; and would have given unspeakable comfort to a mind less disordered than his was. Being thus interrupted in his purpose, he returned, and mounting his horse, rode on to London, and in a short time after shot himself. He dwelt in a house in St. Paul's church-yard, situate on the place where the Chapter-house now stands: old Mr. Reading, mentioned in page 771 of this work, was passing by at the instant the pistol went off, and entering the house found his friend in the agonies of death.

style; the most celebrated of them are, 'I will love 'thee,' printed in the second book of the Harmonia Sacra; 'Bow down thine ear,' and 'Praise the Lord, 'O Jerusalem.'

The only works of Clark published by himself are lessons for the harpsichord, and sundry songs, which are to be found in the collections of that day, particularly in the Pills to purge Melancholy; but they are there printed without the basses. He also composed for D'Urfey's comedy of the Fond Husband or the Plotting Sisters, that sweet ballad air, 'The bonny grey-eyed morn,' which Mr. Gay has introduced into the Beggars Opera, and is sung to the words, ''Tis woman that seduces all mankind.'

JOHN WELDON, a native of Chichester, had his instruction in music under John Walter, organist of Eton college, and afterwards under Henry Purcell. From Eton he went to Oxford, and was made organist of New College. On the sixth day of January, 1701, he was appointed a gentleman extraordinary of the royal chapel; and in 1708 succeeded Dr. Blow as organist thereof. In 1715, upon the establishment of a second composer's place, Weldon was admitted to it:† He had been but a short time in this station before he gave a specimen of his abilities in the composition of the Communion-office, that is to say, the Prefaces, Sanctus, and Gloria in excelsis; and also sundry anthems, agreeably to the condition of his appointment.

At the same time that Weldon was organist of the royal chapel, he was also organist of the church of St. Bride, London; and king George I. having presented the parish of St. Martin in the Fields with an organ, Mr. Weldon, perhaps in compliment to the king, was chosen organist.‡

The studies of Weldon were for the most part in church music; and we do not find that, like Lock and Purcell, and many others of his profession, he ever

† Upon the accession of George I. to the crown, that prince, who was a lover of music, carried into execution the proposal of Dr. Tillotson, mentioned in the foregoing account of Blow, for an establishment of two composers for the chapel; and made some other regulations for the improvement of the service: these appear by the following entries in the Cheque-book of the chapel royal:—
'1715. His majesty having been graciously pleased to add four gentle-'men of the chapel to the old establishment, viz., Mr. Morley, Mr. 'George Carleton, Mr. Tho. Baker, and Mr. Samuel Chittle, and by 'virtue of four several warrants from the right rev. father in God, John, 'lord bishop of London, dean of his majesty's chapel royal, I have 'sworn and admitted the aforesaid gentlemen, gentlemen in ordinary of 'his majesty's chapel royal, to enjoy the same together with all privileges 'and advantages thereunto belonging. Witness my hand this 8th day 'of August, 1715.
'Dan. Williams, clerk            'J. DOLBEN, Subdean.'
'of the Cheque.
'Aug. 8, 1715. That besides the four additional gentlemen of the 'chapel above-mentioned, there was added in king George's establishment 'as follows, viz.:—
'A second composer in ordinary, which place Mr. John Weldon was 'sworn and admitted into.
'A lutenist, which place Mr. John Shore was sworn and admitted into.
'A violist, which place Mr. Francisco Goodsens was sworn and ad-'mitted into.
'All these three were sworn and admitted into their respective places 'by me.
'Witness, Dan. Williams.'            'J. DOLBEN, Subdean.'
'There was likewise inserted in the aforesaid establishment an allowance 'to Dr. William Croft, as master of the children, of eighty pounds per 'annum, for teaching the children to read, write, and accompts, and for 'teaching them to play on the organ and compose music.'
'J. DOLBEN, Subdean.'
‡ The reason that moved the king to this act of munificence was a very singular one; the parish had chosen him their churchwarden, and he executed the office for two months, but at the end thereof, as he well might, he grew tired of it, and presented the parish with that noble instrument which is now in the church.

composed for the theatre, except that in competition with two other masters, namely, Daniel Purcell, John Eccles, and one Franck, or Franco, mentioned in page 763 of this work, and perhaps many others, he set to music Mr. Congreve's masque, the Judgment of Paris. The motive to this undertaking was an advertisement in the London Gazette, offering rewards out of a fund of two hundred guineas advanced by sundry persons of quality, to be distributed in prizes to such masters as should be adjudged to compose the best.* The largest was adjudged to Weldon, and the next to Eccles.

Some songs of Weldon's composition are to be found in a book entitled Mercurius Musicus, and other collections; the following is yet remembered as a favourite air in its time :—

FROM grave lessons and re-straint, I'm stole out to re-vel here; Yet I trem-ble and I pant, in the mid-dle of the fair. O, O, O wou'd for-tune in my way throw a lov-er kind and gay; Now's the time, now's the time, now's the time, he soon may move a young heart un-us'd to Love. Shall I venture? no, no, no! Shall I from the dan-ger go? O no, no, no, no, no, no, no, no, no, no, no, no, no, no, no, I must not try, I can-not fly, I must not, durst not, can-not fly, I must not try, I can-not fly, I must not, durst not, can-not fly. Help me Na-ture, help me Art, why should I de-ny my heart? help me Na-ture

* See the advertisement, page 759 of this work.

help . me Art, . . . . why should I . . . de - ny . . my heart ? If a lo - ver
will . . . pur - sue, like the wi - sest let me do, I will
fit . . him if he's true, if he's false . I'll fit . . him too.

JOHN WELDON.

At the time when Weldon became first of the chapel, Mr. Elford was a singer there, and was celebrated for a very fine counter-tenor voice. Weldon composed for him sundry solo anthems, six of which he published, with a preface acknowledging the advantages they derived from his fine performance. These have their merit, but they fall very far short of his full anthems, particularly those to the words, 'In thee, O Lord,' 'Hear my crying,' of which it is hard to say whether the melody or the harmony of each be its greatest excellence.

Weldon was a very sweet and elegant composer of church music: He died in the year 1736, and lies buried in the church-yard of St. Paul, Covent-garden. His successor in his places in the royal chapel is one whose merits will ever endear him to the lovers and judges of harmony, and particularly of cathedral music, Dr. William Boyce.

JOHN ECCLES was the son of Solomon Eccles, a master of the violin, and the author of sundry grounds with divisions thereon, published in the second part of the Division Violin, printed at London, in 1693, oblong quarto. He was instructed by his father in music, and became a composer for the theatre, of act-tunes, dance-tunes, and such incidental songs as frequently occur in the modern comedies, a collection whereof he published, and dedicated to queen Anne. He composed the music to a tragedy entitled Rinaldo and Armida, written by Dennis, and performed in 1699, in which is a song for a single voice, 'The 'jolly breeze,' which for the florid divisions in it was by many greatly admired. Eccles set to music an

ode for St. Cecilia's Day, written by Mr. Congreve, and performed on the anniversary festival of that saint in 1701; as also his masque entitled the Judgment of Paris, for one of the prizes mentioned in the preceding article; and obtained the second, which was of fifty guineas. His music to the Judgment of Paris is published.

In the collection above mentioned are many excellent songs, particularly one for three voices, 'Inspire us, Genius of the day,' and another, also for three voices, 'Wine does wonders every day,' sung in a comedy entitled Justice Busy, which has long been a favourite with the Gloucestershire singers of catches, and other small proficients in vocal harmony. In it are also contained a very spirited song for two voices, sung in the play of Henry V. to the words 'Fill all your glasses;' and a solo song, which with sundry others the author composed for D'Urfey's play of Don Quixote, the rest being set by Purcell. That of Eccles above mentioned is a mad song, sung by Mrs. Bracegirdle, in the character of Marcella, the words whereof are 'I burn, my brain consumes 'to ashes.' In the Orpheus Britannicus is a song occasioned by Mrs. Bracegirdle's singing 'I burn,' &c.; there are also some pretty tunes of his composing to songs in the Pills to purge Melancholy, published by D'Urfey. Eccles composed the tune to the song 'A soldier and a sailor,' * in Mr. Congreve's comedy of Love for Love, with a bass peculiarly adapted to the manner of singing it as directed by the play; which never having been printed, is here inserted.

* The words of this song are those translated by Dean Aldrich, ' Miles et navigator,' vide page 766 of this work.

JOHN ECCLES.

About the year 1698, upon the decease of Dr. Staggins, Eccles was appointed master of the queen's band; but in the latter part of his life he was known to the musical world only by the New Year and Birth-day Odes, which it was his duty to compose, having retired to Kingston in Surrey for the convenience of angling, a recreation of which he was very fond.

There were three brothers of the name of Eccles, all musicians, viz., the above named John Henry, a violin player in the king of France's band, and the author of twelve excellent solos for that instrument, printed at Paris in 1720, and Thomas,* who was one of those itinerant musicians, perhaps the

last of them, who in winter evenings were used to go about to taverns, and for the sake of a slender subsistence expose themselves to the insults of those who were not inclined to hear them; there are none of this class of mendicant artists now remaining, but in the time of the usurpation they were so numerous, that an ordinance was made declaring them vagrants.†

From the above account of English musicians in

† Vide ante, page 702, in a note.

To the practice of having music in taverns and inns there are numberless allusions in our old English writers. In bishop Earle's character of a poor fiddler, inserted in the note above referred to, we are told that he made it his business to get the names of the worshipful of the inn, in order that he might salute them by their names at their rising in the morning: but it seems that formerly there were to the greater inns, musicians who might be said to be in some sort retainers to the house. Fynes Moryson has given a hint of this in his Itinerary, part III. page 151, in a passage, the whole whereof, as it exhibits a view of the manners of his time, is here inserted. 'As soone as a passenger comes to an Inne, 'the servants run to him, and one takes his horse and walkes him till he 'be cold, then rubs him, and gives him meate, yet I must say that they 'are not much to be trusted in this last point, without the eye of the 'Master or his Servant to oversee them. Another servant gives the 'passenger his private chamber, and kindles his fier, the third pulls of 'his bootes, and makes them cleane. Then the Host or Hostess visits 'him, and if he will eate with the Host, or at a common Table with 'others, his meale will cost him sixpence, or in some places but foure 'pence, (yet this course is less honourable and not used by Gentlemen): 'but if he will eate in his chamber, he commands what meate he will 'according to his appetite, and as much as he thinkes fit for him and his 'company, yea, the kitchen is open to him, to command the meat to 'be dressed as he best likes; and when he sits at the Table, Host or 'Hostess will accompany him, or if they have many Guests, will at least 'visit him, taking it for curtesie to be bid sit downe: while he eates, if 'he have company especially, he shall be offered musicke, which he may 'freely take or refuse, and if he be solitary, the Musitians will give him 'the good day with Musicke in the morning. It is the custome and no 'way disgracefull to set up part of supper for his breakfast: in the 'evening or in the morning after breakefast, (for the common sort use 'not to dine, but ride from breakfast to supper time, yet comming early 'to the Inne for better resting of their Horses) he shall have a reckoning 'in writing, and if it seeme unreasonable, the Host will satisfie him, 'either for the due price, or by abaiting part, especially if the servant 'deceive him any way, which one of experience will soone find. I will 'now onely adde that a Gentleman and his Man shall spend as much, as 'if he were accompanied with another Gentleman and his Man, and if 'Gentlemen will in such sort joyne together, to eate at one Table, the 'expenses will be much diminished. Lastly, a Man cannot more freely 'command at home in his owne House, then he may doe in his Inne, 'and at parting if he give some few pence to the Chamberlin and Ostler, 'they wish him a happy journey.'

* This person was living about thirty years ago. A good judge of music, who had heard him play, gives the following account of him and his performance. 'It was about the month of November, in the year '1735, that I with some friends were met to spend the evening at a 'tavern in the city, when this man, in a mean but decent garb, was in- 'troduced to us by the waiter; immediately upon opening the door 'I heard the twang of one of his strings from under his coat, which was 'accompanied with the question, "Gentlemen will you please to hear '"any music?" Our curiosity, and the modesty of the man's deportment, 'inclined us to say yes; and music he gave us, such as I had never heard 'before, nor shall again under the same circumstances: with as fine and 'delicate a hand as I ever heard, he played the whole fifth and ninth 'solo of Corelli, two songs of Mr. Handel, Del minnaciar in Otho, and 'Spero si mio caro bene, in Admetus; in short, his performance was 'such as would command the attention of the nicest ear, and left us his 'auditors much at a loss to guess what it was that constrained him to 'seek his living in a way so disreputable: he made no secret of his 'name; he said he was the youngest of three brothers, and that Henry, 'the middle one, had been his master, and was then in the service of the 'king of France: we were very little disposed to credit the account he 'gave us of his brother's situation in France, but the collection of solos 'above-mentioned to have been published by him at Paris, puts it out of 'question.' Upon inquiry some time after, it appeared that he was idle, and given to drinking. He lodged in the Butcher-row near Temple bar, and was well known to the musicians of his time, who thought themselves disgraced by this practice of his, for which they have a term of reproach not very intelligible; they call it *going a-busking.* By the *Leges Conviviales of the academy of Ben Jonson, held in the Apollo Room, at the Devil Tavern, Temple bar,* such persons as these were forbidden admittance into that assembly.

*Fidiun, nisi accersitus, non venito.*

*Let no saucy fiddler dare to intrude unless he is sent for to vary our bliss. Vide second part of Miscellany Poems, published by Mr. Dryden, 12mo. 1716, page 148-150.*

succession, it is necessary here to digress to make way for the relation of a discovery, the result of a series of experiments made by Sir Isaac Newton, tending to demonstrate what has often been asserted in the course of this work, viz., that the principles of harmony are discoverable in so great a variety of instances, that they seem to pervade the universe. Many arguments in favour of this opinion are deducible from geometry, as particularly from the Helicon of Ptolemy, the famous theorem of Archimedes,* and that other of Pythagoras, contained in the 47th Proposition of the first book of Euclid, with the observations thereon by Mr. Harrington and Sir Isaac Newton, mentioned previously. But, which was little to be expected, farther demonstration of this general principle results from the analogy between colours and sounds. This noble discovery we owe to the sagacity of Sir Isaac Newton, whose relation of it is here given in his own words :—

‘ When I had caused the rectilinear line sides A F, ‘ G M, of the spectrum of colours made by the prism ‘ to be distinctly defined, as in the fifth experiment ‘ of the first book is described, there were found in ‘ it all the homogeneal colours in the same order ‘ and situation one among another as in the spectrum ‘ of simple light, described in the fourth experiment ‘ of that book. For the circles of which the spec- ‘ trum of compound light P T is composed, and ‘ which in the middle parts of the spectrum inter- ‘ fere and are intermixt with one another, are not ‘ intermixt in their outmost parts where they touch ‘ those rectilinear sides A F and G M. And therefore ‘ in those rectilinear sides when distinctly defined, ‘ there is no new colour generated by refraction. ‘ I observed also, that if any where between the ‘ two outmost circles T M F and P G A a right line, ‘ as $\gamma\,\delta$, was cross to the spectrum, so as at both ends ‘ to fall perpendicularly upon its rectilinear sides, ‘ there appeared one and the same colour and degree ‘ of colour from one end of this line to the other. ‘ I delineated therefore in a paper the perimeter of ‘ the spectrum F A P G M T, and in trying the third ‘ experiment of the first book, I held the paper so ‘ that the spectrum might fall upon this delineated ‘ figure, and agree with it exactly, whilst an assistant, ‘ whose eyes for distinguishing colours were more ‘ critical than mine, did by right lines $\alpha\beta$, $\gamma\delta$, $\varepsilon\zeta$, ‘ &c. drawn cross the spectrum, note the confines ‘ of the colours, that is of the red M $\alpha\,\beta$ F of the ‘ orange $\alpha\,\gamma\,\delta\,\beta$, of the yellow $\gamma\,\varepsilon\,\zeta\,\delta$, of the green ‘ $\varepsilon\,\eta\,\theta\,\zeta$, of the blue $\eta\,\iota\,\kappa\,\theta$, of the indigo $\iota\,\lambda\,\mu\,\kappa$, and ‘ of the violet $\lambda$ G A $\mu$. And this operation being ‘ divers times repeated both in the same and in ‘ several papers, I found that the observations agreed ‘ well enough with one another, and that the rec- ‘ tilinear sides M G and F A were by the said cross

* Of this theorem of Archimedes mention is made in page 10, in a note. It seems he thought the discovery of such importance to man- kind, that he caused a diagram thereof to be engraven on his sepulchre. Cicero, in the Tusculan Disputations, book V. sect. 23, glories in his having discovered at Syracuse, without one of the city gates, the sepulchre of Archimedes covered with brambles and thorns, and says that he knew it by the figure of a cylinder and a sphere carved on the stone.

‘ lines divided after the manner of a musical chord. ‘ Let G M be produced to X, that M X may be ‘ equal to G M, and conceive G X, $\lambda$ X, $\iota$ X, $\eta$ X, ‘ $\varepsilon$ X, $\gamma$ X, $a$ X, M X, to be in proportion to one ‘ another, as the numbers $1, \frac{8}{9}, \frac{5}{6}, \frac{3}{4}, \frac{2}{3}, \frac{3}{5}, \frac{9}{16}, \frac{1}{2}$, and ‘ so to represent the chords of the key, and of a tone ‘ a third minor, a fourth, a fifth, a sixth major, ‘ a seventh, and an eighth above that key : And ‘ the intervals M $a$, $a\,\gamma$, $\gamma\,\varepsilon$, $\varepsilon\,\eta$, $\eta\,\iota$, $\iota\,\lambda$. and $\lambda$ G, will ‘ be the spaces which the several colours (red, ‘ orange, yellow, green, blue, indico, violet) take ‘ up.’ Sir Isaac Newton’s Optics, book I. part II. prop. iii. prob. i. exper. vii.

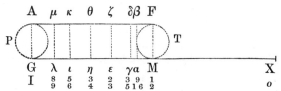

From the relation of this curious and important discovery in the theory, we proceed to relate the farther progress of music in such particulars as respect the practice.

The concert of Britton, the small-coal man at Clerkenwell, continued to flourish till the end of the century in which it was established, and onward into the next, completing a period of more than forty years, when his death put an end to it. Many particulars relating to the life and character of this extraordinary man, are to be met with in books published about and after the time when he lived ; but the most authentic account of him, so far as it goes, is contained in Hearne’s Appendix to his Hemingi Chartularii Ecclesiæ Wygorniensis, page 665, which, as it was drawn up by one that was well acquainted with him, and he a man of the most scrupulous accuracy, is entitled to the highest degree of credit. Some pains have been taken by searches, and inquiries of persons in his neigh- bourhood, and of others who remember him, to collect those suppletory anecdotes which here follow Hearne’s account of him, and furnish a copious memoir of this extraordinary person.

## CHAP. CLXV.

‘ Mr. Thomas Britton, *(a Portrait)*, the famous ‘ Musical Small-Coal Man, was born at or near ‘ Higham Ferrers in Northamptonshire. From ‘ thence he went to London, where he bound himself ‘ Apprentice to a Small-Coal Man in St. John ‘ Baptist’s Street. After he had served his full ‘ time of seven Years, his Master gave him a Sum ‘ of Money not to set up. Upon this Tom went in- ‘ to Northamptonshire again, and, after he had spent ‘ his Money, he returned again to London, set up ‘ the Small-Coal Trade (notwithstanding his Master ‘ was still living) and, withal, he took a Stable, and ‘ turned it into a House, which stood the next Door ‘ to the little Gate of St. John’s of Jerusalem next ‘ Clarken-Well-Green. Some time after he had ‘ settled here, he became acquainted with Dr. Ga-

J. Wollaston pinxit.    C. Grignion sculpsit.

**THOMAS BRITTON**

**SMALL-COAL-MAN.**

'renciers, his near Neighbour, by which means he
'became an excellent Chymist, and perhaps, he
'performed such Things in that Profession, as had
'never been done before, with little Cost and Charge,
'by the help of a moving Elaboratory, that was
'contrived and built by himself, which was much
'admired by all of that Faculty, that happened to
'see it; insomuch that a certain Gentleman of Wales
'was so much taken with it, that he was at the
'Expense of carrying him down into that Country,
'on purpose to build him such another, which Tom
'performed to the Gentleman's very great satis-
'faction, and for the same he received of him a very
'handsome and generous Gratuity. Besides his
'great skill in Chymistry, he was as famous for his
'knowledge in the Theory of Musick; in the Practick
'Part of which Faculty he was likewise very con-
'siderable. He was so much addicted to it, that
'he pricked with his own Hand (very neatly and
'accurately) and left behind him a valuable Col-
'lection of Musick, mostly pricked by himself, which
'was sold upon his Death for near an hundred
'Pounds. Not to mention the excellent Collection
'of printed Books, that he also left behind him,
'both of Chymistry and Musick. Besides these
'Books that he left behind him, he had, some Years
'before his Death, sold by Auction a noble Col-
'lection of Books, most of them in the Rosacrucian
'Faculty (of which he was a great Admirer) whereof
'there is a printed Catalogue extant (as there is of
'those that were sold after his Death) which I have
'often looked over with no small surprize and
'wonder, and particularly for the great Number of
'MSS. in the before mentioned Faculties that are
'specified in it. He had, moreover, a considerable
'Collection of Musical instruments, which were sold
'for fourscore Pounds upon his Death, which hap-
'pened in September 1714, being upwards of three-
'score Years of Age, and lyes buried in the Church-
'Yard of Clarken-Well, without Monument or
'Inscription, being attended to his Grave, in a very
'solemn and decent manner, by a great Concourse
'of People, especially of such as frequented the
'Musical Club, that was kept up for many Years
'at his own Charges (he being a Man of a very
'generous and liberal Spirit) at his own little Cell.
'He appears by the Print of him (done since his
'Death) to have been a Man of an ingenious Coun-
'tenance and of a sprightly Temper. It also re-
'presents him as a comely Person, as indeed he was,
'and, withal, there is a modesty expressed in it
'every way agreeable to him. Under it are these
'Verses, which may serve instead of an Epitaph:—

   'Tho' mean thy Rank, yet in thy humble Cell
   'Did gentle Peace and Arts unpurchas'd dwell;
   'Well pleas'd Apollo thither led his Train,
   'And Musick warbled in her sweetest Strain.
   'Cyllenius so, as Fables tell, and Jove
   'Came willing Guests to poor Philemon's Grove.
   'Let useless Pomp behold, and blush to find
   'So low a Station, such a liberal Mind.*

* These verses were written by Mr. John Hughes, who was a frequent
performer on the violin at Britton's concert: they are printed in the first
volume of his Poems, published in 1735; and are also under one of two
mezzotinto prints of Britton.

'In short, he was an extraordinary and very valuable
'Man, much admired by the Gentry, even those of
'the best Quality, and by all others of the more
'inferiour Rank, that had any manner of Regard
'for Probity, Sagacity, Diligence, and Humility.
'I say Humility, because, tho' he was so much fam'd
'for his Knowledge, and might, therefore, have lived
'very reputably without his Trade, yet he continued
'it to his Death, not thinking it to be at all beneath
'him. Mr. Bagford and he used frequently to con-
'verse together, and when they met they seldom
'parted very soon. Their Conversation was often
'about old MSS. and the Havock made of them.
'They both agreed to retreive what Fragments of
'Antiquity they could, and, upon that occasion, they
'would frequently divert themselves in talking of
'old Chronicles, which both loved to read, tho'
'among our more late Chronicles, printed in English,
'Isaackson's was what they chiefly preferr'd for
'a general knowledge of Things, a Book which
'was much esteem'd also by those two eminent
'Chronologers, Bp. Lloyd and Mr. Dodwell. By
'the way, I cannot but observe, that Isaackson's
'Chronicle is really, for the most part, Bp. Andrews's,
'Isaackson being Amanuensis to the Bishop.'

Hearne seems to have understood but very little
of music, and we are therefore not to wonder that
his curiosity extended not to an inquiry into the
order and economy of that musical club, as he calls
it, which he says Britton for many years kept up in
his own little cell. The truth is, that it was nothing
less than a musical concert; and so much the more
does it merit our attention, as it was the first meeting
of the kind, and the undoubted parent of some of the
most celebrated concerts in London. The time when
Britton lived is not so remote, but that there are
some now living who are able to give an account of
this extraordinary institution, of the principal persons that performed at his concert, and of the company that frequented it: many of these have been
sought out and conversed with, for the purpose of
collecting all that could be known of him: inquiries
have been made in his neighbourhood, of particulars
touching his life, his character, and general deportment; and the result of these will furnish out such
a supplement to what has been said of this extraordinary man in print, as can hardly fail to gratify the
curiosity of such as take pleasure in this kind of
information.

Of the origin of Britton's concert we have an
account written by a near neighbour of his, one who
dwelt in the same parish, and indeed but a small distance from him, namely, the facetious Mr. Edward
Ward, the author of the London Spy, and many
doggrel poems, coarse, it is true, but not devoid of
humour and pleasantry. Ward at that time kept
a public-house in Clerkenwell, and there sold ale of
his own brewing. From thence he removed to a
house in an alley on the west side of Moorfields,
between the place called Little Moorfields and the
end of Chiswell-street, and sold the same kind of
liquor His house, as we are given to understand by
the notes on the Dunciad, was for a time the great

resort of high churchmen. In a book of his writing, entitled Satirical Reflections on Clubs, he has bestowed a whole chapter on the small-coal man's club: from the account therein given we learn that 'this club was first begun, or at least confirmed, by 'Sir Roger L'Estrange, a very musical gentleman, 'and who had a tolerable perfection on the bass viol.' Ward says that 'the attachment of Sir Roger and 'other ingenious gentlemen, lovers of the Muses, to 'Britton, arose from the profound regard that he had 'in general to all manner of literature: that the pru- 'dence of his deportment to his betters procured him 'great respect, and that men of the best wit, as well as some of the best quality, honoured his musical 'society with their company: that Britton was so 'much distinguished, that when passing the streets 'in his blue linen frock, and with his sack of small- 'coal on his back, he was frequently accosted with 'such expressions as these, " There goes the famous " small-coal man, who is a lover of learning, a per- " former in music, and a companion for gentlemen." Ward adds, and speaks of it as of his own knowledge, and indeed the fact is indisputable, that he had made a very good collection of ancient and modern music by the best masters; that he also had collected a very handsome library, which he had publicly disposed of to a very considerable advantage; and that he had remaining by him many valuable curiosities. He farther says that, at the first institution of it, his concert was performed at his own house, but that some time after he took a convenient room out of the next to it. What sort of a house Britton's own was, and the spot where it stood, shall now be related.

It was situated on the south side of Aylesbury-street, which extends from Clerkenwell-green to St. John's-street, and was the corner house of that passage leading by the old Jerusalem tavern, under the gateway of the priory, into St. John's-square;* on the ground floor was a repository for small-coal; over that was the concert-room, which was very long and narrow, and had a ceiling so low, that a tall man could but just stand upright in it. The stairs to this room were on the outside of the house, and could scarce be ascended without crawling. The house itself was very old and low-built, and in every respect so mean, as to be a fit habitation for only a very poor man. Notwithstanding all, this mansion, despicable as it may seem, attracted to it as polite an audience as ever the opera did; and a lady of the first rank in this kingdom, the duchess of Queensbury, now living, one of the most celebrated beauties of her time, may yet remember that in the pleasure which she manifested at hearing Mr. Britton's concert, she seemed to have forgotten the difficulty with which she ascended the steps that led to it.

Britton was in his person a short, thickset man, with a very honest, ingenuous countenance. There are two pictures of him extant, both painted by his friend Mr. Woolaston, and from both there are mezzotinto prints; one of the pictures is now in the British Museum; the occasion of painting it, as related by Mr. Woolaston himself, to the author of

this work, was as follows: Britton had been out one morning, and having nearly emptied his sack in a shorter time than he expected, had a mind to see his friend Mr. Woolaston; but having always been used to consider himself in two capacities, viz., as one who subsisted by a very mean occupation, and as a companion for persons in a station of life above him, he could not, consistently, with this distinction, dressed as he then was, make a visit; he therefore in his way home varied his usual round, and passing through Warwick-lane, determined to cry small-coal so near Mr. Woolaston's door as to stand a chance of being invited in by him. Accordingly he had no sooner turned into Warwick-court, and cried small-coal in his usual tone,[†] than Mr. Woolaston, who had never heard him there before, flung up the sash and beckoned him in. After some conversation Mr. Woolaston intimated a desire to paint his picture, which Britton modestly yielding to, Mr. Woolaston then, and at a few subsequent sittings, painted him in his blue frock, and with his small-coal measure in his hand, as he appears in the picture at the Museum. A mezzotinto print was taken from this picture, for which Mr. Hughes wrote those lines inserted in page 789; and this is the print which Hearne speaks of. But there was another picture of him painted by the same person, upon what occasion is not known: from that a mezzotinto print was also taken, which being very scarce, has been made use of for the engraving of Britton inserted in this work: in this he is represented tuning a harpsichord, a violin hanging on the side of the room, and shelves of books before him. Under the print are the following lines :—

> Tho' doom'd to small-coal, yet to arts ally'd,
> Rich without wealth, and famous without pride;
> Musick's best patron, judge of books and men,
> Belov'd and honour'd by Apollo's train;
> In Greece or Rome sure never did appear
> So bright a genius in so dark a sphere;
> More of the man had artfully been sav'd,
> Had Kneller painted and had Vertue grav'd.

The above verses were scribbled by Prior with a view to recommend Vertue, then a young man, and patronised by Edward earl of Oxford, though they are little less than a sarcasm on Woolaston and Johnson, who scraped the plate. It is suspected that the insignificant adverb *artfully* was inserted by a mistake of the transcriber, and that it originally stood *probably*.

## CHAP. CLXVI.

THE account above given of Britton will naturally awaken a curiosity to know of what kind was the music with which his audience was entertained, and who were the persons that performed in his concert: an answer the first of these queries may be collected from the catalogue of his music, which follows this account of him; to the latter an answer is at hand: Dr. Pepusch, and frequently Mr. Handel, played the harpsichord, Mr. Banister, and also Mr. Henry

---

* It has long since been pulled down and rebuilt: at this time is an alehouse, known by the sign of the Bull's Head.

† *The goodness of his ear directed him to the use of the most perfect of all musical intervals, the diapason; his cry being, as some relate that remember it :—*

Small coal.

Needler, of the Excise-office, and other capital performers for that time, the first violin; Mr. John Hughes, author of the Siege of Damascus, Mr. Woolaston, the painter, Mr. Philip Hart, Mr. Henry Symonds, Mr. Abiell Whichello, and Mr. Obadiah Shuttleworth, a fine player on the violin, some constantly, and others frequently, performed there. That fine performer Mr. Matthew Dubourg was then but a child, but the first solo that ever he played in public, and which probably was one of Corelli's, he played at Britton's concert, standing upon a joint-stool; but so terribly was the poor child awed at the sight of so splendid an assembly, that he was near falling to the ground.* It has been questioned whether Britton had any skill in music or not; but those who remember him say that he could tune a harpsichord, and that he frequently played the viol da gamba in his own concert.

Britton's skill in ancient books and manuscripts is mentioned by Hearne; and indeed in the preface to his edition of Robert of Gloucester he refers to a curious manuscript copy of that historian in Britton's possession. The means used by him and other collectors of ancient books and manuscripts about that time, as related by one of that class lately deceased, were as follow, and these include an intimation of Britton's pursuits and connexions :—

About the beginning of this century a passion for collecting old books and manuscripts reigned among the nobility. The chief of those who sought after them were Edward earl of Oxford, the earls of Pembroke, Sunderland, and Winchelsea, and the duke of Devonshire. These persons in the winter season, on Saturdays, the Parliament not sitting on that day, were used to resort to the city, and dividing themselves, took several routes, some to Little Britain, some to Moorfields, and others to different parts of the town, inhabited by booksellers; there they would inquire in the several shops as they passed along for old books and manuscripts, and some time before noon would assemble at the shop of one Christopher Bateman, a bookseller, at the corner of Ave Maria-lane, in Paternoster-row; and here they

were frequently met by Mr. Bagford and other persons engaged in the same pursuits, and a conversation always commenced on the subject of their inquiries. Bagford informed them where anything curious was to be seen or purchased, and they in return obliged him with a sight of what they from time to time collected. While they were engaged in this conversation, and as near as could be to the hour of twelve by St. Paul's clock, Britton, who by that time had finished his round, arrived clad in his blue frock, and pitching his sack of small-coal on the bulk of Mr. Bateman's shop window, would go in and join them; and after a conversation which generally lasted about an hour, the noblemen above mentioned adjourned to the Mourning Bush at Aldersgate,† where they dined and spent the remainder of the day.

The singularity of his character, the course of his studies, and the collections he made, induced suspicions that Britton was not the man he seemed to be : and what Mr. Walpole says as to this particular is very true; some thought his musical assembly only a cover for seditious meetings, others for magical purposes, and that Britton himself was taken for an atheist, a presbyterian, a Jesuit; but these were ill-grounded conjectures, for he was a plain, simple, honest man, perfectly innoffensive, and highly esteemed by all who knew him, and, notwithstanding the meanness of his occupation, was called Mr. Britton.

The circumstances of this man's death are not less remarkable than those of his life. There dwelt in Britton's time, near Clerkenwell-close, a man named Robe, who frequently played at his concert, and who, being in the commission of the peace for the county of Middlesex, was usually called Justice Robe; at the same time one Samuel Honeyman, a blacksmith by trade, and who lived in Bear-street, near Leicester-square, became very famous for a faculty which he possessed of speaking as if his voice proceeded from some distant part of the house where he stood; in short, he was one of those men called Ventriloqui, i. e., those that speak as it were from their bellies, and are taken notice of by Reginald Scott in his Discovery of Witchcraft, page 111, for which reason he was called the Talking Smith. The pranks played by this man, if collected, would fill a volume.‡ During the time that Dr. Sacheverell was under censure, and had a great resort of friends to his house, near the church in Holborn, he had the confidence to get himself admitted, by pretending that he came from a couple who wished to be married by the doctor. He stayed not long in the room, but made so good use of his time, that the doctor, who was a large man, and one of the stoutest and most athletic then living, was

---

* Mr. Walpole, in his account of Woolaston the painter, Anecdotes of Painting, vol. III., has taken occasion to mention some particulars of Britton, which he says he received from the son of Mr Woolaston, who, as well as his father, was a member of Britton's musical club : it is there said that Britton found the instruments, that the subscription was ten shillings a year, and that they had coffee at a penny a dish.

It seems by this passage that Britton had departed from his original institution, for at first no coffee was drunk there, nor would he receive, in any way whatever, any gratuity from his guests : on the contrary, he was offended whenever it was offered him. This is the account of a very ancient person now living, a frequent performer at Britton's concert; and it seems to be confirmed by the following stanza of a song written by Ward in praise of Britton, printed at the end of his description of the small-coal man's club above cited :—

Upon Thursdays repair
To my palace, and there
Hobble up stair by stair,
But I pray ye take care
That you break not your shins by a stumble :

And without e'er a souse
Paid to me or my spouse,
Sit as still as a mouse
At the top of the house,
And there you shall hear how we fumble.

And it is farther confirmed by a manuscript diary of Mr. Thomas Rowe, the husband of the famous Mrs. Elizabeth Rowe, and the author of some supplemental lives to Plutarch, in which there is this memorandum, 'Thomas Britton, the musical small-coal man, had con-'certs at his house in Clerkenwell forty-six years, to which he admitted 'gentlemen gratis. He died October, 1714.'

† A bush was anciently the sign of a tavern, as may be inferred from the proverb 'Good wine needs no bush.' This was succeeded by a thing intended to resemble a bush, consisting of three or four tier of hoops fastened one above another; with vine leaves and grapes richly carved and gilt, and a Bacchus bestriding a tun at top. The owner of this house, at the time when king Charles I. was beheaded, was so affected upon that event, that he put his bush in mourning by painting it black.

‡ The following one is related by Dr. Shaw in his edition of the Philosophical Works of Lord Bacon, Vol. III. page 112, in nota. 'Tis said that he once counterfeited a man's voice coming out of a large cask, in a cart loaded with empty casks, as it was going along the streets, to the great astonishment and perplexity of the carman.

almost terrified into fits. Dr. Derham, of Upminster, that sagacious enquirer into the works of nature, had a great curiosity to see Honeyman, but the person he employed to bring about the meeting, and who communicated this anecdote, contrived always to disappoint him, knowing full well that, had it taken effect, it must have terminated in the disgrace of the doctor, whose reputation as a divine and a philosopher he thought a subject too serious to be sported with.

This man, Robe was foolish and wicked enough to introduce, unknown, to Britton, for the sole purpose of terrifying him, and he succeeded in it: Honeyman, without moving his lips, or seeming to speak, announced, as from afar off, the death of poor Britton within a few hours, with an intimation that the only way to avert his doom was for him to fall on his knees immediately and say the Lord's Prayer. The poor man did as he was bid, went home and took to his bed, and in a few days died, leaving his friend Mr. Robe to enjoy the fruits of his mirth.

Hearne says that his death happened in September, 1714. Upon searching the parish-books, it is found that he was buried on the first day of October following.

Britton's wife survived her husband He left little behind him besides his books, his collection of manuscript and printed music, and musical instruments. The former of these were sold by auction at Tom's coffee-house, Ludgate-hill. Sir Hans Sloane was a purchaser of sundry articles, and catalogues of them are in the hands of many collectors of such things as matters of curiosity. His music-books were also sold in the month of December, in the year of his death, by a printed catalogue, of which the following is a copy:—

' A CATALOGUE of extraordinary musical instruments made
' by the most eminent workmen both at home and abroad.
' Also divers valuable compositions, ancient and modern,
' by the best masters in Europe; a great many of which
' are finely engrav'd, neatly bound, and the whole care-
' fully preserv'd in admirable order; being the entire
' collection of Mr. Thomas Britton of Clerkenwell, small-
' coal man, lately deceased, who at his own charge
' kept up so excellent a consort forty odd years at his
' dwelling-house, that the best masters were at all times
' proud to exert themselves therein; and persons of the
' highest quality desirous of honouring his humble cottage
' with their presence and attention: but death having
' snatched away this most valuable man that ever enjoyed
' so harmonious a life in so low a station, his music books
' and instruments, for the benefit of his widow, are to be
' sold by auction on Monday, Tuesday, and Wednesday,
' the 6th, 7th, and 8th Decemb. at Mr. Ward's, house in
' Red Bull-Yard, in Clerkenwell, near Mr. Britton's,
' where Catalogues are to be had gratis; also at most
' Music-shops about town. Conditions of sale as usual.

' 1. Two sets of books, one of three, and one of four parts,
' by divers authors. 2. Two sets of ditto in 4 parts by Jen-
' kins, Lock, Lawes, &c. 3. Two sets ditto by Robert Smith,
' Brewer, and other authors. 4. Two sets ditto by Mr. Richard
' Cobb, and other authors. 5. Two Lyra consorts by Loose-
' more, Wilson, &c. 6. Three sets of books by Baptist, &c.
' 7. Two sets ditto by old Mr. Banister, Akeroyd, &c. 8. Two
' sets of books by Mr. Paisible, Grabu, &c. 9. Three ditto,
' two by Mr. Courteville and one by Mr. Banister. 10. Two
' ditto, four parts, by Chr. Simpson and Mr Wilson. 11. Two
' ditto, Jenkins's Pearl consort and Dr. Rogers. 12. Two
' ditto of Lyra consorts by Jenkins and Wilson. 13. Three
' ditto by Jenkins, Simpson, and Cuts. 14. Nicola's 1st, 2nd,

' 3d, and 4th books, original plates, with second trebles and
' tenors. 15. Three sets of three parts by Dr. Gibbons and
' other authors. 16. Two ditto of four parts by Mr. Eccles.
' Mr. Courteville, and Dr. Coleman. 17. Three printed operas
' by Vitali, Grossi, and one by divers authors, Italian. 18.
' Two sets in three parts by Jenkins, Mr. Paisible, &c. 19.
' Four sets ditto by Vitali, &c. 20. Corelli's Opera Quarta,
' and Ravenscroft's Ayres. 21. 25 Sonatas by Corelli, Bassani,
' &c. Italian writing. 22. Ditto. 23. 16 Concertos by Carlo
' Catrilio, Carlo Ambrosio, Corelli ditto. 24. 25 Sonatas by
' Melani, Bassani, Ambrosio, &c. 25. Mr. H. Purcell's
' musick in Dioclesian with trumpets, Mr. Finger. 9 books
' with ditto. 26. Trumpet pieces in 4 and 5 parts by Dr.
' Pepusch, &c. 27. Two sets of books ayres by Mr. Eccles,
' Barret, Bassani, Gabrielli. 28. Desnier's Overtures, Ayres,
' &c. engraved and neatly bound, another set by divers. 29.
' Fantasies, &c. by Ferabosco, &c. 30. Ayres in 2, 3, and 4
' parts by Lenton, Tollet, Jenkins, &c. 31. 13 Sonatas of 2,
' 3, and 4 parts by Corelli, Italian writing. 32. Five books of
' Pavans, Ayres, &c. neatly bound. 33. Four sets of Ayres
' of 3 and 4 parts by Jenkins, &c. 34. Three sets of Lyra
' books by Wilson and Simpson. 35. Two sets of books by
' Mr. Jenkins in 3 parts. 36. Three sets ditto by Vitali, R.
' Smith, &c. 3 parts. 37. Three sets ditto by Mr. Courteville,
' Finger, Grabu, &c. 4 parts. 38. Six sets ditto by Mr. H.
' Purcell, Mr. Paisible, Mr. Demoivre, &c. Duos for flutes and
' violins. 39. Three sets ditto by Sign. Baptist, Lock, &c.
' 3 parts. 40. One set ditto of Gillier of his last and best
' works. 41. 12 Sonatas by Batt. Gigli for the marriage of
' the Duke of Tuscany. 42. Simpson's Division Violist in
' English, neatly bound. 43. Simpson's ditto in English
' and Latin, ditto. 44. Three sets by Orl. Gibbons, Mons. la
' Voles, and Lock, 3 parts. 45. Six sets of books of Redding's
' Lyra, 2 violins, &c. and divers authors. 46. A set of
' Sonatas in three parts with two basses. 47. Mr Sherard's
' Opera prima on the best large paper, and finely bound and
' lettered. 48. A set of Grabu in 5 parts, and a set of Vitali
' in 6 parts. 49. Two sets of Sonatas by Carlo Manelli and
' Cav. Tarq. Merula. 50. Three sets by Vitali, Uccellini,
' and Adson, printed in 5 parts. 51. 17 Sonatas by Mr.
' Finger. two of them with a high violin. 52. Canzonette for
' 3 and 4 voices, with a harpsichord and lute part. 53. Mace's
' Musick's Monument. 54. 12 Sonatas by Fiorenzo a Kempis
' for a violin, and viol da gamba and bass. 55. A set of
' Sonatas by Baltzar for a lyra violin, treble violin, and bass.
' 56. 2 sets ditto by Coperario, Lupo, Dr. Gibbons, &c. and
' Fancies, 3 parts, also a set by Baptist. 57. 2 sets ditto by
' Vitali, and 1 set by Hernels, 3 parts. 58. 12 Sonatas by
' Mr. Novel finely engraved and on good paper. 59. 2 sets
' of fancies of 3 and 4 parts by Ferabosco, Lupo, and other
' excellent authors. 60. Mr. Finger's printed Sonatas, 2 first
' violins and 2 basses. 61. 3 sets ditto by Vitali, Opera 14,
' and Lock, &c. 62. The opera of Isis, and a set of 5 parts
' by several authors. 63. A collection of many divisions, &c.
' by Baltzar, Mell, &c. 64. Concertos by P. Romolo and
' Nicola. 65. Overtures and tunes, 4 parts, by Mr. Paisible,
' Mr. Courteville, &c. 66. 3 sets of ditto and fancies by
' Jenkins, Gibbons. 67. 12 Solos by Torelli for a violin and
' bass, and 10 Solos by Corelli. 68. 16 Solos by Corelli, Dr.
' Croft, &c. some for flutes and some for violins. 69. 4 sets
' by Lock, and Young's Sonatas, Farmer's Ayres, &c. 70.
' 18 Sonatas by Dr. Pepusch, Carlo Ruggiero. 71. 3 sets of
' books of Sonatas by divers authors 72. Krieger's 12 Sonatas.
' 73. 3. sets of Sonatas, and one set by Lawes, 5 and 6 parts,
' and 2 sets by Birchenshaw. 74. 4 sets of Sonatas and Ayres
' by divers authors. 75. Caldara's 1st and 2d operas. 76.
' Mr. H. Purcell's 2 operas of Sonatas, and Bassani's opera 5ta
' printed. 77. Bassani's opera quinta, and a set of sonatas.
' 78. 4 sets of books for 2 violins by Finger, Courteville, &c.
' 79. Merula and Bleyer's sonatas, 3 parts. 80. Grassi's
' sonatas of 3, 4, and 5 parts. 81. Walter's Solos finely
' engrav'd and neatly bound. 82. Mr. H. Purcell's Overtures
' and Ayres in his Operas, Tragedies and Comedies, 8 books,
' printed in Holland. 83. Ditto fairly printed here. 84.
' Bassani's best Sonatas well wrote. 85. A large and good
' collection of Ayres in 3 and 4 parts, by the best modern
' masters. 86. Nicolini Cosmi's solo book neatly bound. 87.

' Corelli's solo book, Dutch print. 88. Ditto. 89. Senallio's
' Solos finely engrav'd. 90. Danrieu's Solos ditto. 91. Biber's
' Sonatas, 5 parts. 92. Lock's Fancies, 4 parts : Cobb's 3 parts,
' Vitali 3 parts, &c. 93. 6 Concertos for trumpets, hautboys,
' and Mr. Eccles's Coronation of Q. Anne. 94. Hely's Sonatas
' for 3 viols, and ditto by several authors. 95 to 98. Corelli's
' Opera terza finely wrote. 98. Corelli Opera terza in sheets.
' 99. Corelli Opera prima. 100. Playhouse tunes of 3 and
' 4 parts. 101. 12 Concertos and Sonatas, 10 of them by
' Dr. Pepusch. 102. 12 Concertos by Dr. Pepusch, young
' Mr. Babel, Vivaldi. 103. Albinoni's Concertos, Dutch print.
' 104. Biber's Solo book finely engrav'd. 105. A curious
' collection of Concertos by Dr. Pepusch, &c. 106. Mr. Corbet's
' 3d and 4th Operas, Mr. Williams's 6 Sonatas, and Mr.
' Finger's 9 Sonatas. 107. Mr. Keller's Sonatas for Trumpets,
' Flutes, Hautboys, &c. Dutch print. 108. Pez Opera prima
' engrav'd in Holland. 109. 3 sets of books in 3 parts. 110.
' 9 sets ditto of tunes. 111. 7 sets ditto for 4, 5, 6, 7, 8, and
' 10 instruments. 112. 5 sets ditto for violins, lyra viols, with
' basses by Jenkins. 113 to 115. 6 sets ditto of 2 and 3 parts.
' 116. Lawes's Royal Consort, Jenkins, Simpson, &c. 4 parts.
' 117 to 120. Sets of books, viz. Jenkin's Pearl Consort, and
' most by him, and other in 3 and 4 parts. 121 to 124. Sets
' of books of fancies, &c. 2 and 3 parts by Jenkins, &c. 125.
' 8 sets ditto of lyra pieces, most by Jenkins, in 2, 3, 4, and 5
' parts. 126. 5 sets ditto of 3 parts, most by Jenkins. 127.
' 6 sets ditto for the organ by Bird, Bull, Gibbons, &c. 128.
' A great collection of divisions on grounds. 129. 6 sets of
' Duos by Veracini and other authors. 130. 9 books of in-
' structions for the Psalmody, Flute and Mock-trumpet. 131.
' 15 ditto for the Lute, Guitar, Citharen, &c. 132. 2 sets by
' Becker, Rosenmuller, in 2, 3, 4, and 5 parts. 133. 5 sets for
' 2 viols and violins by Jenkins, Simpson, &c. 134. 8 sets for
' Lyra viols and other instruments by Jenkins, &c. 135.
' Bononcini's Ayres, and a great collection with them. 136.
' 5 sets Pavans, Fancies, &c. by Jenkins, Mico, &c. in 4 and
' 5 parts. 137. 5 books of instructions and lessons for the
' harpsichord. 138. 2 sets of books of Concertos &c. by Dr.
' Pepusch, &c. 139. 8 Concertos, Italian writing, for Trum-
' pets, &c. divers authors. 140. 2 sets for three lyra viols,
' and one set for a lyra viol, violin and bass, Jenkins. 141.
' Des Cartes, Butler, Bath, &c. 6 books of the theory of
' Musick. 142. Cazzati's Sonatas and pieces for lyra viols,
' and Sonatas, Ayres, &c. 143. Sonatas for 3 flutes, and
' several Solos and Sonatas for flutes and violins, Dr. Pepusch,
' &c. 144. Country dances with the basses, and other books.
' 145. 2 books finely bound, most plain paper. 146. Several
' excellent Sonatas, with a great parcel of other music. 147.
' Romolo's 2 Choirs in 6 books, Uccellini and Becker's So-
' natas. 148. Corelli's first, second, and third operas printed.
' 149. Plain paper of several sizes. 150. 3 sets of books, most
' plain paper. 151. 12 Sonatas by an unknown author. 152.
' Morley's Introduction. 153. Ditto. 154. Lawes's Treasury
' of Music. 155. Butler's Principles of Music. 156. 6 books
' full of Opera Overtures, Sonatas, &c. of the best authors.
' 157. 6 books of Trumpet Sonatas and Tunes for 2 flutes and
' 2 hautboys. 158. 6 books Overture of Hercules, and a Con-
' certo of Corelli. 159. 5 books of Morgan's best Overtures,
' Cibels, and tunes, and some by Mr. Clark. 160. Simpson's
' Months and Seasons; a bundle of cases for books; odd
' books and papers.

### ' VOCAL MUSICK.

' 1. Divine Companion, Canons, Catches, Godeaus French
' Psalms, &c. 2. Nine books of the theory of musick by
' divers authors. 3. The first and second sets of Madrigals
' of that excellent author John Wilbye. 4. The Gentleman's
' Journal for almost three years, with songs at the end. 5.
' 3 Different Catch Books by Mr. Purcell and the best masters.
' 6. Anthems in 4, 5, and 6 parts in English and Latin, in 6
' books neatly bound. 7. The Treasury of Musick in 5 books,
' by H. Purcell, &c. neatly bound. 8. Orpheus Britannicus,
' the 2 volumes in one book, well bound. 9. Several little
' books of Songs. 10. Orpheus Britannicus, the first book,
' with new additions. 11. Amphion Angelicus by Dr. Blow,
' for 1, 2, 3, and 4 voices, to a thorow bass. 12. The opera
' Pyrrhus and Demetrius with the Symphonies. 13. The
' opera of Antiochus with the Symphonies. 14. The opera of

' Hydaspes with the Symphonies. 15. A great collection of
' ancient and modern songs, some by Bassani, &c. 16.
' Bassani's Motetts, Opera 8 with Symphonies. 17. Ditto
' Opera 13. 18. Pietro Reggio's Song book. 19. The operas
' of Camilla and Thomyris with Symphonies. 20. Several
' Catch-books. 21. The opera of Clotilda with Symphonies.
' 22. The opera of Almahide ditto. 23. Dr. Pepusch's
' Cantatas. 24 to 25. A great collection of Song-books by
' divers authors. 26. Services and anthems by Tallis, Bird,
' Gibbons, &c. the part for the organ. 27. The 2 Harmonia
' Sacras by Mr. H. Purcell. 28. A very large collection of
' sheet songs. 29. A collection of song books. 30. Nine
' song books by divers authors. 31. Bird's Psalms in 5 parts,
' and Lawes's Psalms in 3 parts, and 9 Canons of 3 and 4.
' 32. Several divine pieces in 3 and 4 parts, and Child's
' Psalms. 33. Seven song-books, &c. 34. One set for 2 and
' 3 voices : and one set for 5 voices by Dr. Gibbons. 35. 2
' sets of books for 2, 3, 4, and 5 voices, by Dumont, Jones, &c.
' 36. Six sets of books, most of Dowland, for many parts.
' 37. 5 books of Playford's Psalms in 4 parts, folio, proper for
' a shopkeeper. 38 An old book finely wrote of Latin church
' musick. 39. Several books and sets of songs. 40. Lawes's
' Psalms, and several ditto. 41. Four new Psalm books.
' 42. 2 Harmonia Sacras, first part.

### ' SCORES.

' 1. Mr. Jenkins, Dr. Gibbons, and another author, 3 books.
' 2. Mr. Purcell's Cecilia, Lock's opera of Psyche, and 15
' sheets. 3. By Baptist Lully, Lock, Smith, &c. 4. Songs
' for 2 and 3 voices by Dr. Wilson. 5. Albion and Albanius
' by Mr. Grabu. 6. Mr. Purcell's Te Deum and Jubilate.
' 7. Mr. Purcell's opera of Dioclesian. 8. Ditto. 9. A large
' book of Sonatas. 10. A noble book by Gasparini and the
' best Italian authors, 168 folios. 11. Ditto by Melani and
' the best Italian authors, 166 folios.

### ' INSTRUMENTS.

' 1. A fine Guittar in a case. 2. A good Dulcimer. 3. Five
' instruments in the shape of fish. 4. A curious ivory Kitt
' and bow in a case. 5. A good Violin by Ditton. 6. Another
' very good one. 7. One said to be a Cremona. 8. An ex-
' traordinary Rayman.* 9. Ditto. 10. Ditto. 11. Ditto.
' 12. One very beautiful one by Claud, Pieray of Paris, as
' good as a Cremona. 13. One ditto. 14. Another very
' good one. 15. Another ditto. 16. A very good one for a
' high violin. 17. Another ditto. 18. An excellent tenor.
' 19. Another ditto by Mr. Lewis. 20. A fine viol by Mr.
' Baker of Oxford. 21. Another excellent one, bellied by Mr.
' Norman.† 22. Another, said to be the neatest that Jay
' ever made. 23. A fine bass violin, new neck'd and bellied
' by Mr. Norman. 24. Another rare good one by Mr. Lewis.
' 25. A good harpsichord by Philip Jones. 26. A Rucker's
' Virginal, thought to be the best in Europe. 27. An Organ
' of five stops, exactly consort pitch, fit for a room, and with
' some adornments may serve for any chapel, being a very
' good one.
' N. B. There is not one book or instrument here men-
' tioned that was not his own : and as it will be the best sale
' that hath been made in its kind, so it shall be the fairest. All
' persons that are strangers to pay 5s. in the pound for what
' they buy, and to take away all by Friday night following.
' There are a great many books that Mr. Britton had
' collected in most parts of learning, the whole consisting of
' 14 or 1500 books, which will shortly be sold at his late
' dwelling house. But the manner and method of sale is not
' yet concluded on.'

## CHAP. CLXVII.

BEFORE we proceed to give an account of sundry
concerts and musical meetings which may be said to
have taken their rise from that of Britton, it will be
necessary to mention one of a very different kind, as

* Jacob Rayman dwelt in Bell-yard, Southwark, about the year 1650.
The tenor violins made by him are greatly valued.

† Barah Norman was one of the last of the celebrated makers of viols
in England : he lived in Bishopsgate, and afterwards in St. Paul's church-
yard. He had two daughters, who were actresses of the lower class at
the theatre in Goodman's-fields.

being conducted at a great expense, namely, that of the duchess of Mazarine, who came into England in the reign of Charles II., and for a series of years contrived by various methods to make her house the resort of all that had any pretensions to wit, gallantry, or politeness. To understand the nature of the entertainment above mentioned a sketch of this lady's history will hardly be thought improper.

HORTENSIA MANCINI was one of the four daughters of Lorenzo Mancini by Jeronima Mazarine, sister of Cardinal Mazarine. She had been in France from the time that she was six years of age, and improving in wit and beauty, attracted the regard of the whole court. King Charles II. saw her at Paris, and more than once demanded her in marriage; but the cardinal, seeing no prospect of his restoration, refused his consent, though he lived to repent it, and in 1661 married her to the duke de la Meilleraie, with whom she lived about four years without reproach; but, upon a disagreement with him, she left him, possessed of the fortune which the cardinal had bequeathed to her, amounting to twenty millions of livres; and in 1675, having been invited hither with a view to supplant the duchess of Portsmouth in the king's affections, she came into England, where she was scarce arrived before the king settled on her an annual pension of four thousand pounds; and there was little doubt but she would have answered the end of her being sent for, but in the following year the prince of Monaco arriving here, she was so negligent of her business as to engage in an amour with him, which coming to the king's ear, he withdrew her pension, and was hardly prevailed on to restore it. She had other intrigues upon her hands at different times, which are not to be wondered at, seeing that she was even in her youth, or rather infancy, so great a libertine as not to have the least tincture of religion. In the memoirs of her life, written by the Abbé de St. Real, but under her own immediate direction, it is related that the cardinal her uncle was much displeased with her, and her sister Madame de Bouillon, for their want of devotion; and that once complaining to them that they did not hear mass every day, he told them that they had neither piety nor honour; adding this exhortation, which deserves to be remembered to his credit, 'At least, if you will not hear mass for God's sake, do it for the world's.'

But the want of religious principle in this lady seems, in the opinion of her panegyrists, especially Mons. St. Evremond, to have been amply atoned for by her wit and beauty. This person, who had a considerable hand in the laudable business of bringing her hither, might almost be said to have resided in her house (*Lindsay House*), which was at Chelsea; and, if we may believe the accounts that are given of her manner of living, was a kind of academy, and daily frequented by the principal nobility, and persons distinguished for wit and genius, where, in the style of free conversation, were discussed subjects of the deepest speculation, such as philosophy and religion, as also history, poetry, criticism on dramatic and other ingenious compositions, and the niceties of

the French language. And that nothing might be wanting to increase the attractions of this bower of bliss, the game of basset was introduced, and an obscure man, named Morin permitted to keep a bank in it;* and concerts were given there, in which St. Everemond himself set the music: indeed, if we come to inquire into his share of the musical composition, his attempts in this way must appear ridiculous; for we are told, though he composed tunes to his own verses, and particularly to sundry Idyls, Prologues, and other pieces of his writing, yet that as to overtures, chorusses, and symphonies, he left them to some able musician, who we elsewhere learn was Mr. Plaisible, the famous composer for the flute, already spoken of in this work.

St. Evremond, though an old man, was blind to the follies, and even vices of this woman, whom we may style the modern Cleopatra, and has disgraced himself by the fulsome praises of her with which his works abound. He wrote the words to most of the vocal compositions performed at her house, and generally presided at the performance. The duchess died in 1699, aged fifty-two.

The musical representations at the duchess of Mazarine's were chiefly dramatic, and are celebrated for their magnificence. The singers in them were women from the theatres, whose names have been mentioned in the preceding part of this work, and the instrumental performers the most eminent masters of the time. It is supposed that the design of introducing the Italian opera into England was first concerted in this assembly: the death of the duchess retarded but for a few years the carrying of it into execution, for in 1707 the opera of Arsinoe, consisting of English words adapted to Italian airs by Mr. Thomas Clayton, was performed at Drurylane theatre; and a succession of entertainments of this kind terminated in the establishment of an opera properly so called, in which the drama was written in the Italian language, and the music in the Italian style of composition. This important era in the history of music, as it respects England, will be noticed in a succeeding page: in the interim it is found necessary to continue the account of eminent church musicians who flourished in this period.

The encouragement given to church music by the establishment of two composers for the chapel, had excited but little emulation in the young men to distinguish themselves in this kind of study, so that after the decease of Blow there were but few that addicted themselves to the composition of anthems, and of these the most considerable were Tudway, Croft, Creighton, Dr. Turner, Heseltine, Godwin, King, and Greene.

THOMAS TUDWAY received his education in music in the chapel royal, under Dr. Blow, being one of

* *In a song of Sir George Etherege's on Basset, is this stanza :—*
Let equipage and dress despair,
Since Bassett has come in;
For nothing can oblige the fair,
Like Money and Morin.

*Morin is also mentioned in Bruyere's Characters. Sidney earl of Godolphin told Sir Robert Walpole that he had played at the duchess of Mazarine's, and that, in consideration of her poverty, it was customary to leave a guinea under the carpet on the table.*

those called the second set of chapel children, and a fellow-disciple of Turner, Purcell, and Estwick. On the twenty-second day of April, 1664, he was admitted to sing a tenor in the chapel at Windsor. After that, viz., in 1671, he went to Cambridge, to which university he was invited by the offer of the place of organist of King's College chapel, and in 1681 was admitted to the degree of bachelor in his faculty. In the year 1705 queen Anne made a visit to the university of Cambridge, upon which occasion he composed an anthem, ' Thou, O God, hast heard my vows,' which he performed as an exercise for the degree of doctor in music, and was created accordingly, and honoured with the title of public professor of music in that university.* He also composed an anthem, ' Is it true that God will dwell with men on earth?' on occasion of her Majesty's first going to her royal chapel at Windsor; and for these compositions, and perhaps some others on similar occasions, he obtained permission to style himself composer and organist extraordinary to queen Anne.

A few songs and catches are the whole of Dr. Tudway's works in print; nevertheless it appears that he was a man studious in his profession, and a composer of anthems to a considerable number. He had a son, intended by him, as it seems, for his own profession; for his information and use the doctor drew up, in the form of a letter, such an account of music and musicians as his memory enabled him to furnish. Many very curious particulars are related in it, and some facts which but for him must have been buried in oblivion; among which are the contest between father Smith and Harris about the making of the Temple organ, and the decision of it by Jefferies, afterwards Lord Chancellor—a fact scarcely known to any person living except such as have perused the letter.

His intimacy with Purcell, who had been his school-fellow, furnished him with the means of forming a true judgment, as well of his character as his abilities, and he has borne a very honourable testimony to both in the following passage :—' I knew ' him perfectly well; he had a most commendable ' ambition of exceeding every one of his time, and ' he succeeded in it without contradiction, there ' being none in England, nor anywhere else that ' I know of, that could come in competition with him ' for compositions of all kinds. Towards the latter ' end of his life he was prevailed with to compose ' for the English stage; there was nothing that ever ' had appeared in England like the representations ' he made of all kinds, whether for pomp or solem- ' nity; in his grand chorus, &c., or that exquisite ' piece called the freezing piece of music; in repre- ' senting a mad couple, or country swains making ' love, or indeed any other kind of musick whatever. ' But these are trifles in comparison of the solemn ' pieces he made for the church, in which I will ' name but one, and that is his Te Deum. &c., with ' instruments, a composition for skill and invention

* The professorship of music in the university of Cambridge is merely honorary, there being no endowment for it; Dr. Staggins was the first professor, being appointed in 1684, and Dr. Tudway the second.

' beyond what was ever attempted in England before ' his time.'

In his sentiments touching music, as delivered in his letter, Dr. Tudway is somewhat singular, inasmuch as he manifests an almost uniform dislike to the practice of fuguing in vocal music, alledging as a reason that it obscures the sense of the words, which is either the case or not, according as the point is managed. Certain it is, that the practice of the ablest masters, both before and since his time, is against him; and it is perhaps owing to this singularity of opinion that the best of his compositions do not rise above mediocrity, and that scarce any of them are in use at this day.

In the latter part of his life Dr. Tudway was mostly resident in London. Having a general acquaintance with music, and being personally intimate with the most eminent of the profession, he was employed by Edward, earl of Oxford, in collecting for him musical compositions, chiefly of the Italians, and in making a collection of the most valuable services and anthems, the work of our own countrymen. Of these he scored with his own hand as many as filled seven thick quarto volumes, which are now deposited in the British Museum, and answer to Numb. 7337, et seq. in the printed catalogue of that collection.

The favour shown him by Lord Oxford, together with his merit in his profession, procured him admittance into a club, consisting of Prior, Sir James Thornhill, Christian the seal engraver, Bridgman the gardener, and other ingenious artists, which used to meet at Lord Oxford's once a week. Sir James Thornhill drew all their portraits in pencil, and amongst the rest that of Dr. Tudway playing on the harpsichord, and Prior scribbled verses under the drawings. These portraits were in the collection of Mr. West, the late president of the Royal Society.

In the music-school at Oxford is a painting of Dr. Tudway, with the anthem performed on the queen's coming to Cambridge in his hand. The picture was a present from the late Dr. Rawlinson. Dr. Tudway is yet remembered at Cambridge for his singular style in conversation, and for that, like Daniel Purcell, he could scarce ever speak without a pun.

SAMUEL MARSHALL, *a young man of a promising genius and amiable character, merits a place among the church musicians of this time. He was a scholar of Blow, and organist of St. Catherine Cree Church, London. An anthem, ' Behold how good and joyful,' in the key of C with the greater third, extant only in manuscript, and a few Songs, printed with his name, are all of his compositions that at this day are known: among them is one for two voices, ' Earth's Treasure', which being sung at a concert at Stationers' Hall, was received with great applause. It was reprinted about twenty years ago, but without a name, in a collection entitled The Essex Harmony. He died in 1714, at the age of twenty-seven, and lies buried under the organ of his church. Over the place of his interment is a marble tablet, erected by the Rev. Mr. Prat, at that time minister of St. Botolph's, Aldgate, with an encomiastic inscription too long to be here inserted, but which is given at length in Strype's edition of Ston's Survey, Book II. Page 63.*

William Croft *(a Portrait)*, a native of Nether Eatington, in the county of Warwick, was educated in the royal chapel under Dr. Blow; and upon the erection of an organ in the parish church of St. Anne, Westminster, was elected organist of that church. In 1700 he was admitted a gentleman extraordinary of the chapel royal, and in 1704 was appointed joint-organist of the same with Jeremiah Clark, upon whose decease in 1707 he obtained the whole place. In the year 1708 he succeeded Dr. Blow as master of the children and composer to the chapel royal, as also in his place of organist of the collegiate church of St. Peter, Westminster.

In the year 1711 he resigned his place of organist of St. Anne, Westminster, in favour of Mr. John Isham, who was elected in his room, and in the following year published, but without his name, 'Divine 'Harmony, or a new Collection of select Anthems 'used at her Majesty's Chapels Royal, Westminster Abbey, St. Paul's, &c.' This collection, like that of Clifford, so often mentioned in the course of this work, contains only the words and not the music of the several anthems selected. Before it is a preface, containing a brief account of church music, and an encomium on Tallis and Bird, the former of whom is therein said to have been famous all over Europe. And here the author takes occasion to mention, that although the first anthem in the collection, 'O Lord, the maker of all things,' had been printed with the name of Munday to it, yet that Dr. Aldrich had restored it to its proper author, king Hen. VIII.

In 1713 Croft was created doctor in music in the university of Oxford. His exercise for that degree was an English and also a Latin ode, written by Mr. Joseph Trapp, afterwards Dr. Trapp, which were performed by gentlemen of the chapel, and others from London, in the theatre, on Monday, 13 July, 1713. Both the odes with the music were afterwards curiously engraved in score, and published with the title of Musicus Apparatus Academicus.

In the same year an addition was made to the old establishment of the royal chapel of four gentlemen, a second composer, a lutenist, and a violist, in which was inserted an allowance to Dr. William Croft, as master of the children, of eighty pounds per annum, for teaching the children to read, write, and accompts, and for teaching them to play on the organ and to compose music.

In the year 1724 Dr. Croft published by subscription a noble work of his composition, entitled 'Musica 'Sacra, or select Anthems in score,' in two volumes, the first containing the burial service, which Purcell had begun, but lived not to complete. In the preface the author observes of this work that it is the first essay in music-printing of the kind, it being in score, engraven and stamped on plates; and that for

want of some such contrivance, the music formerly printed in England had been very incorrectly published; as an instance whereof he mentions the Te Deum and Jubilate of Purcell, in which he says the faults and omissions are so gross, as not to be amended but by some skilful hand.

He professes himself ignorant of the state of church music before the reformation, as the same does not appear from any memorials or entries thereof in books remaining in any of our cathedral churches, from whence it is to be inferred that he had never seen or heard of that formula of choral service the Boke of Common Praier noted, composed by John Marbeck, of which, and also of the author, an account has already been given.

He celebrates, in terms of high commendation, for skill and a fine voice, Mr. Elford, of whom he says, 'he was a bright example of this kind, exceeding all 'as far as is known, that ever went before him, and 'fit to be imitated by all that come after him; he 'being in a peculiar manner eminent for his giving 'a due energy and proper emphasis to the words of 'his music.'

The anthems contained in this collection are in that grand and solemn style of composition which should ever distinguish music appropriated to the service of the church. Many of the anthems were made on the most joyful occasions, that is to say, thanksgivings for victories obtained over our enemies during a war in which the interests of all Europe were concerned: upon the celebration of which solemnities it was usual for queen Anne to go in state to St. Paul's Cathedral.* Others are no less worthy to be admired for that majestic and sublime style in which they are written, and of which the following, viz. 'O Lord rebuke me not,' 'Praise the 'Lord, O my soul,' 'God is gone up,' and 'O Lord 'thou hast searched me out,' are shining examples.

Dr. Croft died in August 1727, of an illness occasioned by his attendance on his duty at the coronation of the late king George II. A monument was erected for him at the expence of one of his most intimate friends and great admirers, Humphrey Wyrley Birch, Esq., a gentleman of good estate, and a lawyer by profession,† whereon is inscribed the following character of him:—

---

* As 'I will always give thanks,' for the victory Oudenarde; 'Sing 'unto the Lord,' for the success of our arms in the year 1708. Many other anthems were composed by Dr. Croft and others on the like occasions, which are not in print. *See Bayley's Collection of Anthems.*

† This person was remarkable for the singularity of his character. He was a man of abilities in his profession: he was of counsel for Woolston in the prosecution against him for his blasphemous publications against the miracles of our blessed Saviour, and made for him as good a defence as so bad a cause would admit of. He was possessed of a good estate, and therefore at liberty to gratify his passion for music, which was a very strange one, for he chiefly affected that which had a tendency to draw tears. Of all compositions he most admired the funeral service by Purcell and Croft, and would leave the circuit and ride many miles to Westminster Abbey to hear it. At the funeral of queen Caroline, for the greater convenience of hearing it, he, with another lawyer, who was afterwards a judge, though neither of them could sing a note, walked among the choirmen of the abbey, each clad in a surplice, with a music paper in one hand and a taper in the other. Dr. Croft was a countryman of Mr. Wyrley Birch, which circumstance, together with his great merit in his profession, was Mr. Birch's inducement to the above-mentioned act of munificence, the erection of a monument for him.

GULIELMUS CROFT MUS. DOCT.

NATUS APUD EATINGTON INFERIOREM

IN AGRO WARWICENSI.

Hic juxta Sepultus est
GULIELMUS CROFT
Musicæ Doctor,
Regiiq; Sacelli et hujusce Ecclesiæ Collegiatæ
Organista.
Harmoniam,
A præclarissimo Modulandi Artifice,
Cui alterum jam claudit latus,
Feliciter derivavit;
Suisq; celebratis Operibus,
Quæ Deo consecravit plurima,
Studiose provexit:
Nec Solennitate tantùm Numerorum,
Sed et Ingenii, et Morum, et Vultûs etiam Suavitate,
Egregiè commendavit.
Inter Mortalia
Per quinquaginta fere Annos
Cum summo versatus Candore,
(Nec ullo Humanitatis Offici conspectior
Quàm erga suos quotquot instituerit Alumnos
Amicitiâ et charitate verè Paternâ)
XIV Die Augusti, A. D. M.DCC. XXVII.
Ad Cœlitum demigravit Chorum,
Præsentior Angelorum Concentibus
Suum adstiturus HALLELUJAH.

Expergiscere, mea GLORIA;
Expergiscere, Nablium et cithara;
Expergiscar ego multo mane.

Thus translated: 'Near this place lies interred 'William Croft, doctor in music, organist of the 'royal chapel and this collegiate church. His 'harmony he happily derived from that excellent 'artist in modulation who lies on the other side of 'him.* In his celebrated works, which for the

'most part he consecrated to God, he made a dili-'gent progress; nor was it by the solemnity of the 'numbers alone, but by the force of his ingenuity, 'and the sweetness of his manners, and even his 'countenance, that he excellently recommended 'them. Having resided among mortals for fifty 'years, behaving with the utmost candour (not 'more conspicuous for any other office of humanity 'than a friendship and love truly paternal towards 'all whom he had instructed), he departed to the 'heavenly choir on the fourteenth day of August, '1727, that, being near, he might add his own 'Hallelujah to the concert of angels. Awake up 'my glory, awake psaltery and harp, I myself will 'awake right early.'†

Dr. Croft was a grave and decent man, and being a sincere lover of his art, devoted himself to the study and practice of it. The bent of his genius led him to church music; nevertheless he composed and published six sets of tunes for two violins and a bass, which in his youth he made for several plays. He also composed and published six Sonatas for two flutes, and six Solos for a flute and a bass. The flute, as we have already observed, being formerly a favourite instrument in this kingdom.

There are also extant in print songs of his composition to a considerable number, and some in manuscript, that have never yet appeared; among the latter is that well-known song of Dr. Byrom, 'My time O ye Muses,'‡ first published in the Spectator, No. 603, to which Dr. Croft made the following tender and pathetic air:—

MY time, O ye mu-ses, was hap-pi-ly spent, When Phœbe went with me where-e-ver I went; Ten thou-sand sweet pleasures I felt in my breast, Sure ne-ver fond shepherd, sure ne-ver fond shep-herd like Co-lin was blest. But now she is gone and has left me be-hind, What a mar-vellous change on a sud-den I find; When things were as fine as could

---

* Dr. Blow.          † Psalm lvii. verse 9.

‡ The lady the subject of the above ballad, was the eldest daughter of the famous Dr. Richard Bentley, and a university beauty at the time when the author was at college; she was married to Dr. Richard Cumberland, late bishop of Kilmore, a son of Dr. Cumberland, bishop of Peterborough, the author of that noble antidote against the poison of Hobbes's philosophy, 'De Legibus Naturæ Disquisitio Philosophica,' and died a few months ago.

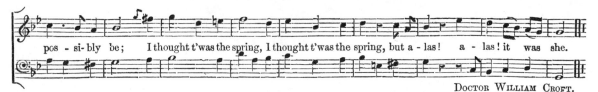

pos - si- bly be;    I thought t'was the spring, I thought t'was the spring, but a - las!    a - las! it was she.

DOCTOR WILLIAM CROFT.

## BOOK XVIII.    CHAP. CLXVIII.

ROBERT CREIGHTON, doctor in divinity, was the son of Dr. Robert Creighton of Trinity college, Cambridge, who was afterwards bishop of Bath and Wells, and attended Charles II. during his exile. In his youth he had been taught the rudiments of music, and entering into holy orders, he sedulously applied himself to the study of church music; he attained to such a degree of proficiency therein, as entitled him to a rank among the ablest masters of his time. In the year 1674 he was appointed a canon residentiary, and also chanter of the cathedral church of Wells; and, being an unambitious man, and in a situation that afforded him opportunities of indulging his passion for music, he made sundry compositions for the use of his church, some of which are remaining in the books thereof. He died at Wells in the year 1736, having attained the age of ninety-seven. Dr. Boyce has given to the world an anthem for four voices, 'I will arise and go to ' my father,' composed by Dr. Creighton, which no one can peruse without regretting that it is so short.

WILLIAM TURNER, one of the second set of chapel children, and a disciple of Blow; when he was grown up, his voice broke into a fine countertenor, a circumstance which procured him an easy admittance into the royal chapel, of which he was sworn a gentleman on the eleventh day of October, 1669, and afterwards was appointed a vicar choral in the cathedral church of St. Paul, and a lay vicar of the collegiate church of St. Peter at Westminster. In the year 1696 he commenced doctor of his faculty in the university of Cambridge.

In the choir-books of the royal chapel, and of many cathedrals, is an anthem, 'I will alway give thanks,' called the club anthem, as having been composed by Humphrey, Blow, and Turner, in conjunction, and intended by them as a memorial of the strict friendship that subsisted between them.

Dr. Turner died at the age of eighty-eight, on the thirteenth day of January, 1740, and was buried in the cloister of Westminster Abbey, in the same grave and at the same time with his wife Elizabeth, whose death happened but four days before his own. They had been married but a few years short of seventy, and in their relation exhibited to the world an illustrious example of conjugal virtue and felicity. The daughter and only child of these two excellent persons was married to Mr. John Robinson, organist of Westminster Abbey, and also of two parish churches in London, namely, St. Lawrence Jewry, and St. Magnus, and of her further mention will be made hereafter. She had a good voice, and sang in the opera of Narcissus, performed at the Haymarket in 1720.*

* In the Memoranda of Anthony Wood mention is made of a William

JOHN GOLDWIN was a disciple of Dr. William Child, and on the 12th day of April, 1697, succeeded him as organist of the free chapel of St. George at Windsor. In the year 1703 he was appointed master of the choristers there; in both which stations he continued till the day of his death, which was the 7th of November, 1719. Of the many anthems of his composition, Dr. Boyce has selected one for four voices, 'I have set God alway before me,' which, in respect of the modulation, answers precisely to the character which the doctor has given of the music of Goldwin, viz., that it is singular and agreeable.

CHARLES KING, bred up in the choir of St. Paul's, under Dr. Blow, was at first a supernumerary singer in that cathedral for the small stipend of 14l. a year. In the year 1704 he was admitted to the degree of bachelor in music in the university of Oxford, and, upon the death of Jeremiah Clark, whose sister was his first wife, was appointed Almoner and master of the children of St. Paul's, continuing to sing for his original stipend, until 31 Oct. 1730, when he was admitted a vicar choral of that cathedral, according to the customs and statutes thereof. Besides his places in the cathedral, he was permitted to hold one in a parish church in the city, being organist of St. Bennet Fink, London: in which several stations he continued till the time of his death, which happened on the seventeenth day of March, 1745. With his second wife he had a fortune of seven or eight thousand pounds, which was left her by the widow of Mr. Primatt the chemist, who lived in Smithfield, and also in that house at Hampton which is now Mr. Garrick's. But, notwithstanding this accession of wealth, he left his family in but indifferent circumstances. King composed some anthems, and also services to a great number, and thereby gave occasion to Dr. Greene to say, and indeed he was very fond of saying it, as he thought it a witty sentiment, that 'Mr. King was a very serviceable man.' As a musician he is but little esteemed; his compositions are uniformly restrained within the bounds of mediocrity; they are well known, as being frequently performed, yet no one cares to censure or commend them, and they leave the mind just as they found it. Some who were intimate with him say he was not devoid of genius, but averse to study; which character seems to agree with that general indolence and apathy which were visible in his look

Turner, the son of a cook of Pembroke college, Oxon. who had been bred a chorister in Christ-church under Mr. Low, and was afterwards a singing-man in that cathedral: this might be Dr. Turner; and upon searching the books of the parish of St. Margaret, Westminster, it appears that on the sixth day of April, 1708, Henry Turner was elected organist of that church in the room of Bernard Smith, being recommended by Mr. John Robinson: probably, therefore, this Henry Turner was a brother of the doctor.

and behaviour at church, where he seemed to be as little affected by the service as the organ-blower.

JOHN ISHAM, or, as his name is sometimes corruptly spelt, Isum, though little known in the musical world, was a man of abilities in his profession. Where he received his instruction in music is not known. He was the deputy of Dr. Croft for several years, and was one of the many persons who went from London to Oxford to assist in the performance of his exercise for his doctor's degree. It appears that Mr. Isham, together with William Morley, a gentleman of the royal chapel, were admitted to the degree of bachelor in music at the same time that Croft commenced doctor. In the year 1711 Dr. Croft resigned the place of organist of St. Anne's, Westminster, and by his interest in the parish Isham was elected in his stead.

Isham had no cathedral employment, nor any place in the royal chapel; for which, considering his merit in his profession, no better reason can be suggested, than that perhaps he had not the recommendation of a good voice; at least this is the only way in which we are able to account for his being so frequently a candidate for the place of organist to several churches in and about London. To that of St. Anne, Westminster, he was chosen on the twenty-second day of January, 1711. On the third day of April, 1718, he was elected organist of St. Andrew, Holborn, with a salary of fifty pounds a year; upon which occasion Dr. Pelling, the rector of St. Anne's, moved in vestry that he might be permitted to retain his place in that church, which motion being rejected, Isham quitted the place; and a vacancy at St. Margaret's, Westminster, happening soon after, he stood for organist of that church, and was elected.

He died about the month of June, 1726, having, with very little encouragement to such studies, made sundry valuable compositions for the use of the church. The words of two anthems composed by him, viz., 'Unto thee, O Lord,' and 'O sing unto the Lord a new song,' are in the collection heretofore mentioned to have been made by Dr. Croft, and published in 1712. He joined with William Morley, above mentioned, in the publication of a collection of songs composed by them both, among which is the following one for two voices:—

all ... her charms are such, we think her some-thing so di - vine, we can - not

all .... her charms are such, we think her some-thing so di - vine, we can - not

gaze, .... not gaze, .... we can - not, can - - not gaze too much.

gaze, ... not gaze, .... we can - not, can - - not gaze too much.

JOHN ISHAM.

DANIEL HENSTRIDGE, organist of the cathedral church of Canterbury about the year 1710, composed sundry anthems. The words of some of them are in the collection entitled Divine Harmony, herein before mentioned to have been published by Dr. Croft in 1712.

JAMES HESLETINE, a disciple of Blow, was organist of the cathedral church of Durham, and also of the collegiate church of St. Catherine, near the Tower, the duty of which latter office he executed by deputy. He was an excellent cathedral musician, and composed a great number of anthems, a few whereof, namely, 'Behold how good and joyful,' and some others, are to be found in the choir books of many of the cathedrals of this kingdom; others, to a great number, he caused to be copied into the books of his own cathedral; but having, as he conceived, been slighted, or otherwise illtreated by the dean and chapter, he in revenge tore out of the church-books all his compositions that were there to be found. He died in an advanced age about twenty years ago.

MAURICE GREENE was the son of a London clergy-man, viz., Mr. Thomas Greene, vicar of St. Olave Jewry, and nephew of John Greene, serjeant at law. He was brought up in St. Paul's choir under Mr. King, and upon the breaking of his voice was taken apprentice by Mr. Richard Brind, then organist of that cathedral. Being an ingenious and studious young man, he was very soon distinguished, as well for his skill in musical composition, as for an elegant and original style in performing on the organ. About the year 1716, his uncle then being a member of Sergeant's-Inn, which is situate in the parish of St. Dunstan in the West, London, had interest enough to procure for his nephew, though under twenty years of age, the place of organist of that parish church. In February, 1717, Daniel Purcell, organist of St. Andrew's, Holborn, being then lately dead, and the parish having agreed to make the salary fifty pounds a year, Greene stood for the place, and carried it; but the year following Brind dying, Greene was by the dean and chapter of St. Paul's appointed his successor; and upon this his preferment he quitted both his places. The dean of St. Paul's at this time was Dr. Godolphin, a musical man, and a friend of Greene, and he by his influence with the chapter procured, in augmen-

tation of the ancient appointment or salary of the organist, the addition of a lay vicar's stipend.

In the year 1730 Mr. Greene was created doctor in music of the university of Cambridge, and at the same time was honoured with the title of public professor of music in that university, in the room of Tudway, who it is supposed died some short time before. As there will be farther occasion to speak of Dr. Greene, the conclusion of this memoir concerning him is postponed.

Frequent occasion has been taken, in the course of this work, to mention Estienne Roger, and Michael Charles Le Cene, two booksellers of Amsterdam. These persons were the greatest publishers of music in Europe; and as they greatly improved the method of printing music on copper plates, are entitled to particular notice. And here it must be observed that the practice now spoken of is supposed to have begun at Rome about the time of Frescobaldi, whose second book of Toccatas was printed there in the year 1637, on copper plates engraven. The practice was adopted by the Germans and the French. The English also gave into it, as appears by a collection of lessons by Dr. Bull, Bird, and others, entitled 'Parthenia, or the Maidenhead of the first Music 'that ever was printed for the Virginals.' Not-withstanding these instances, it appears in general that music continued in most countries to be printed on letter-press types; and, to speak of England only, it prevailed so greatly here, that but for the single songs engraven by one Thomas Cross,* who dwelt in Catherine-wheel-court near Holborn, or as it was also called, Snow-hill Conduit, and published from time to time, about the beginning of this century, to a great number, we should scarce have known that any other method of printing music existed among us.

Playford, whose shop, during the space of near half a century, was the resort of all musicians and practitioners in and about London, seems actually to have been himself a printer of music, at least for a great part of his life. His printing-house was in Little Britain,† and there he bred up to the business

* This person is mentioned by Harry Hall in some verses of his prefixed to the second part of the Orpheus Britannicus; and in his verses addressed to Dr. Blow upon the publication of his Amphion Anglicus is this humorous distich :—
  'While at the shops we daily dangling view
  'False concord by Tom Cross engraven true.'

† In the London Gazette, Numb. 2136, of 6 May, 1686, is an advertise-

his elder son named John, who printed several books published by his brother Henry. His successors in that business have been mentioned in page 736 of this work, and there are a few persons who follow it at this time.

As to printing on copper plates, it had in many respects the advantage of letter-press; the great objection was the expence of it, but this the Dutch artificers found means to reduce; for they contrived by some method, which to others is yet a secret, so to soften the copper, as to render it susceptible of an impression from the stroke of a hammer on a punch, the point whereof had the form of a musical note. The success of this invention is only to be judged of by the numerous articles contained in the Dutch catalogues of music published between the year 1700 and the present time, which seem to indicate little less than that the authors of this discovery had a monopoly of that business.

The difficulty in getting music from abroad, and the high duty on the importation of it, were motives to an attempt of a somewhat similar kind in England. Two persons, namely John Walsh and John Hare, engaged together about the year 1710, to print music on stamped pewter plates. The one had a shop in Catherine-street in the Strand, the other kept a shop, the sign of the Viol, in St. Paul's church-yard,* and another in Freeman's-yard, or court, in Cornhill. They imported from time to time music from Holland, and reprinting it here, circulated it throughout the kingdom to their very great emolument. They were both very illiterate men, neither of them was able to form a title-page according to the rules of grammar, and they seemed both to be too penurious to employ others for the purpose. Their publications were in numberless instances a disgrace to the science and its professors; but they got money, and no one complained.

There lived about this time one Richard Mears, a maker of musical instruments, an ingenious but whimsical man; he had been bred up under his father to that business,† and seeing the slovenly manner in which music was published by Walsh and Hare, and being desirous to participate in so gainful a trade, he became their rival, and proposed to himself and the public to print in a fairer character than pewter would admit of, and to sell his books at a

ment for the sale of Playford's printing-house and utensils. The industry of this man, and the pains he took to get an honest livelihood for himself and his family, are very remarkable; and it seems he had a wife who came not behind him in that virtue. At the end of one of his publications in 1679, is an advertisement purporting 'that at Islington, over-against 'the church, Mrs. Playford then kept a boarding-school, where young 'gentlewomen might be instructed in all manner of curious works, as 'also reading, writing, musick, dancing, and the French tongue.'

* In St. Paul's church-yard were formerly many shops where music and musical instruments were sold, for which at this time no better reason can be given, than that the service at that cathedral drew together twice a day all the lovers of music in London; not to mention that the choirmen were wont to assemble there, where they were met by their friends and acquaintance. The rebuilding of the church was but little interruption to these meetings; for though the church was not finished till 1710, divine service was performed in it as soon as the choir was completed, which was in 1697, *for on the second day of December in that year the same was opened, and a solemn thaksgiving celebrated therein on occasion of the peace of Ryswic.*

† The elder Mears kept a shop for the sale of musical instruments opposite the Catherine-wheel inn without Bishopsgate; and in the London Gazette, Numb. 2433, for March 7, 1688, advertised from thence lutes and viols fretted according to Mr. Salmon's proposal, of which an account is given, page 716, in a note, and also page 724.

price little above what they were sold for by the others.

In prosecution of this design he procured of Mattheson, of Hamburgh, who had married an English woman, and was besides secretary to the British resident in that city, the manuscript of two collections of lessons composed by him. These he caused to be engraven on copper in a handsome character, and printed in a thin folio volume. Some years after, Mr. Handel, having composed for the practice of the princess Anne sundry suits of lessons for the harpsichord, made a collection of them, and gave it to Mears to print; but, properly speaking, it was published by the author's amanuensis, Christopher Smith, who then lived at the sign of the Hand and Music-book in Coventry-street, the upper end of the Haymarket. Mears also printed Mr. Handel's opera of Radamistus, and Coriolanus, composed by Attilio. The next undertaking of Mears was an edition of the works of Corelli; for the four operas of Sonatas he had the assistance of a subscription; the work he completed in an elegant manner, but Walsh and Hare damped the sale of it by lowering the price of an edition published by them some years before. Nevertheless Mears continued to go on. He printed the Opera quinta of Corelli in the same character, and undertook to print his Concertos; but in this work he failed; only the first and second violin parts were engraven, the others were stamped, and that in a worse character than had been made use of by Walsh and his colleague.

After a variety of projects, Mears found himself unable to stand his ground; he quitted his shop in St. Paul's church-yard, and some years after set up in Birchin-lane; he continued there about two years, and then removed to London-house-yard in St. Paul's church-yard, where he died about the year 1743, leaving a son of Walsh in possession of almost the whole trade of the kingdom.

There were two other persons, namely J. Cluer and Benjamin Creake, co-partners; the former dwelt in Bow church-yard, and besides being a printer, was a vender of quack medicines; the latter lived in Jermyn-street. These men undertook to stamp music, and printed many of Handel's operas, that is to say, Admetus, Siroe, Scipio, Rodelinda, Julius Cæsar, Tamerlane, Alexander, and some others, but generally in a character singularly coarse and difficult to read. Thomas Cross, junior, a son of him above mentioned, stamped the plates of Geminiani's Solos, and a few other publications, but in a very homely and illegible character, of which he was so little conscious that he set his name to everything he did, even to single songs. William Smith, who had been an apprentice of Walsh, and lived at the sign of Corelli's head, opposite Norfolk-street, in the Strand, and Benjamin Cooke, in New-street, Coventgarden, were printers of music: the former was chiefly employed by such authors as Festing and a few others, who published their works themselves, and had a type of his own, remarkably steady and uniform.

But the last and great improver of the art of

stamping music in England was one Phillips, a Welchman, who might be said to have stolen it from one Fortier, a Frenchman, and a watchmaker, who stamped some of the parts of Martini's first opera of Concertos, and a few other things. This man, Phillips, by repeated essays arrived at the methods of making types of all the characters used in music. With these he stamped music on pewter plates, and taught the whole art to his wife and son. In other respects he improved the practice of stamping to so great a degree, that music is scarce anywhere so well printed as in England.

About ten years ago one Fougt, a native of Lapland, arrived here, and taking a shop in St. Martin's-lane, obtained a patent for the sole printing of music on letter-press types of his own founding, which were very neat. This patent, had it been contested at law, would undoubtedly have been adjudged void, as the invention was not a new one. He published several collections of lessons and sonatas under it, but the music sellers in London copied his publications on pewter plates, and by underselling, drove him out of the kingdom.

## CHAP. CLXIX.

ANDREA ADAMI (a Portrait), surnamed da Bolsena, Maestro della Cappella Pontificia, was the author of a book entitled 'Osservationi per ben re- ' golare il Coro de i Cantori della Cappella Pontificia, ' tanto nelle Funzioni ordinarie, che straordinairie,' printed at Rome in 1711, 4to; containing, first, a formula of the several functions performed as well on solemn as on ordinary occasions in the pontifical chapel; and, secondly, a brief account of the principal musicians and singers, members of the college of the same chapel.

The preface to this work is a history of the college above mentioned. It begins with an enumeration of the suffrages of the fathers in favour of church music,* in substance as follows :—

'After the death of our Saviour, the singing of ' psalms and hymns was introduced into the church ' by the apostles themselves, according to the docu- ' ments of their Master. During the reigns of the ' Roman emperors, in all the eastern and western ' temples, the ecclesiastical functions were performed ' in Canto figurato, till St. Athanasius introduced ' into the church of Alexandria the Canto piano.

' St. Augustine, in his Confessions, lib. ix. Con- ' fess. 7, assures us, as does also Dominicus Macrus, ' in his Lexicon,† that St. Ambrose introduced into ' his church at Milan the Canto soave e figurato, in ' imitation of that of the Greek church, commonly ' called χροματιζομενος. About a century after, that ' is to say, in 460, pope St. Hilary introduced at ' Rome the true Cantus Ecclesiasticus, and founded ' an academy for singers. This is also said by ' Macrus in his Lexicon, but Johannes Diaconus,

* Next to the exhortations in St. Paul's Epistles to St. James and to the Colossians to sing psalms and spiritual songs, the following passage in the Confessions of St. Augustine, lib. x. cap. 33, is most frequently adduced in favour of church music. 'Verumtamen cum reminiscor 'lacrymas meas, quas fudi ad cantus ecclesiæ tuæ in primordiis re- 'cuperatæ fidei meæ; et nunc ipso, quod moveor non cantu, sed rebus, 'quæ cantantur, (cum liquidâ voce, et convenientissimâ modulatione 'cantantur,) magnam institui hujus utilitatem rursus agnosco.'

† Hierolexicon, sive Dictionarium sacrum, in quo Ecclesiasticæ voces, &c. elucidantur. Rom. 1677.

'with more probality, ascribes it to St. Gregory ' the Great.

' In the year 590, St. Gregory reformed the ' Cantus Ecclesiasticus, and instituted the Cantus ' Gregorianus, which is still used in the pontifical ' chapel. This great man instituted also a school for ' singers, from which the college of pontifical singers ' now existing derives its origin, and appointed sala- ' ries and proper habitations for all the performers. ' St. Gregory took upon himself to preside in the ' school thus founded and endowed by him; after his ' decease one of the most skilful scholars was elected ' Primicerius Scholæ Cantorum, answering to the ' προτωψάλτης or λαοσυνακτης in the Greek church.

' Upon the decease of St. Gregory music lost its ' principal support, and declined greatly, until ' Vitalianus, in 683, Leo II., the Sicilian, and ' chiefly venerable Bede, revived and restored it. ' Notwithstanding these eminent men, church music ' fell again into disuse, not less by the incursions of ' barbarians than by the little attention paid to it at ' that time. And although Guido Aretinus, Josquin ' del Prato, and Christopher Morales, a Spaniard, ' supported it in the eleventh and sixteenth centu- ' ries by many inventions and improvements, the ' true spirit of it was lost at the time of Marcellus ' II., when Palestrina manifested to that pontiff and ' the world the great powers of sacred music.

' The sacred college, however, maintained itself ' always with great decorum and splendour, even ' when the holy see was transferred to Avignon; but ' it flourished greatly upon the return of Gregory ' IX. to Rome.

' The singers in the pontifical chapel have ever ' been held in great veneration and esteem, even by ' monarchs. Pope Agatho sent John, the principal ' singer in the church of St. Peter, and abbot of the ' monastery of St. Martin, to England, to inquire ' into the state of the catholic religion; and at a ' synod convened by Theodore, archbishop of Can- ' terbury, he assisted as the pope's legate.

' All this may be seen at large in the Ecclesiastical ' History of Bede, lib. IV., cap. xviii., where it is ' related that the aforesaid John taught the English ' to sing after the Roman and Gregorian manner, ' and that he died at Tours, and was buried there on ' his return to Italy. The pontifical singers were in ' such estimation, that for particular purposes they ' were the delegates of the pope himself. By a bull ' of Clement IV. it appears that one of the singers of ' the chapel was sent by that pope to Lando, bishop ' of Anagni.

' Mabillon, in his Museo Italico, tom. II., shows ' the pre-eminence due to the college of singers, and ' relates that on a certain occasion, in reading the ' mattin lecture before the pope, on Candlemas-day, ' the singers were preferred to the canons, and that ' the primicerius, or first singer, bore the pontiff's ' mantle : that on Easter-day they received the ' ceremony of the Pax before the subdean and acoly- ' thites, and all other inferior orders. Besides that, ' the pope on that day used to administer to them ' the cup, &c., with many other ceremonies.'

ANDREA ADAMI DA BOLSENA CITTADINO ORIGINARIO
VENEZIANO BENEFIZIATO DI S.M.MAGGIORE E
MAGISTRO DELLA CAPPELLA PONTIFICIA.

Adami observes that these marks of distinction declare the good opinion and esteem which the holy see entertained of the singers in the pontifical chapel in former ages. He adds, that when the French singers who accompanied Charlemagne to Rome contended with the sacred college for pre-eminence in music, that emperor could not help deciding in favour of the Roman singers, saying that the rivulets should not be larger than the fountains, and requested Adrian I. to send two Roman singers to France, to teach throughout the kingdom the true Cantus Gregorianus. For this he cites Cardinal Bona, lib. 1. cap. xxv.

In after times it was the uniform endeavour of the Roman pontiffs to procure the ablest singers for the service of the papal chapel, to which end they frequently made instances to secular princes to send to Rome the most celebrated singers in their dominions; as a proof whereof he inserts the following letter from Leo X. to the marquis of Mantua :—

'Quoniam ad sacra conficienda, precesque divinas 'celebrandas cantore mihi opus est, qui graviori 'voce concinat. Velim, si tibi incommodum non est, 'ut ad me Michælum Lucensem cantorem tuum 'mittas, ut eo nostris in sacris, atque templo, quod 'est omnium celeberrimum, atque sanctissimum, com- 'munemque totius orbis terrarum suavitatem et læti- 'tiam continet, uti possim. Datum 3 Kal. Augusti 'anno 2. Romæ.'

He proceeds, 'Many are the privileges and immu- 'nities granted to singers of the pontifical chapel; 'but unhappily few of the instruments by which 'they were granted escaped the flames in the de- 'plorable sack of Rome in the pontificate of Clement 'VII. There are existing, however, in the archives 'of the Vatican, and of the castle of St. Angelo, 'a brief of Honorius III., a bull of Clement IV., and 'another of Eugenius IV., in which the singers 'are mentioned with great distinction; and in one 'of Eugenius IV. they are styled the pope's 'companions, and the constant attendants on his 'person. Calixtus III., Pius II., and Sixtus IV. 'ratify and confirm the said brief and bulls. Inno- 'cent VIII. forbids all lawyers, notaries, or attorneys 'taking any fee of the pontifical singers, and em- 'powers the bishop maestro di capella to present 'the singers of the chapel to the benefices of the de- 'ceased members, that they may perpetually remain 'in the possession of the sacred college. This pri- 'vilege was confirmed by Alexander VI. and Julius 'II., and Leo X. ordained that every cardinal that 'says mass in the pontifical chapel should pay four 'ducats to the singers, instead of the usual collation, 'and every bishop or prelate attendant two ducats, 'and granted them many perquisites at a cardinal's 'funeral. Clement VII. and Paul III. enacted several 'laws in favour of the singers. Farther, Julius III. 'declared the college of singers equal in every re- 'spect to that of the apostolic writers, and limited it 'to the number of twenty-four.

'Sixtus V. endowed the sacred singers with the 'revenues of the monastery of Santa Maria in Cris- 'piano, in the diocese of **Taranto** of Saint Salvador's 'church in Perugia, and of Santa Maria in Felonica, 'in the diocese of Mantua. He reduced their 'number to twenty-one, and appointed a cardinal for 'their patron and judge in all causes. He also pro- 'vided for the old and infirm members by a grant of 'the same allowances as they enjoyed when in actual 'service of the chapel; but Gregory IV. repealed all 'these bulls of Sixtus V. and made an aggregate 'fund for the college, by which the singers enjoy 'a handsome stipend to this day, with all their former 'privileges and immunities.'

Who was the first maestro di cappella Signor Adami thinks it is impossible to ascertain; he how- ever says, that originally the maestro was always a bishop; and this appears by the succession of maestri di cappella, which he gives from the year 1507 to 1574.

He mentions also a Cardinal, Protettore del Col- legio de Cantori della Cappella Pontificia, the first of whom he says was Decio Azzolino, in the pon- tificate of Sixtus V. and continues the succession down to his own time, concluding with Cardinal Pietro Ottoboni, elected 27 Nov. 1700.

The foregoing particulars are contained in the preface to Adami's book; the book itself exhibits an inside view of the pontifical chapel, otherwise called La Cappella Sistina, as having been built by pope Sixtus IV., *and will be found in the supple- mentary Volume with the Portraits.* After which follows a description of the several functions per- formed in that chapel, as well upon ordinary as solemn occasions; from which it appears that by the usage of the chapel, motets, and other offices of sundry masters by name are appropriated to peculiar days: thus for instance, Alla Messa dell' Epifania, is sung a motet of Palestrina, 'Surge illuminare 'Jerusalem.' Nella terza Domenica di Quaresima, a motet of Cristoforo Morales, 'Lamentabatur Jacob;' and on Wednesday and Friday in the Holy Week the Miserere of Allegri, referring to the books of the chapel where the several compositions are to be found.

The several functions described by Adami are performed agreeably to the ancient usage of the Romish church: that in which the Nativity is celebrated seems to be of the dramatic kind, and accounts for that note prefixed to the eighth concerto of Corelli, 'Fatto per la Notte di Natale.' The function itself is thus described: 'Primo Vespero 'di Natale. Il regolamento di questa funzione di- 'pende dal sapere, se il Papa nel seguente giorno 'di Natale vuol celebrare egli stesso la messa, perchè 'in tal caso il vespero và ordinato nella stessa guisa 'di quello di S. Pietro, quando che nò, come quello 'di tutt' i Santi.

'Terminato il vespero, restano nel Palazzo Apos- 'tolico quelli eminentissimi Cardinali, che nella se- 'guente notte vogliono assistere al mattutino, ed 'alla messa, alla quali li ministri del detto Palazzo, 'a spese della reverenda camera danno una lautissima 'cena, con un apparecchio nobile di varj trionfi, che 'rappresentano i fatti della Natività del nostro Re- 'dentore. Prima della cena è costume dare ancora

' alli detti eminentissimi un virtuoso divertimento
' di musica, con una cantata volgare sopra la Nati-
' vità del Bambino Gesù, la quale si dee regolare
' dal nostro Signor Maestro di Cappella, e però pre-
' ventivamente dovrà egli portarsi da Monsignor
' Maggiordomo, a cui spetta la direzone di tutta
' questa funzione, per intender da esso l'elezione
' tanto del poeta, quanto del compositore della musica;
' e poi dovrà scieglier i migliori cantori del nostro
' collegio per cantarla; e dopo terminata, unito alli
' cantori, e egli stromenti dovrà portarsi al luogo
' destinato per la cena, che ancora essi suol dare la
' reverenda camera apostolica.'

The second part contains a description of the extraordinary functions, namely these that follow:—

Nella Creazione del nuovo Pontefice. Nella Consagrazione del nuovo Pontefice. Nella Consagrazione che fa il Papa di qualche Vescovo. Nella Coronazione del nuovo Pontefice. Nel Possesso del nuovo Pontefice. Nell' Anniversario della Creazione del Pontefice. Nell' Anniversario della Coronazione del Pontefice. Nel Consistoro pubblico. Nell' aprire la Porta Santa. Nel serrare la Porta Santa. Nella Canonizazione de' Santi. Nel Battesimo di qualche Ebreo. Nelle Processioni straordinarie per Giubilei, o Indulgenze. Nell' Essequie de' Sommi Pontefici. Settima Essequie. Decimo Giorno. Nell' Anniversario del Sommo Pontefice Defonto. Nell' Essequie degli Eminentissimi Cardinali Defonti. Nell' Essequie d'un nostro Compagno Defonto, ed altri Anniversarj della Cappella. Nell' Anniversario di Marazzoli, e de' nostri Compagni Defonti a S. Gregorio. Nelle Cappelle Cardinalizie di San Tomasso d'Aquino, e San Bonaventura. Nella Festa della Annunziata. Per S. Marta Festa di Palazzo alla sua Chiesa vicino a S. Pietro.

The remainder of the book consists of an account of the pontifical singers from the time of Paul III. to that of the then reigning pope, Clement XI. extracted from the books of the chapel, and other authentic memorials, with sundry historical particulars relating to such of them as were celebrated for their compositions. The following is the substance of this account, so far as it regards the most eminent of them :—

' Many are the singers who distinguish themselves
' in the pontifical chapel since the first institution
' thereof; amongst them was Jacopo Pratense, who
' flourished in the sixteenth century, and was ad-
' mitted a singer in the said chapel under Sixtus IV.
' His name is engraven in the choir of the Vatican
' palace. His works, consisting of Masses, were
' published at Fossombrone, in three volumes, in
' the years 1515 and 1516, by Ottavio de Petrucci,
' the first inventor of printing music.

' Giacomo Arcadelt, maestro di cappella to Cardinal
' di Lorena, was esteemed one of the first of his
' time of the composers of madrigals, five books
' whereof composed by him were printed at Venice;
' one of the finest among them is that celebrated
' one, "Il bianco e dolce Cigno cantando muore."

' In 1544, under Paul III. was admitted into the
' sacred college, Christoforo Morales of Sevil.' The

particulars respecting this person, as also Palestrina, are already inserted in this work.

' In this century, under Pius IV. flourished Ales-
' sandro Romano. He was for his skill in playing
' on the viol called Alessandro della Viola. He was
' the inventor of Canzonets for four and five voices.
' Upon leaving the chapel he changed his name to
' that of Julius Cæsar, and embraced the monastic
' life in the Olivetan congregation.

' About the year 1562 the reverend Father Fran-
' cesco Soto da Langa, by birth a Spaniard, and
' a soprano singer, began to display his musical
' talents. He was of the congregation of St. Philip
' Neri, and the thirteenth priest in succession after
' that saint; and founded a nunnery at Rome in
' honour of St. Teresa. He died in 1619, aged 85.

' Arcangelo Crivelli Bergamasco, a tenor, admitted
' in 1583, published divers works highly esteemed,
' and particularly a book of Masses. Many of his
' compositions are sung in the apostolic chapel.

' In 1631 the reverend father Girolamo Rosini da
' Perugia, a soprano, was esteemed for his voice and
' fine manner of singing. He stood candidate for
' a place of singer in the pontifical chapel; and
' although heard and approved of by Clement VIII.
' the Spanish singers contrived to get him excluded,
' for no other reason than that he was not of their
' country,* and elected in his stead a man very much
' his inferior. At which repulse being highly mor-
' tified he took the habit of St. Francis, and became
' a brother in a convent of Capuchins. But the
' pontiff being informed of the injustice done him,
' severely reprimanded the Spanish singers, and re-
' called the Perugian, annulling the solemn vow he
' had taken upon his entering into the monastic life.
' He was received afterwards into the congregation
' of St. Philip Neri in 1606, eleven years after the
' death of that saint; and, being a man of exemplary
' goodness, was favoured by all the popes to the
' time of his death.

' Teofilo Gargano da Gallese, a contralto, was
' admitted in 1601. He left a legacy to maintain
' four students, natives of this country, to enable
' them to prosecute the study of music at Rome, and
' died in 1648.

' Vincenzo de Grandis da Monte Albotto, a con-
' tralto, was admitted in 1605, under Paul V. and
' published many works, particularly a set of Psalms,
' printed by Philip Kespeol.

' In 1610 the reverend Martino Lamotta, a Sicilian,
' and a tenor; in 1612, Giovanni Domenico Poliaschi,
' a Roman tenor; and in 1613 Francesco Severi
' Perugino, a soprano, were severally admitted; the
' two latter distinguished themselves by their several
' compositions dedicated to Cardinal Borghesi in
' 1618 and 1615.

' The reverend Santi Naldino, a Roman contralto,
' is mentioned in 1617. He was a Silvestrine monk,
' and a good composer, as may be seen by his printed
' Motets. He died in 1666, and was buried in S.
' Stefano del Cacco, as appears by a monument in

---

* It seems that till his time no native Italian had ever been a soprano singer in the chapel.

' the said church, where there is a fine canon of his
' composition.

' Under Gregory XV. 1662, was admitted as a
' soprano, Cavalier Loreto Vittori da Spoleti, an
' excellent composer of airs and cantatas. He set
' to music the favorite drama of Galatea, which
' was received with uncommon applause, and printed
' with a dedication to Cardinal Barberini. He was
' buried in the church of Santa Maria sopra Minerva,
' where is a monument for him.

' In 1628, under Urban VIII. the reverend
' Odoardo Ceccarelli da Mevania was admitted a
' tenor; he was a man of letters, and collected
' several rules about our constitution for the use of
' the Puntatore; and was famous for setting music
' to Latin words.

' In 1639, Stefano Landi, a Roman contralto, a
' beneficiary clerk of St. Peter's, published the first
' book of Masses for four and five voices.

' In 1636 the reverend Filippo Vitali, a Florentine
' tenor, and an excellent church composer, was ad-
' mitted. He published Hymns and Psalms.

' In 1637 Marco Marazzoli, a tenor. He composed
' several oratorios, which were much applauded,
' and the same had been many times performed in
' the Chiesa Nuova, in the hearing of Adami himself.
' He was an excellent player on the harp, and has
' left many compositions behind him.

' In 1642 Marco Savioni, a Roman contralto. He
' published several chamber-compositions in parts,
' and sundry other works very much esteemed by
' the judges of harmony.

' Under pope Innocent X. in 1645, was admitted
' Bonaventura Argenti Perugino, a soprano. He
' was highly favoured by cardinal Pio Mori. For
' defraying the expences of finishing the church of
' St. Mary Vallicella, he bequeathed six thousand
' crowns to the fathers of the Oratory, and they out
' of gratitude buried him in their own vault.

' The reverend Domenico del Pane, a Roman
' soprano, was admitted into the college in 1654;
' an excellent composer in the grand style. He left
' many valuable compositions.*

' And under Alexander VII. the reverend father
' Antonio Cesti, a Florentine, and a tenor, was ad-
' mitted into the college 1 Jan. 1660.' A memoir
of this person has a place in page 595 of this work.
Adami says that he excelled both in the chamber
and the theatric styles; and that he composed an
opera, La Dori, reckoned a masterpiece in its kind.

In the course of this work are contained accounts
of the following persons, members of the college
of pontifical singers, viz., Christopher Morales,
Palestrina, Gio. Maria Nanino, Felice Anerio, Luca
Marenzio, Ruggiero Giovanelli, Tomasso Lodovico
da Vittoria, Antimo Liberati, and Matteo Simonelli.
The substance of these severally is herein before
inserted in the article respecting each person.

* Of these one of the most celebrated is a work entitled ' Messe dell'
' Abbate Domenico dal Pane, Soprano della Cappella Pontificia, à quattro,
' cinque, sei, ed otto Voci, estratte da exquisiti Mottetti del Palestrina.
' In Roma, 1687.' This is a collection of masses made on the following motets of Palestrina, ' Doctor bonus,' *from which the anthem ' We have heard
with our ears' is taken,* and ' Domine quando veneris,' à 4 voci. ' Stella
' quam viderant Magi,' ' O Beatum Virum,' and ' Jubilat Deo,' à 5 voci,
' Canite Tuba in Sion,' and ' Fratres ego enim accepi,' à 6 voci.

The design of Adami is evidently to exalt into
importance the college of pontifical singers. A work
of this kind afforded the author a fair opportunity
of deducing the history of choral singing and church
music, from the time of its first introduction, through
a variety of periods, in some whereof it was in
danger of an almost total repudiation : The materials for such an historical account are very copious,
and lie dispersed in the writings of the ecclesiastical
historians, ritualists, and the Corpus Juris Canonici ;
and, above all, in the Lexicon of Dominicus Macrus,
cited by him ; besides what was to be extracted
from Bulls, Breviates, and other pontifical instruments, containing grants in their favour. It seems
that Adami was aware of the information that these
would afford, for he has cited Durandus, Cardinal
Bona, and other writers on the subject ; but his
extracts from them are very brief and unsatisfactory.
The account of the contest between the Roman and
French singers in the time of Charlemagne, though
related by Baronius and the French chroniclers,
with a variety of curious particulars, Adami has
but slightly mentioned ; which is the more to be
wondered at, seeing that the issue of the contest was
a triumph of the Roman over the Gallican ritual.

The description of the several functions performed
in the pontifical chapel we may suppose to be very
accurate ; and we learn from it that many compositions of great antiquity, and which are in the
collections of the curious in this kingdom, are still
held in high estimation.

The lives of such of the pontifical singers as he
has thought proper to distinguish, are simple narra-
tions of uninteresting facts ; they can no way be
considered as portraits of the persons whom they
are intended to represent ; and they are greatly
deficient in respect of those reflections, which a paucity of events renders necessary in biographical
writings ; so that, upon the whole, Adami's work is
little more than an obituary, or at best a register ;
and if we allow it to be a correct one, we give it
all due praise.

## CHAP. CLXX.

THE Italian music had for near fifty years been
making its way in this country, and at the beginning
of this century many persons of distinction, and gentlemen, had attained to great proficiency in the performance on the viol da gamba, the violin, and the
flute. In the year 1710 a number of those, in conjunction with some of the most eminent masters of
the time, formed a plan of an academy for the study
and practice of vocal and instrumental harmony, to
be held at the Crown and Anchor tavern, opposite
St. Clement's church, in the Strand, in which was a
spacious room, in every respect proper for musical
performances. The principal persons engaged in
this laudable design were Mr. Henry Needler, a gentleman who held a considerable post in the excise ;
Mr. John Christopher Pepusch, Mr. John Ernest
Galliard, a fine performer on the hautboy, and a very
elegant composer ; Mr. Bernard Gates, of the queen's

chapel; and many other persons, whose names at this distance of time are not to be recovered.

The foundation of this society was laid in a library, consisting of the most celebrated compositions, as well in manuscript as in print, that could be procured either at home or abroad; these were a voluntary donation from several of the members of the society. With the assistance of the gentlemen of the chapel royal, and the choir of St. Paul's, and the boys belonging to each, and the small contribution of half a guinea a member, the academy set out, and greatly to the improvement of themselves, and the delight of such as heard their performances, this institution continued to flourish till the year 1728, when an accident happened that went very near to destroy them, of which, and other particulars of their history, a relation will be given hereafter.

Mr. HENRY NEEDLER *(a Portrait)*, was the grandson of a gentleman in the army, Colonel Needler, a royalist, who served under General Monk about the time of the restoration, and a brother's son of Mr. Henry Needler of the Navy-office, a collection of whose poems was published in 1724. His father was a good performer on the violin, and instructed him in the practice of that instrument; but having attained in a short time to a considerable proficiency on it, he was committed to the care of Purcell, by whom he was instructed in the principles of harmony. After that he became a pupil of Mr. John Banister, who played the first violin at Drury-lane theatre, and was esteemed one of the best performers in his time.

Being an excellent penman and arithmetician, before he had attained the age of twenty-five he was promoted to the place of Accountant-general of the Excise, the duties of which he discharged with the utmost care and fidelity. Notwithstanding that multiplicity of business in which his office involved him, and the close attendance which it obliged him to, having acquired in his youth a habit of industry and application, he found means to prosecute his musical studies, and to form connections of the best kind. At that time there were weekly concerts at the houses of the duke of Rutland, the earls of Burlington and Essex, lord Percival, father of the late earl of Egmont, and others of the nobility, at which Mr. Needler was always a welcome visitant as a gentleman performer. The soundness of his judgment and the goodness of his taste led him to admire the music of Corelli, and it is said that no person of his time was equal to him in the performance of it, and he stands distinguished by this remarkable circumstance, that he was the first person that ever played the concertos of Corelli in England, and that upon the following occasion. He was used to frequent a weekly concert at the house of Mr. John Loeillet, in Hart-street, Covent-garden. There lived at that time opposite Southampton-street, in the Strand, where Mr. Elmsley now resides, Mr. Prevost, a bookseller, who dealt largely to Holland. It happened that one day he had received a large consignment of books from Amsterdam, and among them the concertos of Corelli, which had just then been published; upon looking at them he thought

of Mr. Needler, and immediately went with them to his house in Clement's-lane, behind St. Clement's church in the Strand, but being informed that Mr. Needler was then at the concert at Mr. Loeillet's, he went with them thither. Mr. Needler was transported with the sight of such a treasure; the books were immediately laid out, and he and the rest of the performers played the whole twelve concertos through, without rising from their seats.*

Mr. Needler was one of that association which gave rise to the establishment of the Academy of Ancient Music, and being a zealous friend to the institution, attended constantly on the nights of performance, and played the principal violin part. The toils of business he alleviated by the study of music, and in his leisure hours employed himself in putting into score the works of the most celebrated Italian masters, with a view to improve himself, and enrich the stores of the academy.

He dwelt for the greatest part of his life in an old-fashioned house in Clement's-lane, behind St. Clement's church, in the Strand, and was there frequently visited by Mr. Handel, and other the most eminent masters of his time. He married late, and having no children, nor any worldly pursuits to engage him, other than the discharge of the duties of his office, in which he was very punctual, he indulged himself in his love of music to such a degree, as to forego all other pleasures for the sake of it; and the delight he took in it seemed to have such an effect upon his mind, as to induce in him a habit of cheerfulness and good-humour. When he was at the Academy he seemed to be at home; strangers that came as visitors were introduced to him at their first entrance: he did the honours of the society in a manner becoming a gentleman, and was in his deportment courteous and obliging to all.

He was a very fine and delicate performer on the violin, and, till he was advanced in years, when his arm grew stiff, was equal, in point of execution, to the performance of any composition that was not too difficult to be good for anything, and in the performance of Corelli's music, in particular, he was not exceeded by any master of his time.

* Besides Mr. Needler, other gentlemen, not of the profession of music, have been distinguished for their skill and performance. Mr. Valentine Oldys, an apothecary in Black-Friars, was the author of several compositions in Court Ayres, published in 1655. Lord Keeper North, when young, was one of the greatest violists of his time, and afterwards became a good composer, and an excellent theorist. Dr. Nathaniel Crew, afterwards lord Crew, bishop of Durham, when at Oxford played his part in concert on the viol da gamba. The family of the Harringtons, descendants of Sir John Harrington, has produced several both theoretic and practical musicians. Sir Roger L'Estrange was an excellent violist. Mr. Sherard, an apothecary in Crutched-Friars, played finely on the violin, and composed two operas of Sonatas. Dr. Cæsar, a physician of an ancient family at Rochester, many of whose ancestors are interred in that cathedral, composed two excellent Ca'ches, printed in the Pleasant Musical Companion, published in 1726. Col. Blathwayt, whose picture when a boy, painted by Kneller, hangs in the music-school, Oxford, was a prodigy on the harpsichord at fourteen. He had been taught that instrument abroad by Alessandro Scarlatti. Dr. Arbuthnot composed an anthem: the words of it ' As pants the hart,' are in a collection printed in 1712. without a name, but made by Dr. Croft, who wrote the preface to the book. In the collection of services and anthems made by Dr. Tudway for the earl of Oxford, in seven volumes, now in the British Museum, is a Te Deum and Jubilate composed by the hon. and rev. Mr. Edward Finch, afterwards dean of York, temp. Anne. Mr. Bendall Martyn, secretary to the commisioners of the Excise, played on the violin, and composed fourteen Sonatas for that instrument which were published upon his decease about fifteen years ago. And lastly, Capt. Marcellus Laroon, the son of old Laroon the painter, played on the violoncello, and composed Solos for that instrument. This gentleman died at Oxford in 1772

HENRY NEEDLER ESQ;

This ingenious and amiable man died on the eighth day of August, 1760, aged seventy-five, and was buried at Frinsbury, near Rochester.*

During the time that Britton's concert subsisted, it was resorted to by the most eminent masters, who gave their performance gratis. Upon the absence of such performers as Banister, Corbett, or such others as usually played the principal violin, that part was taken by Mr. Woolaston, the portrait painter, of whom mention has been made before. He was a sound performer on that instrument, as also on the flute. Being but an indifferent painter, he, upon Britton's decease, with a view to the increase of his acquaintance, and consequently his business, gave a concert on Wednesday evenings at his house in Warwick-court, in Warwick-lane, Newgate-street, which was frequented by the best families in the city, especially Dissenters, till the establishment of the concert at the Castle tavern in Paternoster-row, of which there will shortly be occasion to speak. In the interim it is necessary to take notice that upon the beaking up of Britton's concert, the persons that frequented it formed themselves into little societies, that met at taverns in different parts of the town for the purpose of musical recreation. One of these was at the Angel and Crown tavern in White-chapel, where the performance was both vocal and instrumental : the persons that frequented it were Mr. Peter Prelleur, then a writing-master in Spital-fields, but who played on the harpsichord, and afterwards made music his profession, and by study and application became such a proficient in it as to be ranked among the first masters of his time. Mr. John Gilbert, a mathematical instrument maker, and clerk to a Dissenters' meeting in Eastcheap, and Mr. John Stephens, a carpenter in Goodman's-fields, two persons with good voices, and who had been used to sing Purcell's songs, were also of the number. Others of Britton's friends accepted a hospitable invitation to the house of Mr. William Caslon, the letter founder. This person had been bred to the business of engraving letters on gun-barrels, and served his apprenticeship in the Minories ; but, being an ingenious man, he betook himself to the business of letter-founding, and by diligence and unwearied application, not only freed us from the necessity of importing printing types from Holland, but in the beauty and elegance of those made by him surpassed the best productions of foreign artificers.

Mr. Caslon meeting with encouragement suitable to his deserts, settled in Ironmonger-row, in Old-street, and being a great lover of music, had frequent concerts at his house, which were resorted to by many eminent masters : to these he used to invite his friends, and those of his old acquaintance, the companions of his youth. He afterwards removed to a large house in Chiswell-street, and had an organ in his concert-room : after that he had stated monthly concerts, which for the convenience of his friends, and that they might walk home in safety when the performance was over, were on that Thursday in the month which was nearest the full moon, from which circumstance his guests were wont humorously to call themselves Lunatics. The performers at Mr. Caslon's concert were Mr. Woolaston, and oftentimes Mr. Charles Froud, organist of Cripplegate church, to whom, whenever he came, Mr. Woolaston gave place, and played the second violin ; Mr. William De Santhuns, who had been an organist in the country, and succeeded Mr. Prelleur as organist of Spitalfields ; Mr. Samuel Jeacock, a baker at the corner of Berkeley-street in Red Lion-street, Clerkenwell, and many others, who occasionally resorted thither. The performance consisted mostly of Corelli's music, intermixed with the overtures of the old English and Italian operas, namely, Clotilda, Hydaspes, Camilla, and others, and the more modern ones of Mr. Handel. In the intervals of the performance the guests refreshed themselves at a sideboard, which was amply furnished ; and, when it was over, sitting down to a bottle of wine, and a decanter of excellent ale, of Mr. Caslon's own brewing, they concluded the evening's entertainment with a song or two of Purcell's sung to the harpsichord, or a few catches, and about twelve retired.

These and a few others for the same purpose were select meetings, but there were also about this time, though but very few in comparison with the present, public concerts, to which all were admitted that brought either tickets or money. Performances of this kind had been exhibited from about the year 1700, at the great room in York-buildings and other places, but these were discontinued about the year 1720, and Stationers' Hall in the city, and the Devil tavern at Temple-bar, were the places from whence concerts were most frequently advertised. The method of announcing them was by advertisement in the papers, and bills posted up, in which the names of the principal singers were generally inserted. There was one Mr. Charles Young, organist of the church of Allhallows, Barking, who had three daughters, namely, Cecilia, Esther, and Isabella ;† the first of these had an excellent voice, and was a good singer ; at the concert here spoken of she was generally the first performer ; and as few people then resorted to concerts but such as were real lovers of music, three or four performances of this kind in a winter were found to be as many as the town would bear ; and these were in a great measure discontinued upon the establishment, in 1724, of the Castle concert in Paternoster-row, of which the following is the history :—

There dwelt at the west corner of London-house-yard, in St. Paul's church-yard, at the sign of the Dolphin and Crown, one John Young, a maker of violins and other musical instruments ; this man had a son whose Christian name was Talbot, who had been brought up with Greene in St. Paul's choir, and had attained to great proficiency on the violin, as Greene had on the harpsichord. The merits of the two Youngs, father and son, are celebrated in the following quibbling verses, which were set to music in the form of a catch, printed in the Pleasant Musical Companion, published in 1726 :—

<hr>

* On Tuesday se'nnight died, at Dorking in Surrey, Mrs. Hester Needler, relict of Henry Needler Esq. in the 91st year of her age ; a lady greatly beloved by all who knew her, for her benevolent disposition.—St. James' Chronicle, June 5, 1783.

† Afterwards Mrs. Arne and Mrs. Lampe.

You scrapers that want a good fiddle well strung,
You must go to the man that is old while he's young,
But if this same fiddle you fain would play bold,
You must go to his son, who'll be young when he's old.
There's old Young and young Young, both men of renown,
Old sells and young plays the best fiddle in town,
Young and old live together, and may they live long,
Young to play an old fiddle, old to sell a new song.

This young man, Talbot Young, together with Greene and several persons, had weekly meetings at his father's house for the practice of music. The fame of this performance spread far and wide, and in a few winters the resort of gentlemen performers was greater than the house would admit of; a small subscription was set on foot, and they removed to the Queen's Head tavern in Paternoster-row. Here they were joined by Mr. Woolaston and his friends, and also by a Mr. Franchville, a fine performer on the viol da gamba. And after a few winters, being grown rich enough to hire additional performers, they removed in the year 1724, to the Castle in Paternoster-row, which was adorned with a picture of Mr. Young painted by Woolaston.

The Castle concert continuing to flourish for many years, auditors as well as performers were admitted subscribers, and tickets were delivered out to the members in rotation for the admission of ladies. Their fund enabling them, they hired second-rate singers from the opera; and many young persons of professions and trades that depended upon a numerous acquaintance, were induced by motives of interest to become members of the Castle concert.

Mr. Young continued to perform in this society till the declining state of his health obliged him to quit it; after which time Prospero Castrucci, and other eminent performers in succession continued to lead the band. About the year 1744, at the instance of an alderman of London, now deservedly forgotten, the subscription was raised from two guineas to five, for the purpose of performing oratorios. From the Castle this society removed to Haberdashers' hall, where they continued for fifteen or sixteen years; from thence they removed to the King's Arms in Cornhill, where they now remain.

Upon the plan of the Castle concert another society was formed at the Swan tavern, now the King's Arms, in Exchange Alley, Cornhill. The master of the house, one Barton, had been a dancing-master, and loved music; the great room in his house was one of the best for the purpose of any in London; a great number of merchants and opulent citizens raised a subscription for a concert about the year 1728: Mr. Obadiah Shuttleworth played the first violin; after him Mr. John Clegg, then Mr. Abraham Brown, and after him Mr. Michael Christian Festing. This society flourished for about twelve years, but it broke into factions, which were put an end to by the melancholy accident of a fire, which, on the evening of a performance, on the twenty-fourth day of March, 1748, consumed the books and instruments, and among the latter a fine organ made by Byfield, and laid the house and adjacent buildings in ashes.

## CHAP. CLXXI.

IT is now necessary, in order to lay a foundation for an account of the introduction of the Italian opera into this kingdom, to recur to the beginning of the century, and, having mentioned Scarlatti, Gasparini, Bononcini, Conti, and some other composers in the theatric style, to take notice of some of the most eminent instrumental performers of the time, as also of a few of the most applauded singers of both sexes.

At this time there were many performers in Italy, who for their excellence on various instruments were celebrated throughout Europe; namely, for the harpsichord, BERNARDO PASQUINI, and his scholar BERNARDO GAFFI, as also ALESSANDRO SCARLATTI; these were settled at Rome. At Venice were POLLAROLI, and a son of Scarlatti, called SCARLATTINO, the wonder of his time. For the violin at Rome Corelli was without a rival: next to him his scholar MATTEO and ANTONIO MONTENARI were most esteemed. At Florence MARTINO BITTI was reckoned the most famous, and at Venice ALBINONI; at Naples GIOVANNI CARLO CAITO and PEDRILLO, as also GIOVANNI ANTONIO GUIDO; and above all, CARLO AMBROSIO LUNATI, of Milan, surnamed Il Gobbo della Regina, who with Sifacio, a famous singer, was here in England in the reign of James II.

For the violoncello BUONONCINI was indisputably the first; at Turin, FIORE; at Bologna, GIUSEPPE JACHINI; and at Rome, PIPPO AMADIO were in the highest degree of reputation.

On the theorbo, TEDESCHINO of Florence was esteemed a most capital performer; but he was afterwards excelled by Conti, he who was in England in the year 1708, and had a hand in the opera of Clotilda.

Contemporary with Corelli and Pasquini at Rome was GAETANO, an admirable master on the theorbo, who died very young. These three persons were performers at the same time in the opera at Rome. PETRUCCIO and DOMENICO SARRI of Naples were at the same time celebrated for their performance on that instrument; and GALLETTI on the cornet was deemed the greatest performer in the world.

Of singers, he that was known by the name of SIFACIO, from his having appeared in the character of Syphax in some opera abroad, was reckoned the first. He had been in England a singer in the chapel of James II., but, after a short stay, returned to Italy; and about the year 1699, in his passage from Bologna to Ferrara, was murdered; he had a very fine voice, and was remarkable for a very chaste and pure manner of singing, and fine expression.

LUIGINO, a singer in the chapel of the emperor Joseph, was also in high repute. He died in 1707, and had been a scholar of Pistocchi, who, as having by the introduction of a chaste, elegant, and pathetic style, greatly improved the practice of vocal music among the Italians, was of such eminence, that he merits to be particularly noticed.

FRANCESCO ANTONIO PISTOCCHI had a very fine

soprano voice, which by a dissolute life he lost, together with a fortune which he had acquired by the exercise of it. In this distress he was reduced to the necessity of becoming a copyist, in which employment, by his attention and assiduity, he arrived at such a degree of skill in music, as to be able himself to compose. In the course of a few years he discovered that his voice was returning; and having experienced great misery while he was deprived of that faculty, he practised incessantly till it settled into a fine contralto. With this valuable acquisition he determined to travel, and accordingly visited most of the courts in Europe; and from a variety of manners in singing formed that elegant style, which the more modern refinements in singing render it difficult to conceive of. The encouragement he met with, and the offer of the employment of chapel-master to the Margrave of Anspach, with a handsome stipend, induced him to settle at that court, where in the possession of a newly acquired fortune he continued many years. At length he returned to Italy, and retired to a convent, in which he died about the year 1690.

There is extant of Pistocchi's composition, a collection of cantatas, duets, and songs, entitled 'Scherzi-Musicali,' dedicated to Frederic III., Margrave of Brandenburg Anspach, published by Estienne Roger of Amsterdam; at the end are two airs, one to French the other to German words; in the former he professes to have imitated the style of Lully, in the latter that of the German composers.

There were about the beginning of this century many other fine singers, but by some it is said that the excellences of them all were united in NICOLINI GRIMALDI, called Signor Nicolini di Napoli, who, not more for his singing than his personal merit, had been dignified with the title of Cavaliero di San Marco.

This person came into England in the year 1708, and made his first appearance in the opera of Camilla. Mr Galliard, in a note in his translation of Tosi's Opinioni de' Cantori, says that he was both a fine actor and a good singer. Mr. Addison in the Spectator, No. 405, has given him the same character, and complimented him on the generous approbation he had given to an English opera, Calypso and Telemachus, written by Mr. Hughes, and set by Mr. Galliard, when the other Italians were in a confederacy to ruin it. Nicolini seems to have enjoyed the friendship both of Steele and Addison. He entertained an affection for them and their writings, and was inclined to study the English language, for the pleasure of reading the Tatler.* He was in England at two or three different periods: upon his quitting it the first time it was supposed he meant not to return; and the assurance thereof gave occasion to the following verses, published in Steele's Miscellany, which bespeaks the general sentiments of the English with regard to the Italian opera and singers :—

Begone, our nation's pleasure and reproach!
Britain no more with idle trills debauch,

Back to thy own unmanly Venice sail,
Where luxury and loose desires prevail;
There thy emasculating voice employ,
And raise the triumphs of the wanton boy.
Long, ah! too long the soft enchantment reign'd,
Seduc'd the wise, and ev'n the brave enchain'd;
Hence with thy curst deluding song! away!
Shall British freedom thus become thy prey;
Freedom which we so dearly used to prize,
We scorn'd to yield it—but to British eyes.
    Assist ye gales, with expeditious care,
Waft this prepost'rous idol of the fair;
Consent ye fair, and let the trifler go,
Nor bribe with wishes adverse winds to blow:
Nonsense grew pleasing by his syren arts,
And stole from Shakespeare's self our easy hearts.†

VALENTINI was a singer on the opera stage in London at the same time with Nicolini. He had been a scholar of Pistocchi, and was, in the opinion of Mr. Galliard, though not so powerful in voice or action as Nicolini, much more chaste in his singing.

Of the female singers the following were in the first degree of eminence at the end of the last century, and at the beginning of this.

SIGNORA GIORGINA, a great favourite of Christina queen of Sweden, as also of the vice-queen of Naples, to whom she was first lady of honour, and by whose interest she was ennobled with the dignity of a marchioness of Spain.

MARGARITINA SAN NICOLA, she was the principal singer in the court of Dresden, and was highly favoured by the elector of Saxony. In Italy Signora POLLACINI and Signora MARCHESINA; as also those other females, BOMBACE, MIGNATTA, BARBARUCCI, DIAMANTINA, and CECCA, were highly celebrated.

SIGNORA SANTINI sang in several of the courts of Germany with great applause; afterwards she went to Venice, where Sig. Antonio Lotti, the famous chapel-master of St. Mark's, married her.

FRANCESCA VANINI BOSCHI and her husband were in England in 1710, and sang in Mr. Handel's opera of Rinaldo: she continued here only one season, at the end whereof she went to Venice, leaving her husband behind her: She was at this time in years, and her voice upon the decline. Signor Giuseppe Boschi had a fine bass voice. He sang here in the opera of Hydaspes after his wife left England. Mr. Handel composed songs on purpose for him, and among many others, those two fine ones, ' Del min-'nacciar in vento,' in Otho, and 'Deh Cupido,' in Rodelinda.

There was also a woman, who had sung in many of the courts of Europe, yet was known by no other appellation than that of the Baroness. Some have supposed her to be the unfortunate relict of Stradella, see page 653 of this work, but this is a mistake. She was a German, a very fine singer, and, being in

† It seems that he was used to frequent Bath, and that he sang in public there. In Tony Aston's song entitled 'The Bath Medley,' is the following line:—
'Here's half a guinea to hear Nicolini!'
Mus. Misc. Vol. III. page 162.
And among Durfey's songs is one entitled 'The Bath Teazers,' with this stanza:—
'Then comes Nicolini to teaze them the more,
'Subscribe your two guineas to make up fourscore.
'I never performed at so low rate before.'
Pills to Purge Melancholy, Vol. VI. page 283.

England, sang in the operas of Camilla, the Triumph of Love, and Pyrrhus and Demetrius.

From the account herein before given of the progress of music in this country after the Restoration, it evidently appears that the taste of the English was accommodating itself to that of the Italians, not to say of the French, who in this respect were then as little worthy of imitation as they are now. Cibber, in the Apology for his Life, says, that about the beginning of this century the Italian opera began to steal into England; and that the new theatre in the Haymarket opened with a translated opera to Italian music called the Triumph of Love. That this account is erroneous in many respects will presently be shewn: it is true that entertainments of a similar kind to the opera were known among us soon after the Restoration; but these were in strictness no more than musical dramas; tragedies with interludes set to music, such as the Tempest, Oedipus, the Indian Queen, Timon of Athens, Dioclesian, and some others by Purcell, Circe by Banister, and Psyche by Matthew Lock. These for a series of years were performed at the theatre in Drury-lane, designed by Sir Christopher Wren, and furnished with all the conveniencies and accommodations requisite in a building of that kind. But the first opera, truly and properly so called, exhibited on the English stage, was that of Arsinoe, set to music by Mr. Thomas Clayton, and performed at Drury-lane theatre in 1707. The merit of this work, as also of its author, may be judged of by the following memoir, and the account hereafter given of his Rosamond:—

THOMAS CLAYTON was one of the royal band of music in the reign of king William and queen Mary; there are two of the name of Clayton in the list of the royal band in Chamberlayne's present State of England, published in 1694, the one William, the other Thomas. The one of them is mentioned in Shadwell's comedy of Bury Fair, act III. scene 1. in this speech: '——They sing Charon, O gentle 'Charon, and Come my Daphne [two famous old 'dialogues] better than Singleton and Clayton did.' The latter, a man of no account in his profession, travelled into Italy with a view to improvement; and returning from thence into England, possessed people with an high opinion of his abilities, insomuch that men were persuaded into a belief that by means of Mr. Clayton's assistance the rusticity of the English music would no longer be its characteristic, and that, due encouragement being given to him, it would in a short time emulate that of the Italians themselves. This is an artifice that has been practised more than once in this kingdom, but never with such success as in this instance. With the hope of great advantages, Clayton associated to him two persons, namely, Signor Nicolino Haym and Mr. Charles Dieupart, both of them good musicians, and either of them, in respect of abilities, far his superior. Clayton had brought with him a collection of Italian airs, which he set a high value on; these he mangled and sophisticated, and adapting them to the words of an English drama, *written for the purpose by Motteux*, and entitled Arsinoe

Queen of Cyprus, called it an opera, composed by himself. There will be farther occasion to speak of this man; in the interim it may be observed that Mr. Addison says that Arsinoe was the first opera that gave us a taste of the Italian music; and as he intimates that it met with great success, and afterwards suffered Clayton to set his opera of Rosamond, it may be inferred that he thought it a fine composition: But a better judge than himself[*] pronounces of it, that excepting Rosamond, it is one of the most execrable performances that ever disgraced the stage.

In the year 1706 Sir John Vanbrugh designed, and, with the help of a subscription, erected a theatre in the Haymarket, and opened it with a pastoral entertainment entitled the Loves of Ergasto,[†] set to music after the manner of the Italian opera, that is to say, in recitative, with airs intermixed, by a German musician, who had studied in Italy, and called himself Signor Giacomo Greber. This man brought with him from Tuscany Signora Margarita de l'Epine, and gave occasion to her being called Greber's Peg. This entertainment, though but ill received, was succeeded by another of the same kind, the Temple of Love, composed by Signor Saggioni, a Venetian, and a performer on the double bass, which pleased as little as the former.

The bad success of these entertainments at the Haymarket induced the managers of Drury-lane theatre to attempt, in good earnest, the exhibition of an Italian opera; they fixed upon that of Camilla, *the words whereof were written by Silvio Stampiglia, a Roman by birth, and poet to his Cæsarean Majesty, and the music* composed by Bononcini, then resident in the court of the emperor. To accommodate the singers of our own country, many of the recitatives and airs were translated into English; the conduct of the whole was referred to Nicolino Haym, who was himself an able musician; Valentini performed the part of Turnus; and, notwithstanding the glaring absurdity of so motley a performance, it is said that the opera of Camilla never met with so good a reception abroad as it did here.

To Camilla succeeded Rosamond, an entertainment of which the town had for some considerable time conceived a longing expectation, as well from the character of Mr. Addison as the supposed abilities of the musical composer. The names of the singers and the cast of the parts were as follow:—

| | |
|---|---|
| Queen Eleanor, | Mrs. Tofts. |
| Page, | Mr. Holcombe. |
| Sir Trusty, | Mr. Leveridge. |
| Grideline, | Mrs. Linsey. |
| Rosamond, | Signora Maria Gallia. |
| King Henry, | Mr. Hughs. |
| War, | Mr. Lawrence. |
| Peace, | Miss Reading. |

[*] The translator of the Abbé Raguenet's Parallel of the French and Italian Musick and Operas, in his Critical Discourse on Operas and Musick in England, printed at the end thereof. Supposed to be Mr. Galliard.

[†] *A prologue written by Dr. Garth was spoken on the occasion, in which is this line—*

'*By beauty founded and by wit designed,*'

*Alluding to lady Sunderland who laid the first stone, and Sir John Vanbrugh the architect.*

A criticism on this most wretched performance is more than it deserves, but, to account for the bad reception it met with, it is necessary to mention that the music preponderating against the elegance and humour of the poetry, and the reputation of its author, bore it down the third night of representation.

To begin with the overture; it is in three parts, and in the key of D with the greater third; the first movement pretends to a great deal of spirit, but is mere noise. The two violin parts are simple counterpoint, and move in thirds almost throughout; and the last movement intended for an air is the most insipid ever heard. As to the songs, they have neither air nor expression. There is one that sings thus :—

O the pleasing, pleasing, pleasing, pleasing, pleasing anguish.

An ingenious and sensible writer, mentioned in a preceding note, who was present at the performance, says of Rosamond that it is a confused chaos of music, and that its only merit is its shortness. The overture and the succeeding duetto are given as a specimen of the work :—

THOMAS CLAYTON.

THOMAS CLAYTON.

We meet, in a critical discourse on operas and music in England, published by way of appendix to an English translation of the Abbé Raguenet's Parallel between the French and Italians in regard to their Music, with the mention of a person by the name of the Swiss Count; this was John James Heidegger, by birth a Fleming, as is supposed, who arriving in England in 1708, undertook the conduct of the opera in the Haymarket, and continued it with various success till about 1730, by which he acquired a large fortune, which he lived to enjoy for twenty years after. What were his pretensions to the title ascribed to him is not known; he was a man of a projecting head, possessed of such talents as enabled him to gratify those whose chief pursuits were pleasure, which he exercised in the introduction of masquerades into this country.*

This man, who is represented as in necessitous circumstances at the time of his arrival in England, had the address to procure a subscription, with which he was enabled to furnish out the opera of Thomyris, which, like the former was in English; the music, however, was Italian, that is to say, airs selected from sundry of the foreign operas by Bononcini, Scarlatti, Steffani, Gasparini, and Albinoni. It was performed at the Queen's Theatre in the Haymarket in 1709.

Most of the songs in Thomyris were excellent, those by Bononcini especially; Valentini, Margarita, and Mrs. Tofts sang in it; and Heidegger by this performance alone was a gainer of five hundred guineas.† The following is one of the songs composed by Bononcini, and was sung by Mrs. Tofts:—

* In a collection of letters of several eminent persons deceased, including the correspondence of Mr. John Hughes, vol. III., is a humorous dedication of his Vision of Charon or the Ferry-boat, printed in his works, to the Swiss Count [Heidegger.]

† Camilla and Thomyris were revived at Lincoln's-Inn fields in 1726, but the taste of the town was improved, and they did not succeed.

GIOVANNI BONONCINI.

## CHAP. CLXXII.

THE good success of Thomyris was an inducement with Valentini soon after to undertake an exhibition at the same theatre of a pastoral called the Triumph of Love. This pastoral was written by Cardinal Ottoboni, and set to music by Carlo Cesarini Giovanni, surnamed del Violone, and Francesco Gasparini, and was intended to introduce a kind of drama, wherein certain little wooden figures were the actors, which by means of springs, contrived by two famous mechanics, the Count St. Martini and the Cavalier Acciaioli, were made to move with surprising grace and agility: the expense of this singular exhibition may in some measure be guessed at, when it is known that each of these little figures cost the cardinal an hundred pistoles. The music to this entertainment Valentini found means to procure, and having got it, he contrived to get it set to English words; he rejected almost all the recitatives, to make room for a great number of noisy airs and chorusses, with dances after the French manner, and endeavoured to suit the performance, which was calculated for chamber amusement, to the opera stage; but the bad success that attended the representation convinced him of his error, and determined him to confine himself to his profession of a singer, and never more act as a manager.

In the winter of 1709 the opera of Pyrrhus and Demetrius, written by Owen Mac Sweney and set to music of Alessandro Scarlatti, was performed at the Haymarket theatre. Haym fitted the music to the words, and added many airs of his own composition, one whereof is inserted in the account hereafter given of him. It was received with general applause, and, in the opinion of very good judges, was held to be superior even to Camilla.

Clotilda, represented also in 1709, was the next opera that appeared. This was made up by Heidegger; the airs were of Bononcini, Scarlatti, and Signor Francesco Conti, already spoken of, who made the overture. To these succeeded the opera of Almahide, consisting of songs both in Italian and English, adapted to Italian airs; the latter were sung by Dogget the comedian. And with these the town were in general pleased till the arrival of Mr. Handel in England, whose coming announced the production of operas, such as were performed at the theatres in Italy; that is to say, the drama being in the Italian language, and the music in the modern Italian style.

At this time Mr. Aaron Hill was in the direction of the Haymarket theatre. Mr. Handel, then a very young man, had received pressing invitations from some of the principal nobility to come and settle in England; to these he yielded, and arrived in the year 1710. Mr. Hill received him with open arms; he immediately concerted with him the plan of an opera entitled Rinaldo, and in a very short time wrought it into form; in short, he wrote the whole drama, and got it translated into Italian by a Signor Rossi, and Mr. Handel set it; an extract from the preface is inserted in the Spectator, No. 5, in which we are told that Mr. Handel composed this opera in a fortnight. It is needless to point out the beauties of this excellent composition, as the overture and the airs are in print; the applause it met with was greater than had been given to any musical performance in this kingdom: in a word, it established Mr. Handel's character on a firm and solid basis.

The success of Rinaldo was in some measure injurious to the interests of those whose employment it had been to furnish out operas by collections from various Italian masters, and torturing music to a sense that it was never intended to bear; for in the Spectator, No. 258, for 26 Dec. 1711, and in another of the same papers, No. 278, Clayton, Haym, and Charles Dieupart, in a letter signed by them all, complain of their dismission, and solicit the public to favour a musical performance for their joint benefit at the house of Mr. Clayton in York-buildings.*

The principal performers before this time were Valentini and Nicolini, Signora Margarita de l'Epine, and Mrs. Tofts, singers: in the band of instrumental performers were Dieupart above-mentioned, Mr. Pepusch, and Mr. Leoillet, masters of the harpsichord; Mr. John Banister, a son of him of that name, formerly mentioned; Mr. William Corbet, and Signor Claudio, violin masters; Haym for the violoncello, and Saggioni for the double bass. The alteration that immediately followed Mr. Handel's coming to the Haymarket is no otherwise noticed than by the above letter, notwithstanding which, and the applause given to Rinaldo, other operas of the like kind with the former, particularly in 1712, Hydaspes, composed by Francesco Mancini, was represented at the Haymarket: the decorations of this opera were very splendid; the scenes were painted by Morco Ricci, and the words of the songs were all Italian.

From this time the opera was conducted in a manner less liable to exception than at first; and to this reformation it is probable the ridicule of Mr. Addison, and the censures of critics less humorously disposed than himself, might not a little contribute; for though in Rinaldo we are told that sparrows were introduced,[†] and in Hydaspes a lion, which part was performed by a man, and gave occasion to some of the most diverting papers in the Spectator,[‡] we hear no more of these absurdities after the performance of Hydaspes, and the opera was freed from all objections, save only those to which the entertainment itself was at all times obnoxious.

To understand the force of Mr. Addison's satire, if it merits to be called by so harsh a name, it is necessary for us to take a view of the opera at the time of its first introduction among us. Of the nature of this entertainment in general, a judgment may be formed from the account herein before given of the invention of recitative by the Italians, of the musical representations of the same people, and of the establishment of the Royal Academy of Paris; as also from the memoirs of eminent French musicians, inserted in the preceding pages of this work; but of the English Italian opera no mortal can form a judgment, that is not acquainted with the circumstances of its introduction among us, or has not with a critical eye perused the several productions, which in the short space of four or five years at most, were obtruded on the world under that denomination. To take them in their order, Arsinoe consisted of English words fitted to Italian music, originally adapted to Italian poetry, of which the English does not so much as pretend to be a translation; no wonder then if the hearers sought in vain for that correspondence between the sound and the sense, which in the opinion of some make so considerable a part of the merit of vocal composition. The case was the same in Camilla, Thomyris, Pyrrhus and Demetrius, and the rest, with this difference, that for the sake of those singers, who, as being foreigners, were strangers to our language, many of the songs were sung in the original Italian, to which a great part of the audience must at least at that time be

---

* In the preface to the poems of Mr. John Hughes is a letter from Sir Richard Steele, in the name of himself and Mr. Clayton, requesting him to alter Dryden's Alexander's Feast for music, in order to its being performed in York-buildings. He complied, and Clayton had the courage to attempt it, but failed, as Mr. Hughes relates in a letter to Sir Richard Steele, mentioned in the preface above cited. It is printed as altered, in Mr. Hughes's poems, and was performed in 1711.

† Spectator, No. 5.

‡ The humour of these papers is so strong and pointed, that it is said the Pope, on reading them, laughed till his sides shook. Mr. Addison, perhaps from the bad success of Rosamond, was led to think that only nonsense was fit to be set to music; and this error is farther to be accounted for by that want of taste, not to say of skill, in music, which he manifests in his preference of the French to the Italian composers, and in his general sentiments of music and musicians, in which he is ever wrong.

supposed to be utter strangers. But this was not all; in the adapting English words to the Italian airs, not one circumstance was adverted to, except that of a correspondence, in respect of measure and cadence, between the words and the music; sentiment and sense were held unnecessary, and these being neglected, what must the poetry have been but such nonsense as the following?

> So sweet an air, so high a mien
>  Was never seen.  ARSINOE.

> For thy ferry boat Charon I thank thee,
> But thrust me not out for I come in a hurry. Ibid.

> Since you from death thus save me,
>  I'll live for you alone,
> The life you freely gave me,
>  That life is not my own.  CAMILLA.

> Charming fair,
>  For thee I languish,
>   But bless the hand that gave the blow;
>  With equal anguish
> Each swain despairs,
> And when she appears
>   Streams forget to flow.  Ibid.

> My delight, my dear, my princess,
> With desire I lose my senses,
> I before you feel with fury,
>  My blood hurry
>   Through every vein,
>   At my heart
>   I feel a smart,
> Dying thus who can complain.

> I had vow'd to play the rover,
> Fool with love or give it over,
> But who can though grave and wise,
> 'Scape those dimples, lips, and eyes,
>  Then to bless you
> I'll caress you,
>  Press you,
>  Kiss you,
>  And caress you,
> Till like me you cry 'tis vain,
> O my dear to frown and feign,
> Dying thus who can complain.  THOMYRIS.

> Away you rover,
> For shame give over,
> So bold a lover
>  Never will pass;
> You press and thunder
> To bring us under,
> Then all you plunder,
>  And leave the place.
> Though you are for storming,
> And think you are charming,
> Your faint performing
>  We read in your face.  Ibid.

>  No more trial,
>  Nor denial,
>  Be more kind,
>  And tell your mind;
>   So tost,
>   So crost,
>   I'm sad,
>   I'm mad,
> No more then hide your good nature
>  Thou dear creature;

>  Baulk no longer,
>  Love nor hunger,
>  Both grow stronger
>  When they're younger;
>   But pall,
>   And fall
>   At last,
> If long we fast.  LOVE'S TRIUMPH.*

It must be confessed that, as musical compositions, such of the operas as were compiled from the works of Italian masters had great merit. As to Camilla, though wholly the work of Bononcini, it was but a puerile essay, the author being scarce eighteen when he set it, and seems to have been greatly overrated; the airs are so very short, that they admit of no variety. The first air, 'I was born of royal race,' is but fourteen bars in length, and is no sooner heard than the idea of it is effaced by a succeeding one in a different key. In Thomyris, and Pyrrhus and Demetrius this fault seems to have been avoided; besides which the airs appear to have been selected with great care from the works of a variety of great masters, such as Scarlatti, Bononcini, Cesarini, Gasparini, and others; and where these have failed, as they do in the latter, the defect has been ably supplied by Haym: so that upon the whole those entertainments were not destitute of merit, but it was of such a kind as no audience composed of persons promiscuously assembled, some with an ear for music, and others without, could be supposed capable of discerning; and this circumstance co-operating with the others abovementioned, seems to lead to the true reason why the opera was less favourably received here than in Italy and France. In these and many of the subsequent operas some of the principal female singers were natives of this country, and among them Mrs. Barbier and Mrs. Anastasia Robinson, afterwards countess of Peterborough, were the most celebrated. Mrs. Tofts, of whom we shall presently have occasion to speak, sang in Arsinoe, the first opera performed in England, but she quitted the stage in a short time; the others continued to perform long after the opera had been supplied with Italian women: in her voice and manner she so far surpassed the rest of the English women, as to be able to divide the applause of the town with Margarita; but between any other of our countrywomen and the Italians we hear of no competition; the reason whereof may perhaps be, that, in respect of their performance, the Italian women had so much the advantage over the English, that the latter could not but consider themselves as their scholars. The most celebrated English women singers about the end of the last century, were Mrs. Davis, Mrs. Cross, Mrs.

* Love's Triumph, from whence the above air is taken, is a different drama from the Triumph of Love mentioned in page 810 of this work; it was written by Motteux, as were also the operas of Arsinoe, Thomyris, the Temple of Love, and most of the musical dramas and interludes that preceded the introduction of the Italian opera on the English stage. This man kept what in his time was called an India shop, in Leadenhall-street, which was then much frequented by the old duchess of Marlborough, and other ladies of queen Anne's court; and sold tea, fans, screens, Japan cabinets, silks, and other commodities imported by the India Company: it was also the staple of city news, and in the opinion of many a place of intrigue. The numerous publications of Motteux have entitled him to a rank among the English dramatic poets; but of them he must be said to have been one of the most vulgar. He died in 1717-18, and was interred in the parish church of St. Andrew Undershaft, London.

Cibber, Mrs. Bracegirdle, and Miss Campion,* all of whom have been already spoken of; but it is easy to discover that their perfections were confined to perhaps a beautiful person, graceful and easy action, and a fine voice, the gift of nature, and that owed little of its fascinating power to the improvements of art; if this fact should be doubted, let any one look into the songs of that day, particularly those of Purcell, where he will find the graces written at length, a manifest proof that in the performance of them little was meant to be trusted to the singer.

The two following ladies, as they contributed by their performance to establish the Italian opera in this country, merit our notice :—

Mrs. Tofts, although a native of this country, is celebrated as a singer little inferior, either for her voice or her manner, to the best Italian women. Cibber, who was well acquainted with her, speaks thus of her in the Apology for his Life, page 226. ' Mrs. Tofts, who took her first grounds of musick ' here in her own country, before the Italian taste ' had so highly prevail'd, was then but an adept in ' it : yet, whatever defect the fashionably skilful ' might find in her manner, she had, in the general ' sense of her spectators, charms that few of the most ' learned singers ever arrive at. The beauty of her ' fine proportioned figure, and the exquisitely sweet, ' silver tone of her voice, with that peculiar, rapid ' swiftness of her throat, were perfections not to be ' imitated by art or labour.' She sang in the operas of Arsinoe, Camilla, Rosamond, Thomyris, and Love's Triumph.

The author of the following epigram, supposed to be Mr. Pope, at the same time that he celebrates her beauty and fine singing, has taken care to contrast these her excellencies with two vices, which, supposing him to speak truth, must have considerably abated the power of her charms.

So bright is thy beauty, so charming thy song,
As had drawn both the beasts and their Orpheus along;
But such is thy avarice, and such is thy pride,
That the beasts must have starv'd, and the poet have died.

In the opera of Camilla she performed the part of Camilla; and it is conjectured that the dignity which she was obliged to assume in that character, had an effect upon her mind; for in the Tatler, No. 20, for Thursday, May 26, 1709, there is this plain intimation that her brain was turned : ' The unfortunate ' Camilla has had the ill-luck to break before her ' voice, and to disappear at a time when her beauty ' was in the height of its bloom. This lady enter'd ' so thoroughly into the great characters she acted, ' that when she had finished her part, she could not ' think of retrenching her equipage, but would appear ' in her own lodgings with the same magnificence ' that she did upon the stage. This greatness of soul ' has reduced that unhappy princess to an involuntary ' retirement, where she now passes her time among ' the woods and forests, thinking on the crowns and

' scepters she has lost, often humming over in her ' solitude,

' I was born of royal race,
' Yet must wander in disgrace.†

' But for fear of being overheard, and her quality known, she usually sings it in Italian.

' Nacqui al regno, nacqui al trono,
' E pur sono
' Sventurata.'

It seems that this disorder had taken deep root in her mind : nevertheless, by the help of medicines and other proper remedies, she was restored to the use of her reason.

In the meridian of her beauty, and possessed of a large sum of money, which she had acquired by singing, Mrs. Tofts quitted the stage, and was married to Mr. Joseph Smith, a gentleman, who being appointed consul for the English nation at Venice, she went thither with him. Mr. Smith was a great collector of books, and patron of the arts; he procured engravings to be made from pictures and designs of Amiconi, Marco Ricci, Piazetta, and other masters. He lived in great state and magnificence; but the disorder of his wife returning, she dwelt sequestered from the world in a remote part of the house, and had a large garden to range in, in which she would frequently walk, singing and giving way to that innocent frenzy which had seized her in the earlier part of her life. She was living about the year 1735. Mr. Smith died about five years ago, and left a numerous and valuable collection of books, which was brought over into England, and sold by auction by Mr. Baker of Yorkstreet.

Francesca Margarita de L'Epine, a native of Tuscany, and also a celebrated singer, performed in some of the first of the Italian operas that were represented in England. She came hither with one Greber, a German, but who had studied some few years in Italy,‡ and appeared first in a musical entertainment of his composition, called the Loves of Ergasto, but better known by the name of Greber's Pastoral.§ The most memorable circumstance relating to it is that it was performed in the year 1706, at the opening of the Haymarket theatre, and was the first entertainment of any kind there exhibited.

From the connection between Margarita and Greber, she became distinguished by the invidious appellation of Greber's Peg. After it was ended she commenced a new one with Daniel, earl of Nottingham, which, in an imitation of an ode of Horace, ' Ne sit ancillæ tibi amor pudori,' by Mr. Rowe, is thus alluded to :—

Did not base Greber's Peg inflame
The sober earl of Nottingham,
Of sober Sire descended ?
That, careless of his soul and fame,
To playhouses he nightly came,
And left church undefended.||

* Miss Campion sang in the Island Princess, as altered by Motteux, together with Mr. Magnus's boy, as he is called, a dialogue beginning ' Must I a girl for ever be?' set by Jerry Clark. She also sang at the theatre, and at the concert in York-buildings, many songs set by Weldon purposely for her.

† A song of her's in Camilla, the first in the opera.

‡ Vide ante, page 810.

§ In the Catalogue de la Musique of Estienne Roger, page 20, is the following article : ' Six Sonates à une Flûte et une Basse continué, com- ' posées par Messrs. Greber et Fede.'

|| The earl had written against Whiston on the doctrine of the Trinity.

And there is extant the following shrewd epigram relating to her, written by lord Halifax :—

On Orpheus and Signora Francesca Margarita.*

Hail, tuneful pair ! say by what wondrous charms,
One scap'd from Hell, and one from Greber's arms ?
When the soft Thracian touch'd the trembling strings,
The winds were hush'd, and curl'd their airy wings ;
And when the tawny Tuscan † raised her strain,
Rook furls the sails, and dares it on the main.
Treaties unfinish'd in the office sleep,
And Shovell yawns for orders on the deep.
Thus equal charms and equal conquests claim, }
To him high woods, and bending timber came, }
To her shrub-hedges, and tall Nottingham. }

Margarita sang in many of the earlier operas, particularly Thomyris, in which she did the part of the queen ; and in Love's Triumph, in which she performed the character of Olinda. In Mr. Hughes's opera of Calypso and Telemachus she appeared in the character of Calypso. She also sang in concerts at York-buildings and Stationers'-hall, and once in the hall of the Middle Temple, in a musical performance at the Christmas revels of that society. She continued to sing on the stage, and occasionally at concerts and other public entertainments, till about the year 1718, when having, as Downes relates, got, at a modest computation, above ten thousand guineas, she retired, and was married to Mr. afterwards Dr. Pepusch.

The two singers abovementioned were rivals for the public favour, and it seems divided pretty equally the applause of the town. The following verses of Mr. John Hughes are a proof of this fact, and point out who of the principal nobility were at the head of the two parties that severally patronized them :—

Music has learn'd the discords of the state,
And concerts jar with Whig and Tory hate.
Here Somerset and Devonshire attend
The British Tofts, and every note commend ,
To native merit just, and pleas'd to see
We've Roman arts, from Roman bondage free.
There fam'd L'Epine does equal skill employ,
While list'ning peers crowd to th' ecstatic joy :
Bedford to hear her song his dice forsakes,
And Nottingham is raptur'd when she shakes :
Lull'd statesmen melt away their drowsy cares
Of England's safety in Italian airs.
Who would not send each year blank passes o'er,
Rather than keep such strangers from our shore.

Mrs. Barbier, a native of England, was also celebrated among the female singers at the beginning of this century. Her first appearance was in the opera of Almahide, represented in the year 1711, upon which occasion she is said to have discovered a more than ordinary concern, that recommended her no less than her agreeable voice and just performance.‡ She sang in many of the subsequent operas, and in that of Calypso and Telemachus, represented at the Haymarket in 1712. She also performed the part of Daphne in Mr. Hughes's masque of Apollo and Daphne, set to music by Dr.

* Collection of the works of celebrated authors, published by Tonson in three volumes duodecimo.
† This epithet of tawny is very characteristic of her, for she was remarkably swarthy, and in general so destitute of personal charms, that Dr. Pepusch, who afterwards married her, seldom called her by any other name than Hecate, which she answered to very readily.
‡ See a letter in the Spectator, No. 231.

Pepusch, and performed at Drury-lane theatre in 1716. Notwithstanding her attachment to the stage, she remained under the protection of her parents, residing at her father's house till the year 1717, when, being no longer able to resist the solicitations of one that pretended love to her, she left it, and gave occasion to Mr. Hughes to write the following verses :—

O yes !—hear, all ye beaux and wits,
Musicians, poets, 'squires, and cits,
All, who in town or country dwell,
Say, can you tale or tidings tell
Of Tortorella's hasty flight ?
Why in new groves she takes delight,
And if in concert, or alone,
The cooing murmurer makes her moan ?
Now learn the marks by which you may
Trace out and stop the lovely stray !
Some wit, more folly, and no care,
Thoughtless her conduct, free her air ;
Gay, scornful, sober, indiscreet,
In whom all contradictions meet ;
Civil, affronting, peevish, easy,
Form'd both to charm you and displease you ;
Much want of judgment, none of pride,
Modish her dress, her hoop full wide ;
Brown skin, her eyes of sable hue,
Angel, when pleas'd, when vex'd a shrew.
Genteel her motion, when she walks,
Sweetly she sings, and loudly talks ;
Knows all the world, and its affairs,
Who goes to court, to plays, to prayers,
Who keeps, who marries, fails, or thrives,
Leads honest, or dishonest lives ;
What money match'd each youth or maid,
And who was at each masquerade ;
Of all fine things in this fine town,
She's only to herself unknown.
By this description, if you meet her,
With lowly bows and homage greet her ;
And if you bring the vagrant beauty
Back to her mother and her duty,
Ask for reward a lover's bliss,
And (if she'll let you) take a kiss ;
Or more, if more you wish and may, }
Try if at church the words she'll say, }
Then make her, if you can—" obey." }

After this elopement Mrs. Barbier returned to the stage, and attaching herself to Mr. Rich, sang in most of his pantomime operas; and, upon the revival of Camilla and Thomyris at Lincoln's-Inn fields in 1726, sang in both of them. Her last appearance on the stage was in the pantomime of Perseus and Andromeda, composed by Rich, in conjunction with Mr. Thurmond, a dancing-master, and represented about the year 1729. In a note on the above poem, which is printed among the letters of Mr. Hughes, herein before cited, it is said that the late John, earl of Corke, who knew her well, expressed his opinion of her as follows : ' She never could rest long in a ' place ; her affectations increased with her years. I ' remember her in the parts of Turnus and Orontes, ' when the operas of Camilla and Thomyris were ' represented at Lincoln's-Inn fields. She loved ' change so well, that she liked to change her sex.' There is an affectation of wit in this puerile sentiment that renders it totally unintelligible.

## CHAP. CLXXIII.

THE opera was an entertainment calculated for the better sort of people in this country: to say the truth, the practice of singing had never till lately been cultivated with any great assiduity among us; and the best that is said of any of our most celebrated vocal performers from the time of Mr. Hales, in queen Elizabeth's, down to the end of queen Anne's reign, is that they were severally endowed with the gift of a fine voice, but as to grace and elegance, or what is called a manner in singing, their panegyrists are silent. In Italy we hear of schools of singers, wherein different styles were cultivated, by which the students of each were as much discriminated as were the disciples of the several schools of painters, the Roman, the Florentine, the Venetian, the Lombard, and the Flemish. In England we have none such; no wonder then if the generality of the people had but little relish for those refinements which the Italian opera was productive of. Those who had a natural taste for music, were content with the plain harmony of vocal composition; or, to speak of vocal performance, with such singing as the playhouses afforded, which consisted for the most part in occasional songs set to music by English masters; with these the stage was competently supplied, and the success of them was a perpetual incentive to poets of an inferior class, and the musicians, to furnish the public with compositions of the like kind. The subjects of these were generally love and rural gallantry, or the delights of the bottle: in short, their general tendency was to promote mirth, to alleviate the toils of labour, and superinduce a temporary oblivion of care. Among the poets of this class, the authors of popular songs, one stands so eminently distinguished as to claim a regard from all lovers of vocal melody, and merit that eulogium which is given him in the ensuing article.

THOMAS D'URFEY (a Portrait), was a native of Devonshire, and bred to the profession of the law, which he forsook under a persuasion, which some poets, and even players, have been very ready to entertain as an excuse for idleness, and an indisposition to sober reflection, viz., that the law is a study so dull, that no man of genius can submit to it. With the full confidence in the powers of a mind thus liberally formed, D'Urfey enlisted himself in the service of the stage, and became an author of tragedies, comedies, and operas, of which he wrote near thirty. The success of his dramatic productions far exceeded their deserts; for whether we consider the language, the sentiments, or the morals of his plays, they are in all these respects so exceptionable, as to be below criticism, and to leave him in possession of that character only which he seemed most to affect, to wit, that of a pleasant companion. The time when D'Urfey lived was very favourable to men of his facetious, and, we may say, licentious turn of manners: he came into the world a few years after the Restoration, when all was joy and merriment, and when to be able to drink and to sing were reckoned estimable qualities; D'Urfey could do both; and, superadded to these

gifts, he had a talent of poetry, which he could adapt to any occasion: he wrote songs, and, though unskilled in music, and labouring under the impediment of stammering in his speech, having a tolerable voice, sang them himself frequently at public feasts and meetings, and not seldom in the presence of king Charles II., who, laying aside all state and reserve, would lean on his shoulder and look over the paper.* The compositions of D'Urfey are so many, and so singularly humorous, that they elude all description, save that they are in general mirthful in the highest degree; so that such of them as were not liable to exception, on account of their indelicacy, became favourites with the whole kingdom. Mr. Addison, in a paper in the Guardian, No. 67, after exhibiting a lively portrait of D'Urfey, whom he is pleased to call his old friend and contemporary, speaking to the ladies his disciples, says that he had often made their grandmothers merry; and that his sonnets had perhaps lulled asleep many a toast among the ladies then living, when she lay in her cradle. And in No. 82 of the same paper is a notification to the reader that a play of D'Urfey's, the Plotting Sisters, which had been honoured with the presence of king Charles the Second three of its first five nights, was then shortly to be acted for his benefit, concluding with a recommendation of it as a pleasant entertainment. But nothing distinguishes his songs more than the uncouthness and irregularity of the metre in which they are written; the modern Pindaric odes, which are humorously resembled to a comb with the teeth broken by frequent use, are nothing to them. Besides that he was able to set English words to Italian airs, as in the instance of 'Blouzabella my buxom doxy,' which he made to an air of Bononcini, beginning 'Pastorella che trà le selve,' he had the art of jumbling long and short quantities so dexterously together, that they counteracted each other, so that order resulted from confusion. Of this happy talent he has given us various specimens, in adapting songs to tunes composed in such measures as scarce any instrument but the drum would express; and, to be even with the musicians for giving him so much trouble, he composed songs in metres so broken and intricate, that few could be found that were able to suit them with musical notes. It is said that he once challenged Purcell to set to music such a song as he would write, and gave him that well-known ballad 'One long Whitsun holiday,' which cost the latter more pains to fit with a tune than the composition of his Te Deum.

Three volumes, consisting mostly of songs written by D'Urfey, were by him published early in this century, with the title of 'Laugh and be fat, or Pills to Purge Melancholy;' but in the year 1719, he, with the assistance of a numerous subscription of lords, ladies, and gentry, as he styles them, republished them, with the addition of three volumes, including a great number of Orations, Poems, Pro-

* See Pills to Purge Melancholy, vol. I. page 246, the song 'Remember 'ye Whigs what was formerly done,' which is thus entitled, 'Advice to 'the City, a famous song: set to a tune of Signor Opdar, so remarkable, 'that I had the honour to sing it with king Charles at Windsor, he 'holding one part of the paper with me.'

F. Gouge pinx.

C. Grignion sculp.

THOMAS DURFEY

POETA LYRICUS.

logues, and Epilogues written by him, and gave the whole collection the title of ' Wit and Mirth, or Pills to Purge Melancholy ; being a Collection of the best merry Ballads and Songs, old and new, fitted to all Humours ; having each their proper Tune for either Voice or Instrument.'

In this collection, besides a great number of singularly humorous songs, are many that bespeak the political sentiments of their author ; Tom, at least in the early part of his life, was a Tory by principle, and never let slip an opportunity of representing his adversaries the Whigs as a set of sneaking rascals. Mr. Addison says that the song of ' Joy to great Cæsar,' gave them such a blow as they were never able to recover during the reign of King Charles II.* This song is set to a tune called Farinel's Ground, of which we have had occasion to speak in a preceding page ; divisions were made upon it by some English master ; it became a favourite tune, and D'Urfey set words to it, in which he execrates the Papists, and their attempts to disturb the peace of the kingdom. Farinelli was a papist, a circumstance which gave occasion for that shrewd remark of Mr. Addison, that his friend Tom had made use of Italian tunes and sonatas for promoting the protestant interest, and turned a considerable part of the pope's music against himself. The paper in which these and other passages, equally humorous, respecting D'Urfey and his compositions are contained, was written by Mr. Addison with a view to fill the house at a play, the Plotting Sisters, acted for his benefit on the fifteenth day of June, 1713, concluding with a character of him :—

' As my friend, after the manner of the Old ' Lyricks, accompanies his works with his own voice, ' he has been the delight of the most polite com- ' panies and conversations from the beginning of ' king Charles the Second's reign to our present ' times. Many an honest gentleman has got a repu- ' tation in his country by pretending to have been in ' company with Tom D'Urfey.

' I might here mention several other merits in my ' friend, as his enriching our language with a multi- ' tude of rhimes, and bringing words together, that ' without his good offices would never have been ac- ' quainted with one another so long as it had been a ' tongue. But I must not omit that my old friend ' angles for a trout the best of any man in England. ' May-flies come in late this season, or I myself ' should before now have had a trout of his hooking.

' After what I have said, and much more that I ' might say on this subject, I question not but the ' world will think that my old friend ought not to ' pass the remainder of his life in a cage like a ' singing-bird, but enjoy all that Pindarick liberty ' which is suitable to a man of his genius. He has ' made the world merry, and I hope they will make ' him easy so long as he stays among us. This ' I will take upon me to say, they cannot do a kind- ' ness to a more diverting companion, or a more ' chearful, honest, and good-natured man.' †

D'Urfey was a great frequenter of places of public

* Guardian, No. 67.     † Ibid.

resort, and, among the rest, Epsom, where in his time many of the best fashion were induced to pass a few weeks in the summer for the sake of the waters ; being there one season, a quarrel commenced between him and a person named Bell, a musician, and a duel ensued, which was the occasion of some mirth at the place. It seems that neither of the combatants had much stomach for fighting ; and a wit of the time maliciously compared this rencounter with the famous single combat of Clinias and Dametas in Sir Philip Sidney's Arcadia, in the following verses :—

' I sing of a duel in Epsom befel
' 'Twixt fa sol la D'Urfey and sol la mi Bell :
' But why do I mention the scribbling brother,
' For naming the one you may guess at the other ?
' Betwixt them there happen'd a horrible clutter,
' Bell set up the loud pipes, and D'Urfey did sputter
' " Draw, Bell wert thou dragon, I'll spoil thy soft note ; "
' "Thy squealing," said t'other, "for, I'll cut thy throat."
' With a scratch on the finger the duel's dispatch'd,
' Thy Clinias (O Sidney) was never so match'd.'
           Ex. MS. Harl. No. 7319, page 625.

Of D'Urfey it may be said as of Falstaff, that he not only had wit himself, but was also the cause of it in other men. In the Miscellanies of Pope and Swift are some humorous verses, occasioned by an &c. at the end of his name, in the title to one of his plays, and also a prologue designed for his last play : and in the fourth volume of the works of Tom Brown are three stanzas on him, wherein for presuming to call his ballads Lyric Odes, this judgment is denounced against him :—

' Horace shall pluck thee by the nose,
  ' And Pindar beat thy brains out.'

This merry fellow died, in a very advanced age, on the twenty-sixth day of February, 1723, and lies buried in the church-yard of St. James's, Westminster.

## CHAP. CLXXIV.

Nicola Francesco Haym, by birth a Roman, was settled at London as a professor of music, and engaged with Clayton and Dieupart in an attempt to establish an Italian opera here. It does not appear that he had any hand in the opera of Arsinoe, represented at Drury-lane theatre in 1707 ; that doughty performance being a collection of Italian airs adapted to English words by Clayton himself ; but in the opera of Camilla, performed at the same place in the year following, he lent his assistance, by fitting the airs to English words, and otherwise rendering it a proper entertainment for an English audience. He did the same by Pyrrhus and Demetrius, and added to it an overture, and sundry songs of his own composition, which rank with the best in the work. He continued thus employed, sharing with his colleagues the profits arising from these and other representations of the like kind, till the year 1710, when Mr. Handel arrived in England, and performed the opera of Rinaldo at the Haymarket. The superior merit of Rinaldo over every representation of this nature, that till then had been exhibited on the English stage, had such an effect as to silence all the attempts of Clayton and his associates to entertain the town with dramatic music; and of this they heavily complain in a joint letter, printed in the Spectator, No. 258, for Wednesday, December 26, 1711, and also in another, printed in No. 278 of the same paper, for January 8, in the following year, wherein they claim the merit of having introduced Italian music into England, and solicit the encouragement of the public to a musical entertainment for their joint benefit at the house of Mr. Clayton, in York-buildings. For the success of this application we are to seek; and we only know with certainty that Clayton precipitated into contempt;* that

Haym had little to do with the opera, or indeed with music, after the year 1712; and that Dieupart, who was a very fine performer on the violin, enlisted himself into the opera band, and became a teacher of the harpsichord.

The merit of Haym as a musician entitled him to better encouragement than he seems to have met with. He published two operas of Sonatas for two violins and a bass, which shew him to have been an able master; and his talent for dramatic music may be judged of by the following air in Pyrrhus and Demetrius, composed by him, and sung by Mrs. Tofts:—

* Mr. Tickell, in his life of Mr. Addison, speaking of the opera of Rosamond, says, 'that as the Italian taste prevailed, the musick was 'thought sufficiently inexcusable because it was the composition of an 'Englishman.' This it is for men to talk of what they do not understand; and it is for the sake of refuting this injudicious charge, that the overture, and also a duet in this opera, are inserted in a preceding part of this work; to those two compositions the intelligent reader is referred, and upon perusal of them is left to judge for himself, whether for the failure of Rosamond a better reason might not be assigned, than that the music to it was composed by an Englishman.

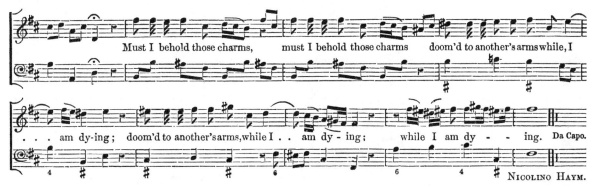

Must I behold those charms, must I behold those charms doom'd to another's arms while, I

. . . am dy-ing; doom'd to another's arms, while I . . am dy - ing; while I am dy - - ing. Da Capo.

NICOLINO HAYM.

Haym was a man of learning, and is to be regarded in other respects than as a mere musician; he was well skilled in medals, and published a work entitled 'Il Tesoro delle Medaglie antiche,' in two volumes in quarto, Italian and English. He also wrote La Merope and La Demodice, two tragedies, and published a fine edition of the Gierusalemme Liberata of Tasso, in two volumes in quarto, with cuts; and was the compiler of a very useful book to the lovers of Italian literature, entitled 'Notizia de' Libri rari Italiani.'

This person published also, about the year 1730, proposals for printing by subscription the whole history of music in two volumes in quarto, which he had written in Italian, and was to have been translated into English; but it is to be presumed that he met with small encouragement, seeing that the work was never published, so that of the nature of it we can only judge by the proposals, in which the author first declares his intention in these words :—

'The author's design is, I. to render his subject 'intelligible and agreeable to all readers, even to 'those that do not understand music. II. From 'ancient writers, antique statues, bass relievos, and 'medals, to collect whatever is most material to 'ancient music : To give an account of its origin, 'and the esteem in which it was in the several 'periods of time : The lives of their musicians, 'and the use they made of music in their games, 'sacrifices, &c , with some explications of the ancient 'fables concerning it. III. The progress and decay 'of the said science in the different ages down to 'the present time. IV. The introduction of operas 'into several parts of Europe, and particularly into 'England; with an accurate account of their pro-'gress and success. V. The lives of all the eminent 'masters and professors of this art in all times, with 'their effigies.'

This is the substance of the printed proposals circulated among the author's friends; but besides these the following table, showing the order of the work, has come to hand :—

'Contents of the History of Musick in two Volumes.

'Volume I. Book I. Begins from the earliest 'antiquity to the restoring of Music in the Temple 'after the captivity of the Jews ; to which is 'annexed an account of twenty gods of the Gen-'tiles, who were all musicians, and the most 'remarkable medals concerning them.

'Book II. The introduction of music into Greece 'in the time of Cadmus, down to the siege of Troy; 'wherein mention in also made of 44 persons who 'exercised music and poetry in those ages; together 'with all the monuments relating to them that are 'now extant.

'Book III. From the siege of Troy to the first 'Olympiad, with an account of forty persons who 'flourished during that period; and the effigies 'of such of them as have been transmitted to pos-'terity. In these three books several ancient fables, 'necessary for the illustration of this history, are 'explained.

'Book IV. From the first Olympiad to Alexander 'the Great, containing the history of 84 musicians, 'with several other particulars relating to the science 'they professed ; as also their effigies, and other 'antique monuments as above. N.B. To this period 'the reader will have a complete history of poetry 'as well as music, it being proved that all poets 'were hitherto musicians also.

'Book V. From Alexander the Great to the 'emperor Alexander Severus, when the music of 'the Gentiles ends; containing the fall of ancient 'music, and an account of 40 other musicians as 'before; to which is annexed 50 apophthegms of 'ancient musicians.

'Book VI. Treats of all those solemnities, &c. 'in which music was employed by the ancients, 'as sacrifices, wars, triumphs, nuptials, banquets, 'tragedies, comedies, pantomimic entertainments, 'dancings, funerals, festivals, and games, all proved 'and illustrated by medals, gems, bass reliefs, and 'other antique monuments.

'Book VII. Treats of the several instruments 'used by the ancients in a manner altogether new, 'and much clearer than has been done hitherto ; 'with such of their instruments, as could be deli-'neated from antiquities now existing, engraved on 'copper. The whole making the most complete 'collection of that kind yet published.

'Book VIII. Includes a curious enquiry into 'ancient music in the several periods of time, with 'its excellency; wherein the ancient musicians ex-'celled the moderns ; and also those particulars in 'which the latter surpassed them ; and concludes 'with judging the palm to the ancient music.

'Vol. II. Book I. Begins from Christ, with the 'institution of music in the Christian churches; and 'comprehends also the invention of the notes now

'used, and harmony; their introduction into all
'parts of Europe; with the institution of doctors
'of music in England; and several other curious
'matters that occurred during the space of 1550
'years.

'Book II. An account of the greatest masters in
'all parts of Europe during the fifty years following,
'with several other particulars.

'Book III. Beginning with the xvii. century,
'gives an accurate account of the invention of
'operas in imitation of the Greeks, with several
'important particulars; and a series of masters to
'anno 1650.

'Book IV. Another series of masters for the
'succeeding 25 years; the introduction of operas
'and other kind of music into different parts of
'Europe.

'Book V. The continuation as before for the next
'25 years.

'Book VI. Beginning at 1700, with an account
'of the introduction of Italian operas into England,
'and the progress they have since made; the founding
'of the royal academy, and several other curious
'matters.

'Book VII. Some account of the principal masters
'now living, and the present state of music in all
'parts of Europe.

'Book VIII. A curious dissertation or enquiry
'in what manner music may be carried to a greater
'perfection than it hath hitherto attained to.'

Haym met with but small encouragement for this
undertaking, as appears by a printed copy of the
proposals and plan, with a list of subscribers in his
own hand-writing, scarce amounting to forty in
number; for this reason he dropped the design, and,
abandoning the profession of music, betook himself
to another, viz., that of a collector of pictures; and
in that capacity was employed by Sir Richard Walpole, Dr. Mead, and other persons. Besides his
talent in music, which was no inconsiderable one,
he possessed the faculty of poetry: in a collection
of Mr. Galliard's compositions, in his own hand-
writing, are two Italian Cantatas written by Haym.
He was also the author of Etearco, an opera represented at the Haymarket in the year 1711.

CHARLES DIEUPART, a Frenchman by birth, and
a fine performer on the violin, and also on the
harpsichord, together with Clayton and Haym promoted the introduction of the Italian opera into
England, and greatly assisted the former in bringing
on the stage the first opera ever performed here,
namely Arsinoe, represented at the theatre in Drury-
lane in 1707. At the performance of that and the
subsequent operas of Camilla, and Pyrrhus and
Demetrius, he played the harpsichord, and Haym
the violoncello. Upon Mr. Handel's first arrival in
England in the year 1710, and the representation of
Rinaldo at the Haymarket theatre, it was received
with such applause, that the managers of the opera
at Drury-lane were discouraged from any farther
attempts of that kind; the consequence thereof was
that Clayton, Haym, and Dieupart were necessitated
to solicit the encouragement of the town in behalf

of a concert, which they proposed jointly to carry
on at Clayton's house in York-buildings, in which
was a large room, where concerts had been usually
performed before. Their proposals for this undertaking are contained in two letters printed in the
Spectator, Numb. 258 and 278.

This association continued but a short time, for
in 1711 we find him engaged with Sir Richard
Steele in the performance of concerts there.* Haym
went to the Haymarket, and became a performer in
the opera band, and farther assisted in bringing on
that stage sundry musical performances. Dieupart
betook himself wholly to teaching the harpsichord,
and in the capacity of a master of that instrument,
had admission into some of the best families in the
kingdom. In the latter part of his life he grew
negligent, and frequented concerts performed at
ale-houses, in obscure parts of the town, and distinguished himself not more there, than he would
have done in an assembly of the best judges, by his
neat and elegant manner of playing the solos of
Corelli. He died far advanced in years, and in very
necessitated circumstances, about the year 1740.
There are extant of Dieupart's composition, 'Six
'Suittes de Clavessin, divisées en Ouvertures, Alle-
'mandes, Courantes, Sarabandes, Gavottes, Minuets,
'Rondeaux, et Gigues, composées et mises en Con-
'cert pour un Violin et Flûte, avec une Basse de
'Viole et un Archilut.'

GODFREY KELLER was a celebrated master of the
harpsichord about this time. He, together with
Finger, published Sonatas in five parts for flutes
and hautboys, and was the author of Six Sonatas
for violins, trumpets, hautboys and flutes. The
titles at large of these two several publications may
be seen in the Dutch catalogue. At present Keller
is known only by a work which he had prepared
for the press, but was prevented from publishing by
an immature death: it was however printed a short
time after by John Cullen, at the Buck, between the
two Temple-gates, in Fleet-street, with the title of
'A compleat Method for attaining to play a Tho-
'rough-Bass upon either Organ, Harpsichord, or
'Theorbo-Lute, by the late famous Mr. Godfry
'Keller, with Variety of proper Lessons and Fugues,
'explaining the several Rules throughout the whole
'Work; and a Scale for tuneing the Harpsichord
'or Spinnet, all taken from his own copies, which
'he did design to print.'

It was afterwards reprinted by Pearson of Aldersgate-street, as an Appendix to Dr. Holder's Treatise
of the natural Grounds and Principles of Harmony,
to which it must be owned it is but an awkward
supplement, as being altogether practical. Matthew
Lock's Melothesia is the first book on the subject of
thorough-bass published in England, this of Keller
is the next; since his time there have been others
without number.

WILLIAM CORBETT, one of the king's band, was
a celebrated performer on the violin, and leader of
the first opera orchestra at the Haymarket, at the
time when Arsinoe was performed there. Of this

* Vide ante, page 814.

person there are some particulars worth noting. He was a good composer, and a great collector of music and musical instruments. When the Italian opera, properly so called, was established at London, that is to say in the year 1710, when Rinaldo was performed at the Haymarket, a new set of instrumental performers were introduced; and Corbett, though in the service of the king, was permitted to go abroad. Accordingly he went to Italy, and resided at Rome many years, during which time he made a valuable collection of music and musical instruments. Those who, as being acquainted with his circumstances, were otherwise at a loss to account for his being able to lay out such sums as he was observed to do in the purchase of books and instruments, confidently asserted that besides his salary he had an allowance from the government, and that his business at Rome was to watch the motions of the Pretender.

In his younger days, and before he left England, he had published two or three sets of Sonatas for violins and flutes, twelve Concertos for all instruments, and sundry sets of tunes made for plays; but upon his return, about the year 1740, he brought over with him a great quantity of music of his composing during his residence abroad, from the publication of which here he hoped to derive considerable advantage: accordingly he published proposals for printing by subscription his Opera VIII. a work which he entitled 'Concertos or Universal ' Bizzarries, composed on all the new Gustos during 'many years residence in Italy,' in three books, containing thirty-five Concertos of seven parts, in which the styles of the various kingdoms in Europe, and of divers cities and provinces in Italy are professed to be imitated; that is to say, to give a few of them, the several styles of Milan, Rome, Naples, Florence, Bologna, Brescia, Tyrol, England, Ireland, Scotland, Flanders, Hungary, Denmark, Muscovy, &c. The proposal was ridiculous; for in music, composed according to the principles generally known and received, there can be no such discrimination of style as will enable the hearer to distinguish the music of one country, much less one city, from another. However the author was determined to try the experiment; and to make the proposal to go down, he advertised that any person of quality willing to encourage the publication of these compositions, should, upon notice, be waited on by the author and a band of performers, in order, as he phrases it, ' that they might hear the idea of them.' With little or no encouragement Corbett proceeded to publish this his work; but, not being able to vend the many copies of it which he had caused to be printed, they in a short time became waste paper, and lay exposed on booksellers' stalls.

Corbett died at an advanced age in the year 1748. By his will he bequeathed the best of his musical instruments, by the description of his 'Serys ' or Gallery of Cremonys and Stainers,' mentioned in an inventory, part of the will,* to the managers, as he calls them, of Gresham college, with a view

as it seems that they should remain for inspection under certain rules. He also bequeathed 10l. a year to a female servant to show these instruments; and directed that the rest of his personal estate should be sold 'for the establishment of the rules of ' Gresham college;'† and farther gave to the same college many sets of the concertos composed by him, with directions that four copies should be presented every year to foreigners that were good performers. How far this whimsical disposition was complied with we know not,‡ but in a short time after the testator's decease, there was a sale by auction of his instruments at Mercer's-hall, where many curious violins were knocked down at prices far beneath their value. His collection of music-books and manuscripts was also sold by auction at his house in Silver-street, near Pulteney-street, Golden-square.

JOHN LOEILLET, a relation, as it is supposed, of John Baptist Loeillet, of Ghent, a famous master of the flute, and the author of four operas of Solos for that instrument, was a celebrated master of the harpsichord, and a performer in the opera band at the same time with Corbett and the others above mentioned. He was a man well respected by those of his profession; and dwelling in a house in Hart-street, Covent-garden, in which was a large room, had a weekly concert there, which was frequented chiefly by gentlemen performers, who gratified him very handsomely for his assistance in conducting it. It was at this concert that the concertos of Corelli were first performed in England, the particular circumstances whereof are related in the account herein before given of Mr. Henry Needler.

Loeillet was a teacher of the harpsichord, and an excellent composer for that instrument. *He was also celebrated for his performance on the hautboy.* There is extant among his printed lessons a minuet in the key of A, with the minor third, which was a great favourite with the ladies of the last age. The vulgar pronunciation of Loeillet's name led the world into a mistake, so that it was universally ascribed to Jean Baptiste Lully, and few are sensible of the error. In the latter part of his life he dwelt in New North-street, near Red Lion-square. He died about the year 1728, having by his industry acquired a fortune of 16,000l. The works published by him, and printed for Walsh, are six suits of lessons for the harpsichord, six Sonatas for variety of instruments, viz., flutes, hautboys, German flutes, and violins, Opera prima. Twelve Sonatas for violins, German flutes, and common flutes, Opera secunda. Twelve Solos for a German flute, common flute, and violin, Opera terza.

## CHAP. CLXXV.

PIER FRANCESCO TOSI was an Italian singer greatly celebrated in his time. Having resided in most of the courts of Europe, and being an attentive hearer of others, and a person of reflection, he attained to

* In the inventory one of the violins is said to have been formerly Corelli's.

† i. e. the rules by him prescribed, touching the custody of the instruments, and the use to be made of them.
‡ Repeated applications have been made to the clerk of the Mercer's Company for information in this respect, but to no purpose.

such a degree of skill and judgment in the practice of singing, as enabled him to compose a treatise on the subject, which he published at Bologna in the year 1723, with this title, ' Opinioni de' Cantori ' antichi e moderni, o sieno Osservazioni sopra il ' Canto Figurato di Pier Francesco Tosi, Academico ' Filarmonico,' and dedicated to the earl of Peterborough.

Tosi not only visited England, but had made London his residence from the latter end of king William's reign to the end of that of George I. except during such short intervals as either business, or the desire of seeing his friends and relations called him hence : nevertheless it does not appear that he ever sang in the opera here, which is the more to be wondered at, seeing that he had concerts for his benefit.\* During his abode in England he was greatly favoured by the principal nobility ; and upon lord Peterborough's return from Spain, and final settlement in England, was much at his house at Parson's-green, where he had opportunities of conversing with Mrs. Anastasia Robinson, then a singer in the opera, afterwards countess of Peterborough.

The treatise of Tosi above mentioned is altogether practical, and contains a great number of particulars respecting the management of the voice, and the method of singing with grace and elegance. Moreover, it contains short memoirs and general characters of the most celebrated singers, male and female, of the author's time. Of Pistocchi in particular he speaks in terms of high commendation, and scruples not to say that he excelled not only those of his own, but of all former times. Mr. Galliard, in the year 1743, published a translation into English of this book, with notes thereon ; but by adhering too closely to the original, and adopting those rhapsodical expressions of the author, which, though they suit well enough with the Italian language, disgust an English reader, he has rather degraded than recommended the art which it is the design of the book to teach.

Tosi was, it seems, not only a very fine singer, but also a composer. Mr. Galliard relates, that after his voice had left him he composed sundry cantatas of an exquisite taste, especially in the recitatives, wherein he says the author excels, in the pathetic and expression, all others. To Galliard's translation is a prefatory discourse, containing a brief account of the author, wherein it is said that he died soon after the late king's accession to the crown, having attained above the age of fourscore.

JOHN BANISTER (a Portrait), was the son of that Banister mentioned before to have been sent into France by king Charles II. for his improvement on the violin. The father died in the year 1679, and the son, who had been educated under him, played the first violin at Drury-lane theatre, as well when the opera was performed there, as ordinarily. He too was a composer, and made several Grounds, with

divisions thereon, published in the Division Violin ; and in the London Gazette, Numb. 2712, for November 5, 1691, is an advertisement of a collection of music, composed by Godfrey Finger and himself, to be sold at Banister's house in Brownlow-street, Drury-lane. That he was a man eminent in his profession may be inferred from the mezzotinto of him by Smith, from which the engraving is taken. Banister continued at the head of the band at Drurylane till about the year 1720, when he was succeeded by Carbonelli. He died in or about the year 1725. A son of his taught the flute, and was it seems a celebrated performer ; for in Brightland's English Grammar, published about the year 1710, this sentence is given as an example, to show that the particle at is frequently used for on or upon,

' Banister is good at the flute.'

He was famous for playing on two flutes at once.

THOMAS ROSEINGRAVE was the son of Daniel Roseingrave already spoken of,† who, having been organist of Salisbury, went to Ireland, and in the year 1698 was appointed organist, and also one of the vicars choral of the cathedral church of St. Patrick in Dublin. He had two sons, whom he brought up to music, the one named Thomas, the other Ralph ; Thomas, of whom we are about to speak, being a young man of a promising genius, was favoured by the chapter of St. Patrick with a pension, to enable him to travel for improvement ; and accordingly he went to Rome in the year 1710, where he became acquainted with Alessandro Scarlatti, and his son Domenico, with whom he contracted a friendship, which subsisted for many years.

How long Roseingrave continued abroad is not certainly known, but in 1720 he had some concern in the management of the opera at the Haymarket : for in that year he brought upon the stage the opera of Narcissus, written by Rolli, and set to music by Domenico Scarlatti, with additional songs composed by Roseingrave himself. A short time after this representation the management of the opera got into other hands, and Roseingrave became a teacher of music, in the principles whereof he was looked upon to be profoundly skilled ; notwithstanding which, his style both of playing and composing was harsh and disgusting, manifesting great learning, but void of elegance and variety. About the year 1725, an organ having been erected in the new church of St. George, Hanover-square, Roseingrave offered himself for the place. The parish being determined to choose the person best qualified, required that each of the candidates should give a specimen of his abilities by a performance, of which Mr. Handel and Geminiani were requested to be judges ; the test of which was by them settled to be a point or subject of a fugue, which the performer was to conduct at his pleasure : this kind of trial was so suited to the talents of Roseingrave, that he far exceeded his competitors, and obtained the place, with a salary of fifty pounds a year. With few other motives than the love of his art, Roseingrave pursued the study of music with

---

\* Vide ante, page 764, an advertisement in the Gazette for April 3, 1693, of a concert for Signor Tosi's benefit in Charles-street, Covent-Garden ; and another in the Gazette for October 26, in the same year, purporting that Signor Tosi's concert would be performed weekly during the winter in York-buildings.

† Vide ante, page 771.

T. Murray pinx.    C. Grignion sculp.

Mᴿ JOHN BANNISTER.

intense application, but so greatly to the injury of his mental faculties, that he refused to teach even persons of the first quality. He was an enthusiastic admirer of Palestrina, and the furniture of his bed-chamber was scraps of paper, containing select passages from the works of that author. His brother Ralph having been bred to music, their father, in the year 1718, obtained permission of the dean and chapter of St. Patrick's to resign his place of organist in favour of him; and in April, 1719, Ralph Roseingrave was elected in his room. This person died in October, 1747, and left a son, William Roseingrave, Esq., who is now living in Dublin, and enjoys several considerable employments under the government in Ireland.

Thomas Roseingrave died about the year 1750, having subsisted for some years chiefly on the bounty of his nephew above mentioned. Some time before his death he published a collection of lessons of his friend Domenico Scarlatti, in which is a composition or two of his own. His other works in print are, Additional Songs to the opera of Narcissus, Voluntaries and Fugues for the organ and harpsichord, to the number of fifteen; and twelve Solos for the German flute, with a thorough-bass for the harpsichord. He was a frequent visitant of the reverend Mr. Woodeson, master of the free-school at Kingston-upon-Thames, and would often leave his bed in the night to go to the harpsichord. Mr. Woodeson wrote an epitaph for him, which Roseingrave was so pleased with that he set it to music. It was an elegant composition, but is irrecoverably lost.

JOHN BARRETT was music-master to the boys in Christ's hospital, London,* and organist of the church of St. Mary-at-Hill. He was a skilful musician, and made the tunes to songs in sundry plays; excelling most of his time in the composition of songs and ballad airs. In the Pills to Purge Melancholy are many songs composed by him. He was the author of that sweet air to the song of 'Ianthe the lovely,' made on queen Anne and prince George of Denmark, to which tune a song is adapted in the Beggar's Opera, 'When he holds up his hand.' Some verses of Barrett, prefixed to the Amphion Anglicus, bespeak him to have been a pupil of Blow.

LEWIS RAMONDON was a singer in sundry of the English Italian operas. His first appearance was in that of Arsinoe. In Camilla he performed the part of Metius, and in Pyrrhus and Demetrius that of Cleartes. He had attained to some skill in music, and composed the tunes to some songs in a collection published in 1716, entitled the 'Merry Musician, or 'a Cure for the Spleen,' among which is a hymn upon the execution of two criminals, beginning 'All you 'that must take a leap in the dark.' It is there printed with only the song part, but there are other copies with the bass, which shew it to be a perpetual

fugue, or composition in canon. Gay, in the Beggar's Opera, has adapted a song to this fine tune.

PHILIP HART, supposed to be the son of Mr. James Hart, one of king William's band, and whose name frequently occurs in the Treasury of Music, and other collections of that time, was organist of the church of St. Andrew Undershaft, and also of St. Michael's, Cornhill, which latter place he quitted upon a disagreement with the churchwardens, who were so mean as to contend that during a repair of the organ, which took up a year, his salary should cease, and was elected organist to the neighbouring church of St. Dionis Backchurch. He was a sound musician, but entertained little relish for those refinements in music which followed the introduction of the Italian opera into this country, for which reason he was the idol of the citizens, especially such of them as were old enough to remember Blow and Purcell. He was a grave and decent man, remarkable for his affability and gentlemanly deportment. There are extant of his composition a collection of Fugues for the organ, and the Morning Hymn from the fifth book of the Paradise Lost, which latter work he published in March, 1728-9. Mr. Galliard had set this hymn, and published it by subscription in 1728; and it is said that Mr. Hart meant to emulate him by a composition to the same words; but if he did, he failed in the attempt, for Mr. Galliard's hymn is a fine and elegant composition, admired at this day, whereas that of Mr. Hart is forgotten. He died about the year 1750, at a very advanced age.

GEORGE MONRO was an organist, and a competitor with Roseingrave for the place at St. George's, Hanover-square: failing in this application, he became organist of the church of St. Peter, in Cornhill. He played the harpsichord at Goodman's-fields theatre from the time when it was first opened, in 1729, till his death, which happened in a year or two afterwards. Monro had a happy talent in composing song tunes and ballad airs, of which he made many that were greatly admired. Sundry of them are printed in the Musical Miscellany, an elegant collection of songs with the music, in six volumes, printed and published by Watts in the year 1731.

GEORGE HAYDEN was organist of the church of St. Mary Magdalen, Bermondsey; he composed and published, about the year 1723, three Cantatas, the first whereof was sung by one Bat, or Bartholomew Platt, a favourite singer with the vulgar, in a pantomime called Harlequin Director, performed at Sadler's Wells; the first words of it are 'A cypress grove, whose melancholy shade,' a composition which would have done honour to some of the ablest masters of the time. He also composed a song called New Mad Tom, beginning 'In my triumphant chariot hurl'd,' which the same Bat. Platt was used to sing at Sadler's Wells, dressed in the character of a madman,† to the great delight of all who mistook roaring for singing. There is also extant of Hayden's composition a pretty song in two parts, 'As I saw

---

* In this Hospital, anno. 3 Jac. a free singing school was founded and endowed by Robert Dow, whose many charitable donations are recorded by Stow in his Survey, edit. Strype, book II. page 18-19, book V. page 62; wherein, as in the college at Dulwich founded by Allen the Player, the children were to be taught prick-song. These, as far as can be recollected, are the only endowments of the kind since the Reformation. At Dulwich the boys are taught the musical notes, and are able to chant; but at Christ's Hospital they sing only psalm tunes, and those by ear.

† Songs of this kind, such as Tom of Bedlam, and others set by Lawes, of which there are perhaps more in the English than any other language, were frequently sung in character. In Shadwell's comedy of Bury Fair, act III. scene I. Sir Humphrey Noddy says of a fellow, one of the Thetford music, that he acts Tom of Bedlam to a miracle.

fair Chlora walk alone,' which is well known to the proficients in vocal harmony.

VANBRUGH composed and published two elegant collections of songs, some of which became great favourites. Of this person very little, not even his Christian name, is known: though by the title-page of the second book it appears that the author's house was next door to the Black Lion, near Serjeants'-Inn, Fleet-street.

MAGNUS, organist of the church of St. Giles-in-the-Fields, was esteemed a great master of harmony, and had a style which none could imitate. In his voluntaries on the organ he despised the use of single stops, and attained to so great a command of the instrument as to be able to conduct four parts in fugue. Excessive study and application brought on a disorder in his mind, and he died a young man.

WILLIAM BABELL, organist of the church of All-hallows, Bread-street, and of his majesty's private music, was the son of a musician, who played the bassoon at Drury-lane theatre till he was eighty years of age. He was instructed by his father in the rudiments of music, and *by Dr. Pepusch in the practice of Composition*; and taking to the harpsichord, he became an admirable proficient. Coming into the world about the time when the opera began to get footing in England, he made it his study to emulate the Italians. His first essay in composition was to make the favourite airs in the operas of Pyrrhus and Demetrius, Hydaspes, and some others, into lessons for the harpsichord. After that he did the same by Mr. Handel's opera of Rinaldo, and succeeded so well in the attempt, as to make from it a book of lessons, which few could play but himself, and which has long been deservedly celebrated. He also composed twelve Solos for a violin or haut-boy, twelve Solos for a German flute or hautboy, six Concertos for small flutes and violins, and some other works, enumerated in Walsh's catalogue. Babell died *at about the age of thirty three, on the twenty-third of September,* 1723, *at Canonbury House, Islington, and was buried in the Church of which he was Organist.* It seems the fame of Babell's abilities had reached Hamburgh, for Mattheson says he was a pupil of Handel; but in this he is mistaken, for Handel disdained to teach his art to any but princes.

ROBERT WOODCOCK, a famous performer on the flute, composed twelve concertos, so contrived, as that flutes of various sizes, having the parts transposed, might play in concert with the other instruments*. He had a brother named Thomas, who kept a coffee-house at Hereford, an excellent performer on the violin, and played the solos of Corelli with exquisite neatness and elegance. In that country his merits were not known, for his employment was playing country-dances, and his recreation angling. He died about the year 1750.

JOHN SHEELES was a harpsichord master, and the author of two collections of lessons for that in-

* When the flute was an instrument in vogue this was a very common practice. Corelli's concertos had been in like manner fitted for flutes by Schickard of Hamburgh, a great performer on, and composer for, that instrument.

strument. He, together with Mr. Monro, before mentioned, Mr. Whichello, who will be spoken of hereafter, and Mr. Galliard, were great contributors to the Musical Miscellany, a collection of songs published in the year 1731, and mentioned in a preceding article.

## CHAP. CLXXVI.

OBADIAH SHUTTLEWORTH, organist of the church of St. Michael, Cornhill, London, was elected to that place upon Mr. Hart's quitting it, and a few years after was appointed one of the organists of the Temple church. He was the son of old Mr. Shuttleworth of Spitalfields, the father of a musical family, and who had acquired a little fortune, partly by teaching the harpsichord, and partly by copying Corelli's music before it was printed in England. There were three sons of this family, and also a daughter. The father had frequent concerts at his house for the entertainment of a few select friends, in which the sons played the violin, the daughter the harpsichord, and the old gentleman the viol da gamba. Obadiah in particular played the violin to such a degree of perfection, as gave him a rank among the first masters of his time. He played the first violin at the Swan concert in Cornhill, from the first institution of that society till the time of his death, which was about the year 1735. He was besides a very good composer, and made twelve Concertos, and sundry Sonatas for violins, of which some of his friends were favoured with manuscript copies. Nothing of his composition is extant in print, except two Concertos made from the first and eleventh Solos of Corelli. Of his two brothers, the one was a clerk in the South-Sea-house, a very gay man; the other had a place in some other of the public offices, and was as remarkably grave; they were both excellent performers on the violin, and used to be at all concerts in the city. Obadiah Shuttleworth was celebrated for his fine finger on the organ, and drew numbers to hear him, especially at the Temple church, where he would frequently play near an hour after evening service.

HENRY SYMONDS, one of the king's band of musicians, and organist of the church of St. Martin, Ludgate, and also of the chapel of St. John, at the end of James-street, near Bedford-row, was a celebrated master of the harpsichord in his time. He published Six suites of lessons for the harpsichord, in the dedication whereof to the duchess of Marlborough he intimates that they had been seen and approved by Bononcini. He died about the year 1730.

ABIELL WHICHELLO had been for some years deputy to Mr. Hart, who being a pluralist, had need of an assistant; after that he became organist of the church of St. Edmund the King, and taught the harpsichord in some of the best families in the city. He composed many songs, which have been separately printed, and a collection of lessons for the harpsichord or spinet, containing Almands, Courants, Sarabands, Airs, Minuets, and Jigs. He was one of those masters that used to frequent the concert of Britton the small-coal man, and became there acquainted with Mr. John Hughes, for whose memory he was used to profess a sincere regard. He died about the year 1745.

JOHN ROBINSON, organist of Westminster-abbey, and also of the parish churches of St. Laurence Jewry, and St. Magnus, London; educated in the royal chapel under Blow, was a very florid and elegant performer on the organ, insomuch that crowds resorted to hear him. His wife was the daughter of Dr. William Turner, already spoken of in this work, who as it seems, sang in the opera of Narcissus; and to distinguish her from Mrs. Anastasia Robinson, a singer in the same opera, was called Mrs. Turner Robinson. He had a daughter, who sang for Mr. Handel in Hercules, and some other of his oratorios. Being a very active and industrious man, and highly celebrated as a master of the harpsichord, he was in full employment for many years of his life; and had a greater number of scholars than any one of his time. He died at an advanced age in the year 1762. There is a good print of him sitting at a harpsichord, engraved by Vertue.

RICHARD LEVERIDGE, a young man possessed of a deep and firm bass voice, became a very early retainer to the theatres. In Dryden's tragedy of the Indian Queen he performed the part of Ismeron, a conjurer, and in it sang that fine song 'Ye twice ten hundred deities,' composed by Purcell on purpose for him. He also sang in the opera of Arsinoe, composed by Clayton; and afterwards in Camilla, Rosamond, Thomyris, and Love's Triumph. When the opera came to be entirely Italian, the bass parts were sung by singers of that country, of whom Boschi was one of the first; and Leveridge became a singer in Lincoln's-Inn fields playhouse, under Rich, where he made himself very useful by performing such characters as Pluto, Faustus, Merlin, or, in short, any part in which a long beard was necessary, in the pantomimes and other exhibitions of that kind, of which Rich was the contriver. Mr. Galliard, who made the music to the best of these entertainments, composed many songs purposely for him, and one in particular in the Necromancer, or Harlequin Dr. Faustus, which Leveridge valued himself much upon singing, 'Arise ye subtle forms that sport.' He had a talent both for poetical and musical composition; the first he manifested by sundry songs of the jovial kind, made to well-known airs; the latter by the songs in the play of the Island Princess, altered by Motteux, which have great merit, and various others. Though he had been a performer in the opera at the same time with Nicolino and Valentini, he had no notion of grace or elegance in singing; it was all strength and compass; and at one time, viz., in the year 1730, he thought his voice so good, that he offered, for a wager of a hundred guineas, to sing a bass song with any man in England.

About the year 1726, he opened a coffee-house in Tavistock-street, Covent-Garden, and published a collection of his songs in two pocket volumes, neatly engraved. In Rowe's edition of Shakespeare the music in the second act of Macbeth is said to be set by Leveridge; and perhaps we are to understand that the rest of the songs in that tragedy were also set by him: but whether that editor did not mistake the musick of Matthew Lock for Leveridge, may deserve enquiry. Being a man of rather coarse manners, and able to drink a great deal, he was by some thought a good companion. The humour of his songs, and indeed of his conversation, consisted in exhortation to despise riches and the means of attaining them; to drown care by drinking; to enjoy the present hour, and to set reflection and death at defiance.* With such a disposition as this, Leveridge could not fail to be a welcome visitor at all clubs and assemblies, where the avowed purpose of meeting was an oblivion of care; and being ever ready to contribute to the promotion of social mirth, he made himself many friends, from whose bounty he derived all the comforts that in an extreme old age he was capable of enjoying. A physician in the city procured from a number of persons an annual contribution for his support, which he continued to receive till about seven years ago, when he died, having nearly attained the age of ninety.

HENRY CAREY (a Portrait), was a man of facetious temper, resembling Leveridge in many respects. He was a musician by profession, and one of the lower order of poets; his first preceptor in music was Olaus Westeinson Linnert, a German; he received some farther instructions from Roseingrave; and, lastly, was in some sort a disciple of Geminiani.† But with all the advantages he might be supposed to have derived from these instructors, the extent of his abilities seems to have been the composition of a ballad air, or at most a little cantata, to which he was just able to set a bass. Being thus slenderly accomplished in his art, his chief employment was teaching at boarding-schools, and among people of middling rank in private families. Though he had but little skill in music, he had a prolific invention, and very early in his life distinguished himself by the composition of songs, being the author both of the words and the music: one of these, beginning 'Of all the girls that are so smart,' he set to an air so very pretty, and withal so original, that it was sung by everybody. The subject of it is the love of an apprentice for a young girl in the lowest station of life, and, as the author relates, was founded on a real incident; and, mean as the subject

* Sentiments of this kind are predominant in almost all his songs, but in no one of them are they more closely compacted than in the following:—

Should I die by the force of good wine,
'Tis my will that a tun be my shrine;
And for the age to come
Engrave this story on my tomb:—
Here lies a body once so brave,
Who with drinking made his grave.
Since thus to die will purchase fame,
And raise an everlasting name,
　　Drink, drink away,
　　Drink, drink away;
And there let's be nobly interr'd;
　　Let misers and slaves
　　Pop into their graves,
And rot in a dirty church-yard.

† See his Poems, edit. 1729, pages 118, 111, 113.

may appear, Carey relates that Mr. Addison was pleased with that natural ease and simplicity of sentiment which distinguishes the ballad, and more than once vouchsafed to commend it.

With a small stock of reputation thus acquired, Carey continued to exercise his talent in poetry and music. He published, in the year 1720, a little collection of poems, and, in 1732, six Cantatas, written and composed by himself; he also composed sundry songs for modern comedies, particularly those in the Provoked Husband, and thereby commenced a relation to the theatres; soon after which he wrote a farce called the Contrivances, in which were several little songs to very pretty airs of his own composition : he also made two or three little dramas for Goodman's-fields theatre, which were very favourably received. In 1729 he published, by subscription, his poems much enlarged, with the addition of one entitled 'Namby Pamby;' the occasion of it was as follows: Ambrose Phillips being in Ireland at the time when lord Carteret was lord lieutenant of Ireland, wrote a poem on his daughter, lady Georgina, now the dowager lady Cowper, then in the cradle ; in such a kind of measure, and with such infantine sentiments, as were a fair subject for ridicule : Carey laid hold of this, and wrote a poem, in which all the songs of children at play are wittily introduced, and called it by a name by which children might be supposed to call the author, whose name was Ambrose, Namby Pamby. Carey's talent lay in humour and unmalevolent satire; in ridicule of the rant and bombast of modern tragedies he wrote one, to which he gave the strange title of Chrononhotonthologos, acted, in 1734, at the Little Theatre in the Haymarket, of which it is the least praise to say that no one can read it and preserve a serious countenance; he also wrote a farce called the Honest Yorkshireman; two interludes, the one called Nancy, or the Parting Lovers, the other Thomas and Sally; and two serious operas, viz., Amelia, set to music by Mr. John Frederick Lampe; and Teraminta, set by Mr. John Christopher Smith.

Carey was an Englishman, and entertained an excusable partiality for his country and countrymen; in consequence whereof he had an unsurmountable aversion to the Italian opera and the singers in it; which throughout his poems, and in some of his musical compositions, he has taken care to express. Farther, in pursuance of a hint in a little book called 'The Touchstone, or historical, critical, poli- 'tical, philosophical, and theological Essays on the ' reigning diversions of the town.' duod. 1728, written by the late Mr. James Ralph, he wrote a burlesque opera on the subject of the Dragon of Wantley, and gave it to a friend of his, the above mentioned Mr. John Frederick Lampe, a native of Saxony, but who had been some years in England, to set to music; Lampe undertook it, and did such justice to the work, that it may be said to be the truest burlesque of the Italian opera that was ever represented, at least in this country. Carey wrote a sequel to it, entitled the Dragoness, which Lampe also set, and is in no respect inferior to the Dragon of Wantley.

As the qualities that Carey was endowed with

were such as rendered him an entertaining companion, it is no wonder that he should be, as he frequently was, in straits. He had experienced the bounty of his friends by their readiness to assist him with little subscriptions to the works by him from time to time published. Encouraged by these, he republished, in 1740, all the songs he had ever composed, in a collection entitled 'The Musical ' Century, in one hundred English Ballads on various ' subjects and occasions, adapted to several characters ' and incidents in human life, and calculated for ' innocent conversation, mirth, and instruction.' In 1743 he published his dramatic works in a small quarto volume, and as well to this as his collection of songs, was favoured with a numerous subscription.

With all his mirth and good humour, Carey seems to have been at times deeply affected with the malevolence of some of his own profession, who, for reasons that no one can guess at, were his enemies : It is true that in some of his poems he manifests a contempt for them, but it is easy to discover that it is dissembled. Unable to resist the shafts of envy, and labouring under the pressure of his circumstances, about the year 1744, in a fit of desperation he laid violent hands on himself, and at his house in Warner-street, Coldbath fields, put a period to a life which had been led without reproach.

As a musician Carey seems to have been one of the first of the lowest rank; and as a poet, the last of that class of which D'Urfey was the first, with this difference, that in all the songs and poems written by him on wine, love, and such kind of subjects, he seems to have manifested an inviolable regard for decency and good manners.

Henry Holcombe was a singer in the opera at its first introduction into this country. In that of Camillo he performed the part of Prenesto; and being very young at the time, is in the printed copy of the music called the boy. In Rosamond he did the page, and is called by his name. He continued not long after a singer on the stage, but took to the profession of a harpsichord master, and taught in the families of some of the chief citizens of London. One, and but one song of his composition, 'Happy hours all hours excelling,' is printed in the Musical Miscellany, the words whereof were written by Dr. Wright, a dissenting teacher, minister to a congregation in Carter-lane. Mr. Holcombe also set to music the song of Arno's Vale, written by Charles earl of Middlesex, afterwards duke of Dorset, and addressed to a favourite of his, Signora Muscovita, a singer, on occasion of the death, in the year 1737, of John Gaston, the last duke of Tuscany of the house of Medici. It is printed in a collection of twelve songs set by Mr. Holcombe, and published by himself a few years before his death, which happened about the year 1750.

## CHAP. CLXXVII.

John Ernest Galliard was the son of a perruquier, and a native of Zell; he was born in or about the year 1687, and received his instructions in the practice of musical composition from Farinelli, the

J. Worsdale Pinx.                    C. Grignion sculp.

HARRY CAREY.

director of the concerts at Hanover, and of Steffani,[*] who was resident there in another capacity. After he had finished his studies he applied himself to the practice of the hautboy and the flute, which latter instrument was then the recreation of well-bred gentlemen, and was taken into the service of prince George of Denmark, who appointed him one of his chamber music. Upon the marriage of the prince with the lady, afterwards queen Anne, Galliard came over to England; at that time Baptist Draghi, who had been her master, was chapel-master to the queen dowager Catherine, the relict of Charles II., at Somerset House, but upon her death this place became a sinecure, and Draghi dying soon after her, it was bestowed on Mr. Galliard.

It appears by his own manuscript collection of his works, in which he has carefully noted down the times and occasions of his several compositions, that Mr. Galliard was much about the court; and many of them are there said to have been made at Richmond and Windsor, the places of the royal residence. He composed a Te Deum and Jubilate, and three anthems performed at St. Paul's and at the royal chapel at St. James's, upon thanksgiving for victories obtained in the course of the war;[†] and was in general esteemed an elegant and judicious composer.

The merits of Mr. Galliard, together with his interest at court, afforded reason at one time to suppose that he would have had the direction of the musical performances in this kingdom; but he was not able to stand in competition with either Bononcini or Handel, and wisely declined it. Nevertheless, in compliance with the request of his friend Mr. John Hughes, he set to music his opera of Calypso and Telemachus, which in the year 1712 was performed at the Haymarket theatre; the singers were Signora Margarita, Signora Manina, Mrs. Barbier, Mrs. Pearson, and Mr. Leveridge. Notwithstanding the goodness both of the poetry and the music, and that Nicolini himself had the generosity to applaud it, the friends of the Italian opera formed a resolution to condemn it; so that it was represented under the greatest discouragements; but some years afterwards it was revived with better success at Lincoln's Inn fields.

As Mr. Galliard led a retired and studious life, and had little intercourse with the musical world, there will be but little occasion to mention him hereafter, wherefore the particulars relating to him are here collected in one point of view.

From the time of Mr Handel's final settlement in this kingdom, he was occasionally the author of many elegant compositions, particularly six Cantatas, five of them written by Mr. John Hughes, and the sixth by Mr. Congreve; to the first impression of this work is a preface, containing sundry curious particulars respecting this species of musical composition; three other Cantatas written by Mr. Hughes, and printed in his works; six Solos for the flute, with a thorough-bass; six Solos for the violoncello or bassoon, composed at the request of one Kennedy, a fine player on the bassoon, and by him often performed in public. He also set to music, and published by subscription in 1728, the Morning Hymn of Adam and Eve, taken from the fifth book of Paradise lost; and in 1742 published a translation of Tosi's 'Opinioni de' Cantori antichi e moderni,' with the title of 'Observations on the Florid Song, or Sentiments on the ancient and modern singers.' Of the merits of this translation mention is made in the account hereinbefore given of Pier Francesco Tosi.[‡]

But his principal employment for a series of years was composing for the stage. He set to music an opera of one act, called Pan and Syrinx, written by Mr. Lewis Theobald, and performed at Lincoln's Inn fields in 1717; and in virtue of his engagements with Mr. Rich, was doomed to the task of composing the music to such entertainments as that gentleman from time to time thought proper to set before the public at his theatre in Lincoln's Inn fields, and afterwards at that of Covent-garden, consisting of a strange conjunction of opera and pantomime, the highest and lowest species of dramatic representation. Those of Mr. Galliard's composition, as far as can now be collected, were Jupiter and Europa; the Necromancer, or Harlequin Dr. Faustus; the Loves of Pluto and Proserpine, with the Birth of Harlequin; Apollo and Daphne, or the Burgomaster tricked. One of the last of his works of this kind was the music to an entertainment called the Royal Chace, or Merlin's Cave, in which is that famous song 'With early horn,' by the singing whereof, for some hundred nights, Mr. Beard first recommended himself to the public. He also composed the music for the tragedy of Œdipus, which had before been set by Purcell. This was never printed, but is in the library of the Academy of Ancient Music. Mr. Galliard was a great contributor by songs of his composition to the Musical Miscellany, in six volumes, printed by Watts, and mentioned in a preceding page. He also published, about 1740, in a separate volume, twelve songs composed by him at sundry times.

A letter from Mr. Galliard to Mr. John Hughes is printed in the preface to Mr. Hughes's Poems in two volumes, duodecimo, published in the year 1735.

About the year 1745 he had a concert for his benefit at Lincoln's Inn fields theatre, in which were

---

* See the printed catalogue of his music, in which, lot 65 of the manuscripts, is thus described: 'Mr. Galliard's first lessons for composition under the tuition of Sig. Farinelli and Abbate Steffani, at the age of 15 or 16, in 1702;' and in a manuscript collection of many of his compositions is a Sonata for a hautboy and two bassoons, with this note in his own hand-writing, 'Jaij fait cet Air a Hannover, que Jaij Joué a la Serenade de Monsieur Farinelli ce 22me Juin, 1704.'

† The words of these severally are, 'I will magnify thee, O Lord,' 'O Lord God of hosts,' and 'I am well pleased.'

‡ Mr. Galliard, though a foreigner, had attained to such a degree of proficiency in the English language, as to be able to write it correctly; but he was not enough acquainted with the niceties of it to know that we have no term that answers to the appellative Canto figurato, and consequently that that of the florid song could convey to an Englishman scarce any other idea than of the song of a bird, the nightingale for instance, and it happened accordingly that upon the publication of his translation men wondered what was meant by the term. Mr. Galliard has illustrated his author by notes of his own, which are curious and entertaining; and it is upon the use of certain phrases and peculiar modes of expression, common to the translation of the Abbé Raguenet's Parallel, published in 1709, with the title of 'A comparison between the French and Italian Musick and Operas, with Remarks,' and this of Tosi's book, that we found a conjecture that Mr. Galliard was the translator of both, and also the author of 'A Critical Discourse upon Operas in England, and a means proposed for their improvement,' printed at the end of the translation of the Parallel.

performed the chorusses to Sheffield duke of Buckingham's two tragedies of Brutus and Julius Cæsar, set to music by Mr. Galliard, and an instrumental piece for twenty-four bassoons and four double basses.

Mr. Galliard died in the beginning of the year 1749, leaving behind him a small but very curious collection of music, containing, among other things, a great number of scores of valuable compositions in his own hand-writing, which has been inspected for the purpose of compiling this article; and an Italian opera of his composition, not quite completed, entitled 'Oreste e Pilade, overo la Forza dell' Amicizia.' This collection, together with his instruments, was sold by auction at Mr. Prestage's, a few months after his decease.

The following duet in the hymn of Adam and Eve is inserted as a specimen of that natural and elegant style which distinguishes the compositions of this ingenious master :—

JOHN ERNEST GALLIARD.

John Christopher Pepusch (*a Portrait*), one of the greatest theoretic musicians of the modern times, was born at Berlin about the year 1667. His father, a minister of a protestant congregation in that city, discovering in him an early propensity to music, employed at the same time two different masters to instruct him, the one in the theory, the other in the practice of the science; the former of these was

Klingenberg, the son of Gottlieb Klingenberg, componist and organist of the churches of St. James and St. John, at Stettin in Pomerania, the latter, one Grosse, a Saxon, and an exceedingly fine performer on the organ.*

Under the care of these two masters Pepusch continued but the short space of one year, the strait circumstances of his father not affording him the means of farther instruction; but labouring incessantly at his studies, he profited so greatly under them, that he acquired an early reputation for his skill and performance; for at the age of fourteen he was sent for to court, and by accompanying one of the ladies who sang before the queen, so recommended himself, that he was immediately appointed to teach the prince, the father of the present king of Prussia, on the harpsichord, and that very day gave him a lesson.

Encouraged by a patronage so honorable, Pepusch prosecuted his studies with unremitted diligence; nor were his pursuits confined to that kind of knowledge, which is sufficient for a practical composer. He had an inquisitive disposition, that led him to investigate the principles of his art; and being competently skilled in the learned languages, he applied himself to the study of the ancient Greek writers, and acquired the character of a deep theorist in music. He continued at Berlin a professor of Music, and in the service of the court, till about the thirtieth year of his age, when, being in the royal palace, he became an eye-witness of a transaction which determined him to quit the country of his nativity. An officer in the service of his Prussian majesty had at a levee made use of some expression which so exasperated the king, that he ordered the offender into immediate custody, and, without a trial, or any other judicial proceeding, his head was struck off. Mr. Pepusch, who was present, conceived the life of every subject so precarious in a country where in the punishment of offences the forms of public justice were dispensed with, that he determined to abandon it, and put himself under the protection of a government founded on better principles.

In pursuance of this resolution he quitted Berlin, and arriving in England about the year 1700, was retained as a performer at Drury-lane. It is probable that he assisted in fitting the operas for the stage that were performed there, for in that of Thomyris is an additional song of his composition, to the words 'How blest is a soldier.'

While he was thus employed, he forbore not to prosecute his private studies, and these led him to an enquiry into the music of the ancients, and the perusal of the Greek writers, in which he persisted so inflexibly, that he arrived at a greater knowledge of the ancient system, than perhaps any theorist since the time of Salinas; and at length entertained an opinion that the science, instead of improving, had for many years been degenerating, and that what is now known of it, either in principle or practice, bears little proportion to that which is lost. Nevertheless this persuasion wrought not so upon his mind, as to prevent him from the exercise of his inventive faculty, nor of directing his studies to that kind of composition which was best suited to gratify the public ear, as appears by the works published by him at different times.

It is well known that at the beginning of this century the state of dramatic music was very low; and of the opera in particular, that it was scarce able to stand its ground against the ridicule of Mr. Addison, and other writers in the Spectator. Nevertheless there were so many who affected to discover charms in the Italian music, particularly that novel species of it, Recitative, as gave great encouragement to the composers of the time to study it: trusting to this disposition in its favour, Mr. Pepusch set to music six Cantatas for a voice and instruments, the words whereof were written by Mr. John Hughes; and afterwards six others by different authors. The several compositions contained in these two collections are evidently in the style of the Italian opera, as consisting of airs intermixed with recitative; and he must be but very moderately skilled in music who cannot discover between them and the cantatas of Alessandro Scarlatti a very near resemblance. They were received with as much applause as the novelty of this kind of music could well entitle them to; but the remembrance of this work exists only in the cantata 'See from the silent grove,' which is yet heard with delight.

The abilities of Pepusch as a practical composer were not likely to become a source of wealth to him; his music was correct, but it wanted variety of modulation; besides which Mr. Handel had gotten possession of the public ear, and the whole kingdom were forming their taste for harmony and melody by the standard of his compositions. Pepusch, who soon became sensible of this, wisely betook himself to another course, and became a teacher of music, not the practice of any particular instrument, but music in the strict sense of the word, that is to say, the principles of harmony and the science of practical composition; and this not to children or novices, but in very many instances to professors of music themselves.

In the year 1713, at the same time with Croft, Mr. Pepusch was admitted to the degree of doctor in music in the university of Oxford,† and continued

---

* Probably Severus Grosse of Hildesheim, a bishopric in the circle of Lower Saxony. He was organist of the cathedral church at Groningen, a town situate in the principality of Halberstadt.

† To assist in the performance of the exercise for his degree, he took from London many of the performers from the theatres, and had concerts in the city for his benefit, which was censured as a very unacademical practice, and unwarranted by any precedent. His conduct in this respect

to prosecute his studies with great assiduity. Having taken upon himself to teach the rudiments of music, and the art of composition, he reverted to the system of Guido, and revived the practice of solmisation by the hexachords, which for almost a century had been disused in favour of a method far less certain and perfect, viz., that in which only the syllables SOL, LA, MI, FA, were used.*

His manner of inculcating the precepts of musical composition, and the method he took with his pupils to form their style, was somewhat singular. From the time that the works of Corelli first became known to the public, he entertained a most exalted opinion of their merit; and conceiving that they contained the perfection of melody and harmony, he formed a kind of musical code, consisting of rules extracted from the works of this his favourite author; and the exercises which he enjoined his disciples were divisions on, and harmonies adapted to, basses selected from his works.

In the course of his studies Dr. Pepusch had discovered the error of those, who seemed to resolve the efficacy of music and its influence on the human mind solely into novelty; he saw with concern persons who made pretensions to great skill in the science, treat with indifference and contempt the music of the preceding century; and being himself persuaded of its superior excellence, he laboured to retrieve and exhibit it to public view. To this end, about the year 1710, he concerted with some of the most eminent masters then living, and a number of gentlemen distinguished for their performance on various instruments, the plan of an academy for the practice of ancient vocal and instrumental music. The origin of this institution has already been spoken of; the farther history of it is reserved for another part of this work.

About the year 1712, the duke of Chandois having built himself a house near Edgware in Middlesex, which he named Cannons, in pursuance of a plan which he had formed of living in a state of regal magnificence,† determined on having divine service

being contrasted with that of Croft, whose exercise was performed by singers from the chapel royal, and who declined all pecuniary emoluments on the occasion, gave great offence to the university.

* Touching the syllables used in solmisation, it may not be amiss to remark that they were originally six, UT, RE, MI, FA, SOL, LA. See page 155, et seq. The Italians finding the syllable UT rather difficult to pronounce, rejected it, and instead of it, made use of DO; and we find it adopted in the Armonia Gregoriana of Gerolamo Cantone, published in 1678. Some years before this, that is to say, upon the Restoration, when the masters throughout this kingdom were employed in training up children for cathedral service, which had been abolished in the time of the usurpation, they, as thinking it more easy, introduced a practice of solfaing by the tetrachords, using only the syllables, SOL, LA, MI, FA; which method Dr. Wallis has followed in the several examples by him given in his Appendix to Ptolemy; but it having been found in some respects less true and certain than the former, Dr. Pepusch revived the practice of solmisation by the hexachords; which at first appeared so difficult, that few could be prevailed on to learn it. Stanesby the flute-maker, a very ingenious man, in the year 1736, declared that besides Dr. Pepusch he never met with but one person who could solfa by the hexachords, namely Mr. John Grano, the author of sundry Trumpet-tunes, and a celebrated performer on that instrument. *Mr. Bernard Gates, master of the chapel children, first introduced the practice into his school,* and since that time the boys of St. Paul's choir have been taught to do it with great facility.

† The very short period that intervened between the time of the

performed in his chapel, with all the aids that could be derived from vocal and instrumental music. To this end he retained some of the most celebrated performers of both kinds, and engaged the greatest masters of the time to compose anthems and services with instrumental accompaniments, after the manner of those performed in the churches of Italy. It is well known that Mr. Handel's anthems, to the number of near twenty, were made for the duke's chapel. It is also certain that the morning and evening services performed there were for the most part the compositions of Dr. Pepusch; many of these, among which is a very fine Magnificat, as also some anthems composed by him at the request of the duke, are now in the library of the Academy of Ancient Music, and are occasionally performed in that society.

About the year 1722 Signora Margarita de l'Pine having quitted the stage with a large sum of money, Dr. Pepusch married her, and went to reside in Boswell-court, Carey-street. Her mother also lived with him. The house where they dwelt was sufficiently noted by a parrot, which was used to be set out at the window, and had been taught to sing the air 'Non e si vago e bello,' in Julius Cæsar. The farther particulars respecting Dr. Pepusch are referred to a future page.

erection and demolition of that fabric, Cannons, affords an example of the instability of human grandeur that history can hardly parallel.

James Bridges, duke of Chandois, was paymaster of the forces during queen Anne's war; and having accumulated an immense sum of money, determined on the building of two magnificent houses, the one for a town, the other for a country residence: for the situation of the former he made choice of Cavendish-square, but proceeded no farther in that design than the building of two pavilions, which are the two houses at the extremities of the north side of that quadrangle, and may be distinguished by the similarity of their form, and the roofs, which are somewhat singular. For the site of his country house, the place he fixed on was a little west of Brentford, about half a mile north of the great road, and on the right hand side of the lane where lord Holderness's house now stands; and there are yet remaining the stone piers for the gates, and some other erections, which mark the very spot fixed on; but upon some disagreement with Charles, duke of Somerset, who did not choose that in his manor of Sion a mansion should be erected that was likely to vie with Sion-house itself, the duke of Chandois changed his intention, and went to Edgware in the county of Middlesex, from which place he had married his duchess, and there erected that splendid edifice, which for a few years was known by the name of Cannons. Three architects were employed in the design of it, namely Gibbs, James of Greenwich, and one Sheppard, who had been a plaisterer, but having built in and about Grosvenor-square with some success, professed himself an architect, and designed Goodman's-fields theatre, and after that Covent-Garden. The fabric, the costly furniture, and the mode of living at this place, subjected the owner of it to the censure of Mr. Pope, who has been pretty free in pronouncing, that, unless for vain expence and inelegant profusion, the duke had no taste at all; he might have included in the exception his grace's taste for music, of which he gave the best proofs; but panegyric and satire sort but ill together. It may be said that Mr. Pope in one of his letters to Mr. Aaron Hill, has denied that his Epistle on Taste is a satire on the duke of Chandois; but how far he may be credited, they only can judge who are able to point out, who but his Grace is meant by Lord Timon. Mr. Pope had the comfort to see the cause of his uneasiness removed in the change of the duke's circumstances, occasioned by the misfortunes of the year 1720, which in a short time obscured the splendour of Cannons; and had he lived to the year 1747, he might have enjoyed the pleasure of seeing this magnificent structure, which cost 200,000l. erecting and furnishing, sold at such a price, as afforded the purchaser a temptation to pull it down, and dispose of the materials in lots, one of which, namely, the marble staircase, was bought by the late earl of Chesterfield for his house near Hyde park, and is now there.

Of the order and economy of his Grace's expenditure it is not so difficult to judge, as of the proportion which it bore to his fortune; this however is certain, that when the plan of living at Cannons was originally concerted, the utmost abilities of human prudence were exerted to guard against profusion. One of the ablest accomptants in England, Mr. Watts, master of the academy in Little Tower-street, was employed by the duke to draw a plan which ascertained, and by inspection declared, the total of a year's, a month's, a week's, and even a day's expenditure. The scheme was engraved on a very large copper plate; and those who have seen impressions from it, pronounce it a very extraordinary effort of economical wisdom.

Tho. Hudson pinxit.

C. Grignion sculpsit.

JOHANNES CHRISTOPHORUS PEPUSCH.

MUS.DOCT. OXON.

## BOOK XIX.   CHAP. CLXXVIII.

In the year 1715 was published 'Histoire de la 'Musique, et de ses Effets, depuis son Origine jusqu' 'à présent.' The editor of this work was Bonnet, paymaster of the salaries of the lords of the parliament of Paris, who finding among the manuscripts of his uncle the Abbé Bourdelot, and also among those of his own brother Bonnet Bourdelot, physician to the king of France, certain memoirs on the subject of music, was induced to publish them.* The first edition of the book, and which was printed in 1705, seems to contain only so much as was written by the Abbé, but a later, printed in 1715, and at Amsterdam in 1725,† extends it to four volumes, and comprehends the papers of Bonnet Bourdelot.

The author begins his history with an account of the invention of the lyre by Mercury, and the establishment of a system by Pythagoras, founded on a division of the monochord. The relation which he gives is taken chiefly from Boetius, and needs not here to be repeated. In tracing the subsequent improvements by Gregory the Great, Guido Aretinus, and De Muris, he agrees in general with other writers.

It is to be observed that this work is written in a very desultory manner, by no means containing a regular deduction of the history of the science: all the use thereof that will be here made of it, will be to give from it such particulars respecting music as are worth noticing, and are not to be found elsewhere, and of these there are many.

In delivering the sentiments of the ancient philosophers, poets, and musicians, touching the use of music, and its effects on the passions, the author takes occasion to mention the marriage of our Henry VIII. with Anne Boleyn, who, he says, and cites Mezeray for his purpose, could sing and dance too well to be wise or staid, of which the king was well convinced when he discovered an intrigue between her and Mark Smeton, one of her musicians.‡ He cites from the memoirs of the Abbé Victorio Siry, a relation that queen Elizabeth of England, in the hour of her departure, ordered her musicians into her chamber, and died hearing them: and says that he had been informed by a friend of his, one of the attendants on the prince of Orange, afterwards king William III. that in the year 1688, the prince being then at the Hague, and, as it may be supposed, deeply engaged in reflections on the critical situation of his affairs at that time, had three choice musicians to play to him whenever he was disposed to be melancholy or over thoughtful.

Another instance, and that a very affecting one, of the power of music to assuage grief, he cites from the life of the emperor Justinian to this effect:

Ricimer, king of the Vandals,§ having been defeated in a great battle by Belisarius, was constrained to fly to the mountains, and was there with his army invested by him. Overwhelmed with grief, he made to the general this moving request : 'Send me,' says he, 'a loaf of bread, lest I perish with hunger; 'a spunge to dry up my tears ; and a musical instru-'ment to console me under my afflictions.'

Other particulars respecting music in general occur in this order. The ancient chronicles of France mention that Cherebert, king of Paris, about the year 562, married successively two of the maids of honour of his queen Ingoberge ; their names were Meroflede and Marcouefe, his inducement to it being that they were both fine singers.‖ Dagobert, king of France, in the year 630 divorced his queen Gomatrude upon pretence of barrenness, and married Nantilde, a nun, and a fine singer. William, duke of Normandy, in his expedition to England had singers at the head of his army. Francis I. king of France had music both for his chamber and his chapel : the musicians of his chapel followed him to Milan, and, jointly with those of pope Leo X. sang high mass, in the year 1515, at Bologna. Great numbers of Italian musicians followed Catherine de Medicis into France, upon her marriage with Henry II. and raised an emulation among the French, which contributed greatly to the improvement of their music. In the reign of Charles IX. king of France, Jean-Antoine de Baïf established an academy of music in his house, to which the king resorted once a week, and assisted at it in his own person, as did also his successor Henry III. till the civil wars of France obliged Baïf to break up the academy. At this time Eustache du Carroys, a native of Beauvais, was chapel-master to Charles IX. who dying, he was continued in his employment by his successor.¶ In the year 1580, Baltzarina, an Italian, afterwards called Beaujoyeux, came into France with a band of violins, and was made first valet-de-chambre to the queen. He was esteemed the finest performer on the violin then in Europe. Lewis XIII. of France is said to have composed a book of airs.** In 1630 a musician named Du Manoir, a fine performer on the violin, was by letters patent appointed King of the violins, with power to licence performers on that instrument in all the provinces in France. In 1684, cardinal Mazarine having sent for musicians from Italy, entertained the court at the Louvre with a representation of an Italian opera; the subject of it was the amours of Hercules : Lully composed the Entrées, and thereby gave proofs

---

* Of the authors that cite this book, some, not adverting to the circumstances of its publication, refer to it as the work of Bonnet, who was in truth but the editor.

† *I have it* 1743.

‡ Of this supposed intrigue Burnet has given the circumstances, which amount to no more than that Smeton was used to play on the virginals to the queen ; that one day standing in a window of her apartments, very pensive, she asked him why he was so sad ; he said it was no matter. She answered, 'You must not expect I should speak to you as if you 'were a nobleman, since you are an inferior person.' 'No, no, Madam,' says he, 'a look suffices me.' Vide Burn. Hist. Reform. vol. I. page 199.

§ The author seems to have mistaken this name for Gilimer, one of the nephews of Genseric, king of the Vandals, who claimed to be successor to his uncle. Justinian engaged in a war with him in behalf of Yldericus, another nephew of Genseric, and a competitor for his crown, and drove Gilimer into the mountains of Numidia. Of such a person as Ricimer we meet with no mention in the history of those times.

‖ Cherebert had by his queen Ingoberge, a daughter, named Bertha, who was married to Ethelbert, king of Kent, and greatly favoured the arrival of Austin the monk, when he came to teach the hristian religion

¶ Some compositions of his are to be found both in the French and the Latin work of Mersennus.

** This may be true, for see an air of his composition in page 638.

of his genius for music. In 1660 Lambert, master of the king's music, brought singing to perfection in France, by introducing the shake, and other graces, to which the French till his time were strangers. In 1669 the king granted to Cambert his letters patent for an opera, he having a short time before set to music a pastoral of Perrin, which was represented at Vincennes with great applause. The dialogues in the operas performed under the direction of Cambert, were composed by Lambert, Martin, Pordigal, Boisset, and himself, and were the models after which the French recitative was formed. Lewis XIV. understood music in perfection; he was also the best dancer in his court; cardinal Mazarine sent to Italy for a master to teach him the guitar, and in eighteen months the king excelled his master. All the foreign embassadors at the court of France allowed that the music of the king's chapel, as also of his chamber, excelled that of any prince in Europe. Few nations have a greater passion for music than the Spaniards; there are few of them that do not play on the guitar, and with this instrument at night they serenade their mistresses. At Madrid, and in other cities of Spain, it is common to meet in the streets, young men equipped with a guitar and a dark lanthorn, who taking their station under the windows, sing, and accompany themselves on their instrument; and there is scarce an artificer or labourer in any of the cities or principal towns, who when his work is over does not go to some of the public places and entertain himself with his guitar: nevertheless few Spaniards are composers of music; their operas are Italian, and the performers come chiefly from Milan, Naples, or Venice. Upon the marriage of the king of Spain, Charles II. with Mademoiselle d'Orleans, sundry operas of Lully were represented at Madrid, but the Spaniards were but little pleased with them. The emperor Charles V. was a great lover and judge of music. Guerrino, the best musician in all Spain, composed motets, and, with a licence which some great masters have at times used, had made free with the compositions of others; this the emperor discovered, although none of the musicians of his court were able to do it. The court of Vienna was the last that admitted the Italian music: upon the marriage of the emperor Leopold in the year 1660, an Italian opera was represented; the subject was the story of Orpheus and Eurydice; and since that time the emperor's musicians have been Italians. The marquis Santinella, an excellent musician, composed five or six Italian operas, one whereof was represented at the emperor's own expence, and was therefore entitled Opera Regia. Scarlatti composed an opera for the birth-day of the electoral prince of Bavaria; the subject of it was 'The Triumph of Bavaria over 'Heresy.' The English are said to owe their music to the French, for in 1668 Cambert left France, and went into England, and at London performed his opera of Pomone; but although he was favoured by the king, he was envied by the English musicians, envy being inseparable from merit. Some Englishmen had composed music to operas in their own

language, but these not succeeding, the Italian opera has taken place in that kingdom. Some years ago certain French musicians attempted an opera at London, which was well received by the audience; but the English musicians being determined to interrupt the performance, began a quarrel, in which five or six were killed on one side or the other, and the survivors of the French musicians went back to their own country.* In England are concerts at all the places resorted to for the benefit of mineral waters. The king of England's band of music is either good or otherwise, accordingly as he cares for the expence of it. That of James II. was very indifferent, for this reason, that the king chose rather to employ his superfluous money in charity than in music.

These and other particulars contained in the first tome of this work, make the whole of the history of music, as given by the author; the remainder of it has not the least pretence to that character, it being a miscellaneous collection of dissertations, dialogues, discourses, and reflections on the subject of music, without the least regard to the order and course of historical narration. Many of those it is to be suspected are not the work of the author, seeing that the second tome begins with and contains the whole of the 'Comparaison de la Musique Italienne et de 'la Musique Françoise,' written by Mons. de la Viéuville de Freneuse, in answer to the 'Paralele 'des Italiens et des François,' &c., and mentioned in a preceding page of this work.

The first of these detached pieces, and which makes the twelfth chapter of the first tome of the 'Histoire de la Musique et de ses Effets,' is entitled 'Dissertation sur le bon Goût de la Musique d' Italie, de la Musique Françoise, et sur les Opera.' It begins with a remark that the admirers of the Italian music are a small sect of demi-sçavans in the art, notwithstanding they are persons of condition, and that they absolutely condemn the French music as insipid. But that there is another party more deeply skilled in the science, who are faithful to their country, and cannot without indignation suffer that the French music should be despised; and these look upon the Italian music as wild, capricious, and contrary to the rules of art. Between these two parties the author professes to be a moderator: of his impartiality a judgment may be formed from the following sentiments. The harmony of the Italian musicians is learned, especially in their Cantatas and Sonatas; but the style of the French is more natural: besides that, the French performers exceed the Italians in point of execution. The music of the Italians is like Gothic architecture, abounding with ornaments that obscure the work. The Italians express all the passions alike; their symphonies are but echoes of the song. They change the key too frequently, and repeat the same passages too often. Their Cantatas are fit only for the chamber,

* Of this quarrel no mention is made in any of the accounts extant of the English drama, nor any traces of it to be met with in any of the newspapers of the time, which we allow to comprehend all that interval between the first publication of the Gazette in king Charles the Second's reign and the year 1715, when the book now citing was first published.

and their Sonatas of two parts should be played by one violin only. Their thorough-basses doubled and chorded, and their Arpeggios are calculated to deceive the ignorant; and they are like dust thrown into the eyes of men to prevent their seeing; with a deal more to the same purpose. He says that the Abbé de la Louette made certain compositions for a concert at Rome, performed at the palace of the princess Colonna in 1689, which were so difficult to execute, that the famous Francisci was twice out in playing them; from hence he says it appears that the Italian performers are not infallible when they attempt to play or sing at sight.

In the thirteenth and last chapter of the 'Histoire 'de la Musique et de ses Effets,' that is to say, the history of music properly so called, the author treats of the sensibility of some animals, and of the effects of music upon many of them. He says that, being in Holland in the year 1688, he went to see a villa of Milord Portland, and was struck with the sight of a very handsome gallery in his great stable. 'At 'first,' says he, 'I concluded it was for the grooms to 'lye in, but the master of the horse told me that it 'was to give a concert to the horses once a week to 'chear them, which they did, and the horses seemed 'to be greatly delighted therewith.' He says that naturalists observe that hinds are so ravished with the sound of a fine voice, that they will lie down and hearken to it with the more attention; and that some of them are so enraptured with music, as to suffer themselves frequently to be taken without resistance.* It is not uncommon, he adds, to see nightingales, at the time of their making love, assemble themselves in a wood when they hear the sound of instruments or the singing of a fine voice, which they will answer by warbling with so much violence, as often to fall down expiring at the feet of the performer; and as a proof of this fact, he relates that in the month of May the people of Paris go to play in the gardens of the Tuilleries upon lutes and guitars, and that the nightingales and linnets there will perch upon the necks of the instruments, and listen with great attention and delight.

The second tome begins with and contains the whole of the Comparaison de la Musique Italienne et de la Musique Françoise, with a letter of the author to one of his friends on the same subject.

The third tome contains a letter to a lady on the subject of music and the French opera, with some songs adapted to well-known airs in the French operas, and a pastoral drama entitled L'Innocente. This is followed by several dialogues on music in general, containing many curious particulars respecting the French musicians, more particularly Lully, of which a due use has been made in the memoir herein before inserted of that musician.

In tome IV. the author re-assumes the style of history, interspersing a variety of observations upon church music, on the qualifications of a master of

music, and on music in general; and relates that Henry II. of France sang with the chanters of his chapel, as did also Charles IX., who, as Brantome asserts, sang his part very well; and for an encouragement to the study and practice of church music, founded the school of St. Innocent. He adds that Henry III. also sang, and that both he and his predecessor, Henry II., were composers of music.

The rest of this tome is taken up with an examen of the Italians and French with respect to the music of each. And herein the author takes occasion to observe on the liberty which some of the Italian musicians have assumed in the composition of motets, to alter the words of the vulgate translation; and of this he gives as an instance a motet of Carissimi, 'Peccavi Domine,' &c., in which he severely censures him for the use of the word Culpas, though he allows the motet to be a beautiful one. Again he remarks that the Italian musicians seldom regard the expression of the words; as an instance whereof he refers to the Judicium Salomonis of this author, upon which he observes, that the setting of the word Discernere, in the prayer of Solomon, is shocking, as containing a melody in which all the chords are taken, which he condemns as a puerile effort. Nevertheless, he commends very highly other parts of this composition, particularly the chidings of the two mothers; and, above all, the dignity and majesty with which Solomon is made to pronounce his decree. The author adds, that this composition is the finest of Carissimi's works that he had ever seen, and that he looks upon this musician as the least unworthy adversary whom the Italians have to oppose Lully.

He observes that, for want of attention, the expression of a particular word in music may become ridiculous, and may even be a burlesque of the sentiment. And to this purpose he relates the following story: 'In 1680 or 82, when Dumont 'died, and Robert retired, instead of the two masters 'of music which the king had at his chapel, he 'chose to have four; and to the end that these 'places should be filled by musicians that were 'worthy of them, he sent into the provinces a 'circular letter, by which all the masters at cathe-'drals were invited to Versailles, in order to give 'proofs of their several abilities. Among many 'that offered themselves was Le Sueur, chapel-'master of the church of Notre Dame at Rouen, 'a man of a happy and fruitful genius, one who 'had a very good knowledge of the Latin tongue, 'and merited this post as well as any. As he had 'no great patrons, he endeavoured to recommend 'himself by the performance of a studied com-'position, previous to that which was to be the test 'of his abilities: to that end he prepared a piece 'to be sung one day at the king's mass: it was the 'seventieth psalm, "Qui habitat in adjutorio," &c.† 'an admirable one, and equal to the text; and the 'king and all his court heard it with great attention. 'At the seventh verse, "Cadent a latere tuo," &c., 'Le Sueur had represented the falling, signified by

---

* That horses are sensible of the effects of music is remarked by the duke of Newcastle in his treatise of Horsemanship; and that deer are rendered tame by it, is no less confidently asserted: Playford relates that he saw a herd of stags, twenty in number, who were drawn by the sound of a bagpipe and a violin, from Yorkshire to Hampton-Court. See page 402, in note.

† This is a mistake of the author, the psalm is the ninetieth in the Vulgate, and the ninety-first in our translation.

'the word Cadent, by a chorus in fugue, which made
' a rumbling through seven or eight notes descending;
' and when the deep basses had run over the noisy
' octave, resting upon the last note, there was no
' auditor but must be supposed, according to Le Sueur,
' whom this invention had charmed, to have repre-
' sented to himself the idea of a man rolling down
' stairs, and falling with great violence to the bottom.
' This description struck but too much one of the
' courtiers, who, upon hearing the rumblings of the
' fugue, at one of those Ca-a-a-dents, cried out,
" There is somebody down that will never get up
" again." This pleasantry disturbed the gravity and
' the silence of the whole assembly. The king
' laughed at it, and the rest appeared to wait only
' for permission to second him. A long uninterrupted
' hearty laugh ensued, at the end whereof the king
' made a sign with his hand, and the music went on.
' At the tenth verse, " Et flagellum non appropin-
" quabit," &c., poor Le Sueur, whose misfortune was
' that of not having exalted himself above those
' puerilities, had set a new fugue upon the word
' Flagellum, in notes that represented the lashing of
' scourges, and that in so lively a manner, that a
' hearer must have thought himself in the midst of
' fifty Capuchins, who were whipping each other with
' all their might. " Alas !" cried another courtier,
' tired with this hurly burly, " these people have
' been scourging each other so long, that they must
" be all in blood." The king was again taken with
' a fit of laughter, which soon became general. The
' piece was finished, and Le Sueur was in hopes that
' the exceptionable passages in it would have been
' forgot. The time of trial drawing on, the candi-
' dates were shut up in a house, and for five or six
' days maintained at the king's expence, but under a
' strict command that none of them should be per-
' mitted to communicate with any person. Each
' tried his utmost efforts upon a psalm appointed for
' the competition, which was the thirty-first, " Beati
" quorum remissæ sunt," &c. But as soon as those
' of the chapel began to sing the work of Le Sueur,
' instead of attending to the beauties of the compo-
' sition, the courtiers recalling to mind the idea of the
' two obnoxious passages in his former master-piece,
' and the jests passed thereupon, cried out, " This is
" the Ca-a-a-dent," and a general laughter ensued.
' The consequence was, that Colasse, La Lande,
' Minoret, and Coupillet were chosen; the three first
' worthy without a doubt, of this post, the last not ;*
' and Le Sueur returned home melancholy to his
' house, to execute in the choir of his church an
' excellent " Beati quorum," which no one would
' hear at Versailles, though it received a thousand
' applauses at Rouen. This adventure, which Le
' Sueur after recounted with a very lively resentment
' against the court, had nevertheless so well cured
' him of trifling and false expression, that he passed
' over almost to the opposite extreme. He threw all
' his old music into the fire, fine and pleasing as it
' was ; and, during the remainder of his life, com-
' posed new upon every occasion, sober even to
' dryness.'

* For a reason that will be given hereafter.

Throughout his book the author takes every occasion that offers to censure the practice of fugue ;
and, taking advantage of the story above related, he
says that although in their church-music, and in their
opera, fugues are the delight of the Italians, they are
tiresome, and in church-music improper ; for that
there are few passages in scripture which allow us to
repeat them so many times as the fugue would demand. It is even difficult, adds he, for one to find
words in the church-service with which these frequent repetitions can agree. As to double fugues,
which are made to differ at the same time, good sense
requires that they should be sung by two choirs.

He says of the profane music of France, that it
was originally too intricate and elaborate ; but that
Lully reformed it, and left a shining example of that
medium, which ought ever to be preserved between
the extremes of simplicity and refinement. Yet he
observes that the music of Dumont, who flourished
before Lully, though his motets were not printed till
1688, is of an extreme simplicity. He farther says
of this author, that it was he who brought in, or at
least established in France, the use of continued
basses ; and that the art and high skill which appear
in the more modern compositions, have not rendered
those of Dumont contemptible, but that they are yet
bought ; their respective graces are yet felt ; and his
dialogue between an angel and a sinner, ' Peccator
' ubi es ?' is still heard with pleasure.

He says that Desmarets, author of the fine opera,
Æneas and Dido, ought to be reckoned among the
church musicians, it being certain that he composed
all that music which Coupillet caused to be performed:
as a proof whereof he relates the following fact.
' After Coupillet had been named for the king's cha-
' pel, merely because Madam the Dauphiness, whom
' Mons. Bossuet had solicited, desired it ; he soon
' became sensible of his inability to discharge the
' duties of it, and had recourse to Desmarets, a young
' man then needy and unknown. A bargain was
' made between them, and during ten or a dozen
' years Coupillet held his employment with reputation
' and esteem, till upon breach of the agreement on
' the part of Coupillet, Desmarets made a discovery
' of the secret, and Coupillet retired.'

Towards the close of this work we meet with a
tract, that appears to be an answer to a reply of the
Abbé Raguenet to the Comparaison de la Musique
Italienne et de la Musique Françoise ; and by this
author's recognition of the Comparaison, we know it
to be the work of Mons. de la Viéuville de Freneuse.
In this answer it appears that the applauses which in
the Parellel are given to the Italians, more particularly Corelli and Bononcini, had greatly irritated him,
and even bereft him of every source of argument,
excepting personal reflection. Of Corelli he does
but repeat the censures contained in the Comparaison,
but Bononcini is made the subject of a distinct tract,
entitled ' Eclaircissement sur Buononcini.' In this
senseless libel, for it deserves no better a name, the
author enters into an examination of the duets and
cantatas of Bononcini, which he says have no other
fault than that they cannot be sung ; which impossi-

bility he makes to arise from the use of fugues, counter-fugues, and intervals but little used, most of them false and irregular; objections, he says, which are equally to be made against the compositions both of Corelli and Bononcini. He then proceeds to examine a Cantata of Bononcini, as he has done a Sonata of Corelli, that he may equally satisfy, as he professes to do, the friends of these two heroes in different kinds of music. To this end he remarks on a cantata of Bononcini, 'Arde il mio petto amante;' for the choice whereof he gives this notable reason, that it is very short, and therefore one of the best of the many which that author had composed: and after a great number of idle objections to the expression of the poet's sentiments, the conduct of the melody and harmony, and the use of the tritone in the recitatives, he expresses his sentiments in the following modest terms: 'Ces jolis traits de Corelli et de 'Buononcini, dont vous êtes enchantez, choquent, 'renversent toutes les régles et de la musique et du 'bon sens: on vous défie de trouver quoi que ce soit 'de pareil dans Boesset, Lambert, Camus, dans tous 'les ouvrages de Lulli, et dans les ouvrages de 'Campra, de Desmarets, de M. des Touches, qui ont 'eu du succès; toute la France, les gens de la cour, 'les connoisseurs ont jusqu'ici méprisé, abhorré de si 'fausses beautez.'

He concludes his invective with an assertion, that, let his adversary, with all his skill in music, choose any sonata of Corelli, or cantata of Bononcini, and correct it at his pleasure, he will not be able to accommodate it to the taste of a Frenchman; which assertion may be very true, and no reflection on the merit of either of these two persons.

And lastly, to express his contempt, he exhorts the people, as it seems is the custom in Italy, to throw apples, medlars, and oranges at the heads of such musicians as those whom he has so freely censured in the passage above quoted.

Traits du peuple en corroux, pommes, nefles, oranges,
Sifflets de toute espèce et de toute grandeur,
Volez sur ce compositeur,
Célebréz ses louanges.

No one that reflects on this controversy can wonder that nothing decisive is produced by it, seeing that in questions of this kind, those of one party generally reason upon principles which are denied by the other. In such a case there can be no appeal but to the general sense of mankind, which has long determined the question, and given to the Italian music that preference, which upon principles universally admitted, is allowed to be its due.

## CHAP. CLXXIX.

BARON DE ASTORGA was eminently skilled in music, and a celebrated composer. Of his history little is known, save that he was a Sicilian by birth, and was at the court of Vienna at the beginning of this century, where he was greatly favoured by the emperor Leopold, from whence it is presumed he went to Spain,* and had that title conferred upon him, which,

* Astorga is a city in the province of Leon in Spain, and a bishop's see.

for want of his family name, is the only known designation of him. He was at Lisbon some time, and after that at Leghorn, where being exceedingly caressed by the English merchants there, he was induced to visit England, and passed a winter or two in London, from whence he went to Bohemia; and at Breslaw, in the year 1726, composed a pastoral entitled Daphne, which was performed there with great applause. He excelled altogether in vocal composition; his cantatas in particular are by the Italians esteemed above all others. He never travelled without a great number of them, and, though very short-sighted, was used to sing them, accompanying himself on the harpsichord. The anonymous author of Remarks on Mr. Avison's Essay on Musical Expression, says that the Cantatas of the Baron d'Astorga have in general too much of that extravagant gusto, which he condemns, at the same time that he celebrates a Stabat Mater of his as a composition to which he says he scarcely ever met with an equal. This hymn, he adds, had lately been performed at Oxford with universal approbation. The Academy of Ancient Music are in possession of it, and it now frequently makes a part of their entertainment on Thursday evenings.

ANTONIO VIVALDI (a Portrait), Maestro de' Concerti del Pio Ospitale della Pieta in Venetia, and Maestro di Capella dà Camera to Philip, landgrave of Hesse Darmstadt, was a celebrated composer for the violin, as also a great master of that instrument. He composed Solos, Sonatas, and Concertos to a great number; but his principal works are his third and eighth operas; the latter of these consists of two books of concertos, entitled 'Il Cimento dell Armonia e dell' Inventione;' but the common name of them is the Seasons. The plan of this work must appear very ridiculous; for the four first concertos are a pretended paraphrase, in musical notes, of so many sonnets on the four seasons, wherein the author endeavours, by the force of harmony, and particular modifications of air and measure, to excite ideas correspondent with the sentiments of the several poems. The subsequent compositions have a similar tendency, but are less restrained; whether it be that the attempt was new and singular, or that these compositions are distinguished for their peculiar force and energy, certain it is that the Opera VIII. is the most applauded of Vivaldi's works. Indeed the peculiar characteristic of Vivaldi's music, speaking of his Concertos—for as to his Solos and Sonatas they are tame enough—is, that it is wild and irregular; and in some instances it seems to have been his study that it should be so; some of his compositions are expressly entitled Extravaganzas, as transgressing the bounds of melody and modulation; as does also that concerto of his in which the notes of the cuckoo's song are frittered into such minute divisions as in the author's time few but himself could express on any instrument whatsoever. From this character of his compositions it will necessarily be inferred that the harmony of them, and the artful contexture of the parts, is their least merit; but against this conclusion there are a few exceptions;

the eleventh of his first twelve Concertos being, in the opinion of the judicious author of Remarks on Mr. Avison's Essay on Musical Expression, a very solid and masterly composition, and an evidence that the author was possessed of a greater degree of skill and learning than his works in general discover. For these his singularities, no better reason can be given than this: Corelli, who lived a few years before him, had introduced a style which all the composers of Italy affected to imitate: as Corelli formed it, it was chaste, sober, and elegant, but with his imitators it degenerated into dulness; this Vivaldi seemed to be aware of, and for the sake of variety, gave into a style which had little but novelty to recommend it.*

The account herein before given of the progress of music in England respects solely this island, where only it had been cultivated as a liberal science. Mention has occasionally been made of the state of music in Wales, in Ireland, and in Scotland; and a particular account has been given of the origin of those melodies which distinguish the music of this latter kingdom from that of every other country. In the principality of Wales, and the kingdom of Ireland, it appears that music derived very little assistance from those precepts which it had been the endeavour of learned and ingenious men to disseminate throughout Europe; the consequence whereof has been, that, submitting to no regulation but the simple dictates of nature, the music of those countries has for many centuries remained the same; and can hardly be said to have received the least degree of improvement.

In Scotland the case has been somewhat different: a manuscript is now extant,† written in the Scottish dialect, entitled 'The art of Music collectit out of 'all ancient Doctouris of Music,' wherein all the modern improvements respecting the composition of music in parts are adopted; and the precepts of Franchinus, Zarlino, and other eminent writers, are enforced by arguments drawn from the principles of the science, and the practice of those countries where it had been first improved, and has continued to flourish in the greatest degree. The study of the mathematics has in these later years been cultivated in Scotland; and at the beginning of this century some faint essays were made in that country towards an investigation of the principles of music: the result of these we are strangers to; but of the success of the pursuit in general we are enabled to form a judgment by means of a learned and valuable work, entitled 'A Treatise of Music, speculative, 'practical, and historical, by ALEXANDER MALCOLM,' printed at Edinburgh in 1721, of which it is here proposed to give an account.

This book contains fourteen chapters, subdivided into sections.

Chap. I. contains an account of the object and end of music, and the nature of the science. In the definition and division of it under this head, the author considers the nature of sound, a word he says that stands for every perception that comes immediately by the ear; and which he explains to be the effect of the mutual collision, and consequent tremulous motions in bodies, communicated to the circumambient fluid of the air, and propagated through it to the organs of hearing. He then enquires into the various affections of sound, so far as they respect music, of which he makes a two-fold division, that is to say, into

I. The knowledge of the Materia Musica.

II. The art of Composition.

Chap. II. treats of tune, or the relation of acuteness and gravity in sounds. The author says that sounds are produced in chords by their vibratory motions, which, though they are not the immediate cause of sound, yet they influence those insensible motions that immediately produce it; and, for any reason we have to doubt of it, are always proportional to them; and therefore he infers that we may measure sounds as justly in these as we could do in the other, if they fell under our measures; but as the sensible vibrations of whole chords cannot be measured in the act of producing sound, the proportions of vibrations of different chords must be sought in another way, that is to say, by chords of different tensions, or grossness, or lengths, being in all other respects equal. And for the effect of these differences he cites Vincentio Galilei, who asserts that there are three ways by which we may make the sound of a chord acuter, viz., by shortening it, by a greater tension, and by making it smaller, cæteris paribus. By shortening it, the ratio of an octave is $1 : 2$; by tension it is $1 : 4$; and by lessening the thickness it is also $1 : 4$; meaning in the last case when the tones are measured by the weights of the chord.

The vibrations of chords in either of the cases above put, in order to ascertain the degrees of acuteness and gravity, are insensible; and being by necessary consequence immeasurable, can only be judged by analogy. In order however to form some conclusion about them, the author cites from Dr. Holder's treatise, the following passage; on which he says the whole theory of his natural grounds and principles of harmony is founded. 'The first 'and great principle upon which the nature of har-'monical sounds is to be found out and discovered 'is this: That the tune of a note (to speak in our 'vulgar phrase) is constituted by the measure and 'proportions of vibrations of the sonorous body; 'I mean of the velocity of these vibrations in their 'recourses; for the frequenter these vibrations are, 'the more acute is the tune: the slower and fewer 'they are in the same space of time, by so much 'more grave is the tune. So that any given note of 'a tune is made by one certain measure of velocity 'of vibrations, viz., such a certain number of courses 'and recourses, e. g. of a chord or string in such 'a certain space of time, doth constitute such a de-'terminate tune.'

* The Opera terza of Vivaldi, containing twelve Concertos for violins, was reprinted in England, and published by Walsh and Hare, with the following title, which is here inserted as a proof of the assertion in page '801 of this work, that they were both illiterate men; 'Vivaldi's most 'celebrated Concertos in all their parts for violins and other instruments, 'with a Thorough-Bass for the Harpsichord, Compos'd by Antonia 'Vivaldi, Opera terza.'

† Penes Authorem.

EFFIGIES ANTONII VIVALDI

Upon this passage Malcolm observes, that though we want experiments to prove that the difference of the numbers of vibrations in a given time is the true cause on the part of the object of our perceiving a difference of tune, yet we find by experience and reason both, that the differences of tunes are inseparably connected with the number of vibrations; and therefore these, or the lengths of chords to which they are proportional, may be taken for the true measure of different tunes.

Chap. III. contains an enquiry into the nature of concord and discord. The several effects of these on the mind are too obvious to need any remark; but the causes of those different sensations of pleasure and distaste severally excited by them, he resolves into the will of God, as other philosophers do the principle of gravitation. Yet upon what he calls the secondary reason of things, arising from the law or rule of that order which the divine wisdom has established, he proceeds to investigate the ratios of the several intervals of the diapason, distinguishing them into concords and discords: and concludes this chapter with a relation of some remarkable phœnomena respecting concord and discord; such as the mutual vibration of consonant strings; the breaking of a drinking-glass by the sound of the human voice adjusted to the tune of it, and gradually encreased to the greatest possible degree of loudness;* and to these, which are the effects of concord, he adds an instance of a different kind, that is to say, of an effect produced by discordant sounds: the relation is taken from Dr. Holder, a person of sound judgment in music, and of unquestionable veracity, and is well worthy of attention.

‘ Being in an arched sounding room near a shrill ‘ bell of a house-clock, when the alarm struck I ‘ whistled to it, which I did with ease in the same ‘ tune with the bell; but endeavouring to whistle ‘ a note higher or lower, the sound of the bell and ‘ its cross motions were so predominant, that my ‘ breath and lips were checked so, that I could not ‘ whistle at all, nor make any sound of it in that ‘ discordant tune. After, I sounded a shrill whistling ‘ pipe, which was out of tune to the bell, and their ‘ motions so clashed that they seemed to sound like ‘ switching one another in the air.’†

Chap. IV. is on the subject of harmonical arithmetic, and contains an explanation of the nature of arithmetical, geometrical, and harmonical proportion, with rules for the addition, subtraction, multiplication, and division of ratios and intervals.

Chap. V. contains the uses and application of the preceding theory, explaining the nature of the original concords, and also of the compound concords.

Chap. VI. explains the geometrical part of music, and the method of dividing right lines, so as their sections or parts one with another, or with the whole, shall contain any given interval of sound.

Chap. VII. treats of harmony, and explains the

nature and variety of it, as it depends upon the various combinations of concording sounds.

Chap. VIII. treats of concinnous intervals, and the scale of music, and herein are shewn the necessity and use of discords, and their original dependence on the concords. Farther it explains the use of degrees in the construction of the scale of music.

Chap. IX. treats of the mode or key in music, and of the office of the scale of music.

Chap. X. treats of the defects of instruments, and of the remedy thereof in general, by the means of sharps and flats.

In order to shew these defects he exhibits in the first place the series of tones and semitones in the Systema Maxima, taking it from C, and extending it to cc, as hereunder given; upon which it is to be observed that the colon between two letters is the sign of a greater tone, 8 : 9; a semicolon the sign of a lesser tone, 9 : 10; and a point the sign of a semitone, 15 : 16; supposing the letters to represent the several notes of an instrument tuned according to the relations marked by those tones and semitones.

C : D ; E . F : G ; A : B . c : d ; e . f : g ; a : b . cc.

Upon which he makes the following observation: ‘ Here we have the diatonick series with the 3d ‘ and 6th greater proceeding from C; and therefore ‘ if only this series is expressed, some songs com- ‘ posed with a flat melody, i. e. whose key has a ‘ lesser 3d, &c. could not be performed on the organ ‘ or harpsichord, because no one of the octaves of ‘ this series has all the natural intervals of the ‘ diatonick series, with a 3d lesser.’

To remedy these and other defects of instruments whose intervals depend not upon the will of the performer, but are determined by the tuning, he says a scale of semitones was invented, which he exhibits in this form :—

c.  c♯.  d.  d♯.  e.  f.  f♯.  g.  g♯.  a.  b.  ♮.  cc.

$\frac{15}{16}$  $\frac{128}{135}$  $\frac{15}{16}$  $\frac{24}{25}$  $\frac{15}{16}$  $\frac{128}{135}$  $\frac{15}{16}$  $\frac{15}{16}$  $\frac{24}{25}$  $\frac{15}{16}$  $\frac{128}{135}$  $\frac{15}{16}$

And upon it he observes that it contains the diatonic series in the key C, with both the greater and lesser third, with their accompaniments in all their just proportions; and that it corrects the errors of the tritone between F and ♮, and the defective fifth between ♮ and F.

This division corresponds in theory with the Systema Participato mentioned by Bontempi, and spoken of in page 415, and elsewhere in the course of this work.

Malcolm also gives a second division of the octave into semitones in the following form :—

c.  c♯.  d.  d♯.  e.  f.  f♯.  g.  g♯.  a.  b.  ♮.  cc.

$\frac{16}{17}$  $\frac{17}{18}$  $\frac{18}{19}$  $\frac{19}{20}$  $\frac{15}{16}$  $\frac{16}{17}$  $\frac{17}{18}$  $\frac{18}{19}$  $\frac{19}{20}$  $\frac{16}{17}$  $\frac{17}{18}$  $\frac{15}{16}$

being that invented by Mr. Thomas Salmon, and inserted in the Philosophical Transactions; upon which Malcolm observes, that having calculated the ratios thereof, he found more of them false than in the preceding scale, but that their errors were

---

* It is said that Mr. Francis Hughes, a gentleman of the royal chapel in the reign of king George I. who had a very strong counter-tenor voice, could with ease break a drinking-glass in this manner.

† Treatise of the Natural Grounds and Principles of Harmony, page 34.

considerably fewer; so that upon the whole the merits of both seem to be nearly equal.

This chapter of Malcolm's book contains many curious observations upon the necessity of a temperature, arising from that surd quantity, which for many centuries, even from the time of Boetius, it has been the study of musicians to dispose of. The author concludes with a general approbation of the semitonic division, and of the present practice in tuning the organ and harpsichord, corresponding as nearly to it as the judgment of the ear will enable men. As to the pretences of the nicer kind of musicians, he demonstrates that they tend to introduce more errors than those under which the present system labours.

Chap. XI. describes the method and art of writing music, and shews how the differences in tune are represented. Under this head the author explains the nature and use of the cliffs; as also the nature of transposition, both by a change of the cliff and of the key or mode. He also explains the practice of solmisation, and makes some remarks on the names of notes. Lastly he enters into an examination of Salmon's proposal for reducing all music to one cliff, as delivered in his Essay to the Advancement of Music. This proposal Malcolm not only approves of, but expresses himself with no little acrimony against that ignorance and superstition which haunts little minds, and the pride and vanity of the possessors of the art; all which he says have concurred in the rejection of so beneficial an invention.

Chap. XII. treats of the time or duration of sounds in music, and herein, 1. Of time in general, and its subdivision into absolute and relative; and particularly of the names, signs, and proportions in relative measures of notes as to time. 2. Of absolute time, and the various modes or constitution of parts of a piece of melody, on which the different airs in music depend; and particularly of the distinction of common and triple time; and the description of the Chronometer for measuring it. 3. Concerning rests and pauses of time, with some other necessary remarks in writing music.

The Chronometer mentioned in this chapter is an invention of Mons. Loulie, a French musician, and is described in the account herein before given of him, and of a book of his writing, entitled 'Elemens ou Principes de Musique.'

Chap. XIII. contains the general rules and principles of harmonic composition.

The whole of this chapter, as Malcolm acknowledges in the introduction to his work, was communicated to him by a friend, whom he is forbidden to name. The rules are such as are to be found in almost every book on the subject of musical composition.

The account given in Chap. XIV. of the ancient music, is, considering the brevity of it, very entertaining and satisfactory. Speaking of the tones or modes, he says there are four different senses in which the term is accepted, that is to say, it is used to signify, 1. A single sound, as when we say the lyre had seven tones. 2. A certain interval, as for example, the difference between the diatessaron and diapente. 3. The tension of the voice, as when we say one sings with an acute or a grave voice.* 4. A certain system, as when they say the Doric or Lydian mode or tone.

In the consideration of this latter sense of the word Mode, he observes that Boetius has given a very ambiguous definition of the term; for, to give the remark in his own words, Malcolm says he first tells us 'that the modes depend on the seven 'different species of the diapason, which are also 'called Tropi; and these, says he, are 'Con-'stitutiones in totis vocum ordinibus vel gravitate 'vel acumine differentes.' Again he says, 'Con-'stitutio est plenum veluti modulationis corpus, ex 'consonantiarum conjunctione consistens, quale est 'Diapason, &c. Has igitur constitutiones, si quis 'totas faciat acutiores, vel in gravius totas remittat 'secundum supradictas Diapason consonantiæ species, 'efficiet modes septem.' This is indeed a very 'ambiguous determination, for if they depend on 'the species of 8ves, to what purpose is the last 'clause? and if they differ only by the tenor or 'place of the whole 8ve, i. e. as it is taken at a 'higher or lower pitch, what need the species of '8ves be at all brought in? His meaning perhaps 'is only to signify that the different orders or 'species of 8ves lie in different places, i. e. higher 'and lower in the scale. Ptolemy makes them the 'same with the species of diapason; but at the 'same time he speaks of their being at certain 'distances from one another.'

Upon this seeming ambiguity it may be remarked, that the two definitions of a mode or tone above cited from Boetius, are reconcileable with each other; for the proof whereof we refer to a dissertation on this subject by Sir Francis Haskins Eyles Stiles, published in the Philosophical Transactions, vol. LI. part ii. for the year 1760, and abridged in book II. chap. 11, 12, of this work.

In a short history of the improvements in music, which makes part of the fourteenth chapter, the author takes particular notice of the reformation of the ancient scale by Guido, and adopts the sentiments of some very ingenious man, who scruples not to say of his contrivance of six syllables to denote the position of the two semitones in the diatonic series of an octave, that it is 'Crux tenellorum ingeniorum.'†

In the comparison between the ancient and modern music, contained in this chapter, this author says that the latter has the preference; and upon that controverted question, whether the ancients were acquainted with music in consonance or not, he cites

---

* Acuteness and gravity are affections of sound: and note of tone, that both the grave and acute pipes of any given stop in an organ, the vox humana and cornet, for instance, have, comparing pipe with pipe, the same tone, or rather that peculiarity of sound which distinguishes the voice of one person from another, or the sound of the cornet from another instrument.

† This censure is grounded on the opinion of some very ingenious man, whom Malcolm has not thought fit to name, and probably never heard of. Great pains have been taken to find out the author of it, but to no purpose. All that can be said of it is, that it occurs in Brossard's Dictionaire de Musique, voce SYSTEME, as the sentiment of an illustrious writer of the last age. Dr. Pepusch has given it an answer in his Treatise of Harmony, edit. 1731, page 70.

a variety of passages from Aristotle, Seneca, and Cassiodorus, to the purpose, and scruples not to determine in the negative.

From this general view of its contents, it must appear that the work above mentioned is replete with musical erudition. Extensive as the subject is, the author has contrived to bring under consideration all the essential parts of the science. His knowledge of the mathematics has enabled him to discuss, with great clearness and perspicuity, the doctrine of ratios, and other abstract speculations, in the language of a philosopher and a scholar. In a word, it is a work from which a student may derive great advantage, and may be justly deemed one of the most valuable treatises on the subject of theoretical and practical music to be found in any of the modern languages.

## CHAP. CLXXX.

John Francis De La Fond, a singing-master, and a teacher of the principal instruments, and also of the Latin and French tongues, published in 1725, at London, an octavo volume, entitled 'A new 'System of Music both theoretical and practical, 'and yet not mathematical,' wherein he undertakes to make the practice of music easier by three quarters, and to teach a new and easier method than any yet known of figuring and playing thorough, or, as he affects to call it, compound bass.

The first of these ends he attempts to effect by an indiscriminate charge of folly and absurdity on all that had written on music before him, and an assertion that mathematics have little or nothing to do with music; the second by an argument tending to prove, what no one ever yet denied, to wit, that in the semitonic scale, which divides the octave into tones and semitones, there are twelve intervals. His proposition of teaching thorough-bass consists not in the rejection of the figures with which it is necessarily encumbered, but in the assigning to them severally, powers different from what they now possess; it is conceived in the following terms: 'Nature teaches us to call the first or unison, the 'unison; the flat 2nd the 2nd; the sharp 2nd the '3rd, the flat 3rd the 4th; the sharp third the 5th, 'the 4th the 6th, the flat 5th the 7th, the natural '5th the 8th, the sharp 5th or flat 6th the 9th, the 'sharp 6th the 10th, the flat 7th the 11th, the sharp '7th the 12th; the 8th, which according to their 'notions should be either natural, flat, or sharp, or 'sometimes one of them, and sometimes another; 'the 8th I say is the 13th, the flat 9th the 14th, 'and the sharp 9th the 15th, all which I mark thus, '1, 2, 3, 4, 5, 6, 7, 8, 9, o, u, d, t, q, Q, using 'letters for the five last, not only for the sake of 'keeping to one figure only, but because those letters 'are the initials of the proper names of those con- 'cords; and I make the last a capital, to distinguish 'it from the last but one. The concords I think 'proper to call by the Latin names, as being more 'musical than the English ones. And these terms 'I write here at length for the sake of the Non- 'Latinists; Unison or Prime, Second, Terce, Quart,

'Quint, Sexte, Septime, Octave, None, Decime, 'Undecime, Duodecime, Tredecime, Quatuordecime, 'and Quindecime. Nor can this be thought a great 'innovation, for three of those names are received 'already.

'All these denominations are plain, self-consistent, 'and free from the very shadow of ambiguity. The 'scholar, counting his concords from the bass note, 'as is now done, and minding his plain figures, 'without troubling himself about the naturalness, 'flatness, or sharpness of any note, will at once find 'all his concords, let the mode be soft or gay, or 'the piece run over all their flats and sharps.'*

To illustrate this whimsical scheme of notation, the author gives an example in the sixth Sonata of the fourth opera of Corelli, figured according to the above directions.

Another improvement of music suggested by this author, and which he means to refer to the first head, of an easier practice, is the rejection of the cliffs, for which innovation the following is his modest apology:—'At my first setting out, I have 'complained of a veil that has for many ages hung 'before the noble science of music. This complaint 'I have repeated since; but this is the place where 'it ought to be repeated with the most passionate 'tone. For indeed the business of clefs is the thickest 'part of that thick veil. This veil, or rather this 'worst part of it, is so much the more intolerable, 'as it seems to have been wilfully made. We have 'seen that the authors of the seven pretended notes, '&c. have probably been misled into that absurd 'notion by their idle remark that the voice naturally 'sings eight notes. But I think it impossible to 'assign any cause of mistake in the introducing of 'the clefs into the tablature.'† His proposal for getting rid of the cliffs is in truth a notable one, and is nothing more than that we should suppose the three parts of a musical composition to be comprehended within the compass of one cliff, viz., the treble, in which case, to use his own words, 'I call 'the note upon the second line G, (as it is now 'called in the trebles) not only in the treble, but 'likewise in the tenor and the bass * * * In short, 'I reduce both the tenor and the bass to the treble, 'because there are a great many more trebles played 'than there are tenors and basses, both put together.'‡

With regard to his system, as he calls it, so far as it tends to establish a division of the octave into twelve notes, omitting the blunder of notes for intervals,§ it is not his own, but is the systema participato, mentioned by Bontempi, explained in the foregoing part of this work, and referred to at the bottom of the page. His method of figuring thorough-bass is less intelligible than that now in use; and as to his proposal for rejecting the cliffs,

* Page 113, et seq.

† Page 40. The Tablature is that method of notation in which the sounds are signified by the letters of the alphabet, and not by the musical notes: here the author substituted the term in the place of the word Scale, and adds one instance more to the many others that occur in his book, of his ignorance of the subject he is writing on.

‡ The Systema participato, or semitonic scale, divides the octave into thirteen sounds or notes, comprehending twelve intervals of a semitone each. See page 401 of this work, in note, 415, in note, 455, in note.

§ Page 146.

there is no end to the confusion which it has a tendency to introduce; nor can any one without the cliffs be capable of understanding the nature and office of the scale of music. And, after all, the arguments urged in favour of these several innovations, are none of them of weight sufficient to justify them, seeing, that with all the difficulties imputed to it, the modern system of notation is a language that we find by experience

'Girls may read, and boys may understand.' POPE.

But allowing it to be otherwise, it might admit of a question what would be gained by an innovation that would render the compositions of all former musicians as generally unintelligible as is at this day a Saxon manuscript.

To enumerate all the arrogant assertions in favour of his own notions, and the contemptuous expressions with respect to the discoveries and improvements of others, that occur in the course of this work, would be in effect to transcribe the whole of a book now deservedly consigned to oblivion.

In the year 1724, the lovers of music were gratified with a work, the only one of the kind, and which, for the circumstances attending it, may be considered as the grandest and most splendid of any musical publication at this day extant; the title of it, to give it at length, is as follows: 'Estro 'poetico-armonico Parafrasi sopra li primi venti-'cinque Salmi. Poesia di Girolamo Ascanio Gius-'tiniani, Musica di Benedetto Marcello, Patrizi 'Veneti.' This work, consisting of no fewer than eight volumes in folio, has the recommendation of some of the most eminent musicians of the time in all the several countries of Europe; and these accompany not only the first, but each of the several volumes, in such sort, that it appears to have been the occasion of a correspondence, in which some of the most eminent poets and musicians were engaged, ultimately tending to celebrate the work and its author. The letters that passed on this occasion, and are prefixed to the several volumes, abound with a variety of curious particulars respecting music, and have the signatures of the following persons, viz., Domenico Lazzarini, Francesco Gasparini, Antonio Bononcini, Francesco Conti, Francesco Rosellini, Carlo Baliani, Francesca-Antonio Calegari, Giovanni Bononcini, Tommaso Carapella, Domenico Sarri, John Mattheson, Steffano Andrea Fiorè, Giuseppe Bencini, Geminiani Jacomelli, and George Philip Telemann. Thus much must serve for a general character of the work, a particular account of it is referred to a memoir of the author, which it is here proposed to give.

BENEDETTO MARCELLO, a noble Venetian, was born on the twenty-fourth day of July, 1686. His father, Agostino Marcello, was a senator of Venice; his mother, Paolino, was of the honourable family of Cappello, being the daughter of Girolamo Cappello, and the aunt of Pietro Andrea Cappello, ambassador from the state of Venice to the court of Spain, Vienna, and Rome, and who also was resident in England in that capacity about the year 1743, and afterwards.

The male issue of these two persons were Alessandro, a son next to him whose Christian name is unknown, and the above mentioned Benedetto Marcello. The elder of them addicted himself to the study of natural philosophy and the mathematical sciences, as also music, in which he attained to great proficiency; his younger brother Benedetto had been well instructed in classical literature, and having gone through a regular course of education under proper masters, was committed to the tuition of his elder brother, and by him taken into his house, with a view to his farther improvement in philosophy and the liberal arts.

Alessandro Marcello dwelt at Venice; he had a musical academy in his house, holden regularly on a certain day in every week, in which were frequently performed his own compositions. Being a man of rank, and eminent for his great endowments, his house was the resort of all strangers that came to visit the city. It happened at a certain time that the princes of Brunswic were there, who being invited to a musical performance in the academy above mentioned, took particular notice of Benedetto, at that time very young, and among other questions, asked him, in the hearing of his brother, what were the studies that most engaged his attention; 'O,' said his brother, 'he is a very 'useful little fellow to me, for he fetches my books 'and papers; the fittest employment for such a one 'as he is.' The boy was nettled at this answer, which reflected as much upon his supposed want of genius, as his youth, he therefore resolved to apply himself to music and poetry; which his brother seeing, committed him to the care of Francesco Gasparini, to be instructed in the principles of music;* for poetry he had other assistances, and at length became a great proficient in both arts.

In the year 1716, the birth of the first son of the emperor Charles VI. was celebrated at Vienna with great magnificence; and upon this occasion a Serenata, composed by Benedetto Marcello, was performed there with great applause. In the year 1718, he published a little collection of Sonnets under the title of 'Driante, Sacreo Pastor Arcade,' which he dedicated to the celebrated Giovanni Mario Crescimbeni of Macerata, by his assumed name of Alfesibeo Cario, one of the founders of the Academy of Arcadians, into which Benedetto, from his great reputation, had been some time before elected.†

In the year 1722, he published an elegant little work, intitled 'Teatro alla moda,' of which there have been many editions. The judgment which the Marquis Scipio Maffei has given of this excellent performance, which is in the gay, lively, and facetious style, may be seen in the third volume of his Literary Observations, page 308, of the Verona edition, printed in 1738, and in the letters of Apostolo Zeno, both of them to the honour of the author.

Benedetto Marcello also published a collection of

* See a letter of this person prefixed to the first volume of Marcello's Psalms, wherein he mentions that Marcello prosecuted his studies under him.

† Vide Le Vite degli Arcade Illustri, in the Istoria della Volgar Poesia of Crescimbeni, printed at Venice in 1730, vol. VI. page 378.

Sonnets intitled 'Sonetti a Dio,' with various other compositions on sacred subjects, of which there were two numerous impressions in a short time. This work he published as a forerunner of a greater, which he did not live to finish. To prepare himself for this learned and sublime undertaking, he employed some years in the study of theology and the holy fathers.

As to his musical compositions, they were many and various; two Cantatas of his, the one intitled 'Il Timoteo,' the other 'La Cassandra,' are celebrated by Signor Abbate Conti, in a letter to Girolamo Ascanio Giustiniani, to this effect: 'Dryden, 'a celebrated English poet, in an ode for music in-'troduces Timotheus, who singing to Alexander, one 'while of wars and victories, another of tenderness 'and love; then of the slain in battle, and their 'ghosts, and of other subjects which move terror or 'pity, raises in him by turns all the softest and most 'furious passions. I was so pleased with the new-'ness of this thought, that so long ago as when 'I was in France, I translated the ode out of English 'into Italian verse, changing the lyric form of the 'poem into the dramatic, by introducing the chorus 'and two persons, one of whom explains the subject 'of the song, the other is Timotheus himself, who 'sings. Benedetto Marcello being pleased with the 'poem, set it to music in the form of a Cantata, dis-'playing therein the fruitfulness, and at the same 'time the depth of his art. Afterwards he desired 'to have the whole variety of passions expressed in 'Timotheus, brought into a poem by means of some 'other fable or story, in which one person only should 'speak; and recollecting that first Euripides, and 'afterwards Lycophron, had introduced Cassandra to 'foretell the misfortunes that should befall, in the 'one case the Greeks, in the other the Trojans, 'I undertook to imitate them; and to give magnifi-'cence and beauty to the imaginations of poetry, 'I put into the mouth of Cassandra, in the form of 'a prophecy, the most remarkable events celebrated 'by Homer in the Iliad. Marcello was pleased with 'the invention, and adorned it with all those colours 'of harmony which are most interesting, surprising, 'and delightful; and I think I say everything when 'I compare the music of the Cassandra, making due 'allowance for the deficiency of the subject, to that 'of the Psalms paraphrased by your excellence, and 'sung with so much applause at Venice, Vienna, 'and Padua.'

Marcello made also a composition for a mass, which is highly celebrated, and was performed for the first time in the church of Santa Maria della Celestia, on occasion of Donna Alessandra Maria Marcello, his brother's daughter, taking the veil in that monastery. He also set to music the Lamentations of Jeremiah, the Miserere, and the Salve: these, with many other sacred compositions, he gave to the clergy of the church of Santa Sophia, and was at the pains of in-structing them in the manner in which they were to be performed.

For many years Marcello was a constant member of a musical academy held at the house of Agostino Coletti, organist of the church of the Holy Apostles, in which he always sat at the harpsichord; and by his authority, which every one acquiesced in, directed and regulated the whole performance.

In the year 1724 came out the first four volumes of the Paraphrase of the Psalms by Giustiniani, in Italian, set to music for one, two, and three voices, by Benedetto Marcello; and in the two subsequent years four more, including in the whole the first fifty of the Psalms. Before the work is a prefatory ad-dress of the poet and the musical composer, explaining the nature and tendency of the work, wherein they observe that it is the first of its kind, and is intro-duced into the world without the advantage of any precedent that might have directed the method and disposition of it. Of the Paraphrase they say, that, although embellished with the ornaments of poetry, it is rather literal than allegorical; and that where the poet has ventured to dilate upon the text, he has followed those interpreters, who have most closely adhered to the letter. Farther, it is said that the verse is without rhyme, and of various metres; in which latter respect it corresponds with that of the Psalms as they stand in the Hebrew text, to which, notwithstanding that the Paraphrase is chiefly founded on the Vulgate translation, as also to the Septuagint version, the poet has in some instances had recourse.

In what regards the music, we must suppose the preface to speak the sentiments of Marcello himself. And herein he observes, that as the subject requires that the words and sentiments be clearly and pro-perly expressed, the music for the most part is composed for two voices only. It was, he says, for this reason, and to move the passions and affections the more forcibly, that the music of the ancients, as namely the Hebrews, the Phœnicians, and Greeks, was altogether unisonous; but in these our days, and now that our ears are accustomed to the harmony of many parts, an attempt to approach too nearly to the happy and simple melody of the ancients, might prove no less difficult than dangerous. It was therefore, he says, judged not improper to compose these Psalms, as he had done, for two, and sometimes for three and four parts; but, after all, the author confesses that this kind of composition, which is ra-ther to be called an ingenious counterpoint, than natural melody, is more likely to please the learned reader, who peruses it in writing, than the ordinary hearer; as well by reason of the perpetual conflict of fugues and imitations in the different parts, as from the multiplicity of mixed consonances which accom-pany them, in order to fill and complete the chorus; and which in fact are not real consonances, according to the undeniable geometric and arithmetic experi-ments of the ancient Greek philosophers, who in the investigation of what is to be admired in this science, have discovered great skill.

On the other hand this author remarks, that during a long series of years, new laws have been given both to the theory and practice of music, to which it is necessary to render obedience.

From this observation the author digresses to the

music of the ancient Greeks, which he commends for its simplicity ; ascribing to it more power to affect the passions than that of the moderns with all its laboured and artificial ornaments. For this, as also for other reasons, Marcello professes that in his work he has not always affected the modern style, though he would not take upon him to reform it ; yet he owns that he has sometimes transgressed against the rules of it, in order to attain to the true simplicity and manly gravity which characterizes that of the ancients.

After lamenting the debasement of music, by its association with vain and trivial poetry ; and the abuse of the science, not only in the theatre, but in places of sacred worship, the author professes that his design is to restore it to its primitive dignity. And that to that end he has chosen for his subject the Psalms of David, which, though by him composed for the most part for two voices, he says may and ought to be sung by a great number, agreeably to the practice recorded in the holy scriptures, which speak of psalms and hymns sung by many companies or chorusses.

He gives his reader to understand that he has introduced in the course of his work several of the most ancient and best known intonations of the Hebrews, which are still sung by the Jews, and are a species of music peculiar to that people. These, which for want of a better word, we are necessitated to call Chants, he says he has sometimes accompanied according to the artificial practice of the moderns, as he has done by certain Cantilenas of the ancient Greeks ; the latter, he says, he has interpreted with the utmost diligence ; and, by the help of those two ancient philosophers, Alypius and Gaudentius, has reduced them to modern practice.

To those mysterious and emphatic sentences, in which the royal prophet has denounced the terrors of divine justice, he says he has thought it not inexpedient to adapt a peculiar kind of music, that is to say, a modulation in the Madrigalesc style, with a commixture of the diatonic and chromatic genera. And in this respect he compares his present labours to those of a pilot, who in a wide and tempestuous ocean avails himself of every wind that may conduct him to his port, yet in a long and dangerous voyage is constrained to vary his course.

A few brief directions for the performance of the several compositions, and a modest apology for the defects in the work, conclude this preface, which, though written under the influence of strong prejudices, is an ingenious and learned dissertation on the subjects of poetry and music.

In the year 1726 this great work was completed by the publication of four volumes more, containing a paraphrase of the second twenty-five psalms ; and as an evidence of the author's skill in that kind of composition, in which some of the most eminent musicians have endeavoured to excel, viz., Canon, he has, at the end of the last volume, given one of a very elaborate contexture.

For the character of this work we must refer to the letters and testimonies of those eminent musicians and other persons above named, who have joined in the recommendation of it in their several addresses to the author. Mattheson of Hamburg, in a letter to him, prefixed to the sixth volume, says that the music to some of the Psalms had been adapted to words in the German language, and had been performed with great applause in the cathedral of that city. And we are farther told, that for the satisfaction of hearing these compositions, the Russians had made a translation of the Italian paraphrase into their own language, associating to it the original music of Marcello,* and that some sheets of the work had been transmitted to the author in his lifetime. At Rome these compositions were held in the highest estimation by all who professed either to understand or love music : at the palace of Cardinal Ottoboni was a musical academy holden on Monday in every week, in which Corelli performed ; at this musical assembly one of the psalms of Marcello made constantly a part of the entertainment ; and for the purpose of performing them there, the author composed to them instrumental parts.† When the news of Marcello's death arrived at Rome, his eminence, as a public testimony of affection for his memory, ordered that on a day appointed for the usual assembly, there should be a solemn musical performance. The room was hung with black ; the performers and all present were in deep mourning ; Father Santo Canal, a Jesuit, made the oration ; and the most eminent of the learned of that time rehearsed their respective compositions upon the occasion in various languages, in the presence of the many considerable personages there assembled. Nor has this country been wanting in respect for the abilities of this great man ; Mr. Charles Avison, organist in Newcastle, had celebrated this work in an Essay on Musical Expression, and had given out proposals for publishing by subscription an edition of it revised by himself ; but it seems that the execution of this design devolved to another person, Mr. John Garth, of Durham, who was at the pains of adapting to the music of Marcello suitable words from our own prose translation of the Psalms, with a view to their being performed as anthems in cathedrals ; and with the assistance of a numerous subscription, the work was completed and published in eight folio volumes.

From the foregoing account of his studies and pursuits it might be supposed that Marcello had wholly devoted himself to a life of ease and retirement ; but in this opinion it seems we should be mistaken, for we find that he held several honourable posts in the state, and as a magistrate was ever ready to contribute his share of attention and labour towards the support of that government under which he lived. He was for many years a judge in one of the councils of forty : from thence he was removed to the charge of Proveditor of Pola. Afterwards he was appointed to the office of chamberlain or treasurer of the city of Brescia, where he gained the affection and esteem of all orders of men, and, above

---

* Life of Marcello prefixed to the English Psalms adapted to the music of Marcello.

† A copy of these was in the collection of the late Mr. Smith, the English consul at Venice, and was sold as part of his library by Messieurs Baker and Leigh, booksellers, in York street, Covent-Garden.

all, of his eminence Cardinal Quirini, who encouraged frequent visits from him in the most familiar manner; and had once a week a literary conference with him.

Marcello died at Brescia in the year 1739. He was buried in the church of the fathers, Minor Observants of St. Joseph of Brescia, with a degree of funeral pomp suited to his rank. On his tombstone of marble, in the middle of the church, is engraved the following inscription :—

BENEDICTO MARCELLO PATRITIO VENETO
SAPIENTISSIMO PHILOLOGO POETÆ MUSICES PRINCIPI
QUESTORI BRIXIENSI UXOR MOESTISSIMA
POSUIT
ANNO MDCCXXXIX VIII KALENDAS AUGUSTI
VIXIT ANNOS LII MENSES XI DIES XXVIII.

While he was at Brescia he wrote a very elegant poem, which he entitled Volo Pindarico Eroi-comico, in which, feigning himself to be carried with a sudden flight to the coffee-house in the square of St. Felice at Venice, which he used to frequent, to meet the many friends he had there, he describes, in a pleasing and lively strain of humour, the peculiar manners and characters of them severally; and then gives them the like information of his own way of life at Brescia, and of the most respectable of those persons whose friendship he there enjoyed.

He left in manuscript some admonitions in prose to his nephew, Lorenzo Alessandro, a son of his brother Alessandro, a young man of great genius and learning: these consist of counsels and precepts that bespeak as well the piety as the wisdom of their author; twenty-five cantos of the poem above-mentioned; a treatise of proportions; another of the musical system; another of the harmonical concords; and a great number of poetical compositions, the manuscripts whereof are in the possession of his above-mentioned nephew.

Of the noble family of Marcello mention is made by all the historians of Venice, and in the oldest chronicles in manuscript. Battista Nani celebrates Lorenzo Marcello, captain of the Venetian Galleasses, who in an engagement at sea, with the fleet of Amurath IV. had his arm broken, and was afterwards by the senate raised to a post of great honour. Among the moderns Casimire, Frescoth, Bruzen, La Martiniere, in his Geographical Dictionary, under the article Venice; and Marco Foscarini, in his excellent treatise of the Italian literature, speak of this family in terms of the greatest respect.

To the foregoing account of the works of Marcello may be added from the Dutch catalogues, VI. Sonate a violoncello solo e basso continuo, opera prima. XII. Sonate a flauto solo e basso continuo, opera seconda; and VI. Sonate a tre, due violoncelli o due viole da gamba, e violoncello o basso continuo, called opera seconda.

Mr Avison, as well in certain remarks on the Psalms of Marcello, prefixed to the English version adapted to his music, as in the proposals for the publication thereof, printed at the end of the second edition of his Essay on Musical Expression, has represented this work as a most perfect exemplar of the grand, the beautiful, and the pathetic in music; with sundry other epithets, not less proper, as applied to music, than fanciful: notwithstanding which, and the numerous testimonies of authors, that accompany the original work, there have not been wanting in this country men of sober judgment, and of great eminence for skill in the science of practical composition, who object to the Psalms of Marcello, that the levity of these compositions in general renders the work a fitter entertainment for the chamber, than an exercise for church service.* That they abound in the evidences of a fertile invention, improved to a high degree by study, all must allow; but whoever shall contemplate that style in music, which in the purest ages has been looked upon as the best adapted to excite devout affections, and understands what in musical speech is meant by the epithets, sublime and pathetic, will be apt to entertain a doubt whether these can with greater propriety be applied to them than to many less celebrated compositions.

The following specimen of Marcello's style is selected from the forty-second of his Psalms :—

DAL Tri-bunal' au-gusto, o-ve tu sie - di O . . di gius-ti - zia Fon-te, O Fonte

di cle-men-za l'al-to giu-di - zio as-pet - - - to l'al-to giu-di-zio aspet-to,

dal Tri-bunal' au-gusto o - ve tu sie - di O . . di gius-ti - zia Fonte, O Fonte di cle-menza

* See Remarks on Mr. Avison's Essay on Musical Expression, Lond. 1743, pag. 113, et seq. The author of these Remarks, in proof of his assertion, has referred to the eighth of Marcello's Psalms, than which a more injudicious association of sound and sentiment can hardly be found: in this poem the psalmist celebrates the power and goodness of God, as manifested in his works of creation and providence; and to one of the most sublime sentiments contained in it, the musical composer has adapted an air in minuet time, the lightest that can be conceived. This psalm, which as it stands in the English version, begins, ' O Lord our governor, how excellent is thy name in all the world!' is now frequently sung as an anthem; and there are persons that will give a boy half a guinea to sing it, who can scarce lend their attention to Gibbons's ' Hosanna,' or Purcell's ' O give thanks.'

l'alto giu-di-zio as - pet - - to, l'alto giu-di-zio l'alto, giu-di-zio aspet - to, Di

la la mia ra-gion d'u-dir-ti de - gna, e si decida al-fin e si de-cida al fin la cau - sa mi -

- a e si decida al - fiin e si decida al - fin la cau - sa mi - a

Largo.

Da un Po-po - lo che a te non fu non . fu mai sacro, per pie-tà, per pie-tà mi di-fen - - -

Allegro.

- di, e dagl'inganni i-niqui e dal-le frodi di quel che lo governa in-giusto Rege fa, che dis-ciolto che disciol - -

Allegro.

- - to fa, che dis - ciolto che disciol - - to fa, che dis - ciol - - -

- - - - - to t. a . . merce-de tua merce-de io res - - ti fa che dis -

- - ciol - - - - - - - - to tua . . mercede tua mercede io res - -

- - ti fa che disciol-to, che dis-ciolto tua merce-de io io res - ti.

BENEDETTO MARCELLO.

J. Jenkins pinxit. C. Grignion sculp.

FRANCESCO GEMINIANI.

## CHAP. CLXXXI.

FRANCESCO GEMINIANI *(a Portrait)*, a native of Lucca, was born about the year 1680. He received his first instructions in music from Alessandro Scarlatti, and after that became a pupil of Carlo Ambrosio Lunati, surnamed Il Gobbo,* a most celebrated performer on the violin; after which he became a disciple of Corelli, and under him finished his studies on that instrument.

In the year 1714 he came to England, where in a short time he so recommended himself by his exquisite performance, that all who professed to understand or love music, were captivated at the hearing him; and among the nobility were many who severally laid claim to the honour of being his patrons; but the person to whom he seemed the most closely to attach himself was the Baron Kilmansegge, chamberlain to king George I. as elector of Hanover, and a favourite of that prince. In the year 1716 he published and dedicated to that nobleman twelve Sonatas, a Violino Violone e Cembalo: the first six with fugues and double stops, as they are vulgarly called; the last with airs of various measures, such as Allemandes, Courants, and Jigs.

The publication of this work had such an effect, that men were at a loss to determine which was the greatest excellence of Geminiani, his performance or his skill and fine style in composition; and, with a due attention to his interest, there is no saying to what degree he might have availed himself of that favour, which his merits had found in this country: this at least is certain, that the publication of his book impressed his patron with such a sense of his abilities, as moved him to endeavour to procure for him a more beneficial patronage than his own; to this end he mentioned Geminiani to the king as an exquisite performer, and the author of a work, which at the same time he produced, and the king had no sooner looked over, than he expressed a desire to hear some of the compositions contained in it performed by the author. The baron immediately communicated the king's pleasure to Geminiani, who, though he was gladly disposed to obey such a command, intimated to the Baron a wish that he might be accompanied on the harpsichord by Mr. Handel, which being signified to the king, both masters had notice to attend at St. James's, and Geminiani acquitted himself in a manner worthy of the expectations that had been formed of him.

It is much to be doubted whether the talents of Geminiani were of such a kind as qualified him to give a direction to the national taste; his compositions, elegant and ornate as they were, carried in them no evidences of that extensive genius which is required in dramatic music; nor did he make the least effort to show that he was possessed of the talent of associating music with poetry, or of adapting corresponding sounds to sentiments: the consequence hereof was, that he was necessitated to rely on the patronage of his friends among the nobility,

Vide ante, page 808.

and to depend for subsistence upon presents, and the profits which accrued to him by teaching, upon terms which himself was permitted to make.

A situation like this must appear little better than humiliating, to one that considers the ease and affluence, and, comparatively speaking, independent situation of Corelli, who through his whole life seems to have enjoyed the blessings of ease, affluence, and fame. Corelli for some years led the orchestra in the opera at Rome; we find not that Geminiani occupied a similar situation at London, nor that he was at any time of his life a public performer: it may therefore be a wonder what were his means of subsistence during his long stay in this country. All that can be said to this purpose is, that he had very many bountiful patrons and pupils, as many in number as he could possibly attend.

The relation between the arts of music and painting is so near, that in numberless instances, those who have excelled in one have been admirers of the other. Geminiani was an enthusiast in painting, and the versatility of his temper was such, that, to gratify this passion, he not only suspended his studies, and neglected the exercise of his talents, but involved himself in straits and difficulties, which a small degree of prudence would have taught him to avoid. To gratify his taste, he bought pictures; and, to supply his wants, he sold them; the necessary consequence of this kind of traffic was loss, and its concomitant, necessity.

In the distress, which by this imprudent conduct he had brought on himself, Geminiani was necessitated, for the security of his person, to avail himself of that protection which the nobility of this country have power to extend in favour of their servants. The late earl of Essex was a lover of music, and had been taught the violin by Geminiani, who at times had been resident in his lordship's family; upon this ground the earl was prevailed on to inroll the name of Geminiani in the list of those servants of his whom he meant to screen from the process of the law.

The notification of the security which Geminiani had thus obtained was not so general as to answer the design of it. A creditor for a small sum of money arrested him, and threw him into the prison of the Marshalsea, from whence, upon an application to his protector, he was, however, in a very short time discharged.[†]

A series of conduct such as that of Geminiani was, the neglecting the improvement of those advantages which would have resulted from his great abilities in his profession; his contracting of debts, and neglect in payment of them, seem to indicate as well a want of principle as discretion: nevertheless that he was in an eminent degree possessed of the former, will appear from the following anecdote.

The place of master and composer of the state music in Ireland had been occupied for several years

† Immediately upon his confinement he sent, by one Forest, an attorney, a letter to a gentleman in lord Essex's family, who, upon shewing it to his lordship, was directed to go to the prison and claim Geminiani as the servant of the earl of Essex, which he did, and the prisoner was accordingly discharged. This fact, together with many others abovementioned, was communicated by the person to whom the letter was sent.

by John Sigismund Cousser, a German musician of great eminence, who will be spoken of hereafter. This person died in the year 1727; and notice of his decease coming to the earl of Essex, he, by means of lord Percival, obtained of the minister, Sir Robert Walpole, a promise of the place; which he had no sooner got, than lord Essex immediately sent for Geminiani, and told him that his difficulties were now at an end, for that he had provided for him an honourable employment, suited to his profession and abilities, and which would afford him an ample provision for life; but upon enquiry into the conditions of the office, Geminiani found that it was not tenable by one of the Romish communion, he therefore declined accepting it, assigning as a reason that he was a member of the catholic church; and that though he had never made great pretensions to religion, the thought of renouncing that faith in which he had been baptized, for the sake of worldly advantage, was what he could in no way answer to his conscience. Upon this refusal on the part of Geminiani, the place was bestowed on Mr. Matthew Dubourg, a young man who had been one of his pupils, and was a celebrated performer on the violin.

Some years had now elapsed since the publication of his Solos, and as well with a view to advantage, as in compliance with his inclinations, he set himself to compose parts to the first part of the Opera quinta of Corelli, or, in other words, to make Concertos of the first six of his Solos. This work he completed, and, with the help of a subscription, at the head of which were the names of the royal family, he published it in the year 1726. A short time after, he made the remaining six of Corelli's Solos also into Concertos; but these having no fugues, and consisting altogether of airs, afforded him but little scope for the exercise of his skill, and met with but an indifferent reception.

He also made Concertos of six of Corelli's Sonatas, that is to say, the ninth in the first opera, and the first, third, fourth, ninth, and tenth of the third. This seems to have been a hasty publication, and is hardly now remembered. In the year 1732 he published what he styled his Opera second, that is to say, VI. Concerti grossi con due Violini, Violoncello, e Viola di Concertino Obligati, e due altri Violini, e basso di Concerto grosso ad arbitrio, with a dedication to Henrietta, duchess of Marlborough. The first of these compositions is celebrated for the fine minuet with which it closes; the first idea of the Concerto was the following Solo, which the author had composed many years before, and has never yet appeared in print:—

FRANCESCO GEMINIANI.

The publication of this work was soon followed by another of the same kind, that is to say, his Opera terza, consisting of six Concertos for violins, the last whereof is looked upon as one of the finest compositions of the kind in the world.

Geminiani was now in the highest degree of estimation as a composer for instruments; for, to say the truth, he was in this branch of music without a rival; but his circumstances were very little mended by the profits that resulted from these several publications. The manuscript of his Opera seconda had been surreptitiously obtained by Walsh, who was about to print it, but thinking it would be the better for the corrections of the author, he gave him the alternative of correcting it, or submitting it to appear in the world with such faults as would have reflected indelible disgrace on the author.

An offer of this kind was nothing less than an insult, and as such Geminiani received it. He therefore not only rejected it with scorn, but instituted a process in the court of chancery for an injunction against the sale of the book, but Walsh compounded the matter, and the work was published under the inspection of the author.

The Opera terza he parted with for a sum of money to Walsh, who printed it, and in an advertisement has given the lovers of music to understand that he came honestly by the copy.

As Geminiani lived to a great age, and published at different times many other of his compositions, the farther particulars of his life are referred to a subsequent part of this work.

The refinements that resulted from the association of music with the drama, were successively adopted by the English and the French; by the former at the restoration of Charles II., and by the latter in the year 1669, when Lewis XIV. established the Royal Academy of Music at Paris. Germany at that time abounded with excellent musicians, viz., deep theorists, and men profoundly skilled in the principles of harmony, and the practice of musical composition; but, excepting the organists of that country, and they must be acknowledged to have been at all times excellent, we hear of few that were distinguished for their performance on any particular instrument; and of still fewer of either sex that were celebrated as fine singers; and it seems that without those adventitious aids, which in other countries were thought necessary to the support of music, that is to say, the blandishments of an effeminate and enervated melody, and the splendour of scenic decoration, in Germany both the science and the practice continued to flourish for many ages in the simple purity of nature, and under regulations so austere, as seemed to bid defiance to innovations of any kind.

It happened, notwithstanding, that the emperor Leopold, being a great lover of music, began to discover an early propensity to the style of the Italians: the recitative of Carissimi exhibited to him a species of composition, in which the powers of eloquence derived new force by the association to speech, of sounds that corresponded to the sense, and were of all others the most melodious. As soon therefore

as a cessation from the toils of war gave him leisure to cultivate the arts of peace, he set himself to introduce the Italian music into Germany; accordingly we find that he had Italian composers in his court; that he gave pensions and rewards to the most excellent of them, as namely, Caldara, Ziani, Lotti, Bononcini, and others; that he had also representations of Italian operas, and that some of the most celebrated singers performed in them, and requited his patronage and bounty with their usual ingratitude and insolence.

Nor was it alone at Vienna that Italian music and the opera were thus introduced and encouraged; the same passion influenced other princes of Germany, and in other cities, namely, Berlin, Hanover, and Hamburg, we find that the Italian musicians were greatly caressed; that the works of some of the most eminent of them, that is to say, Pistocchi, Corelli, Vivaldi, and many others, are dedicated to German princes; that operas were represented in the principal cities in Germany, some whereof were written in the German language; and, lastly, that the German musicians themselves became composers of operas.

From these circumstances we are enabled to ascertain the origin of dramatic music in Germany, and having fixed it, it becomes necessary to give an account of some of the most celebrated composers in the theatric style, natives of that country, including one who chose this kingdom for his residence, and whose loss will long be deplored by its inhabitants.

## CHAP. CLXXXII.

JOHANN SIGISMUND COUSSER, born about the year 1657, was the son of an eminent musician of Presburg, in Hungary; and being initiated by his father in the rudiments of music, and also in the practice of composition, he travelled for improvement into France, and at Paris became a favourite of Lully, and was by him assisted in the prosecution of his studies. After a stay of six years in Paris, Cousser visited Germany, where he was so well received, that in two cities, viz., Wolffenbuttel and Stutgard, he was successively chosen chapel-master; but, being of a roving disposition, he quitted the latter charge, and went to settle at Hamburg, where being chosen director of the opera, he, about the year 1693, introduced the Italian method of singing, to which the Germans had till that time been strangers. About the year 1700 he took a resolution to visit Italy, and made two journies thither in the space of five years. Upon his last return to Germany, failing of that encouragement which he thought due to his merit, he quitted that country, and came to England, and, settling in London, became a private teacher of music; by which profession, and also by the profits arising from an annual public concert, he was enabled to support himself in a decent manner. In the year 1710 he went to Ireland, and obtained an employment in the cathedral church of Dublin, which, though our ecclesiastical constitution knows no such officer, he looked upon as equivalent to that of chapel-master in foreign countries. After some continuance in that city, his merits recommended him to the place of master of the king's band of music in Ireland, which he held till the time of his death. From the time of his first settlement in Ireland, Cousser applied himself to the study of the theory of music, with a view, as it is said, to his attainment of the degree of doctor in that faculty of the university of Dublin. His works in print are Erindo, an opera, 1693 ; Porus, and Pyramus and Thisbe, 1694 ; Scipio Africanus, 1695 ; and Jason, 1697. These several operas had been performed at Hamburg. There was also published at Nuremberg, in 1700, a work of Cousser, entitled ' Apollon enjoüe, con-' tenant six Overtures de Theatre, accompagnées de ' plusieurs airs ;' and in the same year an opera entitled Ariadne ; as also a collection of airs from it, entitled Helicon-**ische Musen-Lust.** He was re-sident in London at the time of the death of Mrs. Arabella Hunt, and set to music an ode written on that occasion by one William Meres, Esq. beginning ' Long have I fear'd that you, my sable muse.'

The last of his publications was, A Serenade represented on the Birth-day of Geo. I. at the castle of Dublin, the 28th of May, 1724, in the title whereof he styles himself 'master of the musick ' attending his Majesty's state in Ireland, and chapel-' master of Trinity-college, Dublin.'

Cousser died at Dublin in the year 1727 ; and, having recommended himself to the people of that city by his great abilities in his profession, and the general tenor of his deportment, his loss was greatly lamented. His successor in the office of master of the king's band was Mr. Matthew Dubourg, a pupil of Geminiani, and a celebrated performer on the violin.

Reinhard Keiser was a native of Saxe-Weissen-fels, and chapel-master to the duke of Mecklenburg. He was a most voluminous writer, and is said to have exceeded Scarlatti in the number of operas composed by him ; which may probably be true, for in the preface to an opera of his, published at Hamburg in 1725, that work is said to be the hundred and seventh opera of his composing. The operas of Keiser were written in the German lan-guage, the music was nevertheless in the style of the Italians ; they were performed at Hamburg, and many of them were by the author himself published in that city. He had the direction of the opera at Hamburg from the time when it was first established, till, being a man of gaiety and expence, he was necessitated to quit it ; after which the composers for that theatre were successively Steffani, Mattheson, and Mr. Handel. From Hamburg, Keiser went to Copenhagen ; and, in 1722, being royal chapel-master in that city, he composed an opera for the king of Denmark's birth-day, entitled Ulysses. An imperfect catalogue of his works, containing an account of such only of them as are printed, is given by Walther in the article Keiser ; they consist of Operas, Oratorios, Hymns, and Cantatas, amounting to an incredible number.

Keiser is ranked with Scarlatti and other the most eminent musicians who flourished at the begin-ning of this century ; and although his compositions could derive but little advantage from the poetry with which his music was associated, such was the native ease and elegance of his style, and such his command over the passions of his hearers, that all became susceptible of their effects.

Dietrich Buxtehude, son of Johann Buxtehude, organist of St. Olaus at Elsineur, was a disciple of John Thiel, and organist of the church of St. Mary at Lubec. Mattheson, in his **Vollkommenen Capellmeister,** page 130, celebrates him as a famous organist and composer, and speaks of six Suites of Lessons for the harpsichord of his, in which the nature of the planets is represented or delineated. With these are printed a choral com-position to German words, being a lamentation on the death of his father. In 1696 he published two operas of Sonatas a Violino, Viola da Gamba, e Cembalo.

Johann Mattheson, a native of Hamburg, was born the twenty-eighth day of September, 1681. In the seventh year of his age he was by his parents placed under the care of different masters, and was by them instructed in the rudiments of learning and the principles of music, in which science he improved so fast, that at the age of nine he was able to sing to the organ at Hamburg, compositions of his own. At the same time that he pursued the study of music he made himself master of the modern languages, and applied himself to attain a knowledge of the civil law ; to which purpose he became a diligent attendant on the public lectures successively read by two eminent doctors in that faculty. At the age of eighteen he composed an opera, and in it performed the principal part. In 1703 an offer was made him of the place of organist of the church at Lubec, but, not liking the conditions of the appointment, which were that he should submit to the yoke of marriage with a young woman whom the magistrates had chosen for him,[*] he thought proper to decline it. In 1704 he visited Holland, and was invited to accept the place of organist at Harlem, with a salary of fifteen hundred florins a year ; but he declined it, choosing to return to his own country, where he became secretary to Sir Cyril Wych, resident at Hamburg for the English court. In this station he made himself master of the English tongue, and, without abandoning the study of music, took up a resolution to quit the opera stage, on which he had been a singer for fifteen years. In 1709 he married Catherine, a daughter of Mr. Jennings, a clergyman, nearly related to the admiral Sir John Jennings.

In the course of his employment as secretary to the resident, he was intrusted with several important

* This expedient to get rid of a burgher's daughter, by yoking her with the town organist, suggests to remembrance a practice nearly similar to it in this country. The road from Putney to Richmond lies through common fields, at the entrance whereof are sundry gates, at each of which a poor man is stationed, who upon opening the gate for passengers, is generally rewarded with a halfpenny. The appointment of these persons is by the parish officers, who, considering that the profits thus arising are more than adequate to the wants of a poor man, annex to their grant a condition that the person appointed shall marry a poor woman out of their workhouse, and rid the parish of the expense of maintaining her.

negotiations, and made frequent journies to Leipsic, Bremen, and divers parts of Saxony, from which he reaped considerable advantages. Upon the death of Sir Cyril Wych, in the year 1712, the care of the English affairs in the circle of Lower Saxony devolved upon Mattheson, and he occupied the office of resident till the son of the late minister was appointed to it. Upon the accession of king George I. to the crown of England, he composed a memorable Serenata ; and in the year 1715 obtained the reversion of the office of chapel-master in the cathedral of Hamburg, with certain other preferments annexed to it. During all this time he continued his station of secretary to the British resident ; and, upon many occasions of his absence, he discharged in his own proper person the functions of the minister. Amidst that multiplicity of business which necessarily sprang from such a situation, Mattheson found means to prosecute his musical studies; he composed music for the church and for the theatre, and was ever present at the performance of it : he practised the harpsichord at his own apartments incessantly, and on that instrument, if not on the organ, was unquestionably one of the first performers of his time. He wrote and translated books to an incredible number, and this without an exclusive attachment to any particular object ; and the versatility of his temper cannot be more strongly marked than by observing that he composed church-music and operas, wrote treatises on music, and upon the longitude ; and translated from the English into the German language, the Chevalier Ramsay's Travels of Cyrus, and the History of Moll Flanders, written by Daniel de Foe. Of his musical treatises his Orchestre, his Critica Musica, his **Musicalische** Patriot, and his **Vollkommenen Capellmeister,** are the best known. His writings in general abound with intelligence communicated in a desultory manner, and are an evidence that the author possessed more learning than judgment.

Mattheson was very well acquainted with Handel. Before the latter came to settle in England they were in some sort rivals, and solicited with equal ardour the favour of the public. Mattheson relates that he had often vied with him on the organ both at Hamburg and Lubec. The terms upon which these two great men lived when they were together, must appear very strange. Handel approved so highly of the compositions of Mattheson, particularly his lessons, that he was used to play them for his private amusement ;* and Mattheson had so great a regard for Handel, that he at one time entertained thoughts of writing his life. In the years 1735 and 1737 he published a work entitled **Die wol=klingende Fin=**

* Mattheson had sent over to England, in order to their being published here, two collections of lessons for the harpsichord, and they were accordingly engraved on copper, and printed for Richard Meares, in St. Paul's church-yard, and published in the year 1714. Handel was at this time in London, and in the afternoon was used to frequent St. Paul's church for the sake of hearing the service, and of playing on the organ after it was over ; from whence he and some of the gentlemen of the choir would frequently adjourn to the Queen's Arms tavern in St. Paul's church-yard, where was a harpsichord : it happened one afternoon, when they were thus met together, Mr. Weely, a gentleman of the choir, came in and informed them that Mr. Mattheson's lessons were then to be had at Mr. Meares's shop ; upon which Mr. Handel ordered them immediately to be sent for, and upon their being brought, played them all over without rising from the instrument.

**ger=Sprache,** i. e. 'The well-sounding Finger 'Language,' consisting of twelve fugues for the organ, on two and three subjects, and dedicated it to Handel, who, upon the publication of it, wrote him a letter, in which is the following passage :—

' ——à present je viens de receivoir votre dernier 'lettre avec votre ouvrage, je vous en remercie 'Monsieur, et je vous assure que j'ai toute l'estime 'pour votre merite.—L'ouvrage est digne de l'atten-'tion des connoisseurs,—et quant a moi je vous rends 'justice.'

And yet these two men were in one moment of their lives at so great enmity, that each had the other opposed to the point of his sword. In short, they, upon a dispute about the feat at the harpsichord at the performance of one of Mattheson's operas, fought a duel in the market-place of Hamburg, which a mere accident prevented from being mortal to one or both of them. Mattheson died at Hamburg in the year 1764. At the beginning of the sixth volume of Marcello's Psalms, is a letter of his to the author, in the Italian language, dated Hamburg, 6 Oct. 1725, with this subscription, ' Giovanni Mattheson di ' S. A. R. il Duca d' Holstein, Secretario Britannico. ' Canonico minore della Chiesa d'Amburgo, e ' Direttore della Musica Catedrale.'

JOHANN BERNHARD BACH, eldest son of Giles Bach, senior musician to the senate of Erfurth, was born November 23, 1676, and was at first organist in the merchants' church there. Afterwards he went to reside at Magdeburg, and in the year 1703 to Eisenach, where he became chamber-musician to the duke.

JOHANN CHRISTOPHER BACH, of the same family, was organist at Eisenach, and continued in that function thirty-eight years. He died in the year 1703, leaving behind him three sons, all musicians, namely, JOHANN NICOLAUS, organist at Jena in the year 1695, and a celebrated maker of harpsichords. JOHANN CHRISTOPHER, who resided first at Erfurth, afterwards at Hamburgh, and after that at Rotterdam and London, in which cities his profession was teaching ; and JOHANN FREDERICK, organist of the church of St. Blase at Muhlhausen.

JOHANN MICHAEL BACH, brother of the above-mentioned John Christopher Bach, of Eisenach, was organist, and also town-clerk of Gehren, a market-town and bailiwick near the forest of Thuringia. He has composed a great many church pieces, concertos, and harpsichord lessons, of which none have ever yet been printed.

JOHANN SEBASTIAN BACH, son of John Ambrose Bach, formerly musician to the court and senate of Eisenach, and a near relation of him last named, was born in that city on the twenty-first day of March, 1685. He was initiated in the practice of the harpsichord by his eldest brother John Christopher Bach, organist and professor of music in the school of Ohrdruff; and in 1703 was appointed first organist of the new church at Arnstadt, which station he quitted in 1707, for the place of organist of the church of St. Blase at Muhlhausen. Here also he stayed but a short time, for in 1708 he went to settle at Weimar, and became chamber-musician, and also court-organist to the duke; and in 1714 was appointed concert-master to that prince. In 1717 he was preferred to the office of chapel-master to the prince of Anhalt Cothen; and in 1723, upon the decease of Kuhnau, to that of music-director at Leipsic; and about the same time was appointed chapel-master to the duke of Weissenfells. Amongst a great variety of excellent compositions for the harpsichord, he published, in 1726, a collection of lessons entitled **Clabier=Ubung,** or Practice for the Harpsichord. He composed a double fugue in three subjects, in one of which he introduces his name.*

This person was celebrated for his skill in the composition of canon, as also for his performance on the organ, especially in the use of the pedals. Mattheson says that on this instrument he was even superior to Handel. His son, Mr. John Christian Bach, now in London, who has furnished some of the anecdotes contained in this article, relates that there are many printed accounts of his father extant in the German language; as also that he had a trial of skill with Marchand, the famous French organist, and foiled him. The particulars of this contest are

as follow: Marchand being at Dresden, and having shewn himself superior to the best organists of France and Italy, made a formal notification that he was ready to play extempore with any German who was willing to engage with him. Upon which the king of Poland sent to Weimar for John Sebastian Bach, who accepting the challenge of Marchand, obtained, in the judgment of all the hearers, a complete victory over him.

John Sebastian Bach died about the year 1749, leaving four sons, who, as if it had been intended that a genius for music should be hereditary in the family, are all excellent musicians: the eldest, Frederic William, is at this time organist of Dresden: the second, Charles Philip Emanuel, is now an organist and music-director at Hamburg; the third, John Frederic Christian, is in the service of the Count de la Lippe; and the fourth, John Christian, after having studied some years in Italy, has chosen London for the place of his residence; and in his profession has the honour to receive the commands of our amiable queen.†

The following composition of John Sebastian Bach is among his lessons above mentioned. :—

ARIA.

* Walther relates that he had observed that the notes B♭, A, C, and ♮ are melodious in their order; the last is by the Germans signified by the letter ♮: taking, therefore, this succession of notes for a point or subject, he wrought it into a fugue, as above is mentioned. Mr. John Christian Bach being applied to for an explanation of this obscure passage in Walther's memoir of his father, gave this account of it, and in the presence of the author of this work, wrote down the point of the fugue.

† Her majesty's master of the harpsichord upon her arrival in England was Mr. Kelway, an Englishman; as is also the dancing-master of the present queen of France, a circumstance so singular as to merit remembrance. At Layton Stone, in Essex, dwells an eminent dancing-master, Mr.      Jay; a few years ago he had an apprentice, the son of a neighbour, a diligent and ingenious lad, and who was generally called by the familiar appellation of Harry Bishop. A person of distinction, who had a seat near Layton Stone, had taken notice of him, and conceiving him to be a youth of great hopes, sent him for improvement to Paris, and in a short time he excelled the most celebrated masters there; and, such are his abilities in a profession in which the French are generally allowed to exceed all Europe, that the queen of France is at this time the scholar of Mr. Bishop, an Englishman, and at the royal palace of Versailles receives from him a stated number of lessons in every week.

JOHANN SEBASTIAN BACH.

## CHAP. CLXXXIII.

GEORGE PHILIPP TELEMANN was born at Magdeburg on the fourteenth day of March, 1681. His father was a minister of the Lutheran church, who dying in the infancy of this his son, left him to the care of his mother. As the child grew up he discovered a strong propensity to music, which his mother endeavoured to get the better of, intending him for the university; but she finding that her son, who had been taught the rudiments of music, as other children in the German schools usually are, was determined to pursue the study of it, gave way to his inclination. As a proof of the early abilities of Telemann, it is said that he composed motets, and other pieces for the church service, in his infancy; and that by the time he was twelve years of age, he had composed almost the whole of an opera.

Having taken a resolution to yield to this inclination of her son, and seeing the progress he had already made in music, the mother of Telemann was easily prevailed on by the friends of the family to encourage him in this course of study; accordingly she placed him first in the school of Zellerfelde, and after four years stay there, removed him to the Gymnasium at Hildesheim, where he perfected his studies in literature; and in music made such great improvements that he was appointed director of the church-music in the monastery of the Godchardins, and in the performance thereof was indulged with the liberty of employing musicians of the Lutheran persuasion.

This was but the beginning of his fame; soon after a wider field opened for him to exhibit his uncommon talents in, for in the year 1701, being sent to Leipsic to study the law, he was appointed to the direction of the operas, and was also chosen first music-director and organist in the new church.

Anno 1704 he became chapel-master to the count of Promniz, which post, in 1709, he exchanged for that of secretary and chapel-master to the duke of Eisenach. In 1712 he was chosen chapel-master to the Carmelite monastery at Francfort-on-the-Mayne. Shortly after he obtained the music direction in St. Catherine's church, and was appointed chapel-master at the court of Saxe Gotha.

In the year 1721, the city of Hamburg, desirous of having such an extraordinary man amongst them, prevailed on him to accept the place of director of their music, as also of the office of chanter in the church of St. John. He had hardly been a year at Hamburg, when an offer was made him of the post of music-director at Leipsic, which by the decease of Kuhnau was then lately become vacant; but being so well settled, he declined accepting it, and it was thereupon conferred on John Sebastian Bach. All this time Telemann continued in the service of the duke of Eisenach, who found him sufficient employment, not only in the way of his profession, but in his post of secretary, to which he had formerly appointed him. The few leisure hours which these his employments left him, he devoted to the service of the Margrave of Bareith, to whom for some years he had presented his compositions, and who had appointed him his chapel-master. However all these numerous avocations could not detain him from pursuing a design, which for many years he had entertained, of seeing Paris; and accordingly about Michaelmas, 1738, he made a journey thither; and as his fame had reached that country, he met upon his arrival there with all the distinguishing marks of esteem due to his character. After a stay of about six months at Paris he returned to Hamburg, where he spent the remainder of his days. The time of his death is variously reported, but the better opinion is that it was about the year 1767.

Telemann was a very voluminous composer, and the greatest church musician in Germany. Handel, speaking of his uncommon skill and readiness, was used to say that he could write a church piece of eight parts with the same expedition as another would write a letter. Telemann was twice married; by both his wives he had ten children, of whom it is remarkable that none of them ever discovered the least genius for music; six of them were living at the time of his decease. To testify his regard for the city of Leipsic, to which he was indebted for his first preferments, he founded a music school there, which still exists. His successor in the office of music-director at Hamburg is the celebrated Charles Philip Emanuel Bach, mentioned in the preceding article.

JOHANN GOTTFRIED WALTHER was one of a family that from the time of Luther downwards, had produced many excellent musicians. The person here spoken of flourished in the present century, and was organist of the church of St. Peter and Paul in the city of Weimar, and is by Mattheson, in his 𝕮𝖔𝖑𝖑𝖐𝖔𝖒𝖒𝖊𝖓𝖊𝖓 𝕮𝖆𝖕𝖊𝖑𝖑𝖒𝖊𝖎𝖘𝖙𝖊𝖗, ranked among the most famous organists and composers for the organ of his time.

Of his musical compositions little is here to be

said, the titles of none of them occurring in any of the catalogues, whence information of this kind has been derived in the course of this work; but the friends of music have the highest obligation to him, as the author of a laborious and most valuable book compiled by him, and published at Leipsic in 1732, entitled **Musicalisches** Lexicon, oder **Musicalische Bibliothec**, in a large octavo volume, containing not only an explanation, in the manner of Brossard, of all the terms used in music, but memoirs of musicians in all ages and all countries, from the first institutors of the science down to his own time. Of the exactness and precision with which this work is executed, a clearer proof cannot be given, than that there is scarce a musician of any eminence, or a parish organist at all celebrated for his performance in this our country, for whom he has not an article.

The book is written in the German language; and no one that is sensible of the copious fund of knowledge contained in it, and the great variety of information it is capable of affording, but must regret that it is not extant in every language in Europe.

The Lexicon of Walther, unlike the History of Music of Printz, contains no account of the author himself, and therefore we are to seek for the particulars of his life. Considering the great variety of learning, and the evidence of long and laborious research displayed in this his work, we cannot suppose him a young man at the time of its publication, and that being now forty-three years ago, it is probable that he has long been at rest from his labours.

GEORGE FREDERIC HANDEL (*a Portrait*), or, if we would recur to the original spelling of his name, HENDEL, was a native of Halle, a city in the circle of Upper Saxony, and born on the twenty-fourth day of February, 1684. His mother was the second wife of his father, then a man advanced in years, being upwards of sixty; a physician, and also a surgeon in that city.

From the time that Handel began to speak he was able to sing, or at least to articulate musical sounds; and as he grew up, his father, who almost from the time of his birth had determined him for the profession of the law, was very much concerned to find in the child such a strong propensity to music, as was at one time or other likely to thwart his endeavours for his welfare. To prevent the effects of this growing inclination, he banished from his house all musical instruments, and by every method in his power endeavoured to check it. As yet Handel, an infant under seven years of age, having never been sent, as most of the German children are, to the public schools, where they learn music as they do grammar, had no idea of the notes or the method of playing on any instrument: he had, perhaps, seen a harpsichord or clavichord, and, with the innocent curiosity of a child, may be supposed to have pressed down a key, which producing a sound, affected him with pleasure; be this as it may, by the exercise of that cunning, which is discoverable very early in children, Handel found means to get a little clavichord conveyed into a

room at the top of his father's house, to which he constantly resorted as soon as the family retired to rest; and, astonishing to say! without any rules to direct his finger, or any instructor than his own ear, he found means to produce from the instrument both melody and harmony.

The father of Handel had a son by his former wife, who was valet de chambre to the duke of Saxe-Weissenfells, and by the time that Handel had nearly attained the age of seven years, he had determined on a journey to see him: his intention was to have gone alone, but Handel having a strong desire to see his half-brother, pressed to be taken with him; his father refused, and accordingly set out by himself; the boy, however, contrived to watch when the chaise set off, and followed it with such resolution and spirit, as to overtake it; and begging with tears to be taken up, the tenderness of a father prevailed, and Handel was made a companion in the journey. Being arrived at the court of the duke, Handel being suffered to go about the apartments, could not resist the temptation to sit down to a harpsichord wherever he met with one. One morning he found means, when the service was just over, to steal to the organ in the duke's chapel, and began to touch it before the people were departed; the duke himself was not gone, and hearing the organ touched in an unusual manner, upon his return to his apartments enquired of his valet what stranger was at it, and was answered his brother; the duke immediately commanded him to be sent for, as also his father: it is needless to repeat the conversation between them, for it terminated in a resolution in the father to yield to the impulse of nature, and give up his son to the profession of music; and accordingly on his return to Halle he placed him under the care of Frederick William Zachau, a sound musician, and organist of the cathedral church of that city.* After having taught him the principles of the science, Zachau put into the hands of his young pupil the works of the greatest among the Italian and German composers, and, without directing his attention to any of them, left him to form a style of his own. Handel had now been under the tuition of Zachau about two years, during which time he had frequently supplied his place, and performed the cathedral duty; the exercises which he had been accustomed to were the composition of fugues and airs upon points or subjects delivered to him from time to time by his master.† At the age of nine he actually composed motets for the service of the church, and continued to make one every week for three years, with scarce any intermission. By the time he was arrived at the age of thirteen, Handel began to look upon Halle as a place not likely to afford him opportunities of much farther improvement; he determined

* See an account of him in page 646 of this work.
† This in Germany is the mode of exercise for young proficients in music, and is also the test of a master. When an organist was to be chosen for the new church of St. George, Hanover-square, Mr. Handel, who lived in the parish, Geminiani, Dr. Pepusch, and Dr. Croft, were the judges to determine of the pretensions of the candidates; they gave them each the same subject for a fugue; and Roseingrave, who acquitted himself the best in the discussion of it, was elected.

GEORGE FREDERIC HANDEL.

to visit Berlin, and arriving in that city in the year 1698, found the opera there in a flourishing condition, under the direction of Bononcini and Attilio; the former of these, a most admirable musician, was yet a haughty and insolent man; the other, his inferior, was of a modest and placid disposition, a proof whereof he gave in the affection shewn by him to this young stranger, whom he would frequently set upon his knee, and listen to with delight while he played on the harpsichord.

Handel had been but a short time at Berlin before the king, the grandfather of the present king of Prussia, took notice of him, and signified to him an intention to send him to Italy; but by the advice of his friends, Handel declined the offer, and returned home to Halle; soon after which he had the misfortune to be deprived of his father. Being by this accident less attached to the city of his nativity than before, Handel began to think of another place of residence. There was at that time an opera at Hamburg, little inferior to that at Berlin: Steffani had composed for it, and Conradina and Mattheson were the principal singers; the former of these was the daughter of a barber at Dresden, named Conradine, but, according to custom, she had given her name an Italian termination.* Mattheson was an indifferent singer, but he was a very good composer, and played finely on the harpsichord and organ.

## CHAP. CLXXXIV.

Upon Handel's arrival at Hamburg he found the opera under the direction of a great master, Reinhard Keiser, a native of Weissenfels, and chapel-master to the duke of Mecklenburgh, who being a man of gaiety and expense, was reduced to the necessity of absconding, to avoid the demands of his creditors. Upon occasion of his absence, the person who had played the second harpsichord thought he had a good title to the first, and accordingly placed himself at it; but Handel, who had hitherto played the violin in the orchestra, and, as it is said, only a Ripieno part, with a promptitude which his inexperience of the world will hardly excuse, put in his claim to Keiser's place, and urged his ability to fill it. The arguments of Handel were seconded by the clamours of a numerous audience, who constrained the substitute of Keiser to yield to his competitor. For the name of this person we are to seek; it is said he was a German; he was deeply affected with the indignity that had been shown him: his honour had sustained an injury, but he comforted himself with the thought that it was in his power to repair it by killing his adversary, a youth but rising to manhood, and who had never worn, nor knew the use of a weapon; and at a time, too, when none were near to assist him. Accordingly one evening, when the opera was over, this assassin followed Handel out of the orchestra, and at a convenient place made a pass at him with his sword; and, had it not been for the

score of the opera which Handel was taking home with him, and had placed in his bosom, under his coat, there is little doubt but that the thrust would have proved mortal.

The absence of Keiser, the merits of Handel, and the baseness of this attempt to deprive him of life, operated so strongly, that those who had the management of the opera looked upon Handel as the only fit person to compose for it: he was then somewhat above fourteen years of age, and being furnished with a drama, he in a very few weeks brought upon the stage his first opera, named Almeria, which was performed thirty nights without intermission.

Handel having continued at Hamburgh about three years, during which time he composed and performed two other operas, namely, Florinda and Nerone, resolved to visit Italy. The prince of Tuscany, brother to the grand duke John Gaston de Medicis, had been present at the performance of the operas of Almeria and Florinda, and had given Handel an invitation to Florence; as soon, therefore, as he found himself in a situation to accept it, he went thither, and composed the opera of Roderigo, being then in his eighteenth year, for which he was honoured by the grand duke with a present of one hundred sequins and a service of plate. The prince's mistress, Vittoria, sang the principal part in it, and, if fame says true, conceived such a passion for Handel, as, if he had been disposed to encourage it, might have proved the ruin of them both. After about a year's stay at Florence, Handel went to Venice, and there composed the opera of Agrippina, which was performed twenty-seven nights successively; from thence he went to Rome, where being introduced to Cardinal Ottoboni, he became acquainted with Corelli and Alessandro Scarlatti; the first of these had apartments in the cardinal's palace, and played the first violin in a concert which the cardinal had there on Monday in every week. From Rome he went to Naples, and after some stay there, having seen as much of Italy as he thought necessary, he determined to return to Germany. He had no particular attachment to any city, but having never seen Hanover, he bent his way thither. Upon his arrival he found Steffani in possession of the place of musician to the court; he might perhaps be styled chapel-master, a title which the foreign musicians are very ambitious of; but he could not be so in fact, for the service in the electoral chapel was according to the Lutheran ritual, and Steffani was a dignitary in the Romish church. The reception which Handel met with from Steffani was such as made a lasting impression upon his mind. The following is the manner in which he related it to the author of this work:—'When I first arrived at 'Hanover I was a young man, under twenty; I was 'acquainted with the merits of Steffani, and he had 'heard of me. I understood somewhat of music, 'and,' putting forth both his broad hands, and extending his fingers, 'could play pretty well on the 'organ; he received me with great kindness, and 'took an early opportunity to introduce me to the 'princess Sophia and the elector's son, giving them

* She was both a fine singer and an excellent actress. She sang in the opera at Berlin in 1708, and in 1711 was married to Count Gruzewska.

'to understand that I was what he was pleased to
'call a virtuoso in music; he obliged me with in-
'structions for my conduct and behaviour during my
'residence at Hanover; and being called from the
'city to attend to matters of a public concern, he left
'me in possession of that favour and patronage
'which himself had enjoyed for a series of years.'

The connection between the court of Hanover and
that of London at this time was growing every day
more close, and Handel, prompted perhaps by curiosity to see a city which was likely one time or other
to become the place of his residence, determined to
visit London. At the time that he was preparing
for his departure, a nobleman at the court of
Hanover, Baron Kilmansegge, was actually soliciting
with the electer the grant of a pension to Handel of
fifteen hundred crowns per annum, which he having
obtained, Handel hesitated to accept, being conscious
of the resolution he had taken to visit England.
Upon this objection the Baron consulted his highness's pleasure, and Handel was then acquainted that
he should not be disappointed in his design by the
acceptance of the pension proposed, for that he had
permission to be absent for a twelvemonth or more,
if he chose it, and to go whithersoever he pleased. On
these easy conditions he thankfully accepted the
electer's bounty. Before he left Germany he made a
visit to his mother at Halle, whom he found labouring
under the accumulated burthen of old age and
blindness; he visited also his preceptor Zachau, and
some other of his friends; and passing through
Dusseldorp to Holland, embarked for England, and
arrived at London in the winter of the year 1710.

The state of the opera in England at this time has
already been spoken of; Mr. Aaron Hill was concerned in the management of it; he gave to Rossi,
an Italian poet, the story of Rinaldo from Tasso's
Gierusalemme; and Rossi having wrought it into the
form of an opera, Mr. Handel set the music to it,
and Hill published it with an English translation.

As to the poem itself, it is neither better nor
worse than most compositions of the kind; Mr.
Addison, in the Spectator, No. 5, is very arch on it,
and has extracted from the preface the following
curious passage: 'Eccoti, benigno Lettore, un Parto
'di poche Sere, che se ben nato di Notte, non e'
'però aborto di Tenebre, mà si farà conoscere
'Figliolo d' Apollo con qualche Raggio di Par-
'nasso;' that is, 'Behold, gentle reader, the birth of a
'few Evenings, which though it be the offspring of
'the Night, is not the abortive of darkness, but will
'make itself known to be the son of Apollo, with a
'certain ray of Parnassus.' The following is the
author's apology for the imperfections of the work :—
'Gradisci, ti prego, discreto lettore, questa mia
'rapida fatica, e se non merita le tue lodi, almeno
'non privarla del tuo compatimento, chi dirò più
'tosto giustizia per un tempo così ristretto, poiche il
'Signor Hendel, Orfeo del nostro secolo, nel porla
'in musica, a pena mi diede tempo di scrivere; e
'viddi con mio grand stupore, in due sole settimane
'armonizata al maggior grado di perfezzione un
'opera intiera.' Mr. Handel is said to have com-

posed the opera of Rinaldo in the short space of
a fortnight; in it is an air, 'Cara sposa,' sung by
Nicolini, which the author would frequently say
was one of the best he ever made. The success
of this opera was greater than can be imagined;
Walsh got fifteen hundred pounds by the printing it.

After this specimen of his abilities, the lovers of
music here used every motive to prevail on Handel
to make London the place of his residence; but, after
a twelvemonth's stay in England, he determined to
return to Hanover. He took leave of the queen,
and, upon expressing his sense of the obligations
which he had to the English nation, and her majesty
in particular, she made him some valuable presents,
and intimated a wish to see him again. Upon his
return to Hanover he composed for the electoral
princess, Caroline, afterwards queen of England,
twelve chamber duets, in imitation, as he professed,
of those of Steffani, but in a style less simple, and in
other respects different from those of that author.
The words of these compositions abound with all the
beauties of poetry, and were written by Abbate
Hortensio Mauro.

After two years stay at Hanover, Mr. Handel obtained leave of the elector to revisit England, upon
condition of his returning within a reasonable time.
He arrived at London about the latter end of the
year 1712, at which time the negociations of the
peace of Utrecht were in great forwardness. In the
following year the treaty was concluded; a public
thanksgiving was ordered for the occasion, and Mr.
Handel received from the queen a command to compose a Te Deum and Jubilate, which were performed
at St. Paul's cathedral, her majesty herself attending
the service. The queen died in 1714, and the elector
of Hanover immediately came over. On his arrival
here, he had two grounds of resentment against
Handel, the one the breach of his engagement to return to Hanover after a reasonable stay here; the
other his having lent the assistance of his art towards
the celebrating as happy and glorious, an event which
by many was looked upon as detrimental to the interests, not only of this kingdom, but of all the
protestant powers of Europe. To avert the king's
displeasure, baron Kilmansegge contrived an expedient, which nothing but his sincere friendship for
Handel could have suggested; the Baron formed
a party, who were to take the pleasure of a fine
summer's day on the Thames, and the king condescended to be of it: Handel had an intimation of the
design, and was advised by the baron to prepare
music for the occasion; and he composed for it that
work, consisting of an overture and a variety of airs
and other movements, which we know by the name
of the Water Music. It was performed in a barge,
attendant on that in which the king and his company
were, and Handel himself conducted it. The king
being little at a loss to guess who was the composer
of music so grand and original as this appeared to
be, anticipated the relation that Mr. Handel was the
author of it. From this time the baron waited with
impatience for an intimation from the king of his
desire to see Handel; at length an opportunity

offered, which he with the utmost eagerness embraced; Geminiani had been in England a short time, during which he had published and dedicated to baron Kilmansegge his Opera prima, consisting of those twelve Solos for the violin, which will be admired as long as the love of melody shall exist, and the king was desirous of hearing them performed by the author, who was the greatest master of the instrument then living; Geminiani was extremely pleased with the thought of being heard, but was fearful of being accompanied on the harpsichord by some performer, who might fail to do justice both to the compositions and the performance of them: in short, he suggested to the baron a wish that Mr. Handel might be the person appointed to meet him in the king's apartment; and upon mentioning it to his majesty, the baron was told that Handel would be admitted for the purpose, and he attended accordingly; and upon expressing his desire to atone for his former misbehaviour, by the utmost efforts of duty and gratitude, he was reinstated in the king's favour; and soon after, as a token of it, received a grant of a pension of 200l. a year, over and above one for the same sum which had been settled on him by queen Anne.

Being now determined to make England the country of his residence, Handel began to yield to the invitations of such persons of rank and fortune as were desirous of his acquaintance, and accepted an invitation from one Mr. Andrews, of Barn-Elms, in Surrey, but who had also a town residence, to apartments in his house. After some months stay with Mr. Andrews, Handel received a pressing invitation from the earl of Burlington, whose love of music was equal to his skill in architecture and his passion for other liberal studies, to make his house in Piccadilly the place of his abode. Into this hospitable mansion was Handel received, and left at liberty to follow the dictates of his genius and invention, assisting frequently at evening concerts, in which his own music made the most considerable part. The course of his studies during three years residence at Burlington-house, was very regular and uniform: his mornings were employed in study, and at dinner he sat down with men of the first eminence for genius and abilities of any in the kingdom. Here he frequently met Pope, Gay, Dr. Arbuthnot,[*] and others of that class: the latter was able to' converse with him on his art, but Pope understood not, neither had he the least ear or relish for music; and he was honest enough to confess it. When Handel had no particular engagements, he frequently went in the afternoon to St. Paul's church, where Mr. Greene, though he was not then organist, was very assiduous in his civilities to him: by him he was introduced to, and made acquainted with the principal performers in the choir. The truth is, that Handel was very fond of St. Paul's organ, built by father Smith, and which was then almost a new instrument; Brind was then the organist, and no very celebrated per-

former: the tone of the instrument delighted Handel; and a little intreaty was at any time sufficient to prevail on him to touch it, but after he had ascended the organ-loft, it was with reluctance that he left it; and he has been known, after evening service, to play to an audience as great as ever filled the choir. After his performance was over it was his practice to adjourn with the principal persons of the choir to the Queen's Arms tavern in St. Paul's church-yard, where was a great room, with a harpsichord in it; and oftentimes an evening was there spent in music and musical conversation.[†]

After three years residence at Burlington-house, during which time he composed three operas, namely, Amadis, Theseus, and Pastor Fido, Mr. Handel received a pressing invitation from the duke of Chandois to undertake the direction of the chapel at his superb mansion, Cannons. Pepusch had had for some years the direction of it, and had composed services and anthems for it to a great number; but, like most other of his compositions, they were merely correct harmony, without either melody or energy; and it suited but ill with the duke's ideas of magnificence, and the immense expence he had been at in building such a house, and furnishing his chapel, to have any other than the greatest musician in the kingdom for his chapel-master. We may suppose that the offers made to induce Handel to exchange the patronage of one nobleman for another, and to enter into engagements that rendered him somewhat less than master of himself and his time, were proportioned as well to the munificence of his new patron as his own merits: whatever they were, he complied with the invitation, and in the year 1718 went to reside with the duke at Cannons, where he was no sooner settled, than he sat himself to compose a suite of anthems for the duke's chapel. In the course of these his studies, he seems to have disdained all imitation, and to have looked with contempt on those pure and elegant models for the church style, the motets of Palestrina, Allegri, and Foggia, and for that of the chamber the Cantatas of Cesti and Pier Simone Agostino; for these he thought, and would sometimes say, were stiff, and void of that sweetness of melody, which he looked upon to be essential as well to choral as theatrical music; much less would he vouchsafe an imitation of those milder beauties which shine so conspicuously in the anthems of the English composers for the church, namely, Tallis, Bird, Gibbons, and others; or, to come near to his own time, those of Wise, Humphrey, Blow, and Purcell: in short, such was the sublimity of his genius, and the copiousness of his invention, that he was persuaded of his ability to form a style of his own: he made the experiment, and it succeeded.

The establishment of the chapel at Cannons consisted in a sufficient number of voices of various pitches, including those of boys, for the performance of any composition merely vocal; but, in imitation

* Dr. Arbuthnot was not only a passionate lover of music, but was well skilled in the science: an anthem of his composition, 'As pants the hart,' is to be found in the books of the chapel royal. See Divine Harmony, or a new Collection of select Anthems. Lond. octavo, 1712.

† At one of these meetings, word being brought that Mattheson's lesson's which had been engraved and printed in London, were just come from the press, the book was immediately sent for, and Handel, without hesitation, played it through.

of the practice in the chapels of foreign countries, the duke retained a band of the best instrumental performers ; the anthems composed by Mr. Handel were made for voices and instruments, and in number are supposed to be little short of twenty : as they have never been printed, it may be some satisfaction to the curious to be told that in the library of the Academy of Ancient Music in London, are the following : ' O praise the Lord,' ' As pants the ' hart,' ' O sing unto the Lord,' ' Have mercy upon ' me,' ' O come let us sing,' ' I will magnify thee,' ' The Lord is my light,' ' My song shall be alway,' ' In the Lord put I my trust,' ' The king shall ' rejoice,' and ' Let God arise.'

The Academy have also an anthem of his, ' Sing ' unto God,' performed at the marriage of Frederic, prince of Wales.

He also composed for the duke of Chandois, his serenata of Acis and Galatea, the words whereof are said to have been written by Mr. Gay. Handel while at Naples had composed and performed a serenata entitled Acide e Galatea ; and it is probable that he might have adapted many parts of the original composition to the English words ; however this particular is to be remarked in the Acis and Galatea, that the fine chorus, ' Behold the monster Poly- ' pheme,' so much admired for expressing horror and affright, is taken from one of his duets, in which the self-same notes are set to words of a very different import.

During the last year of his residence with the duke of Chandois, the principal nobility and gentry of the kingdom formed themselves into a musical academy for the performance of operas at the theatre in the Haymarket, to be composed by Mr. Handel, and performed under his direction. To this end a subscription was raised, amounting to 50,000l. The king subscribed 1000l., and permitted the society thus formed to be dignified with the title of the Royal Academy. It consisted of a governor, deputy governor, and twenty directors, whose names were as follow : Thomas, duke of Newcastle, governor ; lord Bingley, deputy governor ; directors, the dukes of Portland and Queensberry, the earls of Burlington, Stair, and Waldegrave, lord Chetwynd, lord Stanhope, James Bruce, Esq., colonel Blathwayt,* Thomas Coke, of Norfolk, Esq., Conyers D'Arcy, Esq., brigadier-general Dormer, Bryan Fairfax, Esq., colonel O'Hara, George Harrison, Esq., brigadier-general Hunter, William Pulteney, Esq., Sir John Vanbrugh, major-general Wade, and Francis Whitworth, Esq.

Handel being thus engaged, found it necessary to seek abroad for the best singers that could be procured. Accordingly he went to Dresden ; and, having secured Senesino and Signora Margarita Durastanti, returned with them to England. It has been asserted that at this time Bononcini and Attilio were in possession of the opera stage ; but this can no otherwise be true, than that the compositions of those two masters, or rather operas made up of

songs selected from Italian operas composed by them, were represented here : that this was the case with respect to Bononcini, is most evident from what has already been related touching the operas of Camilla and Thomyris. Besides which it may be observed that Bononcini came first to reside in London upon the invitation of the Academy ; and the first entire opera of his, named Astartus, was performed in the year 1720, and Coriolanus, the first of Attilio, in 1723. The fact seems to stand thus : Bononcini, though he had never been in England, had a strong party among the nobility ; and at the institution of the Royal Academy it seems to have been the design of the directors that the entertainment should have all the advantages that could be derived from the studies of men of equal abilities, but different talents, and accordingly Bononcini was included in the resolutions, and Attilio engaged about three or four years after.

## CHAP. CLXXXV.

GIOVANNI BONONCINI (*a Portrait*), or as he affected to spell his name, BUONONCINI, was one of the sons of Giovanni Maria Bononcini, of whom an account has already been given,† and a native of Modena. After having finished his musical studies, probably under his father, who, to judge from the works published by him, particularly a treatise entitled Musico Prattico, must have been an able instructor ; he went to Vienna, and having a very fine hand on the violoncello, was entered in the band of the emperor Leopold, and retained with a very large salary. At this time Alessandro Scarlatti had gained great reputation by the operas which he had composed ; and Bononcini, desirous to emulate him, though but eighteen years of age, composed one entitled Camilla, which was performed at Vienna, and also at divers of the Italian theatres, with greater applause than had ever been given to any work of the kind.

The introduction of the Italian opera into England, and the feeble attempts of Mr. Clayton to recommend it, have already been mentioned ; Mr. Haym, convinced of the merit of Camilla, and of the possibility of adapting it to the taste of an English audience but little sensible of the charms of Italian melody, contrived to fit it with English words ; and, notwithstanding the disadvantages arising from this conjunction, it is said to have been received no less favourably here than abroad. This was about the year 1707 ; and so deep was the impression which the music of Bononcini had made upon the minds of the people here, that till the year 1710, the managers found themselves reduced to a kind of necessity of introducing into every opera they exhibited, more than an equal proportion of Bononcini's airs, selected from a variety of works, which by that time he had composed. In the year above-mentioned Mr. Handel arrived in England, and soon after gave to the English the opera of Rinaldo, and thereby laid the foundation for that

---

* This gentleman, an officer in the army, had when a child been a pupil of Alessandro Scarlatti. His proficiency on the harpsichord at twelve years of age astonished every one. There is a picture of him by Kneller, painted when he was about that age, in the music school, Oxon.

† Page 661.

GIOVANNI BUONONCINI

DA MODENA,

COMPOSITORE

fame which he afterwards acquired, and so long enjoyed in this country, and indeed throughout Europe; but his connections at Hanover did not allow of his making London his residence, wherefore, after a twelvemonth's stay here, he returned.

The nobility and gentry, who were now become sensible of the charms of dramatic music, began to associate in its behalf, and themselves became conductors of the opera. Mr. Handel returned again to England; but having entered into engagements with the earl of Burlington and the duke of Chandois, he was for some years but an occasional composer of operas : as soon as these were determined, the foundation of a royal academy was laid in the manner above related ; Bononcini was then at Rome, and, as he himself expressly asserts, was called from thence to the service of the Royal Academy.* About three years after, Attilio was also sent for from Bologna, and, in virtue of their engagements with the directors, and during an interval of about seven years, they composed and exhibited the following operas; that is to say, Bononcini composed the operas of Astartus, Crispus, Griselda, Pharnaces, Erminia, Calphurnia, and Astyanax ; and Attilio, those of Coriolanus, Vespasian, Artaxerxes, Darius, and Lucius Verus.

It was hardly possible that men possessed of talents so different as were those of Handel and Bononcini, should be equally admired and patronized by the same persons. The style of Bononcini was tender, elegant, and pathetic; Handel's possessed all these qualities, and numberless others, and his invention was inexhaustible. For some or other of these considerations, and perhaps others of a very different kind, two parties were formed among the nobility, the one professing to patronize Handel, and the other Bononcini : as to Attilio, he was an ingenious and modest man, and was therefore left to make his way as he could. Handel was honoured with the favour of the electoral family ; and this might be one, among other reasons, that induced the Marlborough family, as it stood affected at that time, to take his rival under their protection ; and yet, so strange and capricious are the motives of party opposition, Handel was espoused by the Tories, and Bononcini by the Whigs. Upon the death of John, duke of Marlborough, in 1722, Bononcini was employed by the family to compose an anthem, which was performed at his interment in Henry the Seventh's chapel, Westminster-abbey, and published in score ;† and soon after the countess of Godolphin, who upon the decease of her father, by a peculiar limitation of that title, was now become duchess of Marlborough, took him into her family, and settled on him a pension of five hundred pounds a year.‡ Her dwelling was in the Stable-

yard near St. James's palace, in the house lately inhabited by her husband, the earl of Godolphin; and there she had concerts twice a week, in which the music was solely the composition of this her favourite master, and the principal singers in the opera performed in it.

In this easy and honourable situation, Bononcini had leisure and opportunity to pursue his studies ; here he composed most of his operas, as also twelve Sonatas or Chamber Airs for two violins and a bass, printed in the year 1732.

That subscription of the nobility and gentry which has been already mentioned, and which laid the foundation of what was called the Royal Academy of Music, was calculated with a view to the improvement of the science ; but, unluckily for Bononcini, the views of this association were chiefly directed towards Handel, and accordingly he was the first retained in their service, and this notwithstanding that Bononcini had for his friend the governor of the academy, the late duke of Newcastle, who had married the daughter of the countess of Godolphin, his patroness.

The academy was no sooner established, than a contest began between the friends of Handel on the one part, and those of Bononcini on the other, which was brought to a crisis by the performance of the opera of Muzio Scævola, of which Handel, Bononcini, and Attilio composed each an act : the judgment of the public in favour of Handel, put an end to the competition, and left him without a rival for the public favour. This dispute, although it determined the point of precedence between Handel and Bononcini, did not operate in the total exclusion of the latter from the academy. He continued to perform operas there till the year 1727 ; after which he retired, and pursued a life of study and ease in that noble family which had so long afforded him protection ; but, being a man of a haughty and imperious temper, he at length rendered himself unworthy of this honourable patronage ; and finding that he had ruined his fortunes in the Marlborough family, and by a singular instance of folly and disingenuity, forfeited the esteem of his friends in the musical world, he associated himself with a common sharper ; and, finding England no abiding place for them, took leave of it altogether. The motives to this retreat, so far as respected Bononcini, were as follow :—

The Academy of ancient Music, of the establishment whereof an account has been given in a preceding page, continued to flourish, and was become the resort of the most eminent masters, as well foreigners as natives, of the time, and Bononcini himself was a member of it. About the beginning of the year 1731, one of the members had received from Venice a book intitled ' Duetti, Terzetti and ' Madrigali, Consecrati alla Sacra Cesarea Real ' Maestà di Gioseppe I. Imperatore : Da Antonio ' Lotti Veneto, Organista della Ducale di San Marco, ' Venezia, 1705 ;' and, having looked it over, he appointed the eighteenth madrigal in the book, beginning ' In una siepe ombrosa,' to be sung in the

---

* In the dedication of his Cantatas to king George I.

† The initial sentence of it is as follows : ' When Saul was king over ' Israel, thou wast he that leddest out and broughtest in Israel.' This composition, though a fine one, is not uniformly excellent ; but allowances must be made for the short interval to which the author was confined.

‡ This circumstance is mentioned by Rolli in the notes on his translation of the comedy of the Conscious Lovers, and is confirmed by a lady of high rank, the daughter of the duchess, now living, who communicated many of the particulars contained in this memoir.

course of the next evening's performance, which was done accordingly : this madrigal had about four years before, by Dr. Greene, been produced in manuscript as a composition of Signor Giovanni Bononcini, who was then in England, and one of their members ; and he, hearing that it was now performed as the work of another author, writes a letter to the Academy, wherein he makes grievous complaints, accuses the pretended author of plagiarism, and affirms that he himself composed it thirty years before, exactly as it is printed in the book, at the command of the emperor Leopold ; for a proof of which assertion he appeals to the archives of that emperor. This obliged the Academy to write by their secretary to Signor Lotti, who in his answer assures them that he was the author of the madrigal in question, and had formerly given a copy of it to Sig. Ziani, chapel-master to the emperor Leopold, before whom it had been performed ; and that it seemed incredible to him that Signor Bononcini should, in the ' gayeté de coeur,' as he expresses himself, adopt his defects for his own. This letter was delivered into Bononcini's own hands ; but he not thinking fit to answer it, the Academy wrote again to Venice, and procured from Lotti an instrument under the seal of a public notary, wherein, after an invocation of the name of the eternal God, it is certified that four of the most eminent masters of Venice,* and an officer of the emperor, had appeared before him, and, having voluntarily taken their oath, ' tacto pectore, et tactis Scripturis,' had deposed that they knew the madrigal, ' In una siepe ombrosa,' to be the work of the above-named Signor Antonio Lotti ; some of them having seen it composing in the rough draught ; others having sung it, and others having heard it practised before it went to the press. Besides this certificate, there were at the same time transmitted to London divers attestations of persons of undoubted credit living at Vienna, one of whom was the Abbate Pariati, author of the words of the above madrigal, to the same effect. These letters, for the satisfaction of the public, were soon after printed, and thus this remarkable contest ended.†

The consequence of this dispute was very fatal to the interests of Bononcini ; it was thought a very dishonest thing in him to assume, and that in terms so positive and express, the merit of a composition, which he could not but know was the work of another ; to palliate this, it is said that the score of the madrigal delivered in to be sung at the Academy was not subscribed with the name of Bononcini, as others of his compositions had invariably been ; and to this fact a gentleman of undoubted veracity, now living, speaks with great certainty, who was present at the performance, and perused the manuscript of the score ; but whether the letters above referred to

are not evidence of his claim, and also of the injustice of it, will hardly bear a question.‡

Notwithstanding the variety and strength of the evidence against Bononcini, it does not appear that he ever retracted his claim to the madrigal in question, or apologized for his behaviour in any one instance during the contest, but with a sullen kind of pride left his adversaries to pursue their own measures ; all which conduct must seem unaccountable to such as are acquainted with his great abilities ; and the more so, as there are extant sundry compositions of his of this very kind, that is to say, madrigals for five voices, not only equal to this of Lotti, but to any that we know of.

From this time the reputation of Bononcini began to sink in the world ; and, what was worse, he found that his disgrace began to operate upon his interest in the Marlborough family ; indeed his behaviour in it had at no time been such as suited with that generous protection which it had invariably afforded him, for he was haughty and capricious, and was for ever telling such stories of himself as were incredible. From a propensity, that must seem unaccountable, he affected to be thought a much older man than he was ; and in the year 1730, when every circumstance in his person and countenance bespoke the contrary, he scrupled not to assert that he was on the verge of fourscore. About the year 1733 his affairs were come to a crisis in England : there was at that time about the town a man, who with scarce any other recommendation than fine clothes, and a great stock of impudence, appeared at court, and assumed the title of Count Ughi ; it is said that he was a friar, but his pretence here was that he was an Italian nobleman, and a natural son of our king James II. Being a man of parts, and well accomplished, he on the footing of relation, such as it was, gained an easy admission to the duchess of Buckingham, and became so much her favourite, that those who were not aware of the supposed consanguinity between them, hesitated not to say she meant to make him her husband.

This fellow, among various other artifices, pretended to be possessed of the secret of making gold, and Bononcini, who had never in his life known the want of it, was foolish enough to believe him. In short, he was prevailed on to leave the hospitable roof under which he had so long been sheltered, and became a sharer in the fortunes of this egregious impostor ; they quitted the kingdom together, but it is probable that this connexion lasted not long, and that Bononcini was constrained to recur for a livelihood to the exercise of his profession ; for a few years after his leaving England, he was at Paris, and composed for the royal chapel there, a motet, in which was a solo, with an accompaniment for the

* Their names and titles were as follow, viz., the most reverend Antonio Bifi, maestro di capella of the most serene republic of Venice ; Girolamo Melari, musician of the ducal chapel of St. Mark ; Claudio Severo Frangioni, also musician of the said ducal chapel ; the reverend Sig. D. Clemente Leopoldo de Tarsis et Ottavio, late chamberlain of the Golden Key to his Imperial majesty, hereditary postmaster general of the empire at Venice, and Giorgio Gentili, first violin of the said ducal chapel.

† Vide Letters from the Academy of ancient Music at London, to Signor Antonio Lotti of Venice, with his Answers and Testimonies, octavo, Lond. 1732.

‡ Dr. Greene, who had introduced the madrigal in question into the Academy, notwithstanding the evidence to the contrary, was one of the last to believe that it was a composition of any other than his friend Bononcini ; but finding himself almost singular in this opinion, he withdrew from the society, carrying with him the boys of St. Paul's ; and, calling to his assistance Mr. Festling, the first violin of the king's band, he established a concert at the Devil tavern, Temple Bar, which being performed in the great room called the Apollo, was named the Apollo Society ; and the joke upon this occasion among the academicians was, that Dr. Greene was gone to the Devil.

violoncello, which he himself performed in the presence of the late king of France. This composition was printed at Paris.

Upon the conclusion of the peace of Aix la Chapelle, Bononcini was sent for to Vienna by the emperor of Germany, and composed the music for that occasion, and was rewarded with a present of eight hundred ducats. This was in the year 1748; and soon after the rejoicings for the peace were over, he, together with Monticelli, a singer who had appeared in the opera at London, set out for Venice, the one having been engaged as composer, the other as principal singer there. Mr. Carrington, the messenger, was at Vienna at the same time, and saw them both set off in the same post-chaise.

## CHAP. CLXXXVI.

The merits of Bononcini as a musician were very great; and it must be thought no diminution of his character to say that he had no superior but Handel; though, as the talents which each possessed were very different in kind, it is almost a question whether any comparison can justly be made between them. Handel's excellence consisted in the grandeur and sublimity of his conceptions, of which he gave the first proofs in his Te Deum and Jubilate; Bononcini's genius was adapted to the expression of tender and pathetic sentiments. His melodies, the richest and sweetest that we know of, are in a style peculiarly his own; his harmonies are original, and at the same time natural: in his recitatives, those manifold inflexions of the voice, which accompany common speech, with the several interjections, exclamations, and pauses proper thereto, are marked with great exactness and propriety.

Whoever reflects on the divisions and animosities occasioned by the competition between the two great masters, Handel and Bononcini, must wonder at the infatuation of the parties that severally espoused them, in that they were not able to discern in the compositions of both, beauties, of different kinds it is true, but such as every soul susceptible of the charms of music must feel and acknowledge. This animosity may seem to have been owing to the determination of an over-refined judgment; but such as have a true idea of the ridiculous character of an opera connoisseur, or are sensible of the extravagant length to which the affectation of a musical taste will carry silly people of both sexes, will justly impute it to ignorance, and an utter inability to form any judgment or well grounded opinion about the matter.

But where was the reason for competition? Is it not with music as in poetry and painting, where the different degrees of merit are not estimated by an approximation to any one particular style or manner as a standard, and where different styles are allowed to possess peculiar powers of delighting? And, to apply the question to the present case, why was it to be assumed as a principle, that to an ear capable of being affected with the sublimity and dignity of Handel's music, the sweetness and elegance of Bononcini's must necessarily be intolerable? and, vice versa. Milton and Spenser were not contemporaries; but had they been so, could the admirers of one have had any reason for denying praise to the other? In this view of the controversy, the conduct of the parties who severally espoused Handel and Bononcini can be resolved only into egregious folly and invincible prejudice; and that mutual animosity, which men, when they are least in the right, are most disposed to entertain.

The long residence of Handel in this country, the great number of his compositions, and the frequent performance of them, enable us to form a competent judgment of his abilities; but the merits of Bononcini are little known and less attended to. Such as form their opinion of him by his early operas, such as Camilla, and those others from which the airs in Thomyris were taken, will greatly err in the estimation of his talents, these being but puerile essays, while he was under twenty years of age. The works of his riper years carry in them the evidences of a mature judgment; and though his characteristic be elegance, softness, and a fine, easy, flowing fancy, there are compositions of his extant in manuscript, particularly a mass for eight voices, with instruments, a Laudate Pueri, and sundry madrigals for five voices, from which we must conclude that his learning and skill were not inferior to those powers of invention, which in an eminent degree he was allowed to possess.

A person now living, and at the head of the profession of music, and who perfectly remembers Bononcini, inclines to the opinion, that, notwithstanding the suspicions to the contrary, the reports which he made of his very advanced age were founded in truth; and calculates that in the year 1748 he could be but little short of a hundred. He says that his merit in his profession may be inferred from that respect and deference with which he was treated by the singers in the opera, particularly Senesino; as also by the principal instrumental performers, Carbonelli, the elder Castrucci, and Giuseppe San Martini.* A letter of Bononcini, dated from London, in the year 1725, is printed in the fifth volume of Marcello's Psalms, and contains a commendation of that work and its author.

The works of Bononcini published in England are, Cantate e Duetti, dedicati alla sacra Maestà di Giorgio Re della Gran Bretagna, &c. Londra, 1721.† The subscription to this book was two guineas: It was honoured with the names of many of the principal nobility, who were very liberal to the author; the duke and duchess of Queensberry subscribed each for twenty-five books; and the countess of Sunderland alone for fifty-five; and many others for ten and five; and it is computed that this work produced the author near a thousand guineas. The operas of Astartus and Griselda, Divertimenti da Camera pel Violino o Flauto, dedicati all' eccellenza del Duca di Rutland, &c. Londra, 1722. The

* Of these severally an account will hereafter be given.

† Some copies of the book are abroad, with a title-page expressing barely the name of the book and of the author, and with no dedication.

funeral anthem for John, duke of Marlborough, and Twelve Sonatas for the Chamber, for two violins and a bass, dedicated to the duchess of Marlborough, London, 1732. Of these publications the first seems to be the chief; and was the produce of those leisure hours of study, when, without being goaded by the call of the public, he was at liberty to wait the returns of his fancy, and to take advantage of those moments in which he found the powers of his genius and invention at the highest. Certain it is that the Cantatas and Duets contained in the above collection have long been held in high esti-

mation by all good judges of music; and it is some proof thereof, that the preludes to them, consisting of airs for two violins and a bass, till within about the last twelve years, were alternately, with Corelli's Sonatas, the second music before the play at one or other of the theatres.

The following air of Bononcini, taken from his opera of Astyanax, was, at the time when that opera was performed, greatly admired for the sweetness of the air, and the originality of the accompaniment; it was never printed, and may be esteemed a curiosity:—

core   di sospirar  .  .  .  .  .  per un mo - men  -  -  to,   deh lascia o cor  di sospi-

- rar       per un momen  -  -  -  to                                  e

tor - na,     e torna poi con piu do-lor  a la-crimar chio mi conten  -  -  to,       e   tor-na poi con piu do-

lor a lacrimar chio mi contento, chio mi con - ten - - - - to, con piu dolore a lacrimar chio mi conten - to,

chio mi con - ten - - - to

Al segno.

Deh las - cia o

GIOVANNI BONONCINI.

ATTILIO ARIOSTI *(a Portrait)*, an ecclesiastic, and therefore usually called in England and elsewhere Padre Attilio,* was a native of Bologna, and chapel-master to the electress of Brandenburg. In the year 1700, on the anniversary of the nuptials of Frederic, hereditary prince of Hesse Cassel, with the electoral princess of Brandenburg, Louisa Dorothea Sophia, being the first day of June, he performed at Lutzen-burg, a villa of the princess at a small distance from Berlin, a ballet, and on the sixth of the same month, an opera, both of his composition, which were received with great applause. In the former he affected to imitate the style of Lully; but in the latter, following the dictates of his own genius and invention, he exceeded the highest expectations. The title of the opera was Atys, in which a shepherd of that name is represented in the extremity of rage and despair, to which passions Attilio had adapted a composition called Sinfonia Infernale, the modula-tion whereof was so singular, and withal so masterly, that the audience were alternately affected with terror and pity, in an exact correspondence with the sentiments of the poet and the design of the repre-

* It is said that he was a Dominican friar, but that he had a dis-pensation from the pope that exempted him from the rule of his order, and left him at liberty to follow a secular profession.

sentation. He also composed a musical drama entitled 'Amor tra Nemici,' which was performed on the birth-day of the emperor Joseph in that year. The words of this drama were printed for the perusal of the audience during the time of per-formance; and it is from the title-page of this pub-lication only, that the fact of his being an ecclesiastic is ascertained; for as to his profession, it was altogether secular, and he never pretended to the exercise of any ecclesiastical function. Attilio was a celebrated performer on the violoncello; but he was most distinguished for his performance on an instrument, of which if he was not the inventor, he was the great improver, namely, the Viol d'Amore, for which he made many compositions. The re-sidence of Attilio at Berlin in the year 1698, the time when Handel, then but a child, arrived at that city, gave him an opportunity of knowing him, and laid the foundation of a friendship, which, notwith-standing a competition of interests, subsisted for many years after. The occasion of his leaving Berlin was an invitation from the directors of the opera here to come and settle at London; upon his arrival he joined with Bononcini: the consequences of that association are related in the account herein

ATTILIUS ARIOSTI BONONIENSIS.

before given of his colleague and his rival Handel, and leaves little to be said of him farther than regards his works, and his general character as a musician.

Of sundry operas composed by Attilio, only Coriolanus and Lucius Verus are in print, though many of the airs in others of them are to be found in collections published by Walsh. Of his operas Coriolanus was best received, and is the most celebrated; the prison scene in particular is wrought up to the highest degree of perfection that music is capable of, and is said to have drawn tears from the audience at every representation : one of the Newgate scenes in the Beggar's Opera is apparently a parody on it, and Mr. Gay seems to intimate no less in his preface.

The success of Mr. Handel in the composition of operas, and the applause with which his productions were received, not only silenced all competition against him, but drove his opponents to the necessity of relinquishing their claim to the public favour. Bononcini, upon his ceasing to compose for the opera, found a comfortable retreat, and a sovereign remedy for the pangs of disappointed ambition, in the Marlborough family ; the lot of Attilio was less happy, and we know of no patronage extended to him. Pressed by the necessity which followed from his want of encouragement, he not so properly solicited as begged, a subscription from the nobility and gentry to a book of Cantatas, in which he purposed to display the utmost of his abilities. Before this time Bononcini had made the like attempt in a proposal to publish his Duettos and Cantatas ; the subscription to the work was two guineas ; and he succeeded so well, that the profits of the publication were estimated at near a thousand guineas. Attilio, in the hope of like success, applied himself to such as he thought his friends, and, as well where he failed of a promise, as where he obtained one, he inrolled the name of the person applied to, in his list of subscribers, and his book was published with the strange title of ' Alla Maestà di Giorgio Rè della Gran Britagna, &c., &c., &c.,' and only the initials of his name to the dedication. The work consists of six Cantatas, the words whereof are conjectured to have been written by Paolo Rolli ; and a collection of lessons for the Viol d'Amore. The compositions of both kinds contained in it abound with evidences of a fertile invention, and great skill in the art of modulation and the principles of harmony ; and upon the whole, may be said to have merited a better reception than the public vouchsafed to give them. After the publication of this book Attilio took leave of England.

## CHAP. CLXXXVII.

THE account which it is proposed to give of the opera, and of those contentions among the singers, that, in the subsequent history of it will be found to have greatly embarrassed the directors, and divided the supporters of it into parties, will convince every one who reads it, that the profession of an opera singer was become of great importance ; and that the caresses of princes and other great personages, who were slaves to their pleasures, had contributed to make them insolent ; and this consideration makes it necessary to recur some years backwards, and take a view of the profession in its infancy, and to assign the causes that contributed to aggrandize it.

The profession of a public singer was not unknown to the ancient Romans ; but among that people those that followed it were in general the slaves or domestic servants of the Patricians. In after-times it was followed for a livelihood by persons of both sexes, and with the greatest emolument by males, who in their infancy had undergone an operation, which seldom fails to improve the vocal organs. Of the general character and behaviour of this latter class of singers, we have no clear intimation till about the year 1647, when Doni published his treatise De Præstantia Musicæ veteris, in which he gives many instances of their arrogant and licentious behaviour to their superiors, and their general disposition to luxury and extravagance. Of the women the above writer says little but what is to their honour ; two the most celebrated female singers of his time, Hadriana Baroni, and Leonora her daughter, he represents as virtuous and modest women.

The same author informs us, that in his time singers with remarkably fine voices were hired at great rates to sing at the public theatres ; but so servile in his estimation does the profession seem to appear, that he has forborne, except in the instances above mentioned, to distinguish even the most celebrated of them by their names. In proportion as theatric music improved, these people became more and more conspicuous ; but not till the close of the last century were any of the singers in the Italian opera known by their names ; the first that can be readily recalled to memory is Sifacio, who, after having sung abroad for many years with great applause, came into England, and was a singer in the chapel of James II., soon after whom appeared Francesco Antonio Pistocchi, who, to borrow a term from the painters, was the founder of a school, which has produced some of the most celebrated singers in these latter ages. The school of Pistocchi is called the School of Bologna ; but it seems that there was also one more ancient, called the School of Tuscany ; and to this seminary Milton seems to allude in the following lines, part of a sonnet inscribed to Mr. Lawrence :—

What neat repast shall feast us, light and choice,
    Of Attic taste, with wine ; whence we may rise
To hear the lute well toucht, or artful voice
    Warble immortal notes and Tuscan air ?

Mr. Martinelli, in two letters by him written to an English nobleman, on the origin of the Italian opera,* would insinuate that the style of the Tuscan school, even down to the beginning of the present century, retained much of that natural simplicity and austerity which characterized the songs of the church; and that Sifacio,† and La Tilla, both natives of

* Lettere Familiari e Critiche di Vincenzio Martinelli. Londra, 1758.

† This was a name of distinction given to him on his performing the character of Syphax in an opera, and in consequence thereof his true name was forgotten.

Tuscany, and of this ancient school, determined the epocha of this grave and simple music ; and farther that Pistocchi corrupted it.  His character of this person is, ' that he sang at first upon the theatre, but ' being obliged, because of his disagreeable voice and ' ungraceful figure, to quit the stage, he turned priest, ' and undertook to teach an art which he was judged ' unable to practice with success.'

To this opinion of Mr. Martinelli, so far as it respects Pistocchi, we have to oppose that of a much better judge, namely, Mr. Galliard, who gives the following account of him, viz., ' That he refined the ' manner of singing in Italy, which was then a little ' crude ; and that his merit in this is acknowledged ' by all his countrymen, and contradicted by none : ' that when he first appeared to the world, and a ' youth, he had a very fine treble voice, but by a ' dissolute life lost it : that after some years he re- ' covered a little glimpse of voice, which by time ' and practice turned into a fine contralto ; that he ' took care of it, and, travelling all Europe over, ' where hearing different manners and tastes, he ' appropriated them to himself, and formed that ' agreeable mixture which he produced in Italy, ' where he was imitated and admired.'  Mr. Galliard concludes this character of Pistocchi with the mention of a remark, which he seems to acquiesce in, viz., that though several of his disciples shewed the improvement they had from him, yet others made an ill use of it, having not a little contributed to the introduction of the modern taste.

To proceed with the school of Bologna.  Mr. Martinelli adds, the most celebrated scholars of Pistocchi were Bernacchi* and Pasi, both of Bologna, and his countrymen ; the former he says has acquired the applause of a few enthusiasts, who are fond of difficulties, by his skill and ingenuity in running over the most hard passages of music in the short space of an Arietta ; but that he was never so successful as to please the generality, because he often neglected the sentiment which he had to express, in order to give a loose to his fancy ; besides, he adds, his voice was little pleasing, and his figure wanted consequence.  On the contrary, he says, that Pasi retained none of the lessons of his master but what were necessary in order to set off a voice, which, though weak, was exceedingly agreeable ; a circumstance, that, joined to an advantageous figure, procured him in a short time the reputation of the most perfect singer that had appeared upon the stage.  The same author mentions Porpora as the instructor of Farinelli and other celebrated singers, and who, as he taught his pupils a manner of singing till then unknown, is, as well as Bernacchi, considered as the founder of a school which will be mentioned in a future page.†

While the proposal for an academy was under

consideration, and to accelerate the carrying of it into execution, Mr. Handel set himself to compose the opera of Radamistus, and caused it to be represented at the Haymarket theatre in the winter of the year 1720.  The applause with which it was received cannot be better related than in the words of the anonymous author of Memoirs of the Life of Mr. Handel, published in the year 1760, which are as follow : ' If persons who are now living, and who ' were present at that performance, may be credited, ' the applause it received was almost as extravagant ' as his Agrippina had excited ; the crowds and ' tumults of the house at Venice were hardly equal ' to those at London.  In so splendid and fashionable ' an assembly of ladies, to the excellence of their ' taste we must impute it, there was no shadow of ' form or ceremony, scarce indeed any appearance of ' order or regularity, politeness or decency : many, ' who had forced their way into the house with an ' impetuosity but ill suited to their rank and sex, ' actually fainted through the excessive heat and ' closeness of it ; several gentlemen were turned ' back who had offered forty shillings for a seat in ' the gallery, after having despaired of getting any ' in the pit or boxes.'

The performance of the opera of Radamistus had impressed upon the friends of Handel, and indeed upon the public in general, a deep sense of his abilities.  It received great advantages from the performance ; for Senesino sang in it that admirable air, ' Ombra Cara,' and Durastanti others ; but, to remove all suspicion that the applause of the public was paid to the representation, and not to the intrinsic merit of the work, Handel published it himself, having previously obtained a licence under the sign manual, dated 14 June, 1720, for securing to him the property in that, and such other of his works as he should afterwards publish.‡

Whoever peruses the opera of Radamistus, will find abundant reason to acquiesce in the high opinion that was entertained of it.  The airs in it are all excellent, but those of chief note are, ' Deh fuggi un ' traditore,' ' Son contenta di muore,' ' Doppo torbide ' procelle,' ' Ombra Cara,' ' Spero placare,' ' La sorte ' il ciel amor,' and ' Vanne sorella ingrata.'§  The performance and the publication jointly operated in bringing the interests of the three rivals to a crisis.  Neither was disposed to yield, and the friends of each concurred in a proposal that Handel, Bononcini, and Attilio should in conjunction compose an opera, that is to say, each of them an act, as also an overture : the opera was Mutius Scævola ; Bononcini set the first act, Attilio the second, and Handel the third ; the songs and the overture in the first and third are in print, and we are enabled to make a comparison

* Antonio Bernacchi : one of that name sang at London in the opera of Lotharius, represented in the year 1729, but with little applause, though he was allowed to be a great master.

† The cant of all professions is disgusting, and that of the musical connoisseurs most so, as it is ever dictated by ignorance and affectation.  Nevertheless as the term school, as applied to musical performance, may be thought technical, we choose rather to adopt it than express it by a periphrasis.

‡ It was in the title-page said to be published by the author, and printed and sold by Richard Meares, musical instrument maker, and music printer, in St. Paul's church-yard, and by Christopher Smith, at the Hand and Music book in Coventry street, near the Haymarket, and nowhere else in England.

§ There is in this opera a short air, ' Cara Sposa,' in the key of A, with the greater third, which is to be distinguished from one with the same beginning in the opera of Rinaldo in E, with the lesser third, which is a studied composition, for this reason that Mr. Handel looked upon the two airs, ' Cara Sposa,' and ' Ombra Cara,' as the two finest he ever made, and declared this his opinion to the author of this work.

between Handel and Bononcini, but of Attilio's part of the work we can say nothing.

The issue of this contest determined the point of precedence between Handel and his competitors: his act in Mutius Scævola was pronounced superior to the others, and Bononcini's next in merit. This victory however was not productive of those consequences that some might hope for; it did not reduce the adversaries of Handel to the necessity of a precipitate retreat, nor even leave the conqueror in possession of the field of battle, for both Bononcini and Attilio continued to compose for the opera after the dispute; and indeed the finest compositions of each, as namely, Astartus, Crispus, Griselda, Pharnaces, Calphurnia, Erminia, Astyanax, by the former; and Coriolanus, Vespasian, Artaxerxes, Darius, and Lucius Verus, by the latter, were composed and performed with the applause severally due to them, between the years 1721 and 1727.*

Of the singers in the Royal Academy two only have as yet been particularly mentioned, that is to say, Senesino and Durastanti; and these had the greatest share in the performance. There were others however of such distinguished merit, as to deserve to be noticed, as namely, Signor Gaetano Berenstadt, whom Mr. Handel had brought from Dresden with the two former, and Boschi, for whom were composed those two celebrated bass songs, 'Del minacciar del 'vento,' in Otho, and 'Deh Cupido,' in Rodelinda; and when these went off, their places were supplied by Pacini, Borosini, Baldi, Antenori, Palmieri, and others. Of female singers there were also some whose merits were too considerable to be forgotten: there were two of the same name, viz., Robinson, though no way related to each other; one of them, Mrs. Anastasia Robinson, afterwards countess of Peterborough, will be spoken of hereafter; the other was the daughter of Dr. William Turner, and the wife of Mr. John Robinson, organist of Westminster-abbey, already mentioned; for which reason, and to distinguish her from the former, she was called Mrs. Turner Robinson.† Soon after the establishment of the Royal Academy, Mr. Handel had engaged Signora Cuzzoni, who sang with unrivalled applause till the year 1726, when Signora Faustina came hither, and became a competitor with her for the public favour, and succeeded so well in her endeavours to obtain it, as to divide the musical world into two parties, not less violent in their enmity to each other than any that we read of in history.

An account of the dispute between these two famous singers, equally excellent, but in different ways, will be reserved for a future page. In the interim it is to be remarked, that the establishment of the opera gave a new turn to the sentiments and manners of the young nobility and gentry of this kingdom: most of these were great frequenters of the opera; they professed to admire the music, and next to that the language in which they were written;

many of them became the scholars of the instrumental performers, and by them were taught the practice of the violin, the violoncello, and the harpsichord. Others, who were ambitious of being able to converse with the singers, especially with the females; to utter with a grace the exclamations used to testify applause, and to be expert in the use of all the cant phrases which musical connoisseurs affect, set themselves to learn the Italian language; and in proportion to their progress in it were more or less busy behind the scenes, and in other respects troublesome and impertinent.

Who was the first writer in England of Italian operas is now only known in the instance of Etearcus, written by Haym, and represented in 1711; unless it can be supposed that Rossi, the author of Rinaldo, had been sufficiently encouraged to a second attempt of that kind; however, at the time of the establishment of the Academy the directors took care to engage in their service one whose abilities as a poet were never questioned, namely, Paolo Antonio Rolli. This person was a Florentine by birth, and, notwithstanding his pretensions to an honourable descent, was, as it is asserted by a gentleman who knew him in England, originally of a very mean occupation, that is to say, a maker of vermicelli; in plain English a pastry-cook; but having a talent for poetry, he cultivated it with great assiduity; and in some little songs, cantatas, and occasional poems, by him published from time to time, gave proofs of his genius. He came into England about the year 1718, and wrote for the managers the opera of Narcissus; Rolli wrote also Mutius Scævola, Numitor, Floridante, Astartus, Griselda, and Crispus,‡ and, in short, most of the operas exhibited under the direction of the Royal Academy: Elpidia, represented in 1725, was written by Apostolo Zeno. Finding in the English that frequented the opera a propensity to the study of the Italian language, Rolli became a teacher of it to those who were able to make him such gratifications, as men possessed with a high sense of their own merits are wont to require. Being a man of assiduity, he applied himself to the publication of valuable books written in his own language, as namely, the Decameron of Boccace, the Satires of Ariosto, the Opere burlesche of Francesco Berni, Giovanni della Cafa, and other Italian poets, and the translation of Lucretius by Alessandro Marchetti. For the improvement of his scholars he also translated into Italian two of Sir Richard Steele's comedies, viz., the Conscious Lovers and the Funeral, and also the Paradise Lost of Milton; upon which it is to be remarked, that, being of the Romish communion, he has left out the Limbo of Vanity, and that some of the copies were printed on blue paper. In the year 1744 he quitted England, and retired, as it is said,

---

* Elpidia and Elisa were performed in the year 1725, but by whom they were composed is not known.

† She is so called in the opera of Narcissus, composed by Domenico, the son of Alessandro Scarlatti, with additional songs by Roseingrave, and performed at the theatre in the Haymarket in 1720.

‡ The subject of the opera of Griselda is the well known story of the marquis of Saluzzo and Griselda, related by Boccace, and is the Clerk of Oxford's tale in Chaucer. See vol. II. page 29. It is known to the vulgar by an old ballad entitled 'Patient Grisel,' beginning 'A noble marquis as he did ride a hunting.' It seems that at the time of performing the operas of Griselda and Crispus, their comparative merits were the subject of a dispute that divided the ladies into parties, one whereof preferred the former, the other the latter. This difference of opinion is taken notice of by Sir Richard Steele in his comedy of the Conscious Lovers, Act II.

to the enjoyment of a patrimonial estate in the Campania of Rome, assuming the title of a Roman senator.

Besides the singers, the instrumental performers in the opera deserve some notice; Corbett played the first violin at the time when they were first introduced: to him succeeded Claudio, an Italian, a sound and judicious performer; but when the entertainment was put upon a new and better footing, Carbonelli was placed at the head of the orchestra. He continued in that station about seven years, and was succeeded by Pietro Castrucci. Mr. Galliard played the first hautboy, and Kenny, mentioned before in the life of Purcell by the mistaken name of Kennedy, the bassoon.

## BOOK XX.　　CHAP. CLXXXVIII.

MR. HANDEL continued to fulfil his engagements with the directors, until the year 1726, when, having composed a new opera, entitled Alessandro, and engaged a new singer, namely Signora Faustina, he laid the foundation of a dispute, that terminated in the ruin of the whole undertaking.

But before we proceed to relate the circumstances of this event, it may be observed that it seemed to be no more than the necessary consequence of that extravagant applause which the opera audience had shewn itself ever ready to bestow on their favourites among the singers. Senesino was one of the first that discovered this benevolent propensity in the English, and he laboured by a vigorous exertion of all his powers, to cultivate and improve that good opinion which had been conceived of him on his first appearance among us; and it was not long before he began to feel his own importance. Handel was not a proud man, but he was capricious: in his comparison of the merits of a composer and those of a singer, he estimated the latter at a very low rate, and affected to treat Senesino with a degree of indifference that the other could but ill brook; in short, they were upon very ill terms almost from the time of their first coming together; but in a year or two after Faustina's arrival, the flame of civil discord burst forth, and all was disorder and confusion. The two women were soon sensible, from the applause bestowed upon Senesino, that the favour of an English audience was worth courting; and in proportion as it appeared desirable, each of them began to grow jealous of the other: Senesino had no rival, but each of the women was possessed of talents sufficient to engage a very strong party. To render the history of this contest intelligible will require a short digression.

Mrs. ANASTASIA ROBINSON (*a Portrait*) was descended from a good family in the county of Leicester; her father was brought up to the profession of a portrait painter, and having, to perfect himself in his studies, travelled to Rome, he returned to England, and settling in London, married a woman of some fortune, by whom he had *two daughters, Anastasia, the subject of the present article, and another named Margaret. In the infancy of these his children, Mr. Robinson had the misfortune to lose his wife; and needing the assistance of a female to bring them up and manage the concerns of his family, he married a young gentlewoman of the name of Lane.* Soon after this Mr. Robinson contracted a disorder in his eyes, which terminated in the loss of his sight, and deprived him of the means of supporting himself and his family by the exercise of his pencil. Under the heavy pressure of this calamity, he and his wife reflecting on their inability to make a provision for them, resolved to bring up both the children to a profession: Anastasia, the elder, having discovered in her childhood an ear for music, was designed by them for a singer; and other motives, equally cogent at the time, determined them to make of Peggy a miniature painter. The story of this younger daughter is but short, and is, against the order of precedence, here inserted, to prevent a digression in that which is more to our purpose, the the history of her sister.

The second Mrs. Robinson was possessed of a small income, part whereof, under the direction of her husband, was appropriated to the instruction of the two children in the professions they were severally intended for; but all the endeavours of the parents in favour of the younger were in vain; she slighted her studies, and, deviating into her sister's track, would learn nothing but music: yielding, therefore, to this strong propensity, Mr. Robinson placed her under Bononcini, and afterwards sent her to Paris, where, being committed to the tuition of Rameau, and having a most delicate ear, and great powers of execution, she attained to such a degree of perfection in singing as set her upon a level with the most celebrated performers of the time; but having a natural bashfulness, which she could never overcome, and being besides lower in stature than the lowest of her sex, she could never be prevailed on to become a public singer; *yet with these disadvantages she was not destitute of attractions: a gentleman of the army, Colonel Bowles, liked and married her.* On the other hand, Anastasia, who had been committed to the care of Dr. Croft, but was rather less indebted to nature for the gift of a voice than her sister, prosecuted her studies with the utmost industry. With the assistance of her father she became such a mistress of the Italian language, that she was able to converse in it, and to repeat with the utmost propriety passages from the poets. To remedy some defects in her singing, to mend if possible her shake, which was not altogether correct, and, above all, to make the Italian modulation familiar to her, the assistance of Sandoni, a celebrated teacher,* was called in; but all that could be done by him, and the lady called the Baroness, a singer in

* Pier Giuseppe Sandoni; he published, and dedicated to the countess of Pembroke, a work of his entitled 'Cantate da Camera e Sonate per il Cembalo.'

MRS. ANASTASIA ROBINSON.
AFTERWARDS COUNTESS OF PETERBOROUGH.

FRANCESCO BERNARDO SENESINO.

the opera, then greatly caressed, in these respects was but little; she had a fine voice, and an extensive compass, but she wanted a nice and discriminating ear to make her a perfect singer. Her first public appearance was in the concerts performed at that time in York-buildings, and at other places, in which she sang, and generally accompanied herself on the harpsichord. Her father had carefully attended to her education, and had exerted his utmost efforts in the improvement of her mind; the advantages she derived from these instances of his affection, added to her own good sense and amiable qualities, consisting in a strictly virtuous disposition, a conduct full of respect to her superiors, and an undissembled courtesy and affability to others, mixed with a cheerfulness that diffused itself to all around her, were visible in the reception she met with from the public, which was of such a kind as seemed to ensure her success in whatever she undertook. Encouraged by the favour of the public to his daughter, and more especially by the countenance and bounty of some persons of high rank of her own sex, Mr. Robinson took a house in Golden-square, and had concerts, and also conversations on certain days in every week, which were the resort of all who had any pretensions to politeness. *A lady of very high rank now living (the Duchess Dowager of Portland), who honoured Mrs. Anastasia Robinson with her patronage, and was very intimate with her, has condescended to furnish some of the above anecdotes respecting her and her family, which she concludes with saying that it was to support her afflicted father that she became a singer in the opera, and, speaking of her mental endowments, gives her this exalted character:—* 'Mrs. Robinson was most perfectly well bred and 'admirably accomplished, and, in short, one of the 'most virtuous and best of women, but never very 'handsome.' *The same person says that Mr. Robinson had by his second wife a daughter, who was married to Mr. George Arbuthnot, a wine merchant, a brother of Dr. Arbuthnot, the physician and friend of Mr. Pope.*

At the time when Mrs. Tofts and Margarita retired from the stage, scarce any female singers worth hearing were left; Mrs. Linsey, Mrs. Cross, Signora Isabella Girardeau, and the Baroness above mentioned, are the only names that we meet with, except the two former, and Signora Maria Gallia, who sang the part of Rosamond in Mr. Addison's opera of that name, between the time of the first introduction of the opera and the year 1718. Under these favourable circumstances, and the several others above enumerated, Mrs. Robinson was prevailed on to appear on the opera stage. The first opera she sang in was that of Narcissus, mentioned in a preceding page to have been composed by Domenico Scarlatti, and brought on the stage by Roseingrave; in this she sang the part of Echo with great applause. In the succeeding operas of Mutius Scævola, Crispus, Griselda, Otho, Floridante, Flavius, Julius Cæsar, Pharnaces, Coriolanus, and Vespasian, she also sang, and, together with Cuzzoni and Senesino, contributed greatly to the support of the entertainment. Her

salary was a thousand pounds, and her emoluments, arising from benefits and presents of various kinds, were estimated at nearly as much more. She continued to sing in the opera till the year 1723, at the end whereof she retired from the stage, in consequence, as it is supposed, of her marriage with the earl of Peterborough; for she at that time went to reside at his house at Parson's Green, and appeared there the mistress of his family; and the marriage was announced some years after in the public papers, in terms that imported it to be a transaction some years precedent to the time of notifying it, which was not till the year 1735. During this critical interval, in which the earl, for the same reasons that restrained him from publishing his marriage, studiously avoided the styling her his countess, she was visited by persons of the highest rank, under a full persuasion, founded on the general tenor of her life and conduct, that she could be no other than the mistress of the mansion in which she did the family honours, and that she had a legal title to a rank which, for prudential reasons, she was content to decline. This nobleman had a seat called Bevis Mount, situate near Southampton. By a letter from the earl to Mr. Pope, written about the year 1728, it appears that Mrs. Robinson then lived with him, for she is there mentioned by the appellation of the Farmeress of Bevis; and in others from the same person, of a later date, are sundry expressions alluding to the severities which at stated seasons she practised on herself, and plainly indicating that she was of the Romish communion.*

In this exalted station of life she forgot not her obligations to Bononcini; he had improved her manner of singing, and in most of his operas, particularly Crispus and Griselda, had composed songs peculiarly adapted to her powers of execution; for him she obtained the pension of five hundred pounds a year, granted him by the duchess of Marlborough; and for his friend Greene she procured the places of

* Works of Alexander Pope, Esq. Lond. 1739, vol. VI. page 210, et seq. It is conjectured that all her family were of the same persuasion; at least it is certain that Mr. Robinson's second wife was, and that her brother Mr. Lane, resided in the family of the earl of Peterborough, from the time of his marriage with Mrs. Robinson, in the avowed character of a Romish ecclesiastic.

The general character of the above-mentioned nobleman, who is equally celebrated for his bravery and his parts, is well known; he wrote those exquisitely neat and elegant lines in Pope and Swift's Miscellany, beginning 'I said to my heart between sleeping and waking;' four letters in Pope's collection, and a few other things of small account, mentioned in Mr. Walpole's Catalogue of Royal and Noble Authors; but Mrs. Howard, afterwards countess of Suffolk, the subject of the above verses, had seen and read in the manuscript three volumes of his lordship's memoirs, which it is feared are irrecoverably lost. That lady, who knew him very well, used to relate a story, which she had from his own mouth, so singular, that the mention of it here may merit an excuse. Lord Peterborough, when a young man, and about the time of the Revolution, had a passion for a lady who was fond of birds; she had seen and heard a fine canary bird at a coffee-house near Charing-cross, and entreated him to get it for her; the owner of it was a widow, and lord Peterborough offered to buy it at a great price, which she refused: finding there was no other way of coming at the bird, he determined to change it; and getting one of the same colour, with nearly the same marks, but which happened to be a hen, went to the house; the mistress of it usually sat in a room behind the bar, to which he had easy access; contriving to send her out of the way, he effected his purpose; and upon her return took his leave. He continued to frequent the house to avoid suspicion, but forbore saying any thing of the bird till about two years after; when taking occasion to speak of it, he said to the woman, 'I would have bought that bird of you, and you refused my money for it, 'I dare say you are by this time sorry for it.' 'Indeed, Sir,' answered the woman, 'I am not, nor would I now take any sum for him, for would 'you believe it? from the time that our good king was forced to go 'abroad and leave us, the dear creature has not sung a note.'

organist and composer to the royal chapel, vacant by the decease of her master, Dr. Croft.

The earl was very far advanced in years at the time when he married Mrs. Robinson; in 1735, being advised to go to Lisbon for the recovery of his health, he went thither, and on the twenty-fifth day of October, in the same year, died at the advanced age of seventy-seven. The countess surviving him, continued to reside at Bevis Mount till the year 1750, when she also died.

During the residence of Mrs. Robinson at Parson's Green she had a kind of a musical academy there, in which Bononcini, Martini, Tosi, Greene, and others of that party, were frequent performers. His lordship had also frequent dining parties, whom he entertained with music, and, what was little less delightful, the recital of his adventures during his long residence abroad, particularly while he commanded in Spain. In that kingdom, while he was upon journies he was frequently in danger of perishing for want of food; and when he could get it, was so often constrained to dress it himself, that he became a good cook; and, such was the force of habit, that, till disabled by age, his dinner was constantly of his own dressing. Those who have dined with him at Parson's Green say that he had a dress for the purpose, like that of a tavern cook; and that he used to retire from his company an hour before dinner time; and, having despatched his culinary affairs, would return properly dressed, and take his place among them.

## CHAP. CLXXXIX.

FRANCESCO BERNARDO SENESINO (*a Portrait*), a native of Sienna, as his surname imports, was a singer in the opera at Dresden in the year 1719, at the same time with Signora Margarita Durastanti. In consequence of his engagement with the directors of the academy, Mr. Handel went to Dresden, and entered into a contract with both these persons, as also with Berenstadt, to sing in the opera at London, the former at a salary of fifteen hundred pounds for the season. Senesino had a very fine even-toned voice, but of rather a narrow compass; some called it a mezzo soprano, others a contralto; it was nevertheless wonderfully flexible: besides this he was a graceful actor, and in the pronunciation of recitative had not his fellow in Europe. His first appearance was in the opera of Mutius Scævola, represented in the year 1721.

It has been already mentioned, that notwithstanding Senesino was so excellent and useful a singer, as to be in a great measure the support of the opera, Handel and he agreed but ill together; and that a short time after the arrival of Faustina, the disputes among the singers rose to such a height, as threatened the ruin of the opera. Handel suspected that the example of Senesino had given encouragement to that refractory spirit which he found rising in the two contending females; and being determined to strike at the root of the evil, he proposed to the directors to discard Senesino; but they refusing to consent, Handel refused also to compose for him any

longer, or indeed to have any farther concern with him. A year or two afterwards the academy broke up, after having flourished for more than nine years.

The academy being thus dissolved, some of the nobility raised a new subscription for an opera at Lincoln's-Inn fields, in which Porpora was engaged to compose, and Senesino to sing. The success of this undertaking will be the subject of a future page; Senesino continued in the service of the nobility, singing at Lincoln's-Inn fields theatre, and afterwards at the Haymarket, which Handel had quitted, till about the year 1735, when, having acquired the sum of fifteen thousand pounds, he retired to Sienna, the place of his nativity, and built a handsome house, which, upon his decease, he bequeathed, together with the whole of his fortune, to his relations.

Signora MARGARITA DURASTANTI was engaged by Mr. Handel at the same time with Senesino, and came with him into England. She sang in the operas composed by Handel, Bononcini, and Attilio, till the year 1723. For the reason of her quitting England we are to seek, unless we may suppose that the applause bestowed on Cuzzoni, who appeared on the stage for two or three winters with her, was more than she could bear. However, she made a handsome retreat, and, as it seems, took a formal leave of the English nation by singing on the stage a song written for her in haste by Mr. Pope, at the earnest request of the earl of Peterborough, which, together with a burlesque of it by Dr. Arbuthnot, were lately printed in some of the public papers from a volume of poems among the Harleian manuscripts in the British Museum. Both poems are here inserted :—

> Generous, gay, and gallant nation,
> 　Bold in arms, and bright in arts;
> Land secure from all invasion,
> 　All but Cupid's gentle darts!
> From your charms, oh who would run?
> Who would leave you for the sun?
>
> 　Happy soil, adieu, adieu!
> Let old charmers yield to new.
> 　In arms, in arts, be still more shining;
> All your joys be still encreasing;
> 　All your tastes be still refining;
> All your jars for ever ceasing:
> 　But let old charmers yield to new
> 　Happy soil, adieu, adieu!

> Puppies, whom I now am leaving,
> 　Merry sometimes, always mad,
> Who lavish most, when debts are craving,
> 　On fool, and farce, and masquerade!
> Who would not from such bubbles run,
> And leave such blessings for the sun?
>
> 　Happy soil, and simple crew!
> 　Let old sharpers yield to new;
> All your tastes be still refining;
> All your nonsense still more shining:
> Blest in some Berenstadt or Boschi,
> He more aukward, he more husky;
> And never want, when these are lost t'us,
> Another Heidegger and Faustus.
> 　Happy soil, and simple crew!
> 　Let old sharpers yield to new?
> 　Bubbles all, adieu, adieu!

FRANCESCA CUZZONI SANDONI,

DA PARMA.

SIGNORA FAUSTINA.

Francesca Cuzzoni Sandoni *(a Portrait)*, a native of Modena, became a singer in the opera at London soon after the arrival of Senesino; for it appears that she sang in the opera of Otho, which was performed in the year 1722. She continued to sing the principal songs till the year 1726, when Faustina arrived, and becoming a competitor with her for the public favour, gave rise to a contest, which more properly belongs to the next article.

Signora Faustina* *(a Portrait)*, a Venetian by birth, and a young woman with a handsome face, and of a pleasing form, had sung abroad with such applause, that, as it is said, persons labouring under the tortures of the gout left their beds, and resorted to the theatres to hear her; and at Florence, in particular, medals in honour of her were struck. It was thought that the accession of such a distinguished singer would tend greatly to the advantage of the opera in England; accordingly, in the year 1726, she was engaged, and appeared first in the opera of Alexander. In the powers of execution, and a distinct manner of singing quick passages, she exceeded Cuzzoni: the merit of her rival consisted in a fine-toned voice, and a power of expression that frequently melted the audience into tears. For the circumstances of this famous dispute recourse has been had to some persons of distinguished rank, leaders of the two parties which it gave rise to; and as all animosity between them is now subsided, the relation of each appears to be such as may safely be relied on.

Till the time of Faustina's arrival, Cuzzoni as a female singer was in full possession of the public favour; the songs which Mr. Handel gave her were composed with the utmost solicitude to display her talents to advantage, as appears by the songs 'Affanni del pensier,' in Otho, 'Da tanti affanni 'oppressa,' 'Sen vola lo sparvier,' and 'E per monti 'e per piano,' in Admetus, and others. She had driven Durastanti out of the kingdom; Mrs. Robinson quitted the stage about the same time, so that for three seasons she remained without a rival. The consciousness of her great abilities, and the stubborn resistance of Senesino to Handel, had no small effect on the behaviour of Cuzzoni: she too could at times be refractory; for some slight objection that she had to the song 'Falsa imagine,' in Otho, she at the practice of it refused to sing it; when Mr. Handel referring to other instances of her stubbornness, took her round the waist, and swore, if she persisted, to throw her out of the window. It was high time therefore to look out for means of quieting this rebellious spirit, and, to effect his purpose, nothing seemed to bid so fair as the engagement of Faustina.

As Handel had taken the pains to compose songs peculiarly adapted to the powers and excellencies of Cuzzoni, he was not less solicitous to display those of Faustina; accordingly he made for her the air, 'Alla sua gabbia d'oro,' in Alexander, in the performance whereof she emulated the liquid articula-tion of the nightingale, and charmed the unprejudiced part of her hearers into ecstasy; as also 'Vedeste 'mai sul prato,' in Siroe, 'Gelosia spietato alletto,' in Admetus, and many others. *Riccoboni asserts that she invented, but we should rather say introduced, a new manner of singing, and it seems so by the songs composed for her, which abound with long and rapid divisions, such as none but a voice like hers could execute.*

From the account above given of Cuzzoni and Faustina, it appears that they were possessed of very different talents. The design of the directors in producing them both on the same stage, was to form a pleasing contrast between the powers of expression and execution, that of Handel was to get rid of Cuzzoni; but the town no sooner became sensible of the perfections which each was possessed of, than they began to compare them in their own minds, and endeavour to determine to whom of the two the greatest tribute of theatrical applause was due. Some ladies of the first quality entered very deeply into the merits of this competition; a numerous party engaged to support Cuzzoni, and another not less formidable associated on the side of Faustina. Thus encouraged, the behaviour of the rivals to each other was attended with all the circumstances of malevolence that jealousy, hatred, and malice could suggest; private slander and public abuse were deemed weapons too innoxious in this warfare, blows were made use of in the prosecution of it, and, shame to tell! the two Signoras fought. The countess of Pembroke[†] headed the Cuzzoni party, and carried her animosity to such lengths, as gave occasion to the following epigram:—

**Upon Lady Pembroke's promoting the catcalling of Faustina.**

> Old poets sing that beasts did dance
> Whenever Orpheus play'd,
> So to Faustina's charming voice
> Wise Pembroke's asses bray'd.

The chief supporters of Cuzzoni among the men are pointed out in the following epigram, which with that above given is extracted from a volume of poems among the Harleian manuscripts now in the British Museum, Numb. 7316, pages 394, 319.

**Epigram on the Miracles wrought by Cuzzoni.**

> Boast not how Orpheus charm'd the rocks,
> And set a dancing stones and stocks,
>     And tygers' rage appeas'd;
> All this Cuzzoni has surpass'd,
> Sir Wilfred[‡] seems to have a taste,
>     And Smith[§] and Gage[||] are pleas'd.

Faustina's friends among the ladies were Dorothy, countess of Burlington, and Charlotte, lady Delawar; the men in general were on her side, as being by far a more agreeable woman than Cuzzoni.[¶]

---

[*] *Riccoboni in his account of the theatres in Europe, gives her two surnames, calling her Faustina Bardoni Asse. The latter, it is supposed, is meant for that which she acquired by her marriage with Hasse. Vide infra 874.*

[†] Mary Howe, third wife of earl Thomas.

[‡] Sir Wilfred Lawson, Bart.    [§] Simon Smith, Esq.    [||] Sir William Gage, Bart, all subscribers to the Royal Academy.

[¶] *In the contest between Faustina and Cuzzoni, Sir Robert Walpole took part with the former, as being the least assuming of the two. His Lady, that the latter might not be born down by his influence countenanced Cuzzoni; and on Sundays when he was gone to Chelsea would invite them to dinner. She was at first distrest to adjust the precedence between them at her table, but their concessions to each other were mutual.*

The directors, greatly troubled with the dispute, and foreseeing the probable consequences of it, fell upon an odd expedient to determine it. The time for a new contract with each of these singers was at hand, and they agreed among themselves to give as a salary to Faustina one guinea a year more than to her rival. Lady Pembroke and some others, the friends of Cuzzoni, hearing this, made her swear upon the holy gospels never to take less than Faustina, and the directors continuing firm in their resolution not to give her quite so much, Cuzzoni found herself ensnared by her oath into the necessity of quitting the kingdom. The following lines were written by Ambrose Phillips on her departure :—

> Little syren of the stage,
> Charmer of an idle age,
> Empty warbler, breathing lyre,
> Wanton gale of fond desire ;
> Bane of every manly art,
> Sweet enfeebler of the heart ;
> O ! too pleasing is thy strain,
> Hence to southern climes again :
> Tuneful mischief, vocal spell,
> To this island bid farewell ;
> Leave us as we ought to be,
> Leave the Britons rough and free.

About the year 1748 she was engaged to sing at the Haymarket, and appeared in the opera of Mitridate, composed by Terradellas, but, being far advanced in years, she gave but little satisfaction. She returned to Italy at the end of the season, and, as we have been informed, was living about five years ago in a very mean condition, subsisting by the making of buttons. *That she was of a turbulent and obstinate temper may be inferred from a circumstance noted in a preceding page, and that she was ungrateful and insolent is little less certain, if credit be due to the author of the 'Essai sur la 'Musique,' printed at Paris, in four tomes, quarto, who relates that she begged of an English nobleman a suit of lace, but not liking it when sent to her, she threw it into the fire. After her leaving England she was for some time in Holland, where being imprisoned for debt, she was occasionally indulged by her keeper with permission to sing at the theatre, one of his servants attending to conduct her back. By these means she was enabled to pay her debts. Upon her enlargement she went to Bologna, and there, having experienced the miseries of extreme poverty, died.*

A better fate attended Faustina. She remained in England a short time after Cuzzoni, and in 1728 sang in the operas of Admetus and Siroe ; but, upon the disagreement between Handel and the directors of the opera, which terminated in the dissolution of the Royal Academy, she too left England, and went to Dresden, where she was married to Hasse, a musician of some eminence there, and is now living at Vienna.

## CHAP. CXC.

The singing of Senesino, Cuzzoni, and Faustina had captivated the hearers of them to such a degree, that they forgot the advantages which the human voice derives from its association with instruments, so that they could have been well content with mere vocal performance during the whole of the evening's entertainment. The cry was that these persons were very liberally paid, and that the public had not singing enough for their money ; and from a few instances, such as occur in the song 'Lusinghe 'piu care,' in Alexander, 'Luci care,' in Admetus, and some others, in which the song part seems to be overcharged with symphony, it was complained of that compositions thus constructed were not so properly songs as sonatas. In favour of this notion an anonymous pamphlet was published in the year 1728, entitled 'Avviso ai Compositori, ed ai Can-'tanti,' with an English translation ; the design of it was to rectify the errors, real or supposed, in the composition of opera songs, but without any such particular instances as might lead to a suspicion that it was written to serve the interests of either of those masters who had for some time divided the opinion of the public ; in the general drift of it it seems calculated to add as much as possible to the importance of the singers, and to banish from the stage those aids of instrumental performance, which serve as reliefs to the vocal, and enable the singer to display his talent to greater advantage.

To this purpose the author expresses himself in these words : 'Another irregularity is that of en-'cumbering and overcharging the composition with 'too many symphonies. This custom has so much 'grown upon us within these late years, that 'if a stop be not put to it, the singer will be made 'to give place to the instruments, and the orchestra 'will be more regarded than the voices. It cannot 'be denied, that if symphonies are well intermixed 'with the songs, it will have a very good effect, 'especially if the composer rightly understands how 'to make use of them, and is a complete master ; but 'then he must take particular care that they do not 'make his composition any ways confused, and must 'guard himself against running into excess in the use 'of them, remembering that most useful saying 'of Terence, "Ne quid nimis."'

At the time when the opera was in its most flourishing state, that is to say, in the year 1727, was brought on the stage the Beggar's Opera, written by Mr. John Gay. Dean Swift says that this comedy exposeth with great justice that unnatural taste for Italian music among us,[*] which is wholly unsuitable to our northern climate. But there is nothing to warrant this assertion, unless Macheath's appearing in Newgate in fetters can be supposed a ridicule of the prison scene in Coriolanus, which had been represented at the Haymarket a few years before :[†] it was in truth a satire, and that so

---

[*] Intelligencer, No. 3, in Swift's works, printed by Faulkner, vol. I. page 284.

[†] The truest burlesque of the Italian opera is a mean subject, affording a mock hero, wrought into the form of a drama, in a style of bombast, set in recitative, with airs intermixed, in which long divisions are made on insignificant words. In a book entitled the Touchstone, or Historical, Critical, Political, Philosophical, and Theological Essays on the reigning Diversions of the Town, written by Mr. James Ralph ; the Dragon of Wantley, Robinhood and Little John, the London Prentice, Tom Thumb, and Chevy Chase, are proposed as subjects for a mock opera : the plan recommended by this writer was pursued by the facetious Henry Carey, who wrote the Dragon of Wantley, and got it set by Lampe, a Saxon, who was here some years ago, and composed for Covent Garden theatre ; and by the author of Tom Thumb, taken from Fielding's Tragedy of

general, as to include in it all stations and characters, and, in short, every class of men whose rank or situation of life was above that of the author. The motive for writing this piece, and for the many acrimonious expressions and bitter invectives against statesmen, lawyers, priests, and others, contained in it, was the disappointment of Mr. Gay in his application for preferment at court. He had been brought up to the trade of a mercer, but did not choose to follow it; for, having a genius for poetry, he became acquainted with Pope and Swift, who might probably tell him that he was a man of genius, and that such men had a right to places and preferments; and that from the time of the Revolution it had been a matter of contention between the leaders of the Whig and Tory parties, which should provide best for the writers of verses on either side respectively.* The poor man took their advice, and wrote his Fables for the use and instruction of the duke of Cumberland, then a child. He also wrote a tragedy called the Captives, which he was permitted to read to queen Caroline, and which was acted at Lincoln's-Inn fields, in 1720, with tolerable success. As a reward of these his merits, and upon the solicitation of some persons of high rank about the court, an offer was made him of the place of gentleman-usher to the princess Louisa, which he rejected with contempt, and, in the greatness of his soul, preferred to it a life of ease, and servile dependence on the bounty of his friends and the caprice of the town.

The Beggar's Opera had a run of sixty-three nights, during which the operas of Richard I. and Admetus were performing at the Haymarket, and, as it is said, but to thin audiences. The malevolence of the people, and the resentment which they had been taught to entertain against that conduct of administration, which they were equally unqualified to approve or condemn, were amply gratified by the representation of it; but the public were little aware of the injury they were doing to society, by giving countenance to an entertainment, which has been productive of more mischief to this country than any would believe at the time; for, not to

mention that the tendency of it, by inculcating that persons in authority are uniformly actuated by the same motives as thieves and robbers, is to destroy all confidence in ministers, and respect for magistrates, and to lessen that reverence, which, even in the worst state of government, is due to the laws and to public authority, a character is exhibited to view, of a libertine endowed with bravery, generosity, and the qualities of a gentleman, subsisting by the profession of highway robbery, which he defends by examples drawn from the practice of men of all professions. In this view Macheath is as much a hero as the principal agent in an epic poem; but lest this character should not be sufficiently fascinating to young minds, he is farther represented as having attained to some degree of wealth, to keep good company, that is to say, gamesters of fashion; to be a favourite with the women, and so successful in his amours, that one is with child by him, and another he marries. In short, his whole life is represented as an uninterrupted pursuit of criminal gratifications, in which he has the good fortune to succeed, and in the end to escape with impunity. Nevertheless the vox populi was in favour of this immoral drama; and Dr. Herring, the late archbishop of Canterbury, for presuming to censure it in a sermon delivered before the honourable society of Lincoln's-Inn, while he was preaching there, was by Dean Swift stigmatized with the appellation of a stupid, injudicious, and prostitute divine.†

The effects of the Beggar's Opera on the minds of the people have fulfilled the prognostications of many that it would prove injurious to society. Rapine and violence have been gradually increasing ever since its first representation: the rights of property, and the obligation of the laws that guard it, are disputed upon principle. Every man's house is now become what the law calls it, his castle, or at least it may be said that, like a castle, it requires to be a place of defence; young men, apprentices, clerks in public offices, and others, disdaining the arts of honest industry, and captivated with the charms of idleness and criminal pleasure, now betake themselves to the road, affect politeness in the very act of robbery, and in the end become victims to the justice of their country: and men of discernment, who have been at the pains of tracing this evil to its source, have found that not a few of those, who, during these last fifty years have paid to the law the forfeit of their lives, have in the course of their pursuits been emulous to imitate the manners and general character of Macheath.

It has been already mentioned that the consequence of the dispute between the nobility and Mr. Handel, and the determination of the former to support Senesino, was the utter dissolution of the academy; but the nobility raised a new subscription for an opera to be represented at the theatre in Lin-

---

Tragedies, and made into an opera, and set to music, but with less success than the former. The Beggar's Opera is nothing like either of these; the dialogue is common speech, and the airs are old ballad-tunes and country-dances; and yet it is said, but without any foundation in truth, that it contributed more to bring the Italian opera into contempt, than the invectives of the poets and the friends of the drama, and the writings of Dennis, who had been labouring all his life to convince the world of the absurdity of this exotic entertainment.

* In the writings of Swift, particularly in his letters, there occur many such sentiments. In consequence of an opinion that men possessed of a talent for poetry were best qualified for public employment, Mr. Addison was made secretary of state, Prior was secretary to the English plenipotentiaries at the Hague, after under-secretary of state, and, lastly, a lord of trade; and Congreve, Stepney, Steele, and others, had seats at some of the public boards; the error of this opinion was evinced in the case of Mr. Addison, who, with all those talents for which he is justly celebrated, not only made a very mean figure in the office of secretary of state, but shewed himself to be as little fit for active life, as an excess of timidity, even to sheepishness, could render a man. Though a minister, he attempted to speak in the house of commons, but was not able to do it, and was very deservedly removed to make room for one that could. Dr. Mandeville, the author of the Fable of the Bees, who, though of very bad principle, was a man of understanding, and that knew the world, was very frequently with the lord chief justice Parker, afterwards earl of Macclesfield, whom Mr. Addison visited, and expressed to the chief justice a desire to meet him; his lordship brought them together, and, after an evening's conversation, asked the doctor what was his opinion of Mr. Addison; 'I think,' answered the Doctor, 'he is a parson in a 'tye-wig.'

† Intelligencer, No. 3, Dublin edition of Swift's works, vol. I. page 284. This paper is a laboured defence of the Beggar's Opera, addressed to the people of Ireland; and the sentiments therein delivered do very well consist with the character of a man, of whom it may with justice be said, that scarce any one of his profession, whose writings are of an equal bulk with those of Swift, has, as an author, contributed less than he to the promotion of religion, virtue, or the general interests of mankind.

coln's-Inn fields, and established a direction of twelve of their own body, who in the conduct thereof resolved to act without the control of such as should be retained to assist in it, whether composers or singers, although of these latter Senesino was one, and indeed the chief. Seeing this formidable association, Handel had nothing left but to enter into an agreement with Heidegger, who, though old, was yet living, for carrying on an opera in conjunction, for the short term of three years, at the Haymarket. Upon the conclusion of this agreement, Handel found himself under a necessity of going to Italy for the purpose of engaging singers. After a short stay abroad, he returned with Fabri, and another Castrato; Strada, surnamed del Po, and Bertoli; the two last were women, and the former of them a very fine singer. He also engaged a German named Reimschneider, a bass singer, and some other persons of less account. The winter after his arrival Handel began his contest with the nobility by the representation of his opera of Lotharius, on the sixteenth of November, 1729. This was succeeded by Parthenope, with which he closed the season.

Handel continued at the Haymarket till the expiration of the term for which he stood engaged with Heidegger, during which he composed and performed successively the operas of Porus, Sosarmes, Orlando, and Ætius: at the end thereof he, together with old Mr. Smith, went abroad in quest of singers. In Italy he heard Farinelli, a young man of astonishing talents, and also Carestini, and, which is very strange, preferring the latter, he engaged with him, and returned to England. With this assistance he ventured to undertake an opera at the Haymarket on his own bottom.

During all this time the adversaries of Handel went on with but little better success; they performed a variety of operas, composed by sundry authors whose names are now forgotten, but to audiences that were seldom numerous enough to defray the ordinary expenses of the representation. At length they entered into engagements with Porpora, a musician who had distinguished himself abroad, and Farinelli, and took possession of the Haymarket theatre, which Handel at the end of the season had abandoned. Of the success of this new association there will be farther occasion to speak: at present it may suffice to say, that, having two such singers as Farinelli and Senesino at their command, the nobility had greatly the advantage, and for one season at least were great gainers. It is true they were losers in the end, for Cibber, who was living at the time, and kept a watchful eye on the theatres, asserts that Farinelli during his stay here had been known to sing to an audience of five and thirty pounds.*

CARLO BROSCHI FARINELLI (*a Portrait*), was the nephew of that Farinelli whom we have before mentioned to have been concert-master or director of the elector's music at Hanover. He was born at Naples, in the year 1705, and derived great advantage from the instructions of Porpora. He had sung at Rome and at Bologna, at the latter of which cities he had

* Apology for his Life, page 243.

heard Bernacchi; and also at Venice; when the fame of his great talents reaching England, he was engaged to sing in the opera at London, and in the year 1734 came over hither. His arrival in this country was in the newspapers announced to the public as an event worthy of notoriety. As soon as he was enough recovered from the fatigue of his journey, he was introduced to the king at St. James's, and had the honour to sing to him, the princess royal, afterwards princess of Orange, accompanying him on the harpsichord. At the same time with Farinelli arrived in England Porpora, who had been his instructor, and was the companion of his fortunes, and Giacomo Amiconi, the painter.† These three persons seem to have been united together in the bonds of a strict friendship and a communion of interests: at the same time that the nobility under the new subscription engaged with Farinelli, they also agreed with Porpora as a composer for the opera, and with Amiconi to paint the scenes. The operas in which Farinelli sang, were, Ariadne and Polifemo, set by Porpora, and Artaxerxes, by Hasse, who had acquired some reputation in Germany by his compositions for the theatre. He sang also in the oratorio of David, composed by Porpora, and in an opera entitled Demetrius, by Pescetti, both performed at the Haymarket. The world had never seen two such singers upon the same stage as Senesino and Farinelli; the former was a just and graceful actor, and in the opinion of very good judges had the superiority of Farinelli in respect of the tone of his voice; but the latter had so much the advantage in other respects, that few hesitated to pronounce him the greatest singer in the world; this opinion was grounded on the amazing compass of his voice, exceeding that of women, or any of his own class; his shake was just, and sweet beyond expression; and in the management of his voice, and the clear articulation of divisions and quick passages, he passed all description. Such perfections as these were enough for one singer to possess, and indeed they were so evident, and their effects so forcible on the minds of his hearers, that few were disposed to reflect that his person was tall and slender to excess, and by consequence his mien and action ungraceful.

Upon what terms Farinelli was engaged to sing

† Amiconi found employment here as a portrait, and also a history painter. In the former capacity it was the fashion among the friends of the opera and the musical connoisseurs to sit to him; in the latter he exercised his talent in the painting of halls and staircases; and this, notwithstanding that Kent, who, because he was a bad painter himself, had, as an architect, in his construction of stair-cases driven that kind of painting out of the kingdom, Amiconi painted the staircase of Powishouse in Ormond-street with the story of Judith and Holofernes, in three compartments; and the hall in the house at More-park in Hertfortshire, with that of Jupiter and Iö. Of this house the following is a brief history: in 1617 it was granted by the crown to the earl of Bedford, and he by a deed, declaring the uses of a fine, limited the inheritance thereof to himself for life, remainder to Lucy his wife and her heirs. See Chauncy's Historical Antiquities of Hertfordshire, page 479. This Lucy was the famous countess of Bedford, celebrated by Sir Toby Matthews, Dr. Donne, and other writers of those times; and she it is said laid out the gardens in such a manner as induced Sir William Temple, in his Essay on Gardening, to say it was the perfectest figure of a garden he ever saw. Many years after the decease of the countess of Bedford, the duke of Ormond became the owner of More-park; and, after his attainder, Mr. Stiles; who employed Amiconi to paint the hall: the succeeding proprietor of this mansion was lord Anson, and the present, Sir Laurence Dundas. The fondness of Sir William Temple for this place, induced him to give the name of it to his seat near Farnham in Surrey. Hence has arisen a mistaken notion that the More-park mentioned in his Essay on Gardening was in Surrey.

CARLO BROSCHI,

DETTO FARINELLI.

here, is not known to a degree of certainty; his salary however, be it what it might, bore but a small proportion to the annual amount of his profits, which, by a benefit, and rich presents of various kinds, were estimated at five thousand pounds a year. The excessive fondness which the nobility discovered for this person, the caresses they bestowed on, and the presents they made him indicated little less than infatuation; their bounty was prodigality, and their applause adoration.*

That unmanly propensity in persons of high rank to promote and encourage this last refinement of modern luxury which they manifested in these and various other instances, was loudly complained of as derogating from the national character. It was urged that the reputation of this country abroad was founded on the disposition of the people to arms, and their love of letters; and that we were adopting the manners of a people who have long since ceased to be distinguished for either. Indeed it was ridiculous to see a whole people in such a state of fascination as they were in at this time; many pretended to be charmed with the singing of Farinelli, who had not the least ear for music; and who could not, if they had been left to themselves, have distinguished between him and an inferior singer. However the experiment of a few years was sufficient to convince the world of this truth at least, that two operas at a time were more than this metropolis could support; and determined Farinelli to try his success in another country. The particulars of his retreat will be mentioned in a subsequent page. Mr. Martinelli has given the following short character of him, which naturally leads us to give an account of his master Porpora, and also of Hasse, the joint composer with him for the opera, during the residence of Farinelli in London. 'He had a voice proportioned to his 'gigantic stature, extending beyond the ordinary 'compass near an octave, in notes equally clear and 'sonorous. At the same time he possessed such 'a degree of knowledge in the science of music, as 'he might be supposed to have derived from the in- 'structions of the skilful Porpora, bestowed on a 'diligent and favourite pupil: with unexampled 'agility and freedom did he traverse the paths which 'Bernacchi had trod with success, till he became the 'idol of the Italians, and at length of the harmonic 'world.'†

* Mr. Hogarth, in his Rake's Progress, has ridiculed this folly with great humour; in the second plate of that work he represents his rake at his levee in a circle, consisting of a bravo, a jockey, a dancing-master, a fencing-master, a gardener, and other dependents. In a corner of the room sits an opera composer at a harpsichord, with a long roll hanging from the back of his chair, on which is the following inscription: 'A list 'of the rich presents Signor Farinelli the Italian singer condescended to 'accept of the English nobility and gentry for one night's performance in 'the opera of Artaxerxes. A pair of diamond knee-buckles, presented 'by　　　　　a diamond ring by　　　　　A bank-note enclosed 'in a rich gold case by　　　　　A gold snuff box chased with the 'story of Orpheus charming the brutes, by T. Rakewell, Esq. 100*l*. '200*l*. 100*l*.' Many of the above presents were actually made to Farinelli during his stay among us, and were mentioned in the daily papers. On the floor lies a picture representing Farinelli seated on a pedestal, with an altar before him, on which are several flaming hearts; near which stand a number of people with their arms extended, offering him presents: at the foot of the altar is one lady kneeling, tendering her heart, from whose mouth a label issues, inscribed 'One God, one Farinelli;' alluding to a lady of distinction, who being charmed with a particular passage in one of his songs, uttered aloud from the boxes that impious exclamation.

† Lettere familiare e critiche, Carte 361.

## CHAP. CXCI.

Nicolo Porpora is celebrated among the modern musicians, not less as the instructor of some of the most applauded singers, than as a musical composer of the dramatic class. In the early part of his life he was in the service of Augustus, king of Poland, but quitting it, he made a temporary residence in sundry of the German courts, and afterwards in the principal cities of Italy. At Naples he became acquainted with Farinelli, who was then very young, and having a very promising voice, was endeavouring to acquire that style and manner of singing, which it is said Antonio Bernacchi of Bologna took from Pistocchi, and which gave rise to the denomination of the Bernacchi school. Porpora seeing this, and being desirous of correcting those extravagancies which Bernacchi had introduced into vocal practice, he laboured to form a style of greater simplicity, such as was calculated rather to affect than to astonish the hearers. As to Farinelli in particular, he set himself with all his might to improve those great talents which he had discovered in him, and in the end made him the finest singer that had then or has ever since been heard. A degree of success, alike proportioned to their several abilities, had he in the tuition of Salimbelli, Caffarelli, and Mingotti, all of whom were the pupils of Porpora.

The attachments of Porpora to Farinelli were of such a friendly kind, as determined him to become, if not a sharer in his fortunes, at least a witness of that applause which was bestowed on him whithersoever he went: with this view he was the companion of his travels; and it may well be supposed that the English nobility, when they engaged Farinelli to sing here, considered Porpora as so intimately connected with him, that an attempt to separate them would go near to render a treaty for that purpose abortive; accordingly they were both engaged and arrived in England together.

The operas of Porpora, as musical compositions, had little to recommend them: that of Ariadne was looked upon as inferior to the Ariadne of Handel, in which, excepting the minuet at the end of the overture, there is scarce a good air. Dr. Arbuthnot however, in a humorous pamphlet written on occasion of the disputes about the opera, entitled Harmony in an Uproar, calls that of Handel the Nightingale, the other the Cuckoo.‡

In the year 1735 Porpora published and dedicated to Frederic, prince of Wales, who had taken part with him in the dispute with Handel, Twelve Italian Cantatas, which at this day are greatly esteemed. He also published Six Sonatas for two violins and a bass; these compositions are mere symphonies, and, having in them very little of design or contrivance, are now scarcely remembered.

Giovanni Adolfo Hasse was born near Hamburg, and received his first instructions in music in that city. At the age of eighteen he composed an opera entitled Antigono; but, being desirous of farther improvement, he went to Naples, and for a short time

‡ Miscellaneous works of the late Dr. Arbuthnot, vol. II. page 21.

was under the tuition of Porpora, but afterwards became a disciple of Alessandro Scarlatti. Upon his return to Germany he became maestro di cappella to the elector of Saxony, and at Dresden composed operas, some in the German, and others in the Italian language. In the composition of operas he was esteemed abroad the first of the German masters; and the fame of his abilities reaching England at the time of the rupture between Handel and the English nobility, he was employed by them, and composed the opera of Artaxerxes, written by Metastasio, and some others, which were represented here, and received great advantage from the performance of Farinelli. He married Faustina soon after her return from England: it does not appear that he was ever here himself; it seems he was strongly pressed at the time above-mentioned to come to London, but Mr. Handel being then living, he declined the invitation, not choosing to become a competitor with one so greatly his superior.

The abilities of Hasse seem to have been greatly over-rated by some of our countrymen who have taken occasion to mention him. Six Cantatas for a voice, with an accompaniment for the harpsichord, a Salve Regina for a single voice with instruments, a single concerto for French horns, and other instruments, and a few airs selected from his operas performed here, are all of his compositions that have been published in England; and these are so far from affording evidence of any extraordinary talent, that they are a full justification of the author of the Remarks on Mr. Avison's Essay on Musical Expression, who has not hesitated to assert that the distinguishing characteristic of Hasse's compositions is effeminacy.

The contest between Handel and the nobility was carried on with so much disadvantage to the former, that he found himself under the necessity of quitting the Haymarket theatre at the time when his opponents were wishing to get possession of it; and in the issue each party shifted its ground by an exchange of situations. The nobility removed with Farinelli, Senesino, and Montagnana, a bass singer, who had sung for Handel in Sosarmes and other of his operas; and Handel, with Strada, Bertoli, and Waltz, a bass singer, who had been his cook, went to Lincoln's-Inn fields. Here he continued but for a short time; for, finding himself unable singly to continue the opposition, he removed to Covent Garden, and entered into some engagements with Rich, the particulars of which are not known; save that in discharge of a debt that he had contracted with him in consequence thereof, he some years after set to music an English opera entitled Alceste, written by Dr. Smollett, and for which Rich was at great expence in a set of scenes painted by Servandoni; but it was never performed. Handel afterwards adapted this music to Dryden's Song for St. Cecilia's Day, 1687, printed in the fourth part of his Miscellaneous Poems, and performed it together with Alexander's Feast.

Such as are not acquainted with the personal character of Handel, will wonder at his seeming temerity, in continuing so long an opposition which tended

but to impoverish him; but he was a man of a firm and intrepid spirit, no way a slave to the passion of avarice, and would have gone greater lengths than he did, rather than submit to those whom he had ever looked on as his inferiors: but though his ill success for a series of years had not affected his spirit, there is reason to believe that his genius was in some degree damped by it; for whereas of his earlier operas, that is to say, those composed by him between the years 1710 and 1728, the merits are so great, that few are able to say which is to be preferred; those composed after that period have so little to recommend them, that few would take them for the work of the same author. In the former class are Radamistus, Otho, Tamerlane, Rodelinda, Alexander, and Admetus, in either of which scarcely an indifferent air occurs; whereas in Parthenope, Porus, Sosarmes, Orlando, Ætius, Ariadne, and the rest down to 1736, it is a matter of some difficulty to find a good one.

The nobility were no sooner settled at the Haymarket, than Farinelli appeared in the meridian of his glory: all the world resorted thither, even aldermen and other citizens, with their wives and daughters, to so great a degree, that in the city it became a proverbial expression, that those who had not heard Farinelli sing and Foster preach, were not qualified to appear in genteel company.*

But it fared far otherwise with Handel, who, after his engagement with Rich, performed to almost empty houses; and, after a contest, which lasted about three years, during which time he was obliged to draw out of the funds almost the whole of what in his prosperous days he had there invested, he gave out; and discovered to the world that in this dreadful conflict he had not only suffered in his fortune but his health.† To get rid of that dejection

* Mr. James Foster was a dissenting minister of the Anabaptist denomination. In the Old Jewry, during the winter season, on Sunday evenings, he preached a lecture, in which with great clearness and strength of reasoning he enforced the obligations of religion and virtue, chiefly from principles in which all mankind are agreed. The Freethinkers, as they are called, took him for a Deist, and his audiences were somewhat the larger for them; but they were greatly mistaken: on the contrary he was a devout and sincere Christian, as the author of this work can testify, who lived many years with him on terms of strict friendship; and gave ample proof of his faith in an excellent answer to a worthless book, Christianity as old as the Creation; and contributed to put to confusion its more worthless author, Dr. Matthew Tindal. Pope was acquainted with Foster, and, having frequently resorted to the Old Jewry purposely to hear him, complimented him with the following lines :—

Let modest FOSTER, if he will, excel<br>
Ten metropolitans in preaching well.<br>
Epilogue to the Satires, Dialogue I.

Lord Bolingbroke expressed to Mr. Pope a great desire to know Foster, and an appointment was made for a meeting of all the three; but an accident prevented it. Most of the sermons preached at the Old Jewry lecture are extant in four volumes, published by the author himself: they were also preached to a congregation of which he was pastor, in a place situated between Red-cross street and Barbican; but such was the fashion of the time, and such were the different effects of the same discourses at different places, that few but his own congregation resorted to the one, and people, at the risk of their limbs, struggled to get in at the other. In consideration of his great merit, and the estimation in which he was held throughout this kingdom, the university of Aberdeen honoured him with the degree of doctor in divinity. In the year 1746 he was requested to assist in preparing lord Kilmarnock for a submission to that sentence, which, for having been active in the rebellion of 1745, he was doomed to suffer. Dr. Foster complied with this request, and was necessitated to be a spectator of his end; the unspeakable anguish of mind which he felt upon this occasion, and the frequent reflection on all the circumstances of the execution, made such a deep impression on him, as could never be effaced; his mental faculties forsook him, and on the fifth day of November, in the year 1753, he died.

† Upon occasion of this his distress, Strada and others of the singers were content to accept of bonds for the payment of their arrears, and left the kingdom upon Mr. Handel's assurances that they should be discharged; and he paid a due regard to his engagement by remitting them the money

of mind, which his repeated disappointments had brought on him, he was advised to the use of the waters at Tunbridge, and a regimen calculated to assist their operation; but his disorder was so deeply rooted, that by several particulars in his behaviour, which it would give the reader no pleasure to be informed of, he discovered that his mental powers were affected; and, to complete his distress, one of those hands, which had frequently administered such delight to others, was now become useless to himself; in a word, the palsy had seized his right arm, and the whole of the limb was by a sudden stroke rendered incapable of performing its natural functions.

Medicines having been found ineffectual to remove his disorder, he was prevailed on, but with great difficulty, to resort to Aix la Chapelle; accordingly he went thither, and submitted to such sweats, excited by the vapour baths there, as astonished every one. After a few essays of this kind, during which his spirits seemed to rise rather than sink under an excessive perspiration, his disorder left him; and in a few hours after the last operation he went to the great church of the city, and got to the organ, on which he played in such a manner that men imputed his cure to a miracle. Having received so much benefit from the baths, he prudently determined to stay at Aix la Chapelle, till the end of six weeks from the time of his arrival there, and at the end thereof returned to London in perfect health.

Farinelli, during the interval of a few winters, had accumulated great wealth, but it arose chiefly from presents, and crowded houses at his benefits; and as he had experienced what it was to sing to an audience of thirty-five pounds, he began to suspect that his harvest in this country, which, as Mattheson terms it, was a golden one, was pretty well over, and began to think of trying his success in another: he had visited France in the year 1736, and finding at his return to London but little encouragement to engage at the opera, he finally quitted England the following summer, and on the ninth of July, 1737, appeared at Versailles, hoping to derive great advantages from the solemnities which were expected to attend the approaching birth of the duke of Anjou; but in this he was disappointed.

It happened about this time that the king of Spain laboured under a melancholy disorder, for which no relief could be suggested but music; his queen contrived to entertain him with frequent concerts: to make these as delightful to him as possible, she sent for Farinelli, and upon his arrival at Madrid attached him to the service of that court by a pension of 1400 piastres, or 3150l. per annum, and a coach and equipage maintained at the king's expense. Over and above his salary, considerable presents were made him; the king gave him his picture set with diamonds, valued at 5000 dollars: the queen presented him with a gold snuff-box, with two large diamonds on the lid; and the prince of Asturias gave him a diamond button and loop of great value. Upon the death of Philip V., Farinelli was continued in his station by his successor, Ferdinand VI., and in 1750 was honoured with the cross of Calatrava,

the badge of an order of knighthood in Spain of great antiquity. He continued, with the assistance of the best composers and singers, and of Metastasio and Amiconi the painter, which latter had followed him into Spain, to conduct the opera till about the year 1761, when he took a resolution to return to Italy; accordingly he went thither, and had an audience of Benedict XIV., to whom, upon his recounting the riches and honours that had been showered down upon him here and in Spain, the pope made this remark: 'In other words you mean 'to say, that you found abroad what you left here.'

His pension from the court of Spain being still continued to him, Farinelli chose the neighbourhood of Bologna for his residence; and in a house of his own building, near that city, he is now living in ease and great affluence.

It is now necessary to recur to a former period, and in an orderly course of narration to relate such other particulars respecting the subject of this history, as were necessarily postponed to make way for the above account of Mr. Handel.

Greene, who already has been mentioned as an ingenious young man, was got to be organist of St. Paul's; and having, upon the decease of Dr. Croft, in 1727, been appointed organist and composer to the royal chapel in his room, was thereby placed at the head of his profession in England. He courted the friendship of Mr. Handel with a degree of assiduity, that, to say the truth, bordered upon servility; and in his visits to him at Burlington-house, and at the duke of Chandois's, was rather more frequent than welcome. At length Mr. Handel discovering that he was paying the same court to his rival, Bononcini, as to himself, would have nothing more to say to him, and gave orders to be denied whenever Greene came to visit him.

Some particulars respecting Greene and his first appearance in the world have been given towards the commencement of Book XVIII. The busy part he acted at this time, his attachment to Bononcini, and his opposition to Mr. Handel, make it necessary in this place to resume his history.

In the year 1730 he took the degree of doctor in music in the university of Cambridge: his exercise for it was Mr. Pope's ode for St. Cecilia's day, which he set very finely to music.* It was performed with great applause; and, as an additional testimony to

---

* Mr. Pope, to answer Greene's purpose, condescended to make considerable alterations in this poem, and at his request to insert in it one entire new stanza, viz., the third. As he thereby rendered it greatly different from the ode originally published, and as with the variations it has never yet appeared in print, it is here given as a curiosity:—

ODE for St. Cecilia's Day,
As altered by Mr. Pope for Dr. Greene.
I.
Descend ye Nine! descend and sing;
The breathing instruments inspire;
Wake into voice each silent string,
And sweep the sounding lyre!
    In a sadly pleasing strain
    Let the warbling lute complain:
In more lengthen'd notes and slow,
The deep, majestic, solemn organs blow,
    Hark! the numbers soft and clear,
    Gently steal upon the ear;
        Now louder they sound,
        'Till the roofs all around
        The shrill echos rebound:
    'Till, by degrees, remote and small,
        The strains decay,
        And melt away
    In a dying, dying fall.

his merit, he was honoured with the title of professor of music in the university of Cambridge.

The following duett, taken from the doctor's own manuscript, was part of the performance :—

Siciliana.

BY the streams that e - ver

### II.

By music minds an equal temper know,
    Nor swell too high, nor sink too low.
If in the breast tumultous joys arise,
Music her soft, assuasive voice applies ;
    Or when the soul is sunk in cares,
    Exalts her with enlivening airs.
Warriors she fires by sprightly sounds ;
Pours balm into the lover's wounds :
Passions no more the soul engage,
Ev'n factions hear away their rage.

### III.

Amphion thus bade wild dissension cease,
And soften'd mortals learn'd the arts of peace.
    Amphion taught contending kings,
        From various discords to create
        The music of a well-tun'd state ;
    Nor slack nor strain the tender string
        Those usual touches to impart,
        That strike the subject's answ'ring heart,
And the soft silent harmony that springs
From sacred union and consent of things.

### IV.

But when our country's cause provokes to arms,
How martial music every bosom warms !
    When the first vessel dar'd the seas
        The Thracian rais'd his strain,
    And Argo saw her kindred trees
    Descend from Pelion to the main.
Transported demi-gods stood round,
And men grew heroes at the sound,
    Inflam'd with glory's charms !
Each chief his sev'nfold shield display'd,
And half unsheath'd the shining blade :
And seas, and rocks, and skies rebound
    To arms, to arms, to arms !

### V.

But when thro' all th' infernal bounds,
Which flaming Phlegeton surrounds,
**Sad** Orpheus sought his consort lost :
    The adamantine gates were barr'd,
    And nought was seen and nought was heard
**Around** the dreary coast ;
        But dreadful gleams,
        Dismal screams,
        Fires that glow,
        Shrieks of woe,
        Sullen moans,
        Hollow groans,
    And cries of tortur'd ghosts !
But hark ! he strikes the golden lyre ;
And see ! the tortur'd ghosts respire,

See, shady forms advance !
And the pale spectres dance !
The Furies sink upon their iron beds,
And snakes uncurl'd hang list'ning round their heads.

### VI.

By the streams that ever flow,
By the fragrant winds that blow
    O'er th' Elysian flow'rs ;
By those happy souls that dwell
In yellow meads of Asphodel,
    Or Amaranthine bow'rs,
By the heroes' armed shades,
Glitt'ring thro' the gloomy glades,
By the youths that dy'd for love,
Wand'ring in the myrtle grove,
Restore, restore Eurydice to life,
Oh take the husband, or return the wife !

### VII.

He sang, and hell consented
    To hear the poet's pray'r ;
Stern Proserpine relented,
    And gave him back the fair.
        Thus song could prevail
        O'er death and o'er hell,
A conquest how hard and how glorious ?
    Tho' fate had fast bound her
    With Styx nine times round her,
Yet music and love were victorious.

*The earlier writers on music, and even Kircher, a modern, have in their division of music distinguished it into mundane, humane, and political. And Cicero, de Repub. lib. II. says that what in music is termed harmony is in the government of a city styled concord: of the latter of these distinctions it may be observed that Shakespeare has shown himself not a little fond of it, as in Henry V. act 1, scene 2.—*

> *For government though high and low and lower,*
> *Put into parts doth keep in one consent,*
> *Congruing in a full and natural close*
> *Like music.*

*And again in Troilus and Cressida, Act 1, Scene 3.—*

> *Take but degree away, untune that string,*
> *And hark what discord follows.*

*The same fanciful notion we find recognised in the third stanza of the above ode. Milton also seems to allude to it in this passage :—*

> *—— orders and degrees*
> *Jar not with liberty, but well consist.*
> *Par. Lost, Book V. line 792.*

*It may be thought not unworthy of remark, that in the two passages first above cited, and also in Mr. Pope's Ode, the word* consent *is mistaken for* concent, *from the Latin* concentus, *a concert of music.*

flow, By the fra - grant winds that blow   O'er th'e-ly-sian flow'rs,   o'er th'e-ly-sian flow'rs;

By those happy souls who dwell In yellow meads of As-pho-del,   Or A-ma-ranthine

By the he-roes' armed shades, Glitt'ring thro' the gloomy

bow'rs,   or A-maranthine bow'rs.

glades,   Restore,   restore Eu-ry - di-ce   to life, Oh . .

By the youths that dy'd for love wand'ring in the myrtle grove, Restore,   restore Eu-ry - di-ce   to life,

glades,	Restore Eu-ry-di-ce to life,	Oh take the

By the youths that dy'd for love Wand'ring in the myrtle grove, Restore Eu-ry-di-ce to life, Oh . . take the

husband or return, return the wife,	Restore Eu-ry-di-ce to life,	Oh take the

husband or re-turn, return the wife,	Restore Eu-ry-di-ce to life, Oh . . take the

husband or return, re-turn the wife,	oh	take the husband or	return, return the wife, return the wife.

husband or re - turn, return the wife,	oh	take the husband or	return, return the wife, return the wife.

DOCTOR MAURICE GREENE.

In the disputes between Handel and Bononcini, Greene had acted with such duplicity, as induced the former to renounce all intercourse with him; and from that time no one was so industrious as he in decrying the compositions of Handel, or applauding those of his rival. He was a member of the Academy of ancient Music, and, with a view to exalt the character of Bononcini, produced in the year 1728 the madrigal 'In una siepe ombrosa,' which gave rise to a dispute that terminated in the disgrace of his friend. Not able to endure the slights of those who had marked and remembered his pertinacious behaviour in this business, Dr. Greene left the academy, and drew off with him the boys of St. Paul's cathedral, and some other persons, his immediate dependents; and fixing on the great room called the Apollo at the Devil tavern, for the performance of a concert, under his sole management, gave occasion to a saying not so witty as sarcastical, viz., that Dr. Greene was gone to the Devil.

Dr. Greene was happy in the friendship of Bishop Hoadley and his family: he set to music sundry elegant pastoral poems, namely, Florimel, Phœbe, and others, written, as it is said, by Dr. John Hoadley, a son of that prelate. He had also an interest with the late duke of Newcastle, probably through the duchess, who had frequent musical parties at Newcastle-house, at which Greene used to assist; and whose mother, Henrietta, duchess of Marlborough, was the patroness of Bononcini, with whom, as has been related, Greene had contracted a close intimacy. With such connexions as these, Greene stood fair for the highest preferments in his profession, and he attained them; for, upon the decease of Dr. Croft, through the interest of the countess of Peterborough, he succeeded to his places of organist and composer to the royal chapel; and, upon that of Eccles, about 1735, was appointed master of the royal band.

Greene had given some early specimens of his abilities in the composition of a set of lessons for the harpsichord, which he probably meant to publish; but a copy having been surreptitiously obtained by one Daniel Wright, a seller of music and musical instruments, near Furnival's Inn, who never printed any thing that he did not steal, they were published by him in so very incorrect a manner, that the doctor was necessitated to declare that they were not his compositions; and Wright, no less falsely than impudently, asserted in the public papers that they were. Notwithstanding that he was an excellent organist, and not only perfectly understood the nature of the instrument, but was a great master of fugue, he affected in his voluntaries that kind of practice on single stops, the cornet and the vox-humana for instance, which puts the instrument almost on a level with the harpsichord; a voluntary of this kind being in fact little more than a solo for a single instrument, with the accompaniment of a bass; and in this view Greene may be looked on as the father of modern organists. This kind of performance, as it is calculated to catch the ears of the vulgar, who are ever more delighted with melody, or what is called air, than harmony, was beneath one, whose abilities were such, that Mattheson, a man but little disposed to flattery, and who was himself one of the first organists in Europe, has not scrupled to rank him among the best of his time.

## CHAP. CXCII

THE conduct of Pepusch was very different from that of Greene. Upon Mr. Handel's arrival in England, he acquiesced in the opinion of his superior merit, and chose a track for himself in which he was sure to meet with no obstruction, and in which none could disturb him without going out of their way to do it. He had been retained by the duke of Chandois, and assisted as composer to his chapel, till he gave place to Handel; after that he professed the teaching of the principles of musical science, and continued so to do till about the year 1724, when a temptation offered of advancing himself, which he was prevailed on to yield to: few persons conversant in literary history are unacquainted with the character and benevolent spirit of Dr. George Berkeley, the late excellent bishop of Cloyne; or that this gentleman, upon his promotion to the deanery of Londonderry, formed a plan for the propagation of religion and learning in America, in which was included a scheme for erecting a college in the Summer Islands, otherwise called the Isles of Bermudas. With a view to carry this project into execution, Dr. Berkeley obtained permission to found and endow such a college, and also engaged divers persons of distinguished eminence in the several professions and faculties to accompany him, and become professors in his intended college; of these Dr. Pepusch was one. He and his associates embarked for the place of the intended settlement, but the ship was wrecked, and the undertaking frustrated; immediately after which such difficulties arose as put a final end to the design.

Being returned to England, Dr. Pepusch married Signora Margarita de l'Epine, and went to reside in Boswell-court, Carey-street, taking, together with his wife, her mother, a woman as remarkably short as her daughter was tall. The fortune which Margarita had acquired was estimated at ten thousand pounds, and the possession thereof enabled the doctor to live in a style of elegance which till his marriage he had been a stranger to: this change in his circumstances was no interruption to his studies; he loved music, and he pursued the knowledge of it with ardour. He, at the instance of Gay and Rich, undertook to compose, or rather correct, the music to the Beggar's Opera. Every one knows that the music to this drama consists solely of ballad tunes and country dances; it was, nevertheless, necessary to settle the airs for performance, and also to compose basses to such as needed them. This the doctor did, prefixing to the opera an overture, which was printed in the first, and has been continued in every succeeding edition of the work.

The reputation of the doctor was now at a great

height; he had perused with great attention those several ancient treatises on harmonics which Meibomius had given to the world about the middle of the last century, and that of Ptolemy, published by Dr. Wallis with his own learned appendix. In the perusal of these authors, the difficulties which occurred to him were in a great measure removed by his friend Mr. Abraham de Moivre, an excellent mathematician, who assisted him in making calculations for demonstrating those principles which are the foundation of harmonic science; and in consequence of these his studies, Pepusch was esteemed one of the best theoretic musicians of his time.

About the year 1730 he took a house in Fetter-lane, the next door but one to the south corner of the passage leading from thence into Bartlett's-buildings, and fitted up a large room in it for the reception of his books and manuscripts, which were very many, and had been collected by him with great labour and expense. His wife had long quitted the opera stage, and, though rather advanced in years, retained her hand on the harpsichord, and was in truth a fine performer. The doctor had in his library a book which had formerly been queen Elizabeth's, containing a great number of lessons for the harpsichord, composed by Dr. Bull; of the merit of these pieces he entertained a very high opinion; and though they were much more difficult to execute than can be well conceived by those who reflect on their antiquity, yet by a regular course of practice she attained to such perfection in playing them, that great was the resort of persons to hear her. He had one only son, whom he determined to qualify for his own profession, a child of very promising parts; the doctor laboured incessantly in his education, but he lived not to attain the age of thirteen.

Among the many that resorted to him for instruction, lord Paisley, afterwards earl of Abercorn, was one; and to him the doctor had communicated lessons in writing for his private study, with no other obligation not to impart them to the world than is implied in the mutual relation of teacher and disciple; which it seems was so ill understood, that in the year 1730 the substance of the doctor's lessons was by his pupil given to the world with the following title: 'A short treatise on harmony, containing the chief 'rules for composing in two, three, and four parts, 'dedicated to all lovers of music. By an admirer of 'this noble and agreeable science.'

The publisher of this little book had studiously avoided inserting in the book any of those examples in musical notes which the precepts contained in it made it necessary to refer to, for which omission he makes a kind of apology.

The doctor affected to speak of the publication of this book as injurious both to his character and interest; however it did not long, if at all, interrupt the friendship between lord Paisley and him. For proof of the fact that his lordship and the doctor were upon very good terms after the publishing the short treatise on harmony, recourse has been had to the doctor's papers, among which has been found a diary in his own hand-writing, containing an account

of the daily occurrences in his life for a series of years, and, among others, a relation of a visit he made to lord Paisley at his seat at Witham in Essex, in the summer of the year 1733, and of his entertainment during a week's stay there; which may serve to show, either that the surreptitious publication of the book was not the act of his lordship, or that the lapse of less than three years had effaced from his remembrance all sense of injury resulting from it.

The book, as published in the manner above related, was of very little use to the world. It wanted the illustration of examples, and was in other respects obscure and most affectedly perplexed; besides all which, it was written in a style the meanest that can be conceived: the motto in the title-page was that trite passage of Horace, 'Si quid novisti rectius istis,' &c., and the sentence intended to supply the omission of the author's name, contains in it the flattest anti-climax that ever disgraced a literary production.

The doctor spoke the English language but indifferently, and wrote it worse than many foreigners do that have long resided in this country; and it may be doubted whether the lessons which he used to give his pupils were ever digested into the form of a treatise; but seeing that the book could not be recalled, and that he was looked upon by the world as responsible for the subject matter of it, he thought it prudent to adopt it; and accordingly in the year 1731 published a genuine edition, retaining the language of the former, but considerably altered and enlarged, and also illustrated with those examples in notes, which were in truth an essential part of it. The precepts delivered, and the laws of harmonical combination contained in this book, are such only as are warranted by the practice of modern composers; and the rules of transition from key to key are evidently extracted from the works of Corelli; but the most valuable part of the book is the chapter treating of solmisation, which practice is explained with the utmost precision and perspicuity.* In forming the diagrams, it is said that the doctor was assisted by Brooke Taylor, LL.D., author of a well-known treatise on Perspective, who, besides being an excellent mathematician, was eminently skilled in the theory of music.

It has already been mentioned that Pepusch was one of the founders of the Academy of ancient Music. That society, with his assistance, continued to flourish until the year 1734, when, upon some disgust taken by Mr. Gates, master of the children of the royal chapel, it was deprived of the assistance which it was wont to receive from them, and left without boys to sing the soprano parts.† After trying for one winter what could be done without

---

* That of the hexachords, with directions for the mutations by the arrows and daggers, is a great stroke of invention. But the table adjoining to it, for reducing a composition in a transposed key to its natural one, by the help of the slider, is a disingenuous artifice, and calculated rather to blind than enlighten those whom the author professes to teach. Had he, as Loulie has done in his Elements ou Principes de Musique, given the rule to call the last sharp, in the case of sharp keys, B, and the last flat in the flat keys F; and sol-fa upwards and downwards accordingly, the wretched contrivance of a slider to be cut off, and which being lost, would render the table useless and the book imperfect, would have been unnecessary. See page 59, in note.

† Dr. Greene, upon the dispute about the author of the madrigal, 'In 'una siepe ombrosa,' three years before, had retired, and taken with him the boys of St. Paul's choir

treble voices, and finding that their endeavours amounted to nothing, the managers determined to enlarge the plan, and make the Academy a seminary for the instruction of youth in the principles of music and the laws of harmony. Invitations to parents, and offers of such an education for their children as would fit them as well for trades and businesses as the profession of music, were given by advertisements in the public papers; these brought in a great number of children, and such of them as were likely to be made useful were retained.* Upon this occasion Dr. Pepusch generously undertook the care of their instruction, for a stipend greatly disproportionate to his merit, though the largest the circumstances of the Academy could afford, and succeeded so well in his endeavours, that many of those his pupils became afterwards eminent professors in the science.

The above memoir of Dr. Pepusch continues the history of the Academy down to about the year 1735, when the managers had recourse to the expedient of educating boys for their purpose, and that of admitting auditor members, both which answered their ends; and upon that footing, excepting the difference of an increased subscription, the society subsists at this day.

The Academy made it their constant care to keep up a correspondence with the most eminent masters and professors of music in foreign countries; and Steffani having desired to be admitted a member of their society, and having from time to time presented them with compositions of great value, bearing the name of Gregorio Piua, his secretary or copyist, but which were in truth his own, they unanimously chose him their president; and, upon occasion of the dispute about the madrigal 'In una siepe ombrosa,' mentioned in the foregoing memoir of Bononcini; they entered into a correspondence with Signor Antonio Lotti. with which he thought himself so honoured, that he presented them with a madrigal and a mass of his composition, and they in return sent him, as a specimen of the English music, two motets, the one 'Domine quis habitabit,' for five

voices, by Tallis, the other · Tribulationes Civitatum,† also for five voices, by Bird, both which were thankfully accepted.

As an institution designed for the improvement of music, the Academy was generally visited by foreigners of the greatest eminence in the faculty. Many of the opera singers and celebrated masters on particular instruments, by the performance of favourite airs in the operas, and solos calculated to display their various excellencies, contributed to the variety of the evening's entertainment. Tosi frequently sang here; and Bononcini, who was a member, played solos on the violoncello, on which he ever chose to be accompanied by Waber on the lute. Geminiani was a frequent visitor of the Academy, and would often honour it with the performance of his own compositions previous to their publication.

And here it may not be improper to mention an anecdote in musical history, which reflects some credit on this institution. In the interval between the secession of Dr. Greene and Mr. Gates, viz., in the month of February, 1732, when the conflict between Mr. Handel and the nobility had rendered the situation of the former almost desperate, the Academy being in possession of a copy of the oratorio of Esther, originally composed for the duke of Chandois by Mr. Handel, performed it by their own members and the children of the chapel royal; and the applause with which it was there received, suggested to the author the thought of performing it himself, and of exhibiting in future during the Lent season, that species of musical entertainment. So that to this accident it may be said to be in a great measure owing, that the public for a series of years past have not only been delighted with hearing, but are now in possession of, some of the most valuable compositions of that great master.

The advantages that resulted to music from the exercises of the Academy were evident, in that they tended to the establishment of a true and just notion of the science; they checked the wanderings of fancy, and restrained the love of novelty within due bounds; they enabled the students and performers to contemplate and compare styles; to form an idea of classical purity and elegance; and, in short, to fix the standard of a judicious and rational taste. One of the principal ends of the institution was a retrospect to those excellent compositions of former ages, which its very name implies; and in the prosecution thereof were brought forth to public view, the works of very many authors, whose names, though celebrated with all the applauses of panegyric, had else been consigned to oblivion: nor was this all; the spirit that directed the pursuits of this society diffused itself, and gave rise to another, of which here follows an account.

Mr. John Immyns, an attorney by profession, was a member of the Academy, but, meeting with misfortunes, he was occasionally a copyist to the society, and amanuensis to Dr. Pepusch; he had a strong

---

* Among the children who were thus taken into the service of the Academy, was one whose promising genius and early attainments in music render him worthy of notice in this place. His name was Isaac Peirson; his father, a poor man, and master of the charity-school of the parish of St. Giles without Cripplegate, dwelt in the school-house in Redcross-street, and being, as he was used to style himself, a lover of divine music, or, in other words a singer of psalm-tunes after the fashion of those who look upon Playford as one of the greatest among musicians, he gladly laid hold of the opportunity which then offered, and got his son, about seven years old, admitted into the Academy. A very few months tuition of the doctor enabled him to sing his part; and in less than a twelvemonth he had attained to great proficiency on the organ, though his fingers were so weak that he was incapable of making a true shake, and instead thereof was necessitated to make use of a tremulous motion of two keys at once, which he did so well, that the discord arising from it passed unnoticed. In the instruction of this child the doctor took uncommon pains, and shewed great affection, making him the associate of his own son in his studies. He endeavoured to inculcate in him the true organ-style, and succeeded so well, that his pupil, before he was full nine years of age, rejecting the use of set voluntaries, began upon his own stock, and played the full organ extempore, with the learning and judgment of an experienced master. The circumstances of his parents co-operating with his irresistible propensity, determined him to music as a profession; he was therefore taught the violin, and soon became able to execute the most difficult of Geminiani's concertos with great facility. With these attainments, singularly great for one of his years, and a temper of mind in every respect amiable, he gave to his parents and friends the most promising assurances of his becoming a great musician; but his death defeated their hopes before he had quite attained the age of twelve years.

† The first of these is not in print; the latter is the twenty-fourth motett in the Sacræ Cantiones of Bird, printed by Tho. Este in 1589.

counter-tenor voice, which, being not very flexible, served well enough for the performance of madrigals. Of this species of music he in a short time became so fond, that in the year 1741 he formed the plan of a little club, called the Madrigal Society; and got together a few persons who had spent their lives in the practice of psalmody; and who, with a little pains, and the help of the ordinary solmisation, which many of them were very expert in, became soon able to sing, almost at sight, a part in an English, or even an Italian madrigal. They were mostly mechanics; some, weavers from Spitalfields, others of various trades and occupations; they met at first at the Twelve Bells, an alehouse in Bride-lane, Fleet-street, and Immyns was both their president and instructor; their subscription was five shillings and sixpence a quarter, which defrayed their expenses in books and music paper, and afforded them the refreshments of porter and tobacco. After four or five years continuance at the Twelve Bells, the society removed to the Founders' Arms in Lothbury; and from thence, after a short stay, to the Twelve Bells again, and after that to the Queen's Arms in Newgate-street, a house that had been formerly a tavern, but was now an alehouse. In it was a room large enough for the reception of the society, who were about five-and-twenty in number, with a convenient recess for a large press that contained their library. The meetings of the society were on Wednesday evening in every week; their performance consisted of Italian and English madrigals in three, four, and five parts; and, being assisted by three or four boys from the choir of St. Paul's, they sang compositions of this kind, as also catches, rounds, and canons, though not elegantly, with a degree of correctness that did justice to the harmony; and, to vary the entertainment, Immyns would sometimes read, by way of lecture, a chapter of Zarlino translated by himself.

The persons that composed this little academy were men not less distinguished by their love of vocal harmony, than the harmless simplicity of their tempers, and their friendly disposition towards each other. Immyns was a man of a very singular character; and as he was one of the most passionate admirers of music of his time, merits to be taken particular notice of. He had a cracked counter-tenor voice, and played upon the flute, the viol da gamba, the violin, and the harpsichord, but on none of them well: in his younger days he was a great beau, and had been guilty of some indiscretions, which proved an effectual bar to success in his profession, and reduced him to the necessity of becoming a clerk to an attorney in the city. The change in his circumstances had not the least tendency to damp his spirits; he wrote all day at the desk, and frequently spent most part of the night in copying music, which he did with amazing expedition and correctness. At the age of forty he would needs learn the lute, and by the sole help of Mace's book, acquired a competent knowledge of the instrument; but, beginning so late, was never able to attain to any great degree of proficiency on it: having a

family, he lived for some years in extreme poverty, the reflection on which did not trouble him so much as it did his friends; Mr. George Shelvocke, secretary to the general post office, was one of the number, and, upon the decease of Mr. Serjeant Shore, by his interest obtained for Immyns the place of lutenist of the royal chapel, the salary whereof is about forty pounds a year. The taste of Immyns was altogether for old music, which he had been taught to admire by Dr. Pepusch; and this he indulged to such a degree, that he looked upon Mr. Handel and Bononcini as the great corrupters of the science. With these prejudices, it is no wonder that he entertained a relish for madrigals, and music of the driest style: Vincentio Ruffo, Orlando de Lasso, Luca Marenzio, Horatio Vecchi, and, above all, the prince of Venosa, were his great favourites. He was very diligent in collecting their works, and studied them with incredible assiduity; nevertheless he was but meanly skilled in the theory of the science, considering the opportunities which his intimacy with Dr. Pepusch afforded him. He was the founder, and chief support of the Madrigal Society, and, being a man of great good-humour and pleasantry, was much beloved by those that frequented it. In the latter part of his life he began to feel himself in tolerable circumstances, but the infirmities of old age coming on him apace, he died of an asthma at his house in Cold-Bath-fields on the fifteenth day of April, 1764.

Mr. Samuel Jeacocke, another member of this fraternity, was a man not less remarkable for singularities of another kind: this man was a baker by trade, and the brother of Mr. Caleb Jeacocke, now living, and who for many years was president of the Robin Hood disputing society. The shop of Samuel was at the south-west corner of Berkeley-street, in Red-lion street, Clerkenwell. He played on several instruments, but mostly the tenor-violin; and at the Madrigal Society usually sang the bass part. In the choice of his instruments he was very nice, and when a fiddle or a violoncello did not please him, would, to mend the tone of it, bake it for a week in a bed of saw-dust. He was one of the best ringers and the best swimmer of his time; and, even when advanced in years, was very expert in other manly exercises; he was a plain, honest, good-humoured man, and an inoffensive and cheerful companion, and, to the grief of many, died about the year 1748.

The Madrigal Society still subsists, but in a manner very different from its original institution; they meet at a tavern in the city, but under such circumstances, as render its permanency very precarious.

## CHAP. CXCIII.

The music with which the public in general had been formerly entertained, was chiefly that of the theatre, and such as was occasionally performed at concerts; but, in proportion to the increase of wealth in the metropolis, the manners of the people began to relax; the places of public entertainment increased in number, and to these music seemed to be essential. It is curious to reflect on the parsimony of our ancestors in all their recreations and amusements; the playhouses afforded them entertainment during the winter season, and the length of the summer days afforded leisure for a walk in the gardens of the inns of court, the park, or to the adjacent villages. Besides these there were several Mulberry-gardens about the town; and places at the extremities of it distinguished by the name of Spring Gardens and the World's End : some of these were frequented by the better sort of persons of both sexes, for purposes that may be guessed at.

The World's End is mentioned in Congreve's comedy of Love for Love, in a scene where Mrs. Foresight rallies Mrs. Frail for having been seen with a man in a hackney-coach : there is a place so called between Chelsea and Fulham,* another a little beyond Stepney, and another opposite St. George's Fields, in the road to Newington. The reason of this appellation is, that the houses of this sort were generally the last in the neighbourhood; the sign was usually a man and a woman walking together, with the following distich underwrote :—

　　　I'll go with my friend
　　　To the World's End.

A kind of intimation what sort of company were most welcome there.†

Barn-Elms and Vauxhall were also places of great resort for water parties; of the latter of these the history is but little known; all we can learn of it is, that the house so called was formerly the habitation of Sir Samuel Moreland. Aubrey, in his Antiquities of Surrey, gives this account of it : 'At Vauxhall 'Sir Samuel Moreland built a fine room, anno 1667, 'the inside all of looking-glass, and fountains very 'pleasant to behold, which is much visited by 'strangers ; it stands in the middle of the garden, '—— foot square, —— high, covered with Cornish 'slate ; on the point whereof he placed a Punchinello, 'very well carved, which held a dial, but the winds have demolished it.' Vol. I. page 12.

The house seems to have been rebuilt since the time that Sir Samuel Moreland dwelt in it. About the year 1730, Mr. Jonathan Tyers became the occupier of it; and, there being a large garden belonging to it, planted with a great number of stately trees, and laid out in shady walks, it obtained the name of Spring Gardens; and the house being converted into a tavern, or place of entertainment, it was much frequented by the votaries of pleasure. Mr. Tyers opened it with an advertisement of

a Ridotto al Fresco, a term which the people of this country had till that time been strangers to. These entertainments were several times repeated in the course of the summer, and numbers resorted to partake of them ; and this encouraged the proprietor to make his garden a place of musical entertainment for every evening during the summer season ; to this end he was at great expence in decorating the gardens with paintings; he engaged a band of excellent musicians; he issued silver tickets for admission at a guinea each ; and, receiving great encouragement, he set up an organ in the orchestra, and in a conspicuous part of the garden erected a fine statue of Mr. Handel, the work of Mr. Roubiliac.

The success of this undertaking was an encouragement to another of a similar kind; a number of persons purchased the house and gardens of the late earl of Ranelagh ; they erected a spacious building of timber, of a circular form, and within it an organ, and an orchestra capable of holding a numerous band of performers : the entertainment of the auditors during the performance is either walking round the room, or refreshing themselves with tea and coffee in the recesses thereof, which are conveniently adapted to that purpose. Mr. Festing, during his life-time, led the band ; the performance here, as at Vauxhall, is instrumental, intermixed with songs and ballad airs, calculated rather to please the vulgar, than gratify those of a better taste.

The account given of Mr. Handel in the preceding pages, has been continued down to the year 1736, at which time the restoration of his health, which had suffered greatly in the contest with the nobility, engrossed his whole attention. Having happily got the better of that disorder, which boded little less than a privation of his mental faculties, he returned to England, and at Covent-Garden made an effort to regain the public favour by the performance of the operas of Atalanta,‡ Justin, Arminius, and Berenice; these succeeded but ill ; and the indifference of the town towards him may be judged of by the fruitless endeavours of his friends to render the publication of the above compositions beneficial to him, evidenced by a subscription to them severally, that hardly defrayed the expence of printing.

In the composition of the two subsequent operas of Faramond and Alexander Severus, performed in 1737, he was indemnified against all risk of loss by an engagement with the late duke of Dorset, then earl of Middlesex, in virtue whereof he composed them both, and was paid by his lordship the sum of one thousand pounds. Three other operas, namely Xerxes, Hymen, and Deidamia, of his composition, were represented between the years 1737 and 1740, after which Handel gave another direction to his studies, better suited, as he himself used to declare, to the circumstances of a man advancing in years, than that of adapting music to such vain and trivial poetry as the musical drama is generally made to consist of. This resolution led him to reflect on

---

* The sign of the house at this time is the globe of the world in that state of conflagration which is to put an end to its existence ; a pun in painting as singular as the title of a well known song, 'The Cobbler's End.'

† Spring Garden, and the Mulberry Garden, are mentioned as places of Intrigue in Sir George Etherege's Comedy of 'She would if she could ;' and in a comedy of Sir Charles Sedley's, entitled ' The Mulberry Garden,' the scene is in the Mulberry Garden, near St. James's. At the time when the above were places of public resort, there was an edifice built of timber and divided into sundry rooms with a platform and balustrade at top, which floated on the Thames above London Bridge, and was called the Folly : a view of it, anchored opposite Somerset House, is given in Strype's Stow, book IV. page 105 ; and the humours of it are described by Ward in his London Spy. At first it was resorted to for refreshment by persons of fashion ; and queen Mary with some of her courtiers had once the curiosity to visit it. But it sank into a receptacle for companies of loose and disorderly people, for the purposes of drinking and promiscuous dancing ; and at length becoming scandalous, the building was suffered to decay, and the materials thereof became fire-wood.

‡ Originally performed on occasion of the marriage of the prince of Orange with our princess royal.

that kind of representation, the Concerto Spirituale, so frequent in the Romish countries, and which, by the name of the Oratorio, is nearly of as great antiquity as the opera itself, and determined him to the choice of sacred subjects for the exercise of his genius. He was well acquainted with the Holy Scriptures, and was sensible that the sublime sentiments with which they abound would give opportunities of displaying his greatest talents : he had made the experiment in the anthems which he had composed for the duke of Chandois, and in four others performed at the coronation of the late king ; and as to the risk that an entertainment so little known in this country as the oratorio would be disrelished, of that too he was able to form some judgment, for in the year 1733, upon occasion of the solemnization of a public act in the university of Oxford, he performed the oratorio of Athaliah, and the profits thereof were so considerable as in some degree to repair the damage his fortunes had sustained in that dreadful conflict in which he was then engaged.

Other considerations suggested to him the almost certain benefit of such an undertaking : the performance of a sacred drama would consist with the solemnity of the Lent season, during which stage representations in this as in other Christian countries are in general forbidden ; but, above all, this served to recommend it, that it could be conducted at a small expence : no costly scenery was required, nor dresses for the performers, other than a suit of black, with which all persons that appeared in public were supposed to be provided.* Instead of airs that required the delicacy of Cuzzoni, or the volubility of Faustina to execute, he hoped to please by songs, the beauties whereof were within the comprehension of less fastidious hearers than in general frequent the opera, namely, such as were adapted to a tenor voice, from the natural firmness and inflexibility whereof little more is ever expected than an articulate utterance of the words, and a just expression of the melody ; and he was happy in the assistance of a singer† possessed of these and many other valuable qualities. He knew also that he could attach to him the real lovers and judges of music by those original beauties, which he was able to display in the composition of fugue and chorus ; ‡ and these being once gained, the taste of the town was likely to fall in, as it frequently does, with the opinion of those who are best qualified to give a direction to it. To such a performance the talents of a second-rate singer, and persons used to choir service were adequate. Signora Francesina, and afterwards Signora Frasi, and some others in succession, were engaged on terms comparatively easy ; and the chapel royal and

* It is a trivial circumstance to remark upon, but it serves to shew a great change of manners, and the little regard to the decencies of religion in this country of liberty : neither the singers in the oratorio, nor their hearers, make any distinction in their dress between Lent and a season of festivity.

† Mr. Beard.

‡ The chorusses of Mr. Handel's oratorios are of a cast very different from those in his operas ; the latter are simply counterpoint, and are destitute of all art and contrivance ; the former answer to the sublime in poetry ; they are of his own invention, and are the very basis of his reputation.

the choir of St. Paul's furnished boys and chorus singers sufficient in abilities and number to answer his purpose.

The former performances of the oratorios of Athaliah, Deborah, and Esther, were but essays towards the introduction of this kind of entertainment ; and it is upon very good authority asserted, that Mr. Handel was induced to this attempt by the performance of Esther at the academy of ancient Music in the month of February, 1731, which was so greatly applauded, that in the following year, in the Lent season, he performed it, as also Deborah, at Covent Garden theatre. Upon this occasion he also gratified the public with a species of music of which he may be said to be the inventor, namely, the organ-concerto. Few but his intimate friends were sensible that on this instrument he had scarce his equal in the world ; and he could not but be conscious that he possessed a style of performing on it that at least had the charm of novelty to recommend it. From the third of his Sonatas for two violins or hautboys, which he had composed some years before, he had made an overture to Esther ; and of the last movement in the same composition, inserting in it sundry solo passages adapted to the instrument, and adding to it a prelude and an air singularly elegant, he now formed a concerto, the beauties whereof he displayed by his own masterly performance. It must be confessed that this was not that true organ-style which a profound judge of music would admire, and of which Handel had shewn himself a complete master in the voluntaries and fugues for the organ published by him ; but the full harmony of the instrumental parts in this composition, contrasted with those eloquent solo passages interspersed in it, protracting the cadences, and detaining the ear in a delightful suspense, had a wonderful effect.

Having thus made an experiment of the disposition of the town towards these entertainments, Handel determined to rest his future fortunes on the success of them ; accordingly, on his return to London from Aix la Chapelle, he set to music Mr. Dryden's ode for St. Cecilia's Day, entitled Alexander's Feast, and therein introduced a trio, which he had formerly set to the words 'Quel fior che al alba ride,' which, with the addition of another part, he adapted so well to the chorus 'Let old Timotheus yield the prize,' that most men took it for an original composition. The success of this performance determined him in his resolution to addict himself for the future to this species of composition, and accordingly he persisted in it, with a few occasional deviations, for the remainder of his life. And finding that his own performance on the organ never failed to command the attention of his hearers, he set himself to compose, or rather make up, concertos for that instrument,§

§ Of his first six organ concertos, only the first and fourth are original compositions ; both the second and third are taken from his Sonatas ; the fifth was a lesson for the harp, composed for the younger Powel, a fine performer on that instrument ; and the sixth is a solo for the flute, as is apparent from the compass of it, and was made for the practice of a gentleman, one of Handel's friends. The second set of organ concertos is evidently made out of his grand concertos.

There were two persons of the name of Powel, father and son, who played finely on the harp ; the elder was patronized by the duke of Portland, and when that nobleman was appointed governor of Jamaica,

and uniformly interposed one in the course of the evening's performance.

The applause bestowed on the oratorios of Handel, was at least equal to that of the best of his operas; but, such was the taste of the town, that he was constrained to give these entertainments a dramatic form; for he was used to say, that, to an English audience, music joined to poetry was not an entertainment for an evening, and that something that had the appearance of a plot or fable was necessary to keep their attention awake. Perhaps he might be mistaken in this opinion; and the success of Israel in Egypt, L'Allegro ed Il Penseroso, and Messiah, seem to indicate the contrary; nevertheless it determined his conduct with respect to these entertainments, and frequently induced him to have recourse to some small poet for his assistance in forming a drama, which, without regard to sentiment or language, or indeed any thing but the conduct of the drama, was to be the mere vehicle of his music; and such, for instance, are the oratorios of Esther, Saul, Susanna, and many others. Some of the pretended admirers of music were for carrying the illusion still farther, and offered many reasons, such as they were, in favour of a real representation of the history which was the subject of the entertainment; and would have had, to give one instance as an example of the rest, Jacob and Joseph and his brethren personated on the stage, with all the aids of action and scenic decoration. In some of his performances, included under the general denomination of oratorios, such as Alexander's Feast, Israel in Egypt, and L'Allegro ed Il Penseroso, and others equally unsusceptible of a dramatic form, the idea of personal representation would have been absurd, and therefore the audience acquiesced in that disposition of words and sentiments, which in the judgment of the musical composer was best calculated to display the powers of his art; and these never appeared to so great advantage as when he made use of passages selected from Holy Writ for the subjects of his compositions; of this there needs no other evidence than his Israel in Egypt and the Messiah, concerning which latter work there are some particulars, which for his honour deserve to be remembered. It was performed for the first time at Covent Garden in the

year 1741, by the name of a Sacred Oratorio. As it consisted chiefly of chorus, and the airs contained in it were greatly inferior to most in his operas and former oratorios, it was but coldly received by the audience; the consciousness whereof, and a suspicion that the public were growing indifferent towards these entertainments, determined him to try the temper of the people of Ireland; accordingly he went to Dublin in the year 1741, and gave a performance of the Messiah for the benefit of the prisoners in that city. He returned to London in the year 1741-2, and performed an oratorio, consisting of passages selected from the Samson Agonistes of Milton, which was received with such applause, as seemed to insure him success in his future attempts of that kind.

About this time he published by subscription twelve grand Concertos. To this undertaking Handel was probably encouraged by the good success of a former publication of the like kind, namely, Six Concertos composed on occasion of the marriage of the prince of Orange with the princess royal, and distinguished by the name of his Hautboy Concertos, which being made up of fugues taken from his lessons, and from six fugues for the organ, composed by him as studies, had great merit. But as to these twelve Concertos, they appear to have been made in a hurry, and in the issue fell very short of answering the expectations that were formed of them, and inclined men to think that the composition of music merely instrumental, and of many parts, was not Handel's greatest excellence.

In the succeeding year he had a slight return of that disorder which had driven him to seek relief from the baths of Aix-la-Chapelle; and, to add to this misfortune, an opposition to him and his entertainment was set on foot by some persons of distinction, who by card assemblies, and other amusements, at that time not usual in the Lent season, endeavoured to make his audiences as thin as possible. The effects of this association he felt for a season or two, in the course whereof he frequently performed to houses that would not pay his expenses; but at length a change of sentiment in the public began to manifest itself; the Messiah was received with universal applause, and has ever since been considered as one of the most sublime of his compositions. In gratitude for the favour shown him by the public, and actuated by motives of benevolence, he performed the Messiah for the benefit of an institution, which then stood in need of every assistance, the Foundling-hospital; and this he not only continued to do for several years, but, by presenting the charity with a copy of the score and parts of this composition, gave them such a title to it as seemed to import an exclusive right to the performance of it. This act of bounty was so ill understood by some of the governors of that foundation, that they formed a resolution for an application to parliament to establish their supposed right; in short, to prohibit, under penalties, the performance of the Messiah by any others than Mr. Handel and themselves. To facilitate the passing of a law for the

went with him thither. The younger stayed in England, and Mr. Handel being desirous to make him known, composed for him the lesson abovementioned, and introduced it in one or two of his oratorios: as also the song in Esther, 'Tune your harps to cheerful strains,' which has an accompaniment for the harp.

Besides the Powels there was at the same time in London a performer on the harp, who merits to be had in remembrance: his name was Jones, a Welchman, and blind; the old duchess of Marlborough would have retained him with a pension, but he would not endure confinement, and was engaged by one Evans, who kept a home-brewed ale house of great resort, the sign of the Hercules Pillars, opposite Clifford's-Inn passage in Fleet-street, and performed in a great room up-stairs during the winter season. He played extempore voluntaries, the fugues in the Sonatas and Concertos of Corelli, as also most of his Solos, and many of Mr. Handel's opera songs with exquisite neatness and elegance. He also played on the violin, and on that instrument imitated so exactly the irregular intonation, mixed with sobs and pauses, of a quaker's sermon, that none could hear him and refrain from immoderate laughter. The man of the house dying, his widow took Cuper's Garden, in Surrey, opposite Somerset-house, and erected therein an orchestra and an organ, intending it as a place of entertainment for the summer evenings, like Vauxhall, with the addition of fireworks. It subsisted for four or five summers, but, failing at length, Jones, who was supported by her all the time, was turned adrift, and, about the year 1738, died. He was buried in Lambeth church-yard, and his funeral, which was celebrated with a dead march, was attended by a great number of the musical people.

purpose, Mr. Handel's concurrence was asked, but he was so little sensible of the propriety of it, that upon the bare mention of it he broke out into a furious passion, which he vented in the following terms: 'For vat sal de Foundlings put mein oratorio 'in de Parlement? Te Teuffel! mein musik sal not 'go to de Parlement.'

The retreat of Handel to Ireland, and the favourable reception he met with at Dublin, awakened the people of this country to a sense of his merit, and was a kind of reproach on those who had necessitated him to seek protection in that kingdom; so that his return hither was felicitated with every testimony of esteem and respect, and the strongest assurances of future encouragement. His Messiah was frequently performed to such audiences, as he could no otherwise accommodate than by erecting seats on the stage, to such a number as scarcely left room for the performers. In this prosperous state did his affairs go on, till he was afflicted with the misfortune of blindness, which, great as it was, did not totally incapacitate him from study, or the power of entertaining the public. The circumstances of this misfortune, as also of his death, are reserved for that which is meant to be the last period of the memoir here given of him.

## CHAP. CXCIV.

STEFANO CARBONELLI had studied the practice of the violin under Corelli; and coming hither from Rome, was received into the family of the duke of Rutland, a great patron of music. During his residence with this nobleman, he published and dedicated to him twelve Solos for a violin and a bass of his composition, which he frequently played in public with great applause. Upon the institution of the Royal Academy, Carbonelli was placed at the head of the opera band, and soon became so celebrated for his excellent hand, as to give Sir Richard Steele, in his comedy of the Conscious Lovers, occasion of making him a very handsome compliment. The manner of it was this; Carbonelli led the orchestra at the Haymarket in the year 1721, when Bononcini's opera of Griselda was performed there; and in a discourse between Young Bevil and Indiana, the lady is made to commend that opera, particularly the air in it, 'Dolce Sogno;' upon which a conversation ensues on the subject of the opera in general, which is interrupted by a servant, who enters and informs his master that Signor Carbonelli waits his commands in the next room; upon this Bevil tells the lady that she had mentioned the day before, her desire to hear him; accordingly he is introduced, and plays a solo.* About the year 1725, Carbonelli quitted the opera-house, and went to Drury-lane theatre, where he led, and frequently played select pieces between the acts. His successor at the opera-house was Pietro Castrucci. After continuing a few years at Drury-lane, Carbonelli quitted his station there in favour of Mr. Richard Jones, and attached

himself to Mr. Handel at the time when he began to perform oratorios. For a series of years he played at the rehearsal and performance at St. Paul's for the benefit of the sons of the clergy.

At his first coming into England, Carbonelli professed himself to be of the Romish persuasion, but after his arrival he became a protestant, and married the daughter of Mr. Warren, parish-clerk of St. James's, Westminster. In the latter part of his life he in some measure declined the profession of music, and betook himself to that of a merchant, and an importer of wines from France and Germany. By the interest of a powerful friend he obtained the place of one of the purveyors of wine to the king; and died in that employment in the year 1772.

Among the performers on the violin at the time when the Italian opera was first introduced into England, were some whose names are now scarcely remembered; of these Signor Claudio, a native of Lucca, was the chief: he played the second violin at the Haymarket many years; and was the author of six Solos for that instrument, published a few years before his death, that is to say, in or about 1740. Others there were of greater eminence, of whom here follows an account.

PIETRO CASTRUCCI, by birth a Roman, was an excellent performer on the violin. He succeeded Corbett as first violin at the opera-house, and led the opera for many years; but growing old, Handel had a mind to place a young man, named John Clegg, a scholar of Dubourg, at the head of his orchestra; Castrucci being in very necessitous circumstances, and not in the least conscious of any failure in his hand, was unwilling to quit his post; upon which Handel, in order to convince him of his inability to fill it, composed a concerto, in which the second concertino was so contrived, as to require an equal degree of execution with the first;† this he gave to Clegg, who in the performance of it gave such proofs of his superiority, as reduced Castrucci to the necessity of yielding the palm to his rival. Oppressed with years, he immediately sank into oblivion, and at the age of eighty, upon the merit of his past services, became a supplicant to the public for a benefit, at which he performed a solo, and soon after died. He published two sets of Solos for a violin, with a thorough-bass, and twelve Concertos for violins, which, though hardly known, have great merit. He had a brother, younger than himself, named Prospero, who for some years led the concert at the Castle tavern in Paternoster-row, and was author of six Solos for a violin and a bass; but as a musician he was in no respect equal to Pietro.

Clegg succeeded to the favour of Handel, and under his patronage enjoyed the applause of the town. This person had been a pupil of Dubourg in Ireland, and travelling with lord Ferrers to Italy, so greatly improved himself, that at his return he excelled in the leading of a concert, all in England: the strength of his tone, and the most rapid and distinct execution that had ever been heard in this country, were the

---

* Rolli, who translated the Conscious Lovers into Italian in the year 1724, has a note on this passage, indicating that Carbonelli was then in the service of the duke of Rutland.

† It is printed in the fourth collection of Concertos, entitled Select Harmony, published by Walsh.

qualities that recommended him. His intense application and incessant practice had such an effect on his mind, that he became a lunatic, and was confined in the hospital of Bedlam. During his continuance there, he was at times permitted the use of his instrument, and drew crowds to hear him.

Richard Charke was a performer on the violin, and, succeeding as first violin in the band at Drury-lane one who was called Dicky Jones, attained to some degree of eminence. He married Charlotte, the youngest daughter of Colley Cibber, and by his ill usage of her gave occasion to those reflections on him contained in a narrative of her most extraordinary life, written by herself, and published in 1755. Charke was famous for playing the eleventh of Carbonelli's Solos in A♯. Being a loose extravagant fellow, and deeply involved in debt, he was necessitated to quit this country : Jamaica was his asylum, and he died there in the prime of his age. He was the first that composed medley-overtures, which are overtures made up of passages taken from well-known airs and common popular tunes ; and among three or four that are extant, his is reckoned the best : this, and a hornpipe that bears his name, are the only compositions of Charke extant.

Matthew Dubourg was a scholar of Geminiani, and by him was taught the practice of the violin. Upon the death of Cousser, in the year 1728, Geminiani having declined the offer of his place of master and composer of the state music in Ireland, it was conferred on Dubourg. As the duties of this employment did not require his constant residence in that kingdom, he passed much of his time in England, and had the honour to be the instructor in music of the late prince of Wales and the duke of Cumberland. There is nothing of his composition extant that we know of, excepting a set of variations on a minuet of Geminiani, to which the song, ' Gently touch the warbling lyre,' is adapted, and these have never yet been printed ; nay it does not appear that he ever composed solos for his own practice, contenting himself with performing those of Corelli and his master Geminiani.*

Dubourg's performance on the violin was very bold and rapid ; greatly different from that of Geminiani, which was tender and pathetic ; and these qualities it seems he was able to communicate, for Clegg his disciple possessed them in as great perfection as himself. He had many admirers, and among them was Mrs. Martin : this woman was a native of Holland, and the widow of a Dutch burgomaster, but having married an Englishman, and being possessed of a large fortune, she came to reside in London, and dwelt in the house in Sherborn-lane, formerly Sir Gilbert Heathcote's, where during the winter season she had frequent concerts, which were resorted to by citizens of the first rank, and at times by sundry of the nobility. A picture of Dubourg, painted when he was a boy, was a conspicuous object in Mrs. Martin's concert-room, which was very large

* Dubourg must have had some instructor before he became a pupil of Geminiani ; he played a solo, standing upon a joint-stool at Britton's concert : Britton died in 1714, and Geminiani arrived in England in the same year.

and splendid, two sides of it being lined with looking-glass. He died on the third day of July, 1767, aged sixty-four, and lies buried in the church-yard of Paddington, under a monumental stone, whereon is the following inscription :—

> Tho' sweet as Orpheus thou could'st bring
> Soft pleadings from the trembling string,
> Uncharm'd the king of terror stands,
> Nor owns the magic of thy hands.

Michael Christian Festing, a master of the violin, and a very elegant composer for that instrument, was at first a scholar of Dicky Jones, above-mentioned, the successor of Carbonelli at Drury-lane theatre ; but was perfected in his musical studies by Geminiani, under whom he acquired such a degree of skill, as, cultivated by his own natural genius, enabled him, at least so far as regards composition for the violin, to form a style original as it was elegant. Being a man of understanding and knowledge of the world, he found means throughout his life to form such connexions, and to attach to him such patrons of music among the nobility, as were his constant support. He also derived considerable advantage from the friendship of Dr. Greene ; and, being of the royal band, led the performance in the odes of his composing performed at court. He played the first violin in what was called the Philharmonic Society, consisting of noblemen and gentlemen performers, who met on Wednesday nights during the winter season, at the Crown and Anchor tavern in the Strand ; and upon the building of the rotunda in the garden of Ranelagh house at Chelsea, besides that he led the band, he had the sole conduct of the musical performances there. By his interest and indefatigable industry he contributed greatly to the establishment and increase of the fund for the support of decayed musicians and their families, and for some years discharged gratis the duty of secretary to that institution. He had a brother named John, who played on the hautboy, and was a teacher of the German flute, for which latter instrument he had more scholars than any master in London ; *and whose success in this his profession affords a very remarkable instance of what industry and economy are capable of effecting in the exercise of it ; for he died in the year 1772 possessed of the sum of £8000, acquired chiefly by teaching.*

The works of Festing in print were all published by himself, that is to say, he took subscriptions for them, and was not beholden for the circulation of them through the kingdom to the keepers of music-shops ; the consequence whereof is, that they are less known than the compositions of any other master of his time. He died in the year 1752, leaving a son, a clergyman, who married the daughter of Dr. Greene. His goods, books, and instruments were sold at his house in Warwick-street near Golden-square, in the month of September, in the year above-mentioned.

As a performer on the violin, Festing was inferior to many of his time ; but as a composer, particularly of solos for that instrument, the nature and genius whereof he perfectly understood, he had but few equals.

LEWIS MERCY or MERCI, an Englishman by birth, though his name imports him to have been of French extraction,* was a celebrated performer on the flute abec, and an excellent composer for that instrument. He published six Solos, with a preface, containing a very brief history of the scale, and of Guido's reformation of it, taken from Brossard : and after that his Opera seconda, containing also six solos for the same instrument. Mercy lived at the time when the flute was becoming an unfashionable recreation for gentlemen, and the German flute was growing into favour ; he therefore concerted with the younger Stanesby, the wind-instrument-maker, the scheme of a new system, and of making the flute a concert instrument, without an actual transposition, by changing the denomination of the lower note from F to C, by which contrivance a flute of the fifth size was precisely an octave above the other treble instruments. He published twelve Solos, the first six whereof are said to be for the Traverse-flute, Violin, or English Flute, according to Mr. Stanesby's new system, with a preface in recommendation of it, in which he refers to Mersennus, de Instrumentis Harmonicis, and asserts that Stanesby's is in truth the ancient system of the flute ; and so upon a reference to the book it appears to be.† He also makes a comparison between the flute abec and the German flute, and asserts that the former of the two is the best in tune, and in other respects to be preferred. But all the endeavours of Stanesby and Mercy to restore this instrument seem to have failed of their end. Mercy lived in Orange-court in Castle-street near Leicester-fields, and advertised that his works were there to be had. His solos for the flute may be ranked among the best compositions for that instrument extant.

JONATHAN MARTIN had his education in the royal chapel under Dr. Croft, and soon after his decease was committed to the tuition of Roseingrave, then organist of St. George's, Hanover-square; and having under him attained to a great proficiency on the organ, and, with other assistances, qualified himself for choral duty, he became the deputy of Weldon as organist of the chapel ; and, upon his decease in the year 1736, his places of organist and composer to the chapel becoming vacant, Martin was appointed to one, and Dr. William Boyce to the other. Martin had the misfortune to labour under a pulmonic indisposition that suffered him to enjoy his preferment but a short time. In the year 1737, and a few months before his decease, he had a concert for his benefit at Stationers'-hall, at which were present almost every person in London that pretended to any skill in music, and where, though he had scarcely strength to sit upright, by two voluntaries on the organ he gave such proofs of a fine invention and a masterly hand, as astonished all his hearers. His manual performance was his greatest excellence,

there being nothing of his composition extant, save the song in Tamerlane, 'To thee O gentle sleep,' which ever since his decease has been sung to his music at the performance of that tragedy. Martin lies buried in the cloister of Westminster-abbey, but without a stone to point out the place of his interment.‡

JOHN HUMPHRIES, a young man of promising parts, and a good performer on the violin, published, before he was twenty, Six Solos for that instrument ; a puerile effort of a genius that was approaching to maturity. His success in that publication encouraged him to farther attempts, and in the year 1728 he published by subscription twelve Sonatas for two violins and a bass, of a very original cast, in respect that they are in a style somewhat above that of the common popular airs and country-dance tunes, the delight of the vulgar, and greatly beneath what might be expected from the studies of a person at all acquainted with the graces and elegancies of the Italians in their compositions for instruments. To this it must be attributed that the sonatas of Humphries were the common practice of such small proficients in harmony, as in his time were used to recreate themselves with music at alehouse clubs, and places of vulgar resort in the villages adjacent to London : of these there were formerly many, in which six-pence at most was the price of admission.§

Humphries died about the year 1730. Cooke, of New-street, Covent-Garden, a seller of music, published twelve Concertos of Humphries, precisely in the same cast with his sonatas.

JOHN RAVENSCROFT was one of the waits, as they are called, of the Tower Hamlets, and in the band of Goodman's Fields play-house was a Ripieno violin, notwithstanding which, he was a performer good enough to lead in any such concerts as those above described ; and, to say the truth, was able to do justice to a concerto of Corelli, or an overture of Handel. He was much sought after to play at balls and dancing parties ; and was singularly excellent in the playing of hornpipes, in which he had a manner that none could imitate. It seems that this was a kind of music which of all others he most affected ; so that by mere dint of a fancy accommodated to these little essays, he was enabled to compose airs of this kind equal to those of the ablest masters ; and yet so little was he acquainted with the rules of composition, that for suiting them with basses he was indebted to others. As a singular instance of the powers of a limited genius, the following are selected from a collection of hornpipes published by Ravenscroft :—

---

* He seems to have been fearful of being mistaken for a Frenchman, for in the title-page of one of his publications he styles himself ' di Nazione Inglesa.'

† See page 608, in note.

‡ A very elegant inscription was composed by Mr. Vincent Bourne, and intended for a tablet over the spot of his interment ; but as yet it is extant only in his poems, of which there are sundry editions. Together with Martin and very near his grave, was buried Charles Stroud, a disciple of Dr. Croft, a young man of great hopes, known by an anthem of his composition, " Hear my prayer O God."

§ To such readers as are interested in the knowledge of low manners, it may be some gratification to mention that there were concerts of this kind at the following places : the Blacksmith's Arms on Lambeth hill, behind St. Paul's ; the Cock and Lion in St. Michael's alley, Cornhill ; the Coachmakers' Arms in Windmill-street, Piccadilly : at sundry alehouses in Spitalfields, frequented by journeymen weavers ; and at Lambeth Wells, and the Unicorn at Hoxton. The keepers of these houses were generally men that loved music.

JOHN RAVENSCROFT.

Ravenscroft was a very corpulent man, a circumstance which made the neatness of his performance the more remarkable. He died about the year 1745.

GIUSEPPE SAN MARTINI was a native of Milan. He was a performer on the hautboy, an instrument invented by the French, and of small account, till by his exquisite performance, and a tone which he had the art of giving it, he brought it into reputation. Martini arrived in England about the year 1729, and was favoured by Bononcini, Greene, and others of that party, as also by Frederic, prince of Wales, who was his great patron. When Greene went to Cambridge to take his degree, Martini attended him, and performed in the exercise for it; and had there a concert for his benefit, which produced him a considerable sum. He was an admirable composer; and, for instrumental music, may, without injury to either, be classed with Corelli and Geminiani. His first compositions were Sonatas for two flutes, and others for German flutes : these are scarcely known, but the greatness of his talents is manifested in six Concertos and twelve Sonatas, published by himself, the latter dedicated to the late princess of Wales. The first of these works was published in the year 1738, when the concertos of Corelli and Geminiani, and the overtures of Mr. Handel were become familiar, there being scarce any concert in which the compositions of these two masters did not make a considerable part of the evening's entertainment ; and, with respect to those of Corelli, this had been the case for almost thirty years. Martini had therefore a ground to hope that the charm of novelty would recommend these his compositions to the public favour ; but he was disappointed in the expectations he had formed of the immediate sale of the whole impression of his book, and in an evil hour destroyed not only a great number of the copies, but also the plates from which they were wrought. The work being thus rendered scarce, Johnson, of Cheapside, was tempted to republish it ; and it was so well received, that the author soon found reason to repent his rashness, and was encouraged to prepare for the press eight overtures, and six grand concertos for violins, &c., but just as he had completed them he died ; however they were published by Johnson after his decease, with an advertisement in the title-page, that the work was engraved for the author in his life-time, and was by him intended to be published by subscription. The overtures in this collection are called Opera decima, and the concertos, Opera XI.* Walsh also published eight overtures in eight parts, and six grand concertos for violins, &c., by Martini, which, notwithstanding they are a posthumous publication, carry with them undoubted evidence of their genuineness.

The merits of Martini as a composer of music in many parts, were unquestionably very great. He had a fertile invention, and gave into a style of modulation less restrained by rule than that of his predecessors, and by consequence affording greater scope for his fancy. Those who ascribe his deviation from known and established rules to the want of musical erudition, are grossly mistaken ; he was thoroughly skilled in the principles of harmony ; and his singularities can therefore only be ascribed to that boldness and self-possession which are ever the concomitants of genius ; and in most of the licences he has taken, it may be observed that he is in a great measure warranted by the precepts, and indeed by the example, of Geminiani.

He performed on the hautboy in the opera till the time that Bononcini left it ; after that he played at the Castle concert, and occasionally at others ; but being patronized by Frederic, prince of Wales, he was at length received into his family upon the footing of a domestic, and appointed master or director of the chamber music to his royal highness.

In the course of this employment he composed a great number of Sonatas for the practice of the chamber ; and, upon the birth of the princess of Brunswick, set to music a drama written on occasion of that event. He also composed a musical solemnity, which was publicly performed at the chapel of the Bavarian minister. In the honourable and easy station above-mentioned, Martini continued till about the year 1740, when he died.

As a performer on the hautboy, Martini was undoubtedly the greatest that the world had ever known. Before his time the tone of the instrument was rank, and, in the hands of the ablest proficients, harsh and grating to the ear ; by great study and application, and by some peculiar management of the reed, he contrived to produce such a tone as approached the nearest to that of the human voice of any we know of.† It may well be supposed that he was not backward in communicating the improvements which he had made on this his favourite instrument, since a pupil of his, Mr. Thomas Vincent, is known to have possessed most of his excellencies in a very eminent degree ; and we farther observe that the performers on the hautboy at this time are greatly superior to any that can be remembered before the arrival of Martini in England.

JOHN FREDERIC LAMPE was, as he affected to style himself, sometime a student of music at Helmstadt in Saxony ; and arriving in England about the year 1725, obtained employment in the opera band. About the year 1730 he was engaged by Rich, of Covent Garden theatre, to compose the music to his pantomimes, and other entertainments performed there. Carey, who had received from him some instructions, had a high opinion of his abilities, and got him to set to music his burlesque opera of the Dragon of Wantley, as also the sequel to it, entitled Margery, and in his printed dramatic works, the Dragoness, in both which he has happily ridiculed the extravagancies of the modern Italian music, and the affected manner of the opera singers. In 1737 he published, in a quarto volume, 'A plain and ' compendious method of teaching Thorough-bass ' after the most rational manner, with proper rules ' for practice,' and dedicated it to Col. Blathwayt, assigning as a reason for so doing, his elegant taste and sound knowledge of music. There are extant many single songs composed by Lampe at sundry times, some of which are printed in the Musical Miscellany, in six volumes, published by Watts. He set to music, in a burlesque style exactly suited to the words, a Cantata of Swift, beginning ' In ' harmony would you excel,' printed at the end of the eighth volume of Faulkner's edition of Swift's works.‡ His wife was Isabella, one of the daughters of

---

* The intermediate publications of Martini between his first concertos and the Opera decima, are erroneously numbered ; the sonatas are his Opera terza, the rest are sonatas and solos for German flutes, and are of small account.

† About the year 1735 an advertisement appeared in the public papers, offering a reward of ten guineas for a hautboy-reed that had been lost. It was conjectured to be Martini's, and favoured the opinion that he had some secret in preparing or meliorating the reeds of his instrument, though none could account for the offer of a reward so greatly disproportionable to the utmost conceivable value of the thing lost. It seems that the reed was found, and brought to the owner, but in such a condition as rendered it useless.

‡ It was originally printed for Johnson, in Cheapside, with the title of 'The Force of Music and Poetry, a Pindaric Ode,' and, though an anonymous publication, is undoubtedly the work of Lampe.

Mr. Charles Young, who, together with her sister Esther, sang in the Dragon of Wantley. Lampe died in London about twenty years ago.

FRANCESCO BARSANTI, a native of Lucca, born about the year 1690, studied the civil law in the university of Padua; but, after a short stay there, chose music for his profession. Accordingly he put himself under the tuition of some of the ablest masters in Italy, and having attained to a considerable degree of proficiency in the science of practical composition, took a resolution to settle in England, and came hither with Geminiani, who was also a Luccese, in the year 1714. He was a good performer on the hautboy, and also on the flute; in the former capacity he found employment in the opera band; and in the latter derived considerable advantages by teaching. He published, with a dedication to the earl of Burlington, Six Solos for a flute, with a thorough-bass, and afterwards Six Solos for a German flute and a bass. He also made into sonatas for two violins and a bass, the first six solos of Geminiani. He continued many years a performer at the opera-house; at length, reflecting that there was a prospect of advantage for one of his profession in Scotland, he went thither; and, with greater truth than the same is asserted of David Rizzo, may be said to have meliorated the music of that country, by collecting and making basses to a great number of the most popular Scots tunes.

About the year 1750 Barsanti returned to England, but, being advanced in years, he was glad to be taken into the opera band as a performer on the tenor violin; and in the summer season into that of Vauxhall: at this time he published twelve Concertos for violins, and, shortly after, Sei Antifone, in which he endeavoured to imitate the style of Palestrina, and the old composers of motets; but from these publications so little profit resulted, that, towards the end of his life, the industry and œconomy of an excellent wife, whom he had married in Scotland, and the studies and labours of a daughter, whom he had qualified for the profession of a singer, but is now an actress at Covent-Garden, were his chief support.*

PETER PRELLEUR, a person of French extraction, was, in the very early part of his life, a writing-master in Spitalfields; but, having a genius for music, and having been taught the harpsichord, he studied the science with great assiduity, and at length took to music as a profession. About the year 1728 he was elected organist of St. Alban, Wood-street, London; and a short time after, upon the decease of Monro, was taken into the band at the theatre in Goodman's-fields, and there played the harpsichord, till that house was suppressed by the operation of the statute of the tenth of the late king, cap. 28, whereby the acting of plays is restrained to the city of Westminster, and the places of his majesty's residence. His skill in music enabled

* This circumstance in the character of Miss Barsanti, as also her dutiful regard for her surviving parent, are well known; and, to the honour of the present age, it is here mentioned, that the public are not more disposed to applaud her theatrical merit, than to distinguish by their favour so illustrious an example of filial duty and affection.

him to compose the dances, as also interludes of various kinds, for which there is ever a demand at a theatre, and in these his merits were apparent.

About the year 1730 he was employed by Cluer and Dicey, music-printers in Bow church-yard, to compile an Introduction to Singing, as also instructions for the practice of most instruments; this work he completed, and added thereto a brief history of the science, extracted chiefly from Bontempi, containing sundry curious particulars.

About the year 1735, the parish of Christ-Church, Middlesex, had come to a resolution to erect an organ in their church, which is situated in Spitalfields, and Prelleur having many friends in that quarter, made an early interest for the place of organist, but was opposed by a young man who lived in that neighbourhood: the contest was carried on with such spirit by both parties, as was scarce ever known, but in popular elections to some great office. A scurrilous pamphlet was published by his competitor in support of his pretensions, and the inhabitants of the parish were set at enmity; but, notwithstanding all his endeavours and artifices, Prelleur was elected.

Upon the suppression of Goodman's-fields theatre, a place of entertainment was opened in the neighbourhood of it, of a similar kind with Sadler's Wells, and though there was no pretence of a well near it, it was called Goodman's-fields Wells: with the proprietor of this place Prelleur engaged, and during a few seasons that it was suffered, he composed the songs and dances, and also a little interlude, called Baucis and Philemon, in which there is a good overture, and a few pretty songs.

JOHN JAMES, a celebrated organist, was for some years only a deputy, at a salary of about eight pounds a year; but after that was elected to the place of organist of St. Olave, Southwark, which he quitted about the year 1738 for that of St. George, Middlesex. In his performance he was distinguished by the singularity of his style, which was learned and sublime. He paid very little attention to his interest, and was so totally devoid of all solicitude to advance himself in his profession, as to prefer the company and conversation of the lowest of mankind to that of the most celebrated of his own profession. To the wonder of all that knew him, his love of an art, that has a general tendency to improve the mind, had not the least influence on his manners, which were to so great a degree sordid and brutal, that his associates were butchers and bailiffs, and his recreations dog-fighting and bull-baiting. In a perfect consistence with the character he most affected, which was that of a blackguard, he indulged an inclination to spirituous liquors of the coarsest kind, such as are the ordinary means of ebriety in the lowest of the people; and this kind of intemperance he would indulge even while attending his duty at church.

The sole merit of James was his extempore performance; he composed a few voluntaries, which are in the hands of every deputy-organist in London. Three or four songs of his setting are all of his works that are known to be in print. He died about the year 1745; his funeral was attended by great numbers of the musical profession, and was celebrated by the performance of a dead march composed by himself. He left behind him a son, baptized by the name of Handel, who now rows a sculler on the Thames.

## CHAP. CXCV.

THE progress of music in Italy had been very rapid for more than a century, and it was thought that both the science and practice had received nearly the last degree of improvement in the studies of Corelli: it was no small argument in favour of this opinion, that for some years after his decease, such an uniformity of style prevailed, especially in the instrumental compositions of the time, as seemed to indicate that the topics of invention were exhausted. The succeeding race of musicians however gave proofs of the contrary, and, emancipating music from that state of bondage which imitation ever implies, by the introduction of new combinations they added to the fund of harmony, and laid the foundation of a new style.

To bring the proof of this assertion home to ourselves, we need do no more than consult the compositions of Geminiani, and the later Italian musicians, namely, Pergolesi, Tartini, Vinci, Leo, Galuppi, and others which are recent in the memory of persons now living. To enumerate all of this class is unnecessary, but the two first are of such distinguished eminence as to merit a memorial.

GIOVANNI BATTISTA PERGOLESI was born at Naples about the year 1718; and at an age when he could be scarce supposed to have finished his studies, introduced a style of vocal composition, which, for its singular sweetness and power over the affections, has hitherto been inimitable. Those who have analysed his works resolve that original strain of modulation, which characterizes them, into a liberal use of the semitonic intervals, and a studious rejection of passages or musical phrases ready formed, which being adopted by succeeding writers, render a composition little better than a cento. Pergolesi died at the age of twenty-two, just as he had finished the last verse of a Stabat Mater, by which he will ever be remembered: his premature death, and the great reputation he had so suddenly acquired, furnished ground for a suspicion that, to remove him out of the way, his rivals for fame had recourse to poison; but others, better informed, attribute his death to a severe attack of a pleurisy that baffled all attempts to save him. His Cantatas, published at Rome in 1738; two comic interludes, the one entitled La Serva Padrona, the other Il Maestro di Musica, a Salve Regina, and his famous Stabat Mater, the last printed in England, are all of his works that have been published.* There are in print twelve Sonatas for violins that bear his name; but evidence that they are genuine is wanting.

* In the library of the Academy of ancient Music are the following compositions of Pergolesi in manuscript: Two Masses, one for two choirs; A Salve Regina Domine adjuvandum, Confitebor, Laudate Pueri, and a Miserere.

GIUSEPPE TARTINI, of Padua, the last great improver of the practice of the violin, and a most sweet and judicious composer for that instrument, was born in the year 1692, at Pirano, a sea-port town in Istria, a province in the Venetian territory. When he was very young he entertained a passion for a young woman, who being in circumstances inferior to those of his own family, was by his friends thought an improper match for him; and all arguments to induce him to divert his affection proving ineffectual, his father confined him to his room; and, to engage his attention, furnished him with books and musical instruments, in the use whereof he profited so greatly, that when some time after he had got the better of his passion, and determined to make music his profession, being committed to the care of proper instructors, he gave the most promising hopes of becoming, both of the theory and practice, a complete master.

Having effaced from his mind the image of that mistress who had been the innocent cause of his restraint, he settled his affections on another, whom he married; but the object of his choice being but slenderly endowed with those mental qualities that are essential to conjugal happiness, and having no children, nor a prospect of any, he still found himself in a state of solitude, from which he could find no relief but in the pursuit of his studies.

In remarking the improvements that have been made in the practice of instruments, it may be noted, that the later performers have begun, as it were, where their predecessors left off; and that the powers of execution have been amazingly increased of late years: this is no other way to be accounted for, than upon the supposition that those particular energies which constitute perfection on any instrument, have been carefully noted down, and made to serve as common places for succeeding practisers. That Tartini was very assiduous in his remarks of this kind, is manifest from the nature of his performance, which was regulated by such principles as lead to perfection by the shortest road; of his success in these his observations in particular, one example shall suffice.

All men acquainted with music are sensible that the instruments of the fidicinal kind, which are those that are acted upon by a bow, are the most difficult of practice, and that the difference as well in respect of tone, and the powers of execution between one performer and another, is very great; but few have observed that this difference does almost solely arise from the action of the wrist of the right-hand, which being made to hang loose, will shoot the bow at right angles across the strings, and return it in the same line, producing a free and mellow tone, and giving power to execute the quickest passages; when this is not attended to, the shoulder becomes the centre of motion: the bow forms a curve in its passage, the weight of the arm prevents the vibration of the instrument, and by consequence damps the tone, and easy passages become difficult.

Tartini seems to have been the first that discovered this secret in the performance on the violin, and he made it a leading principle in the instruction of his pupils, who invariably adhere to it, and are the best performers in the world.

The perfection to which Tartini had attained on his favourite instrument, was alone sufficient to have established his character as a master, but, following the example of Zarlino, he made the theory of his art his study. Of sundry treatises that he wrote, the most celebrated is one entitled 'Trattata di 'Musica secondo la vera Scienza dell' Armonia,' printed at Padua in 1754, wherein from that well-known phenomenon mentioned by Mersennus and Dr. Wallis, that a chord, besides the sound to which it is tuned, will produce its twelfth, seventh, and, as the former asserts, its twenty-second also, he deduces sundry observations, tending to explain the scale, and, in the opinion of some, to correct sundry of the intervals of which it is composed.

An attempt to explain the doctrines contained in this tract, which all allow to be very obscurely written, was lately made in a book entitled Principles and Power of Harmony, printed in 1771, upon which it may be observed, that wherever the commentator can catch a glimpse of the author's meaning, he is very diffuse in his illustrations; but in others, where the sense is too deep for his powers of investigation, and those occur but too frequently, he, to do him justice, candidly acknowledges the difficulty, or else he offers an explanation that fails of its end. Whoever peruses the preface and introduction to the Principles and Power of Harmony, would expect to find the book a commentary on Tartini's treatise, but instead thereof it is for the most part a collection of miscellaneous observations, made in the course of a transient view of some very able writers on music, whose sense the author has not so often illustrated as mistaken.*

To explain the doctrines delivered in his book, Tartini has recourse to numerical and algebraical calculations, in which he discovers that he was but meanly skilled in even the first of those sciences.

He seems clearly to declare his opinion that the ancient Greeks were unacquainted with music in consonance, in the following passage : 'La loro 'armonia era formata non come la nostra di note 'equitemporance, ma di note successive.'† And in the frequent comparisons which he occasionally makes between the ancient and modern music, generally decides in favour of the latter. To show at least that, in respect of its influence on the passions, the modern is not inferior to the ancient music, he relates that in an opera represented at Ancona in the year 1714, he heard a passage of recitative, with no other accompaniment than that of the bass, which made himself and the others that heard it change colour, and caused a sensible commotion in their minds ; he says that this effect was produced by notes that expressed indignation so forcibly, that they seemed to freeze the blood ; and that it was uniformly the same in a representation thirteen times of the drama.

The residence of Tartini during almost the whole of his life was at Padua, to which city he was attached by the employment of director of the music in the great church of St. Anthony ; thither resorted to him for instruction in music, but chiefly in the practice of the violin, great numbers of young men from various countries. In the early part of his life he published ' Sonate a Violino e Violoncello o Cim-'balo, Opera prima,' with a dedication to Sig. Girolamo Giustiniani, the celebrated paraphrast of those Psalms which Marcello set to music, and are spoken of in the memoir herein before given of him : these, as also his Opera seconda, being six Sonatas or Solos for the same instrument, and another work of his, entitled 'XVIII. Concerti a 5 Stromenti,' are all published by Le Cene of Amsterdam, and shew him to have been as able a composer as he was a theorist.

Towards the end of his life he was afflicted with the palsy. The time of his death is not precisely ascertained in any of the accounts extant that speak of him, but is supposed to be about the beginning of the year 1770.

Among the Germans the successive improvements in music, and the variations of style may be traced in the compositions of Buxtehude, Mattheson, Telemann, Bach, and Handel. The French continued for many years at a stand : Lully had formed a style, which in their opinion was incapable of improvement ; Couperin convinced them of the contrary. Of the true organ-style they had no conception, till Marchand and D'Andrieu displayed the powers of that instrument. Their symphonies and other compositions for violins were of a light and shadowy cast, destitute of invention and contrivance ; and as to theory, the study of it had been discontinued in France from the time of Mersennus and Des Cartes, who, in the general opinion of the musicians of that country, had nearly exhausted the subject. Of these errors they were however at length convinced by the studies of Le Clair and Rameau; the first introduced among them a style of instrumental composition, in

---

* For instance, he asserts in Sect. 59 of his book, that the harp was formerly the favourite instrument of our ancestors ; and Sect. 62, cites sundry passages from Spenser, Shakespeare, Milton, and others, in support of his opinion : that it was so with the Britons, and also with the Saxons, no one can doubt ; but that it was ever in practice among the English, we are not warranted to say, much less that it was a favourite instrument in the time of any of these writers whose testimony is adduced for the purpose. What compositions have we extant for the harp, or who among the English musicians are celebrated for their performance on it ? The truth is, that harp, like lyre, is a poetical term for a string musical instrument ; and in the sense in which these appellatives are used, each is as vague and indefinite as the other. Sect. 85, he says that Tartini has not been more successful in his endeavours to discover the true enarmonic than others. Perhaps he has been less so, for, in the opinion of Dr. Pepusch, Salinas and others have determined this genus of ancient music accurately: see his letter to Mr. Abraham De Moivre in the Philosophical Transactions, Numb. 481, page 266. And again, neither Tartini, nor his expositor, in their elucidation of the ancient modes, seem to have been aware of a passage in Ptolemy, and taken notice of by Dr. Wallis, viz., that they anwered to the seven species of diapason, but that in each a particular tuning of the lyre was necessary, which could not be effected without a dislocation of the semitones. When he says, as he does in Sect. 9, that the discoveries contained in the first chapter of Tartini's book are fully sufficient to account for every thing practised or practicable in art, we think he has asserted too much. And when in his Appendix he gives to the Kamschatcans as good a right to decide against the possibility of foretelling an eclipse, or of representing all the elements of speech by about twenty-four marks, as the moderns have to doubt of the effects of ancient music, he seems rather to rave than reason. These strictures on a book, which, by an ostentatious display of deep and various reading, has raised in some a high opinion of his merit, would have been spared, had not the errors contained in it called for animadversion, and the exceeding confidence and self-sufficiency of the author for reprehension.

† Trattato, pag. 143.

which the suggestions of a wild and irregular fancy were made to give place to a solid and substantial harmony, that spoke to the understanding : and the latter, by a deep investigation of the principles of harmony, and a variety of experiments and numerical calculations, taught them that much remained to be known. Of these eminent professors, as also of some others who flourished in France in the age immediately preceding the present, the following memoirs are extant.

NICOLAS BERNIER was born at Mante on the Seine, in the year 1664. By his merit in his profession he attained to be conductor of the music in the chapel of St. Stephen, and afterwards in that of the king. The regent duke of Orleans admired his works, and patronized their author. This prince having given him a motet of his own composition to examine, and, being impatient for his observations thereon, went to the house of Bernier, and, entering his study, found the Abbé de la Croix there, criticising his piece, while the musician himself was in another room, carousing and singing with a company of his friends. The duke broke in upon and interrupted their mirth, with a reprimand of Bernier for his inattention to the task assigned him. This musician died at Paris in 1734. His five books of Cantatas and Songs for one and two voices, the words of which were written by Rousseau and Fuselier, have procured him great reputation. There are besides of his composition ' Les Nuits de Sceaux,' and many motets, which are still in great esteem.

MICHEL MONTECLAIR was born, in the year 1666, at Andelot, a town of Bassigny, about ten miles from Chaumont. He took his surname from an old castle near the place of his birth. He was at first a teacher of music at Paris ; after that he was taken into the Royal Academy there ; and is said to have first introduced the Violone or double bass into the orchestra of the opera. He died near St. Dennis in 1737. There are extant of his works ' Méthode ' pour apprendre la Musique,' ' Principes pour le ' Violon,' ' Trios de Violons,' Cantatas, Motets, and one Messe de Requiem. He also composed the music to an entertainment entitled ' Les Fêtes de ' l' Eté,' and to the celebrated opera of Jepthé, written by Pellegrin, and represented at Paris in the year 1732.

JEAN-JOSEPH MOURET, born at Avignon in 1682, became remarkable from the age of twenty for his excellent musical compositions : his sense, wit, and taste for music rendered him a favourite with the great ; the duchess of Maine employed him to compose music for the festivals so much celebrated under the name of the Nuits de Sceaux. Ragonde, or la Soirée de Village, represented at the opera-house in Paris with great applause, was one of those entertainments. The levity of Mouret's compositions, and the sprightliness of his airs, were the great recommendations of his music. Towards the close of his life he became subject to some mental disorders, and met with other misfortunes, which hastened his end. Of these the most considerable was the loss of an income of five thousand livres a year, which arose

from the places of director of the Concert Spirituel, Superintendent of the music of the duchess of Maine, and musical composer to the Italian comedy. Mouret died at Charenton near Paris in the year 1738. He composed sundry operas, ballets, and other musical representations, namely, ' Les Fêtes ' de Thalie,' ' Les Amours des Dieux,' ' Le Triomphe ' des Sens,' ' Les Graces,' opera-ballets ; and Ariane, and Pirithous, tragedies, the one represented in 1717, the other in 1723. He also composed three books of songs of various kinds, and other works of less account.

JEAN-FRANÇOIS DANDRIEU, a celebrated musician, was born in the year 1684. He was a masterly performer on the organ and harpsichord, nor were his compositions less excellent. He resembled the celebrated Couperin both in style and execution. Dandrieu died at Paris in 1740, leaving of his works, three volumes of pieces for the harpsichord, and one of pieces for the organ, ' avec un suite de Noels,'* all which are greatly esteemed.

HENRI DESMARETS, born at Paris in the year 1662, was page de la musique to the king, and enjoyed a pension of nine hundred livres a year. Being on a journey to Senlis, he became enamoured with the daughter of the President of Elections, and, without the knowledge of her friends, married her. The father of the young woman instituted a process against Desmarets for seducing and carrying off his daughter ; in consequence of which, by a sentence du Châtelet, he was condemned to death. Desmarets fled into Spain, and from thence to Lorrain ; but, at length succeeding in his solicitations to the parliament for a pardon, he returned to Paris, and became a composer to the opera. When he was a young man he composed those motets which go under the name of Coupillet ;† but the most celebrated of his works are his operas of Didon and Iphigénie in Tauride, represented at Paris in the year 1704, with some alterations of Campra. Desmarets died at Luneville in the year 1741.

CHARLES-HUBERT GERVAIS was intendant of the band of the regent duke of Orleans, and afterwards master of the chapel royal. He died at Paris in the year 1744, aged seventy-two. He composed three operas, namely Meduse, represented in 1702 ; Hypermnestre, in 1716 ; and Les Amours de Protée, in 1720. These, with sundry Motets, and a collection of Cantatas of his composition, are in print.

ANDRE-CARDINAL DESTOUCHES was born at Paris in the year 1672. He accompanied Father Tachard, a Jesuit, in a voyage to Siam, with an intention to enter himself of that society on his return. On his arrival however at Paris, he changed his mind, and betook himself to the profession of a soldier ; but, being passionately fond of music, he quitted the military profession, and became an eminent composer of operas. His first essay of this kind was the opera of Issé, represented at Paris in 1708, with which the king was so pleased, that he gave him a purse of two hundred Louis d'Ors, adding that he meant by

* Carols or Songs celebrating the nativity of our Saviour.
† Vide ante, page 836.

that present only to attach him to his service; for that, excepting the operas of Lully, he had never heard any that delighted him so much as this of Issé. It is said with great confidence that at the time he composed this opera, Destouches had not the least knowledge of the rules of composition, but that nevertheless a happy coincidence of words and expression rendered the recitative part of it peculiarly excellent.* To encourage him in his new profession, the king made him superintendent of his band, and inspector-general of the Royal Academy; upon which Destouches set himself to study the rules of his art, but it was observed that the restrictions which these laid him under, served but to check the flights of his genius, and had a bad effect upon his future compositions, which were the operas, or, as the French call them, the tragedies of Amadis de Grece, Marthesie, Omphale, Télémaque, and Sémiramis, and sundry Ballets, all which were represented in the Royal Academy, but with far less applause than was bestowed on his first production, the opera of Issé. Destouches died in the year 1749 in the employments above-mentioned, having for many years been favoured by the royal bounty with a pension of four thousand livres per annum.

LOUIS-NICOLAS CLERAMBAULT was a native of Paris, and, being a favourite of Louis XIV., was by him appointed director of the private concerts of Madam de Maintenon, and organist of St. Cyr. There are extant of his composition five books of Cantatas, in which there is one entitled Orphée, that is greatly admired; and there are also attributed to him sundry Motets, and other vocal compositions for particular festivals, that shew him to have been a man of considerable abilities in his profession. He died at Paris in the year 1749.

JOSEPH-NICOLAS-PANCRACE ROYER, a native of Savoy, came to reside at Paris about the year 1725, and there acquired much reputation for his manner of singing, and his excellent performance on the organ and harpsichord. Being a well-bred man, and of an amiable character, he formed such connections as led him into the way of preferment at court. By the interest of his friends there, and his own merit, he obtained a reversionary grant of the place of music-master to the royal family of France, and came into the possession of it in the year 1746. In the following year he was appointed director of the Concert Spirituel. In 1754 he was appointed composer of the music for the king's chamber, and inspector-general of the opera. He lived not long to enjoy these lucrative employments, for he died on the eleventh of January, 1755, in the fiftieth year of his age. Royer composed the following operas, viz., Pyrrhus, Zaïde, Le Pouvoir de l'Amour, Amalsis, and Prométhée, and many lessons for the harpsichord, of which only one collection has as yet been published.

FRANCOIS-COLIN DE BLAMONT was born at Versailles in the year 1690, and, for his merit in his profession, was made a chevalier of the order of St. Michael. He was a composer for the opera, and enjoyed the places of superintendent of the king's music, and master of that of his chamber. The operas composed by him are Didon, and Les Fêtes Grecques et Romaines. He died in the year 1760.

JEAN-MARIE LE CLAIR was born at Lyons in 1697. His father was a musician, and with his instructions, and the assistance of able masters, he became a fine performer on the violin. He travelled abroad some years for improvement, and seemed disposed to settle in Holland; but, upon an invitation from the duke de Grammont, who had been his pupil, he went to Paris, and was favoured by him with a handsome pension. By the recommendation of this nobleman, and his own masterly performance, Le Clair attained to the place of symphonist to Louis XV. in which he laboured incessantly to improve the practice of the violin among his countrymen. With this view he composed and published in the year 1723, a collection of Solos for the violin; and soon after that another of the same kind, in both which the author has displayed a perfect knowledge of the instrument, and the powers of a rich and well-regulated fancy.

The character and demeanour of Le Clair were such as attracted the esteem of all that knew him; and, as he affected a retired and contemplative life, he had little reason to fear the shafts of envy: nevertheless it seems that he fell a sacrifice to his own fame, for, without having given offence to any one, being abroad in the streets of Paris, in the evening of the twenty-second day of October, 1764, and returning to his own home, he was assassinated. Besides the two collections of Solos above-mentioned, Le Clair was the author of Six Sonatas for two Violins and a bass, Oeuvre IV. which have this singular circumstance to distinguish them, that in the title-page they are said to be engraved by his wife, 'Gravée par Madam son Epouse.'† Le Clair is celebrated for the spirit and energy of his manual performance, and these compositions are in some sort a proof of it. At least it may be said, that, for grandeur and dignity of style, there are no instrumental compositions of the French musicians, not even of Lully himself, that merit to be compared with them. It is true that they are difficult to be executed, and this for some time was a general objection to the compositions of Le Clair; but the French musicians, like those of other countries, have improved on the violin, and this difficulty has long since vanished. The other works of Le Clair in print are two books of Duos, two of Trios, two of Concertos, two under the title of Récréations, and the opera of Sylla and Glaucus.

JEAN-PHILIPPE RAMEAU was born at Dijon on the twenty-fifth of September, 1683. After having learned the rudiments of music, his taste for the art led him while young to leave his native country, and wander about with the performers of a strolling opera. At the age of eighteen he composed a

---

* This is a most unaccountable relation; all that can be said in defence of it is, that it is taken from the Nouveau Dictionnaire Historique, originally written by Mons. l'Advocat, and improved on by a set of men who had opportunities of the best information.

† He is in the title-page styled Mons. Le Clair l'ainé, from which adjunct it is conjectured that he was the elder of two brothers of the same profession.

musical entertainment, which was represented at Avignon, and was received with as much applause as can be thought due to so puerile an essay : but as this applause was less than the author hoped for, he removed from thence, and, after travelling through a part of Italy and France, corrected his ideas of music by the practice of the harpsichord; on which instrument, by incessant application, he attained a degree of proficiency little inferior to that which distinguished the famous Marchand. In the course of his travels he stopped at Dijon, and performed on the organ of the Holy Chapel; he did the same at Clermont, and played on the organ of that cathedral ; in both places to large audiences, composed of the members of the church, and other good judges of music. The reputation which he by these means acquired, brought Marchand to hear him, who upon that occasion is said to have made use of this expression, ' Rameau a plus de main que moi, mais ' j'ai plus de tête que lui.' Upon hearing this, Rameau, with a view to satisfy himself touching the merits of Marchand's pretensions, went to Paris, where he had no sooner heard him than he became sensible of his own inferiority, and with great candour and modesty professed himself an humble hearer of Marchand, expressing at the same time an ardent desire to become his pupil. Marchand generously condescended to his request, and laboured to the utmost of his power in the improvement of a genius so capable of cultivation. Rameau, by a course of severe study, had in a great measure united the perfections of Marchand with his own ; and upon the strength of these he became a candidate for the place of organist of the church of St. Paul in Paris; but failing to obtain it, he had almost determined to decline that branch of his profession, but was prevented by the offer of the place of organist of the cathedral church of Clermont in Auvergne, which he accepted. In this retirement he studied with the utmost assiduity the theory of his art. His investigations in the course of this pursuit gave birth to his 'Traité de l'Harmonie,' printed at Paris in 1722; and to his ' Nouveau 'Systeme de Musique Theorique,' printed at the same place in 1726. But the work for which Rameau is most celebrated is his 'Démonstration du Principe ' de l'Harmonie,' Paris 1750, in which, as his countrymen say, he has shewn that the whole depends upon one single and clear principle, viz., the fundamental bass : and in this respect he is by them compared to Newton, who by the single principle of gravitation was able to assign reasons for some of the most remarkable phenomena in physics ; for this reason they scruple not to style Rameau the Newton of Harmony.

With such extraordinary talents as these, and a style in musical composition far surpassing, in the opinion of some, that of the greatest among the French musicians, it had been a national reproach had Rameau been suffered to remain organist of a country cathedral. He was called to Paris, and appointed to the management of the opera; in which employment it was his care to procure the ablest performers of all kinds that could be found, and to furnish from the inexhaustible stores of his own invention, compositions worthy of so great a genius. His music was of an original cast, and the performers complained at first that it could not be executed; but he asserted the contrary, and evinced it by experiment. By practice he acquired a great facility in composing, so that he was never at a loss to adapt sounds to sentiments. It was a saying of Quinault, ' that the poet was the musician's servant;' but Rameau would say, ' Qu'on me donne la Gazette ' d'Hollande et je la mettrai en musique.' The king, to reward his extraordinary merit, conferred upon him the ribbon of the order of St. Michael; and a little before his death raised him to the rank of the noblesse. Rameau was a man of pure morals, and lived happily with a wife whom he tenderly loved : there was much simplicity in his character ; and his temper, though not so philosophic as to render him altogether inirascible, was upon the whole mild and placid, and in the offices of friendship and humanity no man went beyond him.

This philosophical artist died at Paris on the twelfth day of September, in the year 1764. His exequies were celebrated by a musical solemnity in the church of the Oratory in the street of St. Honoré, the place of his sepulture, in which several extracts from his own compositions were introduced. Besides the tracts above-mentioned, there are extant of Rameau's writing the following : ' Generation Har- ' monique,' Paris, 1737 ; and ' Nouvelles Reflexions ' sur la Démonstration,' &c. His musical compositions consist of sundry collections of lessons for the harpsichord, and his operas, the names whereof are as follow : Hyppolite et Aricie, les Indes Galantes, Castor et Pollux, les Fêtes d'Hébé, Dardanus, Platée, les Fêtes de Polhimnie, le Temple de la Gloire, les Fêtes de l'Himen, Zaïs, Pigmalion, Naïs, Zoroastre, la Guirlande, Acante et Céphise, Daphnis et Eglé, Lisis et Délie, les Sybarites, la Naissance d'Osiris, Anacréon, les Surprises de l'Amour, and les Paladins.

As a theorist, the character of Rameau stands very high ; and as a testimony to his merit in this particular, it is here mentioned as a fact, that Mr. Handel was ever used to speak of him in terms of great respect. As a musical composer his character remains to be settled : while one set of men celebrate his works for the grace and spirit of them, others object to them that they are either stiff and laboured, or light and trifling even to puerility. Should the latter be the true characteristic of them, it would be no wonder, since a fine style of composition is by no means the necessary consequence of profound skill in the principles of harmony. The poetic faculty does not keep pace with our improvements in the niceties of grammar or the laws of prosody ; and the compositions of those deep theorists, Zarlino and Pepusch, do not rise above mediocrity. As to the French music in general, the merit of it has at different periods been a subject of controversy ; many think that in the art of musical composition the French are an age behind the rest of Europe : and many more are of opinion that, having deviated from the path of nature, they may be two before they find their way back again.

Besides the above persons who were practical musicians, there were many among the French who are distinguished for general skill in the principles of the science ; Pere Antoine Parran, a Jesuit, who flourished about the middle of the last century, is reckoned one of their best writers on the subject of music at large. He published at Paris, in the year 1646, 'Traité de la Musique Theorique et Practique, ' contenant les Preceptes de la Composition.' Some years after Claude Perrault, the architect, and for his great skill therein called the French Vitruvius, published a ' Dissertation de la Musique des ' Anciens,' wherein he denies that the ancients were acquainted with music in consonance. In later times the Abbé Raguenet distinguished himself by his Parallel between the French and Italian Music, and Mons. de la Viéville de Freneuse by his answer to it. Of both these tracts an account has already been given : the latter of these persons is also known by the name of Jean-Laurent le Cerf ; he was keeper of the seals of the parliament of Normandy, and died in 1707. There are several dissertations of his writing in the Journals de Trevoux. The Abbé Chateauneuf in 1725 published a ' Dialogue sur la ' Musique des Anciens ;' others there are who have obliged the world by occasional discourses and dissertations on the subject of music in the Memoirs of the Academy of Inscriptions, printed at the Hague in duodecimo, with the title of ' Memoires de Litera- ' ture tirés des Régistres de l'Académie Royal des ' Inscriptions et Belles-Lettres.' The papers respecting music in this collection most worthy of notice, are those that tend to obviate a doubt that had been raised of the genuineness of Plutarch's Dialogue on Music ; and to settle a question the most embarrassing of all that have arisen on the subject of music, that is to say, whether the ancients were acquainted with, or ignorant of, the practice of music in consonance, polyphonous music, simultaneous harmony, or whatever else is to be understood by the term, music in parts.

The controversy touching Plutarch's Dialogue, as it arose from an inconsiderate remark of Amyot the French translator of his works, made above a hundred years ago, and which no one till of late had thought worthy of a refutation, was terminated by Mons. Jean-Pierre Burette, a physician of Paris, and member of the Academy of Inscriptions, in favour of the piece in question ; but those who disputed its authority, founding their objections upon the circumstance that the mention of music in consonance does not once occur in it, the determination of the question, as to the authenticity of the book, had no other effect than to bring on another of a greater latitude. They who contended that the dialogue was spurious, assumed that the ancients were acquainted with music in consonance ; and it was necessary for them to get rid of a book which was negative evidence of the contrary ; but the authority of it being once established, their adversaries made good use of their advantage, and insisted that the silence of such an author as Plutarch as to any such practice, was a very strong argument in favour of the contrary opinion.

It is not necessary here to repeat what was urged in the course of this dispute, or to recapitulate those arguments respecting the question itself which are stated in an earlier part of this work. It may suffice to say, that Mons. Fraguier, a member of the academy, was the champion of the ancients, and Mons. Burette of the moderns, and that the latter in his ' Dissertation sur la Symphonie des Anciens,' published in the Memoirs abovementioned, tom. V. page 151, gained a complete victory.*

Two other French writers, namely, the fathers Bougeant and Cerceau, have in the principal question taken the side of Burette, as appears by the papers of theirs published in the Journals de Trevoux for April and Oct. 1725, and Jan. and Feb. 1729. In a word this question, to use a phrase of Chaucer, has been ' bolted to the bran ;' and there is very little probability remaining that any argument in favour of the affirmative can in future be adduced that has not been refuted.

## CHAP. CXCVI.

THE termination of the dispute between Handel and his adversaries, as it left him in the quiet possession of that empire, in which it seems to have been his fixed resolution never to admit a rival, though it totally extinguished emulation, was in general favourable to music. Covent-Garden theatre was an excellent seminary ; and by the performance of the oratorio there, the practice of music was greatly improved throughout the kingdom. As to its precepts, the general opinion was that they needed no farther cultivation : Dr. Pepusch had prescribed to the students in harmony a set of rules, which no one was hardy enough to transgress ; the consequence thereof was a disgusting uniformity of style in the musical productions of the time ; while these were adhered to, fancy laboured under the severest restrictions, and all improvement in the science of composition was at a stand.

That we are at this time in a state of emancipation from the bondage of laws imposed without authority, is owing to a new investigation of the principles of harmony, and the studies of a class of musicians, of whom Geminiani seems to have been the chief ; and this consideration makes it necessary to resume the account of him, and to relate, among other particulars, the efforts made by him towards the improvement of the science of harmony.

It is observable upon the works of Geminiani, that his modulations are not only original, but that

---

* Burette seems to have been less sensible of the force of his own reasoning, than many of his readers ; for after he had refuted his adversary, he was provoked to resume the controversy, and made some few concessions, that tended to weaken his former arguments ; particularly, that besides the unison and octave, the ancients made use of the third in consonance ; the latter of which facts has never yet been proved. On the contrary, it is strongly insisted that they never used either the third or sixth, no such practice being mentioned, or even hinted at, in any of the old Greek writers.

his harmonies consist of such combinations as were never introduced into music till his time : the rules of transition from one key to another, which are laid down by those who have written on the composition of music, he not only disregarded, but objected to as an unnecessary restraint on the powers of invention. He has been frequently heard to say, that the cadences in the fifth, the third, and the sixth of the key which occur in the works of Corelli, were rendered too familiar to the ear by the frequent repetition of them : and it seems to have been the study of his life, by a liberal use of the semitonic intervals, to increase the number of harmonic combinations; and into melody to introduce a greater variety than it was otherwise capable of.

In a full persuasion of the advantages that must result to music from the study of variety, he compiled an harmonical code, consisting of a great number of passages composed by himself, connected with and referring to others in a series almost infinite ; and published proposals for printing it, with the title of Guida Armonica, but it was not till several years after that it appeared in the world.

In the year 1739 he published his Opera quarta, consisting of twelve Sonatas for a violin and a bass; and also a new edition of his Opera prima, with considerable additions and improvements; and soon after, what he called 'A Treatise on good Taste;' and also 'Rules for playing in Taste;' a cant phrase much in use with the musical connoisseurs. These two publications contained, besides examples of such graces as himself was used to practice on the violin, variations on some well-known airs, such as that of Purcell in the opera of Dioclesian, 'What shall I do 'to shew how much I love her,' and some select Scots tunes.

About this time he also published the 'Art of 'playing on the Violin,' containing the most minute directions for holding the instrument, and for the use of the bow, the graces, the various shifts of the hand,* and a great variety of examples adapted to the rules.

About the year 1740 he published and dedicated to the Academy of ancient Music his Opera settima, consisting of six Concertos for violins. This work carries with it the evidence of great labour and study, but it is greatly inferior to his former works of the like kind.

In the month of April, 1742, came forth his long expected work, with the title of 'Guida Armonica 'o Dizionario Armonico,' with a preface, wherein, after giving due commendation to Lully, Corelli, and Bononcini, as having been the first improvers of instrumental music, he endeavours to obviate an opinion that the vast foundations of universal harmony can be established upon the narrow and confined modulation of those authors, and remarks on the uniformity of modulation, apparent in the com-

positions that have appeared in different parts of Europe for forty years back.

The publication of this book was attended with circumstances that seemed but little to favour its reception; some suspected that the author's chief view in the publication of it was the getting money to supply his necessities ; many had been made to believe that the author professed by it no less than to teach the art of musical composition to persons totally ignorant of the science, and of consequence ridiculed the attempt; and there were very few that were able to comprehend either the motives to, or the tendency of, the work.

In one of those excursions which Geminiani was frequently making during his residence in England, that is to say, to Italy, France, Holland, and other countries, he visited at Paris a learned and ingenious Jesuit, Pere Castel, a man well skilled in music ;† to whom he shewed his manuscript, and explained the nature and design of it : and with a view to obviate the prejudices that had been entertained against it, this person published in the Journal des Sçavans a dissertation on the Guida Armonica, which Geminiani upon his return hither got translated into English, and published in a pamphlet of about thirty pages.

The author of this dissertation says, that, upon a careful examination of the Guida Armonica, he found that any person able to read and write might by the help thereof become able to compose true, good, and well-modulated music, with proper figures to denote the accompaniment; and that the execution of this contrivance was as simple and infallible as the plan of it was wonderful ; and that it is in reality a set of musical integers ready to be connected into a body.

The facility of this practice appearing at first suspicious, Pere Castel says he took the liberty of opposing it to the author as an objection to his scheme, comparing it to the German organ, which being turned by the most unskilful person, will nevertheless make excellent music. He also compared it in his own mind with an invention of Johannes Trithemius, abbat of Spanheim, who flourished about the year 1490, and wrote a treatise entitled Steganographia, the third book whereof professes to teach a man ignorant of letters, only knowing his mother-

---

* There is reason to suppose that the practice of shifting on the violin was greatly improved by Geminiani ; Baltzar the Lubecker introduced it into England in the time of Charles I.; but with him, and subsequent performers, it answered no other purpose than extending the compass of the instrument to D : the half shift, contrived to avoid the disgusting clangor of an open string, and enable the performer to shake with the third instead of the little finger, is but of late invention.

† Louis-Bertrand Castel was born at Montpelier in 1688, and entered into the society of the Jesuits in 1703. About the end of the year 1720 he removed from Thoulouse to Paris, where he became known to the world by his treatise on Gravitation, published in two volumes in duodecimo in 1727. According to his hypothesis, all things depend upon two principles, the gravity of bodies and the action of spirits ; by means of the former all things tend to rest, while motion proceeds from the latter principle. This system was attacked by the Abbé de St. Pierre, and the dispute was carried on between them for some time with a considerable degree of vivacity. His second work was a concise system of universal mathematics, in one volume quarto, which met with general applause, and procured him an admission into the Royal Society at London. In the course of his pursuits he had discovered a certain analogy between the laws of colours and sound. Upon this principle he proceeded to construct an instrument called by him the Clavecin Oculaire, which by a proper mixture and just succession of the different colours, should be the means of exciting in the mind of the spectator a pleasure similar to that derived from harmony. This attempt, visionary as it was, produced some useful discoveries. The other writings of Castel are of little importance, and are chiefly contained in the Memoires de Trevoux. His style is lively and full of affected refinements, but desultory and incorrect. He died in the year 1757, aged sixty-three.

tongue, in the space of two hours to read, and understand Latin, and write it ornately and eloquently.* But Castel says he thinks that in neither instance the comparison will hold; and finally recommends the Guida Armonica to the students in music in the following terms:

' Mr. Geminiani's book is then a useful work, and ' that even to the masters themselves, since it contains ' all the musical passages, whether regular, or of the ' class of licences and exceptions, that may be, or ' have already been employed by the greatest masters, ' with guides and references that serve to link them ' together in all the various manners in which they ' can be connected. In a word, it is a musical ma-' nual, a library, a repertory; a kind of dictionary, ' though not an alphabetical one, in which is always ' to be found a musical phrase or periphrasis fit to ' be adapted, even with elegance and variety, to any ' other already formed. By it we are enabled to ' determine whether a phrase, a passage, a succession ' of harmony, a certain progression of modulation, ' which the composer is desirous of taking, be regular ' and allowable or not; whether it has its proper ' arithmetical figures, or is preceded by, and followed ' with, proper consonances; in short, what are the ' most eligible and elegant modes of passage from ' one series or compages of sounds to another, and of

' returning again to those from which the deviation ' was made.'

Castel's dissertation is throughout, an eulogium on the Guida Armonica; he was well skilled in music, but by no means a competent judge of musical composition. Such as had made it their study, were unanimously of opinion that it contains very little that was not known before, and is besides so very obscure as to be of small use to any one. The publication of the Guida Armonica was followed by that of a supplement, with examples showing its use.†

Of his performance it is very difficult to convey an idea, there being no master of the violin at this day living with whom he can with any propriety be compared, Jackson excepted, who possesses many of his excellencies, but never came near him in point of tone. It must therefore suffice to say that he had none of the fire and spirit of the modern violinists, but that all the graces and elegancies of melody, all the powers that can engage attention, or that render the passions of the hearer subservient to the will of the artist, were united in his performance. The following solo of Corelli, written as Geminiani used to play it, and copied from a manuscript in his own hand-writing, is here inserted as the best specimen that can be given of the style and manner of his execution.

* The Steganographia was condemned to the flames by the elector palatine Frederic II. This notable art is described by Trithemius himself, in an epistle to Arnoldus Bostius, in these words: ' Tertius ' liber docet, artem per quam possum hominem idiotam, scientem tantum ' linguam maternam, qui nunquam novit verbum Latini sermonis, in ' duabus horis docere, scribere, legere et intelligere Latinum satis ornatè ' et desertè, quantumcunque voluerit, ita ut quicunque viderint ejus ' literas laudent verba, intelligant Latina composita.'

† In the year 1760, GIORGIO ANTONIOTTO, an Italian musician, who :d resided many years in London, published, in a thin folio volume, work entitled ' L'Arte Armonica, or a treatise on the composition of Music, originally written in Italian, and translated under the eye of the author into English.' This, in the opinion of some very good judges, is a work of merit.

CORELLI & GEMINIANI.

## CHAP. CXCVII.

The old musicians who were living at the time when Geminiani published his Guida Armonica, stood aghast at the licences which it allowed, and predicted little less from the work than the utter ruin of the musical science. Not choosing to deviate from the good and wholesome rules which they had been taught in choirs, and had extracted from the compositions of those who were looked on as the classics in harmony, they shook their heads, and hung their harps upon the willows. Pepusch had little at heart but the welfare of his favourite academy, and the investigation of the ancient Rythmus ; and for this and the like studies a favourable opportunity had presented itself in the year 1737, by a vacancy in the place of organist of the Charter-house, occasioned by the death of Mr. Thomas Love. The duchess of Leeds had been his scholar, and at her recommendation he was elected. To apartments assigned him in this venerable mansion, the Doctor, together with his wife, retired. In the year 1739 the place of Gresham professor of music becoming vacant, he solicited to succeed to it ; but finding that his being a married man was a disqualification, he forbore offering himself as a candidate, and one Mr. Thomas Brome was elected.*

About the year 1740 the Doctor's wife died, and he having before lost his son, an only child, had scarce any source of delight left, other than the prosecution of his studies, and the teaching a few favourite pupils, who attended him at his apartments. Here he drew up that account of the ancient genera which was read before the Royal Society, and is published in the Philosophical Transactions for the months of October, November, and December, in the year 1746, the substance whereof is given in an earlier part of this work ; and soon after the publication thereof he was elected a fellow of the Royal Society. During his residence in the Charter-house, notwithstanding his advanced age, he prosecuted his studies with unwearied application : his evening amusements were the game of chess, and the conversation of a few select friends, of whom Mr. John Immyns, the lutenist, mentioned in a preceding page ; Mr. Travers, one of the organists of the royal chapel, and also organist of St. Paul, Covent-Garden ; and Mr. Ephraim Kelner, of the band at Drury-lane theatre, were the most intimate. To the latter two of these persons the Doctor had some obligations ; and shortly before his death he made a disposition which entitled them to his effects, and particularly his valuable library, whenever it

* The right of electing the Gresham music professor is in the mayor and commonalty and citizens of London, and it is curious to reflect on their conduct in the execution of this trust. The first professor, Dr. Bull, was a man eminent in his faculty, but, out of thirteen persons his successors, only two had the least pretence to skill in the science. Dr. Robert Shippen, principal of Brazen-nose college, and rector of White-chapel, was professor for some time, till he resigned in favour of his brother Edward, a physician, who was elected in his room ; and both the brothers made no secret of declaring that they understood not a note of music. Concerning the election of Dr. Robert Shippen there goes the following story. His competitor it seems was a person every way qualified for the place : it happened some time after his disappointment that the place of astronomy professor became vacant, and the electors conscious of the injury they had done him in rejecting his application for the music professorship, determined to repair it, and accordingly made him an offer of the astronomy lecture : but he assigned his reasons for declining it in a bitter sarcasm : 'Gentlemen,' says he, 'I am much obliged 'to you for your offer, but I cannot consistent either with my conscience 'or my reputation accept it, for I understand astronomy as little as 'Dr. Shippen does music.' The other persons whose names appear in the list of professors, were men who had received an academical education, and might be supposed able to compose a lecture on music fit to be heard ; but those who have of late years been elected to the office, grounded their pretensions solely on their being freemen of London ; the last professor was a barber, and the predecessor of him an engraver; hopeful teachers of a liberal science!

should happen. He died in the month of July, in the year 1752, and was buried in the chapel of the Charter-house. By a voluntary subscription of some of his friends, a tablet was erected near the place of his interment, on which is the following memorial of him :—

Near this Place lye the Remains
of
John Christopher Pepusch,
Doctor of Music in the University of Oxford.
He was born at Berlin,
And resided at London, highly esteemed above Fifty Years,
Distinguished as a most learned Master
And Patron of his Profession.
In the Year 1737 he retired to the private Employment
of
Organist to this House,
Where he departed this life,
July 20, 1752, Aged 85.
The Academy of Ancient Music, established in 1710,
Of which he was one of the Original Founders,
And to which he bequeathed a valuable Collection of Music,
In grateful Respect to his Memory
Caused this monument to be erected,
1767.

The history of his library, which contained in it the most valuable treatises on music in various languages that are any where extant, either in manuscript or in print ; as also a noble collection of musical compositions, is attended with some singular circumstances. Immediately upon his decease, in virtue of the disposition which he had previously made of his effects, Travers and Kelner took possession of them, and divided his library into moieties. Travers survived the Doctor but a short time, and his part of it came to the hands of his representative, an old woman ; and after that to a person, who dying, it was sold by auction in July, 1766, and produced a very inconsiderable sum of money. Kelner, who had long assisted the Doctor as his amanuensis, was a man of learning, and a sound musician. He lodged in a house in Martlet-court in Russel-street, Covent-Garden ; having no relations, he gave a man named Cooper, who had been his copyist, and had done him many good offices, reason to hope for a share of the little he should leave at his decease ; but, dying without making any written disposition of his effects, the woman of the house in which they were, laid hands on his instruments, books, and manuscripts, and insisted on keeping them as she had the possession, and there was no legatee or representative to claim them. It was in vain for Cooper to urge the friendly intention of Kelner to him, or, which was the truth, that he had assisted him with money at sundry times, and was therefore a creditor : the right of possession, and the vulgar maxim that it is eleven points of the law, was insisted on, and his claim set at defiance. The man upon this felt his spirit rise, and, taking the advice of a lawyer, applied for and obtained letters of administration as a creditor of the deceased ; commenced a suit in Chancery against the woman, and in a few days time got into his possession the books and manuscripts to the amount of two cart loads ; part of which were disposed of

by private contract ; the rest were sold by auction at Patersons's in Essex-street, on Saturday the twenty-sixth of March, 1763. In this sale were two very curious articles, the one an Antiphonary, which, by a memorandum in an outer leaf of it, appeared to have been found, with almost a cargo of Romish service-books, on board a Spanish man of war, taken at the defeat of the Armada in 1588 ; the other a manuscript very richly bound, that formerly was queen Elizabeth's, most probably written for her own practice, in a fine character, and containing a collection of lessons by Dr. Bull ; the book had been pretty well thumbed by Signora Margarita, who had for many years played out of it, but was otherwise in good preservation.

The manuscript papers of the Doctor, that is to say, his studies for a long course of years, came to the hands of the author of this work, who is sorry to say, that, after a very careful selection and diligent perusal of them, they appear to contain hardly any thing that can tend to the improvement of music, or the gratification of public curiosity. The Doctor for many years before his decease, from a persuasion, which seems to have been uppermost in his mind, that part of the science had been lost,* had endeavoured to recover the ancient genera ; and it appears by a passage in his diary abovementioned, that he was upon that pursuit while on his visit to lord Paisley ; but we see the whole of what he was able to effect towards it in his letter on that subject printed in the Philosophical Transactions.† Towards the end of his life he had adopted the silly notions of Isaac Vossius respecting the rythmus, and endeavoured to introduce into music somewhat that should correspond with the practice of the ancients ; but in this too he failed, for out of a vast number of essays which appear in his own hand-writing, nothing conclusive or satisfactory is deducible. The same may in a great measure be said of his numerous arithmetical calculations of ratios, of which he appears to have been too fond : had he considered how little Salinas, Mersennus, Kircher, and Dr. Wallis have left unsaid on this part of musical science, he might possibly have turned his thoughts another way.

At the time when Pepusch came to settle in England, he found the practice of music in a very low state ; very few but professors being able to play in concert : with a view to the improvement of it he published twenty-four airs for two violins in all the varieties of measure that music is capable of : these seem to be but an introduction to Corelli's Sonatas, which were then deemed much too hard to be put into the hands of learners.‡ To assist the students in music he published the Sonatas and Concertos of Corelli in score.

Pepusch was a voluminous composer, as appears

* Vide Treatise on Harmony, first edit. page 24.

† *This paper, the doctor not being able to write English, was drawn up by Mr. George Lewis Scott, author of the Supplement to Chambers' Dictionary, in two volumes. He was a Barrister of the Inner Temple, and, being a man of science, assisted in the education of his present Majesty (Geo. III.) ; for which he was rewarded with the post of one of the Commissioners of the Excise. He died about the year 1778.*

‡ In the title-page they are expressly said to be for the improvement of Practitioners in Concert.

by the Catalogue of Roger and Le Cene. Little of his music is printed in England; the Airs above mentioned, twenty-four Solos for a violin and a bass, two collections of Cantatas, and a few songs, are all that we know of. His manuscript compositions to a great number he directed to be given to the Academy of Ancient Music, and they remain in the library of that society. He was a learned, but a dry composer, and was apparently deficient in the powers of invention. His cantata 'See from the silent 'grove,' is the only one of all he ever published that has any pretence to elegance. Of his manuscript compositions we know of only one that rises above mediocrity, viz., 'Rejoice in the Lord, O ye righteous,' a full anthem, and in this all the various excellencies of harmony and melody are united.

The contests, which had long divided the votaries of harmony into factions, had in some measure subsided upon the retreat of Cuzzoni and the departure of Bononcini; but the ill success of the opera after the dissolution of the Royal Academy, and the shipwreck of some fortunes engaged in the support of it, induced the people to turn their eyes towards Mr. Handel, and to look on him as the only person from whom, in the way of musical performance, they were to expect any solid and rational entertainment. Greene was sensible of this; and there being in England no competitor of Mr. Handel to whom he could attach himself, he pursued his own track, and endeavoured as a cathedral musician to exalt his character to the utmost. With this view he published in score forty anthems, in a style of composition that furnishes occasion for some remarks. But first it is to be noted that the original formation of the church style, as applied to the English reformed service, was immediately consequent on the establishment of the first liturgy of Edward VI., and in the compositions of Marbeck, Tallis, Bird, Fairfax, Taverner, Shepherd, Redford, and many others, we have the clearest evidence that the whole of our reformed church musical service was borrowed from that which was in use in the age immediately preceding the above-mentioned establishment. To speak more fully to the purpose, the book of Common Prayer noted, is formed on the model of the Roman ritual; and the services and anthems of the authors above named answer to those motets which then were, and at this day are used in the Romish service. This latter is so precisely the fact, that most of the music to the English anthems which bear the name of Tallis and Bird, will upon comparison be found to have been originally set to Latin words in the form of motets, and composed by them for the service of the chapel of Hen. VIII. and Mary; but upon the final settlement of the liturgy at the beginning of queen Elizabeth's reign, the authors thought they could not do better than to adapt the same music to English words, and accordingly these compositions now bear the form of anthems.

The style of these great men was adopted by Tye, Bull, Morley, Gibbons, and Tomkins, and continued to be the standard of church-music till the Restoration, when the king, who, during his abode in France,

had entertained a liking for the music of that country, signified a desire that that of his chapel might partake of the imaginary excellencies of the French music as much as possible.* The chapel composers, though they had no mind to take the French for their masters, relaxed somewhat of the ancient severity of church composition, and in the anthems of Humphrey, Blow, Purcell, Wise, Weldon, and most others, we find a richer vein of melody than in those of their predecessors, but no such resemblance of the French church-music as the king wished for. Most men were of opinion that by this union of melody and harmony our church-music was carried to its utmost degree of perfection; and consequently that in any future variations, the loss on one hand would be equal to the gain on the other. But Greene, who had carefully attended to all those refinements in melody which the opera had introduced, was of opinion that they led to a farther improvement of our church-music; accordingly he formed a style, neat and elegant it is true, but greatly deficient in that dignity and solemnity which are essential in compositions for the church. And this we may call the third, and at present the last, improved style of cathedral music.

The other works of Greene are single songs to a great number, a few Cantatas, Canons, and Catches, published in separate and detached collections; Overtures to his dramatic pastorals, mentioned in a preceding page, and to other of his compositions; the Amoretti of Spenser, that is to say, certain Sonnets selected from the work so called, and a collection of lessons for the harpsichord.

Greene was a man of understanding, and in the exercise of his profession was careful to form connections of the best kind. By his personal civilities to Mrs. Anastasia Robinson, he so recommended himself to her, that when she became countess of Peterborough she procured for him the places of organist and composer to the royal chapel in the room of Dr. Croft.

His wife was a young woman of the name of Dillingham; she, together with her sister, who was married to the Rev. Mr. George Carleton, subdean of the royal chapel,† kept a milliner's shop in Paternoster-row, and had about five hundred pounds when Greene married her. He had but little besides to begin the world with, nevertheless, by industry and œconomy he was enabled to bring up a family of children, and make considerable savings. His uncle, Serjeant Greene, was a single man, and left a natural son of the name of John, who was bred to the bar, and was for some years steward of the manor of Hackney; the Serjeant had by his will devised to him an estate in Essex of about seven hundred pounds a year, called Bois-Hall. This person died about the year 1750, having left by his will to Dr. Greene the whole of his estate.

* Charles II. was but little acquainted with the English church-music, and it is probable that upon his return to England he might conceive a dislike of it. Lock set the music for his public entry, and Capt. Cooke that for his coronation, as Sir Richard Baker asserts: the latter was but a dry composer.

† These two sisters were cousins of the wife of Mr. Charles King, almoner of St. Paul's, and she was a sister of Jerry Clark.

In the state of affluence to which Dr. Greene was raised by this event, he meditated on the corruptions of our church-music, occasioned by the multiplication of copies, and the ignorance and carelessness of transcribers; and resolved to correct, and also secure it against such injuries for the future; accordingly he began with collating a great number of copies of services and anthems, and reducing them into score. By the year 1755, he had made a considerable progress in the work; but his health failing him, he made his will, and remitted the farther prosecution of it to one that had been his disciple, his friend Dr. William Boyce, who, in a manner worthy of himself, completed the work, and thereby gave to the public a collection that has not its fellow in the world. Dr. Greene died on the first day of September, 1755, leaving behind him only one child, a daughter, married to the Rev. Dr. Michael Festing, rector of Wyke Regis, in the county of Dorset, and a son of Mr. Michael Christian Festing, an eminent composer for the violin, and performer on that instrument, mentioned in a preceding chapter of this work.

John Travers received his education in music in the chapel of St. George at Windsor; and, being a favourite boy of Dr. Henry Godolphin, dean of St. Paul's and provost of Eton college, was by him put apprentice to Greene; and about the year 1725 became organist of St. Paul's church, Covent-Garden, and after that of Fulham. Upon the decease of Jonathan Martin in 1737, Travers was appointed organist of the royal chapel; soon after which, upon some disgust, he quitted his place at Fulham. Travers was a sound musician; he commenced an early acquaintance with Dr. Pepusch, and received some assistance from him in the course of his studies, which by a sedulous application he was very careful to improve. In the chapel books are sundry anthems of his composition; but as a composer he is best known to the world by eighteen Canzonets, being verses and songs chiefly taken from the posthumous works of Prior, which he set for two and three voices, in a style as elegant as it is original. Besides these he published the whole book of Psalms for one, two, three, four, and five voices, with a thorough-bass for the harpsichord. He died in the year 1758, and as organist of the royal chapel was succeeded by Dr. William Boyce.

We are now arrived at that which may be considered as the last period of Mr. Handel's life, commencing at that happy conjunction of events, which left him without a competitor, and disposed the public to receive with the utmost approbation whatever he should in future produce for their entertainment.

The oratorio of Sampson, performed in 1743, was followed in the succeeding year by Semele, written by Mr. Congreve, which, though not a sacred composition, but an opera founded on a poetical fiction, was suffered to be performed in that season, during which theatrical representations are forbidden. He had now given a permanent direction to his studies, and composed in succession the entertainments of Susanna, Belshazzar, Hercules, the Occasional Ora-

torio, Judas Maccabæus, Joseph, Alexander Balus, Joshua, Solomon, Theodora,* the Choice of Hercules, Jephtha, and an entertainment called the Triumph of Time and Truth,† most of which were received with general applause. In these he took an ample scope for the exercise of that which was his greatest talent, the sublime in music, and this he displayed to the astonishment of every one in the chorusses to these entertainments.

In the beginning of the year 1751 he was alarmed by a disorder in his eyes, which, upon consulting with *Mr. Samuel Sharp, Surgeon of Guy's Hospital,* he was told was an incipient Gutta serena. From the moment this opinion of his case was communicated to him, his spirits forsook him; and that fortitude which had supported him under afflictions of another kind, deserted him *upon being told* that a freedom from pain in the visual organs was all that he had to hope, for the remainder of his days. In this forlorn state, reflecting on his inability to conduct his entertainments, he called to his aid Mr. Smith, a son of him who had for many years been his copyist and faithful friend; and with this assistance oratorios continued to be performed even to that Lent season in which he died, and this with no other abatement in his own performance than the accompaniment by the harpsichord; the rich vein of his fancy ever supplying him with subjects for extempore voluntaries on the organ, and his hand retaining the power of executing whatever his invention suggested.

The loss of his sight, and the prospect of his approaching dissolution, wrought a great change in his temper and general behaviour. He was a man of blameless morals, and throughout his life manifested a deep sense of religion. In conversation he would frequently declare the pleasure he felt in setting the Scriptures to music; and how much the contemplating the many sublime passages in the Psalms had contributed to his edification; and now that he found himself near his end, these sentiments were improved into solid and rational piety, attended with a calm and even temper of mind. For the last two or three years of his life he was used to attend divine service in his own parish church of St. George, Hanover-square, where, during the prayers, the eyes that at this instant are employed in a faint portrait of his excellencies, have seen him on his knees, expressing by his looks and gesticulations the utmost fervour of devotion.

Towards the beginning of the year 1758 he began to find himself decline apace; and that general debility which was coming on him was rendered still more alarming by a total loss of appetite. When that symptom appeared he considered his recovery as hopeless, and resigning himself to his fate, expired on the fourteenth day of April, 1759. He was buried in Westminster-abbey, the dean, Dr. Pearce, bishop of Rochester, assisted by the choir, performing the funeral solemnity. Over the place of his interment is a monument, designed and

* Founded on the story of the martyrdom of Theodora and Didymus, related by Mr. Boyle in a little book with that title.

† Mostly taken from Il Trionfo del Tempo, composed by Handel at Rome, and there performed.

executed by Roubiliac, representing him at full length, in an erect posture, with a music paper in his hand, inscribed ' I know that my Redeemer liveth,' with the notes to which those words are set in his Messiah. He died worth about twenty thousand pounds, almost the whole whereof he bequeathed to his relations abroad.

Such as were but little acquainted with Handel are unable to characterize him otherwise than by his excellencies in his art, and certain foibles in his behaviour, which he was never studious to conceal : accordingly we are told that he had a great appetite, and that when he was provoked he would break out into profane expressions. These are facts that cannot be denied ; but there are sundry particulars that tend to mark his character but little known, and which may possibly be remembered, when those that serve only to shew that he was subject to human passions are forgotten. In his religion he was of the Lutheran profession ; in which he was not such a bigot as to decline a general conformity with that of the country which he had chosen for his residence ; at the same time that he entertained very serious notions touching its importance. These he would frequently express in his remarks on the constitution of the English government ; and he would often speak of it as one of the great felicities of his life that he was settled in a country where no man suffers any molestation or inconvenience on account of his religious principles.

His attainments in literature cannot be supposed to have been very great, seeing that the studies of his profession absorbed him ; and the prodigious number of his compositions will account for a much greater portion of time than any man could well be supposed able to spare from sleep and the necessary recruits of nature ; and yet he was well acquainted with the Latin and Italian languages ; the latter he had rendered so familiar to him, that few natives seemed to understand it better. Of the English also he had such a degree of knowledge, as to be susceptible of the beauties of our best poets ; so that in the multiplicity of his compositions to English words, he very seldom stood in need of assistance in the explanation of a passage for the purpose of suiting the sense with correspondent sounds. The style of his discourse was very singular ; he pronounced the English as the Germans do, but his phrase was exotic, and partook of the idiom of the different countries in which he had resided, a circumstance that rendered his conversation exceedingly entertaining.*

* Among other particulars in his character, that rendered his conversation very pleasing, one was a talent that enabled him to tell a story with all the circumstances that tend to enliven it. Being one Sunday at court, he was seen engaged with the late Dr. Thomas, bishop of Lincoln : their discourse was in the German language ; and as soon as it was over, and they were parted, a friend of Mr. Handel went up to him, and remarked on the facility with which the bishop spoke high Dutch ; upon which Mr. Handel answered, that, having been chaplain to the English factory at Hamburg, he had made himself master of it ; and that therefore whenever the king went to visit his German dominions, he chose that Dr. Thomas should attend him thither ; and this, says Mr. Handel, brings to my mind a pleasant story, which I will now tell you, and accordingly he related it to this effect. In one of the king's visits to Hanover, the Doctor walking upon deck, a squall of wind blew his hat overboard ; this loss made some diversion among the sailors, and the rumour of it coming to the king's ears, he, the next time they met,

The course of his life was regular and uniform. For some years after his arrival in England his time was divided between study and practice, that is to say, in composing for the opera, and in conducting concerts at the duke of Rutland's, the earl of Burlington's, and the houses of others of the nobility who were patrons of music, and his friends. There were also frequent concerts for the royal family at the queen's library in the Green-Park, in which the princess royal, the duke of Rutland, lord Cowper, and other persons of distinction performed ; of these Handel had the direction.† As these connections dissolved, he gradually retreated into a state of privacy and retirement, and showed no solicitude to form new ones. His dwelling was on the south side of Brooke-street, near Hanover-square, in a house now in the occupation of Sir James Wright, four doors from Bond-street, and two from the passage to the stable-yard. His stated income was six hundred pounds a year, arising from pensions ; that is to say, one of two hundred pounds, granted him by queen Anne, another of two hundred pounds granted by Geo. I., and another of the same amount, for teaching the princesses. The rest was precarious ; for some time it depended upon his engagements with the directors of the Academy, and afterwards upon the profits arising from the musical performances carried on by him on his own account. However, he had at all times the prudence to regulate his expence by his income. At the time of his contest with the nobility he had ten thousand pounds in the funds, and of this he sold out the last shilling, and lived upon his pensions, which, by an interest that he had with the minister, were punctually paid him.‡ Some years after, when he found himself in a state of affluence, and the produce of his oratorios amounted to more than two thousand pounds a season, he continued his wonted course of living, which was equally distant from the extremes of parsimony and profusion. In the latter part of his life he forbore yielding to a temptation, which few in such circumstances as he was then in would, in these times be able to resist, that of keeping a carriage. Indeed, when his sight failed him, he was necessitated occasionally to hire a chariot and horses, especially in his visits to the city for the purpose of investing his money, which he constantly disposed of at the end of the Lent season, under the direction of Mr. Gael Morris, a broker of the first eminence, whom he used to meet and confer with at Garraway's or Batson's coffee-house.

His social affections were not very strong ; and to this it may be imputed that he spent his whole life in a state of celibacy ; that he had no female

affected to condole him upon it ; upon which the Doctor seemed to make light of the accident, by remarking that it was in his majesty's power to repair the loss of his hat by a covering for the head of another kind. The king conceiving that he meant a mitre, answered him only with a smile ; but soon after his return to England nominated him to the vacant see of *St. Asaph, from whence before consecration he was translated to Lincoln, and after that to Salisbury.*

† It is here to be remarked that the king, the queen, and the princesses were the constant patrons of Handel : at the breaking up of the Royal Academy, they continued to favour him, but the prince of Wales took part with the nobility.

‡ *Sir Edward Walpole told me he assisted him in this particular.*

attachment of another kind may be ascribed to a better reason. His intimate friends were but few; those that seemed to possess most of his confidence were Goupy, the painter, and one Hunter, a scarlet-dyer at Old Ford, near Bow, who pretended a taste for music, and at a great expense had copies made for him of all the music of Handel that he could procure. He had others in the city; but he seemed to think that the honour of his acquaintance was a reward sufficient for the kindness they expressed for him.

A temper and conduct like this, was in every view of it favourable to his pursuits; no impertinent visits, no idle engagements to card parties, or other expedients to kill time, were suffered to interrupt the course of his studies. His invention was for ever teeming with new ideas, and his impatience to be delivered of them kept him closely employed. He had a favourite Rucker harpsichord, the keys whereof, by incessant practice, were hollowed like the bowl of a spoon. He wrote very fast, but with a degree of impatience proportioned to the eagerness that possesses men of genius, of seeing their conceptions reduced into form. And here it may not be impertinent to observe, what every person conversant in his works will be inclined to believe, viz. that his style was original and self-formed; and were evidence of the fact wanting, it is capable of proof, by his own testimony, for in a conversation with a very intelligent person now living, on the course of his studies, Mr. Handel declared that, after he became master of the rudiments of his art, he forbore to study the works of others, and ever made it a rule to follow the suggestions of his own fancy.

Like many others of his profession, he had a great love for painting; and, till his sight failed him, among the few amusements he gave into, the going to view collections of pictures upon sale was the chief.

He was in his person a large made and very portly man. His gait, which was ever sauntering, was rather ungraceful, as it had in it somewhat of that rocking motion, which distinguishes those whose legs are bowed. His features were finely marked, and the general cast of his countenance placid, bespeaking dignity attempered with benevolence, and every quality of the heart that has a tendency to beget confidence and insure esteem. Few of the pictures extant of him are to any tolerable degree likenesses, except one painted abroad, from a print whereof the engraving given of him in this work is taken: in the print of him by Houbraken, the features are too prominent; and in the mezzotinto after Hudson there is a harshness of aspect to which his countenance was a stranger; the most perfect resemblance of him is the statue on his monument, and in that the true lineaments of his face are apparent.

As to his performance on the organ, the powers of speech are so limited, that it is almost a vain attempt to describe it otherwise than by its effects. A fine and delicate touch, a volant finger, and a ready delivery of passages the most difficult, are the praise of inferior artists: they were not noticed in Handel, whose excellencies were of a far superior

kind; and his amazing command of the instrument, the fullness of his harmony, the grandeur and dignity of his style, the copiousness of his imagination, and the fertility of his invention were qualities that absorbed every inferior attainment. When he gave a concerto, his method in general was to introduce it with a voluntary movement on the diapasons, which stole on the ear in a slow and solemn progression; the harmony close wrought, and as full as could possibly be expressed; the passages concatenated with stupendous art, the whole at the same time being perfectly intelligible, and carrying the appearance of great simplicity. This kind of prelude was succeeded by the concerto itself, which he executed with a degree of spirit and firmness that no one ever pretended to equal.

Such in general was the manner of his performance; but who shall describe its effects on his enraptured auditory? Silence, the truest applause, succeeded the instant that he addressed himself to the instrument, and that so profound, that it checked respiration, and seemed to controul the functions of nature, while the magic of his touch kept the attention of his hearers awake only to those enchanting sounds to which it gave utterance.

Wonderful as it may seem, this command over the human passions is the known attribute of music; and by effects like these the poets have ever described it, always supposing in the hearers a mind susceptible of its charms. But how are we to account for the influence of that harmony, of which we are now speaking, on those who, so far as regards music, may be said to have no passions, no affections on which it could operate? In all theatrical representations a part only of the audience are judges of the merit of what they see and hear, the rest are drawn together by motives in which neither taste nor judgment have any share: and, with respect to music, it is notorious that the greater number of mankind are destitute, though not of hearing, yet of that sense, which, superadded to the hearing, renders us susceptible of the harmony of musical sounds;* and in times when music was less fashionable than

* Swift remarks of poetry, eloquence, and music, that it is certain that very few have a taste or judgment of the excellencies of the two former; and that if a man succeed in either, it is upon the authority of those few judges that lend their taste to the bulk of readers that have none of their own. And farther, that there are as few good judges in music, and that among those that crowd the operas, nine in ten go thither merely out of curiosity, fashion, or affectation. Intelligencer, No. 3, Faulkner's edition of Swift's works, vol. I. page 278. To these observations we may add, that of all who profess to admire the works of our great dramatic poet, and who talk of nature as if they were privy to her secrets, and judges of her operations upon occasions that do not present themselves in a long course of life to one in a million, few can be supposed to have more than a general sense of the author's meaning; the style of the dialogue being familiar only to those who are well skilled in the English language; these people, in the phrase of Swift, borrow the taste of others, and applaud the sentiment and the action as they are taught, being left to themselves, they are insensible to all that passes, and secretly prefer a ballad opera to the noblest productions of genius.

As to music, there are instances of persons who have entertained a love of the other polite arts, and yet have had no taste for this; and of others with whom it was an object of aversion. Pope once expressed his sentiments of music to a person now living in these words: 'My 'friend Dr. Arbuthnot speaks strongly of the effect that music has on 'his mind, and I believe him; but I own myself incapable of any pleasure 'from it.' The author of a well-known law-book, entitled 'The Office of 'an Executor,' by Thomas Wentworth, but in fact written by Sir John Dodderidge, a judge of the court of King's Bench, temp. Jac. I., prefers a cry of hounds to any other music. Dr. Ralph Bathurst is by Mr. Warton, in his life of him, page 201, said to have had a strong aversion to music; and among the peculiarities of the famous John Philip Barretier, it is in particular noted by Dr. Johnson, in his life of that extraordinary young man, that he could not bear music.

it is now, many of both sexes were ingenuous enough to confess that they wanted this sense, by saying, 'I have no ear for music.' Persons such as these, who, had they been left to themselves, would have interrupted the hearing of others by their talking, were by the performance of Handel not only charmed into silence, but were generally the loudest in their acclamations. This, though it could not be said to be genuine applause, was a much stronger proof of the power of harmony, than the like effect on an audience composed only of judges and rational admirers of his art.

There seems to be no necessary connection between those faculties that constitute a composer of music, and the powers of instrumental performance; on the contrary, the union of them in the same person, seems as extraordinary as if a poet should be able to write a fine hand; nevertheless in the person of Handel all the perfections of the musical art seemed to concenter. He had never been a master of the violin, and had discontinued the practice of it from the time he took to the harpsichord at Hamburg; yet, whenever he had a mind to try the effect of any of his compositions for that instrument, his manner of touching it was such as the ablest masters would have been glad to imitate. But what is more extraordinary, without a voice he was an excellent singer of such music as required more of the pathos of melody than a quick and voluble expression. In a conversation with the author of this work, he once gave a proof that a fine voice is not the principal requisite in vocal performance; the discourse was upon psalmody, when Mr. Handel asserted that some of the finest melodies used in the German churches were composed by Luther, particularly that which in England is sung to the hundredth psalm, and another, which himself sang at the time, and thereby gave occasion to this remark. At a concert at the house of lady Rich he was prevailed on to sing a slow song, which he did in such a manner, that Farinelli, who was present, could hardly be persuaded to sing after him.

The works of Handel come next to be considered; they have been judiciously classed by the author of his life, published in 1760, but are so multifarious, that they elude all but general criticism. This may be remarked of his compositions, that the disparity among them is no way to be accounted for but upon the supposition that he wrote to two sorts of persons, the judicious and the vulgar; and this solicitude to please both seems to have been pretty nearly equal: the former he meant to delight by such airs as the following, viz. : 'Cara Sposa,' in Rinaldo, 'Ombra Cara,' in Radamistus, 'Affanni del pensier,' in Otho, 'Da tempeste,' in Julius Cæsar, 'Di notte il 'Pellegrino,' in Richard I., and 'Spera si,' in Admetus ;* and the latter to fascinate by such as

* Of this air the late Mr. John Lockman relates the following story, assuring his reader that himself was an eye-witness of it, viz., That being at the house of Mr. Lee, a gentleman in Cheshire, whose daughter was a very fine performer on the harpsichord, he saw a pigeon, which, whenever the young lady played this song, and this only, would fly from an adjacent dove-house to the window in the parlour, where she sat, and listen to it with the most pleasing emotions, and the instant the song was over would return to the dove-house. Some Reflexions concerning Operas, &c. prefixed to Roselinda, a Musical Drama by Mr. Lockman, 4to. 1740.

'Si caro,' in Admetus, 'See the conquering hero 'comes,' in Joshua, 'Powerful Guardians,' and 'Come ever smiling Liberty,' in Judas Maccabæus, and very many others.†

At the same time that he laboured to please his hearers, he seems not to have been unmindful of his own gratification ; and if it be said, and of necessity it must be admitted, that many of his compositions were formed in haste,‡ and without any attention to those critical moments, in which the powers of genius are at their spring tide, it is no less true that there are others which must be supposed to have been produced under the influence of the strongest enthusiasm, when the brightest illuminations irradiated his fancy, and he himself felt all that rapture which he meant to excite in others.

In the first and highest class of Handel's works no competent judge of their merits would hesitate to rank his first Te Deum, and the Jublilate, his coronation and other anthems, the Dettingen Te Deum, as it is called, and the chorusses in his oratorios. In many of these compositions, especially those chorusses in his anthems in which the praises of God are celebrated, the power of his harmony is beyond conception ; there is one in the anthem 'O come let us sing unto the Lord,' to the words 'Rejoice in the Lord O ye righteous,' in which nothing less is suggested to the imagination of the hearer than all the powers of the universe associated in the worship of its creator. On the other hand, the music to those passages in the Psalms and in his Oratorios which breathe a spirit of humiliation and contrition, is to the last degree soothing and pathetic ; and, unassociated with the words, could scarce fail to excite sentiments corresponding with those of the poetry.§

† Most of the songs in the opera of Ariadne are calculated to please the many ; and for this deviation from his general conduct, Mr. Handel gave to one of his friends as a reason, that he meant by it to recover the favour of the nobility, whom he was sensible he had displeased in some of his most elaborate compositions for the stage ; but this attempt failed of its end, except that the minuet at the end of the Overture became the most popular air ever known : from those who professed a taste for music the admiration of it descended to the lowest of the people, insomuch that for some years after its publication it was played by the common fiddlers about the streets. The modulation of this air seems to suit but ill with unlearned ears, there being in it some transitions to which they are but little accustomed ; but the circumstance that struck the vulgar was its great compass, extending to two octaves, and this they took for a peculiar excellence.

‡ In the composition of the funeral anthem for queen Caroline he gave an amazing proof of the fecundity of his invention. It was on a Wednesday that he received orders from the king to compose it, the words having been previously selected for the purpose, and approved. On the Saturday se'nnight after it was rehearsed in the morning, and on the evening of the same day it was performed at the solemnity in the chapel of king Hen. VII. The entertainment L'Allegro ed il Penseroso, and a senseless adjunct to it, Il Moderato, were begun and completed in fifteen days.

§ To point out the various excellencies in the choruses of Handel would be an endless task. In general it may be observed that they are fugues, in which the grandest subjects are introduced, and conducted with such art as only himself possessed : some are in the solemn style of the church, as that at the end of the first act in Saul ; others have the natural and easy elegance of madrigals, as 'Then shall they know that 'he whose name Jehovah is,' in Samson ; some again are full of exultation, as that in the anthem 'Have mercy upon me,' 'Thou shalt 'make me to hear of joy and gladness ;' and that other in Israel in Egypt, 'I will sing unto the Lord ;' and these in the Messiah, 'For unto 'us a child is born,' and 'For the Lord God omnipotent reigneth ;' and, lastly, there are others in a style peculiar to himself, and calculated to excite terror, as these, 'He gave them hailstones for rain,' 'But the 'waters overwhelmed their enemies,' and 'Thy right hand O Lord hath 'dashed in pieces the enemy,' in Israel in Egypt. And though it may be said that Handel, agreeably to the practice of his countrymen, has too much affected imitation, particularly in the latter of the above-mentioned productions, by passages broken in the time to express the hopping of frogs, and others calculated to resemble the buzzing of swarms of flies ; and that in Joshua he has endeavoured, by the harmony of one long-extended

In the composition of music merely instrumental it seems that Handel regarded nothing more than the general effect. Of all his productions of this class, scarce any appear to have been real studies, his lessons and fugues for the organ always excepted. His overtures, excellent as they are, were composed as fast as he could write; and the most elaborate of them seldom cost him more than a morning's labour. His concertos for violins are in general wanting in that which is the chief excellence of instrumental music in many parts, harmony and fine modulation: in these respects they will stand no comparison with the concertos of Corelli, Geminiani, and Martini; they seem to indicate that the author attended to little else than the melody of the extreme parts, and that he trusted for their success to the effect that results from the clash of many instruments; and to this only it can be imputed that in the tenor parts of his concertos there are none of those fine binding passages that occur in the music of the authors above-mentioned, and that in general they are destitute of art and contrivance.

His duets and his lessons are of a far more elaborate texture; the former, as also two trios, were composed for the practice of queen Caroline, and are professed imitations of those of Steffani, but their merits are of a different kind; they are thirteen in number, and, although they are all excellent, a preference seems to be due to 'Che vai 'pensando,' 'Conservate raddoppiate avvivate amante 'cori,' 'Tacete ohime tacete,' and 'Tanti strali al 'sen mi scocchi.'*

The lessons of Handel for the harpsichord were composed for the practice of the princess Anne, and consist of suites of airs, with fugues intermixed; the latter perhaps are more proper for the organ, and, because they require a masterly hand, are but little practised. Of the airs, the Allemandes in the third, fifth, and eighth sets are, for the sweetness of the melody, and the rich vein of fancy that runs through them, inimitable; as are the fugues in the second, fourth, and sixth, for the closeness of the harmony, and skilful iteration of their respective subjects. In short, without the hazard of contradiction, or the necessity of an exception, it may be asserted of these compositions, that they are the most masterly productions of the kind that we know of in the world.

The character of an author is but the necessary result of his works, and as the compositions of Handel are many and various, it is but justice to point out such of them as seem the most likely to be the foundation of his future fame. Many of the

note, to impress upon the imagination of his hearers the idea of the great luminary of the universe arrested in its course, or, in other words, to make them hear the sun stand still, it may be said that they abound with examples of the true sublime in music, and that they far surpass in majesty and dignity the productions of every other dead or living author.

* These compositions have never been printed, and are in the hands of only the curious. We may suppose that the author set a value on them, he having borrowed largely from them in his subsequent compositions: for instance, the overture to Judas Maccabeus is taken from the last movement in the first of the Duets; the chorus in Acis and Galatea, 'Behold the monster Polypheme,' from another; and the chorus in Alexander's Feast, 'Let old Timotheus yield the prize,' and that in Il Penseroso, 'These pleasures melancholy give,' from one of the Trios.

excellencies, which as a musician recommended him to the favour and patronage of the public during a residence of fifty years in this country, he might perhaps possess in common with a few of the most eminent of his contemporaries; but, till they were taught the contrary by Handel, none were aware of that dignity and grandeur of sentiment which music is capable of conveying, or that there is a sublime in music as there is in poetry. This is a discovery which we owe to the genius and inventive faculty of this great man; and there is little reason to doubt that the many examples of this kind with which his works abound, will continue to engage the admiration of judicious hearers as long as the love of harmony shall exist.

CHARLES AVISON, organist of Newcastle, and a disciple of Geminiani, was the author of an Essay on Musical Expression, published in the year 1752, in which are some judicious reflections on music in general, but his division of the modern authors into classes is rather fanciful than just. Throughout his book he celebrates Marcello and Geminiani; the latter frequently in prejudice to Mr. Handel, of whose music he vouchsafes no better a character than that 'we often find in it the noblest harmonies, 'and these enlivened with such a variety of modu- 'lation, as could hardly be expected from one who 'had supplied the town with musical entertainments 'of every kind for thirty years together.'

In the year 1753 came out Remarks on Mr. Avison's Essay on Musical Expression, the author whereof first points out sundry errors against the rules of composition in the works of Avison; and, inferring from thence that he was but meanly skilled in the subject of his book, he proceeds to examine it, and, to say the truth, seldom fails to prove his adversary in the wrong. In the same year Avison republished his Essay, with a reply to the author of the Remarks, and a letter, containing a number of loose particulars relating to music, collected in a course of various reading, unquestionably written by Dr. Jortin.

It has already been mentioned that Avison promoted and assisted in the publication of Marcello's music to the Psalms adapted to English words. Of his own composition there are extant five collections of Concertos for violins, forty-four in number, and two sets of Sonatas for the harpsichord and two violins, a species of composition little known in England till his time. The music of Avison is light and elegant, but it wants originality, a necessary consequence of his too close attachment to the style of Geminiani, which in a few particulars only he was able to imitate.

In the year 1748 an attempt towards the farther improvement of music was made by Robert Smith, master of Trinity college, Cambridge, in a book entitled Harmonics, or the Philosophy of Sounds, published in that year, and again in 1758, much improved and augmented; the principal end whereof is a temperament of the scale by calculations of those beats or pulses that attend the vibration of a chord, and which the author gives us to understand are not so minute as to elude the judgment of the ear. It seems that in the second edition of this book the author was assisted by Mr. Harrison, the clockmaker, who by some experiments on the monochord, and certain calculations made by him of the proportion which the circumference of a circle bears to its diameter, had discovered the means of a more correct tuning than at present is known. It is far from being clear that any benefit can result to music from that division of the octave which Dr. Smith recommends; but this is certain, that his book is so obscurely written, that few who have read it can be found who will venture to say they understand it. We are told that Mr. Harrison's sentiments on the division of the monochord are digested into a treatise written by him, entitled 'A short but full account of 'the grounds and foundation of music, particularly ' of the real existence of the natural notes of melody,' and that there is reason to hope for its publication.*

In the year 1762, a society for the improvement of vocal harmony was established by a great number of the nobility and gentlemen, met for that purpose at the Thatched-house tavern in St. James's-street, Westminster, by the name of the Catch Club. As an incentive to the students in music, they gave prize medals to such as were adjudged to excel in the compositions of canons and catches; and rewards of the same kind have with the same view been annually dispensed by them ever since.† These encouragements have contributed greatly to extend the narrow limits of the old harmony; and it is now only to be wished that the plan of this laudable society were adapted to the encouragement of a species of composition too little esteemed in our days, viz., Madrigals, which afford ample scope for the exercise of skill, and all the powers of invention; and for social practice are for many reasons to be preferred to every other kind of vocal harmony.

Of those great musicians who flourished in England at the beginning of this century, Geminiani was the only one living at this time; and, to resume the account herein before given of him and his works, it must be observed, that as he had never attempted dramatic composition of any kind, he drew to him but a small share of the public attention, that being in general awake only to such entertainments as the theatres afford. The consequence whereof was, that the sense of his merits existed only among those who had attained a competent skill in the practice of instrumental harmony to judge of them, and to these his publications were ever acceptable.

In a life so unsettled as that of Geminiani was, spent in different countries, and employed in pursuits that had no connection with his art, and only served to divert his attention from it, we must suppose the number of his friends to be very great, and that they were equally possessed of inclination and abilities to assist him, to account for the means of his support. That in the former part of his life he ex-

perienced the liberality of some persons of distinction is a fact pretty well ascertained; but he was not possessed of the art of forming beneficial connections, on the contrary, he would sometimes decline them;‡ so that as he advanced in years he had the mortification to experience the increase of his wants, and a diminution in the means of supplying them. In general his publications did, in respect of pecuniary advantage, in no degree compensate for his many years' labour and study employed in them, for which reason he had recourse to an expedient for obtaining a sum of money which he had never tried before, viz., a performance by way of benefit at one of the theatres; to this end, in the year 1748, he advertised a Concerto Spirituale, to be performed at Drury-lane theatre, chiefly of compositions of Italian masters of great eminence, but whose names were scarcely known in England.

Geminiani was an utter stranger to the business of an orchestra, and had no idea of the labour and pains that were necessary in the instruction of singers for the performance of music to which they were strangers, nor of the frequent practices which are required previous to an exhibition of this kind. The consequence whereof was, that the singers whom he had engaged for the Concerto Spirituale not being perfect in their parts, the performance miscarried. The particular circumstances that attended this undertaking were these; the advertisements had drawn together a number of persons, sufficient to make what is called a very good house; the curtain drew up, and discovered a numerous band, with Geminiani at their head: by way of overture was performed a concerto of his in a key of D with the minor third, printed in a collection of Concertos published by Walsh, with the title of Select Harmony, in which is a fugue in triple time, perhaps one of the finest compositions of the kind ever heard; then followed a very grand chorus, which, being performed by persons accustomed to sing in Mr. Handel's oratorios, had justice done to it; but when the women, to whom were given the solo airs and duets, rose to sing, they were not able to go on, and the whole band, after a few bars, were necessitated to stop. The audience, instead of expressing resentment in the usual way, seemed to compassionate the distress of Geminiani, and to consider him as a man who had almost survived his faculties, but whose merits were too great to justify their slight of even an endeavour to entertain them: they sat very silent till the books were changed, when the performance was continued with compositions of the author's own, that is to say, sundry of the concertos in his second and third operas, and a solo or two, which notwithstanding his advanced age, he performed in a manner that yet lives in the remembrance of many of the auditors.

The profits which arose from this entertainment enabled Geminiani to gratify that inclination for rambling which he had ever been a slave to; he

* Biographia Britannica, Appendix to the Supplement, page 229.

† The device is a tripod with a lyre, an ewer, and a cup thereon, encircled with a chaplet, Apollo and Bacchus as supporters sitting by it. The motto, taken from a canon of Dr. Hayes, is

LET'S DRINK AND LET'S SING TOGETHER.

‡ The late prince of Wales greatly admired the compositions of Geminiani, and at the same time that he retained Martini in his service, would have bestowed on him a pension of a hundred pounds a year, but the latter affecting an aversion to a life of dependence, declined the offer.

went to France, and took up his residence at Paris. He had formerly experienced the neatness and accuracy of the French artists in the engraving of music; and reflecting that his concertos had never been printed in a manner agreeable to his wishes, he determined to publish them himself, and also to give to the world what had long been earnestly wished for, a score of them. Accordingly he set himself to revise his second and third operas; but here the desire of making improvements, and a passion for refinement betrayed him into errors, for, besides the insertion of a variety of new passages, which did but ill sort with the general design of the several compositions into which they were engrafted, he entirely new modelled some of them, giving in many instances those passages to the second violin which had originally been composed for the tenor. Besides this he frequently made repeats of particular movements, and those so intricately ordered, as to render them very difficult of performance.

He stayed long enough at Paris to get engraven the plates both for the score and the parts of the two operas of concertos; and about the year 1755 returned to England, and took lodgings at the Grange-Inn, in Carey-street,* and advertised them for sale. About the same time he published what he called the Enchanted Forest, an instrumental composition, grounded on a very singular notion, which he had long entertained, namely, that between music and the discursive faculty there is a near and natural resemblance;† and this he was used to illustrate by a

comparison between those musical compositions in which a certain point is assumed in one part, and answered in the other with frequent iterations, and the form and manner of oral conversation. With a view to reduce this notion to practice, Geminiani has endeavoured to represent to the imagination of his hearers the succession of events in that beautiful episode contained in the thirteenth canto of Tasso's Jerusalem, where, by the arts of Ismeno, a pagan magician, a forest is enchanted, and each tree informed with a living spirit, to prevent its being cut down for the purpose of making battering-rams and other engines for carrying on the siege of Jerusalem.

The Enchanted Forest was succeeded by the publication of two numbers of a work entitled 'The 'Harmonical Miscellany, containing sundry modula-'tions on a bass, calculated for the improvement of 'students in music, and the practice of the violin and 'harpsichord.' The author intended to have continued this work by periodical publications, but meeting with little encouragement, he desisted from his purpose.

Notwithstanding the fine talents which as a musician Geminiani possessed, it must be remarked that the powers of his fancy seem to have been limited. His melodies were to the last degree elegant, his modulation original and multifarious, and in their general cast his compositions were tender and pathetic; and it is to the want of an active and teeming imagination that we are to attribute the publication of his works in various forms. Perhaps it was this that moved him to compose his first opera of solos into sonatas for two violins and a bass, notwithstanding that the latter six of them had been made into Sonatas by Barsanti many years before; and also to make into concertos sundry of the solos in his opera quarta. In the same spirit of improvement he employed the latter years of his life in varying and new moulding his former works, particularly he made two books of lessons for the harpsichord, consisting chiefly of airs from his solos; and it was not always that he altered them for the better. Besides those compositions of his which were published by himself, or under his immediate inspection, there are others of Geminiani in print, of which little notice has ever been taken, particularly the concerto above mentioned; as also two others in a collection published by Walsh, with the title of Select Harmony. And in a collection of solos, published by the same person, with the names of Geminiani and Castrucci, are three solos undoubtedly of the former, two whereof are nowhere else to be found.

In the year 1761 he went over to Ireland, and was kindly entertained there by Mr. Matthew Dubourg, who had been his pupil, and was then master of the king's band in Ireland. This person through the course of his life had ever been disposed to render him friendly offices; and it was but a short time after the arrival of Geminiani at Dublin that his humanity was called upon to perform for him the last. It seems that Geminiani had spent many years in compiling an elaborate treatise on

---

* A person who had the curiosity to see him, and went thither to purchase the book, gives this account of him: 'I found him in a room ' at the top of the house half filled with pictures, and in his waistcoat. ' Upon my telling him that I wanted the score and parts of both operas ' of his concertos, he asked me if I loved pictures; and upon my answer-'ing in the affirmative, he said that he loved painting better than music, 'and with great labour drew from among the many that stood upon the 'floor round the room, two, the one the story of Tobit cured of his 'blindness, by Michael Angelo Caravaggio; the other a Venus, by 'Correggio. These pictures, said Geminiani, I bought at Paris, the 'latter was in the collection of the duke of Orleans; they are inestimable, 'and I mean to leave them to my relations: many men are able to 'bequeath to their relations great sums of money, I shall leave to mine 'what is more valuable than money, two pictures that are scarcely to 'be matched in the world.' After some farther conversation, in which it was very difficult to get him to say any thing on the subject of music, the vistor withdrew, leaving Geminiani to enjoy that pleasure which seemed to be the result of frenzy.

† Lord Bacon means somewhat to this purpose in the following passages: 'There be in music certain figures or tropes, almost agreeing 'with the figures of rhetoric. * * * The reports and fugues have an 'agreement with the figures in rhetoric of repetition and traduction.' Nat. Hist. Cent. II. Sect. 113. Upon this sentiment Martinelli has raised a fanciful hypothesis, which seems to have been the motive with Geminiani to this undertaking, and is here given in his own words: 'Le 'sonate d'ogni strumento non fanno che imitare un discorso, rappre-'sentante qualche passione. Il sonatore giudizioso procura sempre di 'scegliere quei tuoni che sono più grati all' orecchio di chi ascolta. Quei 'tuoni delle voci della infanzia acerbi striduli e disgustevoli sono quelli, 'i quali devono maggiormente evitarsi, e i bambini ne i loro vagiti non 'rappresentano che espressioni di quel dolore, al quale quella tenera età 'o per le percussioni troppo violenti dell' aria, o per qualche altro 'accidente gli tiene continuamente soggetti. I sonatori specialmente di 'violino, se avvessero in vista questa considerazione, si guarderebbono 'con molta cura da quei tanti sopracuti de i quali per le loro ingrate e 'insignificanti bravure continuamente si servono. Per le cose allegre l' 'età della gioventù è la più propria, che vale a dire il moderato soprano 'e il contralto, siccome per le amorose, le quali convengono anco al 'tenore, ma con più moderazione. Un discorso serio si sa ordinaria-'mente dalle persone più adulte, e questo il tenore, il baritono e il 'basso lo possono esprimere propriamente. In un concerto dove si 'figura che tutte le voci concorrano in un medesimo discorso, gli accuti 'che figurano le voci più giovani, devono entrar più di rado, siccome 'rappresentanti persone, alle quali è dalla modestia permesso di parler 'più di rado. Di questa filosofia pare che il Corelli più d' ogni altro si 'sia servito perguida ne' suoi componimenti, avendo fatto suo maggior 'negozio delle voci di mezzo, e quindi usati i bassi come regolatori della 'zinfonia, o sia del suo discorso musicale.' Lettere familiare e critiche di Vincenzio Martinelli, Londra, 1758, page 379.

music, which he intended for publication; but, soon after his arrival at Dublin, by the treachery of a female servant, who it is said was recommended to him for no other purpose than that she might steal it, it was conveyed out of his chamber, and could never after be recovered. The greatness of this loss, and his inability to repair it, made a deep impression on his mind, and, as it is conjectured, precipitated his end; at least he survived it but a short time, the seventeenth of September, 1762, being the last day of his life, *which had been prolonged to the age of* 96. The following list comprises the whole of his publications, except two or three articles of small account:—Twelve Solos for a violin, Opera prima; Six Concertos in seven parts, Opera seconda; Six Concertos in seven parts, Opera terza; Twelve solos for a violin, Opera quarta; Six Solos for a violoncello, Opera quinta; the same made into Solos

for a violin; Six Concertos from his Opera quarta; Six Concertos in eight parts, Opera settima; Rules for playing in Taste; a Treatise on good Taste; the Art of playing the Violin; Twelve Sonatas from his first Solos, Opera undecima; Ripieno parts to ditto; Lessons for the Harpsichord; Guida Armonica; Supplement to ditto; the Art of Accompaniment, two books; his two first operas of Concertos in score; and the Enchanted Forest.

These cursory remarks on the compositions of Geminiani may suffice for a description of his style and manner. Of his Solos the Opera prima is esteemed the best. Of his Concertos, some are excellent, others of them scarce pass the bound of mediocrity. The sixth of the third opera not only surpasses all the rest, but, in the opinion of the best judges of harmony, is the finest instrumental composition of the kind extant.

# CONCLUSION.

In the original plan of the foregoing work, it was for reasons, which have yet their weight with the author, determined to continue it no farther than to that period at which it is made to end. It nevertheless appears necessary, on a transient view of the present state of music, to remark on the degree of perfection at which it is at this time arrived; and from such appearances as the general manners of the times, and the uniform disposition of mankind in favour of novelty, to point out, as far as effects can be deduced from causes, the probable changes which hereafter it will be made to undergo; as also those improvements which seem to be but the consequence of that skill in the science to which we have attained.

That we are in possession of a more enlarged theory than that of the ancients will hardly be denied, if the arguments contained in this work, and the opinions and testimonies of the gravest authors are allowed to have any weight; and that we should excel them in our practice seems to be but a necessary consequence; at least the order and course of things, which are ever towards perfection, warrant us in thinking so. Whatever checks are given to the progress of science, or the improvement of manual arts, are accidental and temporary; they do but resemble those natural obstacles that impede the course of a rivulet, which for a short time may occasion a small deviation of its current, but at length are made to yield to its force.

In the comparison of the modern with the ancient music it must evidently appear that that of the present day has the advantage, whether we consider it in theory or practice: the system itself as it is founded in nature, will admit of no variation; consonance and dissonance are the subjects of immutable laws, which when investigated become a rule for all succeeding improvements. Whatever difference is to be found between the modern and ancient musical system, has arisen either from the rejection of those

parts of it which the ancients themselves were willing enough to give up, and which as it were by universal consent, have been suffered to grow into disuse; or such additions to it as reason and experience have at different periods enabled men to make. To instance in a few particulars; the enarmonic and chromatic genera, with all the species or colours of the latter, are no longer recognized as essential parts of music; but the diatonic, attempered as it is with a mixture of chromatic intervals, is found to answer the purpose of all three; and the extension of the scale beyond the limits of the bis-diapason is no more than the extended compass of the modern instruments of all kinds naturally leads to. As to the philosophy of sound, or the doctrine of phonics, it appears that the ancients were almost strangers to it: this is a branch of speculative music; and as it results from the modern discoveries in physics, the moderns only are entitled to the merit of its investigation.

With respect to the relations of the marvellous effects of the ancient music, this remark should ever be uppermost in the minds of such as are inclined to credit them, viz., that men are ever disposed to speak of that which administers delight to them in the strongest terms of applause. At this day we extol the excellencies of a favourite singer, or a celebrated performer on an instrument, in all the hyperbolical terms that fancy can suggest; and these we often think too weak to express those genuine feelings of our own which we mean to communicate to others.

It has been asserted by a set of fanciful reasoners, that there is in the course of things a general and perpetual declination from that state of perfection in which the author of nature originally constituted the world; and, to instance in a few particulars, that men are neither so virtuous, so wise, so ingenious, so active, so strong, so big in stature, or so long lived, as they were even long after the transgression of our first parents, and the subsequent contraction of the period of human life : but no one has ever yet insinuated that the vocal organs have participated in this general calamity ; or that those mechanic arts to which we owe the invention and perfection of the various kinds of musical instruments, are in a less flourishing state than heretofore : till the contrary can be made appear, it may therefore be fairly presumed that in this respect the moderns have sustained no loss.

Farther, if a comparison be made between the instruments of the ancients and those of the moderns, the advantage will be found to be on the side of the latter : the ancient instruments, excepting those of the pulsatile kind, which in strictness are not to be considered as a musical species, as producing no variety of harmonical intervals, are comprehended under two classes, namely, the Lyre and the Tibia ; the former, under all its various modifications, appears to have been extremely deficient in many of those circumstances that contribute to the melioration of sound, and which are common to the meanest instruments of the fidicinal kind ; and, notwithstanding all that is said by Bartholinus and others, of the ancient tibia, and the extravagant elogies which we so frequently meet with of the ancient tibicines, we know very well that the tibia was a pipe greatly inferior to the flutes of modern times, which are incapable of being constructed so as not to be out of tune in the judgment of a nice and critical ear ; and to these no miraculous effects have ever yet been ascribed. To these two classes of instruments of the ancient Greeks, the Romans are said to have added another, viz., the hydraulic organ, for the use whereof we are as much to seek, as we are for a true idea of its structure and constituent parts.

It is true that the instruments in use among the moderns, in the general division of them, like those of the ancients, are comprehended under the tensile and inflatile kinds ; but numberless are the species into which these again are severally divided ; to which it may be added, that they have been improving for at least these five hundred years. And now to begin the comparison ; the instruments of the viol kind are so constructed as to reverberate and prolong that sound, which, when produced from the Lyre, must be supposed to have been wasted in the open air ; the modern flutes, as far as can be judged by a comparison of them with the graphical representations of the ancient Tibiæ, have greatly the advantage ; and as to pipes of other kinds, such as the Hautboy, the Bassoon, the Chalumeau, and others, these, as having the adjunct of a reed, constitute a species new and original, and are an invention unknown to the ancients.

To the hydraulic organ, said to have been invented by Ctesibus of Alexandria, we have to oppose the modern pneumatic organ ; not that rude machine of Saxon construction, a representation whereof is given in page 615 of this work, but such as that noble instrument used in divine worship among us, that of St. Paul's or the Temple church for instance.

Upon a view of the ancient and modern practice of music, and a comparison of one with the other, grounded on the above facts, we cannot but wonder at the credulity of those who give the preference to the former, and lament, as Sir William Temple in good earnest does, that the science of music is wholly lost in the world.*

But this is not the whole of the argument : as far as we can yet learn, it is to the moderns that we owe the invention of music in consonance ; and were it otherwise, and it could be said that we derive it from the Greeks, the multiplication of harmonical combinations must be supposed to be gradual, and is therefore to be ascribed to the moderns ; a circumstance that must necessarily give to the music of any period an advantage over that of the age preceding it. Nor is this kind of improvement any thing more than what necessarily results from practice and experience. In the sciences the accumulated discoveries of one age are a foundation for improvement in the next : and in the manual arts it may be said, that those who begin to learn them, in their noviciate often attain that degree of perfection at which their teachers stopped.†

This is the natural course and order of things ; but how far it is liable to be checked and interrupted may deserve consideration. With respect to music it may be observed, that much of its efficacy is by the vulgar admirers of it attributed to mere novelty ; and as these are a very numerous party, it becomes the interest of those who administer to their delight to gratify them, even against the conviction of their own judgments, and to the injury of the art. If novelty will ensure approbation, what artist will labour at intrinsic excellence, or submit his most arduous studies to the censure of those who neither regard, or indeed are able to judge of their merits ?‡

To this disposition we may impute the gradual declination from the practice and example of the ablest proficients in harmony, discoverable in the

---

* In his Essay upon the ancient and modern Learning.

† This observation will be found to be true in many and various instances : as it respects music, it may suffice to say that the young women of this age are finer performers on the harpsichord than the masters of the last ; and that there are now many better proficients on the violin under twenty, than there were of double their age fifty years ago.

‡ That some persons do not love music is a known fact ; and Dr. Willis, the great physician and anatomist, has endeavoured to account for it by his observations on the structure of the human ear ; and that the majority of those who frequent musical entertainments have no sense of harmony is no less certain. The want of this sense is no ground for reproach, but the affectation of it in those to whom nature has denied it, is a proper subject for ridicule. If it be asked what is the test of a musical ear, the answer is, a general delight in the harmony of sounds. As to those to whom harmony is offensive, and who yet affect a taste for music, their own declarations are often evidence against them, and in general they will be found to be,

Such as having no defect in their vocal organs, are unable to articulate even a short series of musical sounds.

Such as at a musical performance express an uneasiness at the variety and seeming intricacy of the harmony, by a wish that all the instruments played the same tune.

Such as think the quickest music the best, and call that spirit and fire which is but noise and clamour.

Such as by the delight they take in the music of French horns, clarinets, and other noisy instruments, discover that the associated ideas of hunting, and the pleasures of the chase are uppermost in their minds.

Such as think a concert a proper concomitant of a feast.

Such, as having no scruple to it on the score of their religious profession, complain of cathedral music as being dull and heavy.

And lastly, such as at the hearing an adagio movement, or any composition of the pathetic kind, the eighth concerto of Corelli, for instance, complain of an inclination to sleep.

compositions of the present day, which, as they abound in noise and clamour, are totally void of energy. Music of this kind, constructed without art or elegance, awakens no passion : the general uproar of a modern symphony or overture neither engages attention, nor interrupts conversation ; and many persons, in the total absence of thought, flatter themselves that they are merry. To assist this propensity, and as much as possible to banish reflection, the composers of music seem now to act against a fundamental precept of their art, which teaches that variety and novelty are ever to be studied, by reprobating, as they uniformly do, the use of all the keys with the minor third, upon a pretence that they tend to excite melancholy ideas ;* and by rejecting those grave and solemn measures, which, besides that they correspond with the most delightful of our sensations, form a contrast with those of a different kind. Is this to promote variety, or rather is it not contracting the sources of it ? Nor is the structure of their compositions such as can admit of any other than an interchange of little frittered passages and common-place phrases, difficult to execute, and for the most part so rapid in the utterance, that they elude the judgment of the ear ; and, without affecting any one passion, or exciting the least curiosity concerning the composer, leave us to wonder at the art of the performer, and to contemplate the languid effects of misapplied industry.

There can be no better test of the comparative merits of the music of the present day, and that which it has taken place of, than the different effects of each. The impression of the former was deep and is lasting : the compositions of Corelli, Handel, Geminiani, yet live in our memories ; and those of Purcell, though familiarized by the lapse of near a century, still retain their charms ; but who now remembers, or rather does not affect to forget the music that pleased him last year ? Musical publications no longer find a place in our libraries ; and we are as little solicitous for their fate as for the preservation of almanacs or pamphlets.

That music was intended merely to excite that affection of the mind which we understand by the word mirth, is a notion most illiberal, and worthy only of those vulgar hearers who adopt it. On the contrary, that it is an inexhaustible source of entertainment, or, as Milton finely expresses it, 'of sacred 'and home-felt delight,' is known to all that are skilled in its precepts or susceptible of its charms. The passions of grief and joy, and every affection of the human mind, are equally subservient to its call ; but rational admirers of the science experience its effects in that tranquillity and complacency which it

* There is nothing more certain than that those who reason in this manner are ignorant of the structure of the human mind, which is never more delighted than with those images that incline us most to contemplation. Else why do the poets so strenuously labour to awaken the tender passions ? Why are the ravings of Lear, or the sorrows of Hamlet made the subjects of public speculation ? Such as approve only of mirthful music, to be consistent should proclaim aloud their utter aversion to all theatric representations except comedy, farce, and pantomime, and leave the nobler works of genius for the entertainment of better judges.

is calculated to superinduce, and in numberless sensations too delicate for expression.

It is obvious to men of understanding and reflection, that at different periods false notions have prevailed, not only in matters of science, where truth can only be investigated by the improved powers of reason, but in those arts wherein that discriminating faculty, that nameless sense, which, for want of a more proper term to define it by, we call taste, is the sole arbiter. In painting, architecture, and gardening, this truth is most apparent : the love of beauty, symmetry, and elegance, has at times given way to a passion for their contraries ; fashion has interposed in subjects with which fashion has nothing to do : nevertheless it may be observed, that while opinion has been veering round to every point, the principles of these arts, as they are founded in nature and experience, have ever remained in a state of permanency.

To apply this reasoning to the subject before us : we have seen the time when music of a kind the least intelligible has been the most approved. Our forefathers of the last century were witnesses to the union of elegance with harmony, and we of this day behold their separation : let us enquire into the reason of this change.

The prevalence of a corrupt taste in music seems to be but the necesary result of that state of civil policy which enables, and that disposition which urges men to assume the character of judges of what they do not understand. The love of pleasure is the offspring of affluence, and, in proportion as riches abound, not to be susceptible of fashionable pleasures is to be the subject of reproach ; to avoid which men are led to dissemble, and to affect tastes and propensities that they do not possess ; and when the ignorant become the majority, what wonder is it that, instead of borrowing from the judgment of others, they set up opinions of their own ; or that those artists, who live but by the favour of the public, should accommodate their studies to their interests, and endeavour to gratify the many rather than the judicious few ?

But, notwithstanding these evils, it does not appear that the science itself has sustained any loss ; on the contrary, it is certain that the art of combining musical sounds is in general better understood at this time than ever. We may therefore indulge a hope that the sober reflection on the nature of harmony, and its immediate reference to those principles on which all our ideas of beauty, symmetry, order and magnificence are founded ; on the infinitely various modifications of which it is capable ; its influence on the human affections ; and, above all, those nameless delights which the imaginative faculty receives from the artful disposition and succession of concordant sounds, will terminate in a thorough conviction of the vanity and emptiness of that music with which we now are pleased, and produce a change in the public taste, that, whenever it takes place, can hardly fail to be for the better.

# APPENDIX.

No. 1.—Verses supposed to be a complaint of Anne Boleyn, from an ancient MS; the music by Robert Johnson from another.

un-to my fame a mor-tal wounde, un-to my fame a mor - tal, mor - tal

fame a mor-tal wounde, a mor-tal wounde, un-to my fame a mor - tal

wounde, un - to my fame a mor-tal wounde, un - to my fame a mor-tal wounde,

un -to my fame a mor-tal wounde, a mor - tal wounde, un-to my fame a mor -

wounde, say what ye list it will not be, it will not be, say what ye

wounde, say what ye list, say what ye list, say what ye list it will not

say what ye list, say what ye list it will . . . not be, say what ye list, say what ye

- - - tal wounde. say what ye list it will not be, it will not be,

list it will not be, say what ye list it will not be, ye seek for that can-not be founde .

be, say what ye list it will not be, ye seek for that can-not be founde,

list it will not be, say what ye list it will not be, ye seek for that cannot be founde, ye seek . . for that can -

say what ye list it will not be, ye seek for that cannot cannot be founde, ye seek for that can -

. . . ye seek . . . . . for that can-not be founde, De - fyl - ed is my name.

ye seek for that can-not be founde can - not be founde,

- not be founde, ye seek . . for that can - not be founde, . . . . De - fyl -

- not, can-not be founde, ye seek for that can - - not be founde, be founde, de - fyl - ed,

ROBERT JOHNSON.

No. 2.—The Black Sanctus, a song so called, set to music as a canon in the sub-diatessaron and diapason. Concerning which the following account is given in a letter of Sir John Harington to the lord treasurer Burleigh, printed in the Nugæ Antiquæ, vol. I. page 132. 'In an old booke of my 'father's I read a merrie verse, which for lack of my own, I send by Mr. Bellot, to divert your lordshippe, when as you say weighty pain and weightier 'matters will yield to quips and merriment. This verse is called The Blacke Sauntus, or Monkes Hymn to Saunte Satane, made when kynge Henrie 'had spoylede their synginge. My father was wont to say that kynge Henrie was used in pleasaunte moode to singe this verse; and my father, who 'had his good countenance, and a goodlie office in his courte, and also his goodlie Esther [This Esther was a natural daughter of the kyng's, to whom 'he gave as a dower the lands belonging to the Bathe priory, or a part thereof] to wife, did sometyme receive the honour of hearing his own songe, 'for he made the tune which my man Combe hath sent herewith; having been much skilled in musicke, which was pleasing to the kynge, and which 'he learnt in the followship of good Maister Tallis, when a young man.'

No. 2.

O Tu qui dans o - ra-cu-la, Scin-dis co-tem no-va-cu-la, Da nos-tra &c.

O Tu . . qui dans o - ra-cu-la, Scin - dis cotem no-va-cu - la, Da &c.

O Tu . . qui dans o - - ra-cu-la, Scin - - dis cotem no-va-cu - la, Da &c.

JOHN HARINGTON.

'O tu qui dans oracula, scindis cotem novacula,
'Da nostra ut tabernacula, lingua canant vernacula,
'Opima post jentacula, hujusmodi miracula,
'Sit semper plenum poculum, habentes plenum loculum,
'Tu serva nos ut specula, per longa et læta sæcula,
'Ut clerus ut plebecula, nec nocte nec de cula.
'Curent de ulla recula, sed intuentes specula,
'Dura vitemus spicula, jacentes cum amicula,
'Quæ garrit ut cornicula, seu tristis seu ridicula,
'Tum porrigamus oscula, tum colligamus floscula,
'Ornemus ut cœnaculum, et totum habitaculum,
'Tum culy post spiraculum, spectemus hoc spectaculum.'

The foregoing lines are undoubtedly corrupt in more than one place, [In the sixth and twelfth lines perhaps we should read *de pecula* instead of *de cula*, and *culo* in the place of *culy*], but as they are singularly humorous, and nearly resemble the facetious rhymes of Walter de Mapes, archdeacon of Oxford, who lived in the time of Hen. II., and as Camden says, filled England with his merriments, the following translation has been attempted under all the disadvantages that must arise from the obscurity of an original so difficult to be understood:—

O thou who utt'ring mystic notes,
    The whetstone cut'st with razor,
In mother-tongue permit our throats,
    Henceforth to sing and say, Sir!

To rich, material breakfasts join
    These miracles more funny—
Fill all our cups with lasting wine,
    Our bags with lasting money!

To us a guardian tow'r remain,
    Through ages long and jolly;
Nor give our house a moment's pain
    From thought's intrusive folly!

Ne'er let our eyes for losses mourn,
    Nor pore on aught but glasses;
And sooth the cares that still return,
    By toying with our lasses;

Who loud as tatling magpies prate,
    Alternate laugh and lour;
Then kiss we round each wanton mate,
    And crop each vernal flow'r.

To deck our rooms, and chiefly that
    Where supper's charms invite;
Then close in chimney-corner squat,
    To see so blest a sight!

No. 3.—A song set to music by William Bird in the form of a madrigal for three voices. Concerning the words of this song, it has long been a received tradition among musical people, that they were written on some particular occasion by king Henry VIII; and in the Nugæ Antiquæ, vol. II. page 248, is a letter from Sir John Harington to prince Henry, written in 1609, wherein the fact is ascertained by the following passage: 'I will now venture to send to your readinge a special verse of king Henrie the eight, when he conceived love for Anna Bulleign. And 'hereof I entertain no doubt of the author, for if I had no better reason than the rhyme, it were sufficient to think that no other than suche a king 'coud write suche a sonnet; but of this my father oft gave me good assurance. who was in his houshold.' *Notwithstanding this assertion it can never be assented to as a fact, for the whole of the song is to be found in the legend of Jane Shore, written by Thomas Churchyard, and forms a complete Stanza of that poem. It is reprinted in Mr. Cooper's Muses' Library, page 18.* 'This sonnet was sung to the Lady Anne at his commaundment; and here followeth:— "The eagle's force, &c."'
The music is unquestionably Bird's, for the song as given in this Appendix stands the first among the songs in a work published by himself in 1611, entitled 'Psalmes, Songs, and Sonnets: some solemne, others joyful, framed to the life of the words: fit for Voyces or Viols of 3, 4, 5, and 6 parts.'

No. 3.

THE ea-gle's force sub-dues eache byrd that .. flyes; what me-tal
THE ea-gle's force sub-dues eache byrd that flyes, eache byrd that flyes; what me-
THE ea-gle's force sub-dues eache byrd that flyes; what me-tal

can re-sist, re-sist the flam-inge fyre? dothe not the sunne da-
-tal can re-syst the flam-inge fyre? dothe not the sunne da-zle the clear--este
can re-syst the flam--inge fyre? dothe not the sunne da-zle the clear-este

zle the clear-este eyes, the cleareste eyes, the clear-este eyes and melte the ice, and make
eyes, the cleareste eyes, the clear---este eyes, and melte the ice, and
eyes, da--zle the clear--este eyes, and melte the ice, and

.. the froste re-tyre, re--tyre? who can with-stand a puissant
make the froste re-tyre, re--tyre? who can withstand a puissant King's de-sire, ..
make the froste re-tyre, .. re--tyre? who can withstand a puissant King's de-sire,    a

WILLIAM BIRD.

No. 4.—A Song written by Richard Edwards, a gentleman of queen Elizabeth's chapel, and afterwards master of the children there, printed in the Paradyse of daynty Devises, and alluded to in the play of Romeo and Juliet; the music from an ancient manuscript.

In joy it maks our mirth abound,
  In grief it chers our heavy sprights,
The carefull head releaf hath found,
  By Musick's pleasant swete delights;
Our senses, what should I saie more,
  Are subject unto Musick's lore.

The Gods by Musick hath their prayse,
  The soule therin doth joye;
For as the Romaine poets saie,

In seas whom pirats would destroye,
A dolphin sav'd from death moste sharpe,
Arion playing on his harpe.

Oh heavenly gift, that turnes the minde,
  Like as the sterne doth rule the ship,
Of musick whom the Gods assignde,
  To comfort man whom cares would nip,
Sith thou both man and beast doest move,
  What wise man then will thee reprove

No. 5.—Another written by Francis Kindlemarsh, from the Paradyse of daynty Devises; the music by the above Richard Edwards from the same MS.

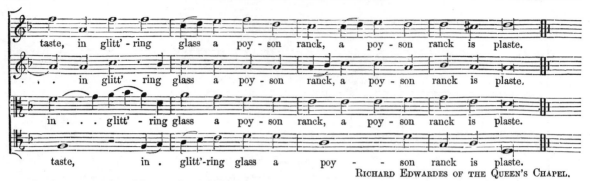

RICHARD EDWARDES OF THE QUEEN'S CHAPEL.

So pleasant woordes, without performing deedes,
May well be deemed to spring of Darnel seedes.
The freendly deede is it, that quickly tryes
Where trusty faith and freendly meaning lyes.
That state therefore most happy seems to be,
Where woordes and deedes most faithfully agree.

  My freend yf thou wilt keepe thy honest name
Fly from the blotte of barking slaunder's blame.
Let not in woord thy promise be more large,
Then thou in deede are wyllyng to discharge.
Abhorred is that false dissembling broode,
That seemes to beare two faces in one hoode.
To say a thing, and not to meane the same,
Wyll turne at length to losse of thy good name.
Wherefore, my freend, let double dealing goe,
In steade whereof let perfect plaineness flowe.
Doo thou no more in idle woordes exceede,
Then thou intendes to doo in very deede.

So goode report shall spread thy woorthy prayse
For being just in woord and deede alwayes.

  You worldly wightes, that worldly dooers are,
Before you let your woord slip foorth too farre,
Consyder well, what inconvenience springes
By breach of promise made in lawfull thinges.
First God mislikes where such deceit dooth swarme;
Next it redoundeth unto thy neighbour's harme;
And last of all, which is not least of all,
For such offence thy conscience suffer shall.
As barren groundes bringe foorth but rotten weedes,
From barren woordes so fruitlesse chaffe proceedes;
As saverie flowres doo spring in fertill ground,
So trusty freendes by tryed freendes are found.
To shunne therefore the woorst that may ensue,
Let deedes alway approve thy sayinges true.

No. 6.—Another from the Paradyse of daynty Devises, written by William Hunnis of the queen's chapel, the successor of Edwards as master
of the children, and set to music by Thomas Tallis; from the same MS.

pi - ning paine,   whose gast - ly lookes, whose blood-ly strems out flow - ing  from each vaine, whose fall - ing

pi - ning paine,   whose gast - ly lookes, whose blood-ly strems out flow - ing  from each vaine, whose fall - ing

pi - ning paine,   whose gast - ly lookes, whose bloodly strems out flow - ing  from each vaine, whose fall - ing

pi - ning paine,   whose gast - ly lookes, whose blood-ly strems out flow - ing  from each vaine, whose fall - ing

from the tree, whose pan-ting on the ground, ex - am - ples be of mine es - tate  tho' there a - pere no wound.

from the tree, whose pan-ting on the ground, ex - am - ples be of mine es - tate tho'  there a - pere no wound.

from the tree, whose pan-ting on the ground, ex - am - ples be of mine es - tate tho'  there a - pere no wound.

from the tree, whose pan-ting on the ground, ex - am - ples be of mine es-tate  tho'  there a - pere no wound.

THOMAS TALLIS.

No. 7.—A Tale from the same collection, written by the above Richard Edwards; the music from the same MS.

**No. 7.**

IN    go - ing to my    na - - ked  bedde,                          as

IN  go - ing to my na - ked bedde,  na - ked  bedde,                as   one that

IN      go - ing to my    na - - - ked bedde, as    one  that would have

IN      go - ing to my      na - - - ked bedde,

one that would have slept,    I heard a    wife    sing  to    her  child that long be - fore had wept.

would have slept,    I heard a    wife sing to  her    child    that    long be - fore    had    wept.

slept, I heard a  wife sing to her  child      that  long      be - fore . . . had wept.

I heard a    wife    sing    to her    child    that  long be - fore    had    wept.

She sigh-ed sore and sang full sweete to bring  the babe to  rest,      that would not cease but

She sigh-ed sore and sang full sweete to bring   the babe to  rest,      that would not cease but

She sigh-ed sore and sang full sweete to bring  the babe to  rest, that would not cease but cri - ed

She sigh-ed sore and sang full sweete to bring  the babe to  rest,      that would not cease but

Then took I paper, penne and ynke,
  This proverbe for to write,
In regester for to remaine
  Of such a worthie wight :
As she proceeded thus in song
  Unto her little bratte,
Muche matter uttered she of waight,
  In place whereas she satte,
And proved plaine there was no beast,
  Nor creature bearing life,
Could well be knowne to live in love,
  Without discorde and strife :
Then kissed shee her little babe,
  And sware by God above,
The falling out of faithfull frends
  Renuing is of love.

She saied that neither king ne prince,
  Ne lord could live aright,
Untill their puissance they did prove,
  Their manhode and their might.
When manhode shal be matched so
  That feare can take no place,
Then wearie works makes warriours
  Eche other to embrace,
And leave their forse that failed them,
  Which did consume the rout,
That might before have lived their tyme,
  And their fulle nature out :
Then did she sing as one that thought
  No man could her reprove,
The falling out of faithfull frends
  Renuing is of love.

She said she sawe no fishe ne foule,
  Nor beast within her haunt,
That mett a straunger in their kinde,
  But could geve it a taunt:
Since fleshe might not indure,
  But rest must wrathe succede,
And forse who fight to fall to play,
  In pasture where they feede.
So noble nature can well ende
  The works she hath begone,
And bridle well that will not cease
  Her tragedy in some;
Thus in her songe she oft reherst,
  As did her well behove,
The falling out of faithfull frends
  Renuing is of love.

I marvaile much pardy quoth she,
  For to beholde the route,
To see man, woman, boy and beast
  To tosse the world about:
Some knele, some crouch, some beck, some chek,
  And some can smothly smile,
And some embrace others in arme,
  And there thinke many a wile.
Some stande aloufe at cap and knee,
  Some humble and some stoute,
Yet are they never frends indeede,
  Untill they once fall out;
Thus ended she her song and saied
  Before she did remove,
The falling out of faithfull frends
  Renuing is of love.

No. 8.—An Anthem composed by John Redford, of St. Paul's, temp. Hen. VIII.

No. 8.

and the peace of God whiche pass-eth all, pass-eth all un-
and the peace of God .... whiche pass-eth all un-der-stand-ing, un-
and the peace of God, whiche pass-eth all un-
and the peace of God whiche pass-eth all un-der-

-der-stand-ing, and the peace of God whiche pass-eth all un-der-stand-
-der-stand-ing, the peace .... of God,
-der-stand-ing, and the peace of God whiche pass-eth all un-der-stand-ing,
-stand-ing, and the peace of God whiche pass-eth all un-der-stand--ing, and the

-ing, ... and the peace of God ... whiche pass-eth all un-der-stan-ding,
and the peace of God whiche pass-eth all un-der-stand-ing, shall
and the peace of God .. whiche pass--eth all un-der-stand-ing, all un-der-stand-ing,
peace of God .. whiche pass---eth all un-der-stand-ing, all un-der-stand-

keepe your heartes and mindes thro' Christ Je - su.
keepe your hearts .... and .. mindes thro' Christ .... Je - su.
... shall keepe your heartes ... and minds thro' Christ .... Je - su.
--ing, shall keepe your heartes ... and mindes thro' Christ Je - su.

JOHN REDFORD.

No. 9.—A Meane composed by William Blitheman, Dr. Bull's master.

No. 9.

WILLIAM BLITHEMAN.

No. 10.—A Poynte.

JOHN SHEPHARD.

No. 11.—A Voluntary.

MASTER ALLWOODE.

No. 12.—The first stanza of the Hymnus Eucharisticus of Dr. Nath. Ingelo, set to music by Dr. Benjamin Rogers, of Oxford, and sung by way of grace after dinner in the hall of Magdalen college.

No. 12.

TE Deum Patrem col - - i - mus, Te lau - di - bus pro - se - qui - mur;

TE De - um Pa - trem col - i - mus, Te lau - di - bus pro - se - qui - mur;

TE De - um Pa - trem col - i - mus, Te lau - di - bus pro - se - - qui - mur;

TE Deum Pa - trem col - i - - mus, Te lau - di - bus pro - se - qui - - mur;

Qui Cor - pus ci - bo re - fi - - cis cœ - les - ti men - tem gra - ti - a.

Qui Cor - pus ci - bo re - fi - - cis cœ - les - ti men - tem gra - ti - a.

Qui Cor - pus ci - bo re - fi - - cis cœ - les - ti men - tem gra - ti - a.

Qui Cor - pus ci - bo re - fi - - cis cœ - les - ti men - tem gra - ti - a.

DOCTOR BENJAMIN ROGERS.

Nos. 13 and 14.—Two very ancient country-dance tunes, viz.: The Shaking of the Shetes, mentioned by Taylor the water-poet, in his character of a bawd; and Trenchmore, mentioned in the Island Princess of Beaumont and Fletcher, and in the Table-talk of Selden.

No. 15.—Paul's Steeple.

No. 16.—Old Simon the King. *This is the tune to an old Song, which see in Pills to purge Melancholy, vol. III, page 144. It is conjectured that the subject of it was Simon Wadloe, who kept the Devil Tavern at the time when Ben Jonson's Club, called the Apollo Club, met there. In the verses over the door of the Apollo Room was this couplet:—*

> " Hang up all the poor hop drinkers,
>   Cries Old Sim, the King of Skinkers."

*A Skinker is one that serves drink.—Johns. Dict. In Camden's remains is the following epitaph on this person:—*

> *Apollo et cohors Musarum,*
> *Bacchus vini et uvarum,*
> *Ceres pro pane et cerevisia*
> *Adeste omnes cum tristitia.*
> *Düque Deæque lamentate cuncti,*
> *Simonis Vadloe funera defuncti*
> *Sub signo malo bene vixit mimbile*
> *Si ad cœlus recessit, gratias Diabole.*

*As to the Song, there is in it nothing characteristic of the man, but it attributes to him the following two strings of Aphorisms; each of them forming that kind of argument which the Logicians call a Sontes:*

> *Drink will make a man drunk,*           *Drinking will make a man quaff,*
> *And drunk will make a man dry,*          *Quaffing will make a man sing,*
> *Dry will make a man sick,*               *Singing will make a man laugh,*
> *And sick will make a man die,*           *And laughing long life will bring,*
>         *Says Old Simon the King.*                *Says Old Simon the King.*

No. 17.—Tollet's Ground.

Thomas Tollet.

No. 18.—John, come kiss me.

No. 18.

No. 19.—Roger of Coverly.

No. 19.

No. 20.—Cold and raw. [An old tune, which makes part of a canon in the unison, by John Hilton, and printed in his Collection of Catches, Rounds, and Canons, published in 1652. It takes the above name from the initial words of an old ballad, which is set to it, and was a favourite tune of queen Mary, the consort of William III. See page 564 of this work, in note.]

No. 20.

No. 21.—Green Sleeves.

No. 21.

No. 22.—The Old Cebell.

No. 22.

GIO. BATT. DRAGHI.

No. 23.—Bellamira, a favourite Ground.

SOLOMON ECCLES.

No. 24.—Farinel's Ground.

No. 25.—Johnny, cock thy beaver.

No. 26.—Hedge-lane, a dance-tune.

JOHN BANISTER.

No. 27.—Mademoiselle Subligny's Minuet.   This person, *whose Christian name was Thérèse, was a Dancer in the Opera at Paris in the year* 1704, *with a pension of* 800 *livres.   Betterton, upon the decline of his company at Lincoln's Inn Theatre, at an extraordinary rate got her over hither, as also at different times Mons. L'Abbé, and Mons. Balon.   She danced for a season or two with great applause, and returned to her own country.—Vide Histoire du Theatre de L'Academie Royale de Musique en France, page* 94.   *Life of Colley Cibber, page* 180.   Before the arrival of these persons, French dancing was unknown on the English stage.

No. 28.—Ballad of John Dory, with the tune; a round for three voices.

**No. 28.** AS it fell on a ho-li-day, as it fell on a ho-li day and up-on a ho-ly-tide a, and up-on a ho-ly-tide a, and up-on a ho-ly-tide a;

John Dory bought him an ambling nag
  to Paris for to ride a.

And when John Dory to Paris was come,
  a little before the gate a;
John Dory was fitted, the porter was witted,
  To let him in thereat a.

The first man that John Dory did meet
  Was good king John of France a;
John Dory con'd well of his courtesie,
  but fell down in a trance a.

A pardon, a pardon, my liege and my king,
  For my merie men and for me a;
And all the churles in merie England
  I'le bring them all bound to thee a.

Sir Nichol was then a Cornish man,
  a little beside Bohyde a;
And he mann'd forth a good blacke barke,
  with fiftie good oares on a side a.

Run up my boy unto the maine top,
  and looke what thou canst spy a:
Who, ho; a goodly ship I do see,
  I trow it be John Dory a.

They hoist their sailes both top and top,
  the mizen and all was tried a;
And every man stood to his lot,
  what ever should betide a.

The roring canons then were plide,
  and dub a dub went the drumme a;
The braying trumpets lowdlie cride
  to 'courage both all and some a.

The grapling hooks were brought at length,
  the browne bill and the sword a;
John Dory at length, for all his strength,
  was clapt fast under board a.

No. 29.—Original tune to the song of Cupes in the Latin comedy of Ignoramus, act iii. scene x.; a Round for three voices.

**No. 29.** UX-OR me-a Ux-or pol-la O si frangat su-a col-la, pol-la col-la, col-la polla.

No. 30.—The tune to the old ballad of Cock Lorrel, written by Ben Jonson, and printed in his masque of the Gypsies metamorphosed.

**No. 30.**

No. 31.—An old ballad tune to which D'Urfey has adapted a song with the words at the end of every stanza, 'Hey boys up go we.'

**No. 31.**

No. 32.—A song, said in an old copy to be written by king Charles II., set by Mr. Pelham Humphrey, master of the children of his chapel.

**No. 32.** I pass all my hours in a sha-dy old Grove, but I live not the day when I see not my

Love: I sur-vey ev'-ry walk now my Phil-lis is gone, and sigh when I think we were there all a-

-lone; O then 'tis O then that I think there's no Hell, like lov - - - ing too well.

But each shade and each conscious bow'r, when I find
Where I once have been happy, and she has been kind ;
When I see the print left of her shape in the green,
And imagin the pleasure may yet come agen ;
   O then 'tis I think no joys are above
     The pleasures of love.

While alone to myself I repeat all her charms,
She I love may be lockt in another man's arms,
She may laugh at my cares, and so false she may be,
To say all the kind things she before said to me ;
   O then 'tis O then that I think there's no hell
     Like loving too well.

But when I consider the truth of her heart,
Such an innocent passion, so kind without art,
I fear I have wrong'd her, and hope she may be
So full of true love to be jealous of me :
   And then 'tis I think that no joys are above
     The pleasures of love.

No. 33.—The tune to the Fandango, a favourite dance of the Spaniards.

No. 34.—A tune for a rope-dance in a singular style, by Mr. John Eccles.

John Eccles.

A COLLECTION OF

# FAC-SIMILES, &c.

OF

# ANCIENT MANUSCRIPTS,

FORMING

APPENDIX, Nos. 35 TO 57.

# COLLECTION OF
# FAC-SIMILES &c.
## FROM
## ANCIENT MANUSCRIPTS.

Nº 37 see page 18. (For Appendix 35 & 36 see following page so placed in order that both may be seen at one view.)

### MONOPHONIA

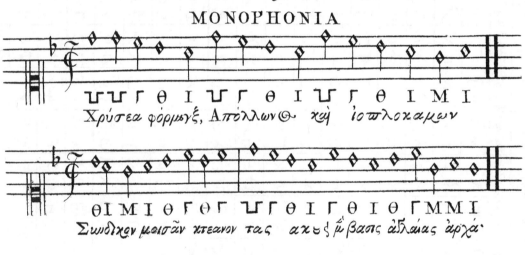

### CHORUS AD CYTHARAM

Musical Fragment from Pindar, and its transcript in modern notation.

Nº 35. ( see page 18.)      Table of Greek Musical Characters.

Column headers (each column: *Charact.* / *Vox.Inftr.*):

Charact. Toni Ionij Lydij · Charact. Toni Hypoly Hyperij · Charact. Toni Hypoly Æolij · Charact. Toni Ionij Hypaco Hyperay · Charact. Toni Ionij Phrygij · Charact. Toni Ionij Hyparao Phrygij · Charact. Toni Ionij Hypoperbar Hypophry · Charact. Toni Ionij Iastij · Charact. Toni Ionij Hyparias Hypias · Charact. Toni Ionij Dorij · Charact. Toni Hyrodo Hyperido

Row labels (with leading note letters):

| | Notæ et Characteres musici veterum iuxta Diatom.Genus |
|---|---|
| aa | Νητη υπερβολαιων |
| g | Υπερβολαιων διατονος |
| f | Τριτη υπερβολαιων |
| e | Νητη διεζευγμενων |
| d | Διεζευγμενων διατονος |
| c | Τριτη διεζευγμενων |
| h | Παραμεση |
| c | Νητη συνημμενων |
| h | Συνημμενων διατονος |
| b | Τριτη συνημμενων |
| a | Μεση |
| G | Μεσων διατονος |
| F | Παρυπατη μεσων |
| E | Υπατη μεσων |
| D | Υπατων διατονος |
| C | Παρυπατη υπατων |
| h | Υπατη υπατων |
| A | Προσλαμβανομενος |

No. 36. (see page 18.)     Table of Greek Musical Characters.

The table lists, for each of the classical Greek tonoi (modes) — *Charact. Toni Lydij*, *Charact. Toni Hyperly*, *Charact. Toni Æolij*, *Charact. Toni Hypoew*, *Charact. Toni Phrygij*, *Charact. Toni Hyperphr*, *Charact. Toni Iastij*, *Charact. Toni Hypoias Hypias*, *Charact. Toni Dorij*, *Charact. Toni Hypodo Hyperdo* — the musical characters (both *Vox. Infer.* and *Vox. Infr.* forms) corresponding to each note of the *Notæ et Characteres musici veterum iuxta Diaton Genus*.

The note names listed in the left-hand column are:

- Νήτη ὑπερβολαίων
- Παράνητη ὑπερβολαίων
- Τρίτη ὑπερβολαίων
- Νήτη διεζευγμένον
- Παράνητη διεζευγμένον
- Τρίτη διεζευγμένον
- Παραμέσος
- Νήτη συνημμένον
- Παράνητη συνημμένον
- Τρίτη συνημμένον
- Μέση
- Λιχανὸς μέσων ο
- Παρυπάτη μέσων
- Ὑπάτη μέσων
- Λιχανὸς ὑπάτων
- Παρυπάτη ὑπάτων
- Ὑπάτη ὑπάτων
- Προσλαμβανόμενος

Appendix No. 37. will be found on the previous page.

Nọ 38 ( see page 144.)

Greek Musical Notation from a Manuscript of the eleventh century.

Nº 39. see page 146.

Initial page from a Greek ritual, found in Buda.

Nº 40. see page 146.

Final page of a Greek ritual found at Buda.

Nº 41. ( see page 169 in note)

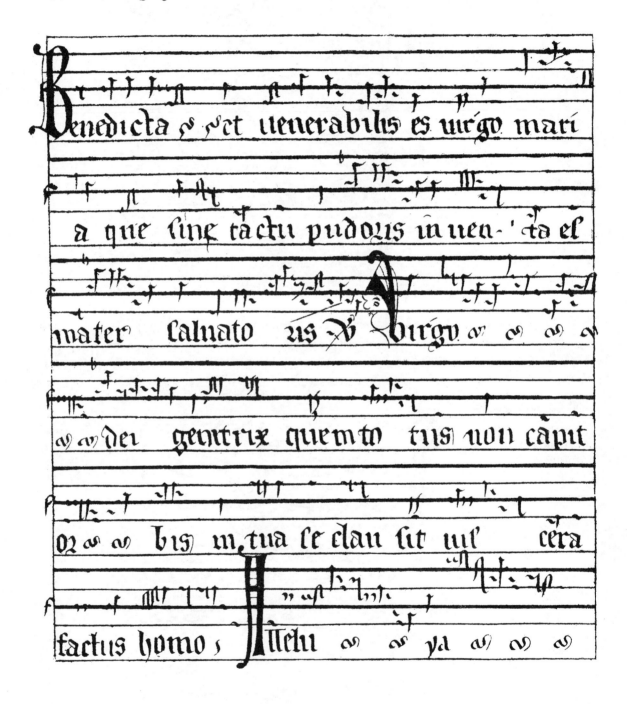

Specimen of Manuscript with thick lines to point out the place of the C & F cleff.

N.º 42 see page 169

Specimen from
Martini.

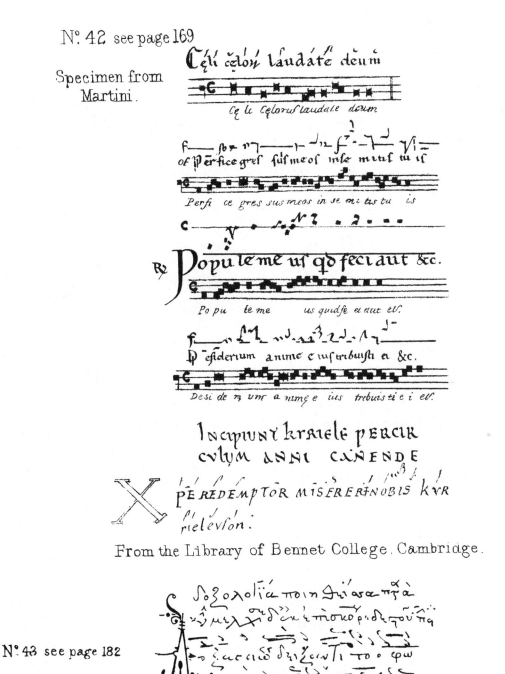

From the Library of Bennet College, Cambridge.

N.º 43 see page 182

Greek Hymn from the Library of Jesus College, Oxon.

Nº 44  see page 181.

ALLELUIA

oﬀ Angelus dni coMicce maﬀum tuam.          *Folio 25.*

Agnus dei quitollis peccata niundi
miserere nobis. Qui patris insolio
residens. persecula  regnas miserere.          *Fo. 75.*

Kirrieleison.   Kirrieleison.  Kirrieleison.

Xpe leison.  Xpe leison. Xpe leison.

Kirrie leison. Kirrie leison.  Kirrie leison.

Kirrie leison. Xpe leison  kirrie leison. Kirrieleison.
*Fo. 182.*

Manuscript by various hands from Bodleian Library Oxford

# Claues medii canticorum aeui.

No. 45.
See Page 379.

*Vocis cantus.*     *Vocis altae primae.*

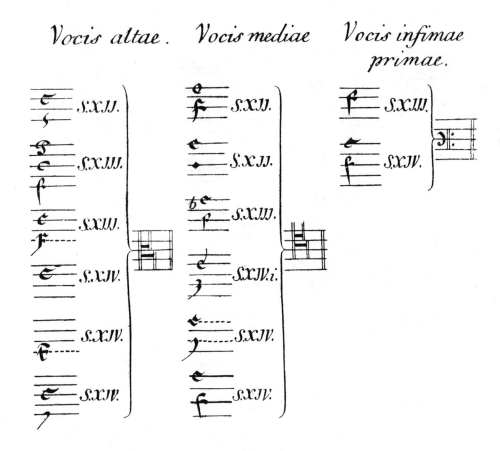

*Vocis altae.*     *Vocis mediae*     *Vocis infimae primae.*

Musical Cleffs in use from the eleventh to the fourteenth Century.

N.º 46. *Notae Musicae.*

See page 379.

| | |
|---|---|
| ‘ o S.XI. | ꝯ oo S.XI. |
| , o S.XI. | ∴ oo S.XI |
| ˙ o S.XII. | oo S.XIII. |
| o S.XII. | o S.XIV. |
| o S.XII. | ꝺ oꝑ S.XI. |
| o S.XII. | oꝑ S.XII. |
| o S.XIII. | ꝧ oꝑ S.XIII. |
| o S.XIII. | oꝑ S.XII. |
| ꞃ ꝑ S.XI. | oꝑ S.XII. |
| ꞅ d S.XI. | oꝑ S.XII. |
| ꝑ S.XII. | oꝑ S.XIV. |
| ꝑ S.XIII. | oꝑ S.XIV. |
| ꝑ S.XIII. | oꝑ S.XIV. |
| ſ ꝑ S.XIV. | oꝑ S.XIV. |
| ꞅ ꝑ S.XIV. | ꝺ od S.XI. |
| ɣ ꝑ S.XIV. | od S.XIV. |
| ꝑ S.XIV. | ɣ ꝑo S.XI. |
| ꝑ S.XIV. | |
| d S.XIV. | |
| ∼ oo S.XI. | |
| ∴ oo S.XI. | |

Musical Characters in use from the eleventh to the fourteenth

Nº 47.  *Notae Musicae.*

See page 379.

Century, with their equivalents in modern notation.

No. 48. see Page 379

Manuscript with Notation previous to the invention of the Staff.

N.º 49. see page 379.

Responsorium. In paupertá - te spi - ri tus serviens chri sto Suit
ber - - - tus. Super terram pauper cum pau - pere in his
quae sur - sum sunt di - ues cum diuite, ubi cor fi xium
hábuit in coe - - - - lo thesauri a - - - - - - - -
- - uit Ae - - - - - uia. Versiculus. Auribus audiendi audi - - ens
dicentem Jesum , ubi est thesaurus tu - us ibi est et cor tu um.
Vbi cor fi - xium.

*Sed expugnatis non longo post tempore Boructuarus a gente antiquorum Saxonum dispersi sunt quotlibet hi qui uerbum receperant. Ipse antistes cum quibusdam Pippinum petiit, qui interpellante Brithtrude coniuge sua, dedit ei locum mansionis in insula Hreni quae lingua illorum uocatur in littore. In qua ipse constructo monasterio quod hactenus possident heredes eius aliquandiu con - tinentissimam gessit uitam, ibique clausit ultimum diem.*

Responsorium. Laudemus Do - - - mi num in be a ti an
- - tisti - - tis Suitber - ti me - ri tis glo - - - ri o - - sus ad -
se pul chrum e - ius aegri ue - - - - ni unt et sa nan - - -
- - - - - - - - - - - - - - - - - - - - - - - - - - - - - - tur. Ae - -
- - uia. Versiculus. Vere mira bilis De us, qui assi du is be a
tum Suitbertum miraculis coru - scare fa - cis Ad se pul
chrum. Gloria patri. Justum deduxit Dominus. Laudes. Serue
bone et fi delis, quia in pauca fu isti fi delis, supra mul - ta
te constituam, in - tra in gaudi um Domini De - i tu
Ae - uia - - - - - - - -

The equivalent of the opposite page in modern characters

Nᵒ 50. see page 379.

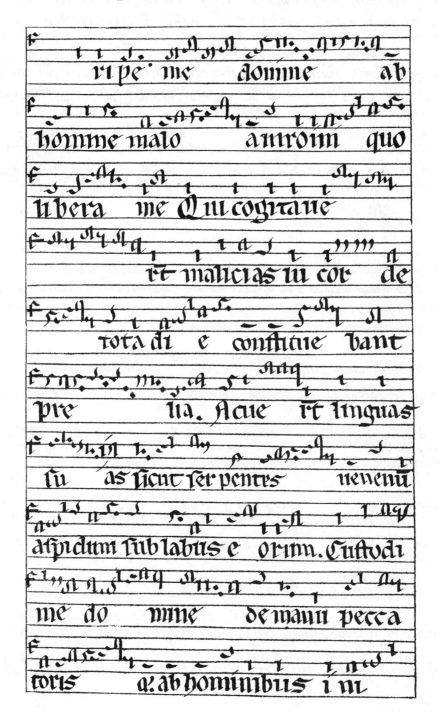

Notation said to be of the Twelfth Century.

N.º 51. see page 379.

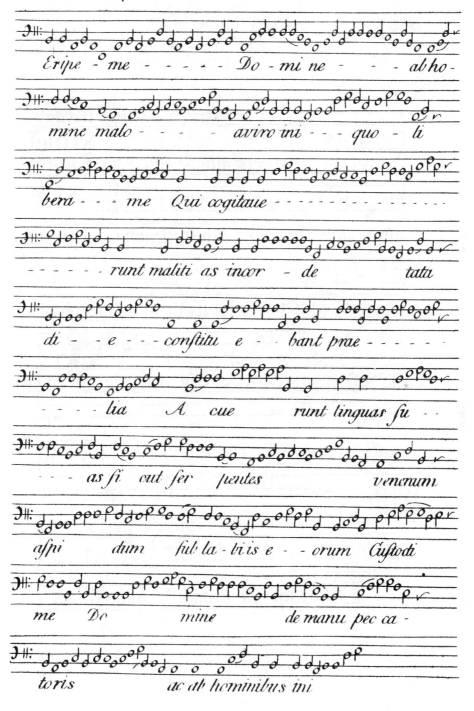

The equivalent of the opposite page in modern notation

N.º 52. see page 379.

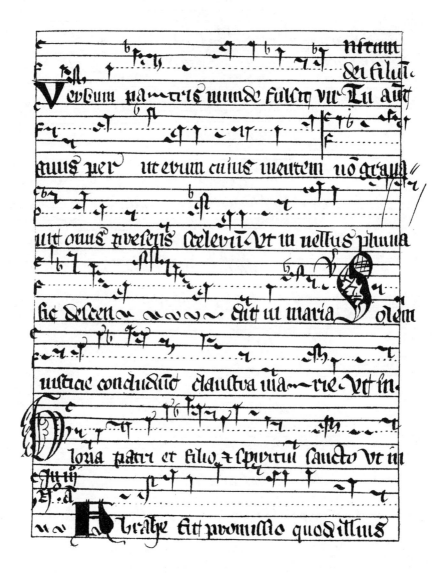

Notation said to be of the Thirteenth Century.

Nº 53. see page 379.

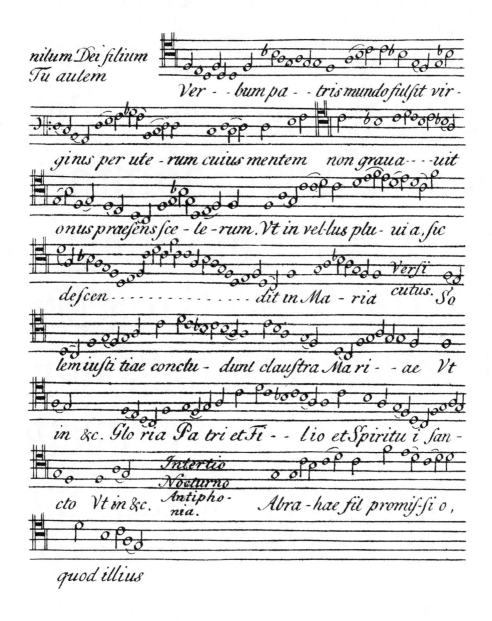

The equivalent of the opposite page in modern notation

Nọ 54 see page 379.

Vere dignum et iustum
est. equum et salutare.
Nos tibi semper et ubiq;
gracias agere. domine
sancte pater omnipotens
eterne deus. Quia per
incarnati uerbi mysterium
             Per quem
maiestatem tuam laudant
angeli. adorant dominationes
ones. tremunt potestates.
Celi celorumq; uirtutes ac

beata seraphyn socia exul
tatione concelebrant.
Cum quibus et nostras uo
ces ut admitti iubeas depre
camur. supplici confessione
dicentes. Sanctus. s. s.

Nº 55.

Vere dignum et iustum est, ae-quum et sa-luta-
re Nos tibi semper et vbi-que grati-as agere, domine
sancte pater omni potens aeterne De-us, Quia per in
carna-ti uerbi mi-ste-rium - - - - - - - - - - - - - Per quem
maiestatem tuam laudant ange-li, ado - - rant dominati-o-
nes, tre-munt po-testa-tes, Coeli coelorum-que uirtutes ac
beatae Se-ra-phim so-cia exulta-ti-o-ne conce-lebrant.
Cum qui-bus et nostras uoces vt ad-mitti iubeas de-pre-
ca-mur sup-plici confes-si-o-ne di - cen-tes San - - ctus,
sanctus, s. s.

Nᵒ 56. see page 160.

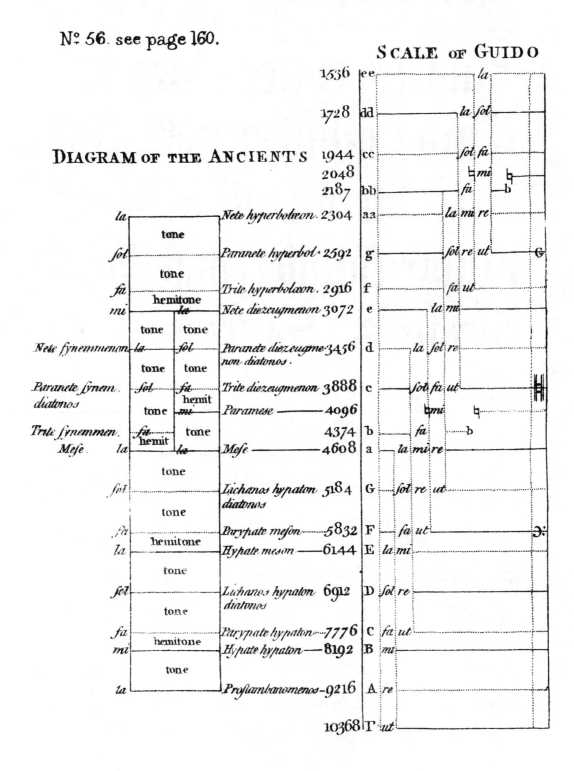

N.° 57  see page 537.

A Lesson of Descant of thirtie eighte Proportions of sundrie kindes made by Master Giles, Master of the children at Windsor.

7 1 Septupla

7 2 Tripla Sesquialtera     7 4 Supertripartiens Quartas     21 4

Quintupla Sesquiquarta

21 8 Dupla Superquintupartiens octavo     Proportio equalis

2 3 Subsesquialtera,    4 3 Sesqui-tertia    8 3 Dupla Superbipartiens tertiens

16 3 Quintupla Sesquitertia

6 1 Sextupla        Proportio equalis

2 5 Subdupla sesquialt.    4 5 Subsesquiquarta    8 5 Supertripartiens Quintas    16 5 Tripla Superbipartiens Quintas

32 5 Sextupla Superbipartiens Quintas

8 1 Octupla        Proportio equalis

MISERERE

DOCTOR NATHANIEL GILES.

# GENERAL INDEX.

N.B. Pages 1 to 486 are in Vol. I.—Pages 487 to end are in Vol. II.

# GENERAL INDEX.

# GENERAL INDEX.

# INDEX

###### TO

# MUSICAL ILLUSTRATIONS.

N.B.   Pages 1 to 486 are in Vol. I.—Pages 487 to end are in Vol. II.

# INDEX

TO

## DIAGRAMS, WOODCUTS, AND MISCELLANEOUS ILLUSTRATIONS.

# INDEX TO DIAGRAMS, WOODCUTS, ETC.

N.B.   Pages 1 to 486 are in Vol. I.—Pages 487 to end are in Vol. II.

# TABLE OF PARALLEL BOOKS, CHAPTERS, AND PAGES,

*To render the New Index available for such Persons as possess the* QUARTO EDITION.